How to Prepare for the

GRE®

Graduate Record Examination

General Test

Eleventh Edition

SAMUEL C. BROWNSTEIN

MITCHEL WEINER

SHARON WEINER GREEN

Author of Special Chapter on Mathematics
STEPHEN HILBERT

BARRON'S

All inquiries should be addressed to:
Barron's Educational Series, Inc.
250 Wireless Boulevard
Hauppauge, New York 11788

Library of Congress Catalog Card No. 94-10409

International Standard Book No. 0-8120-1939-3

Library of Congress Cataloging-in-Publication Data

Brownstein, Samuel C., 1909–
    How to prepare for the graduate record examination : GRE general text /
Samuel C. Brownstein, Mitchel Weiner, Sharon Weiner Green ; author of spe-
cial chapter on mathematics, Stephen Hilbert. — 11th ed.
        p.   cm.
    ISBN 0-8120-1939-3
    1. Graduate Record Examination—Study guides.   I. Weiner,
Mitchel, 1907–   II. Green, Sharon.
III. Hilbert, Stephen.   IV. Title.   V. Title: GRE general test.
LB2367.4.B76 1994
378.'662—dc20   94-10409
                                             CIP

PRINTED IN THE UNITED STATES OF AMERICA

4567   100   9876543

Contents

Acknowledgments

The sample GRE questions in Chapter 1 and GRE test directions are reprinted by permission of Educational Testing Service. GRE test questions selected from *Practicing to Take the GRE General Test — No. 4, 5, 7, & 8*, Educational Testing Service, 1986, 1987, 1989, 1990, and *GRE 1993–94 Information and Registration Bulletin*, Educational Testing Service, © 1993. Reprinted by permission of Educational Testing Service. Permission to reprint the above material does not constitute review or endorsement by Educational Testing Service of this publication as a whole or of any other testing information it may contain.

The authors gratefully acknowledge the following for permission to reprint reading passages:

Page 19: Excerpted from "The Crest of the East Pacific Rise" by Ken C. Macdonald and Bruce P. Luyendyk, *Scientific American*, May 1981. Reprinted in *Volcanoes and the Earth's Interior*, W.H. Freeman & Co. All rights reserved.

Page 22: Reprinted by permission of the publishers from *Century of Struggle: The Women's Rights Movement in the United States* by Eleanor Flexner, Cambridge, Mass: The Belknap Press of Harvard University Press, Copyright 1959, 1975, 1987 by Eleanor Flexner.

Page 23: From Crick, F. *What Mad Pursuit*, 25–26. New York: Basic Books. Copyright © 1988 by Francis Crick. Reprinted with permission.

Page 106: Ladislas Segy, "African Sculpture Speaks," Dover Publications, New York 1958. By permission of Helena Segy.

Page 107: From *The Uses of Enchantment*, by Bruno Bettelheim. Copyright © 1975, 1976 by Bruno Bettelheim. Reprinted by permission of Alfred A. Knopf, Inc.

Page 108: Excerpt from *The Indian in America* (*New American Nations Series*) by Wilcomb E. Washburn. Copyright © 1975 by Wilcomb E. Washburn. Reprinted by permission of HarperCollins Publishers, Inc.

Page 112: From *Black Americans in the Roosevelt Era* by John B. Kirby. Copyright 1980, University of Tennessee Press.

Page 113: From "So Many Female Rivals" by Christine Froula (*The New York Times Book Review*, February 7, 1988). Copyright © 1988 by The New York Times Company. Reprinted by permission.

Page 118: From *The Madwoman in the Attic* by Sandra M. Gilbert and Susan Gubar, © 1979 by Yale University Press, publisher.

Page 391: Reprinted from *The Panda's Thumb: More Reflections in Natural History* by Stephen Jay Gould, with the permission of W.W. Norton & Company, Inc. Copyright © 1980 by Stephen Jay Gould.

Page 394: Elaine Showalter, *A Literature of Their Own: British Women Novelists from Brontë to Lessing*. Copyright © 1977 by Princeton University Press. Excerpt, pp. 10–12 reprinted with permission of Princeton University Press.

Page 395: From *The Soul of the Night* by Chet Raymo. © 1985. Reprinted by permission of the publisher Prentice-Hall, Inc., Englewood Cliffs, New Jersey.

Page 455: From "W.E.B. Du Bois: Protagonist of the Afro-American Protest" by Elliot Rudwick, in *Black Leaders of the Twentieth Century*, edited by John Hope Franklin and August Meier. Copyright 1982, University of Illinois Press.

Page 456: Excerpted from "The Quantum Theory and Reality" by Bernard d'Espagnat, *Scientific American*, November 1979. Copyright © 1979 by Scientific American, Inc. All rights reserved.

Page 488: From *Eyes on the Prize: America's Civil Rights Years*, edited by Clayborne Carson et al. Copyright 1987 by Penguin Books. Blackside, Inc. 1991, with permission.

Page 489: Excerpted from "The Birth of Massive Stars" by Michael Zeilik, *Scientific American*, April 1978. Copyright © 1978 by Scientific American, Inc. All rights reserved.

Page 492: From *The English Novel: Form and Function* by Dorothy Van Ghent. Copyright 1953, Harper & Row Publishers, Inc. By permission of Harcourt Brace & Co.

Page 493: Excerpted from "Transposable Genetic Elements" by Stanley N. Cohen and James A. Shapiro, *Scientific American*, February 1980. Copyright © 1980 by Scientific American, Inc. All rights reserved.

Page 538: From *Literary Women: The Great Writers* by Ellen Moers. Copyright © 1976, 1977 by Ellen Moers. Used by permission of Doubleday, a division of Bantam Doubleday Dell Publishing Group Inc.

Page 538: Excerpted from "Learning by Instinct," by James L. Gould and Peter Marler, *Scientific American*, January 1987. Copyright © 1987 by Scientific American, Inc. All rights reserved.

Page 542: From *From Slavery to Freedom: A History of Negro Americans*, by John Hope Franklin. Copyright 1947, © 1956, 1967, 1974 by Alfred A. Knopf, Inc. Reprinted by permission of Alfred A. Knopf, Inc.

Page 584: From "The Dynamic Abyss" by Charles D. Hollister, Arthur R.M. Nowell, and Peter A. Jumars, *Scientific American*, March 1984. Copyright © 1984 by Scientific American, Inc. All rights reserved.

Page 605: From *Black History and the Historical Profession, 1915–1980* by August Meier and Elliot Rudwick. Copyright 1986, University of Illinois Press.

Page 606: From *Rodents: Their Lives and Habits*, © 1975 by Peter W. Hanney, pp. 103–4. Reprinted by permission of Taplinger Publishing Co., Inc.

Preface

As prospective graduate students concerned with professional advancement, you know the importance of using good tools and drawing on solid research. In this Eleventh Edition of *Barron's How to Prepare for the GRE*, we offer you both.

This revision contains the fruits of our close study of *all* recent GRE General Tests made public by the Graduate Record Examinations Board. We have scrutinized hundreds of actual GRE questions, traced dozens of GRE reading passages to their sources, analyzed subsets of questions by order of difficulty and question type. In the process, we have come up with the following features, which should make this Eleventh Edition particularly helpful to you:

Actual GRE Questions Analyzed
The Eleventh Edition takes you step by step through dozens of verbal, mathematical, and analytical questions from actual published GREs, showing you how to solve them and how to avoid going wrong.

Testing Tactics
The Eleventh Edition provides you with dozens of proven, highlighted testing tactics that will help you attack the different types of questions on the GRE.

High-Frequency Word List
The Eleventh Edition gives you a new, updated 300-word High Frequency Word List, 300 words from *abate* to *zealot* that have been shown by computer analysis to occur and reoccur on actual published GREs, plus Barron's 3,500-word Master Word List, *the* college-level vocabulary list for 40 years.

Comprehensive Mathematics Review
The Eleventh Edition presents you with extensive mathematical review materials that provide a refresher course for students primarily involved in nonscientific disciplines.

GRE-Modeled Tests
The Eleventh Edition offers you a full-length Diagnostic Test geared to the current GRE, a diagnostic test that will enable you to pinpoint your areas of weakness right away and concentrate your review on subjects in which you need most work, plus five additional Model Tests, all with answers completely explained, that in format, difficulty, and content echo today's GRE.

Computer GRE Update
The Eleventh Edition introduces you to the latest fashion in GRE testing—the adaptive, computer-based GRE—informing you of the advantages and disadvantages of the computerized test and helping you determine which form of the GRE suits you.

This Eleventh Edition once more upgrades what has long been a standard text. It reflects the contributions of numerous teachers, editors, and coaches, and the dedication of the staff at Barron's, especially Linda Turner. We, the authors, are indebted to all these individuals and to our publisher, Manuel H. Barron, for their ongoing efforts to make this book America's outstanding GRE study guide.

TIMETABLE FOR THE GRADUATE RECORD EXAMINATION

IMPORTANT NOTE: This is a typical format only. The GRE you take may be slightly different. The order of the sections will probably vary.

Total Time: 3 hours, 40 minutes

Section	Time Allowed	Description
1	30 minutes	*Verbal Ability* 7 sentence completion questions 9 analogy questions 11 reading comprehension questions 11 antonym questions
2	30 minutes	*Verbal Ability* 7 sentence completion questions 9 analogy questions 11 reading comprehension questions 11 antonym questions
3	30 minutes	*Quantitative Ability* 15 quantitative comparison questions 10 discrete quantitative (standard multiple-choice) questions 5 data interpretation questions (tables/graphs)
		10-minute break
4	30 minutes	*Quantitative Ability* 15 quantitative comparison questions 10 discrete quantitative (standard multiple-choice) questions 5 data interpretation questions
5	30 minutes	*Analytical Ability* 19 analytical reasoning questions 6 logical reasoning questions
6	30 minutes	*Analytical Ability* 19 analytical reasoning questions 6 logical reasoning questions
7	30 minutes	*Verbal, Quantitative,* or *Analytical Ability*

1 What You Need to Know About the GRE

■ **An Overview of the GRE General Test**
■ **Commonly Asked Questions About the GRE**
■ **GRE Test Format**
■ **The Verbal Sections**
■ **The Quantitative Sections**
■ **The Analytical Sections**
■ **Testing Tactics**
■ **Sample GRE Questions**

An Overview of the GRE General Test

The GRE General Test is a multiple-choice examination designed to measure the verbal, quantitative, and analytical skills you have developed in the course of your academic career. Because there is a strong correlation between high GRE scores and the probability of success in graduate school, many graduate and professional schools require that their applicants take the GRE General Test. (They may also require their applicants to take the appropriate GRE Subject Test; these tests are offered in seventeen fields.)

There are seven sections on the GRE: two verbal sections, two quantitative sections, two sections testing analytical ability, and one experimental section in one of the three tested areas; this experimental section is not counted in the scoring. The verbal sections measure your ability to use words as tools in reasoning; you are tested not only on the extent of your vocabulary but also on your ability to discern the relationships that exist both within written passages and among individual groups of words. The quantitative sections measure your ability to use and reason with numbers or mathematical concepts; you are tested not on advanced mathematical theory, but on general concepts expected to be part of everyone's academic background. The

analytical sections measure your ability to make rational assessments about unfamiliar, fictitious relationships and to think through arguments logically. You are given 30 minutes to answer the questions in each section; you may not go back to a section once the time for that section has elapsed.

There are three very important points you should be aware of:

1. Each question is worth the same number of points. Whether it was easy or difficult, whether it took you 10 seconds or two minutes to answer, you get the same number of points for each question answered correctly.

2. In each group of questions, the questions tend to go from easy to more difficult. This means that the first analogy question in a group will probably be easier than the seventh analogy question in that group, and so on. (An exception is the reading comprehension questions, which are not ordered by level of difficulty.)

3. The GRE General Test does *not* penalize you for incorrect answers. Leave no question unanswered. When uncertain about an answer, guess—and mark your guesses. You can always come back to them if you have time.

Keep these three points in mind as you learn more about what's on the test, and the tactics and strategies that will help you maximize your test score.

Commonly Asked Questions About the GRE

How Does the GRE Differ from Other Tests?

Most tests students take are achievement tests. They attempt to find out how much the student learned, usually in a specific subject, and how well he or she can apply that information. Without emphasis on memorized information, the GRE General Test measures verbal, mathematical, and analytical reasoning ability that you have developed both in and out of school.

How Can I Determine Which Is the Experimental Section?

Do not waste time in the examination room trying to identify the experimental section. Do your best on all seven sections. Some claim that most often the last section is the experimental part. Others claim that the section with unusual questions is the one that does not count. Ignore the claims: you have no sure way to tell. If you do encounter a series of questions that seem strange, do your best. Either these are experimental and will not count, in which case you have no reason to worry about them, or they will count, in which case they probably will seem just as strange and troublesome to your fellow examinees.

Should I Guess?

Yes, definitely on the *General* Test. Unlike the Subject Tests, which have a guessing penalty, the General Test simply gives credit for correct answers; it does not penalize ones that are incorrect. If you are running out of time, eliminate any answer choices you feel sure are wrong. Then go ahead and guess. On the General Test, guessing at an answer is ALWAYS better than not responding at all.

Is It Advisable to Begin by Doing All the Easy Questions First?

Yes, but don't devote too much time to any one question, even if you think it should be an easy one for you. Usually, the earlier questions of each type, except for the reading comprehension questions, are easier than the later ones. Most tests begin with "warm-up" questions. But what is easy for one person may be hard for another, so it is good advice not to get bogged down with any one question. Remember, all questions carry the same point value. After a reasonable amount of time, guess. Just make sure you make a note of your guesses in your test booklet, so that you can come back to them if you have time.

How Important Is Scrap Work on the GRE?

Scrap work on the GRE is important only to the degree that it is helpful to you. You may write in the test booklet as much as you choose. Don't hesitate to mark key words or phrases in the verbal and analytical sections.

Do any necessary mathematical calculations on or near the problem. Since scrap work is not scored, keep it down to a minimum to save time. Be careful not to do any scrap work or leave any stray markings on your answer sheet. The machine that scores the test may mistake a stray mark for a second answer and give you no credit for a question.

Use your test booklet as your guessing guide. Circle any questions to which you want to return. Cross out any answer choices you are sure are wrong, so that you don't spend time considering them again.

When and Where Is the Test Given?

The GRE is given five times a year at test centers throughout the world. Tests fall on Saturdays in February, April, June, October, and December. In June, only the General Test is given. On the other four dates, the General Test is given in the morning and the Subject Tests are given in the afternoon. Candidates whose religious convictions prohibit their tests on Saturday may arrange for Monday dates.

In New York State, where public disclosure of standardized tests is required by law, a curtailed testing schedule is in effect.

Your college counseling office will have information about the exact test dates and should be able to provide you with a registration form. If a registration form is not available at your school, request one by mail from Graduate Record Examinations, Eucational Testing Service, CN 6000, Princeton, NJ 08541-6000. You will receive with it a copy of the current GRE Information Bulletin, a helpful booklet containing sample questions and information about services and fees.

How and When Are GRE Scores Reported?

The General Test raw score, the number of correct answers, is converted to a score on a scale of 200 to 800. With no correct answers at all, a student would still have a score of 200. With one or two unanswered or incorrectly answered questions, a student could still have a score of 800. Separate scores (from 200 to 800) are given for the verbal, quantitative, and analytical reasoning sections. Your score report will include both your scaled scores and your percentile rank indicating the percent of examinees scoring below your scaled scores on the General Test.

You should recieve your score report in the mail approximately six weeks after the test date.

What is the Computerized GRE Option I've Heard Mentioned

In March 1992 the Graduate Record Examination Board announced a new option for test-takers: the computerized GRE. Refer to Chapter 14 for a complete description of this test.

GRE Test Format

The following seven sections are on the test. You will be given 30 minutes to complete each of them.

38-question verbal section

38-question verbal section

30-question quantitative section

30-question quantitative section

25-question analytical section

25-question analytical section

an experimental section (which can resemble in content any of the six sections described above)

These sections always appear on the GRE, but their order varies. The organization within each section does not vary greatly; sections will tend to be organized as outlined below:

Verbal Section

1–7 sentence completion questions
8–16 analogy questions
17–27 reading comprehension questions
28–38 antonym questions

Quantitative Section

1–15 quantitative comparison questions
16–20 discrete quantitative (standard multiple-choice) questions
21–25 data interpretation questions (tables/graphs)
26–30 discrete quantitative (standard multiple-choice) questions

Analytical Section*

1–5 analytical reasoning questions
6–8 logical reasoning questions
9–22 analytical reasoning questions
23–25 logical reasoning questions

The Verbal Sections

The two verbal sections contain four types of questions: sentence completion, analogy, reading comprehension, and antonym. Your academic success will depend on your verbal abilities—especially your ability to understand scholarly prose and to work with specialized and technical vocabulary.

As in all GRE sections, the questions in the verbal sections progress from easy to difficult within each group of the same type of question. In other words, the first antonym question will probably be easier than the last anto-

---

*The distribution of questions in the analytical ability section varies slightly from section to section. Listed here is one of several possible formats. The total numbers of analytical reasoning questions (19) and logical reasoning questions (6), however, may vary from section to section, depending on whether or not the new analysis of explanations questions are included.

nym question; the first analogy question will probably be easier than the last analogy question, and the first sentence completion question will probably be easier than the last sentence completion question. Reading comprehension questions, however, are not arranged in order of difficulty. They are arranged according to the logic and organization of the passage on which they are based.

Although the amount of time spent on each type of question varies from person to person, in general, antonyms take the least time, then analogies, then sentence completions, and, finally reading comprehension. Since reading comprehension questions take much longer to answer (you have to spend time reading the passage before you can tackle the questions), you should do these questions last.

Sentence Completion Questions

The sentence completion questions ask you to choose the best way to complete a sentence from which one or two words have been omitted. These questions test a combination of reading comprehension skills and vocabulary. You must be able to recognize the logic, style, and tone of the sentence so that you will be able to choose the answer that makes sense in this context. You must also be able to recognize differences in usage. The sentences cover a wide variety of topics from a number of academic fields. They do not, however, test specific academic knowledge. You may feel more comfortable if you are familiar with the topic the sentence is discussing, but you should be able to handle any of the sentences using your knowledge of the English language.

See Chapter 3 for sentence completion question tactics and practice exercises that will help you handle these questions.

Analogy Questions

Analogy questions test your understanding of the relationships among words and ideas. You are given one pair of words and must choose another pair that is related in the same way. Many relationships are possible. The two terms in the pair can be synonyms; one term can be a cause, the other the effect; one can be a tool, the other the worker who uses the tool.

See Chapter 4 for analogy question tactics and practice exercises that will help you handle these questions.

Reading Comprehension Questions

Reading Comprehension questions test your ability to understand and interpret what you read. This is probably the most important ability you will need in graduate school and afterward.

As we already noted, reading comprehension questions take more time than any other questions on the test because you have to read a passage before you can answer them. Therefore, you should do the reading comprehension questions last.

Although the passages may encompass any subject matter, you do not need to know anything about the subject discussed in the passage in order to answer the questions on that passage. The purpose of the questions is to test your reading ability, not your knowledge of history, science, literature, or art. It is true, however, that you might feel more comfortable reading a passage on a topic with which you are familiar. You should, therefore, skim the passages in each section before you start working on the reading comprehension questions, and then start with the questions on the passage with which you feel most comfortable.

See Chapter 5 for reading comprehension question tactics and practice exercises that will help you handle these questions.

Antonym Questions

The antonym questions are always the last group of questions in a verbal section. They are the most straight-forward vocabulary questions on the test. You are given a word and must choose, from the five choices that follow it, the best antonym (opposite). The vocabulary in this section may well include words that are totally unfamiliar to you.

See Chapter 6 for antonym question tactics and practice exercises that will help you handle these questions.

The Quantitative Sections

The two quantitative (mathematics) sections have a total of 60 questions: 30 quantitative comparison questions, 20 discrete quantitative questions (these are actually standard multiple-choice questions), and 10 data interpretation questions. These questions assume that you have had, and remember, arithmetic, elementary algebra, and geometry. You do not need to know any more advanced mathematics. You will be asked to use graphic, spatial, numerical, and symbolic techniques in a variety of problems. The questions are intended to show how well you understand elementary mathematics, how well you can apply your knowledge to solve problems, and how good your mathematical instincts are—how well you can use nonroutine ways of thinking. In one sense, you need some insight to spot the right approach for solving any mathematical question. More important, on the GRE, is the ability to see which answer must be correct, or at least which answers are impossible, without actually solving the problem. This is basically the ability to apply mathematical rules and principles that you already know. For example, imagine that you are asked to multiply $27,654 \times 3,042$. You should see right away that the answer will have to end in 8. When the multiplicand ends in a 4 and the multiplier ends in a 2, then the product must end with an 8. This is a typical illustration of saving time with insight rather than doing lengthy, time-consuming computation, which, incidentally, may lead to computational errors. So not only is insight a time-saver, it may also be an error-saver.

Quantitative Comparison Questions

In quantitative comparison questions, you are given two quantities. Sometimes you are also given information about one or both of them. Then you must decide whether one of the quantities is greater than the other, or whether they are equal. Sometimes there will not be enough information for you to be able to make a decision.

These questions reflect the contemporary emphasis on inequalities in school mathematics courses. In general, these questions require less time than the other mathematics questions, since they require less reading and, usually, less computation. These are the only questions on the GRE that have only four choices.

The testing tactics and practice exercises in Chapter 8 will help you handle these questions.

Discrete Quantitative Questions

The discrete quantitative questions are like the math questions you are familiar with from math textbooks and other standardized tests. They will cover only math concepts that you have learned in school, so if a question seems unusual to you, keep in mind that you probably know the necessary facts, formulas, and concepts to work it out.

The testing tactics and practice exercises in Chapter 9 will help you handle these questions.

Data Interpretation Questions

As you might guess from their name, data interpretation questions are based on information given in graphs or tables. This type of question tests your ability to integrate data, to determine what information is needed to answer a question, or to recognize that you lack sufficient data to answer a question.

The testing tactics and practice exercises in Chapter 10 will help you handle these questions.

The Analytical Sections

The two analytical ability sections have a total of 50 questions, the bulk of which are analytical reasoning questions and a small number of which are logical reasoning questions. One or more of the analytical sections will probably include several questions of a new type involving the analysis of explanations. On the analytical sections, your task is to analyze a passage or set of conditions, reasoning out its implications, and then answer a question or group of questions based upon it. Each section begins with several relatively easy analytical reasoning questions followed by three relatively easy logical reasoning questions. These "warm-up" questions are then followed by additional sets of analytical reasoning questions and three final logical reasoning questions.

Analytical Reasoning Questions

In analytical reasoning questions, the test-makers make up an arbitrary set of conditions and leave it up to you to figure out the relationships ruling them. On the basis of the statements given, you are to make deductions about these relationships. Often it is useful to make charts or diagrams to clarify the relationships and point up conflicts between the statements that have been made. You do not need to have training in formal logic to handle these questions; however, a liking for puzzles may help. Pay particular attention to key words: absolute terms like *always*, *exactly*, and *never*, and relative terms like *sometimes*, *approximately*, and *almost*.

The review of analytical reasoning techniques and practice exercises in Chapter 12 will help you handle these questions.

Logical Reasoning Questions

In logical reasoning questions, you are presented with an argument and must be able to spot its point, recognize the assumptions that lie behind it, and evaluate its worth. You must have a sense of what *necessarily follows* from a given statement as distinguished from what a statement merely suggests without proof. You must be careful here to avoid being influenced by your own personal opinions: your job is to test the argument for its logical soundness, not to testify or bear witness to the argument's ultimate truth.

The review of logical reasoning techniques and practice exercises in Chapter 12 will help you to handle these questions.

Analysis of Explanations Questions

In analysis of explanations questions, you will be presented with a Situation detailing certain events or a scenario and then a Result of something that occurred in this situation. Your task will be to decide whether certain statements provide adequate explanations of how the result could have happened and also whether certain statements are relevant—that is, strengthen or weaken—a possible explanation of the result that occurred. This is a new format for analytic reasoning questions that Educational Testing Service has been experimenting with for about a year. In dealing with this new type of question, you must remain flexible and not be misled by questions that don't resemble the typical five-option multiple-choice items presented in the rest of the test.

The review of analysis of explanations questions and practice exercises in Chapter 12 will help you handle these questions.

Testing Tactics

The easiest way to answer a question correctly is to know the answer. If you know what all the words in an antonym question mean, you won't have any trouble choosing the right answer. If you know exactly how to solve a mathematics question and make no mistakes in arithmetic, you won't have any trouble choosing the right answer. However, some sensible strategies will help you maximize your score.

The tactics in this chapter apply to all sections of the test. In later chapters you will find tactics that apply specifically to each type of question.

Tactic 1

Know what to expect.   By the time you have finished with this preparation program, you will be familiar with all the kinds of questions that will appear on the GRE. You should also be aware of how long the test is going to take. There are seven sections. Each one is 30 minutes long, and there is supposed to be a 10-minute break midway through the session.

Tactic 2

Memorize the directions for each type of question.   These don't change. The test time you would spend reading the directions can be better spent answering the questions.

Tactic 3

Don't get bogged down on any one question. By the time you get to the actual GRE, you should have a fair idea of how much time to spend on each question. If a question is taking too long, guess and go on to the next question. This is no time to show the world that you can stick to a job no matter how long it takes. All the machine that grades the test will notice is the blank space on your answer sheet. However, before you move on, circle the question so that you can locate it quickly if you have time to come back to it at the end.

Tactic 4

On the other hand, don't rush.   Since your score will depend on how many *correct* answers you give *within a definite period* of time, speed and accuracy both count. Don't fall into the common errors born of haste. Read *all* the answer choices*, not just some. Make sure you are answering *the question asked* and not one it may have reminded you of or one you thought was going to be asked. Underline key words like *not* and *except* to make sure that you do not end up trying to answer the exact opposite of the question asked.

Tactic 5

Eliminate as many wrong answers as you can. Deciding between two choices is easier than deciding among five. Even if you have to guess, every answer you eliminate improves your chances of guessing correctly.

Tactic 6

Change answers only if you have a reason for doing so.   It's usually best not to change based on a hunch or a whim.

Tactic 7

Answer every question.   There is no penalty for incorrect answers on the General Test. It's folly to leave any question unanswered.

Tactic 8

Remember that you are allowed to write in the test book.   You can write anything you want in the test book. You can and should do your mathematical computations and analytical diagrams in the booklet. There is absolutely no need to try to do them in your head. And if it helps you to doodle while you think, then doodle away. What you write in the test booklet does not matter to anyone.

Tactic 9

Be careful not to make any stray marks on the answer sheet.   This test is graded by a machine, and a machine cannot tell the difference between an accidental mark and a filled-in answer. When the machine sees two marks, it calls the answer wrong.

Tactic 10

Check frequently to make sure that you are answering the questions in the right spots.

No machine is going to notice that you made a mistake early in the test by answering question 4 in the space for question 5, and that all your subsequent answers are correct, but are in the wrong spaces.

Tactic 11

Get a good night's sleep. The best way to prepare for any test you ever take is to get a good night's sleep before the test so you are well rested and alert.

Tactic 12

Allow plenty of time for getting to the test site. Taking a test is pressure enough. You don't need the extra tension that comes from worrying about whether you will get there on time.

Tactic 13

Bring four sharpened number 2 pencils to the test. The *GRE Information Bulletin* tells you to bring three or four sharpened number 2 pencils to the test. Why skimp? They don't weigh much, and this might be the one day in the decade when two or even three pencil points decide to break. And bring full-size pencils, not little stubs. Bigger ones are easier to write with, and you might as well give yourself every advantage.

Tactic 14

Wear comfortable clothes. This is a test, not a fashion show. And bring a sweater. The test room may be hot, or it may be cold. You can't change the room, but you can put on a sweater.

Tactic 15

Bring an accurate watch. The room in which you take the test may not have a clock, and some proctors are not very good about posting the time on the blackboard. Each time you begin a test section, write down in your booklet the time according to your watch. That way you will always know how much time you have left.

Sample GRE Questions*

The purpose of this section is to familiarize you with the kinds of questions that appear on the GRE by reprinting questions from recent GREs with the permission of Educational Testing Service. Knowing what to expect when you take the examination is an important step in preparing for the test and succeeding in it.

Verbal Section

Sentence Completion Questions

Directions: Each sentence below has one or two blanks, each blank indicating that something has been omitted. Beneath the sentence are five lettered words or sets of words. Choose the word or set of words for each blank that best fits the meaning of the sentence as a whole.

1. The paradoxical aspect of the myths about Demeter, when we consider the predominant image of her as a tranquil and serene goddess, is her ------- search for her daughter.

    (A) extended   (B) agitated   (C) comprehensive
    (D) motiveless   (E) heartless

2. Since she believed him to be both candid and trustworthy, she refused to consider the possibility that his statement had been -------.

    (A) irrelevant   (B) facetious   (C) mistaken
    (D) critical   (E) insincere

3. During the 1960s assessments of the family shifted remarkably, from general endorsement of it as a worthwhile, stable institution to widespread ------ it as an oppressive and bankrupt one whose ------- was both imminent and welcome.

    (A) flight from..restitution
    (B) fascination with..corruption
    (C) rejection of..vogue
    (D) censure of..dissolution
    (E) relinquishment of..ascent

4. The sheer bulk of data from the mass media seems to overpower us and drive us to ------- accounts for an easily and readily digestible portion of news.

    (A) insular
    (B) investigative
    (C) synoptic
    (D) subjective
    (E) sensational

5. People should not be praised for their virtue if they lack the energy to be -------; in such cases, goodness is merely the effect of -------.

   (A) depraved..hesitation
   (B) cruel..effortlessness
   (C) wicked..indolence
   (D) unjust..boredom
   (E) iniquitous..impiety

Analogy Questions

<u>Directions:</u>   In each of the following questions, a related pair of words or phrases is followed by five lettered pairs of words or phrases. Select the lettered pair that best expresses a relationship similar to that expressed in the original pair.

6. AMORPHOUSNESS : DEFINITION ::
   (A) lassitude : energy
   (B) spontaneity : awareness
   (C) angularity : intricacy
   (D) rectitude : drabness
   (E) precision : uniformity

7. PHILATELIST : STAMPS ::
   (A) numismatist : coins
   (B) astrologer : predictions
   (C) geneticist : chromosomes
   (D) cartographer : maps
   (E) pawnbroker : jewelry

8. PROCTOR : SUPERVISE ::
   (A) prophet : rule
   (B) profiteer : consume
   (C) profligate : demand
   (D) prodigal : squander
   (E) prodigy : wonder

9. FLAG : VIGOR ::
   (A) endure : courage
   (B) tire : monotony
   (C) question : perception
   (D) waver : resolution
   (E) flatter : charm

10. EMBROIDER : CLOTH ::
    (A) chase : metal
    (B) patch : quilt
    (C) gild : gold
    (D) carve : knife
    (E) stain : glass

Reading Comprehension Questions

<u>Directions:</u> The passage is followed by questions based on its content. After reading the passage, choose the best answer to each question. Answer all questions following the passage on the basis of what is <u>stated</u> or <u>implied</u> in the passage.

Visual recognition involves storing and retrieving memories. Neural activity, triggered by the eye, forms an image in the brain's memory system that constitutes an internal representation of the viewed object. When an object is encountered again, it is matched with its internal representation and thereby recognized. Controversy surrounds the question of whether recognition is a parallel, one-step process or a serial, step-by-step one. Psychologists of the Gestalt school maintain that objects are recognized as wholes in a parallel procedure: the internal representation is matched with the retinal image in a single operation. Other psychologists have proposed that internal representation features are matched serially with an object's features. Although some experiments show that, as an object becomes familiar, its internal representation becomes more holistic and the recognition process correspondingly more parallel, the weight of evidence seems to support the serial hypothesis, at least for objects that are not notably simple and familiar.

11. The author is primarily concerned with

    (A) explaining how the brain receives images
    (B) synthesizing hypotheses of visual recognition
    (C) examining the evidence supporting the serial-recognition hypotheses
    (D) discussing visual recognition and some hypotheses proposed to explain it
    (E) reporting on recent experiments dealing with memory systems and their relationship to neural activity

12. According to the passage, Gestalt psychologists make which of the following suppositions about visual recognition?

    I.   A retinal image is in exactly the same form as its internal representation.
    II.   An object is recognized as a whole without any need for analysis into component parts.
    III. The matching of an object with its internal representation occurs in only one step.

    (A) II only
    (B) III only
    (C) I and III only
    (D) II and III only
    (E) I, II, and III

13. It can be inferred from the passage that the matching process in visual recognition is

    (A) not a neural activity
    (B) not possible when an object is viewed for the very first time
    (C) not possible if a feature of a familiar object is changed in some way
    (D) only possible when a retinal image is received in the brain as a unitary whole
    (E) now fully understood as a combination of the serial and parallel processes

14. In terms of its tone and form, the passage can best be characterized as

    (A) a biased exposition
    (B) a speculative study
    (C) a dispassionate presentation
    (D) an indignant denial
    (E) a dogmatic explanation

Antonym Questions

Directions: Each question below consists of a word printed in capital letters, followed by five lettered words or phrases. Choose the lettered word or phrase that is most nearly <u>opposite</u> in meaning to the word in capital letters.

15. SYNCHRONOUS ::
   (A) off-key   (B) out-of-shape
   (C) without pity   (D) out-of-phase
   (E) without difficulty

16. LIST :   (A) be upside down
   (B) be upright   (C) slide backward
   (D) sway to and fro   (E) lie flat

17. TRACTABLE :   (A) distraught   (B) irritating
   (C) ruthless   (D) headstrong   (E) lazy

18. PERFIDY :   (A) thoroughness   (B) generosity
   (C) gratitude   (D) tact   (E) loyalty

19. DISSEMBLE: (A) act conventionally
   (B) put together   (C) appear promptly
   (D) behave honestly   (E) obtain readily

Quantitative Section
Quantitative Comparison Questions

Directions: Each of the following questions consists of two quantities, one in Column A and one in Column B. You are to compare the two quantities and choose

   A if the quantity in Column A is greater;
   B if the quantity in Column B is greater;
   C if the two quantities are equal;
   D if the relationship cannot be determined from the information given.

Note: Since there are only four choices, NEVER MARK (E).

Common Information: In a question, information concerning one or both of the quantities to be compared is centered above the two columns. A symbol that appears in both columns represents the same thing in Column A as it does in Column B.

Column A	Column B
$xy < 0$	
1. x	y

The circumference of circle P is greater than the circumference of circle Q.

2. The radius of circle P The diameter of circle Q

$s + t = 6$

3. $s + 2t$ $2s + t$

Column A	Column B

The perimeter of the rectangle is 16.

4. The area of the rectangular region   12

5. The average (arithmetic mean) of 10 numbers is 52. When one of the numbers is discarded, the average of the remaining numbers becomes 53.

The discarded number   51

Discrete Quantitative Questions

Directions: Each of the following questions has five answer choices. For each of these questions, select the best of the answer choices given.

6. A dresser drawer contains 15 garments. If 40 percent of those garments are blouses, how many are <u>not</u> blouses?

   (A) 6   (B) 8   (C) 9   (D) 10   (E) 12

7. $1 + \frac{1}{2} + \frac{1}{3} + \frac{1}{4} + \frac{1}{5} =$

   (A) $\frac{32}{25}$ (B) $\frac{117}{60}$ (C) $\frac{52}{25}$ (D) $\frac{109}{50}$ (E) $\frac{137}{60}$

8. The length of a rectangular floor is 16 feet and its width is 12 feet. If each dimension were reduced by s feet to make the ratio of length to width 3 to 2, what would be the value of s ?

   (A) 0   (B) 2   (C) 4   (D) 6   (E) 8

9. What is the area of the quadrilateral shown above?

   (A) $2\sqrt{3}$ (B) $3\sqrt{3}$ (C) $6\sqrt{3}$ (D) 6   (E) 8

10. If the length of each of the sides of three square garden plots is increased by 50 percent, by what percent is the sum of the areas of the three plots increased?

   (A) 375% (B) 200% (C) 150% (D) 125% (E) 50%

Data Interpretation Questions

<u>Questions 11-15</u> refer to the following graphs.

Distribution of Earnings and Revenues for Company X, 1978–1983
Electronic and Nonelectronic Operations
(1 billion = 1,000,000,000)

Distribution of Earnings from Nonelectronic Operations, 1983
(in millions of dollars)

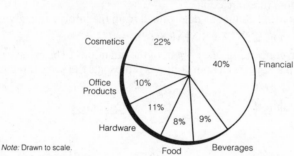

Note: Drawn to scale.

11. Total earnings from operations in 1982 were approximately how much more than total earnings from operations in 1978?

    (A) $100 million
    (B) $125 million
    (C) $180 million
    (D) $340 million
    (E) $475 million

12. For the year in which earnings from electronic operations first exceeded $400 million, <u>total revenues</u> were approximately

    (A) $2.8 billion
    (B) $4.5 billion
    (C) $5.2 billion
    (D) $5.8 billion
    (E) $6.7 billion

13. In 1979, total earnings for Company X were approximately what percent of total revenues?

    (A)   1%
    (B)   5%
    (C) 10%
    (D) 15%
    (E) 60%

14. For the two years in which earnings from electronic operations were most nearly equal, the combined earnings from nonelectronic operations were most nearly

    (A) $340 million
    (B) $520 million
    (C) $670 million
    (D) $780 million
    (E) $1,520 million

15. In 1983 earnings from financial nonelectronic operations accounted for approximately how many millions of dollars?

    (A) 312
    (B) 300
    (C) 180
    (D) 140
    (E) 120

Analytical Ability Section
Analytical Reasoning Questions

<u>Directions:</u> Each question or group of questions is based on a passage or set of conditions. In answering some of the questions, it may be useful to draw a rough diagram. For each question, select the best answer choice given.

Question 1–4

A cryptanalyst must translate into letters all of the digits included in the following two lines of nine symbols each:

9 3 3 4 5 6 6 6 7
2 2 3 3 4 4 5 7 8

The cryptanalyst has already determined some of the rules governing the decoding:

Each of the digits from 2 to 9 represents exactly one of the eight letters A, E, I, O, U, R, S, and T, and each letter is represented by exactly one of the digits.
If a digit occurs more than once, it represents the same letter on each occasion.
The letter T and the letter O are each represented exactly 3 times.
The letter I and the letter A are each represented exactly two times.
The letter E is represented exactly four times.

1. If 2 represents R and 7 represents A, then 5 must represent

(A) I
(B) O
(C) S
(D) T
(E) U

2. Which of the following is a possible decoding of the five-digit message 4 6 5 3 6?

(A) O-T-A-E-T
(B) O-T-E-U-T
(C) O-O-S-E-O
(D) T-O-I-E-T
(E) T-O-R-E-T

3. If 9 represents a vowel, it must represent which of the following?

(A) A
(B) E
(C) I
(D) O
(E) U

4. If 8 represents a vowel, which of the following must represent a consonant?

(A) 2
(B) 4
(C) 5
(D) 7
(E) 9

Questions 5–7

An instructor regularly offers a six-week survey course on film genres. Each time the course is given, she covers six of the following eight genres: adventure films, *cinéma noir*, detective films, fantasy films, horror films, musical comedies, silent films, and westerns. She will discuss exactly one genre per week according to the following conditions:

Silent films are always covered, and always in the first week.
Westerns and adventure films are always covered, with westerns covered in the week immediately preceding the week adventure films are covered.
Musical comedies are never covered in the same course in which fantasy films are covered.
If detective films are covered, they are covered after westerns are covered, with exactly one of the other genres covered between them.
Cinéma noir is not covered unless detective films are covered in one of the previous weeks.

5. Which of the following is an acceptable schedule of genres for weeks one through six of the course?

(A) Silent films, westerns, adventure films, detective films, horror films, musical comedies
(B) Silent films, westerns, adventure films, horror films, detective films, fantasy films
(C) Fantasy films, musical comedies, detective films, *cinéma noir*, westerns, adventure films
(D) Westerns, adventure films, detective films, *cinéma noir*, musical comedies, horror films
(E) Detective films, westerns, adventure films, horror films, fantasy films, *cinéma noir*

6. If musical comedies are covered the week immediately preceding the week westerns are covered, which of the following can be true?

(A) Adventure films are covered the second week.
(B) *Cinéma noir* is covered the fourth week.
(C) Detective films are covered the third week.
(D) Fantasy films are covered the fifth week.
(E) Horror films are covered the sixth week.

7. Which of the following will NEVER be covered in the sixth week of the course?

(A) *Cinéma noir*
(B) Fantasy films
(C) Horror films
(D) Musical comedies
(E) Westerns

Logical Reasoning Questions

Directions: Each question or group of questions is based on a passage or set of conditions. In answering some of the questions, it may be useful to draw a rough diagram. For each question, select the best answer choice given.

8. A study of illusionistic painting inevitably begins with the Greek painter Zeuxis. In an early work, which is the basis for his fame, he painted a bowl of grapes that was so lifelike that birds pecked at the fruit. In an attempt to expand his achievement to encompass human figures, he painted a boy carrying a bunch of grapes. When birds immediately came to peck at the fruit, Zeuxis judged that he had failed.

   Zeuxis' judgment that he had failed in his later work was based on an assumption. Which of the following can have served as that assumption?

   (A) People are more easily fooled by illusionistic techniques than are birds.
   (B) The use of illusionistic techniques in painting had become commonplace by the time Zeuxis completed his later work.
   (C) The grapes in the later painting were even more realistic than the ones in the earlier work.
   (D) Birds are less likely to peck at fruit when they see that a human being is present.
   (E) After the success of his early work, Zeuxis was unable to live up to the expectations of the general public.

9. Dormitories range from two to six stories in height. If a dormitory room is above the second floor, it has a fire escape.

   If the statements above are true, which of the following must also be true?

   (A) Second-floor dormitory rooms do not have fire escapes.
   (B) Third-floor dormitory rooms do not have fire escapes.
   (C) Only dormitory rooms above the second floor have fire escapes.
   (D) Fourth-floor dormitory rooms have fire escapes.
   (E) Some two-story dormitories do not have fire escapes.

10. It is important to teach students to use computers effectively. Therefore, students should be taught computer programming in school.

   Which of the following, if true, most weakens the argument above?

   (A) Only people who use computers effectively are skilled at computer programming.
   (B) Only people skilled at computer programming use computers effectively.
   (C) Some people who use computers effectively cannot write computer programs.
   (D) Some schools teach computer programming more effectively than others.
   (E) Most people who are able to program computers use computers effectively.

11. The Census Bureau reported that the median family income, after adjustment for inflation, increased 1.6 percent in 1983. Poverty normally declines when family income goes up, but the national poverty rate remained at its highest level in eighteen years in 1983. The Census Bureau offered two possible explanations: the lingering effects of the deep and lengthy 1981–1982 recession, and increases in the number of people living in families headed by women and in the number of adults not living with any relatives. Both groups are likely to be poorer than the population as a whole.

   Which of the following conclusions can be properly drawn from this report?

   (A) The national poverty rate has increased steadily over the last eighteen years.
   (B) The national poverty rate will increase when there are lingering effects of an earlier recession.
   (C) The median family income can increase even though the family income of some subgroups within the population declines or fails to increase.
   (D) The category of adults not living with any relatives is the most critical group in the determination of whether the economy has improved.
   (E) The median family income is affected more by the changes in family patterns than by the extent of expansion or recession of the national economy.

12. Literary historians today have rejected conventional analyses of the development of English Renaissance drama. They no longer accept the idea that the sudden achievement of Elizabethan playwrights was a historical anomaly, a sort of magical rediscovery of ancient Greek dramatic form applied to contemporary English subject matter. Instead, most students of the theater now view Elizabethan drama as being organically related to traditional local drama, particularly medieval morality plays.

   Which of the following is NOT consistent with the passage above?

   (A) England had a dramatic tradition before the Renaissance period.
   (B) Elizabethan drama, once thought to be a sudden blossoming forth of creativity, is now seen as part of a historical continuum.
   (C) Historians' views of the antecedents of English Renaissance drama have changed considerably.
   (D) Current scholarship applies an evolutionary model to English Renaissance drama.
   (E) Although English Renaissance drama treats English subject matter, its source of form and method is classical Greek drama.

Answer Key
Verbal Section

1.	B	6.	A	11.	D	16.	B
2.	E	7.	A	12.	D	17.	D
3.	D	8.	D	13.	B	18.	E
4.	C	9.	D	14.	C	19.	D
5.	C	10.	A	15.	D		

Quantitative Section

1.	D	6.	C	11.	D
2.	D	7.	E	12.	E
3.	D	8.	C	13.	C
4.	C	9.	B	14.	C
5.	B	10.	D	15.	E

Analytical Ability Section

1.	A	5.	A	9.	D
2.	A	6.	E	10.	C
3.	E	7.	E	11.	C
4.	E	8.	D	12.	E

2 A DIAGNOSTIC TEST

- ■ **Diagnostic Test**
- ■ **Answer Key**
- ■ **Self-Appraisal**
- ■ **Answer Explanations**

This chapter contains a simulated full-length GRE test. Like the actual GRE that you'll be taking soon, this Diagnostic Test has 7 sections: 2 verbal, 2 quantitative (math), 2 analytical, and 1 experimental (which in this case is another quantitative section). Each section has the same number and type of questions as you'll find on the actual GRE, and each section should be completed in 30 minutes. Taking the Diagnostic Test will provide you with a fairly accurate evaluation of what your GRE score would be barring any special preparation.

After taking the test, score your answers and evaluate your results, using the self-rating guides provided. (Be sure also to read the answer explanations for questions you answered incorrectly and questions you answered correctly but found difficult.)

You should now be in a position to approach your review program realistically and allot your time for study. For example, you should know which topics in mathematics require review and drill. You should also know which of your verbal and analytical skills require concentrated study.

Simulate Test Conditions

Find a quiet place to work, in order to simulate examination conditions. Keep an accurate record of your time. If you complete a section before the suggested time has elapsed, check your work over and do not start another section. Don't be worried, however, if you are not able to answer all questions in the allotted time. This may also occur on the actual test. No one is expected to know the answers to all questions on an aptitude test. Read the questions carefully. Work carefully and as rapidly as possible. Do not spend too much time on questions that seem difficult for you. However, since this is a multiple-choice test, with no penalty imposed for guessing, answer every question even if you have to guess.

Answer Sheet – Diagnostic Test

Start with number 1 for each new section.
If a section has fewer than 38 questions, leave the extra spaces blank.

Section 1

1. Ⓐ Ⓑ Ⓒ Ⓓ Ⓔ	11. Ⓐ Ⓑ Ⓒ Ⓓ Ⓔ	21. Ⓐ Ⓑ Ⓒ Ⓓ Ⓔ	31. Ⓐ Ⓑ Ⓒ Ⓓ Ⓔ
2. Ⓐ Ⓑ Ⓒ Ⓓ Ⓔ	12. Ⓐ Ⓑ Ⓒ Ⓓ Ⓔ	22. Ⓐ Ⓑ Ⓒ Ⓓ Ⓔ	32. Ⓐ Ⓑ Ⓒ Ⓓ Ⓔ
3. Ⓐ Ⓑ Ⓒ Ⓓ Ⓔ	13. Ⓐ Ⓑ Ⓒ Ⓓ Ⓔ	23. Ⓐ Ⓑ Ⓒ Ⓓ Ⓔ	33. Ⓐ Ⓑ Ⓒ Ⓓ Ⓔ
4. Ⓐ Ⓑ Ⓒ Ⓓ Ⓔ	14. Ⓐ Ⓑ Ⓒ Ⓓ Ⓔ	24. Ⓐ Ⓑ Ⓒ Ⓓ Ⓔ	34. Ⓐ Ⓑ Ⓒ Ⓓ Ⓔ
5. Ⓐ Ⓑ Ⓒ Ⓓ Ⓔ	15. Ⓐ Ⓑ Ⓒ Ⓓ Ⓔ	25. Ⓐ Ⓑ Ⓒ Ⓓ Ⓔ	35. Ⓐ Ⓑ Ⓒ Ⓓ Ⓔ
6. Ⓐ Ⓑ Ⓒ Ⓓ Ⓔ	16. Ⓐ Ⓑ Ⓒ Ⓓ Ⓔ	26. Ⓐ Ⓑ Ⓒ Ⓓ Ⓔ	36. Ⓐ Ⓑ Ⓒ Ⓓ Ⓔ
7. Ⓐ Ⓑ Ⓒ Ⓓ Ⓔ	17. Ⓐ Ⓑ Ⓒ Ⓓ Ⓔ	27. Ⓐ Ⓑ Ⓒ Ⓓ Ⓔ	37. Ⓐ Ⓑ Ⓒ Ⓓ Ⓔ
8. Ⓐ Ⓑ Ⓒ Ⓓ Ⓔ	18. Ⓐ Ⓑ Ⓒ Ⓓ Ⓔ	28. Ⓐ Ⓑ Ⓒ Ⓓ Ⓔ	38. Ⓐ Ⓑ Ⓒ Ⓓ Ⓔ
9. Ⓐ Ⓑ Ⓒ Ⓓ Ⓔ	19. Ⓐ Ⓑ Ⓒ Ⓓ Ⓔ	29. Ⓐ Ⓑ Ⓒ Ⓓ Ⓔ	
10. Ⓐ Ⓑ Ⓒ Ⓓ Ⓔ	20. Ⓐ Ⓑ Ⓒ Ⓓ Ⓔ	30. Ⓐ Ⓑ Ⓒ Ⓓ Ⓔ	

Section 2

1. Ⓐ Ⓑ Ⓒ Ⓓ Ⓔ	11. Ⓐ Ⓑ Ⓒ Ⓓ Ⓔ	21. Ⓐ Ⓑ Ⓒ Ⓓ Ⓔ	31. Ⓐ Ⓑ Ⓒ Ⓓ Ⓔ
2. Ⓐ Ⓑ Ⓒ Ⓓ Ⓔ	12. Ⓐ Ⓑ Ⓒ Ⓓ Ⓔ	22. Ⓐ Ⓑ Ⓒ Ⓓ Ⓔ	32. Ⓐ Ⓑ Ⓒ Ⓓ Ⓔ
3. Ⓐ Ⓑ Ⓒ Ⓓ Ⓔ	13. Ⓐ Ⓑ Ⓒ Ⓓ Ⓔ	23. Ⓐ Ⓑ Ⓒ Ⓓ Ⓔ	33. Ⓐ Ⓑ Ⓒ Ⓓ Ⓔ
4. Ⓐ Ⓑ Ⓒ Ⓓ Ⓔ	14. Ⓐ Ⓑ Ⓒ Ⓓ Ⓔ	24. Ⓐ Ⓑ Ⓒ Ⓓ Ⓔ	34. Ⓐ Ⓑ Ⓒ Ⓓ Ⓔ
5. Ⓐ Ⓑ Ⓒ Ⓓ Ⓔ	15. Ⓐ Ⓑ Ⓒ Ⓓ Ⓔ	25. Ⓐ Ⓑ Ⓒ Ⓓ Ⓔ	35. Ⓐ Ⓑ Ⓒ Ⓓ Ⓔ
6. Ⓐ Ⓑ Ⓒ Ⓓ Ⓔ	16. Ⓐ Ⓑ Ⓒ Ⓓ Ⓔ	26. Ⓐ Ⓑ Ⓒ Ⓓ Ⓔ	36. Ⓐ Ⓑ Ⓒ Ⓓ Ⓔ
7. Ⓐ Ⓑ Ⓒ Ⓓ Ⓔ	17. Ⓐ Ⓑ Ⓒ Ⓓ Ⓔ	27. Ⓐ Ⓑ Ⓒ Ⓓ Ⓔ	37. Ⓐ Ⓑ Ⓒ Ⓓ Ⓔ
8. Ⓐ Ⓑ Ⓒ Ⓓ Ⓔ	18. Ⓐ Ⓑ Ⓒ Ⓓ Ⓔ	28. Ⓐ Ⓑ Ⓒ Ⓓ Ⓔ	38. Ⓐ Ⓑ Ⓒ Ⓓ Ⓔ
9. Ⓐ Ⓑ Ⓒ Ⓓ Ⓔ	19. Ⓐ Ⓑ Ⓒ Ⓓ Ⓔ	29. Ⓐ Ⓑ Ⓒ Ⓓ Ⓔ	
10. Ⓐ Ⓑ Ⓒ Ⓓ Ⓔ	20. Ⓐ Ⓑ Ⓒ Ⓓ Ⓔ	30. Ⓐ Ⓑ Ⓒ Ⓓ Ⓔ	

Section 3

1. Ⓐ Ⓑ Ⓒ Ⓓ Ⓔ	11. Ⓐ Ⓑ Ⓒ Ⓓ Ⓔ	21. Ⓐ Ⓑ Ⓒ Ⓓ Ⓔ	31. Ⓐ Ⓑ Ⓒ Ⓓ Ⓔ
2. Ⓐ Ⓑ Ⓒ Ⓓ Ⓔ	12. Ⓐ Ⓑ Ⓒ Ⓓ Ⓔ	22. Ⓐ Ⓑ Ⓒ Ⓓ Ⓔ	32. Ⓐ Ⓑ Ⓒ Ⓓ Ⓔ
3. Ⓐ Ⓑ Ⓒ Ⓓ Ⓔ	13. Ⓐ Ⓑ Ⓒ Ⓓ Ⓔ	23. Ⓐ Ⓑ Ⓒ Ⓓ Ⓔ	33. Ⓐ Ⓑ Ⓒ Ⓓ Ⓔ
4. Ⓐ Ⓑ Ⓒ Ⓓ Ⓔ	14. Ⓐ Ⓑ Ⓒ Ⓓ Ⓔ	24. Ⓐ Ⓑ Ⓒ Ⓓ Ⓔ	34. Ⓐ Ⓑ Ⓒ Ⓓ Ⓔ
5. Ⓐ Ⓑ Ⓒ Ⓓ Ⓔ	15. Ⓐ Ⓑ Ⓒ Ⓓ Ⓔ	25. Ⓐ Ⓑ Ⓒ Ⓓ Ⓔ	35. Ⓐ Ⓑ Ⓒ Ⓓ Ⓔ
6. Ⓐ Ⓑ Ⓒ Ⓓ Ⓔ	16. Ⓐ Ⓑ Ⓒ Ⓓ Ⓔ	26. Ⓐ Ⓑ Ⓒ Ⓓ Ⓔ	36. Ⓐ Ⓑ Ⓒ Ⓓ Ⓔ
7. Ⓐ Ⓑ Ⓒ Ⓓ Ⓔ	17. Ⓐ Ⓑ Ⓒ Ⓓ Ⓔ	27. Ⓐ Ⓑ Ⓒ Ⓓ Ⓔ	37. Ⓐ Ⓑ Ⓒ Ⓓ Ⓔ
8. Ⓐ Ⓑ Ⓒ Ⓓ Ⓔ	18. Ⓐ Ⓑ Ⓒ Ⓓ Ⓔ	28. Ⓐ Ⓑ Ⓒ Ⓓ Ⓔ	38. Ⓐ Ⓑ Ⓒ Ⓓ Ⓔ
9. Ⓐ Ⓑ Ⓒ Ⓓ Ⓔ	19. Ⓐ Ⓑ Ⓒ Ⓓ Ⓔ	29. Ⓐ Ⓑ Ⓒ Ⓓ Ⓔ	
10. Ⓐ Ⓑ Ⓒ Ⓓ Ⓔ	20. Ⓐ Ⓑ Ⓒ Ⓓ Ⓔ	30. Ⓐ Ⓑ Ⓒ Ⓓ Ⓔ	

Section 4

1. Ⓐ Ⓑ Ⓒ Ⓓ Ⓔ	11. Ⓐ Ⓑ Ⓒ Ⓓ Ⓔ	21. Ⓐ Ⓑ Ⓒ Ⓓ Ⓔ	31. Ⓐ Ⓑ Ⓒ Ⓓ Ⓔ
2. Ⓐ Ⓑ Ⓒ Ⓓ Ⓔ	12. Ⓐ Ⓑ Ⓒ Ⓓ Ⓔ	22. Ⓐ Ⓑ Ⓒ Ⓓ Ⓔ	32. Ⓐ Ⓑ Ⓒ Ⓓ Ⓔ
3. Ⓐ Ⓑ Ⓒ Ⓓ Ⓔ	13. Ⓐ Ⓑ Ⓒ Ⓓ Ⓔ	23. Ⓐ Ⓑ Ⓒ Ⓓ Ⓔ	33. Ⓐ Ⓑ Ⓒ Ⓓ Ⓔ
4. Ⓐ Ⓑ Ⓒ Ⓓ Ⓔ	14. Ⓐ Ⓑ Ⓒ Ⓓ Ⓔ	24. Ⓐ Ⓑ Ⓒ Ⓓ Ⓔ	34. Ⓐ Ⓑ Ⓒ Ⓓ Ⓔ
5. Ⓐ Ⓑ Ⓒ Ⓓ Ⓔ	15. Ⓐ Ⓑ Ⓒ Ⓓ Ⓔ	25. Ⓐ Ⓑ Ⓒ Ⓓ Ⓔ	35. Ⓐ Ⓑ Ⓒ Ⓓ Ⓔ
6. Ⓐ Ⓑ Ⓒ Ⓓ Ⓔ	16. Ⓐ Ⓑ Ⓒ Ⓓ Ⓔ	26. Ⓐ Ⓑ Ⓒ Ⓓ Ⓔ	36. Ⓐ Ⓑ Ⓒ Ⓓ Ⓔ
7. Ⓐ Ⓑ Ⓒ Ⓓ Ⓔ	17. Ⓐ Ⓑ Ⓒ Ⓓ Ⓔ	27. Ⓐ Ⓑ Ⓒ Ⓓ Ⓔ	37. Ⓐ Ⓑ Ⓒ Ⓓ Ⓔ
8. Ⓐ Ⓑ Ⓒ Ⓓ Ⓔ	18. Ⓐ Ⓑ Ⓒ Ⓓ Ⓔ	28. Ⓐ Ⓑ Ⓒ Ⓓ Ⓔ	38. Ⓐ Ⓑ Ⓒ Ⓓ Ⓔ
9. Ⓐ Ⓑ Ⓒ Ⓓ Ⓔ	19. Ⓐ Ⓑ Ⓒ Ⓓ Ⓔ	29. Ⓐ Ⓑ Ⓒ Ⓓ Ⓔ	
10. Ⓐ Ⓑ Ⓒ Ⓓ Ⓔ	20. Ⓐ Ⓑ Ⓒ Ⓓ Ⓔ	30. Ⓐ Ⓑ Ⓒ Ⓓ Ⓔ	

Section 5

1. Ⓐ Ⓑ Ⓒ Ⓓ Ⓔ	11. Ⓐ Ⓑ Ⓒ Ⓓ Ⓔ	21. Ⓐ Ⓑ Ⓒ Ⓓ Ⓔ	31. Ⓐ Ⓑ Ⓒ Ⓓ Ⓔ
2. Ⓐ Ⓑ Ⓒ Ⓓ Ⓔ	12. Ⓐ Ⓑ Ⓒ Ⓓ Ⓔ	22. Ⓐ Ⓑ Ⓒ Ⓓ Ⓔ	32. Ⓐ Ⓑ Ⓒ Ⓓ Ⓔ
3. Ⓐ Ⓑ Ⓒ Ⓓ Ⓔ	13. Ⓐ Ⓑ Ⓒ Ⓓ Ⓔ	23. Ⓐ Ⓑ Ⓒ Ⓓ Ⓔ	33. Ⓐ Ⓑ Ⓒ Ⓓ Ⓔ
4. Ⓐ Ⓑ Ⓒ Ⓓ Ⓔ	14. Ⓐ Ⓑ Ⓒ Ⓓ Ⓔ	24. Ⓐ Ⓑ Ⓒ Ⓓ Ⓔ	34. Ⓐ Ⓑ Ⓒ Ⓓ Ⓔ
5. Ⓐ Ⓑ Ⓒ Ⓓ Ⓔ	15. Ⓐ Ⓑ Ⓒ Ⓓ Ⓔ	25. Ⓐ Ⓑ Ⓒ Ⓓ Ⓔ	35. Ⓐ Ⓑ Ⓒ Ⓓ Ⓔ
6. Ⓐ Ⓑ Ⓒ Ⓓ Ⓔ	16. Ⓐ Ⓑ Ⓒ Ⓓ Ⓔ	26. Ⓐ Ⓑ Ⓒ Ⓓ Ⓔ	36. Ⓐ Ⓑ Ⓒ Ⓓ Ⓔ
7. Ⓐ Ⓑ Ⓒ Ⓓ Ⓔ	17. Ⓐ Ⓑ Ⓒ Ⓓ Ⓔ	27. Ⓐ Ⓑ Ⓒ Ⓓ Ⓔ	37. Ⓐ Ⓑ Ⓒ Ⓓ Ⓔ
8. Ⓐ Ⓑ Ⓒ Ⓓ Ⓔ	18. Ⓐ Ⓑ Ⓒ Ⓓ Ⓔ	28. Ⓐ Ⓑ Ⓒ Ⓓ Ⓔ	38. Ⓐ Ⓑ Ⓒ Ⓓ Ⓔ
9. Ⓐ Ⓑ Ⓒ Ⓓ Ⓔ	19. Ⓐ Ⓑ Ⓒ Ⓓ Ⓔ	29. Ⓐ Ⓑ Ⓒ Ⓓ Ⓔ	
10. Ⓐ Ⓑ Ⓒ Ⓓ Ⓔ	20. Ⓐ Ⓑ Ⓒ Ⓓ Ⓔ	30. Ⓐ Ⓑ Ⓒ Ⓓ Ⓔ	

Section 6

1. Ⓐ Ⓑ Ⓒ Ⓓ Ⓔ	11. Ⓐ Ⓑ Ⓒ Ⓓ Ⓔ	21. Ⓐ Ⓑ Ⓒ Ⓓ Ⓔ	31. Ⓐ Ⓑ Ⓒ Ⓓ Ⓔ
2. Ⓐ Ⓑ Ⓒ Ⓓ Ⓔ	12. Ⓐ Ⓑ Ⓒ Ⓓ Ⓔ	22. Ⓐ Ⓑ Ⓒ Ⓓ Ⓔ	32. Ⓐ Ⓑ Ⓒ Ⓓ Ⓔ
3. Ⓐ Ⓑ Ⓒ Ⓓ Ⓔ	13. Ⓐ Ⓑ Ⓒ Ⓓ Ⓔ	23. Ⓐ Ⓑ Ⓒ Ⓓ Ⓔ	33. Ⓐ Ⓑ Ⓒ Ⓓ Ⓔ
4. Ⓐ Ⓑ Ⓒ Ⓓ Ⓔ	14. Ⓐ Ⓑ Ⓒ Ⓓ Ⓔ	24. Ⓐ Ⓑ Ⓒ Ⓓ Ⓔ	34. Ⓐ Ⓑ Ⓒ Ⓓ Ⓔ
5. Ⓐ Ⓑ Ⓒ Ⓓ Ⓔ	15. Ⓐ Ⓑ Ⓒ Ⓓ Ⓔ	25. Ⓐ Ⓑ Ⓒ Ⓓ Ⓔ	35. Ⓐ Ⓑ Ⓒ Ⓓ Ⓔ
6. Ⓐ Ⓑ Ⓒ Ⓓ Ⓔ	16. Ⓐ Ⓑ Ⓒ Ⓓ Ⓔ	26. Ⓐ Ⓑ Ⓒ Ⓓ Ⓔ	36. Ⓐ Ⓑ Ⓒ Ⓓ Ⓔ
7. Ⓐ Ⓑ Ⓒ Ⓓ Ⓔ	17. Ⓐ Ⓑ Ⓒ Ⓓ Ⓔ	27. Ⓐ Ⓑ Ⓒ Ⓓ Ⓔ	37. Ⓐ Ⓑ Ⓒ Ⓓ Ⓔ
8. Ⓐ Ⓑ Ⓒ Ⓓ Ⓔ	18. Ⓐ Ⓑ Ⓒ Ⓓ Ⓔ	28. Ⓐ Ⓑ Ⓒ Ⓓ Ⓔ	38. Ⓐ Ⓑ Ⓒ Ⓓ Ⓔ
9. Ⓐ Ⓑ Ⓒ Ⓓ Ⓔ	19. Ⓐ Ⓑ Ⓒ Ⓓ Ⓔ	29. Ⓐ Ⓑ Ⓒ Ⓓ Ⓔ	
10. Ⓐ Ⓑ Ⓒ Ⓓ Ⓔ	20. Ⓐ Ⓑ Ⓒ Ⓓ Ⓔ	30. Ⓐ Ⓑ Ⓒ Ⓓ Ⓔ	

Section 7

1. Ⓐ Ⓑ Ⓒ Ⓓ Ⓔ	11. Ⓐ Ⓑ Ⓒ Ⓓ Ⓔ	21. Ⓐ Ⓑ Ⓒ Ⓓ Ⓔ	31. Ⓐ Ⓑ Ⓒ Ⓓ Ⓔ
2. Ⓐ Ⓑ Ⓒ Ⓓ Ⓔ	12. Ⓐ Ⓑ Ⓒ Ⓓ Ⓔ	22. Ⓐ Ⓑ Ⓒ Ⓓ Ⓔ	32. Ⓐ Ⓑ Ⓒ Ⓓ Ⓔ
3. Ⓐ Ⓑ Ⓒ Ⓓ Ⓔ	13. Ⓐ Ⓑ Ⓒ Ⓓ Ⓔ	23. Ⓐ Ⓑ Ⓒ Ⓓ Ⓔ	33. Ⓐ Ⓑ Ⓒ Ⓓ Ⓔ
4. Ⓐ Ⓑ Ⓒ Ⓓ Ⓔ	14. Ⓐ Ⓑ Ⓒ Ⓓ Ⓔ	24. Ⓐ Ⓑ Ⓒ Ⓓ Ⓔ	34. Ⓐ Ⓑ Ⓒ Ⓓ Ⓔ
5. Ⓐ Ⓑ Ⓒ Ⓓ Ⓔ	15. Ⓐ Ⓑ Ⓒ Ⓓ Ⓔ	25. Ⓐ Ⓑ Ⓒ Ⓓ Ⓔ	35. Ⓐ Ⓑ Ⓒ Ⓓ Ⓔ
6. Ⓐ Ⓑ Ⓒ Ⓓ Ⓔ	16. Ⓐ Ⓑ Ⓒ Ⓓ Ⓔ	26. Ⓐ Ⓑ Ⓒ Ⓓ Ⓔ	36. Ⓐ Ⓑ Ⓒ Ⓓ Ⓔ
7. Ⓐ Ⓑ Ⓒ Ⓓ Ⓔ	17. Ⓐ Ⓑ Ⓒ Ⓓ Ⓔ	27. Ⓐ Ⓑ Ⓒ Ⓓ Ⓔ	37. Ⓐ Ⓑ Ⓒ Ⓓ Ⓔ
8. Ⓐ Ⓑ Ⓒ Ⓓ Ⓔ	18. Ⓐ Ⓑ Ⓒ Ⓓ Ⓔ	28. Ⓐ Ⓑ Ⓒ Ⓓ Ⓔ	38. Ⓐ Ⓑ Ⓒ Ⓓ Ⓔ
9. Ⓐ Ⓑ Ⓒ Ⓓ Ⓔ	19. Ⓐ Ⓑ Ⓒ Ⓓ Ⓔ	29. Ⓐ Ⓑ Ⓒ Ⓓ Ⓔ	
10. Ⓐ Ⓑ Ⓒ Ⓓ Ⓔ	20. Ⓐ Ⓑ Ⓒ Ⓓ Ⓔ	30. Ⓐ Ⓑ Ⓒ Ⓓ Ⓔ	

Remove answer sheet by cutting on dotted line

DIAGNOSTIC TEST

SECTION 1

Time—30 minutes

38 Questions

Directions: Each sentence below has one or two blanks, each blank indicating that something has been omitted. Beneath the sentence are five lettered words or sets of words. Choose the word or set of words for each blank that best fits the meaning of the sentence as a whole.

1. Any numerical description of the development of the human population cannot avoid -------, simply because there has never been a census of all the people in the world.

   (A) analysis
   (B) conjecture
   (C) disorientation
   (D) corroboration
   (E) statistics

2. Many species of intertidal fish have developed ------- abilities that enable them to ------- a particular location, generally a tide pool, that provides suitable refuge.

   (A) foraging...do without
   (B) compensatory...aspire to
   (C) natural...vanish from
   (D) singular...escape from
   (E) homing...return to

3. There are any number of theories to explain these events and, since even the experts disagree, it is ------- the rest of us in our role as responsible scholars to ------- dogmatic statements.

   (A) paradoxical for...abstain from
   (B) arrogant of...compensate with
   (C) incumbent on...refrain from
   (D) opportune for...quarrel over
   (E) appropriate for...issue forth

4. It may be useful to think of character in fiction as a function of two ------- impulses: the impulse to individualize and the impulse to -------.

   (A) analogous...humanize
   (B) disparate...aggrandize
   (C) divergent...typify
   (D) comparable...delineate
   (E) related...moralize

5. Relatively few politicians willingly forsake center stage, although a touch of ------- on their parts now and again might well increase their popularity with the voting public.

   (A) garrulity
   (B) misanthropy
   (C) self-effacement
   (D) self-dramatization
   (E) self-doubt

6. It is this tightly circumscribed choice of scene that gives to Mrs. Woolf's novels, despite her modernity of technique and insight, their odd and delicious air of -------, as of some small village world, as bright and vivid and perfect in its ------- as a miniature.

   (A) anachronism...transience
   (B) parochialism...tininess
   (C) cynicism...rusticity
   (D) intrigue...antiquity
   (E) fragility...petiteness

7. Lacking the time to examine the treatise in its entirety, the editors asked the author to provide them with ------- instead.

   (A) a compendium
   (B) a dissertation
   (C) an elaboration
   (D) a facsimile
   (E) an exegesis

Directions: In each of the following questions, a related pair of words or phrases is followed by five lettered pairs of words or phrases. Select the lettered pair that best expresses a relationship similar to that expressed in the original pair.

8. CLASP : BRACELET ::
   (A) hook : coat
   (B) buckle : belt
   (C) diamond : ring
   (D) wrist : watch
   (E) cuff : trousers

9. SEDAN : AUTOMOBILE ::
   (A) hangar : airplane
   (B) bedspread : bed
   (C) rocker : chair
   (D) rung : ladder
   (E) marble : statue

10. CIRCUITOUS : ROUTE ::
   (A) problematic : solution
   (B) devious : argument
   (C) elliptical : brevity
   (D) judicious : selection
   (E) profound : depth

11. PARDON : OFFENSE ::
    (A) repent : sin
    (B) detect : violation
    (C) arraign : indictment
    (D) forgive : wrong
    (E) surrender : fugitive

12. NONPLUSSED : BAFFLEMENT ::
    (A) discomfited : embarrassment
    (B) parsimonious : extravagance
    (C) disgruntled : contentment
    (D) despicable : contempt
    (E) surly : harassment

13. GULLY : CANYON ::
    (A) eagle : bird
    (B) cliff : granite
    (C) pebble : boulder
    (D) detour : road
    (E) shore : lake

14. HELPFUL : OFFICIOUS ::
    (A) dutiful : assiduous
    (B) effusive : gushing
    (C) gullible : incredulous
    (D) enigmatic : dumbfounded
    (E) deferential : sycophantic

15. BRONZE : PATINA ::
    (A) wood : veneer
    (B) plaque : honor
    (C) mold : yeast
    (D) iron : rust
    (E) lead : tin

16. MELLIFLUOUS : CACOPHONY ::
    (A) dulcet : euphony
    (B) compliant : obsequiousness
    (C) fragrant : noisomeness
    (D) florid : embellishment
    (E) thrifty : parsimony

Directions: Each passage in this group is followed by questions based on its content. After reading a passage, choose the best answer to each question. Answer all questions following a passage on the basis of what is <u>stated</u> or <u>implied</u> in that passage.

James's first novels used conventional narrative techniques: explicit characterization, action which related events in distinctly phased sequences, settings firmly outlined and specifically described. But this method gradually gave way to a subtler, more deliberate, more diffuse style of accumulation of minutely discriminated details whose total significance the reader can grasp only by constant attention and sensitive inference. His later novels play down scenes of abrupt and prominent action, and do not so much offer a succession of sharp shocks as slow piecemeal additions of perception. The curtain is not suddenly drawn back from shrouded things, but is slowly moved away.

Such a technique is suited to James's essential subject, which is not human action itself but the states of mind which produce and are produced by human actions and interactions. James was less interested in what characters do, than in the moral and psychological antecedents, realizations, and consequences which attend their doings. This is why he more often speaks of "cases" than of actions. His stories, therefore, grow more and more lengthy while the actions they relate grow simpler and less visible; not because they are crammed with adventitious and secondary events, digressive relief, or supernumerary characters, as overstuffed novels of action are; but because he presents in such exhaustive detail every nuance of his situation. Commonly the interest of a novel is in the variety and excitement of visible actions building up to a climactic event which will settle the outward destinies of characters with storybook promise of permanence. A James novel, however, possesses its characteristic interest in carrying the reader through a rich analysis of the mental adjustments of characters to the realities of their personal situations as they are slowly revealed to them through exploration and chance discovery.

17. The passage supplies information for answering which of the following questions?

    (A) Did James originate the so-called psychological novel?
    (B) Is conventional narrative technique strictly chronological in recounting action?
    (C) Can novels lacking overtly dramatic incident sustain the reader's interest?
    (D) Were James's later novels more acceptable to the general public than his earlier ones?
    (E) Is James unique in his predilection for exploring psychological nuances of character?

18. According to the passage, James's later novels differ from his earlier ones in their

    (A) preoccupation with specifically described settings
    (B) ever-increasing concision and tautness of plot
    (C) levels of moral and psychological complexity
    (D) development of rising action to a climax
    (E) subordination of psychological exploration to dramatic effect

19. The author's attitude towards the novel of action appears to be one of

    (A) pointed indignation
    (B) detached neutrality
    (C) scathing derision
    (D) strong partisanship
    (E) decided disapprobation

The theory of plate tectonics describes the motions of the lithosphere, the comparatively rigid outer layer of the earth that includes all the crust and part of the underlying mantle. The lithosphere is divided into a few dozen plates of various sizes and shapes; in general the plates are in motion with respect to one another. A mid-ocean ridge is a boundary between plates where new lithospheric material is injected from below. As the plates diverge from a mid-ocean ridge they slide on a more yielding layer at the base of the lithosphere.

Since the size of the earth is essentially constant, new lithosphere can be created at the mid-ocean ridges only if an equal amount of lithospheric material is consumed elsewhere. The site of this destruction is another kind of plate boundary: a subduction zone. There one plate dives under another and is reincorporated into the mantle. Both kinds of plate boundary are associated with fault systems, earthquakes and volcanism, but the kinds of geologic activity observed at the two boundaries are quite different.

The idea of sea-floor spreading actually preceded the theory of plate tectonics. The sea-floor spreading hypothesis was formulated chiefly by Harry H. Hess of Princeton University in the early 1960s. In its original version it described the creation and destruction of ocean floor, but it did not specify rigid lithospheric plates. The hypothesis was soon substantiated by the discovery that periodic reversals of the earth's magnetic field are recorded in the oceanic crust. An explanation of this process devised by F.J. Vine and D.H. Matthews of Princeton is now generally accepted. As magma rises under the mid-ocean ridge, ferromagnetic minerals in the magma become magnetized in the direction of the geomagnetic field. When the magma cools and solidifies, the direction and the polarity of the field are preserved in the magnetized volcanic rock. Reversals of the field give rise to a series of magnetic stripes running parallel to the axis of the rift. The oceanic crust thus serves as a magnetic tape recording of the history of the geomagnetic field. Because the boundaries between stripes are associated with reversals of the magnetic field that can be dated independently, the width of the stripes indicates the rate of sea-floor spreading. (Precisely how the earth's magnetic field reverses at intervals of from 10,000 to about a million years continues to be one of the great mysteries of geology.)

It follows from the theory of sea-floor spreading that many of the most interesting geologic features of the earth's surface are to be found on the ocean floor. The investigation of such features has been furthered in recent years by the development of deep-diving manned submersibles. In particular the U.S. research submersible *Alvin,* operated by the Woods Hole Oceanographic Institution, has proved to be a valuable tool for studies of the sea bed. A geologist in the *Alvin* can collect rock samples and document in detail the setting of each rock. For the first time a marine geologist can have maps of a site as precise as those of a geologist on land.

20. The author's primary purpose in the passage is to

(A) question established data
(B) describe current explorations
(C) trace the development of a theory
(D) propose an alternative solution
(E) explain the reasons behind a phenomenon

21. The passage would be most likely to appear in a

(A) congressional report advocating the continued funding of oceanographic studies
(B) geological research report focused on the likelihood of volcanism along coastal regions
(C) pamphlet designed to acquaint visitors to Woods Hole with the capabilities of deep-diving manned submersibles
(D) scholarly monograph proposing an explanation for the periodic reversals of the earth's magnetic field
(E) scientific journal article summarizing recent advances in applying plate tectonic theory to marine geology

22. According to the passage, a mid-ocean ridge differs from a subduction zone in that

(A) it marks the boundary line between neighboring plates
(B) only the former is located on the ocean floor
(C) it is a site for the emergence of new lithospheric material
(D) the former periodically disrupts the earth's geomagnetic field
(E) it is involved with lithospheric destruction rather than lithospheric creation

23. It can be inferred from the passage that as new lithospheric material is injected from below

(A) the plates become immobilized in a kind of gridlock
(B) the new material is incorporated into an underwater mountain ridge
(C) the earth's total mass is altered
(D) the magnetic polarity of the new material is reversed
(E) the immediately adjacent plates sink

24. The passage contains information that would answer which of the following questions about the theory of sea-floor spreading and the history of the geomagnetic field?

I. What is the minimum known time span between reversals of the earth's magnetic field?
II. What mechanism is responsible for the magnetic field's changes in polarity?
III. Can the pace of sea-floor spreading be determined from current geomagnetic data?

(A) I only
(B) III only
(C) I and II only
(D) I and III only
(E) I, II, and III

25. It can be inferred from the passage that a large increase in the creation of new lithospheric material would result in

(A) at least a slight decrease in activity along the subduction zones
(B) at the most a slight increase in activity along the subduction zones
(C) a correspondingly large increase in activity along the subduction zones
(D) a cessation of activity along the subduction zones
(E) no change in the level of activity along the subduction zones

26. According to the passage, lithospheric material at the site of a subduction zone

(A) rises and is polarized
(B) sinks and is absorbed
(C) slides and is injected
(D) spreads and is reincorporated
(E) diverges and is consumed

27. The passage most directly suggests that, before the recent underwater explorations involving manned submersibles were undertaken, marine geologists

(A) were negligent in making charts of undersea sites
(B) underestimated the importance of the lithospheric plates
(C) labored under a disadvantage compared to land geologists
(D) had adequate access to those portions of the sea bed under study
(E) were ignorant of the sea-floor spreading hypothesis

Directions: Each question below consists of a word printed in capital letters, followed by five lettered words or phrases. Choose the lettered word or phrase that is most nearly opposite in meaning to the word in capital letters.

Since some of the questions require you to distinguish fine shades of meaning, be sure to consider all the choices before deciding which one is best.

28. DETERIORATE:
(A) hasten
(B) demolish
(C) alter
(D) unify
(E) improve

29. EVASIVE:
(A) frank
(B) serene
(C) pensive
(D) mistaken
(E) exuberant

30. STREW:
(A) deflate
(B) collect
(C) weaken
(D) cleanse
(E) bolster

31. PRODIGAL:
(A) nomad
(B) sycophant
(C) gifted child
(D) economical person
(E) antagonist

32. EQUIVOCATE:
(A) yield
(B) distinguish
(C) condescend
(D) pledge
(E) denounce

33. CRASS:
(A) small
(B) refined
(C) cheerful
(D) modest
(E) liberal

34. ARTIFICE:
(A) edifice
(B) sincerity
(C) prejudice
(D) creativity
(E) affirmation

35. OPULENCE:
(A) transience
(B) penury
(C) solitude
(D) generosity
(E) transparency

36. UNTENABLE:
(A) false
(B) precise
(C) circumscribed
(D) defensible
(E) hypothetical

37. SEDULOUS:
(A) pointless
(B) weighty
(C) lugubrious
(D) cursory
(E) tangential

38. DISABUSE:
(A) maltreat
(B) violate
(C) cancel
(D) deceive
(E) involve

S T O P

IF YOU FINISH BEFORE TIME IS CALLED, YOU MAY CHECK YOUR WORK ON THIS SECTION ONLY.
DO NOT WORK ON ANY OTHER SECTION IN THE TEST.

SECTION 2

Time—30 minutes

38 Questions

Directions: Each sentence below has one or two blanks, each blank indicating that something has been omitted. Beneath the sentence are five lettered words or sets of words. Choose the word or set of words for each blank that best fits the meaning of the sentence as a whole.

1. There was so much ------ material in the argument, ideas dragged in without reference to the case, that it was singularly ------ to grasp the budding lawyer's point.

   (A) exceptional...unrewarding
   (B) variegated...effortless
   (C) hypothetical...superfluous
   (D) superficial...irrelevant
   (E) extraneous...difficult

2. Since the propensity to migrate has persisted in every epoch, its explanation requires a theory ------- any particular period of time.

   (A) tailored to
   (B) unconscious of
   (C) inapplicable to
   (D) independent of
   (E) anomalous in

3. The earth is a planet bathed in light; it is therefore ------- that many of the living organisms that have evolved on the earth have ------- the biologically advantageous capacity to trap light energy.

   (A) anomalous...engendered
   (B) unsurprising...developed
   (C) predictable...forfeited
   (D) problematic...exhibited
   (E) expectable...relinquished

4. According to one optimistic hypothesis, the dense concentration of entrepreneurs and services in the cities would incubate new functions, ------- them, and finally export them to other areas, and so the cities, forever breeding fresh ideas, would ------- themselves repeatedly.

   (A) immunize...perpetuate
   (B) isolate...revitalize
   (C) foster...deplete
   (D) spawn...imitate
   (E) nurture...renew

5. Man is a ------- animal, and much more so in his mind than in his body: he may like to go alone for a walk, but he hates to stand alone in his -------.

   (A) gregarious...opinions
   (B) conceited...vanity
   (C) singular...uniqueness
   (D) solitary...thoughts
   (E) nomadic...footsteps

6. Although Mrs. Proudie ------- an interest in the spiritual well-being of the parishioners, in actuality her concern for their welfare was so ------- as to be practically nonexistent.

   (A) confessed...circumstantial
   (B) manifested...exemplary
   (C) simulated...profound
   (D) feigned...negligible
   (E) expressed...moribund

7. The term *baroque*, originally applied to the lavishly and grotesquely ornamented style of architecture that succeeded the Renaissance, is used generally in literary criticism to describe excessive or grandiloquent works that lack ------- of style.

   (A) diversity
   (B) economy
   (C) prolixity
   (D) adornment
   (E) comprehension

Directions: In each of the following questions, a related pair of words or phrases is followed by five lettered pairs of words or phrases. Select the lettered pair that best expresses a relationship similar to that expressed in the original pair.

8. PROLOGUE : PLAY ::
   (A) chapter : novel
   (B) overture : opera
   (C) intermezzo : symphony
   (D) epilogue : oration
   (E) gesture : pantomime

9. SERRATIONS : SAW ::
   (A) incisions : scalpel
   (B) butchery : cleaver
   (C) mortar : trowel
   (D) cogs : gear
   (E) division : ruler

10. SPIKE : SLEDGE ::
    (A) runner : sleigh
    (B) pole : ski
    (C) nail : hammer
    (D) clip : paper
    (E) trestle : train

11. THIRST : DRIVE ::
    (A) inebriety : excess
    (B) success : ambition
    (C) indifference : passion
    (D) taste : gusto
    (E) smell : sense

12. EPHEMERAL : PERMANENCE ::
    (A) erratic : predictability
    (B) immaculate : cleanliness
    (C) commendable : reputation
    (D) spurious : emulation
    (E) mandatory : obedience

13. CHAFF : WHEAT ::
    (A) mote : dust
    (B) gold : lead
    (C) dregs : wine
    (D) loaf : bread
    (E) yolk : egg

14. OGLE : OBSERVE ::
    (A) haggle : outbid
    (B) clamor : dispute
    (C) discern : perceive
    (D) flaunt : display
    (E) glare : glower

15. ABSTEMIOUS : ABSTINENCE ::
    (A) irascible : militancy
    (B) gregarious : reticence
    (C) truculent : dogmatism
    (D) comatose : sobriety
    (E) pusillanimous : cravenness

16. INELUCTABLE : AVOID ::
    (A) ineffable : utter
    (B) impalpable : desire
    (C) impermeable : endure
    (D) irascible : provoke
    (E) irreconcilable : estrange

Directions: Each passage in this group is followed by questions based on its content. After reading a passage, choose the best answer to each question. Answer all questions following a passage on the basis of what is stated or implied in that passage.

During the decade of 1880–1890 it was becoming increasingly evident that the factors which had brought about the existence of two separate suffrage institutions were steadily diminishing in
(5) importance.

The National Woman Suffrage Association had been launched by the intellectually irrepressible Elizabeth Cady Stanton and the ever catholic Susan B. Anthony. Both were ready to work with any-
(10) one, whatever their views on other matters, as long as they wholeheartedly espoused woman suffrage. Consequently in its earlier years the National was both aggressive and unorthodox. It damned both Republicans and Democrats who brushed the suf-
(15) frage question aside. It was willing to take up the cudgels for distressed women whatever their circumstances, be they "fallen women," divorce cases, or underpaid seamstresses.

The American Woman Suffrage Association, by
(20) contrast, took its tone and outlook from a New England which had turned its back on those fiery days when abolitionists, men and women alike, had stood up to angry mobs. Its advocacy of worthy causes was highly selective. Lucy Stone was not
(25) interested in trade unionism and wished to keep the suffrage cause untarnished by concern with divorce or "the social evil." The very epitome of the American's attitude was its most distinguished convert and leader, Julia Ward Howe – erudite, honored
(30) lay preacher, the revered author of "The Battle Hymn of the Republic," who cast a highly desirable aura of prestige and propriety over the women's cause.

It was not that Mrs. Howe in herself made suf-
(35) frage respectable; she was a symbol of the forces that were drawing the suffrage movement into the camp of decorum. American society was becoming rapidly polarized. The middle class was learning to identify organized labor with social turmoil. A
(40) succession of strikes during the depression of 1873–1878, in textiles, mining, and railroads, culminated in the Great Railroad Strike of 1877 involving nearly 100,000 workers from the Atlantic coast to the Mississippi valley; they did not help
(45) to reassure women taught by press and pulpit to identify any type of militancy with radicalism. Nor was this trend allayed by the hysteria whipped up over the Molly Maguire trials for secret conspiracy among Pennsylvania coal miners, or the alleged
(50) communistic influences at work in such growing organizations as the Knights of Labor and the A.F. of L. The existence of a small number of socialists was used to smear all organized labor with the taint of "anarchism." The crowning touch took place
(55) during the widespread agitation for an eight-hour day in 1886 when a bomb, thrown by a hand unknown to this day into a radical meeting in Chicago's Haymarket Square, touched off a nationwide wave of panic.
(60) The steady trend of the suffrage movement toward the conservative and the conventional during the last twenty years of the nineteenth century must be viewed in this setting, in order to avoid the misconception that a few conservative women took
(65) it over, through their own superior ability and the passivity of the former militants. Even the latter were changing their views, judging by their actions. It was one thing to challenge the proprieties at the Centennial of 1876; ten years later it
(70) would have been inconceivable even to the women who took part in the demonstration. Susan Anthony herself would have thought twice about flouting Federal election laws and going to jail in an era which witnessed the Haymarket hysteria.

17. The author's primary purpose in the passage is to

    (A) contrast Susan B. Anthony with Julia Ward Howe
    (B) recount the advances in the suffrage movement from 1880 to 1890
    (C) account for the changes occurring in the suffrage movement from 1880 to 1890
    (D) explain the growing divisions within the women's movement
    (E) point out aspects of the suffrage movement that exist in contemporary feminism

18. Which of the following statements is most compatible with the early principles of the National as described in the passage?

    (A) Advocates of suffrage should maintain their distance from socially embarrassing "allies."
    (B) Marital and economic issues are inappropriate concerns for the suffrage movement.
    (C) Propriety of behavior should characterize representatives of the women's cause.
    (D) A nominal espousal of woman suffrage is worthy of suffragist support.
    (E) The concerns of all afflicted women are the concerns of the suffrage movement.

19. The passage singles out Julia Ward Howe as an example of

    (A) a venerated figurehead
    (B) an overzealous advocate
    (C) a heterodox thinker
    (D) an ordained cleric
    (E) a militant activist

20. Which of the following titles best describes the content of the passage?

    (A) Trade Unionism and the Suffrage Movement
    (B) Egalitarianism at the Close of the Nineteenth Century
    (C) Rifts in the Woman Suffrage Movement
    (D) Diminution of Radicalism in the Woman Suffrage Movement
    (E) Political Polarization in American Society

21. The author's attitude toward the public reaction to the Molly Maguire trials is that the reaction was

    (A) appropriate
    (B) disorganized
    (C) overwrought
    (D) necessary
    (E) understated

22. As used in the passage, the phrase "ever catholic" (line 8) refers primarily to Anthony's

    (A) deep religious beliefs
    (B) inclusive sympathies
    (C) willingness to work
    (D) wholehearted feminism
    (E) parochial outlook

23. The author stresses the growing antiradical bias of the American middle class during the decade 1880–1890 in order to

    (A) question a trend that proved destructive to the suffrage movement
    (B) explain the unexpected emergence of an able body of conservative leaders
    (C) refute the contention that Anthony was unchanged by her experiences
    (D) correct a misapprehension about changes in the suffrage movement
    (E) excuse the growing lack of militancy on the part of the National

24. The passage suggests that, by 1890, attempts to effect woman suffrage by violating the proprieties and defying Federal laws would probably have been viewed even by movement members with

    (A) indifference
    (B) defiance
    (C) disapprobation
    (D) respect
    (E) optimism

    Perhaps the first point to grasp [about natural selection] is that a complex creature, or even a complex part of a creature, such as the eye, did not arise in one evolutionary step. Rather it evolved through a *series* of small steps. Exactly what is meant by small is not necessarily obvious since the growth of an organism is controlled by an elaborate program, written in its genes. A small change in a key part of the program can make a rather large difference. For example, an alteration in one particular gene in *Drosophila* can produce a fruit fly with legs in the place of its antennae.
    Each small step is caused by a random alteration in the genetic instructions. Many of these random alterations may do the organism no good (some may even kill it before it is born), but occasionally a particular chance alteration may give that particular organism a selective advantage. This means that in the last analysis the organism will, on average, leave more offspring than it would otherwise do. If this advantage persists in its descendants then this beneficial mutant will gradually, over many generations, spread through the population. In favorable cases, every individual will come to possess the improved version of the gene. The older version will have been eliminated. Natural selection is thus a beautiful mechanism for turning rare events (strictly, favorable rare events) into common ones.

25. The author's primary purpose in introducing the reference to *Drosophila* is to

    (A) indicate his familiarity with laboratory experiments on fruit flies
    (B) describe the process by which a genetic alteration transfroms the body
    (C) provide a vivid illustration of extreme effects of a slight genetic change

(D) offer a paradigm of favorable genetic mutation
(E) demonstrate that it took several evolutionary steps for the fruit fly to reach its present form

26. The passage indicates that the nature of a selective advantage is

(A) immutable
(B) reproductive
(C) limited
(D) mental
(E) inequitable

27. The author's attitude towards the process of natural selection can best be described as one of

(A) mild skepticism
(B) puzzled fascination
(C) controlled apprehension
(D) appreciative admiration
(E) lofty detachment

Directions: Each question below consists of a word printed in capital letters, followed by five lettered words or phrases. Choose the lettered word or phrase that is most nearly <u>opposite</u> in meaning to the word in capital letters.

Since some of the questions require you to distinguish fine shades of meaning, be sure to consider all the choices before deciding which one is best.

28. TERMINATE:
   (A) depart
   (B) prevent
   (C) begin
   (D) hasten
   (E) change

29. PROTRACT:
   (A) abbreviate
   (B) distract
   (C) reject
   (D) stabilize
   (E) oppose

30. VOLUBILITY:
   (A) shabbiness
   (B) brevity
   (C) disparity
   (D) subtlety
   (E) lucidity

31. LATE-BLOOMING:
   (A) flourishing
   (B) blatant
   (C) punctilious
   (D) embryonic
   (E) precocious

32. HONE:
   (A) broaden
   (B) twist
   (C) dull
   (D) weld
   (E) break

33. PHLEGMATIC:
   (A) dogmatic
   (B) ardent
   (C) haphazard
   (D) self-assured
   (E) abstracted

34. BANALITY:
   (A) tentative interpretation
   (B) concise summation
   (C) accurate delineation
   (D) laudatory remark
   (E) novel expression

35. ERUDITE:
   (A) unhealthy
   (B) ignorant
   (C) impolite
   (D) indifferent
   (E) imprecise

36. PLETHORA:
   (A) despair
   (B) denial
   (C) avarice
   (D) aversion
   (E) scarcity

37. CURRENCY:
   (A) refractoriness
   (B) obsolescence
   (C) artificiality
   (D) insolvency
   (E) fluency

38. SKIRT:
   (A) embroider
   (B) revert
   (C) address
   (D) disport
   (E) brook

S T O P

IF YOU FINISH BEFORE TIME IS CALLED, YOU MAY CHECK YOUR WORK ON THIS SECTION ONLY.
DO NOT WORK ON ANY OTHER SECTION IN THE TEST.

SECTION 3

Time—30 minutes

30 Questions

Numbers: All numbers used are real numbers.

Figures: Position of points, angles, regions, etc., can be assumed to be in the order shown; and angle measures can be assumed to be positive.

Lines shown as straight can be assumed to be straight.

Figures can be assumed to lie in a plane unless otherwise indicated.

Figures that accompany questions are intended to provide information useful in answering the questions. However, unless a note states that a figure is drawn to scale, you should solve these problems NOT by estimating sizes by sight or by measurement, but by using your knowledge of mathematics (see Example 2 below).

Directions: Each of the Questions 1–15 consists of two quantities, one in Column A and one in Column B. You are to compare the two quantities and choose

        A if the quantity in Column A is greater;
        B if the quantity in Column B is greater;
        C if the two quantities are equal;
        D if the relationship cannot be determined from the information given.

Note: Since there are only four choices, NEVER MARK (E).

Common Information: In a question, information concerning one or both of the quantities to be compared is centered above the two columns. A symbol that appears in both columns represents the same thing in Column A as it does in Column B.

	Column A	Column B	Sample Answers
Example 1:	2×6	$2 + 6$	● Ⓑ Ⓒ Ⓓ Ⓔ

Examples 2-4 refer to △ PQR.

	Column A	Column B	Sample Answers
Example 2:	PN	NQ	Ⓐ Ⓑ Ⓒ ● Ⓔ

(since equal measures cannot be assumed, even though PN and NQ appear equal)

	Column A	Column B	Sample Answers
Example 3:	x	y	Ⓐ ● Ⓒ Ⓓ Ⓔ

(since N is between P and Q)

	Column A	Column B	Sample Answers
Example 4:	$w + z$	180	Ⓐ Ⓑ ● Ⓓ Ⓔ

(since PQ is a straight line)

A if the quantity in Column A is greater;
B if the quantity in Column B is greater;
C if the two quantities are equal;
D if the relationship cannot be determined from the information given.

Column A	Column B	Column A	Column B

$n > 1$

1. $\dfrac{n + 7}{3} + \dfrac{n - 3}{4}$ $\dfrac{7n + 19}{7}$

$0.1y + 0.01y = 2.2$

2. $0.1y$ 20

3. Reciprocal of 4 $\sqrt{\dfrac{1}{16}}$

4. 120 $\sqrt{1440}$

5. 3 feet, 5 inches   1.5 yards

$x = 6 + 7 + 8 + 9 + 10$
$y = 5 + 6 + 7 + 8 + 9$

6. $5(15)$ $x + y$

In this multiplication problem each symbol represents a digit. Assume that the multiplication process is correct.

$$\begin{array}{r} 5678 \\ \times\ 73 \\ \hline 170\triangle4 \\ 3974\bigcirc \\ \hline 414494 \end{array}$$

7. Value of $\triangle$ Value of $\bigcirc$

Sam is older than Mary and Mary is younger than Rose.

8. Sam's age   Rose's age

$4x = 4(14) - 4$

9. x 14

In triangle ABC, $AC = BC$
$BC \parallel DE$ and $x = 65$

10. x y

Area of triangle $ABC = 20$ in?
$AD = 5$ inches and $AD \perp BC$

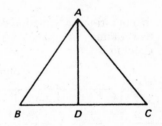

11. 4 inches   Length of DC

$y = 50$

12. $z - y$ 40

Joan covered 36 miles in 45 minutes.

13. Joan's average speed   48 miles per hour
     (in miles per hour)

A if the quantity in Column A is greater;
B if the quantity in Column B is greater;
C if the two quantities are equal;
D if the relationship cannot be determined from the information given.

Column A	Column B

$$a > b > c > d > 0$$

14. $a - d$ $b - c$

Column A	Column B

Area of triangle $ABC = 18$
$AB \perp BC$

15.   Length of AB Length of BC

Directions: Each of the Questions 16-30 has five answer choices. For each of these questions, select the best of the answer choices given.

16. Which of the following has the largest numerical value?

(A) $\dfrac{8}{0.8}$ (B) $\dfrac{0.8}{8}$ (C) $(0.8)^2$ (D) $\sqrt{0.8}$ (E) 0.8π

17. If $17xy + 7 = 19xy$, then $4xy =$

(A) 2   (B) 3   (C) $3\frac{1}{2}$ (D) 7   (E) 14

18. The average of two numbers is XY. If one number is equal to X, the other number is equal to

(A) Y
(B) $2Y$
(C) $XY - X$
(D) $2XY - X$
(E) $XY - 2X$

19. A snapshot $1\frac{7}{8}$ inches $\times$ $2\frac{1}{2}$ inches is to be enlarged so that the longer dimension will be 4 inches. What will be the length (in inches) of the shorter dimension?

(A) $2\frac{3}{8}$ (B) $2\frac{1}{2}$ (C) 3 (D) $3\frac{3}{8}$ (E) $3\frac{1}{2}$

20. The length and width of rectangle $AEFG$ are each $\frac{2}{3}$ of the corresponding parts of $ABCD$. $AEB = 12$; $AGD = 6$. The area of the shaded part is

(A) 24
(B) 32
(C) 36
(D) 40
(E) 48

Questions 21–25 refer to the following graphs.

HOMETOWN SAVINGS BANK

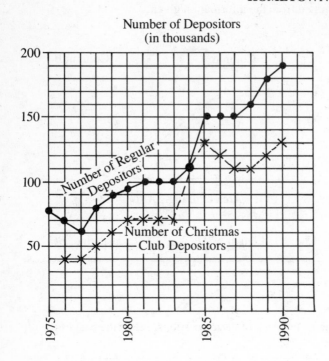

Number of Depositors
(in thousands)

How the Savings Bank Puts
Your Money to Work for You

21. How many thousands of regular depositors did the bank have in 1980?

(A) 70   (B) 85   (C) 95   (D) 100   (E) 950

22. In 1979 what was the ratio of the number of Christmas Club depositors to the number of regular depositors?

(A) $\frac{2}{3}$ (B) $\frac{2}{1}$ (C) $\frac{1}{2}$ (D) $\frac{7}{9}$ (E) $\frac{3}{2}$

23. Which of the following can be inferred from the graphs?

 I. Interest rates were static in the 1980-1983 period.
 II. The greatest increase in the number of Christmas Club depositors over a previous year occurred in 1984.
 III. Hometown Savings Bank invested most of its assets in stocks and bonds.

(A) I only   (B) II only   (C) III only
(D) I and III   (E) II and III

24. About how many degrees (to the nearest degree) are in the angle of the sector representing mortgages?

(A) 59   (B) 106   (C) 211   (D) 246   (E) 318

25. The average annual interest on mortgage investments is m percent and the average annual interest on the bond investment is b percent. If the annual interest on the bond investment is x dollars, how many dollars are invested in mortgages?

(A) $\frac{xm}{b}$

(B) $\frac{xb}{m}$

(C) $\frac{100xb}{m}$

(D) $\frac{bx}{100m}$

(E) $\frac{200x}{b}$

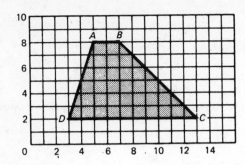

26. What is the area of *ABCD*?

(A) 24
(B) 30
(C) 35
(D) 36
(E) 48

27. The afternoon classes in a school begin at 1:00 P.M. and end at 3:52 P.M. There are 4 afternoon class periods with 4 minutes allowed between periods for passing to classes. The number of minutes in each class period is

(A) 39
(B) 40
(C) 43
(D) 45
(E) 59

28. If $x^2 + 2x - 8 = 0$, then x is either -4 or

(A) -2
(B) -1
(C) $\ \ 0$
(D) $\ \ 2$
(E) $\ \ 8$

29. The distance between two points is correctly expressed as either 720 statute miles or 630 nautical miles. Which of the following most closely approximates the value of one statute mile in terms of nautical miles?

(A) 0.88
(B) 0.89
(C) 0.90
(D) 1.14
(E) 1.25

30. The average of P numbers is x, and the average of N numbers is y. What is the average of all the $(P + N)$ numbers?

(A) $\dfrac{x + y}{2}$

(B) $x + y$

(C) $\dfrac{Py + Nx}{xy(P + N)}$

(D) $\dfrac{x + y}{P + N}$

(E) $\dfrac{Px + Ny}{P + N}$

S T O P

IF YOU FINISH BEFORE TIME IS CALLED, YOU MAY CHECK YOUR WORK ON THIS SECTION ONLY. DO NOT WORK ON ANY OTHER SECTION IN THE TEST.

SECTION 4

Time—30 minutes

30 Questions

Numbers: All numbers used are real numbers.

Figures: Position of points, angles, regions, etc., can be assumed to be in the order shown; and angle measures can be assumed to be positive.

Lines shown as straight can be assumed to be straight.

Figures can be assumed to lie in a plane unless otherwise indicated.

Figures that accompany questions are intended to provide information useful in answering the questions. However, unless a note states that a figure is drawn to scale, you should solve these problems NOT by estimating sizes by sight or by measurement, but by using your knowledge of mathematics (see Example 2 below).

Directions: Each of the Questions 1-15 consists of two quantities, one in Column A and one in Column B. You are to compare the two quantities and choose

A if the quantity in Column A is greater;
B if the quantity in Column B is greater;
C if the two quantities are equal;
D if the relationship cannot be determined from the information given.

Note: Since there are only four choices, NEVER MARK (E).

**Common
Information:**   In a question, information concerning one or both of the quantities to be compared is centered above the two columns. A symbol that appears in both columns represents the same thing in Column A as it does in Column B.

	Column A	Column B	Sample Answers
Example 1:	2×6	$2 + 6$	● Ⓑ Ⓒ Ⓓ Ⓔ

Examples 2-4 refer to $\triangle PQR$.

	Column A	Column B	Sample Answers
Example 2:	PN	NQ	Ⓐ Ⓑ Ⓒ ● Ⓔ (since equal measures cannot be assumed, even though PN and NQ appear equal)
Example 3:	x	y	Ⓐ ● Ⓒ Ⓓ Ⓔ (since N is between P and Q)
Example 4:	$w + z$	180	Ⓐ Ⓑ ● Ⓓ Ⓔ (since PQ is a straight line)

A if the quantity in Column A is greater;
B if the quantity in Column B is greater;
C if the two quantities are equal;
D if the relationship cannot be determined from the information given.

Column A	Column B

2a + 22

$x = y = z$

1. a 7

2. The number of integers | The number of integers
    from -5 to $+5$ | from $+5$ to $+15$

$x - y = 7$

3. $x + y$ 14

The area of square $ABCD$ is 25.

4. $AB + BC + CD$ 20

The area of isosceles right triangle ABC is 18.

5. Length of leg AB | Length of hypotenuse AC

Questions 6 and 7 refer to the following diagram.

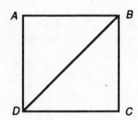

$ABCD$ is a square.   Diagonal $BD = 6\sqrt{2}$

6.   Perimeter of $ABCD$.   24

7.   Area of ABD 18

Column A	Column B

In triangle ABC, $AB = BC$, and the measure of angle $B =$ the measure of angle C.

8. The measure of angle B | The measure of angle B
    + the measure of angle | + the measure of angle
    C | A

$x = 0.5$

9. $4x$ x^4

$x > 1$

10. $\dfrac{x}{1 - x}$ $\dfrac{1}{x - 1}$

The perimeter of triangle $ABC =$ the perimeter of triangle DEF.

11.   Area of triangle ABC Area of triangle DEF

The sum of five consecutive integers is 35.

12. The value of the great-   9
     est of these integers

13. $\sqrt{160}$ $3\sqrt{10}$

$AB = BC = AC$

14. $2x$ y

The gasoline tank is two-thirds full with 12 gallons of gasoline.

15. The capacity of this   20 gallons
     tank

<u>Directions:</u> Each of the <u>Questions 16-30</u> has five answer choices. For each of these questions, select the best of the answer choices given.

16. If four cows produce 4 cans of milk in 4 days, how many days does it take eight cows to produce 8 cans of milk?

    (A) 1   (B) 2   (C) 4   (D) 8   (E) 16

17. A quart of alcohol containing $\frac{1}{2}$ pint of pure alcohol is diluted by the addition of $1\frac{1}{2}$ pints of distilled water. How much pure alcohol is contained in the diluted alcohol?

    (A) $\frac{1}{2}$ pint

    (B) $1\frac{1}{2}$ pints

    (C) 2 pints

    (D) 3 pints

    (E) $3\frac{1}{2}$ pints

18. If 20 teachers out of a faculty of 80 are transferred, what percentage of the original faculty remains?

    (A) 4   (B) 16   (C) 25   (D) 60   (E) 75

19. The total weight of three children is 152 pounds and 4 ounces. The average weight is 50 pounds and

    (A) $\frac{1}{3}$ pound

    (B) $\frac{1}{2}$ pound

    (C) $1\frac{1}{3}$ ounces

    (D) 9 ounces

    (E) 12 ounces

20. Thirty prizes were distributed to 5 percent of the original entrants in a contest. Assuming one prize per person, the number of entrants in this contest was

    (A) 15   (B) 60   (C) 150   (D) 300   (E) 600

Questions 21–25 refer to the following chart and graph.

CALORIES

Composition of Average Diet

	Grams	*Calories*
Carbohydrates	500	2,050
Protein	100	410
Fat	100	930

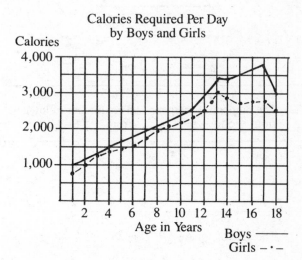

Calories Required Per Day by Boys and Girls

Boys ———
Girls —·—

21. How many calories are there in 1 gram of carbohydrate?

    (A) 0.2   (B) 2   (C) 4.1   (D) 10.25   (E) 1,025

22. What percent (to the nearest %) of the total calories in the average diet is derived from proteins?

    (A) 12   (B) 14   (C) 22   (D) 27   (E) 32

23. How many grams of carbohydrate (to the nearest gram) are needed to yield as many calories as 1,000 grams of fat?

    (A) 1,110
    (B) 2,050
    (C) 2,268
    (D) 4,100
    (E) 4,536

24. Approximately how many more calories per day are required by boys than girls at age 17?

    (A) 800
    (B) 1,000
    (C) 2,500
    (D) 3,500
    (E) 4,000

25. Which of the following can be inferred from the graphs?

    I. Calorie requirements for boys and girls have similar rates of increase until after age 12 to 13.
    II. From ages 4 to 12 calorie requirements for boys and girls are wholly dissimilar.
    III. Calorie requirements for boys and girls reach their peaks at different ages.

    A) I only   (B) II only   (C) III only
    (D) I and III   (E) II and III

26. To cross a ferry the total cost T is 50 cents for the car and driver and c cents for each additional passenger in the car. What is the total cost for a car with n persons in the automobile?

    (A) $n + c$
    (B) $50 + nc$
    (C) cn
    (D) $50 + c(n - 1)$
    (E) $50 + (n + 1)c$

27. Gloria wants to make some candy using a recipe that calls for $1\frac{1}{2}$ cups of sugar, $\frac{1}{2}$ cup of boiling water and several other ingredients. She finds that she has only 1 cup of sugar. How much water will she have to use?

    (A) $\frac{1}{6}$ cup

    (B) $\frac{1}{4}$ cup

    (C) $\frac{1}{3}$ cup

    (D) $\frac{3}{4}$ cup

    (E) 1 cup

28. How many pounds of baggage are allowed for a plane passenger if the European regulations permit 20 kilograms per passenger? (1 kg = 2.2 lb)

    (A) 11   (B) 44   (C) 88   (D) 91   (E) 440

29. Which of the following statements is (are) always true? (a, b, and c are real and not equal to zero.)

    I. $\frac{1}{a}$ is less than a.

    II. $\frac{a + b}{2a}$ equals $\frac{2b}{b + a}$ when a equals b.

    III. $\frac{a + c}{b + c}$ is more than $\frac{a}{b}$.

    (A) II only
    (B) I and II only
    (C) I and III only
    (D) II and III only
    (E) I, II, and III

30. If $\dfrac{y}{s - t} = \dfrac{s + t}{t - s}$, then $y =$

    (A) $- s - t$
    (B) $t - s$
    (C) $t + s$
    (D) $s - t$
    (E) $t^2 - s^2$

S T O P

IF YOU FINISH BEFORE TIME IS CALLED, YOU MAY CHECK YOUR WORK ON THIS SECTION ONLY. DO NOT WORK ON ANY OTHER SECTION IN THE TEST.

SECTION 5

Time—30 minutes

25 Questions

Directions: Each question or group of questions is based on a passage or set of conditions. In answering some of the questions, it may be useful to draw a rough diagram. For each question, select the best answer choice given.

Questions 1–4

Michael attends Saddle Rock School on the 9:00-3:00 session, except on Thursdays, when he is dismissed at noon so the teachers can conduct special help classes and parent conferences. Michael takes a piano lesson at home on Mondays from 3:30 to 4:30. On Tuesdays he goes to a karate class from 4:00 to 6:00. His art class meets from 4:00 to 6:00 on Wednesdays. He remains in school after dismissal on Fridays to participate in a 90-minute club program.

1. The most convenient afternoon for Michael to do library research is

   (A) Tuesday
   (B) Wednesday
   (C) Thursday
   (D) Friday
   (E) Monday

2. Keeping the same 3:30-4:30 schedule, Michael can conveniently change his piano lesson to which of the following days?

   (A) Monday
   (B) Tuesday
   (C) Wednesday
   (D) Thursday
   (E) Friday

3. Michael was invited to replace his 4:00-6:00 P.M. art class with an advanced art class that meets at the same time. He could accept this advancement without interfering with his other activities if the class met on which of the following days?

   (A) Mondays and Wednesdays
   (B) Tuesdays and Wednesdays
   (C) Wednesdays and Thursdays
   (D) Thursdays and Fridays
   (E) Mondays and Thursdays

4. Michael is chosen to play for the varsity basketball team. To attend daily 5:00 P.M. practice sessions, he will have to suspend which of the following activities?

   (A) Piano instruction and karate
   (B) Karate and the club program
   (C) The art class and the club program
   (D) Piano instruction and the art class
   (E) The art class and karate

5. Sarah: Only General Council members sit on the President's Cabinet.
   Charles: That's not true. Dr. Grogan is a General Council member and she's not on the President's Cabinet.

   Charles's response implies that he incorrectly interpreted Sarah's statement to mean that

   (A) all Cabinet members are on the General Council
   (B) Dr. Grogan sits on the President's Cabinet
   (C) all members of the General Council sit on the President's Cabinet
   (D) no General Council members are on the President's Cabinet
   (E) Dr. Grogan is not a General Council manager

6. The only unemployment problem we have is not that people can't find work, but that they won't work. Thousands of jobs go begging every day, but the unemployed are too lazy to go out and find them.

   The above argument would be more persuasive if it were established that

   (A) the majority of available jobs require unusually high levels of skill or experience or both
   (B) unemployed persons tend to be geographically clustered in regions distant from available jobs
   (C) most unemployed persons are back at work within six months
   (D) most unemployed persons do not seek work until their unemployment benefits expire
   (E) a high unemployment rate has been fostered by the government in order to control inflation

7. My father, my three uncles, and both my grandfathers became bald within five years after they began practicing law. I don't want to lose my hair, so I'm going to become a doctor.

   Which of the following most closely resembles the reasoning used in the argument above?

   (A) Every time I drink coffee before going to bed, I have trouble falling asleep. I want to sleep well tonight, so I'm going to take a sleeping pill.
   (B) All of the teenagers in my neighborhood have gotten tickets for speeding on Dole Road within the last year. I don't want to have to pay a fine, so I'm not going to speed on Dole Road.

(C) Everyone else got transferred out of our department within three years after starting work here. I don't want to work in another department, so I'm going to start working harder.

(D) The other punch press operators on my shift each were seriously injured on the job within a week after eating at Rosie's Diner. I want to maintain my safety record, so I'm going to eat at Harry's Luncheonette.

(E) The three other men in my bridge club each became irritable after they quit smoking. I want to be more pleasant, so I'm going to quit my bridge club.

Questions 8–12

The Berkeley-Sothenay Gallery displays seven paintings, one each by Degas, Ernst, Fragonard, Greuze, Hartley, Ingres, and Johns. Each has been valued by the Gallery's curator.

The value of the Johns is three times that of the Ingres.
The Greuze has the lowest valuation of any of the paintings.
The Fragonard and the Degas are valued at the same amount.
The value of the Ernst is as much as that of the Johns and the Ingres together.
The value of the Hartley is as much as that of the Fragonard, the Ernst, and the Johns together.
The value of the Degas is as much as that of the Johns and the Ernst together.

8. Which correctly lists six of the paintings in order of increasing value?

(A) Greuze, Ernst, Fragonard, Johns, Ingres, Hartley
(B) Greuze, Johns, Degas, Ernst, Fragonard, Hartley
(C) Greuze, Ernst, Johns, Degas, Fragonard, Hartley
(D) Greuze, Ingres, Johns, Degas, Ernst, Hartley
(E) Greuze, Ingres, Johns, Ernst, Fragonard, Hartley

9. The value of the Degas is

(A) twice the value of the Johns
(B) twice the value of the Ernst
(C) three times the value of the Johns, less the value of the Ingres
(D) six times the value of the Ingres
(E) half the value of the Hartley

10. A buyer who decided not to buy the Hartley could buy for the same price

I. the Degas, the Ingres, and the Fragonard
II. the Ernst, the Johns, and the Degas
III. the Ingres, the Ernst, and the Johns

(A) I only
(B) II only
(C) I and II only
(D) I and III only
(E) I, II, and III

11. If the Ernst and the Ingres together are valued at ten times the value of the Greuze, the Hartley is valued at how many times the value of the Greuze?

(A) 12
(B) 14
(C) 21
(D) 28
(E) 49

12. The paintings are bought by seven rich collectors who then trade with each other. Which trade represents an exchange of even value?

(A) The Hartley for the Degas, the Ernst, and the Ingres
(B) The Hartley and the Ernst for all the others except the Greuze
(C) The Degas and the Fragonard for the Hartley and the Ingres
(D) The Ingres, the Johns, the Ernst, and the Fragonard for the Hartley
(E) The Johns and the Ernst for the Degas and the Ingres

Questions 13–16

(1) All P and X are N.
(2) All N except P are X.
(3) No P are M.
(4) No R are N.
(5) All M are either X or R.
(6) No Q are X.

13. Which of the following statements must be true if the above six statements are true?

I. No R are P.
II. Some X are P.
III. Some X are M.

(A) I only
(B) I and II only
(C) I and III only
(D) I, II, and III
(E) Neither I, II, nor III

14. Which of the following must be false given the conditions as stated?

(A) No Q are P.
(B) Some Q are neither N nor R.
(C) Some R are X.
(D) All R are M.
(E) Some X are not M.

15. Which of the numbered statements can logically be deduced from one or more of the other statements?

    (A) (2)   (B) (3)   (C) (4)   (D) (5)   (E) (6)

16. If statement (2) were shown to be false, which of the following would necessarily be true?

    (A) Some M are neither X nor R.
    (B) Some P are not N.
    (C) Some Q are X.
    (D) Some N are neither P nor X.
    (E) Either some X are P or some N are neither P nor X, or both.

Questions 17–22

Four persons — Allen, Brian, Carol, and Donna—are camping at four separate campsites — Edmunds, Freeport, Grand Isle, and High Point, not necessarily in that order. The campsites are located on four separate lakes — Indian Point, Jackson, Keewaukett, and Leesville, not necessarily in that order — which are in four separate states — Maine, Nebraska, Ohio, and Pennsylvania, not necessarily in that order.
   Brian is camping on Keewaukett Lake.
   High Point Campsite is on Jackson Lake, which is in Nebraska.
   The person at Indian Point Lake, a native of Pennsylvania, camps only in that state.
   Donna is at Freeport Campsite.
   Allen is camping in Ohio.

17. Where is Brian camping?

    (A) At Edmunds Campsite
    (B) In Maine
    (C) On Leesville Lake
    (D) At Freeport Campsite
    (E) In Nebraska

18. Indian Point Lake is the site of

    (A) Freeport Campsite
    (B) Allen's camp
    (C) the camp in Ohio
    (D) Grand Isle Campsite
    (E) Carol's camp

19. On the basis of the information given, it is possible to deduce that

    I.   Allen is not at High Point Campsite
    II. Carol is in Pennsylvania
    III. Donna is not at Edmunds Campstie

    (A) I only
    (B) II only
    (C) III only
    (D) I and III only
    (E) II and III only

20. Ohio is the site of

    I. Leesville Lake
    II. Freeport Campsite

    (A) I only
    (B) II only
    (C) I and II
    (D) I or II but not both
    (E) Neither I nor II

21. Which is true of Leesville Lake?

    (A) Carol is camping there.
    (B) Donna is camping there.
    (C) It is in Maine
    (D) It is the site of Freeport Campsite.
    (E) Allen is camping there.

22. Which cannot be determined on the basis of the information given?

    (A) What state Keewaukett Lake is in
    (B) Who is at Edmunds Campsite
    (C) What campsite is in Pennsylvania
    (D) Who is camping in Nebraska
    (E) Which states Carol and Donna are in

23. Our new Model EXT Superwash Automatic Dishwasher is the best dishwasher you'll ever own. It comes in any of fourteen decorator colors. It's so quiet you'll find yourself checking to see if it's really on. And best of all, it comes in different widths and heights so that there'll be no need to redesign your present kitchen around it.

    The argument above is most weakened by its failure to mention

    (A) the terms of the warranty
    (B) how well the dishwasher washes dishes
    (C) the specific sizes available
    (D) how much electricity the dishwasher uses
    (E) how many dishes the dishwasher holds

24. Based solely on artifacts recently discovered in ancient Xenian tombs, archeologists claim to have reconstructed the Xenian civilization of that time. What could be more absurd? No hieroglyphs or other written records were unearthed; thus, the archeologists are claiming to have reconstructed a culture without any evidence of how the people who lived in that culture thought.

    The argument above is based on which of the following assumptions?

    (A) Physical artifacts do not provide evidence of how people think.
    (B) Archeologists would be able to translate ancient Xenian writing if it were found.
    (C) Insufficient effort was expended by the archeologists in searching for written records.
    (D) Physical artifacts are of no use in trying to reconstruct a civilization.
    (E) Written records are all that is needed to reconstruct a civilization.

25. I'm afraid that Roger will never be an outstanding football player again. Last year he injured his knee, and the doctors had to remove some of the cartilage.

    The argument above is based upon which of the following assumptions?

    I. One must have healthy knees to play football.
    II. How well one plays football may be influenced by the condition of one's knees.
    III. Healthy knees are necessary for a professional football career.

    (A) I only
    (B) II only
    (C) I and II only
    (D) II and III only
    (E) I, II, and III

S T O P

IF YOU FINISH BEFORE TIME IS CALLED, YOU MAY CHECK YOUR WORK ON THIS SECTION ONLY. DO NOT WORK ON ANY OTHER SECTION IN THE TEST.

SECTION 6

Time — 30 minutes

25 Questions

Directions: Each question or group of questions is based on a passage or set of conditions. In answering some of the questions, it may be useful to draw a rough diagram. For each question, select the best answer choice given.

Questions 1–4

George adores classical music. He always prefers Beethoven to Bartok and Mahler to Mozart. He always prefers Haydn to Hindemith and Hindemith to Mozart. He always prefers Mahler to any composer whose name begins with B, except Beethoven, and he always chooses to listen to a composer he prefers.

1. Which of the following cannot be true?

   (A) George prefers Mahler to Bartok.
   (B) George prefers Beethoven to Mahler.
   (C) George prefers Bartok to Mozart.
   (D) George prefers Mozart to Beethoven.
   (E) George prefers Mahler to Haydn.

2. George's brother gives him one recording by each of the composers mentioned. Which of the following correctly states the order in which George must play some of the records?

   (A) Beethoven, Bartok, Mozart
   (B) Haydn, Hindemith, Mozart
   (C) Beethoven, Mahler, Bartok
   (D) Hindemith, Mahler, Mozart
   (E) Haydn, Hindemith, Mahler

3. George's mother also gives him one recording by each composer mentioned. Which of the following cannot occur?

   (A) George plays the Beethoven first.
   (B) George plays the Haydn first.
   (C) George plays the Mahler third.
   (D) George plays the Beethoven fifth.
   (E) George plays the Bartok last.

4. George's father gives him several records. If the first record he plays is by Berlioz, which of the following must be true?

   (A) There is no record by Hindemith.
   (B) There is no record by Bartok.
   (C) One of the records may be by Haydn.
   (D) If there is a record by Haydn, George will play it second.
   (E) There is no record by Beethoven.

5. The new Spanish film, *The Other Side of the Mirror,* the psychologically probing story of a pair of disturbed lovers, is clearly the best foreign film of the year, since its box office receipts show that even more people are seeing it than have seen *Double Fugue,* the highly acclaimed U.S. film on a similar theme.

The argument above is based on which of the following assumptions?

   (A) *Double Fugue* is the best U.S. film of the year.
   (B) Foreign films should be judged by standards different from those used for U.S. films.
   (C) Foreign films should be judged by the same standards used for U.S. films.
   (D) Psychologically probing stories make the best films.
   (E) The quality of a film can be measured by the number of people who go to see it.

6. By the very nature of their work, scientists must rigorously apply the scientific method. Every conclusion they reach is scrutinized by other scientists and corrected and refined as needed until it can be certified as scientifically valid. No other view of the world is derived in such a manner; neither the theologian nor the sociologist nor the artist makes use of this method. Thus, the scientific worldview must be the most accurate.

Which of the following best describes the flaw in the reasoning used in the argument above?

   (A) The author uses a single term to mean more than one thing.
   (B) The author fails to explain in detail how the scientific method works.
   (C) The truth of the author's conclusion is assumed rather than justified.
   (D) The author ignores the fact that many accepted scientific theories are later disproved.
   (E) The author attacks the people who hold other views, rather than attacking the views themselves.

7. Melinda: George has become a better boxer since he started meditating.
   Alfredo: Impossible. A boxer's most important asset is his aggressiveness.

Alfredo's statement implies that he believes that

   (A) meditation tends to make a person less aggressive
   (B) meditation has little or no effect on the person who practices it
   (C) George was previously a poor boxer because he was not aggressive enough
   (D) George has not really been meditating
   (E) mental attitude has little or nothing to do with a boxer's effectiveness

Questions 8–12

(1) At a baseball game, five men, L, M, N, O, and P, and five women, S, T, U, V, and W, occupy a row of ten seats. The men are in odd-numbered seats, starting from the left; each woman sits to the right of the man she is dating.

(2) O is V's date.

(3) W is not at the right end of the row and the man she is dating is not at the left end of the row.

(4) N is one seat from the right end of the row.

(5) The man dating W likes T best among the other women and insists on being seated to the right of T.

(6) M and his date occupy the middle pair of seats.

(7) V sits next to M.

8. Which of the following lists five persons sitting adjacent to one another, from left to right?

(A) U, V, O, M, T
(B) M, T, L, W, N
(C) O, V, M, T, W
(D) O, V, M, T, and either L or P
(E) L or P, O, V, M, T

9. U's date may be

(A) N or L
(B) L or P
(C) N or P
(D) N, L, or P
(E) M, N, or L

10. Which of the following cannot be determined on the basis of the information given?

I. Who occupies the seat farthest to the left
II. Who occupies the seat farthest to the right
III. Which other women are nearest T

(A) I only
(B) III only
(C) I and II only
(D) II and III only
(E) I, II, and III

11. Which of the following could be determined exactly if the position of either L or P were given?

(A) The identity of L's date
(B) The identity of P's date
(C) The identity of L's date or P's date, but not both
(D) Which woman is not seated between two men
(E) Who is sitting to O's left

12. In order to determine the position of T, it is necessary to use how many of the numbered statements?

(A) 3   (B) 4   (C) 5   (D) 6   (E) 7

Questions 13–16

Seven teenagers at Gateway Amusement Park — Carlos, Leona, Gregor, Ingrid, Naomi, Dave, and Rick — are going to ride the new roller coaster, Dragon's Breath. Two cars are available, but the teens have to split up according to the following conditions:

Carlos and Naomi are boyfriend and girlfriend and must be in the same car.

Dave and Gregor are friends but Ingrid is Gregor's girlfriend, so Dave cannot be in the same car as Gregor unless Ingrid is also in that car.

The roller coaster rules say that the maximum number of riders in each car is four.

Leona is Gregor's sister and Rick is Leona's ex-boyfriend, so neither Leona nor Gregor can ride in the same car as Rick.

13. If Dave rides in the same car as Leona, which of the following must be true?

(A) Rick rides in the other car.
(B) Ingrid rides in the other car.
(C) Gregor rides in the other car.
(D) Naomi rides in the same car as Dave and Leona.
(E) Carlos rides in the same car as Dave and Leona.

14. If Naomi rides in the same car as Gregor, which of the following must be true?

(A) Rick rides in the same car as Naomi and Gregor.
(B) Leona rides in the same car as Rick.
(C) Leona rides in the car other than the one in which Gregor rides.
(D) Naomi and Gregor ride in the car carrying four people.
(E) Carlos rides in the car other than the one in which Gregor rides.

15. If Rick rides in the same car as Ingrid, which of the following must be true?

(A) Dave rides in the same car as Leona.
(B) Dave rides in the same car as Carlos.
(C) Leona rides in the same car as Gregor.
(D) Naomi rides in the same car as Rick and Ingrid.
(E) Dave rides in the same car as Naomi.

16. If Naomi rides in the same car as Dave, which of the following would be a complete and accurate list of the people who must ride in the other car?

(A) Rick, Gregor, Ingrid
(B) Rick, Carlos, Leona
(C) Ingrid, Carlos, Gregor, Rick
(D) Rick, Ingrid, Leona
(E) Ingrid, Leona, Gregor

Questions 17–22

Mathematics 11 is a prerequisite for Mathematics 101,
except for students with advanced placement in mathematics, who may take Mathematics 101 without any
prerequisite.

Chemistry 11 or 21 is a prerequisite for Chemistry 101,
except for students with advanced placement in chemistry, who may take Chemistry 101 without any
prerequisite.

Physics 1, followed by Physics 11 or 21, is a prerequisite
for Physics 101 or 121. There is no advanced placement in physics, but Mathematics 11 is acceptable in
place of Physics 1.

Students who have passed Mathematics 101 may take
Mathematics 202, 211, or 221; students who have
passed Chemistry 101 may take Chemistry 201, 211, or
221, or Mathematics 201 for chemistry credit; students
who have passed Physics 101 or 121 may take Physics
201 or 221, or Chemistry 201 for physics credit.

Students who have passed three or more graduate-level
courses acceptable for credit in a given field may be
admitted to a concentration sequence in that field.
(Courses numbered 200 or higher are considered graduate-level.)

17. A student who has passed Physics 101

   I.   may be admitted to a concentration sequence in
        physics without taking Physics 121
   II. may be admitted to a concentration sequence in
        physics after taking two more physics courses
   III. must have taken Physics 1 or 11 or both

   (A) I only
   (B) III only
   (C) I and II only
   (D) I and III only
   (E) I, II, and III

18. What is the minimum number of courses in mathe-
    matics or chemistry that can satisfy the requirements
    for admission to a concentration sequence in chemis-
    try for a student without advanced placement in
    chemistry?

   (A) 3   (B) 4   (C) 5   (D) 6   (E) 7

19. How many separate ways are there to qualify for
    admission to a concentration sequence in physics?

   (A) 3   (B) 4   (C) 6   (D) 8   (E) 12

20. A student with advanced placement in mathematics
    may qualify for admission to a concentration
    sequence in chemistry by taking which of the
    following?

   I.   Mathematics 101 and 202, Chemistry 11, 201,
        and 211
   II. Chemistry 11, 101, 201, 211, and 221
   III. Mathematics 101 and 211, Chemistry 21, 101,
        201, and 221

   (A) I only
   (B) II only
   (C) III only
   (D) I and III only
   (E) II and III only

21. The maximum number of courses that must be taken
    by any student to qualify for admission to a concen-
    tration sequence is

   (A) 4   (B) 5   (C) 6   (D) 7   (E) 8

22. If all chemistry classes are cancelled following an
    explosion that destroys the chemistry building,
    which of the following must be true?

   I.   No new students will be able to qualify for
        Mathematics 201.
   II. No new students will be able to qualify for a
        concentration sequence in physics.
   III. No graduate-level courses will be open to stu-
        dents who have already passed Chemistry 101.

   (A) I only
   (B) II only
   (C) I and II only
   (D) I and III only
   (E) I, II, and III only

23. None of the stockholders in Elronco who knew
    Ortega and supported her reorganization plan voted
    for the merger with Anaco, but some of them owned
    stock in Anaco.

    If the statement above is true, each of the following
    statements may or must also be true EXCEPT:

   (A) No one who owned Anaco stock supported
       Ortega's reorganization plan.
   (B) Everyone who voted for the merger with Anaco
       owned Anaco stock.
   (C) Some of the Anaco stockholders knew Ortega.
   (D) Some of the Elronco stockholders who opposed
       Ortega's reorganization plan knew Ortega.
   (E) None of the Elronco stockholders voted for the
       Anaco merger.

24. Which of the following contradicts the view that
    only the smart become rich?

   (A) Brian was smart, yet he was poor his whole life.
   (B) Both "smart" and "rich" are relative terms.
   (C) Different people are smart in different ways.
   (D) Some smart people do not desire to become
       rich.
   (E) Peter is stupid, yet he amassed a large fortune
       by the age of 30.

25. Television convinces viewers that the likelihood of their becoming the victims of violent crime is extremely high; at the same time, by its very nature, television persuades viewers to passively accept whatever happens to them.

The argument above leads most logically to the conclusion that

(A) people should not watch television
(B) television promotes a feeling of helpless vulnerability in its viewers
(C) television viewers are more likley to be victimized than other persons
(D) the content of television programs should be changed to avoid fostering the attitudes mentioned
(E) television viewing promotes criminal behavior

S T O P

IF YOU FINISH BEFORE TIME IS CALLED, YOU MAY CHECK YOUR WORK ON THIS SECTION ONLY. DO NOT WORK ON ANY OTHER SECTION IN THE TEST.

SECTION 7

Time—30 minutes

30 Questions

Numbers: All numbers used are real numbers.

Figures: Position of points, angles, regions, etc., can be assumed to be in the order shown; and angle measures can be assumed to be positive.

Lines shown as straight can be assumed to be straight.

Figures can be assumed to lie in a plane unless otherwise indicated.

Figures that accompany questions are intended to provide information useful in answering the questions. However, unless a note states that a figure is drawn to scale, you should solve these problems NOT by estimating sizes by sight or by measurement, but by using your knowledge of mathematics (see Example 2 below).

Directions: Each of the Questions 1-15 consists of two quantities, one in Column A and one in Column B. You are to compare the two quantities and choose

A if the quantity in Column A is greater;
B if the quantity in Column B is greater;
C if the two quantities are equal;
D if the relationship cannot be determined from the information given.

Note: Since there are only four choices, NEVER MARK (E).

Common
Information: In a question, information concerning one or both of the quantities to be compared is centered above the two columns. A symbol that appears in both columns represents the same thing in Column A as it does in Column B.

	Column A	Column B	Sample Answers
Example 1:	2×6	$2 + 6$	● ⓑ ⓒ ⓓ ⓔ

Examples 2-4 refer to $\triangle PQR$.

	Column A	Column B	Sample Answers
Example 2:	PN	NQ	ⓐ ⓑ ⓒ ● ⓔ
			(since equal measures cannot be assumed, even though PN and NQ appear equal)
Example 3:	x	y	ⓐ ● ⓒ ⓓ ⓔ
			(since N is between P and Q)
Example 4:	$w + z$	180	ⓐ ⓑ ● ⓓ ⓔ
			(since PQ is a straight line)

A if the quantity in Column A is greater;
B if the quantity in Column B is greater;
C if the two quantities are equal;
D if the relationship cannot be determined from the information given.

| Column A | Column B | | Column A | Column B |

$$a < b < c$$
$$d < e < f$$

1. a f

$$64 < x < 81$$

2. x 65

$$KA = 6, BCL = 17, \text{ and } BC = 8$$

3.   Length of KL 23

The operation $\triangle$ is defined by the
equation $a \triangle b = a^2 + b^2$.

$$xy \ne 0$$

4. $(x \triangle y)^2$ $x^2 \triangle y^2$

5. $\sqrt{144}$ $\sqrt{100} + \sqrt{44}$

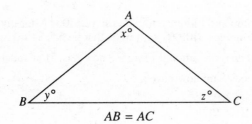

$$AB = AC$$

6. $x + y$ $x + z$

7. $\dfrac{3\sqrt{48}}{\sqrt{3}}$ 12

$$\frac{x}{4} + \frac{x}{3} = \frac{7}{12}$$

8. x -1

$$\frac{9}{a} < \frac{9}{b}$$
$$a > 1$$
$$b > 1$$

9. a b

10.   0.003%   0.0003

11. $\dfrac{k}{400}$ $\dfrac{k}{4}\%$

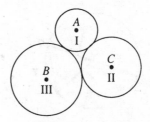

radius of I = 3 inches
radius of II = 4 inches
radius of III = 5 inches

12. Length of perimeter of   2 feet
     triangle ABC, formed
     by joining the centers
     of the three circles

Side BC of parallelogram $ABCE$ is
extended to D.
$$y = 130$$

13. x z

A if the quantity in Column A is greater;
B if the quantity in Column B is greater;
C if the two quantities are equal;
D if the relationship cannot be determined from the information given.

Column A	Column B

$$abc = 0$$
$$c = 1$$

14.   1 ab

Column A	Column B

15. The average of one-   0.111
    tenth, one-hundredth,
    and one-thousandth

Directions: Each of the Questions 16–30 has five answer choices. For each of these questions, select the best of the answer choices given.

---

16. In the figure above, AB is the diameter and $OC = BC$. What is the value of $\frac{x}{2}$?

    (A) 20   (B) 30   (C) 60   (D) 90   (E) 120

17. For which values of n and d is $\frac{n}{d} > 1$?

    (A) $n = 5$ and $d = 6$
    (B) $n = 3$ and $d = 2$
    (C) $n = 1$ and $d = 2$
    (D) $n = 1$ and $d = 1$
    (E) $n = 0$ and $d = 1$

18. One-half of a number is 17 more than one-third of that number. What is the number?

    (A) 52   (B) 84   (C) 102   (D) 112   (E) 204

19. In the figure above, $l \parallel m$. All of the following are true EXCEPT:

    (A) $c = d$
    (B) $a = d$
    (C) $a = e$
    (D) $f = b$
    (E) $f = c$

20. Sam and Florence together have $100. After giving Florence $10.00, Sam finds that he has $4.00 more than $\frac{1}{5}$ the amount Florence now has. How much does Sam now have?

    (A) $18.67
    (B) $20.00
    (C) $21.00
    (D) $27.50
    (E) $35.00

Questions 21–25 refer to the following graphs.

HIGHEST LEVEL OF EDUCATION OF BRIDE-GROOMS IN 24–27 AGE GROUP

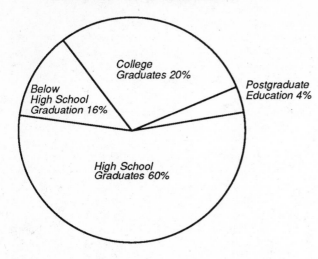

DISTRIBUTION OF 302,000 MARRIAGES ACCORDING TO AGE OF BRIDEGROOM

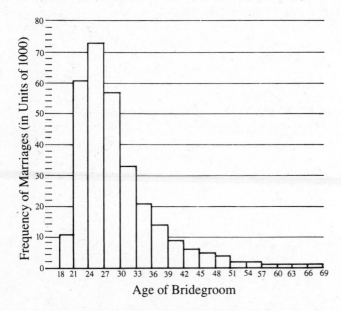

21. In one million marriages, how many thousand (to the nearest thousand) bridegrooms would you expect to be between the ages of 51 and 60?

   (A) 5
   (B) 15
   (C) 16
   (D) 17
   (E) 50

22. Which of the following best represents the percentage of men who married at age 24 or younger?

   (A) 7
   (B) 10
   (C) 24
   (D) 32
   (E) 48

23. Which of the following can be inferred from the graphs?

   I. Almost three times as many marriages occur when bridegrooms are in the 21–24 age bracket as occur when they are aged 33–36.
   II. Most bridegrooms are high school graduates.
   III. About 2920 bridegrooms aged 24–27 receive postgraduate education.

   (A) I only   (B) II only   (C) III only
   (D) I and III   (E) II and III

24. If drawn accurately, how many degrees should there be in the central angle of the sector indicating the number of college graduates?

   (A) 20
   (B) 40
   (C) 60
   (D) 72
   (E) more than 72

25. Approximately what percentage of the men who married were between the ages of 21 and 27 years?

   (A) 7
   (B) 13
   (C) 26
   (D) 44
   (E) 67

26. If 0.6 is the average of the four quantities 0.2, 0.8, 1.0, and x, what is the numerical value of x?

   (A) 0.2
   (B) 0.4
   (C) 0.67
   (D) 1.3
   (E) 2.4

27. $\dfrac{a^2 - b^2}{(a - b)^2}$ is equal to

   (A) $a + b$

   (B) $a - b$

   (C) $\dfrac{a + b}{a - b}$

   (D) $\dfrac{a - b}{a + b}$

   (E) 1

28. If two items cost c¢, how many items can be purchased for x¢?

(A) $\dfrac{x}{2c}$

(B) $\dfrac{2c}{x}$

(C) $\dfrac{2x}{c}$

(D) $\dfrac{cx}{2}$

(E) $2cx$

29. The area of square $EFGH$ is equal to the area of rectangle $ABCD$. If $GH = 6$ feet and $AD = 4$ feet, the perimeter (in feet) of the rectangle is

(A) 13
(B) 16
(C) 24
(D) 26
(E) 36

30. The radius of a pool is twice the radius of a circular flower bed. The area of the pool is how many times the area of the flower bed?

(A) $\dfrac{1}{4}$ (B) $\dfrac{1}{2}$ (C) 2   (D) 4   (E) 8

S T O P

IF YOU FINISH BEFORE TIME IS CALLED, YOU MAY CHECK YOUR WORK ON THIS SECTION ONLY.
DO NOT WORK ON ANY OTHER SECTION IN THE TEST.

Answer Key – Diagnostic Test

Note: The answers to the quantitative sections are keyed to the corresponding review areas in the Mathematics Review (Chapter 11). The numbers in parentheses after each answer refer to the math topic(s) covered by that particular question.

Section 1   Verbal

1.	B	11.	D	21.	E	31.	D
2.	E	12.	A	22.	C	32.	D
3.	C	13.	C	23.	B	33.	B
4.	C	14.	E	24.	D	34.	B
5.	C	15.	D	25.	C	35.	B
6.	B	16.	C	26.	B	36.	D
7.	A	17.	C	27.	C	37.	D
8.	B	18.	C	28.	E	38.	D
9.	C	19.	E	29.	A		
10.	B	20.	C	30.	B		

Section 2   Verbal

1.	E	11.	E	21.	C	31.	E
2.	D	12.	A	22.	B	32.	C
3.	B	13.	C	23.	D	33.	B
4.	E	14.	D	24.	C	34.	E
5.	A	15.	E	25.	C	35.	B
6.	D	16.	A	26.	B	36.	E
7.	B	17.	C	27.	D	37.	B
8.	B	18.	E	28.	C	38.	C
9.	D	19.	A	29.	A		
10.	C	20.	D	30.	B		

Section 3   Quantitative

1.	B (I-B)	9.	B (II-B-4)	17.	E (II-B)	25.	E (II-E, IV)
2.	B (II-B)	10.	A (III-A, D)	18.	D (I-G)	26.	D (III-H)
3.	C (I)	11.	D (III-A, D)	19.	C (II-E)	27.	B (II-C)
4.	A (I-H-4)	12.	C (III-A, D)	20.	D (III-G)	28.	D (II-B)
5.	B (II-E)	13.	C (II-C)	21.	C (IV)	29.	A (II-E)
6.	C (I-A)	14.	A (II-G)	22.	A (II-E, IV)	30.	E (I-G)
7.	B (I-A)	15.	D (III-A)	23.	B (IV)		
8.	D (II-B-4)	16.	A (I-C)	24.	C (IV-B)		

Section 4   Quantitative

1.	C (III-A, D)	9.	A (II-A)	17.	A (II-C)	25.	D (IV)
2.	C (I-A)	10.	B (II-A)	18.	E (I-D)	26.	D (II-C)
3.	D (II-B)	11.	D (III-G)	19.	E (I-G)	27.	C (II-E)
4.	B (III-A)	12.	C (II-B)	20.	E (II-C)	28.	B (II-E)
5.	B (III-G)	13.	A (I-H)	21.	C (IV-C)	29.	A (II-G)
6.	C (III-G)	14.	C (III-D)	22.	A (I-D, IV)	30.	A (II-A)
7.	C (III-G)	15.	B (II-C)	23.	C (II-E, IV)		
8.	C (III-D)	16.	C (II-C)	24.	B (IV)		

Section 5   Analytical

1.	C	8.	E	15.	B	22.	B
2.	D	9.	E	16.	E	23.	B
3.	C	10.	B	17.	B	24.	A
4.	E	11.	D	18.	A	25.	B
5.	C	12.	B	19.	D		
6.	D	13.	A	20.	A		
7.	D	14.	C	21.	E		

Section 6   Analytical

1.	D	8.	D	15.	C	22.	C
2.	B	9.	D	16.	E	23.	A
3.	D	10.	C	17.	C	24.	E
4.	E	11.	C	18.	C	25.	B
5.	E	12.	D	19.	D		
6.	C	13.	A	20.	B		
7.	A	14.	D	21.	C		

Section 7   Quantitative

1.	D (II-G)	9.	A (I-B)	17.	B (I-B)	25.	D (I-D, IV)
2.	D (I-A)	10.	B (I-C, D)	18.	C (II-C-1)	26.	B (I-G)
3.	A (III-B)	11.	C (I-B, D)	19.	A (III-B)	27.	C (II-A)
4.	A (I-H, II-B)	12.	C (III-F)	20.	B (II-B)	28.	C (II-E)
5.	B (I-H)	13.	B (III-C)	21.	D (IV)	29.	D (III-G)
6.	C (III-A)	14.	A (II-A)	22.	C (I-D, IV)	30.	D (III-G)
7.	C (I-H)	15.	B (I-G)	23.	D (IV)		
8.	A (II-A)	16.	C (III-P)	24.	D (III-F, D)		

Self-Appraisal

Now that you have completed the Diagnostic Test, evaluate your performance. Identify your strengths and weaknesses, and then plan a practical study program based on what you have discovered.

Use the Answer Key to check your answers. Your raw score for each section is equal to the number of correct answers you had. Compute your raw score for each ability area (verbal, quantitative, analytical) by adding your raw scores from the two sections on that area. Since on the actual GRE the experimental section does not count in your score, use only two of the three quantitative sections on this Diagnostic Test when computing your raw quantitative score.

Once you have determined your raw score for each ability area, use the conversion chart that follows to get your scaled score. Note that this conversion chart is provided to give you a rough estimate of the GRE score you would achieve if you took the test now without any further preparation. When ETS administers a GRE, a conversion chart for that particular exam is prepared based on statis-tical data. The unofficial conversion chart presented here gives you only an approximate idea of how raw scores convert into scaled scores.

Use this Diagnostic Test to identify areas you may be weak in. You may find that you had trouble with a particular question type (for example, you didn't do well on the analogy questions in either verbal section), or with particular subject matter (for example, you didn't do well on any geometry questions, whether they were quantitative comparisons or discrete quantitative). Determining what you need to concentrate on will help you plan an effective study program.

Remember that, in addition to evaluating your scores and identifying weak areas, you should read all the answer explanations for questions you answered incorrectly, questions you guessed on, and questions you answered correctly but found difficult. Reviewing the answer explanations will help you understand concepts and strategies, and may point out shortcuts.

SCORE CONVERSION CHART

Raw Score	Scaled Scores		
	Verbal Score	Quantitative Score	Analytical Score
75	800		
70	770		
65	710		
60	650	800	
55	590	750	
50	540	690	800
45	490	630	770
40	450	560	700
35	410	500	620
30	360	430	550
25	320	370	470
20	280	310	400

Answer Explanations

Section 1 Verbal

1. **B.** Lacking the information derived from an actual census or population count, a numerical description of the human population would of necessity be a matter of *conjecture* (supposition based on estimate or guesswork).

2. **E.** Given that the tide pool provides suitable refuge, it is likely that the intertidal fish would seek to *return* to it. In such a case, they would be helped by the development of a *homing* instinct.

3. **C.** In a case in which experts disagree, it is *incumbent on* responsible scholars (that is, falls upon them as a scholarly duty or obligation) to *refrain from* making statements that are dogmatic or excessively assertive and arbitrary about the issue.

4. **C.** You are dealing with either similar or contradictory impulses. If the impulses are similar (that is, *analogous*, *comparable*, or *related*), the second missing word should be a synonym or near-synonym for *individualize*. If the impulses are contradictory (that is, *disparate* or *divergent*),

the second missing word should be an antonym or near-antonym for *individualize*. In this case, the latter holds true. The impulses are *divergent*; they are the impulse to individualize and the contradictory impulse to *typify* (treat characters as representatives of a type).

5. **C.** The politicians do not forsake center stage. However, if they did forsake center stage once in a while, the public might like them better for their *self-effacement* (withdrawal from attention).

6. **B.** The key phrase here is "some small village world." To be concerned only with village or parish affairs is to be *parochial*; Mrs. Woolf's novels thus have an air of *parochialism*. Again, it is a *small* world, perfect in its *tininess* as miniature paintings are perfect.
   Choice A is incorrect. It is Mrs. Woolf's choice of scene and not her choice of *period* that gives her novels their special atmosphere. (*Anachronism* has to do with chronological misplacings of persons or events.)
   Choices C and D are incorrect. Nothing in the sentence suggests *cynicism* (pessimistic disbelief) or *intrigue* (love of mystery) to be characteristic of Mrs. Woolf's work.
   Choice E, though tempting, is incorrect. A village world is not necessarily a *fragile* one; it is, however, a provincial, narrow one—in other words, a *parochial* one.

7. **A.** Because they do not have enough time to read the whole treatise, the editors ask for an abridgment or *compendium*.
   Remember, before you look at the answer choices, read the sentence and try to think of a word that makes sense.

8. **B.** A *clasp* is the fastening on a *bracelet*. A *buckle* is the fastening on a *belt*.

   (Function)

9. **C.** A *sedan* is a kind of *automobile*. A *rocker* is a kind of *chair*.

   (Class and Member)

10. **B.** By definition, a *route* that is *circuitous* follows an indirect course. Likewise, an *argument* that is *devious* follows an indirect course.

    (Defining Characteristic)

11. **D.** To *pardon* an *offense* by definition is to give up resentment for it without exacting a penalty. To *forgive* a *wrong* is to give up resentment for it without exacting a penalty.

    (Defining Characteristic)

12. A. To be *nonplussed* (totally at a loss) is to exhibit *bafflement* (perplexity). To be *discomfited* (abashed; disconcerted) is to exhibit *embarrassment*.
    Beware eye-catchers. Choice D is incorrect. To be *despicable* is to be worthy of *contempt*; it is not to *exhibit* contempt.

    (Synonym Variant)

13. C. A *gully* (miniature gorge or valley) is smaller than a *canyon* (deep gorge or valley). Likewise, a *pebble* is smaller than a *boulder*.

    (Degree of Intensity)

14. E. To be *officious* (meddlesome) is to be *helpful* in an excessive, offensive manner. To be *sycophantic* (fawning, obsequious) is to be *deferential* (respectful) in an excessive, offensive manner.

    (Manner)

15. D. *Patina* is the green coating, caused by oxidation, on *bronze* objects. *Rust* is the reddish coating, caused by oxidation, on *iron* objects.

    (Defining Characteristic)

16. C. *Cacophony* (dissonance, harshness of sound) is by definition not *mellifluous* (pleasant-sounding). *Noisomeness* (stench, rankness of smell) is by definition not *fragrant* (pleasant-smelling).

    (Antonym Variant)

17. C. The author states that the later novels of James play down prominent action. Thus they lack *overtly dramatic incident*. However, the author goes on to state that James's novels *do* possess interest; they carry the reader through "a rich analysis of the mental adjustments of the characters to the realities of their personal situations." It is this implicitly dramatic psychological revelation that sustains the reader's interest.

    Question A is unanswerable on the basis of the passage. It is evident that James wrote psychological novels; it is nowhere stated that he originated the genre.

    Question B is unanswerable on the basis of the passage. Although conventional narrative technique relates "events in distinctly phased sequences," clearly separating them, it does not necessarily recount action in *strictly* chronological order.

    Question D is unanswerable on the basis of the passage. The passage does not deal with the general public's reaction to James.

    Question E is unanswerable on the basis of the passage. The passage talks of qualities in James as a novelist in terms of their being *characteristic*, not in terms of their making him *unique*.

18. C. While the stories themselves grow simpler, their moral and psychological aspects become increasingly complex.
    Choice A is incorrect. The passage mentions the specific description of settings as characteristic of James's early, conventional novels, not of his later works.
    Choice B is incorrect. In his later novels James grew less concerned with plot and more concerned with psychological revelation.
    Choice D is incorrect. The "excitement of visible actions building up to a climactic event" is characteristic of the common novel, not of the Jamesian psychological novel.
    Choice E is incorrect. The later novels tend instead to subordinate dramatic effect to psychological exploration and revelation.

19. E. The author refers to novels of action as "overstuffed' and "crammed with *adventitious* events." However, these comments, though stated with assurance, are merely made in passing. Thus, his attitude is best described as one of *decided disapprobation* or disapproval.
    Choice A is incorrect. The author is not *pointedly indignant* or deeply resentful in tone. He is merely making mildly critical remarks in passing.
    Choice B is incorrect. The author does make passing comments that disparage the novel of action. He is not wholly *neutral* on the topic.
    Choice C is incorrect. While the author does disparage the novel of action, he does not ridicule or *deride* it sharply.
    Choice D is incorrect. The author is certainly not a *strong partisan* or advocate of the novel of action.

20. C. The author indicates that the theory of plate tectonics draws upon earlier hypotheses on sea-floor spreading; he provides details about the history of these hypotheses, tracing them from their initial formulation by Hess to their explication by Vine and Matthews and finally to their confirmation by the work of the manned submersibles. Thus, he traces the development of a theory.
    Choice A is incorrect. The author presents data; he does not question data.
    Choice B is incorrect. The author briefly describes current explorations. However, that is not his primary purpose.
    Choice D is incorrect. It is unsupported by the passage.
    Choice E is incorrect. The author mentions the phenomenon of the periodic reversals of the

earth's magnetic field. However, he states this phenomenon "continues to be one of the great mysteries of geology"; he does not explain the reasons behind it.

21. E. The entire thrust of the article is to summarize the current state of knowledge in marine geology. In addition, both the passage's free use of technical terminology and its careful provision of definitions explaining this terminology are characteristic of scientific journal articles aimed at an educated audience of nonspecialists in a field.
Choice A is incorrect. The passage is expository in tone; it is not persuasive or argumentative.

Choice B is incorrect. It mentions volcanism only in passing.
Choice C is incorrect. The passage is far greater in scope.
Choice D is incorrect. The passage indicates no such explanation of "one of the great mysteries of geology" exists.

22. C. The subduction zone is the site of the destruction or consumption of existing lithospheric material. In contrast, the mid-ocean ridge is the site of the creation or emergence of new lithospheric material.
Choice A is incorrect. Both mid-ocean ridges and subduction zones are boundaries between plates.
Choice B is incorrect. Both mid-ocean ridges and subduction zones are located on the ocean floor.
Choice D is incorrect. It is unsupported by the passage.
Choice E is incorrect. The reverse is true.

23. B. Choice B is correct. You are told that the new lithospheric material is injected into a mid-ocean ridge, a suboceanic mountain range. This new material does not disappear; it is added to the material already there. Thus, it is *incorporated into* the existing mid-ocean ridge.
Choice A is incorrect. "In general the plates are in motion with respect to one another." Nothing suggests that they become immobilized; indeed, they are said to diverge from the ridge, sliding as they diverge.
Choice C is incorrect. The passage specifically denies it. ("The size of the earth is essentially constant.")
Choice D is incorrect. It is the earth itself whose magnetic field reverses. Nothing in the passage suggests the new lithospheric material has any such potential.
Choice E is incorrect. At a mid-ocean ridge, the site at which new lithospheric material is injected from below, the plates diverge; they do not sink. (They sink, one plate diving under another, at a subduction zone.)

24. D. You can determine the correct answer by the process of elimination.
Question I is answerable on the basis of the passage. The passage states that the earth's magnetic field "reverses at intervals of from 10,000 to about a million years." Therefore, you can eliminate Choice B. Question II is unanswerable on the basis of the passage. What causes the changes in polarity is still a mystery to geologists. Therefore, you can eliminate Choices C and E.
Question III is answerable on the basis of the passage. The width of the magnetic stripes "indicates the rate" or *pace* of sea-floor spreading. Therefore, you can eliminate Choice A. Only Choice D is left. It is the correct answer.

25. C. Since the passage states that the size of the earth is essentially constant, if large amounts of new lithospheric material are being created at one point, it follows that correspondingly large amounts of lithospheric material are being destroyed at another point. Thus, an increase in activity at a mid-ocean ridge or creation point would be matched by a corresponding increase in activity at a subduction zone or destruction point.

26. B. The third sentence of the second paragraph states that one plate dives under another (*sinks*) and is reincorporated or *absorbed* into the mantle.
Choice A is incorrect. Lithospheric material rises at mid-ocean ridges, not at subduction zones.
Choice C is incorrect. New lithospheric material is injected at a mid-ocean ridge.
Choice D is incorrect. The injection of new lithospheric material causes sea-floor spreading around the mid-ocean ridge.
Choice E is incorrect. The lithospheric plates are described as diverging from a mid-ocean ridge, not from a subduction zone.

27. C. Until the most recent explorations, marine geologists lacked maps "as precise as those of a geologist on land." This suggests that, compared to land geologists, marine geologists were *laboring under a disadvantage*.
Choice A is incorrect. While the marine geologists lacked adequate charts, nothing in the passage suggests they had been *negligent* in their work.
Choice B is incorrect. It is unsupported by the passage.
Choice D is incorrect. The passage suggests that marine geologists had *in*adequate access to the ocean floor before submersibles came into use.
Choice E is incorrect. The sea-floor spreading hypothesis has been known to marine geologists

since the 1960s. Thus, they were aware of it well before the recent explorations involving manned submersibles began.

28. E. The opposite of to *deteriorate* (become worse) is to *improve*.
Think of "deteriorating health."

29. A. The opposite of *evasive* (not direct; shifty; equivocal) is *frank* (candid; open).
Think of "evasive remarks from a politician."

30. B. The opposite of to *strew* or scatter is to *collect*.
Think of "clothes strewn all over the floor."

31. D. The opposite of a *prodigal* (spendthrift; extravagant person) is an *economical person*.
Beware eye-catchers. Choice C is incorrect. A *prodigal* is not a *prodigy* (wonder; gifted person).
Think of "a prodigal squandering his wealth."

32. D. The opposite of to *equivocate* (avoid committing oneself in what one says) is to *pledge* (bind or commit oneself solemnly).
Think of politicians "hedging and equivocating."

33. B. The opposite of *crass* (stupid; vulgar; incapable of appreciating refinement) is *refined*.
Think of "a crass blockhead."

34. B. The opposite of *artifice* (trickery; guile) is *sincerity*.
Think of being "tricked by her skillful artifice."

35. B. The opposite of *opulence* (wealth; affluence) is *penury* or extreme poverty.
Think of "luxurious opulence."

36. D. The opposite of *untenable* (not able to be supported or defended) is *defensible*.
Think of "an untenable argument."

37. D. The opposite of *sedulous* (diligent; exhibiting care) is *cursory* (hasty; inattentive).
Think of "sedulous attention to details."

38. D. The opposite of to *disabuse* (undeceive) is to *deceive*.
Beware eye-catchers. Choice A is incorrect. *Disabuse* is unrelated to physical *maltreatment* or abuse.
Think of "disabusing someone of a misapprehension."

Section 2   Verbal

1. E. The presence of *extraneous* (unrelated; irrelevant) ideas that have been dragged in would make an argument *difficult* to comprehend.
Note that the phrase set off by the commas serves to define the material referred to and thus defines the first missing word.

2. D. *Because* the tendency to migrate exists in all time periods, you cannot fully explain it on the basis of any single time period. Your explanation, like the phenomenon itself, must be *independent of* any particular period of time.
The conjunction *since* here is used as a synonym for *because*; it indicates a cause and effect relationship.

3. B. Given the ubiquity of light, it is *unsurprising* that creatures have *developed* the biologically helpful ability to make use of light energy.
Note the use of *therefore* indicating that the omitted portion of the sentence supports or continues a thought developed elsewhere in the sentence.

4. E. After incubating the new functions, the next step would be to *nurture* or foster their growth until they were ready to be sent out into the world. Their departure, however, would not diminish the cities, for by continuing to breed fresh ideas the cities would *renew* themselves.
Note the metaphoric usage of *incubate* and *breed* that influences the writer's choice of words. Cities do not literally incubate businesses or breed ideas; they do so only figuratively.

5. A. Man is *gregarious* or sociable. However, he is more in need of mental companionship than of physical companionship. The writer plays on words in his conceit that a man may like to go alone for a walk but hates to stand alone in his *opinions*.

6. D. Here the contrast is between reality and pretense. Mrs. Proudie *feigned* or pretended a great interest in the parishioners' welfare. However, her interest was *not* great but actually *negligible* or insignificant, so insignificant as to be almost nonexistent.
Note that the conjunction *although* signals the contrast here. Note also that the phrase "so negligible as to be practically nonexistent" is a cliché, a literary commonplace.

7. B. By definition, an excessive or grandiloquent literary work lacks *economy* or conciseness in verbal expression.
Note that you are dealing with a secondary meaning of *economy* here.

8. B.   A *prologue* precedes a *play*. An *overture* precedes an *opera*.

(Sequence)

9. D.   *Serrations* are the teeth on the edge of a *saw*. *Cogs* are the teeth on the rim of a *gear*.

(Part to Whole)

10. C.   A *sledge* (large, heavy hammer) strikes or pounds in a *spike* (very large nail). A *hammer* strikes or pounds in a *nail*.
Beware eye-catchers. Choice A is incorrect. *Sledge* here is related to *sledgehammers*, not to sleds or *sleighs*.

(Function)

11. E.   *Thirst* is a specific example of a *drive* (state of instinctual need). *Smell* is a specific example of a *sense*.

(Class and Member)

12. A.   Something *ephemeral* (fleeting; transient) lacks *permanence*. Something *erratic* (unpredictable) lacks *predictability*.

(Antonym Variant)

13. C.   Just as the *wheat* is separated from the worthless straw or *chaff*, the *wine* is separated from the worthless sediment or *dregs*.

(Part to Whole)

14. D.   To *ogle* is to *observe* or look at someone provocatively (in an attention-getting manner). To *flaunt* is to *display* or show off something provocatively (in an attention-getting manner).

(Manner)

15. E.   Someone *abstemious* (sparing in drinking and eating) manifests *abstinence* (self-restraint in drinking and eating). Someone *pusillanimous* (cowardly) manifests *cravenness* (cowardice).

(Synonym Variant)

16. A.   Something *ineluctable* (unavoidable) is impossible to *avoid*. Something *ineffable* (inexpressible) is impossible to *utter*.

(Antonym Variant)

17. C.   The passage points out that in this period the differences between the two branches of the suffrage movement were diminishing in importance. Thus, it is *accounting for changes* occurring in the movement.
Choice A is incorrect. Both Anthony and Howe are mentioned (along with other suffragist leaders) in the context of the movements they led, but only the movements, not these two leaders, are directly contrasted.
Choice B is incorrect. The movement did not advance in this period.
Choice D is incorrect. The divisions were becoming less important, not more so, as the two branches became increasingly alike in nature.
Choice E is incorrect. It is unsupported by the passage.

18. E.   The National took up the cudgels for *all* women in distress, whatever their social or economic standing.

19. A.   The revered Mrs. Howe stood for the forces of propriety that were engulfing the suffragist movement. The embodiment of decorum, she was a *venerated figurehead* to be admired and respected, not a revolutionary firebrand to be followed into the battle.
Choice B is incorrect. Nothing in the passage suggests Mrs. Howe was overzealous.
Choice C is incorrect. Mrs. Howe was orthodox in her thinking, not heterodox.
Choice D is incorrect. A lay preacher is by definition not a member of the clergy. Therefore, Mrs. Howe was not an ordained cleric.
Choice E is incorrect. Mrs. Howe was characterized by a lack of militancy.

20. D.   The passage focuses on describing the factors which led to the diminution or lessening of radicalism in the movement for women's suffrage.
Choice A is incorrect. The title is far too limited in scope to cover the entire passage.
Choice B is incorrect. The title is far too general to suit the passage.
Choice C is incorrect. The title is inapt: the passage focuses not on the rifts but on the diminution of radicalism which led to the closing of the rifts.
Choice E is incorrect. The title is far too broad in scope.

21. C.   The author refers to the public's reaction to the Molly Maguire trials as "hysteria" that was "whipped up" or deliberately incited. Clearly, her attitude toward the reaction is that it was *overwrought* or overexcited.
Note how the use of words that convey emotion ("hysteria") helps you to determine the author's attitude to the subject.

22. B.   The passage describes Anthony as "ever catholic": very broad in sympathies; not provincial in outlook. Anthony was willing to work with anyone; her sympathies were *inclusive*, extending

sisterhood to all those who shared her espousal of woman suffrage.

Note that *catholic* here is used in its less familiar sense of "inclusive; universal," not in its common sense of "pertaining to the Roman Catholic church."

23. D.   The first sentence of the final paragraph indicates that the author's concern is to avoid a misconception or *correct a misapprehension* about what caused the trend towards conservatism in the suffrage movement.

24. C.   If even the radical Susan B. Anthony would have had second thoughts about flouting or disregarding Federal election laws, we may logically infer that the ordinary, not quite so militant movement member would have viewed such actions with disapproval or *disapprobation*.

25. C.   Scanning the passage, you easily find the one sentence that mentions *Drosophila*. The sentence immediately preceding it conveys the author's point: "A small change in a key part of the program can make a large difference."
Choice A is incorrect. While the author does indicate that he is familiar with such experiments, his primary purpose in citing *Drosophila* is to support a generalization he has made.
Choice B is incorrect. The author gives an example of a genetic change; he does not describe just how that change took place.
Choice D is incorrect. Any mutation that results in a fly with legs growing out of its head is unlikely to be an advantageous or *favorable* one.
Choice E is incorrect. The passage suggests that the particular fruit fly mutation mentioned took place in one step; it says nothing about how long it took for the fruit fly to reach its present form.

26. B.   The second paragraph indicates that an organism with a "selective advantage" will reproduce more, that is, "on average, leave more offspring." Its advantage is *reproductive*.

27. D.   The author's attitude is most evident in the concluding sentence, in which natural selection is described as "a beautiful mechanism" that increases favorable events. He clearly views the process with *appreciative admiration*.
Choice A is incorrect. The author does not question the process; he believes in it implicitly.
Choice B is incorrect. While the author is fascinated by natural selection, he views the process appreciatively, not with puzzlement.

Choice C is incorrect. The author indicates no fear or *apprehension* of the natural selection process.
Choice E is incorrect. The author is involved with his topic; his attitude is not one of hauteur or *lofty detachment*.

28. C.   The opposite of to *terminate* (end) is to *begin*.
Think of "terminating someone's employment."

29. A.   The opposite of to *protract* or prolong is to *abbreviate* or shorten.
Think of "protracting a lawsuit."

30. B.   The opposite of *volubility* (glibness, talkativeness) is *brevity* (briefness, pithiness).
Think of "unrestrained volubility."

31. E.   The opposite of *late-blooming* is maturing early or *precocious*.
Beware eye-catchers. Choice D is incorrect. Something *embryonic* is in an incipient stage; it has not yet bloomed at all.
Think of Einstein, "a late-blooming genius" who was considered not particularly intelligent as a child.

32. C.   The opposite of to *hone* or sharpen is to *dull* (make blunt).
Think of "honing a razor."

33. B.   The opposite of *phlegmatic* (stolid; undemonstrative) is *ardent* (passionate; eager).
Think of "phlegmatic and uncaring."

34. E.   The opposite of a *banality* (commonplace; trite expression) is a *novel expression*.
Think of "the banality of a greeting card rhyme."

35. B.   The opposite of *erudite* (scholarly; learned) is *ignorant*.
Think of "an erudite scholar."

36. E.   The opposite of *plethora* (overabundance) is *scarcity*.
Think of "a plethora of tax forms."

37. B.   The opposite of *currency* (vogue or prevalence; period of acceptance) is *obsolescence* (process of falling into disuse).
Beware eye-catchers. Choice D is incorrect. *Currency* here is unrelated to money.
Think of "the currency of an idea."

38. C.   The opposite of to *skirt* something (avoid dealing with a topic or question) is to *address* or
deal directly with it.
Think of "skirting an issue."

Section 3   Quantitative

1. B. $\dfrac{n + 7}{3} + \dfrac{n - 3}{4}$

$\dfrac{4n + 28 + 3n - 9}{12}$

$\dfrac{7n + 19}{12}$

The numerators are the same but the fraction in
Column B has a smaller denominator, denoting
a larger quantity.

2. B. $1y + 0.01y = 2.2$
$10y + 1y = 220$
$11y = 220$
$y = 20$
$0.1y = 2$

3. C.   The reciprocal of 4 is $\dfrac{1}{4}$.

$\sqrt{\dfrac{1}{16}} = \dfrac{1}{4}$

4. A. $\sqrt{1440}$ is a two-digit number $(37 +)$. *Note*: for
this test you are required only to estimate
square roots.

5. B.   1 yard = 3 feet
(0.5) or $\dfrac{1}{2}$ yard = 1 foot, 6 inches
(1.5) or $1\dfrac{1}{2}$ yards = 4 feet, 6 inches

6. C.   Observe $10 + 5$; $9 + 6$; $8 + 7$;....
There are five additions with the sum in each
case equal to 15.

7. B. $8 \times 3 = 24$, $7 \times 3 = 21 + 2 = 23$.
Therefore $\triangle = 3$. Since $8 \times 7 = 56$,
then $\bigcirc = 6$.

8. D.   Since Rose is older than Mary, she may be older
or younger than Sam.

9. B. $4x = 4(14) - 4$
$4x = 56 - 4$
$4x = 52$
$x = 13$

10. A.   Since $x = 65$ and $AC = BC$, then the measure
of angle ABC is 65°, and the measure of angle
ACB is 50°. Since $BC \parallel DE$, then $y = 50°$ and
$x > y$.

11. D.   Since $AD = 5$ and the area = 20 square
inches, we can find the value of base BC but not
the value of DC. BC equals 8 inches but BD
will be equal to DC only if $AB = AC$.

12. C.   Since $y = 50$, the measure of angle DCB is
100° and the measure of angle ABC is 80° since
$ABCD$ is a parallelogram. Since $x = 40$:
$z = 180 - 90 = 90$
$z - y = \ \ 90 - 50 = 40$.

13. C.   Rate = Distance ÷ Time
Rate = 36 miles ÷ $\dfrac{3}{4}$ hour
$(36)\left(\dfrac{4}{3}\right) = 48$ miles per hour

14. A.   In Column A, d, the smallest integer, is subtracted from a, the integer with the largest
value.

15. D. $\dfrac{BC \times AB}{2} = 18$, but any of the following may
be true: $BC > AB$, $BC < AB$, or $BC = AB$.

16. A. $\dfrac{8}{0.8} = \dfrac{80}{8} = 10$

$\dfrac{0.8}{8} = \dfrac{8}{80} = \dfrac{1}{10}$

$(0.8)^2 = 0.64$

$\sqrt{0.8} = 0.8 +$

$0.8\pi = (0.8)(3.14) = 2.5 +$

17. E. $17xy + 7 = 19xy$
$7 = 2xy$
$14 = 4xy$

18. D.   Average = XY
Sum ÷ 2 = XY
Sum = $2XY$
$2XY = X + ?$
$? = 2XY - X$

19. C.   This is a direct proportion.
Let x = length of shorter dimension of enlargement.

$$\frac{\text{longer dimension}}{\text{shorter dimension}} = \frac{2\frac{1}{2}}{4} = \frac{1\frac{1}{8}}{x}$$

$$2\frac{1}{2}x = (4)(1\frac{7}{8})$$

$$\frac{5x}{2} = \frac{60}{8}$$

$$40x = 120$$

$$x = 3$$

20. D. $AEB = 12$ $AE = 8$
$AGD = 6$ $AG = 4$
Area $AEFG = 32$
Area $ABCD = 72$
Area of shaded part $= 72 - 32 = 40$

21. C.   Be careful to read the proper line (regular depositors). The point is midway between 90 and 100.

22. A.   Number of Christmas Club depositors $= 60,000$
Number of regular despositors $= 90,000$

$60,000 : 90,000$ or $6 : 9$ or $\frac{6}{9}$ or $\frac{2}{3}$.

23. B.   I is not true; although the number of depositors remained the same, one may not assume that interest rates were the cause. II is true; in 1984 there were 110,000 depositors. Observe the largest angle of inclination for this period. III is not true; the circle graph indicates that more than half of the bank's assets went into mortgages.

24. C.   (58.6%) of $360° = (0.586)(360°) = 210.9°$

25. E.   (Amount invested) $\times$
(Rate of interest) $=$ Interest
or, Amount invested $= \dfrac{\text{Interest}}{\text{Rate of interest}}$

Amount invested in bonds $= \dfrac{x \text{ dollars}}{b\%}$

or $\dfrac{x \text{ dollars}}{b/100}$

or $x \div \dfrac{b}{100}$ or $x \cdot \left(\dfrac{100}{b}\right)$ or $(x)\left(\dfrac{100}{b}\right)$ or $\dfrac{\$100x}{b}$.

Since the amount invested in bonds $= \dfrac{\$100x}{b}$,

the amount invested in mortgages must be 2 $\left(\dfrac{100x}{b}\right)$ dollars or $\$\dfrac{200x}{b}$ since the chart indicates that twice as much (58.6%) is invested in mortgages as is invested in bonds (28.3%).

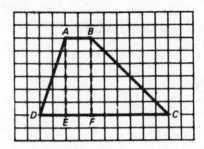

26. D.   Draw altitudes AE and BF.
Area of figure $= \triangle AED + \triangle BFC +$ rectangle $AEFB$
Area of $\triangle AED = \dfrac{bh}{2}$
or $\dfrac{(2 \text{ units})(6 \text{ units})}{2}$ or 6 square units.
Area of $\triangle BCF = \dfrac{bh}{2}$ or $\dfrac{(6 \text{ units})(6 \text{ units})}{2}$
or 18 square units.
Area of rectange $AEFB = lw$.
or (2 units)(6 units) or 12 square units.
Sum $= 36$ square units.
Or apply formula for area of trapezoid:
Area $= \frac{1}{2}h(b + b_l)$
Area $= \frac{1}{2}(6)(10 + 2)$
Area $= 36$ square units.

27. B.   Between 1 P.M. and 3:52 P.M. there are 172 minutes. There are *three* intervals between the 4 classes. 3×4 minutes, or 12 minutes, is the time spent in passing to classes. That leaves $172 - 12$ or 160 minutes for instruction or 40 minutes for each class period.

28. D.   Factor $x^2 + 2x - 8$ into $(x + 4)(x - 2)$. If x is either -4 or 2, $x^2 + 2x - 8 = 0$, and D is the correct answer.

29. A.   This is a case of ratio and proportion.
$\dfrac{\text{nautical}}{\text{statute}} = \dfrac{630}{720} = \dfrac{x}{1}$
$720x = 630$
$x = 0.875$

30. E.   (Average)(Number of cases) $=$ sum
$(x)(P) = Px$
$(y)(N) = Ny$
$\dfrac{\text{Sum}}{\text{Number of cases}} =$ average
$\dfrac{Px + Ny}{P + N} =$ average

Section 4   Quantitative

1. C.   Since the triangle is equilateral
$$3a + 15 = 5a + 1 = 2a + 22$$
$$3a + 15 = 5a + 1$$
$$14 = 2a$$
$$7 = a$$

2. C.   From -5 to zero there are 5 integers and from zero to $+5$ there are 5 integers. Also, from $+5$ to $+15$ there are 10 integers.

3. D.   Since $x - y = 7$, then $x = y + 7$; x and y have many values, and $x + y$ may have many values.

4. B.   Since the area $= 25$, each side $= 5$. The sum of three sides of the square $= 15$.

5. B. $\dfrac{x^2}{2} = 18$

$$x^2 = 36$$
$$x = 6$$
Therefore $AC = 6\sqrt{2}$
$$6\sqrt{2} > 6$$

6. C. $AB = 6$
Perimeter $= 24$

7. C.   Area $= \dfrac{1}{2}(6)(6) = 18$

8. C. $AB = BC$ (given).
Since the measure of angle B equals the measure of angle C, $AB = AC$. Therefore ABC is equilateral and $m\angle A = m\angle B = m\angle C$, and $m\angle B + m\angle C = m\angle B + m\angle A$.

9. A. $x = 0.5$
$4x = (0.5)(4) = 2.0$
$x^4 = (0.5)(0.5)(0.5)(0.5) = 0.0625$
If you prefer to work with fractions:

$$\left(\frac{1}{2}\right)(4) = 2 \text{ and } \left(\frac{1}{2}\right)\left(\frac{1}{2}\right)\left(\frac{1}{2}\right)\left(\frac{1}{2}\right) = \frac{1}{16}$$

10. B.   The fraction in Column A has a denominator with a negative value.

11. D.   The area of a triangle is one-half the product of the lengths of the base and the altitude, and can't be determined from the values of the sides.

12. C.   Let $x =$ the first of the integers, then:
sum $= x + x + 1 + x + 2 + x + 3 + x + 4$
$\qquad = 5x + 10.$
$5x + 10 = 35$ (given), then $5x = 25$.
$x = 5$ and the largest integer, $x + 4 = 9$.

13. A. $\sqrt{160} = \sqrt{16}\sqrt{10} = 4\sqrt{10}$

14. C.   Since the triangle is equilateral, $x = 60$ and exterior angle $y = 120$. Therefore $2x = y$.

15. B.   If $\dfrac{2}{3}$ corresponds to 12 gallons, then $\dfrac{1}{3}$ corresponds to 6 gallons, and $\dfrac{3}{3}$ corresponds to 18 gallons (Column A).

16. C.   Evidently, four cows produce 1 can of milk in 1 day. Therefore, eight cows could produce 2 cans of milk in 1 day. In 4 days, eight cows will be able to produce 8 cans of milk.

17. A.   Visualize the situation. The amount of pure alcohol remains the same after the dilution with water.

18. E.   Note that the question gives information about the transfer of teachers, but asks about the *remaining* teachers.
$$\frac{60}{80} = \frac{3}{4} = 75\%$$

19. E.   152 pounds and 4 ounces $= 152.25$ pounds
$152.25 \div 3 = 50.75$ pounds
0.75 or $\dfrac{3}{4}$ pound $= 12$ ounces

20. E.   Let $x =$ number of contestants.
$$0.05x = 30$$
$$5x = 3{,}000$$
$$x = 600$$

21. C.   500 grams of carbohydrates $= 2{,}050$ calories
100 grams of carbohydrates $= 410$ calories
1 gram of carbohydrate $= 4.1$ calories

22. A.   Total calories = 3,390
          Calories from protein = 410
          $\dfrac{410}{3,390} = \dfrac{41}{339} = 12 + \%$

23. C.   100 grams of fat = 930 calories
          1,000 grams of fat = 9,300 calories
          To obtain 9,300 calories from carbohydrates,
          set up a proportion, letting x = number of
          grams of carbohydrates needed.
          $\dfrac{500 \text{ grams}}{2,050 \text{ calories}} = \dfrac{x}{9,300 \text{ calories}}$
          $2,050x = (9,300)(500)$
          $\qquad x = 2,268$ (to the nearest gram)

24. B.   Boys at 17 require 3,750 calories per day.
          Girls at 17 require 2,750 calories per day.
          Difference = 1,000

25. D.   I is true; observe the regular increase for both
          sexes up to age 13. II is not true; from age 4 to
          12 calorie requirements are generally similar for
          boys and girls. Note that the broken line and the
          solid line are almost parallel. III is true; boys
          reach their peak at 17, while girls reach their
          peak at 13.

26. D.   Since the driver's fee is paid with the car, the
          charge for $n - 1$ person = $c(n - 1)$ cents; cost
          of car and driver = 50¢.
          $T = 50 + c(n - 1)$

27. C.   This is a direct proportion.
          $\dfrac{\text{Cups of sugar}}{\text{Cups of water}} = \dfrac{1.5}{0.5} = \dfrac{1}{x}$
          $1.5x = 0.5$
          $15x = 5$
          $x = \dfrac{1}{3}$

28. B.   1 kilogram = 2.2 lb
          20 kilograms = 44 lb

29. A.   I is not correct because $\dfrac{1}{a}$ is not less than a if a
          is 1 or a fraction less than 1.
          $\left(\text{e.g.,} \dfrac{1}{1} \text{ or } \dfrac{1}{\frac{1}{8}} \text{ is not less than 1 or } \dfrac{1}{8}\right)$. II is correct
          because $\dfrac{a + b}{2a} = \dfrac{2b}{b + a}$ reduces to $\dfrac{2b}{2b} = \dfrac{2b}{2b}$
          (which we know is correct) when $a = b$. III is
          incorrect when a is greater than b $\left(\text{e.g.,} \dfrac{3 + 1}{2 + 1}\right.$
          is not more than $\left.\dfrac{3}{2}\right)$. This statement is also not
          correct when c is negative and a is less than b
          $\left(\text{e.g., if } c \text{ is } -1, \dfrac{2 - 1}{3 - 1} \text{ is not more than } \dfrac{2}{3}\right)$.

          The only correct answer is II.

30. A. $\dfrac{y}{s - t} = \dfrac{s + t}{t - s}$ (given)
          $\dfrac{y}{s - t} = \dfrac{-s - t}{-t + s}$ $\left(\text{multiplying fraction by } -\dfrac{1}{1}\right)$
          $\dfrac{y}{s - t} = \dfrac{-s - t}{s - t}$ (rearrangement of terms)
          $\phantom{\dfrac{y}{s - t}}y = -s - t$ (multiplying by $s - t$)

Section 5   Analytical

1-4.   Summarize Michael's schedule:

Monday	3:30-4:30	Piano Lesson
Tuesday	4:00-6:00	Karate
Wednesday	4:00-6:00	Art Class
Thursday	12:00-	Free
Friday	3:00-	Club Program

1. C.   Note that Thursday is a free afternoon.

2. D.   Since Michael must begin his piano lesson at
          3:30 P.M., Thursday is the only available day.

3. C.   Since Michael would no longer have to attend
          his original Wednesday art class, that day and
          his free Thursday afternoon would be available
          for his new class.

4. E.   Since karate and art meet until 6 P.M., Michael
          will have to give up these activities in order to
          be present at the 5 P.M. basketball sessions.
          After his piano lesson, he will have thirty min-
          utes to get to the basketball court. Thursday
          afternoon is free, and the Friday club program
          is dismissed by 4:30.

5. C.   This question tests an "all/only" confusion.
          Sarah is saying that only members with General
          Council status are eligible for a position in the
          President's cabinet. Charles assumes that Sarah
          is saying all the members on the General Coun-
          cil sit on the President's cabinet. He knows of
          one Council member who doesn't, and refutes
          Sarah's statement. Choice C accurately summa-
          rizes Charles's misinterpretation. Choice A says
          the same thing Sarah says, in reverse; Choice B
          is simply incorrect (Charles says Grogan does
          not sit on the Cabinet); Choice D directly con-
          tradicts Sarah's statement; and Choice E men-
          tions a post—General Council Manager—that
          isn't mentioned in the dialogue.

6. **D.** Analyze the argument: it says that the unemployment problem has one cause, worker laziness. Anything that gives evidence for this strengthens the argument; anything that gives evidence against it or suggests another explanation weakens it. D, if true, *might* be evidence that the unemployed are lazy. Choices A, B, and E all suggest different explanations: A, that the unemployed lack the requisite skills or experience; B, that they are in the wrong places; E, that unemployment has another cause altogether. Choice C tends to weaken the idea that unemployed people are lazy.

7. **D.** Event X (baldness) occurs after Event Y (practicing law). The author of the argument assumes that Event Y caused Event X, and vows to avoid Event X by avoiding Event Y. This is poor reasoning, especially since the author is overlooking at least one far more probable cause for Event X, i.e., heredity. The same kind of poor reasoning is used in choice D, where Event X = injury, Event Y = eating at Rosie's, and the overlooked probable cause is unsafe working conditions. Choice B has the second closest resemblance, but here the reasoning is somewhat more plausible; speeding can lead to one's getting a speeding ticket. Choices A, C, and E all differ from the original argument in the latter portion of their reasoning.

8–12. The only problem in puzzles like this one is to rank the items correctly; the questions are then simple. Use initials, since the seven artists' names begin with different letters. Ignore G, for which no definite value is given, and start with the one whose value seems lowest. This is I. If you call I's value 1, all the others can be expressed as multiples of 1, and we get:

$$G = ?$$
$$I = 1$$
$$J = 3 \text{ times } 1 = 3$$
$$E = J + I = 3 + 1 = 4$$
$$D = J + E = 3 + 4 = 7$$
$$F = D = 7$$
$$H = F + E + J = 7 + 4 + 3 = 14$$

8. **E.** You can tell that the Greuze is worth least and the Hartley most without really figuring out the rest, but all choices include those values. If you've constructed a table like the one shown here, inspection gives choice E.

9. **E.** $D = 7$, $H = 14$. None of the other choices adds up to 7.

10. **B.** $H = 14$. Option I, $D + I + F$, adds up to 15. Option II, $E + J + D$, adds up to 14, which is right. Option III, $I + E + J$, adds up to 8.

11. **D.** $E + I = 5$, so the value of the Greuze, in terms of the value of the Ingres which is our base, is $\frac{1}{2} \cdot H = 14$ or 28 times this.

12. **B.** $H + E = 18$. $I + J + D + F = 18$. Choice A: $14 \neq 12$. Choice C: $14 \neq 15$. Choice D: $15 \neq 14$. Choice E: $7 \neq 8$.

13–16. A diagram of the kind shown here is your best approach to this type of problem.

A circle inside another (like circles P and N) indicates that all members of the first (inner) group belong to the second (outer) group. Overlapping circles (like circles N and M) indicate that the groups have members in common, but neither is contained entirely within the other. Solid lines may be used for relationships that are definitely known; broken lines for relationships that are uncertain. So: statement (1) gives us the two circles N and P; statements (1) and (2) the shaded lines for X. Statement (4) gives us a circle, R, that lies entirely outside N. Why make it border N, instead of being totally separate? Because statement (3) gives us a circle, M, lying outside P, and (5) tells us M lies *inside* the areas of X and R (and outside P). But circle M is made entirely of broken lines because we can't know for sure whether it overlaps the R/N border, lies entirely within the X area of N, or lies entirely within R. Finally, statement (6) gives us a group, Q, that lies either inside P, or outside N (whether inside R or not) or both. Once you have all this admittedly complex information diagrammed, the questions are fairly easy.

13. **A.** I is true, because R lies entirely outside N while P is inside. II contradicts condition (2). III may or may not be true, depending on the location of M.

14. **C.** This is false, because R lies entirely outside N, while X lies inside. Q *may* lie within P (A) or outside both N and R (B), or both; we don't know. D may look impossible, but expand the M circle in your mind until it exactly coincides with the R circle: now, all R are M and vice

versa. No stated condition prevents you from drawing the circle this way, so it is not impossible. No matter how you draw the M circle, it should be apparent that *some* X may not be M (E).

15. B. Statement (5), together with statement (2), indicates that no M can be P, since no X can be P. Statement (2) gives information about X not contained in any other statement; (4) excludes R from N; (5), which may look like the counterpart to (2), contains the additional information that no M are to be found outside X and R; and statement (6) contains the only information about Q.

16. E. Statement (2) could be untrue under either, or both, of two conditions: if some X were P, or if some N that was not P was not X. This is what choice E states. Choice D states only the second possibility; it is not necessarily true if statement (2) is false, because some X that was P would make statement (2) false even if choice D were not true. Choices A, B, and C remain false as long as statements (5), (1), and (6), respectively, are true.

17–22. A four-by-four grid allows you to graph all the information:

Name	Allen	Brian	Carol	Donna
Site			High Point	Freeport
Lake		Keewaukett	Jackson	Indian Point
State	Ohio		Nebraska	Pennsylvania

The other items now follow by elimination. Brian and Keewaukett Lake must be in Maine. Since Donna cannot be at High Point, she, and Freeport Campsite, must be on Indian Point Lake in Pennsylvania. Carol must be at High Point. Allen must be at Leesville, the only remaining lake. Brian and Allen must be at Edmunds and Grand Isle Campsites, but we don't know which person is at which campsite.

17. B. See above. Choice A is possible, but we can't be sure. C is a direct contradiction of the information about Brian. D and E are ruled out once everything is diagrammed.

18. A. See the diagram and the above discussion.

19. D. Allen is at Edmunds or Grand Isle (I). Carol is in Nebraska (II). Donna is at Freeport (III).

20. A. See the diagram.

21. E. See the diagram. Allen is at Leesville Lake , it is in Ohio, and it is the site of either Edmunds or Grand Isle Campsite, but not Freeport Campsite.

22. B. This is the item that remained ambiguous. Keewaukett is in Maine (A); Freeport Campsite is in Pennsylvania (C); Carol is in Nebraska and Donna is in Pennsylvania (D, E).

23. B. The ad states that this dishwasher is the best, but gives only details of its luxury features— its "bells and whistles." The performance of the appliance would show it was the best, so Choice (B) would be the missing part of the ad that most weakens its argument. Warranty terms, sizes, electrical use, and capacity would also be important, but actual dishwashing performance would be most crucial to proving it was the "best."

24. A. It is claimed that the archeologists could not have understood the culture because, without written records, they have no evidence about how people thought. The assumption is that *only* written records provide such evidence, and that physical artifacts do not (A). B and C are side issues: neither one establishes what the argument assumes, that written records are the only clue to what people thought. D and E are too broad: the argument claims neither that the artifacts tell us nothing about other aspects of the civilization (D), nor that written records by themselves are sufficient to reconstruct the civilization (E).

25. B. Statement I is *not* assumed. The conclusion is that Roger will never be an *outstanding* football player, not that he will never play football. Statement II *is* assumed. The injured knee is cited as the reason Roger will never play outstanding football. Statement III is *not* assumed. Nothing was mentioned in the argument about Roger's playing *professional* football.

Section 6   Analytical

1–4. The only problem with this one is that George's preferences regarding Mahler, Beethoven, and Bartok cannot be related exactly to his preferences among Haydn, Hindemith, and Mozart. Note also that while he *definitely* doesn't prefer Mahler to Beethoven, he may or may not prefer Beethoven to Mahler—instead, he may like them equally. (You're never told that George always has a definite preference.) Otherwise, the questions are fairly straightforward.

1. D. George definitely prefers Mahler to Mozart, and likes Beethoven as much as, or more than, Mahler. He definitely prefers Mahler to Bartok (A) and *may* prefer Beethoven to Mahler (B). We know he prefers Mahler to Mozart and to any other composer whose name begins with B, including Bartok, but this doesn't tell us whether or not he prefers Bartok to Mozart (C). We don't know how much he likes Mahler, so he may prefer Mahler to Haydn (E).

2. B. This restates the information in the third sentence; it's the only set of preferences among three composers that we know for certain. George may or may not play Bartok before Mozart (A). We don't know that he prefers Beethoven to Mahler, just that he *doesn't* prefer Mahler to Beethoven (C). D and E may be true but may not be.

3. D. George definitely prefers Beethoven to Bartok. He also prefers Mahler to Mozart, and likes Beethoven; at least as much as Mahler. So among the six, Mozart and Bartok must come after Beethoven. All the other choices are possibilities that cannot be eliminated.

4. E. George prefers Mahler to any composer whose name begins with B (including Berlioz) *except* Beethoven; since he doesn't prefer Mahler to Beethoven but does prefer him to Berlioz, he must prefer Beethoven to Berlioz. If Berlioz is played first, there can be no Beethoven record. None of the other choices is definitely true.

5. E. Examine the structure of the argument: *The Other Side* is best *since* even more people are seeing it…The assumption is that these numbers are a valid measurement of quality (E). All other choices focus on side issues.

6. C. The author is using circular reasoning. He attempts to prove that the scientific worldview is accurate by showing that it has been verified by the scientific method; yet the validity of the scientific method is itself at issue. The author does not commit the errors mentioned in choices A and E. Although choice B is true, it is neither a flaw in nor a necessary part of the author's reasoning. Choice D is wrong because the author claims merely that the scientific worldview is the most accurate, not that it is perfect.

7. A. Alfredo replies to the claim about meditation by stating that aggressiveness is most important to a boxer. The unstated assumption is that meditation somehow lessens aggressiveness (A). B is

off because, clearly, Alfredo assumes that *some* effect results from meditation. Alfredo implies nothing about how good or poor a boxer George was before, and implicitly *accepts* Melinda's testimony that he has been meditating (C, D). E is directly contrary to Alfredo's comment about aggressiveness, which is certainly a mental attitude.

8–12. As in most logical puzzles, a diagram of some sort is the place to start. The simplest is a sketch of the ten seats (below). When you know someone is in a seat, put his/her initial in the box; if a seat is definitely occupied by either of two persons, put both initials there. If someone's position is uncertain, jot the initial below the possible seats. Skip to whichever statements yield the most definite information to start. Here, statements (2), (4), (6), and (7) give this information:

1	2	3	4	5	6	7	8	9	10
		O	V	M				N	

Statement (3) gives an uncertainty: W must be in seat 6 or 8. Statement (5) resolves the question: W's date cannot be M, in seat 5, because M is next to V. So W's date must be in seat 7, W must be in seat 8, and T must be M's date, in seat 6. Nothing else is known definitely. The two remaining women's seats must be occupied by S and U, and the two remaining men's seats by L and P, but we can't tell exactly who is where. Complete your diagram like this:

1	2	3	4	5	6	7	8	9	10
L	S					L			S
		O	V	M	T		W	N	
P	U					P			U

The questions are now easy.

8. D. This can be read from the diagram. Choice A reverses O and V and gives a definite location for U, which we don't know. B puts L in seat 7, when we can't know that. C and E skip a seat— the question specifies persons sitting adjacent to one another.

9. D. U may be in seat 2 or 10. N is in seat 9, and either L or P is in seat 1. Any of these could be U's date.

10. C.   Look at your diagram. Exactly who is in the seats at the two ends of the row (I, II) remains uncertain. The women nearest T (III) are V on the left and W on the right.

11. C.   We know that either L or P is in seat 7, but we don't know which. The other must be in seat 1. If we are told which of the two is in seat 7, we know his date is W. If we are told which of the two is in seat 1, we don't know *his* date (it could be S or U) but we know that the other's date is W.

12. D.   To determine T's position we need statement (1), which gives the conditions for all seating; (3), which gives the seats W may occupy; (2), (6), and (7), which determine where O, V, and M sit; and (5), which determines that T is to the left of W's date and that W must be in seat 8. The one statement that is irrelevant is (4).

13. A.   Leona can't ride in the same car as Rick, so Rick must be in the other car.

14. D.   If Naomi rides in the same car as Gregor, Carlos must be in that car also. This means that Leona is also in that car, since she and Gregor must be together in the car that does not carry Rick.

15. C.   If Rick is in one car, Leona and Gregor must be in another car, together. Choice A is incorrect since Leona and Gregor are together in a car without Rick. Since Dave and Gregor can be together in a car only if Ingrid is in it too, Dave can't be with Leona and Gregor. B and E are incorrect, since Dave, Rick, and Ingrid must be together in the same car, and Carlos and Naomi must be together in one car. Dave, Rick, and Ingrid can't be in that same car because the maximum number of riders in one car is four. Also, Dave and Carlos can't be in a car together.

16. E.   Carlos must be in the same car as Naomi, so Dave, Naomi and Carlos, at least, must be in this car. Gergor can't be in the same car, since he would then be together with Dave, but without Ingrid (and no more than four people can ride in a car). Gregor is then in the other car, and since Gregor and Rick can't be together, Rick is the fourth person in the first car. Leona and Ingrid share a car with Gregor.

17–21.   The information given can be diagrammed in the way shown here. Many of the questions can then be answered by inspection of the diagram, without even looking back at the rules as printed.

17. C.   I is true because Physics 101 and 121 are alternative prerequisites for the 200-level courses in Physics. II is true because Chemistry 201 counts as a graduate-level course, along with Physics 201 and 221. III is not true because Mathematics 11 can substitute for Physics 1, and Physics 21 for Physics 11.

18. C.   To qualify using chemistry courses only, the student must take Chemistry 11 *or* 21, 101, 201, 211, and 221—five in all. Using Mathematics 201 would cut one chemistry course, but to do this the student must take at least two mathematics courses—101 and 201—so the total becomes six.

19. D.   After the Physics 101/121 level, the student *must* take Physics 201 and 221, plus Chemistry 201—but there are eight separate ways to reach this level. You can just follow the separate lines on the diagram: Mathematics 11 *or* Physics 1, followed by Physics 11 *or* 21, followed by Physics 101 *or* 121.

20. B.   I is out because Chemistry 101 must be taken to qualify for the 200-level Chemistry courses. II, though pedestrian, is just fine. III is out because Mathematics 201, not 211, satisfies the chemistry requirement.

21. C.   In physics, one must take Mathematics 11 *or* Physics 1, Physics 11 *or* 21, Physics 101 *or* 121, and three graduate-level courses. In mathematics or chemistry, one can qualify with five courses, or four if one has advanced placement.

22. C.   I is true because Chemistry 101 is the only acceptable prerequisite for Mathematics 201. II is true because only two graduate-level physics courses will be available; the third graduate-level course that could be taken for physics credit is Chemistry 201, which will be cancelled. III is false because Mathematics 201, will still be open to students who have taken Chemistry 101.

23. A.   With a complex statement like this one, a circle diagram similar to those used in some analytical reasoning questions may be a help. In the diagram shown here, those who knew Ortega and those who supported her plan are shown as overlapping circles. The pro-merger votes are shown *not* intersecting the overlapping area (stockholders who knew Ortega *and* supported her plan); the circle for Anaco stock-owners does intersect it, and otherwise is drawn as generally as possible.
         With the aid of the diagram, you can see that choice A is impossible; choices B, D, and E are all possible, while choice C *must* be true.

24. E.   The claim being discussed is that *only* the smart become rich, not that *all* the smart become rich; therefore choice A is wrong. The way to disprove this view would be to point out that some stupid people also become rich (choice E). Choices B, C, and D, while possibly relevant to the issue raised, do not directly contradict the claim.

25. B.   This choice combines the two psychological effects mentioned in the original argument. Choices A and D are wrong because the argument states matters of (alleged) fact and does not, by itself, imply any recommendations. Choices C and E are wrong because the argument (if true) establishes that TV viewers *believe* certain things; it does not imply anything about what actually happens.

Section 7   Quantitative

1. D.   No relationship between a and f is given.

2. D.   The variable x may have a value between 65 and 80.

3. A. $KL = 23 +$ length of AB
        $KL > 23$

4. A. $x \bigtriangleup y = x^2 + y^2$
        $(x \bigtriangleup y)^2 = (x^2 + y^2) = x^4 + 2x^2y^2 + y^4$ (Column A)
        $x^2 \bigtriangleup y^2 = (x^2)^2 + (y^2)^2 = x^4 + y^4$ (Column B)

5. B. $\sqrt{144} = 12;$
        $\sqrt{100} + \sqrt{44} = 10 + 6+ = 16+$

6. C.   Since $y = z$, because $AB = AC$, $x + y = x + z$ (if equals are added to equals the results are equal).

7. C. $\dfrac{3\sqrt{48}}{\sqrt{3}} \times \dfrac{\sqrt{3}}{\sqrt{3}} = \dfrac{3\sqrt{144}}{3} = \dfrac{(3)(12)}{3} = 12$

8. A. $\dfrac{x}{4} + \dfrac{x}{3} = \dfrac{7}{12}$
        $\dfrac{3x}{12} + \dfrac{4x}{12} = \dfrac{7}{12}$
        $3x + 4x = 7$
        $x = 1$
        $1 > -1$

9. A.   The fraction with the larger denominator has the smaller value. Since the value of $\dfrac{9}{b}$ is greater than $\dfrac{9}{a}$, then $a > b$.

10. B. $0.003\% = 0.00003$
         $0.0003 > 0.00003$

11. C. $\dfrac{k}{4}\% = \dfrac{\frac{4}{4}}{100} = \dfrac{k}{4} \div 100 = \dfrac{k}{4} \times \dfrac{1}{100} = \dfrac{k}{400}$

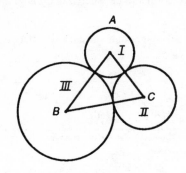

12. C. AB = 3 inches + 5 inches = 8 inches
BC = 5 inches + 4 inches = 9 inches
AC = 4 inches + 3 inches = 7 inches
            Total   24 inches = 2 feet

13. B. Since $y = 130$, $z = 50$.
$m\angle ECD = 180° - 130° = 50°$
$2x = 50°$
$x = 25°$

14. A. Since $abc = 0$ and $c = 1$, then either a or $b = 0$ or a and $b = 0$.

15. B. $0.1 + 0.01 + 0.001 = 0.111$ (sum)
$\text{average} = \dfrac{0.111}{3}$
$0.111 > \dfrac{0.111}{3}$

16. C. Since $OC = BC$ and OC and OB are radii, triangle BOC is equilateral and the measure of angle $BOC = 60°$.
Therefore $x = 120$ and $\dfrac{1}{2}x = 60$.

17. B. Select the choice in which the value of n is greater than the value of d in order to yield a value of $\dfrac{n}{d}$ greater than 1.

18. C. Let x = the number.
$\dfrac{x}{2} = \dfrac{x}{3} + 17$
$3x = 2x + 102$
$x = 102$

19. A. $c + d = 180$ but $c \neq d$
$a = d$ (vertical angles)
$a = e$ (corresponding angles)
$f = b$ (corresponding angles)
$f = c$ (alternate interior angles)

20. B. Let x = amount Florence had.
Let y = amount Sam had.
$x + \$10$ = amount Florence now has.
$y - \$10$ = amount Sam now has.
$x + y = \$100$

$\dfrac{x + \$10}{5} + \$4 = y - 10$

$x + \$10 + \$20 = 5y - \$50$
$x - 5y = -\$80$
$x + y = \$100$
$-x - y = -100$ [multiply by -1]
$x - 5y = -\$80$
$-6y = -\$180$ [subtraction]
$y = \$30$ (amount Sam had)
$\$30 - \$10 = \$20$ (amount Sam now has)

21. D. $6{,}000 : 302{,}000 :: x : 1{,}000{,}000$
$302{,}000x =$
$6{,}000 \times 1{,}000{,}000 = 6{,}000{,}000{,}000$
$x = \dfrac{60{,}000}{3}$ (rounded off) $= 20{,}000$
The closest number is 17.

22. C. $18 - 21$ group $= 11{,}000$
$21 - 24$ group $= 61{,}000$
            Total $= 72{,}000$
$\dfrac{72{,}000}{302{,}000} = 23 + \%$

23. D. I is correct; marriages in 21–24 group = 61,000 and in the 33–36 group = 21,000. II is not correct; the circle graph gives data only for bridegrooms in the 24–27 group. III is correct; the number of bridegrooms aged 24–27 who receive postgraduate education = (73,000) (0.04) or 2920.

24. D. 20% or $\dfrac{1}{5}$ of $360° = 72°$

25. D. Total between 21 and 27 :
$61{,}000 + 73{,}000 = 134{,}000$
$\dfrac{134{,}000}{302{,}000} = \dfrac{134}{302} = \dfrac{44}{100}$ (approx.) $= 44\%$

26. B. Sum $= (0.6)(4)$ or 2.4.
$0.2 + 0.8 + 1 = 2$.
$x = 2.4 - 2$ or 0.4

27. C. $\dfrac{a^2 - b^2}{(a - b)^2} = \dfrac{(a + b)\cancel{(a - b)}}{(a - b)\cancel{(a - b)}} = \dfrac{a + b}{a - b}$

28. C. This is a ratio problem.
$\dfrac{\text{number of items}}{\text{cost in cents}} = \dfrac{2}{c} = \dfrac{?}{x}$
$c(?) = 2x$
$(?) = \dfrac{2x}{c}$

29. D.   Area of square = 36 square feet.
         Area of rectangle = 36 square feet.
         Since $AD = 4$, $DC = 9$ feet,
         and the perimeter of $ABCD$ = 26 feet.

30. D.   Since the formula for the area of a circle is πr^2,
         any change in r will affect the area by the
         square of the amount of the change. Since the
         radius is doubled, the area will be four times as
         much $(2)^2$.

3 Sentence Completion Questions

- ■ **Testing Tactics**
- ■ **Practice Exercises**
- ■ **Answer Key**

GRE sentence completion questions test your ability to use your vocabulary and recognize logical consistency among the elements in a sentence. You need to know more than the dictionary definitions of the words involved. You need to know how the words fit together to make logical and stylistic sense.

Sentence completion questions actually measure one part of reading comprehension. If you can recognize how the different parts of a sentence affect one another, you should do well at choosing the answer that best completes the meaning of the sentence or provides a clear, logical statement of fact. The ability to recognize irony and humor will also stand you in good stead, as will the ability to recognize figurative language and to distinguish between formal and informal levels of speech.

Because the sentence completion questions contain many clues that help you to answer them correctly (far more clues than the antonyms provide, for example), and because analyzing them helps you warm up for the reading passages later on in the test, answer them first. Then go on to tackle the analogies, the antonyms, and, finally, the time-consuming reading comprehension section.

GRE sentence completion questions may come from any of a number of different fields—art, literature, history, philosophy, botany, astronomy, geology, and so on. You cannot predict what subject matter the sentences on your test will involve. However, you can predict what general pattern they will follow.

1. Each GRE verbal section begins with seven sentence completion questions.

2. In each set of sentence completion questions, the first one or two are relatively simple to answer; the last one or two, relatively hard.

A look at the GRE's published tables showing the percentages of examinees answering each question cor-

rectly supports this point. In general, from 80 to 90 percent of the examinees taking a given test will answer the first sentence completion question in a set correctly. On the average, only approximately 35 percent of the examinees taking a given test will answer the last question in that set correctly.

What makes the hard questions hard?

1. **Vocabulary Level.** Sentences contain words like *intransigence*, *nonplussed*, *harbingers*. Answer choices include words like *penchant*, *abeyance*, *eclectic*. Questions employ unfamiliar secondary meanings of words—*brook* as a verb, *economy* with the meaning of *restraint*.

2. **Grammatical Complexity.** Sentences combine the entire range of grammatical possibilities—adverbial clauses, relative clauses, prepositional phrases, gerunds, infinitives, and so on—in convoluted ways. The more complex the sentence, the more difficult it is for you to spot the key words that can unlock its meaning.

3. **Tone.** Sentences reflect the writer's attitude toward the subject matter. It is simple to comprehend material that is presented neutrally. It is far more difficult to comprehend material that is ironic, condescending, playful, somber, or otherwise complex in tone.

4. **Style.** Ideas may be expressed in different manners—ornately or sparely, poetically or prosaically, formally or informally, journalistically or academically, originally or imitatively. An author's style depends on such details as word choice, imagery, repetition, rhythm, sentence structure and length. Many of the most difficult GRE questions hinge on questions of style.

Work through the following tactics and learn the techniques that will help you with vocabulary, grammatical complexity, tone, and style.

Testing Tactics

Before You Look at the Choices, Read the Sentence and Think of a Word That Makes Sense

Your problem is to find the word that best completes the sentence in both thought and style. Before you look at the answer choices, see if you can come up with a word that makes logical sense in the context. Then look at all five choices. If the word you thought of is one of your five choices, select that as your answer. If the word you thought of is not one of your five choices, look for a synonym of that word. Select the synonym as your answer.

This tactic is helpful because it enables you to get a sense of the sentence as a whole without being distracted by any misleading answers among the answer choices. You are free to concentrate on spotting key words or phrases in the body of the sentence and to call on your own "writer's intuition" in arriving at a stylistically apt choice of word.

See how the process works in an example from a recent GRE.

> Since she believed him to be both candid and trustworthy, she refused to consider the possibility that his statement had been -------.
>
> (A) irrelevant   (B) facetious   (C) mistaken
> (D) critical   (E) insincere

This sentence presents a simple case of cause and effect. The key phrase here is *candid and trustworthy*. The woman has found the man to be frank and honest. *Therefore*, she refuses to believe he can say something _____ . What words immediately come to mind? *Dishonest, evasive, hypocritical*? The missing word is, of course, *insincere*. The woman expects openness (*candid*) and sincerity (*trustworthy*). The correct answer is Choice E.

Practice Tactic 1 extensively to develop your intuitive sense of the *mot juste*—the exactly right word. However, do not rely on Tactic 1 alone. On the test, always follow up Tactic 1 with Tactic 2.

Look at All the Possible Answers Before You Make Your Final Choice

Never decide on an answer before you have read all the choices. You are looking for the word that *best* fits the meaning of the sentence as a whole. In order to be sure you have not been hasty in making your decision, substitute all the answer choices for the missing word. Do not spend a lot of time doing so, but do try them all. That way you can satisfy yourself that you have come up with the *best* answer.

See how this tactic helps you deal with another question from a recent GRE.

> People should not be praised for their virtue if they lack the energy to be -------; in such cases, goodness is merely the effect of -------.
>
> (A) depraved..hesitation
> (B) cruel..effortlessness
> (C) wicked..indolence
> (D) unjust..boredom
> (E) iniquitous..impiety

On the basis of a loose sense of this sentence's meaning, you might be tempted to select Choice A. After all, this sentence basically tells you why you should not praise certain people for virtue. Clearly, you should not call people virtuous merely because they *hesitate* to perform a *depraved* or wicked act. However, this reading of the sentence is inadequate: it fails to take into account the sentence's key phrase.

The key phrase here is *lack...energy*. Lack energy for what? The first word of each answer choice is a synonym for *bad*. Thus, goodness is a result of a lack of the necessary energy to be bad. Examine the second word of each answer choice, eliminating those words that carry no suggestion of such a lack of energy. Does indecision or *hesitation* suggest a lack of energy? No, it suggests a lack of decisiveness. Does *effortlessness* or absence of strain suggest a lack of energy? No, it suggests a lack of difficulty. Does *boredom* or monotony suggest a lack of energy? No, it suggests a lack of interest. Does ungodli-

ness or *impiety* suggest a lack of energy? No, it suggests a lack of reverence. Only one word suggests a
lack of energy—*indolence*. Since goodness results from
a lack of the energy to be bad, it is *merely* the effect of
laziness or *indolence*. The correct answer is Choice C.

Note the satiric tone of this epigram, and the use of
merely to point up that this so-called goodness is no
goodness at all.

In Double-Blank Sentences, Go Through the Answers, Testing the *First* Word in Each Choice (and Eliminating Those That Don't Fit)

In a sentence completion question with two blanks, read
through the entire sentence to get a sense of it as a
whole. Then insert the first word of each answer pair in
the sentence's first blank. Ask yourself whether this particular word makes sense in this blank. If the initial word
of an answer pair makes no sense in the sentence, you
can eliminate that answer pair. (*Note*: Occasionally this
tactic will not work. In the preceding question, for example,
the first words of all five answer pairs were near-synonyms. However, the tactic frequently pays off, as it does
in the following example from a recent GRE.)

> During the 1960s assessments of the family
> shifted remarkably, from general endorsement of it
> as a worthwhile, stable institution to widespread
> ------- it as an oppressive and bankrupt one
> whose ------- was both imminent and welcome.
>
> (A) flight from..restitution
> (B) fascination with..corruption
> (C) rejection of..vogue
> (D) censure of..dissolution
> (E) relinquishment of..ascent

For a quick, general sense of the sentence, strip it of all
its modifying phrases. What remains? *Assessments*

*shifted remarkably from endorsement (approval, support)
to _____.*

Since *endorsement* or approval is highly positive, the shift
most likely is in the negative direction of condemnation or
disapproval. The phrase *oppressive and bankrupt* supports this conclusion. Your first missing word must be a
synonym for *disapproval*.

Now eliminate the misfits. Choices A, B, and E fail to
meet the test: *flight*, *fascination*, and *relinquishment* are
not synonyms for *disapproval*. Consider them no further.
Choice C, *rejection*, and Choice D, *censure*, however,
both express disapprobation; they require a second look.

To decide between Choices C and D, consider the second blank. If you viewed the family as a cruel and worthless institution, what destiny for it would you welcome?
You would welcome its *dissolution*, its destruction, not its
popularity or *vogue*. The correct answer is clearly
Choice D.

Remember that, in double-blank sentences, the right
answer must correctly fill **both** blanks. A wrong answer
choice often includes one correct and one incorrect
answer. ALWAYS test both words.

Watch for Signal Words That Link One Part of the Sentence to Another

Writers use transitions to link their ideas logically. These
transitions or signal words are clues that can help you figure out what the sentence actually means.

GRE sentences often contain several signal words, combining them in complex ways.

Cause and Effect Signals

Look for words or phrases explicitly indicating that one
thing **causes** another or logically determines another.

Cause and Effect Signal Words

accordingly	in order to
because	so...that
consequently	therefore
given	thus
hence	when...then
if...then	

Support Signals

Look for words or phrases explicitly indicating that the omitted portion of the sentence **supports** or **continues a thought** developed elsewhere in the sentence. In such cases, a synonym or near-synonym for another word in the sentence may provide the correct answer.

Support Signal Words

additionally	furthermore
also	indeed
and	likewise
as well	moreover
besides	too

Contrast Signals (Explicit)

Look for function words or phrases (conjunctions, sentence adverbs, etc.) that explicitly indicate a **contrast** between one idea and another, setting up a reversal of a thought. In such cases, an antonym or near-antonym for another word in the sentence may provide the correct answer.

Explicit Contrast Signal Words

albeit	nevertheless
although	nonetheless
but	notwithstanding
despite	on the contrary
even though	on the other hand
however	rather than
in contrast	still
in spite of	while
instead of	yet

Contrast Signals (Implicit)

Look for content words whose meanings inherently indicate a contrast. These words can turn a situation on its head. They indicate that something unexpected, possibly even unwanted, has occurred.

Implicit Contrast Signal Words

anomaly	anomalous	anomalously
illogic	illogical	illogically
incongruity	incongruous	incongruously
irony	ironic	ironically
paradox	paradoxical	paradoxically
surprise	surprising	surprisingly
	unexpected	unexpectedly

Note the function of such a contrast signal word in the following GRE question.

> The paradoxical aspect of the myths about Demeter, when we consider the predominant image of her as a tranquil and serene goddess, is her ------- search for her daughter.
>
> (A) extended
> (B) agitated
> (C) comprehensive
> (D) motiveless
> (E) heartless

The ruling image of Demeter is one of tranquillity; we normally think of her as calm and serene. One aspect of the myths about her, however, is *paradoxical*: it contradicts the customary image of her as always calm. This contradictory aspect is her search for her daughter, which is not calm but *agitated*. The correct answer is Choice B.

Use Your Knowledge of Word Parts and Parts of Speech to Figure Out the Meanings of Unfamiliar Words

If a word used by the author is unfamiliar, or if an answer choice is unknown to you, two approaches are helpful.

1. Break the word down into its component parts—prefixes, suffixes, roots—to see whether they provide a clue to its meaning. For example, in the preceding GRE question, the word *predominant* contains two major word parts. *Pre-* here means exceedingly; *domin-* means to rule or command. A *predominant* image, therefore, is a prevailing image, one that has commanding influence or strength.

2. Change the unfamiliar word from one part of speech to another. If the noun *precocity* is unfamiliar to you, think of the adjective *precocious* (maturing early). If the verb *appropriate* is unfamiliar to you, think of the common noun *appropriation* or the still more common noun *misappropriation* (as in the misappropriation of funds).

Note the application of this tactic in the following GRE example.

> The sheer bulk of data from the mass media seems to overpower us and drive us to ------- accounts for an easily and readily digestible portion of news.
>
> (A) insular
> (B) investigative
> (C) synoptic
> (D) subjective
> (E) sensational

First, eliminate any answer choices that are obviously incorrect. If you feel overwhelmed by massive amounts of data provided by the news media, it seems logical that you would seek out *brief* summaries of the news instead.

You would not be particularly tempted to seek out *investigative*, *subjective*, or *sensational* accounts, since none of these are necessarily brief. Thus, you may rule out Choices B, D and E.

The two answer choices remaining may be unfamiliar to you. Analyze them, using what you know of related words. Choice A, *insular*, is related to the noun *peninsula*, a piece of land that juts out so far into the water that it is *almost* an *island*. Thus, an insular account is an islander's account, one that reflects the narrow viewpoint of an isolated, detached writer. Choice C, *synoptic*, is related to the noun *synopsis* (abridgment or summary). A synoptic account provides a summary, a brief but broad overview. Thus, the correct answer is *synoptic*, Choice C.

Break Down Complex Sentences into Simpler Components

In analyzing long, complex sentence completion items, you may find it useful to simplify the sentences by breaking them down. Rephrase dependent clauses and long participial phrases, turning them into simple sentences.

See how this tactic helps you to analyze the following sentence from a recent GRE.

> In failing to see that the judge's pronouncement merely ------- previous decisions rather than actually establishing a precedent, the novice law clerk ------ the scope of the justice's judgment.
>
> (A) synthesized..limited
> (B) overturned..misunderstood
> (C) endorsed..nullified
> (D) qualified..overemphasized
> (E) recapitulated..defined

What do we know?

1. The judge's pronouncement did NOT set a precedent. (Note the use of *rather than* to signal the contrast.)

2. Rather than setting a precedent, the judge's pronouncement did something RELATIVELY UNIMPORTANT to the earlier decisions. (Note the use of *merely* to signal the relative unimportance of what the judge did.)

3. The new law clerk did not understand that the judge had done something relatively unimportant. (He *failed to see*.)

What follows? Because the new clerk failed to see that the judge had done something minor, the clerk believed that the judge had done something major. In other words, the clerk *overemphasized* the scope of what the judge had done. The correct answer is Choice D.

Note that in sentence completion questions a choice may be complicated by an *unusual word order*, such as:

1. *placing the subject after the verb:*
   To the complaints window *strode* the angry *customer*.

2. *placing the subject after an auxiliary of the verb:*
   Only by unending search *could* some few Havana *cigars* be found.

3. *inverting the subject and verb to give the sense of "if":*
   Were defeat to befall him, today's dear friends would be tomorrow's acquaintances, and next week's strangers.

4. *placing a negative word or phrase first, which usually requires at least part of the verb to follow:*
   Never have I encountered so demanding a test!

In all these instances, rephrase the sentence to make it more straightforward. For example:

The angry customer strode to the complaints window.

Some few Havana cigars could be found only by unending search.

If defeat were to befall him, today's dear friends would be tomorrow's acquaintances, and next week's strangers.

I have never encountered so demanding a test!

Tactic 7

If a Sentence Contains a Metaphor, Check to See Whether That Metaphor Controls the Writer's Choice of Words (and Your Answer Choice)

Writers sometimes indulge in extended metaphors, complex analogies that imaginatively identify one object with another. In the following example from a recent GRE, the effect of words on the shape of our thoughts is compared to a common geologic process.

It is strange how words shape our thoughts and trap us at the bottom of deeply ------- canyons of thinking, their imprisoning sides carved out by the ------- of past usage.

(A) cleaved..eruptions
(B) rooted..flood
(C) incised..river
(D) ridged..ocean
(E) notched..mountains

Note how many words in this sentence contribute to the image of the canyon—*bottom, imprisoning sides, sides carved out*. This should alert you that the canyon metaphor greatly affects the writer's choice of words.

The extended metaphor of the canyon unifies this sentence. In choosing an answer, it is necessary to complete the sentence in such a way as to develop that metaphor fully. Choice B does not: one might describe a tree or a tooth as deeply *rooted*, but not a canyon. Similarly, Choice D fails. A canyon is a deep, narrow valley with precipitous sides; one would not describe it as deeply *ridged*. Canyons are carved out of the rock. How? Are they *cleaved, incised*, even *notched*? To choose the correct answer, you must know some elementary geology, plus the precise meanings of these three verbs. To cleave something is to split it in two parts *by means of a cutting blow*. Erosion, the process which creates canyons, involves no cutting blows. To notch something is to *indent* or nick it. It seems almost paradoxical to describe something as *deeply* notched. In contrast, to incise something is to cut into it, to carve it, to *erode* it, in geological terms. A look at the second word of the answer pair confirms the choice. *Rivers* carve out canyons, *incising* them by erosion. Choice C completes the metaphor; it is the correct answer choice.

Practice Exercises

Sentence Completion Exercise A

Directions: Each sentence below has one or two blanks, each blank indicating that something has been omitted. Beneath the sentence are five lettered words or sets of words. Choose the word or set of words for each blank that best fits the meaning of the sentence as a whole.

1. Normally an individual thunderstorm lasts about 45 minutes, but under certain conditions the storm may -------, becoming ever more severe, for as long as four hours.

   (A) wane
   (B) moderate
   (C) persist
   (D) vacillate
   (E) disperse

2. Perhaps because something in us instinctively distrusts such displays of natural fluency, some readers approach John Updike's fiction with -------.

   (A) indifference
   (B) suspicion
   (C) veneration
   (D) recklessness
   (E) bewilderment

3. We lost confidence in him because he never ------- the grandiose promises he had made.

   (A) forgot about
   (B) reneged on
   (C) tired of
   (D) delivered on
   (E) retreated from

4. Ms. Sutcliffe's helpful notes on her latest wine discoveries and her no-nonsense warnings to consumers about ------- wines provide ------- guide to the numbing array of wines of Burgundy.

   (A) excellent…a useful
   (B) overrated…an inadequate
   (C) overpriced…a trusty
   (D) unsatisfactory…a spotty
   (E) vintage…an unreliable

5. We were amazed that a man who had been heretofore the most ------- of public speakers could, in a single speech, electrify an audience and bring them cheering to their feet.

   (A) enthralling
   (B) accomplished
   (C) pedestrian
   (D) auspicious
   (E) masterful

6. If you are trying to make a strong impression on your audience, you cannot do so by being understated, tentative, or ------.

   (A) hyperbolic
   (B) restrained
   (C) argumentative
   (D) authoritative
   (E) passionate

7. Despite the mixture's ------ nature, we found that by lowering its temperature in the laboratory we could dramatically reduce its tendency to vaporize.

   (A) resilient
   (B) volatile
   (C) homogeneous
   (D) insipid
   (E) acerbic

8. No other artist rewards the viewer with more sheer pleasure than Miró: he is one of those blessed artists who combine profundity and ------.

   (A) education
   (B) wisdom
   (C) faith
   (D) fun
   (E) depth

9. Some Central Intelligence Agency officers have ------ their previous statements denying any involvement on their part with the Contra aid network and are now revising their earlier testimony.

   (A) justified
   (B) recanted
   (C) repeated
   (D) protracted
   (E) heeded

10. New concerns about growing religious tension in northern India were ------ this week after at least fifty people were killed and hundreds were injured or arrested in rioting between Hindus and Moslems.

    (A) lessened
    (B) invalidated
    (C) restrained
    (D) dispersed
    (E) fueled

11. In a happy, somewhat boisterous celebration of the European discovery of America, the major phase of the Columbus Cinquecentennial got off to ------ start on Friday.

    (A) a slow
    (B) a rousing
    (C) a reluctant
    (D) an indifferent
    (E) a quiet

12. In one shocking instance of ------ research, one of the nation's most influential researchers in the field of genetics reported on experiments that were never carried out and published deliberately ------ scientific papers on his nonexistent work.

    (A) comprehensive...abstract
    (B) theoretical...challenging
    (C) fraudulent...deceptive
    (D) derivative...authoritative
    (E) erroneous...impartial

13. Measurement is, like any other human endeavor, a complex activity, subject to error, not always used ------, and frequently misinterpreted and ------.

    (A) mistakenly...derided
    (B) erratically...analyzed
    (C) systematically...organized
    (D) innovatively...refined
    (E) properly...misunderstood

14. In a revolutionary development in technology, several manufacturers now make biodegradable forms of plastic: some plastic six-pack rings, for example, gradually ------ when exposed to sunlight.

    (A) harden
    (B) stagnate
    (C) inflate
    (D) propagate
    (E) decompose

15. To alleviate the problem of contaminated chicken, the study panel recommends that the federal government shift its inspection emphasis from cursory bird-by-bird visual checks to a more ------ random sampling for bacterial and chemical contamination.

    (A) rigorous
    (B) perfunctory
    (C) symbolic
    (D) discreet
    (E) dubious

16. Her novel published to universal acclaim, her literary gifts acknowledged by the chief figures of the Harlem Renaissance, her reputation as yet ------ by envious slights, Hurston clearly was at the ------ of her career.

    (A) undamaged...ebb
    (B) untarnished...zenith
    (C) untainted...extremity
    (D) blackened...mercy
    (E) unmarred...brink

17. To the dismay of the student body, the class president was ------ berated by the principal at a school assembly.

    (A) ignominiously
    (B) privately
    (C) magnanimously
    (D) fortuitously
    (E) inconspicuously

18. Aimed at curbing European attempts to seize territory in the Americas, the Monroe Doctrine was a warning to ------ foreign powers.

    (A) pertinacious
    (B) credulous
    (C) remote
    (D) overt
    (E) predatory

19. When Frazer's editors at Macmillan tried to ------ his endless augmentations, he insisted on a type size so small and a page so packed as to approach illegibility; and if that proved ------, thinner paper.

    (A) protract...unwarranted
    (B) expurgate...satisfactory
    (C) reprimand...irrelevant
    (D) restrict...insufficient
    (E) revise...idiosyncratic

20. The authority of voice in Frazer's writing strikes many readers today as ------ colonialism; his prose seems as invulnerable and expansive as something on which the sun was presumed never to set.

    (A) consonant with
    (B) independent of
    (C) ambivalent toward
    (D) cognizant of
    (E) detrimental to

Sentence Completion Exercise B

Directions: Each sentence below has one or two blanks, each blank indicating that something has been omitted. Beneath the sentence are five lettered words or sets of words. Choose the word or set of words for each blank that best fits the meaning of the sentence as a whole.

1. Baldwin's brilliant *The Fire Next Time* is both so eloquent in its passion and so searching in its ------ that it is bound to ------ any reader.

    (A) bitterness...embarrass
    (B) romanticism...appall
    (C) candor...unsettle
    (D) indifference...disappoint
    (E) conception...bore

2. Unlike other examples of ------ verse, Milton's *Lycidas* does more than merely mourn for the death of Edward King; it also denounces corruption in the Church in which King was ordained.

    (A) satiric
    (B) elegiac
    (C) free
    (D) humorous
    (E) didactic

3. Few other plants can grow beneath the canopy of the sycamore tree, whose leaves and pods produce a natural herbicide that leaches into the surrounding soil, ------ other plants that might compete for water and nutrients.

    (A) inhibiting
    (B) distinguishing
    (C) nourishing
    (D) encouraging
    (E) refreshing

4. Although a few years ago the fundamental facts about the Milky Way seemed fairly well ------, now even its mass and its radius have come into ------.

    (A) determined . . . resolution
    (B) ignored . . . danger
    (C) problematic . . . prominance
    (D) diminished . . . disrepute
    (E) established . . . question

5. The officers threatened to take ------ if the lives of their men were ------ by the conquered natives.

    (A) liberties...irritated
    (B) measures...enhanced
    (C) pains...destroyed
    (D) reprisals...endangered
    (E) affront...enervated

6. Despite an affected ------ which convinced casual observers that he was indifferent about his painting and enjoyed only frivolity, Warhol cared deeply about his art and labored at it ------.

    (A) nonchalance...diligently
    (B) empathy...methodically
    (C) fervor...secretly
    (D) gloom...intermittently
    (E) hysteria...sporadically

7. Because she had a reputation for ------ we were surprised and pleased when she greeted us so ------.

    (A) insolence...irately
    (B) insouciance...cordially
    (C) graciousness...amiably
    (D) arrogance...disdainfully
    (E) querulousness...affably

8. The child was so spoiled by her indulgent parents that she pouted and became ------ when she did not receive all of their attention.

    (A) discreet
    (B) suspicious
    (C) elated
    (D) sullen
    (E) tranquil

9. Just as disloyalty is the mark of the renegade, ------ is the mark of the ------.

    (A) timorousness...hero
    (B) temerity...coward
    (C) avarice...philanthropist
    (D) cowardice...craven
    (E) vanity...flatterer

10. He became quite overbearing and domineering once he had become accustomed to the ------ shown to soldiers by the natives; he enjoyed his new sense of power and self-importance.

    (A) disrespect
    (B) apathy
    (C) deference
    (D) culpability
    (E) enmity

11. The ------ of time had left the castle ------; it towered above the village, looking much as it must have done in Richard the Lion-Hearted's time.

    (A) repairs...destroyed
    (B) remoteness...alone
    (C) lack...defended
    (D) status...lonely
    (E) ravages...untouched

12. One of the most ------ educators in New York, Dr. Shalala ignited a controversy in 1984 by calling the city public schools a "rotten barrel" in need of ------ reform.

    (A) disputatious...little
    (B) outspoken...systemic
    (C) caustic...partial
    (D) indifferent...pretentious
    (E) sycophantic...superficial

13. The newest fiber-optic cables that carry telephone calls cross-country are made of glass so ------ that a piece 100 miles thick is clearer than a standard windowpane.

    (A) fragile
    (B) immaculate
    (C) tangible
    (D) transparent
    (E) iridescent

14. The reasoning in this editorial is so ------ that we cannot see how anyone can be deceived by it.

    (A) coherent
    (B) astute
    (C) cogent
    (D) specious
    (E) dispassionate

15. The ------ of evidence was on the side of the plaintiff since all but one witness testified that his story was correct.

    (A) paucity
    (B) propensity
    (C) accuracy
    (D) brunt
    (E) preponderance

16. Glendon provides a dark underside to Frederick Jackson Turner's frontier thesis that saw rugged individualism as the essence of American society—an individualism which she sees ------ atomism.

    (A) antithetical toward
    (B) skeptical of
    (C) degenerating into
    (D) aspiring to
    (E) renewed by

17. Chatwin has devoted his life to a kind of Grail quest, hoping to prove—by study and direct experience with primitive people—that human nature is gentle and defensive rather than ------, and that man is ------, not a predator.

    (A) belligerent...an apostate
    (B) martial...a crusader
    (C) aggressive...a pilgrim
    (D) truculent...a gladiator
    (E) pugnacious...a pawn

18. The texts as we have them were written down and edited carefully by Christians proud of their ancestors but unable to bear the thought of their indulging in heathen practices; thus, all references to the ancient religion of the Celts were ------, if not ------.

    (A) deleted...expunged
    (B) muddied...suppressed
    (C) labored...denigrated
    (D) aggrieved...overawed
    (E) obscure...ironic

19. Because Inspector Morse could not contain his scorn for the police commissioner, he was imprudent enough to make ------ remarks about his superior officer.

    (A) ambiguous
    (B) dispassionate
    (C) unfathomable
    (D) interminable
    (E) scathing

20. In Japanese art, profound emotion is frequently couched in images of nature, observed with ------ conditioned by life in a land of dramatic seasonal change, where perils of earthquake and typhoon make nature's bounty ------ and its processes awesome and beautiful.

    (A) an intimacy...precarious
    (B) a fidelity...munificent
    (C) a skill...excessive
    (D) an indifference...chancy
    (E) a sensitivity...distinctive

Sentence Completion Exercise C

Directions: Each sentence below has one or two blanks, each blank indicating that something has been omitted. Beneath the sentence are five lettered words or sets of words. Choose the word or set of words for each blank that best fits the meaning of the sentence as a whole.

1. A ------ statement is an ------ comparison: it does not compare things explicitly, but suggests a likeness between them.

    (A) sarcastic...unfair
    (B) blatant...overt
    (C) sanguine...inherent
    (D) metaphorical...implied
    (E) bellicose...ardent

2. Modern architecture has discarded the ------ trimming on buildings and has concentrated on an almost Greek simplicity of line.

    (A) flamboyant
    (B) austere
    (C) inconspicuous
    (D) aesthetic
    (E) derivative

3. If you are seeking ------ that will resolve all our ailments, you are undertaking an impossible task.

    (A) a precedent
    (B) a panacea
    (C) an abstraction
    (D) a direction
    (E) a contrivance

4. I have no ------ motive in offering this advice; I seek no personal advantage or honor.

    (A) nominal
    (B) altruistic
    (C) incongruous
    (D) disinterested
    (E) ulterior

5. This park has been preserved in all its ------ wildness so that visitors in future years may see how people lived during the eighteenth century.

    (A) hedonistic
    (B) prospective
    (C) esoteric
    (D) untrammeled
    (E) pristine

6. Though he was theoretically a friend of labor, his voting record in Congress ------ that impression.

    (A) implied
    (B) created
    (C) confirmed
    (D) belied
    (E) maintained

7. The orator was so ------ that the audience became ------.

    (A) soporific...drowsy
    (B) inaudible...elated
    (C) pompous...bombastic
    (D) dramatic...affable
    (E) convincing...moribund

8. If you carry this ------ attitude to the conference, you will ------ any supporters you may have at this moment.

    (A) belligerent...delight
    (B) truculent...alienate
    (C) conciliatory...defer
    (D) supercilious...attract
    (E) ubiquitous...delight

9. The ------ pittance the widow receives from the government cannot keep her from poverty.

    (A) magnanimous
    (B) indulgent
    (C) meticulous
    (D) munificent
    (E) niggardly

10. Harriman, Kennan, and Acheson were part of that inner ------ of the American diplomatic establishment whose distinguished legacy ------ U.S. foreign policy.

    (A) circle...grieved
    (B) sanctum...absorbed
    (C) core...dominated
    (D) life...biased
    (E) coterie...exacerbated

11. The young man was quickly promoted when his employers saw how ------ he was.

    (A) indigent
    (B) indifferent
    (C) assiduous
    (D) lethargic
    (E) cursory

12. For Miró, art became a ------ ritual: paper and pencils were holy objects to him and he worked as though he were performing a religious rite.

    (A) superficial
    (B) sacred
    (C) banal
    (D) cryptic
    (E) futile

13. Because it arrives so early in the season, before many other birds, the robin has been called the ------ of spring.

    (A) hostage
    (B) autocrat
    (C) compass
    (D) newcomer
    (E) harbinger

14. Shy and hypochondriacal, Madison was uncomfortable at public gatherings; his character made him a most ------ lawmaker and practicing politician.

    (A) conscientious
    (B) unlikely
    (C) fervent
    (D) gregarious
    (E) effective

15. The tapeworm is an example of ------ organism, one that lives within or on another creature, deriving some or all of its nutrients from its host.

    (A) a hospitable
    (B) an exemplary
    (C) a parasitic
    (D) an autonomous
    (E) a protozoan

16. In place of the more general debate about abstract principles of government that most delegates probably expected, the Constitutional Convention put ------ proposals on the table.

    (A) theoretical
    (B) vague
    (C) concrete
    (D) tentative
    (E) redundant

17. Overindulgence ------ character as well as physical stamina.

    (A) strengthens
    (B) stimulates
    (C) debilitates
    (D) maintains
    (E) provides

18. We must try to understand his momentary ------ for he has ------ more strain and anxiety than any among us.

    (A) outcry...described
    (B) senility...understood
    (C) vision...forgotten
    (D) generosity...desired
    (E) aberration...undergone

19. He is ------ opponent; you must respect and fear him at all times.

    (A) a redoubtable
    (B) a disingenuous
    (C) a pugnacious
    (D) an insignificant
    (E) a craven

20. Your ------ tactics may compel me to cancel the contract as the job must be finished on time.

    (A) dilatory
    (B) offensive
    (C) repugnant
    (D) infamous
    (E) confiscatory

Sentence Completion Exercise D

Directions: Each sentence below has one or two blanks, each blank indicating that something has been omitted. Beneath the sentence are five lettered words or sets of words. Choose the word or set of words for each blank that best fits the meaning of the sentence as a whole.

1. Truculent in defending their individual rights of sovereignty under the Articles of Confederation, the newly formed states ------ constantly.

    (A) apologized   (B) digressed   (C) conferred
      (D) acquiesced   (E) squabbled

2. If the Titanic had hit the iceberg head on, its watertight compartments might have saved it from ------, but it swerved to avoid the iceberg, and in the collision so many compartments were opened to the sea that disaster was ------.

    (A) foundering...inevitable
    (B) sinking...escaped
    (C) damage...limited
    (D) buoyancy...unavoidable
    (E) collapse...averted

3. Written in an amiable style, the book provides a comprehensive overview of European wines that should prove inviting to both the virtual ------- and the experienced connoisseur.

   (A) prodigal
   (B) novice
   (C) zealot
   (D) miser
   (E) glutton

4. The members of the religious sect ostracized the ------- who had abandoned their faith.

   (A) coward
   (B) suppliant
   (C) litigant
   (D) recreant
   (E) proselyte

5. I am not attracted by the ------- life of the -------, always wandering through the countryside, begging for charity.

   (A) proud...almsgiver
   (B) noble...philanthropist
   (C) affluent...mendicant
   (D) natural...philosopher
   (E) peripatetic...vagabond

6. Her true feelings ------- themselves in her sarcastic asides; only then was her ------- revealed.

   (A) concealed...sweetness
   (B) manifested...bitterness
   (C) hid...sarcasm
   (D) developed...anxiety
   (E) grieved...charm

7. They fired upon the enemy from behind trees, walls, and any other ------- point they could find.

   (A) conspicuous
   (B) definitive
   (C) vantage
   (D) exposed
   (E) indefensible

8. Critics of the movie version of *The Color Purple* ------- its saccharine, overoptimistic mood as out of keeping with the novel's more ------- tone.

   (A) applauded...somber
   (B) condemned...hopeful
   (C) acclaimed...positive
   (D) denounced...sanguine
   (E) decried...acerbic

9. We need more men of culture and enlightenment; we have too many ------- among us.

   (A) visionaries
   (B) students
   (C) philistines
   (D) pragmatists
   (E) philosophers

10. The sugar dissolved in water -------; finally all that remained was an almost ------- residue on the bottom of the glass.

    (A) quickly...lumpy
    (B) immediately...fragrant
    (C) gradually...imperceptible
    (D) subsequently...glassy
    (E) spectacularly...opaque

11. Alec Guinness has few equals among English-speaking actors, and in his autobiography he reveals himself to be an uncommonly ------- prose stylist as well.

    (A) ambivalent
    (B) infamous
    (C) supercilious
    (D) felicitous
    (E) pedestrian

12. Traffic speed limits are set at a level that achieves some balance between the danger of ------- speed and the desire of most people to travel as quickly as possible.

    (A) marginal
    (B) normal
    (C) prudent
    (D) inadvertent
    (E) excessive

13. Although the economy suffers downturns, it also has strong ------- and self-correcting tendencies.

    (A) unstable
    (B) recidivist
    (C) inauspicious
    (D) recuperative
    (E) self-destructive

14. It is foolish to vent your spleen on ------- object; still, you make ------- enemies that way.

    (A) an inanimate...fewer
    (B) an immobile...bitter
    (C) an interesting...curious
    (D) an insipid...dull
    (E) a humane...more

15. Since Cyrano de Bergerac did not wish to be under an obligation to any man, he refused to be a ------- of Cardinal Richelieu.

    (A) proselytizer
    (B) mentor
    (C) protégé
    (D) benefactor
    (E) predecessor

16. The leader of the group is the passionately committed Crimond, whose ------- politics is inversely proportional to his disciples' ------- political faith.

    (A) retreat from...remote
    (B) penchant for...ardent
    (C) indifference to...jaundiced
    (D) engagement in...lapsed
    (E) disinclination for...problematic

17. After the Japanese attack on Pearl Harbor on December 7, 1941, Japanese-Americans were ------- of being spies for Japan, although there was no ------- to back up this accusation.

    (A) acquitted...buttress
    (B) tired...witness
    (C) reminded...reason
    (D) suspected...evidence
    (E) exonerated...money

18. More than one friendly whale has nudged a boat with such ------- that passengers have been knocked overboard.

    (A) enthusiasm
    (B) lethargy
    (C) hostility
    (D) serenity
    (E) animosity

19. The mind of a bigot is like the pupil of the eye: the more light you pour upon it, the more it will -------.

    (A) blink
    (B) veer
    (C) stare
    (D) reflect
    (E) contract

20. We have become so democratic in our habits of thought that we are convinced that truth is determined through ------- of facts.

    (A) a hierarchy
    (B) a transcendance
    (C) a plebiscite
    (D) a repeal
    (E) an ignorance

Sentence Completion Exercise E

Directions: Each sentence below has one or two blanks, each blank indicating that something has been omitted. Beneath the sentence are five lettered words or sets of words. Choose the word or set of words for each blank that best fits the meaning of the sentence as a whole.

1. Studded starfish are well protected from most ------- and parasites by ------- surface whose studs are actually modified spines.

    (A) dangers...a vulnerable
    (B) predators...an armored
    (C) threats...a fragile
    (D) challenges...an obtuse
    (E) exigencies...a brittle

2. Chaotic in conception but not in -------, Kelly's canvases are as neat as the proverbial pin.

    (A) conceit
    (B) theory
    (C) execution
    (D) origin
    (E) intent

3. After having worked in the soup kitchen feeding the hungry, the volunteer began to see her own good fortune as ------- and her difference from the ------- as chance rather than destiny.

    (A) an omen...homeless
    (B) a fluke...impoverished
    (C) a threat...destitute
    (D) a reward...indigent
    (E) a lie...affluent

4. Some students are ------- and want to take only the courses for which they see immediate value.

    (A) theoretical
    (B) impartial
    (C) pragmatic
    (D) idealistic
    (E) opinionated

5. Unlike the Shakespearean plays that lit up the English stage, the "closet dramas" of the nineteenth century were meant to be ------- rather than -------.

    (A) seen..acted
    (B) read...staged
    (C) quiet...raucous
    (D) sophisticated...urbane
    (E) produced...performed

6. Japan's industrial success is ------- in part to its tradition of group effort and -------, as opposed to the emphasis on personal achievement that is a prominent aspect of other industrial nations.

    (A) responsive...independence
    (B) related...introspection
    (C) equivalent...solidarity
    (D) subordinate...individuality
    (E) attributed...cooperation

7. I was so bored with the verbose and redundant style of Victorian novelists that I welcomed the change to the ------- style of Hemingway.

    (A) prolix
    (B) consistent
    (C) terse
    (D) logistical
    (E) florid

8. As ------- head of the organization, he attended social functions and civic meetings but had no ------- in the formulation of company policy.

    (A) titular...voice
    (B) hypothetical...vote
    (C) former...pride
    (D) nominal...competition
    (E) actual...say

9. His listeners enjoyed his ------- wit but his victims often ------- at its satire.

    (A) lugubrious...suffered
    (B) caustic...laughed
    (C) kindly...smarted
    (D) subtle...smiled
    (E) trenchant...winced

10. The first forty years of life give us the text: the next thirty supply the -------.

    (A) abridgement
    (B) bibliography
    (C) commentary
    (D) epitaph
    (E) title

11. The distinctive qualities of African music were not appreciated or even ------- by Westerners until fairly recently.

    (A) deplored
    (B) revered
    (C) ignored
    (D) neglected
    (E) perceived

12. It is only to the vain that all is vanity; and all is ------- only to those who have never been ------- themselves.

    (A) arrogance...proud of
    (B) deception...sincere with
    (C) cowardice...afraid for
    (D) indolence...bored by
    (E) solitude...left to

13. No act of ------- was more pronounced than his refusal of any rewards for his discovery.

    (A) abeyance
    (B) submission
    (C) egoism
    (D) denunciation
    (E) abnegation

14. The evil of class and race hatred must be eliminated while it is still in an ------ state; otherwise it may grow to dangerous proportions.

    (A) amorphous
    (B) embryonic
    (C) uncultivated
    (D) overt
    (E) independent

15. Unlike the gregarious Capote, who was never happier than when he was in the center of a crowd of celebrities, Faulkner, in later years, grew somewhat ------- and shunned company.

    (A) congenial
    (B) decorous
    (C) dispassionate
    (D) reclusive
    (E) ambivalent

16. She is a pragmatist, as ------- to base her future on impractical dreams as she would be to build a castle on shifting sand.

    (A) determined
    (B) disinclined
    (C) quick
    (D) apt
    (E) diligent

17. We are ------- the intellects of the past; or, rather, like children we take it for granted that somebody must supply us with our supper and our -------.

    (A) ungrateful to...ideas
    (B) dependent on...repose
    (C) unfaithful to...needs
    (D) fortunate in...allowance
    (E) generous to...wants

18. This island is a colony; however, in most matters, it is ------- and receives no orders from the mother country.

    (A) submissive
    (B) amorphous
    (C) distant
    (D) autonomous
    (E) aloof

19. Although eighteenth-century English society as a whole did not encourage learning for its own sake in women, nonetheless it illogically ------- women's sad lack of education.

    (A) palliated
    (B) postulated
    (C) decried
    (D) brooked
    (E) vaunted

20. Faced with these massive changes, the government keeps its own counsel; although generally benevolent, it has always been ------- regime.

    (A) an altruistic
    (B) an unpredictable
    (C) a reticent
    (D) a sanguine
    (E) an indifferent

Answer Key

Sentence Completion Exercise A

1.	C	6.	B	11.	B	16.	B
2.	B	7.	B	12.	C	17.	A
3.	D	8.	D	13.	E	18.	E
4.	C	9.	B	14.	E	19.	D
5.	C	10.	E	15.	A	20.	A

Sentence Completion Exercise B

1.	C	6.	A	11.	E	16.	C
2.	B	7.	E	12.	B	17.	C
3.	A	8.	D	13.	D	18.	B
4.	E	9.	D	14.	D	19.	E
5.	D	10.	C	15.	E	20.	A

Sentence Completion Exercise C

1.	D	6.	D	11.	C	16.	C
2.	A	7.	A	12.	B	17.	C
3.	B	8.	B	13.	E	18.	E
4.	E	9.	E	14.	B	19.	A
5.	E	10.	C	15.	C	20.	A

Sentence Completion Exercise D

1.	E	6.	B	11.	D	16.	E
2.	A	7.	C	12.	E	17.	D
3.	B	8.	E	13.	D	18.	A
4.	D	9.	C	14.	A	19.	E
5.	E	10.	C	15.	C	20.	C

Sentence Completion Exercise E

1.	B	6.	E	11.	E	16.	B
2.	C	7.	C	12.	B	17.	A
3.	B	8.	A	13.	E	18.	D
4.	C	9.	E	14.	B	19.	C
5.	B	10.	C	15.	D	20.	C

4 Analogy Questions

- ■ **Testing Tactics**
- ■ **Practice Exercises**
- ■ **Answer Key**

Analogy questions ask you to determine the relationship between the two words in a pair and then to recognize a similar or parallel relationship between the members of a different pair of words. You are given one pair of words and must choose from the five answer choices another pair whose words are related in the same way. The relationship between the words in the original pair will always be specific and precise, as will the relationship between the words in the correct answer pair.

In each GRE verbal section the set of sentence completion questions is followed by nine analogy questions. In each set of analogy questions, the first one or two are relatively simple; the last one or two, relatively hard.

Analogies come from a wide variety of fields. You need to know that musicians study in conservatories and ministers in seminaries, that panegyrics praise and elegies lament. You need to be aware of catalysts and conundrums, augers and auguries, and know in which contexts these words are found. You are not, however, dealing with these words in isolation; you are always dealing with them in relationship to other words.

Once you have analyzed analogy questions, you will find that they fall into certain patterns. You should be able to answer them reasonably rapidly. Tackle them after you have warmed up with the sentence completion questions. Then skip to the antonyms.

Note how a GRE analogy question is set up. First you have the two capitalized words linked by a symbol. Take a look at a few examples.

FRESCO : WALL

A fresco is related to a wall. **How?** A fresco or mural painting is painted on a wall.

STAMMER : TALK

Stammer is related to talk. **How?** To stammer is to make involuntary stops or repetitions when talking. It is to talk in a halting *manner.*

TILE : MOSAIC

Tile is related to mosaic. **How?** A mosaic is made up of tiles. Notice the wording of the last sentence. You could also have said "Tiles are the pieces that make up a mosaic" and maintained the word order of the analogy. Sometimes, however, it is easier to express a relationship if you reverse the order of the words.

Next you come to the five answer choices. See if you can tell which pair best expresses a relationship similar to the relationship of tile to mosaic.

TILE : MOSAIC ::   (A) hoop : embroidery
(B) wick : candle   (C) whalebone : scrimshaw
(D) easel : painting   (E) knot : macrame

The correct answer is Choice E: macrame is made up of knots. Just as the tiles in a mosaic make a pattern, so too the knots in a piece of macrame make a pattern.

Some of the analogy questions on the GRE are as clear-cut as this. Others are more complex. To answer them correctly involves far more than knowing single meanings of individual words: it involves knowing the usual contexts in which they are found, and their connotations as well. Master the tactics that immediately follow. Then proceed to the practice exercises containing both relatively simple and challenging analogies at the chapter's end.

Testing Tactics

Tactic 1

Before You Look at the Choices, Try to State the Relationship Between the Capitalized Words in a Clear Sentence

In answering an analogy question, your first problem is to determine the exact relationship between the two capitalized words. *Before you look at the answer pairs*, make up a sentence that illustrates how these capitalized words are related. Then test the possible answers by seeing how well they fit in your sentence.

Try this tactic on the following two questions from recent GREs.

> DELUGE : DROPLET ::   (A) beach : wave
> (B) desert : oasis   (C) blizzard : icicle
>   (D) landslide : pebble   (E) cloudburst : puddle

A *deluge* (drenching rain or flood) is made up of *droplets*. A *landslide* or fall of rocks is made up of *pebbles*. Choice D is correct.

Don't let Choice E fool you: while a cloudburst, like a deluge, is a drenching rain, it is not made up of puddles; rather, it leaves puddles in its aftermath.

> PHILATELIST : STAMPS ::
> (A) numismatist : coins
> (B) astrologer : predictions
> (C) geneticist : chromosomes
> (D) cartographer : maps
> (E) pawnbroker : jewelry

A *philatelist* collects *stamps*. A *numismatist* collects *coins*. Choice A is correct.

Note how difficult this question would be if you did not know that a philatelist is a stamp collector. You might have guessed that a philatelist primarily *studies* stamps (as, for example, a geneticist studies chromosomes) or even *makes* stamps (as a cartographer makes maps). Knowing the primary relationship between the capitalized words, however, you can go through the answer choices eliminating any pairs that do not express the same relationship. Thus, you can eliminate Choice B: an astrologer may possibly collect predictions; but his primary, dictionary-defined, role is to make predictions, to foretell human affairs by studying the positions of the stars. Similarly, you can eliminate Choice E: a pawnbroker does not collect jewelry; he takes jewelry (and many other sorts of personal property) as a pledge to secure the repayment of money he lends. You can eliminate Choice C as well: a geneticist studies chromosomes. This process of elimination leaves you with two relatively unfamiliar words—*numismatist* and *cartographer*—and a 50 percent chance of guessing the answer correctly.

If you are not sure of the answer, *always* rule out answer choices that you *know* cannot be correct, and then guess among the choices that are left.

Tactic 2

If More Than One Answer Fits the Relationship in Your Sentence, Look for A Narrower Approach

When you try to express the relationship between the two capitalized words in sentence form, occasionally you come up with too simple a sentence, one that fails to include enough details to particularize your analogy. In such cases, more than one answer may fit the relationship, and you will have to analyze the original pair again.

Consider this actual analogy question from the GRE.

> BOUQUET : FLOWERS ::   (A) forest : trees
> (B) husk : corn   (C) mist : rain
>   (D) woodpile : logs   (E) drift : snow

"A bouquet is made up of flowers." You have stated a relationship between the capitalized words in a sentence, but you have not stated a relationship that is precise enough. After all, forests are made up of trees, woodpiles are made up of logs, and even drifts are made of snow. You need to focus on some aspect of the relationship between the words in the original pair that corresponds to an aspect of only *one* of the answer pairs. Go back to the original pair of words for more details. A bouquet is made up of flowers that have been *picked* and *gathered* into a bunch. In contrast, a forest is a tract of land covered with densely growing trees. A drift is a mass of snow driven together by the wind. Neither the relationship in Choice A nor that in Choice E exactly parallels the relationship between the word pair BOUQUET:FLOWERS. Choice D, however, is perfect: a woodpile is made up of logs that have been *cut* and *gathered* into a stack.

In answering analogy questions on the GRE, pay special attention to how a dictionary would define the words involved. Do not settle for what "may be" a good relationship. Precision is important in analogies: a bouquet is not simply made up of flowers, it is made up of flowers that have been cut. Strive to identify the relationship that exists "by definition."

Consider Secondary Meanings of Words As Well As Their Primary Meanings

Frequently, the test-makers attempt to mislead you by using familiar words in relatively uncommon ways. When an apparently familiar word seems incongruous in a particular analogy, consider other definitions of that word.

See how this tactic applies to two examples from recent GREs.

AMORPHOUSNESS : DEFINITION ::
(A) lassitude : energy
(B) spontaneity : awareness
(C) angularity : intricacy
(D) rectitude : drabness
(E) precision : uniformity

What relationship exists between *amorphousness* and *definition*? *Amorphousness* means formlessness or shapelessness; an amorphous idea lacks form or shape. But what does formlessness have to do with *definition*? After all, a definition is a statement of the meaning of a word or phrase.

Look closely at the term *definition*. When you define a word, you distinguish its essential characteristics; you make its features clear. *Definition* in fact possesses a secondary meaning: "sharp demarcation of outlines or limits; distinctness of outline or detail." With this meaning in mind, you can state the essential relationship between the capitalized words: *amorphousness* is a lack of *definition*. Analogously, *lassitude* (listlessness, weariness) is a lack of *energy*. The correct answer is Choice A.

EMBROIDER : CLOTH :: (A) chase : metal
(B) patch : quilt   (C) gild : gold
(D) carve : knife   (E) stain : glass

Ostensibly, this is a simple analogy. One embroiders cloth to ornament it, embellishing it with needlework. The relationship between the capitalized words is clear. However, only 9% of the examinees who answered this question answered it correctly. The problem lies not in the original analogy but in the answer pairs.

Consider the answer choices closely. Choices B, C, D, and E are clear enough: one patches a quilt, either repairing it or putting it together (patch has both senses); one gilds something, overlaying it with gold; one carves with a knife; one stains glass, imparting color to it. Several of these straightforward choices have something to do with ornamentation, but none seems precisely right. But how does one *chase* metal? Certainly not the way one chases an ambulance! Among the straightforward answer choices, Choice A seems strangely out of place.

When an item in an analogy strikes you as out of place, take a second look. Remember that the test-makers usually place more difficult analogies toward the end of the analogy section. Therefore, if one of the final analogy questions in a set looks simple, *suspect a trap*. In this case, the trap is a double one. Choice B, *patch : quilt*, is an eye-catcher: because embroidery and quilt-making both are related to sewing, Choice B has an immediate appeal. Choose it and you fall into the test-makers' trap. Choice A, the odd-seeming choice, is the real answer: *chase*, as used here, means to ornament a metal surface, as silversmiths decorate silver with hammered patterns; chasing metal, thus, is directly analogous to embroidering cloth.

Watch Out for Errors Caused By Eye-Catchers

When you look at answer choices, do you find that certain ones seem to leap right off the page? For instance, when you were looking for an analogy similar to EMBROIDER : CLOTH, did the terms related to stitchery catch your eye? These words are eye-catchers. They look good—but not if you take a second glance.

In an analogy you have two capitalized words that relate in a particular way. In creating eye-catchers, the test-makers tempt you with pairs of words that are related, but in a grammatically or logically different way. See how eye-catchers work in an example from a published GRE.

> PROCTOR : SUPERVISE ::   (A) prophet : rule
> (B) profiteer : consume   (C) profligate : demand
>   (D) prodigal : squander   (E) prodigy : wonder

Just as there are many possible relationships linking word pairs, there are many possible ways an eye-catcher may attract your eye. First, an answer choice may some-how remind you in subject matter of one or both of the terms in the original pair. Thus, Choice A is an eye-catcher: *rule* reminds you of *supervise*; both words feel as if they belong in the same set of words, the same *semantic field*. Second, the answer choice may masquer-ade as a clearcut, precise, dictionary-perfect analogy and yet not be one. Thus, Choice E is an eye-catcher: while there is a clear relationship between the nouns *prodigy* and *wonder*, there is no such clear relationship between the noun *prodigy* and the verb *wonder*. See how this works:

Noun/Noun	A *prodigy* (marvel) is a *wonder*.	CLEAR ANALOGY
Noun/Verb	A *prodigy wonders* (ponders; marvels).	VAGUE ANALOGY

A prodigy excites wonder in others; he is not necessarily astonished or full of wonder himself. The relationship is vague. Eliminate vague analogies when you find them; their only function is to catch your eye.

You have ruled out Choice E; you are suspicious of Choice A. How do you determine the correct answer? In this case, ask yourself **who is doing what to whom.** A *proctor* (monitor) by definition *supervises* students or examinees. You can eliminate Choices A, B, and C because no necessary relationship links the words in these pairs. Prophets prophesy; they do not rule. Profit-eers sell goods (at excessive prices) that others con-sume. Profligates waste their fortunes; they do not necessarily demand.

The correct answer is Choice D. Just as a *proctor super-vises* students, a *prodigal* or wastrel *squanders* wealth.

Look at the Answer Choices to Determine a Word's Part of Speech

Look at the capitalized words. What parts of speech are they? Words often have several forms. You may think of *run* as a verb, for example, but in the phrases "a run in her stocking" and "hit a home run" *run* is a noun.

The GRE plays on this confusion in testing your verbal ability. When you look at a capitalized word, you may not know whether you are dealing with a noun, a verb, or an adjective. *Harbor*, for example, is a very common noun; in "to harbor a fugitive," to give refuge to a runaway, it is a much less common verb.

If you suspect that a capitalized word may represent more than one part of speech, don't worry. Grammatical information built into the question can help you recognize analogy types and spot the use of unfamiliar or second-ary meanings of words. In GRE analogy questions, the relationship between the parts of speech of the capital-ized words and the parts of speech of the answer choices is identical. If your capitalized words are a noun and a verb, each of your answer pairs will be a noun and a verb. If they are an adjective and a noun, each of your answer pairs will be an adjective and a noun. If you can recognize the parts of speech in a single answer pair, you

know the parts of speech of every other answer pair and of the original pair as well. See how this tactic works in a somewhat difficult question from a recently published GRE.

> FLAG : VIGOR ::   (A) endure : courage
> (B) tire : monotony   (C) question : perception
>   (D) waver : resolution   (E) flatter : charm

At first glance, you might think that both *flag* and *vigor* were nouns; *flag*, after all, is a common noun, and *vigor* ends in -*or*, a common noun suffix. However, *endure* is clearly a verb. Simply from looking at the first answer choice, you know *flag* is a verb, not a noun.

What occurs when someone or something flags? Think of an American flag when the breeze dies down. The ban-ner hangs limp; it droops. In a word, the flag *flags*. By extension, the verb *flag* has come to mean to slacken or decline; when vigor flags, it becomes less firm. Only one answer choice conveys this sense of something firm weakening: Choice D. If one's resolution wavers, it declines.

Familiarize Yourself with Common Analogy Types

Analogies tend to fall into certain basic types. If you can discover no apparent relationship between the two capitalized words, try establishing a relationship between them based on the types commonly used on this test.

Common Analogy Types

Definition
REFUGE : SHELTER
A *refuge* (place of asylum) by definition *shelters*.

TAXONOMIST : CLASSIFY
A *taxonomist*, a person who specializes in classification, by definition *classifies*.

HAGGLER : BARGAIN
A *haggler*, a person who argues over prices, by definition *bargains*.

Defining Characteristic
TIGER : CARNIVOROUS
A *tiger* is defined as a *carnivorous* or meat-eating animal.

ENTOMOLOGIST : INSECTS
An *entomologist* is defined as a person who studies *insects*.

APIARY : BEE
An *apiary* is defined as a home for *bees*.

Class and Member
AMPHIBIAN: SALAMANDER
A *salamander* is an example of an *amphibian*.

METAPHYSICS : PHILOSOPHY
Metaphysics belongs to the field of *philosophy*.

SONNET : POEM
A *sonnet* is a specific kind of *poem*.

Antonyms
Antonyms are words that are opposite in meaning. Both words belong to the same part of speech.

CONCERNED : INDIFFERENT
Concerned is the opposite of *indifferent* (unconcerned).

WAX : WANE
Wax, to grow larger, and *wane*, to dwindle, are opposites.

ANARCHY : ORDER
Anarchy is the opposite of *order*.

Antonym Variants
In an Antonym Variant, the words are not strictly antonyms; their meanings, however, are opposed. Take the adjective *nervous*. A strict antonym for the adjective *nervous* would be the adjective *poised*. However, where an Antonym would have the adjective *poised*, an Antonym Variant analogy has the noun *poise*. It looks like this:

NERVOUS : POISE
Nervous means lacking in *poise*.

INIQUITOUS : VIRTUE
Something *iniquitous* lacks *virtue*. It is the opposite of virtuous.

ABSTINENT : GORGE
Abstinent or sparing in eating means not inclined to cram or *gorge*.

Synonyms
Synonyms are words that have the same meaning. Both words belong to the same part of speech.

MAGNIFICENT : GRANDIOSE
Grandiose means *magnificent*.

RATIOCINATE : THINK
To *ratiocinate* is to *think*.

RECIDIVIST : BACKSLIDER
A *recidivist* or habitual offender is a *backslider*.

Synonym Variants
In a Synonym Variant, the words are not strictly synonymous; their meanings, however, are similar. Take the adjective *willful*. A strict synonym for the adjective *willful* would be the adjective *unruly*. However, where a Synonym would have the adjective *unruly*, a Synonym Variant analogy has the noun *unruliness*. It looks like this:

WILLFUL : UNRULINESS
Willful means exhibiting *unruliness*.

VERBOSE : WORDINESS
Someone *verbose* is wordy; he or she exhibits *wordiness*.

SOLICITOUS : CONCERN
Someone *solicitous* is concerned; he or she shows *concern*.

Degree of Intensity
FOND : DOTING
Fond is less extreme than *doting*.

FLURRY : BLIZZARD
A *flurry* or shower of snow is less extreme than a *blizzard*.

GRASPING : RAPACIOUS
To be *grasping* is less extreme than to be *rapacious*.

Part to Whole
ISLAND : ARCHIPELAGO
Many *islands* make up an *archipelago*.

SHARD : POTTERY
A *shard* is a fragment of *pottery*.

CANTO : POEM
A *canto* is part of a *poem*.

Function
ASYLUM : REFUGE
An *asylum* provides *refuge* or protection.

BALLAST : STABILITY
Ballast provides *stability*.

LULL : STORM
A *lull* temporarily interrupts a *storm*.

Manner
MUMBLE : SPEAK
To *mumble* is to *speak* indistinctly.

STRUT : WALK
To *strut* is to *walk* proudly.

STRAINED : WIT
Wit that is *strained* is forced in manner.

Action and Its Significance
WINCE : PAIN
A *wince* is a sign that one feels *pain*.

BLUSH : DISCOMFITURE
A *blush* signifies *discomfiture* or embarrassment.

PROSTRATION : SUBMISSIVENESS
Prostration (assuming a prostrate position, face to the ground) is a sign of *submissiveness* or abasement.

Worker and Article Created
POET : SONNET
A *poet* creates a *sonnet*.

ARCHITECT : BLUEPRINT
An *architect* designs a *blueprint*.

MASON : WALL
A *mason* builds a *wall*.

Worker and Tool
PAINTER : BRUSH
A *painter* uses a *brush*.

SICKLE : REAPER
A *reaper* uses a *sickle* to cut the grain.

CARPENTER : VISE
A *carpenter* uses a *vise* to hold the object being worked on.

Worker and Action
ACROBAT : CARTWHEEL
An *acrobat* performs a *cartwheel*.

FINANCIER : INVEST
A *financier invests*.

TENOR : ARIA
A *tenor* sings an *aria*.

Worker and Workplace
MUSICIAN : CONSERVATORY
A *musician* studies at a *conservatory*.

SCULPTOR : ATELIER
A *sculptor* works in an *atelier* or studio.

MINER : QUARRY
A *miner* works in a *quarry* or pit.

Tool and Its Action
DRILL : BORE
A *drill* is a tool used to *bore* holes.

CROWBAR : PRY
A *crowbar* is a tool used to *pry* things apart.

SIEVE : SIFT
A *sieve* is a tool used to strain or *sift*.

Less Common Analogy Types

Cause and Effect
SOPORIFIC : SLEEPINESS
A *soporific* causes *sleepiness*.

Sex
DOE : STAG
A *doe* is a female deer; a *stag*, a male deer.

Age
COLT : STALLION
A *colt* is a young *stallion*.

Time Sequence
CORONATION : REIGN
The *coronation* precedes the *reign*.

Spatial Sequence
ROOF : FOUNDATION
The *roof* is the highest point of a house; the *foundation*, the lowest point.

Symbol and Quality It Represents
DOVE : PEACE
A *dove* is the symbol of *peace*.

Practice Exercises

Analogy Exercise A

<u>Directions:</u> In each of the following questions, a related pair of words or phrases is followed by five lettered pairs of words or phrases. Select the lettered pair that best expresses a relationship similar to that expressed in the original pair.

1. MASON : WALL ::   (A) artist : easel
    (B) fisherman : trout   (C) author : book
    (D) congressman : senator   (E) sculptor : mallet

2. FIRE : ASHES ::   (A) accident : delay
    (B) wood : splinters   (C) water : waves
    (D) regret : melancholy   (E) event : memories

3. GOOSE : GANDER ::   (A) duck : drake
    (B) hen : chicken   (C) sheep : flock
    (D) dog : kennel   (E) horse : bridle

4. CARPENTER : SAW ::
    (A) stenographer : typewriter   (B) painter : brush
    (C) lawyer : brief   (D) seamstress : scissors
    (E) runner : sneakers

5. CAPTAIN : SHOAL ::   (A) lawyer : litigation
    (B) pilot : radar   (C) soldier : ambush
    (D) doctor : hospital   (E) corporal : sergeant

6. HORNS : BULL ::   (A) mane : lion
    (B) wattles : turkey   (C) antlers : stag
    (D) hoofs : horse   (E) wings : eagle

7. JUDGE : COURTHOUSE ::   (A) carpenter : bench
    (B) lawyer : brief   (C) architect : blueprint
    (D) physician : infirmary   (E) landlord : studio

8. HELMET : HEAD ::   (A) pedal : foot
    (B) gun : hand   (C) breastplate : chest
    (D) pendant : neck   (E) knapsack : back

9. GULLIBLE : DUPED ::   (A) credible : cheated
    (B) careful : cautioned   (C) malleable : molded
    (D) myopic : misled   (E) articulate : silenced

10. DUNGEON : CONFINEMENT ::
    (A) church : chapel   (B) school : truancy
    (C) asylum : refuge   (D) hospital : mercy
    (E) courthouse : remorse

11. HERMIT : GREGARIOUS ::
    (A) miser : penurious
    (B) ascetic : hedonistic
    (C) coward : pusillanimous
    (D) scholar : literate
    (E) crab : crustacean

12. MENDACITY : HONESTY ::
    (A) courage : cravenness
    (B) truth : beauty
    (C) courage : fortitude
    (D) unsophistication : ingenuousness
    (E) turpitude : depravity

13. MARATHON : STAMINA ::
    (A) relay : independence
    (B) hurdle : perseverance
    (C) sprint : celerity
    (D) jog : weariness
    (E) ramble : directness

14. NAIVE : INGENUE ::
    (A) ordinary : genuis
    (B) venerable : celebrity
    (C) urbane : sophisticate
    (D) crafty : artisan
    (E) modest : braggart

15. RETOUCH : PHOTOGRAPH ::
    (A) hang : painting   (B) finger : fabric
    (C) retract : statement   (D) compose : melody
    (E) refine : style

16. INDIGENT : WEALTH ::
    (A) contented : happiness
    (B) aristocratic : stature
    (C) smug : complacency
    (D) emaciated : nourishment
    (E) variegated : variety

17. SHALE : GEOLOGIST ::
    (A) catacombs : entomologist
    (B) aster : botanist
    (C) obelisk : fireman
    (D) love : philologist
    (E) reef : astrologer

18. DIDACTIC : TEACH ::   (A) sophomoric : learn
    (B) satiric : mock   (C) reticent : complain
    (D) chaotic : rule   (E) apologetic : deny

19. HACKNEYED : ORIGINAL ::
    (A) mature : juvenile   (B) trite : morbid
    (C) withdrawn : reserved   (D) evasive : elusive
    (E) derivative : traditional

20. AUGER : CARPENTER ::
    (A) studio : sculptor   (B) awl : cobbler
    (C) seam : seamstress   (D) cement : mason
    (E) apron : chef

Analogy Exercise B

Directions: In each of the following questions, a related pair of words or phrases is followed by five lettered pairs of words or phrases. Select the lettered pair that best expresses a relationship similar to that expressed in the original pair.

1. MUSTER : CREW ::
   (A) convene : committee
   (B) demobilize : troops
   (C) dominate : opposition
   (D) cheer : team
   (E) dismiss : jury

2. DWELL : DENIZEN ::   (A) shun : outcast
   (B) inherit : heir   (C) squander : miser
    (D) obey : autocrat   (E) patronize : protégé

3. MEANDERING : DIRECTNESS ::
   (A) menacing : ambition
   (B) affable : permissiveness
   (C) digressive : conciseness
   (D) circuitous : rotation
   (E) aboveboard : openness

4. CEMENT : TROWEL ::   (A) lawn : rake
   (B) conflagration : match   (C) paint : brush
    (D) floor : polish   (E) wallpaper : ladder

5. PIGHEADED : YIELD ::
   (A) lionhearted : retreat   (B) lily-livered : flee
    (C) dogged : pursue   (D) featherbrained : giggle
     (E) eagle-eyed : discern

6. ALARM : TRIGGER ::   (A) prison : escape
   (B) tunnel : dig   (C) criminal : corner
    (D) fright : allay   (E) trap : spring

7. QUOTATION : QUOTATION MARKS ::
   (A) remark : colon
   (B) sentence : period
   (C) aside : parentheses
   (D) clause : semicolon
   (E) interjection : exclamation point

8. SIGNATURE : ILLUSTRATION ::
   (A) byline : column   (B) alias : charge
    (C) credit : purchase   (D) note : scale
     (E) reference : recommendation

9. SCALES : JUSTICE ::   (A) weights : measures
   (B) laws : courts   (C) torch : liberty
    (D) laurel : peace   (E) balance : equity

10. SURPRISE : EXCLAMATION ::
    (A) insolence : bow   (B) dismay : groan
     (C) happiness : grimace   (D) deference : nod
      (E) contentment : mutter

11. APOSTATE : RELIGION ::
    (A) potentate : kingdom   (B) traitor : country
     (C) bureacrat : government   (D) jailor : law
      (E) teacher : education

12. FOX : CUNNING ::   (A) dog : playful
    (B) hyena : amusing   (C) beaver : industrious
     (D) vixen : cute   (E) colt : sturdy

13. PERJURY : OATH ::   (A) plagiarism : authority
    (B) embezzlement : trust   (C) disrespect : age
     (D) testimony : court   (E) jury : vow

14. EULOGY : BLAME ::   (A) elegy : loss
    (B) satire : mockery   (C) tirade : abuse
     (D) simile : likeness   (E) benediction : curse

15. PRIDE : LIONS ::   (A) gaggle : geese
    (B) honor : thieves   (C) snarl : wolves
     (D) arrogance : kings   (E) lair : bears

16. RANGE : MOUNTAINS ::   (A) atlas : maps
    (B) plain : prairie   (C) string : beads
     (D) novel : short stories   (E) sea : rivers

17. EXCESSIVE : MODERATION ::
    (A) extensive : duration
    (B) arbitrary : courage
    (C) impulsive : reflection
    (D) distinguished : reverence
    (E) expensive : cost

18. DEADBEAT : PAY ::   (A) killjoy : lament
    (B) spoilsport : refrain   (C) daredevil : risk
     (D) diehard : quit   (E) turncoat : betray

19. MENDICANT : IMPECUNIOUS ::
    (A) critic : quizzical   (B) complainer : petulant
     (C) physician : noble   (D) liar : compulsive
      (E) philanthropist : prodigal

20. SNICKER : DISRESPECT ::
    (A) whimper : impatience   (B) chortle : glee
     (C) frown : indifference   (D) sneer : detachment
      (E) glower : cheerfulness

Analogy Exercise C

<u>Directions:</u>   In each of the following questions, a related pair of words or phrases is followed by five lettered pairs of words or phrases. Select the lettered pair that best expresses a relationship similar to that expressed in the original pair.

1. MYTH : LEGENDARY ::   (A) sermon : lengthy
   (B) anecdote : witty   (C) fable : didactic
   (D) epic : comic   (E) allegory : obscure

2. TIRADE : ABUSIVE ::
   (A) monologue : lengthy
   (B) aphorism : boring
   (C) prologue : conclusive
   (D) encomium : laudatory
   (E) critique : insolent

3. EXPEDITIOUS : SPEED ::
   (A) astute : wisdom
   (B) decorous : impropriety
   (C) thoughtful : inanity
   (D) haggard : sturdiness
   (E) portable : frailty

4. ANNOTATE : TEXT ::
   (A) enact : law   (B) prescribe : medication
   (C) caption : photograph   (D) abridge : novel
   (E) censor : film

5. DRUDGERY : IRKSOME ::
   (A) encumbrance : burdensome
   (B) journey : wearisome
   (C) ambivalence : suspicious
   (D) compliance : forced
   (E) dissonance : harmonious

6. IMPROMPTU : REHEARSAL ::
   (A) practiced : technique   (B) makeshift : whim
   (C) offhand : premeditation   (D) glib : fluency
   (E) numerical : calculation

7. ELISION : SYLLABLES ::
   (A) contraction : letters   (B) thesis : ideas
   (C) diagnosis : symptoms   (D) almanac : facts
   (E) abacus : numbers

8. STICKLER : INSIST ::   (A) mumbler : enunciate
   (B) trickster : risk   (C) haggler : concede
   (D) laggard : outlast   (E) braggart : boast

9. DETRITUS : GLACIER ::   (A) thaw : snowfall
   (B) snow : ice cap   (C) silt : river
   (D) range : mountain   (E) foliage : tree

10. DESCRY : DISTANT ::   (A) mourn : lost
    (B) whisper : muted   (C) discern : subtle
    (D) destroy : flagrant   (E) entrap : hostile

11. HORSE : CORRAL ::   (A) oyster : reef
    (B) dog : muzzle   (C) sheep : flock
    (D) pig : sty   (E) deer : stag

12. RUBBER : ELASTIC ::   (A) paper : brittle
    (B) diamond : hard   (C) satin : sheer
    (D) metal : heavy   (E) dust : allergic

13. REAM : PAPER ::   (A) carton : milk
    (B) statue : marble   (C) tablet : clay
    (D) ink : pen   (E) cord : wood

14. HOBBLE : WALK ::   (A) gallop : run
    (B) stammer : speak   (C) stumble : fall
    (D) sniff : smell   (E) amble : stroll

15. DETECTIVE : INFORMER ::
    (A) spy : counterspy   (B) reporter : source
    (C) author : editor   (D) architect : draftsman
    (E) sailor : mutineer

16. SCULPTOR : STONE ::   (A) essayist : words
    (B) painter : turpentine   (C) composer : symphony
    (D) logger : timber   (E) etcher : acid

17. MASTHEAD : NEWSPAPER ::
    (A) footnote : essay   (B) credits : film
    (C) spine : book   (D) ream : paper
    (E) advertisement : magazine

18. FRAYED : FABRIC ::   (A) thawed : ice
    (B) renovated : building   (C) frazzled : nerves
    (D) watered : lawn   (E) cultivated : manner

19. INDOLENT : WORK ::   (A) decisive : act
    (B) gullible : cheat   (C) perceptive : observe
    (D) theatrical : perform   (E) taciturn : speak

20. INFALLIBLE : ERROR ::   (A) irreversible : cure
    (B) invulnerable : emotion   (C) impeccable : flaw
    (D) intolerable : defect   (E) immovable : choice

Analogy Exercise D

<u>Directions:</u>   In each of the following questions, a related pair of words or phrases is followed by five lettered pairs of words or phrases. Select the lettered pair that best expresses a relationship similar to that expressed in the original pair.

1. INFRACTION : LAW ::
   (A) interruption : continuity
   (B) renovation : structure
   (C) establishment : order
   (D) enactment : amendment
   (E) punishment : crime

2. LACHRYMOSE : TEARS ::
   (A) effusive : requests   (B) ironic : jests
   (C) morose : speeches   (D) profound : sighs
   (E) verbose : words

3. MOISTEN : DRENCH ::   (A) enclose : confine
   (B) prick : stab   (C) disregard : ignore
   (D) scrub : polish   (E) heat : chill

4. WITCH : COVEN ::   (A) ogre : castle
   (B) seer : prophecy   (C) actor : troupe
   (D) fairy : spell   (E) doctor : medicine

5. CONTINENT : ISLAND ::   (A) ocean : lake
   (B) isthmus : peninsula   (C) cape : cove
   (D) river : canal   (E) plateau : plain

6. SKINFLINT : STINGY ::
   (A) daredevil : alert
   (B) braggart : carefree
   (C) blackguard : protective
   (D) spendthrift : weak
   (E) diehard : stubborn

7. STORY : BUILDING ::   (A) plot : outline
   (B) rung : ladder   (C) cable : elevator
   (D) foundation : skyscraper   (E) spire : church

8. CANONIZE : SAINT ::   (A) train : athlete
   (B) guard : dignitary   (C) deify : sinner
   (D) lionize : celebrity   (E) humanize : scholar

9. STARE : GLANCE ::   (A) participate : observe
   (B) scorn : admire   (C) hunt : stalk
   (D) gulp : sip   (E) confide : tell

10. PERFORATE : HOLES ::   (A) speckle : spots
    (B) evaporate : perfume   (C) decorate : rooms
    (D) filter : water   (E) repent : sins

11. PUGNACIOUS : BATTLE ::   (A) timorous : beg
    (B) loquacious : drink   (C) tenacious : persist
    (D) veracious : lie   (E) wicked : survive

12. CLEARSIGHTED : PERSPICACITY ::
    (A) daring : temerity
    (B) reserved : impulsiveness
    (C) transparent : opacity
    (D) severe : clemency
    (E) lethargic : energy

13. PLEAD : SUPPLIANT ::
    (A) disperse : rioter
    (B) shun : outcast
    (C) revere : elder
    (D) beg : philanthropist
    (E) translate : interpreter

14. EPIGRAM : PITHY ::   (A) allegory : lengthy
    (B) saga : heroic   (C) anecdote : humorous
    (D) elegy : satiric   (E) proverb : modern

15. BOLT : FABRIC ::   (A) lock : key
    (B) book : paper   (C) roll : film
    (D) needle : thread   (E) light : lamp

16. PROOF : ALCOHOL ::   (A) cream : milk
    (B) canteen : water   (C) tanker : oil
    (D) octane : gasoline   (E) pulp : juice

17. INCUBATOR : INFANT ::
    (A) henhouse : chicken   (B) greenhouse : plant
    (C) archives : document   (D) cooler : wine
    (E) hive : bee

18. CITADEL : DEFENSE ::
    (A) chapel : refreshment
    (B) gazebo : refuge
    (C) marina : contemplation
    (D) warehouse : storage
    (E) rampart : supervision

19. RANCID : TASTE ::   (A) tepid : temperature
    (B) glossy : look   (C) rank : smell
    (D) dulcet : sound   (E) savory : odor

20. TRYST : CLANDESTINE ::
    (A) reverie : dreamy
    (B) acquaintanceship : brief
    (C) expectation : hopeless
    (D) glance : resentful
    (E) journey : leisurely

Analogy Exercise E

Directions: In each of the following questions, a related pair of words or phrases is followed by five lettered pairs of words or phrases. Select the lettered pair that best expresses a relationship similar to that expressed in the original pair.

1. WHISPER : SPEAK ::   (A) brush : touch
   (B) skip : walk   (C) listen : hear
   (D) request : ask   (E) whimper : whine

2. ELUSIVE : CAPTURE ::
   (A) persuasive : convince   (B) elastic : stretch
   (C) headstrong : control   (D) sensible : decide
   (E) gullible : trick

3. LINEAGE : PERSON :   (A) foliage : tree
   (B) derivation : word   (C) adolescence : child
   (D) title : book   (E) landscape : portrait

4. IMPANEL : JUROR ::   (A) accuse : defendant
   (B) convict : culprit   (C) testify : witness
   (D) enroll : student   (E) involve : bystander

5. PECCADILLO : TRIFLING ::
   (A) pariah : popular   (B) diagnosis : accurate
   (C) notion : farfetched   (D) squabble : petty
   (E) pursuit : trivial

6. PHYSIQUE : STURDY ::   (A) intellect : noble
   (B) punctuality : tardy   (C) investment : sound
   (D) fabric : worn   (E) technique : inept

7. TRAILER : MOTION PICTURE ::
   (A) truck : cargo   (B) theater : play
   (C) edition : novel   (D) commercial : product
   (E) libretto : opera

8. SIGN : ZODIAC ::   (A) poster : billboard
   (B) letter : alphabet   (C) prediction : prophecy
   (D) signal : beacon   (E) rhyme : almanac

9. LUMINARY : ILLUSTRIOUS ::
   (A) zealot : intense   (B) miser : prodigal
   (C) atheist : devout   (D) dignitary : conceited
   (E) celebrity : wealthy

10. BUFFOON : DIGNITY ::
    (A) braggart : modesty
    (B) blackguard : strength
    (C) laughingstock : ridicule
    (D) imposter : identification
    (E) gambler : risk

11. ROUT : DEFEAT ::   (A) ovation : applause
    (B) triumph : failure   (C) grief : loss
    (D) pathway : ruin   (E) memory : oblivion

12. METAPHOR : FIGURATIVE ::
    (A) fable : contemporary
    (B) adage : paradoxical
    (C) precept : instructive
    (D) irony : dramatic
    (E) epic : literal

13. CALUMNY : ASPERSIONS ::
    (A) approbation : praise
    (B) slander : mockery
    (C) approval : criticism
    (D) expectation : threats
    (E) satire : lamentations

14. LAST : SHOE ::   (A) cuff : trousers
    (B) finale : curtain   (C) pattern : glove
    (D) buckle : belt   (E) strap : slip

15. INDOLENT : SLOTH ::   (A) wrathful : ire
    (B) arrogant : acuity   (C) covetous : enigma
    (D) gluttonous : loyalty   (E) impatient : apathy

16. GROVEL : SERVILITY ::   (A) titter : arrogance
    (B) fume : anger   (C) yawn : civility
    (D) preen : modesty   (E) snivel : hypocrisy

17. DELICATE : FASTIDIOUS ::
    (A) hard-working : diligent
    (B) altruistic : mercenary
    (C) demonstrative : effusive
    (D) deceptive : fallacious
    (E) blithe : melancholy

18. RICOCHET : BULLET ::   (A) soar : falcon
    (B) aim : crossbow   (C) pierce : dart
    (D) carom : ball   (E) catapult : missile

19. JUGGERNAUT : INEXORABLE ::
    (A) cosmonaut : worldly
    (B) colossus : gigantic
    (C) demagogue : liberal
    (D) philistine : cultivated
    (E) despot : immaculate

20. APOCRYPHAL : AUTHENTICITY ::
    (A) nefarious : wickedness
    (B) dogmatic : assertiveness
    (C) hypocritical : integrity
    (D) perspicacious : discernment
    (E) deceptive : artifice

Answer Key

Analogy Exercise A

1.	C	6.	C	11.	B	16.	D
2.	E	7.	D	12.	A	17.	B
3.	A	8.	C	13.	C	18.	B
4.	D	9.	C	14.	C	19.	A
5.	C	10.	C	15.	E	20.	B

Analogy Exercise B

1.	A	6.	E	11.	B	16.	C
2.	B	7.	C	12.	C	17.	C
3.	C	8.	A	13.	B	18.	D
4.	C	9.	C	14.	E	19.	B
5.	A	10.	B	15.	A	20.	B

Analogy Exercise C

1.	C	6.	C	11.	D	16.	A
2.	D	7.	A	12.	B	17.	B
3.	A	8.	E	13.	E	18.	C
4.	C	9.	C	14.	B	19.	E
5.	A	10.	C	15.	B	20.	C

Analogy Exercise D

1.	A	6.	E	11.	C	16.	D
2.	E	7.	B	12.	A	17.	B
3.	B	8.	D	13.	E	18.	D
4.	C	9.	D	14.	B	19.	C
5.	A	10.	A	15.	C	20.	A

Analogy Exercise E

1.	A	6.	C	11.	A	16.	B
2.	C	7.	D	12.	C	17.	C
3.	B	8.	B	13.	A	18.	D
4.	D	9.	A	14.	C	19.	B
5.	D	10.	A	15.	A	20.	C

5 Reading Comprehension Questions

■ **Testing Tactics**
■ **Practice Exercises**
■ **Answer Key**

GRE reading comprehension questions test your ability to understand what you read—both content and technique. Each verbal section on the GRE includes two passages, one short, one long, the short passage followed by three or four questions, the long passage followed by seven or eight. One passage deals with the **sciences** (including medicine, botany, zoology, chemistry, physics, geology, astronomy); the other deals with the **humanities** (including art, literature, music, philosophy, folklore), or with the **social sciences** (including history, economics, sociology, government). Each test generally contains a passage that is "**ethnic**" in content: whether it is a history passage or a passage on music, art, or literature, it deals with concerns of a particular minority group (including women).

The verbal sections follow two basic patterns.

Section A	Example
1 Science Passage (150 – 200 words)	Geology—Physical Science
1 Nonscience Passage (500–600 words)	Women's Suffrage Movement—Social Sciences
Section B	
1 Science Passage (500 – 600 words)	DNA—Biological Science
1 Nonscience Passage (150 – 200 words)	Thomas Hardy—Literature

The GRE tends to take its reading passages from *Scientific American*, from prestigious university presses (Harvard, Princeton, Oxford), from scholarly journals. Often the test-makers hit academically "hot" topics—sociobiology, plate tectonics, damage to the ozone layer, Arthurian romance, the status of women's literature—that have aroused controversy over the past two decades. Frequently they edit these passages to make them more demanding both in vocabulary level and in grammatical complexity.

Some of the reading comprehension questions on the GRE are factual, asking you about specific details in the passages. Others ask you to interpret the passages, to make judgments about them. Still others ask you to recognize various techniques used by the authors or possible applications of their ideas to other circumstances. Many of the questions include lengthy and complex statements, as lengthy and complex as any sentences in the passage. All require you to read closely, as does the text. Be sure, in answering reading comprehension questions, that you read *all* the answer choices before deciding which is correct.

Unlike the antonym, analogy, and sentence completion questions, the reading comprehension questions following each passage are not arranged in order of difficulty. Their arrangement tends to reflect the way the passage's content is organized. (A question based on information found at the beginning of the passage generally will come before a question based on information at the end.) If you are stumped by a tough reading question, do not skip the other questions on that passage. The next question may be an easy one.

Testing Tactics

Save the Reading Comprehension Questions for Last

To answer an antonym question takes you seconds; to answer a reading comprehension question takes minutes of going over the passage before you ever get to the questions at all.

On the GRE, you get the same points for answering a "quick and easy" question correctly as you do for answering a time-consuming one. The more questions you answer correctly, the higher your score will be. Therefore, it makes sense for you to tackle the quick-to-answer questions—the sentence completions, the analogies, the

antonyms—*first*. Get as many of them right as you can, and then settle down to answering the reading questions, knowing you've done everything possible to maximize your score.

One word of caution: Remember that the reading questions typically occur toward the end of the section, just before the antonyms. If you plan to skip them and come back to them later, *be very careful in marking your answer sheet*.

Tackle Passages with Familiar Subjects Before Passages with Unfamiliar Ones

Just as it is common sense to tackle quick-to-answer questions before time-consuming ones, it is also common sense to tackle reading passages with familiar subjects before reading passages with unfamiliar ones. If you know very little about the physics of elementary particles or are uninterested in it, you are all too likely to run into trouble reading a passage about quantum theory.

It is hard to concentrate when you read about something

wholly unfamiliar to you. Give yourself a break. If you find one reading passage interests you or deals with a topic in which you are well grounded, attack that passage first. There is nothing wrong with skipping questions. Just remember to check the numbering of your answer sheet. You should, of course, go back to the questions you skipped if you have time. If you find you are running out of time, simply guess at random: you get no points for empty spaces on your answer sheet.

First Read the Passage, Then Read the Questions

Students often ask whether it is better to read the passage first or the questions first. Those who want to read the questions before reading the passage think it will save time. Ninety-nine times out of a hundred they are wrong.

Reading the questions before you read the passage will not save you time. It will cost you time. If you read the questions first, when you turn to the passage you will have a number of question words and phrases dancing around in your head. These phrases might possibly focus you; more likely, they will distract you. You will be so involved in trying to spot the places they occur in the passage that you will not be able to concentrate on comprehending the passage as a whole. Why increase your

anxiety and decrease your capacity to think? First read the passage, using the following technique:

1. Read as rapidly as you can with understanding, but do not force yourself. Do not worry about the time element. If you worry about not finishing the test, you will begin to take short cuts and miss the correct answer in your haste. Remember, if you have followed Tactic 1 and answered the quick questions first, you have already maximized your score and made the best use of your time.

2. As you read the opening sentences, try to anticipate what the passage will discuss. Whom or what is the author talking about?

3. As you continue reading, try to identify what *kind* of writing this is, what *techniques* are being used, who the intended *audience* may be, and what *feeling* (if any) the author has toward the subject. Try to retain names, dates, and places for quick reference later. In particular, try to remember where in the passage the author makes *major points*. Then, when you start looking for the phrase or sentence that will justify your choice of answer, you will be able to save time by going back to that section of the passage immediately without having to reread the entire selection. (This is particularly important in dealing with the two 500–600 word passages on the test.)

4. Your first reading of the passage should give you a general impression of the theme of the passage and of the location of its major subdivisions. In order to answer each question properly, *you must go back to the passage* to verify your choice of answer. Do not rely on memory, and, above all, do not rely on knowledge gained from other sources.

5. Underline sparingly, if at all. You may want to circle key words in question stems (words like EXCEPT and LEAST, which the test-makers capitalize for emphasis, and which restrict your answer choice) or put an asterisk (*) or check mark in the margin next to an important word or phrase. You do not, however, want to underline everything in sight, making the passage harder to read.

6. Then read the first question. You may remember where the answer to that question is to be found. If so, go directly to the relevant part of the reading selection. If not, read the entire selection again. Do not jump around, hoping to encounter the answer by chance. Decide on your answer, or, if you cannot be certain you have identified the correct answer, guess. Then go on to the next question.

If you have reservations about this tactic, feel free to try other approaches doing some of the practice exercises at the end of this chapter. Compare the scores you get using each approach. Reading is a highly individual skill. See what approach works best for you. The important thing is to know yourself and to feel comfortable with what you do.

Learn to Spot the Major Reading Question Types

Just as it will help you to know the common types of analogies found on the GRE, it will also help you to familiarize yourself with the major types of reading questions on the test.

If you can recognize just what a given question is asking for, you will be better able to tell which reading tactic to apply.

Here are six categories of reading questions you are sure to face:

1. **Main Idea** Questions that test your ability to find the central thought of a passage or to judge its significance often take the following forms:

   The main point of the passage is to...
   The passage is primarily concerned with...
   The author's primary purpose in this passage is to...
   The chief theme of the passage can best be described as...
   Which of the following titles best states the central idea of the passage?
   Which of the following statements best expresses the main idea of the passage?

2. **Finding Specific Details** Questions that test your ability to understand what the author states *explicitly* are often worded:

   According to the author...

   The author states all of the following EXCEPT . . .
   According to the passage, which of the following is true of the...
   The passage supplies information that would answer which of the following questions?
   Which of the following statements is (are) best supported by the passage?
   Which of the following is NOT cited in the passage as evidence of...

3. **Drawing Inferences** Questions that test your ability to go beyond the author's explicit statements and see what these statements imply may be worded:

   It can be inferred from the passage that...
   The author implies that...
   The passage suggests that...
   Which of the following statements about...can be inferred from the passage?

4. **Application to Other Situations** Questions that test your ability to recognize how the author's ideas might apply to other situations often are worded:

   With which of the following statements would the author of the passage be most likely to agree?
   With which of the following aphorisms would the author be in strongest agreement?
   The author's argument would be most weakened by the discovery of which of the following?
   The author's contention would be most clearly

strengthened if which of the following were found to be true?

Which of the following examples could best be substituted for the author's example of...

Which of the following statements would be most likely to begin the paragraph immediately following the passage?

The author is most probably addressing which of the following audiences?

5. **Tone/Attitude** Questions that test your ability to sense an author's emotional state often take the form:

The author's attitude toward the problem can best be described as...

The author regards the idea that...with...

The author's tone in the passage is that of a person attempting to...

Which of the following best describes the author's tone in the passage?

6. **Technique** Questions that test your ability to recognize a passage's method of organization or technique

often are worded:

Which of the following best describes the development of this passage?

In presenting the argument, the author does all of the following EXCEPT...

The relationship between the second paragraph and the first paragraph can best be described as...

In the passage, the author makes the central point primarily by...

The organization of the passage can best be described as...

7. **Determining the Meaning of Words from Their Context** Questions that test your ability to work out the meaning of unfamiliar words from their context often are worded:

As it is used in the passage, the term...can best be described as...

The phrase...is used in the passage to mean that...

As used by the author, the term...refers to...

The author uses the phrase...to describe...

When Asked to Find the Main Idea, Be Sure to Check the Opening and Summary Sentences of Each Paragraph

Authors typically provide readers with a sentence that expresses a paragraph's main idea succinctly. Although such *topic sentences* may appear anywhere in the paragraph, most often a topic sentence is either the opening or the closing sentence.

Note that in GRE reading passages topic sentences are sometimes implied rather than stated directly. If you cannot find a topic sentence, ask yourself these questions:

1. Who or what is this passage about?
   (The subject of the passage can be a *person*, *place*, or *thing*. It can be something abstract, such as an *idea*. It can even be a *process*, or something in motion, for which no single-word synonym exists.)

2. What aspect of this subject is the author talking about?

3. What is the author trying to get across about this aspect of the subject?
   (Decide the most important thing that is being said about the subject. Either the subject must be *doing* something, or something is *being done* to it.)

Read the following natural science passage from a recent GRE and apply this tactic.

When the same parameters and quantitative theory are used to analyze both termite colonies and troops of rhesus macaques, we will have a unified science of sociobiol-

ogy. Can this ever really happen? As my own studies have advanced, I have been increasingly impressed with the functional similarities between insect and vertebrate societies and less so with the structural differences that seem, at first glance, to constitute such an immense gulf between them. Consider for a moment termites and macaques. Both form cooperative groups that occupy territories. In both kinds of society there is a well-marked division of labor. Members of both groups communicate to each other hunger, alarm, hostility, caste status or rank, and reproductive status. From the specialist's point of view, this comparison may at first seem facile — or worse. But it is out of such deliberate oversimplification that the beginnings of a general theory are made.

[Adapted by ETS from *Sociobiology* by Edward O. Wilson.]

Now look at the GRE's main idea question on this passage.

Which of the following best summarizes the author's main point?

(A) Oversimplified comparisons of animal societies could diminish the likelihood of developing a unified science of sociobiology.

(B) Understanding the ways in which animals as different as termites and rhesus macaques resemble each other requires training in both biology and sociology.

(C) Most animals organize themselves into societies that exhibit patterns of group behavior
similar to those of human societies.
(D) Animals as different as termites and rhesus
macaques follow certain similar and predictable patterns of behavior.
(E) A study of the similarities between insect and
vertebrate societies could provide the basis
for a unified science of sociobiology.

Look at the opening and summary sentences of the passage: "When the same parameters and quantitative theory are used to analyze both termite colonies and troops
of rhesus macaques, we will have a unified science of
sociobiology....it is out of such deliberate oversimplification that the beginnings of a general theory are made."
First, is there a person, place, thing, idea, or process that
is common to both sentences? Are there any words in the
last sentence that repeat something in the first? *A general theory* repeats the idea of *a unified science* of sociobiology. The paragraph's subject seems to be the unified
science of sociobiology. Note as well the words pointing
to expectations for the future—*will have*, *beginnings*. The
tone of both sentences appears positive: when certain
conditions are met, then a specific result will follow—we
will have a unified science or general theory of sociobiol-

ogy. This result, however, is not guaranteed: it can come
about only if the conditions are met.

Now turn to the answer choices. What does Choice A say
about a unified science of sociobiology? It states some
things could make it less likely, not more likely, to come
about. Choice A is incorrect; it contradicts the passage's
sense that a unified science of sociobiology is a *likely* outcome. Choices B, C, and D also may be incorrect: not
one of them mentions a unified science of sociobiology.
On closer inspection, Choice B proves incorrect: it makes
an unsupported statement that one needs biological and
sociological training to understand the resemblances
between insects and vertebrates. Choice C also proves
incorrect: it goes far beyond what the passage actually
states. Where the passage speaks in terms of termites
and rhesus macaques, Choice C speaks in terms of *most*
animals and extends the comparison to include humans
as well. Choice D, while factually correct according to the
passage, is incorrect because it is too narrow in scope. It
ignores the author's main point: it fails to include the
author's interest in the possibility that a study of such
similar patterns of behavior might lead to a general theory of sociobiology. The correct answer is Choice E. It is
the only statement that speaks of a unified science of
sociobiology as a likely possibility.

When Asked to Choose a Title, Watch Out for Choices That Are Too Specific or Too Broad

An appropriate title for a passage must express the central theme developed in the passage. It should be neither
too broad nor too narrow in scope; it should be specific
and yet comprehensive enough to include all the essential ideas presented. For a passage of two or more paragraphs, it should express the thoughts of ALL the
paragraphs.

When you are trying to select the best title for a passage,
watch out for words that come straight out of the passage. They may not always be your best choice.

This second question on the sociobiology passage is a
title question. Note how it resembles questions on the
passage's purpose or main idea.

Which of the following is the best title for the
passage?

(A) Deceptive Comparisons: Oversimplification
in Biological Research
(B) An Uncanny Likeness: Termites and Rhesus
Macaques
(C) Structural Dissimilarities Between Insects and
Vertebrates
(D) Arguments against a Science of Sociobiology
(E) Sociobiology: Intimations of a General
Theory

Choice A is incorrect: it is at once too narrow and too
broad. It is too narrow in that the passage refers to *oversimplification* only in passing. It is too broad in that the
passage emphasizes sociobiology, not the whole realm
of biological research. It is also misleading: the passage
never asserts that the deliberate oversimplification of the
comparison between termites and macaques is intended
to deceive.

Choice B is incorrect: it is too narrow. True, the author
discusses the resemblance between termite and
macaque societies; however, this likeness is not his subject. He discusses it to provide an example of the sort of
comparison that may lay the groundwork for a potential
science of sociobiology.

Choice C is also incorrect because it is not inclusive
enough. It fails to mention the potential science of sociobiology. In addition, while the passage refers to *structural
differences* between insect and vertebrate societies, it
stresses structural similarities, not structural
dissimilarities.

Choices D and E both mention the theory of sociobiology.
Which is the better title for the piece? Clearly, Choice E.
The author is not arguing against the potential science of
sociobiology; he is discussing favorably the likelihood of
sociobiology's emergence as a unified science. Thus, he
finds in the termite-macaque comparison *intimations* or
hints of an incipient general theory.

When Asked to Determine Questions of Attitude, Mood, or Tone, Look for Words That Convey Emotion, Express Values, or Paint Pictures

In determining the attitude, mood, or tone of an author, examine the specific diction used. Is the author using adjectives to describe the subject? If so, are they words like *fragrant*, *tranquil*, *magnanimous*—words with positive connotations? Or are they words like *fetid*, *ruffled*, *stingy*—words with negative connotations?

When we speak, our tone of voice conveys our mood—frustrated, cheerful, critical, gloomy, angry. When we write, our images and descriptive phrases get our feelings across.

The third GRE question on the Wilson passage is an attitude question. Note the range of feelings in the answer choices.

The author's attitude toward the possibility of a unified theory in sociobiology is best described as which of the following?

(A) Guarded optimism
(B) Unqualified enthusiasm
(C) Objective indifference
(D) Resignation
(E) Dissatisfaction

How does the author feel about the possibility of a unified theory of sociobiology? The answer choices range from actively negative (*dissatisfaction*) to actively positive (*unqualified enthusiasm*), with passively negative (*resignation*), neutral (*objective indifference*), and cautiously positive (*guarded optimism*) in between.

Wilson's attitude toward the possibility of a unified theory of sociobiology is implicit in his choice of words. It is clear that he views this possibility positively. The whole thrust

of his argument is that the current studies of the similarities between insect and vertebrate societies could mark the beginnings of such a unified theory and that the specialist should not dismiss these studies as facile or simpleminded. Note, however, in the third sentence how Wilson's specific choice of words conveys his feelings and value judgments. He describes his own studies as having "advanced"—not as having merely continued, but as having progressed and ultimately improved. He implies that he knows better now than he did in earlier years and deprecates less advanced viewpoints with the negative phrases "at first glance" and "seem."

Wilson is certainly not unhappy or *dissatisfied* with this potential unified theory, nor is he merely longsuffering or *resigned* to it. Similarly, he is not *objectively indifferent* to it; he actively involves himself in arguing the case for sociobiology. Thus, you can eliminate Choices C, D, and E. But how do you decide between the two positive terms, *optimism* and *enthusiasm*, Choice A and Choice B? To decide between them, you must look carefully at the adjectives modifying them. Is Wilson's enthusiasm unconditional or *unqualified*? Not absolutely. His opening sentence states a basic condition that must be met before there can be a unified science of sociobiology: the same parameters and quantitative theory must be used to analyze insect and vertebrate societies. *Unqualified enthusiasm* seems to overstate his attitude. Choice B appears incorrect. What of Choice A? Is Wilson's optimism cautious or *guarded*? Yes. He is aware that specialists may well find fault with the sociobiologist's conclusions; he uses terms that convey values, first the negative "facile—or worse" to suggest the specialist's negative attitude toward sociobiology, then the positive "deliberate" to suggest his more positive response. The correct answer is Choice A.

When Asked About Specific Details in the Passage, Spot Key Words in the Question and Scan the Passage to Find Them (or Their Synonyms).

In developing the main idea of a passage, a writer will make statements to support his or her point. To answer questions about such supporting details, you *must* find a word or group of words in the passage supporting your choice of answer. The words "according to the passage" or "according to the author" should focus your attention on what the passage explicitly states. Do not be misled

into choosing an answer (even one that makes good sense) if you cannot find support for it in the text.

Detail questions often ask about a particular phrase or line. In such cases, use the following technique:

1. Look for key words (nouns or verbs) in the answer choices.

2. Run your eye down the passage, looking for those key words or their synonyms. (This is *scanning*. It is what you do when you look up someone's number in the phone directory.)

3. When you find a key word or its synonym, reread the sentence to make sure the test-makers haven't used the original wording to mislead you.

Read the following *Scientific American* passage from a recently published GRE and apply this tactic.

Visual recognition involves storing and retrieving memories. Neural activity, triggered by the eye, forms an image in the brain's memory system that constitutes an internal representation of the viewed object. When an object is encountered again, it is matched with its internal representation and thereby recognized. Controversy surrounds the question of whether recognition is a parallel, one-step process or a serial, step-by-step one. Psychologists of the Gestalt school maintain that objects are recognized as wholes in a parallel procedure: the internal representation is matched with the retinal image in a single operation. Other psychologists have proposed that internal representation features are matched serially with an object's features. Although some experiments show that, as an object becomes familiar, its internal representation becomes more holistic and the recognition process correspondingly more parallel, the weight of evidence seems to support the serial hypothesis, at least for objects that are not notably simple and familiar.

[Adapted by ETS from "Eye Movements and Visual Perception" by David Noton and Lawrence Stark, *Scientific American*, June, 1971]

Now look at a GRE question on a specific detail in the passage.

You can arrive at the correct answer to this question by elimination.

According to the passage, Gestalt psychologists make which of the following suppositions about visual recognition?

   I.   A retinal image is in exactly the same form as its internal representation.
  II. An object is recognized as a whole without any need for analysis into component parts.
 III. The matching of an object with its internal representation occurs in only one step.

(A) II only
(B) III only
(C) I and III only
(D) II and III only
(E) I, II, and III

First, quickly scan the passage looking for the key word *Gestalt*. The sentence mentioning Gestalt psychologists states they maintain that objects are recognized as wholes in a parallel procedure. The sentence immediately preceding defines a parallel procedure as one that takes only one step.

Now examine the statements. Do Gestalt psychologists maintain that a retinal image is in exactly the same form as its internal representation? Statement I is unsupported by the passage. Therefore, you can eliminate Choices C and E.

Statement II is supported by the passage: lines 8–12 indicate that Gestalt psychologists believe objects are recognized as wholes. Therefore, you can eliminate Choice B.

Statement III is supported by the passage: lines 8–12 indicate that Gestalt psychologists believe matching is a parallel process that occurs in one step. Therefore, you can eliminate Choice A.

Only Choice D is left. It is the correct answer.

Note how necessary it is to point to specific lines in the passage when you answer questions on specific details.

When Asked to Make Inferences, Base Your Answers on What the Passage Implies, Not What It States Directly

Inference questions require you to use your own judgment. You must not take anything directly stated by the author as an inference. Instead, you must look for clues in the passage that you can use in deriving your own conclusion. You should choose as your answer a statement that is a logical development of the information the author has provided.

Try this relatively easy GRE inference question, based on the preceding passage about visual recognition.

It can be inferred from the passage that the matching process in visual recognition is

(A) not a neural activity
(B) not possible when an object is viewed for the very first time
(C) not possible if a feature of a familiar object is changed in some way
(D) only possible when a retinal image is received in the brain as a unitary whole
(E) now fully understood as a combination of the serial and parallel processes

Go through the answer choices, eliminating any choices that obviously contradict what the passage states or implies. Remember that in answering inference questions you must go beyond the obvious, beyond what the authors explicitly state, to look for logical implications of what they say.

Choice A is incorrect. Nothing in the passage suggests that the matching process is not a neural activity. Rather, the entire process of visual recognition, including the matching of images, should involve neural activity.

Choice D is incorrect. It can be eliminated because it directly contradicts information in the passage stating that recognition most likely is a serial or step-by-step process rather than a parallel one grasping an image as a unitary whole.

Choice E is incorrect. It is clear from the passage that the matching process is *not* fully understood: the weight of the evidence *seems* to support the serial hypothesis, but controversy still surrounds the entire question.

Choices B and C are left. Which is a possible inference? Choice B seems a possible inference. Although the author never says so, it seems logical that you could not match an object if you had never seen it before. After all, if you had never seen the object before, you would have no prior internal representation of it and would have nothing with which to match it. What of Choice C? Nothing in the passage mentions changing the features of a familiar object. Therefore, *on the basis of the passage* you have no way to deduce whether matching would or would not be possible if such a change took place. There is not enough information in the passage to justify Choice C as an inference. The correct answer is Choice B.

Another, more difficult GRE inference question is based on the excerpt from Wilson's *Sociobiology*, reprinted below. Review the passage briefly and see how you do with a question that only 16 percent of the examinees answered correctly.

When the same parameters and quantitative theory are used to analyze both termite colonies and troops of rhesus macaques, we will have a unified science of sociobiology. Can this ever really happen? As my own studies have advanced, I have been increasingly impressed with the functional similarities between insect and vertebrate societies and less so with the structural differences that seem, at first glance, to constitute such an immense gulf between them. Consider for a moment termites and macaques. Both form cooperative groups that occupy territories. In both kinds of society there is a well-marked division of labor. Members of both groups communicate to each other hunger, alarm, hostility, caste status or rank, and reproductive status. From the specialist's point of view, this comparison may at first seem facile — or worse. But it is out of such deliberate oversimplification that the beginnings of a general theory are made.

In discussing insect and vertebrate societies, the author suggests which of the following?

(A) A distinguishing characteristic of most insect and vertebrate societies is a well-marked division of labor.
(B) The caste structure of insect societies is similar to that of vertebrate societies.
(C) Most insect and vertebrate societies form cooperative groups in order to occupy territory.
(D) The means of communication among members of insect societies is similar to that among members of vertebrate societies.
(E) There are significant structural differences between insect and vertebrate societies.

The reason so many examinees answered this question incorrectly is simple: they confused statements made about specific insect and vertebrate societies with statements made about insect and vertebrate societies in general. They did not see that, in the fourth sentence, the author switches from talking about insect and vertebrate societies in general and considers termites and macaques in particular.

Go through the answer choices one by one. Does the author suggest that a marked division of labor distinguishes *most* insect and vertebrate societies? No. He merely states that it is a characteristic of termite and rhesus macaque societies. Choice A is incorrect: you cannot justify leaping from a single type of insect (*termites*) and a single type of vertebrate (*rhesus macaques*) to most insects and most vertebrates.

Does the author suggest that the caste structure of insect societies is similar to that of vertebrate societies? No. He merely states that termites and macaques both can communicate caste status or rank. Choice B is incorrect. You cannot assume that the caste structure of insect societies is similar to that of vertebrate societies just because termites and rhesus macaques both have some way to communicate caste status or rank.

Does the author suggest that *most* insect and vertebrate societies form cooperative groups in order to occupy territory? No. He merely states that termites and macaques form cooperative groups that occupy territories. Choice C is incorrect: again, you cannot justify leaping from termites and rhesus macaques to most insects and most vertebrates.

Does the author suggest that the means of communication among members of insect societies is similar to that among members of vertebrate societies? No. He merely states that communication among termites and macaques serves similar ends; he says nothing about their means of communication, or about the means of communication used by other insects and vertebrates. Choice D is incorrect.

The correct answer is Choice E. In the passage, the author states that he has grown less impressed "with the structural differences that seem, at first glance, to constitute such an immense gulf between" insect and vertebrate societies. This suggests that, even though Wilson may be unimpressed with them, these differences exist and are *significant*.

When Asked to Apply Ideas from the Passage to a New Situation, Put Yourself in the Author's Place

GRE application questions require you to do three things:

1. *Reason*—If X is true, then Y must also be true.

2. *Perceive Feelings*—If the author feels this way about subject A, he or she probably feels a certain way about subject B.

3. *Sense a Larger Structure*—This passage is part of an argument for a proposal, or part of a description of a process, or part of a critique of a hypothesis.

Like inference questions, application questions require you to go beyond what the author explicitly states. Application questions, however, ask you to go well beyond a simple inference, using clues in the passage to interpret possible reasons for actions and possible outcomes of events. Your concern is to comprehend how the author's ideas might apply to other situations, or be affected by them. To do so, you have to put yourself in the author's place.

Imagine you are the author. What are you arguing for? Given what you have just stated in the passage, what would you want to say next? What might hurt your argument? What might make it stronger? What kind of audience would appreciate what you have to say? Whom are you trying to convince? If you involve yourself personally with the passage, you will be better able to grasp it in its entirety and see its significance.

Answer the following application question based on the same passage from *Sociobiology*.

Which of the following statements would be most likely to begin the paragraph immediately following the passage?

(A) I have raised a problem in ethical philosophy in order to characterize the essence of the discipline of sociobiology.

(B) It may not be too much to say that sociology and the other social sciences are the last branches of biology waiting to be integrated into neo-Darwinist evolutionary theory.

(C) Although behavioral biology is traditionally spoken of as if it were a unified subject, it is now emerging as two distinct disciplines centered on neurophysiology and sociobiology, respectively.

(D) The formulation of a theory of sociobiology constitutes, in my opinion, one of the great manageable problems of biology for the next twenty or thirty years.

(E) In the past, the development of sociobiology has been slowed by too close an identification with ethology and behavioral psychology.

As you know from answering the preceding main idea and attitude questions, Wilson's point is that students of insect and vertebrate societies may be on the verge of devising a general theory of sociobiology. He is optimistic about the likelihood of developing this unified science. At the same time, he is guarded: he does not wish to overstate his case.

Put yourself in Wilson's place. What would you be likely to say next? You have just been talking optimistically about the prospects for putting together a general theory. What would be more natural than to talk in terms of a time frame? Choice D, with its optimistic yet careful view of the formulation of a theory of sociobiology as "one of the great *manageable* problems of biology for the next twenty or thirty years," seems a logical extension of what Wilson has just been saying. While Choices A, B, C, and E all touch on sociobiology in some way, none of them follows as naturally from his immediate argument.

When Asked to Give the Meaning of an Unfamiliar Word, Look for Nearby Context Clues

When a question in the reading comprehension part of an examination asks for the meaning of a word, that meaning can usually be deduced from the word's context. The purpose of this kind of question is to determine how well you can extract meaning from the text, not how extensive your general vocabulary is.

Sometimes the unknown word is a common word used in one of its special or technical meanings. For example:

> He *threw* the pot in an hour. The wheel turned busily and the shape grew quickly as his fingers worked the wet, spinning clay. (*Throw* here means to shape on a potter's wheel.)

At other times, the unknown word may bear a deceptive resemblance to a known word.

> He fell *senseless* to the ground. (He was unconscious. He did not fall foolishly or nonsensically to the ground.)

Just because you know *one* meaning of a word, do not assume that you know its meaning as it is used in a particular passage. You must look within the passage for clues. Often authors will use an unfamiliar word and then immediately define it within the same sentence. The two words or groups of words are juxtaposed—set beside one another—to make their relationship clear. Commas, dashes, and parentheses may be used to signal this relationship.

1. The *rebec*, a medieval stringed instrument played with a bow, has only three strings.

2. *Paleontologists*—students of fossil remains—explore the earth's history.

3. Most mammals are *quadrupeds* (four-footed animals).

Often an unfamiliar word in one clause of a sentence will be defined or clarified in the sentence's other clause.

1. The early morning dew had frozen, and everything was covered with a thin coat of *rime*.

2. Cowards, we use *euphemisms* when we cannot bear the truth, calling our dead "the dear departed," as if they have just left the room.

Refer once more to the *Scientific American* passage to answer the question that follows.

Visual recognition involves storing and retrieving memories. Neural activity, triggered by the eye, forms an image in the brain's memory system that constitutes an internal representation of the
(5) viewed object. When an object is encountered again, it is matched with its internal representation and thereby recognized. Controversy surrounds the question of whether recognition is a parallel, one-step process or a serial, step-by-step one. Psychol-
(10) ogists of the Gestalt school maintain that objects are recognized as wholes in a parallel procedure: the internal representation is matched with the retinal image in a single operation. Other psychologists have proposed that internal representation
(15) features are matched serially with an object's features. Although some experiments show that, as an object becomes familiar, its internal representation becomes more holistic and the recognition process correspondingly more parallel, the weight of evi-
(20) dence seems to support the serial hypothesis, at least for objects that are not notably simple and familiar.

[Adapted by ETS from "Eye Movements and Visual Perception" by David Noton and Lawrence Stark, *Scientific American*, June, 1971]

Which of the following phrases could best be substituted for "becomes more holistic" (line 18) without substantially changing the author's meaning?

(A) increases in complexity
(B) grows less fragmented
(C) diminishes in magnitude
(D) reflects its image
(E) becomes unclear

What words or phrases in the vicinity of "becomes more holistic" give you a clue to the phrase's meaning? Consider the phrase immediately following, "[becomes] more parallel." If the recognition process becomes more parallel as an object becomes more familiar, then matching takes place in one step in which all the object's features are simultaneously transformed into a single internal representation. Thus, to say that an object's internal representation becomes more holistic is to say that it becomes more *integrated* or whole. The correct answer is Choice B.

Look at the words in the immediate vicinity of the word or phrase you are defining. They will often give you a sense of the meaning of the unfamiliar word.

Familiarize Yourself with the Technical Terms Used to Describe a Passage's Organization

Another aspect of understanding the author's point is understanding how the author organizes what he has to say. You have to understand how the author makes his point, figure out whether he begins with his thesis or main idea or works up to it gradually. Often this means observing how the opening sentence or paragraph relates to the passage as a whole.

Here is a technique question based on the last two sentences of the passage from *Sociobiology*. Those lines are repeated here so that you can easily refer to them.

From the specialist's point of view, this comparison
(15) may at first seem facile — or worse. But it is out of such deliberate oversimplification that the beginnings of a general theory are made.

Which of the following statements best describes the organization of the author's discussion of the importance of the termite/macaque comparison in the development of a unified science of sociobiology (lines 14-17)?

(A) He provides an example of a comparison and then rejects its implications.

(B) He concedes that current data are insufficient and modifies his initial assertion of their importance.

(C) He acknowledges hypothetical objections to the comparison, but concludes by reaffirming its significance.

(D) He cites critical appraisals of the comparison, but refrains from making an appraisal of his own.

(E) He notes an ambiguity in the comparison, but finally concedes its validity.

Consider the first clause of each answer choice.

In his comment on how things may seem from the specialist's point of view, does the author *provide an example* of a comparison? No. He refers to a comparison he made earlier. Therefore, you can eliminate Choice A.

Does he *concede the insufficiency* of current data? Not quite. He states that some people may quarrel with the comparison because it seems facile to them; he does not grant that they are right or that the data are inadequate. Therefore, you can eliminate Choice B.

Does he *acknowledge hypothetical objections* to the comparison? Definitely. Make a note to come back later to Choice C.

Does he *cite critical appraisals* of the comparison? Possibly. Again, make a note of Choice D.

Does he *note an ambiguity* in the comparison? No. He notes an objection to the comparison; he mentions no ambiguities within it. Therefore, you can eliminate Choice E.

Now consider the second clause of Choices C and D. Does the author *refrain from making an appraisal* of the comparison? No. He calls it a deliberate oversimplification that may bear fruit. Choice D is incorrect. Does the author conclude by *reaffirming the significance* of the termite/macaque comparison? Clearly he does: his final point is that such oversimplified comparisons can provide the basis for an important general theory. The correct answer is Choice C.

Practice Exercises

Reading Comprehension Exercise A

Directions: Each passage in this group is followed by questions based on its content. After reading a passage, choose the best answer to each question. Answer all questions following a passage on the basis of what is <u>stated</u> or <u>implied</u> in that passage.

One phase of the business cycle is the *expansion phase*. This phase is a twofold one, including recovery and prosperity. During the recovery period there is ever-growing expansion of existing
(5) facilities, and new facilities for production are created. More businesses are created and older ones expanded. Improvements of various kinds are made. There is an ever-increasing optimism about the future of economic growth. Much capital is
(10) invested in machinery or "heavy" industry. More labor is employed. More raw materials are required. As one part of the economy develops, other parts are affected. For example, a great expansion in automobiles results in an expansion of
(15) the steel, glass, and rubber industries. Roads are required; thus the cement and machinery industries are stimulated. Demand for labor and materials results in greater prosperity for workers and sup-

(20) pliers of raw materials, including farmers. This increases purchasing power and the volume of goods bought and sold. Thus prosperity is diffused among the various segments of the population. This prosperity period may continue to rise and rise without an apparent end. However, a time comes (25) when this phase reaches a peak and stops spiralling upwards. This is the end of the expansion phase.

1. Which of the following statements is the best example of the optimism mentioned in line 8 of the passage as being part of the expansion phase?

   (A) Public funds are designated for the construction of new highways designed to stimulate tourism.
   (B) Industrial firms allocate monies for the purchase of machine tools.
   (C) The prices of agricultural commodities are increased at the producer level.
   (D) Full employment is achieved at all levels of the economy.
   (E) As technology advances, innovative businesses replace antiquated firms.

2. It can be inferred from the passage that the author believes that

   (A) when consumers lose their confidence in the market, a recession follows
   (B) cyclical ends to business expansion are normal
   (C) luxury goods such as jewelry are unaffected by industrial expansion
   (D) with sound economic policies, prosperity can become a fixed pattern
   (E) the creation of new products is essential for prosperity

3. Which of the following statements would be most likely to begin the paragraph immediately following the passage?

   (A) Union demands may also have an effect on business cycles.
   (B) Some industries are, by their very nature, cyclical, having regular phases of expansion and recession.
   (C) Inflation is a factor that must be taken into consideration in any discussion of the expansion phase.
   (D) The farmer's role during the expansion phase is of vital importance.
   (E) The other phase of the business cycle is called the recession phase.

The history of mammals dates back at least to Triassic time. Development was retarded, however, until the sudden acceleration of evolutional change that occurred in the oldest Paleocene. This (5) led in Eocene time to increase in average size, larger mental capacity, and special adaptations for different modes of life. In the Oligocene Epoch,

there was further improvement, with appearance of some new lines and extinction of others. (10) Miocene and Pliocene time was marked by culmination of several groups and continued approach toward modern characters. The peak of the career of mammals in variety and average large size was attained in the Miocene.

(15) The adaptation of mammals to almost all possible modes of life parallels that of the reptiles in Mesozoic time, and except for greater intelligence, the mammals do not seem to have done much better than corresponding reptilian forms. The bat is (20) doubtless a better flying animal than the pterosaur, but the dolphin and whale are hardly more fishlike than the ichthyosaur. Many swift-running mammals of the plains, like the horse and the antelope, must excel any of the dinosaurs. The tyrannosaur (25) was a more ponderous and powerful carnivore than any flesh-eating mammal, but the lion or tiger is probably a more efficient and dangerous beast of prey because of a superior brain. The significant point to observe is that different branches of the (30) mammals gradually fitted themselves for all sorts of life, grazing on the plains and able to run swiftly (horse, deer, bison), living in rivers and swamps (hippopotamus, beaver), dwelling in trees (sloth, monkey), digging underground (mole, rodent), (35) feeding on flesh in the forest (tiger) and on the plain (wolf), swimming in the sea (dolphin, whale, seal), and flying in the air (bat). Man is able by mechanical means to conquer the physical world and to adapt himself to almost any set of conditions.

(40) This adaptation produces gradual changes of form and structure. It is biologically characteristic of the youthful, plastic stage of a group. Early in its career, an animal assemblage seems to possess capacity for change, which, as the unit becomes (45) old and fixed, disappears. The generalized types of organisms retain longest the ability to make adjustments when required, and it is from them that new, fecund stocks take origin—certainly not from any specialized end products. So, in the mammals, we (50) witness the birth, plastic spread in many directions, increasing specialization, and in some branches, the extinction, which we have learned from observation of the geologic record of life is a characteristic of the evolution of life.

4. Which of the following would be the most appropriate title for the passage?

   (A) From Dinosaur to Man
   (B) Adaptation and Extinction
   (C) The Superiority of Mammals
   (D) The Geologic Life Span
   (E) Man, Conqueror of the Physical World

5. It can be inferred from the passage that the chronological order of the geologic periods is

   (A) Paleocene, Miocene, Triassic, Mesozoic
   (B) Paleocene, Triassic, Mesozoic, Miocene
   (C) Miocene, Paleocene, Triassic, Mesozoic
   (D) Mesozoic, Oligocene, Paleocene, Miocene
   (E) Mesozoic, Paleocene, Eocene, Miocene

6. It can be inferred from the passage that the pterosaur

   (A) resembled the bat
   (B) was a Mesozoic mammal
   (C) was a flying reptile
   (D) lived in the sea
   (E) evolved during the Miocene period

7. According to the passage, the greatest number of forms of mammalian life is found in the

   (A) Triassic period
   (B) Eocene period
   (C) Oligocene epoch
   (D) Pliocene period
   (E) Miocene period

8. Which of the following statements, if true, would weaken the statement made by the author in lines 15–19?

   (A) Tryannosaur has been found to have a larger brain than was previously thought.
   (B) Mammals will become extinct within the next thousand years.
   (C) Forms of flying ichthyosaurs have recently been discovered.
   (D) The tiger has now been proved to be more powerful than the carnivorous reptiles.
   (E) Computers have been developed that can double human mental capacity.

9. It can be inferred from the passage that the evidence the author uses in discussing the life of past time periods

   (A) was developed by Charles Darwin
   (B) was uncovered by the author
   (C) has been negated by more recent evidence
   (D) was never definitely established
   (E) is based on fossil remains

10. With which of the following proverbial expressions about human existence would the author be most likely to agree?

   (A) It's a cruel world.
   (B) All the world's a stage.
   (C) The more things change, the more they remain the same.
   (D) Footprints in the sands of time.
   (E) A short life, but a merry one.

For me, scientific knowledge is divided into mathematical sciences, natural sciences or sciences dealing with the natural world (physical and biological sciences), and sciences dealing with mankind (psychology, sociology, all the sciences of cultural achievements, every kind of historical knowledge). Apart from these sciences is philosophy, about which we will talk shortly. In the first place, all this is pure or theoretical knowledge, sought only for the purpose of understanding, in order to fulfill the need to understand that is intrinsic and consubstantial to man. What distinguishes man from animal is that he knows and needs to know. If man did not know that the world existed, and that the world was of a certain kind, that he was in the world and that he himself was of a certain kind, he wouldn't be man. The technical aspects of applications of knowledge are equally necessary for man and are of the greatest importance, because they also contribute to defining him as man and permit him to pursue a life increasingly more truly human.

But even while enjoying the results of technical progress, he must defend the primacy and autonomy of pure knowledge. Knowledge sought directly for its practical applications will have immediate and foreseeable success, but not the kind of important result whose revolutionary scope is in large part unforeseen, except by the imagination of the Utopians. Let me recall a well-known example. If the Greek mathematicians had not applied themselves to the investigation of conic sections, zealously and without the least suspicion that it might someday be useful, it would not have been possible centuries later to navigate far from shore. The first men to study the nature of electricity could not imagine that their experiments, carried on because of mere intellectual curiosity, would eventually lead to modern electrical technology, without which we can scarcely conceive of contemporary life. Pure knowledge is valuable for its own sake, because the human spirit cannot resign itself to ignorance. But, in addition, it is the foundation for practical results that would not have been reached if this knowledge had not been sought disinterestedly.

11. The author points out that the Greeks who studied conic sections

   (A) invented modern mathematical applications
   (B) were interested in navigation
   (C) were unaware of the value of their studies
   (D) worked with electricity
   (E) were forced to resign themselves to failure

12. The title below that best expresses the ideas of this passage is

   (A) Technical Progress
   (B) A Little Learning Is a Dangerous Thing
   (C) Man's Distinguishing Characteristics
   (D) Learning for Its Own Sake
   (E) The Difference Between Science and Philosophy

13. It can be inferred from the passage that to the author man's need to know is chiefly important in that it

   (A) allows the human race to progress technically
   (B) encompasses both the physical and social sciences
   (C) demonstrates human vulnerability
   (D) defines man's essential humanity
   (E) has increased as our knowledge of the world has grown

When you first saw a piece of African art, it impressed you as a unit; you did not see it as a collection of shapes or forms. This, of course, means that the shapes and volumes within the sculpture
(5) itself were coordinated so successfully that the viewer was affected emotionally.

It is entirely valid to ask how, from a purely artistic point of view, this unity was achieved. And we must also inquire whether there is a recurrent pat-
(10) tern or rules or a plastic language and vocabulary which is responsible for the powerful communication of emotion which the best African sculpture achieves. If there is such a pattern or rules, are these rules applied consciously or instinctively to obtain
(15) so many works of such high artistic quality?

It is obvious from the study of art history that an intense and unified emotional experience, such as the Christian credo of the Byzantine or 12th or 13th century Europe, when expressed in art forms, gave
(20) great unity, coherence, and power to art. But such an integrated feeling was only the inspirational element for the artist, only the starting point of the creative act. The expression of this emotion and its realization in the work could be done only with dis-
(25) cipline and thorough knowledge of the craft. And the African sculptor was a highly trained workman. He started his apprenticeship with a master when a child, and he learned the tribal styles and the use of tools and the nature of woods so thoroughly that his
(30) carving became what Boas calls "motor action." He carved automatically and instinctively.

The African carver followed his rules without thinking of them; indeed, they never seem to have been formulated in words. But such rules existed,
(35) for accident and coincidence cannot explain the common plastic language of African sculpture. There is too great a consistency from one work to another. Yet, although the African, with amazing insight into art, used these rules, I am certain that
(40) he was not conscious of them. This is the great mystery of such a traditional art: talent, or the ability certain people have, without conscious effort, to follow the rules which later the analyst can discover only from the work of art which has already been
(45) created.

14. The author is primarily concerned with

(A) discussing how African sculptors achieved their effects
(B) listing the rules followed in African art
(C) relating African art to the art of 12th or 13th century Europe
(D) integrating emotion and realization
(E) expressing the beauty of African art

15. According to the passage, one of the outstanding features of African sculpture is

(A) its esoteric subject matter
(B) the emotional content of the work
(C) the education or training of the artists
(D) its "foreignness" when compared to Western art
(E) its high degree of conscious control

16. The author uses the phrase "plastic language" in lines 10 and 36 to refer to African art's

(A) mass reproduction
(B) unrealistic qualities
(C) modernistic orientation
(D) sculptural symbols
(E) repetitive nature

17. The information in the passage suggests that an African carver might best be compared to a

(A) chef following a recipe
(B) fluent speaker of English who is just beginning to study French
(C) batter who hits a homerun in his or her first baseball game
(D) concert pianist performing a well-rehearsed concerto
(E) writer who is grammatically expert but stylistically uncreative

18. Which of the following does the passage imply about art?

(A) Content is more important than form.
(B) There is no room for untrained artists.
(C) Form is more important then content.
(D) Western artists are too concerned with technique.
(E) Great art must be consistent.

19. The author's presentation of the material includes all of the following EXCEPT

(A) comparison
(B) cause and effect
(C) rhetorical questioning
(D) direct quotation
(E) concrete example

20. Which of the following titles best expresses the content of the passage?

(A) The Apprenticeship of the African Sculptor
(B) The History of African Sculpture
(C) How African Art Achieves Unity
(D) Analyzing African Art
(E) The Unconscious Rules of African Art

Reading Comprehension Exercise B

<u>Directions:</u> Each passage in this group is followed by questions based on its content. After reading a passage, choose the best answer to each question. Answer all questions following a passage on the basis of what is <u>stated</u> or <u>implied</u> in that passage.

Both plants and animals of many sorts show remarkable changes in form, structure, growth habits, and even mode of reproduction in becoming adapted to different climatic environment, types of (5) food supply, or mode of living. This divergence in response to evolution is commonly expressed by altering the form and function of some part or parts of the organism, the original identity of which is clearly discernible. For example, the creeping foot (10) of the snail is seen in related marine pteropods to be modified into a flapping organ useful for swimming, and is changed into prehensile arms that bear suctorial disks in the squids and other cephalopods. The limbs of various mammals are modified (15) according to several different modes of life – for swift running (cursorial) as in the horse and antelope, for swinging in trees (arboreal) as in the monkeys, for digging (fossorial) as in the moles and gophers, for flying (volant) as in the bats, for (20) swimming (aquatic) as in the seals, whales and dolphins, and for other adaptations. The structures or organs that show main change in connection with this adaptive divergence are commonly identified readily as homologous, in spite of great altera-(25) tions. Thus, the finger and wristbones of a bat and whale, for instance, have virtually nothing in common except that they are definitely equivalent elements of the mammalian limb.

1. Which of the following is the most appropriate title for the passage, based on its content?

   (A) Adaptive Divergence
   (B) Evolution
   (C) Unusual Structures
   (D) Changes in Organs
   (E) Our Changing Bodies

2. The author provides information that would answer which of the following questions?

   I.   What factors cause change in organisms?
   II. What is the theory of evolution?
   III. How are horses' legs related to seals' flippers?

   (A) I only
   (B) II only
   (C) I and II only
   (D) I and III only
   (E) I, II, and III

3. Which of the following words could best be substituted for "homologous" (line 24) without substantially changing the author's meaning?

   (A) altered
   (B) mammalian
   (C) corresponding
   (D) divergent
   (E) tactile

4. The author's style can best be described as

   (A) humorous
   (B) objective
   (C) patronizing
   (D) esoteric
   (E) archaic

Plato — who may have understood better what forms the mind of man than do some of our contemporaries who want their children exposed only to "real" people and everyday events — knew what intellectual experiences make for true humanity. He suggested that the future citizens of his ideal republic begin their literary education with the telling of myths, rather than with mere facts or so-called rational teachings. Even Aristotle, master of pure reason, said: "The friend of wisdom is also a friend of myth."

Modern thinkers who have studied myths and fairy tales from a philosophical or psychological viewpoint arrive at the same conclusion, regardless of their original persuasion. Mircea Eliade, for one, describes these stories as "models for human behavior [that], by that very fact, give meaning and value to life." Drawing on anthropological parallels, he and others suggest that myths and fairy tales were derived from, or give symbolic expression to, initiation rites or *rites of passage*—such as metaphoric death of an old, inadequate self in order to be reborn on a higher plane of existence. He feels that this is why these tales meet a strongly felt need and are carriers of such deep meaning.

Other investigators with a depth-psychological orientation emphasize the similarities between the fantastic events in myths and fairy tales and those in adult dreams and daydreams — the fulfillment of wishes, the winning out over all competitors, the destruction of enemies — and conclude that one attraction of this literature is its expression of that which is normally prevented from coming to awareness.

There are, of course, very significant differences between fairy tales and dreams. For example, in dreams more often than not the wish fulfillment is disguised, while in fairy tales much of it is openly expressed. To a considerable degree, dreams are the result of inner pressures which have found no relief, of problems which beset a person to which he knows no solution and to which the dream finds none. The fairy tale does the opposite: it projects the relief of all pressures and not only offers ways to solve problems but promises that a "happy" solution will be found.

We cannot control what goes on in our dreams. Although our inner censorship influences what we may dream, such control occurs on an unconscious level. The fairy tale, on the other hand, is very much the result of common conscious and unconscious content having been shaped by the conscious mind, not of one particular person, but the consensus of many in regard to what they view as universal human problems, and what they accept as desirable solutions. If all these elements were not present in a fairy tale, it would not be retold by generation after generation. Only if a fairy tale met the conscious and unconscious requirements of many people was it repeatedly retold, and listened to with great interest. No dream of a person could arouse such persistent interest unless it was worked into a myth, as was the story of the pharaoh's dream as interpreted by Joseph in the Bible.

5. It can be inferred from the passage that the author's interest in fairy tales centers chiefly on their

   (A) literary qualities
   (B) historical background
   (C) factual accuracy
   (D) psychological relevance
   (E) ethical weakness

6. According to the passage, fairy tales differ from dreams in which of the following characteristics?

   I.   The communal nature of their creation
   II. Their convention of a happy ending
   III. Their enduring general appeal

   (A) I only
   (B) II only
   (C) I and II only
   (D) II and III only
   (E) I, II, and III

7. It can be inferred from the passage that Mircea Eliade is most likely

   (A) a writer of children's literature
   (B) a student of physical anthropology
   (C) a twentieth-century philosopher
   (D) an advocate of practical education
   (E) a contemporary of Plato

8. Which of the following best describes the author's attitude toward fairy tales?

   (A) Reluctant fascination
   (B) Wary skepticism
   (C) Scornful disapprobation
   (D) Indulgent tolerance
   (E) Open approval

9. The author quotes Plato and Aristotle primarily in order to

   (A) define the nature of myth
   (B) contrast their opposing points of view
   (C) support the point that myths are valuable
   (D) prove that myths originated in ancient times
   (E) give an example of depth psychology

10. The author mentions all of the following as reasons for reading fairy tales EXCEPT

    (A) emotional catharsis
    (B) behavioral paradigm
    (C) uniqueness of experience
    (D) sublimation of aggression
    (E) symbolic satisfaction

The stability that had marked the Iroquois Confederacy's generally pro-British position was shattered with the overthrow of James II in 1688, the colonial uprisings that followed in Massachusetts, New York, and Maryland, and the commencement of King William's War against Louis XIV of France. The increasing French threat to English hegemony in the interior of North America was signalized by French-led or French-inspired attacks on the Iroquois and on outlying colonial settlements in New York and New England. The high point of the Iroquois response was the spectacular raid of August 5, 1689, in which the Iroquois virtually wiped out the French village of Lachine, just outside Montreal. A counterraid by the French on the English village of Schenectady in March, 1690, instilled an appropriate measure of fear among the English and their Iroquois allies.

The Iroquois position at the end of the war, which was formalized by treaties made during the summer of 1701 with the British and the French, and which was maintained throughout most of the eighteenth century, was one of "aggressive neutrality" between the two competing European powers. Under the new system the Iroquois initiated a peace policy toward the "far Indians," tightened their control over the nearby tribes, and induced both English and French to support their neutrality toward the European powers by appropriate gifts and concessions.

By holding the balance of power in the sparsely settled borderlands between English and French settlements, and by their willingness to use their power against one or the other nation if not appropriately treated, the Iroquois played the game of European power politics with effectiveness. The system broke down, however, after the French became convinced that the Iroquois were compromising the system in favor of the English and launched a full-scale attempt to establish French physical and juridical presence in the Ohio Valley, the heart of the borderlands long claimed by the Iroquois. As a consequence of the ensuing Great War for Empire, in which Iroquois neutrality was dissolved and European influence moved closer, the play-off system lost its efficacy and a system of direct bargaining supplanted it.

11. The author's primary purpose in this passage is to

  (A) denounce the imperialistic policies of the French
  (B) disprove the charges of barbarism made against the Iroquois
  (C) expose the French government's exploitation of the Iroquois balance of power
  (D) describe and assess the effect of European military power on Iroquois policy
  (E) show the inability of the Iroquois to engage in European-style diplomacy

12. It can be inferred from the passage that the author's attitude toward the Iroquois leadership can best be described as one of

  (A) suspicion of their motives
  (B) respect for their competence
  (C) indifference to their fate
  (D) dislike of their savagery
  (E) pride in their heritage

13. With which of the following statements would the author be LEAST likely to agree?

  (A) The Iroquois were able to respond effectively to French acts of aggression.
  (B) James II's removal from the throne caused dissension to break out among the colonies.
  (C) The French begrudged the British their alleged high standing among the Iroquois.
  (D) Iroquois negotiations involved playing one side against the other.
  (E) The Iroquois ceased to hold the balance of power early in the eighteenth century.

14. The author attributes such success as the Iroquois policy of aggressive neutrality had to

  (A) the readiness of the Iroquois to fight either side
  (B) their ties of loyalty to the British
  (C) French physical presence in the borderlands
  (D) the confusion of the European forces
  (E) European reliance on formal treaties

Of the 197 million square miles making up the surface of the globe, 71 percent is covered by the interconnecting bodies of marine water; the Pacific Ocean alone covers half the Earth and averages nearly 14,000 feet in depth. The *continents*—Eurasia, Africa, North America, South America, Australia, and Antarctica—are the portions of the *continental masses* rising above sea level. The submerged borders of the continental masses are the *continental shelves,* beyond which lie the deep-sea basins.

The oceans attain their greatest depths not in their central parts, but in certain elongated furrows, or long narrow troughs, called *deeps*. These profound troughs have a peripheral arrangement, notably around the borders of the Pacific and Indian oceans. The position of the deeps near the continental masses suggests that the deeps, like the highest mountains, are of recent origin, since otherwise they would have been filled with waste from the lands. This suggestion is strengthened by the fact that the deeps are frequently the sites of world-shaking earthquakes. For example, the "tidal wave" that in April, 1946, caused widespread destruction along Pacific coasts resulted from a strong earthquake on the floor of the Aleutian Deep.

The topography of the ocean floors is none too well known, since in great areas the available soundings are hundreds or even thousands of miles apart. However, the floor of the Atlantic is becoming fairly well known as a result of special surveys since 1920. A broad, well-defined ridge—the Mid-Atlantic ridge—runs north and south between Africa and the two Americas, and numerous other major irregularities diversify the Atlantic floor. Closely spaced soundings show that many parts of the oceanic floors are as rugged as mountainous regions of the continents. Use of the recently perfected method of echo sounding is rapidly enlarging our knowledge of submarine topography. During World War II great strides were made in mapping submarine surfaces, particularly in many parts of the vast Pacific basin.

The continents stand on the average 2870 feet—slightly more than half a mile—above sea level. North America averages 2300 feet; Europe averages only 1150 feet; and Asia, the highest of the larger continental subdivisions, averages 3200 feet. The highest point on the globe, Mount Everest in the Himalayas, is 29,000 feet above the sea; and as the greatest known depth in the sea is over 35,000 feet, the maximum *relief* (that is, the difference in altitude between the lowest and highest points) exceeds 64,000 feet, or exceeds 12 miles. The continental masses and the deep-sea basins are relief features of the first order; the deeps, ridges, and volcanic cones that diversify the sea floor, as well as the plains, plateaus, and mountains of the continents, are relief features of the second order. The lands are unendingly subject to a complex of activities summarized in the term *erosion*, which first sculptures them in great detail and then tends to reduce them ultimately to sea level. The modeling of the landscape by weather, running water, and other agents is apparent to the keenly observant eye and causes thinking people to speculate on what must be the final result of the ceaseless wearing down of the lands. Long before there was a science of geology, Shakespeare wrote "the revolution of the times makes mountains level."

15. Which of the following would be the most appropriate title for the passage?

  (A) Features of the Earth's Surface
  (B) Marine Topography
  (C) The Causes of Earthquakes
  (D) Primary Geologic Considerations
  (E) How to Prevent Erosion

16. It can be inferred from the passage that the largest ocean is the

    (A) Atlantic
    (B) Pacific
    (C) Indian
    (D) Antarctic
    (E) Arctic

17. The "revolution of the times" as used in the final sentence means

    (A) the passage of years
    (B) the current rebellion
    (C) the science of geology
    (D) the action of the ocean floor
    (E) the overthrow of natural forces

18. According to the passage, the peripheral furrows or *deeps* are found

    (A) only in the Pacific and Indian oceans
    (B) near earthquakes
    (C) near the shore
    (D) in the center of the ocean
    (E) to be 14,000 feet in depth in the Pacific

19. The passage contains information that would answer which of the following questions?

    I.   What is the highest point on North America?
    II. Which continental subdivision is, on the average, 1150 feet above sea level?
    III. How deep is the deepest part of the ocean?

    (A) I only
    (B) II only
    (C) III only
    (D) I and II only
    (E) II and III only

20. From this passage, it can be inferred that earthquakes

    (A) occur only in the peripheral furrows
    (B) occur more frequently in newly formed land or sea formations
    (C) are a prime cause of soil erosion
    (D) will ultimately "make mountains level"
    (E) are caused by the weight of the water

Reading Comprehension Exercise C

<u>Directions:</u>   Each passage in this group is followed by questions based on its content. After reading a passage, choose the best answer to each question. Answer all questions following a passage on the basis of what is <u>stated</u> or <u>implied</u> in that passage.

An essay which appeals chiefly to the intellect is Francis Bacon's "Of Studies." His careful tripartite division of studies expressed succinctly in aphoristic prose demands the complete attention of the
(5) mind of the reader. He considers studies as they should be: for pleasure, for self-improvement, for business. He considers the evils of excess study: laziness, affectation, and preciosity. Bacon divides books into three categories: those to be read in part,
(10) those to be read cursorily, and those to be read with care. Studies should include reading, which gives depth; speaking, which adds readiness of thought; and writing, which trains in preciseness. Somewhat mistakenly, the author ascribes certain virtues to
(15) individual fields of study: wisdom to history, wit to poetry, subtlety to mathematics, and depth to natural philosophy. Bacon's four-hundred-word essay, studded with Latin phrases and highly compressed in thought, has intellectual appeal indeed.

1. Which of the following is the most appropriate title for the passage, based on its content?

    (A) Francis Bacon and the Appeal of the Essay
    (B) "Of Studies": A Tripartite Division
    (C) An Intellectual Exercise: Francis Bacon's "Of Studies"
    (D) The Categorization of Books According to Bacon
    (E) A Method for Reading Books

2. Which of the following words could best be substituted for "aphoristic" (lines 3–4) without substantially changing the author's meaning?

    (A) abstruse
    (B) pithy
    (C) tripartite
    (D) proverbial
    (E) realistic

3. The passage suggests that the author would be most likely to agree with which of the following statements?

    (A) "Of Studies" belongs in the category of works that demand to be read with care.
    (B) Scholars' personalities are shaped by the academic discipline in which they are engaged.
    (C) It is an affectation to use foreign words in one's writing.
    (D) An author can be more persuasive in a long work than in a shorter one.
    (E) Studies should be undertaken without thought of personal gain.

Rocks which have solidified directly from molten materials are called igneous rocks. Igneous rocks are commonly referred to as primary rocks because they are the original source of material found in sedimentaries and metamorphics. Igneous rocks compose the greater part of the earth's crust, but they are generally covered at the surface by a relatively thin layer of sedimentary or metamorphic rocks. Igneous rocks are distinguished by the following characteristics: (1) they contain no fossils; (2) they have no regular arrangement of layers; and (3) they are nearly always made up of crystals.

Sedimentary rocks are composed largely of minute fragments derived from the disintegration of existing rocks and in some instances from the remains of animals. As sediments are transported, individual fragments are assorted according to size. Distinct layers of such sediments as gravels, sand, and clay build up, as they are deposited by water and occasionally wind. These sediments vary in size with the material and the power of the eroding agent. Sedimentary materials are laid down in layers called strata.

When sediments harden into sedimentary rocks, the names applied to them change to indicate the change in physical state. Thus, small stones and gravel cemented together are known as conglomerates; cemented sand becomes sandstone; and hardened clay becomes shale. In addition to these, other sedimentary rocks such as limestone frequently result from the deposition of dissolved material. The ingredient parts are normally precipitated by organic substances, such as shells of clams or hard skeletons of other marine life.

Both igneous and sedimentary rocks may be changed by pressure, heat, solution, or cementing action. When individual grains from existing rocks tend to deform and interlock, they are called metamorphic rocks. For example, granite, an igneous rock, may be metamorphosed into a gneiss or a schist. Limestone, a sedimentary rock, when subjected to heat and pressure may become marble, a metamorphic rock. Shale under pressure becomes slate.

4. The primary purpose of the passage is to

   (A) differentiate between and characterize igneous and sedimentary rocks
   (B) explain the factors that may cause rocks to change in form
   (C) show how the scientific names of rocks reflect the rocks' composition
   (D) define and describe several diverse kinds of rocks
   (E) explain why rocks are basic parts of the earth's structure

5. All of the following are sedimentary rocks EXCEPT

   (A) shale
   (B) gravel
   (C) sand
   (D) limestone
   (E) schist

6. The passage would be most likely to appear in a

   (A) technical article for geologists
   (B) teaching manual accompanying an earth science text
   (C) pamphlet promoting conservation of natural resources
   (D) newspaper feature explaining how oil is found
   (E) nonfiction book explaining where to find the results of sedimentation

7. The relationship between igneous and sedimentary rocks may best be compared to the relationship between

   (A) leaves and compost
   (B) water and land
   (C) DNA and heredity
   (D) nucleus and cell wall
   (E) sand and clay

8. The passage contains information that would answer which of the following questions?

   I.   Which elements form igneous rocks?
   II. What produces sufficient pressure to alter a rock?
   III. Why is marble called a metamorphic rock?

   (A) I only   (B) III only   (C) I and II only
   (D) II and III only   (E) I, II, and III

9. Which of the following methods is NOT used by the author?

   (A) inclusion of concrete examples
   (B) classification and discussion
   (C) comparison and contrast
   (D) observation and hypothesis
   (E) cause and effect

10. The author's tone in the passage can best be described as

   (A) meditative
   (B) objective
   (C) ironic
   (D) concerned
   (E) bombastic

Although vocal cords are lacking in cetaceans, phonation is undoubtedly centered in the larynx.

The toothed whales or odontocetes (sperm whale and porpoises) are much more vociferous than the
(5) whalebone whales, or mysticetes. In this country observers have recorded only occasional sounds from two species of mysticetes (the humpback and right whale). A Russian cetologist reports hearing sounds from at least five species of whalebone
(10) whales but gives no details of the circumstances or descriptions of the sounds themselves. Although comparison of the sound-producing apparatus in the two whale groups cannot yet be made, it is interesting to note that the auditory centers of the
(15) brain are much more highly developed in the odontocetes than in the mysticetes, in fact, to a degree unsurpassed by any other mammalian group.

11. The passage contains information that would answer which of the following questions?

    I.   What are odontocetes and mysticetes?
    II. In which part of the body do whales produce sounds?
    III. In which animals is the auditory center of the brain most developed?

    (A) I only   (B) II only   (C) I and II only
    (D) II and III only   (E) I, II, and III

12. The author's attitude toward the observations reported by the Russian cetologist mentioned in lines 8–11 is best described as one of

    (A) admiration
    (B) indignation
    (C) surprise
    (D) skepticism
    (E) pessimism

13. It can be inferred from the passage that

    (A) animals with more highly developed auditory apparatuses tend to produce more sounds
    (B) animals without vocal cords tend to produce as much sound as those with vocal cords
    (C) highly intelligent animals tend to produce more sound than less intelligent species
    (D) the absence of vocal cords has hindered the adaptation of cetaceans
    (E) sound is an important means of communication among whales

---

    *Like her white friends Eleanor Roosevelt and Aubrey Williams, Mary Bethune believed in the fundamental commitment of the New Deal to assist the black American's struggle and in the need for
(5) blacks to assume responsibilities to help win that struggle. Unlike those of her white liberal associates, however, Bethune's ideas had evolved out of a long experience as a "race leader." Founder of a small black college in Florida, she had become
(10) widely known by 1935 as an organizer of black women's groups and as a civil and political rights activist. Deeply religious, certain of her own capabilities, she held a relatively uncluttered view of what she felt were the New Deal's and her own
(15) people's obligations to the cause of racial justice. Unafraid to speak her mind to powerful whites, including the President, or to differing black factions, she combined faith in the ultimate willingness of whites to discard their prejudice and bigotry
(20) with a strong sense of racial pride and commitment to Negro self-help.
    More than her liberal white friends, Bethune argued for a strong and direct black voice in initiating and shaping government policy. She pursued
(25) this in her conversations with President Roosevelt, in numerous memoranda to Aubrey Williams, and in her administrative work as head of the National Youth Administration's Office of Negro Affairs.

With the assistance of Williams, she was success-
(30) ful in having blacks selected to NYA posts at the national, state, and local levels. But she also wanted a black presence throughout the federal government. At the beginning of the war she joined other black leaders in demanding appointments to
(35) the Selective Service Board and to the Department of the Army; and she was instrumental in 1941 in securing Earl Dickerson's membership on the Fair Employment Practices Committee. By 1944, she was still making appeals for black representation in
(40) "all public programs, federal, state, and local," and "in policy-making posts as well as rank and file jobs."
    Though recognizing the weakness in the Roosevelt administration's response to Negro needs,
(45) Mary Bethune remained in essence a black partisan champion of the New Deal during the 1930s and 1940s. Her strong advocacy of administration policies and programs was predicated on a number of factors: her assessment of the low status of black
(50) Americans during the Depression; her faith in the willingness of some liberal whites to work for the inclusion of blacks in the government's reform and recovery measures; her conviction that only massive federal aid could elevate the Negro economi-
(55) cally; and her belief that the thirties and forties were producing a more self-aware and self-assured black population. Like a number of her white friends in government, Bethune assumed that the preservation of democracy and black people's "full
(60) integration into the benefits and the responsibilities" of American life were inextricably tied together. She was convinced that, with the help of a friendly government, a militant, aggressive "New Negro" would emerge out of the devastation of
(65) depression and war, a "New Negro" who would "save America from itself," who would lead America toward the full realization of its democratic ideas.

14. The author's main purpose in this passage is to

    (A) criticize Mary Bethune for adhering too closely to New Deal policies
    (B) argue that Mary Bethune was too optimistic in her assessment of race relations
    (C) demonstrate Mary Bethune's influence on black progress during the Roosevelt years
    (D) point out the weaknesses of the white liberal approach to black needs
    (E) summarize the attainments of blacks under the auspices of Roosevelt's New Deal

15. It can be inferred from the passage that Aubrey Williams was which of the following?

    I.   A man with influence in the National Youth Administration
    II. A white liberal
    III. A man of strong religious convictions

    (A) I only   (B) II only   (C) I and II only
    (D) II and III only   (E) I, II, and III

16. The author mentions Earl Dickerson (line 37) primarily in order to

    (A) cite an instance of Bethune's political impact
    (B) contrast his career with that of Bethune
    (C) introduce the subject of a subsequent paragraph
    (D) provide an example of Bethune's "New Negro"
    (E) show that Dickerson was a leader of his fellow blacks

17. It can be inferred from the passage that Bethune believed the "New Negro" would "save America from itself" (lines 65–66) by

    (A) joining the army and helping America overthrow its Fascist enemies
    (B) helping America accomplish its egalitarian ideals
    (C) voting for administration antipoverty programs
    (D) electing other blacks to government office
    (E) expressing a belief in racial pride

18. The tone of the author's discussion of Bethune is best described as

    (A) adulatory
    (B) sentimental
    (C) ironic
    (D) objective
    (E) recriminatory

19. The author uses all the following techniques in the passage EXCEPT

    (A) comparison and contrast
    (B) development of an extended analogy
    (C) direct quotation
    (D) general statement and concrete examples
    (E) reiteration of central ideas

20. Which of the following statements about the New Deal does the passage best support?

    (A) It was strongly committed to justice for all races.
    (B) It encouraged black participation in making policy decisions.
    (C) It was actively involved in military strategy.
    (D) It was primarily the province of Eleanor Roosevelt.
    (E) It shaped programs for economic aid and growth.

Reading Comprehension Exercise D

Directions: Each passage in this group is followed by questions based on its content. After reading a passage, choose the best answer to each question. Answer all questions following a passage on the basis of what is stated or implied in that passage.

"The emancipation of women," James Joyce told one of his friends, "has caused the greatest revolution in our time in the most important relationship there is—that between men and women." Other modernists agreed: Virginia Woolf, claiming that in about 1910 "human character changed," and, illustrating the new balance between the sexes, urged, "Read the 'Agamemnon,' and see whether...your sympathies are not almost entirely with Clytemnestra." D.H. Lawrence wrote, "perhaps the deepest fight for 2000 years and more, has been the fight for women's independence."

But if modernist writers considered women's revolt against men's domination one of their "greatest" and "deepest" themes, only recently—in perhaps the past 15 years—has literary criticism begun to catch up with it. Not that the images of sexual antagonism that abound in modern literature have gone unremarked; far from it. But what we are able to see in literary works depends on the perspectives we bring to them, and now that women —enough to make a difference—are reforming canons and interpreting literature, the landscapes of literary history and the features of individual books have begun to change.

1. According to the passage, women are changing literary criticism by

    (A) noting instances of hostility between men and women
    (B) seeing literature from fresh points of view
    (C) studying the works of early twentieth-century writers
    (D) reviewing books written by feminists
    (E) resisting masculine influence

2. The author quotes James Joyce, Virginia Woolf, and D.H. Lawrence primarily in order to show that

    (A) these were feminist writers
    (B) although well-meaning, they were ineffectual
    (C) before the twentieth century, there was little interest in women's literature
    (D) modern literature is dependent on the women's movement
    (E) the interest in feminist issues is not new

3. The author's attitude toward women's emancipation can best be described as one of

   (A) ambivalence
   (B) fervor
   (C) detachment
   (D) endorsement
   (E) reservation

4. Which of the following titles best describes the content of the passage?

   (A) Modernist Writers and the Search for Equality
   (B) The Meaning of Literary Works
   (C) Toward a New Criticism
   (D) Women in Literature, from 1910 On
   (E) Transforming Literature

Ocean water plays an indispensable role in supporting life. The great ocean basins hold about 300 million cubic miles of water. From this vast amount, about 80,000 cubic miles of water are sucked into the atmosphere each year by evaporation and returned by precipitation and drainage to the ocean. More than 24,000 cubic miles of rain descend annually upon the continents. This vast amount is required to replenish the lakes and streams, springs and water tables on which all flora and fauna are dependent. Thus, the hydrosphere permits organic existence.

The hydrosphere has strange characteristics because water has properties unlike those of any other liquid. One anomaly is that water upon freezing expands by about 9 percent, whereas most liquids contract on cooling. For this reason, ice floats on water bodies instead of sinking to the bottom. If the ice sank, the hydrosphere would soon be frozen solidly, except for a thin layer of surface melt water during the summer season. Thus, all aquatic life would be destroyed and the interchange of warm and cold currents, which moderates climate, would be notably absent.

Another outstanding characteristic of water is that water has a heat capacity which is the highest of all liquids and solids except ammonia. This characteristic enables the oceans to absorb and store vast quantities of heat, thereby often preventing climatic extremes. In addition, water dissolves more substances than any other liquid. It is this characteristic which helps make oceans a great storehouse for minerals which have been washed down from the continents. In several areas of the world these minerals are being commercially exploited. Solar evaporation of salt is widely practiced, potash is extracted from the Dead Sea, and magnesium is produced from sea water along the American Gulf Coast.

5. The author's main purpose in this passage is to

   (A) describe the properties and uses of water
   (B) illustrate the importance of conserving water
   (C) explain how water is used in commerce and industry
   (D) reveal the extent of the earth's ocean masses
   (E) compare water with other liquids

6. According to the passage, fish can survive in the oceans because

   (A) they do not need oxygen
   (B) ice floats
   (C) evaporation and condensation create a water cycle
   (D) there are currents in the oceans
   (E) water absorbs heat

7. Which of the following characteristics of water does the author mention in the passage?

   I.   Water expands when it is frozen.
   II. Water is a good solvent.
   III. Water can absorb heat.

   (A) I only   (B) II only   (C) I and II only
   (D) II and III only   (E) I, II, and III

8. According to the passage, the hydrosphere is NOT

   (A) responsible for all forms of life
   (B) able to modify weather
   (C) a source of natural resources
   (D) in danger of freezing over
   (E) the part of the earth covered by water

9. The author's tone in the passage can best be described as

   (A) dogmatic
   (B) dispassionate
   (C) speculative
   (D) biased
   (E) fascinated

10. The author organizes the passage by

   (A) comparison and contrast
   (B) juxtaposition of true and untrue ideas
   (C) general statements followed by examples
   (D) hypothesis and proof
   (E) definition of key terms

11. Which of the following statements would be most likely to begin the paragraph immediately following the passage?

   (A) Water has the ability to erode the land.
   (B) Magnesium is widely used in metallurgical processes.
   (C) Now let us consider the great land masses.
   (D) Another remarkable property of ice is its strength.
   (E) Droughts and flooding are two types of disasters associated with water.

The opposite of adaptive divergence is an interesting and fairly common expression of evolution. Whereas related groups of organisms take on widely different characters in becoming adapted to

(5) unlike environments in the case of adaptive divergence, we find that unrelated groups of organisms exhibit adaptive convergence when they adopt similar modes of life or become suited for special sorts of environments. For example, invertebrate marine

(10) animals living firmly attached to the sea bottom or to some foreign object tend to develop a subcylindrical or conical form. This is illustrated by coral individuals, by many sponges, and even by the diminutive tubes of bryozoans. Adaptive con-

(15) vergence in taking this coral-like form is shown by some brachiopods and pelecypods that grew in fixed position. More readily appreciated is the streamlined fitness of most fishes for moving swiftly through water; they have no neck, the con-

(20) tour of the body is smoothly curved so as to give minimum resistance, and the chief propelling organ is a powerful tail fin. The fact that some fossil reptiles (ichthyosaurs) and modern mammals (whales, dolphins) are wholly fishlike in form is an expres-

(25) sion of adaptive convergence, for these air-breathing reptiles and mammals, which are highly efficient swimmers, are not closely related to fishes. Unrelated or distantly related organisms that develop similarity of form are sometimes desig-

(30) nated as homeomorphs (having the same form).

12. The author mentions ichthyosaurs and dolphins (lines 23 and 24) as examples of

(A) modern mammalian life forms that are aquatic
(B) species of slightly greater mobility than brachiopods
(C) air-breathing reptiles closely related to fish
(D) organisms that have evolved into fishlike forms
(E) invertebrate and vertebrate marine animals

13. According to the passage, adaptive convergence and adaptive divergence are

(A) manifestations of evolutionary patterns
(B) hypotheses unsupported by biological phenomena
(C) ways in which plants and animals adjust to a common environment
(D) demonstrated by brachiopods and pelecypods
(E) compensatory adjustments made in response to unlike environments

14. It can be inferred that in the paragraph immediately preceding this passage the author discussed

(A) marine intelligence
(B) adaptive divergence
(C) air-breathing reptiles
(D) environmental impacts
(E) organisms with similar forms

Nearly two thousand years have passed since a census decreed by Caesar Augustus became part of the greatest story ever told. Many things have changed in the intervening years. The hotel industry worries more about overbuilding than overcrowding, and if they had to meet an unexpected influx, few inns would have a manger to accommodate the weary guests. Now it is the census taker that does the traveling in the fond hope that a highly mobile population will stay put long enough to get a good sampling. Methods of gathering, recording, and evaluating information have presumably been improved a great deal. And where then it was the modest purpose of Rome to obtain a simple head count as an adequate basis for levying taxes, now batteries of complicated statistical series furnished by governmental agencies and private organizations are eagerly scanned and interpreted by sages and seers to get a clue to future events. The Bible does not tell us how the Roman census takers made out, and as regards our more immediate concern, the reliability of present-day economic forecasting, there are considerable differences of opinion. They were aired at the celebration of the 125th anniversary of the American Statistical Association. There was the thought that business forecasting might well be on its way from an art to a science, and some speakers talked about newfangled computers and high-falutin mathematical systems in terms of excitement and endearment which we, at least in our younger years when these things mattered, would have associated more readily with the description of a fair maiden. But others pointed to the deplorable record of highly esteemed forecasts and forecasters with a batting average below that of the Mets, and the president-elect of the Association cautioned that "high powered statistical methods are usually in order where the facts are crude and inadequate, the exact contrary of what crude and inadequate statisticians assume." We left his birthday party somewhere between hope and despair and with the conviction, not really newly acquired, that proper statistical methods applied to ascertainable facts have their merits in economic forecasting as long as neither forecaster nor public is deluded into mistaking the delineation of probabilities and trends for a prediction of certainties of mathematical exactitude.

15. The passage would be most likely to appear in

(A) a journal of biblical studies
(B) an introductory college textbook on statistics
(C) the annual report of the American Statistical Association
(D) a newspaper review of a recent professional festivity
(E) the current bulletin of the census bureau

16. According to the passage, taxation in Roman times was based on

(A) mobility
(B) wealth
(C) population
(D) census takers
(E) economic predictions

17. The author refers to the Romans primarily in order to

    (A) prove the superiority of modern sampling methods to ancient ones
    (B) provide a historical framework for the passage
    (C) relate an unfamiliar concept to a familiar one
    (D) show that statistical forecasts have not significantly improved
    (E) cite an authority to support the thesis of the passage

18. The author refers to the Mets primarily in order to

    (A) show that sports do not depend on statistics
    (B) provide an example of an unreliable statistic
    (C) contrast verifiable and unverifiable methods of record keeping
    (D) indicate the changes in attitudes from Roman days to the present
    (E) illustrate the failure of statistical predictions

19. On the basis of the passage, it can be inferred that the author would agree with which of the following statements?

    (A) Computers have significantly improved the application of statistics in business.
    (B) Statistics is not, at the present time, a science.
    (C) It is useless to try to predict the economy.
    (D) Most mathematical systems are inexact.
    (E) Statisticians should devote themselves to the study of probability.

20. The author's tone can best be described as

    (A) jocular
    (B) scornful
    (C) pessimistic
    (D) objective
    (E) humanistic

Reading Comprehension Exercise E

Directions: Each passage in this group is followed by questions based on its content. After reading a passage, choose the best answer to each question. Answer all questions following a passage on the basis of what is stated or implied in that passage.

Observe the dilemma of the fungus: it is a plant, but it possesses no chlorophyl. While all other plants put the sun's energy to work for them combining the nutrients of ground and air into the body
(5) structure, the chlorophylless fungus must look elsewhere for an energy supply. It finds it in those other plants which, having received their energy free from the sun, relinquish it at some point in their cycle either to animals (like us humans)
(10) or to fungi.

In this search for energy the fungus has become the earth's major source of rot and decay. Wherever you see mold forming on a piece of bread, or a pile of leaves turning to compost, or a blown-down
(15) tree becoming pulp on the ground, you are watching a fungus eating. Without fungus action the earth would be piled high with the dead plant life of past centuries. In fact, certain plants which contain resins that are toxic to fungi will last indefinitely;
(20) specimens of the redwood, for instance, can still be found resting on the forest floor centuries after having been blown down.

1. Which of the following words best describes the fungus as depicted in the passage?

    (A) Unevolved
    (B) Sporadic
    (C) Enigmatic
    (D) Parasitic
    (E) Toxic

2. The passage states all the following about fungi EXCEPT:

    (A) They are responsible for the decomposition of much plant life.
    (B) They cannot live completely apart from other plants.
    (C) They are vastly different from other plants.
    (D) They are poisonous to resin-producing plants.
    (E) They cannot produce their own store of energy.

3. The author's statement that "you are watching a fungus eating" (lines 15–16) is best described as

    (A) figurative
    (B) ironical
    (C) parenthetical
    (D) erroneous
    (E) contradictory

4. The author is primarily concerned with

    (A) warning people of the dangers of fungi
    (B) writing a humorous essay on fungi
    (C) relating how most plants use solar energy
    (D) describing the actions of fungi
    (E) explaining the long life of some redwoods

The establishment of the Third Reich influenced events in American history by starting a chain of events which culminated in war between Germany and the United States. The complete destruction of democracy, the persecution of Jews, the war on religion, the cruelty and barbarism of the Nazis, and especially, the plans of Germany and her allies, Italy and Japan, for world conquest caused great indignation in this country and brought on fear of another world war. While speaking out against Hitler's atrocities, the American people generally favored isolationist policies and neutrality. The Neutrality Acts of 1935 and 1936 prohibited trade with any belligerents or loans to them. In 1937 the President was empowered to declare an arms embargo in wars between nations at his discretion.

American opinion began to change somewhat after President Roosevelt's "quarantine the aggressor" speech at Chicago (1937), in which he severely criticized Hitler's policies. Germany's seizure of Austria and the Munich Pact for the partition of Czechoslovakia (1938) also aroused the American people. The conquest of Czechoslovakia in March 1939 was another rude awakening to the menace of the Third Reich. In August 1939 came the shock of the Nazi-Soviet Pact and in September the attack on Poland and the outbreak of European war. The United States attempted to maintain neutrality in spite of sympathy for the democracies arrayed against the Third Reich. The Neutrality Act of 1939 repealed the arms embargo and permitted "cash and carry" exports of arms to belligerent nations. A strong national defense program was begun. A draft act was passed (1940) to strengthen the military services. A Lend-Lease Act (1941) authorized the President to sell, exchange, or lend materials to any country deemed necessary by him for the defense of the United States. Help was given to Britain by exchanging certain overage destroyers for the right to establish American bases in British territory in the Western Hemisphere. In August 1941 President Roosevelt and Prime Minister Churchill met and issued the Atlantic Charter, which proclaimed the kind of a world that should be established after the war. In December 1941 Japan launched an unprovoked attack on the United States at Pearl Harbor. Immediately thereafter, Germany declared war on the United States.

5. The author is primarily concerned with

(A) evaluating various legislative efforts to strengthen national defense
(B) summarizing the events that led up to America's involvement in the war
(C) criticizing the atrocities perpetrated by the Third Reich
(D) explaining a basic distinction between American and German policy
(E) describing the social and psychological effects of war

6. During the years 1933–36, American foreign policy may best be described as being one of

(A) overt belligerence
(B) deliberate uninvolvement
(C) moral indignation
(D) veiled contempt
(E) reluctant admiration

7. According to the passage, the United States, while maintaining neutrality, showed its sympathy for the democracies by which of the following actions?

I. It came to the defense of Poland.
II. It conscripted recruits for the armed forces.
III. It supplied weapons to friendly countries.

(A) I only   (B) III only   (C) I and II only
(D) II and III only   (E) I, II, and III

8. According to the passage, all of the following events occurred in 1939 EXCEPT

(A) the invasion of Poland
(B) the invasion of Czechoslovakia
(C) the annexation of Austria
(D) passage of the Neutrality Act
(E) the beginning of the war in Europe

9. With which of the following statements would the author of the passage be most likely to agree?

(A) American neutrality during the 1930s was a natural consequence of the course of world events.
(B) Every nation should be free to determine its own internal policy without interference.
(C) The United States, through its aggressive actions, invited an attack on its territory.
(D) Americans were slow to realize the full danger posed by Nazi Germany.
(E) President Roosevelt showed undue sympathy for Britain.

10. Which of the following best decribes the organization of the passage?

(A) The author presents a thesis and then lists events that support that thesis in chronological order.
(B) The author presents a thesis and then cites examples that support the thesis as well as evidence that tends to negate it.
(C) The author summarizes a historical study and then discusses an aspect of the study in detail.
(D) The author describes historical events and then gives a personal interpretation of them.
(E) The author cites noted authorities as a means of supporting his or her own opinion.

Not a few of Jane Austen's personal acquaintances might have echoed Sir Samuel Egerton Brydges, who noticed that "she was fair and handsome, slight and elegant, but with cheeks a little too full," while "never suspect[ing] she was an authoress." For this novelist whose personal obscurity was more complete than that of any other famous writer was always quick to insist either on complete anonymity or on the propriety of her limited craft, her delight in delineating just "3 or 4 Families in a Country Village." With her self-deprecatory remarks about her inability to join "strong manly, spirited sketches, full of Variety and Glow" with her "little bit (two Inches wide) of Ivory," Jane Austen perpetuated the belief among her friends that her art was just an accomplishment "by a lady," if anything "rather too light and bright and sparkling." In this respect she resembled one of her favorite contemporaries, Mary Brunton, who would rather have "glid[ed] through the world unknown" than been "suspected of literary airs — to be shunned, as literary women are, by the more pretending of their own sex, and abhorred, as literary women are, by the more pretending of the other! —my dear, I would sooner exhibit as a ropedancer."

Yet, decorous though they might first seem, Austen's self-effacing anonymity and her modest description of her miniaturist art also imply a criticism, even a rejection, of the world at large. For, as Gaston Bachelard explains, the miniature "allows us to be world conscious at slight risk." While the creators of satirically conceived diminutive landscapes seem to see everything as small because they are themselves so grand, Austen's analogy for her art—her "little bit (two Inches wide) of Ivory"—suggests a fragility that reminds us of the risk and instability outside the fictional space. Besides seeing her art metaphorically, as her critics would too, in relation to female arts severely devalued until quite recently (for painting on ivory was traditionally a "ladylike" occupation), Austen attempted through self-imposed novelistic limitations to define a secure place, even as she seemed to admit the impossibility of actually inhabiting such a small space with any degree of comfort. And always, for Austen, it is women—because they are too vulnerable in the world at large—who must acquiesce in their own confinement, no matter how stifling it may be.

11. The passage focuses primarily on

    (A) Jane Austen's place in English literature
    (B) the literary denigration of female novelists
    (C) the implications of Austen's attitude to her work
    (D) critical evaluations of the novels of Jane Austen
    (E) social rejection of professional women in the 18th and 19th centuries

12. According to the passage, Austen concentrated on a limited range of subjects because

    (A) she had a limited degree of experience in life
    (B) her imagination was incapable of creating other worlds
    (C) women in her time were discouraged from writing about significant topics
    (D) she wanted to create a special niche for her talents
    (E) she did not wish to be acknowledged as an author

13. Which of the following best expresses the relationship of the first sentence to the rest of the passage?

    (A) Specific instance followed by generalizations
    (B) Assertion followed by analysis
    (C) Objective statement followed by personal opinion
    (D) Quotation from an authority followed by conflicting views
    (E) Challenge followed by debate

The atmosphere is a mixture of several gases. There are about ten chemical elements which remain permanently in gaseous form in the atmosphere under all natural conditions. Of these permanent gases, oxygen makes up about 21 percent and nitrogen about 78 percent. Several other gases, such as argon, carbon dioxide, hydrogen, neon, krypton, and xenon, comprise the remaining 1 percent of the volume of dry air. The amount of water vapor, and its variations in amount and distribution, are of extraordinary importance in weather changes. Atmospheric gases hold in suspension great quantities of dust, pollen, smoke, and other impurities which are always present in considerable, but variable amounts.

The atmosphere has no definite upper limits but gradually thins until it becomes imperceptible. Until recently it was assumed that the air above the first few miles gradually grew thinner and colder at a constant rate. It was also assumed that upper air had little influence on weather changes. Recent studies of the upper atmosphere, currently being conducted by earth satellites and missile probings, have shown these assumptions to be incorrect. The atmosphere has three well-defined strata.

The layer of the air next to the earth, which extends upward for about 10 miles, is known as the *troposphere*. On the whole, it makes up about 75 percent of all the weight of the atmosphere. It is the warmest part of the atmosphere because most of the solar radiation is absorbed by the earth's surface, which warms the air immediately surrounding it. A steady decrease of temperature with increasing elevation is a most striking characteristic. The upper layers are colder because of their greater distance from the earth's surface and rapid radiation of heat into space. The temperatures within the troposphere decrease about 3.5 degrees per 1,000-foot increase in altitude. Within the troposphere, winds and air currents distribute heat and moisture. Strong winds, called jet streams, are located at the upper levels of the troposphere. These jet streams are both complex and widespread in occurrence. They normally show a wave-shaped pattern and move from west to east at velocities of 150 mph, but velocities as high as 400 mph have been noted. The influences of changing locations and strengths of jet streams upon weather conditions and patterns are no doubt considerable. Current intensive research may eventually reveal their true significance.

Above the troposphere to a height of about 50 miles is a zone called the *stratosphere*. The stratosphere is separated from the troposphere by a zone of uniform temperatures called the tropopause. Within the lower portions of the stratosphere is a layer of ozone gases which filters out most of the ultraviolet rays from the sun. The ozone layer varies with air pressure. If this zone were not there, the full blast of the sun's ultraviolet light would burn our skins, blind our eyes, and eventually result in our destruction. Within the stratosphere, the temperature and atmospheric composition are relatively uniform.

The layer upward of about 50 miles is the most fascinating but the least known of these three strata. It is called the *ionosphere* because it consists of electrically charged particles called ions, thrown from the sun. The northern lights (*aurora borealis*) originate within this highly charged portion of the atmosphere. Its effect upon weather conditions, if any, is as yet unknown.

14. Which of the following titles best expresses the ideas of the passage?

   (A) The Makeup of the Atmosphere
   (B) Studying the Atmosphere
   (C) Atmosphere and Weather
   (D) Temperature in the Stratosphere
   (E) The Sun's Rays

15. The passage supplies information that would answer which of the following questions?

   I. How do the troposphere and the stratosphere differ?
   II. How does the ionosphere affect the weather?
   III. How do earth satellites study the atmosphere?

   (A) I only   (B) III only   (C) I and II only
   (D) I and III only   (E) I, II , and III

16. According to the passage, life as we know it exists on the earth because the atmosphere

   (A) contains a layer of ozone gases
   (B) contains electrically charged particles
   (C) is warmest at the bottom
   (D) carries the ultraviolet rays of the sun
   (E) provides the changes in weather

17. It can be inferred from the passage that a jet plane will usually have its best average rate of speed on its run from

   (A) New York to San Francisco
   (B) Los Angeles to New York
   (C) Boston to Miami
   (D) Bermuda to New York
   (E) London to Washington, D.C.

18. It can be inferred from the passage that at the top of Jungfrau, which is 12,000 feet above the town of Interlaken in Switzerland, the temperature is usually

   (A) below freezing
   (B) about 42 degrees colder than on the ground
   (C) warmer than in Interlaken
   (D) affected by the ionosphere
   (E) about 75 degrees colder than in Interlaken

19. The passage states that the troposphere is the warmest part of the atmosphere because it

   (A) is closest to the sun
   (B) contains electrically charged particles
   (C) radiates heat into space
   (D) has winds and air current that distribute the heat
   (E) is warmed by the earth's heat

20. According to the passage, the atmosphere consists of all of the following EXCEPT

   (A) 21 percent oxygen
   (B) a definite amount of water vapor
   (C) ten permanent elements
   (D) less than 1 percent of xenon
   (E) considerable waste products

Answer Key
Reading Comprehension Exercise A

1.	B	6.	C	11.	C	16.	D
2.	B	7.	E	12.	D	17.	D
3.	E	8.	A	13.	D	18.	C
4.	B	9.	E	14.	A	19.	E
5.	E	10.	D	15.	B	20.	E

Reading Comprehension Exercise B

1.	A	6.	E	11.	D	16.	B
2.	D	7.	C	12.	B	17.	A
3.	C	8.	E	13.	E	18.	C
4.	B	9.	C	14.	A	19.	E
5.	D	10.	C	15.	A	20.	B

Reading Comprehension Exercise C

1.	C	6.	B	11.	C	16.	A
2.	B	7.	A	12.	B	17.	B
3.	A	8.	B	13.	A	18.	D
4.	D	9.	D	14.	C	19.	B
5.	E	10.	B	15.	C	20.	E

Reading Comprehension Exercise D

1.	B	6.	B	11.	A	16.	C
2.	E	7.	E	12.	D	17.	D
3.	D	8.	D	13.	A	18.	E
4.	C	9.	B	14.	B	19.	B
5.	A	10.	C	15.	D	20.	A

Reading Comprehension Exercise E

1.	D	6.	B	11.	C	16.	A
2.	D	7.	D	12.	A	17.	B
3.	A	8.	C	13.	B	18.	B
4.	B	9.	D	14.	C	19.	E
5.	B	10.	A	15.	A	20.	B

6 Antonym Questions

- **Testing Tactics**
- **Practice Exercises**
- **Answer Key**

Your task in answering antonym questions is straightforward: you are given a word and must choose, from the five choices that follow it, the best antonym (opposite). Antonym questions range from relatively easy ones at the beginning of a set to extremely difficult ones at the set's end. Do not expect to recognize every word—not even professional writers would be familiar with all of them.

The eleven antonym questions always make up the last group of questions in a verbal section. Do not, however, answer them last. Right after you have finished answering the analogy questions, skip to the antonyms and go through them quickly. Answer them all, but do not linger too long on any given one. The time you save by answering the antonym questions quickly will help you when you get to the time-consuming reading comprehension questions.

Testing Tactics

Tactic 1 — Think of a Context for the Capitalized Word

Take a quick look at the word in capital letters. If you don't recollect its meaning right away, try to think of a phrase or sentence in which you have heard it used. The context may help you come up with the word's meaning. For example:

> MAGNIFY: (A) forgive (B) comprehend
> (C) extract (D) diminish (E) electrify

The term "magnifying glass" should immediately come to mind. A magnifying glass enlarges things. The opposite of enlarging something is to make it smaller or *diminish* it. The correct answer is Choice D.

Now apply this tactic to a question from a recent GRE.

> ABERRANT: (A) attractive (B) predictive
> (C) blissful (D) normal (E) precise

What phrase comes to your mind? "Aberrant behavior." "Aberrant data." In both cases you should have an impression of something deviating from what is expected, an impression of something *abnormal,* in fact. Aberrant behavior strays from the norm; *aberrant,* thus, is an antonym for *normal.* The correct answer is Choice D.

Tactic 2 — Before You Look at the Choices, Think Of Antonyms for the Capitalized Word

Suppose your word is *industrious*, hard-working. What opposites come to your mind? You might come up with *lazy, idle, slothful, inactive*—all words that mean lacking industry and energy.

Now look at the choices:

> INDUSTRIOUS: (A) stupid (B) harsh
> (C) indolent (D) complex (E) inexpensive

121

Lazy, idle, and *slothful* all are synonyms for *indolent.* Your correct answer is Choice C.

This tactic will help you even when you have to deal with unfamiliar words among your answer choices. Suppose you do not know the meaning of the word *indolent.* You know that one antonym for your key word *industrious* is *lazy.* Therefore, you know that you are looking for a word that means the same as *lazy.* At this point you can go through the answer choices eliminating answers that don't work. Does *stupid* mean the same as *lazy?* No, smart people can be lazy, too. Does *harsh* mean the same as *lazy?* No, *harsh* means cruel or rough. Does *indolent* mean the same as *lazy?* You don't know; you should check the other choices and then come back. Does *complex* mean the same as *lazy?* No, *complex*

means complicated or intricate. Does *inexpensive* mean the same as *lazy?* No. So what is left? *Indolent.* Once again, your correct answer is Choice C.

Apply this tactic to a question from a recent GRE:

> GARRULITY: (A) servility   (B) forbearance
> (C) peacefulness   (D) constancy
> (E) taciturnity

Garrulity means talkativeness. In thinking of possible antonyms for *garrulity,* you may have come up with words like *untalkativeness, curtness,* and *reticence,* words signifying briefness of speech. *Untalkativeness, curtness,* and *reticence* are all synonyms for *taciturnity.* The correct answer is Choice E.

Read All the Choices Before You Decide Which Is Best

On the GRE you are working under time pressure. You may be tempted to mark down the first answer that seems right and ignore the other choices given. Don't do it. Consider each answer. Only in this way can you be sure to distinguish between two possible answers and come up with the best answer for the question.

Words have shades of meaning. In matching a word with its opposite, you must pay attention to these shades of meaning. Try this example from an actual GRE test to see how this rule works.

> TRACTABLE: (A) distraught   (B) irritating
> (C) ruthless   (D) headstrong   (E) lazy

Suppose you have only a vague sense of the meaning of *tractable.* You associate it with such vaguely positive terms as *gentle, docile, amiable.* For this reason, you stop short when you come to Choice C. Reasoning that

someone gentle and docile is *not* ruthless or merciless, you look no further and mark down Choice C.

Choice C, however, is incorrect. True, a tractable person is docile and easily guided, even mild. Someone who lacks docility, however, is not necessarily ruthless. Such a person is difficult to guide, obstinate, in fact *headstrong.* The correct answer is Choice D.

Now try a second example from a recent GRE.

> PERFIDY: (A) thoroughness   (B) generosity
> (C) gratitude   (D) tact   (E) loyalty

Perfidy means treachery; someone perfidious betrays those who have faith in him. Choice C has an immediate appeal: someone perfidious is ungrateful for the trust shown him; in committing perfidy, he lacks *gratitude.* However, strictly speaking, in committing perfidy, the traitor's crime is not thanklessness but *disloyalty.* The best antonym for *perfidy* is Choice E, *loyalty.*

Look at the Answer Choices to Determine the Main Word's Part Of Speech

Look at the capitalized word. What part of speech is it? Words often exist in several forms. You may think of *run* as a verb, for example, but in the phrases "a run in her stocking" and "hit a home run" *run* is a noun.

The GRE plays on this confusion in testing your verbal ability. When you look at a particular capitalized word, you may not know whether you are dealing with a noun, a verb, or an adjective. *Harbor,* for example, is a very common noun; in "to harbor a fugitive," to give refuge to a runaway, it is a much less common verb.

If you suspect that a capitalized word may have more than one part of speech, don't worry. Just look at the first couple of answer choices and see what part of speech they are. That part of speech will be the capitalized word's part of speech.

In GRE Antonym Questions, **all** *the answer choices have the same part of speech.* You can always tell what that part of speech is by a quick glance at the first answer choice or two.

See how this tactic works in answering a relatively simple question from a published GRE.

> CARDINAL: (A) abstract   (B) elusive
> (C) subtle   (D) minor   (E) miniature

Are you dealing with *cardinal* the noun or *cardinal* the adjective?

A quick look at the answers assures you that they are all adjectives. *Cardinal* here is neither a church leader nor a bird. The adjective *cardinal* means central or principal in importance, as in "the cardinal element" of a plan. Its opposite is *minor*. The correct answer is Choice D.

Now try a second example from a recent GRE.

> APPROPRIATE: (A) create a void
> (B) rectify an error   (C) sanction
> (D) surrender   (E) lend

Is the word in capitals the adjective *appropriate* (suitable, proper) or the verb *appropriate* (to set aside, acquire)?

A quick look at the answer choices reveals that it is a verb. (The *-ate* and *-ify* word endings are common verb endings.) One definition of the verb *appropriate* is to take something or make it particularly one's own, as in *appropriating money* or *appropriating land*. Thus, its opposite is to yield or *surrender* something, Choice D.

Consider Secondary Meanings of the Capitalized Word as Well as Its Primary Meaning

If none of the answer choices seems right to you, take another look at the capitalized word. It may have more than one meaning. The GRE often constructs questions that make use of secondary, less well-known meanings of deceptively familiar words. Take, for example, this typical GRE question.

> LIST: (A) be upside down   (B) be upright
> (C) slide backward   (D) sway to and fro
> (E) lie flat

List here has nothing to do with making lists or enumerating. It has to do with moving. When it *lists* to starboard, a ship simply leans to one side or tilts. The best antonym for this meaning of *list* is Choice B, *be upright*.

Try a second, more difficult GRE question involving a less familiar meaning of a familiar word.

> REDUNDANT: (A) consistent   (B) complex
> (C) diffuse   (D) insightful   (E) economical

Only 38 percent of the examinees tested on this question answered in correctly. Why?

The problem lies not in the capitalized word but in the answer choices. *Redundant* means superfluous, repetitive, wordy. Thus, its antonym means succinct and concise. Not immediately spotting succinct or concise among the answer choices, and looking for a positive term to contrast with *redundant*, some examinees may settle for Choice A, *consistent,* or Choice D, *insightful.* In doing so, they fail to consider that words have secondary meanings. In this case, *economical* does not mean thrifty of profitable, as in "an economical housewife" or "an economical business venture." Instead, it means sparing in quantity, as in "an economical use of words." The correct answer is Choice E.

Break Down Unfamiliar Words into Recognizable Parts

When you come upon a totally unfamiliar word, don't give up. Break it down and see if you recognize any of its parts. Pay particular attention to prefixes—word parts added to the beginning of a word—and to roots, the building blocks of the language.

Look once more at the following question from the GRE.

> ABERRANT: (A) attractive   (B) predictive
> (C) blissful   (D) normal   (E) precise

Suppose you had never seen *aberrant* before. You have seen dozens of other words beginning with *ab-*: *absent, abnormal, abduct*. Take *abduct*. What do you do when you abduct someone? You kidnap him, or steal him away. *Ab-* means *away*.

What about the root, *err*? To *err* is to be wrong or to wander, as in wandering from the right path. Thus, *aberrant* means wandering away, straying from what is right or normal, and its opposite is of course Choice D, *normal*.

Now try a second example from a recently published GRE.

> SYNCHRONOUS:
> (A) off-key
> (B) out-of-shape
> (C) without pity
> (D) out-of-phase
> (E) without difficulty

Syn- means together. *Chron-* means time. Something *synchronous* must have to do with occurring together in time, like the *synchronous* movements of swimmers keeping time with one another. The antonym for *synchronous* thus is Choice D, *out-of-phase*.

The word part approach can help you interpret new words you encounter. However, apply it cautiously. In many words the roots, prefixes, and suffixes have lost their original meanings. In others, the same root occurs, but with markedly differing effects. It would not do to call a *philanthropist* a *philanderer*, for instance, though both words contain the root for love.

If you find the word part approach appealing, try to spend some time working with the Basic Word Parts List in Chapter 7. Remember, however, there is no substitute for learning the exact meaning of a word as it is used today.

In Eliminating Answer Choices, Test Words for Their Positive or Negative Connotations

When you are dealing with a partially unfamiliar word, a word that you cannot define or use in a sentence but that you know you have seen previously, try to remember in what sort of context you have seen that word. Did it have positive connotations, or did it have a negative feel? If you are certain the capitalized word has positive connotations, then, since you are looking for its antonym, you *know* the correct answer must have negative ones. Thus, you can eliminate any answer choices that have positive connotations and guess among the answer choices that are negative in tone.

See how this approach applies in the following example from a recent GRE.

> CHARY: (A) brisk (B) bold (C) untidy
> (D) ungenerous (E) unfriendly

You cannot define *chary*. You would hesitate to use it in a sentence of your own. And yet, you are sure the word has a slightly negative feel to it. A person is *chary about* something. You have a sense of someone holding back.

Look at the answer choices. Which of them have negative connotations? *Untidy*? *Ungenerous*? *Unfriendly*? Eliminate all three. You have narrowed down your choices to *brisk* and *bold*, both words that have a positive feel. You are in an excellent position to guess. As it turns out, *chary* means hesitant or reluctant to proceed. Its opposite is Choice B, *bold*.

Watch Out for Errors Caused by Eye-Catchers

When you look at answer choices, do you find that certain ones seem to leap right off the page? These words are eye-catchers. They look good—but be sure to take a second look.

Try these next GRE antonym questions to see just how an eye-catcher works. First, an easy one.

> GAUCHENESS: (A) probity (B) sophistry
> (C) acumen (D) polish (E) vigor

What comes to mind when you think of synonyms for *gauche* (socially awkward)? *Unsophisticated*? This common association of *gaucheness* with lack of sophistication can hurt you here, for it may cause your eye to be attracted by Choice B, *sophistry*, the eye-catcher here.

Sophistry (superficially plausible, but actually specious reasoning) is not a synonym for *sophistication* or worldliness. Both words share a common root, however, and resemble one another enough that someone unsure of the correct answer might select *sophistry* as a sort of "educated guess." The only way to avoid this error is to read all the answer choices carefully and note that *sophistication's* true synonym here is *polish*.

Here's a more difficult GRE example. See if you can spot the eye-catcher.

> DISSEMBLE: (A) act conventionally
> (B) put together   (C) appear promptly
> (D) behave honestly   (E) obtain readily

Only 10 percent of the test-takers who attempted this question (the last in its set) answered it correctly. Why? Once more an early answer choice has been set up to tempt the hasty reader. In this case, the resemblance of the unfamiliar word *dissemble* to the familiar word *disas-*

semble sets up the confusion. Hurried, the reader glances at *dissemble* and thinks *disassemble*. What's the opposite of *disassemble?* Why, to assemble or *put together* — that's Choice B! Choice B seems like a quick and easy answer. Too quick and easy — it's wrong.

To *dissemble* is to present a false appearance, to try to seem what one is not, like the child accused of stealing cookies who tries to appear innocent even though she's got cookie crumbs on her face. A dissembler lies or dissimulates: she does not *behave honestly*. The opposite of *dissemble* is Choice D.

A word of warning: when you reach the final antonyms of a set, be wary. Suspect questions whose answers seem too easy. There are no easy answers when you get to the last questions of a set.

Practice Exercises

Antonym Exercise A

<u>Directions</u>: Each question below consists of a word printed in capital letters, followed by five lettered words or phrases. Choose the lettered word or phrase that is most nearly <u>opposite</u> in meaning to the word in capital letters.

Since some of the questions require you to distinguish fine shades of meaning, be sure to consider all the choices before deciding which one is best.

1. MOURNFUL: (A) informal   (B) sympathetic
   (C) private   (D) appropriate   (E) joyous

2. SCAD: (A) parsimony   (B) allocation
   (C) dearth   (D) restraint   (E) provision

3. GRANDIOSE: (A) docile   (B) unlikely to occur
   (C) simple and unimposing   (D) light in weight
   (E) uncommunicative

4. ENTRENCH: (A) defy   (B) oust
   (C) extinguish   (D) squander   (E) intercede

5. LACKLUSTER: (A) superficial
   (B) courteous   (C) vibrant
   (D) complex   (E) abundant

6. CENSURE: (A) augment   (B) eradicate
   (C) enthrall   (D) commend   (E) reform

7. TRANSIENCE: (A) slowness   (B) permanence
   (C) lack of caution   (D) desire for perfection
   (E) original nature

8. DESICCATE: (A) lengthen   (B) hallow
   (C) exonerate   (D) saturate   (E) anesthetize

9. PROTRUSION: (A) deep recess
   (B) strong dislike   (C) growing scarcity
   (D) illusion   (E) chaos

10. ENTICE: (A) repel   (B) authorize
    (C) baffle   (D) misplace   (E) diminish

11. ORTHODOXY: (A) renown   (B) trepidation
    (C) unconventionality   (D) inquisitiveness
    (E) remoteness

12. SUMPTUOUS: (A) dank   (B) frequent
    (C) partial   (D) restrained   (E) open

13. DISSOLUTION: (A) retribution
    (B) compliance   (C) futility
    (D) persuasion   (E) establishment

14. IRK: (A) pry   (B) tinge
    (C) beguile   (D) convince   (E) soothe

15. LIMBER: (A) sturdy   (B) orderly
    (C) durable   (D) stiff   (E) gloomy

16. OBLIQUITY: (A) praise
    (B) straightforwardness   (C) conformity
    (D) self-righteousness   (E) depreciation

17. SLUR: (A) sensitivity   (B) sacrifice
    (C) understatement   (D) challenge
    (E) commendation

18. APOTHEOSIS: (A) departure from tradition
    (B) impatience with stupidity
    (C) demotion from glory
    (D) surrender to impulse
    (E) cause for grief

19. ENERVATE : (A) narrate (B) enrage
(C) accomplish (D) invigorate (E) acquiesce

20. NIGGARDLY : (A) appropriate (B) generous
(C) complete (D) radiant (E) ongoing

Antonym Exercise B

<u>Directions:</u> Each question below consists of a word printed in capital letters, followed by five lettered words or phrases. Choose the lettered word or phrase that is most nearly <u>opposite</u> in meaning to the word in capital letters.

Since some of the questions require you to distinguish fine shades of meaning, be sure to consider all the choices before deciding which one is best.

1. HEDGE :

(A) act on impulse
(B) refuse to represent
(C) state without qualification
(D) make a foolish comment
(E) establish a connection

2. ABROGATE : (A) transgress (B) signify
(C) alleviate (D) question (E) ratify

3. INDUSTRY : (A) cleanliness (B) pragmatism
(C) sloth (D) promptness (E) abasement

4. SPUNK : (A) success (B) timidity
(C) growing awareness (D) lack of intelligence
(E) loss of prestige

5. SAGE : (A) zealot (B) miser
(C) braggart (D) fool (E) tyrant

6. ADMONITION : (A) premonition
(B) hallucination (C) escape
(D) commendation (E) trepidation

7. CHARY : (A) lugubrious (B) brash
(C) indifferent (D) graceful (E) scornful

8. STUPEFY : (A) lie (B) bend
(C) enliven (D) talk nonsense
(E) consider thoughtfully

9. COGENT : (A) contemplative
(B) unpersuasive (C) expository (C) stable
(D) inconceivable

10. FICKLE : (A) spotless (B) industrious
(C) welcome (D) urgent (E) loyal

11. COMPLY : (A) simplify (B) strive
(C) rebel (D) unite (E) appreciate

12. CREDIT : (A) believe false
(B) treat as equal (C) make more difficult
(D) underemphasize (E) forget

13. STILTED : (A) informal
(B) verbose (C) secretive
(D) senseless (E) tentative

14. UNGAINLY : (A) slender
(B) graceful (C) restrained
(D) inaccurate (E) unnoticed

15. QUIXOTIC : (A) slow
(B) abstemious (C) pragmatic
(D) benevolent (E) grave

16. DISPARITY: (A) timidity (B) complacency
(C) bigotry (D) likeness (E) influence

17. CRITICAL: (A) unimportant (B) uncertain
(C) silent (D) coherent (E) destructive

18. SOBRIETY: (A) influence (B) nonchalance
(C) holiness (D) civility (E) mirth

19. RESTIVENESS: (A) completeness
(B) conviction (C) concern (D) docility
(E) petulance

20. HALLOW : (A) keep silence
(B) prove incorrect (C) accuse openly
(D) desecrate (E) instigate

Antonym Exercise C

<u>Directions:</u> Each question below consists of a word printed in capital letters, followed by five lettered words or phrases. Choose the lettered word or phrase that is most nearly <u>opposite</u> in meaning to the word in capital letters.

Since some of the questions require you to distinguish fine shades of meaning, be sure to consider all the choices before deciding which one is best.

1. HARBINGER: (A) ascetic (B) miser
(C) counselor (D) follower (E) braggart

2. SPUR: (A) embitter (B) discourage
(C) impress (D) mislead (E) ignore

3. DISJOINTED: (A) responsible (B) connected
(C) implied (D) useful (E) imprecise

4. MEALYMOUTHED: (A) hungry
(B) indefinite (C) tightlipped (D) sincere
(E) apathetic

5. PREVARICATE: (A) postulate
(B) emphasize (C) support in theory
(D) consider thoughtfully (E) state truthfully

6. LUMINARY: (A) impostor (B) nonentity
(C) pilgrim (D) braggart (E) mutineer

7. TESTY: (A) erroneous (B) uncommunicative (C) even-tempered (D) quick-witted (E) industrious

8. NEFARIOUS: (A) lackadaisical (B) eccentric (C) exemplary (D) corrigible (E) hypocritical

9. BEGRUDGE: (A) mourn silently (B) grant freely (C) hunger for (D) advance rapidly (E) fight back

10. BILK: (A) reduce in size (B) make famous (C) roughen (D) renovate (E) pay in full

11. COMPOSE: (A) disturb (B) reveal (C) strengthen (D) isolate (E) prevent

12. OCCLUDE: (A) determine (B) transcend (C) surround (D) open (E) regulate

13. AMBIGUITY: (A) extent (B) success (C) clarity (D) normality (E) expression

14. AMELIORATION: (A) prevention (B) aggravation (C) distraction (D) indifference (E) dissuasion

15. CAVIL: (A) discern (B) disclose (C) introduce (D) flatter (E) commend

16. SKEPTICAL: (A) theoretical (B) indifferent (C) ready to believe (D) eager for change (E) lost in thought

17. FLEDGLING: (A) experienced person (B) shy onlooker (C) social outcast (D) fugitive (E) adversary

18. CRASS: (A) boastful (B) temporary (C) cheerful (D) refined (E) extensive

19. RECALCITRANT: (A) tractable (B) erratic (C) intuitive (D) vigorous (E) rambling

20. PROTRACT: (A) defy (B) supplement (C) postpone (D) shorten (E) design

Antonym Exercise D

Directions: Each question below consists of a word printed in capital letters, followed by five lettered words or phrases. Choose the lettered word or phrase that is most nearly opposite in meaning to the word in capital letters.

Since some of the questions require you to distinguish fine shades of meaning, be sure to consider all the choices before deciding which one is best.

1. PRIM: (A) rare (B) careful (C) unnecessary (D) improper (E) decisive

2. REPUGNANCE: (A) attraction (B) lethargy (C) blame (D) virtue (E) awe

3. NETTLE: (A) disentangle (B) mollify (C) magnify (D) muffle (E) recompense

4. REPLETE: (A) unwrinkled (B) devoid (C) vulgar (D) matchless (E) unsympathetic

5. UNASSUAGED: (A) presumed (B) deceptive (C) singular (D) faulty (E) soothed

6. PALTRY: (A) munificent (B) improvident (C) random (D) cautious (E) obsolete

7. CONCLUSIVE: (A) difficult to express (B) bringing bad luck (C) easy to solve (D) lacking merit (E) open to question

8. RESOURCEFULNESS: (A) wealth (B) gratitude (C) melancholy (D) incompetence (E) frustration

9. DISSUADE: (A) extol (B) exhort (C) intensify (D) complicate (E) precede

10. SPLENETIC: (A) lackluster (B) heartless (C) diffident (D) constant (E) cordial

11. VIRULENCE: (A) pallor (B) orderliness (C) femininity (D) harmlessness (E) cowardice

12. ADHERENT: (A) fugitive (B) dissembler (C) opponent (D) educator (E) witness

13. OSCILLATE: (A) entreat (B) intensify (C) remain fixed (D) expand gradually (E) wither away

14. ASPERITY: (A) gentility (B) superiority (C) kindness (D) clarity (E) vagueness

15. UNSCATHED: (A) honest (B) gathered (C) injured (D) cleansed (E) forgiven

16. FETTER: (A) diminish (B) enervate (C) liberate (D) return (E) cure

17. AUTONOMY: (A) dependence (B) animation (C) renown (D) altruism (E) antipathy

18. SLACK: (A) rough (B) active (C) liberal (D) dependent (E) familiar

19. RECOIL : (A) plunge forward (B) cease firing (C) skirt an issue (D) facilitate (E) surrender

20. ENCUMBER : (A) disburden (B) perform easily (C) challenge boldly (D) observe with care (E) suppress

Antonym Exercise E

Directions: Each question below consists of a word printed in capital letters, followed by five lettered words or phrases. Choose the lettered word or phrase that is most nearly opposite in meaning to the word in capital letters.

Since some of the questions require you to distinguish fine shades of meaning, be sure to consider all the choices before deciding which one is best.

1. OPACITY : (A) iridescence (B) firmness
   (C) transparence (D) poverty (E) slum

2. PREDILECTION : (A) postponement
   (B) afterthought (C) lamentation
   (D) reoccurrence (E) aversion

3. SEEDY : (A) elegant (B) intricate
   (C) tranquil (D) irregular (E) slow

4. BOGGLE : (A) disentangle
   (B) repudiate (C) ascertain
   (D) remain unruffled (E) lack planning

5. HIDEBOUND : (A) strong-willed
   (B) open-minded (C) thin-skinned
   (D) tenderhearted (E) scatterbrained

6. CASTIGATE : (A) diminish (B) imitate
   (C) compare (D) reward (E) misjudge

7. GAMBOL : (A) dodge (B) masquerade
   (C) digress (D) plod (E) vex

8. RAUCOUS : (A) orderly (B) absorbent
   (C) mellifluous (D) contentious (E) buoyant

9. TAPER : (A) emphasize (B) restore
   (C) split (D) broaden (E) modify

10. HIGH-HANDED : (A) dejected
    (B) reasonable (C) hard-handed
    (D) short-handed (E) dynamic

11. DIMINUTION : (A) measurement
    (B) proximity (C) augmentation
    (D) orderliness (E) inclination

12. DISTEND : (A) tell the truth
    (B) respond as expected (C) approximate
    (D) collect (E) shrink

13. EMBROIL:
    (A) disengage
    (B) remonstrate
    (C) refute thoroughly
    (D) answer hypothetically
    (E) consider genuinely

14. VOUCHSAFE : (A) postpone (B) dissemble
    (C) endanger (D) prohibit (E) justify

15. JETTISON : (A) salvage (B) decelerate
    (C) muffle (D) distract (E) anchor

16. STOIC : (A) savant (B) herald
    (C) whiner (D) victor (E) bystander

17. GAMELY : (A) fearfully (B) diligently
    (C) clumsily (D) gloomily (E) respectfully

18. CRESTFALLEN : (A) haughty (B) impolite
    (C) frivolous (D) tentative (E) rough

19. DESULTORY : (A) apologetic
    (B) independent (C) laudatory
    (D) questionable (E) methodical

20. PULCHRITUDE : (A) antipathy
    (B) unsightliness (C) inexperience
    (D) languor (E) rancor

Answer Key

Antonym Exercise A

1.	E	6.	D	11.	C	16.	B
2.	C	7.	B	12.	D	17.	E
3.	C	8.	D	13.	E	18.	C
4.	B	9.	A	14.	E	19.	D
5.	C	10.	A	15.	D	20.	B

Antonym Exercise B

1.	C	6.	D	11.	C	16.	D
2.	E	7.	B	12.	A	17.	A
3.	C	8.	C	13.	A	18.	E
4.	B	9.	B	14.	B	19.	D
5.	D	10.	E	15.	C	20.	D

Antonym Exercise C

1.	D	6.	B	11.	A	16.	C
2.	B	7.	C	12.	D	17.	A
3.	B	8.	C	13.	C	18.	D
4.	D	9.	B	14.	B	19.	A
5.	E	10.	E	15.	E	20.	D

Antonym Exercise D

1.	D	6.	A	11.	D	16.	C
2.	A	7.	E	12.	C	17.	A
3.	B	8.	D	13.	C	18.	B
4.	B	9.	B	14.	C	19.	A
5.	E	10.	E	15.	C	20.	A

Antonym Exercise E

1.	C	6.	D	11.	C	16.	C
2.	E	7.	D	12.	E	17.	A
3.	A	8.	C	13.	A	18.	A
4.	D	9.	D	14.	D	19.	E
5.	B	10.	B	15.	A	20.	B

7 REVIEWING VOCABULARY

- **GRE High-Frequency Words**
- **Master Word List**
- **Basic Word Parts**

Now that you have mastered the appropriate strategies for dealing with the four basic types of questions on the Graduate Record Examination that test your verbal ability, you have the opportunity to spend some time refining your vocabulary and acquainting yourself with the fine shades of meaning that words possess. Studies show that, where the average high school graduate recognizes about 50,000 words, the average college graduate recognizes around 70,000. The increase indicates that during your four years of college you have rapidly acquired about 20,000 new words (many of them technical terms from a variety of disciplines), some of which may have connotations and nuances that still escape you.

The best way to develop a powerful vocabulary is to read extensively and well. However, it is possible to fine-tune your vocabulary by exploring unabridged dictionaries, in which usage notes make clear the fine distinctions between related words, and by studying high-level vocabulary lists, such as our 3,500-word Master Word List.

This chapter presents the Master Word List and a Basic Word Parts List, a chart of prefixes, roots, and suffixes that may provide you with clues to the meanings of unfamiliar words. The chapter begins with the GRE High-Frequency Word List, 300 words that have occurred and reoccurred on GREs published in the 1980s and 1990s.

The GRE High-Frequency Word List

How many of the following words do you think you know? Half? Even more? First, check off those words that you recognize. Then, look up all 300 words and their definitions in our Master Word List. Pay particular attention to the following:

1. Words you recognize but cannot use in a sentence or define. You have a feel for these words—you are on the brink of knowing them. Effort you put into mastering these "borderline" words will pay off soon.

2. Words you thought you knew—but didn't. See whether any of them are defined in an unexpected way. If they are, make a special note of them. As you know from the preceding chapters, the GRE often stumps students with questions based on unfamiliar meanings of familiar-looking words.

In the course of your undergraduate career, you have undoubtedly developed your own techniques for building your vocabulary. One familiar technique—flash cards—often is used less than effectively. Students either try to cram too much information onto a flash card or try to cram too many flash cards into a practice session. If you wish to work with flash cards, try following these suggestions:

Writing the Flash Card   Be brief—but include all the information you need. On one side write the word. On the other side write a *concise* definition—two or three words at most—for each major meaning of the word you want to learn. Include an antonym, too: the synonym-antonym associations can help you remember both words. To fix the word in your mind, use it in a short phrase. Then write that phrase down.

Memorizing the Flash Card   Carry a few of your flash cards with you every day. Look them over whenever you have a spare moment or two. Work in short bursts. Try going through five flash cards at a time, shuffling through them quickly so that you can build up your rapid sight recognition of the words for the test. You want these words and their antonyms to spring to your mind instantaneously.

Test your memory: don't look at the back of the card unless you must. Go through your five cards several times a day. Then, when you have mastered two or three of the cards and have them down pat, set those cards aside and add a couple of new ones to your working pile. That way you will always be working with a limited group, but you won't be wasting time reviewing words you already recognize on sight.

Never try to master a whole stack of flash cards in one long cram session. It won't work.

GRE High-Frequency Words

abate	cogent	divest	imperturbable	paradigm
aberrant	collusion	dogmatic	impervious	paragon
abeyance	commensurate	dormant	implacable	parsimonious
abscond	complaisant	ebullient	implicit	partisan
abstemious	compliant	eclectic	inadvertently	pathological
adamant	conciliatory	efficacy	inchoate	paucity
adulterate	condone	elegy	incongruity	pedantic
adversity	conducive	elicit	indeterminate	penchant
aesthetic	connoisseur	embellish	indigence	penury
aggregate	consensus	emulate	indolence	perennial
alleviate	contentious	endemic	inertia	perfidious
amalgamate	conundrum	enervate	ingenuous	perfunctory
ambiguous	converge	engender	inherent	permeable
ambivalence	convoluted	ephemeral	insensible	pervasive
ameliorate	daunt	equivocate	insipid	phlegmatic
anachronism	decorum	erudite	insularity	piety
analogous	deference	esoteric	intractable	placate
anarchy	delineate	eulogy	intransigence	platitude
anomalous	denigrate	euphemism	intrepid	plethora
antipathy	deprecate	euphoria	intrinsically	plummet
apathy	derision	exculpate	inundate	pragmatic
appease	derivative	exigency	invective	precarious
approbation	desiccate	extrapolation	irascible	precipitate (ADJ.)
appropriate (v.)	despotism	facetious	irresolute	precipitate (v.)
arduous	desultory	facilitate	itinerary	precursor
ascetic	deterrent	fallacious	judicious	presumptuous
assuage	devoid	fawning	laconic	pretentious
audacious	diatribe	felicitous	lassitude	prevaricate
austere	dichotomy	fervor	latent	pristine
autonomous	diffidence	flag (v.)	laudatory	probity
aver	diffusion	fledgling	lethargic	problematic
banal	digression	foment	levity	prodigal
belie	disabuse	forestall	lucid	profligate
beneficent	discerning	frugality	luminous	proliferate
bolster	discordant	furtive	magnanimity	prolific
bombast	discredit	gainsay	malingerer	propensity
boorish	discrepancy	garrulity	malleable	propriety
burgeon	discrete	gratuitous	maverick	proscribe
burnish	disingenuous	gregarious	meticulous	pundit
buttress	disinterested	grudging	misanthrope	pungency
cacophony	disjointed	guileless	mitigate	qualified
capitulate	disparage	hamper	mollify	qualms
capricious	disparate	harangue	mundane	quiescent
castigation	dissemble	homogeneous	obdurate	rarefied
catalyst	disseminate	hyperbole	obsequious	recalcitrant
centrifuge	dissolution	iconoclastic	obviate	recant
chauvinist	dissonance	immutable	officious	recluse
coagulate	distill	impair	oscillate	recondite
coda	diverge	impassive	ostentatious	refractory

refute	saturate	sporadic	tacit	ubiquitous
relegate	savor	spurious	tangential	vacillate
reprobate	scapegoat	stigma	tenuous	venerate
repudiate	secrete	stint	tirade	veracity
rescind	secular	stolidity	torpor	verbose
resolution	shard	striated	torque	viable
resolve	skeptic	strut (N.)	tortuous	viscous
reticent	solicitous	subside	tractable	welter
reverent	◆ sophistry	substantiate	transgression	whimsical
salubrious	soporific	supersede	truculence	zealot
sanction	specious	supposition	turbid	

The 3,500 Master Word List

The 3,500-word Master Word List begins on the following page. As a graduate student you should be familiar with the majority of these words. You do not, however, need to memorize every word.

The best way to enlarge your vocabulary is to read extensively in a variety of fields. You can, however, assess the extent of your vocabulary by exploring specialized word lists such as this one.

For those of you who wish to work your way through the word list and feel the need for a plan, we recommend that you follow the procedure described below in order to use the lists and the exercises most profitably:

1. Allot a definite time each day for the study of a list.

2. Devote at least one hour to each list.

3. First go through the list looking at the short, simple-looking words (six letters at most). Mark those you don't know. In studying, pay particular attention to them.

4. Go through the list again looking at the longer words. Pay particular attention to words with more than one meaning and familiar-looking words with unusual definitions that come as a surprise to you. Many tests make use of these secondary definitions.

5. List unusual words on index cards, which you can shuffle and review from time to time. (Use the flash card technique described earlier in this chapter.)

6. Using the illustrative sentences in the list as models, make up new sentences of your own.

7. Take the test that follows each list at least one day after studying the words. In this way, you will check your ability to remember what you have studied.

8. If you can answer correctly 12 of the 15 questions in the test, you may proceed to the next list; if you cannot answer this number, restudy the list.

9. Keep a record of your guesses and of your success as a guesser.

For each word, the following is provided:

1. The word (printed in heavy type).

2. Its part of speech (abbreviated).

3. A brief definition.

4. A sentence or sentences illustrating the word's use.

5. Whenever appropriate, related words together with their parts of speech.

The word lists are arranged in strict alphabetical order. In each list, words that appear also on the High-Frequency GRE Word List are marked with a square bullet (■).

Master Word List

Word List 1   abase-adroit

abase V. lower; degrade; humiliate. Anna expected to have to curtsy to the King of Siam; when told to cast herself down on the ground before him, however, she refused to *abase* herself.

abash V. embarrass. He was not at all *abashed* by her open admiration.

■ **abate** V. subside or moderate. Rather than leaving immediately, they waited for the storm to *abate*.

abbreviate V. shorten. Because we were running out of time, the lecturer had to *abbreviate* her speech.

abdicate V. renounce; give up. When Edward VII *abdicated* the British throne, he surprised the entire world.

■ **aberrant** ADJ. abnormal or deviant. Given the *aberrant* nature of the data, we came to doubt the validity of the entire experiment.

aberration N. deviation from the expected or the normal; mental irregularity or disorder. Survivors of a major catastrophe are likely to exhibit *aberrations* of behavior because of the trauma they have experienced.

abet V. assist, usually in doing something wrong; encourage. She was unwilling to *abet* him in the swindle he had planned.

■ **abeyance** N. suspended action. The deal was held in abeyance until her arrival.

abhor V. detest; hate. She *abhorred* all forms of bigotry. abhorrence, N.

abject ADJ. wretched; lacking pride. On the streets of New York the homeless live in *abject* poverty, huddling in doorways to find shelter from the wind.

abjure V. renounce upon oath. He *abjured* his allegiance to the king. abjuration, N.

ablution N. washing. His daily *ablutions* were accompanied by loud noises that he humorously labeled "Opera in the Bath."

abnegation N. renunciation; self-sacrifice. Though Rudolph and Duchess Flavia loved one another, their love was doomed, for she had to wed the king; their act of *abnegation* was necessary to preserve the kingdom.

abolish V. cancel; put an end to. The president of the college refused to *abolish* the physical education requirement. abolition, N.

abominate V. loathe; hate. Moses scolded the idol worshippers in the tribe because he *abominated* the custom. abominable, ADJ.

aboriginal ADJ., N. being the first of its kind in a region; primitive; native. Her studies of the primitive art forms of the *aboriginal* Indians were widely reported in the scientific journals. aborigine, N.

abortive ADJ. unsuccessful; fruitless. We had to abandon our *abortive* attempts.

abrasive ADJ. rubbing away; tending to grind down. Just as *abrasive* cleaning powders can wear away a shiny finish, *abrasive* remarks can wear away a listener's patience. abrade, V.

abridge V. condense or shorten. Because the publishers felt the public wanted a shorter version of *War and Peace,* they proceeded to *abridge* the novel.

abrogate V. abolish. He intended to *abrogate* the decree issued by his predecessor.

■ **abscond** V. depart secretly and hide. The teller *absconded* with the bonds and was not found.

absolute ADJ. complete; totally unlimited; certain. Although the King of Siam was an *absolute* monarch, he did not want to behead his unfaithful wife without *absolute* evidence of her infidelity.

absolve V. pardon (an offense). The father confessor *absolved* him of his sins. absolution, N.

abstain V. refrain; withhold from participation. After considering the effect of alcohol on his athletic performance, he decided to *abstain* from drinking while he trained for the race.

■ **abstemious** ADJ. sparing in eating and drinking; temperate. The drunkards mocked him because of his *abstemious* habits.

abstinence N. restraint from eating or drinking. The doctor recommended total *abstinence* from salted foods. abstain, V.

abstract ADJ. theoretical; not concrete; nonrepresentational. To him, hunger was an *abstract* concept; he had never missed a meal.

abstruse ADJ. obscure; profound; difficult to understand. Baffled by the *abstruse* philosophical texts assigned in class, Dave asked Lexy to explain Kant's *Critique of Pure Reason.*

abusive ADJ. coarsely insulting; physically harmful. An *abusive* parent damages a child both mentally and physically.

abut V. border upon; adjoin. Where our estates *abut,* we must build a fence.

abysmal ADJ. bottomless. His arrogance is exceeded only by his *abysmal* ignorance.

accede V. agree. If I *accede* to this demand for blackmail, I am afraid that I will be the victim of future demands.

accelerate V. move faster. In our science class, we learn how falling bodies *accelerate.*

accessible ADJ. easy to approach; obtainable. We asked our guide whether the ruins were *accessible* on foot.

accessory N. additional object; useful but not essential thing. She bought an attractive handbag as an *accessory* for her dress. also ADJ.

acclaim V. applaud; announce with great approval. The sportscasters *acclaimed* every American victory in the Olympics and decried every American defeat. acclamation, N.

acclimate V. adjust to climate or environment; adapt. One of the difficulties of our present air age is the need of travelers to *acclimate* themselves to their new and often strange environments.

acclivity N. sharp upslope of a hill. The car could not go up the *acclivity* in high gear.

accolade N. award of merit. In Hollywood, an "Oscar" is the highest *accolade*.

accommodate V. oblige or help someone; adjust or bring into harmony; adapt. Mitch always did everything possible to *accommodate* his elderly relatives, from driving them to medical appointments to helping them with paperwork. (secondary meaning)

accomplice N. partner in crime. Because he had provided the criminal with the lethal weapon, he was arrested as an *accomplice* in the murder.

accord N. agreement. She was in complete *accord* with the verdict.

accost V. approach and speak first to a person. When the two young men *accosted* me, I was frightened because I thought they were going to attack me.

accoutre V. equip. The fisherman was *accoutred* with the best that the sporting goods store could supply. accoutrement, N.

accretion N. growth; increase. The *accretion* of wealth marked the family's rise in power.

accrue V. come about by addition. You must pay the interest that has *accrued* on your debt as well as the principal sum. accrual, N.

acerbity N. bitterness of speech and temper. The meeting of the United Nations Assembly was marked with such *acerbity* that little hope of reaching any useful settlement of the problem could be held. acerbic, ADJ.

acetic ADJ. vinegary. The salad had an exceedingly *acetic* flavor.

acidulous ADJ. slightly sour; sharp; caustic. James was unpopular because of his sarcastic and *acidulous* remarks.

acknowledge V. recognize; admit. When pressed for an answer, she *acknowledged* the existence of another motive for the crime.

acme N. peak; pinnacle; highest point. Welles's success in *Citizen Kane* marked the *acme* of his career as an actor; never again did he achieve such popular acclaim.

acoustics N. science of sound; quality that makes a room easy or hard to hear in. Carnegie Hall is liked by music lovers because of its fine *acoustics*.

acquiesce V. assent; agree passively. Although she appeared to *acquiesce* to her employer's suggestions, I could tell she had reservations about the changes he wanted made. acquiescence, N.; acquiescent, ADJ.

acquittal N. deliverance from a charge. His *acquittal* by the jury surprised those who had thought him guilty. acquit, V.

acrid ADJ. sharp; bitterly pungent. The *acrid* odor of burnt gunpowder filled the room after the pistol had been fired.

acrimonious ADJ. stinging; caustic. His tendency to utter *acrimonious* remarks alienated his audience. acrimony, N.

actuarial ADJ. calculating; pertaining to insurance statistics. According to recent *actuarial* tables, life expectancy is greater today than it was a century ago.

actuate V. motivate. I fail to understand what *actuated* you to reply to this letter so nastily.

acuity N. sharpness. In time his youthful *acuity* of vision failed him, and he needed glasses.

acumen N. mental keenness. His business *acumen* helped him to succeed where others had failed.

acute ADJ. quickly perceptive; keen; brief and severe. The *acute* young doctor realized immediately that the gradual deterioration of her patient's once-*acute* hearing was due to a chronic illness, not an *acute* one.

adage N. wise saying; proverb. There is much truth in the old *adage* about fools and their money.

■ **adamant** ADJ. hard; inflexible. He was *adamant* in his determination to punish the wrongdoer. adamancy, N.

adapt V. alter; modify. Some species of animals have become extinct because they could not *adapt* to a changing environment.

addendum N. addition; appendix to book. Jane's editor approved her new comparative literature text but thought it would be even better with an *addendum* on recent developments in literary criticism.

addiction N. compulsive, habitual need. His *addiction* to drugs caused his friends much grief.

addle V. muddle; drive crazy; become rotten. This idiotic plan is confusing enough to *addle* anyone. addled ADJ.

address V. direct a speech to; deal with or discuss. Due to *address* the convention in July, Brown planned to *address* the issue of low-income housing in his speech.

adept ADJ. expert at. She was *adept* at the fine art of irritating people. also N.

adhere V. stick fast. I will *adhere* to this opinion until proof that I am wrong is presented. adhesion, N.; adherence, N.

adherent N. supporter; follower. In the wake of the scandal, the senator's one-time *adherents* quietly deserted him.

adjunct N. something attached to but holding an inferior position. I will entertain this concept as an *adjunct* to the main proposal.

adjuration N. solemn urging. Her *adjuration* to tell the truth did not change the witnesses' testimony. adjure, V.

adjutant N. staff officer assisting the commander; assistant. Though Wellington delegated many tasks to his chief *adjutant*, Lord Fitzroy Somerset, Somerset was in no doubt as to who made all major decisions.

admonish v. warn; reprove. He *admonished* his listeners to change their wicked ways. admonition, N.

adorn v. decorate. Wall paintings and carved statues *adorned* the temple. adornment, N.

adroit ADJ. skillful. His *adroit* handling of the delicate situation pleased his employers.

Word List 1   *Synonyms*

Each of the questions below consists of a word in capital letters, followed by five lettered words or phrases. Choose the lettered word or phrase that is most nearly similar in meaning to the word in capital letters and write the letter of your choice on your answer paper.

1. ABASE (A) incur (B) tax (C) estimate (D) elope (E) humiliate
2. ABERRATION (A) deviation (B) abhorrence (C) dislike (D) absence (E) anecdote
3. ABET (A) conceive (B) wager (C) encourage (D) evade (E) protect
4. ABEYANCE (A) obedience (B) discussion (C) excitement (D) suspended action (E) editorial
5. ABJURE (A) discuss (B) renounce (C) run off secretly (D) perjure (E) project
6. ABLUTION (A) censure (B) forgiveness (C) mutiny (D) survival (E) washing
7. ABNEGATION (A) blackness (B) self-denial (C) selfishness (D) cause (E) effectiveness
8. ABORIGINE (A) first design (B) absolution (C) finale (D) concept (E) primitive inhabitant
9. ABORTIVE (A) unsuccessful (B) consuming (C) financing (D) familiar (E) fruitful
10. ABSTINENCE (A) restrained eating or drinking (B) vulgar display (C) deportment (D) reluctance (E) population
11. ABSTRUSE (A) profound (B) irrespective (C) suspended (D) protesting (E) not thorough
12. ABUT (A) stimulate (B) grasp (C) oppose (D) widen (E) adjoin
13. ABYSMAL (A) bottomless (B) eternal (C) meteoric (D) diabolic (E) internal
14. ACCEDE (A) fail (B) compromise (C) correct (D) consent (E) mollify
15. ACCLIVITY (A) index (B) report (C) upslope of a hill (D) character (E) negotiator

---

Word List 2   adulation-amend

adulation N. flattery; admiration. The rock star thrived on the *adulation* of his groupies and yes-men. adulate, v.

■ **adulterate** v. make impure by mixing with baser substances. It is a crime to *adulterate* foods without informing the buyer.

advent N. arrival. Most Americans were unaware of the *advent* of the Nuclear Age until the news of Hiroshima reached them.

adventitious ADJ. accidental; casual. He found this *adventitious* meeting with his friend extremely fortunate.

adversary N. opponent; enemy. Batman struggled to save Gotham City from the machinations of his wicked *adversary,* the Joker.

adverse ADJ. unfavorable; hostile. *Adverse* circumstances compelled him to close his business.

■ **adversity** N. poverty; misfortune. We must learn to meet *adversity* gracefully.

advert v. refer (to). Since you *advert* to this matter so frequently, you must regard it as important.

advocate v. urge; plead for. The abolitionists *advocated* freedom for the slaves. also N.

aegis N. shield; defense. Under the *aegis* of the Bill of Rights, we enjoy our most treasured freedoms.

■ **aesthetic** ADJ. artistic; dealing with or capable of appreciating the beautiful. The beauty of Tiffany's stained glass appealed to Alice's *aesthetic* sense. aesthete, N.

affable ADJ. courteous. Although he held a position of responsibility, he was an *affable* individual and could be reached by anyone with a complaint.

affected ADJ. artificial; pretended. His *affected* mannerisms irritated many of us who had known him before his promotion. affectation, N.

affidavit N. written statement made under oath. The court refused to accept his statement unless he presented it in the form of an *affidavit.*

affiliation N. joining; associating with. His *affiliation* with the political party was of short duration for he soon disagreed with his colleagues.

affinity N. kinship. She felt an *affinity* with all who suffered; their pains were her pains.

affirmation N. positive assertion; confirmation; solemn pledge by one who refuses to take an oath. Despite Tom's *affirmations* of innocence, Aunt Polly still suspected he had eaten the pie.

affix v. attach or add on; fasten. First the registrar had to *affix* his signature to the license; then he had to *affix* his official seal.

affluence N. abundance; wealth. Foreigners are amazed by the *affluence* and luxury of the American way of life.

affront v. insult; offend. Accustomed to being treated with respect, Miss Challoner was *affronted* by Vidal's offensive behavior. also N.

agape ADJ. openmouthed. She stared, *agape,* at the many strange animals in the zoo.

agenda N. items of business at a meeting. We had so much difficulty agreeing upon an *agenda* that there was very little time for the meeting.

agglomeration N. collection; heap. It took weeks to assort the *agglomeration* of miscellaneous items she had collected on her trip.

aggrandize V. increase or intensify; raise in power, wealth, rank or honor. The history of the past quarter century illustrates how a President may *aggrandize* his power to act aggressively in international affairs without considering the wishes of Congress.

■ **aggregate** ADJ. sum; total. The *aggregate* wealth of this country is staggering to the imagination. also V, N.

aghast ADJ. horrified. He was *aghast* at the nerve of the speaker who had insulted his host.

agility N. nimbleness. The *agility* of the acrobat amazed and thrilled the audience.

agitate V. stir up; disturb. Her fiery remarks *agitated* the already angry mob.

agnostic N. one who is skeptical of the existence or knowability of a god or any ultimate reality. The *agnostic* demanded proof before she would accept the statement of the minister. also ADJ.

agog ADJ. highly excited; intensely curious. We were all *agog* at the news that the celebrated movie star was giving up his career in order to enter a monastery.

agrarian ADJ. pertaining to land or its cultivation. As a result of its recent industrialization, the country is gradually losing its *agrarian* traditions.

alacrity N. cheerful promptness. He demonstrated his eagerness to serve by his *alacrity* in executing the orders of his master.

alchemy N. medieval chemistry. The changing of baser metals into gold was the goal of the students of *alchemy*. alchemist, N.

alcove N. nook; recess. Though their apartment lacked a full-scale dining room, an *alcove* adjacent to the living room made an adequate breakfast nook for the young couple.

alias N. an assumed name. John Smith's *alias* was Bob Jones. also ADV.

alienate V. make hostile; separate. Her attempts to *alienate* the two friends failed because they had complete faith in each other.

alimentary ADJ. supplying nourishment. The *alimentary* canal in our bodies is so named because digestion of foods occurs there.

alimony N. payments made to an ex-spouse after divorce. Because Tony had supported Tina through medical school, on their divorce he asked the court to award him $500 a month in *alimony*.

allay V. calm; pacify. The crew tried to *allay* the fears of the passengers by announcing that the fire had been controlled .

allege V. state without proof. It is *alleged* that she had worked for the enemy. allegation, N.

allegory N. story in which characters are used as symbols; fable. *Pilgrim's Progress* is an *allegory* of the temptations and victories of the human soul. allegorical, ADJ.

■ **alleviate** V. relieve. This should *alleviate* the pain; if it does not, we shall have to use stronger drugs.

alliteration N. repetition of beginning sound in poetry. "The furrow followed free" is an example of *alliteration*.

allocate V. assign. Even though the Red Cross had *allocated* a large sum for the relief of the sufferers of the disaster, many people perished.

alloy N. a mixture as of metals. *Alloys* of gold are used more frequently than the pure metal.

allude V. refer indirectly. Try not to *allude* to this matter in his presence because the topic annoys him.

allure V. entice; attract. *Allured* by the song of the sirens, the helmsman steered the ship toward the reef. also N.

allusion N. indirect reference. The *allusions* to mythological characters in Milton's poems bewilder the reader who has not studied Latin.

alluvial ADJ. pertaining to soil deposits left by running water. The farmers found the *alluvial* deposits at the mouth of the river very fertile.

aloof ADJ. apart; reserved. Shy by nature, she remained *aloof* while all the rest conversed.

aloft ADV. upward. The sailor climbed *aloft* into the rigging.

altercation N. noisy quarrel. Throughout the *altercation*, not one sensible word was uttered.

altruistic ADJ. unselfishly generous; concerned for others. In providing tutorial assistance and college scholarships for hundreds of economically disadvantaged youths, Eugene Lang performed a truly *altruistic* deed. altruism, N.

■ **amalgamate** V. combine; unite in one body. The unions will attempt to *amalgamate* their groups into one national body.

amass V. collect. The miser's aim is to *amass* and hoard as much gold as possible.

amazon N. female warrior. Ever since the days of Greek mythology we refer to strong and aggressive women as *amazons*.

ambidextrous ADJ. capable of using either hand with equal ease. A switch-hitter in baseball should be naturally *ambidextrous*.

ambience N. environment; atmosphere. She went to the restaurant not for the food but for the *ambience*.

■ **ambiguous** ADJ. unclear or doubtful in meaning. His *ambiguous* instructions misled us; we did not know which road to take. ambiguity, N.

■ **ambivalence** N. the state of having contradictory or conflicting emotional attitudes. Torn between loving her parents one minute and hating them the next, she was confused by the *ambivalence* of her feelings. ambivalent, ADJ.

amble N. moving at an easy pace. When she first mounted the horse, she was afraid to urge the animal to go faster than a gentle *amble*. also V.

ambrosia N. food of the gods. *Ambrosia* was supposed to give immortality to any human who ate it.

ambulatory ADJ. able to walk. He was described as an *ambulatory* patient because he was not confined to his bed.

■ **ameliorate** V. improve. Many social workers have attempted to *ameliorate* the conditions of people living in the slums.

amenable ADJ. readily managed; willing to be led. He was *amenable* to any suggestions that came from those he looked up to; he resented advice from his inferiors.

amend V. correct; change, generally for the better. Hoping to *amend* his condition, he left Vietnam for the United States.

Test

Word List 2   *Antonyms*

Each of the questions below consists of a word in capital letters, followed by five lettered words or phrases. Choose the lettered word or phrase that is most nearly opposite in meaning to the word in capital letters and write the letter of your choice on your answer paper.

16. ADULATION (A) youth (B) purity (C) brightness (D) defense (E) criticism
17. ADVOCATE (A) define (B) oppose (C) remove (D) inspect (E) discern
18. AFFABLE (A) rude (B) ruddy (C) needy (D) useless (E) conscious
19. AFFECTED (A) weary (B) unfriendly (C) divine (D) unfeigned (E) slow
20. AFFLUENCE (A) poverty (B) fear (C) persuasion (D) consideration (E) neglect
21. AGILITY (A) awkwardness (B) solidity (C) temper (D) harmony (E) warmth
22. ALACRITY (A) slowness (B) plenty (C) filth (D) courtesy (E) despair
23. ALLEVIATE (A) endure (B) worsen (C) enlighten (D) maneuver (E) humiliate
24. ALLURE (A) hinder (B) repel (C) ignore (D) leave (E) wallow
25. ALOOF (A) triangular (B) gregarious (C) comparable (D) honorable (E) savory
26. AMALGAMATE (A) equip (B) separate (C) generate (D) materialize (E) repress
27. AMBIGUOUS (A) salvageable (B) corresponding (C) responsible (D) clear (E) auxiliary
28. AMBLE (A) befriend (B) hasten (C) steal (D) browse (E) prattle
29. AMBULATORY (A) convalescent (B) valedictory (C) bedridden (D) emergency (E) congenital
30. AMELIORATE (A) make slow (B) make sure (C) make young (D) make worse (E) make able

Word List 3   amenities-apothecary

amenities N. convenient features; courtesies. In addition to the customary *amenities* for the business traveler—fax machines, modems, a health club—the hotel offers the services of a butler versed in the social *amenities*.

amiable ADJ. agreeable; lovable. His *amiable* disposition pleased all who had dealings with him.

amicable ADJ. friendly. The dispute was settled in an *amicable* manner with no harsh words.

amiss ADJ. wrong; faulty. Seeing her frown, he wondered if anything were *amiss*. also ADV.

amity N. friendship. Student exchange programs such as the Experiment in International Living were established to promote international *amity*.

amnesia N. loss of memory. Because she was suffering from *amnesia*, the police could not get the young girl to identify herself.

amnesty N. pardon. When his first child was born, the king granted *amnesty* to all in prison.

amoral ADJ. nonmoral. The *amoral* individual lacks a code of ethics; he should not be classified as immoral.

amorous ADJ. moved by sexual love; loving. Don Juan was known for his *amorous* adventures.

amorphous ADJ. shapeless; vague; indeterminate. John was subject to panic attacks that left him prey to vague, *amorphous* fears: he knew he was terrified, but could neither define nor explain the cause of his terror.

amphibian ADJ. able to live both on land and in water. Frogs are classified as *amphibian*. also N.

amphitheater N. oval building with tiers of seats. The spectators in the *amphitheater* cheered the gladiators.

ample ADJ. abundant. He had *ample* opportunity to dispose of his loot before the police caught up with him.

amplify V. enlarge. Her attempts to *amplify* her remarks were drowned out by the jeers of the audience.

amputate V. cut off part of body; prune. When the doctors had to *amputate* Ted Kennedy's leg to prevent the spread of cancer, he did not let the loss of his leg keep him from participating in sports.

amok (also **amuck**) ADV. in a state of rage. The police had to be called in to restrain him after he ran *amok* in the department store.

amulet N. charm; talisman. Around her neck she wore the *amulet* that the witch doctor had given her.

■ **anachronism** N. something or someone misplaced in time. Shakespeare's reference to clocks in *Julius Caesar* is an *anachronism;* no clocks existed in Caesar's time. anachronistic, ADJ.

analgesic ADJ. causing insensitivity to pain. The *analgesic* qualities of this lotion will provide temporary relief.

■ **analogous** ADJ. comparable. She called our attention to the things that had been done in an *analogous* situation and recommended that we do the same.

analogy N. similarity; parallelism. Your *analogy is* not a good one because the two situations are not similar.

anarchist   N. person who rebels against the established order. Only the total overthrow of all governmental regulations would satisfy the *anarchist*.

■ anarchy   N. absence of governing body; state of disorder. The assassination of the leaders led to a period of *anarchy*.

anathema   N. solemn curse; someone or something that is despised. He heaped *anathema* upon his foe.

anathematize   V. curse. The high priest *anathematized* the heretic.

anchor   V. secure or fasten firmly; be fixed in place. We set the post in concrete to *anchor* it in place. anchorage, N.

ancillary   ADJ. serving as an aid or accessory; auxiliary. In an *ancillary* capacity Doctor Watson was helpful; however, Holmes could not trust the good doctor to solve a perplexing case on his own. also N.

anecdote   N. short account of an amusing or interesting event. Rather than make concrete proposals for welfare reform, President Reagan told *anecdotes* about poor people who became wealthy despite their impoverished backgrounds.

anemia   N. condition in which blood lacks red corpuscles. The doctor ascribes her tiredness to *anemia*. anemic, ADJ.

anesthetic   N. substance that removes sensation with or without loss of consciousness. His monotonous voice acted like an *anesthetic*; his audience was soon asleep. anesthesia, N.

anguish   N. acute pain; extreme suffering. Visiting the site of the explosion, Premier Gorbachev wept to see the *anguish* of the victims and their families.

angular   ADJ. sharp-cornered; stiff in manner. His features, though *angular*, were curiously attractive.

animadversion   N. critical remark. He resented the *animadversions* of his critics, particularly because he realized they were true.

animated   ADJ. lively. Her *animated* expression indicated a keenness of intellect. animation, N.

animosity   N. active enmity. He incurred the *animosity* of the ruling class because he advocated limitations of their power.

animus   N. hostile feeling or intent. The *animus* of the speaker became obvious to all when he began to indulge in sarcastic and insulting remarks.

annals   N. records; history. In the *annals* of this period, we find no mention of democratic movements.

anneal   V. reduce brittleness and improve toughness by heating and cooling. After the glass is *annealed*, it will be less subject to chipping and cracking.

annihilate   V. destroy. The enemy in its revenge tried to *annihilate* the entire population.

annotate   V. comment; make explanatory notes. In the appendix to the novel, the critic sought to *annotate* many of the more esoteric references.

annuity   N. yearly allowance. The *annuity* he set up with the insurance company supplements his social security benefits so that he can live very comfortably without working.

annul   V. make void. The parents of the eloped couple tried to *annul* the marriage.

anodyne   N. drug that relieves pain; opiate. His pain was so great that no *anodyne* could relieve it.

anoint   V. consecrate. The prophet Samuel *anointed* David with oil, crowning him king of Israel.

■ anomalous   ADJ. abnormal; irregular. He was placed in the *anomalous* position of seeming to approve procedures that he despised.

anomaly   N. irregularity. A bird that cannot fly is an *anomaly*.

anonymity   N. state of being nameless; anonymousness. The donor of the gift asked the college not to mention him by name; the dean readily agreed to respect his *anonymity*. anonymous, ADJ.

antagonistic   ADJ. hostile; opposed. Despite his lawyers' best efforts to stop him, the angry prisoner continued to make *antagonistic* remarks to the judge. antagonism, N.

antecede   V. precede. The invention of the radiotelegraph *anteceded* the development of television by a quarter of a century.

antecedents   N. preceding events or circumstances that influence what comes later; early life; ancestors. Before giving permission for Drummle to marry Estella, Miss Havisham had a few questions about the young man's birth and *antecedents*.

antediluvian   ADJ. antiquated; ancient. The *antediluvian* customs had apparently not changed for thousands of years. also N.

anthropoid   ADJ. manlike. The gorilla is the strongest of the anthropoid animals. also N.

anthropologist   N. student of the history and science of humankind. *Anthropologists* have discovered several relics of prehistoric humans in this area.

anthropomorphic   ADJ. having human form or characteristics. Primitive religions often have deities with *anthropomorphic* characteristics.

anticlimax   N. letdown in thought or emotion. After the fine performance in the first act, the rest of the play was an anticlimax. anticlimactic, ADJ.

■ antipathy   N. aversion; dislike. His extreme *antipathy* to dispute caused him to avoid argumentative discussions with his friends.

antiquated   ADJ. obsolete; outdated. Accustomed to editing his papers on word processors, Philip thought typewriters were too *antiquated* for him to use.

antiseptic   N. substance that prevents infection. It is advisable to apply an *antiseptic* to any wound, no matter how slight or insignificant. also ADJ.

antithesis   N. contrast; direct opposite of or to. This tyranny was the *antithesis* of all that he had hoped for, and he fought it with all his strength. antithetical or antithetic, ADJ.

anvil   N. iron block used in hammering out metals. After heating the iron horseshoe in the forge, the blacksmith picked it up with his tongs and set it on the *anvil*.

apathetic   ADJ. indifferent. He felt *apathetic* about the conditions he had observed and did not care to fight against them. apathy, N.

■ **apathy** N. lack of caring; indifference. A firm believer in democratic government, she could not understand the *apathy* of people who never bothered to vote.

ape V. imitate or mimic. He was suspended for a week because he had *aped* the principal in front of the whole school.

aperture N. opening; hole. She discovered a small *aperture* in the wall, through which the insects had entered the room.

apex N. tip; summit; climax. He was at the *apex* of his career.

aphasia N. loss of speech due to injury or illness. After the automobile accident, the victim had periods of *aphasia* when he could not speak at all or could only mumble incoherently.

aphorism N. pithy maxim. An *aphorism* differs from an adage in that it is more philosophical or scientific. aphoristic, ADJ.

apiary N. a place where bees are kept. Although he spent many hours daily in the *apiary*, he was very seldom stung by a bee.

aplomb N. poise; composure. Wellington's nonchalance and *aplomb* in the heat of battle always heartened his followers.

apocalyptic ADJ. prophetic; pertaining to revelations; especially of disaster. His *apocalyptic* remarks were dismissed by his audience as wild surmises.

apocryphal ADJ. untrue; made up. To impress his friends, Tom invented *apocryphal* tales of his adventures in the big city.

apogee N. highest point. When the moon in its orbit is furthest away from the earth, it is at its *apogee*.

apoplexy N. stroke; loss of consciousness followed by paralysis. He was crippled by an attack of *apoplexy*.

apostate N. one who abandons his religious faith or political beliefs. Because he switched from one party to another, his former friends shunned him as an *apostate*. apostasy, N.

apothecary N. druggist. In Holland, *apothecaries* still sell spices as well as ointments and pills.

Test

Word List 3   *Antonyms*

Each of the questions below consists of a word in capital letters, followed by five lettered words or phrases. Choose the lettered word or phrase that is most nearly opposite in meaning to the word in capital letters and write the letter of your choice on your answer paper.

31. AMICABLE (A) penetrating (B) compensating (C) unfriendly (D) zigzag (E) inescapable
32. AMORAL (A) unusual (B) unfriendly (C) ethical (D) suave (E) firm
33. AMORPHOUS (A) nauseous (B) obscene (C) providential (D) definite (E) happy
34. AMPLIFY (A) distract (B) infer (C) publicize (D) decrease (E) pioneer
35. ANALOGOUS (A) not comparable (B) not capable (C) not culpable (D) not corporeal (E) not congenial
36. ANATHEMATIZE (A) locate (B) deceive (C) regulate (D) radiate (E) bless

37. ANEMIC (A) pallid (B) cruel (C) red-blooded (D) ventilating (E) hazardous
38. ANIMATED (A) worthy (B) dull (C) humorous (D) lengthy (E) realistic
39. ANIMUS (A) pterodactyl (B) bastion (C) giraffe (D) grimace (E) favor
40. ANOMALY (A) desperation (B) requisition (C) registry (D) regularity (E) radiation
41. ANONYMOUS (A) desperate (B) signed (C) defined (D) expert (E) written
42. ANTEDILUVIAN (A) transported (B) subtle (C) isolated (D) celebrated (E) modern
43. ANTIPATHY (A) profundity (B) objection (C) willingness (D) abstention (E) fondness
44. ANTITHESIS (A) velocity (a) maxim (C) similarity (D) acceleration (E) reaction
45. APHASIA (A) volubility (B) necessity (C) pain (D) crack (E) prayer

Word List 4   apothegm-astigmatism

apothegm N. pithy, compact saying. Proverbs are *apothegms* that have become familiar sayings.

apotheosis N . deification; glorification. The Roman empress Livia envied the late emperor his *apotheosis*; she hoped that on her death she, too, would be exalted to the rank of a god.

appall V. dismay; shock. We were *appalled* by the horrifying conditions in the city's jails.

apparition N. ghost; phantom. Hamlet was uncertain about the identity of the *apparition* that had appeared and spoken to him.

■ **appease** V. pacify; soothe. We have discovered that, when we try to *appease* our enemies, we encourage them to make additional demands.

appellation N. name; title. He was amazed when the witches hailed him with his correct *appellation*.

append V. attach. I shall *append* this chart to my report.

application N. diligent attention. Pleased with how well Tom had whitewashed the fence, Aunt Polly praised him for his *application*. (secondary meaning) apply, V.

apposite ADJ. appropriate; fitting. He was always able to find the *apposite* phrase, the correct expression for every occasion.

appraise V. estimate value of. It is difficult to *appraise* old paintings; it is easier to call them priceless. appraisal, N.

appreciate V. be thankful for; increase in worth; be thoroughly conscious of. Little Orphan Annie truly *appreciated* the stocks Daddy Warbucks gave her, whose value *appreciated* considerably over the years.

apprehend V. arrest (a criminal); dread; perceive. The police will *apprehend* the culprit and convict him before long.

apprehensive ADJ. fearful; discerning. His *apprehensive* glances at the people who were walking in the street revealed his nervousness.

apprise V. inform. When he was *apprised* of the dangerous weather conditions, he decided to postpone his trip.

■ **approbation** N. approval. Wanting her parents' regard, she looked for some sign of their *approbation*.

■ **appropriate** V. acquire; take possession of for one's own use. The ranch owners *appropriated* the lands that had originally been set aside for the Indians' use.

appurtenances N. subordinate possessions. He bought the estate and all its *appurtenances*.

apropos PREP. with reference to; regarding. I find your remarks *apropos* of the present situation timely and pertinent. also ADJ. and ADV.

aptitude N. fitness; talent. The counselor evaluated his *aptitudes* before advising him about the career he should follow.

aquiline ADJ. curved, hooked. He can be recognized by his *aquiline* nose, curved like the beak of the eagle.

arable ADJ. fit for plowing. The land was no longer *arable;* erosion had removed the valuable topsoil.

arbiter N. person with power to decide a matter in dispute; judge. As an *arbiter* in labor disputes, she has won the confidence of the workers and the employers.

arbitrary ADJ. unreasonable or capricious; tyrannical. The coach claimed the team lost because the umpire made some *arbitrary* calls.

arbitrate V. act as judge. She was called upon to *arbitrate* the dispute between the union and the management.

arboretum N. place where different varieties of trees and shrubs are studied and exhibited. Walking along the treelined paths of the *arboretum,* Rita noted poplars, firs, and some particularly fine sycamores.

arcade N. a covered passageway, usually lined with shops. The *arcade* was popular with shoppers because it gave them protection from the summer sun and the winter rain.

arcane ADJ. secret; mysterious. What was *arcane* to us was clear to the psychologist.

archaeology N. study of artifacts and relics of early mankind. The professor of *archaeology* headed an expedition to the Gobi Desert in search of ancient ruins.

archaic ADJ. antiquated. "Methinks," "thee," and "thou" are *archaic* words that are no longer part of our normal vocabulary.

archetype N. prototype; primitive pattern. The Brooklyn Bridge was the *archetype* of the many spans that now connect Manhattan with Long Island and New Jersey.

archipelago N. group of closely located islands. When he looked at the map and saw the *archipelagoes* in the South Seas, he longed to visit them.

archives N. public records; place where public records are kept. These documents should be part of the *archives* so that historians may be able to evaluate them in the future.

ardor N. heat; passion; zeal. Katya's *ardor* was contagious; soon all her fellow demonstrators were busily making posters and handing out flyers, inspired by her *ardent* enthusiasm for the cause. ardent, ADJ.

■ **arduous** ADJ. hard; strenuous. Her *arduous* efforts had sapped her energy.

argot N. slang. In the *argot of* the underworld, she "was taken for a ride."

aria N. operatic solo. At her Metropolitan Opera audition, Marian Anderson sang an *aria* from *Norma.*

arid ADJ. dry; barren. The cactus has adapted to survive in an *arid* environment.

aristocracy N. hereditary nobility; privileged class. Americans have mixed feelings about hereditary *aristocracy*: we say all men are created equal, but we describe particularly outstanding people as natural *aristocrats.*

armada N. fleet of warships. Queen Elizabeth's navy was able to defeat the mighty *armada* that threatened the English coast.

aromatic ADJ. fragrant. Medieval sailing vessels brought *aromatic* herbs from China to Europe,

arraign V. charge in court; indict. After his indictment by the Grand Jury, the accused man was *arraigned* in the County Criminal Court.

array V. marshal; draw up in order. His actions were bound to *array* public sentiment against him. also N.

array V. clothe; adorn. She liked to watch her mother *array* herself in her finest clothes before going out for the evening. also N.

arrears N. being in debt. He was in *arrears* with his payments on the car.

arrogance N. pride, haughtiness. The *arrogance* of the nobility was resented by the middle class.

arroyo N. gully. Until the heavy rains of the past spring, this *arroyo* had been a dry bed.

articulate ADJ. effective; distinct. Her *articulate* presentation of the advertising campaign impressed her employers. also V.

artifacts N. products of primitive culture. Archaeologists debated the significance of the *artifacts* discovered in the ruins of Asia Minor and came to no conclusion.

artifice N. deception; trickery. The Trojan War proved to the Greeks that cunning and *artifice* were often more effective than military might.

artisan N. a manually skilled worker. Artists and *artisans* alike are necessary to the development of a culture.

artless ADJ. without guile; open and honest. Red Riding Hood's *artless* comment, "Grandma, what big eyes you have!" indicates the child's innocent surprise at her "grandmother's" changed appearance.

ascendancy N. controlling influence. President Marcos failed to maintain his *ascendancy* over the Philippines.

ascertain V. find out for certain. Please *ascertain* her present address.

■ **ascetic** ADJ. practicing self-denial; austere. The wealthy young man could not understand the *ascetic* life led by the monks. also N.

asceticism N. doctrine of self-denial. We find *asceticism* practiced in many monasteries.

ascribe V. refer; attribute; assign. I can *ascribe* no motive for her acts.

aseptic ADJ. preventing infection; having a cleansing effect. Hospitals succeeded in lowering the mortality rate as soon as they introduced *aseptic* conditions.

ashen ADJ. ash-colored; deadly pale. Her face was *ashen* with fear.

asinine ADJ. stupid. Your *asinine* remarks prove that you have not given this problem any serious consideration.

askance ADV. with a sideways or indirect look. Looking *askance* at her questioner, she displayed her scorn.

askew ADV. crookedly; slanted; at an angle. When he placed his hat *askew* upon his head, his observers laughed .

asperity N. sharpness (of temper). These remarks, spoken with *asperity*, stung the boys to whom they had been directed.

aspersion N. slanderous remark. Do not cast *aspersions* on her character.

aspirant N. seeker after position or status. Although I am an *aspirant* for public office, I am not willing to accept the dictates of the party bosses. also ADJ.

aspiration N. noble ambition Youth's *aspirations* should be as lofty as the stars.

assail V. assault. He was *assailed* with questions after his lecture.

assay V. analyze; evaluate. When they *assayed* the ore, they found that they had discovered a very rich vein. also N.

assent V. agree; accept. It gives me great pleasure to *assent* to your request. also N.

assert V. state strongly or positively; insist on or demand recognition of (rights, claims, etc.). When Jill *asserted* that nobody else in the junior class had such an early curfew, her parents *asserted* themselves, telling her that if she didn't get home by nine o'clock she would be grounded for the week. assertion, N.

assessment N. estimation; appraisal. I would like to have your *assessment* of the situation in South Africa.

assiduous ADJ. diligent. It took Rembrandt weeks of *assiduous* labor before he was satisfied with his portrait of his son.

assimilate V. absorb; cause to become homogenous. The manner in which the United States was able to *assimilate* the hordes of immigrants during the nineteenth and early part of the twentieth centuries will always be a source of pride.

■ **assuage** V. ease; lessen (pain). Your messages of cheer should *assuage* her suffering. assuagement, N.

assumption N. something taken for granted; the taking over or taking possession of. The young princess made the foolish *assumption* that the regent would not object to her *assumption* of power. assume, V.

assurance N. promise or pledge; certainty; self-confidence. When Guthrie gave Guinness his *assurance* that rehearsals were going well, he spoke with such *assurance* that Guinness was convinced. assure, V. assured, ADJ.

asteroid N. small planet. *Asteroids* have become commonplace to the readers of interstellar travel stories in science fiction magazines.

astigmatism N. eye defect that prevents proper focus. As soon as his parents discovered that the boy suffered from *astigmatism,* they took him to the optometrist for corrective glasses.

Test

Word List 4   *Synonyms and Antonyms*

Each of the following questions consists of a word in capital letters, followed by five lettered words or phrases. Choose the lettered word or phrase that is most nearly similar or opposite in meaning to the word in capital letters and write the letter of your choice on your answer paper.

46. APPEASE (A) agitate (B) qualify (C) display (D) predestine (E) interrupt

47. APPOSITE (A) inappropriate (B) diagonal (C) exponential (D) unobtrusive (E) discouraging

48. APPREHEND (A) obviate (B) set free (C) shiver (D) understand (E) contrast

49. APTITUDE (A) sarcasm (B) inversion (C) adulation (D) lack of talent (E) gluttony

50. AQUILINE (A) watery (B) hooked (C) refined (D) antique (E) rodentlike

51. ARCHAIC (A) youthful (B) cautious (C) antiquated (D) placated (E) buttressed

52. ARDOR (A) zeal (B) paint (C) proof (D) group (E) excitement

53. ARRAY (A) swindle (B) lighten (C) strip bare (D) set free (E) cleanse

54. ARROYO (A) crevice (B) gully (C) value (D) food (E) fabric

55. ARTIFICE (A) spite (B) exception (C) anger (D) candor (E) loyalty

56. ARTISAN (A) educator (B) decider (C) sculptor (D) discourser (E) unskilled laborer

57. ASCERTAIN (A) amplify (B) master (C) discover (D) retain (E) explode

58. ASPERITY (A) anguish (B) absence (C) innuendo (D) good temper (E) snake

59. ASSUAGE (A) stuff (B) describe (C) wince (D) worsen (E) introduce

60. ASTEROID (A) Milky Way (B) radiance (C) large planet (D) rising moon (E) setting moon

Word List 5 astral-barb

astral ADJ. relating to the stars. She was amazed at the number of *astral* bodies the new telescope revealed.

astringent ADJ. binding; causing contraction; harsh or severe. The *astringent* quality of the unsweetened lemon juice made swallowing difficult. also N.

astronomical ADJ. enormously large or extensive. The government seemed willing to spend *astronomical* sums on weapons development.

astute ADJ. wise; shrewd. That was a very *astute* observation. I shall heed it.

asunder ADV. into parts; apart. Their points of view are poles *asunder*.

asylum N. place of refuge or shelter; protection. The refugees sought *asylum* from religious persecution in a new land.

asymmetric ADJ. not identical on both sides of a dividing central line. Because one eyebrow was set markedly higher than the other, William's face had a particularly *asymmetric* appearance. asymmetry, N.

atavism N. resemblance to remote ancestors rather than to parents; reversion to an earlier type; throwback. In his love for gardening, Martin seemed an *atavism* to his Tuscan ancestors who lavished great care on their small plots of soil. atavistic, ADJ.

atheistic ADJ. denying the existence of God. His *atheistic* remarks shocked the religious worshippers.

atone V. make amends for; pay for. He knew no way in which he could *atone* for his brutal crime.

atrocity N. brutal deed. In time of war, many *atrocities* are committed by invading armies.

atrophy N. wasting away. Polio victims need physiotherapy to prevent the *atrophy* of affected limbs. also V.

attenuate V. make thin; weaken. By withdrawing their forces, the generals hoped to *attenuate* the enemy lines.

attest V. testify; bear witness. Having served as a member of a grand jury, I can *attest* that our system of indicting individuals is in need of improvement.

attribute N. essential quality. His outstanding *attribute* was his kindness.

attribute V. ascribe; explain. I *attribute* her success in science to the encouragement she received from her parents.

attrition N. gradual wearing down. They decided to wage a war of *attrition* rather than to rely on an all-out attack.

atypical ADJ. not normal. You have cited an *atypical* case. It does not prove anything.

■ **audacious** ADJ. daring; bold. Audiences cheered as Luke Skywalker and Princess Leia made their *audacious,* death-defying leap to freedom and escaped Darth Vader's troops. audacity, N.

audit N. examination of accounts. When the bank examiners arrived to hold their annual *audit,* they discovered the embezzlements of the chief cashier. also V.

augment V. increase. How can we hope to *augment* our forces when our allies are deserting us?

augury N. omen; prophecy. He interpreted the departure of the birds as an *augury* of evil. augur, V.

august ADJ. impressive; majestic. Visiting the palace at Versailles, she was impressed by the *august* surroundings in which she found herself.

aureole N. sun's corona; halo. Many medieval paintings depict saintly characters with *aureoles* around their heads.

auroral ADJ. pertaining to the aurora borealis. The *auroral* display was particularly spectacular that evening.

auspicious ADJ. favoring success. With favorable weather conditions, it was an *auspicious* moment to set sail.

■ **austere** ADJ. strict, stern. His *austere* demeanor prevented us from engaging in our usual frivolous activities.

austerity N. sternness; severity; lack of luxuries. The *austerity* and dignity of the court were maintained by the new justices, who were a strict and solemn group.

authenticate V. prove genuine. An expert was needed to *authenticate* the original Van Gogh painting, distinguishing it from its imitation.

authoritarian ADJ. favoring or exercising total control; non-democratic. The people had no control over their own destiny; they were forced to obey the dictates of the *authoritarian* regime. also N.

authoritative ADJ. having the weight of authority; dictatorial. We accepted her analysis of the situation as *authoritative*.

autocrat N. monarch with supreme power. He ran his office like an *autocrat,* giving no one else any authority.

automaton N. mechanism that imitates actions of humans. Long before science fiction readers became aware of robots, writers were creating stories of *automatons* who could outperform humans.

■ **autonomous** ADJ. self-governing. This island is a colony; however, in most matters, it is *autonomous* and receives no orders from the mother country. autonomy, N.

autopsy N. examination of a dead body; postmortem. The medical examiner ordered an *autopsy* to determine the cause of death. also V.

auxiliary ADJ. offering or providing help; additional or subsidiary. To prepare for the emergency, they built an *auxiliary* power station. also N.

avarice N. greed for wealth. King Midas's *avarice* has been famous for centuries. avaricious, ADJ.

■ **aver** V. state confidently. I wish to *aver* that I am certain of success.

averse ADJ. reluctant. He was *averse to* revealing the sources of his information.

aversion N. firm dislike. Their mutual *aversion* was so great that they refused to speak to one another.

avert v. prevent; turn away. She *averted* her eyes from the dead cat on the highway.

aviary N. enclosure for birds. The *aviary* at the zoo held nearly 300 birds.

avid ADJ. greedy; eager for. He was *avid* for learning and read everything he could get. avidity, N.

avocation N. secondary or minor occupation. His hobby proved to be so fascinating and profitable that gradually he abandoned his regular occupation and concentrated on his *avocation*.

avow v. declare openly. I must *avow* that I am innocent.

avuncular ADJ. like an uncle. *Avuncular* pride did not prevent him from noticing his nephew's shortcomings.

awe N. solemn wonder. The tourists gazed with *awe* at the tremendous expanse of the Grand Canyon.

awl N. pointed tool used for piercing. She used an *awl* to punch additional holes in the leather belt she had bought.

awry ADV. distorted; crooked. He held his head *awry*, giving the impression that he had caught cold in his neck during the night. also ADJ.

axiom N. self-evident truth requiring no proof. Before a student can begin to think along the lines of Euclidean geometry, he must accept certain principles or *axioms*. axiomatic, ADJ.

azure ADJ. sky blue. *Azure* skies are indicative of good weather.

babble v. chatter idly. The little girl *babbled* about her doll. also N.

bacchanalian ADJ. drunken. Emperor Nero attended the *bacchanalian* orgy.

badger v. pester; annoy. She was forced to change her telephone number because she was *badgered* by obscene phone calls.

badinage N. teasing conversation. Her friends at work greeted the news of her engagement with cheerful *badinage*.

baffle v. frustrate; perplex. The new code *baffled* the enemy agents.

bait v. harass; tease. The soldiers *baited* the prisoners, terrorizing them.

baleful ADJ. menacing; deadly. Casting a *baleful* eye at his successful rival, the rejected suitor stole off, vowing to have his revenge.

balk v. stop short, as if faced with an obstacle, and refuse to continue. The chief of police *balked* at sending his officers into the riot-torn area.

balk v. foil. When the warden learned that several inmates were planning to escape, he took steps to *balk* their attempt.

ballast N. heavy substance used to add stability or weight. The ship was listing badly to one side; it was necessary to shift the *ballast* in the hold to get her back on an even keel. also v.

balm N. something that relieves pain. Friendship is the finest *balm* for the pangs of disappointed love.

balmy ADJ. mild; fragrant. A *balmy* breeze refreshed us after the sultry blast.

■ **banal** ADJ. hackneyed; commonplace; trite. His frequent use of clichés made his essay seem *banal*. banality, N.

bandy v. discuss lightly; exchange blows or words. The President refused to *bandy* words with the reporters at the press conference.

bane N. cause of ruin. Lack of public transportation is the *bane* of urban life. baneful, ADJ.

bantering ADJ. good-naturedly ridiculing. They resented his *bantering* remarks because they misinterpreted his teasing as sarcasm.

barb N. sharp projection from fishhook, etc.; pointed comment. The *barb* from the fishhook caught in his finger as he grabbed the fish. barbed, ADJ.

Test

Word List 5 *Synonyms*

Each of the questions below consists of a word in capital letters, followed by five lettered words or phrases. Choose the lettered word or phrase that is most nearly similar in meaning to the word in capital letters and write the letter of your choice on your answer paper.

61. ASTUTE (A) sheer (B) noisy (C) astral (D) unusual (E) clever
62. ATROCITY (A) endurance (B) fortitude (C) session (D) heinous act (E) hatred
63. ATROPHY (A) capture (B) waste away (C) govern (D) award prize (E) defeat
64. ATTENUATE (A) appear (B) be absent (C) weaken (D) testify (E) soothe
65. ATYPICAL (A) superfluous (B) fortitude (C) unusual (D) clashing (E) lovely
66. AUDACITY (A) boldness (B) asperity (C) strength (D) stature (E) anchorage
67. AUGMENT (A) make noble (B) anoint (C) increase (D) harvest (E) reach
68. AUXILIARY (A) righteous (B) prospective (C) assistant (D) archaic (E) mandatory
69. AVARICE (A) easiness (B) greed (C) statement (D) invoice (E) power
70. AVERT (A) entertain (B) transform (C) turn away (D) lead toward (E) displease
71. AWRY (A) recommended (B) commiserating (C) startled (D) crooked (E) psychological
72. BALEFUL (A) doubtful (B) virtual (C) deadly (D) conventional (E) virtuous
73. BALMY (A) venturesome (B) dedicated (C) mild (D) fanatic (E) memorable
74. BANAL (A) philosophical (B) trite (C) dramatic (D) heedless (E) discussed
75. BANEFUL (A) intellectual (B) thankful (C) decisive (D) poisonous (E) remorseful

Word List 6   bard-bluff

bard N. poet. The ancient *bard* Homer sang of the fall of Troy.

barefaced ADJ. shameless; bold; unconcealed. Shocked by Huck Finn's *barefaced* lies, Miss Watson prayed the good Lord would give him a sense of his unregenerate wickedness.

baroque ADJ. highly ornate. Accustomed to the severe, angular lines of modern skyscrapers, they found the flamboyance of *baroque* architecture amusing.

barrage N. barrier laid down by artillery fire; overwhelming profusion. The company was forced to retreat through the *barrage* of heavy cannons.

barrister N. counselor-at-law. Galsworthy started as *a barrister*, but, when he found the practice of law boring, turned to writing.

barterer N. trader. The *barterer* exchanged trinkets for the natives' furs.

bask V. luxuriate; take pleasure in warmth. *Basking* on the beach, she relaxed so completely that she fell asleep.

bastion N. stronghold; something seen as a source of protection. The villagers fortified the town hall, hoping this improvised *bastion* could protect them from the guerrilla raids.

bate V. let down; restrain. Until it was time to open the presents, the children had to *bate* their curiosity. bated, ADJ.

bauble N. trinket; trifle. The child was delighted with the *bauble* she had won in the grab bag.

bawdy ADJ. indecent; obscene. She took offense at his *bawdy* remarks.

beatific ADJ. giving bliss; blissful. The *beatific* smile on the child's face made us very happy.

beatitude N. blessedness; state of bliss, Growing closer to God each day, the mystic achieved a state of indescribable *beatitude.*

bedizen V. dress with vulgar finery. The witch doctors were *bedizened* in their gaudiest costumes.

bedraggle V. wet thoroughly. We were so *bedraggled* by the severe storm that we had to change into dry clothing. bedraggled, ADJ.

befuddle V. confuse thoroughly. His attempts to clarify the situation succeeded only in *befuddling* her further.

beget V. father; produce; give rise to. One good turn may deserve another; it does not necessarily *beget* another.

begrudge V. resent. I *begrudge* every minute I have to spend attending meetings.

beguile V. amuse; delude; cheat. He *beguiled* himself during the long hours by playing solitaire.

behemoth N. huge creature; something of monstrous size or power. Sportscasters nicknamed the linebacker "The *Behemoth.*"

beholden ADJ. obligated; indebted. Since I do not wish to be *beholden* to anyone, I cannot accept this favor.

behoove V. be suited to; be incumbent upon. In this time of crisis, it *behooves* all of us to remain calm and await the instructions of our superiors.

belabor V. explain or go over excessively or to a ridiculous degree; assail verbally. The debate coach warned her student not to bore the audience by *belaboring* his point.

belated ADJ. delayed. He apologized for his *belated* note of condolence to the widow of his friend and explained that he had just learned of her husband's untimely death.

beleaguer V. besiege. As soon as the city was *beleaguered*, life became more subdued as the citizens began their long wait for outside assistance. beleaguered, ADJ.

■ **belie** V. contradict; give a false impression. His coarse, hard-bitten exterior *belied* his innate sensitivity.

belittle V. disparage; depreciate. Parents should not *belittle* their children's early attempts at drawing, but should encourage their efforts.

bellicose ADJ. warlike. His *bellicose* disposition alienated his friends. bellicosity, N.

belligerent ADJ. quarrelsome. Whenever he had too much to drink, he became *belligerent* and tried to pick fights with strangers. belligerence, N.

bemused ADJ. confused; lost in thought; preoccupied. Jill studied the garbled instructions with a *bemused* look on her face.

benediction N. blessing. The appearance of the sun after the many rainy days was like a *benediction.*

benefactor N. gift giver; patron. Scrooge later became Tiny Tim's *benefactor* and gave him gifts.

■ **beneficent** ADJ. kindly; doing good. The overgenerous philanthropist had to curb his *beneficent* impulses before he gave away all his money and left himself with nothing.

beneficiary N. person entitled to benefits or proceeds of an insurance policy, government program, or will. You may change your *beneficiary* as often as you wish.

benevolent ADJ. generous; charitable. His *benevolent* nature prevented him from refusing any beggar who accosted him. benevolence, N.

benign ADJ. kindly; favorable; not malignant. The old man was well liked because of his *benign* attitude toward friend and stranger alike.

benison N. blessing. Let us pray that the *benison* of peace once more shall prevail among the nations of the world.

bent ADJ.; N. determined; natural talent or inclination. *Bent* on advancing in the business world, the secretary-heroine of *Working Girl* had a true *bent* for high finance.

bequeath V. leave to someone by means of a will; hand down. In his will, Father *bequeathed* his watch to Philip; the *bequest* meant a great deal to the boy. bequest, N.

berate v. scold strongly. He feared she would *berate* him for his forgetfulness.

bereavement N. state of being deprived of something valuable or beloved. His friends gathered to console him upon his sudden *bereavement*.

bereft ADJ. deprived of; lacking. The foolish gambler soon found himself *bereft of* funds.

berserk ADV. frenzied. Angered, he went *berserk* and began to wreck the room.

beset v. harass; trouble. Many problems *beset* the American public school system.

besmirch v. soil, defile. The scandalous remarks in the newspaper *besmirch* the reputations of every member of the society.

bestial ADJ. beastlike; brutal; inhuman. The Red Cross sought to put an end to the *bestial* treatment of prisoners of war.

bestow v. confer. He wished to *bestow* great honors upon the hero.

betroth v. become engaged to marry. The announcement that they had become *betrothed* surprised their friends who had not suspected any romance. betrothal, N.

bevy N. large group. The movie actor was surrounded by a *bevy of* starlets.

bicameral ADJ. two-chambered, as a legislative body. The United States Congress is a *bicameral* body.

bicker v. quarrel. The children *bickered* morning, noon and night, exasperating their parents.

biennial ADJ. every two years. The group held *biennial* meetings instead of annual ones.

bifurcated ADJ. divided into two branches; forked. With a *bifurcated* branch and a piece of elastic rubber, he made a crude but effective slingshot.

bigotry N. stubborn intolerance. Brought up in a democratic atmosphere, the student was shocked by the *bigotry* and narrowness expressed by several of his classmates.

bilious ADJ. suffering from indigestion; irritable. His *bilious* temperament was apparent to all who heard him rant about his difficulties.

bilk v. swindle; cheat. The con man specialized in *bilking* insurance companies.

bivouac N. temporary encampment. While in *bivouac*, we spent the night in our sleeping bags under the stars. also v.

bizarre ADJ. fantastic; violently contrasting. The plot of the novel was too *bizarre* to be believed.

blanch v. bleach; whiten. Although age had *blanched* his hair, he was still vigorous and energetic.

bland ADJ. soothing; mild. She used a *bland* ointment for her sunburn. blandness, N.

blandishment N. flattery. Despite the salesperson's *blandishments*, the customer did not buy the outfit.

blasé ADJ. bored with pleasure or dissipation. Your *blasé* attitude gives your students an erroneous impression of the joys of scholarship.

blasphemous ADJ. profane; impious. The people in the room were shocked by his *blasphemous* language. blasphemy, N.

blatant ADJ. extremely obvious; loudly offensive. Caught in a *blatant* lie, the scoundrel had only one regret: he wished that he had lied more subtly. blatancy, N.

bleak ADJ. cold; cheerless. The Aleutian Islands are *bleak* military outposts.

blighted ADJ. suffering from a disease; destroyed. The extent of the *blighted* areas could be seen only when viewed from the air.

blithe ADJ. gay; joyous. Shelley called the skylark a "*blithe* spirit" because of its happy song.

bloated ADJ. swollen or puffed as with water or air. Her *bloated* stomach came from drinking so much water.

blowhard N. talkative boaster. After all Sol's talk about his big show business connections led nowhere, Sally decided he was just another *blowhard*.

bludgeon N. club; heavy-headed weapon. His walking stick served him as a *bludgeon* on many occasions. also v.

bluff N. pretense (of strength); deception; high cliff. Claire thought Lord Byron's boast that he would swim the Hellespont was just a *bluff*; she was astounded when he dove from the high *bluff* into the waters below.

Test

Word List 6   *Antonyms*

Each of the questions below consists of a word in capital letters, followed by five lettered words or phrases. Choose the lettered word or phrase that is most nearly opposite in meaning to the word in capital letters and write the letter of your choice on your answer paper.

76. BAROQUE (A) polished (B) constant (C) transformed (D) simple (E) aglow
77. BEATIFIC (A) glorious (B) dreadful (C) theatrical (D) crooked (E) handsome
78. BELITTLE (A) disobey (B) forget (C) magnify (D) extol (E) envy
79. BELLICOSE (A) peaceful (B) naval (C) amusing (D) piecemeal (E) errant
80. BENIGN (A) tenfold (B) peaceful (C) blessed (D) wavering (E) malignant
81. BENISON (A) curse (B) bachelor (C) wedding (D) orgy (E) tragedy
82. BERATE (A) grant (B) praise (C) refer (D) purchase (E) deny
83. BESTIAL (A) animated (B) noble (C) zoological (D) clear (E) dusky
84. BIGOTRY (A) arrogance (B) approval (C) mourning (D) promptness (E) tolerance

85. BIZARRE (A) roomy (B) veiled (C) subdued
   (D) triumphant (E) normal
86. BLANCH (A) bleach (B) scatter (G) darken
   (D) analyze (E) subdivide
87. BLAND (A) caustic (B) meager (C) soft
   (D) uncooked (E) helpless
88. BLASÉ (A) fiery (B) clever (C) intriguing
   (D) slim (E) ardent
89. BLEAK (A) pale (B) sudden (C) dry (D) narrow
   (E) cheerful
90. BLITHE (A) spiritual (B) profuse (C) cheerless
   (D) hybrid (E) comfortable

Word List 7   blunder-canter

blunder N. error. The criminal's fatal *blunder* led to his capture. also V.

blurt V. utter impulsively. Before she could stop him, he *blurted* out the news.

bode V. foreshadow; portend. The gloomy skies and the sulfurous odors from the mineral springs seemed to *bode* evil to those who settled in the area.

bogus ADJ. counterfeit; not authentic. The police quickly found the distributors of the *bogus* twenty-dollar bills.

boisterous ADJ. violent; rough; noisy. The unruly crowd became even more *boisterous* when he tried to quiet them.

■ **bolster** V. support; reinforce. The debaters amassed file boxes full of evidence to *bolster* their arguments.

■ **bombast** N. pompous, inflated language. Filled with *bombast,* the orator's speech left the audience more impressed with his pomposity than with his logic.

boon N. blessing; benefit. The recent rains that filled our empty reservoirs were a *boon* to the whole community.

boorish ADJ. rude; insensitive. Though Mr. Potts constantly interrupted his wife, she ignored his *boorish* behavior, for she had lost hope of teaching him courtesy.

bouillon N. clear beef soup. The cup of *bouillon* served by the stewards was welcomed by those who had been chilled by the cold ocean breezes.

bountiful ADJ. generous; showing bounty. She distributed gifts in a *bountiful* and gracious manner.

bourgeois N. middle class. The French Revolution was inspired by the *bourgeois,* who resented the aristocracy. also ADJ.

bovine ADJ. cowlike; placid and dull. Nothing excites Esther; even when she won the state lottery, she still preserved her air of *bovine* calm.

bowdlerize V. expurgate. After the film editors had *bowdlerized* the language in the script, the motion picture's rating was changed from "R" to "PG."

brackish ADJ. somewhat saline. He found the only wells in the area were *brackish*; drinking the water made him nauseous.

braggadocio N. boasting. He was disliked because his manner was always full of *braggadocio.*

braggart N. boaster. Modest by nature, she was no *braggart,* preferring to let her accomplishments speak for themselves.

bravado N. swagger; assumed air of defiance. The *bravado* of the young criminal disappeared when he was confronted by the victims of his brutal attack.

brawn N. muscular strength; sturdiness. It takes *brawn* to become a champion weight-lifter. brawny, ADJ.

brazen ADJ. insolent. Her *brazen* contempt for authority angered the officials.

breach N. breaking of contract or duty; fissure; gap. They found a *breach* in the enemy's fortifications and penetrated their lines. also V.

breadth N. width; extent. We were impressed by the *breadth* of her knowledge.

brevity N. conciseness. *Brevity is* essential when you send a telegram or cablegram; you are charged for every word.

brindled ADJ. tawny or grayish with streaks or spots. He was disappointed in the litter because the puppies were *brindled;* he had hoped for animals of a uniform color.

bristling ADJ. rising like bristles; showing irritation. The dog stood there, *bristling* with anger.

brittle ADJ. easily broken; difficult. My employer's *brittle* personality made it difficult for me to get along with her.

broach V. open up. He did not even try to *broach* the subject of poetry.

brocade N. rich, figured fabric. The sofa was covered with expensive *brocade.*

brochure N. pamphlet. This *brochure* on farming was issued by the Department of Agriculture.

brooch N. ornamental clasp. She treasured the *brooch* because it was an heirloom.

brook V. tolerate; endure. The dean would *brook* no interference with his disciplinary actions. (secondary meaning)

browbeat V. bully; intimidate. Billy resisted Ted's attempts to *browbeat* him into handing over his lunch money.

brusque ADJ. blunt; abrupt. She was offended by his *brusque* reply.

bucolic ADJ. rustic; pastoral. The meadow was the scene of *bucolic* gaiety.

buffoonery N. clowning. John Candy's *buffoonery* in *Uncle Buck* was hilarious.

bugaboo N. bugbear; object of baseless terror. If we become frightened by such *bugaboos,* we are no wiser than the birds who fear scarecrows.

bullion N. gold and silver in the form of bars. Much *bullion* is stored in the vaults at Fort Knox.

bulwark N. earthwork or other strong defense; person who defends. The navy is our principal *bulwark* against invasion.

bungle v. spoil by clumsy behavior. I was afraid you would *bungle* this assignment but I had no one else to send.

bureaucracy N. government by bureaus. Many people fear that the constant introduction of federal agencies will create a government by *bureaucracy*.

■ **burgeon** v. grow forth; send out buds. In the spring, the plants that *burgeon* are a promise of the beauty that is to come.

burlesque v. give an imitation that ridicules. In his caricature, he *burlesqued* the mannerisms of his adversary.

burly ADJ. husky; muscular. The *burly* mover lifted the packing crate with ease.

■ **burnish** v. make shiny by rubbing; polish. The maid *burnished* the brass fixtures until they reflected the lamplight.

■ **buttress** v. support; prop up. Just as architects *buttress* the walls of cathedrals with flying *buttresses*, debaters *buttress* their arguments with facts. also N.

buxom ADJ. full-bosomed; plump; jolly. High-fashion models usually are slender rather than *buxom*.

cabal N. small group of persons secretly united to promote their own interests. The *cabal* was defeated when its scheme was discovered.

cache N. hiding place. The detectives followed the suspect until he led them to the *cache* where he had stored his loot. also V.

■ **cacophony** N. discord. Some people seem to enjoy the *cacophony* of an orchestra that is tuning up. cacophonous, ADJ. .

cadaver N. corpse. In some states, it is illegal to dissect *cadavers*.

cadaverous ADJ. like a corpse; pale. From his *cadaverous* appearance, we could see how the disease had ravaged him.

cadence N. rhythmic rise and fall (of words or sounds); beat. Marching down the road, the troops sang out, following the *cadence* set by the sergeant.

cajole v. coax; wheedle. I will not be *cajoled* into granting you your wish. cajolery, N.

calamity N. disaster; misery. As news of the *calamity* spread, offers of relief poured in to the stricken community.

caliber N. ability; capacity. A man of such *caliber* should not be assigned such menial tasks.

calligraphy N. beautiful writing; excellent penmanship. As we examine ancient manuscripts, we become impressed with the *calligraphy* of the scribes.

callous ADJ. hardened; unfeeling. He had worked in the hospital for so many years that he was *callous to* the suffering in the wards. callus, N.

callow ADJ. youthful; immature. In that youthful movement, the leaders were only a little less *callow* than their immature followers.

calorific ADJ. heat-producing. Coal is much more *calorific* than green wood.

calumny N. malicious misrepresentation; slander. He could endure his financial failure, but he could not bear the *calumny* that his foes heaped upon him.

camaraderie N. good-fellowship. What he loved best about his job was the sense of *camaraderie* he and his co-workers shared.

cameo N. shell or jewel carved in relief. Tourists are advised not to purchase *cameos* from the street peddlers of Rome who sell poor specimens of the carver's art.

canard N. unfounded rumor; exaggerated report. It is almost impossible to protect oneself from such a base *canard*.

candor N. frankness. The *candor* and simplicity of his speech impressed all; it was clear he held nothing back. candid, ADJ.

canine ADJ. related to dogs; doglike. Some days the *canine* population of Berkeley seems almost to outnumber the human population.

canker N. any ulcerous sore; any evil. Poverty is a *canker* in the body politic; it must be cured.

canny ADJ. shrewd; thrifty. The *canny* Scotsman was more than a match for the swindlers.

cant N. pious phraseology; jargon of criminals. Angry that the president had slashed the education budget, we dismissed his speech on the importance of education as mere *cant*.

cantankerous ADJ. ill-humored; irritable. Constantly complaining about his treatment and refusing to cooperate with the hospital staff, he was a *cantankerous* patient.

cantata N. story set to music, to be sung by a chorus. The choral society sang the new *cantata* composed by its leader.

canter N. slow gallop. Because the racehorse had outdistanced its competition so easily, the reporter wrote that the race was won in a *canter*. also V.

Test

Word List 7 *Synonyms*

Each of the questions below consists of a word in capital letters, followed by five lettered words or phrases. Choose the lettered word or phrase that is most nearly similar in meaning to the word in capital letters and write the letter of your choice on your answer paper.

91. BOISTEROUS (A) conflicting (B) noisy (C) testimonial (D) grateful (E) adolescent
92. BOMBASTIC (A) sensitive (B) pompous (C) rapid (D) sufficient (E) expensive
93. BOORISH (A) brave (B) oafish (C) romantic (D) speedy (E) dry

94. BOUILLON (A) insight (B) chowder (C) gold (D) clear soup (E) stew
95. BRACKISH (A) careful (B) salty (C) chosen (D) tough (E) wet
96. BRAGGADOCIO (A) weaponry (B) boasting (C) skirmish (D) encounter (E) position
97. BRAZEN (A) shameless (B) quick (C) modest (D) pleasant (E) melodramatic
98. BRINDLED (A) equine (B) pathetic (C) hasty (D) spotted (E) mild tasting
99. BROCHURE (A) opening (B) pamphlet (C) censor (D) bureau (E) pin
100. BUCOLIC (A) diseased (B) repulsive (C) rustic (D) twinkling (E) cold
101. BUXOM (A) voluminous (B) indecisive (C) convincing (D) plump (E) bookish
102. CACHE (A) lock (B) hiding place (C) tide (D) automobile (E) grappling hook
103. CACOPHONY (A) discord (B) dance (C) applause (D) type of telephone (E) rooster
104. CALLOW (A) youthful (B) holy (C) mild (D) colored (E) seated
105. CANDID (A) vague (B) outspoken (C) experienced (D) anxious (E) sallow

---

Word List 8   canto–chameleon

canto N. division of a long poem. Dante's poetic masterpiece *The Divine Comedy* is divided into *cantos*.

canvass V. determine or seek opinions, votes, etc. After *canvassing* the sentiments of his constituents, the congressman was confident that he represented the majority opinion of his district. also N.

capacious ADJ. spacious. In the *capacious* areas of the railroad terminal, thousands of travelers lingered while waiting for their train.

capillary ADJ. having a very fine bore. The changes in surface tension of liquids in *capillary* vessels is of special interest to physicists. also N.

■ **capitulate** V. surrender. The enemy was warned to *capitulate* or face annihilation.

caprice N. whim. She was an unpredictable creature, acting on *caprice*, never taking thought of the consequences.

■ **capricious** ADJ. fickle; incalculable. The storm was *capricious* and changed course constantly.

caption N. title; chapter heading; text under illustration. I find the *captions* that accompany these cartoons very clever and humorous. also V.

captious ADJ. faultfinding. His criticisms were always *captious* and frivolous, never offering constructive suggestions.

carafe N. glass water bottle; decanter. With each dinner, the patron receives a *carafe* of red or white wine.

carapace N. shell covering the back (of a turtle, crab, etc.). At the children's zoo, Richard perched on top of the giant turtle's hard *carapace* as it slowly made its way around the enclosure.

carat N. unit of weight for precious stones; measure of fineness of gold. He gave her a diamond that weighed three *carats* and was mounted in an eighteen-*carat* gold band.

carcinogenic ADJ. causing cancer. Many supposedly harmless substances have been revealed to be *carcinogenic*.

cardinal ADJ. chief. If you want to increase your word power, the *cardinal* rule of vocabulary-building is to read.

careen V. lurch; sway from side to side. The taxicab *careened* wildly as it rounded the corner.

caricature N. distortion; burlesque. The *caricatures* he drew always emphasized personal weaknesses of the people he burlesqued. also V.

carillon N. a set of bells capable of being played. The *carillon* in the bell tower of the Coca-Cola pavilion at the New York World's Fair provided musical entertainment every hour.

carnage N. destruction of life. The *carnage* that can be caused by atomic warfare adds to the responsibilities of our statesmen.

carnal ADJ. fleshly. The public was more interested in *carnal* pleasures than in spiritual matters.

carnivorous ADJ. meat-eating. The lion is a *carnivorous* animal. carnivore, N.

carousal N. drunken revel. The party degenerated into an ugly *carousal*.

carping N. petty criticism; fault-finding. Welcoming constructive criticism, Lexy appreciated her editor's comments, finding them free of *carping*. also ADJ.

carrion N. rotting flesh of a dead body. Buzzards are nature's scavengers; they eat the *carrion* left behind by other predators.

cartographer N. map-maker. Though not a professional *cartographer*, Tolkien was able to construct a map of his fictional world.

cascade N. small waterfall. We could not appreciate the beauty of the many *cascades* as we made detours around each of them to avoid getting wet. also V.

caste N. one of the hereditary classes in Hindu society; social stratification; prestige. The differences created by *caste* in India must be wiped out if true democracy is to prevail in that country.

■ **castigation** N. punishment; severe criticism. Sensitive even to mild criticism, Woolf could not bear the *castigation* that she found in certain reviews. castigate, V.

casualty N. serious or fatal accident. The number of automotive *casualties* on this holiday weekend was high.

cataclysm N. deluge; upheaval. A *cataclysm* such as the French Revolution affects all countries. cataclysmic, ADJ.

■ **catalyst** N. agent that brings about a chemical change while it remains unaffected and unchanged. Many chemical reactions cannot take place without the presence of a *catalyst*.

catapult N. slingshot; hurling machine. Airplanes are sometimes launched from battleships by *catapults*. also V.

cataract N. great waterfall; eye abnormality. She gazed with awe at the mighty *cataract* known as Niagara Falls.

catastrophe N. calamity. The Johnstown flood was a *catastrophe*.

catechism N. book for religious instruction; instruction by question and answer. He taught by engaging his pupils in a *catechism* until they gave him the correct answer.

categorical ADJ. without exceptions; unqualified; absolute. Though the captain claimed he was never, never sick at sea, he finally qualified his *categorical* denial: he was "hardly ever" sick at sea.

catharsis N. purging or cleansing of any passage of the body. Aristotle maintained that tragedy created a *catharsis* by purging the soul of base concepts.

cathartic N. purgative. Some drugs act as laxatives when taken in small doses but act as *cathartics* when taken in much larger doses. ADJ.

catholic ADJ. universal; wide-ranging liberal. He was extremely *catholic* in his taste and read everything he could find in the library.

caucus N. private meeting of members of a party to select officers or determine policy. At the opening of Congress the members of the Democratic Party held a *caucus* to elect the majority leader of the House and the party whip.

caulk V. to make watertight (by plugging seams). When water from the shower leaked into the basement, we knew it was time to *caulk* the tiles at the edges of the shower stall.

causal ADJ. implying a cause-and-effect relationship. The psychologist maintained there was a *causal* relationship between the nature of one's early childhood experiences and one's adult personality. causality, N.

caustic ADJ. burning; sarcastically biting. The critic's *caustic* remarks angered the hapless actors who were the subjects of his sarcasm.

cauterize V. burn with hot iron or caustic. In order to prevent infection, the doctor *cauterized* the wound.

cavalcade N. procession; parade. As described by Chaucer, the *cavalcade* of Canterbury pilgrims was a motley group.

cavalier ADJ. casual and offhand; arrogant. Sensitive about having her ideas taken lightly, Marcia felt insulted by Mark's *cavalier* dismissal of her suggestion.

cavil V. make frivolous objections. I respect your sensible criticisms, but I dislike the way you *cavil* about unimportant details. also N.

cede V. transfer; yield title to. I intend to *cede* this property to the city.

celerity N. speed; rapidity. Hamlet resented his mother's *celerity* in remarrying within a month after his father's death.

celestial ADJ. heavenly. She spoke of the *celestial* joys that awaited virtuous souls in the hereafter.

celibate ADJ. abstaining from sexual intercourse; unmarried. Though the late Havelock Ellis wrote extensively about sexual customs and was considered an expert in such matters, recent studies maintain he was *celibate* throughout his life. celibacy, N.

censor N. overseer of morals; person who eliminates inappropriate matter. Soldiers dislike having their mail read by a *censor* but understand the need for this precaution. also V.

censorious ADJ. critical. *Censorious* people delight in casting blame.

censure V. blame; criticize. He was *censured* for his inappropriate behavior. also N.

centaur N. mythical figure, half man and half horse. I was particularly impressed by the statue of the *centaur* in the Roman Hall of the museum.

centigrade ADJ. denoting a widely used temperature scale (basically same as Celsius). On the *centigrade* thermometer, the freezing point of water is zero degrees.

centrifugal ADJ. radiating; departing from the center. Many automatic drying machines remove excess moisture from clothing by *centrifugal* force.

■ **centrifuge** N. machine that separates substances by whirling them. At the dairy, we employ a *centrifuge* to separate cream from milk. also V.

centripetal ADJ. tending toward the center. Does *centripetal* force or the force of gravity bring orbiting bodies to the earth's surface?

centurion N. Roman army officer. Because he was in command of a company of one hundred soldiers, he was called a *centurion*.

cerebral ADJ. pertaining to the brain or intellect. The content of philosophical works is *cerebral* in nature and requires much thought.

cerebration N. thought. Mathematics problems sometimes require much *cerebration*.

ceremonious ADJ. marked by formality. Ordinary dress would be inappropriate at so *ceremonious* an affair.

cessation N. stopping. The workers threatened a *cessation* of all activities if their demands were not met. cease, V.

cession N. yielding to another; ceding. The *cession* of Alaska to the United States is discussed in this chapter.

chafe V. warm by rubbing; make sore by rubbing. The collar *chafed* his neck. also N.

chaff N. worthless products of an endeavor. When you separate the wheat from the *chaff*, be sure you throw out the *chaff*.

chaffing ADJ. bantering; joking. Sometimes his flippant and *chaffing* remarks annoy us.

chagrin N. vexation; disappointment. Her refusal to go with us filled us with *chagrin*.

chalice N. goblet; consecrated cup. In a small room adjoining the cathedral, many ornately decorated *chalices* made by the most famous European goldsmiths were on display.

chameleon N. lizard that changes color in different situations. Like the *chameleon*, he assumed the political coloration of every group he met.

Test

Word List 8 *Antonyms*

Each of the questions below consists of a word in capital letters, followed by five lettered words or phrases. Choose the lettered word or phrase that is most nearly opposite in meaning to the word in capital letters and write the letter of your choice on your answer paper.

106. CAPACIOUS (A) warlike (B) cordial (C) curious (D) not spacious (E) not capable
107. CAPRICIOUS (A) satisfied (B) insured (C) photographic (D) scattered (E) steadfast
108. CAPTIOUS (A) tolerant (B) capable (C) frivolous (D) winning (E) recollected
109. CARNAL (A) impressive (B) minute (C) spiritual (D) actual (E) private
110. CARNIVOROUS (A) gloomy (B) tangential (C) productive (D) weak (E) vegetarian
111. CARPING (A) rapid (B) uncritical (C) unintellectual (D) illegal (E) terse
112. CASTIGATION (A) commendation (B) patience (C) generosity (D) understatement (E) honesty
113. CATEGORICAL (A) negative (B) ironic (C) impartial (D) qualified (E) permanent
114. CATHOLIC (A) religious (B) pacific (C) narrow (D) weighty (E) funny
115. CELERITY (A) assurance (B) state (C) acerbity (D) delay (E) infamy
116. CELIBATE (A) investing (B) married (C) retired (D) commodious (E) dubious
117. CENSURE (A) process (B) enclose (C) interest (D) praise (E) penetrate
118. CENTRIFUGAL (A) centripetal (B) ephemeral (C) lasting (D) barometric (E) algebraic
119. CESSATION (A) premium (B) gravity (C) beginning (D) composition (E) apathy
120. CHAFFING (A) achieving (B) serious (C) capitalistic (D) sneezing (E) expensive

Word List 9 champion-colander

champion V. support militantly. Martin Luther King, Jr., won the Nobel Peace Prize because he *championed* the oppressed in their struggle for equality. also N.

chaotic ADJ. in utter disorder. He tried to bring order into the *chaotic* state of affairs. chaos, N.

charisma N. divine gift; great popular charm or appeal. Political commentators have deplored the importance of a candidate's *charisma* in these days of television campaigning.

charlatan N. quack; pretender to knowledge. When they realized that the Wizard didn't know how to get them back to Kansas, Dorothy and her friends were sure they'd been duped by a *charlatan*.

chary ADJ. cautious; sparing or restrained about giving. A prudent, thrifty New Englander, DeWitt was as *chary* of investing money in junk bonds as he was *chary* of paying people unnecessary compliments.

chase V. ornament a metal surface by indenting. With his hammer, he carefully *chased* an intricate design onto the surface of the chalice. (secondary meaning)

chasm N. abyss. They could not see the bottom of the *chasm*.

chassis N. framework and working parts of an automobile. Examining the car after the accident, the owner discovered that the body had been ruined but that the *chassis* was unharmed.

chaste ADJ. pure. Her *chaste* and decorous garb was appropriately selected for the solemnity of the occasion. chastity, N.

chasten V. discipline; punish in order to correct. Whom God loves, God *chastens*.

chastise V. punish. I must *chastise* you for this offense.

■ **chauvinist** N. blindly devoted patriot. A *chauvinist* cannot recognize any faults in his country, no matter how flagrant they may be. chauvinistic, ADJ.

check V. stop motion; curb or restrain. Thrusting out her arm, Grandma *checked* Bobby's lunge at his sister. "Young man," she said, "you'd better *check* your temper."(secondary meaning)

checkered ADJ. marked by changes in fortune. During his *checkered* career he had lived in palatial mansions and in dreary boardinghouses.

cherubic ADJ. angelic; innocent-looking. With her cheerful smile and rosy cheeks, she was a particularly *cherubic* child.

chicanery N. trickery. Your deceitful tactics in this case are indications of *chicanery*.

chide V. scold. Grandma began to *chide* Steven for his lying.

chimerical ADJ. fantastic; highly imaginative. Poe's *chimerical* stories are sometimes too morbid for reading in bed. chimera, N.

chivalrous ADJ. courteous; faithful; brave. *Chivalrous* behavior involves noble words and good deeds.

choleric ADJ. hot-tempered. His flushed, angry face indicated a *choleric* nature.

choreography N. art of dancing. Martha Graham introduced a form of *choreography* that seemed awkward and alien to those who had been brought up on classic ballet.

chronic ADJ. long established, as a disease. The doctors were finally able to attribute his *chronic* headaches and nausea to traces of formaldehyde gas in his apartment.

chronicle V. report; record (in chronological order). The gossip columnist was paid to *chronicle* the latest escapades of the socially prominent celebrities. also N.

churlish ADJ. boorish; rude. Dismayed by his *churlish* manners at the party, the girls vowed never to invite him again.

ciliated ADJ. having minute hairs. The paramecium is a *ciliated,* one-celled animal.

cipher N. nonentity; worthless person or thing. She claimed her ex-husband was a total *cipher* and wondered why she had ever married him.

cipher N. secret code. Lacking his code book, the spy was unable to decode the message sent to him in *cipher.*

circlet N. small ring; band. This tiny *circlet* is very costly because it is set with precious stones.

circuitous ADJ. roundabout. Because of the traffic congestion on the main highways, she took a *circuitous* route. circuit, N.

circumlocution N. indirect or roundabout expression. He was afraid to call a spade a spade and resorted to *circumlocutions* to avoid direct reference to his subject.

circumscribe V. limit; confine. Although I do not wish to *circumscribe* your activities, I must insist that you complete this assignment before you start anything else.

circumspect ADJ. prudent; cautious. Investigating before acting, she tried always to be *circumspect.*

circumvent V. outwit; baffle. In order to *circumvent* the enemy, we will make two preliminary attacks in other sections before starting our major campaign.

citadel N. fortress. The *citadel* overlooked the city like a protecting angel.

cite V. quote; commend. She could *cite* passages in the Bible from memory. citation, N.

civil ADJ. having to do with citizens or the state; courteous and polite. Although Internal Revenue Service agents are *civil* servants, they are not always *civil* to suspected tax evaders.

clairvoyant ADJ., N. having foresight; fortuneteller. Cassandra's *clairvoyant* warning was not heeded by the Trojans. clairvoyance, N.

clamber V. climb by crawling. She *clambered* over the wall.

clamor N. noise. The *clamor* of the children at play outside made it impossible for her to take a nap. also V.

clandestine ADJ. secret. After avoiding their chaperon, the lovers had a *clandestine* meeting.

clangor N. loud, resounding noise. The blacksmith was accustomed to the *clangor of* hammers on steel.

clapper N. striker (tongue) of a bell. Wishing to be undisturbed by the bell, Dale wound his scarf around the *clapper* to muffle its striking.

clarion ADJ. shrill, trumpetlike sound. We woke to the *clarion* call of the bugle.

claustrophobia N. fear of being locked in. His fellow classmates laughed at his *claustrophobia* and often threatened to lock him in his room.

clavicle N. collarbone. Even though he wore shoulder pads, the football player broke his *clavicle* during a practice scrimmage.

cleave V. split asunder. The lightning *cleaves* the tree in two. cleavage, N. cloven, ADJ.

cleft N. split. Erosion caused a *cleft* in the huge boulder. also ADJ.

clemency N. disposition to be lenient; mildness, as of the weather. The lawyer was pleased when the case was sent to Judge Smith's chambers because Smith was noted for her *clemency* toward first offenders.

cliché N. phrase dulled in meaning by repetition. High school compositions are often marred by such *clichés* as "strong as an ox."

clientele N. body of customers. The rock club attracted a young, stylish *clientele.*

climactic ADJ. relating to the highest point. When he reached the *climactic* portions of the book, he could not stop reading. climax, N.

clime N. region; climate. His doctor advised him to move to a milder *clime.*

clique N. small, exclusive group. She charged that a *clique* had assumed control of school affairs.

cloister N. monastery or convent. The nuns lived in the *cloister.*

clout N. great influence (especially political or social). Gatsby wondered whether he had enough *clout* to be admitted to the exclusive club.

cloying ADJ. distasteful (because excessive); excessively sweet or sentimental. Disliking the *cloying* sweetness of standard wedding cakes, Jody and Tom chose a homemade carrot cake for their reception. cloy, V.

■ **coagulate** V. thicken; congeal; clot. Even after you remove the pudding from the burner, it will continue to *coagulate* as it stands. coagulant, N.

coalesce V. combine; fuse. The brooks *coalesce* into one large river.

■ **coda** N. concluding section of a musical or literary composition. The piece concluded with a distinctive *coda* that strikingly brought together various motifs.

coddle V. treat gently; pamper. Don't *coddle* the children so much; they need a taste of discipline.

codicil N. supplement to the body of a will. This *codicil* was drawn up five years after the writing of the original will.

codify V. arrange (laws, rules) as a code; classify. We need to take the varying rules and regulations of the different health agencies and *codify* them into a national health code.

coercion N. use of force. They forced him to obey, but only by great *coercion.* coerce, V.

coeval ADJ. living at the same time as; contemporary. *Coeval* with the dinosaur, the pterodactyl flourished during the Mesozoic era.

cog N. tooth projecting from a wheel. A bicycle chain moves through a series of *cogs* in order to propel the bike.

■ **cogent** ADJ. convincing. She presented *cogent* arguments to the jury.

cogitate V. think over. *Cogitate* on this problem; the solution will come.

cognate ADJ. related linguistically; allied by blood; similar or akin in nature. The English word "mother" is *cognate* to the Latin word "mater," whose influence is visible in the words "maternal" and "maternity." also N.

cognitive ADJ. having to do with knowing or perceiving related to the mental processes. Though Jack was emotionally immature, his *cognitive* development was admirable; he was very advanced intellectually.

cognizance N. knowledge. During the election campaign, the two candidates were kept in full *cognizance* of the international situation.

cohere V. stick together. Solids have a greater tendency to *cohere* than liquids.

cohesion N. tendency to keep together. A firm believer in the maxim "Divide and conquer," the emperor, by lies and trickery, sought to disrupt the *cohesion* of the free nations.

cohorts N. armed band. Caesar and his Roman *cohorts* conquered almost all of the known world.

coiffure N. hairstyle. You can make a statement with your choice of *coiffure*: in the '60's many African-Americans affirmed their racial heritage by wearing their hair in Afros.

coincident ADJ. occurring at the same time. Some people find the *coincident* events in Hardy's novels annoyingly improbable. coincidence, N.

colander N. utensil with perforated bottom used for straining. Before serving the spaghetti, place it in a *colander* to drain it.

Word List 9   *Synonyms*

Each of the questions below consists of a word in capital letters, followed by five lettered words or phrases. Choose the lettered word or phrase that is most nearly similar in meaning to the word in capital letters and write the letter of your choice on your answer paper.

121. CHASTE (A) loyal (B) timid (C) curt (D) pure (E) outspoken
122. CHIDE (A) unite (B) fear (C) record (D) skid (E) scold
123. CHIMERICAL (A) developing (B) brief (C) distant (D) economical (E) fantastic
124. CHOLERIC (A) musical (B) episodic (C) hotheaded (D) global (E) seasonal
125. CHURLISH (A) marine (B) economical (C) impolite (D) compact (E) young
126. CILIATED (A) foolish (B) swift (C) early (D) constructed (E) hairy
127. CIRCUITOUS (A) indirect (B) complete (C) obvious (D) aware (E) tortured

128. CITE (A) galvanize (B) visualize (C) locate (D) quote (E) signal
129. CLANDESTINE (A) abortive (B) secret (C) tangible (D) doomed (E) approved
130. CLAUSTROPHOBIA (A) lack of confidence (B) fear of spiders (C) love of books (D) fear of grammar (E) fear of closed places
131. CLEFT (A) split (B) waterfall (C) assembly (D) adherence (E) surplus
132. CLICHÉ (A) increase (B) vehicle (C) morale (D) platitude (E) pique
133. COERCE (A) recover (B) begin (C) force (D) license (E) ignore
134. COGNIZANCE (A) policy (B) knowledge (C) advance (D) omission (E) examination
135. COHERE (A) hold together (B) occur simultaneously (C) recollect (D) materialize (E) understand

Word List 10   **collaborate-congenital**

collaborate V. work together. Two writers *collaborated* in preparing this book.

collage N. work of art put together from fragments. Scraps of cloth, paper doilies, and old photographs all went into her *collage*.

collate V. examine in order to verify authenticity; arrange in order. They *collated* the newly found manuscripts to determine their age.

collateral N. security given for loan. The sum you wish to borrow is so large that it must be secured by *collateral*.

collation N. a light meal. Tea sandwiches and cookies were offered at the *collation*.

colloquial ADJ. pertaining to conversational or common speech. Your use of *colloquial* expressions in a formal essay such as the one you have presented spoils the effect you hope to achieve.

colloquy N. informal discussion. I enjoy our *colloquies*, but I sometimes wish that they could be made more formal and more searching.

■ **collusion** N. conspiring in a fraudulent scheme. The swindlers were found guilty of *collusion*.

colossal ADJ. huge. Radio City Music Hall has a *colossal* stage.

colossus N. gigantic statue. The legendary *Colossus* of Rhodes, a bronze statue of the sun god that dominated the harbor of the Greek seaport, was one of the Seven Wonders of the World.

comatose ADJ. in a coma; extremely sleepy. The long-winded orator soon had his audience in a *comatose* state.

combustible ADJ. easily burned. After the recent outbreak of fires in private homes, the fire commissioner ordered that all *combustible* materials be kept in safe containers. also N.

comely ADJ. attractive; agreeable. I would rather have a poor and *comely* wife than a rich and homely one.

comestible N. something fit to be eaten. The roast turkey and other *comestibles,* the wines, and the excellent service made this Thanksgiving dinner particularly memorable.

comeuppance N. rebuke; deserts. After his earlier rudeness, we were delighted to see him get his *comeuppance.*

comity N. courtesy; civility. A spirit of *comity* should exist among nations.

commandeer V. to draft for military purposes; to take for public use. The policeman *commandeered* the first car that approached and ordered the driver to go to the nearest hospital.

commemorative ADJ. remembering; honoring. The new *commemorative* stamp honors the late Martin Luther King, Jr.

■ **commensurate** ADJ. equal in extent. Your reward will be *commensurate* with your effort.

commiserate V. feel or express pity or sympathy for. Her friends *commiserated* with the widow.

commodious ADJ. spacious and comfortable. After sleeping in small roadside cabins, they found their hotel suite *commodious.*

communal ADJ. held in common; of a group of people. When they were divorced, they had trouble dividing their *communal* property.

compact N. agreement; contract. The signers of the Mayflower *Compact* were establishing a form of government.

compact ADJ. tightly packed; firm; brief. His short, *compact* body was better suited to wrestling than to basketball.

compatible ADJ. harmonious; in harmony with. They were *compatible* neighbors, never quarreling over unimportant matters. compatibility, N.

compelling ADJ. overpowering; irresistible in effect. The prosecutor presented a well-reasoned case, but the defense attorney's *compelling* arguments for leniency won over the jury.

compendium N. brief, comprehensive summary. This text can serve as a *compendium* of the tremendous amount of new material being developed in this field.

compensatory ADJ. making up for; repaying. Can a *compensatory* education program make up for the inadequate schooling he received in earlier years?

compilation N. listing of statistical information in tabular or book form. The *compilation* of available scholarships serves a very valuable purpose.

complacent ADJ. self-satisfied. There was a *complacent* look on his face as he examined his paintings. complacency, N.

■ **complaisant** ADJ. trying to please; obliging. The courtier obeyed the king's orders in a *complaisant* manner.

complement V. complete; consummate; make perfect. The waiter recommended a glass of port to *complement* the cheese. also N.

compliance N. conformity in fulfilling requirements; readiness to yield. The design for the new school had to be in *compliance* with the local building code.

■ **compliant** ADJ. yielding. He was *compliant* and ready to go along with his friends' desires.

complicity N. participation; involvement. You cannot keep your *complicity* in this affair secret very long; you would be wise to admit your involvement immediately.

component N. element; ingredient. I wish all the *components* of my stereo system were working at the same time.

comport V. bear one's self; behave. He *comported* himself with great dignity.

composure N. mental calmness. Even the latest work crisis failed to shake her *composure.*

compound V. combine; constitute; pay interest; increase. The makers of the popular cold remedy *compounded* a nasal decongestant with an antihistamine. also N.

comprehensive ADJ. thorough; inclusive. This book provides a *comprehensive* review of verbal and math skills for the SAT.

compress V. close; squeeze; contract. She *compressed* the package under her arm.

comprise V. include; consist of. If the District of Columbia were to be granted statehood, the United States of America would *comprise* fifty-one states, not just fifty.

compromise V. adjust; endanger the interests or reputation of. Your presence at the scene of the dispute *compromises* our claim to neutrality in this matter. also N.

compunction N. remorse. The judge was especially severe in his sentencing because he felt that the criminal had shown no *compunction* for his heinous crime.

compute V. reckon; calculate. He failed to *compute* the interest, so his bank balance was not accurate.

concatenate V. link as in a chain. It is difficult to understand how these events could *concatenate* as they did without outside assistance.

concave ADJ. hollow. The back-packers found partial shelter from the storm by huddling against the *concave* wall of the cliff.

concede V. admit; yield. Despite all the evidence Monica had assembled, Mark refused to *concede* that she was right.

conceit N. whimsical idea; extravagant metaphor. He was an entertaining companion, always expressing himself in amusing *conceits* and witty turns of phrase. (secondary meaning)

concentric ADJ. having a common center. The target was made of *concentric* circles.

conception N. beginning; forming of an idea. At the first *conception* of the work, he was consulted. conceive, V.

concerted ADJ. mutually agreed on; done together. The Girl Scouts in the troop made a concerted effort to raise funds for their annual outing, and emitted a concerted sigh when their leader announced that they had reached their goal.

concession N. an act of yielding. Before they could reach an agreement, both sides had to make certain concessions.

■ **conciliatory** ADJ. reconciling; soothing. She was still angry despite his conciliatory words. conciliate, V.

concise ADJ. brief and compact When you define a new word, be concise: the shorter the definition, the easier it is to remember.

conclave N. private meeting. He was present at all their conclaves as an unofficial observer.

conclusive ADJ. decisive; ending all debate. When the stolen books turned up in John's locker, we finally had conclusive evidence of the identity of the mysterious thief.

concoct V. prepare by combining; make up in concert. How did the inventive chef ever concoct such a strange dish? concoction, N.

concomitant N. that which accompanies. Culture is not always a concomitant of wealth. also ADJ.

concord N. harmony. Watching Tweedledum and Tweedledee battle, Alice wondered why the two brothers could not manage to live in concord.

concur V. agree. Did you concur with the decision of the court or did you find it unfair?

concurrent ADJ. happening at the same time. In America, the colonists were resisting the demands of the mother country; at the concurrent moment in France, the middle class was sowing the seeds of rebellion.

condescend V. bestow courtesies with a superior air. The king condescended to grant an audience to the friends of the condemned man. condescension, N.

condign ADJ. adequate; deservedly severe. The public approved the condign punishment for the crime.

condiments N. seasonings; spices. Spanish food is full of condiments.

condole V. express sympathetic sorrow. His friends gathered to condole with him over his loss. condolence, N.

■ **condone** V. overlook; forgive; give tacit approval; excuse. Unlike Widow Douglass, who condoned Huck's minor offenses, Miss Watson did nothing but scold.

conducive ADJ. helpful; contributive. Rest and proper diet are conducive to good health.

conduit N. aqueduct; passageway for fluids. Water was brought to the army in the desert by an improvised conduit from the adjoining mountain.

confidant N. trusted friend. He had no confidants with whom he could discuss his problems at home.

confiscate V. seize; commandeer. The army confiscated all available supplies of uranium.

conflagration N. great fire. In the conflagration that followed the 1906 earthquake, much of San Francisco was destroyed.

confluence N. flowing together; crowd. They built the city at the confluence of two rivers.

conformity N. harmony; agreement. In conformity with our rules and regulations, I am calling a meeting of our organization.

confound V. confuse; puzzle. No mystery could confound Sherlock Holmes for long.

congeal V. freeze; coagulate. His blood congealed in his veins as he saw the dread monster rush toward him.

congenial ADJ. pleasant; friendly. My father loved to go out for a meal with congenial companions.

congenital ADJ. existing at birth. His congenital deformity disturbed his parents.

Test

Word List 10 *Synonyms and Antonyms*

Each of the following questions consists of a word in capital letters, followed by five lettered words or phrases. Choose the lettered word or phrase that is most nearly similar or opposite in meaning to the word in capital letters and write the letter of your choice on your answer paper.

136. COLLATION (A) furor (B) emphasis (C) distillery (D) spree (E) lunch

137. COLLOQUIAL (A) burnt (B) polished (C) political (D) gifted (E) problematic

138. COLLOQUY (A) dialect (B) diversion (C) announcement (D) discussion (E) expansion

139. COMATOSE (A) cozy (B) restrained (C) alert (D) dumb (E) grim

140. COMBUSTIBLE (A) flammable (B) industrious (C) waterproof (D) specific (E) plastic

141. COMELY (A) yielding (B) unattractive (C) extremely sleepy (D) equal in extent (E) roving

142. COMMISERATE (A) communicate (B) expand (C) repay (D) diminish (E) sympathize

143. COMMODIOUS (A) numerous (B) yielding (C) leisurely (D) limited (E) expensive

144. COMPLIANT (A) numerous (B) veracious (C) soft (D) adamant (E) livid

145. CONCILIATE (A) defend (B) activate (C) integrate (D) quarrel (E) react

146. CONCOCT (A) thrive (B) wonder (C) intrude (D) drink (E) invent

147. CONDONE (A) build (B) evaluate (C) pierce (D) infuriate (E) overlook

148. CONFISCATE (A) discuss (B) discover (C) seize (D) exist (E) convey

149. CONFORMITY (A) agreement (B) ambition (C) confinement (D) pride (E) restraint

150. CONGENITAL (A) slight (B) obscure (C) thorough (D) existing at birth (E) classified

Word List 11   conglomeration-countermand

conglomeration N. mass of material sticking together. In such a *conglomeration* of miscellaneous statistics, it was impossible to find a single area of analysis.

congruence N. correspondence of parts; harmonious relationship. The student demonstrated the *congruence* of the two triangles by using the hypotenuse-arm theorem.

conifer N. pine tree; cone-bearing tree. According to geologists, the *conifers* were the first plants to bear flowers.

conjecture N. surmise; guess. I will end all your *conjectures;* I admit I am guilty as charged. also V.

conjugal ADJ. pertaining to marriage. Their dreams of *conjugal* bliss were shattered as soon as their temperaments clashed.

conjure V. summon a devil; practice magic; imagine; invent. He *conjured* up an image of a reformed city and had the voters completely under his spell.

connivance N. pretense of ignorance of something wrong; assistance; permission to offend. With the *connivance* of his friends, he plotted to embarrass the teacher. connive, V.

■ **connoisseur** N. person competent to act as a judge of art, etc.; a lover of an art. She had developed into a *connoisseur* of fine china.

connotation N. suggested or implied meaning of an expression. Foreigners frequently are unaware of the *connotations* of the words they use.

connubial ADJ. pertaining to marriage or the matrimonial state. In his telegram, he wished the newlyweds a lifetime of *connubial* bliss.

consanguinity N. kinship. The lawsuit developed into a test of the *consanguinity* of the claimant to the estate.

conscientious ADJ. scrupulous; careful. A *conscientious* editor, she checked every definition for its accuracy.

conscript N. draftee; person forced into military service. Did Rambo volunteer to fight in Vietnam, or was he a *conscript*, drafted against his will? also V.

consecrate V. dedicate; sanctify. We shall *consecrate* our lives to this noble purpose.

■ **consensus** N. general agreement. The *consensus* indicates that we are opposed to entering into this pact.

consequential ADJ. pompous; self-important. Convinced of his own importance, the actor strutted about the dressing room with a *consequential* air.

conservatory N. school of the fine arts (especially music or drama). A gifted violinist, Marya was selected to study at the *conservatory.*

consign V. deliver officially; entrust; set apart. The court *consigned* the child to her paternal grandmother's care. consignment, N.

consistency N. absence of contradictions; dependability; uniformity; degree of thickness. Holmes judged puddings and explanations on their *consistency:* he liked his puddings without lumps and his explanations without improbabilities.

console V. lessen sadness or disappointment; give comfort. When her father died, Marius did his best to *console* Cosette. consolation, N.

consonance N. harmony; agreement. Her agitation seemed out of *consonance* with her usual calm.

consort V. associate with. We frequently judge people by the company with whom they *consort.*

consort N. husband or wife. The search for a *consort* for the young Queen Victoria ended happily.

conspiracy N. treacherous plot. Brutus and Cassius joined in the *conspiracy* to kill Julius Caesar.

constituent N. supporter. The congressman received hundreds of letters from angry *constituents* after the Equal Rights Amendment failed to pass.

constraint N. compulsion; repression of feelings. There was a feeling of *constraint* in the room because no one dared to criticize the speaker. constrain, V.

construe V. explain; interpret. If I *construe* your remarks correctly, you disagree with the theory already advanced.

consummate ADJ. complete. I have never seen anyone who makes as many stupid errors as you do; you must be a *consummate* idiot. also V.

contagion N. infection. Fearing *contagion,* they took drastic steps to prevent the spread of the disease.

contaminate V. pollute. The sewage system of the city so *contaminated* the water that swimming was forbidden.

contempt N. scorn; disdain. Even if you feel superior to others, it is unwise to show your *contempt* for them. contemptuous, contemptible, ADJ.

contend V. struggle; compete; assert earnestly. In *Revolt of the Black Athlete,* sociologist Harry Edwards *contends* that young black athletes have been exploited by some college recruiters. contention, N.

■ **contentious** ADJ. quarrelsome. We heard loud and *contentious* noises in the next room.

contest V. dispute. The defeated candidate attempted to *contest* the election results.

context N. writings preceding and following the passage quoted. Because these lines are taken out of *context,* they do not convey the message the author intended.

contiguous ADJ. adjacent to; touching upon. The two countries are *contiguous* for a few miles; then they are separated by the gulf.

continence N. self-restraint; sexual chastity. She vowed to lead a life of *continence.* continent, ADJ.

contingent ADJ. conditional. The continuation of this contract is *contingent* on the quality of your first output. contingency, N.

contortions N. twistings; distortions. As the effects of the opiate wore away, the *contortions* of the patient became more violent and demonstrated how much pain she was enduring.

contraband N. illegal trade; smuggling; smuggled goods. The Coast Guard tries to prevent *contraband* in U.S. waters. also ADJ.

contravene V. contradict; oppose: infringe on or transgress. Mr. Barrett did not expect his frail daughter Elizabeth to *contravene* his will by eloping with Robert Browning.

contrite ADJ. penitent. Her *contrite* tears did not influence the judge when he imposed sentence. contrition, N.

contrived ADJ. forced; artificial; not spontaneous. Feeling ill at ease with his new in-laws, James made a few *contrived* attempts at conversation and then retreated into silence.

controvert V. oppose with arguments; contradict. To *controvert* your theory will require much time but it is essential that we disprove it.

contumacious ADJ. disobedient; resisting authority. The *contumacious* mob shouted defiantly at the police. contumacy, N.

contusion N. bruise. She was treated for *contusions* and abrasions.

■ **conundrum** N. riddle; difficult problem. During the long car ride, she invented *conundrums* to entertain the children.

convene V. assemble. Because much needed legislation had to be enacted, the governor ordered the legislature to *convene* in special session by January 15.

convention N. social or moral custom; established practice. Flying in the face of *convention*, George Sand (Amandine Dudevant) shocked her contemporaries by taking lovers and wearing men's clothes.

conventional ADJ. ordinary; typical. His *conventional* upbringing left him wholly unprepared for his wife's eccentric family.

■ **converge** V. come together. Marchers *converged* on Washington for the great Save Our Cities—Save Our Children March.

conversant ADJ. familiar with. The lawyer is *conversant* with all the evidence.

converse N. opposite. The inevitable *converse* of peace is not war but annihilation.

convert N. one who has adopted a different religion or opinion. On his trip to Japan, though the President spoke at length about the merits of American automobiles, he made few *converts* to his beliefs. also V.

convex ADJ. curving outward. He polished the *convex* lens of his telescope.

conveyance N. vehicle; transfer. During the transit strike, commuters used various kinds of *conveyances*.

conviction N. strongly held belief. Nothing could shake his *conviction* that she was innocent. (secondary meaning)

convivial ADJ. festive; gay; characterized by joviality. The *convivial* celebrators of the victory sang their college songs.

convoke V. call together. Congress was *convoked* at the outbreak of the emergency. convocation, N.

■ **convoluted** ADJ. coiled around; involved; intricate. His argument was so *convoluted* that few of us could follow it intelligently.

copious ADJ. plentiful. She had *copious* reasons for rejecting the proposal.

coquette N. flirt. Because she refused to give him an answer to his proposal of marriage, he called her a *coquette*. also V.

cordial ADJ. gracious; heartfelt. Our hosts greeted us at the airport with a *cordial* welcome and a hearty hug.

cordon N. extended line of men or fortifications to prevent access or egress. The police *cordon* was so tight that the criminals could not leave the area. also V.

cornice N. projecting molding on building (usually above columns). Because the stones forming the *cornice* had been loosened by the storms, the police closed the building until repairs could be made.

cornucopia N. horn overflowing with fruit and grain; symbol of abundance. The encyclopedia salesman claimed the new edition was a veritable *cornucopia* of information, an inexhaustible source of knowledge for the entire family.

corollary N. consequence; accompaniment. Brotherly love is a complex emotion, with sibling rivalry its natural *corollary*.

corporeal ADJ. bodily; material. He was not a churchgoer; he was interested only in *corporeal* matters.

corpulent ADJ. very fat. The *corpulent* man resolved to reduce. corpulence, N.

correlation N. mutual relationship. He sought to determine the *correlation* that existed between ability in algebra and ability to interpret reading exercises. correlate, V., N.

corroborate V. confirm. Unless we find a witness to *corroborate* your evidence, it will not stand up in court.

corrosive ADJ. eating away by chemicals or disease. Stainless steel is able to withstand the effects of *corrosive* chemicals. corrode, V. corrosion, N.

corrugated ADJ. wrinkled; ridged. She wished she could smooth away the wrinkles from his *corrugated* brow.

cosmic ADJ. pertaining to the universe; vast. *Cosmic* rays derive their name from the fact that they bombard the earth's atmosphere from outer space. cosmos, N.

coterie N. group that meets socially; select circle. After his book had been published, he was invited to join the literary *coterie* that lunched daily at the hotel.

countenance V. approve; tolerate. He refused to *countenance* such rude behavior on their part.

countenance N. face. When José saw his newborn daughter, a proud smile spread across his *countenance*.

countermand V. cancel; revoke. The general *countermanded* the orders issued in his absence.

Test

Word List 11   *Synonyms*

Each of the questions below consists of a word in capital letters, followed by five lettered words or phrases. Choose the lettered word or phrase that is most nearly similar in meaning to the word in capital letters and write the letter of your choice on your answer paper.

151. CONJECTURE (A) magic (B) guess (C) position (D) form (E) place
152. CONNOISSEUR (A) gourmand (B) lover of art (C) humidor (D) delinquent (E) interpreter
153. CONSANGUINITY (A) kinship (B) friendship (C) bloodletting (D) relief (E) understanding
154. CONSENSUS (A) general agreement (B) project (C) insignificance (D) sheaf (E) crevice
155. CONSTRUE (A) explain (B) promote (C) reserve (D) erect (E) block
156. CONTAMINATE (A) arrest (B) prepare (C) pollute (D) beam (E) inform
157. CONTENTIOUS (A) squealing (B) surprising (C) quarrelsome (D) smug (E) creative
158. CONTINENCE (A) humanity (B) research (C) embryology (D) bodies of land (E) self-restraint
159. CONTRABAND (A) purpose (B) rogue (C) rascality (D) difficulty (E) smuggling
160. CONTRITE (A) smart (B) penitent (C) restful (D) recognized (E) perspiring
161. CONTROVERT (A) turn over (B) contradict (C) mind (D) explain (E) swing
162. CONVENE (A) propose (B) restore (C) question (D) gather (E) motivate
163. CONVERSANT (A) ignorant (B) speaking (C) incorporated (D) familiar (E) pedantic
164. COPIOUS (A) plentiful (B) cheating (C) dishonorable (D) adventurous (E) inspired
165. CORPULENT (A) regenerate (B) obese (C) different (D) hungry (E) bloody

Word List 12   counterpart-decelerate

counterpart N. a thing that completes another; things very much alike. Night and day are *counterparts*.

coup N. highly successful action or sudden attack. As the news of his *coup* spread throughout Wall Street, his fellow brokers dropped by to congratulate him.

couple v. join; unite. The Flying Karamazovs *couple* expert juggling and amateur joking in their nightclub act.

courier N. messenger. The publisher sent a special *courier* to pick up the manuscript.

covenant N. agreement. We must comply with the terms of the *covenant*.

covert ADJ. secret; hidden; implied. She could understand the *covert* threat in the letter.

covetous ADJ. avaricious; eagerly desirous of. The child was *covetous* by nature and wanted to take the toys belonging to his classmates. covet, v.

cow v. terrorize; intimidate. The little boy was so *cowed* by the hulking bully that he gave up his lunch money without a word of protest.

cower v. shrink quivering, as from fear. The frightened child *cowered* in the corner of the room.

coy ADJ. shy; modest; coquettish. She was *coy* in her answers to his offer.

cozen v. cheat; hoodwink; swindle. He was the kind of individual who would *cozen* his friends in a cheap card game but remain eminently ethical in all his business dealings.

crabbed ADJ. sour; peevish. The children avoided the *crabbed* old man because he scolded them when they made noise.

crass ADJ. very unrefined; grossly insensible. The philosophers deplored the *crass* commercialism.

craven ADJ. cowardly. When he saw the enemy troops advancing, he had a *craven* impulse to run for his life.

credence N. belief. Do not place any *credence* in his promises.

credo N. creed. I believe we may best describe his *credo* by saying that it approximates the Golden Rule.

credulity N. belief on slight evidence. The witch doctor took advantage of the *credulity* of the superstitious natives. credulous, ADJ.

creed N. system of religious or ethical belief. In any loyal American's *creed*, love of democracy must be emphasized.

crescendo N. increase in the volume or intensity, as in a musical passage; climax. The overture suddenly changed from a quiet pastoral theme to a *crescendo* featuring blaring trumpets and clashing cymbals.

crestfallen ADJ. dejected; dispirited. We were surprised at his reaction to the failure of his project; instead of being *crestfallen*, he was busily engaged in planning new activities.

crevice N. crack; fissure. The mountain climbers found footholds in the tiny *crevices* in the mountainside.

cringe v. shrink back, as if in fear. The dog *cringed*, expecting a blow.

criteria N. standards used in judging. What *criteria* did you use when you selected this essay as the prize winner? criterion, SING.

crone N. hag. The toothless *crone* frightened us when she smiled.

crotchety ADJ. eccentric; whimsical. Although he was reputed to be a *crotchety* old gentleman, I found his ideas substantially sound and sensible.

crux N. crucial point. This is the *crux* of the entire problem.

crypt N. secret recess or vault usually used for burial. Until recently only bodies of rulers and leading statesmen were interred in this *crypt*.

cryptic ADJ. mysterious; hidden; secret. His *cryptic* remarks could not be interpreted.

cubicle N. small chamber used for sleeping. After his many hours of intensive study in the library he retired to his *cubicle*.

cuisine N. style of cooking. French *cuisine* is noted for its use of sauces and wines.

culinary ADJ. relating to cooking. Many chefs attribute their *culinary* skill to the wise use of spices.

cull V pick out; reject. Every month the farmer *culls* the nonlaying hens from his flock and sells them to the local butcher. also N.

culmination N. attainment of highest point. His inauguration as President of the United States marked the *culmination* of his political career.

culpable ADJ. deserving blame. Corrupt politicians who condone the activities of the gamblers are equally *culpable*.

culvert N. artificial channel for water. If we build a *culvert* under the road at this point, we will reduce the possibility of the road's being flooded during the rainy season.

cumbersome ADJ. heavy; hard to manage. He was burdened down with *cumbersome* parcels.

cumulative ADJ. growing by addition. Vocabulary-building is a *cumulative* process: as you go through your flash cards, you will add new words to your vocabulary, one by one.

cupidity N. greed. The defeated people could not satisfy the *cupidity* of the conquerors, who demanded excessive tribute.

curator N. superintendent; manager. The members of the board of trustees of the museum expected the new *curator* to plan events and exhibitions that would make the museum more popular.

curmudgeon N. churlish, miserly individual. Although he was regarded by many as a *curmudgeon*, a few of us were aware of the many kindnesses and acts of charity that he secretly performed.

cursive ADJ. flowing, running. In normal writing we run our letters together in *cursive* form; in printing, we separate the letters.

cursory ADJ. casual; hastily done. A *cursory* examination of the ruins indicates the possibility of arson; a more extensive study should be undertaken.

curtail V. shorten; reduce. During the coal shortage, we must *curtail* our use of this vital commodity.

cynical ADJ. skeptical or distrustful of human motives. *Cynical* at all times, he was suspicious of all altruistic actions of others. cynic, N.

cynosure N. object of general attention. As soon as the movie star entered the room, she became the *cynosure* of all eyes.

dais N. raised platform for guests of honor. When he approached the *dais*, he was greeted by cheers from the people who had come to honor him.

dally V. trifle with; procrastinate. Laertes told Ophelia that Hamlet could only *dally* with her affections.

dank ADJ. damp. The walls of the dungeon were *dank* and slimy.

dapper ADJ. neat and trim. In "The Odd Couple," Tony Randall played Felix Unger, an excessively *dapper* soul who could not stand to have a hair out of place.

dappled ADJ. spotted. The sunlight filtering through the screens created a *dappled* effect on the wall.

daub V. smear (as with paint). From the way he *daubed* his paint on the canvas, I could tell he knew nothing of oils. also N.

■ **daunt** V. intimidate. Your threats cannot *daunt* me.

dauntless ADJ. bold. Despite the dangerous nature of the undertaking, the *dauntless* soldier volunteered for the assignment.

dawdle V. loiter; waste time. Inasmuch as we must meet a deadline, do not *dawdle* over this work.

deadlock N. standstill; stalemate. The negotiations had reached a *deadlock*. also v.

deadpan ADJ. wooden; impassive. We wanted to see how long he could maintain his *deadpan* expression.

dearth N. scarcity. The *dearth* of skilled labor compelled the employers to open trade schools.

debacle N. breaking up; downfall. This *debacle* in the government can only result in anarchy.

debase V. reduce to lower state. Do not *debase* yourself by becoming maudlin. debasement, N.

debauch V. corrupt; make intemperate. A vicious newspaper can *debauch* public ideals. debauchery, N.

debilitate V. weaken; enfeeble. Overindulgence *debilitates* character as well as physical stamina.

debonair ADJ. friendly; aiming to please. The *debonair* youth was liked by all who met him, because of his cheerful and obliging manner.

debris N. rubble. A full year after the earthquake in Mexico City, workers were still carting away the *debris*.

debunk V. expose as false, exaggerated, worthless, etc.; ridicule. Pointing out that he consistently had voted against strengthening antipollution legislation, reporters *debunked* the candidate's claim that he was a fervent environmentalist.

debutante N. young woman making formal entrance into society. As a *debutante*, she was often mentioned in the society columns of the newspapers.

decadence N. decay. The moral *decadence* of the people was reflected in the lewd literature of the period.

decant V. pour off gently. Be sure to *decant* this wine before serving it.

decapitate V. behead. They did not hang Lady Jane Grey; they *decapitated* her.

decelerate V. slow down. Seeing the emergency blinkers in the road ahead, he *decelerated* quickly.

Test

Word List 12 *Antonyms*

Each of the questions below consists of a word in capital letters, followed by five lettered words or phrases. Choose the lettered word or phrase that is most nearly opposite in meaning to the word in capital letters and write the letter of your choice on your answer paper.

166. COY (A) weak (B) airy (C) brazen (D) old (E) tiresome
167. COZEN (A) amuse (B) treat honestly (C) prate (D) shackle (E) vilify
168. CRAVEN (A) desirous (B) direct (C) bold (D) civilized (E) controlled
169. CRUX (A) affliction (B) spark (C) events (D) trivial point (E) belief
170. CRYPTIC (A) tomblike (B) futile (C) famous (D) candid (E) indifferent
171. CUPIDITY (A) anxiety (B) tragedy (C) generosity (D) entertainment (E) love

172. CURTAIL (A) mutter (B) lengthen (C) express (D) burden (E) shore up
173. CYNICAL (A) trusting (B) effortless (C) conclusive (D) gallant (E) vertical
174. DANK (A) dry (B) guiltless (C) warm (D) babbling (E) reserved
175. DAPPER (A) unintelligent (B) untidy (C) uncertain (D) ungrateful (E) unhealthy
176. DAUNTLESS (A) stolid (B) cowardly (C) irrelevant (D) peculiar (E) particular
177. DEARTH (A) life (B) abundance (C) brightness (D) terror (E) width
178. DEBACLE (A) progress (B) refusal (C) masque (D) cowardice (E) traffic
179. DEBILITATE (A) bedevil (B) repress (C) strengthen (D) animate (E) deaden
180. DEBONAIR (A) awkward (B) windy (C) balmy (D) strong (E) stormy

Word List 13 deciduous-dermatologist

deciduous ADJ. falling off, as of leaves. The oak is a *deciduous* tree.

decimate V. kill, usually one out of ten. We do more to *decimate* our population in automobile accidents than we do in war.

decipher V. decode. I could not *decipher* the doctor's handwriting.

declivity N. downward slope. The children loved to ski down the *declivity*.

décolleté ADJ. having a low-cut neckline. Fashion decrees that evening gowns be *décolleté* this season; bare shoulders are again the vogue.

decomposition N. decay. Despite the body's advanced state of *decomposition,* the police were able to identify the murdered man.

■ **decorum** N. propriety; seemliness. Shocked by the unruly behavior, the teacher criticized the class for its lack of *decorum*. decorous, ADJ.

decoy N. lure or bait. The wild ducks were not fooled by the *decoy*. also V.

decrepitude N. state of collapse caused by illness or old age. I was unprepared for the state of *decrepitude* in which I had found my old friend; he seemed to have aged twenty years in six months.

decry V. express strong disapproval of; disparage. The founder of the Children's Defense Fund, Marian Wright Edelman, strongly *decries* the lack of financial and moral support for children in America today.

deducible ADJ. derived by reasoning. If we accept your premise, your conclusions are easily *deducible*.

deface V. mar; disfigure. If you *deface* a library book, you will have to pay a hefty fine.

defamation N. harming a person's reputation. Such *defamation* of character may result in a slander suit.

default N. failure to do. As a result of her husband's failure to appear in court, she was granted a divorce by *default*. also V.

defeatist ADJ. resigned to defeat; accepting defeat as a natural outcome. If you maintain your *defeatist* attitude, you will never succeed. also N.

defection N. desertion. The children, who had made him an idol, were hurt most by his *defection* from our cause.

■ **deference** N. courteous regard for another's wish. In *deference* to his desires, the employers granted him a holiday. defer, V.

defile V. pollute; profane. The hoodlums *defiled* the church with their scurrilous writing.

definitive ADJ. most reliable or complete. Carl Sandburg's *Abraham Lincoln* may be regarded as the *definitive* work on the life of the Great Emancipator.

deflect V. turn aside. His life was saved when his cigarette case *deflected* the bullet.

defoliate V. destroy leaves. In Vietnam the army made extensive use of chemical agents to *defoliate* the woodlands.

defray V. provide for the payment of. Her employer offered to *defray* the costs of her postgraduate education.

defrock V. to strip a priest or minister of church authority. We knew the minister had violated church regulations, but we had not realized his offense was serious enough to cause him to be *defrocked*.

deft ADJ. neat; skillful. The *deft* waiter uncorked the champagne without spilling a drop.

defunct ADJ. dead; no longer in use or existence. The lawyers sought to examine the books of the *defunct* corporation.

degenerate V. become worse; deteriorate. As the fight dragged on, the champion's style *degenerated* until he could barely keep on his feet.

degraded ADJ. lowered in rank; debased. The *degraded* wretch spoke only of his past glories and honors.

dehydrate V. remove water from; dry out. Vigorous dancing quickly *dehydrates* the body; between dances, be sure to drink more water than normal.

deify V. turn into a god; idolize. Admire the rock star all you want; just don't *deify* him.

deign V. condescend. He felt that he would debase himself if he *deigned* to answer his critics.

delete V. erase; strike out. If you *delete* this paragraph, the composition will have more appeal.

deleterious ADJ. harmful. Workers in nuclear research must avoid the *deleterious* effects of radioactive substances.

deliberate V. consider; ponder. Offered the new job, she asked for time to *deliberate* before she made her decision.

■ **delineate** V. portray. He is a powerful storyteller, but he is weakest when he attempts to *delineate* character. delineation, N.

delirium N. mental disorder marked by confusion. The drunkard in his *delirium* saw strange animals.

delta N. flat plain of mud or sand between branches of a river. His dissertation discussed the effect of intermittent flooding on the fertility of the Nile *delta*.

delude V. deceive. Do not *delude* yourself into believing that he will relent.

deluge N. flood; rush. When we advertised the position, we received a *deluge* of applications. also V.

delusion N. false belief; hallucination. This scheme is a snare and a *delusion*.

delusive ADJ. deceptive; raising vain hopes. Do not raise your hopes on the basis of his *delusive* promises.

delve V. dig; investigate. *Delving* into old books and manuscripts is part of a researcher's job.

demagogue N. person who appeals to people's prejudice; false leader. He was accused of being a *demagogue* because he made promises that aroused futile hopes in his listeners.

demean V. degrade; humiliate. He felt that he would *demean* himself if he replied to the scurrilous letter.

demeanor N. behavior; bearing. His sober *demeanor* quieted the noisy revelers.

demented ADJ. insane. She became increasingly *demented* and had to be hospitalized.

demise N. death. Upon the *demise* of the dictator, a bitter dispute about succession to power developed.

demographic ADJ. related to population balance. In conducting a survey, one should take into account *demographic* trends in the region. demography, N.

demolition N. destruction. One of the major aims of the air force was the complete *demolition* of all means of transportation by the bombing of rail lines and terminals. demolish, V.

demoniac ADJ. fiendish. The Spanish Inquisition devised many *demoniac* means of torture. demon, N.

demotic ADJ. pertaining to the people. He lamented the passing of aristocratic society and maintained that a *demotic* society would lower the nation's standards.

demur V. delay; object. To *demur* at this time will only worsen the already serious situation; now is the time for action.

demure ADJ. grave; serious; coy. She was *demure* and reserved.

■ **denigrate** V. blacken. All attempts to *denigrate* the character of our late President have failed; the people still love him and cherish his memory.

denizen N. inhabitant of. Ghosts are *denizens* of the land of the dead who return to earth.

denotation N. meaning; distinguishing by name. A dictionary will always give us the *denotation* of a word; frequently, it will also give us its connotation.

denouement N. outcome; final development of the plot of a play or other literary work. The play was childishly written; the *denouement* was obvious to sophisticated theatergoers as early as the middle of the first act.

denounce V. condemn; criticize. The reform candidate *denounced* the corrupt city officers for having betrayed the public's trust. denunciation, N.

depict V. portray. In this book, the author *depicts* the slave owners as kind and benevolent masters.

deplete V. reduce; exhaust. We must wait until we *deplete* our present inventory before we order replacements.

deplore V. regret. Although I *deplore* the vulgarity of your language, I defend your right to express yourself freely.

deploy V. move troops so that the battle line is extended at the expense of depth. The general ordered the battalion to *deploy* in order to meet the offensive of the enemy.

depose V. dethrone; remove from office. The army attempted to *depose* the king and set up a military government.

deposition N. testimony under oath. He made his *deposition* in the judge's chamber.

depravity N. corruption; wickedness. The *depravity* of the tyrant's behavior shocked all. deprave, V.

■ **deprecate** V. express disapproval of; protest against; belittle. A firm believer in old-fashioned courtesy, Miss Post *deprecated* the modern tendency to address new acquaintances by their first names. deprecatory, ADJ.

depreciate V. lessen in value. If you neglect this property, it will *depreciate*.

depredation N. plundering. After the *depredations* of the invaders, the people were penniless.

deranged ADJ. insane. He had to be institutionalized because he was *deranged*.

derelict ADJ. neglectful of duty; abandoned. The corporal who fell asleep while on watch was thrown into the guardhouse for being *derelict* in his duty. also N.

deride V. scoff at. The people *derided* his grandiose schemes.

■ **derision** N. ridicule. They greeted his proposal with *derision* and refused to consider it seriously. derisive, ADJ.

■ **derivative** ADJ. unoriginal; obtained from another source. Although her early poetry was clearly *derivative* in nature, the critics thought she had promise and eventually would find her own voice.

dermatologist N. one who studies the skin and its diseases. I advise you to consult a *dermatologist* about your acne.

Test

Word List 13 *Synonyms*

Each of the questions below consists of a word in capital letters, followed by five lettered words or phrases. Choose the lettered word or phrase that is most nearly similar in meaning to the word in capital letters and write the letter of your choice on your answer paper.

181. DECIMATE (A) kill (B) disgrace (C) search (D) collide (E) deride
182. DECLIVITY (A) trap (B) quadrangle (C) quarter (D) activity (E) downward slope
183. DECOLLETÉ (A) flavored (B) demure (C) flowery (D) low-necked (E) sweet
184. DECOROUS (A) momentary (B) emotional (C) suppressed (D) proper (E) unexpected
185. DECREPITUDE (A) feebleness (B) disease (C) coolness (D) melee (E) crowd
186. DEFAULT (A) failure to act (B) tendency to err (C) desire to remedy (D) debt (E) misunderstanding

187. DEFECTION (A) determination (B) desertion (C) invitation (D) affection (E) reservation
188. DEFILE (A) manicure (B) ride (C) pollute (D) assemble (E) order
189. DEGRADED (A) surprised (B) lowered (C) ascended (D) learned (E) prejudged
190. DELETERIOUS (A) delaying (B) experimental (C) harmful (D) graduating (E) glorious
191. DELUGE (A) confusion (B) deception (C) flood (D) mountain (E) weapon
192. DENIGRATE (A) refuse (B) blacken (C) terrify (D) admit (E) review
193. DENOUEMENT (A) action (B) scenery (C) resort (D) character (E) solution
194. DEPRAVITY (A) wickedness (B) sadness (C) heaviness (D) tidiness (E) seriousness
195. DERANGED (A) insane (B) systematic (C) neighborly (D) alphabetical (E) surrounded

Word List 14 derogatory-disgruntle

derogatory ADJ. expressing a low opinion. I resent your *derogatory* remarks.

descry V. catch sight of. In the distance, we could barely *descry* the enemy vessels.

desecrate V. profane; violate the sanctity of. The soldiers *desecrated* the temple.

■ **desiccate** V. dry up. A tour of this smokehouse will give you an idea of how the pioneers used to *desiccate* food in order to preserve it.

desolate V. rob of joy; lay waste to; forsake. The bandits *desolated* the countryside, burning farms and carrying off the harvest. also ADJ.

desperado N. reckless outlaw. Butch Cassidy was a bold *desperado* with a price on his head.

despicable ADJ. contemptible. Your *despicable* remarks call for no reply.

despise V. scorn. I *despise* your attempts at a reconciliation at this time and refuse to meet you.

despoil V. plunder. If you do not yield, I am afraid the enemy will *despoil* the countryside.

despondent ADJ. depressed; gloomy. To the dismay of his parents, he became more and more *despondent* every day. despondency, N.

■ **despotism** N. tyranny. The people rebelled against the *despotism* of the king.

destitute ADJ. extremely poor. The costs of the father's illness left the family *destitute*.

■ **desultory** ADJ. aimless; haphazard; digressing at random. In prison Malcolm X set himself the task of reading straight through the dictionary; to him, reading was purposeful, not *desultory*.

detached ADJ. emotionally removed; calm and objective; indifferent. A psychoanalyst must maintain a *detached* point of view and stay uninvolved with her patients' personal lives. detachment, N. (secondary meaning)

determinate ADJ. having a fixed order of procedure; invariable. At the royal wedding, the procession of the nobles followed a *determinate* order of precedence.

■ **deterrent** N. something that discourages; hindrance. Does the threat of capital punishment serve as a *deterrent* to potential killers? also ADJ.

detonation N. explosion. The *detonation* of the bomb could be heard miles away.

detraction N. slandering; aspersion. He is offended by your frequent *detractions* of his ability as a leader.

detrimental ADJ. harmful; damaging. Your acceptance of her support will ultimately prove *detrimental* rather than helpful to your cause. detriment, N.

deviate V. turn away from. Do not *deviate* from the truth; you must face the facts.

devious ADJ. going astray; erratic. Your *devious* behavior in this matter puzzles me since you are usually direct and straightforward.

■ **devoid** ADJ. lacking. He was *devoid* of any personal desire for gain in his endeavor to secure improvement in the community.

devolve V. deputize; pass to others. It *devolved* upon us, the survivors, to arrange peace terms with the enemy.

devotee N. enthusiastic follower. A *devotee* of the opera, he bought season tickets every year.

devout ADJ. pious. The *devout* man prayed daily.

dexterous ADJ. skillful. The magician was so *dexterous* that we could not follow his movements as he performed his tricks.

diabolical ADJ. devilish. This scheme is so *diabolical* that I must reject it.

diadem N. crown. The king's *diadem* was on display at the museum.

dialectic N. art of debate. I am not skilled in *dialectic* and, therefore, cannot answer your arguments as forcefully as I wish.

diaphanous ADJ. sheer; transparent. They saw the burglar clearly through the *diaphanous* curtain.

■ **diatribe** N. bitter scolding; invective. During the lengthy *diatribe* delivered by his opponent he remained calm and self-controlled.

■ **dichotomy** N. branching into two parts. The *dichotomy* of our legislative system provides us with many safeguards.

dictum N. authoritative and weighty statement. She repeated the statement as though it were the *dictum* of the most expert worker in the group.

didactic ADJ. teaching; instructional; preaching or moralizing. The *didactic* qualities of his poetry overshadow its literary qualities; the lesson he teaches is more memorable than the lines.

die N. device for stamping or impressing; mold. In coining pennies, workers at the old mint squeezed sheets of softened copper between two *dies*.

■ **diffidence** N. shyness. You must overcome your *diffidence* if you intend to become a salesperson.

■ **diffusion** N. wordiness; spreading in all directions like a gas. Your composition suffers from a *diffusion* of ideas; try to be more compact. diffuse, ADJ. and V.

■ **digression** N. wandering away from the subject. Nobody minded when Professor Renoir's lectures wandered away from their official theme; his *digressions* were always more fascinating than the topic of the day. digress, V.

dilapidated ADJ. ruined because of neglect. We felt that the *dilapidated* building needed several coats of paint. dilapidation, N.

dilate V. expand. In the dark, the pupils of your eyes *dilate*.

dilatory ADJ. delaying. Your *dilatory* tactics may compel me to cancel the contract.

dilemma N. problem; choice of two unsatisfactory alternatives. In this *dilemma*, he knew no one to whom he could turn for advice.

dilettante N. aimless follower of the arts; amateur; dabbler. He was not serious in his painting; he was rather a *dilettante*

diligence N. steadiness of effort; persistent hard work. Her employers were greatly impressed by her *diligence* and offered her a partnership in the firm.

dilute V. make less concentrated; reduce in strength. She preferred her coffee *diluted* with milk.

diminution N. lessening; reduction in size. The blockaders hoped to achieve victory as soon as the *diminution* of the enemy's supplies became serious.

din N. continued loud noise. The *din* of the jackhammers outside the classroom window drowned out the lecturer's voice. also V.

dinghy N. small boat (often ship's boat). In the film *Lifeboat,* an ill-assorted group of passengers from a sunken ocean liner are marooned at sea in a *dinghy*.

dingy ADJ. dull; not fresh; cheerless. Refusing to be depressed by her *dingy* studio apartment, Bea spent the weekend polishing the floors and windows and hanging bright posters on the walls.

dint N. means; effort. By *dint* of much hard work, the volunteers were able to control the raging forest fire.

diorama N. life-size, three-dimensional scene from nature or history. Because they dramatically pose actual stuffed animals against realistic painted landscapes, the *dioramas* at the Museum of Natural History particularly impress high school biology students.

dire ADJ. disastrous. People ignored her *dire* predictions of an approaching depression.

dirge N. lament with music. The funeral *dirge* stirred us to tears.

■ **disabuse** V. correct a false impression; undeceive. I will attempt to *disabuse* you of your impression of my client's guilt; I know he is innocent.

disaffected ADJ. disloyal. Once the most loyal of Gorbachev's supporters, Sheverdnaze found himself becoming increasingly *disaffected*.

disapprobation N. disapproval; condemnation. The conservative father viewed his daughter's radical boyfriend with *disapprobation*.

disarray N. a disorderly or untidy state. After the New Year's party, the once orderly house was in total *disarray*.

disavowal N. denial; disclaiming. His *disavowal* of his part in the conspiracy was not believed by the jury. disavow, V.

disband V. dissolve; disperse. The chess club *disbanded* after its disastrous initial season.

disburse V. pay out. When you *disburse* money on the company's behalf, be sure to get a receipt.

discernible ADJ. distinguishable; perceivable. The ships in the harbor were not *discernible* in the fog.

■ **discerning** ADJ. mentally quick and observant; having insight. Because he was considered the most *discerning* member of the firm, he was assigned the most difficult cases. discern, V. discernment, N.

disclaim V. disown; renounce claim to. If I grant you this privilege, will you *disclaim* all other rights?

disclose V. reveal. Although competitors offered him bribes, he refused to *disclose* any information about his company's forthcoming product. disclosure, N.

discombobulated ADJ. confused; discomposed. The novice square dancer became so *discombobulated* that he wandered into the wrong set.

discomfit V. put to rout; defeat; disconcert. This ruse will *discomfit* the enemy. discomfiture, N. discomfited, ADJ.

disconcert V. confuse; upset; embarrass. The lawyer was *disconcerted* by the evidence produced by her adversary.

disconsolate ADJ. sad. The death of his wife left him *disconsolate*.

■ **discordant** ADJ. inharmonious; conflicting. She tried to unite the *discordant* factions.

discount V. disregard. Be prepared to *discount* what he has to say about his ex-wife.

discourse N. formal discussion; conversation. The young Plato was drawn to the Agora to hear the philosophical *discourse* of Socrates and his followers. also V.

■ **discredit** V. defame; destroy confidence in; disbelieve. The campaign was highly negative in tone; each candidate tried to *discredit* the other.

■ **discrepancy** N. lack of consistency; difference. The police noticed some *discrepancies* in his description of the crime and did not believe him.

■ **discrete** ADJ. separate; unconnected. The universe is composed of *discrete* bodies.

discretion N. prudence; ability to adjust actions to circumstances. Use your *discretion* in this matter and do not discuss it with anyone. discreet, ADJ.

discrimination N. ability to see differences; prejudice. They feared he lacked sufficient *discrimination* to judge complex works of modern art. (secondary meaning) discriminating, ADJ.

discursive ADJ. digressing; rambling. They were annoyed and bored by her *discursive* remarks.

disdain V. treat with scorn or contempt. You make enemies of all you *disdain*. also N.

disembark V. go ashore; unload cargo from a ship. Before the passengers could *disembark*, they had to pick up their passports from the ship's purser.

disenfranchise V. deprive of a civil right. The imposition of the poll tax effectively *disenfranchised* poor Southern blacks, who lost their right to vote.

disengage V. uncouple; separate; disconnect. A standard movie routine involves the hero's desperate attempt to *disengage* a railroad car from a moving train.

disfigure V. mar the appearance of; spoil. An ugly frown *disfigured* his normally pleasant face.

disgorge V. surrender something; eject; vomit. Unwilling to *disgorge* the cash he had stolen from the pension fund, the embezzler tried to run away.

disgruntle V. make discontented. The passengers were *disgruntled* by the numerous delays.

Test

Word List 14   *Antonyms*

Each of the questions below consists of a word in capital letters, followed by five lettered words or phrases. Choose the lettered word or phrase that is most nearly opposite in meaning to the word in capital letters and write the letter of your choice on your answer paper.

196. DEROGATORY (A) roguish (B) immediate
     (C) opinionated (D) praising (E) conferred
197. DESECRATE (A) desist (B) integrate (C) confuse
     (D) intensify (E) consecrate
198. DESPICABLE (A) steering (B) worthy of esteem
     (C) inevitable (D) featureless (E) incapable
199. DESTITUTE (A) affluent (B) dazzling (C) stationary
     (D) characteristic (E) explanatory
200. DEVOID (A) latent (B) eschewed (C) full of
     (D) suspecting (E) evident
201. DEVOUT (A) quiet (B) dual (C) impious
     (D) straightforward (E) wrong

202. DIABOLICAL (A) mischievous (B) lavish
     (C) seraphic (D) azure (E) redolent
203. DIATRIBE (A) mass (B) range (C) eulogy
     (D) elegy (E) starvation
204. DIFFIDENCE (A) sharpness (B) boldness
     (C) malcontent (D) dialogue (E) catalog
205. DILATE (A) procrastinate (B) contract
     (C) conclude (D) participate (E) divert
206. DILATORY (A) narrowing (B) prompt (C) enlarging
     (D) portentous (E) sour
207. DIMINUTION (A) expectation (B) context
     (C) validity (D) appreciation (E) difficulty
208. DIN (A) lightness (B) safety (C) silence
     (D) hunger (E) promptness
209. DISABUSE (A) crash (B) violate (C) renege
     (D) control (E) deceive
210. DISCONSOLATE (A) unprejudiced (B) thankful
     (C) theatrical (D) joyous (E) prominent

Word List 15   dishearten-duplicity

dishearten V. discourage. His failure to pass the bar exam *disheartened* him.

disheveled ADJ. untidy. Your *disheveled* appearance will hurt your chances in this interview.

disinclination N. unwillingness. Some mornings I feel a great *disinclination* to get out of bed.

■ **disingenuous** ADJ. not naive; sophisticated. Although he was young, his remarks indicated that he was *disingenuous*.

disinter V. dig up; unearth. They *disinterred* the body and held an autopsy.

■ **disinterested** ADJ. unprejudiced. The only *disinterested* person in the room was the judge.

■ **disjointed** ADJ. disconnected. His remarks were so *disjointed* that we could not follow his reasoning.

dislodge V. remove (forcibly). Thrusting her fist up under the choking man's lower ribs, Margaret used the Heimlich maneuver to *dislodge* the food caught in his throat.

dismantle V. take apart. When the show closed, they *dismantled* the scenery before storing it.

dismember V. cut into small parts. When the Austrian Empire was *dismembered*, several new countries were established .

dismiss V. eliminate from consideration; reject. Believing in John's love for her, she *dismissed* the notion that he might be unfaithful. (secondary meaning)

■ **disparage** V. belittle. Do not *disparage* anyone's contribution; these little gifts add up to large sums.

■ **disparate** ADJ. basically different; unrelated. It is difficult, if not impossible, to organize these *disparate* elements into a coherent whole.

disparity N. difference; condition of inequality. The *disparity* in their ages made no difference at all.

dispassionate ADJ. calm; impartial. In a *dispassionate* analysis of the problem, he carefully examined the causes of the conflict and proceeded to suggest suitable remedies.

dispatch N. speediness; prompt execution; message sent with all due speed. Young Napoleon defeated the enemy with all possible *dispatch*; he then sent a *dispatch* to headquarters, informing his commander of the great victory. also V.

dispel V. scatter; drive away; cause to vanish. The bright sunlight eventually *dispelled* the morning mist.

disperse V. scatter. The police fired tear gas into the crowd to *disperse* the protesters. dispersion, N.

dispirited ADJ. lacking in spirit. The coach used all the tricks at his command to buoy up the enthusiasm of his team, which had become *dispirited* at the loss of the star player.

disport V. amuse. The popularity of Florida as a winter resort is constantly increasing; each year, thousands more *disport* themselves at Miami and Palm Beach.

disputatious ADJ. argumentative; fond of argument. People avoided discussing contemporary problems with him because of his *disputatious* manner.

disquisition N. a formal systematic inquiry; an explanation of the results of a formal inquiry. In his *disquisition*, he outlined the steps he had taken in reaching his conclusions.

dissection N. analysis; cutting apart in order to examine. The *dissection* of frogs in the laboratory is particularly unpleasant to some students.

■ **dissemble** V. disguise; pretend. Even though John tried to *dissemble* his motive for taking modern dance, we all knew he was there not to dance but to meet girls.

■ **disseminate** V. scatter (like seeds). The invention of the radio helped propagandists to *disseminate* their favorite doctrines very easily.

dissent V. disagree. In a landmark Supreme Court decision, Justice Marshall *dissented* from the majority opinion. also N.

dissertation N. formal essay. In order to earn a graduate degree from many of our universities, a candidate is frequently required to prepare a *dissertation* on some scholarly subject.

dissident ADJ. dissenting; rebellious. In the purge that followed the student demonstrations at Tianamen Square, the government hunted down the *dissident* students and their supporters. also N.

dissimulate V. pretend; conceal by feigning. She tried to *dissimulate* her grief by her exuberant attitude.

dissipate V. squander. The young man quickly *dissipated* his inheritance and was soon broke.

■ **dissolution** N. disintegration; looseness in morals. The profligacy and *dissolution* of life in Caligula's Rome appall some historians. dissolute, ADJ.

■ **dissonance** N. discord. Some contemporary musicians deliberately use *dissonance* to achieve certain effects.

dissuade V. advise against. He could not *dissuade* his friend from joining the conspirators. dissuasion, N.

distant ADJ. reserved or aloof; cold in manner. His *distant* greeting made me feel unwelcome from the start. (secondary meaning)

distend V. expand; swell out. I can tell when he is under stress by the way the veins *distend* on his forehead.

■ **distill** V. purify; refine; concentrate. A moonshiner *distills* mash into whiskey; an epigrammatist *distills* thoughts into quips.

distortion N. twisting out of shape. It is difficult to believe the newspaper accounts of this event because of the *distortions* and exaggerations of the reporters.

distrait ADJ. absentminded. Because of his concentration on the problem, the professor often appeared *distrait* and unconcerned about routine.

distraught ADJ. upset; distracted by anxiety. The *distraught* parents frantically searched the ravine for their lost child.

diurnal ADJ. daily. A farmer cannot neglect his *diurnal* tasks at any time; cows, for example, must be milked regularly.

diva N. operatic singer; prima donna. Although world famous as a *diva*, she did not indulge in fits of temperament.

■ **diverge** V. vary; go in different directions from the same point. The spokes of the wheel *diverge* from the hub.

divergent ADJ. differing; deviating. The two witnesses presented the jury with remarkably *divergent* accounts of the same episode. divergence, N.

diverse ADJ. differing in some characteristics; various. There are *diverse* ways of approaching this problem.

diversion N. act of turning aside; pastime. After studying for several hours, he needed a *diversion* from work. divert, V.

diversity N. variety; dissimilitude. The *diversity* of colleges in this country indicates that many levels of ability are being served.

■ **divest** V. strip; deprive. He was *divested of* his power to act and could no longer govern. divestiture, N.

divine V. perceive intuitively; foresee the future. Nothing infuriated Tom more than Aunt Polly's ability to *divine* when he was not telling the truth.

divulge V. reveal. I will not tell you this news because I am sure you will *divulge* it prematurely.

docile ADJ. obedient; easily managed. As *docile* as he seems today, that old lion was once a ferocious, snarling beast. docility, N.

docket N. program as for trial; book where such entries are made. The case of *Smith v. Jones* was entered in the *docket* for July 15. also V.

doctrinaire ADJ. unable to compromise about points of doctrine; dogmatic; unyielding. Weng had hoped that the student-led democracy movement might bring about change in China, but the repressive response of the *doctrinaire* hard-liners crushed his dreams of democracy.

document V. provide written evidence. She kept all the receipts from her business trip in order to *document* her expenses for the firm. also N.

doddering ADJ. shaky; infirm from old age. Although he is not as yet a *doddering* and senile old man, his ideas and opinions no longer can merit the respect we gave them years ago.

doff V. take off. A gentleman used to *doff* his hat to a lady.

dogged ADJ. determined; stubborn. *Les Miserables* tells of Inspector Javert's long, *dogged* pursuit of the criminal Jean Valjean.

doggerel N. poor verse. Although we find occasional snatches of genuine poetry in her work, most of her writing is mere *doggerel*.

■ **dogmatic** ADJ. positive; arbitrary. Do not be so *dogmatic* about that statement; it can be easily refuted.

doldrums N. blues; listlessness; slack period. Once the excitement of meeting her deadline was over, she found herself in the *doldrums*.

dolorous ADJ. sorrowful. He found the *dolorous* lamentations of the bereaved family emotionally disturbing and he left as quickly as he could.

dolt N. stupid person. I thought I was talking to a mature audience; instead, I find myself addressing a pack of *dolts*.

domicile N. home. Although his legal *domicile* was in New York City, his work kept him *away* from his residence for many years. also V.

domineer V. rule over tyrannically. Students prefer teachers who guide, not ones who *domineer.*

don V. put on. When Clark Kent had to *don* his Superman outfit, he changed clothes in a convenient phone booth. phone booth.

■ **dormant** ADJ. sleeping; lethargic; torpid. Sometimes *dormant* talents in our friends surprise those of us who never realized how gifted our acquaintances really are. dormancy, N.

dormer N. window projecting from roof. In remodeling the attic into a bedroom, we decided that we needed to put in *dormers* to provide sufficient ventilation for the new room.

dorsal ADJ. relating to the back of an animal. A shark may be identified by its *dorsal* fin, which projects above the surface of the ocean.

dossier N. file of documents on a subject. Ordered by J. Edgar Hoover to investigate the senator, the FBI compiled a complete *dossier* on him.

dotage N. senility. In his *dotage,* the old man bored us with long tales of events in his childhood.

dote V. be excessively fond of; show signs of mental decline. Not only grandmothers bore you with stories about their brilliant grandchildren; grandfathers *dote* on the little rascals, too.

dour ADJ. sullen; stubborn . The man was *dour* and taciturn.

douse V. plunge into water; drench; extinguish. They *doused* each other with hoses and water balloons.

dowdy ADJ. slovenly; untidy. She tried to change her *dowdy* image by buying a fashionable new wardrobe.

downcast ADJ. disheartened; sad. Cheerful and optimistic by nature, Beth was never *downcast* despite the difficulties she faced.

drab ADJ. dull; lacking color; cheerless. The Dutch woman's *drab* winter coat contrasted with the distinctive, colorful native costume she wore beneath it.

dregs N. sediment; worthless residue. David poured the wine carefully to avoid stirring up the *dregs*.

droll ADJ. queer and amusing. He was a popular guest because his *droll* anecdotes were always entertaining.

drone N. idle person; male bee. Content to let his wife support him, the would-be writer was in reality nothing but a *drone*.

drone V. talk dully; buzz or murmur like a bee. On a gorgeous day, who wants to be stuck in a classroom listening to the teacher *drone*.

dross N. waste matter; worthless impurities. Many methods have been devised to separate the valuable metal from the *dross*.

drudgery N. menial work. Cinderella's fairy godmother rescued her from a life of *drudgery*.

dubious ADJ. doubtful. He has the *dubious* distinction of being the lowest man in his class.

ductility N. malleability; flexibility; ability to be drawn out. Copper wire has many industrial uses because of its extreme *ductility*. ductile, ADJ.

dulcet ADJ. sweet sounding. The *dulcet* sounds of the birds at dawn were soon drowned out by the roar of traffic passing our motel.

dupe N. someone easily fooled. While the gullible Watson often was made a *dupe* by unscrupulous parties, Sherlock Holmes was far more difficult to fool.

duplicity N. double-dealing; hypocrisy. People were shocked and dismayed when they learned of his *duplicity* in this affair, as he had always seemed honest and straightforward.

Test

Word List 15   *Synonyms and Antonyms*

Each of the following questions consists of a word in capital letters, followed by five lettered words or phrases. Choose the lettered word or phrase that is most nearly similar or opposite in meaning to the word in capital letters and write the letter of your choice on your answer paper.

211. DISINGENUOUS (A) uncomfortable (B) eventual (C) naive (D) complex (E) enthusiastic
212. DISINTERESTED (A) prejudiced (B) horrendous (C) affected (D) arbitrary (E) bored
213. DISJOINTED (A) satisfied (B) carved (C) understood (D) connected (E) evicted
214. DISPARITY (A) resonance (B) elocution (C) relief (D) difference (E) symbolism
215. DISPASSIONATE (A) sensual (B) immoral (C) inhibited (D) impartial (E) scientific
216. DISPIRITED (A) current (B) dented (C) drooping (D) alcoholic (E) dallying

217. DISSIPATE (A) economize (B) clean (C) accept (D) anticipate (E) withdraw
218. DISTEND (A) bloat (B) adjust (C) exist (D) materialize (E) finish
219. DISTRAIT (A) clever (B) industrial (C) absentminded (D) narrow (E) crooked
220. DIVULGE (A) look (B) refuse (C) deride (D) reveal (E) harm
221. DOFF (A) withdraw (B) take off (C) remain (D) control (E) start
222. DOGMATIC (A) benign (B) canine (C) impatient (D) petulant (E) arbitrary
223. DOTAGE (A) senility (B) silence (C) sensitivity (D) interest (E) generosity
224. DOUR (A) sullen (B) ornamental (C) grizzled (D) lacking speech (E) international
225. DROLL (A) rotund (B) amusing (C) fearsome (D) tiny (E) strange

Word List 16   duress-encroachment

duress N. forcible restraint, especially unlawfully. The hostages were held under *duress* until the prisoners' demands were met.

dutiful ADJ. respectful; obedient. The *dutiful* child grew up to be a conscientious adult, aware of his civic obligations.

dwindle V. shrink; reduce. They spent so much money that their funds *dwindled* to nothing.

dynamic ADJ. active; efficient. A *dynamic* government is necessary to meet the demands of a changing society.

dyspeptic ADJ. suffering from indigestion. All the talk about rich food made him feel *dyspeptic*. dyspepsia, N.

earthy ADJ. unrefined; coarse. His *earthy* remarks often embarrassed the women in his audience.

ebb V. recede; lessen. His fortunes began to *ebb* during the recession. also N.

■ ebullient ADJ. showing excitement; overflowing with enthusiasm. His *ebullient* nature could not be repressed; he was always exuberant. ebullience, N.

eccentric ADJ. odd; whimsical; irregular. The comet passed close by the earth in its *eccentric* orbit.

eccentricity N. oddity; idiosyncrasy. Some of his friends tried to account for his rudeness to strangers as the *eccentricity* of genius.

ecclesiastic ADJ. pertaining to the church. The minister donned his *ecclesiastic* garb and walked to the pulpit. also N.

■ eclectic ADJ. selective; composed of elements drawn from disparate sources. His style of interior decoration was *eclectic*: bits and pieces of furnishings from widely divergent periods, strikingly juxtaposed to create a unique decor. eclecticism, N.

eclipse V. darken; extinguish; surpass. The new stock market high *eclipsed* the previous record set in 1985.

ecologist N. person concerned with the interrelationship between living organisms and their environment. The *ecologist* was concerned that the new dam would upset the natural balance of the creatures living in Glen Canyon.

economy N. efficiency or conciseness in using something. Reading the epigrams of Pope, I admire the *economy* of his verse: in few words he conveys worlds of meaning. (secondary meaning)

ecstasy N. rapture, joy; any overpowering emotion. The announcement that the war had ended brought on an *ecstasy* that resulted in many uncontrolled celebrations.

eddy N. swirling current of water, air, etc. The water in the tide pool was still, except for an occasional *eddy*. also V.

edify v. instruct; correct morally. Although his purpose was to *edify* and not to entertain his audience, many of his listeners were amused and not enlightened.

eerie ADJ. weird. In that *eerie* setting, it was easy to believe in ghosts and other supernatural beings.

efface v. rub out. The coin had been handled so many times that its date had been *effaced*.

effectual ADJ. efficient. If we are to succeed, we must seek *effectual* means of securing our goals.

effeminate ADJ. having womanly traits. His voice was high-pitched and *effeminate*.

effervescence N. inner excitement; exuberance. Nothing depressed her for long; her natural *effervescence* soon reasserted itself. effervescent, ADJ.

effete ADJ. worn out; exhausted; barren. The literature of the age reflected the *effete* condition of the writers; no new ideas were forthcoming.

■ **efficacy** N. power to produce desired effect. The *efficacy* of this drug depends on the regularity of the dosage. efficacious, ADJ.

effigy N. dummy. The mob showed its irritation by hanging the judge in *effigy*.

effluvium N. noxious smell. Air pollution has become a serious problem in our major cities; the *effluvium* and the poisons in the air are hazards to life. effluvia, PL.

effrontery N. shameless boldness. She had the *effrontery* to insult the guest.

effusion N. pouring forth. The critics objected to her literary *effusion* because it was too flowery.

effusive ADJ. pouring forth; gushing. Her *effusive* manner of greeting her friends finally began to irritate them.

egoism N. excessive interest in one's self; belief that one should be interested in one's self rather than in others. His *egoism* prevented him from seeing the needs of his colleagues.

egotism N. conceit; vanity. She thought so much of herself that we found her *egotism* unwarranted and irritating. egotistic, ADJ.

egregious ADJ. notorious; conspicuously bad; shocking. She was an *egregious* liar; we all knew better than to believe a word she said.

egress N. exit. Barnum's sign "To the *Egress*" fooled many people who thought they were going to see an animal and instead found themselves in the street.

ejaculation N. exclamation. He could not repress an *ejaculation* of surprise when he heard the news.

elaboration N. addition of details; intricacy. Tell what happened simply, without any *elaboration*. elaborate, v.

elated ADJ. overjoyed; in high spirits. Grinning from ear to ear, Bonnie Blair was clearly *elated* by her Olympic victory. elation, N.

■ **elegy** N. poem or song expressing lamentation. On the death of Edward King, Milton composed the *elegy* "Lycidas." elegiacal, ADJ.

■ **elicit** v. draw out by discussion. The detectives tried to *elicit* where he had hidden his loot.

elixir N. cure-all; something invigorating. The news of her chance to go abroad acted on her like an *elixir*.

ellipsis N. omission of words from a text. Sometimes an *ellipsis* can lead to a dangling modifier, as in the sentence "Once dressed, you should refrigerate the potato salad."

elliptical ADJ. oval; ambiguous, either purposely or because key words have been left out. An *elliptical* billiard ball wobbles because it is not perfectly round; an *elliptical* remark baffles because it is not perfectly clear.

eloquence N. expressiveness; persuasive speech. The crowds were stirred by Martin Luther King's *eloquence*.

elucidate v. explain; enlighten. He was called upon to *elucidate* the disputed points in his article.

elusive ADJ. evasive; baffling; hard to grasp. His *elusive* dreams of wealth were costly to those of his friends who supported him financially. elude, v.

elysian ADJ. relating to paradise; blissful. An afternoon sail on the bay was for her an *elysian* journey.

emaciated ADJ. thin and wasted. His long period of starvation had left him *emaciated*.

emanate v. issue forth. A strong odor of sulfur *emanated* from the spring.

emancipate v. set free. At first, the attempts of the Abolitionists to *emancipate* the slaves were unpopular in New England as well as in the South.

embargo N. ban on commerce or other activity. As a result of the *embargo*, trade with the colonies was at a standstill.

embark v. commence; go on board a boat; begin a journey. In devoting herself to the study of gorillas, Dian Fossey *embarked* on a course of action that was to cost her her life.

embed v. enclose; place in something. Tales of actual historical figures like King Alfred have become *embedded* in legends.

■ **embellish** v. adorn. My mother-in-law's stories about her journey from Russia made us laugh because she *embellished* the bare facts of her travels with humorous anecdotes.

embezzlement N. stealing. The bank teller confessed his *embezzlement* of the funds.

embroil v. throw into confusion; involve in strife; entangle. He became *embroiled* in the heated discussion when he tried to arbitrate the dispute.

embryonic ADJ. undeveloped; rudimentary. The evil of class and race hatred must be eliminated while it is still in an *embryonic* state; otherwise, it may grow to dangerous proportions.

emend v. correct, usually a text. The critic *emended* the book by retranslating several passages.

emendation N. correction of errors; improvement. Please initial all the *emendations* you have made in this contract.

emetic N. substance causing vomiting. The use of an *emetic* like mustard is useful in cases of poisoning.

eminent ADJ. high; lofty. After his appointment to this *eminent* position, he seldom had time for his former friends.

emissary N. agent; messenger. The Secretary of State was sent as the President's special *emissary to* the conference on disarmament.

emollient N. soothing or softening remedy. He applied an *emollient* to the inflamed area. Also ADJ.

emolument N. salary; compensation. In addition to the *emolument* this position offers, you must consider the social prestige it carries with it.

empathy N. ability to identify with another's feelings, ideas, etc. What made Ann such a fine counselor was her *empathy,* her ability to put herself in her client's place and feel his emotions as if they were her own. empathize, v.

empirical ADJ. based on experience. He distrusted hunches and intuitive flashes; he placed his reliance entirely on *empirical* data.

■ **emulate** V. rival; imitate. As long as our political leaders *emulate* the virtues of the great leaders of this country, we shall flourish.

enamored ADJ. in love. Narcissus became *enamored* of his own beauty.

enclave N. territory enclosed within an alien land. The Vatican is an independent *enclave* in Italy.

encomiastic ADJ. praising; eulogistic. Some critics believe that his *encomiastic* statements about Napoleon were inspired by his desire for material advancement rather than by an honest belief in the Emperor's genius.

encomium N. high praise; eulogy. Uneasy with the *encomiums* expressed by his supporters, Tolkien felt unworthy of such high praise.

encompass V. surround. Although we were *encompassed* by enemy forces, we were cheerful for we were well stocked and could withstand a siege until our allies joined us.

encroachment N. gradual intrusion. The *encroachment* of the factories upon the neighborhood lowered the value of the real estate.

Word List 16   *Synonyms*

Each of the questions below consists of a word in capital letters, followed by five lettered words or phrases. Choose the lettered word or phrase that is most nearly similar in meaning to the word in capital letters and write the letter of your choice on your answer paper.

226. DWINDLE (A) blow (B) inhabit (C) spin (D) lessen (E) combine
227. ECSTASY (A) joy (B) speed (C) treasure (D) warmth (E) lack
228. EDIFY (A) mystify (B) suffice (C) improve (D) erect (E) entertain
229. EFFACE (A) countenance (B) encourage (C) recognize (D) blackball (E) rub out
230. EFFIGY (A) requisition (B) organ (C) charge (D) accordion (E) dummy
231. EGREGIOUS (A) pious (B) shocking (C) anxious (D) sociable (E) gloomy

232. EGRESS (A) entrance (B) bird (C) exit (D) double (E) progress
233. ELATED (A) debased (B) respectful (C) drooping (D) gay (E) charitable
234. ELUSIVE (A) deadly (B) eloping (C) evasive (D) simple (E) petrified
235. EMACIATED (A) garrulous (B) primeval (C) vigorous (D) disparate (E) thin
236. EMANCIPATE (A) set free (B) take back (C) make worse (D) embolden (E) run away
237. EMBELLISH (A) doff (B) don (C) abscond (D) adorn (E) equalize
238. EMBROIL (A) cherish (B) overheat (C) entangle (D) assure (E) worry
239. EMENDATION (A) correction (B) interpretation (C) exhumation (D) inquiry (E) fault
240. EMINENT (A) purposeful (B) high (C) delectable (D) curious (E) urgent

Word List 17   encumber-eulogistic

encumber V. burden. Some people *encumber* themselves with too much luggage, when they take short trips.

endearment N. fond word or act. Your gifts and *endearments* cannot make me forget your earlier insolence.

■ **endemic** ADJ. prevailing among a specific group of people or in a specific area or country. This disease is *endemic* in this part of the world; more than 80 percent of the population are at one time or another affected by it.

endorse V. approve; support. Everyone waited to see which one of the rival candidates for the city council the mayor would *endorse.* (secondary meaning) endorsement, N.

endue V. provide with some quality; endow. He was *endued* with a lion's courage.

enduring ADJ. lasting; surviving. Keats believed in the *enduring* power of great art, which would outlast its creators' brief lives.

energize V. invigorate; make forceful and active. Rather than exhausting Maggie, dancing *energized* her.

■ **enervate** V. weaken. She was slow to recover from her illness; even a short walk to the window *enervated* her. enervation, N.

enfranchise V. admit to the rights of citizenship (especially the right to vote). Although blacks were *enfranchised* shortly after the Civil War, women did not receive the right to vote until 1920.

engage V. attract; hire; pledge oneself; confront. "Your case has *engaged* my interest, my lord," said Holmes. "You may *engage* my services."

engaging ADJ. charming; attractive. Everyone liked Nancy's pleasant manners and *engaging* personality.

■ **engender** V. cause; produce. To receive praise for real accomplishments *engenders* self-confidence in a child.

engross V. occupy fully. John was so *engrossed* in his studies that he did not hear his mother call.

enhance v. advance; improve. Your chances for promotion in this department will be *enhanced* if you take some more courses in evening school.

enigma N. puzzle. Despite all attempts to decipher the code, it remained an *enigma*.

enigmatic ADJ. obscure; puzzling. Many have sought to fathom the *enigmatic* smile of the *Mona Lisa.*

enjoin v. command; order; forbid. The owners of the company asked the court to *enjoin* the union from picketing the plant.

enmity N. ill will; hatred. At Camp David President Carter labored to bring an end to the *enmity* that prevented Egypt and Israel from living in peace.

ennui N. boredom. The monotonous routine of hospital life induced a feeling of *ennui* which made him moody and irritable.

enormity N. hugeness (in a bad sense). He did not realize the *enormity* of his crime until he saw what suffering he had caused.

enrapture v. please intensely. The audience was *enraptured* by the freshness of the voices and the excellent orchestration

ensconce v. settle comfortably. The parents thought that their children were *ensconced* safely in the private school and decided to leave for Europe.

ensue v. follow. The evils that *ensued* were the direct result of the miscalculations of the leaders.

enthrall v. capture; enslave. From the moment he saw her picture, he was *enthralled* by her beauty.

entice v. lure; attract; tempt. She always tried to *entice* her baby brother into mischief.

entity N. real being. As soon as the charter was adopted, the United Nations became an *entity* and had to be considered as a factor in world diplomacy.

entomology N. study of insects. I found *entomology* the least interesting part of my course in biology; studying insects bored me.

entrance v. put under a spell; carry away with emotion. Shafts of sunlight on a wall could *entrance* her and leave her spellbound.

entreat v. plead; ask earnestly. She *entreated* her father to let her stay out till midnight.

entree N. entrance; a way in. Because of his wealth and social position, he had *entree* into the most exclusive circles.

entrepreneur N. businessperson; contractor. Opponents of our present tax program argue that it discourages *entrepreneurs* from trying new fields of business activity.

enumerate v. list; mention one by one. Huck hung his head in shame as Miss Watson *enumerated* his many flaws.

enunciate v. speak distinctly. How will people understand you if you do not *enunciate?*

environ v. enclose; surround. In medieval days, Paris was *environed* by a wall. environs, N.

eon N. long period of time; an age. It has taken *eons* for our civilization to develop.

epaulet N. ornament worn on the shoulder (of a uniform, etc.). The shoulder loops on Sam Spade's trench coat are the nonmilitary counterparts of the fringed *epaulets* on George Washington's uniform.

■ **ephemeral** ADJ. short-lived; fleeting. The mayfly is an *ephemeral* creature.

epic N. long heroic poem, novel, or similar work of art. Kurosawa's film *Seven Samurai* is an *epic* portraying the struggle of seven warriors to destroy a band of robbers. also ADJ.

epicure N. connoisseur of food and drink. *Epicures* frequent this restaurant because it features exotic wines and dishes. epicurean, ADJ.

epigram N. witty thought or saying, usually short. Poor Richard's *epigrams* made Benjamin Franklin famous.

epilogue N. short speech at conclusion of dramatic work. The audience was so disappointed in the play that many did not remain to hear the *epilogue*.

episodic ADJ. loosely connected. Though he tried to follow the plot of *Gravity's Rainbow,* John found the novel too *episodic.*

epistemologist N. philosopher who studies the nature of knowledge. "What is more important, a knowledge of nature or the nature of knowledge?" the *epistemologist* asked the naturalist.

epitaph N. inscription in memory of a dead person. In his will, he dictated the *epitaph* he wanted placed on his tombstone.

epithet N. word or phrase characteristically used to describe a person or thing. So many kings of France were named Charles that modern students need *epithets* to tell them apart: Charles the Wise, for example, was someone far different from Charles the Fat.

epitome N. perfect example or embodiment. Singing "I am the very model of a modern Major-General" in *The Pirates of Penzance,* Major-General Stanley proclaimed himself the *epitome* of an officer and a gentleman. epitomize, v.

epoch N. period of time. The glacial *epoch* lasted for thousands of years.

equable ADJ. tranquil; steady; uniform. After the hot summers and cold winters of New England, he found the climate of the West Indies *equable* and pleasant.

equanimity N. calmness of temperament. In his later years, he could look upon the foolishness of the world with *equanimity* and humor.

equestrian N. rider on horseback. These paths in the park are reserved for *equestrians* and their steeds. also ADJ.

equilibrium N. balance. After the divorce, he needed some time to regain his *equilibrium*.

equine ADJ. resembling a horse. His long, bony face had an *equine* look to it.

equinox N. period of equal days and nights; the beginning of spring and autumn. The vernal *equinox is* usually marked by heavy rainstorms.

equipoise N. balance; balancing force; equilibrium. The high-wire acrobat used his pole as an *equipoise* to overcome the swaying caused by the wind.

equitable ADJ. fair; impartial. I am seeking an *equitable* solution to this dispute, one which will be fair and acceptable to both sides.

equity N. fairness; justice. Our courts guarantee *equity* to all.

equivocal ADJ. doubtful; ambiguous. Macbeth was misled by the *equivocal* statements of the witches.

■ **equivocate** V. lie; mislead; attempt to conceal the truth. The audience saw through his attempts to *equivocate* on the subject under discussion and ridiculed his remarks.

erode V. eat away. The limestone was *eroded* by the dripping water. erosion, N.

erotic ADJ. pertaining to passionate love. The *erotic* passages in this novel should be removed as they are merely pornographic.

errant ADJ. wandering. Many a charming tale has been written about the knights-*errant* who helped the weak and punished the guilty during the Age of Chivalry.

erratic ADJ. odd; unpredictable. Investors become anxious when the stock market appears *erratic*.

erroneous ADJ. mistaken; wrong. I thought my answer was correct, but it was *erroneous.*

■ **erudite** ADJ. learned; scholarly. His *erudite* writing was difficult to read because of the many allusions which were unfamiliar to most readers. erudition, N.

escapade N. prank; flighty conduct. The headmaster could not regard this latest *escapade* as a boyish joke and expelled the young man.

eschew V. avoid. He tried to *eschew* all display of temper.

■ **esoteric** ADJ. hard to understand; known only to the chosen few. *New Yorker* short stories often include *esoteric* allusions to obscure people and events: the implication is, if you are in the in-crowd, you'll get the reference; if you come from Cleveland, you won't. esoterica, N.

espionage N. spying. In order to maintain its power, the government developed a system of *espionage* that penetrated every household.

espouse V. adopt; support. She was always ready to *espouse* a worthy cause.

esteem V. respect; value; judge. I *esteem* Ezra Pound both for his exciting poetry and for his acute comments on literature. also N.

estranged ADJ. separated; alienated. The *estranged* wife sought a divorce. estrangement, N.

ethereal ADJ. light; heavenly; fine. Visitors were impressed by her *ethereal* beauty, her delicate charm.

ethnic ADJ. relating to races. Intolerance between *ethnic* groups is deplorable and usually is based on lack of information.

ethnology N. study of humankind. Sociology is one aspect of the science of *ethnology.*

ethos N. underlying character of a culture, group, etc. Seeing how tenderly Spaniards treated her small daughter made author Barbara Kingsolver aware of how greatly children were valued in the Spanish *ethos.*

etymology N. study of word parts. A knowledge of *etymology* can help you on many English tests.

eugenic ADJ. pertaining to the improvement of race. It is easier to apply *eugenic* principles to the raising of racehorses or prize cattle than to the development of human beings.

eulogistic ADJ. praising. To everyone's surprise, the speech was *eulogistic* rather than critical in tone.

Test

Word List 17   *Antonyms*

Each of the questions below consists of a word in capital letters, followed by five lettered words or phrases. Choose the lettered word or phrase that is most nearly opposite in meaning to the word in capital letters and write the letter of your choice on your answer paper.

241. ENERVATE (A) strengthen (B) sputter (C) arrange (D) scrutinize (E) agree
242. ENHANCE (A) degrade (B) doubt (C) scuff (D) gasp (E) avoid
243. ENNUI (A) hate (B) excitement (C) seriousness (D) humility (E) kindness
244. ENUNCIATE (A) pray (B) request (C) deliver (D) wait (E) mumble
245. EPHEMERAL (A) sensuous (B) passing (C) popular (D) distasteful (E) eternal
246. EQUABLE (A) flat (B) decisive (C) stormy (D) dishonest (E) scanty

247. EQUANIMITY (A) agitation (B) stirring (C) volume (D) identity (E) luster
248. EQUILIBRIUM (A) imbalance (B) peace (C) inequity (D) directness (E) urgency
249. EQUITABLE (A) able to leave (B) able to learn (C) unfair (D) preferable (E) rough
250. EQUIVOCAL (A) mistaken (B) quaint (C) azure (D) clear (E) universal
251. ERRATIC (A) unromantic (B) free (C) popular (D) steady (E) unknown
252. ERRONEOUS (A) accurate (B) dignified (C) curious (D) abrupt (E) round
253. ERUDITE (A) professorial (B) stately (C) short (D) unknown (E) ignorant
254. ETHEREAL (A) long-lasting (B) earthy (C) ill (D) critical (E) false
255. EULOGISTIC (A) pretty (B) critical (C) brief (D) stern (E) free

Word List 18   eulogy-faculty

■ **eulogy** N. praise. All the *eulogies* of his friends could not remove the sting of the calumny heaped upon him by his enemies. eulogize, V.

■ **euphemism** N. mild expression in place of an unpleasant one. The expression "he passed away" is a *euphemism* for "he died."

euphony N. sweet sound. Noted for its *euphony* even when it is spoken, the Italian language is particularly pleasing to the ear when sung. euphonious, ADJ.

■ **euphoria** N. feeling of exaggerated (or unfounded) well-being. "Jill's been on cloud nine ever since Jack asked her out," said Betty, dismissing her friend's *euphoria.*

euthanasia N. mercy killing. Many people support *euthanasia* for terminally ill patients who wish to die.

evanescent ADJ. fleeting; vanishing. For a brief moment, the entire skyline was bathed in an orange-red hue in the *evanescent* rays of the sunset.

evasive ADJ. not frank; eluding. Your *evasive* answers convinced the judge that you were withholding important evidence. evade, V.

evince V. show clearly. When he tried to answer the questions, he *evinced* his ignorance of the subject matter.

evenhanded ADJ. impartial; fair. Do men and women receive *evenhanded* treatment from their teachers, or, as recent studies suggest, do teachers pay more attention to male students than to females?

evoke V. call forth. He *evoked* much criticism by his hostile manner. evocation, N.

ewe N. female sheep. The flock of sheep was made up of dozens of *ewes*, together with only a handful of rams.

exacerbate V. worsen; embitter. This latest arrest will *exacerbate* the already existing discontent of the people and enrage them.

exacting ADJ. extremely demanding. The colonies rebelled against the *exacting* financial claims of the mother country. exaction, N.

exalt V. raise in rank or dignity; praise. The actor Alec Guinness was *exalted* to the rank of knighthood by the Queen; he now is known as Sir Alec Guinness.

exasperate V. vex. Johnny often *exasperates* his mother with his pranks.

excerpt N. selected passage (written or musical). The cinematic equivalent of an *excerpt* from a novel is a clip from a film. also V.

exchequer N. treasury. He had been Chancellor of the *Exchequer* before his promotion to the office he now holds.

excise V. cut away; cut out. When you *excise* the dead and dying limbs of a tree, you not only improve its appearance but also enhance its chances of bearing fruit. excision, N.

excoriate V. flay; abrade. These shoes are so ill-fitting that they will *excoriate* the feet and create blisters.

■ **exculpate** V. clear from blame. He was *exculpated* of the crime when the real criminal confessed.

execrable ADJ. very bad. The anecdote was in *execrable* taste and shocked the audience.

execrate V. curse; express abhorrence for. The world *execrates* the memory of Hitler and hopes that genocide will never again be the policy of any nation.

execute V. put into effect; carry out. The choreographer wanted to see how well she could *execute* a pirouette. (secondary meaning) execution, N.

exegesis N. explanation, especially of biblical passages. I can follow your *exegesis* of this passage to a limited degree; some of your reasoning eludes me.

exemplary ADJ. serving as a model; outstanding. Her *exemplary* behavior was praised at commencement.

exemplify V. show by example; furnish an example. Three-time winner of the Super Bowl, Joe Montana *exemplifies* the ideal quarterback.

exertion N. effort; expenditure of much physical work. The *exertion* involved in unscrewing the rusty bolt left her exhausted.

exhort V. urge. The evangelist will *exhort* all sinners in his audience to reform. exhortation, N.

exhume V. dig out of the ground; remove from a grave. Because of the rumor that he had been poisoned, his body was *exhumed* in order that an autopsy might be performed.

■ **exigency** N. urgent situation. In this *exigency,* we must look for aid from our allies. exigent, ADJ.

exiguous ADJ. small; minute. Grass grew there, an *exiguous* outcropping among the rocks.

existential ADJ. pertaining to existence; pertaining to the philosophy of existentialism. To the *existential* philosopher, human reason is inadequate to explain an irrational, meaningless universe.

exodus N. departure. The *exodus* from the hot and stuffy city was particularly noticeable on Friday evenings.

exonerate V. acquit; exculpate. I am sure this letter naming the actual culprit will *exonerate* you.

exorbitant ADJ. excessive. The people grumbled at his *exorbitant* prices but paid them because he had a monopoly.

exorcise V. drive out evil spirits. By incantation and prayer, the medicine man sought to *exorcise* the evil spirits that had taken possession of the young warrior.

exotic ADJ. not native; strange. Because of his *exotic* headdress, he was followed in the streets by small children who laughed at his strange appearance.

expatiate V. talk at length. At this time, please give us a brief résumé of your work; we shall permit you to *expatiate* later.

expatriate N. exile; someone who has withdrawn from his native land. Henry James was an American *expatriate* who settled in England.

expedient ADJ. suitable; practical; politic. A pragmatic politician, he was guided by what was *expedient* rather than by what was ethical. expediency, N.

expedite V. hasten. We hope you will be able to *expedite* delivery because of our tight schedule.

expertise N. specialized knowledge; expert skill. Although she was knowledgeable in a number of fields, she was hired for her particular *expertise* in computer programming.

expiate V. make amends for (a sin). He tried to *expiate* his crimes by a full confession to the authorities.

expletive N. interjection; profane oath. The sergeant's remarks were filled with *expletives* that offended the new recruits.

explicate V. explain; interpret; clarify. Harry Levin *explicated* James Joyce's novels with such clarity that even *Finnegan's Wake* seemed comprehensible to his students.

explicit ADJ. totally clear; definite; outspoken. Don't just hint around that you're dissatisfied: be *explicit* about what's bugging you.

exploit N. deed or action, particularly a brave deed. Raoul Wallenberg was noted for his *exploits* in rescuing Jews from Hitler's forces.

exploit V. make use of, sometimes unjustly. Cesar Chavez fought attempts to *exploit* migrant farmworkers in California. exploitation, N.

expository ADJ. explanatory; serving to explain. The manual that came with my VCR was no masterpiece of *expository* prose: its explanations were so garbled that I couldn't even figure out how to rewind a tape.

expostulation N. protest; remonstrance. Despite the teacher's scoldings and *expostulations,* the class remained unruly.

exposure N. risk, particularly of being exposed to disease or to the elements; unmasking; act of laying something open. *Exposure* to sun and wind had dried out her hair and weathered her face.

expunge V. cancel; remove. If you behave, I will *expunge* this notation from your record.

expurgate V. clean; remove offensive parts of a book. The editors felt that certain passages in the book had to be *expurgated* before it could be used in the classroom.

extant ADJ. still in existence. Although the authorities suppressed the book, many copies are *extant* and may be purchased at exorbitant prices.

extemporaneous ADJ. not planned; impromptu. Because his *extemporaneous* remarks were misinterpreted, he decided to write all his speeches in advance.

extenuate V. weaken; mitigate. It is easier for us to *extenuate* our own shortcomings than those of others.

extirpate V. root up. The Salem witch trials were a misguided attempt to *extirpate* superstition and heresy.

extol V. praise; glorify. The astronauts were *extolled* as the pioneers of the Space Age.

extort V. wring from; get money by threats, etc. The blackmailer *extorted* money from his victim.

extradition N. surrender of prisoner by one state to another. The lawyers opposed the *extradition* of their client on the grounds that for more than five years he had been a model citizen.

extraneous ADJ. not essential; external. Do not pad your paper with *extraneous* matters; stick to essential items only.

■ **extrapolation** N. projection; conjecture. Based on their *extrapolation* from the results of the primaries on Super Tuesday, the networks predicted that George Bush would be the Republican candidate for the presidency. extrapolate, V.

extricate V. free; disentangle. He found that he could not *extricate* himself from the trap.

extrinsic ADJ. external; not inherent; foreign. Do not be fooled by *extrinsic* causes. We must look for the intrinsic reason.

extrovert N. person interested mostly in external objects and actions. A good salesperson is usually an *extrovert,* who likes to mingle with people.

extrude V. force or push out. Much pressure is required to *extrude* these plastics.

exuberant ADJ. abundant; effusive; lavish. His speeches were famous for his *exuberant* language and vivid imagery.

exude V. discharge; give forth. The maple syrup is obtained from the sap that the trees *exude* in early spring. exudation, N.

exult V. rejoice. We *exulted* when our team won the victory.

fabricate V. build; lie. Because of the child's tendency to *fabricate,* we had trouble believing her.

facade N. front of the building. The *facade* of the church had often been photographed by tourists because it was more interesting than the rear.

facet N. small plane surface (of a gem); a side. The stonecutter decided to improve the rough diamond by providing it with several *facets.*

■ **facetious** ADJ. humorous; jocular. Your *facetious* remarks are not appropriate at this serious moment.

facile ADJ. easy; expert. Because he was a *facile* speaker, he never refused a request to address an organization.

■ **facilitate** V. make less difficult. He tried to *facilitate* repayment of the loan by getting a part-time job.

facsimile N. copy. Many museums sell *facsimiles* of the works of art on display.

faction N. party; clique; dissension. The quarrels and bickering of the two small *factions* within the club disturbed the majority of the members.

factious ADJ. inclined to form factions; causing dissension. Your statement is *factious* and will upset the harmony that now exists.

factitious ADJ. artificial; sham. Hollywood actresses often create *factitious* tears by using glycerine.

factotum N. handyman; person who does all kinds of work. Although we had hired him as a messenger, we soon began to use him as a general *factotum* around the office.

faculty N. mental or bodily powers; teaching staff. As he grew old, he feared he might lose his *faculties* and become useless to his employer.

Test

Word List 18   *Antonyms*

Each of the questions below consists of a word in capital letters, followed by five lettered words or phrases. Choose the lettered word or phrase that is most nearly opposite in meaning to the word in capital letters and write the letter of your choice on your answer paper.

256. EUPHONIOUS (A) strident (B) lethargic
(C) literary (D) significant (E) merry

257. EVASIVE (A) frank (B) correct (C) empty
(D) fertile (E) watchful

258. EXASPERATE (A) confide (B) formalize
(C) placate (D) betray (E) bargain

259. EXCORIATE (A) scandalize (B) encourage
(C) avoid (D) praise (E) vanquish

260. EXCULPATE (A) blame (B) prevail (C) acquire
(D) ravish (E) accumulate

261. EXECRABLE (A) innumerable (B) philosophic
(C) physical (D) excellent (E) meditative

262. EXECRATE (A) disobey (B) enact (C) perform
(D) acclaim (E) fidget

263. EXHUME (A) decipher (B) sadden (C) integrate
(D) admit (E) inter

264. EXODUS (A) neglect (B) consent (C) entry
(D) gain (E) rebuke

265. EXONERATE (A) forge (B) accuse (C) record
(D) doctor (E) reimburse

266. EXORBITANT (A) moderate (B) partisan
(C) military (D) barbaric (E) counterfeit

267. EXTEMPORANEOUS (A) rehearsed (B) hybrid
(C) humiliating (D) statesmanlike (E) picturesque

268. EXTRANEOUS (A) modern (B) decisive
(C) essential (D) effective (E) expressive

269. EXTRINSIC (A) reputable (B) inherent (C) swift
(D) ambitious (E) cursory

270. EXTROVERT (A) clown (B) hero (C) ectomorph
(D) neurotic (E) introvert

Word List 19   fallacious-flinch

■ **fallacious** ADJ. misleading. Your reasoning must be *fallacious* because it leads to a ridiculous answer.

fallible ADJ. liable to err. I know I am *fallible,* but I feel confident that I am right this time.

fallow ADJ. plowed but not sowed; uncultivated. Farmers have learned that it is advisable to permit land to lie *fallow* every few years.

falter V. hesitate. When told to dive off the high board, she did not *falter,* but proceeded at once.

fanaticism N. excessive zeal. The leader of the group was held responsible even though he could not control the *fanaticism* of his followers. fanatic, ADJ., N.

fancied ADJ. imagined; unreal. You are resenting *fancied* insults. No one has ever said such things about you.

fancier N. breeder or dealer of animals. The dog *fancier* exhibited her prize collie at the annual Kennel Club show.

fanciful ADJ. whimsical; visionary. This is a *fanciful* scheme because it does not consider the facts.

fanfare N. call by bugles or trumpets; showy display. The exposition was opened with a *fanfare* of trumpets and the firing of cannon.

fantastic ADJ. unreal; grotesque; whimsical. Your fears are *fantastic* because no such animal as you have described exists.

farce N. broad comedy; mockery. Nothing went right; the entire interview degenerated into a *farce.* farcical, ADJ.

fastidious ADJ. difficult to please; squeamish. The waitresses disliked serving him dinner because of his very *fastidious* taste.

fatalism N. belief that events are determined by forces beyond one's control. With *fatalism,* he accepted the hardships that beset him. fatalistic, ADJ.

fathom V. comprehend; investigate. I find his motives impossible to *fathom.*

fatuous ADJ. foolish; inane. He is far too intelligent to utter such *fatuous* remarks.

fauna N. animals of a period or region. The scientist could visualize the *fauna* of the period by examining the skeletal remains and the fossils.

■ **fawning** ADJ. courting favor by cringing and flattering. She was constantly surrounded by a group of *fawning* admirers who hoped to win some favor. fawn, V.

faze V. disconcert; dismay. No crisis could *faze* the resourceful hotel manager.

feasible ADJ. practical. This is an entirely *feasible* proposal. I suggest we adopt it.

febrile ADJ. feverish. In his *febrile* condition, he was subject to nightmares and hallucinations.

fecundity N. fertility; fruitfulness. The *fecundity* of his mind is illustrated by the many vivid images in his poems.

feign V. pretend. Lady Macbeth *feigned* illness in the courtyard although she was actually healthy.

feint N. trick; shift; sham blow. The boxer was fooled by his opponent's *feint* and dropped his guard. also V.

■ **felicitous** ADJ. apt; suitably expressed; well chosen. He was famous for his *felicitous* remarks and was called upon to serve as master-of-ceremonies at many a banquet.

felicity N. happiness; appropriateness (of a remark, choice, etc.). She wrote a note to the newlyweds wishing them great *felicity* in their wedded life.

fell ADJ. cruel; deadly. The newspapers told of the tragic spread of the *fell* disease.

felon N. person convicted of a grave crime. A convicted *felon* loses the right to vote.

ferment N. agitation; commotion. With the breakup of the Soviet Union, much of Eastern Europe was in a state of *ferment.* also V.

ferret V. drive or hunt out of hiding. She *ferreted* out their secret.

fervent ADJ. ardent; hot. She felt that the *fervent* praise was excessive and somewhat undeserved.

fervid ADJ. ardent. Her *fervid* enthusiasm inspired all of us to undertake the dangerous mission.

■ **fervor** N. glowing ardor. Their kiss was full of the *fervor* of first love.

fester V. generate pus. When her finger began to *fester,* the doctor lanced it and removed the splinter that had caused the pus to form.

fester V. rankle, produce irritation or resentment. Joe's insult *festered* in Anne's mind for days, and made her too angry to speak to him.

festive ADJ. joyous; celebratory. Their wedding in the park was a *festive* occasion.

fete V. honor at a festival. The returning hero was *feted* at a community supper and dance. also N.

fetid ADJ. malodorous. The neglected wound became *fetid*.

fetter V. shackle. The prisoner was *fettered* to the wall.

fiasco N. total failure. Our ambitious venture ended in a *fiasco* and we were forced to flee.

fiat N. command. I cannot accept government by *fiat;* I feel that I must be consulted.

fickle ADJ. changeable; faithless. He discovered his supposedly faithful girlfriend was *fickle*.

fictitious ADJ. imaginary. Although this book purports to be a biography of George Washington, many of the incidents are *fictitious*.

fidelity N. loyalty. A dog's *fidelity* to its owner is one of the reasons why that animal is a favorite household pet.

figment N. invention; imaginary thing. That incident never took place; it is a *figment* of your imagination.

figurative ADJ. not literal, but metaphorical; using a figure of speech. "To lose one's marbles" is a *figurative* expression; if you're told Jack has lost his marbles, no one expects you to rush out to buy him a replacement set.

figurine N. small ornamental statuette. In *The Maltese Falcon,* Sam Spade was hired to trace the missing *figurine* of a black bird.

filch V. steal. The boys *filched* apples from the fruit stand.

filial ADJ. pertaining to a son or daughter. Many children forget their *filial* obligations and disregard the wishes of their parents.

filibuster V. block legislation by making long speeches. Even though we disapproved of Senator Foghorn's political goals, we were impressed by his ability to *filibuster* endlessly to keep an issue from coming to a vote.

filigree N. delicate, lacelike metalwork. The pendant with gold *filigree* that she wore round her neck trembled with each breath she took.

finale N. conclusion. It is not until we reach the *finale* of this play that we can understand the author's message.

finesse N. delicate skill. The *finesse* and adroitness of the surgeon impressed the observers in the operating room.

finicky ADJ. too particular; fussy. The old lady was *finicky* about her food and ate very little.

finite ADJ. limited. It is difficult for humanity with its *finite* existence to grasp the infinite.

firebrand N. hothead; troublemaker. The police tried to keep track of all the local *firebrands* when the President came to town.

fissure N. crevice. The mountain climbers secured footholds in tiny *fissures* in the rock.

fitful ADJ. spasmodic; intermittent. After several *fitful* attempts, he decided to postpone the start of the project until he felt more energetic.

flaccid ADJ. flabby. His sedentary life had left him with *flaccid* muscles.

■ **flag** V. droop; grow feeble. When the opposing hockey team scored its third goal only minutes into the first period, the home team's spirits *flagged*. flagging, ADJ.

flagrant ADJ. conspicuously wicked. We cannot condone such *flagrant* violations of the rules.

flail V. thresh grain by hand; strike or slap; toss about. In medieval times, warriors *flailed* their foe with a metal ball attached to a handle.

flair N. talent. She has an uncanny *flair* for discovering new artists before the public has become aware of their existence.

flamboyant ADJ. ornate. Modern architecture has discarded the *flamboyant* trimming on buildings and emphasizes simplicity of line.

flaunt V. display ostentatiously. She is not one of those actresses who *flaunt* their physical charms; she can act.

flay V. strip off skin; plunder. The criminal was condemned to be *flayed* alive.

fleck V. spot. Her cheeks, *flecked* with tears, were testimony to the hours of weeping.

■ **fledgling** ADJ. inexperienced. While it is necessary to provide these *fledgling* poets with an opportunity to present their work, it is not essential that we admire everything they write. also N.

fleece N. wool coat of a sheep. They shear sheep of their *fleece,* which they then comb into separate strands of wool.

fleece V. rob; plunder. The tricksters *fleeced* him of his inheritance.

flick N. light stroke as with a whip. The horse needed no encouragement; only one *flick* of the whip was all the jockey had to apply to get the animal to run at top speed.

flinch V. hesitate; shrink. He did not *flinch* in the face of danger but fought back bravely.

Test

Word List 19 *Synonyms and Antonyms*

Each of the following questions consists of a word in capital letters, followed by five lettered words or phrases. Choose the lettered word or phrase that is most nearly similar or opposite in meaning to the word in capital letters and write the letter of your choice on your answer paper.

271. FANCIFUL (A) imaginative (B) knowing (C) elaborate (D) quick (E) lusty

272. FATUOUS (A) fatal (B) natal (C) terrible (D) sensible (E) tolerable

273. FEASIBLE (A) theoretical (B) impatient (C) constant (D) present (E) impractical

274. FECUNDITY (A) prophecy (B) futility
(C) fruitfulness (D) need (E) dormancy
275. FEIGN (A) deserve (B) condemn (C) condone
(D) attend (E) pretend
276. FELL (A) propitious (B) illiterate (C) uppermost
(D) futile (E) inherent
277. FERMENT (A) stir up (B) fill (C) ferret (D) mutilate
(E) banish
278. FIASCO (A) cameo (B) mansion (C) pollution
(D) success (E) gamble
279. FICKLE (A) fallacious (B) tolerant (C) loyal
(D) hungry (E) stupid

280. FILCH (A) milk (B) purloin (C) itch (D) cancel
(E) resent
281. FINITE (A) bounded (B) established (C) affirmative
(D) massive (E) finicky
282. FLAIL (A) succeed (B) harvest (C) mend
(D) strike (E) resent
283. FLAIR (A) conflagration (B) inspiration (C) bent
(D) egregiousness (E) magnitude
284. FLAMBOYANT (A) old-fashioned (B) restrained
(C) impulsive (D) cognizant (E) eloquent
285. FLEDGLING (A) weaving (B) bobbing
(C) beginning (D) studying (E) flaying

Word List 20 flippancy-gaffe

flippancy N. trifling gaiety. Your *flippancy* at this serious moment is offensive. flippant, ADJ.

flit V. fly; dart lightly; pass swiftly by. Like a bee *flitting* from flower to flower, Rose *flitted* from one boyfriend to the next.

floe N. mass of floating ice. The ship made slow progress as it battered its way through the ice *floes*.

flora N. plants of a region or era. Because she was a botanist, she spent most of her time studying the *flora* of the desert.

florid ADJ. flowery; ruddy. His complexion was even more *florid* than usual because of his anger.

flotsam N. drifting wreckage. Beachcombers eke out a living by salvaging the *flotsam* and jetsam of the sea.

flourish V. grow well; prosper; make sweeping gestures. The orange trees *flourished* in the sun.

flout V. reject; mock. The headstrong youth *flouted* all authority; he refused to be curbed.

fluctuation N. wavering. Meteorologists watch the *fluctuations* of the barometer in order to predict the weather.

fluency N. smoothness of speech. He spoke French with *fluency* and ease.

fluke N. unlikely occurrence; stroke of fortune. When Douglas defeated Tyson for the heavyweight championship, some sportscasters dismissed his victory as a *fluke*.

fluster V. confuse. The teacher's sudden question *flustered* him and he stammered his reply.

fluted ADJ. having vertical parallel grooves (as in a pillar). All that remained of the ancient building were the *fluted* columns.

flux N. flowing; series of changes. While conditions are in such a state of *flux*, I do not wish to commit myself too deeply in this affair.

fodder N. coarse food for cattle, horses, etc. One of Nancy's chores at the ranch was to put fresh supplies of *fodder* in the horses' stalls.

foible N. weakness; slight fault. We can overlook the *foibles* of our friends; no one is perfect.

foil N. contrast. In "Star Wars," dark, evil Darth Vader is a perfect foil for fair-haired, naive Luke Skywalker.

foil V. defeat; frustrate. In the end, Skywalker is able to *foil* Vader's diabolical schemes.

foist V. insert improperly; palm off. I will not permit you to *foist* such ridiculous ideas upon the membership of this group.

foliage N. masses of leaves. Every autumn before the leaves fell he promised himself he would drive through New England to admire the colorful fall *foliage*.

■ **foment** V. stir up; instigate. This report will *foment* dissension in the club.

foolhardy ADJ. rash. Don't be *foolhardy*. Get the advice of experienced people before undertaking this venture.

foppish ADJ. vain about dress and appearance. He tried to imitate the *foppish* manner of the young men of the court.

foray N. raid. The company staged a midnight *foray* against the enemy outpost.

forbearance N. patience. We must use *forbearance* in dealing with him because he is still weak from his illness.

ford N. place where a river can be crossed on foot. Rather than risk using the shaky rope bridge, David walked a half-mile downstream until he came to the nearest *ford*. also V.

forebears N. ancestors. Reverence for one's *forebears* (sometimes referred to as ancestor worship) plays an important part in many Oriental cultures.

foreboding N. premonition of evil. Caesar ridiculed his wife's *forebodings* about the Ides of March.

forensic ADJ. suitable to debate or courts of law. In her best *forensic* manner, the lawyer addressed the jury.

foreshadow V. give an indication beforehand; portend; prefigure. In retrospect, political analysts realized that Yeltsin's defiance of the attempted coup *foreshadowed* his emergence as the dominant figure of the new Russian republic.

foresight N. ability to foresee future happenings; prudence. A wise investor, she had the *foresight* to buy land just before the current real estate boom.

■ **forestall** V. prevent by taking action in advance. By setting up a prenuptial agreement, the prospective bride and groom hoped to *forestall* any potential arguments about money in the event of a divorce.

forgo V. give up; do without. Determined to lose weight for the summer, Ida decided to *forgo* dessert until she could fit into a size eight again.

formality N. adherence to established rules or procedures. Signing this petition is a mere *formality;* it does not obligate you in any way.

formidable ADJ. menacing; threatening. We must not treat the battle lightly for we are facing a *formidable* foe.

forsake V. desert; abandon; renounce. No one expected Foster to *forsake* his wife and children and run off with another woman.

forswear V. renounce; abandon. The captured knight could escape death only if he agreed to *forswear* Christianity and embrace Islam as the one true faith.

forte N. strong point or special talent. I am not eager to play this rather serious role, for my *forte* is comedy.

forthright ADJ. straightforward; direct; frank. I prefer Jill's *forthright* approach to Jack's tendency to beat around the bush.

fortitude N. bravery; courage. He was awarded the medal for his *fortitude* in the battle.

fortuitous ADJ. accidental; by chance. There is no connection between these two events; their timing is entirely *fortuitous.*

foster V. rear; encourage. According to the legend, Romulus and Remus were *fostered* by a she-wolf that raised the abandoned infants as her own. also ADJ.

founder V. fail completely; sink. After hitting the submerged iceberg, the *Titanic* started taking in water rapidly and soon *foundered.*

founder N. person who establishes (an organization, business). Among those drowned when the *Titanic* sank was the *founder* of the Abraham & Straus chain.

fracas N. brawl, melee. The military police stopped the *fracas* in the bar and arrested the belligerents.

fractious ADJ. unruly. The *fractious* horse unseated its rider.

frailty N. weakness. The doctor prescribed vitamin and mineral supplements for the sick old woman because of her *frailty.*

franchise N. right granted by authority. The city issued a *franchise* to the company to operate surface transit lines on the streets for ninety-nine years. also V.

frantic ADJ. wild. At the time of the collision, many people became *frantic* with fear.

fraudulent ADJ. cheating; deceitful. The government seeks to prevent *fraudulent* and misleading advertising.

fraught ADJ. filled. Since this enterprise is *fraught* with danger, I will ask for volunteers who are willing to assume the risks.

fray N. brawl. The three musketeers were in the thick of the *fray.*

frenetic ADJ. frenzied; frantic. His *frenetic* activities convinced us that he had no organized plan of operation.

frenzied ADJ. madly excited. As soon as they smelled smoke, the *frenzied* animals milled about in their cages.

fresco N. painting on plaster (usually fresh). The cathedral is visited by many tourists who wish to admire the *frescoes* by Giotto.

fret V. to be annoyed or vexed. To *fret* over your poor grades is foolish; instead, decide to work harder in the future.

friction N. clash in opinion; rubbing against. At this time when harmony is essential, we cannot afford to have any *friction* in our group.

frieze N. ornamental band on a wall. The *frieze* of the church was adorned with sculpture.

frigid ADJ. intensely cold. Alaska is in the *frigid* zone.

fritter V. waste. He could not apply himself to any task and *frittered* away his time in idle conversation.

frivolous ADJ. lacking in seriousness; self-indulgently carefree; relatively unimportant. Though Nancy enjoyed Bill's *frivolous,* lighthearted companionship, she sometimes wondered whether he could ever be serious. frivolity, N.

frolicsome ADJ. prankish; gay. The *frolicsome* puppy tried to lick the face of its master.

frond N. fern leaf; palm or banana leaf. After the storm the beach was littered with the *fronds* of palm trees.

fructify V. bear fruit. This peach tree should *fructify* in three years.

■ **frugality** N. thrift; economy. In these economically difficult days businesses must practice *frugality* or risk bankruptcy. frugal, ADJ.

fruition N. bearing of fruit; fulfillment; realization. This building marks the *fruition* of all our aspirations and years of hard work.

frustrate V. thwart; defeat. We must *frustrate* this dictator's plan to seize control of the government.

fugitive ADJ. fleeting or transitory; roving. The film brought a few *fugitive* images to her mind, but on the whole it made no lasting impression upon her.

fulcrum N. support on which a lever rests. If we use this stone as a *fulcrum* and the crowbar as a lever, we may be able to move this boulder.

fulminate V. thunder; explode. The people against whom she *fulminated* were innocent of any wrongdoing.

fulsome ADJ. disgustingly excessive. His *fulsome* praise of the dictator annoyed his listeners.

functionary N. official. As his case was transferred from one *functionary* to another, he began to despair of ever reaching a settlement.

fundamental V. basic; primary; essential. The committee discussed all sorts of side issues without ever getting down to addressing the *fundamental* problem.

funereal ADJ. sad; solemn. I fail to understand why there is such a *funereal* atmosphere; we have lost a battle, not a war.

furor N. frenzy; great excitement. The story of her embezzlement of the funds created a *furor* on the stock exchange.

■ **furtive** ADJ. stealthy; sneaky. The boy gave a *furtive* look at his classmate's test paper.

fusillade N. simultaneous firing or outburst (of missiles, questions, etc.). Tchaikovsky's *1812 Overture* concludes with a thunderous *fusillade* of cannon fire.

fusion N. union; coalition. The opponents of the political party in power organized a *fusion* of disgruntled groups and became an important element in the election.

futile ADJ. ineffective; fruitless. Why waste your time on *futile* pursuits? futility, N.

gadfly N. animal-biting fly; an irritating person. Like a *gadfly*, he irritated all the guests at the hotel; within forty-eight hours, everyone regarded him as an annoying busybody.

gaffe N. social blunder. According to Miss Manners, to call your husband by your lover's name is worse than a mere *gaffe*; it is a tactical mistake.

Test

Word List 20 *Synonyms*

Each of the questions below consists of a word in capital letters, followed by five lettered words or phrases. Choose the lettered word or phrase that is most nearly similar in meaning to the word in capital letters and write the letter of your choice on your answer paper.

286. FLORID (A) ruddy (B) rusty (C) ruined (D) patient (E) poetic
287. FOIL (A) bury (B) frustrate (C) shield (D) desire (E) gain
288. FOMENT (A) spoil (B) instigate (C) interrogate (D) spray (E) maintain
289. FOOLHARDY (A) strong (B) unwise (C) brave (D) futile (E) erudite
290. FOPPISH (A) scanty (B) radical (C) orthodox (D) dandyish (E) magnificent
291. FORAY (A) excursion (B) contest (C) ranger (D) intuition (E) fish

292. FORMIDABLE (A) dangerous (B) outlandish (C) grandiloquent (D) impenetrable (E) venerable
293. FOSTER (A) accelerate (B) fondle (C) become infected (D) raise (E) roll
294. FRANCHISE (A) subway (B) discount (C) license (D) reason (E) fashion
295. FRITTER (A) sour (B) chafe (C) dissipate (D) cancel (E) abuse
296. FRUGALITY (A) foolishness (B) extremity (C) indifference (D) enthusiasm (E) economy
297. FULMINATE (A) fulfill (B) contemplate (C) talk nonsense (D) protest loudly (E) meander
298. FUROR (A) excitement (B) worry (C) flux (D) anteroom (E) lover
299. FURTIVE (A) underhanded (B) coy (C) brilliant (D) quick (E) abortive
300. GADFLY (A) humorist (B) nuisance (C) scholar (D) bum (E) thief

Word List 21 gainsay-gossamer

■ **gainsay** V. deny. She was too honest to *gainsay* the truth of the report.

gait N. manner of walking or running; speed. The lame man walked with an uneven *gait*.

galaxy N. the Milky Way; any collection of brilliant personalities. The deaths of such famous actors as Clark Gable, Gary Cooper, Spencer Tracy, and Marlene Dietrich demonstrate that the *galaxy* of Hollywood superstars is rapidly disappearing.

gall N. bitterness; nerve. The knowledge of his failure filled him with *gall*.

gall V. annoy; chafe. Their taunts *galled* him.

galleon N. large sailing ship. The Spaniards pinned their hopes on the *galleon*, the large warship; the British, on the smaller and faster pinnace.

galvanize V. stimulate by shock; stir up. The entire nation was *galvanized* into strong military activity by the news of the attack on Pearl Harbor.

gambit N. opening in chess in which a piece is sacrificed. The player was afraid to accept his opponent's *gambit* because he feared a trap which as yet he could not see.

gambol V. skip; leap playfully. Watching children *gamboling* in the park is a pleasant experience. also N.

gamely ADV. in a spirited manner; with courage. Because he had fought *gamely* against a much superior boxer, the crowd gave him a standing ovation when he left the arena.

gamut N. entire range. In this performance, the leading lady was able to demonstrate the complete *gamut* of her acting ability.

gape V. open widely. The huge pit *gaped* before him; if he stumbled, he would fall in.

garbled ADJ. mixed up; jumbled; distorted. A favorite party game involves passing a whispered message from one person to another; by the time it reaches the last player, the message has become totally *garbled*. garble, V.

gargantuan ADJ. huge; enormous. The *gargantuan* wrestler was terrified of mice.

gargoyle N. waterspout carved in grotesque figures on a building. The *gargoyles* adorning the Cathedral of Notre Dame in Paris are amusing in their grotesqueness.

garish ADJ. gaudy. She wore a *garish* rhinestone necklace.

garner V. gather; store up. She hoped to *garner* the world's literature in one library.

garnish V. decorate. Parsley was used to *garnish* the boiled potato. also N.

■ **garrulity** N. talkativeness. The man who married a dumb wife asked the doctor to make him deaf because of his wife's *garrulity* after her cure.

garrulous ADJ. excessively talkative, especially about unimportant subjects; loquacious; wordy. Many club members avoided the company of the *garrulous* junior executive because his constant chatter bored them to tears.

gastronomy N. science of preparing and serving good food. One of the by-products of his trip to Europe was his interest in *gastronomy*; he enjoyed preparing and serving foreign dishes to his friends.

gauche ADJ. clumsy; boorish. Such remarks are *gauche* and out of place; you should apologize for making them. gaucherie, N.

gaudy ADJ. flashy; showy. Her *gaudy* taste in clothes appalled us.

gaunt ADJ. lean and angular; barren. His once-round face looked surprisingly *gaunt* after he had lost weight.

gawk V. stare foolishly; look in open-mouthed awe. The country boy *gawked* at the skyscrapers and neon lights of the big city.

gazette N. official periodical publication. He read the *gazettes* regularly for the announcement of his promotion.

genealogy N. record of descent; lineage. He was proud of his *genealogy* and constantly referred to the achievements of his ancestors.

generality N. vague statement. This report is filled with *generalities*; you must be more specific in your statements.

generic ADJ. characteristic of an entire class or species. Sue knew so many computer programmers who spent their spare time playing fantasy games that she began to think that playing Dungeons & Dragons was a *generic* trait.

genesis N. beginning; origin. Tracing the *genesis* of a family is the theme of "Roots."

geniality N. cheerfulness; kindliness; sympathy. This restaurant is famous and popular because of the *geniality* of the proprietor, who tries to make everyone happy. genial, ADJ.

genre N. particular variety of art or literature. Both a short story writer and a poet, Langston Hughes proved himself equally skilled in either *genre*.

genteel ADJ. well-bred; elegant. We are looking for a man with a *genteel* appearance who can inspire confidence by his cultivated manner.

gentility N. those of gentle birth; refinement. Her family was proud of its *gentility* and elegance.

gentry N. people of standing; class of people just below nobility. The local *gentry* did not welcome the visits of the summer tourists and tried to ignore their presence in the community.

genuflect V. bend the knee as in worship. A proud democrat, he refused to *genuflect* to any man.

germane ADJ. pertinent; bearing upon the case at hand. The lawyer objected that the testimony being offered was not *germane* to the case at hand.

germinal ADJ. pertaining to a germ; creative. Such an idea is *germinal*; I am certain that it will influence thinkers and philosophers for many generations.

germinate V. cause to sprout; sprout. After the seeds *germinate* and develop their permanent leaves, the plants may be removed from the cold frames and transplanted to the garden.

gerontocracy N. government ruled by old people. Gulliver visited a *gerontocracy* in which the young people acted as servants to their elders, all the while dreaming of the day they would be old enough to have servants of their own.

gerrymander V. change voting district lines in order to favor a political party. The illogical pattern of the map of this congressional district is proof that the state legislature *gerrymandered* this area in order to favor the majority party. also N.

gestate V. evolve, as in prenatal growth. While this scheme was being *gestated* by the conspirators, they maintained complete silence about their intentions.

gesticulation N. motion; gesture. Operatic performers are trained to make exaggerated *gesticulations* because of the large auditoriums in which they appear.

ghastly ADJ. horrible. The murdered man was a *ghastly* sight.

gibberish N. nonsense; babbling. Did you hear that foolish boy spouting *gibberish* about monsters from outer space?

gibe V. mock. As you *gibe* at their superstitious beliefs, do you realize that you, too, are guilty of similarly foolish thoughts?

giddy ADJ. light-hearted; dizzy. He felt his *giddy* youth was past.

gingerly ADV. very carefully. To separate egg whites, first crack the egg *gingerly*. also ADJ.

girth N. distance around something; circumference. It took an extra-large cummerbund to fit around Andrew Carnegie's considerable *girth*.

gist N. essence. She was asked to give the *gist* of the essay in two sentences.

glacial ADJ. like a glacier; extremely cold. Never a warm person, when offended Hugo could seem positively *glacial*.

glaring ADJ. highly conspicuous; harshly bright. *Glaring* spelling or grammatical errors in your résumé will unfavorably impress potential employers.

glaze V. cover with a thin and shiny surface. The freezing rain *glazed* the streets and made driving hazardous. also N.

glean V. gather leavings. After the crops had been harvested by the machines, the peasants were permitted to *glean* the wheat left in the fields.

glib ADJ. fluent. He is a *glib* and articulate speaker.

glimmer V. shine erratically; twinkle. In the darkness of the cavern, the glowworms hanging from the cavern roof *glimmered* like distant stars.

gloat V. express evil satisfaction; view malevolently. As you *gloat* over your ill-gotten wealth, do you think of the many victims you have defrauded?

gloss over V. explain away. No matter how hard he tried to talk around the issue, President Bush could not *gloss over* the fact that he had raised taxes after all.

glossary N. brief explanation of words used in the text. I have found the *glossary* in this book very useful; it has eliminated many trips to the dictionary.

glossy ADJ. smooth and shining. I want this photograph printed on *glossy* paper, not matte.

glower V. scowl. The angry boy *glowered* at his father.

glut V. overstock; fill to excess. The many manufacturers *glutted* the market and could not find purchasers for the many articles they had produced. also N.

glutinous ADJ. sticky; viscous. Molasses is a *glutinous* substance.

glutton N. someone who eats too much. When Mother saw that Bobby had eaten all the cookies, she called him a little *glutton*. gluttonous, ADJ.

gnarled ADJ. twisted. The *gnarled* oak tree had been a landmark for years and was mentioned in several deeds.

gnome N. dwarf; underground spirit. In medieval mythology, *gnomes* were the special guardians and inhabitants of subterranean mines.

goad V. urge on. He was *goaded* by his friends until he yielded to their wishes. also N.

gorge N. narrow canyon; steep, rocky cleft. Terrified of heights, George could not bring himself to peer down into the *gorge* to see the rapids below.

gorge V. stuff oneself. The gluttonous guest *gorged* himself with food as though he had not eaten for days.

gory ADJ. bloody. The audience shuddered as they listened to the details of the *gory* massacre. gore, N.

gossamer ADJ. sheer; like cobwebs. Nylon can be woven into *gossamer* or thick fabrics. also N.

Test

Word List 21   *Synonyms*

Each of the questions below consists of a word in capital letters, followed by five lettered words or phrases. Choose the lettered word or phrase that is most nearly similar in meaning to the word in capital letters and write the letter of your choice on your answer paper.

301. GALLEON (A) liquid measure (B) ship (C) armada (D) company (E) printer's proof
302. GARISH (A) sordid (B) flashy (C) prominent (D) lusty (E) thoughtful
303. GARNER (A) prevent (B) assist (C) collect (D) compute (E). consult
304. GARNISH (A) paint (B) garner (C) adorn (D) abuse (E) banish
305. GARRULITY (A) credulity (B) senility (C) loquaciousness (D) speciousness (E) artistry
306. GARRULOUS (A) arid (B) hasty (C) sociable (D) quaint (E) talkative
307. GAUCHE (A) rigid (B) swift (C) awkward (D) taciturn (E) needy
308. GAUDY (A) holy (B) showy (C) sentimental (D) mild (E) whimsical
309. GAUNT (A) victorious (B) tiny (C) stylish (D) haggard (E) nervous
310. GENUFLECT (A) falsify (B) trick (C) project (D) bend the knee (E) pronounce correctly
311. GERMANE (A) bacteriological (B) Middle European (C) prominent (D) warlike (E) relevant
312. GERMINAL (A) creative (B) excused (C) sterilized (D) primitive (E) strategic
313. GIST (A) chaff (B) summary (C) expostulation (D) expiation (E) chore
314. GLIB (A) slippery (B) fashionable (C) antiquated (D) articulate (E) anticlimactic
315. GNOME (A) fury (B) giant (C) dwarf (D) native (E) alien

Word List 22   gouge-hiatus

gouge V. tear out. In that fight, all the rules were forgotten; the adversaries bit, kicked, and tried to *gouge* each other's eyes out.

gourmand N. epicure; person who takes excessive pleasure in food and drink. *Gourmands* lack self-restraint; if they enjoy a particular cuisine, they eat far too much of it.

gourmet N. connoisseur of food and drink. The *gourmet* stated that this was the best onion soup she had ever tasted.

graduated ADJ. arranged by degrees (of height, difficulty, etc.). Margaret loved her *graduated* set of Russian hollow wooden dolls; she spent hours happily putting the smaller dolls into their larger counterparts.

granary N. storehouse for grain. We have reason to be thankful, for our crops were good and our *granaries* are full.

grandeur N. impressiveness; stateliness; majesty. No matter how often he hiked through the mountains, David never failed to be struck by the *grandeur* of the Sierra Nevada range.

grandiloquent ADJ. pompous; bombastic; using high-sounding language. The politician could never speak simply; she was always *grandiloquent*.

grandiose ADJ. imposing; impressive. His *grandiose* manner impressed those who met him for the first time.

granulate V. form into grains. Sugar that has been *granulated* dissolves more readily than lump sugar. granule, N.

graphic ADJ. pertaining to the art of delineating; vividly described. I was particularly impressed by the *graphic* presentation of the storm.

grapple V. wrestle; come to grips with. He *grappled* with the burglar and overpowered him.

grate v. make a harsh noise; have an unpleasant effect; shred. The screams of the quarreling children *grated* on her nerves.

gratify v. please. Her parents were *gratified* by her success.

gratis ADV. free. The company offered to give one package *gratis* to every purchaser of one of their products. also ADJ.

■ **gratuitous** ADJ. given freely; unwarranted; uncalled for. Quit making *gratuitous* comments about my driving; no one asked you for your opinion.

gratuity N. tip. Many service employees rely more on *gratuities* than on salaries for their livelihood.

gravity N. seriousness. We could tell we were in serious trouble from the *gravity* of her expression. (secondary meaning) grave, ADJ.

■ **gregarious** ADJ. sociable. Typically, party-throwers are *gregarious*; hermits are not.

grievance N. cause of complaint. When her supervisor ignored her complaint, she took her *grievance* to the union.

grill v. question severely. In violation of the Miranda law, the police *grilled the* suspect for several hours before reading him his rights. (secondary meaning)

grimace N. a facial distortion to show feeling such as pain, disgust, etc. Even though he remained silent, his *grimace* indicated his displeasure. also v.

grisly ADJ. ghastly. She shuddered at the *grisly* sight.

grotesque ADJ. fantastic; comically hideous. On Halloween people enjoy wearing *grotesque* costumes.

grotto N. small cavern. The Blue *Grotto* in Capri can be entered only by small boats rowed by natives through a natural opening in the rocks.

grouse v. complain; fuss. Students traditionally *grouse* about the abysmal quality of "mystery meat" and similar dormitory food.

grovel v. crawl or creep on ground; remain prostrate. Even though we have been defeated, we do not have to *grovel* before our conquerors.

■ **grudging** ADJ. unwilling; reluctant; stingy. We received only *grudging* support from the mayor despite his earlier promises of aid.

gruel N. thin, liquid porridge. Our daily allotment of *gruel* made the meal not only monotonous but also unpalatable.

grueling ADJ. exhausting. The marathon is a *grueling* race.

gruesome ADJ. grisly. People screamed when her *gruesome* appearance was flashed on the screen.

gruff ADJ. rough-mannered. Although he was blunt and *gruff* with most people, he was always gentle with children.

guffaw N. boisterous laughter. The loud *guffaws* that came from the closed room indicated that the members of the committee had not yet settled down to serious business. also v.

guile N. deceit; duplicity. She achieved her high position by *guile* and treachery.

■ **guileless** ADJ. without deceit. He is naive, simple, and *guileless*; he cannot be guilty of fraud.

guise N. appearance; costume. In the *guise* of a plumber, the detective investigated the murder case.

gullible ADJ. easily deceived. He preyed upon *gullible* people, who believed his stories of easy wealth.

gustatory ADJ. affecting the sense of taste. The Thai restaurant offered an unusual *gustatory* experience for those used to a bland cuisine.

gusto N. enjoyment; enthusiasm. He accepted the assignment with such *gusto* that I feel he would have been satisfied with a smaller salary.

gusty ADJ. windy. The *gusty* weather made sailing precarious.

gyroscope N. apparatus used to maintain balance, ascertain direction, etc. By using a rotating *gyroscope*, they were able to stabilize the vessel, counteracting the rolling movements of the sea.

hackles N. hairs on back and neck, especially of a dog. The dog's *hackles* rose and he began to growl as the sound of footsteps grew louder.

hackneyed ADJ. commonplace; trite. The English teacher criticized her story because of its *hackneyed* and unoriginal plot.

haggard ADJ. wasted away; gaunt. After his long illness, he was pale and *haggard*.

haggle v. argue about prices. I prefer to shop in a store that has a one-price policy because, whenever I *haggle* with a shopkeeper, I am never certain that I paid a fair price for the articles I purchased.

halcyon ADJ. calm; peaceful. In those *halcyon* days, people were not worried about sneak attacks and bombings.

hale ADJ. healthy. After a brief illness, he was soon *hale*.

hallowed ADJ. blessed; consecrated. She was laid to rest in *hallowed* ground.

hallucination N. delusion. I think you were frightened by a *hallucination* that you created in your own mind.

halting ADJ. hesitant; faltering. Novice extemporaneous speakers often talk in a *halting* fashion as they grope for the right words.

■ **hamper** v. obstruct. The minority party agreed not to *hamper* the efforts of the leaders to secure a lasting peace.

hap N. chance; luck. In his poem *Hap*, Thomas Hardy objects to the part chance plays in our lives. also v.

haphazard ADJ. random; by chance. His *haphazard* reading left him unacquainted with the authors of the books.

hapless ADJ. unfortunate. This *hapless* creature had never known a moment's pleasure.

■ **harangue** N. long, passionate, and vehement speech. In her lengthy *harangue*, the principal berated the offenders. also v.

harass v. annoy by repeated attacks. When he could not pay his bills as quickly as he had promised, he was *harassed* by his creditors.

harbinger N. forerunner. The crocus is an early *harbinger* of spring.

harbor V. provide a refuge for; hide. The church *harbored* illegal aliens who were political refugees. also N.

hardy ADJ. sturdy; robust; able to stand inclement weather. We asked the gardening expert to recommend particularly *hardy* plants that could withstand our harsh New England winters.

harping N. tiresome dwelling on a subject. After he had reminded me several times about what he had done for me I told him to stop his *harping* on my indebtedness to him. harp, V.

harrow V. break up ground after plowing; torture. I don't want to *harrow* you at this time by asking you to recall the details of your unpleasant experience.

harry V. harass, annoy, torment; raid. The guerrilla band *harried* the enemy nightly.

hatch N. deck opening; lid covering a deck opening. The latch on the *hatch* failed to catch, so the *hatch* remained unlatched.

haughtiness N. pride; arrogance. I resent his *haughtiness* because he is no better than we are.

hazardous ADJ. dangerous. Your occupation is too *hazardous* for insurance companies to consider your application.

hazy ADJ. slightly obscure. In *hazy* weather, you cannot see the top of this mountain.

headlong ADJ. hasty; rash. The slave seized the unexpected chance to make a *headlong* dash across the border to freedom.

headstrong ADJ. stubborn; willful; unyielding. Because she refused to marry the man her parents had chosen for her, everyone scolded Minna and called her a foolish, *headstrong* girl.

heckler N. person who verbally harasses others. The *heckler* kept interrupting the speaker with rude remarks. heckle, V.

hedonism N. belief that pleasure is the sole aim in life. *Hedonism* and asceticism are opposing philosophies of human behavior.

heedless ADJ. not noticing; disregarding. He drove on, *heedless* of the warnings that the road was dangerous. heed, V.

hegemony N. dominance, especially of one nation over others. As one Eastern European nation after another declared its independence, commentators marveled at the sudden breakdown of the once monolithic Soviet *hegemony*.

heinous ADJ. atrocious; hatefully bad. Hitler's *heinous* crimes will never be forgotten.

herbivorous ADJ. grain-eating. Some *herbivorous* animals have two stomachs for digesting their food.

heresy N. opinion contrary to popular belief or to accepted religion. He was threatened with excommunication because his remarks were considered to be pure *heresy*. heretical, ADJ.

heretic N. person who maintains opinions contrary to the doctrines of the church. She was punished by the Spanish Inquisition because she was a *heretic*.

hermetic ADJ. sealed by fusion so as to be airtight. After these bandages are sterilized, they are placed in *hermetic* containers.

hermetic ADJ. obscure and mysterious; occult. It is strange to consider that modern chemistry originated in the *hermetic* teachings of the ancient alchemists. (secondary meaning)

hermitage N. home of a hermit. Even in his remote *hermitage* he could not escape completely from the world.

herpetologist N. one who studies reptiles. As a boy, Indiana Jones had a traumatic experience involving snakes; sensibly enough, he studied to be an archaeologist, not a *herpetologist*.

heterodox ADJ. unorthodox; unconventional. To those who upheld the belief that the earth did not move, Galileo's theory that the earth circled the sun was disturbingly *heterodox*.

heterogeneous ADJ. dissimilar. In a *heterogeneous* group, we have an unassorted assemblage, while in a homogeneous group we have people or things that have common traits. heterogeneity, N.

hew V. cut to pieces with ax or sword. The cavalry rushed into the melee and *hewed* the enemy with their swords.

heyday N. time of greatest success; prime. In their *heyday,* the San Francisco Forty-Niners won the Super Bowl two years running.

hiatus N. gap; pause. Except for a brief two-year *hiatus,* during which she enrolled in the Peace Corps, Ms. Clements has devoted herself to her medical career.

Test

Word List 22 *Antonyms*

Each of the questions below consists of a word in capital letters, followed by five lettered words or phrases. Choose the lettered word or phrase that is most nearly opposite in meaning to the word in capital letters and write the letter of your choice on your answer paper.

316. GRANDIOSE (A) false (B) ideal (C) proud (D) simple (E) functional

317. GRATUITOUS (A) warranted (B) frank (C) ingenuous (D) frugal (E) pithy

318. GREGARIOUS (A) antisocial (B) anticipatory (C) glorious (D) horrendous (E) similar

319. GRISLY (A) suggestive (B) doubtful (C) untidy (D) pleasant (E) bearish

320. GULLIBLE (A) incredulous (B) fickle (C) tantamount (D) easy (E) stylish

321. GUSTO (A) noise (B) panic (C) atmosphere (D) gloom (E) distaste
322. GUSTY (A) calm (B) noisy (C) fragrant (D) routine (E) gloomy
323. HACKNEYED (A) carried (B) original (C) banned (D) timely (E) oratorical
324. HAGGARD (A) shrewish (B) inspired (C) plump (D) maidenly (E) vast
325. HALCYON (A) wasteful (B) prior (C) subsequent (D) puerile (E) martial

326. HAPHAZARD (A) safe (B) indifferent (C) deliberate (D) tense (E) conspiring
327. HAPLESS (A) cheerful (B) consistent (C) fortunate (D) considerate (E) shapely
328. HEED (A) ignore (B) hope (C) overtake (D) nurture (E) depart
329. HERETIC (A) sophist (B) believer (C) interpreter (D) pacifist (E) owner
330. HETEROGENEOUS (A) orthodox (B) pagan (C) unlikely (D) similar (E) banished

Word List 23   hibernal-imbue

hibernal ADJ. wintry. Bears prepare for their long *hibernal* sleep by overeating.

hibernate V. sleep throughout the winter. Bears are one of the many species of animals that *hibernate*. hibernation, N.

hierarchy N. body divided into ranks. It was difficult to step out of one's place in this *hierarchy*. hierarchical, ADJ.

hieroglyphic N. picture writing. The discovery of the Rosetta Stone enabled scholars to read the ancient Egyptian *hieroglyphics*.

hilarity N. boisterous mirth. This *hilarity* is improper on this solemn day of mourning. hilarious, ADJ.

hindmost ADJ. furthest behind. The coward could always be found in the *hindmost* lines whenever a battle was being waged.

hindrance N. block; obstacle. Stalled cars along the highway are a *hindrance* to traffic that tow trucks should remove without delay. hinder, V.

hinterlands N. back country. They seldom had visitors, living as they did way out in the *hinterlands*.

hireling N. one who serves for hire (usually used contemptuously). In a matter of such importance, I do not wish to deal with *hirelings;* I must meet with the chief.

hirsute ADJ. hairy. He was a *hirsute* individual with a heavy black beard.

histrionic ADJ. theatrical. He was proud of his *histrionic* ability and wanted to play the role of Hamlet. histrionics, N.

hoard V. stockpile; accumulate for future use. Whenever there are rumors of a food shortage, people are tempted to *hoard* food. also N.

hoary ADJ. white with age. The man was *hoary* and wrinkled when he was 70.

hoax N. trick; practical joke. Embarrassed by the *hoax,* he reddened and left the room. also V.

holocaust N. destruction by fire. Citizens of San Francisco remember that the destruction of the city was caused not by the earthquake but by the *holocaust* that followed.

holster N. pistol case. Even when he was not in uniform, he carried a *holster* and pistol under his arm.

homage N. honor; tribute. In her speech she tried to pay *homage* to a great man.

homeostasis N. tendency of a system to maintain relative stability. A breakdown of the body's immune system severely undermines the body's ability to maintain *homeostasis.*

homespun ADJ. domestic; made at home. *Homespun* wit, like *homespun* cloth, was often coarse and plain.

homily N. sermon; serious warning. His speeches were always *homilies,* advising his listeners to repent and reform. homiletic, ADJ.

■ **homogeneous** ADJ. of the same kind. Many educators try to put pupils of similar abilities in the same class because they believe that this *homogeneous* grouping is advisable. homogeneity, N.

hone V. sharpen. To make shaving easier, he *honed* his razor with great care.

hoodwink V. deceive; delude. Having been *hoodwinked* once by the fast-talking salesman, he was extremely cautious when he went to purchase a used car.

horde N. crowd. Just before Christmas the stores are filled with *hordes* of shoppers.

hortatory ADJ. encouraging; exhortive. The crowd listened to his *hortatory* statements with ever-growing excitement; finally they rushed from the hall to carry out his suggestions.

horticultural ADJ. pertaining to cultivation of gardens. When he bought his house, he began to look for flowers and decorative shrubs, and began to read books dealing with *horticultural* matters.

hovel N. shack; small, wretched house. He wondered how poor people could stand living in such a *hovel.*

hover V. hang about; wait nearby. The police helicopter *hovered* above the accident.

hubbub N. confused uproar. The marketplace was a scene of *hubbub* and excitement; in all the noise, we could not distinguish particular voices.

hubris N. arrogance; excessive self-conceit. Filled with *hubris*, Lear refused to heed his friends' warnings.

hue N. color; aspect. The aviary contained birds of every possible *hue.*

hue and cry N. outcry. When her purse was snatched, she raised such a *hue and cry* that the thief was captured.

humane ADJ. kind. His *humane* and considerate treatment of the unfortunate endeared him to all.

humdrum ADJ. dull; monotonous. After his years of adventure, he could not settle down to a *humdrum* existence.

humid ADJ. damp. She could not stand the *humid* climate and moved to a drier area.

humility N. humbleness of spirit. He spoke with a *humility* and lack of pride that impressed his listeners.

hummock N. small hill. The ascent of the *hummock* is not difficult and the view from the hilltop is ample reward for the effort.

humus N. substance formed by decaying vegetable matter. In order to improve his garden, he spread *humus* over his lawn and flower beds.

hurtle V. crash; rush. The runaway train *hurtled* toward disaster.

husbandry N. frugality; thrift; agriculture. He accumulated his small fortune by diligence and *husbandry*. husband, V.

hybrid N. mongrel; mixed breed. Mendel's formula explains the appearance of *hybrids* and pure species in breeding. also ADJ.

hydrophobia N. fear of water; rabies. A dog that bites a human being must be observed for symptoms of *hydrophobia*.

■ **hyperbole** N. exaggeration; overstatement. This salesman is guilty of *hyperbole* in describing his product; it is wise to discount his claims. hyperbolic, ADJ.

hypercritical ADJ. excessively exacting. You are *hypercritical* in your demands for perfection; we all make mistakes.

hypochondriac N. person unduly worried about his health; worrier without cause about illness. The doctor prescribed chocolate pills for his patient who was a *hypochondriac*.

hypocritical ADJ. pretending to be virtuous; deceiving. I resent his *hypocritical* posing as a friend for I know he is interested only in his own advancement. hypocrisy, N.

hypothetical ADJ. based on assumptions or hypotheses. Why do we have to consider *hypothetical* cases when we have actual case histories that we may examine? hypothesis, N.

ichthyology N. study of fish. Jacques Cousteau's programs about sea life have advanced the cause of *ichthyology*.

icon N. religious image; idol. The *icons* on the walls of the church were painted in the 13th century.

■ **iconoclastic** ADJ. attacking cherished traditions. George Bernard Shaw's *iconoclastic* plays often startled more conventional people. iconoclasm, N.

ideology N. ideas of a group of people. That *ideology* is dangerous to this country because it embraces undemocratic philosophies.

idiom N. special usage in language. I could not understand their *idiom* because literal translation made no sense.

idiosyncrasy N. peculiarity; eccentricity. One of his personal *idiosyncrasies* was his habit of rinsing all cutlery given him in a restaurant.

idiosyncratic ADJ. private; peculiar to an individual. Such behavior is *idiosyncratic*, it is as easily identifiable as a signature.

idolatry N. worship of idols; excessive admiration. Such *idolatry* of singers of country music is typical of the excessive enthusiasm of youth.

idyllic ADJ. charmingly carefree; simple. Far from the city, she led an *idyllic* existence in her rural retreat.

igneous ADJ. produced by fire; volcanic. Lava, pumice, and other *igneous* rocks are found in great abundance around Mount Vesuvius near Naples.

ignite V. kindle; light. When Desi crooned, "Baby, light my fire," literal-minded Lucy looked around for some paper to *ignite*.

ignoble ADJ. of lowly origin; unworthy. This plan is inspired by *ignoble* motives and I must, therefore, oppose it.

ignominious ADJ. disgraceful. The country smarted under the *ignominious* defeat and dreamed of the day when it would be victorious. ignominy, N.

illicit ADJ. illegal. The defense attorney claimed that the police had entrapped his client; that is, they had elicited the *illicit* action of which they now accused him.

illimitable ADJ. infinite. Human beings, having explored the far corners of the earth, are now reaching out into *illimitable* space.

illuminate V. brighten; clear up or make understandable; enlighten. Just as a lamp can *illuminate* a dark room, a perceptive comment can *illuminate* a knotty problem.

illusion N. misleading vision. It is easy to create an optical *illusion* in which lines of equal length appear different.

illusive ADJ. deceiving. This is only a mirage; let us not be fooled by its *illusive* effect.

illusory ADJ. deceptive; not real. Unfortunately, the costs of running the lemonade stand were so high that Tom's profits proved *illusory*.

imbalance N. lack of balance or symmetry; disproportion. Because of the great *imbalance* between the number of men and women invited, the dance was unsuccessful.

imbecility N. weakness of mind. I am amazed at the *imbecility* of the readers of these trashy magazines.

imbibe V. drink in. The dry soil *imbibed* the rain quickly.

imbroglio N. complicated situation; perplexity; entanglement. He was called in to settle the *imbroglio* but failed to bring harmony into the situation.

imbue V. saturate, fill. His visits to the famous Gothic cathedrals *imbued* him with feelings of awe and reverence.

Test

Word List 23   *Antonyms*

Each of the questions below consists of a word in capital letters, followed by five lettered words or phrases. Choose the lettered word or phrase that is most nearly opposite in meaning to the word in capital letters and write the letter of your choice on your answer paper.

331. HIBERNAL (A) musical (B) summerlike (C) local (D) seasonal (E) discordant
332. HILARITY (A) gloom (B) heartiness (C) weakness (D) casualty (E) paucity
333. HIRSUTE (A) scaly (B) bald (C) erudite (D) quiet (E) long
334. HORTATORY (A) inquiring (B) denying (C) killing (D) frantic (E) dissuading
335. HOVER (A) commence (B) soothe (C) leave (D) transform (E) solidify
336. HUBBUB (A) calm (B) fury (C) capital (D) axle (E) wax
337. HUMMOCK (A) unmusical (B) scorn (C) wakefulness (D) vale (E) vestment
338. HUSBANDRY (A) sportsmanship (B) dishonesty (C) wastefulness (D) friction (E) cowardice

339. HYBRID (A) productive (B) special (C) purebred (D) oafish (E) genial
340. HYPERBOLE (A) velocity (B) climax (C) curve (D) understatement (E) expansion
341. HYPERCRITICAL (A) tolerant (B) false (C) extreme (D) inarticulate (E) cautious
342. HYPOCRITICAL (A) sincere (B) narrow-minded (C) shameful (D) amiable (E) modest
343. HYPOTHETICAL (A) rational (B) fantastic (C) wizened (D) opposed (E) axiomatic
344. IGNOBLE (A) produced by fire (B) worthy (C) given to questioning (D) huge (E) known
345. ILLUSIVE (A) not deceptive (B) not certain (C) not obvious (D) not coherent (E) not brilliant

Word List 24   immaculate-incessant

immaculate ADJ. pure; spotless. The West Point cadets were *immaculate* as they lined up for inspection.

imminent ADJ. near at hand; impending. Rosa was such a last-minute worker that she could never start writing a paper till the deadline was *imminent*.

immobility N. state of being immovable. Modern armies cannot afford the luxury of *immobility,* as they are vulnerable to attack while standing still.

immolate V. offer as a sacrifice. The tribal king offered to *immolate* his daughter to quiet the angry gods.

immune ADJ. exempt. He was fortunately *immune* from the disease and could take care of the sick.

immure V. imprison; shut up in confinement. For the two weeks before the examination, the student *immured* himself in his room and concentrated upon his studies.

■ **immutable** ADJ. unchangeable. Scientists are constantly seeking to discover the *immutable* laws of nature.

■ **impair** V. worsen; diminish in value. This arrest will *impair* her reputation in the community.

impale V. pierce. He was *impaled* by the spear hurled by his adversary.

impalpable ADJ. imperceptible; intangible. The ash is so fine that it is *impalpable* to the touch but it can be seen as a fine layer covering the window ledge.

impasse N. predicament from which there is no escape. In this *impasse,* all turned to prayer as their last hope.

■ **impassive** ADJ. without feeling; not affected by pain. The Native American has been incorrectly depicted as an *impassive* individual, undemonstrative and stoical.

impeach V. charge with crime in office; indict. The angry congressman wanted to *impeach* the President for his misdeeds.

impeccable ADJ. faultless. He was proud of his *impeccable* manners.

impecunious ADJ. without money. Now that he was wealthy, he gladly contributed to funds to assist *impecunious* and disabled persons.

impede V. hinder; block. The special prosecutor determined that the Attorney General, though inept, had not intentionally set out to *impede* the progress of the investigation.

impediment N. hindrance; stumbling-block. She had a speech *impediment* that prevented her from speaking clearly.

impending ADJ. nearing; approaching. The entire country was saddened by the news of his *impending* death.

impenetrable ADJ. not able to be pierced or entered; beyond understanding. How could the murderer have gotten into the locked room? To Watson, the mystery, like the room, was *impenetrable.*

impenitent ADJ. not repentant. We could see by his brazen attitude that he was *impenitent.*

imperial ADJ. like an emperor; related to an empire. When hotel owner Leona Helmsley appeared in ads as Queen Leona standing guard over the Palace Hotel, her critics mocked her *imperial* fancies.

imperiousness N. lordliness; domineering manner; arrogance. His *imperiousness* indicated that he had long been accustomed to assuming command. imperious, ADJ.

impermeable ADJ. impervious; not permitting passage through its substance. This new material is *impermeable* to liquids.

impertinent ADJ. insolent. I regard your remarks as *impertinent* and I resent them.

■ **imperturbable** ADJ. calm; placid. Wellington remained *imperturbable* and in full command of the situation in spite of the hysteria and panic all around him. imperturbability, N.

■ **impervious** ADJ. not penetrable; not permitting passage through. You cannot change their habits for their minds are *impervious* to reasoning.

impetuous ADJ. violent; hasty; rash. We tried to curb his *impetuous* behavior because we felt that in his haste he might offend some people.

impetus N. moving force; incentive; stimulus. A new federal highway program would create jobs and give added *impetus* to our economic recovery.

impiety N. irreverence; wickedness. We must regard your blasphemy as an act of *impiety*.

impinge V. infringe; touch; collide with. How could they be married without *impinging* on one another's freedom?

impious ADJ. irreverent. The congregation was offended by her *impious* remarks.

■ **implacable** ADJ. incapable of being pacified. Madame Defarge was the *implacable* enemy of the Evremonde family.

implausible ADJ. unlikely; unbelievable. Though her alibi seemed *implausible,* it in fact turned out to be true.

implement V. put into effect; supply with tools. The mayor was unwilling to *implement* the plan until she was sure it had the governor's backing. also N.

implication N. that which is hinted at or suggested. If I understand the *implications* of your remark, you do not trust our captain.

■ **implicit** ADJ. understood but not stated. Jack never told Jill he adored her; he believed his love was *implicit* in his deeds.

implore V. beg. He *implored* her to give him a second chance.

imply V. suggest a meaning not expressed; signify. Even though your statement does not declare that you are at war with that country, your actions *imply* that that is the actual situation.

impolitic ADJ. not wise. I think it is *impolitic* to raise this issue at the present time because the public is too angry.

imponderable ADJ. weightless. I can evaluate the data gathered in this study; the *imponderable* items are not so easily analyzed.

import N. significance. I feel that you have not grasped the full *import* of the message sent to us by the enemy.

importunate ADJ. urging; demanding. He tried to hide from his *importunate* creditors until his allowance arrived.

importune V. beg persistently. Democratic and Republican phone solicitors *importuned* her for contributions so frequently that she decided to give nothing to either party.

imposture N. assuming a false identity; masquerade. She was imprisoned for her *imposture* of a doctor.

impotent ADJ. weak; ineffective. Although he wished to break the nicotine habit, he found himself *impotent* in resisting the craving for a cigarette.

imprecation N. curse. Roused from bed at what he considered an ungodly hour, Roy muttered *imprecations* under his breath.

impregnable ADJ. invulnerable. Until the development of the airplane as a military weapon, the fort was considered *impregnable*.

impromptu ADJ. without previous preparation. Her listeners were amazed that such a thorough presentation could be made in an *impromptu* speech.

impropriety N. state of being inappropriate. Because of the *impropriety* of his costume, he was denied entrance into the dining room.

improvident ADJ. thriftless. He was constantly being warned to mend his *improvident* ways and begin to "save for a rainy day." improvidence, N.

improvise V. compose on the spur of the moment. She would sit at the piano and *improvise* for hours on themes from Bach and Handel.

■ **imprudent** ADJ. lacking caution; injudicious. It is *imprudent* to exercise vigorously and become overheated when you are unwell.

impugn V. doubt; challenge; gainsay. I cannot *impugn* your honesty without evidence.

impuissance N. powerlessness; feebleness. The lame duck President was frustrated by his shift from enormous power to relative *impuissance*.

impunity N. freedom from punishment. The bully mistreated everyone in the class with *impunity* for he felt that no one would dare retaliate.

impute V. attribute; ascribe. If I wished to *impute* blame to the officers in charge of this program, I would state my feelings definitely and immediately.

■ **inadvertently** ADV. carelessly; unintentionally; by oversight. She *inadvertently* omitted two questions on the examination and mismarked her answer sheet.

inalienable ADJ. not to be taken away; nontransferable. The Declaration of Independence mentions the *inalienable* rights that all of us possess.

inane ADJ. silly; senseless. Such comments are *inane* because they do not help us solve our problem. inanity, N.

inanimate ADJ. lifeless. She was asked to identify the still and *inanimate* body.

inarticulate ADJ. speechless; producing indistinct speech. He became *inarticulate* with rage and uttered sounds without meaning.

inaugurate V. begin formally; install in office. The candidate promised that he would *inaugurate* a new nationwide health care plan as soon as he was *inaugurated* as president. inauguration, N.

incandescent ADJ. strikingly bright; shining with intense heat. If you leave on an *incandescent* light bulb, it quickly grows too hot to touch.

incantation N. singing or chanting of magic spells; magical formula. Uttering *incantations* to make the brew more potent, the witch doctor stirred the liquid in the caldron.

incapacitate V. disable. During the winter, many people were *incapacitated* by respiratory ailments.

incarcerate V. imprison. The warden will *incarcerate* the felon after conviction.

incarnate ADJ. endowed with flesh; personified. Your attitude is so fiendish that you must be a devil *incarnate*.

incarnation N. act of assuming a human body and human nature. The *incarnation* of Jesus Christ is a basic tenet of Christian theology.

incendiary N. arsonist. The fire spread in such an unusual manner that the fire department chiefs were certain that it had been set by an *incendiary*. also ADJ.

incense V. enrage; infuriate. Unkindness to children *incensed* her.

incentive N. spur; motive. Students who dislike school must be given an *incentive* to learn.

inception N. start; beginning. She was involved with the project from its *inception*.

incessant ADJ. uninterrupted. The crickets kept up an *incessant* chirping that disturbed our attempts to fall asleep.

Test

Word List 24   *Synonyms and Antonyms*

Each of the following questions consists of a word in capital letters, followed by five lettered words or phrases. Choose the lettered word or phrase that is most nearly similar or opposite in meaning to the word in capital letters and write the letter of your choice on your answer paper.

346. IMMOLATE (A) debate (B) scour (C) sacrifice (D) sanctify (E) ratify

347. IMMUTABLE (A) silent (B) changeable (C) articulate (D) loyal (E) varied

348. IMPAIR (A) separate (B) make amends (C) make worse (D) falsify (E) cancel

349. IMPALPABLE (A) obvious (B) combined (C) high (D) connecting (E) lost

350. IMPASSIVE (A) active (B) demonstrative (C) perfect (D) anxious (E) irritated

351. IMPECCABLE (A) unmentionable (B) quotable (C) blinding (D) faulty (E) hampering

352. IMPECUNIOUS (A) affluent (B) afflicted (C) affectionate (D) affable (E) afraid

353. IMPERVIOUS (A) impenetrable (B) perplexing (C) chaotic (D) cool (E) perfect

354. IMPETUOUS (A) rash (B) inane (C) just (D) flagrant (E) redolent

355. IMPOLITIC (A) campaigning (B) advisable (C) aggressive (D) legal (E) fortunate

356. IMPORTUNE (A) export (B) plead (C) exhibit (D) account (E) visit

357. IMPROMPTU (A) prompted (B) appropriate (C) rehearsed (D) foolish (E) vast

358. INALIENABLE (A) inherent (B) repugnant (C) closed to immigration (D) full (E) accountable

359. INANE (A) passive (B) wise (C) intoxicated (D) mellow (E) silent

360. INCARCERATE (A) inhibit (B) acquit (C) account (D) imprison (E) force

Word List 25   inchoate-infraction

■ **inchoate** ADJ. recently begun; rudimentary; elementary. Before the Creation, the world was an *inchoate* mass.

incidence N. rate of occurrence; particular occurrence. Health professionals expressed great concern over the high *incidence* of infant mortality in major urban areas.

incidental ADJ. not essential; minor. The scholarship covered his major expenses at college and some of his *incidental* expenses as well.

incipient ADJ. beginning; in an early stage. I will go to sleep early for I want to break an *incipient* cold.

incisive ADJ. cutting; sharp. His *incisive* remarks made us see the fallacy in our plans. incision, N.

incite V. arouse to action. The demagogue *incited* the mob to take action into its own hands.

inclement ADJ. stormy; unkind. I like to read a good book in *inclement* weather.

incline N. slope; slant. The architect recommended that the nursing home's ramp be rebuilt because its *incline* was too steep for wheelchairs.

inclined ADJ. tending or leaning toward; bent. Though I am *inclined* to be skeptical, the witness's manner *inclines* me to believe his story. also V.

inclusive ADJ. tending to include all. The comedian turned down the invitation to join the Players' Club, saying any club that would let him in was too *inclusive* for him.

incognito ADV. with identity concealed; using an assumed name. The monarch enjoyed traveling through the town *incognito* and mingling with the populace. also ADJ.

incoherent ADJ. unintelligible; muddled; illogical. The bereaved father sobbed and stammered, his words becoming almost *incoherent* in his grief. incoherence, N.

incommodious ADJ., not spacious; inconvenient. In their *incommodious* quarters, they had to improvise for closet space.

incompatible ADJ. inharmonious. The married couple argued incessantly and finally decided to separate because they were *incompatible*. incompatibility, N.

■ **incongruity** N. lack of harmony; absurdity. The *incongruity* of his wearing sneakers with formal attire amused the observers. incongruous, ADJ.

inconsequential ADJ. insignificant; unimportant. Brushing off Ali's apologies for having broken the wine glass, Tamara said, "Don't worry about it; it's *inconsequential*."

inconsistency N. state of being self-contradictory; lack of uniformity or steadiness. How are lawyers different from agricultural inspectors? Where lawyers check *inconsistencies* in witnesses' statements, agricultural inspectors check *inconsistencies* in Grade A eggs. inconsistent, ADJ.

incontinent ADJ. lacking self-restraint; licentious. His *incontinent* behavior off stage shocked many people and they refused to attend the plays and movies in which he appeared.

incontrovertible ADJ. indisputable. We must yield to the *incontrovertible* evidence that you have presented and free your client.

incorporate V. introduce something into a larger whole; combine; unite. Breaking with precedent, President Truman ordered the military to *incorporate* blacks into every branch of the armed services. also ADJ.

incorporeal ADJ. immaterial; without a material body. We must devote time to the needs of our *incorporeal* mind as well as our corporeal body.

incorrigible ADJ. uncorrectable. Though Widow Douglass hoped to reform Huck, Miss Watson pronounced him *incorrigible* and said he would come to no good end.

incredulity N. a tendency to disbelief. Your *incredulity* in the face of all the evidence is hard to understand.

incredulous ADJ. withholding belief; skeptical. When Jack claimed he hadn't eaten the jelly doughnut, Jill took an *incredulous* look at his smeared face and laughed.

increment N. increase. The new contract calls for a 10 percent *increment* in salary for each employee for the next two years.

incriminate V. accuse; serve as evidence against. The witness's testimony against the racketeers *incriminates* some high public officials as well.

incubate V. hatch; scheme. Inasmuch as our supply of electricity is cut off, we shall have to rely on the hens to *incubate* these eggs.

incubus N. burden; mental care; nightmare. The *incubus* of financial worry helped bring on her nervous breakdown.

inculcate V. teach. In an effort to *inculcate* religious devotion, the officials ordered that the school day begin with the singing of a hymn.

incumbent N. officeholder. The newly elected public official received valuable advice from the present *incumbent*. also ADJ.

incur V. bring upon oneself. His parents refused to pay any future debts he might *incur*.

incursion N. temporary invasion. The nightly *incursions* and hit-and-run raids of our neighbors across the border tried the patience of the country to the point where we decided to retaliate in force.

indefatigable ADJ. tireless. He was *indefatigable* in his constant efforts to raise funds for the Red Cross.

indemnify V. make secure against loss; compensate for loss. The city will *indemnify* all home owners whose property is spoiled by this project.

indenture V. bind as servant or apprentice to master. Many immigrants could come to America only after they had *indentured* themselves for several years. also N.

■ **indeterminate** ADJ. uncertain; not clearly fixed; indefinite. That interest rates shall rise appears certain; when they will do so, however, remains *indeterminate*.

indicative ADJ. suggestive, implying. A lack of appetite may be *indicative* of a major mental or physical disorder.

indict V. charge. If the grand jury *indicts* the suspect, he will go to trial. indictment, N.

indifferent ADJ. unmoved; lacking concern. Because she felt no desire to marry, she was *indifferent* to his constant proposals.

■ **indigence** N. poverty. Neither the economists nor the political scientists have found a way to wipe out the inequities of wealth and eliminate *indigence* from our society. indigent, ADJ., N.

indigenous ADJ. native. Tobacco is one of the *indigenous* plants that the early explorers found in this country.

indignation N. anger at an injustice. He felt *indignation* at the ill-treatment of the helpless animals.

indignity N. offensive or insulting treatment. Although he seemed to accept cheerfully the *indignities* heaped upon him, he was inwardly very angry.

indiscriminate ADJ. choosing at random; confused. She disapproved of her son's *indiscriminate* television viewing and decided to restrict him to educational programs.

indisputable ADJ. too certain to be disputed. In the face of these *indisputable* statements, I withdraw my complaint.

indissoluble ADJ. permanent. The *indissoluble* bonds of marriage are all too often being dissolved.

indite V. write; compose. Cyrano *indited* many letters for Christian.

■ **indolence** N. laziness. He outgrew his youthful *indolence* to become a model of industry and alertness on the job. indolent, ADJ.

indomitable ADJ. unconquerable. The founders of our country had *indomitable* willpower.

indubitably ADV. beyond a doubt. Because her argument was *indubitably* valid, the judge accepted it.

induce V. persuade; bring about. After the quarrel, Tina said nothing could *induce* her to talk to Tony again. inducement, N.

inductive ADJ. pertaining to induction or proceeding from the specific to the general. The discovery of the planet Pluto is an excellent example of the results that can be obtained from *inductive* reasoning.

indulgent ADJ. humoring; yielding; lenient. *Indulgent* parents spoil their children by giving in to their every whim.

inebriety N. habitual intoxication. Because of his *inebriety*, he was discharged from his position as family chauffeur.

ineffable ADJ. unutterable; cannot be expressed in speech. Such *ineffable* joy must be experienced; it cannot be described.

ineffectual ADJ. not effective; weak. Because the candidate failed to get across his message to the public, his campaign was *ineffectual*.

ineluctable ADJ. irresistible; not to be escaped. He felt that his fate was *ineluctable* and refused to make any attempt to improve his lot.

inept ADJ. lacking skill; inadequate; inappropriate. *Inept* as a carpenter, Ira was all thumbs.

inequity N. unfairness. In demanding equal pay for equal work, women protest the basic *inequity* of a system that allots greater financial rewards to men. inequitable, ADJ.

inerrancy N. infallibility. Jane refused to believe in the pope's *inerrancy,* reasoning: "All human beings are capable of error. The pope is a human being. Therefore, the pope is capable of error."

■ **inertia** N. state of being inert or indisposed to move. Our *inertia* in this matter may prove disastrous; we must move to aid our allies immediately.

inevitable ADJ. unavoidable. Death and taxes are both *inevitable.*

inexorable ADJ. relentless; unyielding; implacable. After listening to the pleas for clemency, the judge was *inexorable* and gave the convicted man the maximum punishment allowed by law.

infallible ADJ. unerring. We must remember that none of us is *infallible;* we all make mistakes.

infamous ADJ. notoriously bad. Jesse James was an *infamous* outlaw.

infantile ADJ. childish; infantlike. When will he outgrow such *infantile* behavior?

infer V. deduce; conclude. We must be particularly cautious when we *infer* that a person is guilty on the basis of circumstantial evidence. inference, N.

infernal ADJ. pertaining to hell; devilish. They could think of no way to hinder his *infernal* scheme.

infidel N. unbeliever. The Saracens made war against the *infidels.*

infiltrate V. pass into or through; penetrate (an organization) sneakily. In order to *infiltrate* enemy lines at night without being seen, the scouts darkened their faces and wore black coveralls. infiltrator, N.

infinitesimal ADJ. very small. In the twentieth century, physicists have made their greatest discoveries about the characteristics of *infinitesimal* objects like the atom and its parts.

infirmity N. weakness. Her greatest *infirmity* was lack of willpower.

inflated ADJ. exaggerated; pompous; enlarged (with air or gas). His claims about the new product were *inflated;* it did not work as well as he had promised.

influx N. flowing into. The *influx* of refugees into the country has taxed the relief agencies severely.

infraction N. violation. Because of his many *infractions* of school regulations, he was suspended by the dean.

Test

Word List 25   *Synonyms*

Each of the questions below consists of a word in capital letters, followed by five lettered words or phrases. Choose the lettered word or phrase that is most nearly similar in meaning to the word in capital letters and write the letter of your choice on your answer paper.

361. INCLEMENT (A) unfavorable (B) abandoned (C) kindly (D) selfish (E) active
362. INCOMPATIBLE (A) capable (B) reasonable (C) faulty (D) indifferent (E) alienated
363. INCONSEQUENTIAL (A) disorderly (B) insignificant (C) subsequent (D) insufficient (E) preceding
364. INCONTINENT (A) insular (B) complaisant (C) crass (D) wanton (E) false
365. INCORRIGIBLE (A) narrow (B) straight (C) inconceivable (D) unreliable (E) unreformable
366. INCRIMINATE (A) exacerbate (B) involve (C) intimidate (D) lacerate (E) prevaricate

367. INCULCATE (A) exculpate (B) educate (C) exonerate (D) prepare (E) embarrass
368. INDIGENT (A) lazy (B) pusillanimous (C) penurious (D) affluent (E) contrary
369. INDIGNITY (A) pomposity (B) bombast (C) obeisance (D) insult (E) message
370. INDOLENCE (A) sloth (B) poverty (C) latitude (D) aptitude (E) anger
371. INDUBITABLY (A) flagrantly (B) doubtfully (C) carefully (D) carelessly (E) certainly
372. INEBRIETY (A) revelation (B) drunkenness (C) felony (D) starvation (E) gluttony
373. INEPT (A) outward (B) spiritual (C) foolish (D) clumsy (E) abundant
374. INFALLIBLE (A) final (B) unbelievable (C) perfect (D) inaccurate (E) inquisitive
375. INFIRMITY (A) disability (B) age (C) inoculation (D) hospital (E) unity

Word List 26   infringe-invert

infringe V. violate; encroach. I think your machine *infringes* on my patent and I intend to sue.

ingenious ADJ. clever. He came up with a use for Styrofoam packing balls that was so *ingenious* that his business school professors declared it was marketable. ingenuity, N.

■ **ingenuous** ADJ. naive; young and unsophisticated. Although she was over forty, the movie star still insisted that she be cast as an *ingenuous* sweet young thing. ingenue, N.

ingrained ADJ. deeply established; firmly rooted. Try as they would, the missionaries were unable to uproot the *ingrained* superstitions of the natives.

ingrate N. ungrateful person. That *ingrate* Bob sneered at the tie I gave him.

ingratiate V. become popular with. He tried to *ingratiate* himself into her parents' good graces.

■ **inherent** ADJ. firmly established by nature or habit. His *inherent* love of justice compelled him to come to their aid.

inhibit v. prohibit; restrain. The child was not *inhibited* in her responses. inhibition, N.

inimical ADJ. unfriendly; hostile. She felt that they were *inimical* and were hoping for her downfall.

inimitable ADJ. matchless; not able to be imitated. We admire Auden for his *inimitable* use of language; he is one of a kind.

iniquitous ADJ. unjust; wicked. I cannot approve of the *iniquitous* methods you used to gain your present position. iniquity, N.

initiate v. begin; originate; receive into a group. The college is about to *initiate* a program for reducing math anxiety among students.

injurious ADJ. harmful. Smoking cigarettes can be *injurious* to your health.

inkling N. hint. This came as a complete surprise to me as I did not have the slightest *inkling* of your plans.

innate ADJ. inborn. His *innate* talent for music was soon recognized by his parents.

innocuous ADJ. harmless. Let him drink it; it is *innocuous* and will have no ill effect.

innovation N. change; introduction of something new. She loved *innovations* just because they were new. innovative, ADJ.

innuendo N. hint; insinuation. I can defend myself against direct accusations; *innuendos* and oblique attacks on my character are what trouble me.

inopportune ADJ. untimely; poorly chosen. A rock concert is an *inopportune* setting for a quiet conversation.

inordinate ADJ. unrestrained; excessive. She had an *inordinate* fondness for candy.

inquisitor N. questioner (especially harsh); investigator. Fearing being grilled ruthlessly by the secret police, Marsha faced her *inquisitors* with trepidation.

insalubrious ADJ. unwholesome; not healthful. The mosquito-ridden swamp was an *insalubrious* place, a breeding ground for malarial contagion.

insatiable ADJ. not easily satisfied; greedy. Welty's thirst for knowledge was *insatiable;* she was in the library day and night.

inscrutable ADJ. impenetrable; not readily understood; mysterious. Experienced poker players try to keep their expressions *inscrutable,* hiding their reactions to the cards behind a so-called poker face.

insensate ADJ. without feeling. She lay there as *insensate* as a log.

■ **insensible** ADJ. unconscious; unresponsive. Sherry and I are very different; at times when I would be covered with embarrassment, she seems *insensible* to shame.

insidious ADJ. treacherous; stealthy; sly. The fifth column is *insidious* because it works secretly within our territory for our defeat.

insinuate v. hint; imply. What are you trying to *insinuate* by that remark?

■ **insipid** ADJ. lacking in flavor; dull. Flat prose and flat ginger ale are equally *insipid:* both lack sparkle.

insolence N. impudent disrespect; haughtiness. How dare you treat me so rudely! The manager will hear of your *insolence.* insolent, ADJ.

insolvent ADJ. bankrupt; lacking money to pay. When rumors that he was *insolvent* reached his creditors, they began to press him for payment of the money due them. insolvency, N.

insomnia N. wakefulness; inability to sleep. He refused to join us in a midnight cup of coffee because he claimed it gave him *insomnia.*

insouciant ADJ. indifferent; without concern or care. Your *insouciant* attitude at such a critical moment indicates that you do not understand the gravity of the situation.

instigate v. urge; start; provoke. I am afraid that this statement will *instigate* a revolt.

insubordinate ADJ. disobedient. The *insubordinate* private was confined to the barracks.

insubstantial ADJ. lacking substance; insignificant; frail. His hopes for a career in acting proved *insubstantial*; no one would cast him, even in an *insubstantial* role.

■ **insularity** N. narrow-mindedness; isolation. The *insularity* of the islanders manifested itself in their suspicion of anything foreign. insular, ADJ.

insuperable ADJ. insurmountable; invincible. In the face of *insuperable* difficulties they maintained their courage and will to resist.

insurgent ADJ. rebellious. We will not discuss reforms until the *insurgent* troops have returned to their homes. also N.

insurrection N. rebellion; uprising. Given the current state of affairs in South Africa, an *insurrection* seems unavoidable.

intangible ADJ. not able to be perceived by touch; vague. Though the financial benefits of his Oxford post were meager, Lewis was drawn to it by its *intangible* rewards: prestige, intellectual freedom, the fellowship of his peers.

integral ADJ. complete; necessary for completeness. Physical education is an *integral* part of our curriculum; a sound mind and a sound body are complementary.

integrate v. make whole; combine; make into one unit. She tried to *integrate* all their activities into one program.

integrity N. uprightness; wholeness. Lincoln, whose personal *integrity* has inspired millions, fought a civil war to maintain the *integrity* of the republic, that these United States might remain undivided for all time.

intellect N. higher mental powers. He thought college would develop his *intellect.*

intelligentsia N. intellectuals; members of the educated elite [often used derogatorily]. She preferred discussions about sports and politics to the literary conversations of the *intelligentsia.*

inter v. bury. They are going to *inter* the body tomorrow at Broadlawn Cemetry. interment, N.

interdict v. prohibit; forbid. Civilized nations must *interdict* the use of nuclear weapons if we expect our society to live.

interim N. meantime. The company will not consider our proposal until next week; in the *interim,* let us proceed as we have in the past.

interloper N. intruder. The merchant thought of his competitors as *interlopers* who were stealing away his trade.

interminable ADJ. endless. Although his speech lasted for only twenty minutes, it seemed *interminable* to his bored audience.

intermittent ADJ. periodic; on and off. Our picnic was marred by *intermittent* rains.

internecine ADJ. mutually destructive. The rising death toll on both sides indicates the *internecine* nature of this conflict.

interpolate V. insert between. She talked so much that I could not *interpolate* a single remark.

interregnum N. period between two reigns. Henry VIII desperately sought a male heir because he feared the civil strife that might occur if any prolonged *interregnum* succeeded his death.

interrogate V. question closely; cross-examine. Knowing that the Nazis would *interrogate* him about his background, the secret agent invented a cover story that would help him meet their questions.

intervene V. come between. She *intervened* in the argument between her two sons. *intervention*, N.

intimate V. hint. She *intimated* rather than stated her preferences.

intimidation N. fear. A ruler who maintains his power by *intimidation* is bound to develop clandestine resistance.

■ **intractable** ADJ. unruly; refractory. The horse was *intractable* and refused to enter the starting gate.

■ **intransigence** N. state of stubborn unwillingness to compromise. The *intransigence* of both parties in the dispute makes an early settlement almost impossible to obtain. *intransigent*, ADJ.

■ **intrepid** ADJ. fearless. For his *intrepid* conduct in battle, he was promoted.

■ **intrinsically** ADV. essentially; inherently; naturally. Although my grandmother's china has *intrinsically* little value, I shall always cherish it for the memories it evokes. *intrinsic*, ADJ.

introspective ADJ. looking within oneself. We all have our *introspective* moments during which we examine our souls.

introvert N. one who is introspective; inclined to think more about oneself. In his poetry, he reveals that he is an *introvert* by his intense interest in his own problems. also V.

intrude V. trespass; enter as an uninvited person. She hesitated to *intrude* on their conversation.

intuition N. power of knowing without reasoning. She claimed to know the truth by *intuition*. *intuitive*, ADJ.

■ **inundate** V. overflow; flood. The tremendous waves *inundated* the town.

inured ADJ. accustomed; hardened. She became *inured* to the Alaskan cold.

invalidate V. weaken; destroy. The relatives who received little or nothing sought to *invalidate* the will by claiming that the deceased had not been in his right mind when he signed the document.

■ **invective** N. abuse. He had expected criticism but not the *invective* that greeted his proposal.

inveigh V. denounce; utter censure or invective. He *inveighed* against the demagoguery of the previous speaker and urged that the audience reject his philosophy as dangerous.

inveigle V. lead astray; wheedle. She was *inveigled* into joining the club after an initial reluctance.

inverse ADJ. opposite. There is an *inverse* ratio between the strength of light and its distance.

invert V. turn upside down or inside out. When he *inverted* his body in a hand stand, he felt the blood rush to his head.

Test

Word List 26 *Synonyms*

Each of the questions below consists of a word in capital letters, followed by five lettered words or phrases. Choose the lettered word or phrase that is most nearly similar in meaning to the word in capital letters and write the letter of your choice on your answer paper.

376. INGENUOUS (A) clever (B) stimulating (C) naive (D) worried (E) cautious
377. INIMICAL (A) antagonistic (B) anonymous (C) fanciful (D) accurate (E) atypical
378. INNOCUOUS (A) not capable (B) not dangerous (C) not eager (D) not frank (E) not peaceful
379. INSINUATE (A) resist (B) suggest (C) report (D) rectify (E) lecture
380. INSIPID (A) witty (B) flat (C) wily (D) talkative (E) lucid
381. INTEGRATE (A) tolerate (B) unite (C) flow (D) copy (E) assume

382. INTER (A) bury (B) amuse (C) relate (D) frequent (E) abandon
383. INTERDICT (A) acclaim (B) dispute (C) prohibit (D) decide (E) fret
384. INTERMITTENT (A) heavy (B) fleet (C) occasional (D) fearless (E) responding
385. INTRACTABLE (A) culpable (B) flexible (C) unruly (D) efficient (E) base
386. INTRANSIGENCE (A) lack of training (B) stubbornness (C) novelty (D) timidity (E) cupidity
387. INTREPID (A) cold (B) hot (C) understood (D) callow (E) courageous
388. INTRINSIC (A) extrinsic (B) abnormal (C) above (D) abandoned (E) basic
389. INUNDATE (A) abuse (B) deny (C) swallow (D) treat (E) flood
390. INVEIGH (A) speak violently (B) orate (C) disturb (D) apply (E) whisper

Word List 27   inveterate-laggard

inveterate ADJ. deep-rooted; habitual. She is an *inveterate* smoker and cannot break the habit.

invidious ADJ. designed to create ill will or envy. We disregarded her *invidious* remarks because we realized how jealous she was.

invincible ADJ. unconquerable. Superman is *invincible.*

inviolability N. security from being destroyed, corrupted or profaned. They respected the *inviolability* of her faith and did not try to change her manner of living.

invoke V. call upon; ask for. She *invoked* her advisor's aid in filling out her financial aid forms.

invulnerable ADJ. incapable of injury. Achilles was *invulnerable* except in his heel.

iota N. very small quantity. She hadn't an *iota* of common sense.

■ **irascible** ADJ. irritable; easily angered. Her *irascible* temper frightened me.

irate ADJ. angry. When John's mother found out that he had overdrawn his checking account for the third month in a row, she was so *irate* that she could scarcely speak to him.

iridescent ADJ. exhibiting rainbowlike colors. She admired the *iridescent* hues of the oil that floated on the surface of the water. iridescence, N.

irksome ADJ. annoying; tedious. He found working on the assembly line *irksome* because of the monotony of the operation he had to perform. irk, V.

ironic ADJ. occurring in an unexpected and contrary manner. It is *ironic* that his success came when he least wanted it.

irony N. hidden sarcasm or satire; use of words that convey a meaning opposite to the literal meaning. Gradually his listeners began to realize that the excessive praise he was lavishing was merely *irony*; he was actually denouncing his opponent.

irreconcilable ADJ. incompatible; not able to be resolved. Because the separated couple were *irreconcilable,* the marriage counselor recommended a divorce.

irrelevant ADJ. not applicable; unrelated. This statement is *irrelevant* and should be disregarded by the jury.

irremediable ADJ. incurable; uncorrectable. The error she made was *irremediable*; she could see no way to repair it.

irreparable ADJ. not able to be corrected or repaired. Your apology cannot atone for the *irreparable* damage you have done to her reputation.

irrepressible ADJ. unable to be restrained or held back. Her high spirits were *irrepressible.*

■ **irresolute** ADJ. uncertain how to act; weak. She had no respect for him because he seemed weak-willed and *irresolute.*

irreverent ADJ. lacking proper respect. The worshippers resented her *irreverent* remarks about their faith.

irrevocable ADJ. unalterable. Let us not brood over past mistakes since they are *irrevocable.*

isotope N. varying form of an element. The study of the *isotopes* of uranium led to the development of the nuclear bomb.

isthmus N. narrow neck of land connecting two larger bodies of land. In a magnificent feat of engineering, Goethals and his men cut through the *isthmus* of Panama in constructing the Panama Canal.

itinerant ADJ. wandering; traveling. He was an *itinerant* peddler and traveled through Pennsylvania and Virginia selling his wares. also N.

■ **itinerary** N. plan of a trip. Before leaving for his first visit to France and England, he discussed his *itinerary* with people who had been there and with his travel agent.

jaded ADJ. fatigued; surfeited. He looked for exotic foods to stimulate his *jaded* appetite.

jargon N. language used by special group; gibberish. We tried to understand the *jargon* of the peddlers in the marketplace but could not find any basis for comprehension.

jaundiced ADJ. yellowed; prejudiced; envious. She gazed at the painting with *jaundiced* eyes; she knew it was better than hers.

jaunt N. trip; short journey. He took a quick *jaunt to* Atlantic City.

jaunty ADJ. lighthearted; animated; easy and carefree. In *Singing in the Rain,* Gene Kelly sang and danced his way through the lighthearted title number in a properly *jaunty* style.

jeopardy N. exposure to death or danger. Legally, one cannot be placed in double *jeopardy.*

jettison V. throw overboard. In order to enable the ship to ride safely through the storm, the captain had to *jettison* much of his cargo.

jingoism N. extremely aggressive and militant patriotism. We must be careful to prevent a spirit of *jingoism* from spreading at this time; the danger of a disastrous war is too great.

jocose ADJ. given to joking. The salesman was so *jocose* that many of his customers suggested that he become a stand-up comic.

jocular ADJ. said or done in jest. Do not take my *jocular* remarks seriously.

jocund ADJ. merry. Santa Claus is always vivacious and *jocund.*

jollity N. gaiety; cheerfulness. The festive Christmas dinner was a merry one, and old and young alike joined in the general *jollity.*

jostle V. shove; bump. In the subway he was *jostled* by the crowds.

jovial ADJ. good-natured; merry. A frown seemed out of place on his invariably *jovial* face.

jubilation N. rejoicing. There was great *jubilation* when the armistice was announced.

■ **judicious** ADJ. sound in judgment; wise. At a key moment in his life, he made a *judicious* investment that was the foundation of his later wealth.

juggernaut N. irresistible crushing force. Nothing could survive in the path of the *juggernaut.*

juncture N. crisis; joining point. At this critical *juncture,* let us think carefully before determining the course we shall follow.

junket N. trip, especially one taken for pleasure by an official at public expense. Though she maintained she had gone abroad to collect firsthand data on the Common Market, the opposition claimed that her trip was merely a political *junket.*

junta N. group of persons joined in political intrigue; cabal. As soon as he learned of its existence, the dictator ordered the execution of all of the members of the *junta.*

jurisprudence N. science of law. He was more a student of *jurisprudence* than a practitioner of the law.

juxtapose V. place side by side. Comparison will be easier if you *juxtapose* the two objects.

kaleidoscope N. tube in which patterns made by the reflection in mirrors of colored pieces of glass, etc., produce interesting symmetrical effects. People found a new source of entertainment while peering through the *kaleidoscope;* they found the ever-changing patterns fascinating.

ken N. range of knowledge. I cannot answer your question since this matter is beyond my *ken.*

killjoy N. grouch; spoilsport. At breakfast we had all been enjoying our bacon and eggs until that *killjoy* John started talking about how bad animal fats and cholesterol were for our health.

kindle V. start a fire; inspire. Her teacher's praise *kindled* a spark of hope inside her.

kindred ADJ. related; similar in nature or character. Tom Sawyer and Huck Finn were two *kindred* spirits. also N.

kinetic ADJ. producing motion. Designers of the electric automobile find that their greatest obstacle lies in the development of light and efficient storage batteries, the source of the *kinetic* energy needed to propel the vehicle.

kismet N. fate. *Kismet* is the Arabic word for "fate."

kleptomaniac N. person who has a compulsive desire to steal. They discovered that the wealthy customer was a *kleptomaniac* when they caught her stealing some cheap trinkets.

knavery N. rascality. We cannot condone such *knavery* in public officials.

knead V. mix; work dough. Her hands grew strong from *kneading* bread.

knell N. tolling of a bell, especially to indicate a funeral, disaster, etc.; sound of the funeral bell. "The curfew tolls the *knell* of parting day." also V.

knit V. contract into wrinkles. Whenever David worries, his brow *knits* in a frown. (secondary meaning)

knoll N. little, round hill. Robert Louis Stevenson's grave is on a *knoll* in Samoa; to reach the grave site, you must climb uphill and walk a short distance along a marked path.

knotty ADJ. intricate; difficult; tangled. What to Watson had been a *knotty* problem to Sherlock Holmes was simplicity itself.

kudos N. honor; glory; praise. The singer complacently received *kudos* on his performance from his entourage.

labile ADJ. likely to change; unstable. Because the hormonal changes they undergo affect their spirits, adolescents may become emotionally *labile* and experience sudden shifts of mood. lability, N.

laborious ADJ. demanding much work or care; tedious. In putting together his dictionary of the English language, Doctor Johnson undertook a *laborious* task.

labyrinth N. maze. Tom and Becky were lost in the *labyrinth* of secret caves.

lacerate V. mangle; tear. Her body was *lacerated* in the automobile crash.

lachrymose ADJ. producing tears. His voice has a *lachrymose* quality that is more appropriate at a funeral than a class reunion.

lackadaisical ADJ. affectedly languid. He was *lackadaisical* and indifferent about his part in the affair.

lackluster ADJ. dull. We were disappointed by the *lackluster* performance.

■ **laconic** ADJ. brief and to the point. Many of the characters portrayed by Clint Eastwood are *laconic* types: strong men of few words.

laggard ADJ. slow; sluggish. The sailor had been taught not to be *laggard* in carrying out orders. lag, N., V.

Test

Word List 27 *Antonyms*

Each of the questions below consists of a word in capital letters, followed by five lettered words or phrases. Choose the lettered word or phrase that is most nearly opposite in meaning to the word in capital letters and write the letter of your choice on your answer paper.

391. IRKSOME (A) interesting (B) lazy (C) tireless (D) devious (E) excessive

392. IRRELEVANT (A) lacking piety (B) fragile (C) congruent (D) pertinent (E) varied

393. IRREPARABLE (A) legible (B) correctable (C) proverbial (D) concise (E) legal

394. IRREVERENT (A) related (B) mischievous (C) respective (D) pious (E) violent

395. JADED (A) upright (B) stimulated (C) aspiring (D) applied (E) void

396. JAUNDICED (A) whitened (B) inflamed (C) quickened (D) aged (E) unbiased

397. JAUNTY (A) youthful (B) ruddy (C) strong (D) untraveled (E) sedate

398. JEOPARDY (A) patience (B) courage (C) safety (D) willingness (E) liberty

399. JETTISON (A) salvage (B) submerge (C) descend (D) decelerate (E) repent

400. JOCULAR (A) arterial (B) bloodless (C) verbose (D) serious (E) blind

401. JUDICIOUS (A) punitive (B) unwise (C) criminal (D) licit (E) temporary

402. KINDLE (A) dislike (B) quench (C) gather (D) sparkle (E) estrange

403. LACHRYMOSE (A) cheering (B) smooth (C) passionate (D) curt (E) tense

404. LACKADAISICAL (A) monthly (B) possessing time (C) ambitious (D) pusillanimous (E) intelligent

405. LACONIC (A) milky (B) verbose (C) wicked (D) flagrant (E) derelict

---

Word List 28   lagoon-loquacious

lagoon N. shallow body of water near a sea; lake. They enjoyed their swim in the calm *lagoon*.

laity N. laypersons; persons not connected with the clergy. The *laity* does not always understand the clergy's problems.

lambaste V. beat; thrash verbally or physically. It was painful to watch the champion *lambaste* his opponent, tearing into him mercilessly.

lament V. grieve; express sorrow. Even advocates of the war *lamented* the loss of so many lives in combat. lamentation, N.

lampoon V. ridicule. This article *lampoons* the pretensions of some movie moguls. also N.

languid ADJ. weary; sluggish; listless. Her siege of illness left her *languid* and pallid.

languish V. lose animation; lose strength. In stories, lovelorn damsels used to *languish* and pine away.

languor N. lassitude; depression. His friends tried to overcome the *languor* into which he had fallen by taking him to parties and to the theater.

lank ADJ. long and thin. *Lank,* gaunt, Abraham Lincoln was a striking figure.

larceny N. theft. Because of the prisoner's record, the district attorney refused to reduce the charge from grand *larceny* to petit *larceny*.

larder N. pantry; place where food is kept. The first thing Bill did on returning home from school was to check what snacks his mother had in the *larder*.

largess N. generous gift. Lady Bountiful distributed *largess* to the poor.

lascivious ADJ. lustful. Because they might arouse *lascivious* impulses in their readers, the lewd books were banned by the clergy.

■ **lassitude** N. languor; weariness. The hot, tropical weather created a feeling of *lassitude* and encouraged drowsiness.

■ **latent** ADJ. dormant; hidden. Her *latent* talent was discovered by accident. latency, N.

lateral ADJ. coming from the side. In order to get good plant growth, the gardener must pinch off all *lateral* shoots.

latitude N. freedom from narrow limitations. I think you have permitted your son too much *latitude* in this matter.

laudable ADJ. praiseworthy; commendable. His *laudable* deeds will be remembered by all whom he aided.

■ **laudatory** ADJ. expressing praise. The critics' *laudatory* comments helped to make her a star.

lavish ADJ. liberal; wasteful. The actor's *lavish* gifts pleased her. also V.

lax ADJ. careless. We dislike restaurants where the service is *lax* and inattentive.

leaven V. cause to rise or grow lighter; enliven. As bread dough is *leavened*, it puffs up, expanding in volume.

lechery N. gross lewdness; lustfulness. In his youth he led a life of *lechery* and debauchery; he did not mend his ways until middle age. lecherous, ADJ.

lectern N. reading desk. The chaplain delivered his sermon from a hastily improvised *lectern*.

leery ADJ. suspicious; cautious. Don't eat the sushi at this restaurant; I'm a bit *leery* about how fresh it is.

leeway N. room to move; margin. When you set a deadline, allow a little *leeway*.

legacy N. a gift made by a will. Part of my *legacy* from my parents is an album of family photographs.

legend N. explanatory list of symbols on a map. The *legend* at the bottom of the map made it clear which symbols stood for rest areas along the highway and which stood for public camp sites. (secondary meaning)

legerdemain N. sleight of hand. The magician demonstrated his renowned *legerdemain*.

leniency N. mildness; permissiveness. Considering the gravity of the offense, we were surprised by the *leniency* of the sentence. lenient, ADJ.

leonine ADJ. like a lion. He was *leonine* in his rage.

lethal ADJ. deadly. It is unwise to leave *lethal* weapons where children may find them.

■ **lethargic** ADJ. drowsy; dull. The stuffy room made her *lethargic:* she felt as if she was about to nod off. lethargy, N.

levee N. earthen or stone embankment to prevent flooding. As the river rose and threatened to overflow the *levee,* emergency workers rushed to reinforce the walls with sandbags.

levitate V. float in the air (especially by magical means). As the magician passed his hands over the recumbent body of his assistant, she appeared to rise and *levitate* about three feet above the table.

■ **levity** N. lack of seriousness or steadiness; frivolity. Stop giggling and wriggling around in the pew: such *levity* is improper in church.

levy V. impose (a fine); collect (a payment). Crying "No taxation without representation!," the colonists demonstrated against England's power to *levy* taxes.

lewd ADJ. lustful. They found his *lewd* stories objectionable.

lexicographer N. compiler of a dictionary. The new dictionary is the work of many *lexicographers* who spent years compiling and editing the work.

lexicon N. dictionary. I cannot find this word in any *lexicon* in the library.

liability N. drawback; debts. Her lack of an extensive vocabulary was a *liability* that she was able to overcome.

liaison N. officer who acts as go-between for two armies; intermediary. As the *liaison,* he had to avoid offending the leaders of the two armies. also ADJ.

libelous ADJ. defamatory; injurious to the good name of a person. He sued the newspaper because of its *libelous* story.

libertine N. debauched person, roué. Although she was aware of his reputation as a *libertine,* she felt she could reform him and help him break his dissolute way of life.

libidinous ADJ. lustful. They objected to his *libidinous* behavior.

libido N. emotional urges behind human activity. The psychiatrist maintained that suppression of the *libido* often resulted in maladjustment and neuroses.

libretto N. text of an opera. The composer of an opera's music is remembered more frequently than the author of its *libretto.*

licentious ADJ. wanton; lewd; dissolute. The *licentious* monarch helped bring about his country's downfall.

lien N. legal claim on a property. There was a delay before Ralph could take possession of his late uncle's home; apparently, another claimant had a *lien* upon the estate.

ligneous ADJ. like wood. Petrified wood may be *ligneous* in appearance, but it is stonelike in composition.

lilliputian ADJ. extremely small. Tiny and delicate, the model was built on a *lilliputian* scale. also N.

limber ADJ. flexible. Hours of ballet classes kept him *limber.*

limbo N. region near heaven or hell where certain souls are kept; a prison (slang). Among the divisions of Hell are Purgatory and *Limbo.*

limn V. draw; outline; describe. Paradoxically, the more realistic the details this artist chooses, the better able she is to *limn* her fantastic, other-worldly landscapes.

limpid ADJ. clear. A *limpid* stream ran through his property.

lineage N. descent; ancestry. He traced his *lineage* back to *Mayflower* days.

lineaments N. features, especially of the face. She quickly sketched the *lineaments* of his face.

linguistic ADJ. pertaining to language. The modern tourist will encounter very little *linguistic* difficulty as English has become an almost universal language.

lionize V. treat as a celebrity. She enjoyed being *lionized* and adored by the public.

liquidate V. settle accounts; clear up. He was able to *liquidate* all his debts in a short period of time.

list V. tilt; lean over. That flagpole should be absolutely vertical; instead, it *lists* to one side. (secondary meaning) also N.

listless ADJ. lacking in spirit or energy. We had expected him to be full of enthusiasm and were surprised by his *listless* attitude.

litany N. supplicatory prayer. On this solemn day, the congregation responded to the prayers of the priest during the *litany* with fervor and intensity.

lithe ADJ. flexible; supple. Her figure was *lithe* and willowy.

litigation N. lawsuit. Try to settle this amicably; I do not want to start *litigation.* litigant, N.

litotes N. understatement for emphasis. To say, "He little realizes," when we mean that he does not realize at all, is an example of the kind of understatement we call *litotes.*

livid ADJ. lead-colored; black and blue; ashen; enraged. His face was so *livid* with rage that we were afraid that he might have an attack of apoplexy.

loath ADJ. averse; reluctant. They were both *loath* for him to go.

loathe V. detest. We *loathed* the wicked villain.

lode N. metal-bearing vein. If this *lode* that we have discovered extends for any distance, we have found a fortune.

lofty ADJ. very high. They used to tease him about his *lofty* ambitions.

loiter V. hang around; linger. The policeman told him not to *loiter* in the alley.

loll V. lounge about. They *lolled* around in their chairs watching television.

longevity N. long life. When he reached ninety, the old man was proud of his *longevity.*

lope V. gallop slowly. As the horses *loped* along, we had an opportunity to admire the ever-changing scenery.

loquacious ADJ. talkative. She is very *loquacious* and can speak on the telephone for hours. loquacity, N.

Test

Word List 28   *Antonyms*

Each of the questions below consists of a word in capital letters, followed by five lettered words or phrases. Choose the lettered word or phrase that is most nearly opposite in meaning to the word in capital letters and write the letter of your choice on your answer paper.

406. LAMPOON (A) darken (B) praise (C) abandon
     (D) sail (E) fly

407. LANGUOR (A) vitality (B) length
     (C) embarrassment (D) wine (E) avarice

408. LATENT (A) trim (B) forbidding (C) execrable
     (D) early (E) obvious

409. LAVISH (A) hostile (B) unwashed (C) timely
     (D) decent (E) frugal

410. LAUDATORY (A) dirtying (B) disclaiming
     (C) defamatory (D) inflammatory (E) debased

411. LAX (A) salty (B) strict (C) shrill
(D) boring (E) cowardly

412. LECHERY (A) trust (B) compulsion (C) zeal
(D) addiction (E) purity

413. LETHARGIC (A) convalescent (B) beautiful
(C) enervating (D) invigorating (E) interrogating

414. LEVITY (A) bridge (B) dam (C) praise
(D) blame (E) solemnity

415. LILLIPUTIAN (A) destructive (B) proper
(C) gigantic (D) elegant (E) barren

416. LIMPID (A) erect (B) turbid (C) tangential
(D) timid (E) weary

417. LITHE (A) stiff (B) limpid (C) facetious
(D) insipid (E) vast

418. LIVID (A) alive (B) mundane (C) positive
(D) undiscolored (E) vast

419. LOATH (A) loose (B) evident (C) deliberate
(D) eager (E) tiny

420. LOQUACIOUS (A) taciturn (B) sentimental
(C) soporific (D) soothing (E) sedate

Word List 29   lout-maul

lout N. clumsy person. The delivery boy is an awkward *lout.* loutish, ADJ.

low V. moo. From the hilltop, they could see the herd like ants in the distance; they could barely hear the cattle *low.*

■ **lucid** ADJ. easily understood; clear; intelligible. Her explanation was *lucid* enough for a child to grasp. lucidity, N.

lucrative ADJ. profitable. He turned his hobby into a *lucrative* profession.

lucre N. money. Preferring *lucre* to undying fame, he wrote stories of popular appeal.

ludicrous ADJ. laughable; trifling. Let us be serious; this is not a *ludicrous* issue.

lugubrious ADJ. mournful. The *lugubrious* howling of the dogs added to our sadness.

lull N. moment of calm. Not wanting to get wet, they waited under the awning for a *lull* in the rain.

lumber V. move heavily or clumsily. Still somewhat torpid after its long hibernation, the bear *lumbered* through the woods .

lumen N. unit of light energy (one candle's worth). In buying light bulbs, she checked not only their power, as measured in watts, but their brightness, as measured in *lumens.*

luminary N. celebrity; dignitary. A leading light of the American stage, Ethel Barrymore was a theatrical *luminary* whose name lives on.

■ **luminous** ADJ. shining; issuing light. The sun is a *luminous* body.

lunar ADJ. pertaining to the moon. *Lunar* craters can be plainly seen with the aid of a small telescope.

lurid ADJ. wild; sensational. The *lurid* stories he told shocked his listeners.

lurk V. stealthily lie in waiting; slink; exist unperceived. "Who knows what evils *lurk* in the hearts of men? The Shadow knows."

luscious ADJ. pleasing to taste or smell. The ripe peach was *luscious.*

luster N. shine; gloss. The soft *luster* of the silk in the dim light was pleasing.

lustrous ADJ. shining. Her large and *lustrous* eyes gave a touch of beauty to an otherwise drab face.

luxuriant ADJ. fertile; abundant; ornate. Farming was easy in this *luxuriant* soil.

macabre ADJ. gruesome; grisly. The city morgue is a *macabre* spot for the uninitiated.

mace N. ceremonial staff; clublike medieval weapon. The Grand Marshal of the parade raised his *mace* to signal that it was time for the procession to begin.

macerate V. soften by soaking in liquid; waste away. The strawberries had been soaking in the champagne for so long that they had begun to *macerate*: they literally fell apart at the touch of a spoon.

Machiavellian ADJ. crafty; double-dealing. I do not think he will be a good ambassador because he is not accustomed to the *Machiavellian* maneuverings of foreign diplomats.

machinations N. schemes. I can see through your wily *machinations.*

maculated ADJ. spotted; stained. Instead of writing that Gorbachev had a birthmark on his forehead, the pompous young poet sang of the former premier's *maculated* brow.

madrigal N. pastoral song. His program of folk songs included several *madrigals* which he sang to the accompaniment of a lute.

maelstrom N. whirlpool. The canoe was tossed about in the *maelstrom.*

magisterial ADJ. authoritative; imperious. The learned doctor laid down the law to his patient in a *magisterial* tone of voice.

■ **magnanimity** N. generosity. Noted for his *magnanimity,* philanthropist Eugene Lang donated millions to charity. magnanimous, ADJ.

magnate N. person of prominence or influence. The steel *magnate* decided to devote more time to city politics.

magniloquent ADJ. boastful, pompous. In their stories of the trial, the reporters ridiculed the *magniloquent* speeches of the defense attorney.

magnitude N. greatness; extent. It is difficult to comprehend the *magnitude* of his crime.

maim V. mutilate; injure. The hospital could not take care of all who had been mangled or *maimed* in the railroad accident.

maladroit ADJ. clumsy; bungling. In his usual *maladroit* way, he managed to upset the cart and spill the food.

malaise N. uneasiness; distress. She felt a sudden vague *malaise* when she heard sounds at the door.

malapropism N. comic misuse of a word. When Mrs. Malaprop criticizes Lydia for being "as headstrong as an allegory on the banks of the Nile," she confuses "allegory" and "alligator" in a typical *malapropism.*

malcontent   N. person dissatisfied with existing state of affairs. He was one of the few *malcontents* in Congress; he constantly voiced his objections to the Presidential program. also ADJ.

malediction   N. curse. The witch uttered *maledictions* against her captors.

malefactor   N. criminal. We must try to bring these *malefactors* to justice.

malevolent   ADJ. wishing evil. We must thwart his *malevolent* schemes.

malfeasance   N. wrongdoing. The authorities did not discover the campaign manager's *malfeasance* until after he had spent most of the money he had embezzled.

malicious   ADJ. dictated by hatred or spite. The *malicious* neighbor spread the gossip.

malign   V. speak evil of; defame. Because of her hatred of the family, she *maligns* all who are friendly to them.

malignant   ADJ. having an evil influence; virulent. This is a *malignant* disease; we may have to use drastic measures to stop its spread.

■ **malingerer**   N. one who feigns illness to escape duty. The captain ordered the sergeant to punish all *malingerers* and force them to work. malinger, V.

■ **malleable**   ADJ. capable of being shaped by pounding. Gold is *a malleable* metal.

malodorous   ADJ. foul-smelling. The compost heap was most *malodorous* in summer.

mammal   N. vertebrate animal whose female suckles its young. Many people regard the whale as a fish and do not realize that it is a *mammal.*

mammoth   ADJ. gigantic. The *mammoth* corporations of the twentieth century are a mixed blessing.

manacle   V. restrain; handcuff. The police immediately *manacled* the prisoner so he could not escape. also N.

mandate   N. order; charge. In his inaugural address, the President stated that he had a *mandate* from the people to seek an end to social evils such as poverty and poor housing. also V.

mandatory   ADJ. obligatory. These instructions are *mandatory*; any violation will be severely punished.

mangy   ADJ. shabby; wretched. We finally threw out the *mangy* rug that the dog had destroyed.

maniacal   ADJ. raving mad. His *maniacal* laughter frightened us.

manifest   ADJ. understandable; clear. His evil intentions were *manifest* and yet we could not stop him. also V.

manifestation   N. outward demonstration; indication. Mozart's early attraction to the harpsichord was the first *manifestation* of his pronounced musical bent.

manifesto   N. declaration; statement of policy. The *Communist Manifesto* by Marx and Engels proclaimed the principles of modern communism.

manifold   ADJ. numerous; varied. I cannot begin to tell you how much I appreciate your *manifold* kindnesses.

manipulate   V. operate with the hands; control or change by artful means. How do you *manipulate* these puppets?

mannered   ADJ. affected; not natural. Attempting to copy the style of his wealthy neighbors, Gatsby adopted a *mannered,* artificial way of speech.

manumit   V. emancipate; free from bondage. Enlightened slave owners were willing to *manumit* their slaves and thus put an end to the evil of slavery in the country.

marital   ADJ. pertaining to marriage. After the publication of his book on *marital* affairs, he was often consulted by married people on the verge of divorce.

maritime   ADJ. bordering on the sea; nautical. The *Maritime* Provinces depend on the sea for their wealth.

marked   ADJ. noticeable; targeted for vengeance. He walked with a *marked* limp, a souvenir of an old IRA attack. As British ambassador, he knew he was a *marked* man.

marred   ADJ. damaged; disfigured. She had to refinish the *marred* surface of the table. mar, V.

marshal   V. put in order. At a debate tournament, extemporaneous speakers have only a minute or two to *marshal* their thoughts before addressing their audience.

marsupial   N. one of a family of mammals that nurse their offspring in a pouch. The most common *marsupial* in North America is the opossum.

martial   ADJ. warlike. The sound of *martial* music was always inspiring to the young cadet.

martinet   N. strict disciplinarian. The commanding officer was a *martinet* who observed each regulation to the letter.

masochist   N. person who enjoys his own pain. The *masochist* begs, "Hit me." The sadist smiles and says, "I won't."

masticate   V. chew. We must *masticate* our food carefully and slowly in order to avoid digestive disorders.

materialism   N. preoccupation with physical comforts and things. By its nature, *materialism* is opposed to idealism, for where the materialist emphasizes the needs of the body, the idealist emphasizes the needs of the soul.

maternal   ADJ. motherly. Many animals display *maternal* instincts only while their offspring are young and helpless. maternity, N.

matriarch   N. woman who rules a family or larger social group. The *matriarch* ruled her gypsy tribe with a firm hand.

matrix   N. point of origin; array of numbers or algebraic symbols; mold or die. Some historians claim the Nile Valley was the *matrix* of Western civilization.

maudlin   ADJ. effusively sentimental. I do not like such *maudlin* pictures. I call them tearjerkers.

maul   V. handle roughly. The rock star was *mauled* by his overexcited fans.

Test

Word List 29   *Synonyms and Antonyms*

Each of the following questions consists of a word in capital letters, followed by five lettered words or phrases. Choose the lettered word or phrase that is most nearly similar to or opposite of the word in capital letters and write the letter of your choice on your answer paper.

421. LUGUBRIOUS (A) frantic (B) cheerful (C) burdensome (D) oily (E) militant
422. LURID (A) dull (B) duplicate (C) heavy (D) painstaking (E) intelligent
423. MACABRE (A) musical (B) frightening (C) chewed (D) wicked (E) exceptional
424. MAGNILOQUENT (A) loquacious (B) bombastic (C) rudimentary (D) qualitative (E) minimizing
425. MAGNITUDE (A) realization (B) fascination (C) enormity (D) gratitude (E) interference
426. MALADROIT (A) malicious (B) starving (C) thirsty (D) tactless (E) artistic

427. MALEDICTION (A) misfortune (B) hap (C) fruition (D) correct pronunciation (E) benediction
428. MALEFACTOR (A) quail (B) lawbreaker (C) beneficiary (D) banker (E) female agent
429. MALEVOLENT (A) kindly (B) vacuous (C) ambivalent (D) volatile (E) primitive
430. MALIGN (A) intersperse (B) vary (C) emphasize (D) frighten (E) eulogize
431. MALLEABLE (A) brittle (B) blatant (C) brilliant (D) brownish (E) basking
432. MANIACAL (A) demoniac (B) saturated (C) sane (D) sanitary (E) handcuffed
433. MANIFEST (A) limited (B) obscure (C) faulty (D) varied (E) vital
434. MANUMIT (A) print (B) impress (C) enslave (D) endeavor (E) fail
435. MARTIAL (A) bellicose (B) celibate (C) divorced (D) quiescent (E) planetary

Word List 30   mausoleum-misnomer

mausoleum N. monumental tomb. His body was placed in the family *mausoleum.*

mauve ADJ. pale purple. The *mauve* tint in the lilac bush was another indication that spring had finally arrived.

■ **maverick** N. rebel; nonconformist. To the masculine literary establishment, George Sand with her insistence on wearing trousers and smoking cigars was clearly a *maverick* who fought her proper womanly role.

mawkish ADJ. sickening; insipid. Your *mawkish* sighs fill me with disgust.

maxim N. proverb; a truth pithily stated. Aesop's fables illustrate moral *maxims.*

mayhem N. injury to body. The riot was marked not only by *mayhem,* with its attendant loss of life and limb, but also by arson and pillage.

meager ADJ. scanty; inadequate. His salary was far too *meager* for him to afford to buy a new car.

mealymouthed ADJ. indirect in speech; hypocritical; evasive. Rather than tell Jill directly what he disliked, Jack made a few *mealymouthed* comments and tried to change the subject.

meander V. to wind or turn in its course. It is difficult to sail up this stream because of the way it *meanders* through the countryside .

meddlesome ADJ. interfering. He felt his marriage was suffering because of his *meddlesome* mother-in-law.

mediate V. settle a dispute through the services of an outsider. Let us *mediate* our differences rather than engage in a costly strike.

mediocre ADJ. ordinary; commonplace. We were disappointed because he gave a rather *mediocre* performance in this role.

meditation N. reflection; thought. She reached her decision only after much *meditation.*

medley N. mixture. The band played a *medley* of Gershwin tunes.

meek ADJ. submissive; patient and long-suffering. Mr. Barrett never expected his *meek* daughter would dare to defy him by eloping with her suitor.

megalomania N. mania for doing grandiose things. Developers who spend millions trying to build the world's tallest skyscraper suffer from *megalomania.*

melee N. fight. The captain tried to ascertain the cause of the *melee* that had broken out among the crew members.

mellifluous ADJ. flowing smoothly; smooth. Italian is a *mellifluous* language.

memento N. token; reminder. Take this book as a *memento* of your visit.

memorialize V. commemorate. Let us *memorialize* his great contribution by dedicating this library in his honor.

mendacious ADJ. lying; false. He was a pathological liar, and his friends learned to discount his *mendacious* stories.

mendicant N. beggar. From the moment we left the ship, we were surrounded by *mendicants* and peddlers. mendicancy, N.

menial ADJ. suitable for servants; low. I cannot understand why a person of your ability and talent should engage in such *menial* activities. also N.

mentor N. counselor; teacher. During this very trying period, she could not have had a better *mentor,* for the teacher was sympathetic and understanding.

mercantile ADJ. concerning trade. I am more interested in the opportunities available in the *mercantile* field than I am in those in the legal profession.

mercenary ADJ. motivated solely by money or gain. "I'm not in this war because I get my kicks waving flags," said the *mercenary* soldier. "I'm in it for the dough." also N.

mercurial ADJ. fickle; changing. He was of a *mercurial* temperament and therefore unpredictable.

meretricious ADJ. flashy; tawdry. Her jewels were inexpensive but not *meretricious.*

merger N. combination (of two business corporations). When the firm's president married the director of financial planning, the office joke was that it wasn't a marriage, it was a *merger.*

mesmerize V. hypnotize. The incessant drone seemed to *mesmerize* him and place him in a trance.

metallurgical ADJ. pertaining to the art of removing metals from ores. During the course of his *metallurgical* research, the scientist developed a steel alloy of tremendous strength.

metamorphosis N. change of form. The *metamorphosis* of caterpillar to butterfly is typical of many such changes in animal life. metamorphose, V.

metaphor N. implied comparison. "He soared like an eagle" is an example of a simile; "He is an eagle in flight," a *metaphor.*

metaphysical ADJ. pertaining to speculative philosophy. The modern poets have gone back to the fanciful poems of the *metaphysical* poets of the seventeenth century for many of their images. metaphysics, N.

mete V. measure; distribute. He tried to be impartial in his efforts to *mete* out justice.

meteoric ADJ. swift; momentarily brilliant. We all wondered at his *meteoric* rise to fame.

methodical ADJ. systematic. An accountant must be *methodical* and maintain order among his financial records.

■ **meticulous** ADJ. excessively careful. He was *meticulous* in checking his accounts and never made mistakes.

metropolis N. large city. Every evening this terminal is filled with the thousands of commuters who are going from this *metropolis* to their homes in the suburbs.

mettle N. courage; spirit. When challenged by the other horses in the race, the thoroughbred proved its *mettle* by its determination to hold the lead. mettlesome, ADJ.

miasma N. swamp gas; heavy, vaporous atmosphere, often emanating from decaying matter; pervasive corrupting influence. The smog hung over Victorian London like a dark cloud; noisome, reeking of decay, it was a visible *miasma.*

microcosm N. small world. In the *microcosm* of our rural village, we find illustrations of all the evils that beset the universe.

migrant ADJ. changing its habitat; wandering. These *migrant* birds return every spring. also N.

migratory ADJ. wandering. The return of the *migratory* birds to the northern sections of this country is a harbinger of spring.

milieu N. environment; means of expression. His *milieu* is watercolors, although he has produced excellent oil paintings and lithographs.

militant ADJ. combative; bellicose. Although at this time he was advocating a policy of neutrality, one could usually find him adopting a more *militant* attitude. also N.

militate V. work against. Your record of lateness and absence will *militate* against your chances of promotion.

millennium N. thousand-year period; period of happiness and prosperity. I do not expect the *millennium* to come during my lifetime.

mimicry N. imitation. Her gift for *mimicry* was so great that her friends said that she should be in the theater.

minatory ADJ. menacing; threatening. Jabbing a *minatory* forefinger at Dorothy, the Wicked Witch cried, "I'll get you, and your little dog, too!"

mincing ADJ. affectedly dainty. Yum-Yum walked across the stage with *mincing* steps.

minion N. a servile dependent. He was always accompanied by several of his *minions* because he enjoyed their subservience and flattery.

minuscule ADJ. extremely small. Why should I involve myself with a project with so *minuscule* a chance for success?

minute ADJ. extremely small. The twins resembled one another closely; only *minute* differences set them apart.

minutiae N. petty details. She would have liked to ignore the *minutiae* of daily living.

mirage N. unreal reflection; optical illusion. The lost prospector was fooled by a *mirage* in the desert.

mire V. entangle; stick in swampy ground. Their rear wheels became *mired* in mud. also N.

mirth N. merriment; laughter. Sober Malvolio found Sir Toby's *mirth* improper.

misadventure N. mischance; ill luck. The young explorer met death by *misadventure.*

■ **misanthrope** N. one who hates mankind. We thought the hermit was a *misanthrope* because he shunned our society. misanthropic, ADJ.

misapprehension N. error; misunderstanding. To avoid *misapprehension,* I am going to ask all of you to repeat the instructions I have given.

miscellany N. mixture of writings on various subjects. This is an interesting *miscellany* of nineteenth-century prose and poetry.

mischance N. ill luck. By *mischance,* he lost his week's salary.

misconstrue V. interpret incorrectly; misjudge. She took the passage seriously rather than humorously because she *misconstrued* the author's ironic tone.

miscreant N. wretch; villain. His kindness to the *miscreant* amazed all of us who had expected to hear severe punishment pronounced.

misdemeanor N. minor crime. The culprit pleaded guilty to a *misdemeanor* rather than face trial for a felony.

miserly ADJ. stingy; mean. The *miserly* old man hoarded his coins not out of prudence but out of greed. miser, N.

misgivings N. doubts. Hamlet described his *misgivings* to Horatio but decided to fence with Laertes despite his foreboding of evil.

mishap N. accident. With a little care you could have avoided this *mishap*.

misnomer N. wrong name; incorrect designation. His tyrannical conduct proved to all that his nickname, King Eric the Just, was a *misnomer*.

Word List 30   *Synonyms*

Each of the questions below consists of a word in capital letters, followed by five lettered words or phrases. Choose the lettered word or phrase that is most nearly similar in meaning to the word in capital letters and write the letter of your choice on your answer paper.

436. MAWKISH (A) sentimental (B) true (C) certain (D) devious (E) carefree
437. MEDIOCRE (A) average (B) bitter (C) medieval (D) industrial (E) agricultural
438. MELEE (A) heat (B) brawl (C) attempt (D) weapon (E) choice
439. MELLIFLUOUS (A) porous (B) honeycombed (C) strong (D) smooth (E) viscous
440. MENIAL (A) intellectual (B) clairvoyant (C) servile (D) arrogant (E) laudatory
441. MENTOR (A) guide (B) genius (C) talker (D) philosopher (E) stylist
442. MESMERIZE (A) remember (B) hypnotize (C) delay (D) bore (E) analyze
443. METICULOUS (A) steadfast (B) recent (C) quaint (D) painstaking (E) overt
444. MIASMA (A) dream (B) noxious fumes (C) scenario (D) quantity (E) total
445. MILITANT (A) combative (B) dramatic (C) religious (D) quaint (E) paternal
446. MINION (A) monster (B) quorum (C) majority (D) host (E) dependent
447. MIRAGE (A) dessert (B) illusion (C) water (D) mirror (E) statement
448. MISANTHROPE (A) benefactor (B) philanderer (C) man-hater (D) aesthete (E) epicure
449. MISCHANCE (A) gamble (B) ordinance (C) aperture (D) anecdote (E) adversity
450. MISDEMEANOR (A) felony (B) peccadillo (C) indignity (D) fiat (E) illiteracy

---

Word List 31   misogamy-nascent

misogamy N. hatred of marriage. He remained a bachelor not because of *misogamy* but because of ill fate: his fiancee died before the wedding.

misogynist N. hater of women. She accused him of being a *misogynist* because he had been a bachelor all his life.

missile N. object to be thrown or projected. Scientists are experimenting with guided *missiles*.

missive N. letter. The ambassador received a *missive* from the Secretary of State.

mite N. very small object or creature; small coin. Gnats are annoying *mites* that sting.

■ **mitigate** V. appease. Nothing he did could *mitigate* her wrath; she was unforgiving.

mnemonic ADJ. pertaining to memory. He used *mnemonic* tricks to master new words.

mobile ADJ. movable; not fixed. The *mobile* blood bank operated by the Red Cross visited our neighborhood today. mobility, N.

mode N. prevailing style. She was not used to their lavish *mode* of living.

modicum N. limited quantity. Although his story is based on a *modicum* of truth, most of the events he describes are fictitious.

modish ADJ. fashionable. She always discarded all garments that were no longer *modish*.

modulation N. toning down; changing from one key to another. When she spoke, it was with quiet *modulation* of voice.

mogul N. powerful person. The oil *moguls* made great profits when the price of gasoline rose.

molecule N. the smallest particle (one or more atoms) of a substance that has all the properties of that substance. In chemistry, we study how atoms and *molecules* react to form new substances.

■ **mollify** V. soothe. We tried to *mollify* the hysterical child by promising her many gifts. mollification, N.

mollycoddle V. pamper; indulge excessively. Don't *mollycoddle* the boy, Maud! You'll spoil him.

molt V. shed or cast off hair or feathers. The male robin *molted* in the spring.

molten ADJ. melted. The city of Pompeii was destroyed by volcanic ash rather than by *molten* lava flowing from Mount Vesuvius.

momentous ADJ. very important. On this *momentous* occasion, we must be very solemn.

momentum N. quantity of motion of a moving body; impetus. The car lost *momentum* as it tried to ascend the steep hill.

monarchy N. government under a single hereditary ruler with varying degrees of power. England today remains a *monarchy*.

monastic ADJ. related to monks. Wanting to live a religious life, he took his *monastic* vows.

monetary ADJ. pertaining to money. Jane held the family purse strings: she made all *monetary* decisions affecting the household.

monochromatic ADJ. having only one color. Most people who are color blind actually can distinguish several colors; some, however, have a truly *monochromatic* view of a world all in shades of gray.

monolithic ADJ. solidly uniform; unyielding. Knowing the importance of appearing resolute, the patriots sought to present a *monolithic* front.

monotheism N. belief in one God. Abraham was the first to proclaim his belief in *monotheism.*

monotony N. sameness leading to boredom. He took a clerical job, but soon grew to hate the *monotony* of his daily routine.

monumental ADJ. massive. Writing a dictionary is a *monumental* task.

moodiness N. fits of depression or gloom. We could not discover the cause of her recurrent *moodiness.*

moratorium N. legal delay of payment. If we declare a *moratorium* and delay collection of debts for six months, I am sure the farmers will be able to meet their bills.

morbid ADJ. given to unwholesome thought; gloomy. These *morbid* speculations are dangerous; we must lighten our spirits by emphasizing more pleasant matters.

mordant ADJ. biting; sarcastic; stinging. Actors feared the critic's *mordant* pen.

mores N. customs. The *mores* of Mexico are those of Spain with some modifications.

moribund ADJ. at the point of death. The doctors called the family to the bedside of the *moribund* patient.

morose ADJ. ill-humored; sullen. When we first meet Hamlet, we find him *morose* and depressed.

mortician N. undertaker. The *mortician* prepared the corpse for burial.

mortify V. humiliate; punish the flesh. She was so *mortified* by her blunder that she ran to her room in tears.

mosaic N. picture made of small, colorful inlaid tiles. The mayor compared the city to a beautiful *mosaic* made up of people of every race and religion on earth. also ADJ.

mote N. small speck. The tiniest *mote* in the eye is very painful.

motif N. theme. This simple *motif* runs throughout the score.

motility N. ability to move spontaneously. Certain organisms exhibit remarkable *motility; motile* spores, for example, may travel for miles before coming to rest. motile, ADJ.

motley ADJ. parti-colored; mixed. The captain had gathered a *motley* crew to sail the vessel.

mottled ADJ. spotted. When he blushed, his face took on a *mottled* hue.

mountebank N. charlatan; boastful pretender. The patent medicine man was a *mountebank.*

muddle V. confuse; mix up. His thoughts were *muddled* and chaotic. also N.

muggy ADJ. warm and damp. August in New York City is often *muggy.*

mulct V. defraud a person of something. The lawyer was accused of trying to *mulct* the boy of his legacy.

multifarious ADJ. varied; greatly diversified. A career woman and mother, she was constantly busy with the *multifarious* activities of her daily life.

multiform ADJ. having many forms. Snowflakes are *multiform* but always hexagonal.

multilingual ADJ. having many languages. Because they are bordered by so many countries, the Swiss people are *multilingual.*

multiplicity N. state of being numerous. He was appalled by the *multiplicity* of details he had to complete before setting out on his mission.

■ **mundane** ADJ. worldly as opposed to spiritual. He was concerned only with *mundane* matters, especially the daily stock market quotations.

munificent ADJ. very generous. The *munificent* gift was presented to the bride by her rich uncle. munificence, N.

murkiness N. darkness; gloom. The *murkiness* and fog of the waterfront that evening depressed me.

muse V. ponder. For a moment he *mused* about the beauty of the scene, but his thoughts soon changed as he recalled his own personal problems. also N.

musky ADJ. having the odor of musk. She left a trace of *musky* perfume behind her.

muster V. gather; assemble. Washington *mustered* his forces at Trenton.

musty ADJ. stale; spoiled by age. The attic was dark and *musty.*

mutable ADJ. changing in form; fickle. His opinions were *mutable* and easily influenced by anyone who had any powers of persuasion.

muted ADJ. silent; muffled; toned down. In the funeral parlor, the mourners' voices had a *muted* quality. mute, V.

mutilate V. maim. The torturer threatened to *mutilate* his victim.

mutinous ADJ. unruly; rebellious. The captain had to use force to quiet his *mutinous* crew. mutiny, N.

myopic ADJ. nearsighted. In thinking only of your present needs and ignoring the future, you are being rather *myopic.*

myriad N. very large number. *Myriads* of mosquitoes from the swamps invaded our village every twilight. also ADJ.

nadir N. lowest point. Although few people realized it, the Dow-Jones averages had reached their *nadir* and would soon begin an upward surge.

naiveté N. quality of being unsophisticated. I cannot believe that such *naiveté* is unassumed in a person of her age and experience. naive, ADJ.

narcissist N. conceited person. A *narcissist* is his own best friend.

narrative ADJ. related to telling a story. A born teller of tales, Olsen used her impressive *narrative* skills to advantage in her story "I Stand Here Ironing." also N. narration, N.

nascent ADJ. incipient; coming into being. If we could identify these revolutionary movements in their *nascent* state, we would be able to eliminate serious trouble in later years.

Test

Word List 31   *Synonyms*

Each of the questions below consists of a word in capital letters, followed by five lettered words or phrases. Choose the lettered word or phrase that is most nearly similar in meaning to the word in capital letters and write the letter of your choice on your answer paper.

451. MODISH (A) sentimental (B) stylish (C) vacillating (D) contrary (E) adorned
452. MOLLIFY (A) avenge (B) attenuate (C) attribute (D) mortify (E) appease
453. MONETARY (A) boring (B) fascinating (C) fiscal (D) stationary (E) scrupulous
454. MORATORIUM (A) burial (B) gathering (C) delay (D) refusal (E) suspicion
455. MORDANT (A) dying (B) trenchant (C) fabricating (D) controlling (E) avenging
456. MORIBUND (A) dying (B) appropriate (C) leather bound (D) answering (E) undertaking

457. MOTLEY (A) active (B) disguised (C) variegated (D) somber (E) sick
458. MUGGY (A) attacking (B) fascinating (C) humid (D) characteristic (E) gelid
459. MULCT (A) swindle (B) hold (C) record (D) print (E) fertilize
460. MULTILINGUAL (A) variegated (B) polyglot (C) multilateral (D) polyandrous (E) multiplied
461. MUNDANE (A) global (B) futile (C) spatial (D) heretic (E) worldly
462. MUNIFICENT (A) grandiose (B) puny (C) philanthropic (D) poor (E) gracious
463. MUSTY (A) flat (B) necessary (C) indifferent (D) nonchalant (E) vivid
464. MYOPIC (A) visionary (B) nearsighted (C) moral (D) glassy (E) blind
465. NASCENT (A) incipient (B) ignorant (C) loyal (D) treacherous (E) unnamed

Word List 32   natation-obsidian

natation N. swimming. The Red Cross emphasizes the need for courses in *natation*.

natty ADJ. neatly or smartly dressed. Priding himself on being a *natty* dresser, the gangster Bugsy Siegel collected a wardrobe of imported suits and ties.

nauseate V. cause to become sick; fill with disgust. The foul smells began to *nauseate* him.

nautical ADJ. pertaining to ships or navigation. The Maritime Museum contains many models of clipper ships, logbooks, anchors and many other items of a *nautical* nature.

nebulous ADJ. vague; hazy; cloudy. She had only a *nebulous* memory of her grandmother's face.

necromancy N. black magic; dealings with the dead. Because he was able to perform feats of *necromancy*, the natives thought he was in league with the devil.

nefarious ADJ. very wicked. He was universally feared because of his many *nefarious* deeds.

negation N. denial. I must accept his argument since you have been unable to present any *negation* of his evidence.

negligence N. carelessness. *Negligence* can prove costly near complicated machinery.

negligible ADJ. so small, trifling, or unimportant as to be easily disregarded. Because the damage to his car had been *negligible*, Michael decided he wouldn't bother to report the matter to his insurance company.

nemesis N. revenging agent. Captain Bligh vowed to be Christian's *nemesis*.

neologism N. new or newly coined word or phrase. As we invent new techniques and professions, we must also invent *neologisms* such as "microcomputer" and "astronaut" to describe them.

neophyte N. recent convert; beginner. This mountain slope contains slides that will challenge experts as well as *neophytes*.

nepotism N. favoritism (to a relative). John left his position with the company because he felt that advancement was based on *nepotism* rather than ability.

nether ADJ. lower. Tradition locates hell in the *nether* regions.

nettle V. annoy; vex. Do not let him *nettle* you with his sarcastic remarks.

nexus N. connection. I fail to see the *nexus* that binds these two widely separated events.

nib N. beak; pen point. The *nibs* of fountain pens often become clotted and corroded.

nicety N. precision; minute distinction. I cannot distinguish between such *niceties* of reasoning. nice, ADJ. (secondary meaning)

niggardly ADJ. meanly stingy; parsimonious. The *niggardly* pittance the widow receives from the government cannot keep her from poverty.

niggle v. spend too much time on minor points; carp. Let's not *niggle* over details. niggling, ADJ.

nihilism N. denial of traditional values; total skepticism. *Nihilism* holds that existence has no meaning.

nirvana N. in Buddhist teachings, the ideal state in which the individual loses himself in the attainment of an impersonal beatitude. Despite his desire to achieve *nirvana*, the young Buddhist found that even the buzzing of a fly could distract him from his meditation.

nocturnal ADJ. done at night. Mr. Jones obtained a watchdog to prevent the *nocturnal* raids on his chicken coops.

noisome ADJ. foul smelling; unwholesome. I never could stand the *noisome* atmosphere surrounding the slaughter houses.

nomadic ADJ. wandering. Several *nomadic* tribes of Indians would hunt in this area each year. nomad, N.

nomenclature N. terminology; system of names. She struggled to master scientific *nomenclature*.

nominal ADJ. in name only; trifling. He offered to drive her to the airport for only a *nominal* fee.

nonchalance N. indifference; lack of interest. Few people could understand how he could listen to the news of the tragedy with such *nonchalance*; the majority regarded him as callous and unsympathetic.

noncommittal ADJ. neutral; unpledged; undecided. We were annoyed by his *noncommittal* reply for we had been led to expect definite assurances of his approval.

nondescript ADJ. undistinctive; ordinary. The private detective was a short, *nondescript* fellow with no outstanding features, the sort of person one would never notice in a crowd.

nonentity N. person of no importance; nonexistence. Don't dismiss John as a *nonentity*; in his quiet way, he's very important to the firm.

nonplus v. bring to a halt by confusion; perplex. Jack's uncharacteristic rudeness *nonplussed* Jill, leaving her uncertain how to react.

nostalgia N. homesickness; longing for the past. The first settlers found so much work to do that they had little time for *nostalgia*.

nostrum N. questionable medicine. No quack selling *nostrums* is going to cheat me.

notoriety N. disrepute; ill fame. To the starlet, any publicity was good publicity: if she couldn't have a good reputation, she'd settle for *notoriety*. notorious, ADJ.

novelty N. something new; newness. The computer is no longer a *novelty* around the office. novel, ADJ.

novice N. beginner. Even a *novice* can do good work if he follows these simple directions.

noxious ADJ. harmful. We must trace the source of these *noxious* gases before they asphyxiate us.

nuance N. shade of difference in meaning or color. The unskilled eye of the layperson has difficulty in discerning the *nuances* of color in the paintings.

nubile ADJ. marriageable. Mrs. Bennet, in *Pride and Prejudice* by Jane Austen, was worried about finding suitable husbands for her five *nubile* daughters.

nugatory ADJ. futile; worthless. This agreement is *nugatory* for no court will enforce it.

nullify v. to make invalid. Once the contract was *nullified*, it no longer had any legal force.

numismatist N. person who collects coins. The *numismatist* had a splendid collection of antique coins.

nuptial ADJ. related to marriage. Their *nuptial* ceremony was performed in Golden Gate Park.

nurture v. nourish; educate; foster. The Head Start program attempts to *nurture* prekindergarten children so that they will do well when they enter public school. also N.

nutrient N. nourishing substance. As a budding nutritionist, Kim has learned to design diets that contain foods rich in important basic *nutrients*. also ADJ.

oaf N. stupid, awkward person. He called the unfortunate waiter a clumsy *oaf*.

■ **obdurate** ADJ. stubborn. He was *obdurate* in his refusal to listen to our complaints.

obeisance N. bow. She made an *obeisance* as the king and queen entered the room.

obelisk N. tall column tapering and ending in a pyramid. Cleopatra's Needle is an *obelisk* in New York City's Central Park.

obese ADJ. excessively fat. It is advisable that *obese* people try to lose weight. obesity, N.

obfuscate v. confuse; muddle. Do not *obfuscate* the issues by dragging in irrelevant arguments.

obituary N. death notice. I first learned of her death when I read the *obituary* in the newspaper. also ADJ.

objective ADJ. not influenced by emotions; fair. Even though he was her son, she tried to be *objective* about his behavior.

objective N. goal; aim. A degree in medicine was her ultimate *objective*.

obligatory ADJ. binding; required. It is *obligatory* that books borrowed from the library be returned within two weeks.

oblique ADJ. slanting; deviating from the perpendicular or from a straight line. The sergeant ordered the men to march "*Oblique* Right."

obliterate v. destroy completely. The tidal wave *obliterated* several island villages.

oblivion N. forgetfulness. Her works had fallen into a state of *oblivion*; no one bothered to read them. oblivious, ADJ.

obloquy N. slander; disgrace; infamy. I resent the *obloquy* that you are casting upon my reputation.

obnoxious ADJ. offensive. I find your behavior *obnoxious*; please mend your ways.

obscure ADJ. dark; vague; unclear. Even after I read the poem a fourth time, its meaning was still *obscure*. obscurity, N.

obscure v. darken; make unclear. At times he seemed purposely to *obscure* his meaning, preferring mystery to clarity.

■ **obsequious** ADJ. slavishly attentive; servile; sycophantic. Helen valued people who behaved as if they respected themselves; nothing irritated her more than an excessively *obsequious* waiter or a fawning salesclerk.

obsequy N. funeral ceremony. Hundreds paid their last respects at his *obsequies*.

obsession N. fixed idea; continued brooding. This *obsession* with the supernatural has made him unpopular with his neighbors.

obsidian N. black volcanic rock. The deposits of *obsidian* on the mountain slopes were an indication that the volcano had erupted in ancient times.

Test

Word List 32   *Antonyms*

Each of the questions below consists of a word in capital letters, followed by five lettered words or phrases. Choose the lettered word or phrase that is most nearly opposite in meaning to the word in capital letters and write the letter of your choice on your answer paper.

466. NEBULOUS (A) starry (B) clear (C) cold (D) fundamental (E) porous
467. NEFARIOUS (A) various (B) lacking (C) benign (D) pompous (E) futile
468. NEGATION (A) postulation (B) hypothecation (C) affirmation (D) violation (E) anticipation
469. NEOPHYTE (A) veteran (B) satellite (C) desperado (D) handwriting (E) violence
470. NIGGARDLY (A) protected (B) biased (C) prodigal (D) bankrupt (E) placated
471. NOCTURNAL (A) harsh (B) marauding (C) patrolling (D) daily (E) fallow

472. NOISOME (A) quiet (B) dismayed (C) fragrant (D) sleepy (E) inquisitive
473. NOTORIOUS (A) fashionable (B) renowned (C) inactive (D) intrepid (E) invincible
474. OBDURATE (A) yielding (B) fleeting (C) finite (D) fascinating (E) permanent
475. OBESE (A) skillful (B) cadaverous (C) clever (D) unpredictable (E) lucid
476. OBJECTIVE (A) indecisive (B) apathetic (C) markedly inferior (D) emotionally involved (E) authoritative
477. OBLIGATORY (A) demanding (B) optional (C) facile (D) friendly (E) divorced
478. OBLOQUY (A) praise (B) rectangle (C) circle (D) dialogue (E) cure
479. OBSEQUIOUS (A) successful (B) democratic (C) supercilious (D) ambitious (E) lamentable
480. OBSESSION (A) whim (B) loss (C) phobia (D) delusion (E) feud

Word List 33   obsolete-overweening

obsolete ADJ. outmoded. "Hip" is an *obsolete* expression; it went out with love beads and tie-dye shirts.

obstetrician N. physician specializing in delivery of babies. Unlike midwives, who care for women giving birth at home, *obstetricians* generally work in a hospital setting.

obstinate ADJ. stubborn. We tried to persuade him to give up smoking, but he was *obstinate* and refused to change.

obstreperous ADJ. boisterous; noisy. The crowd became *obstreperous* and shouted their disapproval of the proposals made by the speaker.

∙usive ADJ. pushing forward. I found her a very *obtrusive* ∙son, constantly seeking the center of the stage. obtrude, V.

obtuse ADJ. blunt; stupid. Because he was so *obtuse,* he could not follow the teacher's reasoning and asked foolish questions.

■ **obviate** V. make unnecessary; get rid of. I hope this contribution will *obviate* any need for further collections of funds.

Occident N. the West. It will take time for the *Occident* to understand the ways and customs of the Orient.

occlude V. shut; close. A blood clot *occluded* an artery to the heart. occlusion, N.

occult ADJ. mysterious; secret; supernatural. The *occult* rites of the organization were revealed only to members. also N.

oculist N. physician who specializes in treatment of the eyes. In many states, an *oculist* is the only one who may

apply medicinal drops to the eyes for the purpose of examining them.

odious ADJ. hateful. I find the task of punishing you most *odious*.

odium N. repugnance; dislike. I cannot express the *odium* I feel at your heinous actions.

odoriferous ADJ. giving off an odor. The *odoriferous* spices stimulated her jaded appetite.

odorous ADJ. having an odor. This variety of hybrid tea rose is more *odorous* than the one you have in your garden.

odyssey N. long, eventful journey. The refugee's journey from Cambodia was a terrifying *odyssey*.

offensive ADJ. attacking; insulting; distasteful. Getting into street brawls is no minor offense for professional boxers, who are required by law to restrict their *offensive* impulses to the ring.

offhand ADJ. casual; done without prior thought. Expecting to be treated with due propriety by her hosts, Great-Aunt Maud was offended by their *offhand* manner.

■ **officious** ADJ. meddlesome; excessively pushy in offering one's services. After her long flight, Jill just wanted to nap, but the *officious* bellboy was intent on showing her all the special features of the deluxe suite.

ogle V. glance coquettishly at; make eyes at. Sitting for hours at the sidewalk cafe, the old gentleman would *ogle* the young girls and recall his youthful romances.

olfactory ADJ. concerning the sense of smell. The *olfactory* organ is the nose.

oligarchy N. government by a few. The feudal *oligarchy* was supplanted by an autocracy.

ominous ADJ. threatening. Those clouds are *ominous;* they suggest that a severe storm is on the way.

omnipotent ADJ. all-powerful. The monarch regarded himself as *omnipotent* and responsible to no one for his acts.

omnipresent ADJ. universally present; ubiquitous. On Christmas Eve, Santa Claus is *omnipresent.*

omniscient ADJ. all-knowing. I do not pretend to be *omniscient,* but I am positive about this fact.

omnivorous ADJ. eating both plant and animal food; devouring everything. Some animals, including humans, are *omnivorous* and eat both meat and vegetables; others are either carnivorous or herbivorous.

onerous ADJ. burdensome. He asked for an assistant because his work load was too *onerous.*

onomatopoeia N. words formed in imitation of natural sounds. Words like "rustle" and "gargle" are illustrations of *onomatopoeia.*

onslaught N. vicious assault. We suffered many casualties during the unexpected *onslaught* of the enemy troops.

onus N. burden; responsibility. The emperor was spared the *onus* of signing the surrender papers; instead, he relegated the assignment to his generals.

opalescent ADJ. iridescent. The Ancient Mariner admired the *opalescent* sheen on the water.

opaque ADJ. dark; not transparent. The *opaque* window kept the sunlight out of the room. opacity, N.

opiate N. sleep producer; deadener of pain. By such *opiates,* she made the people forget their difficulties and accept their unpleasant circumstances.

opportune ADJ. timely; well chosen. You have come at an *opportune* moment for I need a new secretary.

opportunist N. individual who sacrifices principles for expediency by taking advantage of circumstances. Forget about ethics! He's such an *opportunist* that he'll vote in favor of any deal that will give him a break.

opprobrium N. infamy; vilification. He refused to defend himself against the slander and *opprobrium* hurled against him by the newspapers; he preferred to rely on his record.

optician N. maker and seller of eyeglasses. The patient took the prescription given him by his oculist to the *optician.*

optimist N. person who looks on the bright side. The pessimist says the glass is half-empty; the *optimist* says it is half-full.

optimum ADJ. most favorable. If you wait for the *optimum* moment to act, you may never begin your project. also N.

optional ADJ. not compulsory; left to one's choice. I was impressed by the range of *optional* accessories for my microcomputer that were available. option, N.

optometrist N. one who fits glasses to remedy visual defects. Although an *optometrist* is qualified to treat many eye disorders, she may not use medicines or surgery in her examinations.

opulence N. extreme wealth; luxuriousness; abundance. The glitter and *opulence* of the ballroom took Cinderella's breath away. opulent, ADJ.

opus N. work. Although many critics hailed his Fifth Symphony, he did not regard it as his major *opus.*

oracular ADJ. foretelling; mysterious. Oedipus could not understand the *oracular* warning he received. oracle, N.

oratorio N. dramatic poem set to music. The Glee Club decided to present an *oratorio* during their recital.

ordain V. command; arrange; consecrate. The king *ordained* that no foreigner should be allowed to enter the city.

ordeal N. severe trial or affliction. Terry Anderson spoke movingly of his long *ordeal* as a hostage in Lebanon.

ordinance N. decree. Passing a red light is a violation of a city *ordinance.*

ordination N. ceremony conferring holy orders. The candidate for *ordination* had to meet with the bishop and the diocesan officers before being judged ready to be ordained a deacon. ordain, V.

orient V. get one's bearings; adjust. Philip spent his first day in Denver *orienting* himself to the city.

orientation N. act of finding oneself in society. Freshman *orientation* provides the incoming students with an opportunity to learn about their new environment and their place in it.

orifice N. mouthlike opening; small opening. The Howe Caverns were discovered when someone observed that a cold wind was issuing from an *orifice* in the hillside.

ornate ADJ. excessively or elaborately decorated. Furniture of the Baroque period can be recognized by its *ornate* carvings.

ornithologist N. scientific student of birds. Audubon's drawings of American bird life have been of interest not only to the *ornithologists* but also to the general public.

orthodox ADJ. traditional; conservative in belief. Faced with a problem, he preferred to take an *orthodox* approach rather than shock anyone. orthodoxy, N.

orthography N. correct spelling. Many of us find English *orthography* difficult to master because so many of our words are not written phonetically.

■ **oscillate** V. vibrate pendulumlike; waver. It is interesting to note how public opinion *oscillates* between the extremes of optimism and pessimism.

osseous ADJ. made of bone; bony. The hollow "soft spot" found at the top of the infant's skull gradually closes as new *osseous* tissue fills in the gap.

ossify V. change or harden into bone. When he called his opponent a "bonehead," he implied that his adversary's brain had *ossified* and that he was not capable of clear thinking.

ostensible ADJ. apparent; professed; pretended. Although the *ostensible* purpose of this expedition is to discover new lands, we are really interested in finding new markets for our products.

■ **ostentatious** ADJ. showy; pretentious; trying to attract attention. Trump's latest casino in Atlantic City is the most *ostentatious* gambling palace in the East: it easily out-glitters its competitors. ostentation, N.

ostracize V. exclude from public favor; ban. As soon as the newspapers carried the story of his connection with the criminals, his friends began to *ostracize* him. ostracism, N.

oust v. expel; drive out. The world wondered if Aquino would be able to *oust* Marcos from office.

outlandish ADJ. bizarre; peculiar; unconventional. The eccentric professor who engages in markedly *outlandish* behavior is a stock figure in novels with an academic setting.

outmoded ADJ. no longer stylish; old-fashioned. Unconcerned about keeping in style, Lenore was perfectly happy to wear *outmoded* clothes as long as they were clean and unfrayed.

outskirts N. fringes; outer borders. Living on the *outskirts* of Boston, Sarah sometimes felt as if she were cut off from the cultural heart of the city.

outspoken ADJ. candid; blunt. The candidate was too *outspoken* to be a successful politician; he had not yet learned to weigh his words carefully.

outstrip v. surpass; outdo. Jesse Owens easily *outstripped* his competitors to win the gold medal at the Olympic Games.

outwit v. outsmart; trick. By disguising himself as an old woman, Holmes was able to *outwit* his pursuers and escape capture.

ovation N. enthusiastic applause. When Placido Domingo came on stage in the first act of *La Boheme,* he was greeted by a tremendous *ovation.*

overbearing ADJ. bossy; arrogant; decisively important. Certain of her own importance and of the unimportance of everyone else, Lady Bracknell was intolerably *overbearing* in manner. "In choosing a husband," she said, "good birth is of *overbearing* importance; compared to that, neither wealth nor talent signifies."

overt ADJ. open to view. According to the United States Constitution, a person must commit an *overt* act before he may be tried for treason.

overweening ADJ. presumptuous; arrogant. His *overweening* pride in his accomplishments was not justified.

Test

Word List 33   *Antonyms*

Each of the questions below consists of a word in capital letters, followed by five lettered words or phrases. Choose the lettered word or phrase that is most nearly opposite in meaning to the word in capital letters and write the letter of your choice on your answer paper.

481. OBSOLETE (A) heated (B) desolate (C) renovated (D) frightful (E) automatic
482. OBSTREPEROUS (A) turbid (B) quiet (C) remote (D) lucid (E) active
483. OBTUSE (A) sheer (B) transparent (C) tranquil (D) timid (E) shrewd
484. ODIOUS (A) fragrant (B) redolent (C) fetid (D) delightful (E) puny
485. ODIUM (A) noise (B) liking (C) dominant (D) hasty (E) atrium
486. OMNIPOTENT (A) weak (B) democratic (C) despotic (D) passionate (E) late

487. OMNISCIENT (A) sophisticated (B) ignorant (C) essential (D) trivial (E) isolated
488. OPIATE (A) distress (B) sleep (C) stimulant (D) laziness (E) despair
489. OPPORTUNE (A) occasional (B) fragrant (C) fragile (D) awkward (E) neglected
490. OPPORTUNIST (A) man of destiny (B) man of principle (C) changeling (D) adversary (E) colleague
491. OPPROBRIUM (A) delineation (B) aptitude (C) majesty (D) freedom (E) praise
492. OPTIMUM (A) pessimistic (B) knowledgeable (C) worst (D) minimum (E) chosen
493. OPULENCE (A) pessimism (B) patriotism (C) potency (D) passion (E) poverty
494. OSTENTATIOUS (A) inactive (B) unassuming (C) impolite (D) illicit (E) irrational
495. OVERWEENING (A) humble (B) impotent (C) avid (D) acrimonious (E) exaggerated

Word List 34   overwrought-peccadillo

overwrought ADJ. extremely agitated; hysterical. When Kate heard the news of the sudden tragedy, she became too *overwrought* to work and had to leave the office early.

ovoid ADJ. egg-shaped. At Easter she had to cut out hundreds of brightly colored *ovoid* shapes.

pachyderm N. thick-skinned animal. The elephant is probably the best-known *pachyderm.*

pacifist N. one opposed to force; antimilitarist. The *pacifists* urged that we reduce our military budget and recall our troops stationed overseas.

pacify v. soothe; make calm or quiet; subdue. Dentists criticize the practice of giving fussy children sweets to *pacify* them.

paean N. song of praise or joy. *Paeans* celebrating the victory filled the air.

painstaking ADJ. showing hard work; taking great care. The new high-frequency word list is the result of *painstaking* efforts on the part of our research staff.

palatable ADJ. agreeable; pleasing to the taste. Neither Jack's underbaked opinions nor his overcooked casseroles were *palatable* to me.

palatial ADJ. magnificent. He proudly showed us through his *palatial* home.

paleontology N. study of prehistoric life. The professor of *paleontology* had a superb collection of fossils.

palette N. board on which a painter mixes pigments. At the present time, art supply stores are selling a paper *palette* that may be discarded after use.

palimpsest N. parchment used for second time after original writing has been erased. Using chemical reagents, scientists have been able to restore the original writings on many *palimpsests*.

pall V. grow tiresome. The study of word lists can eventually *pall* and put one to sleep.

pallet N. small, poor bed. The weary traveler went to sleep on his straw *pallet*.

palliate V. ease pain; make less severe or offensive. If we cannot cure this disease at present, we can, at least, try to *palliate* the symptoms. palliation, N.

pallid ADJ. pale; wan. Because his occupation required that he work at night and sleep during the day, he had an exceptionally *pallid* complexion.

palpable ADJ. tangible; easily perceptible. I cannot understand how you could overlook such a *palpable* blunder.

palpitate V. throb; flutter. As he became excited, his heart began to *palpitate* more and more erratically.

paltry ADJ. insignificant; petty. This is a *paltry* sum to pay for such a masterpiece.

pan V. criticize harshly. Hoping for a rave review of his new show, the playwright was miserable when the critics *panned* it unanimously.

panacea N. cure-all; remedy for all diseases. There is no easy *panacea* that will solve our complicated international situation.

panache N. flair; flamboyance. Many performers imitate Noel Coward, but few have his *panache* and sense of style.

pandemic ADJ. widespread; affecting the majority of people. They feared the AIDS epidemic would soon reach *pandemic* proportions.

pandemonium N. wild tumult. When the ships collided in the harbor, *pandemonium* broke out among the passengers.

pander V. cater to the low desires of others. The reviewer accused the makers of *Lethal Weapon* of *pandering* to the masses' taste of violence.

panegyric N. formal praise. The modest hero blushed to hear the speakers delivering *panegyrics* about his valorous act.

panoramic ADJ. denoting an unobstructed and comprehensive view. On a clear day, from the top of the World Trade Center you can get a *panoramic* view of New York City and neighboring stretches of New Jersey and Long Island. panorama, N.

pantomime N. acting without dialogue. Because he worked in *pantomime,* the clown could be understood wherever he appeared. also V.

papyrus N. ancient paper made from stem of papyrus plant. The ancient Egyptians were among the first to write on *papyrus*.

parable N. short, simple story teaching a moral. Let us apply to our own conduct the lesson that this *parable* teaches.

■ **paradigm** N. model; example; pattern. Pavlov's experiment in which he trains a dog to salivate on hearing a bell is a *paradigm* of the conditioned-response experiment in behavioral psychology. paradigmatic, ADJ.

paradox N. statement that looks false but is actually correct; a contradictory statement. Wordsworth's "The child is father to the man" is an example of *paradox.*

■ **paragon** N. model of perfection. The class disliked him because the teacher was always pointing him out as a *paragon* of virtue.

parallelism N. state of being parallel; similarity. There is a striking *parallelism* between the twins.

parameter N. limit; independent variable. We need to define the *parameters* of the problem.

paramount ADJ. foremost in importance; supreme. Proper nutrition and hygiene are of *paramount* importance in adolescent development and growth.

paramour N. illicit lover. She sought a divorce on the grounds that her husband had a *paramour* in another town.

paranoia N. psychosis marked by delusions of grandeur or persecution. Suffering from *paranoia,* he claimed everyone was out to get him; ironically, his claim was accurate: even *paranoids* have enemies. paranoid, paranoiac, N. and ADJ.

paraphernalia N. equipment; odds and ends. His desk was cluttered with paper, pen, ink, dictionary and other *paraphernalia* of the writing craft.

paraphrase V. restate a passage in one's own words while retaining thought of author. In 250 words or less, *paraphrase* this article. also N.

parasite N. animal or plant living on another; toady; sycophant. The tapeworm is an example of the kind of *parasite* that may infest the human body.

parched ADJ. extremely dry; very thirsty. The *parched* desert landscape seemed hostile to life.

pariah N. social outcast. I am not a *pariah* to be shunned and ostracized.

parity N. equality; close resemblance. I find your analogy inaccurate because I do not see the *parity* between the two illustrations.

parlance N. language; idiom. All this legal *parlance* confuses me; I need an interpreter.

parley N. conference. The peace *parley* has not produced the anticipated truce. also V.

parochial ADJ. narrow in outlook; provincial; related to parishes. Although Jane Austen writes novels set in small rural communities, her concerns are universal, not *parochial.*

parody N. humorous imitation; travesty. We enjoyed the clever *parodies* of popular songs that the chorus sang.

paroxysm N. fit or attack of pain, laughter, rage. When he heard of his son's misdeeds, he was seized by a *paroxysm* of rage.

parquet N. floor made of wood strips inlaid in a mosaic-like pattern. In laying the floor, the carpenters combined redwood and oak in an elegant *parquet*.

parry V. ward off a blow. He was content to wage a defensive battle and tried to *parry* his opponent's thrusts.

■ **parsimonious** ADJ. stingy; excessively frugal. His *parsimonious* nature did not permit him to enjoy any luxuries. parsimony, N.

partial ADJ. (1) incomplete. In this issue we have published only a *partial* list of contributors because we lack space to acknowledge everyone. (2) biased; having a liking for something. I am extremely *partial* to chocolate eclairs.

partiality N. inclination; bias. As a judge, not only must I be unbiased, but I must also avoid any evidence of *partiality* when I award the prize.

■ **partisan** ADJ. one-sided; prejudiced; committed to a party. On certain issues of conscience, she refused to take a *partisan* stand. also N.

passé ADJ. old-fashioned; past the prime. Her style is *passé* and reminiscent of the Victorian era.

passive ADJ. not active; acted upon. Mahatma Gandhi urged his followers to pursue a program of *passive* resistance as he felt that it was more effective than violence and acts of terrorism.

pastiche N. imitation of another's style in musical composition or in writing. We cannot even say that her music is a *pastiche* of this or that composer; it is, rather, reminiscent of many musicians.

pastoral ADJ. rural. In these stories of *pastoral* life, we find an understanding of the daily tasks of country folk.

patent ADJ. open for the public to read; obvious. It was *patent* to everyone that the witness spoke the truth.

pathetic ADJ. causing sadness, compassion, pity; touching. Everyone in the auditorium was weeping by the time he finished his *pathetic* tale about the orphaned boy.

■ **pathological** ADJ. pertaining to disease. As we study the *pathological* aspects of this disease, we must not overlook the psychological elements.

pathos N. tender sorrow; pity; quality in art or literature that produces these feelings. The quiet tone of *pathos* that ran through the novel never degenerated into the maudlin or the overly sentimental.

patina N. green crust on old bronze works; tone slowly taken by varnished painting. Judging by the *patina* on this bronze statue, we can conclude that this is the work of a medieval artist.

patois N. local or provincial dialect. His years of study of the language at the university did not enable him to understand the *patois* of the natives.

patriarch N. father and ruler of a family or tribe. In many primitive tribes, the leader and lawmaker was the *patriarch*.

patrician ADJ. noble; aristocratic. We greatly admired her well-bred, *patrician* elegance. also N.

patronize V. support; act superior toward. Experts in a field sometimes appear to *patronize* people who are less knowledgeable of the subject.

■ **paucity** N. scarcity. They closed the restaurant because the *paucity* of customers made it uneconomical to operate.

pauper N. very poor person. Though Widow Brown was living on a reduced income, she was by no means a *pauper*.

peccadillo N. slight offense. If we examine these escapades carefully, we will realize that they are mere *peccadilloes* rather than major crimes.

Test

Word List 34   *Synonyms and Antonyms*

Each of the following questions consists of a word in capital letters, followed by five lettered words or phrases. Choose the lettered word or phrase that is most nearly similar or opposite in meaning to the word in capital letters and write the letter of your choice on your answer paper.

496. PAEAN (A) serf (B) pealing (C) lien
     (D) lament (E) folly
497. PALLET (A) bed (B) pigment board (C) bench
     (D) spectrum (E) quality
498. PALLIATE (A) smoke (B) quicken (C) substitute
     (D) alleviate (E) sadden
499. PANDEMONIUM (A) calm (B) frustration
     (C) efficiency (D) impishness (E) sophistication
500. PANEGYRIC (A) medication (B) panacea
     (C) rotation (D) vacillation (E) praise
501. PARABLE (A) equality (B) allegory (C) frenzy
     (D) folly (E) cuticle

502. PARADOX (A) exaggeration (B) contradiction
     (C) hyperbole (D) invective (E) poetic device
503. PARAMOUR (A) illicit lover (B) majority
     (C) importance (D) hatred (E) clandestine affair
504. PARANOIA (A) fracture (B) statement (C) quantity
     (D) benefaction (E) sanity
505. PARIAH (A) village (B) suburb (C) outcast
     (D) disease (E) benefactor
506. PARITY (A) duplicate (B) miniature (C) golf tee
     (D) similarity (E) event
507. PARSIMONIOUS (A) grammatical (B) syntactical
     (C) effective (D) extravagant (E) esoteric
508. PARTIALITY (A) completion (B) equality (C) bias
     (D) divorce (E) reflection
509. PASSÉ (A) scornful (B) rural (C) out-of-date
     (D) silly (E) barbaric
510. PASTICHE (A) imitation (B) glue (C) present
     (D) greeting (E) family

Word List 35   pecuniary-philanderer

pecuniary ADJ. pertaining to money. I never expected a *pecuniary* reward for my work in this activity.

pedagogue N. teacher. He could never be a stuffy *pedagogue*; his classes were always lively and filled with humor.

pedagogy N. teaching; art of education. Though Maria Montessori gained fame for her innovations in *pedagogy*, it took years before her teaching techniques became common practice in American schools.

pedant N. scholar who overemphasizes book learning or technicalities. Her insistence that the book be memorized marked the teacher as a *pedant* rather than a scholar.

■ **pedantic** ADJ. showing off learning; bookish. Leavening his decisions with humorous, down-to-earth anecdotes, Judge Walker was not at all the *pedantic* legal scholar. pedantry, N.

pedestrian ADJ. ordinary; unimaginative. Unintentionally boring, he wrote page after page of *pedestrian* prose.

pediatrician N. physician specializing in children's diseases. The family doctor advised the parents to consult a *pediatrician* about their child's ailment.

pejorative ADJ. negative in connotation; having a belittling effect. Instead of criticizing Clinton's policies, the Republicans made *pejorative* remarks about his character.

pell-mell ADV. in confusion; disorderly. The excited students dashed *pell-mell* into the stadium to celebrate the victory.

pellucid ADJ. transparent; limpid; easy to understand. After reading these stodgy philosophers, I find his *pellucid* style very enjoyable.

penance N. self-imposed punishment for sin. The Ancient Mariner said, "I have *penance* done and *penance* more will do," to atone for the sin of killing the albatross.

■ **penchant** N. strong inclination; liking. He had a strong *penchant* for sculpture and owned many statues.

pendant ADJ. hanging down from something. Her *pendant* earrings glistened in the light.

pendant N. ornament (hanging from a necklace, etc.). The grateful team presented the coach with a silver chain and *pendant* engraved with the school's motto.

pendulous ADJ. hanging; suspended. The *pendulous* chandeliers swayed in the breeze as if they were about to fall from the ceiling.

penitent ADJ. repentant. When he realized the enormity of his crime, he became remorseful and *penitent*. also N.

pensive ADJ. dreamily thoughtful; thoughtful with a hint of sadness. The *pensive* youth gazed at the painting for a long time and then sighed.

penumbra N. partial shadow (in an eclipse). During an eclipse, we can see an area of total darkness and a lighter area, which is the *penumbra*.

penurious ADJ. stingy; parsimonious. He was a *penurious* man, averse to spending money even for the necessities of life.

■ **penury** N. extreme poverty. When his pension fund failed, George feared he would end his days in *penury*.

peon N. landless agricultural worker; bond servant. The land reformers sought to liberate the *peons* and establish them as independent farmers. peonage, N.

perceptive ADJ. insightful; aware; wise. Although Maud was a generally *perceptive* critic, she had her blind spots: she could never see flaws in the work of her friends.

percussion ADJ. striking one object against another sharply. The drum is a *percussion* instrument. also N.

perdition N. damnation; complete ruin. Praying for salvation, young Daedalus feared he was damned to eternal *perdition*.

peregrination N. journey. Auntie Mame was a world traveler whose *peregrinations* took her from Tiajuana to Timbuctoo.

peremptory ADJ. demanding and leaving no choice. From Jack's *peremptory* knock on the door, Jill could tell he would not give up until she let him in.

■ **perennial** N. something long-lasting. These plants are hardy *perennials* and will bloom for many years. also ADJ.

■ **perfidious** ADJ. treacherous; disloyal. When Caesar realized that Brutus had betrayed him, he reproached his *perfidious* friend. perfidy, N.

perforate V. pierce; put a hole through. Before you can open the aspirin bottle, you must first *perforate* the plastic safety seal that covers the cap.

■ **perfunctory** ADJ. superficial; not thorough; lacking interest, care, or enthusiasm. The auditor's *perfunctory* inspection of the books overlooked many errors.

perigee N. point of moon's orbit when it is nearest the earth. The rocket which was designed to take photographs of the moon was launched as the moon approached its *perigee*.

perimeter N. outer boundary. To find the *perimeter* of any quadrilateral, we add the lengths of the four sides.

peripatetic ADJ. walking about; moving. The *peripatetic* school of philosophy derives its name from the fact that Aristotle walked with his pupils while discussing philosophy with them.

peripheral ADJ. marginal; outer. We lived, not in central London, but in one of those *peripheral* suburbs that spring up on the outskirts of a great city.

periphery N. edge, especially of a round surface. He sensed that there was something just beyond the *periphery* of his vision.

perjury N. false testimony while under oath. When several witnesses appeared to challenge his story, he was indicted for *perjury*.

■ **permeable** ADJ. porous; allowing passage through. Glass is *permeable* to light. permeate, V.

pernicious ADJ. very destructive. He argued that these books had a *pernicious* effect on young and susceptible minds.

peroration N. conclusion of an oration. The *peroration* was largely hortatory and brought the audience to its feet clamoring for action at its close.

perpetrate V. commit an offense. Only an insane person could *perpetrate* such a horrible crime.

perpetual ADJ. everlasting. Ponce de Leon hoped to find *perpetual* youth.

perquisite N. any gain above stipulated salary. The *perquisites* attached to this job make it even more attractive than the salary indicates.

personable ADJ. attractive. The man I am seeking to fill this position must be *personable* since he will be representing us before the public.

perspicacious ADJ. having insight; penetrating; astute. The brilliant lawyer was known for his *perspicacious* deductions.

perspicuity N. clearness of expression; freedom from ambiguity. One of the outstanding features of this book is the *perspicuity* of its author; her meaning is always clear.

perspicuous ADJ. plainly expressed. Her *perspicuous* comments eliminated all possibility of misinterpretation.

pert ADJ. impertinent; forward. I think your *pert* and impudent remarks call for an apology.

pertinacious ADJ. stubborn; persistent. He is bound to succeed because his *pertinacious* nature will not permit him to quit.

pertinent ADJ. suitable; to the point. The lawyer wanted to know all the *pertinent* details.

perturb V. disturb greatly. I am afraid this news will *perturb* him and cause him grief. perturbation, N.

perusal N. reading. I am certain that you have missed important details in your rapid *perusal* of this document. peruse, V.

■ pervasive ADJ. spread throughout. Despite airing them for several hours, she could not rid her clothes of the *pervasive* odor of mothballs that clung to them. pervade, V.

perverse ADJ. stubbornly wrongheaded; wicked and unacceptable. When Jack was in a *perverse* mood, he would do the opposite of whatever Jill asked him. When Hannibal Lecter was in a *perverse* mood, he ate the flesh of his victims. perversity, N.

perversion N. corruption; turning from right to wrong. Inasmuch as he had no motive for his crimes, we could not understand his *perversion*.

pessimism N. belief that life is basically bad or evil; gloominess. The good news we have been receiving lately indicates that there is little reason for your *pessimism*.

pestilential ADJ. causing plague; baneful. People were afraid to explore the *pestilential* swamp. pestilence, N.

pestle N. tool for mashing or grinding substances in a hard bowl. From the way in which the elderly pharmacist pounded the drug with his *pestle,* young George could tell that his employer was agitated about something.

petrify V. turn to stone. His sudden and unexpected appearance seemed to *petrify* her.

petty ADJ. trivial; unimportant; very small. She had no major complaints to make about his work, only a few *petty* quibbles that were almost too minor to state.

petulant ADJ. touchy; peevish. The feverish patient was *petulant* and restless.

pharisaical ADJ. pertaining to the Pharisees, who paid scrupulous attention to tradition; self-righteous; hypocritical. Walter Lippmann has pointed out that moralists who do not attempt to explain the moral code they advocate are often regarded as *pharisaical* and ignored.

phenomena N. observable facts; subjects of scientific investigation. We kept careful records of the *phenomena* we noted in the course of these experiments. phenomenon, SING.

philanderer N. faithless lover; flirt. Swearing he had never so much as looked at another woman, Jack assured Jill he was no *philanderer*.

Test

Word List 35 *Antonyms*

Each of the questions below consists of a word in capital letters, followed by five lettered words or phrases. Choose the lettered word or phrase that is most nearly opposite in meaning to the word in capital letters and write the letter of your choice on your answer paper.

511. PEJORATIVE (A) positive (B) legal (C) determining (D) delighting (E) declaiming
512. PELLUCID (A) logistical (B) philandering (C) incomprehensible (D) vagrant (E) warranted
513. PENCHANT (A) distance (B) imminence (C) dislike (D) attitude (E) void
514. PENURIOUS (A) imprisoned (B) captivated (C) generous (D) vacant (E) abolished
515. PERFUNCTORY (A) official (B) thorough (C) insipid (D) vicarious (E) distinctive
516. PERIGEE (A) eclipse (B) planet (C) apogee (D) refugee (E) danger
517. PERIPATETIC (A) worldly (B) stationary (C) disarming (D) seeking (E) inherent
518. PERMEABLE (A) perishable (B) effective (C) plodding (D) impenetrable (E) lasting
519. PERNICIOUS (A) practical (B) comparative (C) harmless (D) tangible (E) detailed
520. PERPETUAL (A) momentary (B) standard (C) serious (D) industrial (E) interpretive
521. PERSPICUITY (A) grace (B) feature (C) review (D) difficulty (E) vagueness
522. PERT (A) polite (B) perishable (C) moral (D) deliberate (E) stubborn
523. PERTINACIOUS (A) vengeful (B) consumptive (C) superficial (D) skilled (E) advertised
524. PERTINENT (A) understood (B) living (C) discontented (D) puzzling (E) irrelevant
525. PETULANT (A) angry (B) moral (C) declining (D) underhanded (E) uncomplaining

Word List 36 philanthropist-precedent

philanthropist N. lover of mankind; doer of good. As he grew older, he became famous as a *philanthropist* and benefactor of the needy.

philatelist N. stamp-collector. When she heard the value of the Penny Black stamp, Phyllis was inspired to become a *philatelist*.

philistine N. narrow-minded person, uncultured and exclusively interested in material gain. We need more men of culture and enlightenment; we have too many *philistines* among us.

philology N. study of language. The professor of *philology* advocated the use of Esperanto as an international language.

■ **phlegmatic** ADJ. calm; not easily disturbed. The nurse was a cheerful but *phlegmatic* person, unexcited in the face of sudden emergencies.

phobia N. morbid fear. Her fear of flying was more than mere nervousness; it was a real *phobia*.

physiognomy N. face. He prided himself on his ability to analyze a person's character by studying his *physiognomy*.

physiological ADJ. pertaining to the science of the function of living organisms. To understand this disease fully, we must examine not only its *physiological* aspects but also its psychological elements.

piebald ADJ. of different colors; mottled; spotted. You should be able to identify Polka Dot in this race; he is the only *piebald* horse running.

pied ADJ. variegated; multicolored. The *Pied* Piper of Hamelin got his name from the multicolored clothing he wore.

■ **piety** N. devoutness; reverence for God. Living her life in prayer and good works, Mother Teresa exemplifies the true spirit of *piety*. pious, ADJ.

pigment N. coloring matter. Van Gogh mixed various *pigments* with linseed oil to create his paints.

pillage V. plunder. The enemy *pillaged* the quiet village and left it in ruins. also N.

pillory V. punish by placing in a wooden frame; subject to criticism and ridicule. Even though he was mocked and *pilloried*, he maintained that he was correct in his beliefs. also N.

pine V. languish, decline; long for, yearn. Though she tried to be happy living with Clara in the city, Heidi *pined* for the mountains and for her gruff but loving grandfather.

pinion V. restrain. They *pinioned* his arms against his body but left his legs free so that he could move about. also N.

pinnacle N. peak. We could see the morning sunlight illuminate the *pinnacle* while the rest of the mountain lay in shadow.

pious ADJ. devout. The *pious* parents gave their children a religious upbringing. piety, N.

piquant ADJ. pleasantly tart-tasting; stimulating. The *piquant* sauce added to our enjoyment of the meal. piquancy, N.

pique N. irritation; resentment. She showed her *pique* by her refusal to appear with the other contestants at the end of the contest.

piscatorial ADJ. pertaining to fishing. He spent many happy hours at the lake in his *piscatorial* activities.

pithy ADJ. concise; meaty. I enjoy reading his essays because they are always compact and *pithy*. pith, N.

pittance N. a small allowance or wage. He could not live on the *pittance* he received as a pension and had to look for an additional source of revenue.

pivotal ADJ. central; critical. De Klerk's decision to set Nelson Mandela free was *pivotal*; without Mandela's release, there was no possibility that the African National Congress would entertain talks with the South African government.

■ **placate** V. pacify; conciliate. The teacher tried to *placate* the angry mother.

placebo N. harmless substance prescribed as a dummy pill. In a controlled experiment, fifty volunteers were given erythromycin tablets; the control group received only *placebos*.

placid ADJ. peaceful; calm. After his vacation in this *placid* section, he felt soothed and rested.

plagiarize V. steal another's ideas and pass them off as one's own. The editor could tell that the writer had *plagiarized* parts of the article; he could recognize whole paragraphs from the original source. plagiarism, N.

plaintive ADJ. mournful. The dove has a *plaintive* and melancholy call.

plasticity N. ability to be molded. When clay dries out, it loses its *plasticity* and becomes less malleable.

■ **platitude** N. trite remark; commonplace statement. The *platitudes* in his speech were applauded by the vast majority in his audience; only a few people perceived how trite his remarks were. platitudinous, ADJ.

platonic ADJ. purely spiritual; theoretical; without sensual desire. Accused of impropriety in his dealings with female students, the professor maintained he had only a *platonic* interest in the women involved.

plauditory ADJ. approving; applauding. The theatrical company reprinted the *plauditory* comments of the critics in its advertisement.

plausible ADJ. having a show of truth but open to doubt; specious. Even though your argument is *plausible*, I still would like to have more proof.

plebeian ADJ. common; pertaining to the common people. His speeches were aimed at the *plebeian* minds and emotions; they disgusted the more refined.

plenary ADJ. complete; full. The union leader was given *plenary* power to negotiate a new contract with the employers.

plenitude N. abundance; completeness. Looking in the pantry, we admired the *plenitude* of fruits and pickles we had preserved during the summer.

■ **plethora** N. excess; overabundance. She offered a *plethora* of excuses for her shortcomings.

pliable ADJ. flexible; yielding; adaptable. In remodeling the bathroom, we replaced all the old, rigid lead pipes with new, *pliable* copper tubing.

pliant ADJ. flexible; easily influenced. Catherine's disposition was *pliant:* she was like putty in her suitor's hands.

pluck N. courage. Even the adversaries of young Indiana Jones were impressed by the boy's *pluck* in trying to rescue the archeological treasure they had stolen.

plumb ADJ. vertical. Before hanging wallpaper it is advisable to drop a *plumb* line from the ceiling as a guide. also N. and V.

■ **plummet** V. fall sharply. Stock prices *plummeted* as Wall Street reacted to the rise in interest rates.

plutocracy N. society ruled by the wealthy. From the way the government caters to the rich, you might think our society is a *plutocracy* rather than a democracy.

podiatrist N. doctor who treats ailments of the feet. He consulted a *podiatrist* about his fallen arches.

podium N. pedestal; raised platform. The audience applauded as the conductor made his way to the *podium.*

poignancy N. quality of being deeply moving; keenness of emotion. Watching the tearful reunion of the long-separated mother and child, the social worker was touched by the *poignancy* of the scene. poignant, ADJ.

polarize V. split into opposite extremes or camps. The abortion issue has *polarized* the country into pro-choice and anti-abortion camps.

polemic N. controversy; argument in support of point of view. Her essays were, for the main part, *polemics* for the party's policy.

politic ADJ. expedient; prudent; well devised. Even though he was disappointed, he did not think it *politic* to refuse this offer.

polity N. form of government of nation or state. Our *polity* should be devoted to the concept that the government should strive for the good of all citizens.

polygamist N. one who has more than one spouse at a time. He was arrested as a *polygamist* when his two wives filed complaints about him.

polyglot ADJ. speaking several languages. New York City is a *polyglot* community because of the thousands of immigrants who settle there.

pomposity N. self-important behavior; acting like a stuffed shirt. Although the commencement speaker had some good things to say, we had to laugh at his *pomposity* and general air of parading his own dignity. pompous, ADJ.

ponderous ADJ. weighty; unwieldy. His humor lacked the light touch; his jokes were always *ponderous.*

pontifical ADJ. pertaining to a bishop or pope; pompous or pretentious. From the very beginning of his ministry it was clear from his *pontifical* pronouncements that John was destined for a high *pontifical* office.

pore V. study industriously; ponder; scrutinize. Determined to become a physician, Beth spends hours *poring* over her anatomy text.

porous ADJ. full of pores; like a sieve. Dancers like to wear *porous* clothing because it allows the ready passage of water and air.

portend V. foretell; presage. The king did not know what these omens might *portend* and asked his soothsayers to interpret them.

portent N. sign; omen; forewarning. He regarded the black cloud as a *portent* of evil.

portly ADJ. stout; corpulent. The salesclerk tactfully referred to the overweight customer as *portly* rather than fat.

poseur N. person who pretends to be sophisticated, elegant, etc., to impress others. Some thought Dali was a brilliant painter; others dismissed him as a *poseur.*

posterity N. descendants; future generations. We hope to leave a better world to *posterity.*

posthumous ADJ. after death (as of child born after father's death or book published after author's death). The critics ignored his works during his lifetime; it was only after the *posthumous* publication of his last novel that they recognized his great talent.

postulate N. self-evident truth. We must accept these statements as *postulates* before pursuing our discussions any further. also V.

posture V. assume an affected pose; act artificially. No matter how much Arnold boasted or *postured,* I could not believe he was as important as he pretended to be.

potable ADJ. suitable for drinking. The recent drought in the Middle Atlantic States has emphasized the need for extensive research in ways of making sea water *potable.* also N.

potent ADJ. powerful; persuasive; greatly influential. The jury was swayed by the highly *potent* testimony of the crime's sole eyewitness. potency, N.

potentate N. monarch; sovereign. The *potentate* spent more time at Monte Carlo than he did at home on his throne.

potential ADJ. expressing possibility; latent. This juvenile delinquent is a *potential* murderer. also N.

potion N. dose (of liquid). Tristan and Isolde drink a love *potion* in the first act of the opera.

potpourri N. heterogeneous mixture; medley. He offered a *potpourri* of folk songs from many lands.

poultice N. soothing application applied to sore and inflamed portions of the body. He was advised to apply a flaxseed *poultice* to the inflammation.

practicable ADJ. feasible. The board of directors decided that the plan was *practicable* and agreed to undertake the project.

practical ADJ. based on experience; useful. He was a *practical* man, opposed to theory.

■ **pragmatic** ADJ. practical (as opposed to idealistic); concerned with the practical worth or impact of something. This coming trip to France should provide me with a *pragmatic* test of the value of my conversational French class.

pragmatist N. practical person. No *pragmatist* enjoys becoming involved in a game that he can never win.

prate V. speak foolishly; boast idly. Let us not *prate* about our qualities; rather, let our virtues speak for themselves.

prattle V. babble. The children *prattled* endlessly about their new toys. also N.

preamble N. introductory statement. In the *Preamble* to the Constitution, the purpose of the document is set forth.

■ **precarious** ADJ. uncertain; risky. I think this stock is a *precarious* investment and advise against its purchase.

precedent N. something preceding in time that may be used as an authority or guide for future action. This decision sets a *precedent* for future cases of a similar nature.

precedent ADJ. preceding in time, rank, etc. Our discussions, *precedent* to this event, certainly did not give you any reason to believe that we would adopt your proposal.

Test

Word List 36   *Synonyms*

Each of the questions below consists of a word in capital letters, followed by five lettered words or phrases. Choose the lettered word or phrase that is most nearly similar in meaning to the word in capital letters and write the letter of your choice on your answer paper.

526. PHLEGMATIC (A) calm (B) cryptic (C) practical (D) salivary (E) dishonest
527. PHYSIOGNOMY (A) posture (B) head (C) physique (D) face (E) size
528. PIEBALD (A) motley (B) coltish (C) hairless (D) thoroughbred (E) delicious
529. PILLAGE (A) hoard (B) plunder (C) versify (D) denigrate (E) confide
530. PINION (A) express (B) report (C) reveal (D) submit (E) restrain
531. PINNACLE (A) foothills (B) card game (C) pass (D) taunt (E) peak
532. PIOUS (A) historic (B) devout (C) multiple (D) fortunate (E) authoritative
533. PIQUE (A) pyramid (B) revolt (C) resentment (D) struggle (E) inventory
534. PLACATE (A) determine (B) transmit (C) pacify (D) allow (E) define
535. PLAGIARISM (A) theft of funds (B) theft of ideas (C) belief in God (D) arson (E) ethical theory
536. PLAINTIVE (A) mournful (B) senseless (C) persistent (D) rural (E) evasive
537. PLATITUDE (A) fatness (B) bravery (C) dimension (D) trite remark (E) strong belief
538. POLEMIC (A) blackness (B) lighting (C) magnetism (D) controversy (E) grimace
539. PONDEROUS (A) contemplative (B) moist (C) rambling (D) bulky (E) erect
540. PRECARIOUS (A) priceless (B) premature (C) primitive (D) hazardous (E) unwelcome

Word List 37   precept-propitiate

precept N. practical rule guiding conduct. "Love thy neighbor as thyself" is a worthwhile *precept*.

precipice N. cliff; dangerous position. Suddenly Indiana Jones found himself dangling from the edge of a *precipice*.

■ **precipitate** ADJ. headlong; rash. Do not be *precipitate* in this matter; investigate further.

■ **precipitate** V. throw headlong; hasten. The removal of American political support appeared to have *precipitated* the downfall of the Marcos regime.

precipitous ADJ. steep; overhasty. This hill is difficult to climb because it is so *precipitous;* one slip, and our descent will be *precipitous* as well.

precise ADJ. exact. If you don't give me *precise* directions and a map, I'll never find your place.

preclude V. make impossible; eliminate. This contract does not *preclude* my being employed by others at the same time that I am working for you.

precocious ADJ. advanced in development. By her rather adult manner of discussing serious topics, the child demonstrated that she was *precocious*. precocity, N.

■ **precursor** N. forerunner. Though Gray and Burns share many traits with the Romantic poets who followed them, most critics consider them *precursors* of the Romantic Movement, not true Romantics.

predatory ADJ. plundering. The hawk is a *predatory* bird. predation, N.

predecessor N. former occupant of a post. I hope I can live up to the fine example set by my late *predecessor* in this office.

predilection N. partiality; preference. Although the artist used various media from time to time, she had a *predilection* for watercolors.

preeminent ADJ. outstanding; superior. The king traveled to Boston because he wanted the *preeminent* surgeon in the field to perform the operation.

preempt V. head off; forestall by acting first; appropriate for oneself; supplant. Hoping to *preempt* any attempts by the opposition to make educational reform a hot political issue, the candidate set out her own plan to revitalize the public schools. preemptive, ADJ.

■ **preen** V. make oneself tidy in appearance; feel self-satisfaction. As Kitty *preened* before the mirror, carefully smoothing her shining hair, she couldn't help *preening* herself on her good looks.

prefatory ADJ. introductory. The chairman made a few *prefatory* remarks before he called on the first speaker.

prehensile ADJ. capable of grasping or holding. Monkeys use not only their arms and legs but also their *prehensile* tails in traveling through the trees.

prelate N. church dignitary. The archbishop of Moscow and other high-ranking *prelates* visited the Russian Orthodox seminary.

prelude N. introduction; forerunner. I am afraid that this border raid is the *prelude* to more serious attacks.

premeditate V. plan in advance. She had *premeditated* the murder for months, reading about common poisons and buying weed killer that contained arsenic.

premise N. assumption; postulate. Because Jack had based his argument upon a faulty *premise*, his opponent cheerfully pointed out the holes in his logic.

premonition N. forewarning. We ignored these *premonitions* of disaster because they appeared to be based on childish fears.

premonitory ADJ. serving to warn. You should have visited a doctor as soon as you felt these *premonitory* chest pains.

preponderance N. superiority of power, quantity, etc. The rebels sought to overcome the *preponderance* of strength of the government forces by engaging in guerrilla tactics. preponderate, V. preponderant, ADJ.

preposterous ADJ. absurd; ridiculous. When the candidate tried to downplay his youthful experiments with marijuana by saying he hadn't inhaled, we all thought, "What a *preposterous* excuse!"

prerogative N. privilege; unquestionable right. The President cannot levy taxes; that is the *prerogative* of the legislative branch of government.

presage V. foretell. The vultures flying overhead *presaged* the discovery of the corpse in the desert.

prescience N. ability to foretell the future. Given the current wave of Japan-bashing, it does not take *prescience* for me to foresee problems in our future trade relations with Japan.

presentiment N. premonition; foreboding. Hamlet felt a *presentiment* about his meeting with Laertes.

prestige N. impression produced by achievements or reputation. The wealthy man sought to obtain social *prestige* by contributing to popular charities. prestigious, ADJ.

■ **presumptuous** ADJ. arrogant; taking liberties. It seems *presumptuous* for one so relatively new to the field to challenge the conclusions of its leading experts. presumption, N.

■ **pretentious** ADJ. ostentatious; ambitious. I do not feel that your limited resources will permit you to carry out such a *pretentious* program.

preternatural ADJ. beyond that which is normal in nature. John's mother's total ability to tell when he was lying struck him as almost *preternatural*.

pretext N. excuse. He looked for a good *pretext* to get out of paying a visit to his aunt.

prevail V. induce; triumph over. He tried to *prevail* on her to type his essay for him.

prevalent ADJ. widespread; generally accepted. A radical committed to social change, Reed had no patience with the conservative views *prevalent* in the America of his day.

■ **prevaricate** V. lie. Some people believe that to *prevaricate* in a good cause is justifiable and regard the statement as a "white lie."

prey N. target of a hunt; victim. In *Stalking the Wild Asparagus,* Euell Gibbons has as his *prey* not wild beasts but wild plants. also V.

prim ADJ. very precise and formal; exceedingly proper. Many people commented on the contrast between the *prim* attire of the young lady and the inappropriate clothing worn by her escort.

primogeniture N. seniority by birth. By virtue of *primogeniture,* in some cultures the first-born child has many privileges denied his brothers and sisters.

primordial ADJ. existing at the beginning (of time); rudimentary. The Neanderthal Man is one of our *primordial* ancestors.

primp V. dress or groom oneself with care. She *primps* for hours before a dance.

■ **pristine** ADJ. characteristic of earlier times; primitive, unspoiled. This area has been preserved in all its *pristine* wildness.

privation N. hardship; want. In his youth, he knew hunger and *privation*.

privy ADJ. secret; hidden; not public. We do not care for *privy* chamber government.

probe V. explore with tools. The surgeon *probed* the wound for foreign matter before suturing it. also N.

■ **probity** N. uprightness; incorruptibility. Everyone took his *probity* for granted; his defalcations, therefore, shocked us all.

■ **problematic** ADJ. perplexing; unsettled: questionable. Given the many areas of conflict still awaiting resolution, the outcome of the peace talks remains *problematic*.

proclivity N. inclination; natural tendency. The cross old lady has a *proclivity* to grumble.

procrastinate V. postpone; delay. It is wise not to *procrastinate;* otherwise, we find ourselves bogged down in a mass of work that should have been finished long ago.

procurement N. obtaining. The personnel department handles the *procurement* of new employees.

prod V. poke; stir up; urge. If you *prod* him hard enough, he'll eventually clean his room.

■ **prodigal** ADJ. wasteful; reckless with money. The *prodigal* son squandered his inheritance. also N.

prodigious ADJ. enormous; marvelous. He marveled at her *prodigious* appetite when he saw all the food she ate.

prodigy N. highly gifted child; marvel. Menuhin was a *prodigy,* performing wonders on his violin when he was barely eight years old.

profane V. violate; desecrate. Tourists are urged not to *profane* the sanctity of holy places by wearing improper garb. also ADJ.

■ **profligate** ADJ. dissipated; wasteful; licentious. In this *profligate* company, she lost all sense of decency. also N. profligacy, N.

profound ADJ. deep; not superficial; complete. Freud's remarkable insights into human behavior caused his fellow scientists to honor him as a *profound* thinker. profundity, N.

profusion N. lavish expenditure; overabundant condition. Seldom have I seen food and drink served in such *profusion* as at the wedding feast.

progenitor N. ancestor. The Roth family, whose *progenitors* emigrated from Germany early in the nineteenth century, settled in Peru, Illinois.

progeny N. children; offspring. He was proud of his *progeny* but regarded George as the most promising of all his children.

prognosis N. forecasted course of a disease; prediction. If the doctor's *prognosis* is correct, the patient will be in a coma for at least twenty-four hours.

prognosticate V. predict. I *prognosticate* disaster unless we change our wasteful ways.

projectile N. missile. Man has always hurled *projectiles* at his enemy whether in the form of stones or of highly explosive shells.

proletarian N. member of the working class. The aristocrats feared mob rule and gave the right to vote only to the wealthy, thus depriving the *proletarians* of a voice in government. also ADJ.

■ **proliferate** v. grow rapidly; spread; multiply. Times of economic hardship inevitably encourage countless get-rich-quick schemes to *proliferate.* proliferation, N.

■ **prolific** ADJ. abundantly fruitful. She was a *prolific* writer who produced as many as three books a year.

prolix ADJ. verbose; drawn out. Her *prolix* arguments irritated and bored the jury. prolixity, N.

prolong v. extend; draw out; lengthen. In their determination to discover ways to *prolong* human life, doctors fail to take into account that longer lives are not always happier ones.

prominent ADJ. conspicuous; notable; protruding. Have you ever noticed that Prince Charles's *prominent* ears make him resemble the big-eared character in *Mad* comics?

promiscuous ADJ. mixed indiscriminately; haphazard; irregular, particularly sexually. In the opera *La Boheme,* we get a picture of the *promiscuous* life led by the young artists of Paris. promiscuity, N.

promontory N. headland. They erected a lighthouse on the *promontory* to warn approaching ships of their nearness to the shore.

prompt v. cause; provoke; provide a cue for an actor. Whatever *prompted* you to ask for such a big piece of cake when you're on a diet?

promulgate v. make known by official proclamation or publication. As soon as the Civil Service Commission *promulgates* the names of the successful candidates, we shall begin to hire members of our staff.

prone ADJ. inclined to; prostrate. She was *prone* to sudden fits of anger.

propagate v. multiply; spread. Since bacteria *propagate* more quickly in unsanitary environments, it is important to keep hospital rooms clean.

propellant N. substance that propels or drives forward. The development of our missile program has forced our scientists to seek more powerful *propellants.* also ADJ.

■ **propensity** N. natural inclination. Convinced of his own talent, Sol has an unfortunate *propensity* to belittle the talents of others.

prophetic ADJ. having to do with predicting the future. In interpreting Pharaoh's *prophetic* dream, Joseph said that the seven fat cows eaten by the seven lean cows represented seven years of plenty followed by seven years of famine. prophecy, N.

prophylactic ADJ. used to prevent disease. Despite all *prophylactic* measures introduced by the authorities, the epidemic raged until cool weather set in. prophylaxis, N.

propinquity N. nearness; kinship. Their relationship could not be explained as being based on mere *propinquity:* they were more than relatives; they were true friends.

propitiate v. appease. The natives offered sacrifices to *propitiate* the gods.

Test

Word List 37   *Antonyms*

Each of the questions below consists of a word in capital letters, followed by five lettered words or phrases. Choose the lettered word or phrase that is most nearly opposite in meaning to the word in capital letters and write the letter of your choice on your answer paper.

541. PRECIPITATE (A) dull (B) anticipatory (C) cautious (D) considerate (E) welcome

542. PREFATORY (A) outstanding (B) magnificent (C) conclusive (D) intelligent (E) predatory

543. PRELUDE (A) intermezzo (B) diva (C) aria (D) aftermath (E) duplication

544. PRESUMPTION (A) assertion (B) activation (C) motivation (D) proposition (E) humility

545. PRETENTIOUS (A) ominous (B) calm (C) unassuming (D) futile (E) volatile

546. PRIM (A) informal (B) prior (C) exterior (D) private (E) cautious

547. PRISTINE (A) cultivated (B) condemned (C) irreligious (D) cautious (E) critical

548. PROBITY (A) regret (B) assumption (C) corruptibility (D) extent (E) upswing

549. PRODIGAL (A) large (B) thrifty (C) consistent (D) compatible (E) remote

550. PRODIGIOUS (A) infinitesimal (B) indignant (C) indifferent (D) indisposed (E) insufficient

551. PROFANE (A) sanctify (B) desecrate (C) define (D) manifest (E) urge

552. PROLIFIC (A) unworkable (B) backward (C) barren (D) controversial (E) unfocussed

553. PROLIX (A) stupid (B) indifferent (C) redundant (D) livid (E) pithy

554. PROPHYLACTIC (A) causing growth (B) causing disease (C) antagonistic (D) brushing (E) favorable

555. PROPINQUITY (A) remoteness (B) uniqueness (C) health (D) virtue (E) simplicity

Word List 38   propitious-quarry

propitious ADJ. favorable; kindly. I think it is advisable that we wait for a more *propitious* occasion to announce our plans; this is not a good time.

proponent N. person who supports or proposes (an idea). After the bill had been amended and re-amended in committee, even its original *proponents* didn't want to vote in its favor.

propound v. put forth for analysis. In your discussion, you have *propounded* several questions; let us consider each one separately.

■ **propriety** N. fitness; correct conduct. I want you to behave at this dinner with *propriety;* don't embarrass me.

propulsive ADJ. driving forward. The jet plane has a greater *propulsive* power than the engine-driven plane.

prosaic ADJ. dull and unimaginative; matter-of-fact; factual. Though the ad writers had come up with a highly creative campaign to publicize the company's newest product, the head office rejected it for a more *prosaic,* down-to-earth approach.

proscenium N. part of stage in front of curtain. In the theater-in-the-round there can be no *proscenium* or *proscenium* arch. also ADJ.

■ **proscribe** v. ostracize; banish; outlaw. Antony, Octavius and Lepidus *proscribed* all those who had conspired against Julius Caesar.

proselytize v. induce someone to convert to a religion or belief. In these interfaith meetings, there must be no attempt to *proselytize;* we must respect all points of view.

prosody N. the art of versification. This book on *prosody* contains a rhyming dictionary as well as samples of the various verse forms.

prosperity N. good fortune; financial success; physical well-being. Promising to stay together "for richer, for poorer," the newlyweds vowed to be true to one another in *prosperity* and hardship alike.

prostrate v. stretch out full on ground. He *prostrated* himself before the idol. also ADJ.

protean ADJ. versatile; able to take on many forms. A remarkably *protean* actor, Alec Guinness could take on any role.

protocol N. diplomatic etiquette. We must run this state dinner according to *protocol* if we are to avoid offending any of our guests.

prototype N. original work used as a model by others. The crude typewriter on display in this museum is the *prototype* of the elaborate machines in use today.

protract v. prolong. Seeking to delay the union members' vote, the management team tried to *protract* the negotiations endlessly, but the union representatives saw through their strategy.

protrude v. stick out. His fingers *protruded* from the holes in his gloves.

protuberance N. protrusion; bulge. A ganglionic cyst is a fluid-filled tumor (generally benign) that develops near a joint membrane or tendon sheath, and that bulges beneath the skin, forming a *protuberance.*

provenance N. origin or source of something. I am not interested in its *provenance;* I am more concerned with its usefulness than with its source.

provender N. dry food; fodder. I am not afraid of a severe winter because I have stored a large quantity of *provender* for the cattle.

provident ADJ. displaying foresight; thrifty; preparing for emergencies. In his usual *provident* manner, he had insured himself against this type of loss.

provincial ADJ. pertaining to a province; limited in outlook; unsophisticated. As *provincial* governor, Sir Henry administered the Queen's law in his remote corner of Canada. Caught up in local problems, out of touch with London news, he became sadly *provincial.*

provisional ADJ. tentative. The appointment is *provisional;* only on the approval of the board of directors will it be made permanent.

proviso N. stipulation. I am ready to accept your proposal with the *proviso* that you meet your obligations within the next two weeks.

provoke v. stir to anger; cause retaliation. In order to prevent a sudden outbreak of hostilities, we must not *provoke* our foe. provocation, N.

proximity N. nearness. The deer sensed the hunter's *proximity* and bounded away.

proxy N. authorized agent. Please act as my *proxy* and vote for this slate of candidates in my absence.

prude N. excessively modest or proper person. The X-rated film was definitely not for *prudes.*

prudent ADJ. cautious; careful. A miser hoards money not because he is *prudent* but because he is greedy. prudence, N.

prune v. cut away; trim. With the help of her editor, she was able to *prune* her manuscript into publishable form.

pseudonym N. pen name. Samuel Clemens' *pseudonym* was Mark Twain.

psyche N. soul; mind. It is difficult to delve into the *psyche* of a human being.

psychiatrist N. a doctor who treats mental diseases. A *psychiatrist* often needs long conferences with his patient before a diagnosis can be made.

psychopathic ADJ. pertaining to mental derangement. The *psychopathic* patient suffers more frequently from a disorder of the nervous system than from a diseased brain.

psychosis N. mental disorder. We must endeavor to find an outlet for the patient's repressed desires if we hope to combat this *psychosis.* psychotic, ADJ.

pterodactyl N. extinct flying reptile. The remains of *pterodactyls* indicate that these flying reptiles had a wingspan of as much as twenty feet.

puerile ADJ. childish. His *puerile* pranks sometimes offended his more mature friends.

pugilist N. boxer. The famous *pugilist* Cassius Clay changed his name to Muhammed Ali.

pugnacious ADJ. combative; disposed to fight. As a child he was *pugnacious* and fought with everyone.

puissant ADJ. powerful; strong; potent. We must keep his friendship for he will make a *puissant* ally.

pulchritude N. beauty; comeliness. I do not envy the judges who have to select this year's Miss America from this collection of female *pulchritude.*

pulmonary ADJ. pertaining to the lungs. In his researches on *pulmonary* diseases, he discovered many facts about the lungs of animals and human beings.

pulsate v. throb. We could see the blood vessels in his temple *pulsate* as he became more angry.

pulverize v. crush or grind into very small particles. Before sprinkling the dried herbs into the stew, Michael first *pulverized* them into a fine powder.

pummel v. beat. The severity with which he was *pummeled* was indicated by the bruises he displayed on his head and face.

punctilious ADJ. laying stress on niceties of conduct or form; precise. We must be *punctilious* in our planning of this affair, for any error may be regarded as a personal affront.

■ **pundit** N. learned Hindu; any learned person; authority on a subject. Even though he discourses on the matter like a *pundit,* he is actually rather ignorant about this topic.

■ **pungency** N. sharpness; stinging quality. The *pungency* of the cigarette smoke made me cough. pungent, ADJ.

punitive ADJ. punishing. He asked for *punitive* measures against the offender.

puny ADJ. insignificant; tiny; weak. Our *puny* efforts to stop the flood were futile.

purchase N. firm grasp or footing. The mountaineer struggled to get a proper *purchase* on the slippery rock.

purgatory N. place of spiritual expiation. In this *purgatory,* he could expect no help from his comrades.

purge V. clean by removing impurities; clear of charges. If you are to be *purged* of the charge of contempt of Congress, you must be willing to answer the questions previously asked. also N.

purport N. intention; meaning. If the *purport* of your speech was to arouse the rabble, you succeeded admirably. also V.

purveyor N. furnisher of foodstuffs; caterer. As *purveyor* of rare wines and viands, he traveled through France and Italy every year in search of new products to sell.

pusillanimous ADJ. cowardly; fainthearted. You should be ashamed of your *pusillanimous* conduct during this dispute. pusillanimity, N.

putative ADJ. supposed; reputed. Although there are some doubts, the *putative* author of this work is Massinger.

putrid ADJ. foul; rotten; decayed. The gangrenous condition of the wound was indicated by the *putrid* smell when the bandages were removed. putrescence, N. putrefaction, N.

pyromaniac N. person with an insane desire to set things on fire. The detectives searched the area for the *pyromaniac* who had set these costly fires.

quack N. charlatan; impostor. Do not be misled by the exorbitant claims of this *quack*; he cannot cure you.

quadruped N. four-footed animal. Most mammals are *quadrupeds.*

quaff V. drink with relish. As we *quaffed* our ale, we listened to the gay songs of the students in the tavern.

quagmire N. soft, wet, boggy land; complex or dangerous situation from which it is difficult to free oneself. Up to her knees in mud, Myra wondered how on earth she was going to extricate herself from this *quagmire.*

quail V. cower; lose heart. He was afraid that he would *quail* in the face of danger.

quaint ADJ. odd; old-fashioned; picturesque. Her *quaint* clothes and old-fashioned language marked her as an eccentric.

■ **qualified** ADJ. limited; restricted. Unable to give the candidate full support, the mayor gave him only a *qualified* endorsement. (secondary meaning)

■ **qualms** N. misgivings. His *qualms* of conscience had become so great that he decided to abandon his plans.

quandary N. dilemma. When the two colleges to which he had applied accepted him, he was in a *quandary* as to which one he should attend.

quarantine N. isolation of a person, place, or ship to prevent spread of infection. We will have to place this house under *quarantine* until we determine the exact nature of the disease. also V.

quarry N. victim; object of a hunt. The police closed in on their *quarry.*

quarry V. dig into. They *quarried* blocks of marble out of the hillside.

Test

Word List 38   *Antonyms*

Each of the questions below consists of a word in capital letters, followed by five lettered words or phrases. Choose the lettered word or phrase that is most nearly opposite in meaning to the word in capital letters and write the letter of your choice on your answer paper.

556. PROPITIOUS (A) rich (B) induced (C) promoted (D) indicative (E) unfavorable

557. PROSAIC (A) pacified (B) reprieved (C) pensive (D) imaginative (E) rhetorical

558. PROTEAN (A) amateur (B) catholic (C) unchanging (D) rapid (E) unfavorable

559. PROTRACT (A) make circular (B) shorten (C) further (D) retrace (E) involve

560. PROVIDENT (A) unholy (B) rash (C) miserable (D) disabled (E) remote

561. PROVINCIAL (A) wealthy (B) crass (C) literary (D) aural (E) sophisticated

562. PSYCHOTIC (A) dangerous (B) clairvoyant (C) criminal (D) soulful (E) sane

563. PUERILE (A) fragrant (B) adult (C) lonely (D) feminine (E) masterly

564. PUGNACIOUS (A) pacific (B) feline (C) mature (D) angular (E) inactive

565. PUISSANT (A) pouring (B) fashionable (C) articulate (D) healthy (E) weak

566. PULCHRITUDE (A) ugliness (B) notoriety (C) bestiality (D) masculinity (E) servitude

567. PUNCTILIOUS (A) happy (B) active (C) vivid (D) careless (E) futile

568. PUNITIVE (A) large (B) humorous (C) rewarding (D) restive (E) languishing

569. PUSILLANIMOUS (A) poverty-stricken (B) chained (C) posthumous (D) courageous (E) strident

570. PUTATIVE (A) colonial (B) quarrelsome (C) undisputed (D) powerful (E) unremarkable

Word List 39   quash-recurrent

quash V. subdue; crush; squash. The authorities acted quickly to *quash* the student rebellion, sending in tanks to cow the demonstrators.

quay N. dock; landing place. Because of the captain's carelessness, the ship crashed into the *quay*.

queasy ADJ. easily nauseated; squeamish. As the ship left the harbor, he became *queasy* and thought that he was going to suffer from seasickness.

quell V. put down; quiet. The police used fire hoses and tear gas to *quell* the rioters.

querulous ADJ. fretful; whining. His classmates were repelled by his *querulous* and complaining statements.

queue N. line. They stood patiently in the *queue* outside the movie theatre.

quibble V. equivocate; play on words. Do not *quibble*; I want a straightforward and definite answer. also N.

■ **quiescent** ADJ. at rest; dormant. After this geyser erupts, it will remain *quiescent* for twenty-four hours. quiescence, N.

quietude N. tranquillity. He was impressed by the air of *quietude* and peace that pervaded the valley.

quintessence N. purest and highest embodiment. Noel Coward displayed the *quintessence* of wit.

quip N. taunt. You are unpopular because you are too free with your *quips* and sarcastic comments. also V.

quirk N. startling twist; caprice, By a *quirk* of fate, he found himself working for the man whom he had discharged years before.

quisling N. traitor who aids invaders. In his conquest of Europe, Hitler was aided by the *quislings* who betrayed their own people and served in the puppet governments established by the Nazis.

quiver N. case for arrows. Robin Hood reached back and plucked one last arrow from his *quiver*. (secondary meaning)

quixotic ADJ. idealistic but impractical. His head is in the clouds; he is constantly presenting these *quixotic* schemes.

quizzical ADJ. bantering; comical; humorously serious. Will Rogers' *quizzical* remarks endeared him to his audiences.

quorum N. number of members necessary to conduct a meeting. The senator asked for a roll call to determine whether a *quorum* was present.

quotidian ADJ. daily; commonplace; customary. To Philip, each new day of his internship was filled with excitement; he could not dismiss his rounds as merely *quotidian* routine.

rabid ADJ. like a fanatic; furious. He was a *rabid* follower of the Dodgers and watched them play whenever he could go to the ball park.

raconteur N. story-teller. My father was a gifted *raconteur* with an unlimited supply of anecdotes.

ragamuffin N. person wearing tattered clothes. He felt sorry for the *ragamuffin* who was begging for food and gave him money to buy a meal.

rail V. scold; rant. You may *rail* at him all you want; you will never change him.

raiment N. clothing. "How can I go to the ball?" asked Cinderella. "I have no *raiment* fit to wear."

rakish ADJ. stylish; sporty. He wore his hat at a *rakish* and jaunty angle.

ramble V. wander aimlessly (physically or mentally). Listening to the teacher *ramble*, Judy wondered whether he'd ever get to his point. also N.

ramification N. branching out; subdivision. We must examine all the *ramifications* of this problem.

ramify V. divide into branches or subdivisions. When the plant begins to *ramify*, it is advisable to nip off most of the new branches.

ramp N. slope; inclined plane. The house was built with *ramps* instead of stairs in order to enable the man in the wheelchair to move easily from room to room and floor to floor.

rampant ADJ. rearing up on hind legs; unrestrained. The *rampant* weeds in the garden killed all the flowers that had been planted in the spring. rampancy, N.

rampart N. defensive mound of earth. "From the *ramparts* we watched" as the fighting continued.

ramshackle ADJ. rickety; falling apart. The boys propped up the *ramshackle* clubhouse with a couple of boards.

rancid ADJ. having the odor of stale fat. A *rancid* odor filled the ship's galley and nauseated the crew.

rancor N. bitterness; hatred. Let us forget our *rancor* and cooperate in this new endeavor.

random ADJ. without definite purpose, plan, or aim; haphazard. Although the sponsor of the raffle claimed all winners were chosen at *random*, people had their suspicions when the grand prize went to the sponsor's brother-in-law.

rankle V. irritate; fester. The memory of having been jilted *rankled* him for years.

rant V. rave; speak bombastically. As we heard him *rant* on the platform, we could not understand his strange popularity with many people.

rapacious ADJ. excessively grasping; plundering. Hawks and other *rapacious* birds prey on a variety of small animals.

rapport N. emotional closeness; harmony. In team teaching, it is important that all teachers in the group have good *rapport* with one another.

■ **rarefied** ADJ. made less dense [of a gas]. The mountain climbers had difficulty breathing in the *rarefied* atmosphere. rarefy, V. rarefaction, N.

raspy ADJ. grating; harsh. The sergeant's *raspy* voice grated on the recruits' ears.

ratify V. approve formally; verify. Before the treaty could go into effect, it had to be *ratified* by the president.

ratiocination N. reasoning; act of drawing conclusions from premises. While Watson was a man of average intelligence, Holmes was a genius, whose gift for *ratiocination* made him a superb detective.

rationalization N. bringing into conformity with reason. All attempts at *rationalization* at this time are doomed to failure; tempers and emotions run too high for intelligent thought to prevail.

rationalize V. reason; justify an improper act. Do not try to *rationalize* your behavior by blaming your companions.

raucous ADJ. harsh and shrill. His *raucous* laughter irritated me and grated on my ears.

ravage V. plunder; despoil. The marauding army *ravaged* the countryside.

rave N. overwhelmingly favorable review. Though critic John Simon seldom has a good word to say about contemporary plays, his review of *All in the Timing* was a total *rave*.

ravel V. fall apart into tangles; unravel or untwist; entangle. A single thread pulled loose, and the entire scarf started to *ravel*.

ravenous ADJ. extremely hungry. The *ravenous* dog upset several garbage pails in its search for food.

ravine N. narrow valley with steep sides. Steeper than a gully, less precipitous than a canyon, a *ravine* is, like them, the product of years of erosion.

raze V. destroy completely. The owners intend to *raze* the hotel and erect an office building on the site.

reactionary ADJ. recoiling from progress; retrograde. His program was *reactionary* since it sought to abolish many of the social reforms instituted by the previous administration. also N.

realm N. kingdom; sphere. The *realm* of possibilities for the new invention was endless.

reaper N. one who harvests grain. Death, the Grim *Reaper*, cuts down mortal men and women, just as a farmer cuts down the ripened grain.

rebate N. discount. We offer a *rebate* of ten percent to those who pay cash.

rebuff V. snub; beat back. She *rebuffed* his invitation so smoothly that he did not realize he had been snubbed. also N.

rebus N. puzzle in which pictures stand for words. A coven of witches beside a tree is a possible *rebus* for the town Coventry.

rebuttal N. refutation; response with contrary evidence. The defense lawyer confidently listened to the prosecutor sum up his case, sure that she could answer his arguments in her *rebuttal*.

■ **recalcitrant** ADJ. obstinately stubborn. Donkeys are reputed to be the most *recalcitrant* of animals.

■ **recant** V. repudiate; withdraw previous statement. Unless you *recant* your confession, you will be punished severely.

recapitulate V. summarize. Let us *recapitulate* what has been said thus far before going ahead.

receptive ADJ. quick or willing to receive ideas, suggestions, etc. Adventure-loving Huck Finn proved a *receptive* audience for Tom's tales of buried treasure and piracy.

recession N. withdrawal; retreat; time of low economic activity. The slow *recession* of the flood waters created problems for the crews working to restore power to the area.

recidivism N. habitual return to crime. Prison reformers in the United States are disturbed by the high rate of *recidivism*; the number of persons serving second and third terms indicates the failure of the prisons to rehabilitate the inmates.

recipient N. receiver. Although he had been the *recipient* of many favors, he was not grateful to his benefactor.

reciprocal ADJ. mutual; exchangeable; interacting. The two nations signed a *reciprocal* trade agreement.

reciprocate V. repay in kind. If they attack us, we shall be compelled to *reciprocate* and bomb their territory. reciprocity, N.

■ **recluse** N. hermit. The *recluse* lived in a hut in the forest. reclusive, ADJ.

reconcile V. correct inconsistencies; become friendly after a quarrel. Every time we try to *reconcile* our checkbook with the bank statement, we quarrel. However, despite these monthly lovers' quarrels, we always manage to *reconcile*.

■ **recondite** ADJ. abstruse; profound; secret. He read many *recondite* books in order to obtain the material for his scholarly thesis.

reconnaissance N. survey of enemy by soldiers; reconnoitering. If you encounter any enemy soldiers during your *reconnaissance*, capture them for questioning.

recount V. narrate or tell; count over again. About to *recount* the latest adventure of Sherlock Holmes, Watson lost track of exactly how many cases Holmes had solved and refused to begin his tale until he'd *recounted* them one by one.

recourse N. resorting to help when in trouble. The boy's only *recourse* was to appeal to his father for aid.

recrimination N. countercharges. Loud and angry *recriminations* were her answer to his accusations.

rectify V. correct. I want to *rectify* my error before it is too late.

rectitude N. uprightness. He was renowned for his *rectitude* and integrity.

recumbent ADJ. reclining; lying down completely or in part. The command "AT EASE" does not permit you to take a *recumbent* position.

recuperate V. recover. The doctors were worried because the patient did not *recuperate* as rapidly as they had expected.

recurrent ADJ. occurring again and again. These *recurrent* attacks disturbed us and we consulted a physician.

Test

Word List 39 *Synonyms and Antonyms*

Each of the following questions consists of a word in capital letters, followed by five lettered words or phrases. Choose the lettered word or phrase that is most nearly similar or opposite in meaning to the word in capital letters and write the letter of your choice on your answer paper.

571. QUEASY (A) toxic (B) easily upset (C) chronic (D) choleric (E) false

572. QUELL (A) boast (B) incite (C) reverse (D) wet (E) answer

573. QUIXOTIC (A) rapid (B) exotic (C) longing (D) timid (E) idealistic

574. RAGAMUFFIN (A) dandy (B) miser (C) exotic dance (D) light snack (E) baker

575. RAUCOUS (A) mellifluous (B) uncooked (C) realistic (D) veracious (E) anticipating

576. RAVAGE (A) rankle (B) revive (C) plunder (D) pillory (E) age

577. RAZE (A) shave (B) heckle (C) finish (D) tear down (E) write

578. REACTIONARY (A) conservative (B) retrograde (C) dramatist (D) militant (E) chemical

579. REBATE (A) relinquish (B) settle (C) discount (D) cancel (E) elicit

580. RECALCITRANT (A) grievous (B) secretive (C) cowardly (D) thoughtful (E) cooperative

581. RECLUSE (A) learned scholar (B) mocker (C) social person (D) careful worker (E) daredevil

582. RECONDITE (A) unfriendly (B) easily comprehensible (C) closely juxtaposed (D) broadminded (E) sardonic

583. RECTIFY (A) remedy (B) avenge (C) create (D) assemble (E) attribute

584. RECUPERATE (A) reenact (B) engage (C) recapitulate (D) recover (E) encounter

585. RECURRENT (A) happening repeatedly (B) flowing backward (C) healing quickly (D) eventful (E) timely

Word List 40 redolent-requite

redolent ADJ. fragrant; odorous; suggestive of an odor. Even though it is February, the air is *redolent* of spring.

redoubtable ADJ. formidable; causing fear. During the Cold War period, neighboring countries tried not to offend the Russians because they could be *redoubtable* foes.

redress N. remedy; compensation. Do you mean to tell me that I can get no *redress* for my injuries? also V.

redundant ADJ. superfluous; excessively wordy; repetitious. Your composition is *redundant*; you can easily reduce its length. redundancy, N.

reek V. emit (odor). The room *reeked* with stale tobacco smoke. also N.

refectory N. dining hall. In this huge *refectory*, we can feed the entire student body at one sitting.

refraction N. bending of a ray of light. When you look at a stick inserted in water, it looks bent because of the *refraction* of the light by the water.

■ **refractory** ADJ. stubborn; unmanageable. The *refractory* horse was eliminated from the race when he refused to obey the jockey.

refrain V. abstain from; resist. N. chorus. Whenever he heard a song with a lively chorus, Sol could never *refrain* from joining in on the *refrain*.

refurbish V. renovate; make bright by polishing. The flood left a deposit of mud on everything; it was necessary to *refurbish* our belongings.

■ **refute** V. disprove. The defense called several respectable witnesses who were able to *refute* the false testimony of the prosecution's only witness. refutation, N.

regal ADJ. royal. Prince Albert had a *regal* manner.

regale V. entertain. John *regaled* us with tales of his adventures in Africa.

regatta N. boat or yacht race. Many boating enthusiasts followed the *regatta* in their own yachts.

regeneration N. spiritual rebirth. Modern penologists strive for the *regeneration* of the prisoners.

regicide N. murder of a king or queen. The beheading of Mary Queen of Scots was an act of *regicide*.

regime N. method or system of government. When a Frenchman mentions the Old *Regime*, he refers to the government existing before the revolution.

regimen N. prescribed diet and habits. I doubt whether the results warrant our living under such a strict *regimen*.

rehabilitate V. restore to proper condition. We must *rehabilitate* those whom we send to prison.

reimburse V. repay. Let me know what you have spent and I will *reimburse* you.

reiterate V. repeat. He *reiterated* the warning to make sure everyone understood it.

rejoinder N. retort; comeback; reply. When someone has been rude to me, I find it particularly satisfying to come up with a quick *rejoinder*.

rejuvenate V. make young again. The charlatan claimed that his elixir would *rejuvenate* the aged and weary.

■ **relegate** V. banish; consign to inferior position. If we *relegate* these experts to minor posts because of their political persuasions, we shall lose their valuable services.

relent V. give in. When her stern father would not *relent* and allow her to marry Robert Browning, Elizabeth Barrett eloped with her suitor. relentless, ADJ.

relevant ADJ. pertinent; referring to the case in hand. Teri was impressed by how *relevant* Virginia Woolf's remarks were to her as a woman writer; it was as if Woolf had been writing with Teri's situation in mind. relevance, N. relevancy, N.

relic N. surviving remnant; memento. Egypt's Department of Antiquities prohibits tourists from taking mummies and other ancient *relics* out of the country. Mike keeps his photos of his trip to Egypt in a box with other *relics* of his travels.

relinquish V. abandon. I will *relinquish* my claims to this property if you promise to retain my employees.

relish V. savor; enjoy. I *relish* a good joke as much as anyone else. also N.

remediable ADJ. reparable. Let us be grateful that the damage is *remediable.*

reminiscence N. recollection. Her *reminiscences* of her experiences are so fascinating that she ought to write a book.

remiss ADJ. negligent. He was accused of being *remiss* in his duty when the prisoner escaped.

remission N. temporary moderation of disease symptoms; cancellation of a debt; forgiveness or pardon. Though Senator Tsongas had been treated for cancer, his symptoms were in *remission,* and he was considered fit to handle the strains of a Presidential race.

remnant N. remainder. I suggest that you wait until the store places the *remnants* of these goods on sale.

remonstrance N. protest; objection. The authorities were deaf to the pastor's *remonstrances* about the lack of police protection in the area. remonstrate, V.

remorse N. guilt; self-reproach. The murderer felt no *remorse* for his crime.

remunerative ADJ. compensating; rewarding. I find my new work so *remunerative* that I may not return to my previous employment. remuneration, N.

rend V. split; tear apart. In his grief, he tried to *rend* his garments. rent, N.

render V. deliver; provide; represent. He *rendered* aid to the needy and indigent.

rendezvous N. meeting place. The two fleets met at the *rendezvous* at the appointed time. also V.

rendition N. translation; artistic interpretation of a song, etc. The audience cheered enthusiastically as she completed her *rendition* of the aria.

renegade N. deserter; traitor. Because he had abandoned his post and joined forces with the Indians, his fellow officers considered the hero of *Dances with Wolves* a *renegade.* also ADJ.

renege V. deny; go back on. He *reneged* on paying off his debt.

renounce V. abandon; disown; repudiate. Even though she knew she would be burned at the stake as a witch, Joan of Arc refused to *renounce* her belief that her voices came from God. renunciation, N.

renovate V. restore to good condition; renew. They claim that they can *renovate* worn shoes so that they look like new ones.

renown N. fame. For many years an unheralded researcher, Barbara McClintock gained international *renown* when she won the Nobel Prize in Physiology and Medicine. renowned, ADJ.

rent N. tear or rip; split. The conflict over abortion threatens to split our nation, creating a *rent* in the social fabric that will be difficult to mend. rend, V.

reparable ADJ. capable of being repaired. Fortunately, the damages we suffered in the accident were *reparable* and our car looks brand new.

reparation N. amends; compensation. At the peace conference, the defeated country promised to pay *reparations* to the victors.

repartee N. clever reply. He was famous for his witty *repartee* and his sarcasm.

repeal V. revoke; annul. What would the effect on our society be if we decriminalized drug use by *repealing* the laws against the possession and sale of narcotics?

repellent ADJ. driving away; unattractive. Mosquitoes find the odor so *repellent* that they leave any spot where this liquid has been sprayed. also N.

repercussion N. rebound; reverberation; reaction. I am afraid that this event will have serious *repercussions.*

repertoire N. list of works of music, drama, etc., a performer is prepared to present. The opera company decided to include *Madame Butterfly* in its *repertoire* for the following season.

repine V. fret; complain. There is no sense *repining* over the work you have left undone.

replenish V. fill up again. Before she could take another backpacking trip, Carla had to *replenish* her stock of freeze-dried foods.

replete ADJ. filled to capacity; abundantly supplied. This book is *replete* with humorous situations.

replica N. copy. Are you going to hang this *replica* of the Declaration of Independence in the classroom or in the auditorium?

replicate V. reproduce; duplicate. To the chagrin of the scientists, they were unable to *replicate* the results of their controversial experiment.

repository N. storehouse. Libraries are *repositories* of the world's best thoughts.

reprehensible ADJ. deserving blame. Your vicious conduct in this situation is *reprehensible.*

repress V. restrain; crush; oppress. Anne's parents tried to curb her impetuosity without *repressing* her boundless high spirits.

reprieve N. temporary stay. During the twenty-four-hour *reprieve,* the lawyers sought to make the stay of execution permanent. also V.

reprimand V. reprove severely. I am afraid that my parents will *reprimand* me when I show them my report card. also N.

reprisal N. retaliation. I am confident that we are ready for any *reprisals* the enemy may undertake.

reprise N. recurrent action; musical repetition; repeat performance. At Waterloo, it was not the effect of any one skirmish that exhausted Colonel Audley; rather, it was the cumulative effect of the constant *reprises* that left him spent.

reproach N. blame; censure. I want my work to be above *reproach* and without error. also V.

■ **reprobate** N. person hardened in sin, devoid of a sense of decency. I cannot understand why he has so many admirers if he is the *reprobate* you say he is.

reprobation N. severe disapproval. The students showed their *reprobation* of his act by refusing to talk with him.

reprove V. censure; rebuke. The principal *reproved* the students when they became unruly in the auditorium. reproof, N.

■ **repudiate** V. disown; disavow. He announced that he would *repudiate* all debts incurred by his wife.

repugnance N. loathing. She looked at the snake with *repugnance.*

repulsion N. act of driving back; distaste. The *repulsion* of the enemy forces was not accomplished bloodlessly; many of the defenders were wounded in driving the enemy back.

reputable ADJ. respectable. If you want to buy antiques, look for a *reputable* dealer; far too many dealers today pass off fakes as genuine antiques.

reputed ADJ. supposed. He is the *reputed* father of the child. repute, V. repute, N.

requiem N. mass for the dead; dirge. They played Mozart's *Requiem* at the funeral.

requisite N. necessary requirement. Many colleges state that a student must offer three years of a language as a *requisite* for admission.

requite V. repay; revenge. The wretch *requited* his benefactors by betraying them.

Test

Word List 40   *Synonyms*

Each of the questions below consists of a word in capital letters, followed by five lettered words or phrases. Choose the lettered word or phrase that is most nearly similar in meaning to the word in capital letters and write the letter of your choice on your answer paper.

586. REFRACTORY (A) articulate (B) sinkable (C) vaunted (D) useless (E) unmanageable
587. REGAL (A) oppressive (B) royal (C) major (D) basic (E) entertaining
588. REITERATE (A) gainsay (B) revive (C) revenge (D) repeat (E) return
589. RELISH (A) desire (B) nibble (C) savor (D) vindicate (E) avail
590. REMISS (A) lax (B) lost (C) foolish (D) violating (E) ambitious
591. REMONSTRATE (A) display (B) restate (C) protest (D) resign (E) reiterate

592. REPARTEE (A) witty retort (B) willful departure (C) spectator (D) monologue (E) sacrifice
593. REPELLENT (A) propulsive (B) unattractive (C) porous (D) stiff (E) elastic
594. REPERCUSSION (A) reaction (B) restitution (C) resistance (D) magnificence (E) acceptance
595. REPLENISH (A) polish (B) repeat (C) reinstate (D) refill (E) refuse
596. REPLICA (A) museum piece (B) famous site (C) battle emblem (D) facsimile (E) replacement
597. REPRISAL (A) reevaluation (B) assessment (C) loss (D) retaliation (E) nonsense
598. REPROVE (A) prevail (B) rebuke (C) ascertain (D) prove false (E) draw back
599. REPUDIATE (A) besmirch (B) appropriate (C) annoy (D) reject (E) avow
600. REPUGNANCE (A) belligerence (B) tenacity (C) renewal (D) pity (E) loathing

Word List 41   rescind-sacrosanct

■ **rescind** V. cancel. Because of public resentment, the king had to *rescind* his order. rescission, N.

reserve N. self-control; formal but distant manner. Although some girls were attracted by Mark's *reserve*, Judy was put off by it, for she felt his aloofness indicated a lack of openness. reserved, ADJ.

residue N. remainder; balance. In his will, he requested that after payment of debts, taxes, and funeral expenses, the *residue* be given to his wife.

resignation N. patient submissiveness; statement that one is quitting a job. If Bob Cratchit had not accepted Scrooge's bullying with timid *resignation,* he might have gotten up the nerve to hand in his *resignation.* resigned, ADJ.

resilient ADJ. elastic; having the power of springing back. Highly *resilient,* steel makes excellent bedsprings. resilience, N.

■ **resolution** N. determination. Nothing could shake his *resolution* to succeed despite all difficulties. resolute, ADJ.

■ **resolve** N. determination. Nothing could shake his *resolve* that his children would get the best education that money could buy. also v.

resolve V. decide; settle; solve. Homes *resolved* to travel to Bohemia to *resolve* the dispute between Irene Adler and the King.

resonant ADJ. echoing; resounding; deep and full in sound. The deep, *resonant* voice of the actor James Earl Jones makes him particularly effective when he appears on stage.

respiration N. breathing; exhalation. The doctor found that the patient's years of smoking had adversely affected both his lung capacity and his rate of *respiration*.

respite N. delay in punishment; interval of relief; rest. The judge granted the condemned man a *respite* to enable his attorneys to file an appeal.

resplendent ADJ. brilliant; lustrous. The toreador wore a *resplendent* costume called a suit of lights.

responsiveness N. state of reacting readily to appeals, orders, etc. The audience cheered and applauded, delighting the performers by its *responsiveness*.

restitution N. reparation; indemnification. He offered to make *restitution* for the window broken by his son.

restive ADJ. restlessly impatient; obstinately resisting control. Waiting impatiently in line to see Santa Claus, even the best-behaved children grow *restive* and start to fidget.

restraint N. controlling force. She dreamt of living an independent life, free of all *restraints*.

resumption N. taking up again; recommencement. During the summer break, Don had not realized how much he missed university life: at the *resumption* of classes, however, he felt marked excitement and pleasure. resume, V.

resurgent ADJ. rising again after defeat, etc. The *resurgent* nation surprised everyone by its quick recovery after total defeat. resurge, V.

resuscitate V. revive. The lifeguard tried to *resuscitate* the drowned child by applying artificial respiration.

retain V. keep; employ. Fighting to *retain* his seat in Congress, Senator Foghorn *retained* a new manager to head his reelection campaign.

retaliate V. repay in kind (usually for bad treatment). Fear that we will *retaliate* immediately deters our foe from attacking us.

retentive ADJ. holding; having a good memory. The pupil did not need to spend much time in study as he had a *retentive* mind.

■ **reticent** ADJ. reserved; uncommunicative; inclined to silence. Hughes preferred *reticent* employees to loquacious ones, noting that the formers' dislike of idle chatter might ensure their discretion about his affairs. reticence, N.

retinue N. following; attendants. The queen's *retinue* followed her down the aisle.

retiring ADJ. modest; shy. Given Susan's *retiring* personality, no one expected her to take up public speaking; surprisingly enough, she became a star of the school debate team.

retort N. quick, sharp reply. Even when it was advisable for her to keep her mouth shut, she was always ready with a *retort*. also v.

retraction N. withdrawal. He dropped his libel suit after the newspaper published a *retraction* of its statement.

retrench V. cut down; economize. If they were to be able to send their children to college, they would have to *retrench*.

retribution N. vengeance; compensation; punishment for offenses. The evangelist maintained that an angry deity would exact *retribution* from the sinners.

retrieve V. recover; find and bring in. The dog was intelligent and quickly learned to *retrieve* the game killed by the hunter. retrieval, N.

retroactive ADJ. taking effect before its enactment (as a law) or imposition (as a tax). Because the new pension law was *retroactive* to the first of the year, even though Martha had retired in February she was eligible for the pension.

retrograde V. go backwards; degenerate. Instead of advancing, our civilization seems to have *retrograded* in ethics and culture. also ADJ.

retrospective ADJ. looking back on the past. It is only when we become *retrospective* that we can appreciate the tremendous advances made during this century. retrospection, N.

revelry N. boisterous merrymaking. New Year's Eve is a night of revelry.

reverberate V. echo; resound. The entire valley *reverberated* with the sound of the church bells.

■ **reverent** ADJ. respectful. His *reverent* attitude was appropriate in a house of worship. revere, V. reverence, N.

reverie N. daydream; musing. He was awakened from his *reverie* by the teacher's question.

revile V. slander; vilify. He was avoided by all who feared that he would *revile* and abuse them if they displeased him.

revoke V. cancel; retract. Repeat offenders who continue to drive under the influence of alcohol face having their driver's licenses permanently *revoked*. revocation, N.

revulsion N. sudden violent change of feeling; negative reaction. Many people in this country who admired dictatorships underwent a *revulsion* when they realized what Hitler and Mussolini were trying to do.

rhapsodize V. to speak or write in an exaggeratedly enthusiastic manner. She greatly enjoyed her Hawaiian vacation and *rhapsodized* about it for weeks.

rhetoric N. art of effective communication; insincere or grandiloquent language. All writers, by necessity, must be skilled in *rhetoric*. rhetorical, ADJ.

ribald ADJ. wanton; profane. He sang a *ribald* song that offended many of the more prudish listeners. ribaldry, N.

rider N. amendment or clause added to a legislative bill. Senator Foghorn said he would support Senator Filibuster's tax reform bill only if Filibuster agreed to add an antipollution *rider* to the bill.

rife ADJ. abundant; current. In the face of the many rumors of scandal, which are *rife* at the moment, it is best to remain silent.

rift N. opening; break. The plane was lost in the stormy sky until the pilot saw the city through a *rift* in the clouds.

rig V. fix or manipulate. The ward boss was able to *rig* the election by bribing people to stuff the ballot boxes with ballots marked in his candidate's favor.

rigid ADJ. stiff and unyielding; strict; hard and unbending. By living with a man to whom she was not married, George Eliot broke Victorian society's most *rigid* rule of respectable behavior.

rigor N. severity. Many settlers could not stand the *rigors* of the New England winters.

rile V. vex; irritate; muddy. Red had a hair-trigger temper: he was an easy man to *rile*.

riveting ADJ. absorbing; engrossing. The reviewer described Byatt's novel *Possession* as a *riveting* tale: absorbed in the story, he had finished it in a single evening.

rivulet N. small stream. As the rains continued, the trickle of water running down the hillside grew into a *rivulet* that threatened to wash away a portion of the slope.

robust ADJ. vigorous; strong. The candidate for the football team had a *robust* physique.

rococo ADJ. ornate; highly decorated. The *rococo* style in furniture and architecture, marked by scrollwork and excessive decoration, flourished during the middle of the eighteenth century.

roil V. to make liquids murky by stirring up sediment; to disturb. Be careful when you pour not to *roil* the wine; if you stir up the sediment you'll destroy the flavor.

roseate ADJ. rosy; optimistic. I am afraid you will have to alter your *roseate* views in the light of the distressing news that has just arrived.

roster N. list. They print the *roster* of players in the season's program.

rostrum N. platform for speech-making; pulpit. The crowd murmured angrily and indicated that they did not care to listen to the speaker who was approaching the *rostrum*.

rote N. repetition. He recited the passage by *rote* and gave no indication he understood what he was saying. also ADJ.

rotunda N. circular building or hall covered with a dome. His body lay in state in the *rotunda* of the Capitol.

rotundity N. roundness; sonorousness of speech. Washington Irving emphasized the *rotundity* of the governor by describing his height and circumference.

rousing ADJ. lively; stirring. "And now, let's have a *rousing* welcome for TV's own Roseanne Arnold, who'll lead us in a *rousing* rendition of 'The Star-Spangled Banner.'"

rout V. stampede; drive out. The reinforcements were able to *rout* the enemy. also N.

rubble N. fragments. Ten years after World War II, some of the *rubble* left by enemy bombings could still be seen.

rubric N. title or heading (in red print); directions for religious ceremony; protocol. In ordaining the new priests, the bishop carefully observed all the *rubrics* for the ordination service.

ruddy ADJ. reddish; healthy-looking. His *ruddy* features indicated that he had spent much time in the open.

rudimentary ADJ. not developed; elementary. His dancing was limited to a few *rudimentary* steps.

rueful ADJ. regretful; sorrowful; dejected. The artist has captured the sadness of childhood in his portrait of the boy with the *rueful* countenance.

ruffian N. bully; scoundrel. The *ruffians* threw stones at the police.

ruminate V. chew the cud; ponder. We cannot afford to wait while you *ruminate* upon these plans.

rummage V. ransack; thoroughly search. When we *rummaged* through the trunks in the attic, we found many souvenirs of our childhood days. also N.

runic ADJ. mysterious; set down in an ancient alphabet. Tolkien's use of Old English words and inscriptions in the *runic* alphabet give *The Lord of the Rings* its atmosphere of antiquity.

ruse N. trick; stratagem. You will not be able to fool your friends with such an obvious *ruse*.

rustic ADJ. pertaining to country people; uncouth. The backwoodsman looked out of place in his *rustic* attire.

rusticate V. banish to the country; dwell in the country. I like city life so much that I can never understand how people can *rusticate* in the suburbs.

ruthless ADJ. pitiless. The escaped convict was a dangerous and *ruthless* murderer.

saboteur N. one who commits sabotage; destroyer of property. Members of the Resistance acted as *saboteurs,* blowing up train lines to prevent supplies from reaching the Nazi army.

saccharine ADJ. cloyingly sweet. She tried to ingratiate herself, speaking sweetly and smiling a *saccharine* smile.

sacrilegious ADJ. desecrating; profane. His stealing of the altar cloth was a very *sacrilegious* act.

sacrosanct ADJ. most sacred; inviolable. The brash insurance salesman invaded the *sacrosanct* privacy of the office of the president of the company.

Test

Word List 41   *Antonyms*

Each of the questions below consists of a word in capital letters, followed by five lettered words or phrases. Choose the lettered word or phrase that is most nearly opposite in meaning to the word in capital letters and write the letter of your choice on your answer paper.

601. RESILIENT (A) pungent (B) foolish (C) worthy (D) insolent (E) unyielding

602. RESTIVE (A) buoyant (B) placid (C) remorseful (D) resistant (E) retiring

603. RETENTIVE (A) forgetful (B) accepting (C) repetitive (D) avoiding (E) fascinating
604. RETICENCE (A) fatigue (B) fashion (C) treachery (D) loquaciousness (E) magnanimity
605. RETROGRADE (A) progressing (B) inclining (C) evaluating (D) concentrating (E) directing
606. REVERE (A) advance (B) dishonor (C) age (D) precede (E) wake
607. RIFE (A) direct (B) scant (C) peaceful (D) grim (E) mature
608. ROBUST (A) weak (B) violent (C) vicious (D) villainous (E) hungry
609. ROTUNDITY (A) promenade (B) nave (C) grotesqueness (D) slimness (E) impropriety
610. RUBBLE (A) artificial facade (B) unbroken stone (C) pale complexion (D) strong defense (E) glib answer
611. RUDDY (A) robust (B) witty (C) wan (D) exotic (E) creative
612. RUDIMENTARY (A) pale (B) polite (C) asinine (D) developed (E) quiescent
613. RUEFUL (A) trite (B) content (C) capable (D) capital (E) zealous
614. RUSTIC (A) urban (B) slow (C) corroded (D) mercenary (E) civilian
615. RUTHLESS (A) merciful (B) majestic (C) mighty (D) militant (E) maximum

Word List 42   sadistic–sepulcher

sadistic ADJ. inclined to cruelty. If we are to improve conditions in this prison, we must first get rid of the *sadistic* warden. sadism, N.

saga N. Scandinavian myth; any legend. This is a *saga* of the sea and the men who risk their lives on it.

sagacious ADJ. keen; shrewd; having insight. He is much too *sagacious* to be fooled by a trick like that. sagacity, N.

sage N. person celebrated for wisdom. Hearing tales of a mysterious Master of All Knowledge who lived in the hills of Tibet, Sandy was possessed with a burning desire to consult the legendary *sage*. also ADJ.

salacious ADJ. lascivious; lustful. Chaucer's monk is not pious but *salacious,* a teller of lewd tales and ribald jests.

salient ADJ. prominent. One of the *salient* features of that newspaper is its excellent editorial page.

saline ADJ. salty. The slightly *saline* taste of this mineral water is pleasant.

sallow ADJ. yellowish; sickly in color. We were disturbed by his *sallow* complexion, which was due to jaundice.

■ **salubrious** ADJ. healthful. Many people with hay fever move to more *salubrious* sections of the country during the months of August and September.

salutary ADJ. tending to improve; beneficial; wholesome. The punishment had a *salutary* effect on the boy, as he became a model student.

salvage V. rescue from loss. All attempts to *salvage* the wrecked ship failed. also N.

sanctimonious ADJ. displaying ostentatious or hypocritical devoutness. You do not have to be so *sanctimonious* to prove that you are devout.

■ **sanction** V. approve; ratify. Nothing will convince me to *sanction* the engagement of my daughter to such a worthless young man.

sanguinary ADJ. bloody. The battle of Iwo Jima was unexpectedly *sanguinary* with many casualties.

sanguine ADJ. cheerful; hopeful. Let us not be too *sanguine* about the outcome; something could go wrong.

sap V. diminish; undermine. The element kryptonite had an unhealthy effect on Superman: it *sapped* his strength.

sarcasm N. scornful remarks, stinging rebuke. His feelings were hurt by the *sarcasm* of his supposed friends. sarcastic, ADJ.

sarcasm N. scornful remarks; stinging rebuke. His feelings were hurt by the *sarcasm* of his supposed friends.

sardonic ADJ. disdainful; sarcastic; cynical. The *sardonic* humor of nightclub comedians who satirize or ridicule patrons in the audience strikes some people as amusing and others as rude.

sartorial ADJ. pertaining to tailors. He was as famous for the *sartorial* splendor of his attire as he was for his acting.

sate V. satisfy to the full; cloy. Its hunger *sated*, the lion dozed.

satellite N. small body revolving around a larger one. During the first few years of the Space Age, hundreds of *satellites* were launched by Russia and the United States.

satiate V. surfeit; satisfy fully. The guests, having eaten until they were *satiated,* now listened inattentively to the speakers. satiety, N.

satire N. form of literature in which irony, sarcasm, and ridicule are employed to attack vice and folly. *Gulliver's Travels,* which is regarded by many as a tale for children, is actually a bitter *satire* attacking human folly.

satirical ADJ. mocking. The humor of cartoonist Gary Trudeau often is *satirical;* through the comments of the Doonesbury characters, Trudeau ridicules political corruption and folly.

■ **saturate** V. soak. Their clothes were *saturated* by the rain. saturation, N.

saturnine ADJ. gloomy. Do not be misled by his *saturnine* countenance; he is not as gloomy as he looks.

satyr N. half-human, half-bestial being in the court of Dionysus, portrayed as wanton and cunning. He was like a *satyr* in his lustful conduct.

saunter V. stroll slowly. As we *sauntered* through the park, we stopped frequently to admire the spring flowers.

savant N. scholar. Our faculty includes many world-famous *savants*.

■ **savor** V. enjoy; have a distinctive flavor, smell, or quality. Relishing his triumph, Costner especially *savored* the chagrin of the critics who had predicted his failure.

savory ADJ. tasty; pleasing, attractive, or agreeable. Julia Child's recipes enable amateur chefs to create *savory* delicacies for their guests.

scabbard N. case for a sword blade; sheath. The drill master told the recruit to wipe the blood from his sword before slipping it back into the *scabbard*.

scad N. a great quantity. Refusing Dave's offer to lend him a shirt, Phil replied, "No, thanks; I've got *scads* of clothes."

scaffold N. temporary platform for workers; bracing framework; platform for execution. Before painting the house, the workers put up a *scaffold* to allow them to work on the second story.

scale V. climb up; ascend. To locate a book on the top shelf of the stacks, Lee had to *scale* an exceptionally rickety ladder.

scanty ADJ. meager; insufficient. Thinking his helping of food was *scanty*, Oliver Twist asked for more.

■ **scapegoat** N. someone who bears the blame for others. After the Challenger disaster, NASA searched for *scapegoats* on whom they could cast the blame.

scavenge V. hunt through discarded materials for usable items; search, especially for food. If you need car parts that the dealers no longer stock, try *scavenging* for odd bits and pieces at the auto wreckers' yards. scavenger, N.

scenario N. plot outline; screenplay; opera libretto. Scaramouche startled the other actors in the commedia troupe when he suddenly departed from their customary *scenario* and began to improvise.

schematic ADJ. relating to an outline or diagram; using a system of symbols. In working out the solution to an analytical logic question, you may find it helpful to construct a simple *schematic* diagram illustrating the relationships between the items of information given in the question. schema, N.

schism N. division; split. Let us not widen the *schism* by further bickering.

scintilla N. shred; least bit. You have not produced a *scintilla* of evidence to support your argument.

scintillate V. sparkle; flash. I enjoy her dinner parties because the food is excellent and the conversation *scintillates*.

scoff V. mock; ridicule. He *scoffed* at dentists until he had his first toothache.

scotch V. stamp out; thwart; hinder. Heather tried to *scotch* the rumor that she had stolen her best friend's fiancé.

scourge N. lash; whip; severe punishment. They feared the plague and regarded it as a deadly *scourge*. also V.

scruple V. fret about; hesitate, for ethical reasons. Fearing that her husband had become involved in an affair, she did not *scruple* to read his diary. also N.

scrupulous ADJ. conscientious; extremely thorough. I can recommend him for a position of responsibility for I have found him a very *scrupulous* young man.

scrutinize V. examine closely and critically. Searching for flaws, the sergeant *scrutinized* every detail of the private's uniform.

scuffle V. struggle confusedly; move off in a confused hurry. The twins briefly *scuffled,* wrestling to see which of them would get the toy. When their big brother yelled, "Let go of my Gameboy!" they *scuffled* off down the hall.

scurrilous ADJ. obscene; indecent. Your *scurrilous* remarks are especially offensive because they are untrue.

scurry V. move briskly. The White Rabbit had to *scurry* to get to his appointment on time.

scurvy ADJ. despicable; contemptible. Peter Pan sneered at Captain Hook and his *scurvy* crew.

scuttle V. sink. The sailors decided to *scuttle* their vessel rather than surrender it to the enemy.

seamy ADJ. sordid; unwholesome. In *The Godfather*, Michael Corleone is unwilling to expose his wife and children to the *seamy* side of his life as the son of a Mafia don.

sear V. char or burn; brand. Accidentally brushing against the hot grill, she *seared* her hand badly.

seasoned ADJ. experienced. Though pleased with her new batch of rookies, the basketball coach wished she had a few more *seasoned* players on the team.

secession N. withdrawal. The *secession* of the Southern states provided Lincoln with his first major problem after his inauguration. secede, V.

seclusion N. isolation; solitude. One moment she loved crowds; the next, she sought *seclusion*.

■ **secrete** V. hide away or cache; produce and release a substance into an organism. The pack rat *secretes* odds and ends in its nest; the pancreas *secretes* insulin in the islets of Langerhans.

sectarian ADJ. narrow-minded; limited in scope. As university chaplain, she sought to address universal religious issues and not limit herself to mere *sectarian* concerns.

■ **secular** ADJ. worldly; not pertaining to church matters; temporal. The church leaders decided not to interfere in *secular* matters.

sedate ADJ. composed; grave. The parents were worried because they felt their son was too quiet and *sedate*.

sedentary ADJ. requiring sitting. Because he had a *sedentary* occupation, he decided to visit a gymnasium weekly.

sedition N. resistance to authority; insubordination. His words, though not treasonous in themselves, were calculated to arouse thoughts of *sedition*.

sedulous ADJ. diligent. The young woman was so *sedulous* that she received a commendation for her hard work. sedulity, N.

seedy ADJ. run-down; decrepit; disreputable. I would rather stay in dormitory lodgings in a decent youth hostel than have a room of my own in a *seedy* downtown hotel.

seemly ADJ. proper; appropriate. Lady Bracknell did not think it was *seemly* for Ernest to lack a proper family: no baby abandoned on a doorstep could grow up to marry *her* daughter.

seep V. ooze; trickle. During the rainstorm, water *seeped* through the crack in the basement wall and damaged the floor boards. seepage, N.

seethe V. be disturbed; boil. The nation was *seething* with discontent as the noblemen continued their arrogant ways.

seine N. net for catching fish. When the shad run during the spring, you may see fishermen with *seines* along the banks of our coastal rivers.

seismic ADJ. pertaining to earthquakes. The Richter scale is a measurement of *seismic* disturbances.

semblance N. outward appearance; guise. Although this book has a *semblance* of wisdom and scholarship, a careful examination will reveal many errors and omissions.

seminal ADJ. germinal; influencing future developments; related to seed or semen. Although Freud has generally been regarded as a *seminal* thinker who shaped the course of psychology, his psychoanalytic methods have come under attack recently.

seminary N. school for training future ministers; secondary school, especially for young women. Sure of his priestly vocation, Terrence planned to pursue his theological training at the local Roman Catholic *seminary.*

senility N. old age; feeble mindedness of old age. Most of the decisions are being made by the junior members of the company because of the *senility* of the president. senile, ADJ.

sensual ADJ. devoted to the pleasures of the senses; carnal; voluptuous. I cannot understand what caused him to drop his *sensual* way of life and become so ascetic.

sensuous ADJ. pertaining to the physical senses; operating through the senses. He was stimulated by the sights, sounds and smells about him; he was enjoying his *sensuous* experience.

sententious ADJ. terse; concise; aphoristic. After reading so many redundant speeches, I find his *sententious* style particularly pleasing.

sentinel N. sentry; lookout. Though camped in enemy territory, Bledsoe ignored the elementary precaution of posting *sentinels* around the encampment.

septic ADJ. putrid; producing putrefaction. The hospital was in such a filthy state that we were afraid that many of the patients would suffer from *septic* poisoning. sepsis, N.

sepulcher N. tomb. Annabel Lee was buried in a *sepulcher* by the sea.

Test

Word List 42   *Antonyms*

Each of the questions below consists of a word in capital letters, followed by five lettered words or phrases. Choose the lettered word or phrase that is most nearly opposite in meaning to the word in capital letters and write the letter of your choice on your answer paper.

616. SADISTIC (A) happy (B) quaint (C) kindhearted (D) vacant (E) fortunate
617. SAGACIOUS (A) foolish (B) bitter (C) voracious (D) veracious (E) fallacious
618. SALLOW (A) salacious (B) ruddy (C) colorless (D) permitted (E) minimum
619. SALUBRIOUS (A) salty (B) bloody (C) miasmic (D) maudlin (E) wanted
620. SALVAGE (A) remove (B) outfit (C) burn (D) lose (E) confuse
621. SANCTIMONIOUS (A) hypothetical (B) paltry (C) mercenary (D) pious (E) grateful

622. SANGUINE (A) choleric (B) sickening (C) warranted (D) irritated (E) pessimistic
623. SATIETY (A) emptiness (B) warmth (C) erectness (D) ignorance (E) straightness
624. SCANTY (A) collected (B) remote (C) invisible (D) plentiful (E) straight
625. SCURRILOUS (A) savage (B) scabby (C) decent (D) volatile (E) major
626. SECULAR (A) vivid (B) clerical (C) punitive (D) positive (E) varying
627. SEDENTARY (A) vicarious (B) loyal (C) accidental (D) active (E) afraid
628. SEDULOUS (A) indolent (B) guileless (C) vindictive (D) upright (E) incorrect
629. SENILITY (A) virility (B) loquaciousness (C) forgetfulness (D) youth (E) majority
630. SENTENTIOUS (A) paragraphed (B) positive (C) posthumous (D) pacific (E) wordy

Word List 43   sequester-somatic

sequester V. retire from public life; segregate; seclude. Although he had hoped for a long time to *sequester* himself in a small community, he never was able to drop his busy round of activities in the city.

sere ADJ. parched; dry. After the unseasonably dry winter the Berkeley hills looked dusty and *sere.*

serendipity N. gift for finding valuable or desirable things by accident; accidental good fortune or luck. Many scientific discoveries are a matter of *serendipity:* Newton was not sitting there thinking about gravity when the apple dropped on his head.

serenity N. calmness; placidity. The *serenity* of the sleepy town was shattered by a tremendous explosion.

serpentine ADJ. winding; twisting. The car swerved at every curve in the *serpentine* road.

serrated ADJ. having a sawtoothed edge. The beech tree is one of many plants that have *serrated* leaves.

servile ADJ. slavish; cringing. Constantly fawning on his employer, humble Uriah Heap was a *servile* creature. servility, N.

servitude N. slavery; compulsory labor. Born a slave, Douglass resented his life of *servitude* and plotted to escape to the North.

severance N. division; partition; separation. The *severance* of church and state is a basic principle of our government.

severity N. harshness; plainness. The newspapers disapproved of the *severity* of the sentence.

sextant N. navigation tool used to determine a ship's latitude and longitude. Given a clear night, with the aid of his *sextant* and compass he could keep the ship safely on course.

shackle V. chain; fetter. The criminal's ankles were *shack-*
shackle V. chain; fetter. The criminal's ankles were *shackled* to prevent his escape. also N.

sham V. pretend. He *shammed* sickness to get out of going to school. also N.

shambles N. slaughterhouse; scene of carnage. By the time the police arrived, the room was a *shambles*.

■ **shard** N. fragment, generally of pottery. The archaeologist assigned several students the task of reassembling earthenware vessels from the *shards* he had brought back from the expedition.

sheaf N. bundle of stalks of grain; any bundle of things tied together. The lawyer picked up a *sheaf* of papers as he rose to question the witness.

sheathe V. place into a case. As soon as he recognized the approaching men, he *sheathed* his dagger and hailed them as friends.

sherbet N. flavored dessert ice. I prefer raspberry *sherbet* to ice cream since it is less fattening.

shimmer V. glimmer intermittently. The moonlight *shimmered* on the water as the moon broke through the clouds for a moment. also N.

shirk V. avoid (responsibility, work, etc.); malinger. Brian has a strong sense of duty; he would never *shirk* any responsibility.

shoddy ADJ. sham; not genuine; inferior. You will never get the public to buy such *shoddy* material.

shrew N. scolding woman. No one wanted to marry Shakespeare's Kate because she was a *shrew*.

shrewd ADJ. clever; astute. A *shrewd* investor, he took clever advantage of the fluctuations of the stock market.

shun V. keep away from. Cherishing his solitude, the recluse *shunned* the company of other human beings.

shunt V. turn aside; divert; sidetrack. If the switchman failed to *shunt* the Silver Streak onto a side track, the train would plow right into Union Station.

shyster N. lawyer using questionable methods. On *L.A. Law*, respectable attorney Brackman was horrified to learn that his newly discovered half brother was a cheap *shyster*.

sibling N. brother or sister. We may not enjoy being *siblings,* but we cannot forget that we still belong to the same family.

sibylline ADJ. prophetic; oracular. Until their destruction by fire in 83 B.C., the *sibylline* books were often consulted by the Romans.

sidereal ADJ. relating to the stars. Although hampered by optical and mechanical flaws, the orbiting *Hubble* space telescope has relayed extraordinary images of distant *sidereal* bodies.

silt N. sediment deposited by running water. The harbor channel must be dredged annually to remove the *silt*.

simian ADJ. monkeylike. Lemurs are nocturnal mammals and have many *simian* characteristics, although they are less intelligent than monkeys.

simile N. comparison of one thing with another, using the word *like* or *as*. "My love is like a red, red rose" is a *simile*.

simper V. smirk; smile affectedly. Complimented on her appearance, Stella self-consciously *simpered*.

simplistic ADJ. oversimplified. Though Jack's solution dealt adequately with one aspect of the problem, it was *simplistic* in failing to consider various complicating factors that might arise.

simulate V. feign. He *simulated* insanity in order to avoid punishment for his crime.

sinecure N. well-paid position with little responsibility. My job is no *sinecure*; I work long hours and have much responsibility.

sinewy ADJ. tough; strong and firm. The steak was too *sinewy* to chew.

singular ADJ. unique; extraordinary; odd. Though the young man tried to understand Father William's *singular* behavior, he still found it odd that the old man incessantly stood on his head.

sinister ADJ. evil. We must defeat the *sinister* forces that seek our downfall.

sinuous ADJ. winding; bending in and out; not morally honest. The snake moved in a *sinuous* manner.

■ **skeptic** N. doubter; person who suspends judgment until he has examined the evidence supporting a point of view. In this matter, I am a *skeptic;* I want proof. skeptical, ADJ. skepticism, N.

skiff N. small, light sailboat or rowboat. Tom dreamed of owning an ocean-going yacht but had to settle for a *skiff* he could sail in the bay.

skimp V. provide scantily; live very economically. They were forced to *skimp* on necessities in order to make their limited supplies last the winter.

skinflint N. miser. The old *skinflint* refused to give her a raise.

skirmish N. minor fight. Custer's troops expected they might run into a *skirmish* or two on maneuvers; they did not expect to face a major battle. also V.

skittish ADJ. lively; frisky. She is as *skittish* as a kitten playing with a piece of string.

skulduggery N. dishonest behavior. The investigation into municipal corruption turned up new instances of *skulduggery* daily.

skulk V. move furtively and secretly. He *skulked* through the less fashionable sections of the city in order to avoid meeting any of his former friends.

slacken V. slow up; loosen. As they passed the finish line, the runners *slackened* their pace.

slag N. residue from smelting metal; dross; waste matter. The blast furnace had a special opening at the bottom to allow the workers to remove the worthless *slag*.

slake V. quench; sate. When we reached the oasis, we were able to *slake* our thirst.

slander N. defamation; utterance of false and malicious statements. Unless you can prove your allegations, your remarks constitute *slander*. also V.

slapdash ADJ. haphazard; careless; sloppy. From the number of typos and misspellings I've found in it, it's clear that Mario proofread the report in a remarkably *slapdash* fashion.

sleazy ADJ. flimsy; unsubstantial. This is a *sleazy* fabric; it will not wear well.

sleeper N. something originally of little value or importance that in time becomes very valuable. Unnoticed by the critics at its publication, the eventual Pulitzer Prize winner was a classic *sleeper.*

sleight N. dexterity. The magician amazed the audience with his *sleight* of hand.

slight N. insult to one's dignity; snub. Hypersensitive and ready to take offense at any discourtesy, Bertha was always on the lookout for real or imaginary *slights.* also v.

slither V. slip or slide. During the recent ice storm, many people *slithered* down this hill as they walked to the station.

sloth N. laziness. Such *sloth* in a young person is deplorable; go to work!

sloth N. slow-moving tree-dwelling mammal. Note how well the somewhat greenish coat of the *sloth* enables it to blend in with its arboreal surroundings. (secondary meaning)

slough V. cast off. Each spring, the snake *sloughs* off its skin. also N.

slovenly ADJ. untidy; slipshod. Such *slovenly* work habits will never produce good products.

sluggard N. lazy person. "You are a *sluggard,* a drone, a parasite," the angry father shouted at his lazy son.

sluggish ADJ. slow; lazy; lethargic. After two nights without sleep, she felt *sluggish* and incapable of exertion.

sluice N. artificial channel for directing or controlling the flow of water. In times of drought, this *sluice* enables farmers to obtain water for irrigation.

slur N. insult to one's character or reputation; slander. Polls revealed that the front-runner's standing had been damaged by the *slurs* and innuendoes circulated by his opponent's staff. also v. (secondary meaning)

smattering N. slight knowledge. I don't know whether it is better to be ignorant of a subject or to have a mere *smattering* of information about it.

smirk N. conceited smile. Wipe that *smirk* off your face! also v.

smolder V. burn without flame; be liable to break out at any moment. The rags *smoldered* for hours before they burst into flame.

snicker N. half-stifled laugh. The boy could not suppress a *snicker* when the teacher sat on the tack. also v.

snivel V. run at the nose; snuffle; whine. Don't you come *sniveling* to me complaining about your big brother.

sobriety N. moderation (especially regarding indulgence in alcohol); seriousness. Neither drunkards nor comics are noted for *sobriety.* sober, ADJ.

sodden ADJ. soaked; dull, as if from drink. He set his *sodden* overcoat near the radiator to dry.

sojourn N. temporary stay. After his *sojourn* in Florida, he began to long for the colder climate of his native New England home.

solace N. comfort in trouble. I hope you will find *solace* in the thought that all of us share your loss.

solder V. repair or make whole by using a metal alloy. The plumber fixed the leak in the pipes by *soldering* a couple of joints from which water had been oozing.

solecism N. construction that is flagrantly incorrect grammatically. I must give this paper a failing mark because it contains many *solecisms.*

solemnity N. seriousness; gravity. The minister was concerned that nothing should disturb the *solemnity* of the marriage service.

solicit V. request earnestly; seek. Knowing she needed to have a solid majority for the budget to pass, the mayor telephoned all the members of the city council to *solicit* their votes.

■ **solicitous** ADJ. worried, concerned. The employer was very *solicitous* about the health of her employees as replacements were difficult to get. solicitude, N.

soliloquy N. talking to oneself. The *soliloquy* is a device used by the dramatist to reveal a character's innermost thoughts and emotions.

solstice N. point at which the sun is farthest from the equator. The winter *solstice* usually occurs on December 21.

solvent ADJ. able to pay all debts. By dint of very frugal living, he was finally able to become *solvent* and avoid bankruptcy proceedings. solvency, N.

somatic ADJ. pertaining to the body; physical. Why do you ignore the spiritual aspects and emphasize only the corporeal and the *somatic* ones?

Test

Word List 43   *Synonyms and Antonyms*

Each of the following questions consists of a word in capital letters, followed by five lettered words or phrases. Choose the lettered word or phrase that is most nearly similar or opposite in meaning to the word in capital letters and write the letter of your choice on your answer paper.

631. SEQUESTER (A) request (B) preclude (C) seclude (D) witness (E) evolve

632. SERRATED (A) riddled (B) diagonal (C) sawtoothed (D) grooved (E) linear

633. SERVILE (A) moral (B) puerile (C) futile (D) foul (E) haughty

634. SHODDY (A) superior (B) barefoot (C) sunlit (D) querulous (E) garrulous

635. SINGULAR (A) silent (B) angular (C) ordinary (D) desirable (E) garrulous

636. SINISTER (A) unwed (B) ministerial (C) good (D) returned (E) splintered

637. SKITTISH (A) tractable (B) inquiring (C) dramatic (D) vain (E) frisky

638. SLEAZY (A) fanciful (B) creeping (C) substantial
     (D) uneasy (E) warranted
639. SLOTH (A) penitence (B) filth (C) futility
     (D) poverty (E) industry
640. SLOUGH (A) toughen (B) trap (C) violate
     (D) cast off (E) depart quickly
641. SLOVENLY (A) half-baked (B) loved
     (C) inappropriate (D) tidy (E) rapid
642. SOBRIETY (A) inebriety (B) aptitude
     (C) scholasticism (D) monotony (E) aversion
643. SOLECISM (A) praise (B) embarrassment
     (C) concise phrase (D) inaccurate count
     (E) correct expression
644. SOLSTICE (A) equinox (B) sunrise (C) pigsty
     (D) interstices (E) iniquity
645. SOLVENT (A) enigmatic (B) bankrupt (C) fiducial
     (D) puzzling (E) gilded

Word List 44   somber-sublime

somber ADJ. gloomy; depressing. From the doctor's grim expression, I could tell he had *somber* news.

somnambulist N. sleepwalker. The most famous *somnambulist* in literature is Lady Macbeth; her monologue in the sleepwalking scene is one of the highlights of Shakespeare's play.

somnolent ADJ. half asleep. The heavy meal and the over-heated room made us all *somnolent* and indifferent to the speaker. somnolence, N.

sonorous ADJ. resonant. His *sonorous* voice resounded through the hall.

sophist N. teacher of philosophy; quibbler; employer of fallacious reasoning. You are using all the devices of a *sophist* in trying to prove your case; your argument is specious.

sophistication N. artificiality; unnaturalness; act of employing sophistry in reasoning. *Sophistication* is an acquired characteristic, found more frequently among city dwellers than among residents of rural areas.

■ **sophistry** N. seemingly plausible but fallacious reasoning. Instead of advancing valid arguments, he tried to overwhelm his audience with a flood of *sophistries*.

sophomoric ADJ. immature; shallow. Your *sophomoric* remarks are a sign of your youth and indicate that you have not given much thought to the problem.

■ **soporific** ADJ. sleep producing. I do not need a sedative when I listen to one of his *soporific* speeches. also N.

sordid ADJ. filthy; base; vile. The social worker was angered by the *sordid* housing provided for the home-less.

spangle N. small metallic piece sewn to clothing for ornamentation. The thousands of *spangles* on her dress sparkled in the glare of the stage lights.

spartan ADJ. lacking luxury and comfort; sternly disciplined. Looking over the bare, unheated room with its hard cot, he wondered what he was doing in such *spartan* quarters. Only his *spartan* sense of duty kept him at his post.

spasmodic ADJ. fitful; periodic. The *spasmodic* coughing in the auditorium annoyed the performers.

spat N. squabble; minor dispute. What had started out as a mere *spat* escalated into a full-blown argument.

spate N. sudden flood. I am worried about the possibility of a *spate* if the rains do not diminish soon.

spatial ADJ. relating to space. It is difficult to visualize the *spatial* extent of our universe.

spatula N. broad-bladed instrument used for spreading or mixing. The manufacturers of this frying pan recommend the use of a rubber *spatula* to avoid scratching the specially treated surface.

spawn V. lay eggs. Fish ladders had to be built in the dams to assist the salmon returning to *spawn* in their native streams. also N.

■ **specious** ADJ. seemingly reasonable but incorrect. Let us not be misled by such *specious* arguments.

spectral ADJ. ghostly. We were frightened by the *spectral* glow that filled the room.

spectrum N. colored band produced when a beam of light passes through a prism. The visible portion of the *spectrum* includes red at one end and violet at the other.

spendthrift N. someone who wastes money. Easy access to credit encourages people to turn into *spendthrifts* who shop till they drop.

sphinx-like ADJ. enigmatic; mysterious. The Mona Lisa's *sphinx-like* expression has puzzled art lovers for centuries.

splice V. fasten together; unite. Before you *splice* two strips of tape together, be sure to line them up evenly. also N.

spontaneity N. impulsiveness; absence of premeditation. What I liked best about Dale's parties was their *spontaneity*: a couple of friends would drop by, someone would pull out a fiddle or guitar, and before you knew it the party would be in full swing. spontaneous, ADJ.

spoonerism N. accidental transposition of sounds in successive words. When the radio announcer introduced the President as Hoobert Herver, he was guilty of a *spoonerism*.

■ **sporadic** ADJ. occurring irregularly. Although there are still *sporadic* outbursts of shooting in the streets, the rebellion is essentially over.

sportive ADJ. playful. Such a *sportive* attitude is surprising in a person as serious as you usually are.

spruce ADJ. neat and trim. Every button buttoned, tie firmly in place, young Alex Keaton looked *spruce* and tidy for his job interview at the bank. also V.

spry ADJ. vigorously active; nimble. She was eighty years old, yet still *spry* and alert.

■ **spurious** ADJ. false; counterfeit; forged; illogical. The hero of Jonathan Gash's mystery novels is an antique dealer who gives the reader advice on how to tell *spurious* antiques from the real thing.

spurn V. reject; scorn. The heroine *spurned* the villain's advances.

squabble N. minor quarrel; bickering. Children invariably get involved in petty *squabbles*; wise parents know when to interfere and when to let the children work things out on their own.

squalid ADJ. dirty; neglected; poor. It is easy to see how crime can breed in such a *squalid* neighborhood.

squander V. waste. The prodigal son *squandered* the family estate.

squat ADJ. stocky; short and thick. Tolkien's hobbits are somewhat *squat*, sturdy little creatures, fond of good ale, good music, and good food.

staccato ADJ. played in an abrupt manner; marked by abrupt, sharp sound. His *staccato* speech reminded one of the sound of a machine gun.

stagnant ADJ. motionless; stale; dull. The *stagnant* water was a breeding ground for disease. stagnate, V.

staid ADJ. sober; sedate. Her conduct during the funeral ceremony was *staid* and solemn.

stalemate N. deadlock. Negotiations between the union and the employers have reached a *stalemate*; neither side is willing to budge from previously stated positions.

stalwart ADJ. strong, brawny; steadfast. His consistent support of the party has proved that he is a *stalwart* and loyal member. also N.

stamina N. strength; staying power. I doubt that she has the *stamina* to run the full distance of the marathon race.

stanch V. check flow of blood. It is imperative that we *stanch* the gushing wound before we attend to the other injuries.

stanza N. division of a poem. Do you know the last *stanza* of "The Star-Spangled Banner"?

static ADJ. unchanging; lacking development. Nothing had changed at home; things were *static* there. statis, N.

statute N. law. We have many *statutes* in our law books which should be repealed.

statutory ADJ. created by statute or legislative action. The judicial courts review and try *statutory* crimes.

steadfast ADJ. loyal; unswerving. Penelope was *steadfast* in her affections, faithfully waiting for Ulysses to return from his wanderings.

stealth N. slyness; sneakiness; secretiveness. Fearing detection by the sentries on duty, the scout inched his way toward the enemy camp with great *stealth*.

steep V. soak; saturate. Be sure to *steep* the fabric in the dye bath for the full time prescribed.

stellar ADJ. pertaining to the stars. He was the *stellar* attraction of the entire performance.

stem V. check the flow. The paramedic used a tourniquet to *stem* the bleeding from the slashed artery.

stem from V. arise from. Milton's problems in school *stemmed from* his poor study habits.

stentorian ADJ. extremely loud. The town crier had a *stentorian* voice.

stereotyped ADJ. oversimplified; lacking individuality; seen as a type. My chief objection to the book is that the characters are *stereotyped*; they come across as ethnic caricatures, not as real people with individual quirks, fears, and dreams. stereotype, N., V.

stickler N. perfectionist; person who insists things be exactly right. The Internal Revenue Service agent was a *stickler* for accuracy; no approximations or rough estimates would satisfy him.

stifle V. suppress; extinguish; inhibit. Halfway through the boring lecture, Laura gave up trying to *stifle* her yawns.

■ **stigma** N. token of disgrace; brand. I do not attach any *stigma* to the fact that you were accused of this crime; the fact that you were acquitted clears you completely. stigmatize, N.

stilted ADJ. bombastic; stiffly pompous. His *stilted* rhetoric did not impress the college audience; they were immune to bombastic utterances.

■ **stint** V. be thrifty; set limits. "Spare no expense," the bride's father said, refusing to *stint* on the wedding arrangements.

stint N. supply; allotted amount; assigned portion of work. He performed his daily *stint* cheerfully and willingly.

stipend N. pay for services. There is a nominal *stipend* for this position.

stipple V. paint or draw with dots. Seurat carefully *stippled* dabs of pure color on the canvas, juxtaposing dots of blue and yellow that the viewer's eye would interpret as green.

stipulate V. make express conditions, specify. Before agreeing to reduce American military forces in Europe, the president *stipulated* that NATO teams be allowed to inspect Soviet bases.

stodgy ADJ. stuffy; boringly conservative. For a young person, Winston seems remarkably *stodgy:* you'd expect someone his age to have a little more life.

stoic N. person who is indifferent to pleasure or pain. The doctor called her patient a *stoic* because he had borne the pain of the examination without whimpering. also ADJ.

stoke V. stir up a fire; feed plentifully. As a Scout, Marisa learned how to light a fire, how to *stoke* it if it started to die down, and how to extinguish it completely.

■ **stolidity** N. dullness; impassiveness. The earthquake shattered his usual *stolidity;* trembling, he crouched on the no longer stable ground.

stratified ADJ. divided into classes; arranged into strata. As the economic gap between the rich and the poor increased, Roman society grew increasingly *stratified*. stratify, V.

stratum N. layer of earth's surface; layer of society. Unless we alleviate conditions in the lowest *stratum* of our society, we may expect grumbling and revolt. strata, PL.

strew V. spread randomly; sprinkle; scatter. Preceding the bride to the altar, the flower girl will *strew* rose petals along the aisle.

■ **striated** ADJ. marked with parallel bands; grooved. The glacier left many *striated* rocks. striate, V.

stricture N. critical comments; severe and adverse criticism. His *strictures* on the author's style are prejudiced and unwarranted.

strident ADJ. loud and harsh. She scolded him in a *strident* voice.

stringent ADJ. binding; rigid. I think these regulations are too *stringent*.

■ **strut** N. pompous walk. His *strut* as he marched about the parade ground revealed him for what he was: a pompous buffoon. also v.

■ **strut** N. supporting bar. The engineer calculated that the *strut* supporting the rafter needed to be reinforced. (secondary meaning)

studied ADJ. unspontaneous; deliberate; thoughtful. Given Jill's previous slights, Jack felt that the omission of his name from the guest list was a *studied* insult.

stultify V. cause to appear or become stupid or inconsistent; frustrate or hinder. His long hours in the blacking factory left young Dickens numb and incurious, as if the menial labor had *stultified* his mind.

stupefy V. make numb; stun; amaze. Disapproving of drugs in general, Laura refused to take sleeping pills or any other medicine that might *stupefy* her.

stupor N. state of apathy; daze; lack of awareness. In his *stupor,* the addict was unaware of the events taking place around him.

stymie V. present an obstacle; stump. The detective was *stymied* by the contradictory evidence in the robbery investigation.

suavity N. urbanity; polish. He is particularly good in roles that require *suavity* and sophistication. suave, ADJ.

subaltern N. subordinate. The captain treated his *subalterns* as though they were children rather than commissioned officers.

subjective ADJ. occurring or taking place within the mind; unreal. Your analysis is highly *subjective*; you have permitted your emotions and your opinions to color your thinking.

subjugate V. conquer; bring under control. It is not our aim to *subjugate* our foe; we are interested only in establishing peaceful relations.

sublimate V. refine; purify. We must strive to *sublimate* these desires and emotions into worthwhile activities.

sublime ADJ. exalted; noble; uplifting. Mother Teresa has been honored for her *sublime* deeds.

Test

Word List 44   *Synonyms and Antonyms*

Each of the following questions consists of a word in capital letters, followed by five lettered words or phrases. Choose the lettered word or phrase that is most nearly similar or opposite in meaning to the word in capital letters and write the letter of your choice on your answer paper.

646. SONOROUS (A) resonant (B) reassuring (C) repetitive (D) resinous (E) sisterly
647. SOPHOMORIC (A) unprecedented (B) mature (C) insipid (D) intellectual (E) illusionary
648. SOPORIFIC (A) dining (B) caustic (C) memorial (D) awakening (E) springing
649. SPASMODIC (A) intermittent (B) fit (C) inaccurate (D) violent (E) physical
650. SPORADIC (A) seedy (B) latent (C) vivid (D) inconsequential (E) occasional
651. SPORTIVE (A) competing (B) playful (C) indignant (D) foppish (E) fundamental

652. SPURIOUS (A) genuine (B) angry (C) mitigated (D) interrogated (E) glorious
653. SQUANDER (A) fortify (B) depart (C) roam (D) preserve (E) forfeit
654. STACCATO (A) musical (B) long (C) legato (D) sneezing (E) pounded
655. STAMINA (A) patience (B) pistils (C) weakness (D)fascination (E) patina
656. STEREOTYPED (A) original (B) antique (C) modeled (D) repetitious (E) continued
657. STILTED (A) candid (B) pompous (C) modish (D) acute (E) inarticulate
658. STRINGENT (A) binding (B) reserved (C) utilized (D) lambent (E) indigent
659. SUAVITY (A) ingeniousness (B) indifference (C) urbanity (D) constancy (E) paucity
660. SUBLIME (A) unconscious (B) respected (C) exalted (D) sneaky (E) replaced

Word List 45   subliminal-tantamount

subliminal ADJ. below the threshold. We may not be aware of the *subliminal* influences that affect our thinking.

submissive ADJ. yielding; timid. Crushed by his authoritarian father, Will had no defiance left in him; he was totally *submissive* in the face of authority.

suborn V. persuade to act unlawfully (especially to commit perjury). In *The Godfather,* the mobsters used bribery and threats to *suborn* the witnesses against Don Michael Corleone.

subpoena N. writ summoning a witness to appear. The prosecutor's office was ready to serve a *subpoena* on the reluctant witness. also v.

subsequent ADJ. following; later. In *subsequent* lessons, we shall take up more difficult problems.

subservient ADJ. behaving like a slave; servile; obsequious. He was proud and dignified; he refused to be *subservient* to anyone. subservience, N.

■ **subside** V. settle down; descend; grow quiet. The doctor assured us that the fever would eventually *subside*.

subsidiary ADJ. subordinate; secondary. This information may be used as *subsidiary* evidence but is not sufficient by itself to prove your argument. also N.

subsidy N. direct financial aid by government, etc. Without this *subsidy*, American ship operators would not be able to compete in world markets.

subsistence N. existence; means of support; livelihood. In those days of inflated prices, my salary provided a mere *subsistence*.

■ **substantiate** V. verify; support. I intend to *substantiate* my statement by producing witnesses.

substantive ADJ. essential; pertaining to the substance. Although the delegates were aware of the importance of the problem, they could not agree on the *substantive* issues.

subsume V. include; encompass. Does the general theory of relativity contradict Newtonian physics, or is Newton's law of gravity *subsumed* into Einstein's larger scheme?

subterfuge N. pretense; evasion. As soon as we realized that you had won our support by a *subterfuge,* we withdrew our endorsement of your candidacy.

subtlety N. nicety; cunning; guile; delicacy. The *subtlety* of his remarks was unnoticed by most of his audience. subtle, ADJ.

subversive ADJ. tending to overthrow; destructive. At first glance, the notion that Styrofoam cups may actually be more ecologically sound than paper cups strikes most environmentalists as *subversive*.

succinct ADJ. brief; terse; compact. His remarks are always *succinct* and pointed.

succor N. aid; assistance; relief. We shall be ever grateful for the *succor* your country gave us when we were in need. also V.

succulent ADJ. juicy; full of richness. To some people, Florida citrus fruits are more *succulent* than those from California. also N.

succumb V. yield; give in; die. I *succumb* to temptation whenever it comes my way.

suffragist N. advocate of voting rights (for women). In recognition of her efforts to win the vote for women, Congress authorized coining a silver dollar honoring the *suffragist* Susan B. Anthony.

suffuse V. spread over. A blush *suffused* her cheeks when we teased her about her love affair.

sully V. tarnish; soil. He felt that it was beneath his dignity to *sully* his hands in such menial labor.

sultry ADJ. sweltering. He could not adjust himself to the *sultry* climate of the tropics.

summation N. act of finding the total, summary. In his *summation*, the lawyer emphasized the testimony given by the two witnesses.

sumptuous ADJ. lavish; rich. I cannot recall when I have had such a *sumptuous* Thanksgiving feast.

sunder V. separate; part. Northern and southern Ireland are politically and religiously *sundered*.

sundry ADJ. various; several. My suspicions were aroused when I read *sundry* items in the newspapers about your behavior.

superannuated ADJ. retired or disqualified because of age. The *superannuated* man was indignant because he felt that he could still perform a good day's work.

supercilious ADJ. contemptuous; haughty. I prefer Jill's modesty to Jack's *supercilious* and arrogant attitude.

supererogatory ADJ. superfluous; more than needed or demanded. We have more than enough witnesses to corroborate your statement; to present any more would be *supererogatory*.

superficial ADJ. trivial; shallow. Since your report gave only a *superficial* analysis of the problem, I cannot give you more than a passing grade.

superfluous ADJ. excessive; overabundant, unnecessary. Please try not to include so many *superfluous* details in your report; just give me the bare facts. superfluity, N.

superimpose V. place over something else. Your attempt to *superimpose* another agency in this field will merely increase the bureaucratic nature of our government.

supernumerary N. person or thing in excess of what is necessary; extra. His first appearance on the stage was as a *supernumerary* in a Shakespearean tragedy.

■ **supersede** V. cause to be set aside; replace. This regulation will *supersede* all previous rules.

supine ADJ. lying on back. The defeated pugilist lay *supine* on the canvas.

supplant V. replace; usurp. Corazon Aquino *supplanted* Ferdinand Marcos as president of the Philippines.

supple ADJ. flexible; pliant. The angler found a *supple* limb and used it as a fishing rod.

suppliant ADJ. entreating; beseeching. He could not resist the dog's *suppliant* whimpering, and he gave it some food. also N.

supplicate V. petition humbly; pray to grant a favor. We *supplicate* Your Majesty to grant him amnesty.

■ **supposition** N. hypothesis; surmise. I based my decision to confide in him on the *supposition* that he would be discreet. suppose, V.

supposititious ADJ. assumed; counterfeit; hypothetical. I find no similarity between your *supposititious* illustration and the problem we are facing.

surfeit V. satiate; stuff; indulge to excess in anything. Every Thanksgiving we are *surfeited* with an overabundance of holiday treats. also N.

surly ADJ. rude; cross. Because of his *surly* attitude, many people avoided his company.

surmise V. guess. I *surmise* that he will be late for this meeting. also N.

surmount V. overcome. He had to *surmount* many obstacles in order to succeed.

surpass V. exceed. Her SAT scores *surpassed* our expectations.

surreptitious ADJ. secret. News of their *surreptitious* meeting gradually leaked out.

surrogate N. substitute. For a fatherless child, a male teacher may become a father *surrogate*.

surveillance N. watching; guarding. The FBI kept the house under constant *surveillance* in the hope of capturing all the criminals at one time.

susceptible ADJ. impressionable; easily influenced; having little resistance, as to a disease. He was a very *susceptible* young man, and so his parents worried that he might fall into bad company.

sustain V. experience; support; nourish. He *sustained* such a severe injury that the doctors feared he would be unable to work to *sustain* his growing family.

sustenance N. means of support, food, nourishment. In the tropics, the natives find *sustenance* easy to obtain because of all the fruit trees.

suture N. stitches sewn to hold the cut edges of a wound or incision; material used in sewing. We will remove the *sutures* as soon as the wound heals. also V.

swarthy ADJ. dark; dusky. Despite the stereotype, not all Italians are *swarthy;* many are fair and blond.

swathe V. wrap around; bandage. When I visited him in the hospital, I found him *swathed* in bandages.

swelter V. be oppressed by heat. I am going to buy an air conditioning unit for my apartment as I do not intend to *swelter* through another hot and humid summer.

swerve V. deviate; turn aside sharply. The car *swerved* wildly as the driver struggled to regain control of the wheel.

swill V. drink greedily. Singing "Yo, ho, ho, and a bottle of rum," Long John Silver and his fellow pirates *swilled* their grog.

swindler N. cheat. She was gullible and trusting, an easy victim for the first *swindler* who came along.

sybarite N. lover of luxury. Rich people are not always *sybarites*; some of them have little taste for a life of luxury.

sycophant N. servile flatterer. The king enjoyed the servile compliments and attentions of the *sycophants* in his retinue. sycophantic, ADJ.

syllogism N. logical formula consisting of a major premise, a minor premise and a conclusion; deceptive or specious argument. There must be a fallacy in this *syllogism*; I cannot accept its conclusion.

sylvan ADJ. pertaining to the woods; rustic. His paintings of nymphs in *sylvan* backgrounds were criticized as oversentimental.

symbiosis N. interdependent relationship (between groups, species), often mutually beneficial. Both the crocodile bird and the crocodile derive benefit from their *symbiosis;* pecking away at food particles embedded in the crocodile's teeth, the bird derives nourishment; the crocodile, meanwhile, derives proper dental hygiene. symbiotic, ADJ.

symmetry N. arrangement of parts so that balance is obtained; congruity. The addition of a second tower will give this edifice the *symmetry* that it now lacks.

synchronous ADJ. similarly timed; simultaneous with. We have many examples of scientists in different parts of the world who have made *synchronous* discoveries.

synoptic ADJ. providing a general overview; summary. The professor turned to the latest issue of *Dissertation Abstracts* for a *synoptic* account of what was new in the field. synopsis, N.

synthesis N. combining parts into a whole. Now that we have succeeded in isolating this drug, our next problem is to plan its *synthesis* in the laboratory. syntheses, PL., synthesize, V.

synthetic ADJ. artificial; resulting from synthesis. During the twentieth century, many *synthetic* products have replaced the natural products. also N.

■ **tacit** ADJ. understood; not put into words. We have a *tacit* agreement based on only a handshake.

taciturn ADJ. habitually silent; talking little. New Englanders are reputedly *taciturn* people.

tactile ADJ. pertaining to the organs or sense of touch. His callused hands had lost their *tactile* sensitivity.

tainted ADJ. contaminated; corrupt. Health authorities are always trying to prevent the sale and use of *tainted* food.

talisman N. charm. She wore the *talisman* to ward off evil.

talon N. claw of bird. The falconer wore a leather gauntlet to avoid being clawed by the hawk's *talons*.

■ **tangential** ADJ. peripheral; only slightly connected; digressing. Despite Clark's attempts to distract her with *tangential* remarks, Lois kept on coming back to her main question: why couldn't he come out to dinner with Superman and her?

tangible ADJ. able to be touched; real; palpable. Although Tom did not own a house, he had several *tangible* assets—a car, a television, a PC—that he could sell if he needed cash.

tanner N. person who turns animal hides into leather. Using a solution of tanbark, the *tanner* treated the cowhide, transforming it into supple leather.

tantalize V. tease; torture with disappointment. Tom loved to *tantalize* his younger brother with candy; he knew the boy was forbidden to have it.

tantamount ADJ. equal. Your ignoring their pathetic condition is *tantamount* to murder.

Test

Word List 45 *Synonyms and Antonyms*

Each of the following questions consists of a word in capital letters, followed by five lettered words or phrases. Choose the lettered word or phrase that is most nearly similar or opposite in meaning to the word in capital letters and write the letter of your choice on your answer paper.

661. SUBLIMINAL (A) radiant (B) indifferent (C) obvious (D) domestic (E) horizontal

662. SUPERANNUATED (A) senile (B) experienced (C) retired (D) attenuated (E) accepted

663. SUPERCILIOUS (A) haughty (B) highbrow (C) angry (D) inane (E) philosophic

664. SUPERFICIAL (A) abnormal (B) portentous (C) shallow (D) angry (E) tiny

665. SUPERNUMERARY (A) miser (B) extra (C) associate (D) astronomer (E) inferiority

666. SUPPLIANT (A) intolerant (B) swallowing (C) beseeching (D) finishing (E) flexible

667. SURFEIT (A) belittle (B) cloy (C) drop (D) estimate (E) claim

668. SURREPTITIOUS (A) secret (B) snakelike (C) nightly (D) abstract (E) furnished

669. SUTURE (A) stitch (B) reflection (C) knitting (D) tailor (E) past

670. SWATHED (A) wrapped around (B) waved (C) gambled (D) rapt (E) mystified

671. SYCOPHANTIC (A) quiet (B) reclusive (C) servilely flattering (D) frolicsome (E) eagerly awaiting

672. SYNTHETIC (A) simplified (B) doubled (C) tuneful (D) artificial (E) fiscal

673. TACIT (A) spoken (B) allowed (C) neutral (D) impertinent (E) unwanted

674. TALISMAN (A) chief (B) juror (C) medicine man (D) amulet (E) gift

675. TANTALIZE (A) tease (B) wax (C) warrant (D) authorize (E) summarize

Word List 46   tantrum-tome

tantrum N. fit of petulance; caprice. The child learned that he could have almost anything if he went into *tantrums*.

taper N. candle. He lit the *taper* on the windowsill.

tarantula N. venomous spider. We need an antitoxin to counteract the bite of the *tarantula*.

tarry V. delay; dawdle. We can't *tarry* if we want to get to the airport on time.

taut ADJ. tight; ready. The captain maintained that he ran a *taut* ship.

tautological ADJ. needlessly repetitious. In the sentence "It was visible to the eye," the phrase "to the eye" is *tautological*. tautology, N.

tawdry ADJ. cheap and gaudy. He won a few *tawdry* trinkets in Coney Island.

taxonomist N. specialist in classifying (animals, etc.). Dental patterns often enable the *taxonomist* to distinguish members of one rodent species from those of another.

tedium N. boredom; weariness. We hope this radio will help overcome the *tedium* of your stay in the hospital. tedious, ADJ.

temerity N. boldness; rashness. Do you have the *temerity* to argue with me?

temper V. moderate; tone down or restrain; toughen (steel). Not even her supervisor's grumpiness could *temper* Nancy's enthusiasm for her new job.

temperament N. characteristic frame of mind; disposition; emotional excess. Although the twins look alike, they differ markedly in *temperament:* Tod is calm, but Rod is excitable.

temperate ADJ. restrained; self-controlled. Noted for his *temperate* appetite, he seldom gained weight.

tempo N. speed of music. I find the conductor's *tempo* too slow for such a brilliant piece of music.

temporal ADJ. not lasting forever; limited by time; secular. At one time in our history, *temporal* rulers assumed that they had been given their thrones by divine right.

temporize V. avoid committing oneself; gain time. I cannot permit you to *temporize* any longer; I must have a definite answer today.

tenacious ADJ. holding fast. I had to struggle to break his *tenacious* hold on my arm.

■ **tenacity** N. firmness; persistency; adhesiveness. It is extremely difficult to overcome the *tenacity* of a habit such as smoking.

tendentious ADJ. having an aim; biased; designed to further a cause. The editorials in this periodical are *tendentious* rather than truth-seeking.

tender V. offer; extend. Although no formal charges had been made against him, in the wake of the recent scandal the mayor felt he should *tender* his resignation.

tenet N. doctrine; dogma. The agnostic did not accept the *tenets* of their faith.

tensile ADJ. capable of being stretched. Mountain climbers must know the *tensile* strength of their ropes.

tentative ADJ. provisional; experimental. Your *tentative* plans sound plausible; let me know when the final details are worked out.

■ **tenuous** ADJ. thin; rare; slim. The allegiance of our allies is held by rather *tenuous* ties; let us hope they will remain loyal.

tenure N. holding of an office; time during which such an office is held. He has permanent *tenure* in this position and cannot be fired.

tepid ADJ. lukewarm. During the summer, I like to take a *tepid* bath, not a hot one.

terminate V. to bring to an end. When his contract was *terminated* unexpectedly, he desperately needed a new job.

terminology N. terms used in a science or art. The special *terminology* developed by some authorities in the field has done more to confuse laypersons than to enlighten them.

terminus N. last stop of railroad. After we reached the railroad *terminus,* we continued our journey into the wilderness on saddle horses.

terrestrial ADJ. on or relating to the earth. We have been able to explore the *terrestrial* regions much more thoroughly than the aquatic or celestial regions.

terse ADJ. concise; abrupt; pithy. I admire his *terse* style of writing; he comes directly to the point.

tertiary ADJ. third. He is so thorough that he analyzes *tertiary* causes where other writers are content with primary and secondary reasons.

tesselated ADJ. inlaid; mosaic. I recall seeing a table with a *tesselated* top of bits of stone and glass in a very interesting pattern.

testator N. maker of a will. The attorney called in his secretary and his partner to witness the signature of the *testator*.

testy ADJ. irritable; short-tempered. My advice is to avoid discussing this problem with him today as he is rather *testy* and may shout at you. testiness, N.

tether V. tie with a rope. Before we went to sleep, we *tethered* the horses to prevent their wandering off during the night.

thematic ADJ. relating to a unifying motif or idea. Those who think of *Moby Dick* as a simple adventure story about whaling miss its underlying *thematic* import.

theocracy N. government of a community by religious leaders. Some Pilgrims favored the establishment of a *theocracy* in New England.

theoretical ADJ. not practical or applied; hypothetical. Bob was better at applied engineering and computer programming than he was at *theoretical* physics and math. While I can still think of some *theoretical* objections to your plan, you've convinced me of its basic soundness.

therapeutic ADJ. curative. Now better known for its racetrack, Saratoga Springs first gained attention for the *therapeutic* qualities of its famous "healing waters."

thermal ADJ. pertaining to heat. The natives discovered that the hot springs gave excellent *thermal* baths and began to develop their community as a health resort. also N.

thespian ADJ. pertaining to drama. Her success in the school play convinced her she was destined for a *thespian* career. also N.

thrall N. slave; bondage. The captured soldier was held in *thrall* by the conquering army.

thrifty ADJ. careful about money; economical. A *thrifty* shopper compares prices before making major purchases.

thrive V. prosper; flourish. Despite the impact of recession on the restaurant trade, Philip's cafe *thrived*.

throes N. violent anguish. The *throes* of despair can be as devastating as the spasms accompanying physical pain.

throng N. crowd. *Throngs* of shoppers jammed the aisles. also V.

throttle V. strangle. The criminal tried to *throttle* the old man with his bare hands.

thwart V. baffle; frustrate. He felt that everyone was trying to *thwart* his plans and prevent his success.

tightwad N. excessively frugal person; miser. Jill called Jack a *tightwad* because he never picked up the check.

tiller N. handle used to move boat's rudder (to steer). Fearing the wind might shift suddenly and capsize the skiff, Tom kept one hand on the *tiller* at all times.

timbre N. quality of a musical tone produced by a musical instrument. We identify the instrument producing a musical sound by its *timbre*.

timidity N. lack of self-confidence or courage. If you are to succeed as a salesperson, you must first lose your *timidity* and fear of failure.

timorous ADJ. fearful; demonstrating fear. His *timorous* manner betrayed the fear he felt at the moment.

tipple V. drink (alcoholic beverages) frequently. He found that his most enjoyable evenings occurred when he *tippled* with his friends at the local pub. N.

■ **tirade** N. extended scolding; denunciation. Long before he had finished his *tirade*, we were sufficiently aware of the seriousness of our misconduct.

titanic ADJ. gigantic. *Titanic* waves beat against the shore during the hurricane.

tithe N. tax of one-tenth. Because he was an agnostic, he refused to pay his *tithes* to the clergy. also V.

titillate V. tickle. I am here not to *titillate* my audience but to enlighten it.

title N. right or claim to possession; mark of rank; name (of a book, film, etc.). Though the penniless Duke of Ragwort no longer held *title* to the family estate, he still retained his *title* as head of one of England's oldest families.

titter N. nervous laugh. Her aunt's constant *titter* nearly drove her mad. also V.

titular ADJ. having the title of an office without the obligations. Although he was the *titular* head of the company, the real decisions were made by his general manager.

toady N. servile flatterer; yes man. Never tell the boss anything he doesn't wish to hear: he doesn't want an independent adviser, he just wants a *toady*. also V.

toga N. Roman outer robe. Marc Antony pointed to the slashes in Caesar's *toga*.

tome N. large volume. He spent much time in the libraries poring over ancient *tomes*.

Test

Word List 46   *Synonyms*

Each of the questions below consists of a word in capital letters, followed by five lettered words or phrases. Choose the lettered word or phrase that is most nearly similar in meaning to the word in capital letters and write the letter of your choice on your answer paper.

676. TARRY (A) polish (B) restrain (C) surpass (D) linger (E) disturb

677. TAUTOLOGY (A) memory (B) repetition (C) tension (D) simile (E) lack of logic

678. TAWDRY (A) orderly (B) meretricious (C) reclaimed (D) filtered (E) proper

679. TEMERITY (A) timidity (B) resourcefulness (C) boldness (D) tremulousness (E) caution

680. TEMPORAL (A) priestly (B) scholarly (C) secular (D) sleepy (E) sporadic

681. TENACIOUS (A) fast running (B) intentional (C) obnoxious (D) holding fast (E) collecting

682. TENACITY (A) splendor (B) perseverance (C) tendency (D) ingratitude (E) decimation

683. TENDENTIOUS (A) biased (B) likely (C) absurd (D) festive (E) literary

684. TENTATIVE (A) prevalent (B) portable (C) mocking (D) wry (E) experimental

685. TENUOUS (A) vital (B) thin (C) careful (D) dangerous (E) necessary

686. TEPID (A) boiling (B) lukewarm (C) freezing (D) gaseous (E) cold

687. TERSE (A) brief in speech (B) bold in manner (C) under strain (D) without honor (E) beyond fear

688. TESSELATED (A) striped (B) made of mosaics (C) piebald (D) uniform (E) trimmed

689. THESPIAN (A) foreigner (B) skeptic (C) daydreamer (D) magician (E) actor

690. TITILLATE (A) hasten (B) fasten (C) stimulate (D) incorporate (E) enlarge

Word List 47   tonsure-ubiquitous

tonsure N. shaving of the head, especially by person entering religious orders. His *tonsure*, even more than his monastic garb, indicated that he was a member of the religious order.

topography N. physical features of a region. Before the generals gave the order to attack, they ordered a complete study of the *topography* of the region.

■ **torpor** N. lethargy; sluggishness; dormancy. Nothing seemed to arouse him from his *torpor*: he had wholly surrendered himself to lethargy. torpid, ADJ.

■ **torque** N. twisting force; force producing rotation. With her wrench she applied sufficient *torque* to the nut to loosen it.

torrent N. rushing stream; flood. Day after day of heavy rain saturated the hillside until the water ran downhill in *torrents*. torrential, ADJ.

torso N. trunk of statue with head and limbs missing; human trunk. This *torso,* found in the ruins of Pompeii, is now on exhibition in the museum in Naples.

■ **tortuous** ADJ. winding; full of curves. Because this road is so *tortuous,* it is unwise to go faster than twenty miles an hour on it.

touchstone N. stone used to test the fineness of gold alloys; criterion. What *touchstone* can be used to measure the character of a person?

touchy ADJ. sensitive; irascible. Do not discuss this phase of the problem as he is very *touchy* about it.

tout V. publicize; praise excessively. I lost confidence in my broker after he *touted* some junk bonds that turned out to be a bad investment.

toxic ADJ. poisonous. We must seek an antidote for whatever *toxic* substance he has eaten. toxicity, N.

tract N. pamphlet; a region of indefinite size. The King granted William Penn a *tract* of land in the New World.

■ **tractable** ADJ. docile. You will find the children in this school very *tractable* and willing to learn.

traduce V. expose to slander. His opponents tried to *traduce* the candidate's reputation by spreading rumors about his past.

trajectory N. path taken by a projectile. The police tried to locate the spot from which the assassin had fired the fatal shot by tracing the *trajectory* of the bullet.

tranquillity N. calmness; peace. After the commotion and excitement of the city, I appreciate the *tranquillity* of these fields and forests.

transcend V. exceed; surpass. This accomplishment *transcends* all our previous efforts. transcendental, ADJ.

transcribe V. copy. When you *transcribe* your notes, please send a copy to Mr. Smith and keep the original for our files. transcription, N.

■ **transgression** N. violation of a law; sin. Forgive us our *transgressions;* we know not what we do.

transient ADJ. momentary; temporary; staying for a short time. Lexy's joy at finding the perfect Christmas gift for Phil was *transient;* she still had to find presents for the cousins and Uncle Bob. Located near the airport, this hotel caters to the largely *transient* trade. also N.

transition N. going from one state of action to another. During the period of *transition* from oil heat to gas heat, the furnace will have to be shut off.

transitoriness N. impermanence. Conscious that all things pass, the psalmist relates the *transitoriness* of happiness and fame. transitory, ADJ.

translucent ADJ. partly transparent. We could not recognize the people in the next room because of the *translucent* curtains that separated us.

transmute V. change; convert to something different. He was unable to *transmute* his dreams into actualities.

transparent ADJ. permitting light to pass through freely; easily detected. Your scheme is so *transparent* that it will fool no one.

transpire V. be revealed; happen. When Austen writes the sentence "It had just *transpired* that he had left gaming debts behind him," her meaning is not that the debts had just been incurred, but that the shocking news had just leaked out.

transport N. strong emotion. Margo was a creature of extremes, at one moment in *transports* of joy over a vivid sunset, at another moment in *transports* of grief over a dying bird. also V. (secondary meaning)

trappings N. outward decorations; ornaments. He loved the *trappings* of success: the limousines, the stock options, the company jet.

traumatic ADJ. pertaining to an injury caused by violence. In his nightmares, he kept on recalling the *traumatic* experience of being wounded in battle. trauma, N.

travail N. painful labor. How long do you think a man can endure such *travail* and degradation without rebelling?

traverse V. go through or across. When you *traverse* this field, be careful of the bull.

travesty N. comical parody; treatment aimed at making something appear ridiculous. The ridiculous decision the jury has arrived at is a *travesty* of justice.

treatise N. article treating a subject systematically and thoroughly. He is preparing a *treatise* on the Elizabethan playwrights for his graduate degree.

trek N. travel; journey. The tribe made their *trek* further north that summer in search of game. also V.

tremor N. trembling; slight quiver. She had a nervous *tremor* in her right hand.

tremulous ADJ. trembling; wavering. She was *tremulous* more from excitement than from fear.

trenchant ADJ. cutting; keen. I am afraid of his *trenchant* wit for it is so often sarcastic.

trepidation N. fear; trembling agitation. We must face the enemy without *trepidation* if we are to win this battle.

tribulation N. distress; suffering. After all the trials and *tribulations* we have gone through, we need this rest.

tribunal N. court of justice. The decision of the *tribunal* was final and the prisoner was sentenced to death.

tribute N. tax levied by a ruler; mark of respect. The colonists refused to pay *tribute* to a foreign despot.

trident N. three-pronged spear. Neptune is usually depicted as rising from the sea, carrying his *trident* on his shoulder.

trigger V. set off. John is touchy today; say one word wrong and you'll *trigger* an explosion.

trilogy N. group of three works. Romain Rolland's novel *Jean Christophe* was first published as a *trilogy*.

trinket N. knickknack; bauble. Whenever she traveled abroad, Ethel would pick up costume jewelry and other *trinkets* as souvenirs.

trite ADJ. hackneyed; commonplace. The *trite* and predictable situations in many television programs alienate many viewers.

trivia N. trifles; unimportant matters. Too many magazines ignore newsworthy subjects and feature *trivia*.

troth N. pledge of good faith especially in betrothal. He gave her his *troth* and vowed to cherish her always.

trough N. container for feeding farm animals; lowest point (of a wave, business cycle, etc.). The hungry pigs struggled to get at the fresh swill in the *trough*. The surfer rode her board, coasting along in the *trough* between two waves.

■ **truculence** N. aggressiveness; ferocity. Tynan's reviews were noted for their caustic attacks and general tone of *truculence*. truculent, ADJ.

truism N. self-evident truth. Many a *truism* is well expressed in a proverb.

truncate V. cut the top off. The top of the cone that has been *truncated* in a plane parallel to its base is a circle.

tryst N. meeting. The lovers kept their *tryst* even though they realized their danger. also V.

tumid ADJ. swollen; pompous; bombastic. I especially dislike his *tumid* style; I prefer writing which is less swollen and bombastic.

tumult N. commotion; riot; noise. She could not make herself heard over the *tumult* of the mob.

tundra N. rolling, treeless plain in Siberia and arctic North America. Despite the cold, many geologists are trying to discover valuable mineral deposits in the *tundra*.

■ **turbid** ADJ. muddy; having the sediment disturbed. The water was *turbid* after the children had waded through it.

turbulence N. state of violent agitation. We were frightened by the *turbulence* of the ocean during the storm.

tureen N. deep dish for serving soup. The waiters brought the soup to the tables in silver *tureens*.

turgid ADJ. swollen; distended. The *turgid* river threatened to overflow the levees and flood the countryside.

turmoil N. confusion; strife. Conscious he had sinned, he was in a state of spiritual *turmoil*.

turncoat N. traitor. The British considered Benedict Arnold a loyalist; the Americans considered him a *turncoat*.

turpitude N. depravity. A visitor may be denied admittance to this country if she has been guilty of moral *turpitude*.

tutelage N. guardianship; training. Under the *tutelage* of such masters of the instrument, she made rapid progress as a virtuoso.

tutelary ADJ. protective; pertaining to a guardianship. I am acting in my *tutelary* capacity when I refuse to grant you permission to leave the campus.

tycoon N. wealthy leader. John D. Rockefeller was a prominent *tycoon*.

tyranny N. oppression; cruel government. Frederick Douglass fought against the *tyranny* of slavery throughout his entire life.

tyro N. beginner; novice. For a mere *tyro*, you have produced some marvelous results.

■ **ubiquitous** ADJ. being everywhere; omnipresent. That Christmas "The Little Drummer Boy" seemed *ubiquitous*: Justin heard the tune everywhere he went. ubiquity, N.

Test

Word List 47   *Antonyms*

Each of the questions below consists of a word in capital letters, followed by five lettered words or phrases. Choose the lettered word or phrase that is most nearly opposite in meaning to the word in capital letters and write the letter of your choice on your answer paper.

691. TRACTABLE (A) unmanageable (B) irreligious (C) mortal (D) incapable (E) unreal

692. TRADUCE (A) exhume (B) increase (C) purchase (D) extol (E) donate

693. TRANQUILLITY (A) lack of sleep (B) lack of calm (C) emptiness (D) renewal (E) closeness

694. TRANSIENT (A) carried (B) close (C) permanent (D) removed (E) certain

695. TREMULOUS (A) steady (B) obese (C) young (D) healthy (E) unkempt

696. TRENCHANT (A) lacking bite (B) imperious (C) inessential (D) unafraid (E) narrow-minded
697. TREPIDATION (A) slowness (B) amputation (C) fearlessness (D) adroitness (E) death
698. TRITE (A) correct (B) original (C) distinguished (D) premature (E) certain
699. TRUCULENT (A) juicy (B) overflowing (C) peaceful (D) determined (E) false
700. TUMULT (A) scarcity (B) defeat (C) coolness (D) density (E) serenity

701. TURBID (A) clear (B) improbable (C) invariable (D) honest (E) turgid
702. TURBULENCE (A) reaction (B) approach (C) impropriety (D) calm (E) hostility
703. TURGID (A) rancid (B) shrunken (C) cool (D) explosive (E) painful
704. TURPITUDE (A) amplitude (B) heat (C) wealth (D) virtue (E) quiet
705. TYRO (A) infant (B) rubber (C) personnel (D) idiot (E) expert

Word List 48   ulterior-vehement

ulterior ADJ. situated beyond; unstated and often questionable. You must have an *ulterior* motive for your behavior, since there is no obvious reason for it.

ultimate ADJ. final; not susceptible to further analysis. Scientists are searching for the *ultimate* truths.

ultimatum N. last demand; warning. Since they have ignored our *ultimatum,* our only recourse is to declare war.

umbrage N. resentment; anger; sense of injury or insult. She took *umbrage* at his remarks and stormed away in a huff.

unanimity N. complete agreement. We were surprised by the *unanimity* with which our proposals were accepted by the different groups. unanimous, ADJ.

unassuaged ADJ. unsatisfied; not soothed. Her anger is *unassuaged* by your apology.

unassuming ADJ. modest. He is so *unassuming* that some people fail to realize how great a man he really is.

unbridled ADJ. violent. She had a sudden fit of *unbridled* rage.

uncanny ADJ. strange; mysterious. You have the *uncanny* knack of reading my innermost thoughts.

unconscionable ADJ. unscrupulous; excessive. She found the loan shark's demands *unconscionable* and impossible to meet.

uncouth ADJ. outlandish; clumsy; boorish. Most biographers portray Lincoln as an *uncouth* and ungainly young man.

unction N. the act of anointing with oil. The anointing with oil of a person near death is called extreme *unction.*

unctuous ADJ. oily; bland; insincerely suave. Uriah Heep disguised his nefarious actions by *unctuous* protestations of his "'umility."

undermine V. weaken; sap. The recent corruption scandals have *undermined* many people's faith in the city government.

underscore V. emphasize. Addressing the jogging class, Kim *underscored* the importance to runners of good nutrition.

undulate V. move with a wavelike motion. The flag *undulated* in the breeze.

unearth V. dig up. When they *unearthed* the city, the archeologists found many relics of an ancient civilization.

unearthly ADJ. not earthly; weird. There is an *unearthly* atmosphere in her work that amazes the casual observer.

unequivocal ADJ. plain; obvious. My answer to your proposal is an *unequivocal* and absolute "No."

unerringly ADV. infallibly. My teacher *unerringly* pounced on the one typographical error in my essay.

unfaltering ADJ. steadfast. She approached the guillotine with *unfaltering* steps.

unfeigned ADJ. genuine; real. She turned so pale that I am sure her surprise was *unfeigned.*

unfettered ADJ. liberated; freed from chains. Chained to the wall for months on end, the hostage despaired that he would ever be *unfettered.* unfetter, V.

unfledged ADJ. immature. It is hard for an *unfledged* writer to find a sympathetic publisher.

unfrock V. to strip a priest or minister of church authority. To disbar a lawyer, to *unfrock* a priest, to suspend a doctor's license to practice—these are extreme steps that the authorities should take only after careful consideration.

ungainly ADJ. awkward. He is an *ungainly* young man; he trips over everything.

unguent N. ointment. Apply this *unguent* to the sore muscles before retiring.

uniformity N. sameness; consistency; monotony. After a while, the *uniformity* of TV situation comedies becomes boring.

unilateral ADJ. one-sided. This legislation is *unilateral* since it binds only one party in the controversy.

unimpeachable ADJ. blameless and exemplary. Her conduct in office was *unimpeachable* and her record is spotless.

uninhibited ADJ. unrepressed. The congregation was shocked by her *uninhibited* laughter during the sermon.

unintimidating ADJ. unfrightening. Though Phil had expected to feel overawed when he met Joe Montana, he found

unique ADJ. without an equal; single in kind. You have the *unique* distinction of being the first student whom I have had to fail in this course.

unison N. unity of pitch; complete accord. The choir sang in *unison.*

universal ADJ. characterizing or affecting all; present everywhere. At first, no one shared Christopher's opinions; his theory that the world was round was met with *universal* disdain.

unkempt ADJ. disheveled; with uncared-for appearance. The beggar was dirty and *unkempt.*

unobtrusive ADJ. inconspicuous; not blatant. The secret service agents in charge of protecting the President tried to be as *unobtrusive* as possible.

unprecedented ADJ. novel; unparalleled. Margaret Mitchell's book *Gone with the Wind* was an *unprecedented* success.

unprepossessing ADJ. unattractive. During adolescence many attractive young people somehow acquire the false notion that their appearance is *unprepossessing*.

unravel V. disentangle; solve. With equal ease Miss Marple *unraveled* tangled balls of yarn and baffling murder mysteries.

unrequited ADJ. not reciprocated. Suffering the pangs of *unrequited* love, Olivia rebukes Cesario for his hardheartedness.

unruly ADJ. disobedient; lawless. The only way to curb this *unruly* mob is to use tear gas.

unsavory ADJ. distasteful; morally offensive. People with *unsavory* reputations should not be allowed to work with young children.

unscathed ADJ. unharmed. They prayed he would come back from the war *unscathed*.

unseemly ADJ. unbecoming; indecent. Your levity is *unseemly* at this time of mourning.

unsightly ADJ. ugly. Although James was an experienced emergency room nurse, he occasionally became queasy when faced with a particularly *unsightly* injury.

unsullied ADJ. untarnished. I am happy that my reputation is *unsullied*.

untenable ADJ. unsupportable. I find your theory *untenable* and must reject it.

untoward ADJ. unfortunate; annoying. *Untoward* circumstances prevent me from being with you on this festive occasion.

unwarranted ADJ. unjustified; groundless; undeserved. We could not understand Martin's *unwarranted* rudeness to his mother's guests.

unwieldy ADJ. awkward; cumbersome; unmanageable. The large carton was so *unwieldy* that the movers had trouble getting it up the stairs.

unwitting ADJ. unintentional; not knowing. She was the *unwitting* tool of the swindlers.

unwonted ADJ. unaccustomed. He hesitated to assume the *unwonted* role of master of ceremonies at the dinner.

upbraid V. scold; reproach. I must *upbraid* him for his unruly behavior.

uproarious ADJ. marked by commotion; extremely funny; very noisy. The *uproarious* comedy hit *Home Alone* featured Macaulay Culkin, whose mugging and comic antics provoked gales of *uproarious* laughter from audiences coast to coast.

upshot N. outcome. The *upshot* of the rematch was that the former champion proved that he still possessed all the skills of his youth.

urbane ADJ. suave; refined; elegant. The courtier was *urbane* and sophisticated. urbanity, N.

urchin N. mischievous child (usually a boy). Get out! This store is no place for grubby *urchins*!

ursine ADJ. bearlike; pertaining to a bear. Because of its *ursine* appearance, the great panda has been identified with the bears; actually, it is closely related to the raccoon.

usurp V. seize power; supplant. The revolution ended when the victorious rebel leader *usurped* the throne. usurpation, N.

usury N. lending money at illegal rates of interest. The loan shark was found guilty of *usury*.

utopia N. imaginary land with perfect social and political system. Shangri-la was the name of James Hilton's Tibetan *utopia*.

uxorious ADJ. excessively devoted to one's wife. His friends laughed at him because he was so *uxorious* and submissive to his wife's desires.

■ **vacillate** V. waver; fluctuate. Uncertain which suitor she ought to marry, the princess *vacillated*, saying now one, now the other. vacillation, N.

vacuous ADJ. empty; lacking in ideas; stupid. The candidate's *vacuous* remarks annoyed the audience, who had hoped to hear more than empty platitudes. vacuity, N.

vagabond N. wanderer; tramp. In summer, college students wander the roads of Europe like carefree *vagabonds*. also ADJ.

vagary N. caprice; whim. She followed every *vagary* of fashion.

vagrant ADJ. stray; random. He tried to study, but could not collect his *vagrant* thoughts.

vagrant N. homeless wanderer. Because he was a stranger in town with no visible means of support, Martin feared he would be jailed as a *vagrant*. vagrancy, N.

vainglorious ADJ. boastful; excessively conceited. She was a *vainglorious* and arrogant individual.

valedictory ADJ. pertaining to farewell. I found the *valedictory* address too long; leave-taking should be brief. also N.

valid ADJ. logically convincing; sound; legally acceptable. You're going to have to come up with a better argument if you want to convince me that your reasoning is *valid*.

validate V. confirm; ratify. I will not publish my findings until I *validate* my results.

valor N. bravery. He received the Medal of Honor for his *valor* in battle.

vampire N. ghostly being that sucks the blood of the living. Children were afraid to go to sleep at night because of the many legends of *vampires*.

vanguard N. forerunners; advance forces. We are the *vanguard* of a tremendous army that is following us.

vantage N. position giving an advantage. They fired upon the enemy from behind trees, walls and any other point of *vantage* they could find.

vapid ADJ. insipid; inane. She delivered an uninspired and *vapid* address.

variegated ADJ. many-colored. Without her glasses, Gretchen saw the fields of tulips as a *variegated* blur.

vassal N. in feudalism, one who held land of a superior lord. The lord demanded that his *vassals* contribute more to his military campaign.

vaunted ADJ. boasted; bragged; highly publicized. This much *vaunted* project proved a disappointment when it collapsed.

veer v. change in direction. After what seemed an eternity, the wind *veered* to the east and the storm abated.

vegetate v. live in a monotonous way. I do not understand how you can *vegetate* in this quiet village after the adventurous life you have led.

vehement ADJ. impetuous; with marked vigor. He spoke with *vehement* eloquence in defense of his client. vehemence, N.

Test

Word List 48   *Antonyms*

Each of the questions below consists of a word in capital letters, followed by five lettered words or phrases. Choose the lettered word or phrase that is most nearly opposite in meaning to the word in capital letters and write the letter of your choice on your answer paper.

706. UNEARTH (A) conceal (B) gnaw (C) clean (D) fling (E) react

707. UNFEIGNED (A) pretended (B) fashionable (C) wary (D) switched (E) colonial

708. UNGAINLY (A) ignorant (B) graceful (C) detailed (D) dancing (E) pedantic

709. UNIMPEACHABLE (A) fruitful (B) rampaging (C) faulty (D) pensive (E) thorough

710. UNKEMPT (A) bombed (B) washed (C) neat (D) showy (E) tawdry

711. UNRULY (A) chatting (B) obedient (C) definite (D) lined (E) curious

712. UNSEEMLY (A) effortless (B) proper (C) conducive (D) pointed (E) informative

713. UNSULLIED (A) tarnished (B) countless (C) soggy (D) papered (E) homicidal

714. UNTENABLE (A) supportable (B) tender (C) sheepish (D) tremulous (E) adequate

715. UNWITTING (A) clever (B) intense (C) sensitive (D) freezing (E) intentional

716. VACILLATION (A) remorse (B) relief (C) respect (D) steadfastness (E) inoculation

717. VALEDICTORY (A) sad (B) collegiate (C) derivative (D) salutatory (E) promising

718. VALOR (A) admonition (B) injustice (C) cowardice (D) generosity (E) repression

719. VANGUARD (A) regiment (B) rear (C) echelon (D) protection (E) loyalty

720. VAUNTED (A) unvanquished (B) fell (C) belittled (D) exacting (E) believed

Word List 49   velocity-vogue

velocity N. speed. The train went by at considerable *velocity*.

venal ADJ. capable of being bribed. The *venal* policeman accepted the bribe offered him by the speeding motorist whom he had stopped.

vendetta N. blood feud. The rival mobs engaged in a bitter *vendetta*.

vendor N. seller. The fruit *vendor* sold her wares from a stall on the sidewalk.

veneer N. thin layer; cover. Casual acquaintances were deceived by his *veneer* of sophistication and failed to recognize his fundamental shallowness.

venerable ADJ. deserving high respect. We do not mean to be disrespectful when we refuse to follow the advice of our *venerable* leader.

■ **venerate** v. revere. In China, the people *venerate* their ancestors.

venial ADJ. forgivable; trivial. We may regard a hungry man's stealing as a *venial* crime.

venison N. the meat of a deer. The hunters dined on *venison*.

vent N. small opening; outlet. The wine did not flow because the air *vent* in the barrel was clogged.

vent v. express; utter. He *vented* his wrath on his class.

ventral v. abdominal. We shall now examine the *ventral* plates of this serpent, not the dorsal side.

ventriloquist N. someone who can make his or her voice seem to come from another person or thing. This *ventriloquist* does an act in which she has a conversation with a wooden dummy.

venturesome ADJ. bold. A group of *venturesome* women were the first to scale Mt. Annapurna.

venue N. location. The attorney asked for a change of *venue*; he thought his client would do better if the trial were held in a less conservative county.

■ **veracious** ADJ. truthful. I can recommend him for this position because I have always found him *veracious* and reliable. veracity, N.

veracity N. truthfulness. Trying to prove Hill a liar, Senator Spector repeatedly questioned her *veracity*. veracious, ADJ.

verbalize v. put into words. I know you don't like to talk about these things, but please try to *verbalize* your feelings.

verbatim ADV. word for word. He repeated the message *verbatim*. also ADJ.

verbiage N. pompous array of words. After we had waded through all the *verbiage*, we discovered that the writer had said very little.

■ **verbose** ADJ. wordy. This article is too *verbose;* we must edit it. verbosity, N.

verdant ADJ. green; lush in vegetation. Monet's paintings of the *verdant* meadows were symphonies in green.

verdigris N. green coating on copper which has been exposed to the weather. Despite all attempts to protect the statue from the elements, it became coated with *verdigris*.

verge N. border; edge. Madame Curie knew she was on the *verge* of discovering the secrets of radioactive elements. also v.

verisimilitude N. appearance of truth; likelihood. Critics praised her for the *verisimilitude* of her performance as Lady Macbeth. She was completely believable.

verity N. truth; reality. The four *verities* were revealed to Buddha during his long meditation.

vernacular N. living language; natural style. Cut out those old-fashioned "thee's" and "thou's" and write in the *vernacular*. also ADJ.

vernal ADJ. pertaining to spring. We may expect *vernal* showers all during the month of April.

versatile ADJ. having many talents; capable of working in many fields. He was a *versatile* athlete; at college he had earned varsity letters in baseball, football, and track.

vertex N. summit. Let us drop a perpendicular line from the *vertex* of the triangle to the base. vertices, PL.

vertigo N. dizziness. We test potential plane pilots for susceptibility to spells of *vertigo*.

verve N. enthusiasm; liveliness. She approached her studies with such *verve* that it was impossible for her to do poorly.

vestige N. trace; remains. We discovered *vestiges* of early Indian life in the cave.

vex N. annoy; distress. Please try not to *vex* your mother; she is doing the best she can.

■ **viable** ADJ. capable of maintaining life; practicable; workable. The infant, though prematurely born, is *viable* and has a good chance to survive.

viand N. food. There was a variety of *viands* at the feast.

vicarious ADJ. acting as a substitute; done by a deputy. Many people get a *vicarious* thrill at the movies by imagining they are the characters on the screen.

vicissitude N. change of fortune. Humbled by life's *vicissitudes,* the last emperor of China worked as a lowly gardener in the palace over which he had once ruled.

victuals N. food. I am very happy to be able to provide you with these *victuals;* I know you are hungry.

vie V. contend; compete. Politicians *vie* with one another, competing for donations and votes.

vigilance N. watchfulness. Eternal *vigilance* is the price of liberty. vigilant, ADJ.

vigor N. active strength. Although he was over seventy years old, Jack had the *vigor* of a man in his prime. vigorous, ADJ.

vignette N. picture; short literary sketch. The *New Yorker* published her latest *vignette.*

vilify V. slander. She is a liar and is always trying to *vilify* my reputation. vilification, N.

vindicate V. clear of charges. I hope to *vindicate* my client and return him to society as a free man.

vindictive ADJ. revengeful. She was very *vindictive* and never forgave an injury.

vintner N. winemaker; seller of wine. The poet wondered what the *vintners* could buy that would be half as precious as the wine they sold.

viper N. poisonous snake. The habitat of the horned *viper*, a particularly venomous snake, is in sandy regions like the Sahara or the Sinai peninsula.

virile ADJ. manly. I do not accept the premise that a man is *virile* only when he is belligerent.

virtual ADJ. in essence; for practical purposes. She is a *virtual* financial wizard when it comes to money matters.

virtue N. goodness; moral excellence; good quality. A *virtue* carried to extremes can turn into something resembling vice; humility, for example, can degenerate into servility and spinelessness.

virtuoso N. highly skilled artist. The child prodigy Yehudi Menuhin grew into a *virtuoso* whose *virtuosity* on the violin thrilled millions. virtuosity, N.

virulent ADJ. extremely poisonous. The virus is highly *virulent* and has made many of us ill for days.

virus N. disease communicator. The doctors are looking for a specific medicine to control this *virus.*

visage N. face; appearance. The stern *visage* of the judge indicated that she had decided to impose a severe penalty.

visceral ADJ. felt in one's inner organs. She disliked the *visceral* sensations she had whenever she rode the roller coaster.

viscid ADJ. adhesive; gluey. The trunk of the maple tree was *viscid* with sap.

■ **viscous** ADJ. sticky, gluey. Melted tar is a *viscous* substance. viscosity, N.

vise N. tool for holding work in place. Before filing its edges, the keysmith took the blank key and fixed it firmly between the jaws of a *vise.*

visionary ADJ. produced by imagination; fanciful; mystical. She was given to *visionary* schemes that never materialized. also N.

vital ADJ. vibrant and lively; critical; living, breathing. The *vital*, highly energetic first aid instructor stressed that it was *vital* in examining accident victims to note their *vital* signs.

vitiate V. spoil the effect of; make inoperative. Fraud will *vitiate* the contract.

vitreous ADJ. pertaining to or resembling glass. Although this plastic has many *vitreous* qualities such as transparency, it is unbreakable.

vitriolic ADJ. corrosive; sarcastic. Such *vitriolic* criticism is uncalled for.

vituperative ADJ. abusive; scolding. He became more *vituperative* as he realized that we were not going to grant him his wish.

vivacious ADJ. lively or animated; sprightly. She had always been *vivacious* and sparkling.

vivisection N. act of dissecting living animals. The Society for the Prevention of Cruelty to Animals opposed *vivisection* and deplored the practice of using animals in scientific experiments.

vixen N. female fox; ill-tempered woman. Aware that she was right once again, he lost his temper and called her a shrew and a *vixen.*

vociferous ADJ. clamorous; noisy. The crowd grew *vociferous* in its anger and threatened to take the law into its own hands.

vogue N. popular fashion. Jeans became the *vogue* on many college campuses.

Test

Word List 49 *Synonyms and Antonyms*

Each of the following questions consists of a word in capital letters, followed by five lettered words or phrases. Choose the lettered word or phrase that is most nearly similar or opposite in meaning to the word in capital letters and write the letter of your choice on your answer paper.

721. VENAL (A) springlike (B) honest (C) angry (D) indifferent (E) going
722. VENERATE (A) revere (B) age (C) reject (D) reverberate (E) degenerate
723. VENIAL (A) unforgivable (B) unforgettable (C) unmistaken (D) fearful (E) fragrant
724. VERACIOUS (A) worried (B) slight (C) alert (D) truthful (E) instrumental
725. VERDANT (A) poetic (B) green (C) red (D) autumnal (E) frequent
726. VERITY (A) sanctity (B) reverence (C) falsehood (D) rarity (E) household
727. VESTIGE (A) trek (B) trail (C) trace (D) trial (E) tract
728. VIABLE (A) moribund (B) salable (C) useful (D) foolish (E) inadequate
729. VIAND (A) wand (B) gown (C) food (D) orchestra (E) frock
730. VICARIOUS (A) substitutional (B) aggressive (C) sporadic (D) reverent (E) internal
731. VIGILANCE (A) bivouac (B) guide (C) watchfulness (D) mob rule (E) posse
732. VILIFY (A) erect (B) eulogize (C) better (D) magnify (E) horrify
733. VINDICTIVE (A) revengeful (B) fearful (C) divided (D) literal (E) convincing
734. VIRULENT (A) sensuous (B) malignant (C) masculine (D) conforming (E) approaching
735. VISAGE (A) doubt (B) personality (C) hermitage (D) face (E) armor

Word List 50 volatile–zephyr

volatile ADJ. changeable; explosive; evaporating rapidly. The political climate today is extremely *volatile:* no one can predict what the electorate will do next. Ethyl chloride is an extremely *volatile* liquid: it evaporates instantly. volatility, N.

volition N. act of making a conscious choice. She selected this dress of her own *volition*.

voluble ADJ. fluent; glib. She was a *voluble* speaker, always ready to talk.

voluminous ADJ. bulky; large. Despite her family burdens, she kept up a *voluminous* correspondence with her friends.

voluptuous ADJ. gratifying the senses. The nobility during the Renaissance led *voluptuous* lives.

voracious ADJ. ravenous. The wolf is a *voracious* animal, its hunger never satisfied.

vortex N. whirlwind; whirlpool; center of turbulence; predicament into which one is inexorably plunged. Sucked into the *vortex* of the tornado, Dorothy and Toto were carried from Kansas to Oz.

vouchsafe V. grant condescendingly; guarantee. I can safely *vouchsafe* you fair return on your investment.

voyeur N. Peeping Tom. Jill called Jack a *voyeur* when she caught him aiming his binoculars at a bedroom window of the house next door.

vulnerable ADJ. susceptible to wounds. Achilles was *vulnerable* only in his heel.

vulpine ADJ. like a fox; crafty. She disliked his sly ways, but granted him a certain *vulpine* intelligence.

waffle V. speak equivocally about an issue. When asked directly about the governor's involvement in the savings and loan scandal, the press secretary *waffled,* talking all around the issue.

waft V. moved gently by wind or waves. Daydreaming, he gazed at the leaves that *wafted* past his window.

waggish ADJ. mischievous; humorous; tricky. He was a prankster who, unfortunately, often overlooked the damage he could cause with his *waggish* tricks. wag, N.

waif N. homeless child or animal. Although he already had eight cats, he could not resist adopting yet another feline *waif*.

waive V. give up temporarily; yield. I will *waive* my rights in this matter in order to expedite our reaching a proper decision.

wallow V. roll in; indulge in; become helpless. The hippopotamus loves to *wallow* in the mud.

wan ADJ. having a pale or sickly color; pallid. Suckling asked, "Why so pale and *wan,* fond lover?"

wane V. grow gradually smaller. From now until December 21, the winter solstice, the hours of daylight will *wane*.

wangle V. wiggle out; fake. She tried to *wangle* an invitation to the party.

wanton ADJ. unrestrained; willfully malicious; unchaste. Pointing to the stack of bills, Sheldon criticized Sarah for her *wanton* expenditures. In response, Sara accused Sheldon of making an unfounded, *wanton* attack.

warble V. sing; babble. Every morning the birds *warbled* outside her window. also N.

warrant V. justify; authorize. Before the judge issues the injunction, you must convince her this action is *warranted*.

warranty N. guarantee; assurance by seller. The purchaser of this automobile is protected by the manufacturer's *warranty* that he will replace any defective part for five years or 50,000 miles.

warren N. tunnels in which rabbits live; crowded conditions in which people live. The tenement was a veritable *warren*, packed with people too poor to live elsewhere.

wary ADJ. very cautious. The spies grew *wary* as they approached the sentry.

wastrel N. profligate. He was denounced as a *wastrel* who had dissipated his inheritance.

wax V. increase; grow. With proper handling, his fortunes *waxed* and he became rich.

waylay V. ambush; lie in wait. They agreed to *waylay* their victim as he passed through the dark alley going home.

wean V. accustom a baby not to nurse; give up a cherished activity. He decided he would *wean* himself away from eating junk food and stick to fruits and vegetables.

weather V. endure the effects of weather or other forces. He *weathered* the changes in his personal life with difficulty, as he had no one in whom to confide.

welt N. mark from a beating or whipping. The evidence of child abuse was very clear; Jennifer's small body was covered with *welts* and bruises.

welter N. turmoil; bewildering jumble. The existing *welter* of overlapping federal and state proclaims cries out for immediate reform.

welter V. wallow. At the height of the battle, the casualties were so numerous that the victims *weltered* in their blood while waiting for medical attention.

wheedle V. cajole; coax; deceive by flattery. She knows she can *wheedle* almost anything she wants from her father.

whelp N. young wolf, dog, tiger, etc. This collie *whelp* won't do for breeding, but he'd make a fine pet.

whet V. sharpen; stimulate. The odors from the kitchen are *whetting* my appetite; I will be ravenous by the time the meal is served.

whiff N. puff or gust (of air, scent, etc.); hint. The slightest *whiff* of Old Spice cologne brought memories of George to her mind.

■ **whimsical** ADJ. capricious; fanciful. He dismissed his generous gift to his college as a sentimental fancy, an old man's *whimsical* gesture. whimsy, N.

whinny V. neigh like a horse. When he laughed through his nose, it sounded as if he *whinnied*.

whit N. smallest speck. There is not a *whit* of intelligence or understanding in your observations.

whittle V. pare; cut off bits. As a present for Aunt Polly, Tom *whittled* some clothespins out of a chunk of wood.

whorl N. ring of leaves around stem; ring. Identification by fingerprints is based on the difference in shape and number of the *whorls* on the fingers.

willful ADJ. intentional; headstrong. Donald had planned to kill his wife for months; clearly, her death was a case of deliberate, *willful* murder, not a crime of passion committed by a hasty, *willful* youth unable to foresee the consequences of his deeds.

wily ADJ. cunning; artful. She is as *wily* as a fox in avoiding trouble.

wince V. shrink back; flinch. The screech of the chalk on the blackboard made her *wince*.

windfall N. fallen fruit; unexpected lucky event. This huge tax refund is quite a *windfall*.

winnow V. sift; separate good parts from bad. This test will *winnow* out the students who study from those who don't bother.

winsome ADJ. agreeable; gracious; engaging. By her *winsome* manner, she made herself liked by everyone who met her.

wispy ADJ. thin; slight; barely discernible. Worried about preserving his few *wispy* tufts of hair, Walter carefully massaged his scalp and applied hair restorer every night.

wistful ADJ. vaguely longing; sadly pensive. With a last *wistful* glance at the happy couples dancing in the hall, Sue headed back to her room to study for her exam.

withdrawn ADJ. introverted; remote. Rebuffed by his colleagues, the initially outgoing young researcher became increasingly *withdrawn*.

wither V. shrivel; decay. Cut flowers are beautiful for a day, but all too soon they *wither*.

witless ADJ. foolish; idiotic. Such *witless* and fatuous statements will create the impression that you are an ignorant individual.

witticism N. witty saying; facetious remark. What you regard as *witticisms* are often offensive to sensitive people.

wizardry N. sorcery; magic. Merlin amazed the knights with his *wizardry*.

wizened ADJ. withered; shriveled. The *wizened* old man in the home for the aged was still active and energetic.

wont N. custom; habitual procedure. As was his *wont*, he jogged two miles every morning before going to work.

worldly ADJ. engrossed in matters of this earth; not spiritual. You must leave your *worldly* goods behind you when you go to meet your Maker.

wrangle V. quarrel; obtain through arguing; herd cattle. They *wrangled* over their inheritance.

wrath N. anger; fury. She turned to him, full of *wrath*, and said, "What makes you think I'll accept lower pay for this job than you get?"

wreak V. inflict. I am afraid he will *wreak* his vengeance on the innocent as well as the guilty.

wrench V. pull; strain; twist. She *wrenched* free of her attacker and landed a powerful kick to his kneecap.

wrest V. pull away; take by violence. With only ten seconds left to play, our team *wrested* victory from their grasp.

writ N. written command issued by a court. The hero of Leonard's novel is a process server who invents unorthodox ways of serving *writs* on reluctant parties.

writhe V. squirm, twist. He was *writhing* in pain, desperate for the drug his body required.

wry ADJ. twisted; with a humorous twist. We enjoy Dorothy Parker's verse for its *wry* wit.

xenophobia N. fear or hatred of foreigners. When the refugee arrived in America, he was unprepared for the *xenophobia* he found there.

yen N. longing; urge. She had a *yen* to get away and live on her own for a while.

yeoman N. man owning small estate; middle-class farmer. It was not the aristocrat but the *yeoman* who determined the nation's policies.

yield N. amount produced; crop; income on investment. An experienced farmer can estimate the annual *yield* of his acres with surprising accuracy. also V.

yield V. give in; surrender. The wounded knight refused to *yield* to his foe.

yoke V. join together, unite. I don't wish to be *yoked* to him in marriage, as if we were cattle pulling a plow. also N.

yokel N. country bumpkin. At school, his classmates regarded him as a *yokel* and laughed at his rustic mannerisms.

yore N. time past. He dreamed of the elegant homes of *yore*, but gave no thought to their inelegant plumbing.

zany ADJ. crazy; comic. I can watch the Marx brothers' *zany* antics for hours.

zeal N. eager enthusiasm. Wang's *zeal* was contagious; soon all his fellow students were busily making posters, inspired by his ardent enthusiasm for the cause. zealous, ADJ.

■ **zealot** N. fanatic; person who shows excessive zeal. It is good to have a few *zealots* in our group for their enthusiasm is contagious.

zenith N. point directly overhead in the sky; summit. When the sun was at its *zenith,* the glare was not as strong as at sunrise and sunset.

zephyr N. gentle breeze; west wind. When these *zephyrs* blow, it is good to be in an open boat under a full sail.

Test

Word List 50   *Synonyms*

Each of the questions below consists of a word in capital letters, followed by five lettered words or phrases. Choose the lettered word or phrase that is most nearly similar in meaning to the word in capital letters and write the letter of your choice on your answer paper.

736. VOLUBLE (A) worthwhile (B) serious (C) terminal (D) loquacious (E) circular

737. VORACIOUS (A) ravenous (B) spacious (C) truthful (D) pacific (E) tenacious

738. VOUCHSAFE (A) borrow (B) grant (C) punish (D) desire (E) qualify

739. WAIF (A) soldier (B) urchin (C) surrender (D) breeze (E) spouse

740. WANTON (A) needy (B) passive (C) rumored (D) oriental (E) unchaste

741. WARRANTY (A) threat (B) guarantee (C) order for arrest (D) issue (E) fund

742. WASTREL (A) refuse (B) spendthrift (C) mortal (D) tolerance (E) song

743. WAYLAY (A) ambush (B) journey (C) rest (D) roadmap (E) song

744. WELTER (A) heat (B) greeting (C) recovery (D) universe (E) tumult

745. WHINNY (A) complain (B) hurry (C) request (D) neigh (E) gallop

746. WINDFALL (A) unexpected gain (B) widespread destruction (C) calm (D) autumn (E) wait

747. WINSOME (A) victorious (B) gracious (C) married (D) permanent (E) pained

748. WIZENED (A) magical (B) clever (C) shriveled (D) swift (E) active

749. YEOMAN (A) masses (B) middle-class farmer (C) proletarian (D) indigent person (E) man of rank

750. ZEALOT (A) beginner (B) patron (C) fanatic (D) murderer (E) leper

Answer Key

Test—Word List 1

1. E	6. E	11. A
2. A	7. B	12. E
3. C	8. E	13. A
4. D	9. A	14. D
5. B	10. A	15. C

Test—Word List 2

16. E	21. A	26. B
17. B	22. A	27. D
18. A	23. B	28. B
19. D	24. B	29. C
20. A	25. B	30. D

Test—Word List 3

31. C	36. E	41. B
32. C	37. C	42. E
33. D	38. B	43. E
34. D	39. E	44. C
35. A	40. D	45. A

Test—Word List 4

46. A	51. C	56. E
47. A	52. A	57. C
48. B	53. C	58. D
49. D	54. B	59. D
50. B	55. D	60. C

Test—Word List 5

61. E	66. A	71. D
62. D	67. C	72. C
63. B	68. C	73. C
64. C	69. B	74. B
65. C	70. C	75. D

Test—Word List 6

76. D	81. A	86. C
77. B	82. B	87. A
78. D	83. B	88. E
79. A	84. E	89. E
80. E	85. E	90. C

Test—Word List 7

91. B	96. B	101. D
92. B	97. A	102. B
93. B	98. D	103. A
94. D	99. B	104. A
95. B	100. C	105. B

Test—Word List 8

106. D	111. B	116. B
107. E	112. A	117. D
108. A	113. D	118. A
109. C	114. C	119. C
110. E	115. D	120. B

Test—Word List 9

121. D	126. E	131. A
122. E	127. A	132. D
123. E	128. D	133. C
124. C	129. B	134. B
125. C	130. E	135. A

Test—Word List 10

136. E	141. B	146. E
137. B	142. E	147. E
138. D	143. D	148. C
139. C	144. D	149. A
140. A	145. D	150. D

Test—Word List 11

151. B	156. C	161. B
152. B	157. C	162. D
153. A	158. E	163. D
154. A	159. E	164. A
155. A	160. B	165. B

Test—Word List 12

166. C	171. C	176. B
167. B	172. B	177. B
168. C	173. A	178. A
169. D	174. A	179. C
170. D	175. B	180. A

Test—Word List 13

181. A	186. A	191. C
182. E	187. B	192. B
183. D	188. C	193. E
184. D	189. B	194. A
185. A	190. C	195. A

Test—Word List 14

196. D	201. C	206. B
197. E	202. C	207. D
198. B	203. C	208. C
199. A	204. B	209. E
200. C	205. B	210. D

Test—Word List 15

211. C	216. C	221. B
212. A	217. A	222. E
213. D	218. A	223. A
214. D	219. C	224. A
215. D	220. D	225. B

Test—Word List 16

226. D	231. B	236. A
227. A	232. C	237. D
228. C	233. D	238. C
229. E	234. C	239. A
230. E	235. E	240. B

Test—Word List 17

241. A	246. C	251. D
242. A	247. A	252. A
243. B	248. A	253. E
244. E	249. C	254. B
245. E	250. D	255. B

Test—Word List 18

256. A	261. D	266. A
257. A	262. D	267. A
258. C	263. E	268. C
259. D	264. C	269. B
260. A	265. B	270. E

Test—Word List 19

271. A	276. A	281. A
272. D	277. A	282. D
273. E	278. D	283. C
274. C	279. C	284. B
275. E	280. B	285. C

Test—Word List 20

286. A	291. A	296. E
287. B	292. A	297. D
288. B	293. D	298. A
289. B	294. C	299. A
290. D	295. C	300. B

Test—Word List 21

301. B	306. E	311. E
302. B	307. C	312. A
303. C	308. B	313. B
304. C	309. D	314. D
305. C	310. D	315. C

Test—Word List 22

316. D	321. E	326. C
317. A	322. A	327. C
318. A	323. B	328. A
319. D	324. C	329. B
320. A	325. E	330. D

Test—Word List 23

331. B	336. A	341. A
332. A	337. D	342. A
333. B	338. B	343. E
334. E	339. C	344. B
335. C	340. D	345. A

Test—Word List 24

346. C	351. D	356. B
347. B	352. A	357. C
348. C	353. A	358. A
349. A	354. A	359. B
350. B	355. B	360. D

Test—Word List 25

361. A	366. B	371. E
362. E	367. B	372. B
363. B	368. C	373. D
364. D	369. D	374. C
365. E	370. A	375. A

Test—Word List 26

376. C	381. B	386. B
377. A	382. A	387. E
378. B	383. C	388. E
379. B	384. C	389. E
380. B	385. C	390. A

Test—Word List 27

391. A	396. E	401. B
392. D	397. E	402. B
393. B	398. C	403. A
394. D	399. A	404. C
395. B	400. D	405. B

Test—Word List 28

406. B	411. B	416. B
407. A	412. E	417. A
408. E	413. D	418. D
409. E	414. E	419. D
410. C	415. C	420. A

Test—Word List 29

421. B	426. D	431. A
422. A	427. E	432. C
423. B	428. B	433. B
424. B	429. A	434. C
425. C	430. E	435. A

Test—Word List 30

436. A	441. A	446. E
437. A	442. B	447. B
438. B	443. D	448. C
439. D	444. B	449. E
440. C	445. A	450. B

Test—Word List 31

451. B	456. A	461. E
452. E	457. C	462. C
453. C	458. C	463. A
454. C	459. A	464. B
455. B	460. B	465. A

Test—Word List 32

466. B	471. D	476. D
467. C	472. C	477. B
468. C	473. B	478. A
469. A	474. A	479. C
470. C	475. B	480. A

Test—Word List 33

481. C	486. A	491. E
482. B	487. B	492. C
483. E	488. C	493. E
484. D	489. D	494. B
485. B	490. B	495. A

Test—Word List 34

496. D	501. B	506. D
497. A	502. B	507. D
498. D	503. A	508. C
499. A	504. E	509. C
500. E	505. C	510. A

Test—Word List 35

511. A	516. C	521. E
512. C	517. B	522. A
513. C	518. D	523. C
514. C	519. C	524. E
515. B	520. A	525. E

Test—Word List 36

526. A	531. E	536. A
527. D	532. B	537. D
528. A	533. C	538. D
529. B	534. C	539. D
530. E	535. B	540. D

Test—Word List 37

541. C	546. A	551. A
542. C	547. A	552. C
543. D	548. C	553. E
544. E	549. B	554. B
545. C	550. A	555. A

Test—Word List 38

556. E	561. E	566. A
557. D	562. E	567. D
558. C	563. B	568. C
559. B	564. A	569. D
560. B	565. E	570. C

Test—Word List 39

571. B	576. C	581. C
572. B	577. D	582. B
573. E	578. A	583. A
574. A	579. C	584. D
575. A	580. E	585. A

Test—Word List 40

586. E	591. C	596. D
587. B	592. A	597. D
588. D	593. B	598. B
589. C	594. A	599. D
590. A	595. D	600. E

Test—Word List 41

601. E	606. B	611. C
602. B	607. B	612. D
603. A	608. A	613. B
604. D	609. D	614. A
605. A	610. B	615. A

Test—Word List 42

616. C	621. D	626. B
617. A	622. E	627. D
618. B	623. A	628. A
619. C	624. D	629. D
620. D	625. C	630. E

Test—Word List 43

631. C	636. C	641. D
632. C	637. E	642. A
633. E	638. C	643. E
634. A	639. E	644. A
635. C	640. D	645. B

Test—Word List 44

646. A	651. B	656. A
647. B	652. A	657. B
648. D	653. D	658. A
649. A	654. C	659. C
650. E	655. C	660. C

Test—Word List 45

661. C	666. C	671. C
662. C	667. B	672. D
663. A	668. A	673. A
664. C	669. A	674. D
665. B	670. A	675. A

Test—Word List 46

676. D	681. D	686. B
677. B	682. B	687. A
678. B	683. A	688. B
679. C	684. E	689. E
680. C	685. B	690. E

Test—Word List 47

691. A	696. A	701. A
692. D	697. C	702. D
693. B	698. B	703. B
694. C	699. C	704. D
695. A	700. E	705. E

Test—Word List 48

706. A	711. B	716. D
707. A	712. B	717. D
708. B	713. A	718. C
709. C	714. A	719. B
710. C	715. E	720. C

Test—Word List 49

721. B	726. C	731. C
722. A	727. C	732. B
723. A	728. A	733. A
724. D	729. C	734. B
725. B	730. A	735. D

Test—Word List 50

736. D	741. B	746. A
737. A	742. B	747. B
738. B	743. A	748. C
739. B	744. E	749. B
740. E	745. D	750. C

Basic Word Parts

Words are made up of word parts: prefixes, suffixes and roots. A knowledge of these word parts and their meanings can help you determine the meanings of unfamiliar words.

Common Prefixes

A *prefix* is a syllable that precedes the root or stem and changes or refines its meaning.

Prefix	Meaning	Illustration
ab, abs	from, away from	*abduct* lead away, kidnap *abjure* renounce
ad, ac, af, ag, an, **ap, ar, as, at**	to, forward	*adit* entrance *accord* agreement, harmony *affliction* cause of distress *aggregation* collection *annexation* addition *appease* bring toward peace *arraignment* indictment *assumption* arrogance, taking for granted *attendance* presence, the persons present
ambi	both	*ambiguous* of double meaning *ambivalent* having two conflicting emotions
an, a	without	*anarchy* lack of government *amoral* without moral sense
ante	before	*antecedent* preceding event or word *antediluvian* ancient (before the flood)
anti	against, opposite	*antipathy* hatred *antithetical* exactly opposite
arch	chief, first	*archetype* original *archbishop* chief bishop
be	over, thoroughly	*bedaub* smear over *befuddle* confuse thoroughly
bi	two	*bicameral* composed of two houses (Congress) *biennial* every two years
cata	down	*catastrophe* disaster *cataract* waterfall *catapult* hurl (throw down)
circum	around	*circumnavigate* sail around (the globe) *circumspect* cautious (looking around) *circumscribe* limit (place a circle around)
com, co, col, con, **cor**	with, together	*combine* merge with *coeditor* joint editor *collateral* subordinate, connected *conference* meeting *corroborate* confirm

Prefix	Meaning	Illustration
contra, contro	against	*contravene* conflict with *controversy* dispute
de	down, away	*debase* lower in value *decadence* deterioration
demi	partly, half	*demigod* partly divine being
di	two	*dichotomy* division into two parts *dilemma* choice between two bad alternatives
dia	across	*diagonal* across a figure *diameter* distance across a circle
dis, dif	not, apart	*discord* lack of harmony *differ* disagree (carry apart)
dys	faulty, bad	*dyslexia* faulty ability to read *dyspepsia* indigestion
ex, e	out	*expel* drive out *eject* throw out
extra, extro	beyond, outside	*extracurricular* beyond the curriculum *extraterritorial* beyond a nation's bounds *extrovert* person interested chiefly in external objects and actions
hyper	above; excessively	*hyperbole* exaggeration *hyperventilate* breathe at an excessive rate
hypo	beneath; lower	*hypoglycemia* low blood sugar
in, il, im, ir	not	*inefficient* not efficient *inarticulate* not clear or distinct *illegible* not readable *impeccable* not capable of sinning; flawless *irrevocable* not able to be called back
in, il, im, ir	in, on, upon	*invite* call in *illustration* something that makes clear *impression* effect upon mind or feelings *irradiate* shine upon
inter	between, among	*intervene* come between *international* between nations *interjection* a statement thrown in
intra, intro	within	*intramural* within a school *introvert* person who turns within himself
macro	large, long	*macrobiotic* tending to prolong life *macrocosm* the great world (the entire universe)
mega	great, million	*megalomania* delusions of grandeur *megaton* explosive force of a million tons of TNT
meta	involving change	*metamorphosis* change of form
micro	small	*microcosm* miniature universe *microscopic* extremely small

Prefix	Meaning	Illustration
mis	bad, improper	*misdemeanor* minor crime; bad conduct *mischance* unfortunate accident
mis	hatred	*misanthrope* person who hates mankind *misogynist* woman-hater
mono	one	*monarchy* government by one ruler *monotheism* belief in one god
multi	many	*multifarious* having many parts *multitudinous* numerous
neo	new	*neologism* newly coined word *neophyte* beginner; novice
non	not	*noncommittal* undecided
ob, oc, of, op	against	*obloquy* infamy; disgrace *occlude* close; block out *offend* insult *opponent* someone who struggles against; foe
olig	few	*oligarchy* government by a few
pan	all, every	*panacea* cure-all *panorama* unobstructed view in all directions
para	beyond, related	*parallel* similar *paraphrase* restate; translate
per	through, completely	*permeable* allowing passage through *pervade* spread throughout
peri	around, near	*perimeter* outer boundary *periphery* edge
poly	many	*polyglot* speaking several languages
post	after	*posthumous* after death
pre	before	*preamble* introductory statement *premonition* forewarning
prim	first	*primordial* existing at the dawn of time *primogeniture* state of being the first born
pro	forward, in favor of	*propulsive* driving forward *proponent* supporter
proto	first	*prototype* first of its kind
pseudo	false	*pseudonym* pen name
re	again, back	*reiterate* repeat *reimburse* pay back
retro	backward	*retrospect* looking back *retroactive* effective as of a past date
se	away, aside	*secede* withdraw *seclude* shut away
semi	half, partly	*semiconscious* partly conscious

Prefix	Meaning	Illustration
sub, suc, suf, sug, sup, sus	under, less	*subjugate* bring under control *succumb* yield; cease to resist *suffuse* spread through *suggest* hint *suppress* put down by force *suspend* delay; temporarily cease
super, sur	over, above	*supernatural* above natural things *surtax* additional tax
syn, sym, syl, sys	with, together	*synchronize* time together *sympathize* pity; identify with *syllogism* explanation of how ideas relate *system* network
tele	far	*telegraphic* communicated over a distance
trans	across	*transport* carry across
ultra	beyond, excessive	*ultracritical* exceedingly critical
un	not	*unkempt* not combed; disheveled
under	below	*underling* someone inferior
uni	one	*unison* oneness of pitch; complete accord
vice	in place of	*viceroy* governor acting in place of a king
with	away, against	*withstand* stand up against; resist

Common Roots and Stems

Roots are basic words which have been carried over into English. *Stems* are variations of roots brought about by changes in declension or conjugation.

Root or Stem	Meaning	Illustration
ac, acr	sharp	*acrimonious* bitter; caustic *acerbity* bitterness of temper *acidulate* make somewhat acid or sour
aev, ev	age, era	*primeval* of the first age *coeval* of the same age or era *medieval* or *mediaeval* of the Middle Ages
ag, act	to do	*act* deed *agent* doer
agog	leader	*demagogue* false leader of people *pedagogue* teacher (leader of children)
agri, agrari	field	*agrarian* one who works in the field *agriculture* cultivation of fields *peregrination* wandering (through fields)

Root or Stem	Meaning	Illustration
ali	another	*alias* assumed (another) name *alienate* estrange (turn away from another)
alt	high	*altitude* height *altimeter* instrument for measuring height
alter	other	*altruistic* unselfish, considering others *alter ego* a second self
am	love	*amorous* loving, especially sexually *amity* friendship *amicable* friendly
anim	mind, soul	*animadvert* cast criticism upon *unanimous* of one mind *magnanimity* greatness of mind or spirit
ann, enn	year	*annuity* yearly remittance *biennial* every two years *perennial* present all year; persisting for several years
anthrop	human beings	*anthropology* study of human beings *misanthrope* hater of humankind *philanthropy* love of humankind; charity
apt	fit	*aptitude* skill *adapt* make suitable or fit
aqua	water	*aqueduct* passageway for conducting water *aquatic* living in water *aqua fortis* nitric acid (strong water)
arch	ruler, first	*archaeology* study of antiquities (study of first things) *monarch* sole ruler *anarchy* lack of government
aster	star	*astronomy* study of the stars *asterisk* starlike type character (*) *disaster* catastrophe (contrary star)
aud, audit	to hear	*audible* able to be heard *auditorium* place where people may be heard *audience* hearers
auto	self	*autocracy* rule by one person (self) *automobile* vehicle that moves by itself *autobiography* story of one's own life
belli	war	*bellicose* inclined to fight *belligerent* inclined to wage war *rebellious* resisting authority
ben, bon	good	*benefactor* one who does good deeds *benevolence* charity (wishing good) *bonus* something extra above regular pay
biblio	book	*bibliography* list of books *bibliophile* lover of books *Bible* The Book

Root or Stem	Meaning	Illustration
bio	life	*biography* writing about a person's life *biology* study of living things *biochemist* student of the chemistry of living things
breve	short	*brevity* briefness *abbreviate* shorten *breviloquent* marked by brevity of speech
cad, cas	to fall	*decadent* deteriorating *cadence* intonation, musical movement *cascade* waterfall
cap, capt, cept, cip	to take	*capture* seize *participate* take part *precept* wise saying (originally a command)
capit, capt	head	*decapitate* remove (cut off) someone's head *captain* chief
carn	flesh	*carnivorous* flesh-eating *carnage* destruction of life *carnal* fleshly
ced, cess	to yield, to go	*recede* go back, withdraw *antecedent* that which goes before *process* go forward
celer	swift	*celerity* swiftness *decelerate* reduce swiftness *accelerate* increase swiftness
cent	one hundred	*century* one hundred years *centennial* one-hundredth anniversary *centipede* many-footed, wingless animal
chron	time	*chronology* timetable of events *anachronism* a thing out of time sequence *chronicle* register events in order of time
cid, cis	to cut, to kill	*incision* a cut (surgical) *homicide* killing of a human being *fratricide* killing of a brother
cit, citat	to call, to start	*incite* stir up, start up *excite* stir up *recitation* a recalling (or repeating) aloud
civi	citizen	*civilization* society of citizens, culture *civilian* member of community *civil* courteous
clam, clamat	to cry out	*clamorous* loud *declamation* speech *acclamation* shouted approval
claud, claus, clos, clud	to close	*claustrophobia* fear of close places *enclose* close in *conclude* finish

Root or Stem	Meaning	Illustration
cognosc, cognit	to learn	*agnostic* lacking knowledge, skeptical *incognito* traveling under assumed name *cognition* knowledge
compl	to fill	*complete* filled out *complement* that which completes something *comply* fulfill
cord	heart	*accord* agreement (from the heart) *cordial* friendly *discord* lack of harmony
corpor	body	*incorporate* organize into a body *corporeal* pertaining to the body, fleshly *corpse* dead body
cred, credit	to believe	*incredulous* not believing, skeptical *credulity* gullibility *credence* belief
cur	to care	*curator* person who has the care of something *sinecure* position without responsibility *secure* safe
curr, curs	to run	*excursion* journey *cursory* brief *precursor* forerunner
da, dat	to give	*data* facts, statistics *mandate* command *date* given time
deb, debit	to owe	*debt* something owed *indebtedness* debt *debenture* bond
dem	people	*democracy* rule of the people *demagogue* (false) leader of the people *epidemic* widespread (among the people)
derm	skin	*epidermis* skin *pachyderm* thick-skinned quadruped *dermatology* study of skin and its disorders
di, diurn	day	*dairy* a daily record of activities, feelings, etc. *diurnal* pertaining to daytime
dic, dict	to say	*abdicate* renounce *diction* speech *verdict* statement of jury
doc, doct	to teach	*docile* obedient; easily taught *document* something that provides evidence *doctor* learned person (originally, teacher)
domin	to rule	*dominate* have power over *domain* land under rule *dominant* prevailing

Root or Stem	Meaning	Illustration
duc, duct	to lead	*viaduct* arched roadway *aqueduct* artificial waterway
dynam	power, strength	*dynamic* powerful *dynamite* powerful explosive *dynamo* engine making electric power
ego	I	*egoist* person who is self-interested *egotist* selfish person *egocentric* revolving about self
erg, urg	work	*energy* power *ergatocracy* rule of the workers *metallurgy* science and technology of metals
err	to wander	*error* mistake *erratic* not reliable, wandering *knight-errant* wandering knight
eu	good, well, beautiful	*eupeptic* having good digestion *eulogize* praise *euphemism* pleasant way of saying something blunt
fac, fic, fec, fect	to make, to do	*factory* place where things are made *fiction* manufactured story *affect* cause to change
fall, fals	to deceive	*fallacious* misleading *infallible* not prone to error, perfect *falsify* lie
fer, lat	to bring, to bear	*transfer* bring from one place to another *translate* bring from one language to another *conifer* bearing cones, as pine trees
fid	belief, faith	*infidel* nonbeliever, heathen *confidence* assurance, belief
fin	end, limit	*confine* keep within limits *finite* having definite limits
flect, flex	to bend	*flexible* able to bend *deflect* bend away, turn aside
fort	luck, chance	*fortuitous* accidental, occurring by chance *fortunate* lucky
fort	strong	*fortitude* strength, firmness of mind *fortification* strengthening *fortress* stronghold
frag, fract	to break	*fragile* easily broken *infraction* breaking of a rule *fractious* unruly, tending to break rules
fug	to flee	*fugitive* someone who flees *refuge* shelter, home for someone fleeing
fus	to pour	*effusive* gushing, pouring out *diffuse* widespread (poured in many directions)

Root or Stem	Meaning	Illustration
gam	marriage	*monogamy* marriage to one person *bigamy* marriage to two people at the same time *polygamy* having many wives or husbands at the same time
gen, gener	class, race	*genus* group of animals or plants with similar traits *generic* characteristic of a class *gender* class organized by sex
grad, gress	to go, to step	*digress* go astray (from the main point) *regress* go backward *gradual* step by step, by degrees
graph, gram	writing	*epigram* pithy statement *telegram* instantaneous message over great distance *stenography* shorthand (writing narrowly)
greg	flock, herd	*gregarious* tending to group together as in a herd *aggregate* group, total *egregious* conspicuously bad; shocking
helio	sun	*heliotrope* flower that faces the sun *heliograph* instrument that uses the sun's rays to send signals
it, itiner	journey, road	*exit* way out *itinerary* plan of journey
jac, jact, jec	to throw	*projectile* missile; something thrown forward *trajectory* path taken by thrown object *ejaculatory* casting or throwing out
jur, jurat	to swear	*perjure* testify falsely *jury* group of men and women sworn to seek the truth *adjuration* solemn urging
labor, laborat	to work	*laboratory* place where work is done *collaborate* work together with others *laborious* difficult
leg, lect, lig	to choose, to read	*election* choice *legible* able to be read *eligible* able to be selected
leg	law	*legislature* law-making body *legitimate* lawful *legal* lawful
liber, libr	book	*library* collection of books *libretto* the "book" of a musical play *libel* slander (originally found in a little book)
liber	free	*liberation* the fact of setting free *liberal* generous (giving freely); tolerant
log	word, study	*entomology* study of insects *etymology* study of word parts and derivations *monologue* speech by one person

Root or Stem	Meaning	Illustration
loqu, locut	to talk	*soliloquy* speech by one individual *loquacious* talkative *elocution* speech
luc	light	*elucidate* enlighten *lucid* clear *translucent* allowing some light to pass through
magn	great	*magnify* enlarge *magnanimity* generosity, greatness of soul *magnitude* greatness, extent
mal	bad	*malevolent* wishing evil *malediction* curse *malefactor* evil-doer
man	hand	*manufacture* create (make by hand) *manuscript* written by hand *emancipate* free (let go from the hand)
mar	sea	*maritime* connected with seafaring *submarine* undersea craft *mariner* seafarer
mater, matr	mother	*maternal* pertaining to motherhood *matriarch* female ruler of a family, group, or state *matrilineal* descended on the mother's side
mit, miss	to send	*missile* projectile *dismiss* send away *transmit* send across
mob, mot, mov	to move	*mobilize* cause to move *motility* ability to move *immovable* not able to be moved
mon, monit	to warn	*admonish* warn *premonition* foreboding *monitor* watcher (warner)
mori, mort	to die	*mortuary* funeral parlor *moribund* dying *immortal* not dying
morph	shape, form	*amorphous* formless, lacking shape *metamorphosis* change of shape *anthropomorphic* in human shape
mut	to change	*immutable* not able to be changed *mutate* undergo a great change *mutability* changeableness, inconstancy
nat	born	*innate* from birth *prenatal* before birth *nativity* birth
nav	ship	*navigate* sail a ship *circumnavigate* sail around the world *naval* pertaining to ships

Root or Stem	Meaning	Illustration
neg	to deny	*negation* denial *renege* deny, go back on one's word *renegade* turncoat, traitor
nomen	name	*nomenclature* act of naming, terminology *nominal* in name only (as opposed to actual) *cognomen* surname, distinguishing nickname
nov	new	*novice* beginner *renovate* make new again *novelty* newness
omni	all	*omniscient* all knowing *omnipotent* all powerful *omnivorous* eating everything
oper	to work	*operate* work *cooperation* working together
pac	peace	*pacify* make peaceful *pacific* peaceful *pacifist* person opposed to war
pass	to feel	*dispassionate* free of emotion *impassioned* emotion-filled *impassive* showing no feeling
pater, patr	father	*patriotism* love of one's country (fatherland) *patriarch* male ruler of a family, group, or state *paternity* fatherhood
path	disease, feeling	*pathology* study of diseased tissue *apathetic* lacking feeling; indifferent *antipathy* hostile feeling
ped, pod	foot	*impediment* stumbling-block; hindrance *tripod* three-footed stand *quadruped* four-footed animal
ped	child	*pedagogue* teacher of children *pediatrician* children's doctor
pel, puls	to drive	*compulsion* a forcing to do *repel* drive back *expel* drive out, banish
pet, petit	to seek	*petition* request *appetite* craving, desire *compete* vie with others
phil	love	*philanthropist* benefactor, lover of humanity *Anglophile* lover of everything English *philanderer* one involved in brief love affairs
pon, posit	to place	*postpone* place after *positive* definite, unquestioned (definitely placed)
port, portat	to carry	*portable* able to be carried *transport* carry across

Root or Stem	Meaning	Illustration
poten	able, powerful	*omnipotent* all-powerful
psych	mind	*psychology* study of the mind
put, putat	to trim, to calculate	*computation* calculation *amputate* cut off
quer, ques, quir, quis	to ask	*inquiry* investigation *inquisitive* questioning *query* question
reg, rect	to rule	*regent* ruler *insurrection* rebellion; overthrow of a ruler
rid, ris	to laugh	*derision* scorn *ridiculous* deserving to be laughed at
rog, rogat	to ask	*interrogate* question
rupt	to break	*interrupt* break into *rupture* a break
sacr	holy	*sacrilegious* impious, violating something holy *sacrament* religious act
sci	to know	*omniscient* knowing all *conscious* aware
scop	to watch, to see	*periscope* device for seeing around corners *microscope* device for seeing small objects
scrib, script	to write	*transcribe* make a written copy *script* written text
sect	cut	*dissect* cut apart *bisect* cut into two pieces
sed, sess	to sit	*sedentary* inactive (sitting)
sent, sens	to think, to feel	*resent* show indignation *sensitive* showing feeling
sequi, secut, seque	to follow	*consecutive* following in order *sequence* arrangement *sequel* that which follows *nonsequitur* something that does not follow logically
solv, solut	to loosen	*absolve* free from blame *dissolute* morally lax
somn	sleep	*insomnia* inability to sleep
soph	wisdom	*philosopher* lover of wisdom
spec, spect	to look at	*spectator* observer *circumspect* cautious (looking around)
spir	to breathe	*respiratory* pertaining to breathing *spirited* full of life (breathe)
string, strict	bind	*stringent* strict *stricture* limit, something that restrains

Root or Stem	Meaning	Illustration
stru, struct	to build	*constructive* helping to build *construe* analyze (how something is built)
tang, tact, ting	to touch	*tangent* touching *contact* touching with, meeting *contingent* depending upon
tempor	time	*contemporary* at same time
ten, tent	to hold	*tenable* able to be held *retentive* holding; having a good memory
term	end	*interminable* endless *terminate* end
terr	land	*terrestrial* pertaining to earth *subterranean* underground
therm	heat	*thermostat* instrument that regulates heat
tors, tort	to twist	*distort* twist out of true shape or meaning *torsion* act of twisting
tract	to drag, to pull	*distract* pull (one's attention) away *intractable* stubborn, unable to be dragged
trud, trus	to push, to shove	*intrude* push one's way in *protrusion* something sticking out
urb	city	*urban* pertaining to a city
vac	empty	*vacuous* lacking content, empty-headed *evacuate* compel to empty an area
vad, vas	to go	*invade* enter in a hostile fashion *evasive* not frank; eluding
veni, vent, ven	to come	*intervene* come between *prevent* stop *convention* meeting
ver	true	*veracious* truthful *verisimilitude* appearance of truth
verb	word	*verbose* wordy
vers, vert	to turn	*vertigo* turning dizzy *revert* turn back (to an earlier state) *diversion* something causing one to turn aside
via	way	*deviation* departure from the way *viaduct* roadway (arched)
vid, vis	to see	*vision* sight *evidence* things seen
vinc, vict, vanq	to conquer	*invincible* unconquerable *victory* winning *vanquish* defeat
viv, vit	alive	*vivacious* full of life *vitality* liveliness

Root or Stem	Meaning	Illustration
voc, vocat	to call	*avocation* calling, minor occupation *provocation* calling or rousing the anger of
vol	wish	*malevolent* wishing someone ill *voluntary* of one's own will
volv, volut	to roll	*revolve* roll around *convolution* coiled state

Common Suffixes

A *suffix* is a syllable that is added to a word. Occasionally, it changes the meaning of the word; more frequently, it serves to change the grammatical form of the word (noun to adjective, adjective to noun, noun to verb).

Suffix	Meaning	Illustration
able, ible	capable of (adjective suffix)	*portable* able to be carried *legible* able to be read
ac, ic	like, pertaining to (adjective suffix)	*cardiac* pertaining to the heart *aquatic* pertaining to the water
acious, icious	full of (adjective suffix)	*audacious* full of daring *avaricious* full of greed
al	pertaining to (adjective or noun suffix)	*maniacal* insane *portal* doorway *logical* pertaining to logic
ant, ent	full of (adjective or noun suffix)	*eloquent* pertaining to fluid, effective speech *suppliant* pleader (person full of requests) *verdant* green
ary	like, connected with (adjective or noun suffix)	*dictionary* book connected with words *honorary* with honor *luminary* celestial body
ate	to make (verb suffix)	*consecrate* to make holy *enervate* to make weary *mitigate* to make less severe
ation	that which is (noun suffix)	*exasperation* irritation *irritation* annoyance
cy	state of being (noun suffix)	*democracy* government ruled by the people *obstinacy* stubbornness
eer, er, or	person who (noun suffix)	*mutineer* person who rebels *lecher* person who lusts *censor* person who deletes improper remarks
escent	becoming (adjective suffix)	*evanescent* tending to vanish *pubescent* arriving at puberty

Suffix	Meaning	Illustration
fic	making, doing (adjective suffix)	*terrific* arousing great fear *soporific* causing sleep
fy	to make (verb suffix)	*magnify* enlarge *petrify* turn to stone
iferous	producing, bearing (adjective suffix)	*pestiferous* carrying disease *vociferous* bearing a loud voice
il, ile	pertaining to, capable of (adjective suffix)	*puerile* pertaining to a boy or child *civil* polite
ism	doctrine, belief (noun suffix)	*monotheism* belief in one god *fanaticism* excessive zeal; extreme belief
ist	dealer, doer (noun suffix)	*realist* one who is realistic *artist* one who deals with art
ity	state of being (noun suffix)	*credulity* state of being unduly willing to believe *sagacity* wisdom
ive	like (adjective suffix)	*quantitative* concerned with quantity *effusive* gushing
ize, ise	to make (verb suffix)	*harmonize* make harmonious *enfranchise* make free or set free
oid	resembling, like (adjective suffix)	*ovoid* like an egg *anthropoid* resembling a human being *spheroid* resembling a sphere
ose	full of (adjective suffix)	*verbose* full of words
osis	condition (noun suffix)	*psychosis* diseased mental condition *hypnosis* condition of induced sleep
ous	full of (adjective suffix)	*nauseous* full of nausea *ludicrous* foolish
tude	state of (noun suffix)	*fortitude* state of strength *certitude* state of sureness

8 Quantitative Comparison Questions

■ Testing Tactics
■ Practice Exercises
■ Answer Key

One-half of the questions on the quantitative sections of the GRE General Test are of the quantitative comparison type. These 15 questions are designed to test your ability to reason quickly about the magnitudes of two quantities. Some questions require simple computation; others ask you to reason more and to consider special cases. In this type of question you are given two quanti- ties, with information regarding either or both, and are asked to decide which, if either, is the greater quantity. Actually, these questions require the same basic knowl- edge of high school level arithmetic, plane geometry, and algebra that you need for the other types of multiple- choice math questions. However, these questions involve less reading and less computation than the other types.

TESTING TACTICS

Memorize the Directions to Save Time in the Examination Room

You may expect to find the following directions:

<u>Directions:</u> Each of the <u>Questions 1–15</u> consists of two quantities, one in Column A and one in Column B. You are to compare the two quantities and choose

        A if the quantity in Column A is greater;
        B if the quantity in Column B is greater;
        C if the two quantities are equal;
        D if the relationship cannot be determined from the information given.

<u>Note:</u>   Since there are only four choices, NEVER MARK (E).

<u>Common Information:</u>   In a question, information concerning one or both of the quantities to be compared is centered above the two columns. A symbol that appears in both columns represents the same thing in Column A as it does in Column B.

Do Not Spend Too Much Time on These Questions

Quantitative comparison questions require less time than the other types of math questions. Do not spend more than 30 seconds on any one question. The following question is typical.

Column A	Column B
3^2	2^3

In about 30 seconds or less you should realize that you are not asked to multiply 3×2 or 2×3 but that the value in Column A is 3×3 (9) and in Column B is $2 \times 2 \times 2$ (8). The correct answer is (A).

Expect the Early Questions to Be Relatively Easy

These are warm-up questions. If you find you cannot reach an answer quickly, perhaps you missed a point. You may expect to find relatively easy questions in the first segment of any section of the test. For example, the question discussed above under Tactic 2 is actually a warm-up question. Be prepared for these questions, and don't begin wondering whether you were given the correct examination booklet. The questions that follow further illustrate the point.

Column A	Column B
	$xy < 0$	
x	y

Column A	Column B
The average (arithmetic mean) of 10 numbers is 52. When one of the numbers is discarded, the average of the remaining numbers becomes 53.	
The discarded number	51

The first question, answered correctly by 93% of the people taking the test, can be done quickly by realizing that, since the product of x and y is negative (less than 0), either x is negative and y is positive, or x is positive and y is negative. The correct answer is (D).

Compare that with the next question, which appeared near the end of the quantitative comparison questions and gave trouble to more than half of those who took this test.

The solution: Average × Number of cases = Sum.
The original sum = (52) (10), or 520.
The resulting sum = (53) (9), or 477.
The difference that results from discarding a number is 43, which is less than 51. The correct answer is (B).

Do Not Spend Time with Unnecessary Computations

Consider the following question:

Column A	Column B
$\dfrac{n+a}{a}$	$\dfrac{n}{a} + 1$

There is no need for lengthy computation.

$$\frac{n + a}{a} = \frac{n}{a} + 1,$$

which is the value also in Column B. The correct answer is (C).

Eliminate from Consideration Any Quantity That Appears in Both Columns

Column A	Column B
(7)(5)(8)(9)	(63)(4)(10)

In this example note that 63 appears in both columns, for (7)(9) = 63. Consider only (5)(8) in Column A and (10)(4) in Column B. The correct answer is (C).

Do Not Choose (D) If the Quantities in Both Columns Have No Variables

If the quantities in both columns have no variables, (D) is not possible. Therefore in such cases you have only three choices. See explanations under Tactics 2 and 5.

Consider All Types of Numbers as Possible Values for Variables

If you find that the relationship between the quantities depends upon the kind of numbers you use, the correct answer is (D). You must consider whether the relationship is affected by using positive or negative values, zero, 1, fractions less than 1, etc. Consider this example, which was troublesome to only 28% of those who took this test.

Column A	Column B
$s + t = 6$	
$s + 2t$	$2s + t$

Note that various values for s and t may yield a sum of 6. Therefore $s + t$ and $2s + t$ may have many possible values. The correct answer is (D).

Do Not Hesitate to Mark Up a Given Diagram in Your Test Booklet

Column A	Column B

The perimeter of the rectangle is 16.

The area of the rectangular region	12

Evidently 53% of those taking the test correctly applied the formulas required:

$$\text{Perimeter} = 2(s) + 2\frac{s}{3} = 16$$

$$2s + \frac{2s}{3} = 16$$

$$6s + 2s = 48$$

Therefore $s = 6$.

$$\text{Area} = (s)\frac{s}{3} \text{ or } (6)\frac{6}{3} \text{ or } 12$$

The correct answer is (C).

Make Rough Sketches or Diagrams to Help You Visualize the Situation Presented

The following example can best be done by making a rough sketch.

Column A	Column B
In triangle *ABC*, the measure of ∠*A* is greater than that of ∠*B*, and ∠*C* has a measure of 60 degrees.	
Length of *AC*	Length of *AB*

The information given tells us that the measure of ∠*A* is greater than the measure of ∠*B*. Since *A* + *B* =120, the measure in degrees of ∠*A* is greater than 60 and ∠*B* has a measure of less than 60. Since ∠*C* > ∠*B*, *AB* (side opposite ∠*C*) > *AC* (side opposite ∠*B*). The correct answer is (B).

Column A	Column B
The circumference of circle *P* is greater than the circumference of circle *Q*.	
The radius of circle *P*	The diameter of circle *Q*

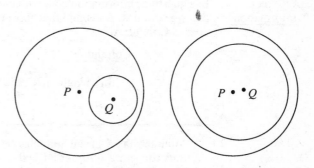

This example, answered correctly by 74% of those taking the test, can also best be done by making a rough sketch. The sketch shows that, if circle *P* is larger than circle *Q*, then its radius can be longer or shorter than the diameter of circle *Q*. The correct answer is (D).

Practice Exercise

Quantitative Comparison Exercise A

<u>Directions:</u> Each of the <u>Questions 1–50</u> consists of two quantities, one in Column A and one in Column B. You are to compare the two quantities and choose

      A if the quantity in Column A is greater;
      B if the quantity in Column B is greater;
      C if the two quantities are equal;
      D if the relationship cannot be determined from the information given.

<u>Note:</u>   Since there are only four choices, NEVER MARK (E).

<u>Common Information:</u>   In a question, information concerning one or both of the quantities to be compared is centered above the two columns. A symbol that appears in both columns represents the same thing in Column A as it does in Column B.

	Column A	Column B
	In triangle ABC, the measure of $\angle ACB = 60°$.	
1.	$\angle B$	$\angle A$
2.	Michael has 5 green marbles and the same number of red marbles. The number of red marbles in his collection is $\frac{1}{2}$ the number of white marbles and $\frac{1}{3}$ the number of blue ones.	Philip has 35 marbles in his collection.
3.	The number of posts needed by Mr. A to hold a wire fence 120 feet long if he places posts 12 feet apart in a straight line	The 10 posts used by Mr. B to support a similar wire fence
	$0 < x < 10$ $0 < y < 12$	
4.	x	y
	$a = 1$ and $b = -1$	
5.	$\dfrac{x(a+b)}{v}$	$\dfrac{2x(a+b)}{v}$
	Triangle ABC	
6.	$AB + BC$	AC

| 7. | $\angle 4$ | $\angle 3$ |

<u>Column A</u>   <u>Column B</u>

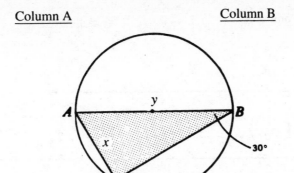

$$\angle B = 30°$$

8.   **2x**   **y**

(This concerns Questions 9 and 10.)

In triangle *ABC*, *AC*<*AB* and *AC*>*BC*.

9.   Angle *B*   Angle *A*

10.   Angle *B*   Angle *C*

11.   *b*   *d − a*

12.   (5)(144)(6)   (12²)(5²)

13.   7 × 5 × 8 × 9   63 × 4 × 10

14. $\dfrac{(369)(72)}{(3)(4)(5)}$ $\dfrac{(10)(8)(369)}{(2)(3)(4)}$

15. $\dfrac{0.9}{2}$ $\dfrac{3}{10}$

16. $\sqrt{14.4}$ 1.2

17. $\sqrt{\dfrac{1}{9} + \dfrac{1}{16}}$ $\sqrt{\dfrac{1}{16}} + \sqrt{\dfrac{1}{9}}$

	<u>Column A</u>	<u>Column B</u>
18.	$\dfrac{1}{0.5}$	$\sqrt{4}$

| 19. | $\left(\dfrac{1}{0.07}\right)^{2}$ | $\dfrac{1}{7}$ |

$$3^{n+2} = 27$$

| 20. | n | 3 |

| 21. | $\sqrt{0.16}$ | $0.1\,\pi$ |

| 22. | $\dfrac{1}{\sqrt{25}}$ | $\dfrac{1}{(0.5)}$ |

$$3 - 2x < 9$$

| 23. | x | -3 |

$$a < 0 \text{ and } b < 0$$

| 24. | $a - b$ | $a + b$ |

$$x > 0 \text{ and } y > 0$$

$$\dfrac{x}{y} > 2$$

| 25. | $2y$ | x |

| 26. | $\sqrt{9} + \sqrt{16}$ | $\sqrt{49}$ |

$$\dfrac{9}{a} < \dfrac{9}{b}$$

$$a > 0 \text{ and } b > 0$$

| 27. | a | b |

$$3^{x+1} = 81$$

| 28. | x | 4 |

$$x > 1 \text{ and } y > 1$$

$$x \neq y$$

| 29. | $\dfrac{x}{y} + 1$ | $\dfrac{x + y}{y}$ |

Column A	Column B

Questions 30–31 refer to $\triangle ABC$.

$x = 40$

30. Length of side AB Length of side BC

31. x y

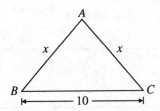

32. $\dfrac{BC}{AB} \cdot \dfrac{AC}{BC}$ 1

$$x^2 + 2xy + y^2 = 25$$
$$xy = 6$$

33. $x^2 + y^2$ $(x + y)^2$

$$a^2 = ab$$
$$a \neq 0$$

34. a b

$$x^2 + y^2 = 100$$

35. x y

$$ab = 0$$

36. a b

$$1 \text{ kilometer} = \frac{5}{8} \text{ mile}$$

37. $\dfrac{5}{8}$ kilometer   3 miles

38. $\dfrac{1274}{7}$ inches   5 yards, 2 inches

39. $(0.2)^3$ $\sqrt{0.64}$

	Column A	Column B

<u>Column A</u>   <u>Column B</u>

40.   50% $\dfrac{1}{0.02}$

It takes x men to complete a job in 12 days, but $x - 4$ men require A days to do the same job.

41. A 12

$$y = \dfrac{k}{x}$$

42. x y

$$\dfrac{a}{b} > \dfrac{a^2}{b^2}$$

$a > 0$ and $b > 0$

43. b a

$$\left(\dfrac{1}{2}\right)^x = 2^y$$

44. x 4

The average weight of Mark, Philip, and Lori is 50 pounds.

45.   Weight of Mark and Lori   Weight of Philip and Lori

---

46. The distance covered going at the average rate of 40 miles per hour for 3 hours   The distance covered in 3 hours going at 50 miles per hour for the first hour and then going at the average rate of 30 miles per hour for the next 2 hours

---

Martin is 5 times as old as Sara.
Michael's age is $\dfrac{1}{6}$ of Martin's age.

47.   Michael's age   Sara's age

Questions 48–50 refer to the following figure.

ABC is a straight line

48. $d + c$ $a + b + c$

49. d b

50. $a + b$ d

Quantitative Comparison Exercise B

<u>Directions:</u> Each of the <u>Questions 1-50</u> consists of two quantities, one in Column A and one in Column B. You are to compare the two quantities and choose

A if the quantity in Column A is greater;
B if the quantity in Column B is greater;
C if the two quantities are equal;
D if the relationship cannot be determined from the information given.

<u>Note:</u>   Since there are only four choices, NEVER MARK (E).

<u>Common Information:</u> In a question, information concerning one or both of the quantities to be compared is centered above the two columns. A symbol that appears in both columns represents the same thing in Column A as it does in Column B.

	<u>Column A</u>	<u>Column B</u>
1.	$\dfrac{1}{2}$	$\dfrac{1}{0.02}$
2.	48	102% of 40
3.	$\sqrt{\dfrac{1}{16} + \dfrac{1}{9}}$	$\dfrac{7}{12}$
4.	0.01π	$\sqrt{0.3}$

5. $a > 0$ and $b > 0$

	Column A	Column B
5.	$a^2 + b^2$	$(a - b)^2$

$x + y = 5$
$x + z = 6$

	Column A	Column B
6.	x	1

7. The average of $(30 + 2x - y)$ and $(10 + y)$ — The average of $(x - 120)$ and $(160 + x)$

8. Area of square with perimeter of 32 feet — Area of isosceles right triangle with hypotenuse of $10\sqrt{2}$ feet

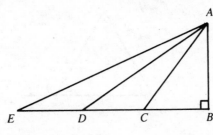

In triangle ABE, $BC = CD = DE$

9. Area of $\triangle ABC$ + Area of $\triangle ACD$ — Area of $\triangle ACD$ + Area of $\triangle ADE$

	<u>Column A</u>	<u>Column B</u>
10.	The length of side *AB* of square *ABCD* with a perimeter of 8 units	The length of side *KL* of square *KLMN* with an area of 4 units

Note: Not drawn to scale.

In quadrilateral *KLMN*, *b* = 80 and *d* = 110.

11.	*a*	*c*

12.	The volume of a cube is 27.	The volume of a cube in which the length of a diagonal of one face is $3\sqrt{2}$

13.	*AB*	*BC*

14.	∠4	∠1 + ∠2

Column A   Column B

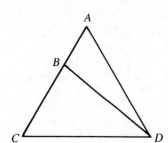

Note: Not drawn to scale.

15.   ∠ACD   ∠ADC

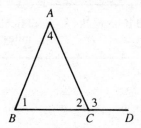

16.   ∠3   ∠1

Questions 17–24 refer to the following figure.

17.   ∠3   ∠4

18.   ∠z   ∠y

19.   ∠x   ∠y

20.   ∠3   ∠2

21.   ∠x + ∠y   ∠z

22.   BC   CD

23.   ∠1 + ∠2   ∠3 + ∠4 + ∠z

24.   BC + CD   AB + AD

<u>Column A</u>   <u>Column B</u>

25. $(c + a)°$ $90°$

$$2a = 3b - 4$$
$$a = b$$

26. b 4

---

27. Martin's average speed if he walks 8 miles in 2 hours   Michael's average speed if he walks 5 miles in an hour and 30 minutes

---

$$x \neq 0$$

28. $\dfrac{2 + 3 + 4 + 5 + 6}{5x}$ $\dfrac{4}{x}$

---

29. a^5 a^4

---

x, y, and z are consecutive integers, and $x + y + z = 12$.

30. xyz 60

$$b \neq -c$$
$$\frac{a}{-b - c} = \frac{-5}{c + b}$$

31. 5 a

---

32. 2 hours, 40 minutes   The elapsed time from 8:55 P.M. to 10:15 the same evening

---

The distance from Mark's house to the Waban school is 3 miles; the distance from Sara's house to this school is 4 miles.

33. The distance from Mark's house to Sara's house   5 miles

---

34. $(0.1)(\pi)$ $\sqrt{0.17}$

---

35. $\dfrac{2 + 2 + 2}{2 - 2 - 2}$ $\dfrac{3 + 3 + 3}{3 - 3 - 3}$

---

36. $\sqrt{1.44}$ 0.12

Column A	Column B

$$X^2 = 100$$

37. X $\qquad\qquad$ 10

$$a > 0 \text{ and } x > 0;$$
$$\frac{a}{x} < 1$$

38. a $\qquad\qquad$ x

$$0 < a < b$$

39. $\dfrac{1}{a}$ $\qquad\qquad$ $\dfrac{1}{b}$

---

40. 105% of 500 $\qquad\qquad$ 50% of 1000

$$5x = 23 = y$$

41. x $\qquad\qquad$ y

$$X > Y \text{ and } Y > Z$$

42. $2X$ $\qquad\qquad$ $Y + Z$

$$x > 0 \text{ and } y > 0$$

43. $\dfrac{1}{x + y}$ $\qquad\qquad$ $\dfrac{\frac{1}{xy}}{\frac{1}{x} + \frac{1}{y}}$

---

44. $\sqrt{\dfrac{1}{25}}$ $\qquad\qquad$ $\left(\dfrac{1}{5}\right)^2$

---

45. 15% $\qquad\qquad$ $\dfrac{0.3}{2}$

$$0 < x < y < z$$

46. $\dfrac{z}{y}$ $\qquad\qquad$ $\dfrac{z}{x}$

---

47. The percentage increase from \$5 to \$7 $\qquad$ The percentage increase from \$7 to \$9

---

48. $a + 1$ $\qquad\qquad$ $a - 1$

$$\frac{1}{a} < 0$$

49. zero $\qquad\qquad$ a

$$1 \text{ kilometer} = \frac{5}{8} \text{ mile}$$

50. 1.6 kilometers $\qquad\qquad$ 1 mile

Answer Key

Quantitative Comparison Exercise A

1.	D	14.	B	27.	A	40.	B
2.	C	15.	A	28.	B	41.	A
3.	A	16.	A	29.	C	42.	D
4.	D	17.	B	30.	A	43.	A
5.	C	18.	C	31.	B	44.	B
6.	A	19.	A	32.	C	45.	D
7.	A	20.	B	33.	B	46.	A
8.	C	21.	A	34.	C	47.	B
9.	A	22.	B	35.	D	48.	C
10.	B	23.	A	36.	D	49.	A
11.	C	24.	A	37.	B	50.	C
12.	A	25.	B	38.	C		
13.	C	26.	C	39.	B		

Quantitative Comparison Exercise B

1.	B	14.	C	27.	A	40.	A
2.	A	15.	B	28.	C	41.	B
3.	B	16.	A	29.	D	42.	A
4.	B	17.	D	30.	C	43.	C
5.	A	18.	A	31.	C	44.	A
6.	D	19.	D	32.	A	45.	C
7.	C	20.	B	33.	D	46.	B
8.	A	21.	C	34.	B	47.	A
9.	C	22.	D	35.	C	48.	A
10.	C	23.	C	36.	A	49.	A
11.	D	24.	B	37.	D	50.	C
12.	C	25.	C	38.	B		
13.	A	26.	C	39.	A		

9 Discrete Quantitative Questions

- ■ Testing Tactics
- ■ Practice Exercises
- ■ Answer Key
- ■ Answer Explanations

The discrete quantitative questions are like the standard multiple-choice questions you have encountered in math classes and on other standardized tests. They cover basic arithmetic operations, elementary algebra, and plane geometry. They test your knowledge of basic mathematical concepts and also, in some cases, your ability to apply that knowledge, as in questions that ask you to solve a problem involving an actual or an abstract situation. The arithmetic questions deal with operations on numbers and finding powers, roots of powers, percents, and averages. The algebra questions include linear equations, factorization, inequalities, exponents, and radicals. Also, some questions test the ability to set up an equation in order to solve a problem. The topics in geometry include properties of lines, circles, triangles, rectangles, and other polygons. Also, some questions test knowledge of measurement-related concepts, the Pythagorean theorem, and coordinate geometry.

There are 10 discrete quantitative questions in each quantitative section of the test—usually questions 16–20 and 26–30, with a set of 5 data interpretation questions in between. Generally, the first 5 discrete quantitative questions are easier than the last 5. The tactics and practice exercises that follow will help you answer these questions.

TESTING TACTICS

Use Your Time Wisely

You have 30 minutes for 30 questions. The 15 quantitative comparison questions should be done in 10 minutes. That leaves 20 minutes to do 5 data interpretation questions and 10 discrete quantitative questions. Thus, it is logical to expect to allow a minute or a minute and a half for each question. If you find that you are spending as much as two minutes on a question, you must come to some decision about your answer right then and there. However, mark the question in some way so that you can return to it when you have completed the section. At that time the question may read differently or perhaps some item that came up since you left the question will help you answer it. In any event do not leave it blank. There is no penalty for guessing on the GRE.

Expect to encounter relatively easy questions in the early part of the test. Don't be surprised to find a beginning question such as the following:

> If $2x - 3 = 2$, then $x - \frac{1}{2} =$
>
> (A) 2 (B) $2\frac{1}{2}$ (C) 3 (D) $4\frac{1}{2}$ (E) $5\frac{1}{2}$

This is a warm-up question and should be done in a few seconds.
If $2x = 2 + 3$, then

$$x = 2\frac{1}{2} \quad \text{and} \quad 2\frac{1}{2} - \frac{1}{2} = 2,$$

Choose (A).

The example that follows was question 30 on a recent test, and only 22% of the people who took the test chose the correct answer. The solution uses a time-saving strategy of representing variable quantities by convenient numbers of your own choice.

If the length of each of the sides of three square garden plots is increased by 50 percent, by what percent is the sum of the areas of the three plots increased?

(A) 375%
(B) 200%
(C) 150%
(D) 125%
(E) 50%

Let the sides of the original three squares be 4, 6, and 8, respectively. The enlarged squares would have sides 6, 9, and 12, respectively. The sum of the areas of the original squares would be 16 + 36 + 64 for a total of 116 square units. The sum of the areas of the three enlarged squares would be 36 + 81 + 144 for a total of 261 square units, which is an increase of 145 square units:

$$\text{Percent Increase} = \frac{\text{Amount of increase}}{\text{Original amount}} \times 100\%$$

$$= \frac{145}{116} \times 100\%$$

$$= 1.25 \times 100\%$$

$$= 125\%$$

Choose (D).

Avoid Lengthy Computations

Time saved on a question permits more time for the challenging questions. Remember that all questions carry the same weight. In general, GRE questions do not involve lengthy, time-consuming computation. Therefore, if you come to a question that seems to require straightforward but complex computation, look for a shortcut; there almost always is one. Consider this question. Can you arrive at the answer in less than 30 seconds, including time to read the question?

$\dfrac{1.116963}{0.369}$ is exactly equal to

(A) 3.023
(B) 3.024
(C) 3.025
(D) 3.026
(E) 3.027

In a question such as this one, your ability to do complicated division is not being tested. Since the question indicates that the quotient is *exactly* one of the answers, the correct answer must obviously have, as its last digit, 7, which when multiplied by 9 (the last digit of the denominator) will yield 3 (the last digit of the numerator). Choose (E).

Here's another question on which you can save time:

$$1 + \frac{1}{2} + \frac{1}{3} + \frac{1}{4} + \frac{1}{5} =$$

(A) $\dfrac{32}{25}$

(B) $\dfrac{117}{60}$

(C) $\dfrac{52}{25}$

(D) $\dfrac{109}{50}$

(E) $\dfrac{137}{60}$

This question was answered correctly by 81% of those who recently took this test. Observe that in adding the fractions the least common denominator is 60. Do you see that as a clue that the correct answer is (B) or (E)?

Since $1 = \dfrac{60}{60}, \dfrac{1}{2} = \dfrac{30}{60}, \dfrac{1}{3} = \dfrac{20}{60}, \dfrac{1}{4} = \dfrac{15}{60}$, and $\dfrac{1}{5} = \dfrac{12}{60}$, the sum is equal to $\dfrac{137}{60}$.

Choose (E).

Read the Questions Carefully

Read each question carefully to make sure you answer the question that was asked and not the one you expected to be asked. Also, make sure you take all relevant information into consideration and that you work with the correct units.

> A dresser drawer contains 15 garments. If 40 percent of those garments are blouses, how many are NOT blouses?
>
> (A) 6
> (B) 8
> (C) 9
> (D) 10
> (E) 12

This is a relatively easy question but the 82% that did not choose (C) carelessly overlooked the word NOT.

Visualize the Situation Presented; make Sketches

Here is the type of question that can be solved easily if you make a pictorial representation of the facts.

> The length of a rectangular floor is 16 feet and its width is 12 feet. If each dimension were reduced by s feet to make the ratio of length to width 3 to 2, what would be the value of s?
>
> (A) 0
> (B) 2
> (C) 4
> (D) 6
> (E) 8

Caution: The sketches you make need not be works of art. Don't spend time showing off; your test booklet will not be inspected.

SOLUTION: $\dfrac{\text{Length}}{\text{Width}} = \dfrac{16-s}{12-s} = \dfrac{3}{2}$

$$32 - 2s = 36 - 3s$$
$$s = 4$$

Choose (C).

Here is another question that requires you to visualize a situation.

> Point B is on line segment AC, and point E is on line segment DF. If $AB > DE$ and $BC = EF$, then
>
> (A) $AC < DF$ (B) $AC = DF$ (C) $AC > DF$
> (D) $DF > AC$ (E) $EF > DF$

To obtain the correct answer quickly, use the following solution and sketch:

> If equal quantities are added to unequal quantities, the sums are unequal in the same order.

Choose (C).

Mark Up Diagrams Given in the Test Booklet

See how this tactic works with a former, very challenging GRE question.

What is the area of the quadrilaterial shown above?

(A) $2\sqrt{3}$ (B) $3\sqrt{3}$ (C) $6\sqrt{3}$

(D) 6   (E) 8

SOLUTION: On the marked-up diagram, $AE \perp FC$ and $BD \perp FC$.

$$(AE)^2 + (FE)^2 = (AF)^2$$
$$(AE)^2 + 1 = 4$$
$$(AE)^2 = 3$$
$$AE = \sqrt{3} = \text{height}$$

Since $ABCF$ is an isosceles trapezoid; its area = (average of bases) × height

$$= \frac{2 + 4}{2} \times \sqrt{3}$$

$$= 3\sqrt{3}$$

Choose (B).

Be Prepared to Apply Basic Rules, Formulas, and Concepts

Examinees are expected to have basic mathematical knowledge of arithmetic, algebra, and geometry, and to be able to apply that knowledge in some cases. In the problem discussed under Tactic 5 the Pythagorean theorem was applied, as well as the formula for the area of an isosceles trapezoid.

Look at the Answer Choices Before Attempting to Answer Complex Problems

This tactic is important for several reasons.

1. Looking at the answer choices may show you a quick way of solving the problem, as in the first example for Tactic 1.

2. The answer choices give you an idea of how exact your figuring has to be. For example, if the choices are 3, 4, 5, 6, 7, you know you have to get a pretty exact answer, whereas if the choices are 9, 18, 40, 80, 90, you do not. This should alert you to several possibilities: you may be able to save time by estimating, there is a good chance that a shortcut is involved, and you may be able to get the correct answer by eliminating choices that just are not reasonable.

3. The answer choices show you the form that is required. This information will keep you from wasting time putting your answer in a form that is not given. For example, if the answers are all decimals, you do not want to compute your answer in terms of fractions.

If You Can't Answer a Question, Try to Work Back from the Answer Choices

Sometimes this is easier and faster than trying to solve the problem through other means. For example, in the following question the best way to do this is to start with answer choice (A) and substitute the values of the table in each of the possible answers.

R	1	2	3	4	5	6
S	2	5	8	11	14	17

Which of the following equations gives the relationship between R and S in the table above?

(A) $S = 2R$
(B) $S = R^2 + 1$
(C) $S = R^2 - 1$
(D) $S = 3R - 1$
(E) $S = 2R + 5$

Choice (A) is not correct because, when $R = 2$, S does not $= 5$. Choice (B) is not correct because, when $R = 3$, S does not $= 8$. Choice (C) is not correct because, when $R = 1$, S does not $= 2$. Choice (D), $S = 3R - 1$, is satisfied by all values in the table: $(3 \times 1) - (1) = 2$, $(3 \times 2) - 1 = 5$, $(3 \times 3) - 1 = 8$, $(4 \times 3) - 1 = 11$ $(5 \times 3) - 1 = 14$, and $(6 \times 3) - 17$. Choice (E) is not correct because, when $R = 1$, S does not $= 2$. Choose (D).

Practice Exercises

Discrete Quantitative Exercise A

<u>Directions:</u> Each of the <u>Questions 1–25</u> has five answer choices. For each of these questions, select the best of the answer choices given.

1. In 1970, it cost $12 to purchase 100 pounds of fertilizer. In 1990, it cost $34 to purchase 100 pounds of fertilizer. The price of 100 pounds of fertilizer increased how many dollars between 1970 and 1990?

   (A) 1.20
   (B) 2.20
   (C) 3.40
   (D) 22
   (E) 34

2. A house cost Ms. Jones C dollars in 1989. Three years later she sold the house for 25% more than she paid for it. She has to pay a tax of 50% of the gain. (The gain is the selling price minus the cost.) How much tax must Ms. Jones pay?

   (A) $\frac{1}{24}C$

   (B) $\frac{C}{8}$

   (C) $\frac{1}{4}C$

   (D) $\frac{C}{2}$

   (E) $0.6C$

3. If the length of a rectangle is increased by 20%, and the width of the same rectangle is decreased by 20%, then the area of the rectangle

   (A) decreases by 20%
   (B) decreases by 4%
   (C) is unchanged
   (D) increases by 20%
   (E) increases by 40%

4. Eight percent of the people eligible to vote are between 18 and 21. In an election, 85% of those eligible to vote who were between 18 and 21 actually voted. In that election, people between 18 and 21 who actually voted were what percent of those people eligible to vote?

   (A) 4.2
   (B) 6.4
   (C) 6.8
   (D) 8
   (E) 8.5

5. If n and p are both odd numbers, which of the following numbers *must* be an even number?

   (A) $n + p$
   (B) np
   (C) $np + 2$
   (D) $n + p + 1$
   (E) $2n + p$

6. It costs g cents a mile for gasoline and m cents a mile for all other costs to run a car. How many *dollars* will it cost to run the car for 100 miles?

   (A) $\dfrac{g + m}{100}$

   (B) $100g + 100m$
   (C) $g + m$
   (D) $g + 0.1m$
   (E) g

7. In the figure above, what is the length of the line segment that connects A to B?

   (A) $\sqrt{3}$
   (B) 2
   (C) $2\sqrt{2}$
   (D) 4
   (E) 8

8. A cab driver's income consists of his salary and tips. His salary is $50 a week. During one week his tips were $\frac{5}{4}$ of his salary. What fraction of his income for the week came from tips?

   (A) $\frac{4}{9}$ (B) $\frac{1}{2}$ (C) $\frac{5}{9}$ (D) $\frac{5}{8}$ (E) $\frac{5}{4}$

9. Given that x and y are real numbers, let $S(x,y) = x^2 - y^2$. Then $S\left(3, S(3,4)\right) =$

(A) -40
(B) -7
(C) 40
(D) 49
(E) 56

10. Eggs cost 90¢ a dozen. Peppers cost 20¢ each. An omelet consists of 3 eggs and $\frac{1}{4}$ of a pepper. How much will the ingredients for 8 omelets cost?

(A) $0.90
(B) $1.30
(C) $1.80
(D) $2.20
(E) $2.70

11. It is 185 miles from Binghamton to New York City. If a bus takes 2 hours to travel the first 85 miles, how many minutes must the bus take to travel the final 100 miles in order to average 50 miles an hour for the entire trip?

(A) 60
(B) 75
(C) 94
(D) 102
(E) 112

12. What is the area of the figure above, if $ABDC$ is a rectangle and BDE is an isosceles right triangle?

(A) ab

(B) ab^2

(C) $b\left(a + \dfrac{b}{2}\right)$

(D) cab

(E) $\frac{1}{2}bc$

13. If $2x + y = 5$, then $4x + 2y =$

(A) 5
(B) 8
(C) 9
(D) 10
(E) none of these

14. In 1967, a new boat cost $2,500; in 1992, the same type of boat cost $4,800. The cost of that type of boat increased by what percent between 1967 and 1992?

(A) 48 (B) 52 (C) 92 (D) 152 (E) 192

15. What is the area of the square $ABCD$ in the figure above?

(A) 10
(B) 18
(C) 24
(D) 36
(E) 48

16. If $x + y = 6$ and $3x - y = 4$, then $x - y =$

(A) -1
(B) 0
(C) 2
(D) 4
(E) 6

17. If $\dfrac{x}{y} = \dfrac{2}{3}$ then $\dfrac{y^2}{x^2}$ is equal to

(A) $\frac{4}{9}$ (B) $\frac{2}{3}$ (C) $\frac{3}{2}$ (D) $\frac{9}{4}$ (E) $\frac{5}{2}$

18. In the figure above, BD is perpendicular to AC. BA and BC have length a. What is the area of the triangle ABC?

(A) $2x\sqrt{a^2 - x^2}$
(B) $x\sqrt{a^2 - x^2}$
(C) $a\sqrt{a^2 - x^2}$
(D) $2a\sqrt{x^2 - a^2}$
(E) $x\sqrt{x^2 - a^2}$

19. If two places are one inch apart on a map, then they are actually 160 miles apart. (The scale on the map is one inch equals 160 miles). If Seton is $2\frac{7}{8}$ inches from Monroe on the map, how many miles is it from Seton to Monroe?

(A) 3
(B) 27
(C) 300
(D) 360
(E) 460

20. In the figure above, $ABCD$ is a rectangle. The area of isosceles right triangle $ABE = 7$, $EC = 3(BE)$. The area of $ABCD$ is

    (A) 21   (B) 28   (C) 42   (D) 56   (E) 84

21. An automobile tire has two punctures. The first puncture by itself would make the tire flat in 9 minutes. The second puncture by itself would make the tire flat in 6 minutes. How long will it take for both punctures together to make the tire flat? (Assume the air leaks out at a constant rate.)

    (A) $3\frac{3}{5}$ minutes

    (B) 4 minutes

    (C) $5\frac{1}{4}$ minutes

    (D) $7\frac{1}{2}$ minutes

    (E) 15 minutes

22. For the integer n, if n^3 is odd, which of the following statements is (are) true?

    I. n is odd.
    II. n^2 is odd.
    III. n^2 is even.

    (A) I only
    (B) II only
    (C) III only
    (D) I and II only
    (E) I and III only

23. There are 50 students enrolled in Business 100. Of the enrolled students, 90% took the final exam. Two-thirds of the students who took the final exam passed the final exam. How many students passed the final exam?

    (A) 30   (B) 33   (C) 34   (D) 35   (E) 45

24. If a is less than b, which of the following numbers is greater than a and less than b?

    (A) $\dfrac{a + b}{2}$

    (B) $\dfrac{ab}{2}$

    (C) $b^2 - a^2$

    (D) ab

    (E) $b - a$

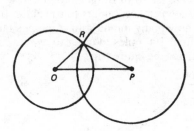

25. In the figure above, OR and PR are radii of circles. PR is tangent to the circle with center O. The length of OP is 4. If $OR = 2$, what is the length of PR?

    (A) 2

    (B) $\dfrac{5}{2}$

    (C) 3

    (D) $2\sqrt{3}$

    (E) $3\sqrt{2}$

Discrete Quantitative Exercise B

Directions: Each of the <u>Questions 1–25</u> has five answer choices. For each of these questions, select the best of the answer choices given.

1. A bus uses one gallon of gasoline to travel 15 miles. After a tune-up, the bus travels 15% farther on one gallon. How many gallons of gasoline (to the nearest tenth) will it take for the bus to travel 150 miles after a tune-up?

    (A) 8.5   (B) 8.7   (C) 8.9   (D) 9.0   (E) 10.0

2. If $x + 2y = 4$ and $\frac{x}{y} = 2$, then $x =$

    (A) 0   (B) $\frac{1}{2}$ (C) 1   (D) $\frac{3}{2}$ (E) 2

3. It costs $1,000 to make the first thousand copies of a book and x dollars to make each subsequent copy. If it costs a total of $7,230 to make the first 8,000 copies of a book, what is x?

    (A) 0.89
    (B) 0.90375
    (C) 1.00
    (D) 89
    (E) 90.375

4. If 16 workers can finish a job in 3 hours, how long should it take 5 workers to finish the same job?

   (A) $3\frac{1}{2}$ hours

   (B) 4 hours

   (C) 5 hours

   (D) $7\frac{1}{16}$ hours

   (E) $9\frac{3}{5}$ hours

5. A box contains 12 poles and 7 pieces of net. Each piece of net weighs 0.2 pound; each pole weighs 1.1 pounds. The box and its contents together weigh 16.25 pounds. How much does the empty box weigh?

   (A) 1.2 pounds
   (B) 1.65 pounds
   (C) 2.75 pounds
   (D) 6.15 pounds
   (E) 16 pounds

6. If $a + b + c + d$ is a positive number, a minimum of x of the numbers a, b, c, and d must be positive where x is equal to

   (A) 0
   (B) 1
   (C) 2
   (D) 3
   (E) 4

7. Consider the accompanying diagram. Which of the following statements is true?

   (A) $KM < KL$
   (B) $KM < LM$
   (C) $KL + LM < KM$
   (D) $KL < LM$
   (E) $KL > LM$

8. Which of the following numbers is the largest?

   (A) $(2 + 2 + 2)^2$
   (B) $[(2 + 2)^2]^2$
   (C) $(2 \times 2 \times 2)^2$
   (D) $2 + 2^2 + (2^2)^2$
   (E) 4^3

9. In a survey of the town of Waso, it was found that 65% of the people polled watched the news on television, 40% read a newspaper, and 25% read a newspaper and watched the news on television. What percent of the people surveyed neither watched the news on television nor read a newspaper?

   (A) 0%
   (B) 5%
   (C) 10%
   (D) 15%
   (E) 20%

10. A worker is paid d dollars an hour for the first 8 hours she works in a day. For every hour after the first 8 hours, she is paid c dollars an hour. If she works 12 hours in one day, what is her average hourly wage for that day?

    (A) $\dfrac{2d + c}{3}$

    (B) $8d + 4c$

    (C) $\dfrac{8d + 12c}{12}$

    (D) $\dfrac{4d + 8c}{12}$

    (E) $d + \left(\dfrac{1}{3}\right)c$

11. A screwdriver and a hammer currently have the same price. If the price of a screwdriver rises by 5% and the price of a hammer goes up by 3%, by what percent will the cost of 3 screwdrivers and 3 hammers rise?

    (A) 3%
    (B) 4%
    (C) 5%
    (D) 8%
    (E) 24%

12. If the radius of a circle is increased by 6%, then the area of the circle is increased by

    (A) 0.36%
    (B) 3.6%
    (C) 6%
    (D) 12.36%
    (E) 36%

13. Given that a and b are real numbers, let $f(a,b) = ab$ and let $g(a) = a^2 + 2$. Then $f[3, g(3)] =$

    (A) $3a^2 + 2$
    (B) $3a^2 + 6$
    (C) 27
    (D) 29
    (E) 33

14. A share of stock in Ace Enterprises cost D dollars on Jan. 1, 1992. One year later, a share increased to Q dollars. The fraction by which the cost of a share of stock has increased in the year is

(A) $\dfrac{Q - D}{D}$

(B) $\dfrac{D - Q}{Q}$

(C) $\dfrac{D}{Q}$

(D) $\dfrac{Q}{D}$

(E) $\dfrac{Q - D}{Q}$

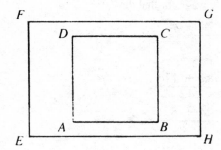

15. In the figure above, $ABCD$ is a square, $EFGH$ is a rectangle. $AB = 3$, $EF = 4$, $FG = 6$. The area of the region outside of $ABCD$ and inside $EFGH$ is

(A) 6
(B) 9
(C) 12
(D) 15
(E) 24

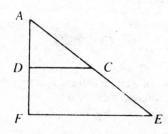

16. In the triangle above, DC is parallel to FE. $AD = DF$, $DC = 4$, and $DF = 3$. What is FE?

(A) 4
(B) 5
(C) 6
(D) 7
(E) 8

17. Which of the following fractions is the largest?

(A) $\dfrac{5}{6}$ (B) $\dfrac{11}{14}$ (C) $\dfrac{12}{15}$ (D) $\dfrac{17}{21}$ (E) $\dfrac{29}{35}$

18. How much simple interest will $2,000 earn in 18 months at an annual rate of 6%?

(A) $ 120
(B) $ 180
(C) $ 216
(D) $1,800
(E) $2,160

19. If $x + y > 5$ and $x - y > 3$, then which of the following gives all possible values of x and only possible values of x?

(A) $x > 3$
(B) $x > 4$
(C) $x > 5$
(D) $x < 5$
(E) $x < 3$

20. If the average (or arithmetic mean) of 6 numbers is 4.5, what is the sum of the numbers?

(A) 4.5
(B) 24
(C) 27
(D) 30
(E) cannot be determined

21. A silo is filled to capacity with W pounds of wheat. Rats eat r pounds a day. After 25 days, what percent of the silo's capacity have the rats eaten?

(A) $\dfrac{25r}{W}$

(B) $\dfrac{25r}{100W}$

(C) $2,500\left(\dfrac{r}{W}\right)$

(D) $\dfrac{r}{W}$

(E) $\dfrac{r}{25W}$

22. If $x^2 + 2x - 8 = 0$, then x is either -4 or

(A) -2
(B) -1
(C) 0
(D) 2
(E) 8

23. The interest charged on a loan is p dollars per $1,000 for the first month and q dollars per $1,000 for each month after the first month. How much interest will be charged during the first three months on a loan of $10,000?

(A) $30p$
(B) $30q$
(C) $p + 2q$
(D) $20p + 10p$
(E) $10p + 20q$

24. In rectangle $ACDF$, $AB = BC$ and $FE = ED$. G is any point on AF. The ratio of the area of $BCDE$ to the area of triangle GCD is

(A) 2:1   (B) 1:2   (C) 1:1   (D) 2:3   (E) 3:2

25. If $3x = \frac{5}{6}y$, then $5y =$

(A) $\frac{1}{2}x$

(B) $2x$

(C) $3.6x$

(D) $5x$

(E) $18x$

Answer Key

The letter following each question number is the correct answer. The numbers in parentheses refer to the sections of Chapter 11: Mathematics Review that explain the necessary mathematics principles. A more detailed explanation of all answers follows.

Discrete Quantitative Exercise A

1.	D (I-A)	8.	C (I-B)	14.	C (I-D)	20.	D (III-G)
2.	B (I-D)	9.	A (II-A)	15.	D (III-H, III-G)	21.	A (II-C)
3.	B (III-G, I-D)	10.	D (I-B)	16.	A (II-B)	22.	D (I-A)
4.	C (I-D)	11.	D (II-C)	17.	D (I-H)	23.	A (I-D, I-B)
5.	A (I-A)	12.	C (III-G, II-A, I-H)	18.	B (III-D, III-G)	24.	A (II-G)
6.	C (II-A)	13.	D (II-B)	19.	E (II-E)	25.	D (III-F, III-D)
7.	C (III-H, I-H)						

Discrete Quantitative Exercise B

1.	B (I-D)	8.	B (I-G)	14.	A (I-B)	20.	C (I-G)
2.	E (II-B)	9.	E (II-D)	15.	D (III-G)	21.	C (I-D)
3.	A (II-A)	10.	A (I-G, II-A)	16.	E (III-D)	22.	D (II-A, II-B)
4.	E (II-B)	11.	B (I-D)	17.	A (I-A, I-B, III-G)	23.	E (II-A)
5.	B (I-C)	12.	D (III-G)	18.	B (I-D)	24.	C (III-G)
6.	B (II-G, I-F)	13.	E (II-A)	19.	B (II-G)	25.	E (II-A)
7.	E (III-D)						

Answer Explanations

Discrete Quantitative Exercise A

1. D.   The price increased by $34 - 12 = 22$ dollars.

2. B.   Ms. Jones sold the house for 125% of C or $\frac{5}{4}C$.

Thus, the gain is $\frac{5}{4}C - C = \frac{C}{4}$. She must pay a

tax of 50% of $\frac{C}{4}$ or $\frac{1}{2}$ of $\frac{C}{4}$. Therefore, the tax is $\frac{C}{8}$.

Notice that the three years has nothing to do with the problem. Sometimes a question contains unnecessary information.

3. B.   The area of a rectangle is length times width. Let L and W denote the original length and width. Then the new length is $1.2L$ and the new width is $0.8W$. Therefore, the new area is $(1.2L)(0.8W) = 0.96LW$ or 96% of the original area. So the area has decreased by 4%.

4. C.   Voters between 18 and 21 who voted were 85% of the 8% of eligible voters. Thus, $(0.08)(0.85) = 0.068$, so people between 18 and 21 who actually voted were 6.8% of the eligible voters.

5. A. Odd numbers are of the form $2x + 1$ where x is an integer. Thus if $n = 2x + 1$ and $p = 2k + 1$, then $n + p = 2x + 1 + 2k + 1 = 2x + 2k + 2$, which is even. Using $n = 3$ and $p = 5$, all the other choices give an odd number. In general, if a problem involves odd or even numbers, try using the fact that odd numbers are of the form $2x + 1$ and even numbers of the form $2y$ where x and y are integers.

6. C. To run a car 100 miles will cost $100(g + m)$ cents. Divide by 100 to convert to dollars. The result is $g + m$.

7. C. Using the distance formula, the distance from A to B is
$\sqrt{(1 - (-1))^2 + (3 - 5)^2} = \sqrt{4 + 4} = \sqrt{8} = \sqrt{4 \times 2} = \sqrt{4}\sqrt{2} = 2\sqrt{2}$. You have to be able to simplify $\sqrt{8}$ in order to obtain the correct answer.

8. C. Tips for the week were $\frac{5}{4} \times 50$, so the driver's total income was $50 + \frac{5}{4}(50) = \frac{9}{4}(50)$.

Therefore,
tips made up $\dfrac{\frac{5}{4}(50)}{\frac{9}{4}(50)} = \dfrac{\frac{5}{4}}{\frac{9}{4}} = \frac{5}{9}$ of his income.

Don't waste time figuring out the total income and the tip income. You can use the time saved to answer other questions.

9. A. $S(3,4) = 3^2 - 4^2 = 9 - 16 = -7$. Therefore, $S(3,S(3,4)) = S(3,-7) = 3^2 - (-7)^2 = 9 - 49 = -40$.

10. D. 8 omelets will use $8 \times 3 = 24$ eggs and $8 \times \frac{1}{4} = 2$ peppers. Since 24 is two dozen, the cost will be $(2)(90¢) + (2)(20¢) = 220¢$ or $2.20.

11. D. In order to average 50 mph for the trip, the bus must make the trip in $\frac{185}{50} = 3\frac{7}{10}$ hours, which is 222 minutes. Since 2 hours or 120 minutes were needed for the first 85 miles, the final 100 miles must be completed in $222 - 120$, which is 102 minutes.

12. C. The area of a rectangle is length times width so the area of $ABDC$ is ab. The area of a triangle is one-half of the height times the base. Since BDE is an isosceles right triangle, the base and height both are equal to b. Thus, the area of BDE is $\frac{1}{2}b^2$. Therefore, the area of the figure is $ab + \frac{1}{2}b^2$, which is equal to $b\left(a + \frac{b}{2}\right)$. You have to express your answer as one of the possible answers, so you need to be able to simplify.

13. D. Since $4x + 2y$ is equal to $2(2x + y)$ and $2x + y = 5$, $4x + 2y$ is equal to $2(5)$ or 10.

14. C. The cost increased by $4,800 minus $2,500 or $2,300 between 1967 and 1975. So the cost increased by $\frac{2,300}{2,500}$, which is 0.92 or 92%. Answer (E) is incorrect. The price in 1975 is 192% of the price in 1967, but the *increase* is 92%.

15. D. The distance from $(-1, 2)$ to $(5, 2)$ is 6. (You can use the distance formula or just count the blocks in this case.) The area of a square is the length of a side squared, so the area is 6^2 or 36.

16. A. Since $x + y = 6$ and $3x - y = 4$, we may add the two equations to obtain $4x = 10$, or $x = 2.5$. Then, because $x + y = 6$, y must be 3.5. Therefore, $x - y = -1$.

17. D. If $\frac{x}{y}$ is $\frac{2}{3}$, then $\frac{y}{x}$ is $\frac{3}{2}$. Since $\left(\frac{y}{x}\right)^2$ is equal to $\frac{y^2}{x^2}$, $\frac{y^2}{x^2}$ is $\left(\frac{3}{2}\right)^2$ or $\frac{9}{4}$.

18. B. The area of a triangle is $\frac{1}{2}$ altitude times base. Since BD is perpendicular to AC, x is the altitude. Using the Pythagorean theorem, $x^2 + (AD)^2 = a^2$ and $x^2 + (DC)^2 = a^2$. Thus, $AD = DC$, and $AD = \sqrt{a^2 - x^2}$. So the base is $2\sqrt{a^2 - x^2}$. Therefore, the area is $\frac{1}{2}(x)(2\sqrt{a^2 - x^2})$, which is choice B.

19. E. $1 : 160 :: 2\frac{7}{8} : x$. $x = 2\frac{7}{8}(160)$. $2\frac{7}{8}$ is $\frac{23}{8}$ so the distance from Seton to Monroe is $\frac{23}{8}(160) = 460$ miles.

20. D. Let $EF = FG = GC$. Therefore, $BE = EF = FG = GC$. Draw perpendiculars EH, FI, GJ. Draw diagonals HF, IG, JC. The 8 triangles are equal in area since they each have the same altitude (AB or DC) and equal bases (BE, EF, FG, GC, AH, HI, IJ, JD). Since the area of $ABE = 7$, the area of $ABCD = (8)(7)$ or 56.

21. A. In each minute the first puncture will leak $\frac{1}{9}$ of the air and the second puncture will leak $\frac{1}{6}$ of the air. Together $\frac{1}{9} + \frac{1}{6} = \frac{5}{18}$. So $\frac{5}{18}$ of the air will leak out in each minute. In $\frac{18}{5}$ or $3\frac{3}{5}$ minutes the tire will be flat.

22. D. Since an even number times any number is even, and n times n^2 is odd, neither n nor n^2 can be even. Therefore, n and n^2 must both be odd for n^3 to be odd. I and II are true, and III is false.

23. A. 90% of 50 is 45, so 45 students took the final. $\frac{2}{3}$ of 45 is 30. Therefore, 30 students passed the final.

24. A. The average of two different numbers is always between the two. If $a = 2$ and $b = 3$, then $b^2 - a^2 = 5$, $ab = 6$, and $b - a = 1$ so C, D, and E must be false. If $a = \frac{1}{2}$ and $b = 1$, then $\frac{(ab)}{2} = \frac{1}{4}$, so B is also false.

25. D. Since the radius to the point of tangency is perpendicular to the tangent, OR must be perpendicular to PR. Therefore, ORP is a right triangle, and $(PO)^2 = (OR)^2 + (PR)^2$. Then, $(PR)^2 = (PO)^2 - (OR)^2$. Thus, $(PR)^2 = 4^2 - 2^2$, and $PR = \sqrt{16 - 4} = \sqrt{12} = \sqrt{4}\sqrt{3} = 2\sqrt{3}$.

Discrete Quantitative Exercise B

1. B. After the tune-up, the bus will travel $(1.15)(15) = 17.25$ miles on a gallon of gas. Therefore, it will take $150 \div 17.25 = 8.7$ (to the nearest tenth) gallons of gasoline to travel 150 miles.

2. E. If $\frac{x}{y} = 2$, then $x = 2y$, so $x + 2y = 2y + 2y = 4y$. But $x + 2y = 4$, so $4y = 4$, or $y = 1$. Since $x = 2y$, x must be 2.

3. A. The cost of producing the first 8,000 copies is $1,000 + 7,000x$. $1,000 + 7,000x = \$7,230$. Therefore, $7,000x = 6,230$ and $x = 0.89$.

4. E. Assume all workers work at the same rate unless given different information. Since 16 workers take 3 hours, each worker does $\frac{1}{48}$ of the job an hour. Thus, the 5 workers will finish $\frac{5}{48}$ of the job each hour. $\frac{5}{48}x = \frac{48}{48}$. It will take $\frac{48}{5} = 9\frac{3}{5}$ hours for them to finish the job.

5. B. The 12 poles weigh $(12)(1.1) = 13.2$ pounds and the 7 pieces of net weigh $7(0.2) = 1.4$ pounds, so the contents of the box weigh $13.2 + 1.4 = 14.6$ pounds. Therefore, the box by itself must weigh $16.25 - 14.6 = 1.65$ pounds.

6. B. If all the numbers were not positive, then the sum could not be positive so A is incorrect. If a, b, and c were all -1 and d were 5, then $a + b + c + d$ would be positive so C, D, and E are incorrect.

7. E. Since the measure of angle M is 55°, the measure of angle K is 35°. Therefore, $KL > LM$ since the larger side is opposite the larger angle.

8. B. Choice A gives 6^2 or 36. Choice B gives 4^4 or 256. Choice C is 8^2 or 64. Choice D is $2 + 4 + 16 = 22$. Choice E is 4^3 or 64.

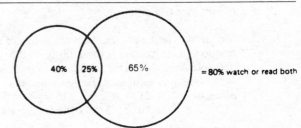

9. E. Since 25% read the newspaper and watched the news on television and 40% read the newspaper, $40\% - 25\%$ or 15% read the newspaper but did not watch the news on television. Thus $65\% + 15\%$ or 80% read the newspaper or watched the news on television, so $100\% - 80\%$ or 20% neither read the newspaper nor watched the news on television.

10. A. For the first 8 hours, the worker is paid a total of $8d$. For the final 4 hours $(12 - 8)$, she is paid $4c$. Therefore, her total pay is $8d + 4c$. To find the average hourly pay, divide by 12. To find the correct answer among the choices, you have to reduce the fraction. Divide the numerator by 4 and the denominator by 4.

11. B. If the price of one screwdriver increases by 5%, then the price of three screwdrivers increases by 5% (not 15%). The percentage change is the same regardless of the number sold. Since a screwdriver and a hammer currently cost the same, the screwdrivers and the hammers each cost one-half of the total price. So one-half of the total is increased by 5%. The other half is increased by 3%. Therefore, the total price is increased by $\frac{1}{2}(5\%) + \frac{1}{2}(3\%)$ = 4%.

12. D. After the radius is increased by 6%, the radius will be 1.06 times the original radius. Since the area of a circle is πr^2, the new area will be $\pi(1.06r)^2 = \pi(1.1236r^2)$ or $1.1236\pi r^2$. Thus, the area has been increased by 0.1236 or by 12.36%.

13. E. Since $g(a) = a^2 + 2$, $g(3)$ is $3^2 + 2$ or 11. So $f[3,g(3)]$ is $f(3,11) = 3 \times 11$ or 33.

14. A. The difference in the price is $Q - D$. So the fraction by which it has increased is $\frac{Q - D}{D}$. Note that the denominator is the *original* price.

15. D. Since $ABCD$ is a square, the area of $ABCD$ is 3^2 or 9. The area of the rectangle $EFGH$ is *length* times *width* or $4 \times 6 = 24$. Thus, the area outside the square and inside the rectangle is $24 - 9$ or 15.

16. E. Since CD is parallel to EF, the triangles ACD and AEF are similar. Therefore, corresponding sides are proportional. So CD is to EF as AD is to AF. Since $AD = DF$, $\frac{AD}{AF}$ is $\frac{1}{2}$. Therefore, EF is twice CD or 8.

17. A. You need to find a common denominator for the fractions. One method is to multiply all the denominators. A quicker method is to find the least common multiple of the denominators. Since $6 = 3 \times 2$, $14 = 2 \times 7$, $15 = 3 \times 5$, $21 = 3 \times 7$, and $35 = 5 \times 7$, the least common multiple is $2 \times 3 \times 5 \times 7 = 210$. $\frac{5}{6}$ is $\frac{175}{210}$, $\frac{11}{14}$ is $\frac{165}{210}$, $\frac{12}{15}$ is $\frac{168}{210}$, $\frac{17}{21}$ is $\frac{170}{210}$, and $\frac{29}{35}$ is $\frac{174}{210}$. $\frac{5}{6}$, written as $\frac{175}{210}$, has the largest numerator.

18. B. 18 months is $\frac{3}{2}$ of a year. Interest = Amount × Time × Rate. $(\$2,000)\left(\frac{3}{2}\right)(0.06) = \$180$.

19. B. If $x + y > 5$ and $x - y > 3$, then, since both inequalities are of the same type, the corresponding sides can be added to obtain $2x > 8$ or $x > 4$.

20. C. The average of 6 numbers is the sum of the numbers divided by 6. Thus, the sum of the numbers is the average multiplied by 6, or 4.5 × 6, which is 27.

21. C. After 25 days the rats have eaten $25r$ pounds of wheat. So $\frac{25r}{W}$ is the fraction of the capacity eaten by the rats. To change this to percent, multiply by 100. $\frac{25r}{W} \times 100 = 2,500\left(\frac{r}{W}\right)$.

22. D. Factor $x^2 + 2x - 8$ into $(x + 4)(x - 2)$. If x is either -4 or 2, $x^2 + 2x - 8 = 0$, and D is the correct answer.

23. E. The interest on the $10,000 for the first month will be $10p$. For the next 2 months the interest will be $20q$. The total interest is $10p + 20q$.

24. C. Area of rectangle $ACDF = (AC)(CD)$. Area of rectangle $BCDE = (BC)(CD)$ or $\left(\frac{1}{2}\right)(AC)(CD)$ Area of triangle $GCD = \left(\frac{1}{2}\right)(AC)(CD)$.

25. E. A time-consuming method would be to solve for y in terms of x and to substitute that value in $5y$. A superior method would be to multiply both sides of the equation by 6 in order to obtain a value of $5y$.

$$3x = \frac{5}{6}y$$
$$(6)(3x) = \left(\frac{5}{6}y\right)(6)$$
$$18x = 5y$$

10 Data Interpretation Questions

Data interpretation questions are based on information given in tables or graphs. These questions test your ability to interpret the information presented and to select the appropriate data for answering a question. There are usually five data interpretation questions in each quantitative section. They are generally questions 21–25.

TESTING TACTICS

The five questions that follow were part of an actual GRE test. These questions will be used to illustrate the data interpretation testing tactics.

Questions 21–25 refer to the following graphs.

DISTRIBUTION OF EARNINGS AND REVENUES FOR COMPANY X, 1978-1983
ELECTRONIC AND NONELECTRONIC OPERATIONS

(1 billion = 1,000,000,000)

Distribution of Earnings from Nonelectronic Operations, 1983
(in millions of dollars)

Note: Drawn to scale.

21. Total earnings from operations in 1982 were approximately how much more than total earnings from
operations in 1978?

(A) $100 million
(B) $125 million
(C) $180 million
(D) $340 million
(E) $475 million

22. For the year in which earnings from electronic operations first exceeded $400 million, <u>total revenues</u>
were appoximately

(A) $2.8 billion
(B) $4.5 billion
(C) $5.2 billion
(D) $5.8 billion
(E) $6.7 billion

23. In 1979, total earnings for Company X were
approximately what percent of total revenues?

(A)   1%
(B)   5%
(C) 10%
(D) 15%
(E) 60%

24. For the two years in which earnings from electronic
operations were most nearly equal, the combined
earnings from nonelectronic operations were most
nearly

(A) $340 million
(B) $520 million
(C) $670 million
(D) $780 million
(E) $1,520 million

25. In 1983 earnings from financial nonelectronic
operations accounted for approximately how
many millions of dollars?

(A) 312
(B) 300
(C) 180
(D) 140
(E) 120

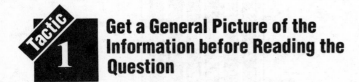

Get a General Picture of the Information before Reading the Question

Read the titles. In the case of the preceding former GRE
questions, note that the upper bar graphs present two
kinds of data.

The bar graph at the left deals with earnings, while the
other bar graph deals with revenues. Note that earnings
are given in millions of dollars, and revenues are expressed in billions. Also notice that each bar deals with
two kinds of company operations. Observe that the pie
chart below the bar graphs takes up the details of nonelectronic operations for one particular year.

Avoid Lengthy Computations

Do not expect to be asked to do extensive computations in
data interpretation questions. Most questions simply require reading the data correctly and putting them to use
with common sense. For example, to obtain the correct
answer for question 21, use the bar graph to the left. For
1978 the bar reaches a point of $430 million; for 1982,
$770 million. If the reading is accurate, the rest of this ex-
ample involves simple subtraction: 770 − 430 = $340
million. The correct choice (D) was picked by 87% of the
people who took this test recently.

Break Down Lengthy Questions into Smaller Parts and Eliminate Impossible Choices

Question 25 is challenging. Only 29% of the people who took this test chose the correct answer (E). First consider the pie chart, and note that 40% of the earnings for 1983 were from financial operations. Now consider earnings, shown in the bar graph at the left. Concentrate on the up-per part of the bar, for nonelectronic operations. The entire bar for 1983 reaches $780 million, and the electronic oper-ations part reaches $480 million. The difference repre-sents the nonelectronic part, or $300 million. 40% of $300 million = $120 million.

Use Only the Information Given

Use only the information given and your knowledge of everyday facts, such as the number of hours in a day, to answer these questions. You must use the data provided even if these data contradict real-life facts that you already know.

Answer the Questions Asked, Not What You Think the Questions Should Be

Question 25 does not ask for all the earnings from non-electronic operations, only the earnings from financial nonelectronic operations.

Be Careful to Use Proper Units

In answering question 23, you must keep in mind that earnings are given in millions, while revenues are in bil-lions. Hence,

$$\frac{\text{1979 earnings}}{\text{1979 total revenues}} = \frac{500 \text{ million}}{5.2 \text{ billion}} = \frac{0.5 \text{ billion}}{5.2 \text{ billion}} = \frac{1}{10.4}, \text{ or approximately 10\%.}$$

Choice (C) is correct.

Use Your Answer Sheet as a Straight Edge to Help You Read the Graph

To make reading easier and to avoid errors, use the edge of your answer sheet to locate the position you are looking for on the graph.

Make Sure Your Answer Is Reasonable

In question 25, answers (A) and (B) are unreasonable since the earnings from financial nonelectronic operations must be less than the *total* earnings of 300 million of *all* nonelectronic operations.

Be Prepared to Apply Basic Mathematical Rules, Principles, and Formulas

Questions 21, 23, 24, and 25 call for careful reading and application of simple arithmetic principles (subtraction and finding a percent). Other questions may require the application of simple algebraic methods and geometric principles.

Whenever Possible, Answer the Question by Visualizing Rather Than by Computing

Since one of the major benefits of graphs and tables is that they present data in a form that enables you to readily see relationships and to make quick comparisons, use this visual attribute of graphs and tables to help you answer the questions. Where possible, use your eye instead of your computational skills. For example, in 1979 the total earnings were $500 million. In answering question 25, however, you need to estimate the 1983 earnings as about $480 million for the electronic operations and $780 million for the total earnings.

Practice Exercises

Directions: Each of the Questions 1–24 has five answer choices. For each of these questions, select the best of the answer choices given.

Questions 1 and 2 refer to the following graphs.

Distribution of Degrees
By Sex, Year 1 and Year 2
Per Cent Distribution

Sources: U.S. Office of Education; The Conference Board

1. The number of women earning Ph.D.'s in Year 2 (to the nearest hundred) was

   (A) 200 (B) 500 (C) 1,500 (D) 13,000
   (E) 15,000

2. Which of the following statements best describes the distribution of master's degrees for Year 1 and Year 2?

   (A) Fewer women received master's degrees in Year 2 than in Year 1.

(B) The increase in the number of males who received master's degrees in Year 2 may be represented by the decimal 0.064.

(C) The number of master's degrees received in Year 2 was more than a 300% increase over the number received in Year 1.

(D) The ratio of men to women receiving master's degrees was the same for both years.

(E) Fewer men received master's degrees in Year 2 than in Year 1.

Questions 3 and 4 refer to the following data.

Territorial Expansion

1	ORIGINAL 13 STATES 1790	888,685
2	LOUISIANA PURCHASE 1803	827,192
3	FLORIDA AND OTHER 1819	72,003
4	TEXAS 1845	390,144
5	OREGON TERRITORY 1846	285,580
6	MEXICAN CESSION 1848	529,017
7	GADSEN PURCHASE 1853	26,640
8	ALASKA 1867	586,412
9	HAWAII 1898	6,450
	UNITED STATES TOTAL	3,615,123
	GUAM AND PUERTO RICO 1899	212 and 3,435
	AMERICAN SAMOA 1500	76
	VIRGIN ISLANDS 1917	133
	OTHER	9,083
	U.S. AND OUTLYING AREAS, TOTAL	3,678,062

GROSS AREA Land and Water, square miles

3. After the Louisiana Purchase the area of the United States had

(A) roughly tripled
(B) roughly doubled
(C) increased slightly
(D) stayed the same
(E) decreased slightly

4. Which of the following percentages is closest to the percent of the United States total area that is Alaska?

(A) 10
(B) 15
(C) 20
(D) 25
(E) 30

Questions 5–9 refer to the following table.

INCOME (IN DOLLARS)	TAX (IN DOLLARS)
0–4,000	1% of income
4,000–6,000	40 + 2% of income over 4,000
6,000–8,000	80 + 3% of income over 6,000
8,000–10,000	140 + 4% of income over 8,000
10,000–15,000	220 + 5% of income over 10,000
15,000–25,000	470 + 6% of income over 15,000
25,000–50,000	1,070 + 7% of income over 25,000

5. How much tax is due on an income of $7,500?

(A) $ 75
(B) $ 80
(C) $125
(D) $150
(E) $225

6. Your income for a year is $26,000. You receive a raise so that next year your income will be $29,000. How much *more* will you pay in taxes next year if the tax rate remains the same?

(A) $ 70
(B) $180
(C) $200
(D) $210
(E) $700

7. Joan paid $100 in taxes. If X was her income, which of the following statements is true?

(A) $0 < X < 4,000$
(B) $4,000 < X < 6,000$
(C) $6,000 < X < 8,000$
(D) $8,000 < X < 10,000$
(E) $10,000 < X < 15,000$

8. The town of Zenith has a population of 50,000. The average income of a person who lives in Zenith is $3,700 per year. What is the total amount paid in taxes by the people of Zenith? Assume each person pays tax on $3,700.

(A) $ 37
(B) $ 3,700
(C) $ 50,000
(D) $ 185,000
(E) $1,850,000

9. A person who has an income of $10,000 pays what percent (to the nearest percent) of his or her income in taxes?

(A) 1
(B) 2
(C) 3
(D) 4
(E) 5

Questions 10–14 refer to the following graph.

Women in the Labor Force

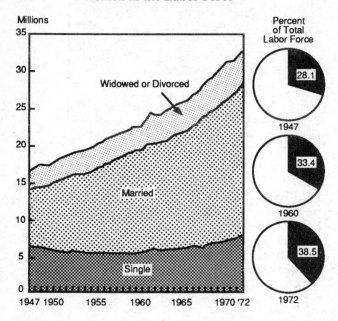

Sources: Pocket Data Book U.S.A. 1973. Bureau of the Census.

10. The total labor force in 1960 was about *y* million with *y* equal to about

    (A) 22
    (B) 65
    (C) 75
    (D) 80
    (E) 85

11. In 1947, the percent of women in the labor force who were married was about

    (A) 28
    (B) 33
    (C) 38
    (D) 50
    (E) 65

12. What was the first year when more than 20 million women were in the labor force?

    (A) 1950
    (B) 1953
    (C) 1956
    (D) 1958
    (E) 1964

13. Between 1947 and 1972, the number of women in the labor force increased by about

    (A) 50%
    (B) 100%
    (C) 150%
    (D) 200%
    (E) 250%

14. Which of the following statements about the labor force can be inferred from the graphs?

    I. Between 1947 and 1957, there were no years when more than 5 million widowed or divorced women were in the labor force.

    II. In every year between 1947 and 1972, the number of single women in the labor force has increased.

    III. In 1965, women made up more than $\frac{1}{3}$ of the total labor force.

    (A) I only
    (B) II only
    (C) I and II only
    (D) I and III only
    (E) I, II, and III

Questions 15–18 refer to the following table.

Participation in National Elections

Persons in millions. Civilian noninstitutional population as of Nov. 1. Based on post-election surveys of persons reporting whether or not they voted; differs from table 103 data which are based on actual vote counts.

Characteristic	1964		1968		1972	
	Persons of voting age	Percent voted	Persons of voting age	Percent voted	Persons of voting age	Percent voted
Total	111	69	117	68	136	63
Male	52	72	54	70	64	64
Female	58	67	62	66	72	62
White	99	71	105	69	121	64
Negro and other	11	57	12	56	15	51
Negro	10	58	11	58	13	52
Region:						
North and West	78	75	82	71	94	66
South	32	57	35	60	43	55
Age:						
18–24 years	10	51	12	50	25	50
25–44 years	45	69	46	67	49	63
45–64 years	38	76	40	75	42	71
65 years and over	17	66	18	66	20	63

Source: U.S. Bureau of the Census.

15. Which of the following groups had the highest percentage of voters in 1968?

    (A) 18–24 years
    (B) Female
    (C) South
    (D) 25–44 years
    (E) Male

16. In 1972, what percent (to the nearest percent) of persons of voting age were female?

    (A) 52
    (B) 53
    (C) 62
    (D) 64
    (E) 72

17. In 1968, how many males of voting age voted?

    (A) 37,440,000
    (B) 37,800,000
    (C) 42,160,000
    (D) 62,000,000
    (E) 374,400,000

18. Let X be the number (in millions) of persons of voting age in the 25–44 year range who lived in the North and West in 1964. Which of the following includes all possible values and only possible values of X?

(A) $0 \lesseqgtr X \lesseqgtr 45$

(B) $13 \lesseqgtr X \lesseqgtr 45$

(C) $13 \lesseqgtr X \lesseqgtr 78$

(D) $45 \lesseqgtr X \lesseqgtr 78$

(E) $75 \lesseqgtr X \lesseqgtr 78$

Questions 19–21 refer to the following table.

SPEED OF A TRAIN OVER A 3-HOUR PERIOD								
TIMED PERIOD (in minutes)	0	30	45	60	90	120	150	180
SPEED AT TIME (in m.p.h.)	40	45	47.5	50	55	60	65	70

19. How fast was the train traveling $2\frac{1}{2}$ hours after the beginning of the timed period?

(A) 50 m.p.h.

(B) 55 m.p.h.

(C) 60 m.p.h.

(D) 65 m.p.h.

(E) 70 m.p.h.

20. During the three hours shown on the table, the speed of the train increased by

(A) 25%

(B) 50%

(C) 75%

(D) 100%

(E) 125%

21. At time t, measured in minutes after the beginning of the time period, which of the following gives the speed of the train in accordance with the table?

(A) $\frac{1}{6}t$

(B) $10t$

(C) $40 + t$

(D) $40 + \frac{1}{6}t$

(E) $40 + 10t$

Questions 22–24 refer to the following table.

	% OF PROTEIN	% OF CARBOHYDRATES	% OF FAT	COST PER 100 GRAMS
FOOD A	10	20	30	$1.80
FOOD B	20	15	10	$3.00
FOOD C	20	10	40	$2.75

22. If you purchase x grams of Food A, y grams of Food B, and z grams of Food C, the cost will be

(A) $\left(\dfrac{9}{5}x + 3y + \dfrac{11}{4}z\right)$¢

(B) $\$\left(\dfrac{9}{5}x + 3y + \dfrac{11}{4}z\right)$

(C) $\$(1.8x + 3z + 2.75y)$

(D) $(3x + 1.8y + 2.75z)$¢

(E) $\$(x + y + z)$

23. Which of the following diets would supply the most grams of protein?

(A) 500 grams of A

(B) 250 grams of B

(C) 350 grams of C

(D) 150 grams of A and 200 grams of B

(E) 200 grams of B and 200 grams of C

24. All of the following diets would supply at least 75 grams of fat. Which of the diets costs the least?

(A) 200 grams of A, 150 grams of B

(B) 500 grams of B, 100 grams of A

(C) 200 grams of C

(D) 150 grams of A, 100 grams of C

(E) 300 grams of A

Answer Key

1.	C	7.	C	13.	B	19.	D
2.	C	8.	E	14.	A	20.	C
3.	B	9.	B	15.	E	21.	D
4.	B	10.	B	16.	B	22.	A
5.	C	11.	D	17.	B	23.	E
6.	D	12.	C	18.	B	24.	E

Answer Explanations

1. C.   10.6% of 14,490 = 1,534.94. The closest answer is 1,500.

2. C.   101,122 ÷ 26,731 = 3.78 or 378%.

3. B.   The Louisiana Purchase added about 830,000 square miles. The previous area was about 890,000 square miles, so the area almost doubled.

4. B. Alaska is almost 600,000 square miles, which is about $\frac{1}{6}$ of 3,660,000 square miles. $\frac{1}{6}$ is $16\frac{2}{3}\%$ so the correct answer is 15%. Save time by estimating; don't perform the calculations exactly.

5. C. 7,500 is in the 6,000–8,000 bracket so the tax will be 80 + 3% of the income over 6,000. Since 7,500 − 6,000 = 1,500, the income over 6,000 is 1,500. 3% of 1500 = (0.03)(1500) = 45, so the tax is 80 + 45 = 125.

6. D. The tax on 26,000 is 1,070 + 7% of (26,000 − 25,000). Thus, the tax is 1,070 + 70 = 1,140. The tax on 29,000 is 1,070 + 7% of (29,000 − 25,000). Thus, the tax on 29,000 is 1,070 + 280 = 1,350. Therefore, you will pay 1,350 − 1,140 = $210 more in taxes next year. A faster method is to use the fact that the $3,000 raise is income over 25,000, so it will be taxed at 7%. Therefore, the tax on the extra $3,000 will be (0.07)(3,000) = 210.

7. C. If income is less than 6,000, then the tax is less than 80. If income is greater than 8,000, then the tax is greater than 140. Therefore, if the tax is 100, the income must be between 6,000 and 8,000. You *do not* have to calculate Joan's exact income.

8. E. Each person pays the tax on $3,700, which is 1% of 3,700 or $37. Since there are 50,000 people in Zenith, the total taxes are (37)(50,000) = $1,850,000.

9. B. The tax on 10,000 is 220, so taxes are $\frac{220}{10,000}$ = 0.022 = 2.2% of income. 2.2% is 2% after rounding to the nearest percent.

10. B. In 1960 women made up 33.4% or about $\frac{1}{3}$ of the labor force. Using the line graph, there were about 22 million women in the labor force in 1960. So the labor force was about 3(22) or 66 million. The closest answer among the choices is 65 million.

11. D. In 1947, there were about 16 million women in the labor force, and about 14 − 6 or 8 million of them were married. Therefore, the percent of women in the labor force who were married is $\frac{8}{16}$ or 50%.

12. C. Look at the possible answers first. You can use your pencil and admission card as straight edges.

13. B. In 1947, there were about 16 million women in the labor force. By 1972 there were about 32 million. Therefore, the number of women doubled, which is an increase of 100% (not of 200%).

14. A. I is true since the width of the band for widowed or divorced women was never more than 5 million between 1947 and 1957. II is false since the number of single women in the labor force decreased from 1947 to 1948. III cannot be inferred since there is no information about the total labor force or women as a percent of it in 1965. Thus, only I can be inferred.

15. E. Look in the fourth column.

16. B. In 1972 there were 72 million females out of 136 million persons of voting age. $\frac{72}{136}$ = 0.529, which is 53% to the nearest percent.

17. B. In 1968, 70% of the 54 million males of voting age voted, and (0.7)(54,000,000) = 37,800,000.

18. B. Since 78 million persons of voting age lived in the North and West in 1964, and there were 65 million persons of voting age not in the 25–44 year range, there must be at least 78 − 65 = 13 million people in the North and West in the 25–44 year range. X must be greater than or equal to 13. Since there were 45 million people of voting age in the 25–44 year range, X must be less than or equal to 45.

19. D. $2\frac{1}{2}$ hours is 150 minutes.

20. C. The train's speed increased by 70 − 40 which is 30 miles per hour. $\frac{30}{40}$ is 75%.

21. D. When $t = 0$, the speed is 40, so A and B are incorrect. When $t = 180$, the speed is 70, so C and E are incorrect. Choice D gives all the values that appear in the table.

22. A. The cost of food A is $1.80 per hundred grams or 1.8¢ a gram, so x grams cost $(1.8x)$¢ or $\left(\frac{9}{5}\right)x$¢. Each gram of food B costs 3¢ so y grams of food B will cost $3y$¢. Each gram of food C costs 2.75¢ or $\frac{11}{4}$¢; thus, z grams of food C will cost $\left(\frac{11}{4}\right)z$¢. Therefore, the total cost is $\left[\left(\frac{9}{5}\right)x + 3y + \left(\frac{11}{4}\right)z\right]$¢.

23. E. Since Food A is 10% protein, 500 grams of A will supply 50 grams of protein. Food B is 20% protein, so 250 grams of B will supply 50 grams of protein. 350 grams of Food C will supply 70 grams of protein. 150 grams of Food A and 200 grams of Food B will supply 15 + 40 = 55 grams of protein. 200 grams of Food B and 200 grams of Food C will supply 40 + 40 or 80 grams of protein. Choice E supplies the most protein.

24. E. The diet of Choice A will cost 2($1.80) + $\left(\frac{3}{2}\right)$($3) = $3.60 + $4.50 = $8.10. Choice B will cost 5($3) + $1.80 = $16.80. Choice C costs 2($2.75) = $5.50. Choice D costs $\left(\frac{3}{2}\right)$($1.80) + $2.75 = $2.70 + $2.75 = $5.45. The diet of Choice E costs 3($1.80) or $5.40 so Choice E costs the least.

11 Mathematics Review

■ **Arithmetic**
■ **Algebra**
■ **Geometry**
■ **Tables and Graphs**
■ **Formulas**

The mathematics questions on the GRE General Test require a working knowledge of mathematical principles, including an understanding of the fundamentals of algebra, plane geometry, and arithmetic, as well as the ability to translate problems into formulas and to interpret graphs. The following review covers these areas thoroughly and will prove helpful.

Read through the review carefully. You will notice that each topic is keyed for easy reference. Each of the Practice

Exercises in this chapter, as well as the Diagnostic and five Model Tests, are keyed in the same manner. Therefore, after working the mathematics problems in each area, you should refer to the answer key and follow the mathematics reference key so that you can focus on the topics where you need improvement.

Review the tactics in the preceding chapters for test-taking help.

Review and Practice

I.   Arithmetic

I–A.   Whole Numbers

A–1

The numbers 1, 2, 3, . . . are called the *positive integers*. –1, –2, –3, . . . are called the *negative integers*. An integer is a positive or negative integer or the number 0.

A–2

If the integer k divides m evenly, then we say m is *divisible by k* or *k is a factor of m*. For example, 12 is divisible by 4, but 12 is not divisible by 5. The factors of 12 are 1, 2, 3, 4, 6, and 12.

If k is a factor of m, then there is another integer n such that $m = k \times n$; in this case, m is called a *multiple of k*.

Since $12 = 4 \times 3$, 12 is a multiple of 4 and also 12 is a multiple of 3. For example, 5, 10, 15, and 20 are all multiples of 5 but 15 and 5 are not multiples of 10.

Any integer is a multiple of each of its factors.

A–3

Any whole number is divisible by itself and by 1. If p is a whole number greater than 1, which has *only p* and 1 as factors, then p is called a *prime number*. 2, 3, 5, 7, 11, 13, 17, 19 and 23 are all primes. 14 is not a prime since it is divisible by 2 and by 7.

A whole number that is divisible by 2 is called an *even* number; if a whole number is not even, then it is an *odd* number. 2, 4, 6, 8, and 10 are even numbers, and 1, 3, 5, 7, and 9 are odd numbers.

A–4

Any integer greater than 1 is a prime or can be written as a product of primes.

To write a number as a *product of prime factors*:

❶ Divide the number by 2 if possible; continue to divide by 2 until the factor you get is not divisible by 2.

❷ Divide the result from ❶ by 3 if possible; continue to divide by 3 until the factor you get is not divisible by 3.

❸ Divide the result from ❷ by 5 if possible; continue to divide by 5 until the factor you get is not divisible by 5.

❹ Continue the procedure with 7, 11, and so on, until all the factors are primes.

Express 24 as a product of prime factors.

❶ $24 = 2 \times 12$, $12 = 2 \times 6$, $6 = 2 \times 3$ so $24 = 2 \times 2 \times 2 \times 3$. Since each factor (2 and 3) is prime, $24 = 2 \times 2 \times 2 \times 3$.

A class of 45 students will be seated in rows. Every row will have the same number of students. There must be at least two students in each row, and there must be at least two rows. A row is parallel to the front of the room. How many different arrangements are possible?

Since the number of students = (the number of rows)(the number of students in each row) and the number of students is 45, the question can be answered by finding how many different ways 45 can be written as a product of two positive integers that are both greater than 1. (The integers must be greater than 1 because there are at least two rows and at least two students per row.) Writing 45 as a product of primes makes this easy. $45 = 3 \times 15 = 3 \times 3 \times 5$. Therefore, 3×15, 5×9, 9×5, and 15×3 are the only possibilities, and the correct answer is 4. (The fact that a row is parallel to the front of the room means that 3×15 and 15×3 are different arrangements.)

A–5

A number m is a *common multiple* of two other numbers k and j if it is a multiple of each of them. For example, 12 is a common multiple of 4 and 6, since $3 \times 4 = 12$ and $2 \times 6 = 12$. 15 is not a common multiple of 3 and 6, because 15 is not a multiple of 6.

A number k is a *common factor* of two other numbers m and n if k is a factor of m and k is a factor of n.

The *least common multiple* (L.C.M.) of two numbers is the smallest number that is a common multiple of both numbers. To find the least common multiple of two numbers k and j:

❶ Write k as a product of primes and j as a product of primes.

❷ If there are any common factors *delete* them in *one* of the products.

❸ Multiply the remaining factors; the result is the least common multiple.

Find the L.C.M. of 27 and 63.

---

❶ $27 = 3 \times 3 \times 3$, $63 = 3 \times 3 \times 7$.

❷ $3 \times 3 = 9$ is a common factor so delete it once.

❸ The L.C.M. is $3 \times 3 \times 3 \times 7 = 189$.

You can find the L.C.M. of a collection of numbers in the same way except that, if in step (B) the common factors are factors of more than two of the numbers, then delete the common factor in *all but one* of the products.

It takes Eric 20 minutes to inspect a car. John needs only 15 minutes to inspect a car. If they both start inspecting cars at 9:00 A.M., what is the first time the two mechanics will finish inspecting a car at the same time?

Eric will finish k cars after $k \times 20$ minutes, and John will finish j cars after $j \times 15$ minutes. Therefore, they will both finish inspecting a car at the same time when $k \times 20 = j \times 15$. Since k and j must be integers (they represent the number of cars finished) this question asks you to find a common multiple of 20 and 15. Since you are asked for the first time the two mechanics will finish at the same time, you must find the least common multiple.

❶ $20 = 4 \times 5 = 2 \times 2 \times 5$, $15 = 3 \times 5$.

❷ Delete 5 from one of the products.

❸ The L.C.M. is $2 \times 2 \times 5 \times 3 = 60$.

Eric and John will finish inspecting a car at the same time 60 minutes after they start, or at 10:00 A.M.

A–6

The numbers 0, 1, 2, 3, 4, 5, 6, 7, 8 and 9 are called **digits**. The number 132 is a three-digit number. In the number 132, 1 is the first or hundreds digit, 3 is the second or tens digit, and 2 is the last or units digit.

Find x if x is a two-digit number whose last digit is 2. The difference of the digits of x is 5.

The two-digit numbers whose last digit is 2 are 12, 22, 32, 42, 52, 62, 72, 82, and 92. The difference of the digits of 12 is either 1 or –1, so 12 is not x. Since $7 - 2$ is 5, x is 72.

I-B. Fractions

B-1

A FRACTION is a number that represents a ratio or division of two numbers. A fraction is written in the form $\frac{a}{b}$. The number on the top, *a*, is called the *numerator*; the number on the bottom, *b*, is the *denominator*. The denominator tells how many equal parts there are (for example, parts of a pie); the numerator tells how many of these equal parts are taken. For example, $\frac{5}{8}$ is a fraction whose numerator is 5 and whose denominator is 8; it represents taking 5 of 8 equal parts, or dividing 8 into 5.

> *A fraction cannot have 0 as a denominator since division by 0 is not defined.*

A fraction with 1 as the denominator is the same as the whole number that is its numerator. For example, $\frac{12}{1}$ is 12, $\frac{0}{1}$ is 0.

If the numerator and denominator of a fraction are identical, the fraction represents 1. For example, $\frac{3}{3} = \frac{9}{9} = \frac{13}{13} = 1$. Any whole number, *k*, is represented by a fraction with a numerator equal to *k* times the denominator. For example, $\frac{18}{6} = 3$, and $\frac{30}{5} = 6$.

B-2

Mixed Numbers. A mixed number consists of a whole number and a fraction. For example, $7\frac{1}{4}$ is a mixed number; it means $7 + \frac{1}{4}$ and $\frac{1}{4}$ is called the fractional part of the mixed number $7\frac{1}{4}$. Any mixed number can be changed into a fraction as follows:

❶ Multiply the whole number by the denominator of the fraction.

❷ Add the numerator of the fraction to the result of ❶.

❸ Use the result of ❷ as the numerator, and use the denominator of the fractional part of the mixed number as the denominator. This fraction is equal to the mixed number.

> Write $7\frac{1}{4}$ as a fraction.

❶ $4 \cdot 7 = 28$

❷ $28 + 1 = 29$

❸ $7\frac{1}{4} = \frac{29}{4}$

A fraction whose numerator is larger than its denominator can be changed into a mixed number.

❶ Divide the denominator into the numerator; the result is the whole number of the mixed number.

❷ Put the remainder from step ❶ over the denominator; this is the fractional part of the mixed number.

> If a pizza pie has 8 pieces, how many pizza pies have been eaten at a party where 35 pieces were eaten?

Since there are 8 pieces in a pie, $\frac{35}{8}$ pies were eaten. To find the number of pies, we need to change $\frac{35}{8}$ into a mixed number.

❶ Divide 8 into 35; the result is 4 with a remainder of 3.

❷ $\frac{3}{8}$ is the fractional part of the mixed number.

❸ $\frac{35}{8} = 4\frac{3}{8}$.

> **In calculations with mixed numbers, change the mixed numbers into fractions.**

B-3

Multiplying Fractions. To multiply two fractions, multiply their numerators to form the numerator of the product. Multiply their denominators to form the denominator of the product.

> John saves $\frac{1}{3}$ of $240. How much does he save?

$$\frac{1}{3} \cdot \frac{240}{1} = \frac{240}{3} = \$80, \text{ the amount John saves.}$$

B-4

Dividing Fractions. To divide one fraction (the dividend) by another fraction (the divisor), invert the divisor and multiply. To invert a fraction turn it upside down; for example, if you invert $\frac{3}{4}$, the result is $\frac{4}{3}$.

$$\frac{5}{6} \div \frac{3}{4} = \frac{5}{6} \cdot \frac{4}{3} = \frac{20}{18}$$

A worker makes a basket in $\frac{2}{3}$ of an hour. If she works for $7\frac{1}{2}$ hours, how many baskets will she make?

It takes $\frac{2}{3}$ of an hour to make one basket, so we need to divide $\frac{2}{3}$ into $7\frac{1}{2}$. Since $7\frac{1}{2} = \frac{15}{2}$, we want to divide $\frac{15}{2}$ by $\frac{2}{3}$. Thus

$$\frac{15}{2} \div \frac{2}{3} = \frac{15}{2} \cdot \frac{3}{2} = \frac{45}{4} = 11\frac{1}{4} \text{ baskets.}$$

B–5

Dividing and Multiplying by the Same Number

If you multiply the numerator and denominator of a fraction by the same nonzero number, the value of the fraction remains the same.

If you divide the numerator and denominator of any fraction by the same nonzero number, the value of the fraction remains the same.

Consider the fraction $\frac{3}{4}$. If we multiply 3 by 10 and 4 by 10, then $\frac{30}{40}$ must be equal $\frac{3}{4}$. (In $\frac{30}{40}$, 10 is a common factor of 30 and 40.)

When we multiply fractions, if any of the numerators and denominators have a common factor (see A–2 for factors) we can divide each of them by the common factor and the fraction remains the same. This process is called *cancelling* and can be a great time-saver.

Multiply $\frac{4}{9} \cdot \frac{75}{8}$.

Since 4 is a common factor of 4 and 8, divide 4 and 8 by 4, getting $\frac{4}{9} \cdot \frac{75}{8} = \frac{1}{9} \cdot \frac{75}{2}$. Since 3 is a common factor of 9 and 75, divide 9 and 75 by 3 to get $\frac{1}{9} \cdot \frac{75}{2} = \frac{1}{3} \cdot \frac{25}{2}$.

Therefore $\frac{4}{9} \cdot \frac{75}{8} = \frac{1}{3} \cdot \frac{25}{2} = \frac{25}{6}$.

Cancelling is denoted by striking or crossing out the appropriate numbers. For instance, the example above

would be written as follows:

$$\frac{\overset{1}{\cancel{4}}}{\underset{3}{\cancel{9}}} \cdot \frac{\overset{25}{\cancel{75}}}{\underset{2}{\cancel{8}}} = \frac{1}{3} \cdot \frac{25}{2} = \frac{25}{6}$$

Since you want to work as fast as possible on the GRE, cancel whenever you can.

B–6

Equivalent Fractions. Two fractions are equivalent or equal if they represent the same ratio or number. In Section B–5, you saw that, if you multiply or divide the numerator and denominator of a fraction by the same nonzero number, the result is equivalent to the original fraction.

For example, $\frac{7}{8} = \frac{70}{80}$ since $70 = 10 \times 7$ and $80 = 10 \times 8$.

In a multiple-choice test, your answer to a problem may not be the same as any of the given choices, yet one choice may be equivalent. Therefore, you may have to express your answer as an equivalent fraction.

To find a fraction with a known denominator equal to a given fraction:

❶ Divide the denominator of the given fraction into the known denominator.

❷ Multiply the result of ❶ by the numerator of the given fraction; this is the numerator of the required equivalent fraction.

Your answer is $\frac{2}{5}$. One of the test answers has a denominator of 30. Find a fraction with denominator 30 that is equal to $\frac{2}{5}$.

---

❶ 5 into 30 is 6.

❷ $6 \cdot 2 = 12$, so $\frac{12}{30} = \frac{2}{5}$.

Check your result. Divide numerator and denominator by the same number. $12 \div 6 = 2$ and $30 \div 6 = 5$.

B–7

Reducing a Fraction to Lowest Terms. A fraction has been reduced to lowest terms when the numerator and denominator have no common factors.

For example, $\frac{3}{4}$ is reduced to lowest terms, but $\frac{3}{6}$ is not because 3 is a common factor of 3 and 6.

To reduce a fraction to lowest terms, cancel all the common factors of the numerator and denominator. (Canceling common factors will not change the value of the fraction.)

For example:

$$\frac{\cancel{100}}{\cancel{150}} = \frac{2}{3}$$

Since 2 and 3 have no common factors, $\frac{2}{3}$ is $\frac{100}{150}$ reduced to lowest terms. A fraction is equivalent to its reduction to lowest terms.

Another way to cancel common factors, and hence reduce to lowest terms, is to first write the numerator and denominator as the products of primes.

B–8

Adding Fractions. If the fractions have the same denominator, then the denominator is called a *common denominator.* Add the numerators, and use this sum as the new numerator, retaining the common denominator as the denominator of the new fraction . Reduce the new fraction to lowest terms.

A box of light bulbs contains 24 bulbs. A worker replaces 17 bulbs in the shipping department and 13 bulbs in the accounting department. How many boxes of bulbs did he use?

The worker used $\frac{17}{24}$ of a box in the shipping department and $\frac{13}{24}$ of a box in the accounting department. The total used was $\frac{17}{24} + \frac{13}{24} = \frac{30}{24} = \frac{5}{4} = 1\frac{1}{4}$ boxes.

If the fractions don't have the same denominator, you must first find a common denominator. One way to get a common denominator is to multiply the denominators together.

For example, to find $\frac{1}{2} + \frac{2}{3} + \frac{7}{4}$, note that $2 \cdot 3 \cdot 4 = 24$ is a common denominator.

There are many common denominators; the smallest one is called the *least common denominator.* For the preceding example, 12 is the least common denominator.

Once you have found a common denominator, express each fraction as an equivalent fraction with the common denominator, and add as you did when the fractions had the same denominator.

$$\frac{1}{2} + \frac{2}{3} + \frac{7}{4} = \,?$$

❶ 24 is a common denominator.

❷ $\frac{1}{2} = \frac{12}{24}, \frac{2}{3} = \frac{16}{24}, \frac{7}{4} = \frac{42}{24}.$

❸ $\frac{1}{2} + \frac{2}{3} + \frac{7}{4} = \frac{12}{14} + \frac{16}{24} + \frac{42}{24} = \frac{12 + 16 + 42}{24} = \frac{70}{24} = \frac{35}{12}.$

B–9

Subtracting Fractions. When the fractions have the same denominator, subtract the numerators and place the result over the denominator.

There are five tacos in a lunch box. Jim eats two of the tacos. What fraction of the original tacos are left in the lunch box?

Jim took $\frac{2}{5}$ of the original tacos, so $1 - \frac{2}{5}$ are left. Write 1 as $\frac{5}{5}$; then $\frac{5}{5} - \frac{2}{5} = \frac{(5-2)}{5} = \frac{3}{5}$. Therefore, $\frac{3}{5}$ of the original tacos are left in the lunch box.

When the fractions have different denominators

❶ Find a common denominator.

❷ Express the fractions as equivalent fractions with the same denominator.

❸ Subtract.

$$\frac{3}{5} - \frac{2}{7} = \,?$$

❶ A common denominator is $5 \cdot 7 = 35$.

❷ $\frac{3}{5} = \frac{21}{35}, \frac{2}{7} = \frac{10}{35}.$

❸ $\frac{3}{5} - \frac{2}{7} = \frac{21}{35} - \frac{10}{35} = \frac{21 - 10}{35} = \frac{11}{35}.$

B–10

Complex Fractions. A fraction whose numerator and denominator are themselves fractions is called a *complex fraction*. For example, $\dfrac{\frac{2}{3}}{\frac{4}{5}}$ is a complex fraction. A complex fraction can always be simplified by dividing its numerator by its denominator.

Simplify $\dfrac{\frac{2}{3}}{\frac{4}{5}}$.

$$\frac{2}{3} \div \frac{4}{5} = \frac{2}{3} \cdot \frac{5}{\overset{2}{\cancel{4}}} = \frac{1}{3} \cdot \frac{5}{2} = \frac{5}{6}$$

It takes $2\dfrac{1}{2}$ hours to get from Buffalo to Cleveland traveling at a constant rate of speed. What part of the distance is traveled in $\dfrac{3}{4}$ of an hour?

$$\frac{3/4}{2\ 1/2} = \frac{3/4}{5/2} = \frac{3}{\overset{2}{\cancel{4}}} \cdot \frac{\overset{1}{\cancel{2}}}{5} = \frac{3}{2} \cdot \frac{1}{5} = \frac{3}{10} \text{ of the distance}$$

I–C. Decimals

C–1

A collection of digits (the digits are 0, 1, 2, . . . , 9) after a period (called the *decimal point*) is called a *decimal fraction*. For example, these are all decimal fractions:

0.503   0.32
0.5602   0.4

The zero to the left of the decimal point is optional in a decimal fraction. We will use the zero consistently in this review.

Every decimal fraction represents a fraction. To find the fraction that a decimal fraction represents, keep in mind the following facts:

❶ The denominator is $10 \times 10 \times 10 \times \cdots \times 10$. The number of 10's is equal to the number of digits to the **right** of the decimal point.

❷ The numerator is the number represented by the digits to the **right** of the decimal point.

What fraction does 0.503 represent?

❶ There are three digits to the right of the decimal point, so the denominator is $10 \times 10 \times 10 = 1{,}000$.

❷ The numerator is 503, so the fraction is $\dfrac{503}{1{,}000}$.

Find the fraction that 0.05732 represents.

❶ There are five digits to the right of the decimal point, so the denominator is $10 \times 10 \times 10 \times 10 \times 10 = 100{,}000$.

❷ The numerator is 5,732, so the fraction is $\dfrac{5{,}372}{100{,}000}$.

You can add any number of zeros to the right of a decimal fraction without changing its value.

$$0.3 = \frac{3}{10} = \frac{30}{100} = 0.30 = 0.30000 =$$
$$\frac{30{,}000}{100{,}000} = 0.300000000 \ldots$$

C–2

We call the first position to the right of the decimal point the tenths place, since the digit in that position tells you how many tenths you should take. (It is the numerator of a fraction whose denominator is 10.) In the same way, we call the second position to the right the hundredths place, the third position to the right the thousandths, and so on. This is similar to the way whole numbers are expressed, since 568 means $5 \times 100 + 6 \times 10 + 8 \times 1$. The various digits represent different numbers depending on their positions: the first place to the left of the decimal point represents units, the second place to the left represents tens, and so on.

The following diagram may be helpful:

```
T H T U       T H T
H U E N       E U H
O N N I  •    N N O
U D D S T     T D U
S R   S       H R S
A E           S E A
N D           E N
D S           D D
S             T T
              H H
              S S
```

Thus, 5,342.061 means 5 thousands + 3 hundreds + 4 tens + 2 + 0 tenths + 6 hundredths + 1 thousandth.

C-3

A DECIMAL is a whole number plus a decimal fraction; the decimal point separates the whole number from the decimal fraction. For example, 4,307.206 is a decimal that represents 4,307 added to the decimal fraction 0.206. A decimal fraction is a decimal with zero as the whole number.

C-4

A fraction whose denominator is a multiple of 10 is equivalent to a decimal. The denominator tells you the last place that is filled to the right of the decimal point. Place the decimal point in the numerator so that the number of places to the right of the decimal point corresponds to the number of zeros in the denominator. If the numerator does not have enough digits, add the appropriate number of zeros *before* the numerator.

> Find the decimal equivalent of $\dfrac{5,732}{100}$.

Since the denominator is 100, you need two places to the right of the decimal point, so $\dfrac{5,732}{100} = 57.32$.

> What is the decimal equivalent of $\dfrac{57}{10,000}$?

The denominator is 10,000, so you need four decimal places to the right of the decimal point. Since 57 has only two places, we add two zeros in front of 57; thus

$$\frac{57}{10,000} = 0.0057.$$

Do not make the error of adding the zeros to the right of 57 instead of to the left. The decimal 0.5700 is $\dfrac{5,700}{10,000}$, not $\dfrac{57}{10,000}$.

C-5

Adding Decimals.   Decimals are much easier to add than fractions. To add a collection of decimals:

❶ Write the decimals in a column with the decimal points vertically aligned.

❷ Add enough zeros to the right of the decimal point so that every number has an entry in each column to the right of the decimal point.

❸ Add the numbers in the same way as whole numbers.

❹ Place a decimal point in the sum so that it is directly beneath the decimal points in the decimals added.

> How much is $5 + 3.43 + 16.021 + 3.1$?

❶	❷	❸
5	5.000	5.000
3.43	3.430	3.430
16.021	16.021	16.021
+ 3.1	+ 3.100	+ 3.100
		❹ 27.551

The answer is **27.551.**

> If Mary has $0.50, 3.25, and $6.05, how much does she have altogether?

$0.50
3.25
+ 6.05
$9.80

Mary has $9.80.

C-6

Subtracting Decimals.   To subtract one decimal from another:

❶ Put the decimals in a column so that the decimal points are vertically aligned.

❷ Add zeros so that every decimal has an entry in each column to the right of the decimal point.

❸ Subtract the numbers as you would whole numbers.

❹ Place the decimal point in the result so that it is directly beneath the decimal points of the numbers you subtracted.

> Solve $5.053 - 2.09$.

❶	❷	❸
5.053	5.053	5.053
−2.09	−2.090	− 2.090
		❹ 2.963

The answer is **2.963.**

> If Joe has $12 and he loses $8.40, how much money does he have left?

Since $12.00 − $8.40 = $3.60, Joe has $3.60 left.

C-7

Multiplying Decimals.   Decimals are multiplied like whole numbers. *The decimal point of the product is* placed so that the number of decimal places in the product is equal to the total of the number of decimal places in all of the numbers multiplied.

What is $(5.02)(0.6)$?

$(502)(6) = 3.012$. There are two decimal places in 5.02 and one decimal place in 0.6, so the product must have $2 + 1 = 3$ decimal places. Therefore, $(5.02)(0.6) = 3.012$.

If eggs cost $0.06 each, how much should a dozen eggs cost?

Since $(12)(0.06) = 0.72$, a dozen eggs should cost $0.72.

> **COMPUTING TIP:** To multiply a decimal by 10, just move the decimal point to the right one place; to multiply by 100, move the decimal point two places to the right; and so on.

$$9,983.456 \times 100 = 998,345.6.$$

C–8

Dividing Decimals. To divide one decimal (the dividend) by another decimal (the divisor):

❶ Move the decimal point in the divisor to the right until there is no decimal fraction in the divisor (this is the same as multiplying the divisor by a multiple of 10).

❷ Move the decimal point in the dividend the same number of places to the right as you moved the decimal point in ❶.

❸ Divide the result of ❷ by the result of ❶ as if they were whole numbers.

❹ The number of decimal places in the result (quotient) should be equal to the number of decimal places in the result of ❷.

Divide 0.05 into 25.155.

---

❶ Move the decimal point two places to the right in 0.05; the result is 5.

❷ Move the decimal point two places to the right in 25.155; the result is 2515.5.

❸ Divide 5 into 25155; the result is 5,031.

❹ Since there was one decimal place in the result of ❷; the answer is 503.1.

The work for this example might look like this:

$$0.05\overline{)25.15\,5} \quad \begin{matrix}503.1\end{matrix}$$

You can always check division by multiplying.

$(503.1)(0.05) = 25.155$, so our answer checks.

If you write division as a fraction, the previous example would be expressed as $\dfrac{25.155}{0.05}$.

You can multiply both the numerator and denominator by 100 without changing the value of the fraction, so

$$\frac{25.155}{0.05} = \frac{25.155 \times 100}{0.05 \times 100} = \frac{2515.5}{5}$$

Steps ❶ and ❷ above always change the division of a decimal by a decimal into division by a whole number.

To divide a decimal by a whole number, divide as if both were whole numbers. Then place the decimal point in the quotient so that the quotient has as many decimal places as the dividend.

$$\frac{55.033}{1.1} = \frac{550.33}{11} = 50.03$$

If oranges cost 42¢ each, how many oranges can you buy for $2.52?

Make sure that the units are compatible; 42¢ = $0.42. The number of oranges you can buy $= \dfrac{2.52}{0.42} = \dfrac{252}{42} = 6$.

> **COMPUTING TIP:** To divide a decimal by 10, move the decimal point to the left one place; to divide by 100, move the decimal point two places to the left; and so on.

$$5,637.6471 \div 1,000 = 5.6376471$$

To divide by 1,000 you move the decimal point three places to the left.

C–9

Converting a Fraction into a Decimal. To convert a fraction into a decimal, divide the denominator into the numerator. For example, $\dfrac{3}{4} = 4\overline{)3.00} = 0.75$. Some fractions give an infinite decimal when you divide the denominator into the numerator; for example, $\dfrac{1}{3} = 0.333\ldots$, where the three dots mean you keep on getting 3 with each step of division. 0.033 . . . is an *infinite decimal.*

You should know the following decimal equivalents of fractions:

$\frac{1}{100} = 0.01$	$\frac{1}{5} = 0.2$
$\frac{1}{50} = 0.02$	$\frac{1}{4} = 0.25$
$\frac{1}{25} = 0.04$	$\frac{1}{3} = 0.333 \ldots$
$\frac{1}{20} = 0.05$	$\frac{2}{5} = 0.4$
$\frac{1}{10} = 0.1$	$\frac{1}{2} = 0.5$
$\frac{1}{8} = 0.125$	$\frac{2}{3} = 0.666 \ldots$
$\frac{1}{6} = 0.1666 \ldots$	$\frac{3}{4} = 0.75$

Any decimal ending with three dots is an infinite decimal.

I–D.   Percentage

D–1

PERCENT is another method of expressing fractions or parts of an object. Percents are expressed in terms of hundredths, so 100% means 100 hundredths or 1. In the same way, 50% is 50 hundredths or $\frac{500}{100}$ or $\frac{1}{2}$.

A decimal is converted into a percent by multiplying the decimal by 100. Since multiplying a decimal by 100 is accomplished by moving the decimal point two places to the right, *you convert a decimal into a percent by moving the decimal point two places to the right.* For example, 0.134 = 13.4%.

If you wish to convert a percent into a decimal, you divide the percent by 100. There is a shortcut for this also. To divide by 100 you move the decimal point two places to the left.

Therefore, *to convert a percent into a decimal, move the decimal point two places to the left.* For example, 24% = 0.24.

A fraction is converted into a percent by changing the fraction to a decimal and then changing the decimal to a

percent. A percent is changed into a fraction by first converting the percent into a decimal and then changing the decimal to a fraction. You should know the following fractional equivalents of percents.

$1\% = \frac{1}{100}$	$33\frac{1}{3}\% = \frac{1}{3}$	$100\% = 1$
$2\% = \frac{1}{50}$	$40\% = \frac{2}{5}$	$120\% = \frac{6}{5}$
$4\% = \frac{1}{25}$	$50\% = \frac{1}{2}$	$125\% = \frac{5}{4}$
$5\% = \frac{1}{20}$	$60\% = \frac{3}{5}$	$133\frac{1}{3}\% = \frac{4}{3}$
$10\% = \frac{1}{10}$	$66\frac{2}{3}\% = \frac{2}{3}$	$150\% = \frac{3}{2}$
$20\% = \frac{1}{5}$	$75\% = \frac{3}{4}$	
$25\% = \frac{1}{4}$	$80\% = \frac{4}{5}$	

Note, for example, that $133\frac{1}{3}\% = 1.33\frac{1}{3} = 1\frac{1}{3} = \frac{4}{3}$.

When you compute with percents, it is usually easier to change the percents to decimals or fractions.

> A company has 6,435 bars of soap. If the company sells 20% of its bars of soap, how many bars of soap did it sell?

Change 20% into 0.2. Thus, the company sold (0.2)(6,435) = 1287.0 = 1,287 bars of soap. An alternative method would be to convert 20% to $\frac{1}{5}$. Then, $\frac{1}{5} \times 6,435 = 1,287$.

> In a class of 60 students, 18 students received a grade of B. What percent of the class received a grade of B?

$\frac{18}{60}$ of the class received a grade of B. $\frac{18}{60} = \frac{3}{10} = 0.3$ and 0.3 = 0.30 = 30%, so 30% of the class received a grade of B.

If the population of Dryden was 10,000 in 1980 and increased by 15% between 1980 and 1990, what was the population of Dryden in 1990?

The population increased by 15% between 1980 and 1990, so the increase was (0.15)(10,000), which is 1,500. The population in 1990 was 10,000 + 1,500 = 11,500.

A quicker method: The population increased 15%, so the population in 1990 was 115% of the population in 1980. Therefore, the population in 1990 was 115% of 10,000, which is (1.15)(10,000) = 11,500.

Interest and Discount. Two of the most common uses of percent are in interest and discount problems.

The rate of interest is usually given as a percent. The basic formula for interest problems is:

$$\text{INTEREST} = \text{AMOUNT} \times \text{TIME} \times \text{RATE}$$

You can assume the rate of interest is the annual rate of interest unless the problem states otherwise, so you should express the time in years.

How much interest will $10,000 earn in 9 months at an annual rate of 6%?

9 months is $\frac{3}{4}$ of a year and 6% = $\frac{3}{50}$. Using the formula, we find that the interest is $10,000 $\times \frac{3}{4} \times \frac{3}{50}$ = $50 $\times$ 9 = $450.

What annual rate of interest was paid if $5,000 earned $300 in interest in 2 years?

Since the interest was earned in 2 years, $150 was the interest earned in 1 year. $\frac{150}{5,000}$ = 0.03 = 3%, so the annual rate of interest was 3%.

The type of interest described above is called *simple interest.*

There is another method of computing interest. Interest computed in this way is called *compound interest.* In computing compound interest, the interest is periodically added to the amount (or principal) that is earning interest.

What will $1,000 be worth after 3 years if it earns interest at the rate of 5% compounded annually?

"Compounded annually" means that the interest earned during 1 year is added to the amount (or principal) at the end of each year. The interest on $1,000 at 5% for 1 year is $1(1,000)(0.05) = $50, so you must compute the interest on $1,050 (not $1,000) for the second year. The interest is $(1.050)(0.05) = $52.50. Therefore, during the third year interest will be computed for $1,102.50. During the third year the interest is $(1,102.50)(0.05) = $55.125 = $55.13. Therefore, after 3 years the original $1,000 will be worth $1,157.63.

If you calculated simple interest on $1,000 at 5% for 3 years, the answer would be $(1,000)(0.05)(3) = $150. Therefore, with simple interest, $1,000 is worth $1,150 after 3 years. You can see that you earn more interest with compound interest.

You can assume that interest means simple interest unless a problem states otherwise.

The basic formula for discount problems is:

$$\text{DISCOUNT} = \text{COST} \times \text{RATE OF DISCOUNT}$$

What is the discount if a car that costs $3,000 is discounted 7%?

The discount is $3,000 × 0.07 = $210.00 since 7% = 0.07.

If we know the cost of an item and its discounted price, we can find the rate of discount by using the formula

$$\text{Rate of discount} = \frac{\text{Cost} - \text{Price}}{\text{Cost}}$$

What was the rate of discount if a boat that cost $5,000 was sold for $4,800?

Using this formula, we find that the rate of discount equals

$$\frac{5,000 - 4,800}{5,000} = \frac{200}{5,000} = \frac{1}{25} = 0.04 = 4\%$$

After an item has been discounted once, it may be discounted again. This procedure is called *successive discounting.*

A bicycle originally cost $100 and was discounted 10%. After three months it was sold after being discounted another 15%. How much was the bicycle sold for?

After the 10% discount the bicycle was selling for $100 (0.90) = $90. An item that costs $90 and is discounted 15% will sell for $90(0.85) = $76.50, so the bicycle was sold for $76.50.

Notice that, if you added the two discounts of 10% and

15% and treated the successive discounts as a single discount of 25%, your answer would be that the bicycle sold for $75, which is incorrect. Successive discounts are *not* identical to a single discount that is the sum of the discounts. The preceding example shows that successive discounts of 10% and 15% are not identical to a single discount of 25%.

I–E.   *Rounding Off Numbers*

E–1

Many times an approximate answer can be found more quickly and may be more useful than the exact answer. For example, if a company had sales of $998,875.63 during a year, it is easier to remember that the sales were about $1 million.

Rounding off a number to a decimal place means finding the multiple of the representative of that decimal place that is closest to the original number. Thus, rounding off a number to the nearest hundred means finding the multiple of 100 that is closest to the original number. Rounding off to the nearest tenth means finding the multiple of $\frac{1}{10}$ that is closest to the original number. After a number has been rounded off to a particular decimal place, all the digits to the right of that particular decimal place will be zero.

To round off a number to the *r*th decimal place:

❶ Look at the digit in the place to the right of the *r*th place.

❷ *If the digit is 4 or less, change all the digits in places to the right of the rth place to 0* to round off the number.

❸ *If the digit is 5 or more, add 1 to the digit in the rth place and change all the digits in places to the right of the rth place to 0* to round off the number.

> Round off 3.445 to the nearest tenth.

The digit to the right of the tenths place is 4, so 3.445 is 3.4 to the nearest tenth.

Most problems dealing with money are rounded off to the nearest hundredth or cent if the answer contains a fractional part of a cent.

> If 16 donuts cost $1.00, how much should three donuts cost?

Three donuts should cost $\frac{3}{16}$ of $1.00. Since $\frac{3}{16} \times 1. = 0.1875$, the cost would be $0.1875. In practice, you would round it up to $0.19 or 19¢.

Rounding off numbers can help you get quick, approximate answers. Since many questions require only rough answers, you can sometimes save time on the test by rounding off numbers.

> Round off 43.796 to the nearest tenth.

The place to the right of tenths is hundredths, so look in the hundredths place. Since 9 is bigger than 5, add 1 to the tenths place. The number 43.796 is 43.8 rounded off to the nearest tenth.

If the digit in the *r*th place is 9 and you need to add 1 to the digit to round off the number to the *r*th decimal place, put a zero in the *r*th place and add 1 to the digit in the position to the left of the *r*th place. For example, 298 rounded off to the nearest 10 is 300; 99,752 to the nearest thousand is 100,000.

I–F.   *Signed Numbers*

F–1

A number preceded by either a plus or a minus sign is called a SIGNED NUMBER. For example, +5, –6, –4.2, and $+\frac{3}{4}$ are all signed numbers. If no sign is given with a number, a plus sign is assumed; thus, 5 is interpreted as +5.

Signed numbers can often be used to distinguish different concepts. For example, a profit of $10 can be denoted by +$10 and a loss of $10 by –$10. A temperature of 20 degrees below zero can be denoted as –20°.

F–2

Signed numbers are also called DIRECTED NUMBERS. You can think of numbers arranged on a line, called a *number line*, in the following manner:

Take a line that extends indefinitely in both directions, pick a point on the line and call it 0, pick another point on the line to the right of 0 and call it 1. The point to the right of 1 that is exactly as far from 1 as 1 is from 0 is called 2, the point to the right of 2 just as far from 2 as 1 is from 0 is called 3, and so on. The point halfway between 0 and 1 is called $\frac{1}{2}$, the point halfway between $\frac{1}{2}$ and 1 is called $\frac{3}{4}$. In this way, you can identify any whole number or any fraction with a point on the line.

All the numbers that correspond to points to the right of 0 are called *positive numbers*. The sign of a positive number is +.

If you go to the left of zero the same distance as you did from 0 to 1, the point is called –1; in the same way as before, you can find –2, –3, $-\frac{1}{2}$, $-\frac{3}{2}$, and so on.

$$-2 \qquad -1 \quad -\frac{1}{2} \quad 0 \quad \frac{1}{2} \quad 1 \qquad 2$$

All the numbers that correspond to points to the left of zero are called *negative numbers*. Negative numbers are signed numbers whose sign is –. For example, –3, –5.15, –0.003 are all negative numbers.

> *0 is neither positive nor negative; any nonzero number is positive or negative but not both.*

F–3

Absolute Value.   The absolute value of a signed number is the distance of the number from 0. The absolute value of any nonzero number is *positive.* For example, the absolute value of 2 is 2; the absolute value of –2 is 2. The absolute value of a number a is denoted by $|a|$, so $|-2| = 2$. The absolute value of any number can be found by dropping its sign, $|-12| = 12$, $|4| = 4$. Thus $|-a| = |a|$ *for any number a.* The only number whose absolute value is zero is zero.

F–4

Adding Signed Numbers.

Case I. Adding numbers with the *same sign:*

❶ The sign of the sum is the same as the sign of the numbers being added.

❷ Add the absolute values.

❸ Put the sign from ❶ in front of the number you obtained in ❷.

> What is $-2 + (-3.1) + (-0.02)$?

❶ The sign of the sum will be –.

❷ $|-2| = 2$, $|-3.1| = 3.1$, $|-0.02| = 0.02$, and $2 + 3.1 + 0.02 = 5.12$.

❸ The answer is –5.12.

Case II. Adding *two* numbers with *different signs:*

❶ The sign of the sum is the sign of the number that is largest in absolute value.

❷ Subtract the absolute value of the number with the smaller absolute value from the absolute value of the number with the larger absolute value.

❸ The answer is the number you obtained in ❷ preceded by the sign from ❶.

> How much is $-5.1 + 3$?

❶ The absolute value of –5.1 is 5.1 and the absolute value of 3 is 3, so the sign of the sum will be –.

❷ 5.1 is larger than 3, and $5.1 - 3 = 2.1$.

❸ The sum is –2.1.

Case III. Adding *more than two* numbers with *different signs*:

❶ Add all the positive numbers; the result is positive (this is Case I).

❷ Add all the negative numbers; the result is negative (this is Case I).

❸ Add the result of ❶ to the result of ❷, by using Case II.

> If a store made a profit of $23.50 on Monday, lost $2.05 on Tuesday, lost $5.03 on Wednesday, made a profit of $30.10 on Thursday, and made a profit of $41.25 on Friday, what was its total profit (or loss) for the week? Use + for profit and – for loss.

The total is $23.50 + (-2.05) + (-5.03) + 30.10 + 41.25$, which is $94.85 + (-7.08) = 87.77$. The store made a profit of $87.77.

F–5

Subtracting Signed Numbers.   When subtracting signed numbers:

❶ Change the sign of the number you are subtracting (the subtrahend).

❷ Add the result of ❶ to the number being subtracted from (the minuend), using the rules of Section F–4.

> What is $7.8 - (-10.1)$?

❶ –10.1 becomes 10.1.

❷ $7.8 + 10.1 = 17.9$.

We subtract a negative number by adding a positive number with the same absolute value, and we subtract a positive number by adding a negative number of the same absolute value.

F–6

Multiplying Signed Numbers

Case I. Multiplying *two* numbers:

❶ Multiply the absolute values of the numbers.

❷ If both numbers have the same sign, the result of ❶ is the answer, that is, the product is positive. If the numbers have different signs, then the answer is the result of ❶ with a minus sign.

$$(4)\,(-3) = ?$$

❶ $4 \times 3 = 12$

❷ The signs are different, so the answer is –12.

You can remember the sign of the product in the following way:

$$(-)(-) = +$$
$$(+)(+) = +$$
$$(-)(+) = -$$
$$(+)(-) = -$$

Case II. Multiplying *more than two* numbers:

❶ Multiply the first two factors using Case I.

❷ Multiply the result of ❶ by the third factor.

❸ Multiply the result of ❷ by the fourth factor.

❹ Continue until you have used each factor.

$$(-5)(4)(2)\left(-\frac{1}{2}\right)\left(\frac{3}{4}\right) = ?$$

❶ $(-5)(4) = -20$

❷ $(-20)(2) = -40$

❸ $(-40)\left(-\frac{1}{2}\right) = 20$

❹ $(20)\left(\frac{3}{4}\right) = 15$, so the answer is 15.

F–7

Dividing Signed Numbers. Divide the absolute values of the numbers; the sign of the quotient is determined by the same rules as you used to determine the sign of a product. Thus:

$$+ \div + = +$$
$$- \div - = +$$
$$+ \div - = -$$
$$- \div + = -$$

$$\boxed{\text{Divide } 53.2 \text{ by } -4.}$$

53.2 divided by 4 is 13.3. Since one of the numbers is positive and the other negative, the answer is –13.3.

$$\frac{-5}{-2} = ?$$

–5 divided by –2 = $\frac{5}{2}$. Since both numbers are negative, the answer is positive.

The sign of the product or quotient is + if there are no negative factors or an even number of negative factors. The sign of the product or quotient is – if there are an odd number of negative factors.

I–G.　Averages and Medians

G–1

The Average or Mean.　The *average* or *arithmetic mean* of *N* numbers is the sum of the *N* numbers divided by *N*.

> The scores of 9 students on a test were 72, 78, 81, 64, 85, 92, 95, 60, and 55. What was the average score of the students?

Since there are 9 students, the average is the total of all the scores divided by 9:

$\frac{1}{9}$ of $(72 + 78 + 81 + 64 + 85 + 92 + 95 + 60 + 55) = \frac{1}{9}$ of

$(682) = 75\frac{7}{9}$. Therefore, the average score is $75\frac{7}{9}$.

> The temperature at noon in Coldtown, U.S.A., was 5° on Monday, 10° on Tuesday, 2° below zero on Wednesday, 5° below zero on Thursday, 0° on Friday, 4° Saturday, and 1° below zero on Sunday. What was the average temperature at noon for the week?

Use negative numbers for the temperatures below zero. The average temperature is the average of 5, 10, –2, –5, 0, 4, and –1 divided by 7, the number of days in a week:

$$\frac{5 + 10 + (-2) + (-5) + 0 + 4 + (-1)}{7} = \frac{11}{7} = 1\frac{4}{7}.$$

Therefore, the average temperature at noon for the week is $1\frac{4}{7}^{\circ}$.

If the average annual income of 10 workers is $15,665 and 2 of the workers each made $20,000 for the year, what is the average annual income of the remaining 8 workers?

The total income of all 10 workers is 10 times the average income, or $156,650. The 2 workers who each earned $20,000 made a total of $40,000, so the total income of the remaining 8 workers was $156,650 – $40,000 = $116,650. Therefore, the average annual income of the 8 remaining workers is $\frac{\$116,650}{8} = \$14,581.25$.

G–2

The Median. If we arrange N numbers in order, the *median* is the middle number if N is odd and the average of the two middle numbers if N is even. In the first example in G–1, the median score was 78; in the second example, the median temperature for the week was 0. Notice that the medians are different from the averages. In the third example, we don't have enough data to find the median, although we know the average.

In general, the median and the average of a collection of numbers are different.

I–H.   Powers, Exponents, and Roots

H–1

If b is any number and n is a positive integer, b^n means the product of n factors each of which is equal to b. Thus,

$b^n = b \times b \times b \times \cdots \times b$, where there are n copies of b.

If $n = 1$, there is only one copy of b so $b^1 = b$. Here are some examples.

$2^5 = 2 \times 2 \times 2 \times 2 \times 2 = 32$, $(-4)^3 = (-4) \times (-4) \times (-4) = -64$, $\frac{3^2}{4} = \frac{3 \times 3}{4} = \frac{9}{4}$, $1^n = 1$ for any n, $0^n = 0$ for any n.

b^n is read as "b raised to the nth power." b^2, read as "b squared," is always greater than 0 (positive) if b is not zero, since the product of two negative numbers is positive. b^3, read as "b cubed," can be negative or positive.

You should know the following squares and cubes:

$1^2 = 1$	$8^2 = 64$
$2^2 = 4$	$9^2 = 81$
$3^2 = 9$	$10^2 = 100$
$4^2 = 16$	$11^2 = 121$
$5^2 = 25$	$12^2 = 144$
$6^2 = 36$	$13^2 = 169$
$7^2 = 49$	$14^2 = 196$
	$15^2 = 225$
$1^3 = 1$	$3^3 = 27$
$2^3 = 8$	$4^3 = 64$
	$5^3 = 125$

If you raise a fraction, $\frac{p}{q}$, to a power, then $\left(\frac{p}{q}\right)^n = \frac{p^n}{q^n}$.

For example,

$$\left(\frac{5}{4}\right)^3 = \frac{5^3}{4^3} = \frac{125}{64}.$$

If the value of an investment triples each year, what percent of its value today will the investment be worth in 4 years?

The value increases by a factor of 3 each year. Since the time is 4 years, there will be four factors of 3. The investment will be worth $3 \times 3 \times 3 \times 3 = 3^4$ as much as it is today. $3^4 = 81$, so the investment will be worth 8,100% of its value today in 4 years.

H–2

Exponents. In the expression b^n, b is called the base and n is called the *exponent*. In the expression 2^5, 2 is the base and 5 is the exponent. The exponent tells how many factors there are.

The *two basic formulas for problems involving exponents* are:

❶ $b^n \times b^m = b^{n+m}$

❷ $a^n \times b^n = (a \cdot b)^n$

❶ and ❷ are called *laws of exponents*.

What is 6^3?

Since $6 = 3 \times 2$,

$$6^3 = 3^3 \times 2^3 = 27 \times 8 = 216,$$

$$6^3 = 6 \times 6 \times 6 = 216.$$

> Find the value of $2^3 \times 2^2$.

Using formula ❶, $2^3 \times 2^2 = 2^{2+3} = 2^5$, which is 32. You can check this, since $2^3 = 8$ and $2^2 = 4$; $2^3 \times 2^2 = 8 \times 4 = 32$.

H–3

Negative Exponents. $b^0 = 1$ *for any nonzero number b.* (NOTE: 0^0 is not defined.)

Using the law of exponents once more, you can define b^{-n} where n is a positive number. If ❶ holds, $b^{-n} \times b^n = b^{-n+n} = b^0 = 1$, so $b^{-n} = \dfrac{1}{b^n}$. *Multiplying by b^{-n} is the same as dividing by b^n.*

$$2^{-3} = \frac{1}{2^3} = \frac{1}{8}$$

$$\left(\frac{1}{2}\right)^{-1} = \frac{1}{1/2} = 2$$

H–4

Roots. If you raise a number d to the nth power and the result is b, then d is called the nth root of b, which is usually written as $\sqrt[n]{b} = d$. Since $2^5 = 32$, then $\sqrt[5]{32} = 2$. The second root is called the square root and is written as $\sqrt{\ }$; the third root is called the cube root. If you read the columns of the table on page 313 from right to left, you have a table of square roots and cube roots. For example, $\sqrt{225} = 15$; $\sqrt{81} = 9$; $\sqrt[3]{64} = 4$.

There are two possibilities for the square root of a positive number; the square root of 9 is +3 and –3. The symbol $\sqrt{9}$ stands for the positive square root only; thus $\sqrt{9} = 3$.

Since the square of any nonzero number is positive, *the square root of a negative number is not defined as a real number.* Thus $\sqrt{-2}$ is not a real number. There are cube roots of negative numbers. $\sqrt[3]{-8} = -2$ because $(-2) \times (-2) \times (-2) = -8$.

You can also write roots as exponents; for example,

$$\sqrt[n]{b} = b^{1/n}, \text{ so } \sqrt{b} = b^{1/2}, \sqrt[3]{b} = b^{1/3}$$

Since you can write roots as exponents, formula ❷ in Section H–2 is especially useful.

$$a^{1/n} \times b^{1/n} = (a \cdot b)^{1/n} \text{ or } \sqrt[n]{a \times b} = \sqrt[n]{a} \times \sqrt[n]{b}.$$

This formula is the basic formula for simplifying square roots, cube roots, and so on. *On the GRE you must state your answer in a form that matches one of the choices given.*

> $\sqrt{54} = ?$

Since $54 = 9 \times 6$, $\sqrt{54} = \sqrt{9 \times 6} = \sqrt{9} \times \sqrt{6}$. Since $\sqrt{9} = 3$, $\sqrt{54} = 3\sqrt{6}$.

You cannot simplify by adding square roots unless you are taking square roots of the same number. For example, $\sqrt{3} + 2\sqrt{3} - 4\sqrt{3} = -\sqrt{3}$, but $\sqrt{3} + \sqrt{2}$ is not equal to $\sqrt{5}$.

> Simplify $6\sqrt{12} + 2\sqrt{75} - 3\sqrt{98}$.

Since $12 = 4 \times 3$, $\sqrt{12} = \sqrt{4 \times 3} = \sqrt{4} \times \sqrt{3} = 2\sqrt{3}$; $75 = 25 \times 3$, so $\sqrt{75} = \sqrt{25} \times \sqrt{3} = 5\sqrt{3}$; and $98 = 49 \times 2$, so $\sqrt{98} = \sqrt{49} \times \sqrt{2} = 7\sqrt{2}$. Therefore, $6\sqrt{12} + 2\sqrt{75} - 3\sqrt{98} = 6 \times 2\sqrt{3} + 2 \times 5\sqrt{3} - 3 \times 7\sqrt{2} = 12\sqrt{3} + 10\sqrt{3} - 21\sqrt{2} = 22\sqrt{3} - 21\sqrt{2}$.

> Simplify $27^{1/3} \times 8^{1/3}$.

$27^{1/3} = \sqrt[3]{27} = 3$ and $8^{1/3} = \sqrt[3]{8} = 2$, so $27^{1/3} \times 8^{1/3} = 3 \times 2 = 6$. Notice that 6 is $\sqrt[3]{216}$ and $27^{1/3} \times 8^{1/3} = (27 \times 8)^{1/3} = 216^{1/3}$.

II. Algebra

II–A. Algebraic Expressions

A–1

Often it is necessary to deal with quantities that have unknown numerical value. For example, we may know that Tom's salary is twice as much as Joe's salary. If we let the value of Tom's salary be T and the value of Joe's salary be J, then T and J are numbers that are unknown. However, we do know that the value of T must be twice the value of J, or $T = 2J$.

T and $2J$ are examples of algebraic expressions. An algebraic expression may involve letters in addition to numbers and symbols; however, *in an algebraic expression a letter always stands for a number.* Therefore, you can multiply, divide, add, subtract, and perform other mathematical operations on a letter. Thus, x^2 would mean x times x.

Some examples of algebraic expressions are $2x + y$, $y^3 + 9y$, $z^3 - 5ab$, $c + d + 4$, $5x + 2y(6x - 4y + z)$. When letters or numbers are written together without any sign or symbol between them, multiplication is assumed. Thus $6xy$ means 6 times x times y. $6xy$ is called a term; terms are separated by $+$ or $-$ signs. The expression $5z + 2 + 4x^2$ has three terms, $5z$, 2, and $4x^2$. An expression consisting of one term is called a *monomial* (*mono* = one). If any expression has more than one term, it is called a *polynomial* (*poly* = many). The letters in an algebraic expression are called *variables* or *unknowns*. When a variable is multiplied by a number, the number is called the *coefficient* of the variable. In the expression $5x^2 + 2yz$, the coefficient of x^2 is 5, and the coefficient of yz is 2.

A–2

Simplifying Algebraic Expressions.   *You must be able to recognize algebraic expressions that are equal.* It will also save time when you are working problems if you can change a complicated expression into a simpler one.

Case I. Simplifying expressions that don't contain parentheses:

❶ Perform any multiplications or divisions before performing additions or subtractions. Thus, the expression $6x + y \div x$ means add $6x$ to the quotient of y divided by x. Another way of writing the expression would be $6x + \dfrac{y}{x}$. This is not the same as $\dfrac{6x + y}{x}$.

❷ The order in which you multiply numbers and letters in a term does not matter, so $6xy$ is the same as $6yx$.

❸ The order in which you add terms does not matter; for instance, $6x + 2y - x = 6x - x + 2y$.

❹ If there are roots or powers in any terms, you may be able to simplify the term by using the laws of exponents. For example, $5xy \cdot 3x^2y = 15x^3y^2$.

❺ Combine like terms. *Like terms* (or similar terms) are terms that have exactly the same letters raised to the same powers; x, $-2x$, $\dfrac{1}{3}x$ are like terms. For example, $6x - 2x + x + y$ is equal to $5x + y$. In combining like terms, you simply add or subtract the coefficients of the like terms, and the result is the coefficient of that term in the simplified expression. In our example above, the coefficients of x were $+6$, -2, and $+1$; since $6 - 2 + 1 = 5$, the coefficient of x in the simplified expression is 5.

❻ Algebraic expressions that involve divisions or factors can be simplified by using the techniques for handling fractions and the laws of exponents. Remember: dividing by b^n is the same as multiplying by b^{-n}.

$$3x^2 - 4\sqrt{x} + \sqrt{4x} + xy + 7x^2 = \,?$$

❹ $\sqrt{4x} = \sqrt{4}\sqrt{x} = 2\sqrt{x}$.

❺ $3x^2 + 7x^2 = 10x^2$, $-4\sqrt{x} + 2\sqrt{x} = -2\sqrt{x}$.

The original expression equals $3x^2 + 7x^2 - 4\sqrt{x} + 2\sqrt{x} + xy$.

Therefore, the simplified expression is $10x^2 - 2\sqrt{x} + xy$.

$$\text{Simplify } \frac{21x^4y^2}{3x^6y}.$$

❻ $\dfrac{21}{3}x^4y^2x^{-6}y^{-1}$.

❷ $7x^4x^{-6}y^2y^{-1}$.

❹ $7x^{-2}y$, so the simplified term is $\dfrac{7y}{x^2}$.

$$\text{Write } \frac{2x}{y} - \frac{4}{x} \text{ as a single fraction.}$$

❻ A common denominator is xy so $\dfrac{2x}{y} = \dfrac{2x \cdot x}{y \cdot x} = \dfrac{2x^2}{xy}$, and $\dfrac{4}{x} = \dfrac{4y}{xy}$.

Therefore, $\dfrac{2x}{y} - \dfrac{4}{x} = \dfrac{2x^2}{xy} - \dfrac{4y}{xy} = \dfrac{2x^2 - 4y}{xy}$.

Case II. Simplifying expressions that have parentheses:

The first rule is to perform the operations inside parentheses before doing the others. Thus, $(6x + y) \div x$ means divide the sum of $6x$ and y by x. Notice that $(6x + y) \div x$ is different from $6x + y \div x$.

The main rule for getting rid of parentheses is the *distributive law*, which is expressed as $a(b + c) = ab + ac$. In other words, if any monomial is followed by an expression contained in parentheses, then *each* term of the expression is multiplied by the monomial. Once we have gotten rid of the parentheses, we proceed as we did in Case I.

$$2x(6x - 4y + 2) = (2x)(6x) + (2x)(-4y) + (2x)(2) =$$
$$12x^2 - 8xy + 4x.$$

If an expression has more than one set of parentheses, get rid of the *inner parentheses first* and then *work out* through the rest of the parentheses.

$$2x - (x + 6(x - 3y) + 4y) = ?$$

To remove the inner parentheses we multiply $6(x - 3y)$, getting $6x - 18y$. Now we have $2x - (x + 6x - 18y + 4y)$, which equals $2x - (7x - 14y)$. Distribute the minus sign (multiply by -1), getting $2x - 7x - (-14y) = -5x + 14y$.

Sometimes brackets are used instead of parentheses.

Simplify $-3x\left[\dfrac{1}{2}(3x-2y) - 2(x(3+y) + 4y)\right]$.

$-3x\left[\dfrac{1}{2}(3x-2y) - 2(x(3+y)+4y)\right]$

$= -3x\left[\dfrac{1}{2}(3x-2y) - 2(3x + xy + 4y)\right]$

$= -3x\left[\dfrac{3}{2}x - y - 6x - 2xy - 8y\right]$

$= -3x\left[-\dfrac{9}{2}x - 2xy - 9y\right]$

$= \dfrac{27}{2}x^2 + 6x^2y + 27xy$

A–3

Adding and Subtracting Algebraic Expressions. Since algebraic expressions are numbers, they can be added and subtracted.

The only algebraic terms that can be combined are like terms.

$$(3x + 4y - xy^2) + (3x + 2x(x - y)) = ?$$

$(3x + 4y - xy^2) + (3x + 2x(x - y))$

$= (3x + 4y - xy^2) + (3x + 2x^2 - 2xy)$, removing the inner parentheses;

$= 6x + 4y + 2x^2 - xy^2 - 2xy$, combining like terms.

$$(2a + 3a^2 - 4) - 2(4a^2 - 2(a + 4)) = ?$$

$(2a + 3a^2 - 4) - 2(4a^2 - 2(a + 4))$

$= (2a + 3a^2 - 4) - 2(4a^2 - 2a - 8)$, removing inner parentheses;

$= 2a + 3a^2 - 4 - 8a^2 + 4a + 16$, removing outer parentheses;

$= -5a^2 + 6a + 12$, combining like terms.

A–4

Multiplying Algebraic Expressions. When you multiply two expressions, you multiply *each term of the first by each term of the second.*

$$(b - 4)(b + a) = b(b + a) - 4(b + a) = ?$$

$(b - 4)(b + a) = b^2 + ab - 4b - 4a.$

$$(2h - 4)(h + 2h^2 + h^3) = ?$$

$(2h - 4)(h + 2h^2 + h^3)$

$= 2h(h + 2h^2 + h^3) - 4(h + 2h^2 + h^3)$

$= 2h^2 + 4h^3 + 2h^4 - 4h - 8h^2 - 4h^3$

$= -4h - 6h^2 + 2h^4$, which is the product.

If you need to multiply more than two expressions, multiply the first two expressions, then multiply the result by the third expression, and so on until you have used each factor. Since algebraic expressions can be multiplied, they can be squared, cubed, or raised to other powers.

$$(x - 2y)^3 = (x - 2y)(x - 2y)(x - 2y).$$

Since $(x - 2y)(x - 2y) = x^2 - 2yx - 2yx + 4y^2$

$$= x^2 - 4xy + 4y^2,$$

then $\qquad (x - 2y)^3 = (x^2 - 4xy + 4y^2)(x - 2y)$

$$= x(x^2 - 4xy + 4y^2) - 2y(x^2 - 4xy + 4y^2)$$

$$= x^3 - 4x^2y + 4xy^2 - 2x^2y + 8xy^2 - 8y^3$$

$$= x^3 - 6x^2y + 12xy^2 - 8y^3.$$

The order in which you multiply algebraic expressions does not matter. Thus $(2a + b)(x^2 + 2x) = (x^2 + 2x)(2a + b)$.

If a and b are two-digit numbers and the last digit of a is 7 and the last digit of b is 8, what is the last digit of a times b?

The key to problems such as this one is to think of a number in terms of its digits. Thus, a must be written as $x7$, where x is a digit. This means that $a = 10x + 7$. In the same way, $b = 10y + 8$ for some digit y. Therefore, a times b is $(10x + 7)(10y + 8)$, which is $100xy + 80x + 70y + 56$. The digits x and y are each multiplied by 10 or 100, so they will **not** affect the units place. The only term that will affect the units place is 56, so the unit digit or last digit of a times b is 6.

This pattern works all the time and can be expressed by the following rule: *The last digit of the product of two numbers is the last digit of the product of the last digits of the two numbers.* For example, the last digit of 136 times 157 is 2 because the last digit of 6 times 7 is 2.

A–5

Factoring Algebraic Expressions. If an algebraic expression is the product of other algebraic expressions, then the expressions are called factors of the original expression. For instance, we say that $(2h - 4)$ and $(h + 2h^2 + h^3)$ are factors of $-4h - 6h^2 + 2h^4$. We can always check to see whether we have the correct factors by multiplying. From the second example in A–4, we see that our claim is correct. We need to be able to factor algebraic expressions in order to solve quadratic equations. Factoring also can be helpful in dividing algebraic expressions.

First remove any monomial factor that appears in every term of the expression. Here are some examples:

$3x + 3y = 3(x + y)$:   3 is a monomial factor.

$15a^2b + 10ab = 5ab(3a + 2)$: $5ab$ is a monomial factor.

$$\frac{1}{2}hy - 3h^3 + 4hy = h\left(\frac{1}{2}y - 3h^2 + 4y\right)$$

$$= h\left(\frac{9}{2}y - 3h^2\right): h \text{ is a monomial factor}$$

You may also need to factor expressions that contain squares or higher powers into factors that contain only linear terms. (Linear terms are terms in which variables are raised only to the first power). The first rule to remember is that, since $(a + b)(a - b) = a^2 + ba - ba - b^2 = a^2 - b^2$, the difference of two squares can always be factored.

Factor $(9m^2 - 16)$.

$9m^2 = (3m)^2$ and $16 = 4^2$, so the factors are $(3m - 4)$ $(3m + 4)$.

Since $(3m - 4)(3m + 4) = 9m^2 - 16$, these factors are correct.

Factor $x^4y^4 - 4x^2$.

$x^4y^4 = (x^2y^2)^2$ and $4x^2 = (2x)^2$, so the factors are $x^2y^2 + 2x$ and $x^2y^2 - 2x$.

You also may need to factor expressions that contain squared terms and linear terms, such as $x^2 + 4x + 3$. The factors will be of the form $(x + a)$ and $(x + b)$. Since $(x + a)(x + b) = x^2 + (a + b)x + ab$, you must look for a pair of numbers a and b such that $a \cdot b$ is the numerical term in the expression and $a + b$ is the coefficient of the linear term (the term with exponent 1).

Factor $x^2 + 4x + 3$.

You want numbers whose product is 3 and whose sum is 4. Look at the possible factors of 3 and check whether they add up to 4. Since $3 = 3 \times 1$ and $3 + 1$ is 4, the factors are $(x + 3)$ and $(x + 1)$. Remember to check by multiplying.

Factor $y^2 + y - 6$.

Since -6 is negative, the two numbers a and b must be of opposite sign. Possible pairs of factors for -6 are -6 and $+1$, 6 and -1, 3 and -2, and -3 and 2. Since $-2 + 3 = 1$, the factors are

$(y + 3)$ and $(y - 2)$. Thus, $(y + 3)(y - 2) = y^2 + y - 6$.

Factor $a^3 + 4a^2 + 4a$.

Factor out a, so $a^3 + 4a^2 + 4a = a(a^2 + 4a + 4)$. Consider $a^2 + 4a + 4$; since $2 + 2 = 4$ and $2 \times 2 = 4$, the factors are $(a + 2)$ and $(a + 2)$. Therefore, $a^3 + 4a^2 + 4a = a(a + 2)^2$.

If the term with the highest exponent has a coefficient unequal to 1, divide the entire expression by that coefficient. For example, to factor $3a^3 + 12a^2 + 12a$, factor out 3 from each term, and the result is $a^3 + 4a^2 + 4a$, which is $a(a + 2)^2$. Thus, $3a^3 + 12a^2 + 12a = 3a(a + 2)^2$.

There are some expressions that cannot be factored, for example, $x^2 + 4x + 6$. In general, if you can't factor something by using the methods given above, don't waste a lot of time on the question. Sometimes you may be able to find the correct factors by checking the answer choices.

A–6

Division of Algebraic Expressions. The main things to remember in division are:

❶ When you divide a sum, you can get the same result by dividing each term and adding quotients.
For example:

$$\frac{9x + 4xy + y^2}{x} = \frac{9x}{x} + \frac{4xy}{x} + \frac{y^2}{x} = 9 + 4y + \frac{y^2}{x}.$$

❷ You can cancel common factors, so the results on factoring will be helpful. For example:

$$\frac{x^2 - 2x}{x - 2} = \frac{x(x - 2)}{x - 2} = x.$$

You can also divide one algebraic expression by another using long division.

$$(15x^2 + 2x - 4) \div 3x - 1.$$

$$
\begin{array}{r}
5x + 2 \\
3x - 1 \overline{\smash{)}15x^2 + 2x - 4} \\
\underline{15x^2 - 5x} \\
7x - 4 \\
\underline{6x - 2} \\
x - 2
\end{array}
$$

The answer is $5x + 2$ with a remainder of $x - 2$.

You can check by multiplying,

$$(5x + 2)(3x - 1) = 15x^2 + 6x - 5x - 2$$

$$= 15x^2 + x - 2;\ \text{now add the remainder } x - 2$$

and the result is $15x^2 + x - 2 + x - 2 = 15x^2 + 2x - 4$.

Division problems where you need to use ❶ and ❷ are more likely than problems involving long division.

II–B.   *Equations*

B–1

AN EQUATION is a statement that says two algebraic expressions are equal.

Thus $x + 2 = 3$, $4 + 2 = 6$, $3x^2 + 2x - 6 = 0$, $x^2 + y^2 = z^2$, $\frac{y}{x} = 2 + z$, and $A = LW$ are all examples of equations. We will refer to the algebraic expressions on each side of the equals sign as the left side and the right side of the equation. Thus, in the equation $2x + 4 = 6y + x$, $2x + 4$ is the left side and $6y + x$ is the right side.

B–2

If we assign a specific number to each variable or unknown in an algebraic expression, then the algebraic expression will be equal to a number. This is called *evaluating* the expression. For example, if you evaluate $2x + 4y^2 + 3$ for $x = -1$ and $y = 2$, the expression is equal to $2(-1) + 4 \cdot 2^2 + 3 = -2 + 4 \cdot 4 + 3 = 17$.

If we evaluate each side of an equation and the number obtained is the same for each side of the equation, then the specific values assigned to the unknowns are called a *solution of the equation.* Another way of saying this is that the choices for the unknowns satisfy the equation.

Consider the equation $2x + 3 = 9$.

If $x = 3$, then the left side of the equation becomes $2 \cdot 3 + 3 = 6 + 3 = 9$, so both sides equal 9, and $x = 3$ is a solution of $2x + 3 = 9$. If $x = 4$, then the left side is $2 \cdot 4 + 3 = 11$. Since 11 is not equal to 9, $x = 4$ is *not* a solution of $2x + 3 = 9$.

Consider the equation $x^2 + y^2 = 5x$.

If $x = 1$ and $y = 2$, then the left side is $1^2 + 2^2$, which equals $1 + 4 = 5$. The right side is $5 \cdot 1 = 5$; since both sides are equal to 5, $x = 1$ and $y = 2$ is a solution.

If $x = 5$ and $y = 0$, then the left side is $5^2 + 0^2 = 25$ and the right side is $5 \cdot 5 = 25$, so $x = 5$ and $y = 0$ is also a solution.

If $x = 1$ and $y = 1$, then the left side is $1^2 + 1^2 = 2$ and the right side is $5 \cdot 1 = 5$. Therefore, since $2 \neq 5$, $x = 1$ and $y = 1$ is not a solution.

Some equations *do not have any solutions that are real numbers.* For example, since the square of any real number is positive or zero, the equation $x^2 = -4$ does not have any real-number solutions.

B–3

Equivalence.   One equation is *equivalent* to another equation if the two have exactly the same solutions. The basic idea in solving equations is to transform a given equation into an equivalent equation whose solutions are obvious.

The two main tools for solving equations are:

❶ **If you add or subtract the same algebraic expression to or from *each side* of an equation, the resulting equation is equivalent to the original equation.**

❷ **If you multiply or divide both sides of an equation by the same *nonzero* algebraic expression, the resulting equation is equivalent to the original equation.**

The most common type of equation is the linear equation with only one unknown. For example, $6z = 4z - 3$, $3 + a = 2a - 4$, and $3b + 2b = b - 4b$ are linear equations, each with only one unknown.

Using ❶ and ❷, you can solve a linear equation in one unknown in the following way:

(a) Group all the terms that involve the unknown on one side of the equation and all the purely numerical terms on the other side of the equation. This is called *isolating the unknown.*

(b) Combine the terms on each side.

(c) Divide each side by the coefficient of the unknown.

Solve $6x + 2 = 3$ for x.

(a) Using ❶, subtract 2 from each side of the equation. Then $6x + 2 - 2 = 3 - 2$ or $6x = 3 - 2$.

(b) $6x = 1$

(c) Divide each side by 6. Therefore, $x = \dfrac{1}{6}$.

You should always check your answer in the original equation,

since $6\left(\dfrac{1}{6}\right) + 2 = 1 + 2 = 3$, $x = \dfrac{1}{6}$ is a solution.

Solve $3x + 15 = 3 - 4x$ for x.

(a) Add $4x$ to each side and subtract 15 from each side. Then $3x + 15 - 15 + 4x = 3 - 15 - 4x + 4x$.

(b) $7x = -12$.

(c) Divide each side by 7. Thus, $x = \dfrac{-12}{7}$ is the solution.

CHECK:

$$3\left(\dfrac{-12}{7}\right) + 15 = \dfrac{-36}{7} + 15 = \dfrac{69}{7}$$

$$\text{and } 3 - 4\left(\dfrac{-12}{7}\right) = 3 + \dfrac{48}{7} = \dfrac{69}{7}$$

If you do the same thing to each side of an equation, the result is still an equation but it may not be equivalent to the original equation. Be especially careful if you square each side of an equation. For example, $x = -4$ is an equation; square both sides and you get $x^2 = 16$, which has both $x = 4$ and $x = -4$ as solutions. *Always check your answer in the original equation.*

If the equation you want to solve involves square roots, get rid of the square roots by squaring each side of the equation. Remember to check your answer since squaring each side does not always give an equivalent equations.

Solve $\sqrt{4x + 3} = 5$.

Square both sides: $\left(\sqrt{4x+3}\right)^2 = 4x + 3$ and $5^2 = 25$, so the new equation is $4x + 3 = 25$. Subtract 3 from each side to get $4x = 22$ and now divide each side by 4. The solution is $x = \dfrac{22}{4} = 5.5$. Since $4(5.5) + 3 = 25$ and $\sqrt{25} = 5$,

$x = 5.5$ is a solution to the equation $\sqrt{4x + 3} = 5$.

If an equation involves fractions, multiply through by a common denominator and then solve. Check your answer to make sure you did not multiply or divide by zero.

Solve $\dfrac{3}{a} = 9$ for a.

Multiply each side by a: the result is $3 = 9a$. Divide each side by 9, and you obtain $\dfrac{3}{9} = a$ or $a = \dfrac{1}{3}$. Since $\dfrac{3}{1/3} = 3 \cdot 3 = 9$, $a = \dfrac{1}{3}$ is a solution.

B–4

You may be asked to solve two equations in two unknowns. Use one equation to solve for one unknown in terms of the other. Then change the second equation into an equation in only one unknown, which can be solved by the methods of the preceding section on equivalence.

Solve for x and y: $\begin{cases} \dfrac{x}{y} = 3 \\ 2x + 4y = 20. \end{cases}$

The first equation gives $x = 3y$. Using $x = 3y$, we find that the second equation is $2(3y) + 4y = 6y + 4y$ or $10y = 20$, so $y = \dfrac{20}{10} = 2$. Since $x = 3y$, $x = 6$.

CHECK:

$$\dfrac{6}{2} = 3, \text{ and } 2 \cdot 6 + 4 \cdot 2 = 20,$$

so $x = 6$ and $y = 2$ is a solution.

If $2x + y = 5$ and $x + y = 4$, find x and y.

Since $x + y = 4$, $y = 4 - x$, so $2x + y = 2x + 4 - x = x + 4 = 5$ and $x = 1$. If $x = 1$, then $y = 4 - 1 = 3$, so $x = 1$ and $y = 3$ is the solution.

CHECK:

$$2 \cdot 1 + 3 = 5 \text{ and } 1 + 3 = 4.$$

Sometimes we can solve two equations by adding them or by subtracting one from the other. If we subtract $x + y = 4$ from $2x + y = 5$ in the second example in B–4, we have $x = 1$. However, the method explained above will work in cases where the addition method does not work.

B–5

Solving Quadratic Equations. If the terms of an equation contain squares of the unknown as well as linear terms, the equation is called *quadratic*. Some examples of quadratic equations are $x^2 + 4x = 3$, $2z^2 - 1 = 3z^2 - 2z$, and $a + 6 = a^2 + 6$.

To solve a quadratic equation:

❶ Group all the terms on one side of the equation so that the other side is *zero*.

❷ Combine the terms on the nonzero side.

❸ Factor the expression into linear expressions.

❹ Set the linear factors equal to zero and solve.

The method depends on the fact that if a product of expressions is zero then at least one of the expressions must be zero.

$$\text{Solve } x^2 + 4x = -3.$$

❶ $x^2 + 4x + 3 = 0$

❸ $x^2 + 4x + 3 = (x + 3)(x + 1) = 0$

❹ Then $x + 3 = 0$ or $x + 1 = 0$. Therefore, the solutions are $x = -3$ and $x = -1$.

CHECK:

$$(-3)^2 + 4(-3) = 9 - 12 = -3$$

$$(-1)^2 + 4(-1) = 1 - 4 = -3,$$
so $x = -3$ and $x = -1$ are solutions.

A quadratic equation will usually have two different solutions, but it is possible for a quadratic to have only one solution or even no solution.

$$\text{If } 2z^2 - 1 = 3z^2 - 2z, \text{ what is } z?$$

❶ $0 = 3z^2 - 2z^2 - 2z + 1$

❷ $z^2 - 2z + 1 = 0$

❸ $z^2 - 2z + 1 = (z - 1)^2 = 0$

❹ $z - 1 = 0$ or $z = 1$

CHECK:

$$2 \cdot 1^2 - 1 = 2 - 1 = 1 \text{ and } 3 \cdot 1^2 - 2 \cdot 1 = 3 - 2 = 1,$$
so $z = 1$ is a solution.

Equations that may not look like quadratics may be changed into quadratics.

$$\text{Find } a \text{ if } a - 3 = \frac{10}{a}.$$

Multiply each side of the equation by a to obtain $a^2 - 3a = 10$, which is quadratic.

❶ $a^2 - 3a - 10 = 0$

❸ $a^2 - 3a - 10 = (a - 5)(a + 2)$

❹ Then $a - 5 = 0$ or $a + 2 = 0$

Therefore, $a = 5$ and $a = -2$ are the solutions.

CHECK:

$$5 - 3 = 2 = \frac{10}{5}, \text{ so } a = 5 \text{ is a solution.}$$

$$-2 - 3 = -5 = \frac{10}{-2}, \text{ so } a = -2 \text{ is a solution.}$$

You can also solve quadratic equations by using the *quadratic formula*. The quadratic formula states that the solutions of the quadratic equation $ax^2 + bx + c = 0$ are

$$x = \frac{1}{2a}\left[-b + \sqrt{b^2 - 4ac}\right] \text{ and } x = \frac{1}{2a}\left[-b - \sqrt{b^2 - 4ac}\right],$$

usually written as $x = \frac{1}{2a}\left[-b \pm \sqrt{b^2 - 4ac}\right]$. Use of the quadratic formula would replace ❸ and ❹.

$$\text{Find } x \text{ if } x^2 + 5x = 12 - x^2.$$

❶ $x^2 + 5x + x^2 - 12 = 0$

❷ $2x^2 + 5x - 12 = 0$

Then $a = 2$, $b = 5$ and $c = -12$. Therefore, using the quadratic formula, we find that the solutions are

$$x = \frac{1}{4}[-5 \pm \sqrt{25 - 4 \cdot 2 \cdot -12}] = \frac{1}{4}[-5 \pm \sqrt{25 + 96}] =$$

$$\frac{1}{4}[-5 \pm \sqrt{121}]. \text{ So we have } x = \frac{1}{4}[-5 \pm 11]. \text{ The solu-}$$

tions are $x = \frac{3}{2}$ and $x = -4$.

CHECK:

$$\left(\frac{3}{2}\right)^2 + 5 \cdot \frac{3}{2} = \frac{9}{4} + \frac{15}{2} = \frac{39}{4} = 12 - \frac{9}{4} = 12 - \left(\frac{3}{2}\right)^2$$

$$(-4)^2 + 5(-4) = 16 - 20 = -4 = 12 - 16 = 12 - (-4)^2$$

NOTE: If $b^2 - 4ac$ is negative, then the quadratic equation $ax^2 + bx + c = 0$ has no real solutions because negative numbers do not have real square roots.

The quadratic formula will always give you the solutions to a quadratic equation. If, however, you can factor the equation, factoring will usually give you the solution in less time. Remember: you want to answer as many questions as you can in the time given, so factor if you can. If you don't see the factor immediately, then use the formula.

Practice Exercises

1. If $r = \dfrac{s}{3}$ and $4r = 5t$, what is s in terms of t?

   (A) $\dfrac{4t}{15}$ (B) $\dfrac{15t}{4}$ (C) $4t$ (D) $5t$ (E) $60t$

2. If $\dfrac{1}{r} = 3$ and $s = 3$, what is r in terms of s?

   (A) s (B) $3 - s$ (C) $\dfrac{1}{s}$ (D) $-s$ (E) $9s$

3. $\dfrac{a}{b} = c;\ b = c;\ b = ?$

   (A) $\dfrac{a}{2}$ (B) $\sqrt{a}$ (C) $\dfrac{a}{6}$ (D) $2a$ (E) a^2

4. $z + \dfrac{1}{z} = 2;\ z = ?$

   (A) $\dfrac{1}{2}$ (B) 1 (C) $1\dfrac{1}{2}$ (D) 2 (E) $2\dfrac{1}{2}$

5. If $\dfrac{n}{7} + \dfrac{n}{5} = \dfrac{12}{35}$, what is the numerical value of n?

   (A) 1 (B) $\sqrt{12}$ (C) 6 (D) 17.5 (E) 35

6. $\dfrac{ca^2 - cb^2}{-a - b}$ is equivalent to $cb + ?$

   (A) ac (B) $-ca$ (C) 1 (D) -1 (E) c

7. $x\sqrt{0.09} = 3;\ x = ?$

   (A) $\dfrac{1}{10}$ (B) $\dfrac{3}{10}$ (C) $\dfrac{1}{3}$ (D) 1 (E) 10

8. $7x - 5y = 13$
   $2x - 7y = 26$
   $9x - 12y = ?$

   (A) 13 (B) 26 (C) 39 (D) 40 (E) 52

9. $ab - 2cd = p$
   $ab - 2cd = q$
   $6cd - 3ab = r$
   $ p = (?)r$

   (A) -3 (B) $-\dfrac{1}{3}$ (C) $\dfrac{1}{3}$ (D) 1 (E) 3

10. $\sqrt{\dfrac{16}{36} + \dfrac{1}{4}} = ?$

   (A) $\dfrac{2}{5}$ (B) $\dfrac{1}{3}$ (C) $\dfrac{5}{6}$ (D) $\dfrac{11}{12}$ (E) $\dfrac{7}{6}$

11. $z + \dfrac{2}{z} = 2z;\ z^2 = (?)$

   (A) 0 (B) $\dfrac{1}{2}$ (C) 1 (D) $1\dfrac{1}{2}$ (E) 2

12. $\dfrac{\dfrac{1}{\frac{1}{N}}}{} \div \dfrac{1}{N} = ?$

   (A) 1 (B) $\dfrac{1}{N^2}$ (C) $\dfrac{1}{N}$ (D) N (E) N^2

13. If $\dfrac{1}{x} = \dfrac{a}{b}$, then x equals the

   (A) sum of a and b
   (B) product of a and b
   (C) difference of a and b
   (D) quotient of b and a
   (E) quotient of a and b

14. $x^2 + y = 9$
    $x^2 - y = -1$
    $\phantom{x^2 - {}}y = ?$

   (A) 1 (B) ± 3 (C) 5 (D) 8 (E) 10

15. $2x - 4y = -10$
    $5x - 3y = -3$
    $3x + 7 = ?$

   (A) $\dfrac{3}{5}$ (B) $\dfrac{2}{3}$ (C) -7 (D) ± 7 (E) 7

16. $5x - 3y = 3$
    $2x - 4y = -10$
    $3x + y = (?)$

   (A) -30 (B) -13 (C) -7 (D) 7 (E) 13

17. $4y - x = 10$
    $3x = 2y$
    $xy = ?$

   (A) 2 (B) 3 (C) 6 (D) 12 (E) 24

18. $3x + 10 = 9x - 20$
    $(x + 5)^2 = (?)$

   (A) 5 (B) 10 (C) 15 (D) 25 (E) 100

19. $\frac{a}{b} = c$; $b = c$. Find b in terms of a.

(A) a (B) b (C) $\pm\sqrt{b}$ (D) $\pm\sqrt{a}$ (E) $\pm\sqrt{ac}$

20. $17xy = 22xy - 5$
$x^2y^2 = (?)$

(A) 0 (B) 1 (C) -5 (D) 5 (E) $7\frac{4}{5}$

Answer Key

1.	B	8.	C	15.	E
2.	C	9.	B	16.	E
3.	B	10.	C	17.	C
4.	B	11.	E	18.	E
5.	A	12.	E	19.	D
6.	B	13.	D	20.	B
7.	E	14.	C		

II–C.   Verbal Problems

C–1

The general method for solving word problems is to translate them in to algebraic problems. The quantities you are seeking are the unknowns, which are usually represented by letters. The information you are given in the problem is then turned into equations. Words such as "is," "was," and "were" mean equals, and "of" and "as much as" mean multiplication.

A coat was sold for $75. The coat was sold for 150% of its cost. How much did the coat cost?

You want to find the cost of the coat. Let C be the cost of the coat. You know that the coat was sold for $75 and that $75 was 150% of the cost. Then $75 = 150% of $C or 75 = 1.5C$. Solving for C, you get $C = \frac{75}{1.5} = 50$, so the coat cost $50.

CHECK:

$$(1.5) \ \$50 = \$75.$$

Tom's salary is 125% of Joe's salary. Mary's salary is 80% of Joe's salary. The total of all three salaries is $61,000. What is Mary's salary?

Let M = Mary's salary, J = Joe's salary, and T = Tom's salary. The first sentence says T = 125% of J or $T = \frac{5}{4}J$, and

M = 80% of J or $M = \frac{4}{5}J$. The second sentence says that $T + M + J = \$61,000$. Using the information from the first sentence, we can write

$$T + M + J = \frac{5}{4}J + \frac{4}{5}J + J = \frac{25}{20}J + \frac{16}{20}J + J = \frac{61}{20}J.$$

Therefore, $\frac{61}{20}J = 61,000$; solving for J, we have $J = \frac{20}{61} \times 61,000 = 20,000$. Therefore, $T = \frac{5}{4} \times \$20,000 = \$25,000$ and $M = \frac{4}{5} \times \$20,000 = \$16,000$.

CHECK:

$$\$25,000 + \$16,000 + \$20,000 = \$61,000.$$

Mary's salary is $16,000.

Steve weighs 25 pounds more than Jim. Their combined weight is 325 pounds. How much does Jim weigh?

Let S = Steve's weight in pounds and J = Jim's weight in pounds. The first sentence says $S = J + 25$, and the second sentence becomes $S + J = 325$. Since $S = J + 25$, $S + J = 325$ becomes $(J + 25) + J = 2J + 25 = 325$. So $2J = 300$ and $J = 150$. Therefore, Jim weighs 150 pounds.

CHECK:

If Jim weighs 150 pounds, then Steve weighs 175 pounds and $150 + 175 = 325$.

A carpenter is designing a closet. The floor will be in the shape of a rectangle whose length is 2 feet more than its width. How long should the closet be if the carpenter wants the area of the floor to be 15 square feet?

The area of a rectangle is length times width, usually written as $A = LW$, where A is the area, L is the length, and W is the width. We know $A = 15$ and $L = 2 + W$. Therefore, $LW = (2 + W) W = W^2 + 2W$; this must equal 15. Therefore, we need to solve $W^2 + 2W = 15$ or $W^2 + 2W - 15 = 0$. Since $W^2 + 2W - 15$ factors into $(W + 5)(W - 3)$, the only possible solutions are $W = -5$ and $W = 3$. Since W represents a width, -5 cannot be the answer; therefore the width is 3 feet. The length is the width plus 2 feet, so the length is 5 feet. Since $5 \times 3 = 15$, the answer checks.

Practice Exercises

1. How many cents are there in $2x - 1$ dimes?

   (A) $10x$ (B) $20x - 10$ (C) $19x$ (D) $\dfrac{2x-1}{10}$

   (E) $\dfrac{x}{5} - 1$

2. How many nickels are there in c cents and q quarters?

   (A) $\dfrac{c}{5} + 5q$ (B) $5(c + q)$ (C) $5c + \dfrac{q}{5}$

   (D) $\dfrac{c+q}{5}$ (E) $c + 25q$

3. How many days are there in w weeks and w days?

   (A) $7w^2$ (B) 7 (C) $8w$ (D) $14w$ (E) $7w$

4. How many pupils can be seated in a room with s single seats and d double seats?

   (A) sd (B) $2sd$ (C) $2(s + d)$ (D) $2d + s$
   (E) $2s + d$

5. A classroom has r rows of desks with d desks in each row. On a particular day when all pupils are present 3 seats are left vacant. The number of pupils in this class is

   (A) $dr - 3$ (B) $d + r + 3$ (C) $dr + 3$ (D) $\dfrac{r}{d} + 3$

   (E) $\dfrac{d}{r} + 3$

6. A storekeeper had n loaves of bread. By noon he had s loaves left. How many loaves did he sell?

   (A) $s - n$ (B) $n - s$ (C) $n + s$ (D) $sn - s$

   (E) $\dfrac{n}{s}$

7. A man has d dollars and spends s cents. How many dollars has he left?

   (A) $d - s$ (B) $s - d$ (C) $100d - s$

   (D) $\dfrac{100d - s}{100}$ (E) $\dfrac{d - s}{100}$

8. How much change (in cents) would a woman who purchases p pounds of sugar at c cents per pound receive from a one-dollar bill?

   (A) $100 - p - c$
   (B) $pc - 100$
   (C) $100 - pc$
   (D) $100 - p + c$
   (E) $pc + 100$

9. Sylvia is two years younger than Mary. If Mary is m years old, how old was Sylvia two years ago?

   (A) $m + 2$ (B) $m - 2$ (C) $m - 4$ (D) $m + 4$
   (E) $2m - 2$

10. A storekeeper sold n articles at \$$D$ each and thereby made a profit of r dollars. The cost to the storekeeper for each article was

    (A) $Dn - r$ (B) $D(n - r)$ (C) $\dfrac{Dn - r}{n}$

    (D) $\dfrac{D(n-r)}{n}$ (E) $\dfrac{Dn + r}{n}$

Answer Key

1.	B	5.	A	9.	C
2.	A	6.	B	10.	C
3.	C	7.	D		
4.	D	8.	C		

C–2

Distance Problems.   A common type of word problem is a distance or velocity problem. The basic formula is

   DISTANCE TRAVELED = RATE × TIME

The formula is abbreviated $d = rt$.

The distance an object travels is the product of its *average* speed (rate) and the time it is traveling. This formula can be readily converted to express time in terms of distance and rate by dividing each side by r:

$$t = \frac{d}{r}$$

It can also be changed to a formula for rate by dividing it by t:

$$r = \frac{d}{t}.$$

You should memorize the original formula, $d = rt$, and know how to convert it quickly to the others.

> A train travels at an average speed of 50 miles per hour for $2\frac{1}{2}$ hours and then travels at a speed of 70 miles per hour for $1\frac{1}{2}$ hours. How far did the train travel in the entire 4 hours?

The train traveled for $2\frac{1}{2}$ hours at an average speed of 50 miles per hour, so it traveled $50 \times \dfrac{5}{2} = 125$ miles in the first

$2\frac{1}{2}$ hours. At a speed of 70 miles per hour for $1\frac{1}{2}$ hours, the distance traveled will be equal to $r \times t$, where $r = 70$ miles per hour and $t = 1\frac{1}{2}$, so the distance is $70 \times \frac{3}{2} = 105$ miles. Therefore, the total distance traveled is $125 + 105 = 230$ miles.

The distance from Cleveland to Buffalo is 200 miles. A train takes $3\frac{1}{2}$ hours to go from Buffalo to Cleveland and $4\frac{1}{2}$ hours to go back from Cleveland to Buffalo. What was the average speed of the train for the round trip from Buffalo to Cleveland and back?

The train took $3\frac{1}{2} + 4\frac{1}{2} = 8$ hours for the trip. The distance of a round trip is $2(200) = 400$ miles. Since $d = rt$ then 400 miles $= r \times 8$ hours. Solve for r and you have $r = \frac{400 \text{ miles}}{8 \text{ hours}} = 50$ miles per hour. Therefore the average speed is 50 miles per hour.

The speed in the formula is the average speed. If you know that there are different speeds for different lengths of time, then you must use the formula more than once, as we did in the first example in C–2.

Practice Exercises

1. An automobile travels at the rate of 55 miles per hour on the Pennsylvania Turnpike. How many minutes will it take to travel $\frac{2}{3}$ of a mile at this rate?

   (A) 0.2 (B) 0.72 (C) 2.2 (D) 13.5 (E) 22

2. Miguel leaves by automobile at 9:00 A.M. and stops for repairs at 9:20 A.M. If the distance covered was 18 miles, what was the average velocity, in miles per hour for this part of the trip?

   (A) 5.4 (B) 6 (C) 54 (D) 36 (E) 60

3. A man runs y yards in m minutes. What is his rate, in yards per hour?

   (A) $\frac{y}{60m}$ (B) $\frac{m}{60y}$ (C) $60my$ (D) $\frac{60y}{m}$

   (E) $\frac{60m}{y}$

4. Ten minutes after a plane leaves the airport, it is reported that the plane is 40 miles away. What is the average speed of the plane, in miles per hour?

   (A) 66 (B) 240 (C) 400 (D) 600 (E) 660

5. An automobile passes City X at 9:55 A.M. and City Y at 10:15 A.M. City X is 30 miles from City Y. What is the average rate of the automobile, in miles per hour?

   (A) 10 (B) 30 (C) 90 (D) 120 (E) 360

6. The distance between two cities is 1,800 miles. How many gallons of gasoline will a motorist use with an automobile that uses (on the average) 1 gallon of gasoline for each 12 miles?

   (A) 150 (B) 160 (C) 216 (D) 1,500
   (E) 2,160

7. How many miles does a car travel if it averages a rate of 35 miles per hour for 3 hours and 24 minutes?

   (A) 109 (B) 112 (C) 113 (D) 119 (E) 129

8. Two cars start towards each other from points 400 miles apart. One car travels at 40 miles an hour and the other travels at 35 miles an hour. How far apart, in miles, will the two cars be after 4 hours of continuous traveling?

   (A) 20 (B) 40 (C) 75 (D) 100 (E) 160

9. A motorist travels for 3 hours at 40 miles per hour and then covers a distance of 80 miles in 2 hours and 40 minutes. His average rate for the entire trip was

   (A) 35 m.p.h.
   (B) 35.3 m.p.h.
   (C) 35.5 m.p.h.
   (D) 36 m.p.h.
   (E) 37 m.p.h.

10. A man driving a distance of 90 miles averages 30 miles per hour. On the return trip he averages 45 miles per hour. His average speed for the round trip, in miles per hour, is

    (A) 34 (B) 36 (C) $37\frac{1}{2}$ (D) 40 (E) 75

11. The El Capitan of the Santa Fe traveled a distance of 152.5 miles from La Junta to Garden City in 2 hours. What was the average speed, in miles per hour?

    (A) 15.25 (B) 31.5 (C) 30.5 (D) 71
    (E) 76.3

12. The distance between Portland, Oregon, and Santa Fe, New Mexico is 1,800 miles. How many hours would it take a train with an average speed of 60 miles per hour to make the trip?

    (A) 30 (B) 39 (C) 48 (D) 300 (E) 480

13. A man drives for 5 hours at an average rate of 40 m.p.h. He develops some motor trouble and returns to his original starting point in 10 hours. What was his average rate on the return trip?

    (A) 10 m.p.h.
    (B) 15 m.p.h.
    (C) 20 m.p.h.
    (D) 26.6 m.p.h.
    (E) 40 m.p.h.

14. If a man walks W miles in H hours, and then rides R miles in the same length of time, what is his average rate, in miles per hour, for the entire trip?

    (A) $\dfrac{R+W}{H}$ (B) $\dfrac{2(R+W)}{H}$ (C) $\dfrac{R+W}{2H}$

    (D) $\dfrac{H}{R-W}$ (E) $\dfrac{RW-H}{2}$

15. How long would a car traveling at 30 miles per hour take to cover a distance of 44 feet? (1 mile = 5,280 feet)

    (A) 1 second
    (B) 2.64 seconds
    (C) 5.2 seconds
    (D) 1 minute
    (E) 7.7 minutes

Answer Key

1.	B	6.	A	11.	E
2.	C	7.	D	12.	A
3.	D	8.	D	13.	C
4.	B	9.	B	14.	C
5.	C	10.	B	15.	A

C–3

Work Problems. In this type of problem you can assume that all workers in the same category work at the same rate. The main idea is this: If it takes k workers 1 hour to do a job, then each worker does $\frac{1}{k}$ of the job in an hour or *he works at the rate of $\frac{1}{k}$ of the job per hour*. If it takes m workers h hours to finish a job, then each worker does $\frac{1}{m}$ of the job in h hours, so he does $\frac{1}{h}$ of $\frac{1}{m}$ in an hour. Therefore, each *worker works at the rate of $\frac{1}{mh}$ of the job per hour.*

> If 5 men take an hour to dig a ditch, how long should 12 men take to dig a ditch of the same type?

Since 5 workers took an hour, each worker does $\frac{1}{5}$ of the job in an hour. Therefore, 12 workers will work at the rate of $\frac{12}{5}$ of the job per hour. Thus, if T is the time required for 12 workers to do the job, $\frac{12}{5} \times T = 1$ job and $T = \frac{5}{12} \times 1$, so

$$T = \frac{5}{12} \text{ hour or 25 minutes.}$$

> Worker A takes 8 hours to do a job. Worker B takes 10 hours to do the same job. How long should worker A and worker B working together, but independently, take to do the same job?

Worker A works at a rate of $\frac{1}{8}$ of the job per hour, since he takes 8 hours to finish the job. Worker B finishes the job in 10 hours, so he works at a rate of $\frac{1}{10}$ of the job per hour.

Therefore, if they work together they should complete $\frac{1}{8} + \frac{1}{10} = \frac{18}{80} = \frac{9}{40}$, so they work at a rate of $\frac{9}{40}$ of the job per hour together. If T is the time they take to finish the job,

$\frac{9}{40}$ of the job per hour $\times$ T hours must equal 1 job. Therefore,

$$\frac{9}{40} \times T = 1 \text{ and } T = \frac{40}{9} = 4\frac{4}{9} \text{ hours.}$$

> There are two taps, tap 1 and tap 2, in a keg. If both taps are opened, the keg is drained in 20 minutes. If tap 1 is closed and tap 2 is open, the keg will be drained in 30 minutes. If tap 2 is closed and tap 1 is open, how long will it take to drain the keg?

Tap 1 and tap 2 together take 20 minutes to drain the keg,

so together they drain the keg at a rate of $\frac{1}{20}$ of the keg per minute. Tap 2 takes 30 minutes to drain the keg by itself, so it drains the keg at the rate of $\frac{1}{30}$ of the keg per minute. Let r be the rate at which tap 1 will drain the keg by itself. Then $\left(r+\frac{1}{30}\right)$ of the keg per minute is the rate

at which both taps together will drain the keg, so $r+\frac{1}{30}=\frac{1}{20}$. Therefore, $r=\frac{1}{20}-\frac{1}{30}=\frac{1}{60}$, and tap 1 drains the keg at the rate of $\frac{1}{60}$ of the keg per minute. Tap 1 will take 60 minutes or 1 hour to drain the keg if tap 2 is closed.

Practice Exercises

1. One boy can deliver newspapers on his route in $1\frac{1}{4}$ hours. Another boy who takes his place one day takes 15 minutes longer to deliver these papers. How long would it take to deliver the papers if the two boys worked together?

    (A) $22\frac{1}{4}$ min.   (B) $37\frac{1}{2}$ min.   (C) 40 min.
    (D) 50 min.   (E) 65 min.

2. A contractor estimates that he can paint a house in 5 days by using 6 men. If he actually uses only 5 men for the job, how many days will they take to paint the house?

    (A) 5   (B) $5\frac{1}{4}$ (C) $5\frac{1}{2}$ (D) 6   (E) $6\frac{1}{2}$

3. A club decided to build a cabin. The job can be done by 3 skilled workmen in 20 days or by 5 of the boys in 30 days. How many days will the job take if all work together?

    (A) 10   (B) 12   (C) $12\frac{2}{3}$ (D) 14   (E) 5

4. Andrew can do a piece of work in r days and Bill, who works faster, can do the same work in s days. Which of the following expressions, if any, represents the number of days the two of them would take to do the work if they worked together?

    (A) $\frac{r+s}{2}$ (B) $\frac{1}{r}+\frac{1}{s}$ (C) $r-s$ (D) $\frac{rs}{r+s}$
    (E) none of these

5. Four tractors working together can plow a field in 12 hours. How long will it take 6 tractors to plow a field of the same size, if all tractors work at the same rate?

    (A) 6 hr.   (B) 9 hr.   (C) 10 hr.   (D) 18 hr.
    (E) 8 hr.

6. A small factory with 3 machines has a job of stamping out a number of pan covers. The newest machine can do the job in 3 days, another machine can do it in 4 days, and the third machine can do it in 6 days. How many days will the factory take to do the job, using all three machines?

    (A) $1\frac{1}{3}$ (B) $4\frac{1}{3}$ (C) 6   (D) 13   (E) $1\frac{4}{9}$

7. Steven can mow a lawn in 20 minutes and Bernard can mow the same lawn in 30 minutes. How long will they take, working together, to mow the lawn?

    (A) 10 min.   (B) $12\frac{1}{2}$ min.   (C) 15 min.
    (D) 25 min.   (E) 12 min.

8. It takes Bert an hour to do a job that Harry can do in 40 minutes. One morning they worked together for 12 minutes; then Bert went away and Harry finished the job. How long did it take him to finish?

    (A) 8 min.   (B) 16 min.   (C) 20 min.
    (D) 28 min.   (E) 33 min.

9. One man can paint a house in r days and another man in s days. If together they can do the work in d days, the equation that expresses the amount of work done by both men in one day is

    (A) $d=\frac{1}{r+s}$ (B) $\frac{1}{r}=\frac{d}{r+s}$ (C) $\frac{1}{d}=\frac{r+s}{rs}$
    (D) $\frac{r+s}{d}=1$ (E) $\frac{d}{rs}=1$

10. Linda has m minutes of homework in each of her s subjects. What part of her homework does she complete in an hour?

    (A) $\frac{1}{ms}$ (B) $\frac{ms}{60}$ (C) $\frac{60}{ms}$ (D) $\frac{s}{60m}$
    (E) $\frac{60m}{s}$

11. Sam can mow a lawn in 20 minutes, while Mark takes 10 minutes longer to mow the same lawn. How long will they take to mow the lawn if they work together?

    (A) 10 min.
    (B) 12 min.
    (C) $12\frac{1}{4}$ min.
    (D) 15 min.
    (E) more than 15 min.

12. It takes h hours to mow a lawn. What part of the lawn is mowed in 1 hour?

(A) h (B) $\dfrac{h}{x}$ (C) hx (D) $\dfrac{1}{h}$ (E) $\dfrac{x}{h}$

13. If M men can complete a job in H hours, how long will 5 men take to do this job?

(A) $\dfrac{5M}{H}$ (B) $\dfrac{M}{5H}$ (C) $\dfrac{MH}{5}$ (D) $\dfrac{5}{MH}$

(E) $\dfrac{5H}{M}$

14. Ann can type a manuscript in 10 hours. Florence can type the same manuscript in 5 hours. If they type this manuscript together, it can be completed in

(A) 2 hr. 30 min.
(B) 3 hr.
(C) 3 hr. 20 min.
(D) 5 hr.
(E) 7 hr. 30 min.

15. It was calculated that 75 men could complete a strip on a new highway in 20 days. When work was scheduled to commence, it was found necessary to send 25 men on another road project. How much longer will it take to complete the strip?

(A) 10 days (B) 20 days (C) 30 days
(D) 40 days (E) 60 days

Answer Key

1.	C	6.	A	11.	B
2.	D	7.	E	12.	D
3.	B	8.	C	13.	C
4.	D	9.	C	14.	C
5.	E	10.	C	15.	A

II–D.   Counting Problems

D–1

Here is an example of the first type of counting problem: 50 students signed up for both English and math, and 90 students signed up for either English or math. If 25 students are taking English but are not taking math, how many students are taking math but not taking English?

In these problems, "either . . . or . . ." means that a person can take both, so the people taking both are included among the people taking either math or English.

You must avoid counting the same people twice in these problems. The formula is:

the number taking English or math =
the number taking English + the number taking math –
the number taking both.

You have to subtract the number taking both subjects since they are counted once with those taking English and counted again with those taking math.

A person taking English is either taking math or not taking math, so there are 50 + 25 = 75 people taking English, 50 taking English and math, and 25 taking English but not taking math. Since 75 are taking English, 90 = 75 + number taking math – 50, so 90 – 25 = 65 people are taking math. Of the people taking math, 50 are also taking English, so 65 – 50 or 15 are taking math but not English.

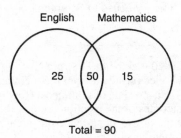

Total = 90

The figure shows what is given. Since 90 students signed up for English or mathematics, 15 must be taking mathematics but not English.

In a survey, 60% of those surveyed owned a car and 80% of those surveyed owned a TV. If 55% owned both a car and a TV, what percent of those surveyed owned a car or a TV but not both?

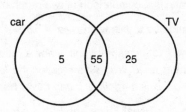

To indicate that 55% is common to both conditions, that is, owning a car and owning a TV, 55 appears in the area common to both circles in the figure. An additional 5% who owned a car but not a TV is indicated by a 5 in the circle at the left, since 60% of those surveyed owned a car. An additional 25% who owned a TV but not a car is indicated by a 25 in the circle at the right, since 80% owned a TV. Therefore 30% owned either a car or a TV, bot not both.

D–2

> If an event can happen in *m* different ways, and each of the *m* ways is followed by a second event that can occur in *k* different ways, then the first event can be followed by the second event in *m · k* different ways. This is called the *fundamental principle of counting.*

> If there are 3 different roads from Syracuse to Binghamton and 4 different roads from Binghamton to Scranton, how many different routes are there from Syracuse to Scranton that go through Binghamton?

There are 3 different ways to go from Syracuse to Binghamton. Once you are in Binghamton, there are 4 different ways to get to Scranton. Using the fundamental principle of counting, you will find that there are $3 \times 4 = 12$ different ways to get from Syracuse to Scranton going through Binghamton.

> A club has 20 members. They are electing a president and a vice president from the members at large; there is no slate of nominees. How many different outcomes of the election are possible? (Assume the president and vice president must be different members of the club.)

There are 20 members, so there are 20 choices for president. Once a president is chosen, 19 members are left who can be vice president. Thus there are $20 \cdot 19 = 380$ different possible outcomes of the election.

II–E.   *Ratio and Proportion*

E–1

Ratio.   A ratio is a comparison of two numbers by division. The ratio of *a* to *b* is written as $a : b = \dfrac{a}{b} = a \div b$. We can handle ratios as fractions, since a ratio is a fraction. In the ratio $a : b$, *a* and *b* are called the *terms* of the ratio. *Since a : b is a fraction, b can never be zero.*

The fraction $\dfrac{a}{b}$ is usually different from the fraction $\dfrac{b}{a}$ $\left(\text{for example, } \dfrac{3}{2} \text{ is not the same as } \dfrac{2}{3}\right)$, so *the order of the terms in a ratio is important.*

> If an orange costs 20¢ and an apple costs 12¢, what is the ratio of the cost of an orange to the cost of an apple?

The ratio is $\dfrac{20¢}{12¢} = \dfrac{5}{3}$ or 5 : 3. Notice that the ratio of the cost of an apple to the cost of an orange is $\dfrac{12¢}{20¢} = \dfrac{3}{5}$ or 3 : 5, so the order of the terms is important.

A ratio is a number, therefore, if you want to find the ratio of two quantities, they must be expressed in the same units.

> What is the ratio of 8 inches to 6 feet?

Change 6 feet into inches. There are 12 inches in a foot, so 6 feet = 6×12 inches = 72 inches. The ratio is $\dfrac{8 \text{ inches}}{72 \text{ inches}} = \dfrac{1}{9}$ or 1 : 9.

If you regard ratios as fractions, the units must cancel out, that is, the two terms in a ratio must be expressed in the same unit of measure. In the above example, if you do not change units, the ratio would be $\dfrac{8 \text{ inches}}{6 \text{ feet}}$ or $\dfrac{4}{3}$ inches per foot, which is not a number.

If two numbers measure different quantities, their quotient is usually called a *rate*. For example, $\dfrac{50 \text{ miles}}{2 \text{ hours}}$, which equal 25 miles per hour, is a rate of speed.

E–2

Proportion.   A proportion is a statement that two ratios are equal. For example, $\dfrac{3}{12} = \dfrac{1}{4}$ is a proportion; it could also be expressed as 3 : 12 = 1 : 4 or 3 : 12 :: 1 : 4.

In the proportion $a : b = c : d$, the terms on the outside, *a* and *d*, are called the *extremes*, and the terms on the inside, *b* and *c*, are called the *means*. Since $a : b$ and $c : d$ are ratios, *b* and *d* are both different from zero, so $bd \neq 0$.

Multiply each side of $\dfrac{a}{b} = \dfrac{c}{d}$ by *bd*; you get $(bd)\left(\dfrac{a}{b}\right) = ad$ and $(bd)\left(\dfrac{c}{d}\right) = bc$. Since $bd \neq 0$, the proportion $\dfrac{a}{b} = \dfrac{c}{d}$ is equivalent to the equation $ad = bc$. This is usually expressed in the following way:

In a proportion the product of the extremes is equal to the product of the means.

Find x if $\dfrac{4}{5} = \dfrac{10}{x}$.

In the proportion $\dfrac{4}{5} = \dfrac{10}{x}$, 4 and x are the extremes and 5 and 10 are the means, so $4x = 5 \cdot 10 = 50$. We solve for x and get $x = \dfrac{50}{4} = 12.5$.

Finding the products ad and bc is also called _cross-multiplying the proportion_: $\dfrac{a}{b} \diagdown\!\!\!\diagup \dfrac{c}{d}$. Cross-multiplying a proportion gives two equal numbers. The proportion $\dfrac{a}{b} = \dfrac{c}{d}$ is read as "a is to b as c is to d."

Two numbers are in the ratio 5 : 4 and their difference is 10. What is the larger number?

Let m and n be the two numbers. Then $\dfrac{m}{n} = \dfrac{5}{4}$ and $m - n = 10$. Cross-multiply the proportion and you get $5n = 4m$ or $n = \dfrac{4}{5}m$. Then $m - n = m - \dfrac{4}{5}m = \dfrac{1}{5}m = 10$ and $m = 50$, which means $n = \dfrac{4}{5} \cdot 50 = 40$. Therefore, the larger number is 50.

CHECK:

$$\dfrac{50}{40} = \dfrac{5}{4} \text{ and } 50 - 40 = 10.$$

Two variables, a and b, are _directly proportional_ if they satisfy a relatioship of the form $a = kb$, where k is a number that is a constant. The distance a car travels in 2 hours and its average speed for the 2 hours are directly proportional, since $d = 2s$, where d is the distance and s is the average speed expressed in miles per hour. Here $k = 2$. Sometimes the word directly is omitted, so "a and b are proportional" means $a = kb$.

If m is proportional to n and $m = 5$ when $n = 4$, what is the value of m when $n = 18$?

There are two different ways to work the problem.

I. Since m and n are directly proportional, $m = kn$; also, $m = 5$ when $n = 4$, so $5 = k \cdot 4$, which means $k = \dfrac{5}{4}$. Therefore, $m = \dfrac{5}{4}n$. When $n = 18$, $m = \dfrac{5}{4} \cdot 18 = \dfrac{90}{4} = 22.5$.

II. Since m and n are directly proportional, $m = kn$. If n' is some value of n, then the value of m

corresponding to n' we will call m', and $m' = kn'$. Then $\dfrac{m}{n} = k$ and $\dfrac{m'}{n'} = k$; therefore, $\dfrac{m}{n} = \dfrac{m'}{n'}$ is a proportion. Since $m = 5$ when $n = 4$, $\dfrac{m}{n} = \dfrac{5}{4} = \dfrac{m'}{18}$. Cross-multiplying, we have $4m' = 90$ or $m' = \dfrac{90}{4} = 22.5$.

If two quantities are proportional, you can always set up a proportion in this manner.

If a machine makes 3 yards of cloth in 2 minutes, how many yards of cloth will the machine make in 50 minutes?

The amount of cloth is proportional to the time the machine operates. Let y be the number of yards of cloth the machine makes in 50 minutes; then $\dfrac{2 \text{ minutes}}{50 \text{ minutes}} = \dfrac{3 \text{ yards}}{y \text{ yards}}$, so $\dfrac{2}{50} = \dfrac{3}{y}$. Cross-multiplying, you have $2y = 150$, so $y = 75$. Therefore, the machine makes 75 yards of cloth in 50 minutes.

Since a ratio is a number, the units must cancel, so put the numbers that measure the same quantity in the same ratio.

Any two units of measurement of the same quantity are directly proportional.

How many ounces are there in $4\dfrac{3}{4}$ pounds?

Let x be the number of ounces in $4\dfrac{3}{4}$ pounds. Since there are 16 ounces in a pound, $\dfrac{x \text{ ounces}}{16 \text{ ounces}} = \dfrac{4\dfrac{3}{4} \text{ pounds}}{1 \text{ pound}}$.

Cross-multiply to get $x = 16 \cdot 4\dfrac{3}{4} = 16 \cdot \dfrac{19}{4} = 76$; so $4\dfrac{3}{4}$ pounds = 76 ounces.

You can always change units by using a proportion. You should know the following measurements:

LENGTH:	**1 foot = 12 inches**
	1 yard = 3 feet
AREA:	**1 square foot = 144 square inches**
	1 square yard = 9 square feet
TIME:	**1 minute = 60 seconds**
	1 hour = 60 minutes
	1 day = 24 hours

1 week = 7 days
1 year = 52 weeks
VOLUME: 1 quart = 2 pints
1 gallon = 4 quarts
WEIGHT: 1 pound = 16 ounces
1 ton = 2,000 pounds

On a map, it is $2\frac{1}{2}$ inches from Harrisburg to Gary.

The actual distance from Harrisburg to Gary is 750 miles. What is the actual distance from town A to town B if they are 4 inches apart on the map?

Let d miles be the distance from A to B; then $\dfrac{2\frac{1}{2}\ \text{inches}}{4\ \text{inches}} =$

$\dfrac{750\ \text{miles}}{d\ \text{miles}}$. Cross-multiplying we have $\left(2\frac{1}{2}\right)d = 4 \times 750$

$= 3{,}000$, so $d = \dfrac{2}{5} \times 3{,}000 = 1{,}200$. Therefore, the distance from A to B is 1,200 miles. Problems like this one are often called scale problems.

Two variables, a and b, are *indirectly proportional* if they satisfy a relationship of the form $k = ab$, where k is a number that is a constant. Thus, the average speed of a car and the time the car takes to travel 300 miles are indirectly proportional, since $st = 300$, where s is the speed and t is the time.

---

m is indirectly proportional to n and $m = 5$ when $n = 4$. What is the value of m when $n = 18$?

Since m and n are indirectly proportional, $m \cdot n = k$, and $k = 5 \cdot 4 = 20$ because $m = 5$ when $n = 4$. Therefore, $18m = k = 20$, so $m = \dfrac{20}{18} = \dfrac{10}{9}$ when $n = 18$.

Other examples of indirect proportion are work problems.

If two quantities are directly proportional, then, when one increases, the other increases. If two quantities are indirectly proportional, then, when one increases, the other decreases.

E–3

It is also possible to compare three or more numbers by using a ratio. "The numbers A, B, and C are in the ratio

2 : 4 : 3" means $A : B = 2 : 4$, $A : C = 2 : 3$, and $B : C = 4 : 3$. The order of the terms is important. $A : B : C$ is read as "A is to B is to C."

What is the ratio of Tom's salary to Martha's salary to Anne's salary if Tom makes \$15,000, Martha makes \$12,000, and Anne makes \$10,000?

The ratio is 15,000 : 12,000 : 10,000, which is the same as 15 : 12 : 10. You can cancel a factor that appears in *every* term.

The angles of a triangle are in the ratio 5 : 4 : 3; how many degrees are there is the largest angle?

The sum of the angles in a triangle is 180°. If the angles are $a°$, $b°$, and $c°$, then $a + b + c = 180$, and $a : b : c = 5 : 4 : 3$. You can find b in terms of a since $\dfrac{a}{b} = \dfrac{5}{4}$, and c in terms of a since $\dfrac{a}{c} = \dfrac{5}{3}$, and then solve the equation for a.

A quicker method for this type of problem is:

❶ Add all the numbers: $5 + 4 + 3 = 12$.

❷ Use each number as the numerator of a fraction whose denominator is the result of ❶, getting $\dfrac{5}{12}$, $\dfrac{4}{12}$, $\dfrac{3}{12}$.

❸ Each quantity is the corresponding fraction, from ❷, of the total. Thus:

$$a = \frac{5}{12}\ \text{of 180 or 75}, \quad b = \frac{4}{12}\ \text{of 180 or 60},$$

$$\text{and } c = \frac{3}{12}\ \text{of 180 or 45}.$$

The largest angle is 75°.

CHECK:

$75 : 60 : 45 = 5 : 4 : 3$ and $75 + 60 + 45 = 180$.

Practice Exercises

1. An Erlenmeyer flask can hold 0.6 liter. How many flasks are necessary to hold 3.6 liters?

   (A) 3   (B) 4.2   (C) 6   (D) 12   (E) 21.6

2. At 13° Centigrade a cubic centimeter of uranium weighs 18.7 grams. What is the weight (in grams) of 0.1 cubic centimeter of uranium at 13° Centigrade?

   (A) 1   (B) 1.87   (C) 0.187   (D) 100   (E) 1870

3. If the cost of 500 articles is d dollars, how many of these articles can be bought for x dollars?

   (A) $\dfrac{500d}{x}$ (B) $\dfrac{500}{dx}$ (C) $\dfrac{dx}{500}$ (D) $\dfrac{500x}{d}$

   (E) $\dfrac{d}{500x}$

4. A man left $5,000.00 to his three sons. For every dollar Abraham received, Benjamin received $1.50 and Charles received $2.50. How much money was left to Benjamin?

   (A) $750   (B) $1,000   (C) $1,100
   (D) $1,500   (E) $3,000

5. The wey of Scotland is equivalent to 40 bushels. How many weys are there in 4 bushels?

   (A) $\dfrac{1}{10}$ (B) 1   (C) 10   (D) 44   (E) 160

6. The Japanese ken is equivalent to 5.97 feet. How many feet are there in 59.7 ken?

   (A) 0.1   (B) 10   (C) 248   (D) 356   (E) 360

7. 640 acres = 1 square mile

   1 acre = 4,840 square yards

   1 square mile = ? square yards

   (A) $\dfrac{16}{121}$ (B) $\dfrac{121}{16}$ (C) 1760   (D) 309,760
   (E) 3,097,600

8. A bag of chicken feed will feed 18 chickens for 54 days. How many days will it feed 12 chickens?

   (A) 36   (B) 37   (C) 53   (D) 72   (E) 81

9. If 9 men need 15 days to complete a task, how many days would it take to complete this task if 3 additional men were employed?

   (A) $4\dfrac{3}{4}$ (B) 10   (C) $11\dfrac{1}{4}$ (D) 12   (E) 6

10. A man works 5 days a week and binds 35 sets of books each week. If there are 7 books in a set, what is the number of books he binds each day?

    (A) 1   (B) 7   (C) 25   (D) 35   (E) 49

11. Three men invested $2,000, $3,000, and $5,000, respectively, upon the formation of a partnership. The net profits at the end of the year amounted to $960.00. How much should the man who invested the least money receive as his share if the profits are divided in accordance with the amount each partner invested?

    (A) $192   (B) $220   (C) $240   (D) $384
    (E) $480

12. Three boys have marbles in the ratio of 19 : 5 : 3. If the boy with the least number has 9 marbles, how many marbles does the boy with the greatest number have?

    (A) 27   (B) 33   (C) 57   (D) 81   (E) 171

13. Snow is accumulating f feet per minute. How much snow will accumulate in h hours if it continues falling at the same rate?

    (A) 60fh (B) fh (C) $\dfrac{60f}{h}$ (D) $\dfrac{60h}{f}$ (E) $\dfrac{f}{h}$

14. A diagram of a plane drawn to the scale of 0.5 inch equals 80 feet. If the length of the diagram is 4.5 inches, the actual length of the plane is

    (A) 320 ft.   (B) 360 ft.   (C) 640 ft.
    (D) 680 ft.   (E) 720 ft.

15. Joan can wire x radios in $\dfrac{3}{4}$ minute. At this rate, how many radios can she wire in $\dfrac{3}{4}$ of an hour?

    (A) $\dfrac{x}{60}$ (B) $\dfrac{60}{x}$ (C) 60x (D) 60   (E) $x + 60$

16. If a light flashes every 6 seconds, how many times will it flash in $\dfrac{3}{4}$ of an hour?

    (A) 225   (B) 250   (C) 360   (D) 450   (E) 480

17. Samuel, Martin, and Miguel invest $5,000, $7,000, and $12,000, respectively, in a business. If the profits are distributed proportionately, what share of a $1,111 profit should Miguel receive?

    (A) $231.40   (B) $264.00   (C) $333.33
    (D) $370.33   (E) $555.50

18. If there are 5 to 8 eggs in a pound, what is the maximum number of eggs in 40 pounds?

    (A) 5   (B) 8   (C) 160   (D) 200   (E) 320

19. 24-carat gold is pure gold.

    18-carat gold is $\frac{3}{4}$ gold.

    20-carat gold is $\frac{5}{8}$ gold.

    The ratio of pure gold in 18-carat gold to pure gold in 20-carat gold is

    (A) 5 : 8   (B) 9 : 10   (C) 15 : 24   (D) 8 : 5
    (E) 10 : 9

20. A cup of oatmeal weighs 3 ounces. A cup of pancake mix weighs 5 ounces. How many cups of oatmeal will have the same weight as 3 cups of pancake mix?

    (A) $\frac{3}{5}$ (B) $1\frac{2}{3}$ (C) 3   (D) 5   (E) 15

Answer Key

1.	C	8.	E	15.	C
2.	B	9.	C	16.	D
3.	D	10.	E	17.	E
4.	D	11.	A	18.	E
5.	A	12.	C	19.	B
6.	D	13.	A	20.	D
7.	E	14.	E		

II–F.   Sequence and Progressions

F–1

A SEQUENCE is an ordered collection of numbers. For example, 2, 4, 6, 8, 10, . . . is a sequence. 2, 4, 6, 8, 10 are called the *terms* of the sequence. We identify the terms by their positions in the sequence; 2 is the first term, 8 is the fourth term, and so on. The dots mean that the sequence continues; you should be able to figure out the succeeding terms. In the example, the sequence is the sequence of even integers, and the next term after 10 is 12.

> What is the eighth term of the sequence 1, 4, 9, 16, 25, . . .?

Since $1^2 = 1$, $2^2 = 4$, $3^2 = 9$, the sequence is the sequence of squares of integers, so the eighth term is $8^2 = 64$.

F–2

An *arithmetical progression* is a sequence of numbers with the property that the *difference* of any two consecutive numbers is always the same. The numbers 2, 6, 10, 14, 18, 22, . . . constitute an arithmetical progression, since each term is 4 more than the term before it. The number 4 is called the common difference of the progression.

If *d* is the common difference and *a* is the first term of the progression, *the nth term will be* $a + (n-1)d$. Thus, a progression with common difference 4 and initial term 5 will have $5 + 6(4) = 29$ as its seventh term. You can check your answer. The sequence would be 5, 9, 13, 17, 21, 25, 29, . . ., so 29 is the seventh term.

To find the sum of the first *n* terms in an arithmetic progression, use the formula $S = \frac{n}{2}(a + l)$, where *l* is the last term.

> In the arithmetic progression 7, 10, 13, 16, . . . what is the sum of 36 terms?

First find the value of *l*:

$l = 1 + d(n - 1)$

$l = 7 + 3(35)$

$l = 112$

Apply the formula $S = \frac{n}{2}(a + l)$:

$S = 18(7 + 112)$

$S = 18(119)$

$S = 2,142$

The sum of 36 terms in the arithmetic progression 7, 10, 13, 16, . . . is 2,142.

A sequence of numbers is called a *geometric progression* if the *ratio* of consecutive terms is always the same. Thus, 3, 6, 12, 24, 48, . . . is a geometric progression since $\frac{6}{3} =$ $2 = \frac{12}{6} = \frac{24}{12} = \frac{48}{24}$, ... *The nth term of a geometric series is* ar^{n-1}, where *a* is the first term and *r* is the common ratio. If a geometric progression starts with 2 and the common ratio is 3, then the fifth term should be $2 \cdot 3^4 = 2 \cdot 81 = 162$. The sequence is 2, 6, 18, 54, 162, . . ., so 162 is indeed the fifth term of the progression.

We can quickly add up the first n terms of a geometric progression that starts with a and has common ratio r. When $r \neq 1$, *the formula for the sum of the first n terms* is $\dfrac{ar^n - a}{r - 1}$. (If $r = 1$, all the terms are the same so the sum is na.)

> Find the sum of the first seven terms of the sequence 5, 10, 20, 40, . . .

Since $\dfrac{10}{5} = \dfrac{20}{10} = \dfrac{40}{20} = 2$, the sequence is a geometric sequence with common ratio 2. The first term is 5, so $a = 5$. The sum of the first seven terms means $n = 7$. Thus, the sum is

$$\frac{5 \cdot 2^7 - 5}{2 - 1} = 5(2^7 - 1) = 5(128 - 1) = 5 \cdot 127 = 635.$$

CHECK:

The first seven terms are 5, 10, 20, 40, 80, 160, 320, and $5 + 10 + 20 + 40 + 80 + 160 + 320 = 635$.

II–G.   Inequalities

G–1

The notation $a > b$ means that the number a is greater than the number b, that is, $a = b + x$, where x is a positive number. If we look at a number line, $a > b$ means that a is to the right of b. The notation $a > b$ can also be read as b is less than a, which is also written as $b < a$. For example, $-5 > -7.5$ because $-5 = -7.5 + 2.5$ and 2.5 is positive.

The notation $a \leq b$ means that a is less than or equal to b, or b is greater than or equal to a. For example, $5 \geq 4$; also $4 \geq 4$. The notation $a \neq b$ means that a is not equal to b.

> **If you need to know whether one fraction is greater than another fraction, put the fractions over a common denominator and compare the numerators.**

> Which is larger, $\dfrac{13}{16}$ or $\dfrac{31}{40}$?

A common denominator is 80.

$$\frac{13}{16} = \frac{65}{80}, \text{ and } \frac{31}{40} = \frac{62}{80};$$

since $65 > 62$,

$$\frac{65}{80} > \frac{62}{80}, \text{ so } \frac{13}{16} > \frac{31}{40}.$$

G–2

Inequalities have certain properties that are similar to those of equations. We can talk about the left side and the right side of an inequality, and we can use algebraic expressions for the sides of an inequality. For example, $6x < 5x + 4$. A value for an unknown *satisfies an inequality* if, when you evaluate each side of the inequality, the numbers satisfy the inequality. Thus, if $x = 2$, then $6x = 12$ and $5x + 4 = 14$, and since $12 < 14$, $x = 2$ satisfies $6x < 5x + 4$. Two inequalities are equivalent if the same collection of numbers satisfies both inequalities.

The following basic principles are used in work with inequalities:

❶ Adding the same expression to *each* side of an inequality gives an equivalent inequality (written as $a < b \leftrightarrow a + c < b + c$, where $\leftrightarrow$ means equivalent).

❷ Subtracting the same expression from *each* side of an inequality gives an equivalent inequality ($a < b \leftrightarrow a - c < b - c$).

❸ Multiplying or dividing *each* side of an inquality by the same *positive* expression gives an equivalent inequality ($a < b \leftrightarrow ca < cb$ for $c > 0$).

❹ Multiplying or dividing each side of an inequality by the same *negative* expression *reverses* the inequality ($a < b \leftrightarrow ca > cb$ for $c < 0$).

❺ If both sides of an inequality have the same sign, inverting both sides of the inequality *reverses* the inequality.

$$0 < a < b \leftrightarrow 0 < \frac{1}{b} < \frac{1}{a}$$

$$a < b < 0 \leftrightarrow \frac{1}{b} < \frac{1}{a} < 0$$

❻ If two inequalities are of the same type (both greater or both less), adding the respective sides gives the same type of inequality.

$$(a < b \text{ and } c < d, \text{ then } a + c < b + d)$$

Note that the inequalities are *not* equivalent.

❼ If $a < b$ and $b < c$, then $a < c$.

> Find the values of x for which $5x - 4 < 7x + 2$.

Using principle ❷, subtract $5x + 2$ from each side; then $(5x - 4 < 7x + 2) \leftrightarrow -6 < 2x$. Now use principle ❸, and divide each side by 2; then $-6 < 2x \leftrightarrow -3 < x$.

Any x greater than -3 satisfies the inequality. It is a good idea to make a spot check. $-1 > -3$; let $x = -1$; then $5x = -4 = -9$ and $7x + 2 = -5$. Since $-9 < -5$, the answer is correct for at least the particular value $x = -1$.

Some inequalities are not satisfied by *any* real number. For example, since $x^2 \geq 0$ for all x, there is no real number x such that $x^2 < -9$.

You may be given an inequality and asked whether other inequalities follow from the original inequality. You should be able to answer such questions by using principles ❶ through ❼.

If there is any property of inequalities you can't remember, try out some specific numbers. If $x < y$, then what is the relation between $-x$ and $-y$? Since $4 < 5$ but $-5 < -4$, the relation is probably $-x > -y$, which is true by ❹.

Probably the most common mistake is forgetting to reverse the inequalities if you multiply or divide by a negative number.

Find the values of a that satisfy $a^2 + 1 > 2a + 4$.

We will solve this using an alternative method:

❶ Group all terms on one side so that the other side will be 0. The result is $a^2 - 2a + 1 - 4 = a^2 - 2a - 3 > 0$.

❷ Find all values of the variable that make the expression equal 0.

Since $a^2 - 2a - 3 = (a - 3)(a + 1) = 0$, the result is $a = 3$ and $a = -1$.

❸ Choose points other than those found in ❷ and check whether the points are solutions. If $a = 0$, then $a^2 - 2a - 3 = -3$, which is less than 0, so $-1 < a < 3$ are not solutions. If $a = 4$, then $a^2 - 2a - 3 = 5$, which is greater than 0, so $a > 4$ are solutions. Use $a = -2$ to see that $a < -1$ are also solutions. Therefore, the solutions are $a > 3$ and $a < -1$.

This method is quicker for solving inequalities that are not linear.

Practice Exercises

1. Point P is on line segment AB. Which of the following is always true?

   (A) $AP = PB$ (B) $AP > PB$ (C) $PB > AP$
   (D) $AB > AP$ (E) $AB > AP + PB$

2. If $x < y$ and $a = b$, then

   (A) $x + a = y + b$ (B) $x + a < y + b$
   (C) $x + a > y + b$ (D) $x + a = y$ (E) $x + a = b$

3. If $x < y$ and $z = \frac{1}{2}x$ and $a = \frac{1}{2}y$, then

   (A) $z > a$ (B) $a > z$ (C) $\frac{1}{2}a = \frac{1}{2}z$ (D) $2x > 2z$

   (E) $2a > y$

4. If $b < d$ and $a = 2b$ and $c = 2d$, then

   (A) $b = d$ (B) $a = c$ (C) $a < c$ (D) $b > d$
   (E) $a > c$

5. If $p < q$ and $r < s$, then

   (A) $p = r > q + s$ (B) $p + r < q + s$ (C) $pr < qs$
   (D) $pr > qs$ (E) $p + r = q + s$

6. If $-1 < x \leq 1$ and x is an integer, then the value of x is

   (A) 0 only   (B) 1 only   (C) 1 and 0
   (D) one value more than 1   (E) one value less than 1

7. In the inequality $5x + 2 < 2x + 5$ all of the following may be values of x except

   (A) 0   (B) 1   (C) -1 (D) -2 (E) -3

8. If $a > b$ and $b > c$, then

   (A) $a < c$ (B) $a > c$ (C) $a = c$ (D) $c > a$
   (E) $b > a$

9. If $a > b > 1$, then which of the following is true?

   (A) $b + a > 2a$ (B) $a^2 < ab$ (C) $a - b < 0$
   (D) $a < b + 1$ (E) $a^2 > b^2$

10. If $2y > 5$, then

    (A) $y > 2.5$ (B) $y < 2.5$ (C) $y = 2.5$
    (D) $y = 10$ (E) $y = 5.2$

11. If $3x - 4 > 8$, then

    (A) $x = 4$ (B) $x = 0$ (C) $x = 4,0$ (D) $x > 4$
    (E) $x < 4$

12. In triangle ABC, $AB = AC$. All of the following statements are true except

    (A) $AB < AC + BC$ (B) $AC < AB + BC$
    (C) $AC < AB + AC$ (D) $AC + BC = AB + BC$
    (E) $BC + AC > AB + BC$

13. In triangle KLM the measure of angle $M >$ the measure of angle L. Which of the following is true?

    (A) $KM > KL$ (B) $KL > KM$ (C) $KL < KM$
    (D) $KM + LM < KL$ (E) $KL + LM < KM$

14. In triangles ABC and DEF, $AC = DF$, $BC = EF$, and $AB > DE$. Then

   (A) m $\angle C$ = m $\angle F$ (B) m $\angle F$ > m $\angle C$
   (C) m $\angle F$ < m $\angle C$ (D) m $\angle A$ = m $\angle D$
   (E) m $\angle B$ = m $\angle E$

15. If $x < y$ and $a < b$, then

   (A) $a + x < b + y$ (B) $a + x > b + y$ (C) $a = y$
   (D) $x = b$ (E) $ax = by$

Answer Key

1.	D	6.	C	11.	D
2.	B	7.	B	12.	E
3.	B	8.	B	13.	B
4.	C	9.	E	14.	C
5.	B	10.	A	15.	A

III. Geometry

III–A.   Angles

A–1

If two straight lines meet at a point, they form an *angle*. The point is called the *vertex* of the angle, and the lines are called the *sides* or *rays* of the angle. The sign for angle is $\angle$, and an angle can be denoted in the following ways:

❶ $\angle ABC$, where B is the vertex, A is a point on one side, and C is a point on the other side.

❷ $\angle B$, where B is the vertex.

❸ $\angle 1$ or $\angle x$, where 1 or x is written inside the angle.

Angles are usually measured in degrees. We say that an angle equals x degrees when its measure is x degrees. Degrees are denoted by °. An angle of 50 degrees is a 50° angle.

A–2

Two angles are *adjacent* if they have the same vertex and a common side, and one angle is not inside the other.

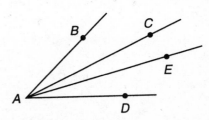

$\angle BAC$ and $\angle CAD$ are adjacent, but $\angle CAD$ and $\angle EAD$ are not adjacent.

If two lines intersect at a point, they form four angles. The angles opposite each other are called *vertical* angles. In the figure below, $\angle 1$ and $\angle 3$ are vertical angles, and $\angle 2$ and $\angle 4$ are vertical angles.

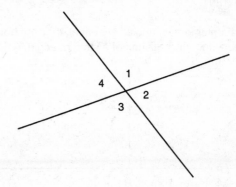

Vertical angles are equal, so, in the figure below,

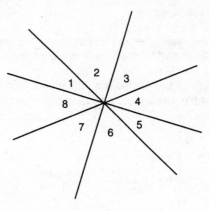

$\angle 1 = \angle 5$, $\angle 2 = \angle 6$, $\angle 3 = \angle 7$, $\angle 4 = \angle 8$.

A–3

A straight angle is an angle whose sides lie on a straight line. *A straight angle equals 180°.*

∠*ABC* is a straight angle.

If the sum of two angles is a straight angle, then the angles are *supplementary* and each angle is the supplement of the other.

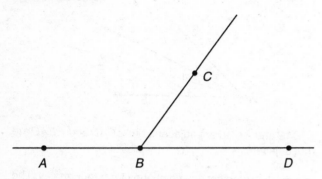

∠*ABC* and ∠*CBD* are supplementary.

If an angle of *x*° and an angle of *y*° are supplements, then *x* + *y* = 180.

If two supplementary angles are equal, they are both *right angles.* A right angle is half of a straight angle. A right angle = 90°.

∠*ABC* = ∠*CBD*, and they are both right angles. A right angle is denoted by ⌐.

When two lines intersect and all four of the angles are equal, then each of the angles is a right angle.

If the sum of two angles is a right angle, then the angles are *complementary* and each angle is a complement of the other.

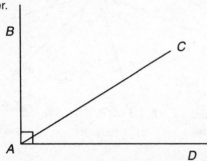

∠*BAC* and ∠*CAD* are complementary.

If an angle of *x*° and an angle of *y*° are complementary, then *x* + *y* = 90.

> If the supplement of angle *x* is three times as much as the complement of angle *x*, how many degrees is angle *x*?

Let *d* be the number of degrees in angle *x*; then the supplement of *x* is (180 − *d*)°, and the complement of *x* is (90 − *d*)°. Since the supplement is 3 times the complement, 180 − *d* = 3(90 − *d*) = 270 − 3*d*, which gives 2*d* = 90, so *d* = 45.

Therefore, angle *x* is 45°.

If an angle is divided into two equal parts by a straight line, then the angle has been *bisected* and the line is called the *bisector* of the angle.

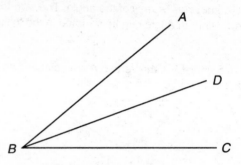

BD bisects ∠*ABC*, so ∠*ABD* = ∠*DBC*.

An *acute angle* is an angle less than a right angle. An *obtuse angle* is an angle greater than a right angle, but less than a straight angle.

∠1 is an acute angle, and ∠2 is an obtuse angle.

III–B.　Lines

B–1

A line is understood to be a straight line. A line is assumed to extend indefinitely in both directions. *There is one and only one line between two distinct points.* There are two ways to denote a line:

❶ by a single letter: *l* is a line;

❷ by two points on the line:

AB is a line.

A *line segment* is the part of a line between two points called *endpoints*. A line segment is denoted by its endpoints.

A   B

AB is a line segment. If a point *P* on a line segment is equidistant from the endpoints, then *P* is called the *midpoint* of the line segment.

A   P   B

P is the midpoint of *AB* if the length of *AP* = the length of *PB*. Two line segments are equal if their lengths are equal, so *AP* = *PB* means that the line segment *AP* has the same length as the line segment *PB*.

When a line segment is extended indefinitely in one direction, it is called a *ray*. A ray has one endpoint.

A   B

AB is a ray that has *A* as its endpoint.

B–2

P is a *point of intersection* of two lines if *P* is a point that is on both of the lines. *Two different lines cannot have more than one point of intersection*, because there is only one line between two points.

P is the point of intersection of *m* and *n*. We also say that *m* and *n* intersect at *P*.

Two lines in the same plane are parallel if they do not intersect no matter how far they are extended.

n

m

k

l

Lines *m* and *n* are parallel, but *k* and *l* are not parallel since, if *k* and *l* are extended, they will intersect. Parallel lines are denoted by the symbol ||, so *m* || *n* means that *m* is parallel to *n*.

If two lines are parallel to a third line, then they are parallel to each other.

If a third line intersects two given lines, it is called a *transversal*. A transversal and the two given lines form eight angles. The four inside angles are called *interior* angles. The four outside angles are called *exterior* angles. If two angles are on opposite sides of the transversal and have different lines for their sides, they are called *alternate* angles.

Line *k* is a transversal of the lines *m* and *n*. Angles 1, 2, 7, and 8 are the exterior angles, and angles 3, 4, 5, and 6 are the interior angles. ∠4 and ∠6 are an example of a pair of alternate angles. ∠1 and ∠5, ∠2 and ∠6, ∠3 and ∠7, and ∠4 and ∠8 are pairs of *corresponding* angles.

If two parallel lines are intersected by a transversal, then:

❶ Alternate interior angles are equal.

❷ Corresponding angles are equal.

❸ Interior angles on the same side of the transversal are supplementary.

If we use the fact that vertical angles are equal, we can replace "interior" by "exterior" in ❶ and ❸.

The fact that *m* is parallel to *n* implies:

❶ ∠4 = ∠6 and ∠3 = ∠5

❷ ∠1 = ∠5, ∠2 = ∠6, ∠3 = ∠7 and ∠4 = ∠8

❸ ∠3 + ∠6 = 180° and ∠4 + ∠5 = 180°

The reverse is also true. Let *m* and *n* be two lines that have *k* as a transversal.

❶ If a pair of alternate interior angles are equal, then *m* and *n* are parallel.

❷ If a pair of corresponding angles are equal, then *m* and *n* are parallel.

❸ If a pair of interior angles on the same side of the transversal are supplementary, then *m* is parallel to *n*.

If ∠3 = ∠5, then *m* ‖ *n*. If ∠4 = ∠6, then *m* ‖ *n*. If ∠2 = ∠6, then *m* ‖ *n*. If ∠3 + ∠6 = 180°, then *m* ‖ *n*.

If *m* and *n* are two parallel lines and angle 1 is 60°, how many degrees is angle 2?

Let ∠3 be the vertical angle equal to ∠2.

∠3 = ∠2. Since *m* and *n* are parallel, corresponding angles are equal. Since ∠1 and ∠3 are corresponding angles, ∠1 = ∠3. Therefore, ∠1 = ∠2, and ∠2 equals 60° since ∠1 = 60°.

B–3

When two lines intersect and all four of the angles formed are equal, the lines are said to be *perpendicular*. If two lines are perpendicular, they are the sides of right angles whose vertex is the point of intersection.

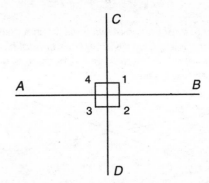

AB is perpendicular to *CD*, and angles 1, 2, 3, and 4 are all right angles. Since ⊥ is the symbol for perpendicular, we can write *AB* ⊥ *CD*.

If two lines in a plane are perpendicular to the same line, then the two lines are parallel.

The fact that *m* ⊥ *k* and *n* ⊥ *k* implies that *m* ‖ *n*.

If *any one* of the angles formed when two lines intersect is a right angle, then the lines are perpendicular.

III–C.   Polygons

A POLYGON is a closed figure in a plane that is composed of line segments that meet only at their endpoints. The line segments are called *sides* of the polygon, and a point where two sides meet is called a *vertex* (plural *vertices*) of the polygon.

A polygon is usually denoted by the vertices given in order.

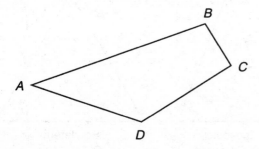

ABCD is a polygon.

A *diagonal* of a polygon is a line segment whose end-points are nonadjacent vertices. The *altitude* from a ver-tex *P* to a side is the line segment with endpoint *P* that is perpendicular to the side.

AC is a diagonal, and *CE* is the altitude from *C* to *AD*.

Polygons are classified by the number of angles or sides they have. A polygon with three angles is called a *trian-gle*; a four-sided polygon is a *quadrilateral*; a polygon with five angles is a *pentagon*; a polygon with six angles is a *hexagon*; an eight-sided polygon is an *octagon*. The num-ber of angles is always equal to the number of sides in a polygon, so a six-sided polygon is a hexagon, which has six angles. The term *n*-gon refers to a polygon with *n* sides.

Triangle

Quadrilateral

Pentagon   Hexagon

If the sides of a polygon are all equal in length and if all the angles of a polygon are equal, the polygon is called a *regular* polygon.

If the corresponding sides and the corresponding angles of two polygons are equal, the polygons are *congruent*. Congruent polygons have the same size and the same shape.

and

are congruent, but

and

are not congruent.

In figures for problems on congruence, sides with the same number of strokes through them are equal.

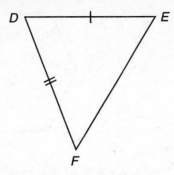

This figure indicates that $AB = DE$ and $AC = DF$.

If all the corresponding angles of two polygons are equal and the lengths of the corresponding sides are proportional, the polygons are said to be *similar*. Similar polygons have the same shape but need not be the same size.

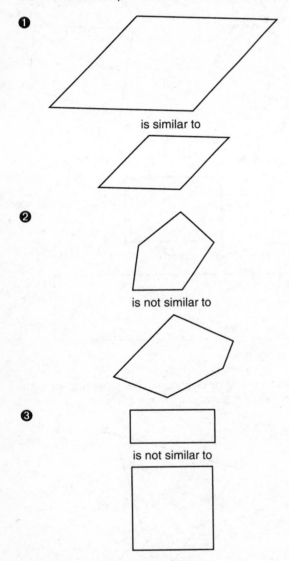

❶

is similar to

❷

is not similar to

❸

is not similar to

In ❸ the corresponding angles are equal, but the corresponding sides are not proportional.

The sum of all the angles of an *n*-gon is $(n - 2)180°$. For example, the sum of the angles in a hexagon is $(6 - 2)180° = 720°$.

III–D.   *Triangles*

D–1

A TRIANGLE is a three-sided polygon. If two sides of a triangle are equal, the triangle is called *isosceles*. If all three sides are equal, the triangle is *equilateral*. When one of the angles in a triangle is a right angle, the triangle is a *right triangle*.

Isosceles   Equilateral

Right

The symbol for a triangle is △, so △*ABC* denotes a triangle whose vertices are *A*, *B*, and *C*.

The sum of the angles in a triangle is 180°.

The sum of the lengths of any two sides of a triangle must be greater than the length of the remaining side.

If two angles in a triangle are equal, then the lengths of the sides opposite the equal angles are equal. If two sides of a triangle are equal, then the angles opposite the two equal sides are equal. In an equilateral triangle all the angles are equal and each angle = 60°. If each of the angles in a triangle is 60°, then the triangle is equilateral.

If $AB = BC$, then $\angle BAC = \angle BCA$.

If one angle in a triangle is larger than another angle, the side opposite the larger angle is longer than the side opposite the smaller angle. If one side is longer than another side, then the angle opposite the longer side is larger than the angle opposite the shorter side.

$AB > AC$ implies $\angle BCA > \angle ABC$.

If a side of a triangle is extended, then the resulting exterior angle is greater than either of the opposite and interior angles. In the triangle above, if we had extended side AC beyond C to a point D, then $\angle BCD$ would be greater than $\angle BAC$ and greater than $\angle ABC$.

In a right triangle, the side opposite the right angle is called the *hypotenuse*, and the remaining two sides are called *legs*.

The Pythagorean theorem states that the square of the length of the hypotenuse is equal to the sum of the squares of the lengths of the legs.

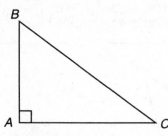

$(BC)^2 = (AB)^2 + (AC)^2$

If $AB = 4$ and $AC = 3$ then $(BC)^2 = 4^2 + 3^2 = 25$ so $BC = 5$.
If $BC = 13$ and $AC = 5$, then $13^2 = 169 = (AB)^2 + 5^2$. So $(AB)^2 = 169 - 25 = 144$ and $AB = 12$.

If the lengths of the three sides of a triangle are a, b, and c and $a^2 = b^2 + c^2$, then the triangle is a right triangle, where a is the length of the hypotenuse.

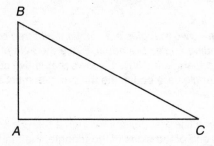

If $AB = 8$, $AC = 15$, and $BC = 17$, then, since $17^2 = 8^2 + 15^2$, $\angle BAC$ is a right angle.

D–2

CONGRUENCE.   Two triangles are congruent if two pairs of corresponding sides and the corresponding *included* angles are equal. This is called *Side-Angle-Side* and is denoted by S.A.S.

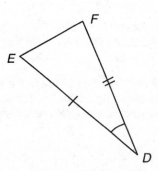

$AB = DE$, $AC = DF$ and $\angle BAC = \angle EDF$ imply that $\triangle ABC \cong \triangle DEF$. The symbol $\cong$ means "is congruent."

Two triangles are congruent if two pairs of corresponding angles and the corresponding *included* side are equal. This is called *Angle-Side-Angle* or A.S.A.

If $AB = DE$, $\angle BAC = \angle EDF$, and $\angle CBA = \angle FED$, then $\triangle ABC \cong \triangle DEF$.

If all three pairs of corresponding sides of two triangles are equal, then the triangles are congruent. This is called *Side-Side-Side* or S.S.S.

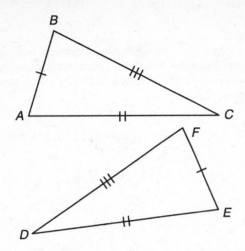

$AB = EF$, $AC = ED$, and $BC = FD$ imply that $\triangle ABC \cong \triangle EFD$.

Because of the Pythagorean theorem, if any two corresponding sides of two right triangles are equal, the third sides are equal and the triangles are congruent.

$AC = DE$ and $BC = EF$ imply $\triangle ABC \cong \triangle DFE$.

In general, if two corresponding sides of two triangles are equal, we cannot infer that the triangles are congruent.

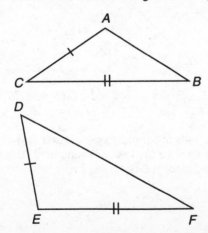

$AC = DE$ and $CB = EF$, but the triangles are not congruent.

If two sides of a triangle are equal, then the altitude to the third side divides the triangle into two congruent triangles.

$AB = BC$ and $BD \perp AC$ implies $\triangle ADB \cong \triangle CDB$.

Therefore, $\angle ABD = \angle CBD$, so BD bisects $\angle ABC$. Since $AD = DC$, D is the midpoint of AC, so BD is the median from B to AC. A *median* is the segment from a vertex to the midpoint of the side opposite the vertex.

If $AB = 4$, $AC = 4.5$, and $BC = 6$, $\angle BAC = \angle EDF$, $DE = 4$, and $DF = 4.5$, what is EF?

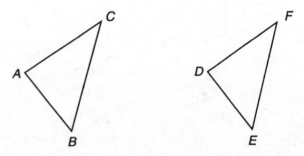

Since two pairs of corresponding sides (AB and DE, AC and DF) and the corresponding included angles ($\angle BAC$, $\angle EDF$) are equal, the triangles ABC and DEF are congruent by S.A.S. Therefore, $EF = BC = 6$.

D–3

Similarity. *Two triangles are similar if all three pairs of corresponding angles are equal.* Since the sum of the angles in a triangle is 180°, it follows that, if two corresponding angles are equal, the third angles must be equal.

If you draw a line that passes through a triangle and is parallel to one of the sides of the triangle, the triangle formed is similar to the original triangle.

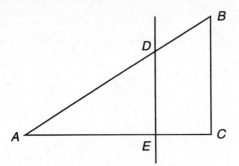

If *DE* ‖ *BC*, then △*ADE* ~ △*ABC*. The symbol ~ means "is similar to."

A man 6 feet tall casts a shadow 4 feet long; at the same time a flagpole casts a shadow 50 feet long. How tall is the flagpole?

The man with his shadow and the flagpole with its shadow can be regarded as the pairs of corresponding sides of two similar triangles.

Let *h* be the height of the flagpole. Since corresponding sides of similar triangles are proportional, $\frac{4}{50} = \frac{6}{h}$.
Cross-multiplying gives $4h = 6 \cdot 50 = 300$, so $h = 75$. Therefore, the flagpole is 75 feet high.

III–E. *Quadrilaterals*

A QUADRILATERAL is a polygon with four sides. The sum of the angles in a quadrilateral is 360°. If the opposite sides of a quadrilateral are parallel, the figure is a *parallelogram*.

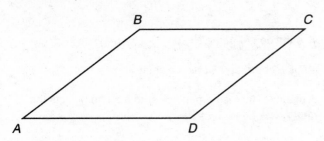

ABCD is a parallelogram.

In a parallelogram:

❶ The opposite sides equal.

❷ The opposite angles are equal.

❸ A diagonal divides the parallelogram into two congruent triangles.

❹ The diagonals bisect each other. (A line *bisects* a line segment if it intersects the segment at the midpoint of the segment.)

ABCD is a parallelogram.

❶ *AB* = *DC*, *BC* = *AD*.

❷ ∠*BCD* = ∠*BAD*, ∠*ABC* = ∠*ADC*.

❸ △*ABC* ≅ △*ADC*, △*ABD* ≅ △*CDB*.

❹ *AE* = *EC* and *BE* = *ED*.

If *any* of the statements ❶, ❷, ❸, and ❹ is true for a quadrilateral, then the quadrilateral is a parallelogram.

If all the angles of a parallelogram are right angles, the figure is a *rectangle*.

ABCD is a rectangle.

Since the sum of the angles in a quadrilateral is 360°, if *all* the angles of a quadrilateral are equal then the figure is a rectangle. The diagonals of a rectangle are equal. The length of a diagonal can be found by using the Pythagorean theorem.

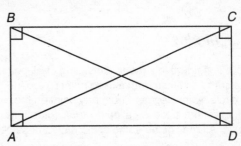

If *ABCD* is a rectangle, $AC = BD$ and $(AC)^2 = (AD)^2 + (DC)^2$.

If all the sides of a rectangle are equal, the figure is a *square*.

ABCD is a square.

The length of the diagonal of a square is $\sqrt{2}\,s$, where *s* is the length of a side.

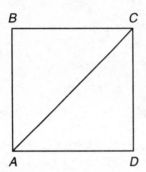

In square *ABCD*, $AC = (\sqrt{2})\,AD$.

A quadrilateral with two parallel sides and two sides that are not parallel is called a *trapezoid*. The parallel sides are called *bases*, and the nonparallel sides are called *legs*.

If *BC* ‖ *AD*, then *ABCD* is a trapezoid; *BC* and *AD* are the bases.

III–F. *Circles*

A CIRCLE is a figure in a plane consisting of all points that are the same distance from a fixed point called the *center* of the circle. A line segment from any point on the circle to the center of the circle is called a *radius* (plural: *radii*) of the circle. All radii of the same circle have the same length.

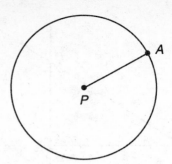

This circle has center *P* and radius *AP*.

A circle is denoted by a single letter, usually its center. Two circles with the same center are *concentric*.

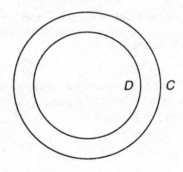

C and *D* are concentric circles.

A line segment whose endpoints are on a circle is called a *chord*. A chord that passes through the center of the circle is a *diameter*. *The length of a diameter is twice the length of a radius.* A diameter divides a circle into two congruent halves called *semicircles*.

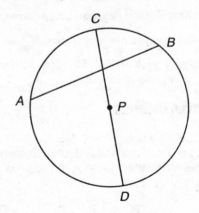

P is the center of the circle.

AB is a chord and *CD* is a diameter.

A diameter that is perpendicular to a chord bisects the chord.

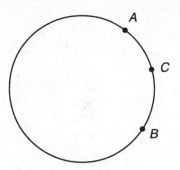

O is the center of this circle, and *AB* ⊥ *CD*; and *AE* = *EB*.

ACB is an arc. Arc *ACB* is written as $\overset{\frown}{ACB}$.

If a line intersects a circle at one and only one point, the line is said to be a *tangent* to the circle. The point common to a circle and a tangent to the circle is called the *point of tangency*. The radius from the center to the point of tangency is perpendicular to the tangent.

If two letters are used to denote an arc, they represent the smaller of the two possible arcs. $\overset{\frown}{AB} = \overset{\frown}{ACB}$.

An arc can be measured in degrees. An entire circle is 360°; thus an arc of 120° is $\frac{1}{3}$ of a circle.

A central angle is equal in measure to the arc it intercepts.

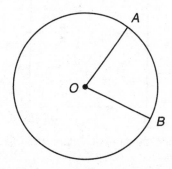

AP is tangent to the circle with center *O*. *P* is the point of tangency, and *OP* ⊥ *PA*.

An angle whose vertex is a point on a circle and whose sides are chords of the circle is called an *inscribed angle*. An angle whose vertex is the center of a circle and whose sides are radii of the circle is called a *central angle*.

m∠*AOB* = m$\overset{\frown}{AB}$ (The measure of ∠*AOB* equals the measure of $\overset{\frown}{AB}$.)

An inscribed angle is equal in measure to $\frac{1}{2}$ the arc it intercepts.

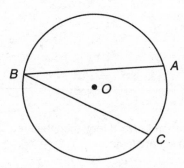

∠*BAC* is an inscribed angle.

∠*DOC* is a central angle.

An *arc* is a part of a circle.

m∠*ABC* = m$\frac{1}{2}$ $\overset{\frown}{AC}$.

An angle inscribed in a semicircle is a *right angle*.

If *BC* is a diameter, then $\angle BAC$ is inscribed in a semicircle; so $m\angle BAC = 90°$.

III–G.   *Area and Perimeter*

G–1

The *area A* of a square equals s^2, where *s* is the length of a side of the square. Thus, $A = s^2$.

If *AD* = 5 inches, the area of square *ABCD* is 25 square inches.

The area of a rectangle equals length times width. If *L* is the length of one side and *W* is the length of a side perpendicular to *L*, then the area $A = LW$.

If AB = 5 feet and *AD* = 8 feet, then the area of rectangle *ABCD* is 40 square feet.

The area of a parallelogram is base × height; $A = bh$, where *b* is the length of the base and *h* is the length of an altitude to the base.

If *AD* = 6 yards and *BE* = 4 yards, then the area of parallelogram *ABCD* is 6 · 4 or 24 square yards.

The area of a trapezoid is the (average of the bases) × height;

$A = \left(\dfrac{b_1 + b_2}{2}\right)h$, where b_1 and b_2 are the lengths of the parallel sides and *h* is the length of an altitude to one of the bases.

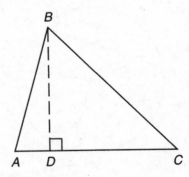

If *BC* = 3 miles, *AD* = 7 miles, and *CE* = 2 miles, then the area of trapezoid *ABCD* is $\left(\dfrac{3+7}{2}\right)2 = 10$ square miles.

The area of a triangle is $\dfrac{1}{2}$ (base × height); $A = \dfrac{1}{2}bh$, where *b* is the length of a side and *h* is the length of the altitude to that side.

If *AC* = 5 miles and *BD* = 4 miles, then the area of the triangle is $\dfrac{1}{2} \times 5 \times 4 = 10$ square miles.

Since the legs of a right triangle are perpendicular to each other, the area of a right triangle is one-half the product of the lengths of the legs.

> If the lengths of the sides of a triangle are 5 feet, 12 feet, and 13 feet, what is the area of the triangle?

Since $5^2 + 12^2 = 25 + 144 = 169 = 13^2$, the triangle is a right triangle and the legs are the sides with lengths 5 feet and 12 feet. Therefore, the area is $\frac{1}{2} \times 5 \times 12 =$ 30 square feet.

If we want to find the area of a polygon that is not of a type already mentioned, we break the polygon up into smaller figures such as triangles or rectangles, find the area of each piece, and add these to get the area of the given polygon.

The area of a circle is πr^2, where r is the length of a radius. Since $d = 2r$, where d is the length of a diameter, $A = \pi \left(\frac{d}{2}\right)^2 = \pi \frac{d^2}{4}$. The number π is equal to approximately $\frac{22}{7}$ or 3.14; however, there is *no fraction that is exactly equal to* π, which is called an *irrational number.*

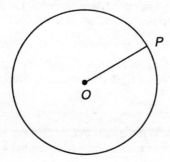

If $OP = 2$ inches, then the area of the circle with center O is $\pi 2^2$ or 4π square inches.

The portion of the plane bounded by a circle and a central angle is called a *sector* of the circle.

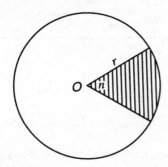

The shaded region is a sector of the circle with center O. The area of a sector with a central angle of $n°$ in a circle of radius r is $\frac{n}{360}\pi r^2$.

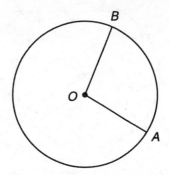

If $OB = 4$ inches and $\angle BOA = 100°$, then the area of the sector is $\frac{100}{360}\pi \cdot 4^2 = \frac{5}{18} \cdot 16\pi = \frac{40}{9}\pi$ square inches.

G–2

The *perimeter of a polygon* is the sum of the lengths of the sides.

> What is the perimeter of a regular pentagon whose sides are 6 inches long?

A pentagon has five sides. Since the pentagon is regular, all sides have the same length, which is 6 inches. Therefore, the perimeter of the pentagon is 5×6, which equals 30 inches or 2.5 feet.

The *perimeter of a rectangle* is $2(L+W)$, where L is the length and W is the width.

The *perimeter of a square* is $4s$, where s is the length of a side of the square.

The *perimeter of a circle* is called the *circumference* of the circle. The *circumference of a circle* is πd or $2\pi r$, where d is the length of a diameter and r is the length of a radius.

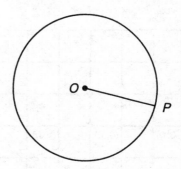

If O is the center of a circle and $OP = 5$ feet, then the circumference of the circle is $2 \times 5\pi$ or 10π feet.

The length of an arc of a circle is $\frac{n}{360}\pi d$, where the central angle of the arc is $n°$.

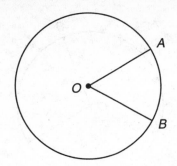

If O is the center of a circle where $OA = 5$ yards and $\angle AOB = 60°$, then the length of arc AB is $\dfrac{60}{360} \pi \times 10 =$

$\dfrac{10}{6} \pi = \dfrac{5}{3} \pi$ yards.

> How far will a wheel of radius 2 feet travel in 500 revolutions? (Assume the wheel does not slip.)

The diameter of the wheel is 4 feet, so the circumference is 4π feet. Therefore, the wheel will travel $500 \times 4\pi$ or $2,000\pi$ feet in 500 revolutions.

III–H.　Coordinate Geometry

In coordinate geometry, every point in the plane is associated with an ordered pair of numbers called *coordinates*. Two perpendicular lines are drawn; the horizontal line is called the *x*-axis, and the vertical line is called the *y*-axis. The point where the two axes intersect is called the *origin*. Both of the axes are number lines with the origin corresponding to zero (see the arithmetic section on signed numbers). Positive numbers on the *x*-axis are to the right of the origin, negative numbers to the left. Positive numbers on the *y*-axis are above the origin, negative numbers below the origin. The coordinates of a point *P* are (x, y) if *P* is located by moving *x* units along the *x*-axis from the origin and then moving *y* units up or down. *The distance along the x-axis is always given first.*

The numbers in parentheses are the coordinates of the point. Thus "$P = (3, 2)$" means that the coordinates of *P* are $(3, 2)$. *The distance d between the point with*

coordinates (x, y) and the point with coordinates (a, b) is $\sqrt{(x-a)^2 + (y-b)^2}$. You should be able to answer most questions by using the distance formula.

$$d = \sqrt{(x-a)^2 + (y-b)^2}$$

> Is $ABCD$ a parallelogram? $A = (3, 2)$, $B = (1, -2)$, $C = (-2, 1)$, $D = (1, 5)$.

The length of AB is $\sqrt{(3-1)^2 + (2-(-2))^2} = \sqrt{2^2 + 4^2}$ $= \sqrt{20}$. The length of CD is $\sqrt{(-2-1)^2 + (1-5)^2} =$ $\sqrt{(-3)^2 + (-4)^2} = \sqrt{25}$. Therefore, $AB \neq CD$, so $ABCD$ cannot be a parallelogram, since in a parallelogram the lengths of opposite sides are equal.

You can often use coordinate geometry to solve problems that do not appear to involve coordinates.

> City A is 5 miles north of City B, and City C is 12 miles west of City B. How far is it from City A to City C?

Set up a coordinate axis with City B at the origin, east-west as the *x*-axis, and north-south as the *y*-axis, as in the diagram.

Then City A has coordinates $(0,5)$, and City C has coordinates $(-12,0)$. The distance from A to C is the square root of $(-12 - 0)^2 + (5 - 0)^2$, or $\sqrt{144 + 25} = \sqrt{169}$, which is 13. It is 13 miles from City A to City C.

Geometry problems occur frequently. *If you are not provided with a diagram, draw one for yourself.* Think of any conditions that will help you answer the question; perhaps you can see how to answer a different question that will lead to an answer to the original question. It may help to draw in some diagonals, altitudes, or other auxiliary lines in your diagram.

Practice Exercises

1. Using these formulas: Circumference $= 2\pi r$, Area $= \pi r^2$ where $r =$ radius, find the area of a circle whose circumference is x.

   (A) $\dfrac{x^2}{4\pi^2}$ (B) $\dfrac{x^2}{4\pi}$ (C) $\dfrac{x^2}{4}$ (D) πx^2 (E) πx

2. One side of a rectangle is x inches. If the perimeter is p inches, what is the length (in inches) of the other side?

   (A) $p - x$ (B) $p - 2x$ (C) $\dfrac{p - x}{2}$ (D) $\dfrac{p - 2x}{2}$
   (E) $2p - 2x$

3. C is the midpoint of line segment AE. B and D are on line segment AE so that $AB = BC$ and $CD = DE$. What percent of AC is AD?

   (A) 33   (B) 50   (C) 66   (D) 133   (E) 150

4. A picture in an art museum is 6 feet wide and 8 feet long. If its frame has a width of 6 inches, what is the ratio of the area of the frame to the area of the picture?

   (A) $\dfrac{5}{16}$ (B) $\dfrac{5}{4}$ (C) $\dfrac{4}{5}$ (D) $\dfrac{5}{12}$ (E) $\dfrac{3\frac{1}{5}}{1}$

5. To represent a family budget on a circle graph, how many degrees of the circle should be used to represent an item that is 20% of the total budget?

   (A) 20   (B) 36   (C) 60   (D) 72   (E) 90

6. What is the maximum number of glass tumblers (each with a circumference of 4π inches) that can be placed rectangularly on a table 48" × 32"?

   (A) 36   (B) 48   (C) 92   (D) 96   (E) 192

7. To avoid paying a toll on a direct road, I go west 10 miles, south 5 miles, west 30 miles, and north 35 miles. What is the length (in miles) of the toll road?

   (A) 30   (B) 45   (C) 50   (D) 70   (E) 85

8. The length of a rectangle is increased by 50%. By what percent would the width have to be decreased to maintain the same area?

   (A) $33\frac{1}{3}$ (B) 50   (C) $66\frac{2}{3}$ (D) 150   (E) 200

9. Area of circle $O = 9\pi$. What is the area of $ABCD$?

   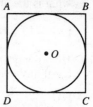

   (A) 24   (B) 30   (C) 35
   (D) 36   (E) 48

10. A man travels 4 miles north, 12 miles east, and then 12 miles north. How far (to the nearest mile) is he from the starting point?

    (A) 17   (B) 20   (C) 21   (D) 24   (E) 28

11. If angle DBA equals 39° and angle FBE equals 79°, then angle GBC has a meaure of

    (A) 39°   (B) 51°
    (C) 62°   (D) 118°   (E) 152°

12. The length of a rectangle is l and the width is w. If the width is increased by 2 units, by how many units will the perimeter be increased?

    (A) 2   (B) 4   (C) $2w$ (D) $2w + 2$ (E) $2w + 4$

13. If the radius of a wheel is f feet, how many revolutions does the wheel make per mile? (1 mile = 5,280 feet.)

    (A) $5,280f$ (B) $\dfrac{2,640}{\pi f}$ (C) $5,280\pi f^2$

    (D) $\dfrac{\pi f}{2,640}$ (E) $\dfrac{\pi f^2}{5,280}$

14. The length of a wire fence around a circular flower bed is 100π feet. What is the area (in square feet) of a two-foot concrete walk surrounding this fence?

    (A) 98π (B) 100π (C) 102π (D) 202π
    (E) 204π

15. How many tiles (each 1 foot square) are necessary to form a 1-foot border around the inside of a room 24 feet by 14 feet?

    (A) 36   (B) 37   (C) 72   (D) 74   (E) 76

16. When the radius of a circle is doubled, the area is multiplied by

    (A) 2   (B) 2π (C) $2\pi r$ (D) 3.14   (E) 4

17. $AD = 14$
    $EF = 6$
    $BC = ?$

    (A) 8   (B) 12
    (C) 20   (D) 26
    (E) 36

18. If the diagonal of a table with a square top is 6 feet, what is the area of the table top (in square feet)?

    (A) $\sqrt{18}$ (B) 9π (C) 18   (D) $18\sqrt{2}$ (E) 36

19. How many spokes are there in the wheel of a sports car if any two spokes form an angle of 15°?

    (A) 12   (B) 15   (C) 22   (D) 24   (E) 36

20. How many degrees are there in an angle formed by the hands of a clock at 2:30?

    (A) 100   (B) 105   (C) 110   (D) 115   (E) 120

21. If $8x$ represents the perimeter of a rectangle and $2x + 3$ represents its length, what is its width?

    (A) $6x + 3$ (B) $6x - 3$ (C) 3   (D) $2x - 3$
    (E) $10x + 3$

22. Base RT of triangle RST is $\frac{4}{3}$ of altitude SV. If SV equals c, which of the following is an expression for the area of triangle RST?

    (A) $\frac{2c}{5}$ (B) $\frac{2c^2}{5}$ (C) $\frac{c^2}{2}$ (D) $\frac{4c^2}{5}$ (E) $\frac{8c^2}{5}$

23. A triangle has a base b and an altitude a. A second triangle has a base twice the altitude of the first triangle, and an altitude twice the base of the first triangle. What is the area of the second triangle?

    (A) $\frac{1}{2}ab$ (B) ab (C) $2ab$ (D) $4ab$

    (E) $\frac{1}{2}a^2b^2$

24. A pond 100 feet in diameter is surrounded by a circular grass walk 2 feet wide. How many square feet of grass are there on the walk? (Answer in terms of π.)

    (A) 98π (B) 100π (C) 102π (D) 202π
    (E) 204π

25. What is the area of $ABCD$?

    (A) 5   (B) 8   (C) 10
    (D) 16   (E) 20

26. The distance from A to C in the square field $ABCD$ is 50 feet. What is the area of field $ABCD$ in square feet?

    (A) $25\sqrt{2}$ (B) 625
    (C) 1250   (D) 2500
    (E) 5000

27. In the figure at the right, $ABCD$ is a square and semicircles are constructed on each side of the square. If AB is 2, what is the area of the entire figure?

    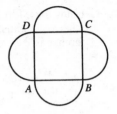

    (A) $2 + 4\pi$ (B) $2 - 4\pi$
    (C) $4 + 8\pi$ (D) $4 - 2\pi$
    (E) $4 + 2\pi$

28. O is the center of the circle at the right, XO is perpendicular to YO and the area of triangle XOY is 32. What is the area of circle O?

    (A) 16π (B) 32π
    (C) 64π (D) 128π
    (E) 256π

29. Square $QRST$ is inscribed in circle O.
    $OV \perp TS$
    $OV = 1$
    The area of the shaded portion is

    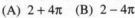

    (A) $\pi - 4$ (B) $4\pi - 4$ (C) $2\pi - 4$ (D) $4\pi - 2$
    (E) $2\pi - 2$

30. $QVR \perp SVT$
    $\angle VSR = x°$
    $\angle VRW = (?)°$

    (A) $90 - x$
    (B) $90 + x$
    (C) $x - 90$
    (D) $180 - x$
    (E) 135

31. $ABJH, JDEF, ACEG$ are squares.
    $\frac{BC}{AB} = 3$

    $\frac{\text{Area } BCDJ}{\text{Area } HJFG} = ?$

    (A) $\frac{1}{9}$ (B) $\frac{1}{3}$ (C) 1   (D) 3   (E) 9

32. Rectangle $ABCD$ is made up of five equal squares. $AD = 30$. Find EF.

    (A) 6   (B) 8   (C) 10   (D) 12   (E) 20

33. Radius $OA = 6.5$
Chord $AC = 5$
Area of triangle ABC equals

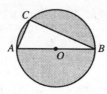

   (A) 16   (B) 18   (C) 24
   (D) 30   (E) 36

34. Angles a, b and c are in ratio
$1 : 3 : 2$. How many degrees are
there in angle b?

   (A) 30   (B) 50   (C) 60
   (D) 90   (E) 100

35. BC equals one half of AB.
The area of right triangle
ABC equals 64 square feet.
Find hypotenuse AC to the
nearest foot.

   (A) 12   (B) 14
   (C) 18   (D) 24   (E) 32

36. $ABCD$ is a square.
$AE = 2$
$GC = 8$
Shaded area $= 44$
Area of $FBEJ = ?$

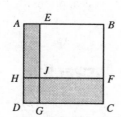

   (A) 36   (B) 56   (C) 64
   (D) 68   (E) 80

37. The area of rectangle $KLMN$
equals 100. Base NM equals 20.
What is the area of triangle ANM
if A is any point on KL?

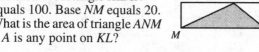

   (A) 25   (B) 50   (C) 75   (D) 100
   (E) cannot be determined

38. $ABCD$ is a rectangle.
$AD = 12$, $AB = 16$, $DE = ?$

   (A) 8   (B) 10   (C) 14
   (D) 15   (E) 20

39. O is the center of the circle.
BC is parallel to AD.
$OA = 5$
$CB = 8$
$\dfrac{AB}{AD} = ?$

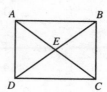

   (A) $\dfrac{3}{4}$ (B) $\dfrac{4}{5}$ (C) 1   (D) $\dfrac{5}{4}$ (E) $\dfrac{4}{3}$

40. $BA = 2BC$
$EA = 2DE$
$BE = 14$
$DC = ?$

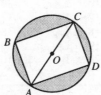

   (A) 7   (B) 18   (C) 21   (D) 24   (E) 28

41. If angle DBG equals 79° and
angle CBE equals 39° then
angle GBE equals

   (A) 51°   (B) 62°   (C) 101°
   (D) 108°   (E) 202°

42. $\angle A = (?)°$

   (A) 15   (B) 45   (C) 60
   (D) 80   (E) 120

43. Four equal circles each of diameter 1 foot touch at four points as
shown in the figure. What is the
area (in square feet) of the shaded
portion?

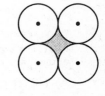

   (A) $1 - \dfrac{\pi}{4}$ (B) $1 - \pi$

   (C) $1 - 4\pi$ (D) π (E) $\dfrac{\pi}{4}$

44. Perimeter of $ABCD = 24$
The area of the shaded portion
is

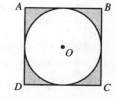

   (A) 27π (B) $9\pi - 36$
   (C) $9\pi - 24$ (D) $36 - 9\pi$
   (E) $24 - 9\pi$

45. $ABIJ$, $BCHI$, $CDGH$, and
$DEFG$ are congruent
rectangles.
$AJ = 21$
$KI = ?$

   (A) 3   (B) 5.25   (C) 7   (D) 10.5   (E) 14

46. The area of the shaded portion
is

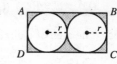

   (A) $2r^2(4 - \pi)$
   (B) $2r^2(2 - 2\pi)$
   (C) $2r^2(\pi - 4)$
   (D) $2r^2(\pi - 2)$
   (E) $r^2(2 - \pi)$

47. How many square units are
there in the shaded triangle?

   (A) 4   (B) 6   (C) 8
   (D) 9   (E) 12

48. $AE \perp ED$ $ED = 13$
$CD \perp ED$ $CD = 3$
$DC \perp CB$ $CB = 2$
$AB = ?$ $AE = 11$

   (A) 8   (B) 13   (C) 14
   (D) 15   (E) 17

49. If an airplane starts at point R and travels 14 miles directly north to S, then 48 miles directly east to T, what is the straight-line distance (in miles) from T to R?

    (A) 25   (B) 34   (C) 50   (D) 62   (E) 2500

50. The area of a circle with radius r is equal to the area of a rectangle with base b. Find the altitude of the rectangle in terms of π, r, and b.

    (A) $\sqrt{\pi r}$ (B) $\dfrac{2\pi r}{b}$ (C) $\pi r^2 b$ (D) $\dfrac{\pi r^2}{b}$

    (E) $\dfrac{\pi r^2}{b^2}$

51. A line segment is drawn from point $(8, -2)$ to point $(4, 6)$. The coordinates of the midpoint of this line segment are

    (A) $(12, 4)$ (B) $(12, 8)$ (C) $(6, 4)$ (D) $(6, 2)$
    (E) $(6, -2)$

52. Lines joining point $(-4, 0)$ with point $(0, 5)$ with point $(4, 0)$ will form

    (A) a circle   (B) a right triangle   (C) a rectangle
    (D) a square   (E) an isosceles triangle

53. Point A $(-3, -4)$ is drawn to point B $(3, 4)$. Which of the following is true?

    (A) The length of $AB = 5$ units.
    (B) AB is parallel to the x-axis.
    (C) AB passes through point $(6, 8)$.
    (D) AB passes through the origin.
    (E) AB is the radius of a circle with center at $(0, 0)$.

54. Triangle ABC has the following vertices: $A(1, 0)$, $B(5, 0)$, and $C(3, 4)$. Which of the following is true?

    (A) $AB = BC$ (B) $AB = AC$ (C) $CA = CB$
    (D) $AC > BC$ (E) $AC < BC$

55. The area of a circle whose center is at $(0, 0)$ is 25π. The circle passes through all of the following points EXCEPT

    (A) $(-5, 0)$ (B) $(5, 5)$ (C) $(5, 0)$ (D) $(0, 5)$
    (E) $(0, -5)$

56. The following points are vertices of quadrilateral $ABCD$: $(0, 4)$, $(4, 0)$, $(0, -4)$ and $(-4, 0)$. The area of $ABCD$ is

    (A) 8   (B) 16   (C) 32   (D) 48   (E) 64

57. The vertices of triangle ABC are $(4, 3)$, $(4, 7)$, and $(8, 3)$. The area of triangle ABC equals

    (A) 4   (B) $4\sqrt{3}$ (C) 8   (D) 12.5   (E) 16

58. A line segment AB is drawn from point $(2, 3)$ to point $(4, 7)$. What are the coordinates of the midpoint?

    (A) $(5, 3)$ (B) $(3, 5)$ (C) $(6, 10)$ (D) $(2, 4)$
    (E) $(4, 2)$

59. What is the distance from point A $(3, 4)$ to point B $(-3, -4)$?

    (A) 0   (B) 5   (C) 10   (D) 13   (E) 14

60. Point P $(4, 2)$ is the midpoint of line OPC, where O is at origin $(0, 0)$. The coordinates of C are

    (A) $(2, 1)$ (B) $(4, 8)$ (C) $(4, 4)$ (D) $(8, 2)$
    (E) $(8, 4)$

Answer Key

1.	B	21.	D	41.	C
2.	D	22.	B	42.	C
3.	E	23.	C	43.	A
4.	A	24.	E	44.	D
5.	D	25.	C	45.	C
6.	D	26.	C	46.	A
7.	C	27.	E	47.	B
8.	A	28.	C	48.	E
9.	D	29.	C	49.	C
10.	B	30.	B	50.	D
11.	C	31.	C	51.	D
12.	B	32.	A	52.	E
13.	B	33.	D	53.	D
14.	E	34.	D	54.	C
15.	C	35.	C	55.	B
16.	E	36.	B	56.	C
17.	D	37.	B	57.	C
18.	C	38.	B	58.	B
19.	D	39.	A	59.	C
20.	B	40.	C	60.	E

IV.   Tables and Graphs

IV–A.   Tables

Tables are often used in reports, magazines, and newspapers to present a set of numerical facts. They enable the reader to make comparisons and to draw quick conclusions. One of the main purposes of tables is to make complicated information easier to understand. The advantage of presenting data in a table is that you can see the information at a glance.

When answering questions based on tables, carefully read the table title and the column headings. The table title gives you a general idea of the type and often the purpose of the information presented. The column headings tell you the specific kind of information given in that column. Both the table titles and the column headings are usually very straightforward; after all, the table is supposed to make it easy for you to grasp this information. Therefore, in a column headed "Hourly Wage," you can expect to find just that—a list of hourly wages. You do have to be careful, however, to choose the appropriate column from which to get the information you need and to take note of the units that are used.

Questions 1 and 2 refer to the following table.

GROWTH OF REGULAR MONTHLY INVESTMENTS
AT 7% RETURN, COMPOUNDED MONTHLY

Number of Years Money Is Invested	Monthly Investment			
	$50	$100	$250	$500
2	$1,292	$2,583	$6,458	$12,915
5	$3,601	$7,201	$18,003	$36,005
10	$8,705	$17,409	$43,524	$87,047
20	$26,198	$52,397	$130,991	$261,983

1. How much interest is earned on a 7% investment for a 5-year period with monthly investments of $100?

(A) $121
(B) $201
(C) $720
(D) $1,201
(E) $6,000

2. How much more is earned on a $50 monthly investment for 10 years than on a $100 monthly investment for 5 years?

(A) $150
(B) $701
(C) $870
(D) $1,504
(E) $1,590

In 5 years, there will be 60 payments, for a total of $6,000. The table indicates that the investment will grow to $7,201, for a return on the investment of $1,201 (Choice D).

In each case the payments amount to $6,000. However, the 10-year program pays $8,705 while the 5-year program yields $7,201, a difference of $1,504 (Choice D).

Questions 3–5 refer to the following table.

PER CAPITA INCOME BY STATE FOR 1991
AND PERCENT INCREASE FROM PRECEDING YEAR

State	Per-capita income	Increase from '90	State	Per-capita income	Increase from '90
Ala.	$15,367	3.8%	Mont.	$16,043	4.8%
Alaska	$21,932	1.3%	Neb.	$17,852	2.1%
Ariz.	$16,401	2.5%	Nev.	$19,175	0.7%
Ark.	$14,733	4.1%	N.H.	$20,951	0.9%
Calif.	$20,592	1.3%	N.J.	$25,372	2.0%
Colo.	$19,440	3.1%	N.M.	$14,844	4.1%
Conn.	$25,881	1.9%	N.Y.	$22,456	1.5%
Del.	$20,349	1.3%	N.C.	$16,642	2.3%
D.C.	$24,439	3.5%	N.D.	$16,088	4.8%
Fla.	$18,880	1.8%	Ohio	$17,916	2.0%
Ga.	$17,364	1.9%	Okla.	$15,827	2.4%
Hawaii	$21,306	4.6%	Ore.	$17,592	2.4%
Idaho	$15,401	1.0%	Pa.	$19,128	2.4%
Ill.	$20,824	1.9%	R.I.	$18,840	0.2%
Ind.	$17,217	1.7%	S.C.	$15,420	1.8%
Iowa	$17,505	1.2%	S.D.	$16,392	3.2%
Kan.	$18,511	2.2%	Tenn.	$16,325	2.9%
Ky.	$15,539	3.6%	Texas	$17,305	3.5%
La.	$15,143	4.2%	Utah	$14,529	3.9%
Maine	$17,306	0.7%	Vt.	$17,747	1.4%
Md.	$22,080	1.0%	Va.	$19,976	1.4%
Mass.	$22,897	1.5%	Wash.	$19,442	3.5%
Mich.	$18,679	1.6%	W. Va.	$14,174	3.1%
Minn.	$19,107	2.0%	Wis.	$18,046	2.6%
Miss.	$13,343	4.0%	Wyo.	$17,118	5.1%
Mo.	$17,842	2.1%	U.S. avg.	$19,082	2.1%

Source: Commerce Dept.

3. How much was the per capita increase in New Jersey in 1991 over 1990?

(A) $498   (B) $507   (C) $2,530   (D) $24,875
(E) $25,372

The $25,372 figure represents a 2% increase over the 1990 per capita income for New Jersey. If x is the 1990 per capita income, then:

$x + 0.02x = \$25,372$

$1.02x = \$25,372$

$102x = \$2,537,200$

$x = \$24,874$ (1990 per capita income)

The difference between the 1991 figure of $25,372 and $24,874 = $498 (Choice A).

4. What was the per capita income for Mississippi for the year 1990?

(A) $513   (B) $1,283   (C) $5,130
(D) $51,237   (E) $12,830

The 1991 per capita income, $13,343, represents a 4% increase over the 1990 figure.

If x = the 1990 per capita income, then:

$x + 0.04x = \$13,343$

$1.04x = \$13,343$

$104x = \$1,334,300$ *Hint:* Estimate and choose E.

The exact answer is $\dfrac{13,343,300}{104} = 12,829.8$. So: $x =$ $12,829.80 (Choice E)

This is the kind of problem that can be solved quickly by estimating. You should be able to see that the only possible answer is E, and you can check your guess by multiplying $1.04 \times 12,830$. The less time you spend on easy questions, the more questions you can try.

5. The per capita income for 1991 in West Virginia is

(A) 2.63% of the national average
(B) 7.37% of the national average
(C) 26.3% of the national average
(D) 73.7% of the national average
(E) 78% of the national average

Let x% or $\dfrac{x}{100}$ of the national average ($19,802) = $14,174.

Hint: Round off $19,802 to $19,000, and $14,174 to $14,000. Then:

$\left(\dfrac{x}{100}\right)\$19,000 = \$14,000$

$190x = \$14,000$

$x = \$73.68$ or 73.7% (Choice D)

Questions 6 and 7 refer to the following table.

ANNUAL INVESTMENTS THAT WILL GROW TO $1000 AT A FUTURE DATE

Year				Rate of Return			
	5%	6%	7%	8%	9%	10%	11%
1	952.38	943.40	934.58	925.93	917.43	909.09	900.90
2	464.58	457.96	451.49	445.16	438.96	432.90	426.97
3	302.10	296.33	290.70	285.22	279.87	274.65	269.56
4	220.96	215.65	210.49	205.48	200.61	195.88	191.29
5	172.36	167.36	162.51	157.83	153.30	148.91	144.66
6	140.02	135.25	130.65	126.22	121.94	117.82	113.85
7	116.97	112.39	107.99	103.77	99.72	95.82	92.09
8	99.74	95.32	91.09	87.05	83.19	79.49	75.96
9	86.37	82.10	78.02	74.15	70.46	66.95	63.61
10	75.72	71.57	67.64	63.92	60.39	57.04	53.88
11	67.04	63.01	59.21	55.63	52.24	49.06	46.05
12	59.83	55.92	52.24	48.79	45.55	42.51	39.66
13	53.77	49.96	46.40	43.08	39.97	37.07	34.37
14	48.59	44.89	41.44	38.24	35.26	32.50	29.94
15	44.14	40.53	37.19	34.10	31.25	28.61	26.18
16	40.26	36.75	33.51	30.53	27.80	25.29	22.99

6. Meri is looking for a 7% investment that will grow to $1000 in 10 years but finds that she will have to accept an investment program that pays 6% for the same period. To realize $1000, how much more will she have to invest at 6% than at 7% over the 10-year period?

   (A) $3.93   (B) $39.30   (C) $67.64   (D) $71.57
   (E) $139.21

In 10 years, on the 6% investment the payments will be $715.70 and on the 7% plan the payments would have been $676.40, for a difference of $39.30 (Choice B).

7. What is the difference to the investor between a 10% investment for 5 years and a similar investment for 10 years?

   (A) The investor pays $174.15 more in the 10-year program.
   (B) The investor pays $174.15 less in the 10-year program.
   (C) The investor pays $744.55 more in the 5-year program.
   (D) The investor pays $570.14 more in the 5-year program.
   (E) The investor pays $91.87 less per month in the 5-year program.

The total payments for the 5-year program = $148.91 × 5 = $744.55.

The total payments for the 10-year program = $57.04 × 10 = $570.40.

The difference = $744.55 − $570.40 = $174.15 (Choice B).

IV–B.   Circle Graphs

Circle graphs are used to show the relationships of various sectors to the whole. Circle graphs often give the percent that each sector represents.

The following graph gives precise figures. It is advisable to convert to percentages, but figures may be rounded out.

Questions 8 and 9 refer to the following graph.

AREAS OF SERVICE OF THE APPROXIMATELY 223,297 WOMEN IN THE U.S. ARMED FORCES

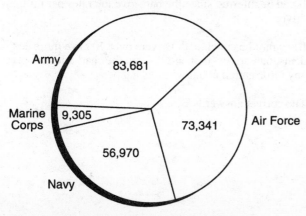

Source: Defense Department's 'Defense Almanac'

8. What is the measure of the central angle of the sector for women in the Air Force?

   (A) 32°   (B) 73°   (C) 92°   (D) 115°   (E) 133°

Hint: Work in thousands.

The Air Force has $\dfrac{73}{223}$ or 0.32 of the circle. It has a measure of (0.32)(360) degrees or 115° (Choice D).

9. What percent of the women in the U.S. Armed Forces are in the Marine Corps?

   (A) 0.04%   (B) 0.14%   (C) 0.4%   (D) 1.4%
   (E) 4%

Hint: Work in thousands.

$\dfrac{9}{223} = 0.04 = 4\%$ (Choice E)

IV–C.   Line Graphs

Line graphs are used to show how a quantity changes continuously. Very often the quantity is measured as time changes. If the line goes up, the quantity is increasing; if the line goes down, the quantity is decreasing; if the line is horizontal, the quantity is not changing. To measure the height of a point on the graph, use your pencil or a piece of paper (for example, the edge of the test booklet) as a straightedge.

Questions 10 and 11 refer to the following graph.

VOLUMES OF SALES FOR A 10-MONTH PERIOD FOR TWO SALESPEOPLE

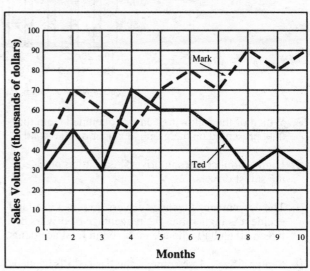

10. In which of the following are the data on the line graph correctly described?

I. The sales in Mark's best month were $50,000 more than in his worst month.

II. The sales in Ted's best month were $20,000 less than the sales in Mark's best month.

III. Ted's sales in his worst months were $10,000 less than Mark's sales in his worst month.

(A) I and II only   (B) II and III only   (C) I only
(D) II only   (E) I, II, and III

Sales in Mark's best months (8 and 10)   = $90,000
Sales in Mark's worst month (1)   = $40,000
Sales in Ted's best month (4)   = $70,000
Sales in Ted's worst months (1, 3, 8, 10) = $30,000

The correct choice is E because:
I. $90,000 – $40,000 = $50,000
II. $90,000 – $70,000 = $20,000
III. $40,000 – $30,000 = $10,000

11. By what percent did Ted's sales increase from month 3 to month 4?

(A) 10%   (B) 30%   (C) 33%   (D) 40%
(E) $133\frac{1}{3}$%

$$\text{Change } \frac{(70,000 - 30,000)}{\text{Original } (\$30,000)} \times 100 = \text{percent change}$$

$\frac{40}{30} = 1\frac{1}{3}$ or $133\frac{1}{3}$% (Choice E)

IV–D.   Bar Graphs

Quantities can be compared by the height or length of a bar in a bar graph. A bar graph can have either vertical or horizontal bars. You can compare different quantities or the same quantity at different times. Use your pencil or a piece of paper to compare bars that are not adjacent to each other.

Question 12 refers to the following graph.

Danger on the Road

Fatalities per one million licensed drivers
in each age group in 1990

Source: National Highway Traffic Safety Administration

12. Which of the following can be concluded from the data presented on the graph "Danger on the Road"?

I. High school courses in drivers' education produce the safest drivers.

II. The percentage of teenage drivers involved in a fatal accident is higher than percentage of drivers between 30 and 40 who are involved in fatal accidents.

III. Senior citizens lose some of the basic skills needed for safe driving.

(A) I only
(B) II only
(C) II and III only
(D) I and III only
(E) I, II, and III

I cannot be inferred since there is no information about whether a teenager involved in a fatal accident took drivers' education.

II can be inferred since the bars give the rates per million drivers.

III cannot be concluded. Drivers over 70 have more accidents than drivers in their 60's, but the chart does not give any information about *why* this happens.

The correct answer is B.

Questions 13 and 14 refer to the following graph.

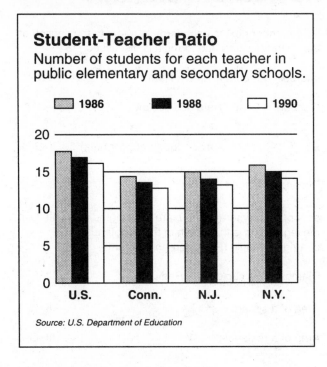

Student-Teacher Ratio
Number of students for each teacher in public elementary and secondary schools.

■ 1986   ■ 1988   □ 1990

Source: U.S. Department of Education

Each Student's Share
Spending per student, in public schools, in 1990 dollars.

■ 1960   ■ 1970   □ 1980   ▦ 1990

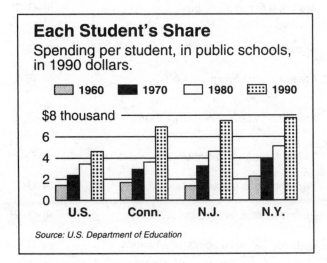

Source: U.S. Department of Education

13. Which of the following had the lowest student-teacher ratio for 1990?

   (A) New York
   (B) New Jersey
   (C) Connecticut
   (D) New York and New Jersey
   (E) New York and Connecticut

For 1990, Connecticut had a ratio of about 12.5 students for each teacher; New Jersey, a ratio of about 13.5; New York, a ratio of almost 15. The correct answer is C.

14. In 1990, how did the spending per public school student in New York and in New Jersey compare with the U.S. average?

   (A) New York and New Jersey spent less than the national average.
   (B) The amount spent by New York and by New Jersey was equal to the national average.
   (C) New York and New Jersey each spent more than $3,000 more per pupil than the U.S. average.
   (D) New York and New Jersey spent $3,000 less per pupil than the national average.
   (E) This question cannot be answered from the information on the graph.

The bars for 1990 for New York and New Jersey indicate that each state spent almost $8,000 per pupil in public schools. The U.S. average is $4,300 per pupil. The correct answer is C.

IV–E.   Cumulative Graphs

You can compare several categories by a graph of the cumulative type. These graphs are usually bar or line graphs where the height of the bar or line is divided proportionately among different quantities.

Questions 15–17 refer to the following graph.

THE BUDGETS OF THREE FAMILES

Family A has an annual income of $20,000. Family B has an annual income of $50,000. Family C has an annual income of $100,000.

FAMILY A   FAMILY B   FAMILY C

■ FOOD
▨ HOUSING
▧ HEALTH
□ SAVINGS
▨ ENTERTAINMENT

15. How does the percent of the total budget spent by Family A for health compare with the percent of the total budget spent by Family B for health?

   (A) Family A spent 200% more of its budget on health than did Family B.
   (B) Family B spent 50% more of its budget on health than did Family A.
   (C) The amounts spent by the two families were unequal, but the percentages of the totals were equal.
   (D) Family A spent 5% less of its budget on health than did Family B.
   (E) Family B spent 5% less of its budget on health than did Family A.

Family A spent 2 of the 20 units, or 10% of the total, on health. Family B spent 1 of the 20 units, or 5%, of the total on health. The correct choice is E.

16. What percent of Family C's budget went for housing and entertainment?

   (A) $16\frac{2}{3}\%$ (B) 25%   (C) $33\frac{1}{3}\%$ (D) 50%
   (E) 75%

For Family C, housing = 4 units and entertainment = 6 units, for a total of 10 units.

$\frac{10}{20} = \frac{1}{2}$, or 50% (Choice D)

17. How does the food bill for Family A compare with the food bill for Family C?

   (A) Family A spent twice as much for food as did Family C.
   (B) Family C spent one-half as much for food as did Family A.
   (C) Family A and Family C spent the same amount for food.
   (D) Family A spent $2\frac{1}{2}$ times as much as did Family C.
   (E) Family C spent $2\frac{1}{2}$ times as much as did Family A.

Though the number of units spent for food is twice as great for Family A, this is a case of a larger part of a smaller whole (annual income of $20,000), compared with a smaller part of a larger whole (annual income of $100,000).

Family A spent $\frac{8}{20}$ or $\frac{4}{10}$ of $20,000 = $8000 for food.

Family C spent $\frac{4}{20}$ or $\frac{2}{10}$ of $100,000 = $20,000 for food.

$\left(2\frac{1}{2}\right)$($8,000) = $20,000. The correct choice is E.

Review of Formulas

(The number next to each formula refers to the section of the chapters where the formula is discussed.)

Interest = Amount × Time × Rate   I–D–2

Discount = Cost × Rate of discount   I–D–2

$x = \frac{1}{2a}\left[-b \pm \sqrt{b^2 - 4ac}\right]$ (quadratic formula)   II–B–5

Distance = Speed × Time   II–C–2

$a^2 + b^2 = c^2$, where a and b are the lengths of   III–D–1
the legs and c is the length of the hypotenuse
of a right triangle (Pythagorean theorem)

Diameter of a circle = 2 × Radius   III–F

Area of a square = s^2 III–G–1

Area of a rectangle = LW III–G–1

Area of a triangle = $\frac{1}{2}bh$ III–G–1

Area of a circle = πr^2 III–G–1

Area of a parallelogram = bh III–G–1

Area of a trapezoid = $\frac{1}{2}(b_1 + b_2)h$ III–G–1

Circumference of a circle = πd III–G–2

Perimeter of a square = $4s$ III–G–2

Perimeter of a rectangle = $2(L + W)$ III–G–2

Distance between points (x, y) and   III–H
$(a, b) = \sqrt{(x - a)^2 + (y - b)^2}$

12 Analytical Ability

- **Analytical Reasoning Tactics**
- **Logical Reasoning Tactics**
- **Analysis of Explanations Tactics**
- **Practice Exercises**
- **Answer Key**
- **Answer Explanations**

The analytical ability portion of the GRE is made up of two types of questions: analytical reasoning (puzzle) questions and logical reasoning (argument analysis) questions; there may also be a third type: analysis of explanations questions. Typically, each analytical ability section consists of twenty-five questions. Nineteen analytical reasoning questions are divided into three to five groups, each containing three to seven questions. Six logical reasoning questions come in two sets of three, one set following the first group of analytical reasoning questions, and one set ending the section.

Analysis of explanations questions are new to the GRE this year. Educational Testing Service is experimenting with this type of question to see whether it provides information about a test-taker's analytical ability that is not provided by the other two types. Exactly how many of these questions will occur on a typical analytical ability section is uncertain. Expect the analytical section to have possibly one less analytic puzzle or one fewer set of logical reasoning problems in order to accommodate this new type of question.

In dealing with analytical ability questions, you should expect to spend most of your time reading and analyzing the puzzle statements and the verbal arguments themselves. Read closely. Once you have worked out a particular structure of relationships, organizing your information in outline or diagram form, you will find the puzzle questions themselves relatively easy. Similarly, once you have critically evaluated a particular verbal argument, noting the assumptions on which it is based and the inferences that can logically be drawn from it, you will find questions concerning the reasoning displayed in that argument readily manageable.

All three types of questions are designed at three different levels of difficulty: easy, moderate, and hard. Of course, your perception of these distinctions will depend on your own level of ability. The tactics presented in this chapter will help you approach questions at all levels. Expect to find some questions in each section relatively easy, and others much more difficult. Do not make the mistake of using all your time on questions that appear extremely difficult.

Analytical Reasoning Tactics

Tactic 1

Tackle Each Group of Analytical Reasoning Questions as a Unit

Analytical reasoning questions require you to think through a complicated set of conditions and to keep these conditions in mind as you answer a group of questions. It therefore makes sense for you to treat each group of questions as a unit and attempt to answer *all* the questions while you still have the conditions clearly in mind. Do not jump from one group to a second before

you answer all the questions in the first group; you will lose time refamiliarizing yourself with the relationships.

Within a given group, you may find it helpful to skip from question to question. In answering the fourth question based on a particular set of conditions, you may gain an insight into the total relationship that will help you answer questions 2 and 3.

Simplify the Information by Using Abbreviations and Symbolic Shorthand

The analytical reasoning questions are not intended to be ambiguous. Far from it—the test-makers take great pains to use language precisely and to word the set of conditions describing a particular relationship so exactly that only one interpretation works. In doing so, however, they use so many words that it is easy to get lost. To see the situation clearly, you need to work with symbols, not words.

Strip away individual names and irrelevant details that confuse the situation. If the test-makers list a lengthy group of items, substitute initials for the individual words. If they take a dozen words to describe a relationship, try to express it in three or four letters and symbols (›, =, +, etc.). In the course of taking lecture notes, you have probably worked up your own personal shorthand, a system of symbolic notation you use to express ideas rapidly. Build on this system, adding to it any of the standard logical symbols found in the following chart.

STANDARD LOGICAL NOTATION

Linking Term	Symbol
and	+
or	V
not	~
if - then	⊃
if and only if	≡
equal to, same as	=
not equal to, not same as	≠
greater than (taller, older, etc.)	>
less than (shorter, younger, etc.)	<

Work with these symbols if and only if they seem useful to you. You may prefer other symbols, such as & for and.

See how this tactic works in dealing with a set of conditions presented on a recent GRE.

Questions 20–22

An instructor regularly offers a six-week survey course on film genres. Each time the course is given, she covers six of the following eight genres: adventure films, *cinema noir*, detective films, fantasy films, horror films, musical comedies, silent films, and westerns. She will discuss exactly one genre per week according to the following conditions:

Silent films are always covered, and always in the first week.
Westerns and adventure films are always covered, with westerns covered in the week immediately preceding the week adventure films are covered.
Musical comedies are never covered in the same course in which fantasy films are covered.
If detective films are covered, they are covered after westerns are covered, with exactly one of the other genres covered between them.
Cinema noir is not covered unless detective films are covered in one of the previous weeks.

Your first task is to reduce this mass of data to manageable proportions. First, substitute initials for the names of the eight genres, as follows:

Adventure films	=	A
Cinema noir	=	C
Detective films	=	D
Fantasy films	=	F
Horror films	=	H
Musical comedies	=	M
Silent films	=	S
Westerns	=	W

Now, note down what you *know* about these genres:

S *always* 1
W⇒A *always* (here⇒means immediately precedes)
If F, no M
If M, no F
If C, D → C (here → means *precedes, but not necessarily immediately*)
If D, W⇒?⇒D

Take a look at the last condition. You *know* that westerns immediately precede adventure films (W⇒ A *always*). Therefore, you can rewrite the last condition to read:

If D, W⇒A⇒D

Whenever detective films are covered, you know the exact order and identity of three of the six film genres discussed in the course.

Highlight Key Words That Limit the Situation Critically

Look at the preceding example. Note the words that limit the relationships presented. Silent films are *always* covered and *always* in the *first* week. Westerns *immediately* precede adventure films. *Exactly one* genre is covered between westerns and detective films. *Cinema noir* is *not* covered *unless* detective films are covered. Musical comedies are *never* covered in the same course in which fantasy films are covered.

These words are critical to your understanding of the situation. Take particular note of them, underlining them or circling them to emphasize their importance.

Frequently Used Key Words

all
always
at least (*at least one member in common* — can be 1, 2, 3...)
at most (*at most two members in common* — can be 0, 1, or 2)
but
can be
cannot be
consecutive (*three consecutive days*)
directly (*directly opposite*; *directly after*)
each
every
exactly (*exactly one*; *exactly once*)
except
if

immediately (*immediately preceding*; *immediately adjacent*)
impossible
must be
never
no fewer than (*no fewer than three*—can be 3, 4, 5...)
no more than (*no more than four*—can be 0, 1, 2, 3, or 4)
none
only (*once and only once*; *if and only if*)
perfectly (*perfectly straight*; *perfectly round*)
possible
same
some
the least (*shortest, smallest, youngest, etc.*)
the most (*tallest, greatest, oldest, etc.*)
unless

Note that certain of these key words have only one function — to rule out a potential ambiguity. These words so precisely define the situation that only one interpretation is possible. Take, for example, *immediately*. What does the statement "John precedes Kenneth" tell you? It tells you that John is somewhere ahead of Kenneth. What does the statement "John immediately precedes Kenneth" tell you? It tells you the exact relationship between John and Kenneth, letting you know that John is the person who comes right before Kenneth, and that nobody else comes between Kenneth and John.

First, Eliminate Answer Choices Ruled Out by Individual Conditions; Then, Work Through Remaining Choices or Guess

Pay special note to any conditions phrased in unambiguous terms—*always, never, all, none*. Because they allow only one interpretation of the situation, you may be able to use them to rule out several answer choices at a glance.

See how a single condition allows you to eliminate three answer choices to a question based on the preceding set of course conditions.

20. Which of the following is an acceptable schedule of genres for weeks one through six of the course?

(A) Silent films, westerns, adventure films, detective films, horror films, musical comedies
(B) Silent films, westerns, adventure films, horror films, detective films, fantasy films
(C) Fantasy films, musical comedies, detective films, *cinema noir*, musical comedies, horror films
(D) Westerns, adventure films, detective films, *cinema noir*, musical comedies, horror films
(E) Detective films, westerns, adventure films, horror films, fantasy films, *cinema noir*

What is the first condition that must be met? "S *always* 1." Therefore, every schedule of genres must begin with S, silent films. Choices A and B begin with S; they deserve further examination. Choices C, D, and E, however, begin with other genres. Eliminate them and give them no further thought.

Go back to Choice A. What pattern do you see?

S W A D H M

S is where it belongs. W A D is an acceptable pattern. In the absence of F, M is acceptable. Choice A works.

Double check yourself. Look over Choice B. Here the pattern is:

S W A H D F

Once again, S is in its place. W A meets the second condition. In the absence of M, F is acceptable. The problem lies in the placement of D. According to the rules, it can exist only in the pattern W A D. It is not enough for westerns merely to precede detective films. The fourth condition states that *exactly* one genre is covered between westerns and detective films. Given the second condition, that one genre must be adventure films. Thus, if detective films are covered, the pattern must be W A D. Choice B is incorrect. The correct answer is Choice A.

In this instance, you narrowed things down to Choices A and B and had time to work out that Choice A was correct. If you run out of time, don't worry. Just guess. In this example, you have a fifty-fifty probability of a correct answer by weeding out Choices C, D, and E. By being able to eliminate some answer choices at a glance, you have improved your chance of selecting the correct choice.

Study Conditions Not Merely for What They State But for What They Imply

Analytical reasoning questions resemble the inference questions you find in reading comprehension tests. To answer them correctly, you must understand not only what the conditions state explicitly but what they imply.

See how this holds true in answering the following question on the preceding GRE example.

22. Which of the following will NEVER be covered in the sixth week of the course?

(A) *Cinema noir*
(B) Fantasy films
(C) Horror films
(D) Musical comedies
(E) Westerns

Look at your list of conditions. Which of them provide information about the order in which the different genres may be covered?

S *always* 1
W⇒A *always* (here⇒means *immediately precedes*)
If C, D → C (here → means *precedes, but not necessarily immediately*)
If D, W⇒A⇒D

Consider the second condition. If westerns and adventure films are always covered, with westerns always immediately preceding adventure films, this implies that

westerns can be covered in only weeks 2, 3, 4, or 5. They cannot be covered in week 1, for that is reserved for silent films (S *always* 1). Likewise, they cannot be covered in week 6, for they must be followed by adventure films. (See table.)

From studying the implications of the conditions, you can see that only four basic configurations are possible. You can also see that westerns will never be covered in the sixth week of the course. The correct answer is Choice E.

Organize Information in List or Table Form

Tactic 6

When you study a set of conditions for its implications, you wind up with a mass of information. You need to organize this information. As in the preceding question, you will find it useful to list the basic conditions and to set down their implications in table form.

Apply this tactic to the following set of conditions from a recent GRE.

Questions 16–19

A cryptanalyst must translate into letters all of the digits included in the following two lines of nine symbols each:

  9 3 3 4 5 6 6 6 7
  2 2 3 3 4 4 5 7 8

The cryptanalyst has already determined some of the rules governing the decoding:
  Each of the digits from 2 to 9 represents exactly one of the eights letters A, E, I, O, U, R, S, and T, and each letter is represented by exactly one of the digits.
  If a digit occurs more than once, it represents the same letter on each occasion.
  The letter T and the letter O are each represented exactly 3 times.
  The letter I and the letter A are each represented exactly two times.
  The letter E is represented exactly four times.

List the digits from 2 to 9. Beside each digit, note the number of times that digit occurs in the two lines being decoded.

Number of Occurrences	Digit
2 x	2
4 x	3
3 x	4
2 x	5
3 x	6
2 x	7
1 x	8
1 x	9

Next, compare the information in this table with the information already determined by the cryptanalyst. Note on the table what you can deduce from this comparison. (For example, the cryptanalyst has determined that the letter E occurs four times. Therefore, you can deduce that the letter E must be represented by the digit 3, the only digit occurring four times.)

Number of Occurrences	Digit	
2 x	2	A or I or ?
4 x	3	E
3 x	4	T or O
2 x	5	A or I or ?
3 x	6	T or O
2 x	7	A or I or ?
1 x	8	?
1 x	9	?

Unassigned Letters R, S, U

See how simple it is to answer the following GRE question by referring to this table of information.

---

16. If 2 represents R and 7 represents A, then 5 must represent

   (A) I
   (B) O
   (C) S
   (D) T
   (E) U

Examine the chart. According to the rules determined by the cryptanalyst, 2, 5 and 7 each represent one (and only one) of three letters: A, I, and an undetermined third letter. This question identifies that third letter as R and stipulates that 2 represents R and 7 represents A. Incorporate this information into your table for the moment. The only letter of the three that remains is I. Thus, 5 *must* represent I. The correct answer is Choice A.

Number of Occurrences	Digit	
2 x	2	R (not A or I)
4 x	3	E
3 x	4	T or O
2 x	5	I
3 x	6	T or O
2 x	7	A (not R or I)
1 x	8	?
1 x	9	?

Unassigned Letters S, U

Organize Information in Map or Diagram Form

One of the best ways to deal with the information in an analytical reasoning question is to construct a simple map or diagram. This is particularly helpful when you are dealing with a problem involving the physical or temporal order of things. It is much easier to tell whether a particular route from point A to point B is possible when you actually see points A and B on a map.

Note how you can construct a map to illustrate the following set of conditions from a recent GRE.

Questions 18–22

On an island there are exactly seven towns: T, U, V, W, X, Y, and Z. All existing and projected roads on the island are two-way and run perfectly straight between one town and the next. All distances by road are distances from the main square of one town to the main square of another town. U is the same distance by road from T, V, and W as Y is from X and Z. The following are all of the currently existing roads and connections by road on the island.

Road 1 goes from T to V via U.
Road 2 goes from U directly to W.
The Triangle Road goes from X to Y, from Y on to Z, and from Z back to X.
Any main square reached by two roads is an interchange between them, and there are no other interchanges between roads.

Draw Road 1, labeling points T, U, and V.

Now draw Road 2, for simplicity's sake making it perpendicular to Road 1.

Above this diagram, and unconnected to it, construct the Triangle Road.

To indicate that they each are the same length (their main squares are the same distance apart), mark the following five line segments with equal signs: UT, UV, UW, YX, and YZ. You now have a diagram that you can use to answer any questions about the physical relationships among the island's seven towns.

Try constructing a second diagram, this one illustrating the way in which five computers are linked.

Questions 14–18

P, Q, R, S, T are the computers in the five overseas offices of a large multinational corporation. The computers are linked in an unusual manner in order to provide increased security for the data in certain offices. Data can be directly requested only from:
   P by Q
   P by T
   Q by P
   R by P
   S by Q
   S by T
   T by R
If a computer can directly request data from another computer, then it can also pass on requests for data to that other computer.

In this situation, you are dealing not with two-way streets, but with "one-way" streets. To say that T can directly request data from P does not imply that P can directly request data from T. Thus, you need to use arrows to indicate the direction in which requests for data may go.

Go through the list, connecting each pair of letters with its arrow or arrows.

You now have a diagram that illustrates exactly how these computers are linked. Note how much information about these relationships you have. For example, you can see that several possible routes allow you to request information from computer R. P can request information directly from R. Alternatively, Q and T may also request information from R via P. Taking this process to extremes, R can even request information from itself by routing its request through T and P.

Individual questions often contain new conditions that affect the determined structure of relationships. To understand how a change in the computer linkup described affects the relationships involved, you have only to make a new diagram or alter your diagram temporarily.

See how readily you can answer the following GRE question by altering your diagram appropriately.

> 17. If computers Q, R, S, and T are the only ones operating, which of the following requests for data can be made, either directly or through one or more of the other computers?
>
> (A) A request by P for data from Q
> (B) A request by Q for data from R
> (C) A request by Q for data from T
> (D) A request by R for data from P
> (E) A request by R for data from S

P is nonfunctional. Therefore, it is out of the linkup: you must delete it and the arrows going to and from it from your diagram. Thus altered, your diagram looks like this:

A quick glance reveals that, of the choices given, only Choice E is possible. Despite the gaps in the linkup, R can still, by going through T, request data from S.

One word of caution: When an analytical reasoning question introduces new information in the form of a stipulation—an additional condition or restriction, or, as in the question above, a suspension of one of the original conditions—be sure you add that information to your diagram or table *temporarily*: apply it to that question alone. Do *not* apply it to other questions in its group.

Tactic 8

Beware of Making Unwarranted Assumptions

Generally, once you have set up your table or completed your diagram based on a particular set of conditions, you should have little difficulty with the group of questions based on those conditions. Sometimes, however, you may misread one of the conditions, drawing an incorrect inference from it. For example, in a set establishing relationships of age and military rank among the members of a squad, you should not assume that a person who is older than another person must hold a higher rank than that person.

Beware of reading too much into a condition. Take the following condition:

If J is selected for a team, K must also be selected for that team.

Or, in brief,

If J, K (J ⊃ K)

Do not assume on the basis of this that if K is selected for a team, J must also be selected for that team. The condition does not work both ways: it has not been imposed on both parties.

Many sets of conditions in analytical reasoning problems include such one-way conditions. The set of conditions for the film course, for example, includes the following condition:

Cinema noir is not covered unless detective films are covered in one of the previous weeks.

In other words,

If C, D → C

However, this restriction does not apply equally to C and D. The same condition has not been imposed on both genres. To say that

Cinema noir is not covered unless detective films are covered in one of the previous weeks

is *not* to say that

Detective films are not covered unless *cinema noir* is covered in one of the following weeks.

In other words,

If C, D → C does NOT imply If D, D → C

It is unfortunately very easy to introduce graphic assumptions into the construction of a diagram. For example, look at the diagram below, based upon the description of road connections in the discussion of Tactic 7.

Questions 18–22

On an island there are exactly seven towns: T, U, V, W, X, Y, and Z. All existing and projected roads on the island are two-way and run perfectly straight between one town and the next. All distances by road are distances from the main square of one town to the main square of another town. U is the same distance by road from T, V, and W as Y is from X and Z. The following are all of the currently existing roads and connections by road on the island.

Road 1 goes from T to V via U.
Road 2 goes from U directly to W.
The Triangle Road goes from X to Y, from Y on to Z, and from Z back to X.
Any main square reached by two roads is an interchange between them, and there are no other interchanges between roads.

The diagram above represents the Triangle Road as an equilateral triangle: visually, XY, YZ, and XZ are equal in length. Unfortunately, this diagram embodies an assumption that may mislead you when you attempt to answer the following question.

---

19. It is possible that the distance by road from X to Y is *unequal* to the distance by road from

(A) T to U
(B) U to V
(C) U to W
(D) X to Z
(E) Y to Z

The question asks that you find a road that *can differ* in length from Road XY.

It is possible that Triangle XYZ is an equilateral triangle, and that lines XY, XZ, and YZ are all equal in length. That, however, is not what you are told. You are told only that XY and YZ are equal in length, as are TU, UV, and UW. You have no information about the length of XZ. By picturing Triangle XYZ as equilateral, you assume a relationship in which all road segments are the same in length and in which no road can differ in length from Road XY. If that were the case, there would be no correct answer to the question.

The test-makers do not create questions for which no correct answers exist. If you can find no correct answer to an analytical reasoning question, go back to the original conditions and re-examine them. You will find that you have misinterpreted one or more of them.

In this case, in constructing your diagram you have assumed incorrectly that the condition defining the length of XY and YZ applies equally to XZ. It does not. XZ can be equal in length to XY. It can be greater in length than XY. It can be shorter in length than XY. Therefore, it follows that the distance by road from X to Y *can be unequal* to the distance by road from X to Z. The correct answer is Choice D.

Logical Reasoning Tactics

Look at the Question Before You Look at the Argument

Analytical reasoning questions come in groups of three to seven questions based on a single set of conditions. It makes sense to analyze the set of conditions carefully before you look at the questions based upon it. One, or at most two, logical reasoning questions, however, are based on a given argument. Rather than jumping in blindly and analyzing each and every aspect of the argument—assumptions, central point, evidence, further application, logical flaws—do no more work than necessary. Look at the question stem. Then examine the argument. Know what aspect of the argument you are to concentrate on, and focus on it. You will save time and effort.

See how this tactic applies to the following logical reasoning question from a recent GRE.

The Census Bureau reported that the median family income, after adjustment, increased 1.6 percent in 1983. Poverty normally declines when family income goes up, but the national poverty rate remained at its highest level in eighteen years in 1983. The Census Bureau offered two possible explanations: the lingering effects of the deep and lengthy 1981-1982 recession, and increases in the number of people living in families headed by women and in the number of adults not living with any relatives. Both groups are likely to be poorer than the population as a whole.

Which of the following conclusions can be properly drawn from this report?

(A) The national poverty rate has increased steadily over the last eighteen years.
(B) The national poverty rate will increase when there are lingering effects of an earlier recession.
(C) The median family income can increase even though the family income of some subgroups within the population declines or fails to increase.
(D) The category of adults not living with any relatives is the most critical group in the determination of whether the economy has improved.
(E) The median family income is affected more by changes in family patterns than by the extent of expansion or recession of the national economy.

Your goal is to select the answer choice that logically follows from specific facts and ideas stated in the passage. You do not have to evaluate the argument for possible flaws in logic or consider the premises on which it is based. You are looking for a proper conclusion. Therefore, you must carefully analyze each answer choice and see how it relates to the passage. You can eliminate any answer choice that contradicts what the passage states as fact. You can also eliminate any answer choice that strays from the subject of the passage or cannot be linked to specific supporting evidence in the passage.

Go through the answer choices, keeping sight of your goal while you think the argument through. Is Choice A a conclusion that can be properly drawn from what is stated in the passage? No. Choice A contradicts something the passage states as fact. In asserting that the national poverty rate has *increased steadily* over the last eighteen years, Choice A contradicts the second sentence, which states that the national poverty rate *remained at its highest level* in 1983. According to the passage, therefore, the national poverty rate did not steadily increase throughout the period in question.

Is Choice B a conclusion that can be properly drawn from what is stated in the passage? No. Choice B goes beyond what the passage states or suggests. In the third sentence, "the lingering effects of the deep and lengthy 1981–1982 recession" are offered as a possible explanation for the failure of the national poverty rate to decline. These lingering effects are not, however, offered as evidence that the national poverty rate will increase.

Is Choice C a conclusion that can be properly drawn from what is stated in the passage? Possibly. Choice C states that the median family income *can* increase *even though* the family income of some subgroups within the population declines or fails to increase. This assertion is in keeping with the facts presented in the passage. The first sentence states that the median family income has increased. The second sentence states that the national poverty rate remained at its highest level. This implies that the income of some families either failed to increase or declined. The third sentence cites two subgroups whose income is likely to fall below the national median. Choice C is probably correct—it appears to be a conclusion that can be drawn from the passage—but, just to be sure, you should check out the remaining answer choices, Choices D and E.

Is Choice D a conclusion that can be properly drawn from what is stated in the passage? No. Choice D goes *far* beyond what the passage suggests or states. Where the passage cites an increase in two subgroups—families headed by women, and adults not living with any relatives—as one *possible* explanation for the lack of improvement in the economy, Choice D pinpoints one of these two subgroups as *the most critical* group in determining whether the economy has improved. There is no evidence in the passage to support singling out one particular subgroup in this way. Therefore, you can eliminate Choice D.

What of Choice E? Is Choice E a conclusion that can be properly drawn from what is stated in the passage? No. Like Choice D, Choice E goes beyond what the passage states or suggests. Nothing in the passage suggests that one factor more than another affects the median family income. In fact, the passage cites changes in family pattern and the effects of recession not as influences on the median family income but as influences on the national poverty rate. Choice E clearly is incorrect.

Of the conclusions listed, the only one that can be properly drawn from the passage is Choice C.

Learn to Spot the Major Logical Reasoning Question Types

Just as it will help you to know the major types of reading questions on the GRE, it will also help you to familiarize yourself with the major types of logical reasoning questions on the test.

If you can recognize just what a given question is asking for, you'll be better able to tell which particular approach to take to the argument at hand.

Here are eight categories of logical reasoning questions you are sure to face.

1. **Assumption**   Questions that test your ability to recognize the premises on which an argument is based often take the following forms:

   The conclusion above depends on which of the following assumptions?
   The author of the passage above makes which of the following assumptions?
   The author of the passage above presupposes that...
   The statement above assumes which of the following?

2. **Inference**   Questions that test your ability to go beyond the author's explicit statements and see what these statements imply may be worded:

   It can be inferred from the passage above that the author believes that...
   Which of the following is implied by the passage above?
   From the information above, which of the following can be most reasonably inferred about...

3. **Conclusion**   Questions that test your ability to determine what claim can logically be made on the basis of the evidence in the passage often take these forms:

   If the statements above are true, which of the following conclusions can be properly drawn?

   Choose the most logical completion for the following paragraph.
   Which of the following would provide the most logical conclusion for the preceding paragraph?
   The statements in the passage, if true, best support which of the following conclusions?

4. **Central Point**   Questions that test your ability to understand the thrust of an argument are often worded:

   The statement cited above conveys which of the following propositions?
   The passage above emphasizes which of the following points?
   The author in the passage above argues that...
   Which of the following expresses the point the author of the passage above makes?

5. **Support**   Questions that test your ability to recognize whether an assertion supports or undermines an argument are often worded:

   Which of the following, if true, does NOT support the claim that...
   Which of the following, if true, would additionally weaken the traditional opinion that...
   Which of the following, if true, would constitute the strongest evidence in support of the claim made above?
   The persuasiveness of the claim made above is most weakened by...

6. **Argument Evaluation**   Questions that test your ability to judge an argument often take these forms:

   Which of the following would be most important to know in evaluating the accuracy of the argument above?
   Which of the following hypotheses, if true, would help resolve the apparent paradox introduced above?

If all of the statements above are correct, an explanation of their apparent contradiction is provided by...
Which of the following identifies a flaw in the speaker's reasoning?
Knowledge of which of the following would be LEAST useful in evaluating the claims made in the passage above?

7. **Application**   Questions that test your ability to apply the principles governing one argument to another argument are often worded:

Which of the following parallels the method of argumentation above?

The argument above is most like which of the following?
Which of the following suffers from a flaw that, in its logical aspects, is most like the difficulty described above?

8. **Technique**   Questions that test your ability to recognize an argument's method of organization or technique may be worded:

The author's point is made primarily by...
The labor negotiator minimizes his differences with management by...
The passage above criticizes the authorities by...

Pay Particular Attention to Signal Words in the Question (and in the Argument as Well)

In answering logical reasoning questions, you must read closely both the argument and the question or questions based on it. When you do so, be on the lookout for certain signal words that can clarify the situation. In particular, be alert for:

Cause and Effect Signal Words

The following words often signal the conclusion of an argument:

accordingly
consequently
hence
therefore
thus

Contrast Signal Words

The following words often signal a reversal of thought within an argument or a question stem:

although
but
despite
even though
however
in contrast
instead
nevertheless
not
on the contrary
on the other hand
rather than
unlike

See how several of these signal words function in the following logical reasoning problem from a recent GRE.

Literary historians today have rejected conventional analyses of the development of English Renaissance drama. They no longer accept the idea that the sudden achievement of Elizabethan playwrights was a historical anomaly, a sort of magical rediscovery of ancient Greek dramatic form applied to contemporary English subject matter. Instead, most students of the theater now view Elizabethan drama as being organically related to traditional local drama, particularly medieval morality plays.

Which of the following is NOT consistent with the passage above?

(A) England had a dramatic tradition before the Renaissance period.
(B) Elizabethan drama, once thought to be a sudden blossoming forth of creativity, is now seen as part of a historical continuum.
(C) Historians' views of the antecedents of English Renaissance drama have changed considerably.
(D) Current scholarship applies an evolutionary model to English Renaissance drama.
(E) Although English Renaissance drama treats English subject matter, its source of form and method is classical Greek drama.

Your job is to decide which answer choice is NOT consistent with the passage above. Therefore, you can eliminate any answer choice that *is* consistent with it.

Go through the answer choices. Is Choice A in keeping with what is stated in the passage? Yes. The concluding sentence states that Elizabethan (i.e., English Renaissance) drama is viewed as "organically related" to the earlier traditional local drama. In other words, there was a dramatic tradition in England before Renaissance times. You can eliminate Choice A.

Is Choice B in keeping with what is stated in the passage? Yes. The second sentence states that the sudden achievement of Elizabethan drama is no longer viewed as a historical anomaly. In other words, it is not seen as something abnormal, something that stands apart from history, but as part of a historical continuum. You can eliminate Choice B.

Is Choice C in keeping with what is stated in the passage? Yes. The opening sentence states that literary historians have rejected the conventional views of how English Renaissance drama developed. Therefore, their views of its antecedents have changed considerably. You can eliminate Choice C.

Is Choice D in keeping with what is stated in the passage? Yes. The concluding sentence speaks of English Renaissance drama as being "organically related" to earlier dramatic forms. In other words, it developed out of or evolved from these earlier forms. The language here is that of evolutionary discourse. You can eliminate Choice D.

Is Choice E in keeping with what is stated in the passage? No. The second sentence states that literary historians have discarded the view that English Renaissance drama owes its form and method to the plays of classical Greece. Choice E asserts the very point that the passage seeks to deny. Thus, Choice E is not consistent with the passage and is the correct answer choice.

In Questions About an Argument's Assumptions, First Pinpoint the Argument's Conclusion and the Grounds on Which It Is Based

When asked about an argument's assumptions, work backwards from what is stated to what is unsaid. Start with the conclusion. Why does the argument's proponent arrive at this conclusion? What evidence supports it? When you are clear exactly what claim has been made and on what grounds it is founded, you are in a position to determine the assumptions underlying the argument. Ask yourself what there is about this particular evidence that justifies this particular claim. In the process, you will uncover the argument's unstated premises.

(A) People are more easily fooled by illusionistic techniques than are birds.
(B) The use of illusionistic techniques in painting had become commonplace by the time Zeuxis had completed his later work.
(C) The grapes in the later painting were even more realistic than the ones in the earlier work.
(D) Birds are less likely to peck at fruit when they see that a human being is present.
(E) After the success of his early work, Zeuxis was unable to live up to the expectations of the general public.

Apply this tactic to the following GRE question.

A study of illusionistic painting inevitably begins with the Greek painter Zeuxis. In an early work, which is the basis for his fame, he painted a bowl of grapes that was so lifelike that birds pecked at the fruit. In an attempt to expand his achievement to encompass human figures, he painted a boy carrying a bunch of grapes. When birds immediately came to peck at the fruit, Zeuxis judged that he had failed.

Zeuxis' judgment that he had failed in his later work was based on an assumption. Which of the following can have served as that assumption?

What is Zeuxis' judgment or conclusion? His conclusion is that he failed to paint human figures with the illusion of life. Why does he draw this conclusion? What evidence does he offer to support it? He concludes that he failed to paint human figures with the illusion of life *because* birds came to peck at the fruit in one of his paintings that included a human figure. Why does he think this evidence supports his conclusion? Given this description, what assumption does he necessarily make about the behavior of birds? He assumes that birds are unlikely to peck at fruit when they realize a person is nearby. In other words, "Birds are less likely to peck at fruit when they see that a human being is present." The correct answer is Choice D.

In Questions About Weakening or Strengthening an Argument, Examine the Argument for Any Unstated Assumptions It Makes

An argument is based upon certain assumptions made by its author. If an argument's basic premises are sound, the argument is strengthened. If the argument's basic premises are flawed, the argument is weakened.

Pinpoint what the argument assumes. Then compare that assumption with the answer choices. If the question asks you to choose an answer that most strengthens the argument, look for the answer choice that is most in keeping with the argument's basic assumption. If the question asks you to choose an answer that most weakens the argument, look for the answer choice that casts the most doubt on that assumption.

Apply this tactic to the following question from a recent GRE.

It is important to teach students to use computers effectively. Therefore, students should be taught computer programming in school.

Which of the following, if true, most weakens the argument above.

(A) Only people who use computers effectively are skilled at computer programming.
(B) Only people skilled at computer programming use computers effectively.
(C) Some people who use computers effectively cannot write computer programs.
(D) Some schools teach computer programming more effectively than others.
(E) Most people who are able to program computers use computers effectively.

The argument claims that, if students are to learn to use computers effectively, they should be taught computer programming in school. It clearly assumes a high correlation between knowledge of computer programming and effective computer use. It assumes at the least that people who have studied computer programming use computers effectively, and, possibly, that people who have not studied computer programming do not.

Choices B and E are in keeping with the argument's assumptions: if true, they would strengthen the argument, not weaken it. Therefore, Choices B and E are incorrect.

Choice A does not cast doubt on an assumption. It reverses it. This particular assumption, however, works only one-way. Think of it in *if-then* terms. Saying "If people are skilled at computer programming, then they can use computers effectively" does not imply "If people can use computers effectively, then they are skilled at computer programming." Likewise, the assumption "Only people skilled at computer programming use computers effectively" does not imply "Only people who use computers effectively are skilled at computer programming." Choice A is incorrect.

Choice D is also incorrect. It neither strengthens nor weakens the argument. It goes off on an entirely different track.

The correct answer is Choice C. It states that people exist who use computers effectively yet are unskilled at computer programming—they cannot write programs. It thus casts doubt upon the assumption that people unskilled at computer programming do not or cannot use computers effectively.

Be on the Lookout for Common Logical Fallacies

If you've studied logic, rhetoric, philosophy, or debating, you may notice some familiar types of fallacies and logical errors turning up on the exam—for example, the *ad hominem* argument, in which the speaker attacks the personality of his or her opponent rather than criticizing the opponent's arguments; the *post hoc ergo propter hoc* argument, in which a simple association between two things is erroneously assumed to imply a cause-and-effect relationship between them; the *hasty generaliza-* *tion*, in which one or two isolated instances are taken as proof of some general rule; *circular reasoning*, in which the argument assumes the truth of what's supposed to be proved; and various kinds of *confusion of logical categories*. Technical terms like the ones just mentioned will NOT be tested or used on the exam. But you will be expected to recognize flaws like these when they appear in arguments and understand why they weaken the arguments based upon them.

Analysis of Explanations Tactics

During 1993, the Educational Testing Service attempted to extend the problem types encountered on the analytical ability sections of the GRE. Students who took the exam that year were presented not only with analytical reasoning questions and logical problems, but also with questions related to what ETS termed "analysis of explanations" and "pattern identification." On the basis of its initial research, ETS is planning to offer only one format, analysis of explanations, during the 1994–95 testing year. There is a good possibility that analytical sections containing this new type of question will constitute the experimental sections of the GRE and won't count toward a student's score. To be on the safe side, however, students should do their best on these questions.

This new type, analysis of explanations, is reasonably similar, in terms of the reasoning skills involved, to the logical problems discussed in the preceding section. Test-takers will be asked to decide whether given statements provide adequate explanations of results based on some situation, and also to decide whether certain other statements help to strengthen or weaken—that is, are relevant to—some explanation. Specialized knowledge of particular subject matter is not necessary to answer questions of this type.

The structure of these questions is as follows: a Situation is described that provides information related to some problem, event, or circumstance; a Result is then presented; and a group of Questions related to the situation follow. At present each question is to answered "Yes" or "No," but don't be surprised if ETS experiments with alternative formats (e.g., three alternatives instead of two). ETS is experimenting not only with the question types but also with the number of answer choices, presently just Choice A ("Yes") or Choice B ("No").

Here are some tactics for the analysis of explanations problems.

Read the result first

By reading the result, you can anticipate relevant and irrelevant information presented in the situation. Notice specific names, events, and other details mentioned in the result. The questions that follow ask for an adequate explanation of how the result occurred or involve factors that may be relevant to a possible explanation. Here is a sample result:

Result: Three years after the acquisition, sales of Hawthorne big-screen televisions had decreased by 50 percent.

Start anticipating what might be adequate explanations of why the sales of Hawthorne big-screen televisions declined. Did the decline have anything to do with the acquisition (whatever that was)? What factors might cause a decline in sales? As you prepare to read the situation next, be primed to focus on the names and events presented in the result and be prepared to discount irrelevant information.

Read the situation

Knowing the result, pay attention, as you read the situation, to the specific names, events, and other details that were mentioned in the result. Try to anticipate how the result could have occurred, given the information in the situation. Notice comparisons and contrasts between entities or information presented in the situation.

Here is the corresponding situation with the result repeated.

1–4

Situation: Five years ago, Smith Consumer Electronics acquired a smaller company, Hawthorne Television Systems. Smith Consumer Electronics sells a variety of products ranging from radios to computers. The corporation has a large sales force and a vast distribution network but has not been able to market successfully its big-screen television sets. Hawthorne Television Systems has only one major product, a big-screen television, whose sales had remained steady for several years. By the terms of the acquisition, the managers of Hawthorne were to continue to oversee their production facilities for a period of five years.

Result: Three years after the acquisition, sales of Hawthorne big-screen televisions had decreased by 50 percent.

We are told that Smith Consumer Electronics bought the smaller company, Hawthorne Television Systems. Smith makes many products and has a large sales force and marketing system. Hawthorne makes only one product, which sold steadily. So why would the sales of Hawthorne TVs decline after the acquisition? Is the reason something to do with the Smith corporation or with the Hawthorne company? Clue into the fact that the situation indicates that the managers at Hawthorne remained the same, indicating that there may be something wrong with the way Smith handled the Hawthorne big-screen televisions.

Do the questions asking for adequate explanations first

These questions will be framed as follows:

Could the following statement, if true, provide the basis for an adequate explanation of the result? An adequate explanation for this purpose does not need to be complete in all details.

By doing these questions first, you can key in to what ETS is offering as reasonable or unreasonable explanations of the result presented. In answering "Yes" or "No" to an adequate-explanation question, the test-taker is urged not to consider extremely unlikely or farfetched explanations.

Here is an example of an adequate-explanation question based on the company acquisition described above. The general directions for answering these questions are as follows:

Directions: Preceding each group of numbered statements is a question that can be answered "Yes" or "No." Answer this question separately for each statement in the group by marking answer choice A on your answer sheet for "Yes" or answer choice B for "No" next to the number for *each* statement. Be careful not to mark answer choices C, D, or E. Do not assume that there are more "Yes" answers or more "No" answers.

Question: Could the following statement, if true, provide the basis for an adequate explanation of the result? An adequate explanation for this purpose does not need to be complete in all details.

1. The sales force at Smith Consumer Electronics primarily marketed to their distributors products that the salespeople had successfully sold in the past.
2. The change in management structure led to a deterioration in the quality of Hawthorne big-screen television sets.

Answers to practice statements 1 and 2

1. The correct answer is A. This statement can adequately explain the result because it indicates that the Smith sales force was efficient only at marketing products it had sold in the past; thus, these salespeople would be inadequate in marketing the new television systems. In fact, we anticipated in our analysis in Tactic 2 that something must have been wrong with the Smith marketing system for sales to decline. Certainly, nothing had changed at Hawthorne. The only other causative factor might be some general problem with Smith Consumer Electronics or something in the economy in general that would account for declining sales.
2. The correct answer is B. This statement cannot adequately explain the result because the management at Hawthorne that oversaw the production (and the quality) of the TV sets did not change. In the complexity of real life, of course, something adverse could have happened to the production facilities at Hawthorne. Given the limited information presented in the situation, however, this explanation does not seem adequate.

Do the relevant-to-explanation questions last

Tactic 4

These questions will be framed as follows:

Is the following statement, if true, relevant to some possible adequate explanation of the result? A statement is relevant to an explanation if it *either* supports *or* weakens that explanation.

On these questions, you will answer "Yes" if the statement presents information that either strengthens or weakens some adequate explanation of the result. You will answer "No" only if the statement appears completely irrelevant to any possible explanation of what occurred.

These questions are independent of the ones just presented and probably will not relate to the explanations of the events in the situation that were presented in the adequate-explanation questions. Also, relevant-to-explanation questions can be trickier, since they ask the test-taker to consider "some" adequate explanation of the events described. The catch is that the test-taker is not to consider "far-fetched" explanations. How to draw the line between the reasonable and the far-fetched is the aspect of these questions that presents the most difficulty.

Answer the question, for each statement, on the basis of the Smith-Hawthorne situation and result presented earlier.

Question: Is the following statement, if true, relevant to some possible adequate explanation of the result? A statement is relevant to an explanation if it *either* supports *or* weakens that explanation.

3. Sales of other products at Smith Consumer Electronics increased by 25 percent over the same three-year period.
4. At a rival company, Josvanger Electronics, sales of multimedia computer systems increased by 35 percent in the same years.

Answers to practice statements 3 and 4

3. The correct answer is A. One possible explanation of the decline in sales of Hawthorne big-screen TVs might be that Smith Consumer Electronics experienced a decline in the sales of all products during the three years in question. The information in statement 3 weakens, and so is relevant to, this hypothesis.
4. The correct answer is B. This statement is irrelevant since the sales of an entirely different product made by a different company are unlikely to have any effect on the sales of Hawthorne television sets. This is too far-fetched an explanation for the information presented.

Let's examine examples of other analysis of explanations questions taken from a recent GRE.

Directions: Preceding each group of numbered statements is a question that can be answered "Yes" or "No."

Answer this question separately for *each* statement in the group by marking answer choice A on your answer sheet for "Yes" or answer choice B for "No" next to the number for *each* statement. Be careful not to mark answer choices C, D, or E. Do not assume that there are more "Yes" answers or more "No" answers.

5–8

Situation: The damming of the Palman River partially flooded the West Kenyan Wildlife Preserve and caused overcrowding of the animal population. Therefore, one hundred of the giraffes and one hundred of the Zimmerman gazelles were moved to the much larger East Kenyan preserve, where identical species of lions and giraffes as in the West Kenyan preserve and one species of gazelles, Allen gazelles, were already living. The only difference in climate was that the East Kenyan preserve averaged about ten inches less rain per year. In both preserves the prevailing winds were from the east, and the terrain was mainly flat.

Result: After three years in the East Kenyan preserve, the population of Zimmerman gazelles there had diminished almost to the point of extinction.

Question: Is the following statement, if true, relevant to some possible adequate explanation of the result? A statement is relevant to an explanation if it *either* supports *or* weakens that explanation.

5. No zoo has succeeded in breeding Allen gazelles in captivity.
6. The weather was normal in East Kenya during the three years after the transfer.

Question: Could the following statement, if true, provide the basis for an adequate explanation of the result? An adequate explanation for this purpose does not need to be complete in all details.

7. The animals successfully rounded up for the transfer included primarily the weaker Zimmerman gazelles, which then lost out in competition for grass with the Allen gazelles.
8. Kenya's efforts to increase hydroelectric power caused the overcrowding in the West Kenyan preserve.

Answers to practice statements 5–8

5. The correct answer is B. This statement is irrelevant because it was Zimmerman gazelles, not Allen gazelles, that suffered the population decline, and because the captivity for the Zimmerman gazelles was not permanent, as in a zoo, but temporary, for the purposes of transportation.
6. The correct answer is A. This statement weakens, and so is relevant to, a possible explanation that there was a drought in the East Kenyan preserve

so severe and protracted that no species of gazelle was able to survive there.

7. The correct answer is A. This statement adequately explains the result, because it shows how the process of transfer worked to diminish the vitality of the stock of transferred Zimmerman gazelles, and how competition with the Allen gazelles was then sufficient to produce the result.

8. The correct answer is B. This statement does not adequately explain the result; rather, it explains the damming of the river, which is only a part of the situation leading up to the result. There is still an unexplained gap between the situation and the result, namely, the reason why Zimmerman gazelles failed to flourish in the new location.

9–12

Situation: Two friends start diets on the same day, each vowing to lose 20 pounds over the next six months. Both choose diet plans that have been advertised to be effective at reducing weight. The first person chooses Plan A, which stresses a reduction in fat intake combined with a moderate exercise program. The second person chooses Plan B, which provides diet supplement tablets to be taken daily to suppress the appetite. Both friends continue on these diet plans for six months.

Result: After a period of one year, the person who had followed Plan A had lost fifteen pounds, while the person who had used Plan B showed no loss in weight.

Question: Could the following statement, if true, provide the basis for an adequate explanation of the result? An adequate explanation for this purpose does not need to be complete in all details.

9. The person on Plan B switched to another diet plan at the end of the six-month period.

10. Only the person on Plan A continued with the diet plan after the end of the six-month period.

Question: Is the following statement, if true, relevant to some possible explanation of the result? A statement is relevant to an explanation if it *either* supports *or* weakens that explanation.

11. Both friends joined a health club at the end of the six-month period.

12. Scientific research has shown that the supplements used in Plan B are effective only over a short period of time.

Answers to practice statements 9–12

9. The correct answer is B. This statement does not adequately explain the result because we are told nothing about the effectiveness of the new diet plan or the length of time it was followed.

10. The correct answer is A. This statement adequately explains the result because the person on Plan A, having continued with the diet plan, could be expected to have lost weight, while the person on Plan B did not continue (note "Only" in statement 10 above).

11. The correct answer is B. This statement is irrele-

vant because it doesn't explain why one person lost weight and the other one didn't. We would need to know more about how much each person used the health club and perhaps other factors as well.

12. The correct answer is A. This statement strengthens, and so is relevant to, an explanation of why Plan B was not as effective as Plan A in causing weight reduction over a period of one year.

13–16

Situation: Salary negotiations between a major league baseball player and the owners of the team for which he plays often result in disputes, with the player asking for more than the owners are willing to pay. If the negotiations cannot be settled by the two parties, the case goes to arbitration. Smith, a catcher, asked for $500,000 for the next year, stating that his performance in the preceding year had been above average compared with the performances of other catchers. The owners offered $300,000, noting that Smith's performance in the past year had improved only slightly over his performance the year before.

Result: The arbitrator decided in favor of the owners.

Question: Could the following statement, if true, provide the basis for an adequate explanation of the result? An adequate explanation for this purpose does not need to be complete in all details.

13. The salary the owners offered was slightly above the average salary for other catchers in the league.

14. Although Smith had improved his performance only slightly over the preceding year, he still outperformed several other players on the team.

Question: Is the following statement, if true, relevant to some possible adequate explanation of the result? A statement is relevant to an explanation if it *either* supports *or* weakens that explanation.

15. The average salary for outfielders in the league was $750,000.

16. In another disputed case with the same team, the same arbitrator decided in favor of a third baseman.

Answers to practice statements 13–16

13. The correct answer is A. This statement adequately explains the result, given that Smith's performance was slightly above average for catchers and the salary offer matched this performance.

14. The correct answer is B. This statement does not adequately explain the result because the owners are comparing Smith's current performance with his previous performance and are not judging it against the performances of other players on the team.

15. The correct answer is B. This statement is irrelevant in the salary dispute since it involves average salaries for outfielders and not catchers.

16. The correct answer is A. This statement weakens, and so is relevant to, an explanation that the arbitrator was biased and tended to decide cases in favor of the owners of Smith's baseball team.

Practice Exercises

Directions: Each questions or group of questions is based on a passage or set of conditions. In answering some of the questions, it may be useful to draw a rough diagram. For each question, select the best answer choice given.

Questions 1-4

An office manager must assign offices to six staff members. The available offices, numbered 1-6 consecutively, are arranged in a row, and are separated only by six-foot-high dividers. Therefore, voices, sounds, and cigarette smoke readily pass from each c ffice to those on either side.

Miss Braun's work requires her to speak on the telephone frequently throughout the day.

Mr. White and Mr. Black often talk to one another in their work, and prefer to have adjacent offices.

Miss Green, the senior employee, is entitled to Office 5, which has the largest window.

Mr. Parker needs silence in the office(s) adjacent to his own.

Mr. Allen, Mr. White, and Mr. Parker all smoke. Miss Green is allergic to tobacco smoke and must have nonsmokers in the office(s) adjacent to her own.

Unless otherwise specified, all employees maintain silence while in their offices.

1. The best location for Mr. White is in Office

    (A) 1   (B) 2   (C) 3   (D) 4   (E) 6

2. The best employee to occupy the office furthest from Mr. Black would be

    (A) Mr. Allen
    (B) Miss Braun
    (C) Miss Green
    (D) Mr. Parker
    (E) Mr. White

3. The three employees who smoke should be placed in Offices

    (A) 1, 2, and 3
    (B) 1, 2, and 4
    (C) 1, 2, and 6
    (D) 2, 3, and 4
    (E) 2, 3, and 6

4. Which of the following events, occurring one month after the assignment of offices, would be most likely to lead to a request for a change in office assignment by one or more employees?

    (A) Miss Braun's deciding that she needs silence in the office(s) adjacent to her own.
    (B) Mr. Black's contracting laryngitis.
    (C) Mr. Parker's giving up smoking.
    (D) Mr. Allen's taking over the duties formerly assigned to Miss Braun.
    (E) Miss Green's installing a noisy teletype machine in her office.

5. Excessive amounts of mercury in drinking water, associated with certain types of industrial pollution, have been shown to cause Hobson's disease. Island R. has an economy based entirely on subsistence-level agriculture; modern industry of any kind is unknown. The inhabitants of Island R. have an unusually high incidence of Hobson's disease.

    Which of the following can be validly inferred from the above statements?
    I.   Mercury in drinking water is actually perfectly safe.
    II. Mercury in drinking water must have sources other than industrial pollution.
    III. Hobson's disease must have causes other than mercury in drinking water.
    (A) II only
    (B) III only
    (C) I or III, but not both
    (D) II or III, but not both
    (E) II or III, or both

6. Those who oppose the new water project claim to have the best interests of this community at heart. Yet they are the same people who, only three years ago, opposed the building of the new state highway, which now provides half a million commuters with fast, easy motoring every day. What could be a better argument in favor of the water project?

    Which of the following statements is most like the argument above?

    (A) Those who oppose nuclear power are unable or simply unwilling to recognize the fact that the nuclear energy industry has a safety record unparalleled by that of any other industry.
    (B) The new gun control law is a misguided and dangerous proposal, which has been denounced by every sportsmen's club and gun-owner's association in the state.
    (C) We must fight the proposed antipornography statute, for its principal sponsors have voted against every major piece of women's rights legislation introduced in the last twenty years.
    (D) The polls show that over 60% of the concerned parents in the state favor the school bond issue; cast your vote with the concerned majority on election day.
    (E) The so-called tax reform bill now before the state senate must be defeated; its only true beneficiaries would be the wealthy corporations, which already pay too little in taxes.

Questions 7–11

The office staff of the XYZ Corporation presently consists of three bookeepers (A, B, and C) and five secretaries (D, E, F, G, and H). Management is planning to open a new office in another city using three secretaries and two book-keepers of the present staff. To do so they plan to separate certain individuals who do not function well together. The following guidelines were established to set up the new office:

1. Bookkeepers A and C are constantly finding fault with one another and should not be sent as a team to the new office.
2. C and E function well alone but not as a team. They should be separated.
3. D and G have not been on speaking terms for many months. They should not go together.
4. Since D and F have been competing for promotion, they should not be a team.

7. If A is to be moved as one of the bookkeepers, which of the following CANNOT be a possible working unit?

   (A) ABDEH
   (B) ABDGH
   (C) ABEFH
   (D) ABEGH
   (E) ABFGH

8. If C and F are moved to the new office, how many combinations are possible?

   (A) 1 (B) 2 (C) 3 (D) 4 (E) 5

9. If C is sent to the new office which member of the staff CANNOT go with C?

   (A) B (B) D (C) F (D) G (E) H

10. Under the guidelines developed, which of the following MUST go to the new office?

    (A) B (B) D (C) E (D) G (E) H

11. If D goes to the new office which of the following is (are) true?

    I.   C cannot go.
    II. A cannot go.
    III. H must also go.

    (A) I only
    (B) II only
    (C) I and II only
    (D) I and III only
    (E) I, II, and III

12. Fran: I want to stay out of Professor Caldwell's classes if I can. I've heard she's very strict when it comes to giving out the grades.

    Sid: That's not true. My friend Phil took her class year, and she gave him an A.

From the conversation above, it can be inferred that Sid interpreted Fran's statement to mean that Professor Caldwell

(A) makes unfair demands on her students
(B) only gives good grades to a few favored students
(C) has become increasingly strict in her grading over the past year
(D) gives out fewer good grades than most teachers in the department
(E) never gives out grades of A

13. The nursing shortage in this country is a phony one, caused by the concentration of nurses in the geo-graphical regions with the highest paid and most generous fringe benefits for nurses. In addition, the League of American Nurses has artificaly worsened the shortage by encouraging nursing schools to keep enrollments low in order to boost nurses' salaries to even higher levels.

All of the following statements, if true, would tend to WEAKEN the argument above except:

(A) Although nurses are paid less in Texas than in Connecticut, there are 35% more nurses in Texas than in Connecticut.
(B) Nationwide, the salaries of nurses have risen at a slower rate than inflation over the last ten years.
(C) The number of students who earned degrees in nursing last year was almost double the num-ber six years ago.
(D) Those areas of the country with the highest pay for nurses also have correspondingly higher living costs.
(E) The League of American Nurses has almost no influence on the policies of American nursing schools.

Questions 14–17

After months of talent searching for an administrative assistant to the president of the college the field of applicants has been narrowed down to five (A, B, C, D, and E). It was announced that the finalist would be cho-sen after a series of all-day group personal interviews were held. The examining committee agreed upon the following procedure:

1. The interviews will be held once a week.
2. Three candidates will appear at any all-day inter-view session.
3. Each candidate will appear at least once.
4. If it becomes necessary to call applicants for addi-tional interviews, no more than one such applicant should be asked to appear the next week.
5. Because of a detail in the written applications, it was agreed that whenever Candidate B appears, A should also be present.
6. Because of travel difficulties, it was agreed that C will appear for only one interview.

14. At the first interview, the following candidates appear: A, B, and D. Which of the following combinations can be called for the interview to be held the next week?

    (A) BCD (B) CDE (C) ABE
    (D) ABC (E) ADE

15. Which of the following is a possible sequence of combinations for interviews in two successive weeks?

    (A) ABC; BDE
    (B) ABD; ABE
    (C) ADE; ABC
    (D) BDE; ACD
    (E) CDE; ABC

16. If A, B, and D appear at the interview and D is called for an additional interview the following week, which two candidates may be asked to appear with D?

    I.   A
    II. B
    III. C
    IV. E

    (A) I and II
    (B) I and III only
    (C) II and III only
    (D) II and IV only
    (E) III and IV only

17. Which of the following correctly state(s) the procedure followed by the search committee?

    I.   After the second interview, all applicants have appeared at least once.
    II. The committee sees each applicant a second time.
    III. If a third session is held it is possible for all applicants to appear at least twice.

    (A) I only
    (B) II only
    (C) I and II only
    (D) III only
    (E) I and III only

Questions 18–21

To obtain a government post in the Republic of Malabar, you must either be a member of the ruling Independence Party or a personal associate of President Zamir.

Party members seeking a government post must either give a substantial donation in gold bullion to the party's campaign fund or make a televised speech denouncing President Zamir's political enemies.

Gold bullion may be purchased only at the National Bank, which does business only with those who have been certified as politically sound by the Minister of Justice.

Only those who either have been certified as politically sound by the Minister of Justice or have donated 300 hours of service to the Independence Party are allowed to make political speeches on television.

To become a personal associate of President Zamir, you must either give a substantial donation in gold bullion to the president's personal expense account or perform personal services for a member of his immediate family.

Before appointing a personal associate to a government post, President Zamir always checks to make sure that he or she has been certified as politically sound by the Minister of Justice.

18. Mr. Mizar is a member of the Independence Party. To obtain a government post, his next step must be to either

    (A) be certified as politically sound by the Minister of Justice, or give a substantial donation in gold bullion to the party's campaign fund
    (B) donate 300 hours of service to the Independence Party, or give a substantial donation in gold bullion to the president's personal expense account
    (C) be certified as politically sound by the Minister of Justice, or donate 300 hours of service to the party
    (D) perform personal services for a member of President Zamir's immediate family, or make a televised speech denouncing the president's political enemies
    (E) be certified as politically sound by the Minister of Justice, or become a personal associate of President Zamir

19. All those who wish to obtain government posts must

    I.   become personal associates of President Zamir
    II. be certified as politically sound by the Minister of Justice
    III. purchase gold bullion at the National Bank

    (A) I only
    (B) II only
    (C) III only
    (D) II and III only
    (E) Neither I, II, nor III

20. Mr. Razim has been certified as politically sound by the Minister of Justice. He may obtain a government post immediately only if he

    (A) has donated 300 hours of service to the Independence Party
    (B) is allowed to make political speeches on television
    (C) is a member of the Independence Party
    (D) is a personal associate of President Zamir
    (E) has purchased gold bullion at the National Bank

21. Becase of a financial crisis, the National Bank is closed indefinitely. Those who wish to obtain government posts during this period must

    (A) either perform some kind of services or make televised speeches denouncing President Zamir's political enemies
    (B) become members of the Independence Party
    (C) donate 300 hours of service to the Independence Party
    (D) become personal associates of President Zamir
    (E) either become members of the Independence Party or perform any services for the party

Questions 22 and 23

In a laboratory study, 160 rabbits in an experimental group were injected with Serum D, while 160 rabbits in a control group were injected with a harmless sugar solution. Within two weeks, 39% of the experimental group rabbits had contracted jungle fever, a highly contagious and usually fatal disease. Therefore, jungle fever must be caused by some substance similar to the substances found in Serum D.

22. The above argument would be most greatly strengthened if it were shown that

    (A) the normal rate of jungle fever among rabbits is less than 0.01%
    (B) 40% of the rabbits in the control group had also contracted jungle fever within two weeks
    (C) Serum D contains substances extracted from the root of a certain poisonous jungle wildflower
    (D) the blood of jungle fever victims invariably contains a high level of a certain toxic substance also found in Serum D
    (E) nearly all the rabbits who contracted jungle fever died within two days of the appearance of the first symptoms

23. The above argument would be most seriously weakened if it were shown that

    (A) none of the substances in Serum D occurs naturally in the habitats of most species of rabbit
    (B) the rabbits in the experimental group had been kept strictly isolated from one another
    (C) jungle fever is usually found only among victims of the bite of the South American Lesser Hooded Viper
    (D) the scientists administering the injections were unaware of the contents of the solutions they were using
    (E) one of the rabbits in the experimental group had had jungle fever prior to the start of the experiment

24. Now Mesa Electronics brings tomorrow's technology to today's home stereo. The same space-age circuitry used by the Wanderer spacecraft to send images of the most distant planets back to earth has been incorporated in the new Mesa X-2700 stereo system. If your home entertainment is important to you, why settle for an old-fashioned stereo system when the Mesa X-2700 is priced at only a few dollars more?

The most serious logical weakness of this argument is its failure to

    (A) provide technical data on the manufacturing specifications of the Mesa X-2700
    (B) show the relevance of space-age circuitry to the requirements of home stereo
    (C) specify the exact price difference between the Mesa X-2700 and old-fashioned stereo systems
    (D) acknowledge the contributions of scientists in the space program to the development of the advanced circuitry mentioned
    (E) explain the precise meaning of the technical terms used

Questions 25–28

Professor Kittredge's literature seminar includes students with varied tastes in poetry. All those in the seminar who enjoy the poetry of Browning also enjoy the poetry of Eliot. Those who enjoy the poetry of Eliot despise the poetry of Coleridge.
Some of those who enjoy the poetry of Eliot also enjoy the poetry of Auden.
All those who enjoy the poetry of Coleridge also enjoy the poetry of Donne.
Some of those who enjoy the poetry of Donne also enjoy the poetry of Eliot.
Some of those who enjoy the poetry of Auden despise the poetry of Coleridge.
All those who enjoy the poetry of Donne also enjoy the poetry of Frost.

25. Miss Garfield enjoys the poetry of Donne. Which of the following must be true?

    (A) She may or may not enjoy the poetry of Coleridge.
    (B) She does not enjoy the poetry of Browning.
    (C) She enjoys the poetry of Auden.
    (D) She does not enjoy the poetry of Eliot.
    (E) She enjoys the poetry of Coleridge.

26. Mr. Huxtable enjoys the poetry of Browning. He may also enjoy any of the following poets except

    (A) Auden
    (B) Coleridge
    (C) Donne
    (D) Eliot
    (E) Frost

27. Miss Inaguchi enjoys the poetry of Coleridge. Which of the following must be false?

    (A) She does not enjoy the poetry of Auden.
    (B) She enjoys the poetry of Donne.
    (C) She enjoys the poetry of Frost.
    (D) She does not enjoy the poetry of Browning.
    (E) She may enjoy the poetry of Eliot.

28. Based on the information provided, which of the following statements concerning the members of the seminar must be true?

    (A) All those who enjoy the poetry of Eliot also enjoy the poetry of Browning.
    (B) None of those who despise the poetry of Frost enjoy the poetry of Auden.
    (C) Some of those who enjoy the poetry of Auden despise the poetry of Coleridge.
    (D) None of those who enjoy the poetry of Browning despise the poetry of Donne.
    (E) Some of those who enjoy the poetry of Frost despise the poetry of Donne.

Questions 29–31

A certain city is served by six subway lines, designated by the letters A, B, and C, and the numbers 1, 2, and 3.
When it snows, morning service on the B line is delayed.
When it rains or snows, service on the A, 2, and 3 lines is delayed both morning and afternoon.
When the temperature drops below 30°F, afternoon service is cancelled on either the A line or the 3 line, but not both.
When the temperature rises above 90°F, afternoon service is cancelled on either the C line or the 3 line, but not both.
When service on the A line is delayed or cancelled, service on the C line, which connects with the A line, is delayed.
When service on the 3 line is cancelled, service on the B line, which connects with the 3 line, is delayed.

29. On January 10, with the temperature at 15°F, it snows all day. On how many lines will service be affected, including both morning and afternoon?

    (A) 2
    (B) 3
    (C) 4
    (D) 5
    (E) 6

30. On August 15, with the temperature at 97°F, it begins to rain at 1 P.M. What is the minimum number of lines on which service will be affected?

    (A) 2
    (B) 3
    (C) 4
    (D) 5
    (E) 6

31. On which of the following occasions would service on the greatest number of lines be disrupted?

    (A) A snowy afternoon with the temperature at 45° F
    (B) A snowy morning with the temperature at 45° F
    (C) A rainy morning with the temperature at 45° F
    (D) A snowy afternoon with the temperature at 20° F
    (E) A rainy afternoon with the temperature at 95° F

Questions 32–36

Seven candidates in a gubernatorial primary election are to speak at a voters' forum. They are named Johnson, Kelleher, Lindsay, Macmillan, Nevins, Oberlander, and Pankhurst, and currently hold the offices of lieutenant governor, attorney general, state comptroller, U.S. Senator, highway commissioner, county supervisor, and schools superintendent, though not necessarily in that order.
The third speaker will be the highway commissioner.
Macmillan, who is not the county supervisor, will speak after the speaker who immediately follows Nevins.
Johnson is the state comptroller.
The lieutenant governor will speak sixth.
The attorney general will speak immediately before the county supervisor.
Pankhurst will speak immediately after Oberlander and immediately before Kelleher.
Schools Superintendent Nevins will speak fifth.

32. The first speaker will be

    (A) Oberlander
    (B) the state comptroller
    (C) Pankhurst
    (D) the county supervisor
    (E) Lindsay

33. The speaker who immediately precedes Macmillan will be

    (A) the highway commissioner
    (B) Johnson
    (C) the lieutenant governor
    (D) Kelleher
    (E) the county supervisor

34. Which of the following correctly pairs a speaker with his or her current office?

    (A) Oberlander—U.S. Senator
    (B) Kelleher—highway commissioner
    (C) Lindsay—county supervisor
    (D) Pankhurst—lieutenant governor
    (E) Macmillan—attorney general

35. Before the forum, Pankhurst drops out of the race, while a new candidate, Quigley, enters the race. If Pankhurst is dropped from the forum, while Quigley is added in the slot immediately after Lindsay, the sixth speaker will be

    (A) Kelleher   (C) Nevins   (E) Macmillan
    (B) Johnson   (D) Quigley

36. If, in addition to the changes described in question 35, the highway commissioner and the U.S. Senator agree to exchange positions in the speaking schedule, which of the following will be true?

    (A) Macmillan will speak after Oberlander and before Johnson.
    (B) Kelleher will be the only candidate to speak after Lindsay.
    (C) There will be an equal number of speakers before and after Johnson.
    (D) Only one candidate will speak after Nevins and before Kelleher.
    (E) The first and last speakers will not be changed.

Questions 37–39

A certain baseball team has four pitchers, named Miller, Craig, Hook, and Mizell. Each of the four is best known for throwing one type of pitch: fastball, curve ball, slider, or screwball.

Each of the four also uses a particular style of delivery in pitching: overhand, three-quarter, sidearm, or underhand.

Hook is best known for throwing the slider.
Neither Craig nor Mizell uses a three-quarter style of delivery.
The pitcher who uses an underhand delivery is best known for throwing the fastball.
Mixell is best known for throwing the screwball.
Miller uses an overhand delivery.

37. Which of the following correctly matches a pitcher with his best-known pitch and his style of delivery?

    (A) Miller—curve ball—three-quarter
    (B) Hook—slider—side arm
    (C) Craig—fastball—underhand
    (D) Mizell—curve ball—underhand
    (E) Miller—screwball—sidearm

38. During a game, if the starting pitcher is ineffective, he will be replaced by another pitcher. All of the following are possible pitching changes except

    (A) the curve ball pitcher being replaced by the pitcher who uses an overhand delivery
    (B) the screwball pitcher being replaced by Hook
    (C) Miller being replaced by the fastball pitcher
    (D) the slider pitcher being replaced by the pitcher who uses a sidearm delivery
    (E) Craig being replaced by the curve ball pitcher

39. In a four-game series, the manager of the team decides to pitch the fastball pitcher first, the pitcher who uses a three-quarter delivery second, the curve ball pitcher third, and the pitcher who uses a sidearm delivery fourth. In which order will the pitchers appear?

    (A) Mizell, Craig, Miller, Hook
    (B) Craig, Hook, Miller, Mizell
    (C) Miller, Craig, Hook, Mizell
    (D) Craig, Miller, Mizell, Hook
    (E) Miller, Hook, Mizell, Craig

Questions 40 and 41

As President of the National Association of Widget Manufacturers, I oppose government handouts to private business. But the present program of federal aid to the widget industry must continue. This is not a handout but rather a system of moderate cash subsidies to enable our beleaguered industry to withstand the shocks of rising costs and high interest rates, and so continue to provide useful employment to thousands of U.S citizens.

40. The major logical weakness of the argument above is the fact that

    (A) the speaker is arguing against his own personal interest
    (B) it makes no attempt to explain the ultimate causes of rising costs and high interest rates
    (C) it draws no meaningful distinction between handouts and subsidies
    (D) it does not explain the significance of the widget industry for the U.S. economy as a whole
    (E) it offers no factual evidence to substantiate the claim that the widget industry is in danger

41. Which of the following persons would be most likely to disagree with the conclusions reached in the above argument?

    (A) The president of a medium-sized widget manufacturing firm
    (B) The patentee of a new device designed to make the widget obsolete
    (C) The federal administrator charged with coordinating the widget industry subsidy program
    (D) A congressional representative from a district containing several large widget manufacturing plants
    (E) The president of the national widget industry employees' union

42. Leafletting and speechmaking on government property should be outlawed. Radicals and fanatics have no right to use public property when peddling their unsavory views.

    The argument above is based on the assumption that

    (A) radicals and fanatics prefer using public property when disseminating their views
    (B) legal restrictions that apply to one group need not apply equally to all
    (C) the general public has a vested interest in the free exchange of varied political views
    (D) political activity that interferes with the orderly functioning of government should not be protected by law
    (E) all those who leaflet and make speeches on government property are radicals and fanatics

Answer Key

1.	C	12.	E	23.	E	33.	C
2.	D	13.	A	24.	B	34.	B
3.	A	14.	B	25.	A	35.	D
4.	D	15.	C	26.	B	36.	A
5.	E	16.	E	27.	E	37.	C
6.	C	17.	A	28.	C	38.	A
7.	B	18.	C	29.	D	39.	B
8.	A	19.	E	30.	C	40.	C
9.	B	20.	D	31.	B	41.	B
10.	A	21.	A	32.	A	42.	E
11.	D	22.	D				

Answer Explanations

1–4: Miss Green is definitely assigned to Office #5. Since no smoker may be near Miss Green, either Miss Braun or Mr. Black are the only ones that may be near #5. Mr. Black cannot go to #6 because he must be close to Mr. White. He must therefore take Office #4 and give Miss Braun #6. Mr. White may have #3 and be close to Mr. Black. Messrs. Allen and Parker have yet to be assigned. At this point the two vacancies are #1 and #2. Mr. Parker cannot be near Mr. White, who often talks to Mr. Black. Mr. Parker should have #1 and leave #2 for Mr. Allen. The assignment of offices may be summarized as follows:

OFFICE #	STAFF MEMBER
1	Mr. Parker
2	Mr. Allen
3	Mr. White
4	Mr. Black
5	Miss Green
6	Miss Braun

1. C. Observe summary chart.

2. D. Observe summary chart.

3. A. Observe summary chart.

4. D. Mr. Allen is a smoker and cannot be near Miss Green, who, because of seniority, must stay in #5. This would cause a complete change of assignments.

5. E. I is denied by the statement that some forms of mercury cause Hobson's disease. II mentions the mercury in drinking water that is associated with industrial pollution. It may be concluded that mercury may get into drinking water by some other means. III alludes to the fact that this island has no industrial wastes and yet has a high incidence of this disease.

6. C. The argument presented here against proposed legislation is based upon unrelated, earlier legislation. Linking the water project and the highway proposal is similar in logic to linking the antipornography proposal and the earlier women's rights legislation.

7–11: This summary with dotted lines indicates combinations to avoid:

BOOKKEEPERS → A B C

SECRETARIES → D E F G H

7. B. See item #3.

8. A. Since C is going, A cannot go, leaving B as the second bookkeeper. To have three secretaries, you cannot use E with C, leaving only D, F, G, and H. If D is used, F and G are ruled out. There is one and only one combination: F, G, and H with C and B.

9. B. If C goes you cannot use D. See explanation above.

10. A. Bookkeeper B has no limitations. A cannot go with C. D cannot go with F or G. E cannot go with C. Although H has no limitations, he could be left in the old office with a combination of E, F, and G. Another way of analyzing this question is to consider that to get two bookkeepers out of the three available ones, you must take either A or C but not both.

11. D. If D goes, the other two secretaries must be E and H. C cannot go with E. Therefore, A and B are the two bookkeepers.

12. E.   If the professor is strict about grades, she might possibly still make unfair demands (A) and also have favorites (B). It is possible that she acquired this tendency recently (C). It is possible that few of her students deserve good grades (D), but the fact that she NEVER gives out grades of A could quite possibly label her as being very strict when it comes to giving out grades.

13. A.   The statement in (A) may not weaken the argument. Texas is a much bigger, more heavily populated state than Connecticut. Even though there are 35% more nurses in Texas than Connecticut, the lower salary in Texas may still cause fewer nurses to go there than would otherwise go.

14. B.   According to procedure item #4, only one candidate may appear on two subsequent weeks.

15. C.   (A) violates item #5. (B) contradicts #4. (D) fails to consider #5. (E) does not take #6 into account.

16. E.   (A) is not correct; see item #4. (B) is not correct because of item #4. (C) and (D) contradict item #5.

17. A.   Since there are five applicants and three appear at each session, after the second session all applicants must have made an appearance (I).

18–21:   In solving this puzzle, a flowchart indicating the various steps which can lead to a government post in Malabar will be useful. It might look something like this:

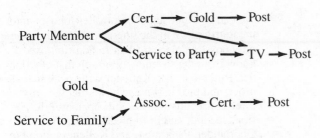

18. C.   As the chart shows, an Independence Party member has two possible routes to a government post. Therefore, as his next step, Mr. Mizar may either be certified by the Minister of Justice or donate 300 hours of service.

19. E.   To answer this question, check the chart to determine whether there is any step which is required by *all* routes to a government post. Since there is no such step, the correct answer is choice E. Note that statement II is not correct; it is possible for a party member to avoid having to be certified by the Minister of Justice by donating 300 hours of service to the party instead.

20. D.   As the chart shows, a personal associate of President Zamir who has been certified by the Minister of Justice is immediately eligible for a government post. Each of the other choices would leave some requirement unfulfilled. Choice E would be correct if Mr. Razim were known to be a party member; however, this is not stated in the question.

21. A.   According to this question, all routes to a government post which require the purchase of gold bullion have been blocked off. The only remaining routes are: the Party Member--Cert. or Services--TV route; and the Service--Assoc.--Cert. route. Both routes require either the performance of some kind of service or the making of a televised speech.

22. D.   The conclusion that some substance found in Serum D causes jungle fever would be greatly strengthened if the substance and the fever were invariably found together, as stated in choice E. Choice A does not help to establish the *cause* of the high rate of jungle fever in the experimental group. Choice B would weaken the original argument, not strengthen it. Choices C and E would neither weaken nor strengthen the argument.

23. E.   Since we are told that jungle fever is a "highly contagious" disease, choice E suggests an alternative explanation for the high rate of jungle fever in the experimental group. Choice A is irrelevant, since we have no idea whether rabbits in general or any particular species of rabbits are frequent victims of jungle fever in the first place. Choice B would strengthen the argument, not weaken it.

24. B.   The force of the argument presented in this advertisement lies in the attractiveness of the promise of "space-age circuitry" in the X-2700 stereo system. Choice B effectively points out the fundamental weakness of this appeal. All the other choices present features of the advertisement which might be regarded as flaws, but which are very minor in comparison to the flaw indicated in choice B.

25–28:   For a puzzle like this one, which relates various interlocking groups to one another, you'll need to draw a *circle diagram* showing the interrelationships of the groups named. Use solid lines to represent groups whose relationships are definitely established; use broken lines to represent groups about which some ambiguity exists. Your diagram should look more or less like this one:

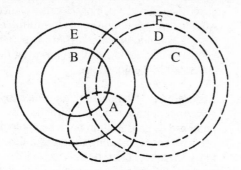

25. A.   If Miss Garfield is within the circle labeled D (lovers of Donne), she may or may not be within the circle labeled C (lovers of Coleridge). Each of the other statements presents as definite fact something which may or may not be true.

26. B.   As the diagram shows, the circle labeled B has no overlap with the circle labeled C. Therefore, there are no Browning-lovers who are also Coleridge-lovers. Browning-lovers may also enjoy Auden, Donne, or Frost; they *definitely* enjoy Eliot, since the circle labeled B is entirely within the circle labeled E.

27. E.   All of the choices are possibly true, with the exception of choice E. Since the circle labeled C and the circle labeled E have no overlap, Miss Inaguchi definitely does not enjoy the poetry of Eliot.

28. C.   Since some Auden-lovers are Eliot-lovers, and since all Eliot-lovers are Coleridge-despisers, there must be some Auden-lovers who are Coleridge-despisers.

29. D.   As shown by the second, third, and sixth statements listed, the A, B, C, 2, and 3 lines will all be affected.

30. C.   The 97° temperature will cancel afternoon service on either the C or the 3 line. The rain will delay service on the A, 2, and 3 lines. When service on the A line is delayed, service on the C line is delayed. Therefore the C line and the 3 line are affected either way, and the delays on the A and the 2 lines raise to four the minimum number of lines affected.

31. B.   On a snowy morning with the temperature at 45° F, the A, B, C, 2, and 3 lines will all be affected. Under each of the other conditions mentioned, only four lines will be affected.

32–36:   Draw a chart providing spaces for the initials of the seven speakers along with abbreviations for the seven offices they hold. Start by filling in the most definite information provided, which is found in the second, fifth, and eighth paragraphs. Your chart now looks like this:

SPEAKER	OFFICE
1.	
2.	
3.	H.C.
4.	
5. N.	S.S.
6.	L.G.
7.	

The third paragraph tells us that Macmillan should be placed in the seventh spot in the line-up. The sixth paragraph tells us that the attorney general will speak immediately before the county supervisor; however, looking at the chart, we see that the only two *consecutive* places still open are the first and the second, so that these two speakers must fit into those two openings. The chart now looks like this:

SPEAKER	OFFICE
1.	A.G.
2.	C.S.
3.	H.C.
4.	
5. N.	S.S.
6.	L.G.
7. M.	

We can now put state comptroller Johnson into the fourth place in the line-up, since this is the only possible place for her. In addition, we know from the seventh paragraph that Oberlander, Pankhurst, and Kelleher will speak in that order, and the chart now shows that the only three consecutive places still open are, the first, second, and third places. Therefore, Oberlander, Pankhurst, and Kelleher belong in those spots. By elimination we can fill in the remaining slots. The questions are now easy.

32. A.   Read directly from the chart

33. C.   Read directly from the chart.

34. B.   Read directly from the chart.

35. D.   If Pankhurst, in the second slot, drops out, those who originally were scheduled to speak third, fourth, fifth, sixth, and seventh will now speak second, third, fourth, fifth, and sixth. If Quigley is to speak following Lindsay, who is now the fifth speaker, Quigley will speak sixth.

36. A. Choice A is correct, since Macmillan will now be the second speaker, and will follow Oberlander and precede Johnson. Choice B is wrong, because Quigley will also speak after Lindsay (see question 35). Choice C is wrong, because only two speakers will precede Johnson but four will follow her. Choice D is wrong, because Lindsay and Quigley will both follow Nevins and precede Kelleher. And choice E is false because the last speaker was changed from Macmillan to Kelleher.

37–39: For this puzzle, you'll need a three-column chart listing pitchers, pitches, and styles of delivery. The information given in the second, fourth, fifth, and sixth paragraphs can be easily charted as follows:

PITCHER	PITCH	DELIVERY
H.	Sl.	
	F.	U.
Miz.	Sc.	
Mil.		O.

Now, using the process of elimination and the information in the third paragraph, you can complete the chart like this:

PITCHER	PITCH	DELIVERY
H.	Sl.	T.
C.	F.	U.
Miz.	Sc.	S.
Mil.	C.	O.

All three questions can be answered by referring to this chart.

37. C. Read directly from the chart.

38. A. Choice A is impossible, because the curve ball pitcher and the pitcher who uses an overhand delivery are one and the same. This difficulty does not apply to any of the other choices.

39. B. Read directly from the chart.

40. C. The only difference between the "handouts" which the author deplores and the "subsidies" he favors is the words used to describe them. In one case, the words used are negatively loaded; in the other, they are positive, or at least neutral. Choice A is directly contrary to fact. Choices B and C are true, but of minor importance. Choice D is probably false; the reference in the argument to the thousands of widget industry jobs does indicate the significance of the industry for the U.S. economy.

41. B. The persons named in choices A, C, D, and E would all have an interest in the continuation of the widget industry subsidy program. The person named in choice B, however, would oppose outside help to an industry with which he or she is in direct competition.

42. E. In this argument, the first sentence states the conclusion; the second sentence states the evidence. However, there is no real connection between the two statements unless the assumption given in choice E is accepted as valid.

13 Test Yourself—Five Practice Tests

■ **5 Full-Length Model Tests**
■ **Answer Keys**
■ **Answer Explanations**

This chapter is designed to give you further experience in what to expect on the verbal, quantitative, and analytical ability sections of the Graduate Record Examination General Test. These tests should serve as a basis for analysis, which for some may signal the need for further drill before taking the other tests, and for others, may indicate that preparation for this part of the test is adequate. For the best results, take these tests only after reviewing your weak areas, found as a result of completing our Diagnostic Test.

Simulate actual test conditions as you take each test. Find a quiet place to work. Keep an accurate record of your time. If you complete a section before the suggested time has elapsed, check your work and do not start another section. Don't be worried, however, if you are not able to answer all questions in the allotted time. This may also occur on the actual test. No one is expected to know the answers to all questions on an aptitude test. Read the questions carefully. Work carefully and as rapidly as possible. Do not spend too much time on questions that

seem difficult for you. If time permits, go back to the ones you left out.

Remember: no penalty is imposed for guessing. Your score is determined by the number of correct answers. Therefore, it is to your advantage to answer every question—even if you have to guess. Of course, you better your odds of answering correctly if you eliminate as many incorrect answer choices as you can and then guess from the remaining choices.

After you have devoted the specified time allowed for each section of a model examination, refer to the correct answers furnished, determine your raw score, judge your progress, and plan further study. You should then carefully study the explanations for the correct answers of those questions that gave you difficulty. If you find that a particular topic needs further review, refer to the earlier part of the book where this topic is treated before attempting to take the next model test. If you follow this procedure, by the time you complete the last test in this chapter you will feel confident about your success.

Answer Sheet – MODEL TEST 1

Start with number 1 for each new section.
If a section has fewer than 38 questions, leave the extra spaces blank.

Section 1

1. Ⓐ Ⓑ Ⓒ Ⓓ Ⓔ
2. Ⓐ Ⓑ Ⓒ Ⓓ Ⓔ
3. Ⓐ Ⓑ Ⓒ Ⓓ Ⓔ
4. Ⓐ Ⓑ Ⓒ Ⓓ Ⓔ
5. Ⓐ Ⓑ Ⓒ Ⓓ Ⓔ
6. Ⓐ Ⓑ Ⓒ Ⓓ Ⓔ
7. Ⓐ Ⓑ Ⓒ Ⓓ Ⓔ
8. Ⓐ Ⓑ Ⓒ Ⓓ Ⓔ
9. Ⓐ Ⓑ Ⓒ Ⓓ Ⓔ
10. Ⓐ Ⓑ Ⓒ Ⓓ Ⓔ

11. Ⓐ Ⓑ Ⓒ Ⓓ Ⓔ
12. Ⓐ Ⓑ Ⓒ Ⓓ Ⓔ
13. Ⓐ Ⓑ Ⓒ Ⓓ Ⓔ
14. Ⓐ Ⓑ Ⓒ Ⓓ Ⓔ
15. Ⓐ Ⓑ Ⓒ Ⓓ Ⓔ
16. Ⓐ Ⓑ Ⓒ Ⓓ Ⓔ
17. Ⓐ Ⓑ Ⓒ Ⓓ Ⓔ
18. Ⓐ Ⓑ Ⓒ Ⓓ Ⓔ
19. Ⓐ Ⓑ Ⓒ Ⓓ Ⓔ
20. Ⓐ Ⓑ Ⓒ Ⓓ Ⓔ

21. Ⓐ Ⓑ Ⓒ Ⓓ Ⓔ
22. Ⓐ Ⓑ Ⓒ Ⓓ Ⓔ
23. Ⓐ Ⓑ Ⓒ Ⓓ Ⓔ
24. Ⓐ Ⓑ Ⓒ Ⓓ Ⓔ
25. Ⓐ Ⓑ Ⓒ Ⓓ Ⓔ
26. Ⓐ Ⓑ Ⓒ Ⓓ Ⓔ
27. Ⓐ Ⓑ Ⓒ Ⓓ Ⓔ
28. Ⓐ Ⓑ Ⓒ Ⓓ Ⓔ
29. Ⓐ Ⓑ Ⓒ Ⓓ Ⓔ
30. Ⓐ Ⓑ Ⓒ Ⓓ Ⓔ

31. Ⓐ Ⓑ Ⓒ Ⓓ Ⓔ
32. Ⓐ Ⓑ Ⓒ Ⓓ Ⓔ
33. Ⓐ Ⓑ Ⓒ Ⓓ Ⓔ
34. Ⓐ Ⓑ Ⓒ Ⓓ Ⓔ
35. Ⓐ Ⓑ Ⓒ Ⓓ Ⓔ
36. Ⓐ Ⓑ Ⓒ Ⓓ Ⓔ
37. Ⓐ Ⓑ Ⓒ Ⓓ Ⓔ
38. Ⓐ Ⓑ Ⓒ Ⓓ Ⓔ

Section 2

1. Ⓐ Ⓑ Ⓒ Ⓓ Ⓔ
2. Ⓐ Ⓑ Ⓒ Ⓓ Ⓔ
3. Ⓐ Ⓑ Ⓒ Ⓓ Ⓔ
4. Ⓐ Ⓑ Ⓒ Ⓓ Ⓔ
5. Ⓐ Ⓑ Ⓒ Ⓓ Ⓔ
6. Ⓐ Ⓑ Ⓒ Ⓓ Ⓔ
7. Ⓐ Ⓑ Ⓒ Ⓓ Ⓔ
8. Ⓐ Ⓑ Ⓒ Ⓓ Ⓔ
9. Ⓐ Ⓑ Ⓒ Ⓓ Ⓔ
10. Ⓐ Ⓑ Ⓒ Ⓓ Ⓔ

11. Ⓐ Ⓑ Ⓒ Ⓓ Ⓔ
12. Ⓐ Ⓑ Ⓒ Ⓓ Ⓔ
13. Ⓐ Ⓑ Ⓒ Ⓓ Ⓔ
14. Ⓐ Ⓑ Ⓒ Ⓓ Ⓔ
15. Ⓐ Ⓑ Ⓒ Ⓓ Ⓔ
16. Ⓐ Ⓑ Ⓒ Ⓓ Ⓔ
17. Ⓐ Ⓑ Ⓒ Ⓓ Ⓔ
18. Ⓐ Ⓑ Ⓒ Ⓓ Ⓔ
19. Ⓐ Ⓑ Ⓒ Ⓓ Ⓔ
20. Ⓐ Ⓑ Ⓒ Ⓓ Ⓔ

21. Ⓐ Ⓑ Ⓒ Ⓓ Ⓔ
22. Ⓐ Ⓑ Ⓒ Ⓓ Ⓔ
23. Ⓐ Ⓑ Ⓒ Ⓓ Ⓔ
24. Ⓐ Ⓑ Ⓒ Ⓓ Ⓔ
25. Ⓐ Ⓑ Ⓒ Ⓓ Ⓔ
26. Ⓐ Ⓑ Ⓒ Ⓓ Ⓔ
27. Ⓐ Ⓑ Ⓒ Ⓓ Ⓔ
28. Ⓐ Ⓑ Ⓒ Ⓓ Ⓔ
29. Ⓐ Ⓑ Ⓒ Ⓓ Ⓔ
30. Ⓐ Ⓑ Ⓒ Ⓓ Ⓔ

31. Ⓐ Ⓑ Ⓒ Ⓓ Ⓔ
32. Ⓐ Ⓑ Ⓒ Ⓓ Ⓔ
33. Ⓐ Ⓑ Ⓒ Ⓓ Ⓔ
34. Ⓐ Ⓑ Ⓒ Ⓓ Ⓔ
35. Ⓐ Ⓑ Ⓒ Ⓓ Ⓔ
36. Ⓐ Ⓑ Ⓒ Ⓓ Ⓔ
37. Ⓐ Ⓑ Ⓒ Ⓓ Ⓔ
38. Ⓐ Ⓑ Ⓒ Ⓓ Ⓔ

Section 3

1. Ⓐ Ⓑ Ⓒ Ⓓ Ⓔ
2. Ⓐ Ⓑ Ⓒ Ⓓ Ⓔ
3. Ⓐ Ⓑ Ⓒ Ⓓ Ⓔ
4. Ⓐ Ⓑ Ⓒ Ⓓ Ⓔ
5. Ⓐ Ⓑ Ⓒ Ⓓ Ⓔ
6. Ⓐ Ⓑ Ⓒ Ⓓ Ⓔ
7. Ⓐ Ⓑ Ⓒ Ⓓ Ⓔ
8. Ⓐ Ⓑ Ⓒ Ⓓ Ⓔ
9. Ⓐ Ⓑ Ⓒ Ⓓ Ⓔ
10. Ⓐ Ⓑ Ⓒ Ⓓ Ⓔ

11. Ⓐ Ⓑ Ⓒ Ⓓ Ⓔ
12. Ⓐ Ⓑ Ⓒ Ⓓ Ⓔ
13. Ⓐ Ⓑ Ⓒ Ⓓ Ⓔ
14. Ⓐ Ⓑ Ⓒ Ⓓ Ⓔ
15. Ⓐ Ⓑ Ⓒ Ⓓ Ⓔ
16. Ⓐ Ⓑ Ⓒ Ⓓ Ⓔ
17. Ⓐ Ⓑ Ⓒ Ⓓ Ⓔ
18. Ⓐ Ⓑ Ⓒ Ⓓ Ⓔ
19. Ⓐ Ⓑ Ⓒ Ⓓ Ⓔ
20. Ⓐ Ⓑ Ⓒ Ⓓ Ⓔ

21. Ⓐ Ⓑ Ⓒ Ⓓ Ⓔ
22. Ⓐ Ⓑ Ⓒ Ⓓ Ⓔ
23. Ⓐ Ⓑ Ⓒ Ⓓ Ⓔ
24. Ⓐ Ⓑ Ⓒ Ⓓ Ⓔ
25. Ⓐ Ⓑ Ⓒ Ⓓ Ⓔ
26. Ⓐ Ⓑ Ⓒ Ⓓ Ⓔ
27. Ⓐ Ⓑ Ⓒ Ⓓ Ⓔ
28. Ⓐ Ⓑ Ⓒ Ⓓ Ⓔ
29. Ⓐ Ⓑ Ⓒ Ⓓ Ⓔ
30. Ⓐ Ⓑ Ⓒ Ⓓ Ⓔ

31. Ⓐ Ⓑ Ⓒ Ⓓ Ⓔ
32. Ⓐ Ⓑ Ⓒ Ⓓ Ⓔ
33. Ⓐ Ⓑ Ⓒ Ⓓ Ⓔ
34. Ⓐ Ⓑ Ⓒ Ⓓ Ⓔ
35. Ⓐ Ⓑ Ⓒ Ⓓ Ⓔ
36. Ⓐ Ⓑ Ⓒ Ⓓ Ⓔ
37. Ⓐ Ⓑ Ⓒ Ⓓ Ⓔ
38. Ⓐ Ⓑ Ⓒ Ⓓ Ⓔ

Section 4

1. A B C D E	11. A B C D E	21. A B C D E	31. A B C D E
2. A B C D E	12. A B C D E	22. A B C D E	32. A B C D E
3. A B C D E	13. A B C D E	23. A B C D E	33. A B C D E
4. A B C D E	14. A B C D E	24. A B C D E	34. A B C D E
5. A B C D E	15. A B C D E	25. A B C D E	35. A B C D E
6. A B C D E	16. A B C D E	26. A B C D E	36. A B C D E
7. A B C D E	17. A B C D E	27. A B C D E	37. A B C D E
8. A B C D E	18. A B C D E	28. A B C D E	38. A B C D E
9. A B C D E	19. A B C D E	29. A B C D E	
10. A B C D E	20. A B C D E	30. A B C D E	

Section 5

1. A B C D E	11. A B C D E	21. A B C D E	31. A B C D E
2. A B C D E	12. A B C D E	22. A B C D E	32. A B C D E
3. A B C D E	13. A B C D E	23. A B C D E	33. A B C D E
4. A B C D E	14. A B C D E	24. A B C D E	34. A B C D E
5. A B C D E	15. A B C D E	25. A B C D E	35. A B C D E
6. A B C D E	16. A B C D E	26. A B C D E	36. A B C D E
7. A B C D E	17. A B C D E	27. A B C D E	37. A B C D E
8. A B C D E	18. A B C D E	28. A B C D E	38. A B C D E
9. A B C D E	19. A B C D E	29. A B C D E	
10. A B C D E	20. A B C D E	30. A B C D E	

Section 6

1. A B C D E	11. A B C D E	21. A B C D E	31. A B C D E
2. A B C D E	12. A B C D E	22. A B C D E	32. A B C D E
3. A B C D E	13. A B C D E	23. A B C D E	33. A B C D E
4. A B C D E	14. A B C D E	24. A B C D E	34. A B C D E
5. A B C D E	15. A B C D E	25. A B C D E	35. A B C D E
6. A B C D E	16. A B C D E	26. A B C D E	36. A B C D E
7. A B C D E	17. A B C D E	27. A B C D E	37. A B C D E
8. A B C D E	18. A B C D E	28. A B C D E	38. A B C D E
9. A B C D E	19. A B C D E	29. A B C D E	
10. A B C D E	20. A B C D E	30. A B C D E	

Section 7

1. A B C D E	11. A B C D E	21. A B C D E	31. A B C D E
2. A B C D E	12. A B C D E	22. A B C D E	32. A B C D E
3. A B C D E	13. A B C D E	23. A B C D E	33. A B C D E
4. A B C D E	14. A B C D E	24. A B C D E	34. A B C D E
5. A B C D E	15. A B C D E	25. A B C D E	35. A B C D E
6. A B C D E	16. A B C D E	26. A B C D E	36. A B C D E
7. A B C D E	17. A B C D E	27. A B C D E	37. A B C D E
8. A B C D E	18. A B C D E	28. A B C D E	38. A B C D E
9. A B C D E	19. A B C D E	29. A B C D E	
10. A B C D E	20. A B C D E	30. A B C D E	

MODEL TEST 1

Directions: Each sentence below has one or two blanks, each blank indicating that something has been omitted. Beneath the sentence are five lettered words or sets of words. Choose the word or set of words for each blank that best fits the meaning of the sentence as a whole.

1. To the cynic, there are no wholly altruistic, unselfish acts; every human deed is ------- an ulterior selfish motive.

    (A) independent of
    (B) emulated by
    (C) disguised as
    (D) founded upon
    (E) similar to

2. Like the theory of evolution, the big-bang model of the universe's formation has undergone modification and -------, but it has ------- all serious challenges.

    (A) alteration...confirmed
    (B) refinement...resisted
    (C) transformation...ignored
    (D) evaluation...acknowledged
    (E) refutation...misdirected

3. We have in America a ------- speech that is neither American, Oxford English, nor colloquial English, but ------- of all three.

    (A) motley...an enhancement
    (B) hybrid...a combination
    (C) nasal...a blend
    (D) mangled...a medley
    (E) formal...a patchwork

4. It has been said that printing does as much harm as good, since it gives us bad books as well as good ones and ------- falsehood and error no less than -------.

    (A) displays...folly
    (B) flaunts...ignorance
    (C) betrays...treachery
    (D) demonstrates...pedantry
    (E) propagates...knowledge

5. A university training enables a graduate to see things as they are, to go right to the point, to disentangle a ------- of thought.

    (A) line
    (B) strand
    (C) mass
    (D) plethora
    (E) skein

6. Rather than portraying Joseph II as a radical reformer whose reign was strikingly enlightened, the play *Amadeus* depicts him as ------- thinker, too wedded to orthodox theories of musical composition to appreciate an artist of Mozart's genius.

    (A) a revolutionary
    (B) an idiosyncratic
    (C) a politic
    (D) a doctrinaire
    (E) an iconoclastic

7. While ------- in his own approach to philosophy, the scholar was, illogically, ------- his colleagues who averred that a seeker of knowledge must be free to select such doctrines as pleased him in every school.

    (A) indiscriminate...supportive of
    (B) eclectic...intolerant of
    (C) speculative...cordial to
    (D) problematical...dismissive of
    (E) theoretic...impatient with

Directions: In each of the following questions, a related pair of words or phrases is followed by five lettered pairs of words or phrases. Select the lettered pair that best expresses a relationship similar to that expressed in the original pair.

8. FANS : BLEACHERS::
    (A) cheerleaders : pompoms
    (B) audience : seats
    (C) team : goalposts
    (D) conductor : podium
    (E) referee : decision

9. AUGER : BORE::
    (A) awl : flatten
    (B) bit : grind
    (C) plane : smooth
    (D) scythe : mash
    (E) mallet : pierce

10. CHAMELEON : HERPETOLOGIST::
    (A) fungi : ecologist
    (B) salmon : ichthyologist
    (C) mongoose : ornithologist
    (D) oriole : virologist
    (E) aphid : etymologist

11. SCURRY : MOVE::
    (A) chant : sing
    (B) chatter : talk
    (C) carry : lift
    (D) sleep : drowse
    (E) limp : walk

12. SONG : CYCLE::
    (A) waltz : dance
    (B) tune : arrangement
    (C) sonnet : sequence
    (D) agenda : meeting
    (E) cadenza : aria

13. OBDURATE : FLEXIBILITY::
    (A) accurate : perception
    (B) turbid : roughness
    (C) principled : fallibility
    (D) diaphanous : transparency
    (E) adamant : submissiveness

14. SARTORIAL : TAILOR::
    (A) pictorial : spectator
    (B) thespian : designer
    (C) histrionic : singer
    (D) rhetorical : questioner
    (E) terpsichorean : dancer

15. SKIRT : ISSUE::
    (A) vest : interest
    (B) rig : wager
    (C) dodge : encounter
    (D) sweep : election
    (E) mask : purpose

16. FEUD : ACRIMONY::
    (A) scuffle : confusion
    (B) crusade : heresy
    (C) duel : brevity
    (D) scrimmage : sparring
    (E) siege : vulnerability

Directions: Each passage in this group is followed by questions based on its content. After reading a passage, choose the best answer to each question. Answer all questions following a passage on the basis of what is stated or implied in the passage.

(This passage was written prior to 1950.)

In the long run a government will always encroach upon freedom to the extent to which it has the power to do so; this is almost a natural law of politics, since, whatever the intentions of the people who exercise political power, the sheer momentum of government leads to a constant pressure upon the liberties of the citizen. But in many countries society has responded by throwing up its own defenses in the shape of social classes or organized corporations which, enjoying economic power and popular support, have been able to set limits to the scope of action of the executive. Such, for example, in England was the origin of all our liberties—won from government by the stand first of the feudal nobility, then of churches and political parties, and latterly of trade unions, commercial organizations, and the societies for promoting various causes. Even in European lands which were arbitrarily ruled, the powers of the monarchy, though absolute in theory, were in their exercise checked in a similar fashion. Indeed the fascist dictatorships of today are the first truly tyrannical governments which Western Europe has known for centuries, and they have been rendered possible only because on coming to power they destroyed all forms of social organization which were in any way rivals to the state.

17. The passage can most accurately be described as a discussion of the

    (A) limited powers of monarchies
    (B) ideal of liberal government
    (C) functions of trade unions
    (D) ruthless methods of dictators
    (E) safeguards of individual liberty

18. According to the passage, the natural relationship between government and individual liberty is one of

    (A) marked indifference
    (B) secret collusion
    (C) inherent opposition
    (D) moderate complicity
    (E) fundamental interdependence

19. Fascist dictatorships differ from monarchies of recent times in

    (A) setting limits to their scope of action
    (B) effecting results by sheer momentum
    (C) rivaling the state in power
    (D) exerting constant pressure on liberties
    (E) eradicating people's organizations

20. The passage suggests which of the following about fascist dictatorships?

    (A) They represent a more efficient form of the executive.
    (B) Their rise to power came about through an accident of history.
    (C) They mark a regression to earlier despotic forms of government.
    (D) Despite superficial dissimilarities, they are in essence like absolute monarchies.
    (E) They maintain their dominance by rechanneling opposing forces in new directions.

Yet, while Darwinian theory extends its domain, some of its cherished postulates are slipping, or at least losing their generality. The "modern synthesis," the contemporary version of Darwinism that
(5) has reigned for thirty years, took the model of adaptive gene substitution within local populations as an adequate account, by accumulation and extension, of life's entire history. The model may work well in its empirical domain of minor, local, adap-
(10) tive adjustment; populations of the moth *Biston betularia* did turn black, by substitution of a single gene, as a selected response for decreased visibility on trees that had been blackened by industrial soot. But is the origin of a new species simply this pro-
(15) cess extended to more genes and greater effect? Are larger evolutionary trends within major lineages just a further accumulation of sequential adaptive changes?

Many evolutionists (myself included) are begin-
(20) ning to challenge this synthesis and to assert the hierarchical view that different levels of evolutionary change often reflect different kinds of causes. Minor adjustment within populations may be sequential and adaptive. But speciation may occur by
(25) major chromosomal changes that establish sterility with other species for reasons unrelated to adaptation. Evolutionary trends may represent a kind of higher-level selection upon essentially static species themselves, not the slow and steady alteration of a
(30) single large population through untold ages.

Before the modern synthesis, many biologists (see Bateson, 1922, in bibliography) expressed confusion and depression because the proposed mechanisms of evolution at different levels seemed
(35) contradictory enough to preclude a unified science. After the modern synthesis, the notion spread (amounting almost to a dogma among its less thoughtful lieutenants) that all evolution could be reduced to the basic Darwinism of gradual, adap-
(40) tive change within local populations. I think that we are now pursuing a fruitful path between the anarchy of Bateson's day and the restriction of view imposed by the modern synthesis. The modern synthesis works in its appropriate arena, but the same
(45) Darwinian processes of mutation and selection may operate in strikingly different ways at higher domains in a hierarchy of evolutionary levels. I think that we may hope for uniformity of causal agents, hence a single, general theory with a Darwinian
(50) core. But we must reckon with a multiplicity of mechanisms that preclude the explanation of higher level phenomena by the model of adaptive gene substitution favored for the lowest level.

At the basis of all this ferment lies nature's irre-
(55) ducible complexity. Organisms are not billiard balls, propelled by simple and measurable external forces to predictable new positions on life's pool table. Sufficiently complex systems have greater richness. Organisms have a history that constrains
(60) their future in myriad, subtle ways. Their complexity of form entails a host of functions incidental to whatever pressures of natural selection superintended the initial construction. Their intricate and largely unknown pathways of embryonic develop-
(65) ment guarantee that simple inputs (minor changes

in timing, for example) may be translated into marked and surprising changes in output (the adult organism).

Charles Darwin chose to close his great book
(70) with a striking comparison that expresses this richness. He contrasted the simpler system of planetary motion, and its result of endless, static cycling, with the complexity of life and its wondrous and unpredictable change through the ages:

(75)   There is grandeur in this view of life, with its several powers, having been originally breathed into a few forms or into one; and that, whilst this planet has gone cycling on according to the fixed law of gravity, from so simple a beginning endless
(80)   forms most beautiful and most wonderful have been, and are being, evolved.

21. According to the author, many contemporary evolutionists find the Darwinian synthesis

(A) wholly unfounded
(B) overly restrictive
(C) essentially contradictory
(D) sadly confusing
(E) strikingly productive

22. In asserting the complexity of nature, the author refers to billiard balls on life's pool table (lines 55–58) as

(A) an illustration of the unpredictable changes of nature
(B) an instance of confusion and mobility
(C) an example of a relatively uncomplicated system
(D) an application of the fixed law of gravity
(E) an accurate model of genetic change

23. It can be inferred that the paragraph immediately preceding this passage most likely discussed

(A) the absence of a unified theory of evolution
(B) individuals challenging the Darwinian synthesis
(C) the expansion of evolutionary theory into new realms
(D) experimental methods of genetic substitution
(E) the place of genetics in the study of natural history

24. With which of the following statements regarding Charles Darwin would the author be most likely to agree?

I.   Darwin left his early successors in some confusion as to the universal applicability of his evolutionary theory.
II. Darwin experienced periods of despondency caused by the thoughtlessness of his lieutenants.
III. Darwin contrasted the simplicity and calculability of planetary cycles favorably to the diversity and unpredictability of living creatures.

(A) I only   (B) III only
(C) I and II only   (D) I and III only
(E) I, II, and III

25. The author does all of the following EXCEPT

   (A) denounce an adversary
   (B) pose a question
   (C) provide an example
   (D) use a metaphor
   (E) refer to an authority

26. Which of the following phrases from the passage best categorizes the transformation undergone by certain members of *Biston betularia?*

   (A) "larger evolutionary trends within major lineages" (line 16)
   (B) "minor adjustment within populations" (line 23)
   (C) "higher-level selection" (line 28)
   (D) "irreducible complexity" (lines 54–55)
   (E) "endless, static cycling" (lines 72–73)

27. The passage supplies information for answering which of the following questions?

   (A) How did the modern synthesis contradict basic Darwinism?
   (B) What effect did industrial pollution have on certain moth populations?
   (C) How did Bateson's theories anticipate the ideas of the modern synthesis?
   (D) What sort of living creature is most likely to evolve into a new species?
   (E) Are instances of speciation less common than the modern synthesis would indicate?

Directions: Each question below consists of a word printed in capital letters, followed by five lettered words or phrases. Choose the lettered word or phrase that is most nearly opposite in meaning to the words in capital letters.

Since some of the questions require you to distinguish fine shades of meaning, be sure to consider all the choices before deciding which one is best.

28. DISREGARD:
   (A) admit
   (B) evade
   (C) heed
   (D) improve
   (E) prevent

29. VERACITY:
   (A) uncertainty
   (B) mendacity
   (C) plausibility
   (D) intuition
   (E) opposition

30. BEDECK:
   (A) erect
   (B) awake
   (C) isolate
   (D) cleanse
   (E) strip

31. SPURIOUS:
   (A) cautious
   (B) fantastic
   (C) modest
   (D) genuine
   (E) pertinent

32. ESTRANGE:
   (A) reconcile
   (B) feign
   (C) perplex
   (D) arbitrate
   (E) commiserate

33. PROVIDENT:
   (A) manifest
   (B) prodigal
   (C) thankful
   (D) tidy
   (E) refuted

34. CAPITULATE:
   (A) initiate
   (B) defame
   (C) exonerate
   (D) resist
   (E) repeat

35. INDIGENOUS:
   (A) affluent
   (B) parochial
   (C) alien
   (D) serene
   (E) inimical

36. SALUBRITY:
   (A) unwholesomeness
   (B) insolvency
   (C) dissatisfaction
   (D) diffidence
   (E) rigidity

37. QUAIL:
   (A) hover
   (B) tolerate
   (C) arouse enmity
   (D) become resolute
   (E) abstain from action

38. TANTAMOUNT:
   (A) not negotiable
   (B) not equivalent
   (C) not ambitious
   (D) not evident
   (E) not relevant

S T O P

IF YOU FINISH BEFORE TIME IS CALLED, YOU MAY CHECK YOUR WORK ON THIS SECTION ONLY.
DO NOT WORK ON ANY OTHER SECTION IN THE TEST.

SECTION 2

Time—30 Minutes

38 Questions

Directions: Each sentence below has one or two blanks, each blank indicating that something has been omitted. Beneath the sentence are five lettered words or sets of words. Choose the word or set of words for each blank that best fits the meaning of the sentence as a whole.

1. The simplest animals are those whose bodies are simplest in structure and which do the things done by all living animals, such as eating, breathing, moving, and feeling, in the most ------- way.

   (A) haphazard
   (B) bizarre
   (C) primitive
   (D) advantageous
   (E) unique

2. Although weeks remain for concessions to be made and for new approaches to be attempted, negotiations have reached such a state that management and union leaders are ------- that their differences can no longer be reconciled.

   (A) encouraged
   (B) bewildered
   (C) apprehensive
   (D) relieved
   (E) skeptical

3. Not only the ------- are fooled by propaganda; we can all be misled if we are not -------.

   (A) ignorant…cynical
   (B) gullible…wary
   (C) credulous…headstrong
   (D) illiterate…mature
   (E) fatuous…intelligent

4. When those whom he had injured accused him of being a -------, he retorted curtly that he had never been a quack.

   (A) libertine
   (B) sycophant
   (C) charlatan
   (D) plagiarist
   (E) reprobate

5. There is an essential ------- in human gestures, and when someone raises the palms of his hands together, we do not know whether it is to bury himself in prayer or to throw himself into the sea.

   (A) economy
   (B) dignity
   (C) insincerity
   (D) reverence
   (E) ambiguity

6. It is somewhat paradoxical that, nine times out of ten, the coarse word is the word that ------- an evil and the ------- word is the word that excuses it.

   (A) condemns…refined
   (B) exonerates…vulgar
   (C) contradicts…crass
   (D) condones…genteel
   (E) admits…clever

7. It has been Virginia Woolf's peculiar destiny to be declared annoyingly feminine by male critics at the same time that she has been ------- by women interested in the sexual revolution as not really eligible to be ------- their ranks.

   (A) lauded…enlisted in
   (B) emulated…counted among
   (C) neglected…helpful to
   (D) dismissed…drafted into
   (E) excoriated…discharged from

Directions: In each of the following questions, a related pair of words or phrases is followed by five lettered pairs of words or phrases. Select the lettered pair that best expresses a relationship similar to that expressed in the original pair.

8. DROPCLOTH : FURNITURE::
   (A) banner : flagpole
   (B) towel : rack
   (C) pillow : bedding
   (D) curtain : theatre
   (E) apron : clothing

9. ARCHIPELAGO : ISLAND::
   (A) arbor : bower
   (B) garden : flower
   (C) mountain : valley
   (D) sand : dune
   (E) constellation : star

10. CROW : BOASTFUL::
   (A) smirk : witty
   (B) conceal : sly
   (C) pout : sulky
   (D) blush : coarse
   (E) bluster : unhappy

11. ASCETIC : SELF-DENIAL::
   (A) nomad : dissipation
   (B) miser : affluence
   (C) zealot : fanaticism
   (D) renegade : loyalty
   (E) athlete : stamina

12. CAMOUFLAGE : DISCERN::
   (A) encipher : comprehend
   (B) adorn : admire
   (C) magnify : observe
   (D) renovate : construct
   (E) embroider : unravel

13. SEER : PROPHECY::
   (A) mentor : reward
   (B) sage : wisdom
   (C) pilgrim : diligence
   (D) diplomat : flattery
   (E) virtuoso : penance

14. BRACKET : SHELF::
   (A) hammer : anvil
   (B) girder : rivet
   (C) strut : rafter
   (D) valve : pipe
   (E) bucket : well

15. TAXONOMY : CLASSIFICATION::
   (A) etymology : derivation
   (B) autonomy : authorization
   (C) economy : rationalization
   (D) tautology : justification
   (E) ecology : urbanization

16. BRUSQUE : UNCEREMONIOUSNESS::
   (A) audacious : trepidation
   (B) obstinate : intractability
   (C) pert : improvidence
   (D) curt : loquacity
   (E) officious : inattentiveness

Directions: Each passage in this group is followed by questions based on its content. After reading a passage, choose the best answer to each question. Answer all questions following a passage on the basis of what is stated or implied in the passage.

As the works of dozens of women writers have been rescued from what E.P. Thompson calls "the enormous condescension of posterity," and consid-
(5) ered in relation to each other, the lost continent of the female tradition has risen like Atlantis from the sea of English literature. It is now becoming clear that, contrary to Mill's theory, women have had a literature of their own all along. The woman novel-
(10) ist, according to Vineta Colby, was "really neither single nor anomalous," but she was also more than a "register and spokesman for her age." She was part of a tradition that had its origins before her age, and has carried on through our own.

Many literary historians have begun to reinter-
(15) pret and revise the study of women writers. Ellen Moers sees women's literature as an international movement, "apart from, but hardly subordinate to the mainstream: an undercurrent, rapid and power-ful. This 'movement' began in the late eighteenth
(20) century, was multinational, and produced some of the greatest literary works of two centuries, as well as most of the lucrative pot-boilers." Patricia Meyer Spacks, in *The Female Imagination*, finds that "for readily discernible historical reasons
(25) women have characteristically concerned them-selves with matters more or less peripheral to male concerns, or at least slightly skewed from them. The differences between traditional female preoc-cupations and roles and male ones make a differ-
(30) ence in female writing." Many other critics are beginning to agree that when we look at women writers collectively we can see an imaginative con-tinuum, the recurrence of certain patterns, themes, problems, and images from generation to
(35) generation.

This book is an effort to describe the female lit-erary tradition in the English novel from the gener-ation of the Brontës to the present day, and to show how the development of this tradition is similar to
(40) the development of any literary subculture. Women have generally been regarded as "sociological cha-meleons," taking on the class, lifestyle, and culture of their male relatives. It can, however, be argued that women themselves have constituted a subcul-
(45) ture within the framework of a larger society, and have been unified by values, conventions, experi-ences, and behaviors impinging on each individual. It is important to see the female literary tradition in these broad terms, in relation to the wider evolu-
(50) tion of women's self-awareness and to the ways any minority group finds its direction of self-expression relative to a dominant society, because we cannot show a pattern of deliberate progress and accumulation. It is true, as Ellen Moers writes,
(55) that "women studied with a special closeness the works written by their own sex"; in terms of influ-ences, borrowings, and affinities, the tradition is strongly marked. But it is also full of holes and hia-tuses, because of what Germaine Greer calls the
(60) "phenomenon of the transience of female literary fame"; "almost uninterruptedly since the Interreg-num, a small group of women have enjoyed daz-zling literary prestige during their own lifetimes, only to vanish without trace from the records of
(65) posterity." Thus each generation of women writers has found itself, in a sense, without a history, forced to rediscover the past anew, forging again and again the consciousness of their sex. Given this perpetual disruption, and also the self-hatred that
(70) has alienated women writers from a sense of col-lective identity, it does not seem possible to speak of a movement.

17. The author of this passage implies that a significant element furthering the woman writer's awareness of a female literary tradition is her

(A) vulnerability to male deprecation
(B) assimilation of the values of her subculture
(C) rejection of monetary gain as an acceptable goal
(D) ability to adopt the culture of the dominant society
(E) sense that fame and prestige are evanescent

18. In the second paragraph of the passage the author's attitude toward the literary critics cited can best be described as one of

(A) irony
(B) ambivalence
(C) disparagement
(D) receptiveness
(E) awe

19. The passage supplies information for answering which of the following questions?

(A) Does the author believe the female literary tradition to be richer in depth than its masculine counterpart?
(B) Are women psychological as well as sociological chameleons?
(C) Does Moers share Greer's concern over the ephemeral nature of female literary renown?
(D) What patterns, themes, images, and problems recur sufficiently in the work of women writers to belong to the female imaginative continuum?
(E) Did Mills acknowledge the existence of a separate female literary tradition?

20. The passage suggests that it might be possible to speak of an actual female literary movement were it not for

(A) masculine suppression of feminist criticism
(B) female lack of artistic autonomy
(C) the ephemeral nature of female literary renown
(D) the absence of proper contemporary role models
(E) female rejection of disruptive male influences

21. In the first paragraph, the author makes use of all the following techniques EXCEPT

(A) extended metaphor
(B) enumeration and classification
(C) classical allusion
(D) direct quotation
(E) comparison and contrast

22. Which of the following words could best be substituted for "forging" (line 67) without substantially changing the author's meaning?

(A) counterfeiting
(B) creating
(C) exploring
(D) diverting
(E) straining

23. It can be inferred from the passage that the author considers Moers' work to be

(A) fallacious and misleading
(B) scholarly and definitive
(C) admirable, but inaccurate in certain of its conclusions
(D) popular, but irrelevant to mainstream female literary criticism
(E) idiosyncratic, but of importance historically

24. Which of the following would be the most appropriate title for the passage?

(A) A Unique Phenomenon: Nineteenth and Twentieth Century Feminine Literary Movements
(B) A Literature of Their Own: The Female Literary Tradition
(C) Adaptive Coloration: Feminine Adoption of Masculine Cultural Criteria
(D) The Emergence of the Contemporary Women's Novel
(E) Fame Versus Fortune: The Dilemma of the Woman Writer

The classical idea of matter was something with solidity and mass, like wet stone dust pressed in a fist. If matter was composed of atoms, then the atoms too must have solidity and mass. At the
(5)   beginning of the twentieth century the atom was imagined as a tiny billiard ball or a granite pebble writ small. Then, in the physics of Niels Bohr, the miniature billiard ball became something akin to a musical instrument, a finely tuned Stradivarius 10
(10)   billion times smaller than the real thing. With the advent of quantum mechanics, the musical instrument gave way to pure music. On the atomic scale, the solidity and mass of matter dissolved into something light and airy. Suddenly physicists were de-
(15)   scribing atoms in the vocabulary of the composer — "resonance," "frequency," "harmony," "scale." Atomic electrons sang in choirs like seraphim, cherubim, thrones, and dominions. Classical distinctions between matter and light became mud-
(20)   dled. In the new physics, light bounced about like particles, and matter undulated in waves like light.
      In recent decades, physicists have uncovered elegant subatomic structures in the music of matter. They use a strange new language to describe the
(25)   subatomic world: *quark, squark, gluon, gauge, technicolor, flavor, strangeness, charm*. There are *up* quarks and *down* quarks, *top* quarks and *bottom* quarks. There are particles with *truth* and *antitruth*, and there are particles with *naked beauty*. The sim-
(30)   plest of the constituents of ordinary matter — the proton, for instance — has taken on the character of a Bach fugue, a four-point counterpoint of matter, energy, space, and time. At matter's heart there are arpeggios, chromatics, syncopation. On the lowest
(35)   rung of the chain of being, Creation dances.

25. Which of the following would be the most appropriate title for the passage?

    (A) Linguistic Implications of Particle Physics
    (B) The Influence of Music on Particle Interactions
    (C) Matter's Transformation: The Music of Subatomic Physics
    (D) Trends in Physics Research: Eliminating the Quark
    (E) The Impossible Dream: Obstacles to Proving the Existence of Matter

26. The author refers to "quarks," "squarks" and "charms" (lines 25–26) primarily in order to

    (A) demonstrate the similarity between these particles and earlier images of the atom
    (B) make a distinction between appropriate and inappropriate terms
    (C) object to theoretical suggestions of similar frivolous names
    (D) provide examples of idiosyncratic nomenclature in contemporary physics
    (E) cite preliminary experimental evidence supporting the existence of subatomic matter

27. The author's tone in the second paragraph can best be described as one of

    (A) sympathetic concern
    (B) moderate indignation
    (C) marked derision
    (D) admiring enthusiasm
    (E) qualified skepticism

Directions: Each question below consists of a word printed in capital letters, followed by five lettered words or phrases. Choose the lettered word or phrase that is most nearly <u>opposite</u> in meaning to the word in capital letters.

Since some of the questions require you to distinguish fine shades of meaning, be sure to consider all the choices before deciding which one is best.

28. RECTIFY:
    (A) apologize
    (B) sanctify
    (C) make worse
    (D) rule illegal
    (E) rebuke

29. APEX:
    (A) smallest amount
    (B) clearest view
    (C) lowest point
    (D) broad plateau
    (E) bright color

30. PROSAIC:
    (A) imaginative
    (B) contradictory
    (C) hesitant
    (D) redundant
    (E) disorderly

31. DISSONANCE:
    (A) amalgamation
    (B) harmony
    (C) neutrality
    (D) resolution
    (E) proximity

32. DOLTISH:
    (A) immature
    (B) coarse
    (C) clever
    (D) stable
    (E) genial

33. CHAGRIN:
    (A) frown
    (B) disguise
    (C) make indifferent
    (D) make aware
    (E) please

34. DISINGENUOUS:
    (A) naive
    (B) accurate
    (C) hostile
    (D) witty
    (E) polite

35. RECALCITRANCE:
    (A) dependability
    (B) submissiveness
    (C) apathy
    (D) incongruity
    (E) eloquence

36. FECUNDITY:
    (A) consideration
    (B) comprehensibility
    (C) barrenness
    (D) gravity
    (E) sanity

37. LUGUBRIOUS:
    (A) transparent
    (B) sedulous
    (C) soporific
    (D) jocose
    (E) querulous

38. ANIMUS:
    (A) hospitality
    (B) probity
    (C) anonymity
    (D) amity
    (E) insularity

S T O P

IF YOU FINISH BEFORE TIME IS CALLED, YOU MAY CHECK YOUR WORK ON THIS SECTION ONLY.
DO NOT WORK ON ANY OTHER SECTION IN THE TEST.

SECTION 3

Time—30 minutes

30 Questions

Numbers: All numbers used are real numbers.

Figures: Position of points, angles, regions, etc., can be assumed to be in the order shown; and angle measures can be assumed to be positive.

Lines shown as straight can be assumed to be straight.

Figures can be assumed to lie in a plane unless otherwise indicated.

Figures that accompany questions are intended to provide information useful in answering the questions. However, unless a note states that a figure is drawn to scale, you should solve these problems NOT by estimating sizes by sight or by measurement, but by using your knowledge of mathematics (see Example 2 below).

Directions: Each of the Questions 1-15 consists of two quantities, one in Column A and one in Column B. You are to compare the two quantities and choose

A if the quantity in Column A is greater;
B if the quantity in Column B is greater;
C if the two quantities are equal;
D if the relationship cannot be determined from the information given.

Note: Since there are only four choices, NEVER MARK (E).

Common
Information: In a question, information concerning one or both of the quantities to be compared is centered above the two columns. A symbol that appears in both columns represents the same thing in Column A as it does in Column B.

	Column A	Column B	Sample Answers
Example 1:	2×6	$2 + 6$	● Ⓑ Ⓒ Ⓓ Ⓔ

Examples 2-4 refer to $\triangle PQR$.

Example 2:	PN	NQ	Ⓐ Ⓑ Ⓒ ● Ⓔ
			(since equal measures cannot be assumed, even though PN and NQ appear equal)
Example 3:	x	y	Ⓐ ● Ⓒ Ⓓ Ⓔ
			(since N is between P and Q)
Example 4:	$w + z$	180	Ⓐ Ⓑ ● Ⓓ Ⓔ
			(since PQ is a straight line)

A if the quantity in Column A is greater;
B if the quantity in Column B is greater;
C if the two quantities are equal;
D if the relationship cannot be determined from the information given.

| Column A | Column B | | Column A | Column B |

<u>Column A</u>   <u>Column B</u>

$$\frac{1}{x} < 0$$

1. x 1

_____

$$x = y^2 - 1 = 3$$

2. x y

_____

Side AB of square $ABCD$ is 2 feet.

3.   Perimeter of $ABCD$ Area of $ABCD$

_____

4. $\dfrac{1}{x} + \dfrac{1}{\frac{1}{x}}$ $\dfrac{1}{x} \cdot \dfrac{1}{x}$

_____

$$0 < x < 31$$
x is divisible by 3 and 9.

5. x 27

_____

Note: Not drawn to scale.

6. $2x$ y

_____

$a \neq b$

7. $90 - b$ $90 - a$

_____

$$x > 0$$

8. $\sqrt{\dfrac{2x}{y}} \times \sqrt{\dfrac{xy}{2}}$ x

_____

$$x = \frac{1}{2}$$

9. $\dfrac{\frac{3}{4}}{1+x}$ x

_____

<u>Column A</u>   <u>Column B</u>

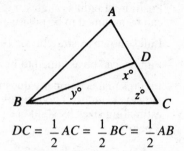

$$DC = \frac{1}{2}AC = \frac{1}{2}BC = \frac{1}{2}AB$$

10. $(BC)^2$ $(DC)^2 + (BD)^2$

_____

| A B | C D |
| (2.8)(3.4) | (5.6)(6.2) |

11.   Length of segment AC Length of segment BD

_____

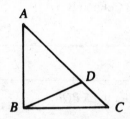

$AB = BD = AD$ and $AB \perp BC$

12. BC DC

_____

a and b are negative integers

13. $a + b$ ab

_____

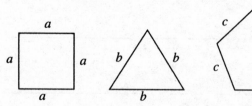

Note: Not drawn to scale.
The perimeters of all the polygons are equal.

14. $5c + 3b$ $4a + 5c$

_____

In triangle ABC, m$\angle A >$ m$\angle B$, and m$\angle C = 60°$.

15.   Side CB Side AB

Each of Questions 16–30 has five choices. For each of these questions, select the best of the answer choices given.

16. A trailer carries 3, 4, or 5 crates on a trip. Each crate weighs no less than 125 pounds and no more than 250 pounds. What is the minimum weight (in pounds) of the crates on a single trip?

    (A)   375
    (B)   600
    (C)   625
    (D)   750
    (E) 1,250

17. In triangle ABC, $\angle B = \angle C$. D is any point on BC. Which of the following statements is true?

    (A) $AB > BC$
    (B) $AB < BC$
    (C) $BD = DC$
    (D) $AC > AD$
    (E) $AC < AD$

18. At a luncheon table where 12 men are seated, one-half of the men belong to Club A, one-third belong to Club B, and one-fourth belong to both clubs. How many men belong to neither?

    (A) 3
    (B) 4
    (C) 5
    (D) 6
    (E) 8

19. A lending library charges c cents for the first week that a book is loaned and f cents for each day over one week. What is the cost for taking out a book for d days, where d is greater than 7?

    (A) $c + fd$
    (B) $c + f(d - 7)$
    (C) cd
    (D) $7c + f(d - 7)$
    (E) $cd + f$

20. The numerator and denominator of a fraction are in the ratio of 2:3. If 6 is subtracted from the numerator, the result will be a fraction that has a value $\frac{2}{3}$ of the original fraction. The numerator of the original fraction is

    (A)   4
    (B)   6
    (C)   9
    (D) 18
    (E) 27

Questions 21–25 refer to the following table and graphs.

WEIGHT DISTRIBUTION IN AVERAGE ADULT	
(Total Body Weight 70,000 Grams)	
Organ	Weight (Grams)
Muscles	30,000
Skeleton	10,000
Blood	5,000
Gastrointestinal tract	2,000
Lungs	1,000
Liver	1,700
Brain	1,500

USE OF WATER BY THE AVERAGE ADULT

DAILY WATER INTAKE
GRAPH I

Solid Food
1000 cc

Fluids
1500 cc

DAILY WATER OUTPUT
GRAPH II

Sweat
500 cc

Lungs
400 cc

Solid Waste
100 cc

Liquid Wastes - Kidneys
1500 cc

21. Which of the following can be inferred from the table and graphs?

    I. Half of the total body weight is the skeleton and blood.
    II. 2.4% of the total body weight is the liver.
    III. The weight of the blood in the average adult is twice the weight of the skeleton.
    (A) I only   (B) II only   (C) III only   (D) I and III
    (E) II and III

22. If the weight of the skeleton is represented as g grams, the total body weight is represented as

    (A) $7g$
    (B) $g + 6$
    (C) $60g$
    (D) $g + 60$
    (E) $70,000g$

23. What is the angle of the sector in Graph I representing daily water intake in solid food?

    (A) 51°
    (B) 72°
    (C) 103°
    (D) 120°
    (E) 144°

24. What percent of daily water output is water expired from the lungs?

   (A) 1.6%
   (B) 4%
   (C) 16%
   (D) 19%
   (E) 40%

25. What percent of the daily water output through the kidneys is the daily water intake in fluids?

   (A) 25%
   (B) 33%
   (C) 60%
   (D) 100%
   (E) 150%

26. If a eggs weigh b ounces, each c eggs weigh from d to e ounces each, and f eggs weigh from g to h ounces each, what is the minimum weight (in ounces) of all the eggs?

   (A) $ab + ce + fg$
   (B) $ab + cd + fg$
   (C) $ab + ce + fh$
   (D) $ab + cd + fh$
   (E) $ab + de + gh$

27. In distributing milk at a summer camp it is found that a quart of milk will fill either 3 large glass tumblers or 5 small glass tumblers. How many small glass tumblers can be filled with one large glass tumbler?

   (A) $\frac{3}{5}$ (B) $1\frac{2}{5}$ (C) $1\frac{2}{3}$ (D) 2   (E) $2\frac{1}{3}$

28. In circle O above, $OA = 4$ and arc $AB = 112°$. How many degrees are in $\angle ABO$?

   (A) 22   (B) 34   (C) 44   (D) 45   (E) 68

29. In the figure above, $AB \perp BC$, $BC \perp CD$, $AB = 8$, $BC = 5$, $CD = 4$. What is the shortest distance from A to D?

   (A) 12   (B) 13   (C) 15   (D) 16   (E) 17

30. There are 27 students in a chemistry class and 22 students in a physics class. Seven of these students take physics and chemistry. What is the ratio of the number of students taking only physics to those taking chemistry?

   (A) 3:4
   (B) 4:3
   (C) 7:6
   (D) 22:27
   (E) 34:29

S T O P

IF YOU FINISH BEFORE TIME IS CALLED, YOU MAY CHECK YOUR WORK ON THIS SECTION ONLY.
DO NOT WORK ON ANY OTHER SECTION IN THE TEST.

SECTION 4

Time—30 minutes

30 Questions

Numbers: All numbers used are real numbers.

Figures: Position of points, angles, regions, etc., can be assumed to be in the order shown; and angle measures can be assumed to be positive.

Lines shown as straight can be assumed to be straight.

Figures can be assumed to lie in a plane unless otherwise indicated.

Figures that accompany questions are intended to provide information useful in answering the questions. However, unless a note states that a figure is drawn to scale, you should solve these problems NOT by estimating sizes by sight or by measurement, but by using your knowledge of mathematics (see Example 2 below).

Directions: Each of the Questions 1-15 consists of two quantities, one in Column A and one in Column B. You are to compare the two quantities and choose

    A if the quantity in Column A is greater;
    B if the quantity in Column B is greater;
    C if the two quantities are equal;
    D if the relationship cannot be determined from the information given.

Note: Since there are only four choices, NEVER MARK (E).

Common
Information: In a question, information concerning one or both of the quantities to be compared is centered above the two columns. A symbol that appears in both columns represents the same thing in Column A as it does in Column B.

	Column A	Column B	Sample Answers
Example 1:	2×6	$2 + 6$	● Ⓑ Ⓒ Ⓓ Ⓔ

Examples 2-4 refer to $\triangle PQR$.

Example 2:	PN	NQ	Ⓐ Ⓑ Ⓒ ● Ⓔ
			(since equal measures cannot be assumed, even though PN and NQ appear equal)
Example 3:	x	y	Ⓐ ● Ⓒ Ⓓ Ⓔ
			(since N is between P and Q)
Example 4:	$w + z$	180	Ⓐ Ⓑ ● Ⓓ Ⓔ
			(since PQ is a straight line)

A if the quantity in Column A is greater;
B if the quantity in Column B is greater;
C if the two quantities are equal;
D if the relationship cannot be determined from the information given.

Column A	Column B	Column A	Column B

$DO \perp OC$ and area of triangle $DOC = 12.5$

1.   Area of circle O 25π

The price of the item is equal to $8 more than $\dfrac{8}{10}$ of its price.

2.   The price of the item $40

In parallelogram $EFGH$, $EF + EH = 20$

3. EH FG

$a > 1, b > 1$

$a \odot b$ is defined by the equation

$$a \odot b = \frac{a+b}{b}.$$

4. $2 \odot 3$ $3 \odot 4$

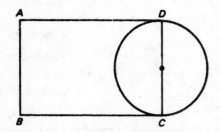

BC of rectangle $ABCD = 2.5\pi$
DC, diameter $= 10$

5.   Area of $ABCD$ Area of circle

$$5 \times 5 \times 5 \times R = 3 \times 3 \times 3 \times 3$$

6.   5   R

---

7. $(-3)^8$ $(-3)^9$

The arithmetic mean (average) of b and c is $60°$.

8. a 60

$$-10 < r < -1$$

9. $\dfrac{1}{r^7}$ $\dfrac{1}{r^6}$

---

10. $\dfrac{c^2 d^2 e^2}{c^3 d^3 e^3}$ $\dfrac{cde}{3}$

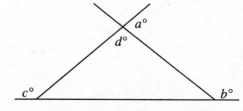

Note: Not drawn to scale.

$d = 70, b = 125$

11. c a

$x \neq 0$
$x^2 = xy$

12. x y

---

13. $\dfrac{1}{2} + \dfrac{1}{3}$ $\dfrac{2}{5}$

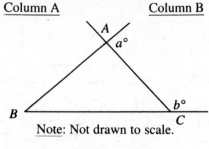

Column A	Column B		Column A	Column B

Note: Not drawn to scale.

Note: Not drawn to scale.

$a = 110$, $b = 125$

Measure of $\angle ABC$ is 80°.

14. AB AC 15. d 100

Directions: Each of the Questions 16–30 has five answer choices. For each of these questions, select the best of the answer choices given.

---

16. Which of the following fractions has the smallest value?

    (A) $\frac{1}{7}$ (B) $\frac{1}{8}$ (C) $\frac{2}{9}$ (D) $\frac{3}{11}$ (E) $\frac{4}{13}$

$AB=BC=AC$

17. In triangle ABC above, if $AB = BC = CA$, then $x + y =$

    (A) 7
    (B) 12
    (C) 19
    (D) 23
    (E) 60

18. In triangle ACD above, the measure of $\angle BAE =$ 50; the length of BE equals the length AE; and $BE \parallel CD$. What is the measure of $\angle ADC$?

    (A)   30
    (B)   50
    (C)   60
    (D)   80
    (E) 100

19. In the figure above, $x =$

    (A) 30
    (B) 40
    (C) 45
    (D) 60
    (E) 80

20. If the operation $\bigcirc$ is defined by the equation $x \bigcirc y = 2x + y$, what is the value of a in the equation $2 \bigcirc a = a \bigcirc 3$?

    (A)   0
    (B) -1
    (C)   1
    (D)   1.5
    (E)   4

Note: Not drawn to scale.

Questions 21–25 are based on the following table.

REQUIRED MONTHLY PAYMENTS NEEDED TO SATISFY
A LOAN MADE AT A RATE OF 10.0%

Amount of Loan (dollars)	Term (Years)						
	13	14	15	16	17	18	19
50	0.58	0.56	0.54	0.53	0.52	0.50	0.50
100	1.15	1.11	1.08	1.05	1.03	1.00	0.99
200	2.30	2.22	2.15	2.10	2.05	2.00	1.97
300	3.45	3.33	3.23	3.14	3.07	3.00	2.95
400	4.60	4.44	4.30	4.19	4.09	4.00	3.93
500	5.74	5.55	5.38	5.23	5.11	5.00	4.91
600	6.89	6.65	6.45	6.28	6.13	6.00	5.89
700	8.04	7.76	7.53	7.33	7.15	7.00	6.87
800	9.19	8.87	8.60	8.37	8.17	8.00	7.86
900	10.34	9.98	9.68	9.42	9.20	9.00	8.84
1,000	11.48	11.09	10.75	10.46	10.22	10.00	9.82
2,000	22.96	22.17	21.50	20.92	20.43	20.00	19.63
3,000	34.44	33.25	32.24	31.38	30.64	30.00	29.44
4,000	45.92	44.33	42.99	41.84	40.85	40.00	39.26
5,000	57.40	55.42	53.74	52.30	51.07	50.00	49.07
6,000	68.88	66.50	64.48	62.76	61.28	60.00	58.88
7,000	80.35	77.58	75.23	73.22	71.49	69.99	68.69
8,000	91.83	88.66	85.97	83.68	81.70	79.99	78.51
9,000	103.31	99.74	96.72	94.14	91.91	89.99	88.32
10,000	114.79	110.83	107.47	104.60	102.13	99.99	98.13

21. At the 10% rate, what would be the monthly payment needed to pay off a $10,000 loan in 15 years?

 (A) $99.74
 (B) $96.72
 (C) $104.60
 (D) $110.83
 (E) $107.47

22. How many years will it take to satisfy a $5000 loan at 10% if the monthly payment is $50?

 (A) 8
 (B) 12
 (C) 16
 (D) 18
 (E) 20

23. What is the difference in each monthly payment between a 17-year loan of $5000 at the 10% rate and an 18-year loan for the same amount at the same rate?

 (A) $0.85
 (B) $1.01
 (C) $1.07
 (D) $1.23
 (E) $1.25

24. According to this table, for an 18-year loan the monthly payment for a $1000 loan is what percent of the amount of the loan?

 (A) 0.1%
 (B) 1.0%
 (C) 1.5%
 (D) 5.1%
 (E) 10.0%

25. How much money will be paid in interest on a $1000 loan at 10% over a period of 18 years?

 (A) $990
 (B) $1000
 (C) $1009
 (D) $1160
 (E) $1890

26. In a class composed of *x* girls and *y* boys what part of the class is composed of girls?

(A) $\dfrac{y}{x + y}$

(B) $\dfrac{x}{xy}$

(C) $\dfrac{x}{x + y}$

(D) $\dfrac{y}{xy}$

(E) $\dfrac{x + y}{y}$

27. If m∠1 = 145 and m∠2 = 125, then m∠3 =

(A) 35
(B) 50
(C) 65
(D) 90
(E) 135

28. What is the maximum number of half-pint bottles of cream that can be filled with a 4-gallon can of cream? (2 pt. = 1 qt., and 4 qt. = 1 gal.)

(A) 16
(B) 24
(C) 30
(D) 32
(E) 64

29. A coffee shop blends 2 kinds of coffee, putting in 2 parts of a 33¢ a pound grade to 1 part of a 24¢ a pound grade. If the mixture is changed to 1 part of the 33¢ a pound grade to 2 parts of the less expensive grade, how much will the shop save in blending 100 pounds?

(A) $0.90
(B) $1.00
(C) $3.00
(D) $8.00
(E) $9.00

30. There are 200 questions on a 3-hour examination. Among these questions are 50 mathematics problems. It is suggested that twice as much time be allowed for each mathematics problem as for each of the other questions. How many minutes should be spent on the mathematics problems?

(A) 36
(B) 60
(C) 72
(D) 100
(E) 120

S T O P

IF YOU FINISH BEFORE TIME HAS ELAPSED, CHECK YOUR WORK ON THIS SECTION OF THE TEST ONLY. DO NOT GO ON TO THE NEXT SECTION OF THE TEST UNTIL TIME IS UP FOR THIS SECTION.

SECTION 5

Time—30 minutes

25 Questions

Directions: Each question or group of questions is based on a passage or set of conditions. In answering some of the questions, it may be useful to draw a rough diagram. For each question, select the best answer choice given.

Questions 1–4

For a motorist there are three ways of going from City A to City C. By way of a bridge the distance is 20 miles and the toll is 75¢. A tunnel between the two cities is a distance of 10 miles and the toll is $1.00 for the vehicle and driver plus 10¢ for each passenger. A two-lane highway without tolls goes east for 30 miles to City B and then 20 miles in a northwest direction to City C.

1. Which of the following is the shortest route from City B to City C?

   (A) Directly on the toll-free highway to City C
   (B) The bridge
   (C) The tunnel
   (D) The tunnel or the bridge
   (E) The bridge only if traffic is heavy on the toll-free highway

2. The most economical way of going from City A to City B, in terms of tolls and distance, is to use the

   (A) tunnel
   (B) bridge
   (C) bridge or tunnel
   (D) toll-free highway
   (E) bridge and highway

3. Martin usually drives alone from City C to City A every working day. His firm deducts a percentage of employee pay for lateness. Which factor would most probably influence his choice of the bridge or the tunnel?

   (A) Whether his wife goes with him
   (B) Scenic interest of each route
   (C) Traffic conditions on the road, bridge, and tunnel
   (D) Saving of 25¢ in tolls
   (E) Price of gasoline consumed in covering the 10 additional miles on the bridge

4. In choosing between the use of the bridge and the tunnel, the chief factor(s) would be

   I.   traffic and road conditions
   II. number of passengers in the car
   III. location of one's home in the center or outskirts of one of the cities
   IV. desire to save 25¢

   (A) I only
   (B) II only
   (C) II and III only
   (D) III and IV only
   (E) I and II only

Questions 5–6

A church's facilities were too small to accommodate the crowd for a special two-day religious service. Church members received a license to use the public park, and a public address system was promptly installed. Citizens who were not members of that church protested the action of the Park Department for having issued this license.

5. What is the best argument used by the church to retain its license?

   (A) Wide publicity had already been given to the location of special service.
   (B) The public address system was installed at great expense.
   (C) The church is a local taxpayer.
   (D) The park had been used before by religious organizations for rallies, concerts, and meetings.
   (E) No one would be excluded from entering the park during the service.

6. Which of the following is the best argument used by the citizens who protested the action by the Park Department?

   (A) Freedom of speech was violated.
   (B) Citizens would be denied the enjoyment of the public park during these two days.
   (C) There would be a violation of the noise-level standards.
   (D) A public referendum should have been held.
   (E) The town would incur expenses to clean up the park after the two-day service.

7. Wilbur is over six feet tall.

   The statement above can be logically deduced from which of the following statements?

   (A) The average height of the members of the basketball team is over six feet; Wilbur is the center on the basketball team.
   (B) If Wilbur was not asked to join the basketball team, then he is not six feet tall; Wilbur was asked to join the basketball team.
   (C) If Wilbur is over six feet tall, then he can see the parade; Wilbur can see the parade.
   (D) In Dr. Gray's seminar, everyone who is not over six feet tall is seated in the first row; Dr. Gray seated Wilbur in the second row.
   (E) Everyone who is over six feet tall has to help stack cartons in the stockroom; Wilbur has to help stack cartons.

Questions 8–12

A project to consolidate the programs of a large university and a small college is set up. It is agreed that the representatives work in small committees of three, with two representatives of the large university. It was also agreed that no committee be represented by faculty members of the same subject area. The large university was represented by the following professors: *J*, who teaches English literature, *K*, who is chairman of the Mathematics Department, and *L*, who is in the Department of Natural Sciences. The small college appointed the following: *M*, who teaches mathematics, *N*, who is a Latin teacher, and *O* and *P*, who teach English literature.

8. Which of the following must be true?

   I.   If *J* serves on a committee, *P* must be assigned to that committee.
   II. If *J* cannot serve on a committee, then *M* cannot be assigned to that committee.
   III. If *J* cannot serve on a committee, then *L* must serve on that committee.

   (A) I only
   (B) II only
   (C) III only
   (D) I and II only
   (E) II and III only

9. Which of the following represents a committee properly composed?

   (A) *K, L, N*
   (B) *K, L, M*
   (C) *J, K, L*
   (D) *J, O, N*
   (E) *J, K, M*

10. Which of the following may serve with *P*?

   (A) *K* and *M*
   (B) *K* and *L*
   (C) *K* and *O*
   (D) *J* and *K*
   (E) *M* and *N*

11. If *L* is not available for service, which of the following must be on the committee?

   (A) *M* and *J*
   (B) *O* and *J*
   (C) *N* and *J*
   (D) *N* and *O*
   (E) *P* and *J*

12. Which of the following must be true?

   I.   *N* and *O* are always on the same committee.
   II. *M* and *O* never serve on the same committee.
   III. When *M* serves, *L* must serve.

   (A) I only
   (B) II only
   (C) I and II only
   (D) III only
   (E) II and III only

Questions 13–16

In a certain society, there are two marriage groups, Red and Brown. No marriage is permitted within a group. On marriage, males become part of their wife's group; women remain in their own group. Children belong to the same group as their parents. Widowers and divorced males revert to the group of their birth. Marriage to more than one person at the same time and marriage to a direct descendant are forbidden.

13. A Brown female could have had

   I.   a grandfather born Red
   II. a grandmother born Red
   III. two grandfathers born Brown

   (A) I only
   (B) III only
   (C) I and II only
   (D) II and III only
   (E) I, II, and III

14. A male born into the Brown group may have

   (A) an uncle in either group
   (B) a Brown daughter
   (C) a Brown son
   (D) a son-in-law born into the Red group
   (E) a daughter-in-law in the Red group

15. Which of the following is not permitted under the rules as stated?

   (A) A Brown male marrying his father's sister
   (B) A Red female marrying her mother's brother
   (C) A man born Red, who is now a widower, marrying his brother's widow
   (D) A widower marrying his wife's sister
   (E) A widow marrying her divorced daughter's ex-husband

16. If widowers and divorced males retained the group they had upon marrying, which of the following would be permissible? (Assume that no previous marriage occurred.)

   (A) A woman marrying her dead sister's husband
   (B) A woman marrying her divorced daughter's ex-husband
   (C) A widower marrying his brother's daughter
   (D) A woman marrying her mother's brother, who is a widower
   (E) A divorced male marrying his ex-wife's divorced sister

Questions 17–22

The letters A, B, C, D, E, F, and G, not necessarily in that order, stand for seven consecutive integers from 1 to 10.
   D is 3 less than A.
   B is the middle term.
   F is as much less than B as C is greater than D.
   G is greater than F.

17. The fifth integer is

    (A) A
    (B) C
    (C) D
    (D) E
    (E) F

18. A is as much greater than F as which integer is less than G?

    (A) A
    (B) B
    (C) C
    (D) D
    (E) E

19. If A = 7, the sum of E and G is

    (A) 8
    (B) 10
    (C) 12
    (D) 14
    (E) 16

20. A − F = ?

    (A) 1
    (B) 2
    (C) 3
    (D) 4
    (E) cannot be determined

21. An integer T is as much greater than C as C is greater than E. T can be written as A + E. What is D?

    (A) 2
    (B) 3
    (C) 4
    (D) 5
    (E) cannot be determined

22. The greatest possible value of C is how much greater than the smallest possible value of D?

    (A) 2
    (B) 3
    (C) 4
    (D) 5
    (E) 6

23. Ellen: I just heard that Julie flunked out of college.
    Nancy: That can't be true; she got straight A's in high school.

    From the conversation above, it can be inferred that

    (A) Nancy thinks Ellen is lying
    (B) Nancy assumes that no one who got straight A's in high school is likely to flunk out of college
    (C) Ellen thinks Julie has flunked out of college
    (D) Nancy thinks Julie is still in college
    (E) Ellen knows that Julie flunked out of college

24. President of the company to the Board of Directors: We are being threatened by a union organizing drive. The workers are trying to wrest control from us. We must take any steps necessary to prevent this takeover, even if some of these measures may not be fully legal.

    If the statements above are true, it follows that

    (A) successful opposition to a union organizing drive must require illegal measures
    (B) the union organizing drive is being conducted illegally
    (C) the board of directors will refuse to recognize the union even if it wins a representation election
    (D) maintaining full control of the company is more important than obeying the law
    (E) successful unionization of any company deprives the company officers of control over the company

25. If you present a purple pass, then you may enter the compound.

    If the statement above is true, which of the following must also be true?

    I.   If you do not present a purple pass, then you may not enter the compound.
    II. If you may enter the compound, then you must have presented a purple pass.
    III. If you may not enter the compound, then you did not present a purple pass.

    (A) I only
    (B) II only
    (C) III only
    (D) I and II only
    (E) I, II, and III

S T O P

IF YOU FINISH BEFORE TIME IS CALLED, YOU MAY CHECK YOUR WORK ON THIS SECTION ONLY.
DO NOT WORK ON ANY OTHER SECTION IN THE TEST.

SECTION 6

Time—30 minutes

25 Questions

<u>Directions:</u> Each question or group of questions is based on a passage or set of conditions. In answering some of the questions, it may be useful to draw a rough diagram. For each question, select the best answer choice given.

<u>Questions 1–4</u>

In country X, the Conservative, Democratic, and Justice parties have fought three civil wars in twenty years. To restore stability, an agreement is reached to rotate the top offices—President, Prime Minister, and Army Chief of Staff—among the parties, so that each party controls one and only one Office at all times. The three top office holders must each have two deputies, one from each of the other parties. Each deputy must choose a staff composed equally of members of his or her chief's party and members of the third party.

1. When the Justice Party holds one of the top offices, which of the following cannot be true?

   (A) Some of the staff members within that Office are Justice Party members.
   (B) Some of the staff members within that Office are Democratic Party members.
   (C) Two of the deputies within the other Offices are Justice Party members.
   (D) Two of the deputies within the other Offices are Conservative Party members.
   (E) Some of the staff members within the other Offices are Justice Party members.

2. When the Democratic Party holds the Presidency, the staffs of the Prime Minister's deputies are composed

   I.   one-fourth of Democratic Party members
   II. one-half of Justice Party members, one-fourth of Conservative Party members
   III. one-half of Conservative Party members, one-fourth of Justice Party members

   (A) I only
   (B) I and II only
   (C) II or III, but not both
   (D) I and II or I and III
   (E) Neither I, II, nor III

3. Which of the following is allowable under the rules as stated?

   (A) More than half of the staff within a given Office belonging to a single party
   (B) Half the staff members within a given Office belonging to a single party
   (C) Any person having a member of the same party as his or her immediate superior
   (D) Half the total number of staff members in all three Offices belonging to a single party
   (E) Half the staff members within a given Office belonging to parties different from the party of the top office holder in that Office

4. The Office of the Army Chief of Staff passes from the Conservative to the Justice Party. Which of the following must be fired?

   (A) The Democratic deputy and all staff members belonging to the Justice Party
   (B) The Justice Party deputy and all his or her staff members
   (C) The Justice Party deputy and half of the Conservative staff members in the chief of staff office
   (D) The Conservative deputy and all of his or her staff members belonging to the Conservative Party
   (E) No deputies, and all staff members belonging to the Conservative Party

5. If Elaine is on the steering committee, then she is on the central committee. This statement can be logically deduced from which of the following statements?

   (A) All members of the central committee are on the steering committee.
   (B) Elaine is on either the central committee or the steering committee.
   (C) Everyone who is on the steering committee is also on the central committee.
   (D) Some members of the central committee are on the steering committee.
   (E) Elaine is on the steering committee.

6. Frank must be a football player; he is wearing a football jersey.

   The conclusion above is valid only if it is true that

   (A) football players often wear football jerseys
   (B) all football players wear football jerseys
   (C) football players never wear any kind of shirt other than football jerseys
   (D) football players are required to wear football jerseys
   (E) only football players wear football jerseys

7. Today's high school students are not being educated, they are being trained. Their teachers demand little of them other than that they memorize facts and follow directions. The current emphasis on training in basic math and verbal skills, while a useful step, rarely leads to the essential second step: development of independent critical thinking.

The author would probably consider which of the following aspects of a student's term paper to be most praiseworthy?

(A) The choice of a challenging topic
(B) The use of grammatically correct sentence structure
(C) Evidence of extensive research prior to writing
(D) Avoidance of clichés and vagueness
(E) Evidence of original insights and freshly developed concepts

Questions 8–11

Tom wishes to enroll in Latin AA, Sanskrit A, Armenian Literature 221, and Celtic Literature 701.

Latin AA meets five days a week, either from 9 to 11 A.M. or from 2 to 4 P.M.

Sanskrit A meets either Tuesday and Thursday from 12 noon to 3 P.M., or Monday, Wednesday, and Friday from 10 A.M. to 12 noon.

Armenian Literature 221 meets either Monday, Wednesday, and Friday from 12:30 to 2 P.M., or Tuesday and Thursday from 10:30 A.M. to 12:30 P.M.

Celtic Literature 701 meets by arrangement with the instructor, the only requirement being that it meet for one four-hour session or two two-hour sessions per week, between 9 A.M. and 4 P.M. from Monday to Friday, beginning on the hour.

8. Which combination is impossible for Tom?

(A) Latin in the morning, Sanskrit on Tuesday and Thursday, and Armenian Literature on Monday, Wednesday, and Friday
(B) Latin in the afternoon and Sanskrit and Armenian Literature on Monday, Wednesday, and Friday
(C) Latin in the afternoon, Sanskrit on Monday, Wednesday, and Friday, and Armenian Literature on Tuesday and Thursday
(D) Latin in the morning and Sanskrit and Armenian Literature on Monday, Wednesday, and Friday
(E) Latin in the afternoon, Armenian Literature on Monday, Wednesday, and Friday, and Celtic Literature on Tuesday

9. Which of the following gives the greatest number of alternatives for scheduling Celtic Literature, assuming that all other courses are scheduled without conflicts?

(A) Latin in the afternoon and Armenian Literature Monday, Wednesday, and Friday
(B) Sanskrit on Tuesday and Thursday and Armenian Literature on Monday, Wednesday and Friday
(C) Latin in the afternoon and Armenian Literature Tuesday and Thursday
(D) Latin in the morning and Sanskrit on Tuesday and Thursday
(E) Sanskrit on Monday, Wednesday, and Friday, and Armenian Literature on Tuesday and Thursday

10. If the Celtic instructor insists on holding at least one session on Friday, in which of the following can Tom enroll?

I.   Armenian Literature on Monday, Wednesday, and Friday
II. Sanskrit on Monday, Wednesday, and Friday

(A) I only
(B) II only
(C) both I and II
(D) I or II but not both
(E) neither I nor II

11. Which of the following additional courses, meeting as indicated, can Tom take?

(A) Old Church Slavonic—Monday, Wednesday, and Friday from 10 A.M. to 12 noon
(B) Intermediate Aramaic—Monday, Wednesday, and Friday from 11 A.M. to 12:30 P.M.
(C) Introductory Acadian—Tuesday and Thursday from 2 to 4 P.M.
(D) Fundamentals of Basque—Tuesday and Thursday from 1 to 3 P.M.
(E) Old Norse-Icelandic—Monday only from 12 to 3 P.M.

Questions 12–18

Joe, Larry, Ned, Mary, Paul, Willy, Crystal, Albert, Bob, Frank, Ellen, and Rick all live in the same six-floor building. There are two apartments per floor. No more than two persons live in any apartment. Some apartments may be empty.

Larry and his roommate live two floors above Albert and his roommate, Crystal.
Joe lives alone, three floors below Willy and two floors below Ellen.
Mary lives one floor below Albert and Crystal.
Ned lives three floors above the floor on which Bob and Frank have single apartments.
Rick and Paul live in single apartments two floors below Mary.

12. Which of the following lists the persons named in the correct order, going from the bottom floor to the top?

(A) Rick, Bob, Mary, Albert, Larry, Ned
(B) Rick, Frank, Ned, Ellen, Larry, Crystal
(C) Paul, Bob, Joe, Crystal, Ned, Larry
(D) Larry, Ellen, Albert, Mary, Frank, Rick
(E) Larry, Joe, Mary, Albert, Bob, Rick

13. Which of the following pairs must live on the same floor?

I.   Ned, Ellen
II. Joe, Mary
III. Albert, Larry

(A) I only
(B) III only
(C) I and II only
(D) II and III only
(E) I, II, and III

14. Larry's roommate, assuming that he or she is one of the persons mentioned, is

    (A) Ellen
    (B) Willy
    (C) Mary
    (D) Ned
    (E) Paul

15. Rick lives on the

    (A) first floor, below Bob or Frank
    (B) second floor, below Joe or Albert and Crystal
    (C) third floor, above Mary or Ellen
    (D) fourth floor, opposite Albert and Crystal
    (E) sixth floor, opposite Larry and his roommate

16. An empty apartment or empty apartments may be found on the

    (A) second floor only
    (B) fourth floor only
    (C) fifth floor only
    (D) third or sixth floor, but not both
    (E) fourth or sixth floor or both

17. Joe arranges to move into an apartment two floors down, whose occupant moves into an apartment one floor up. The occupant of this apartment moves into one three floors up, whose occupant takes Joe's old apartment. The new occupant of Joe's old apartment is

    (A) Bob or Frank
    (B) Ned or Ellen
    (C) Mary
    (D) Rick
    (E) Paul

18. Dorothy lives with a roommate. Her roommate could be any of the following EXCEPT

    (A) Willy
    (B) Mary
    (C) Ned
    (D) Ellen
    (E) Frank

Questions 19–22

(1) A causes B or C, but not both.
(2) F occurs only if B occurs.
(3) D occurs if B or C occurs.
(4) E occurs only if C occurs.
(5) J occurs only if E or F occurs.
(6) D causes G or H or both.
(7) H occurs if E occurs.
(8) G occurs if F occurs.

19. If A occurs, which may occur?

    I.   F and G
    II. E and H
    III. D

    (A) I only
    (B) II only
    (C) III only
    (D) I and III or II and III, but not both
    (E) I, II, and III

20. If B occurs, which must occur?

    (A) F and G
    (B) D and G
    (C) D
    (D) G and H
    (E) J

21. If J occurs, which must have occurred?

    (A) E
    (B) Both E and F
    (C) Either B or C
    (D) G
    (E) Both B and C

22. Which may occur as a result of a cause not mentioned?

    I.   D
    II. A
    III. F

    (A) I only
    (B) II only
    (C) I and II only
    (D) II and III only
    (E) I, II, and III

23. In recommending to the board of trustees a tuition increase of $500 per year, the President of the university said: "There were no student demonstrations over the previous increases of $300 last year and $200 the year before."

    If the President's statement is accurate, which of the following can be validly inferred from the information given?

    I.   Most students in previous years felt that the increases were justified because of increased operating costs.
    II. Student apathy was responsible for the failure of students to protest the previous tuition increases.
    III. Students are not likely to demonstrate over the new tuition increases.

    (A) I only
    (B) II only
    (C) I or II, but not both
    (D) I, II, and III
    (E) Neither I, II, nor III

24. A meadow in springtime is beautiful, even if no one is there to appreciate it.

   The statement above would be a logical rebuttal to which of the following claims?

   (A) People will see only what they want to see.
   (B) Beauty is only skin deep.
   (C) There's no accounting for taste.
   (D) Beauty exists only in the eye of the beholder.
   (E) The greatest pleasure available to mankind is the contemplation of beauty.

25. Since it is possible that substances contained in certain tree roots may provide a cure for cancer, the government must provide sufficient funds to allow thorough testing of this possibility.

   The argument above assumes that

   (A) substances contained in certain tree roots will probably cure cancer
   (B) the line of research mentioned offers at present the most promising possibility for finding a cure for cancer
   (C) the possibility of finding a cure is sufficient reason for funding research into possible cancer cures
   (D) a cure for cancer would be extremely valuable to society
   (E) the government is the only possible source of funds for the research described

S T O P

IF YOU FINISH BEFORE TIME IS CALLED, YOU MAY CHECK YOUR WORK ON THIS SECTION ONLY.
DO NOT WORK ON ANY OTHER SECTION IN THE TEST.

SECTION 7

Time—30 Minutes

38 Questions

Directions: Each sentence below has one or two blanks, each blank indicating that something has been omitted. Beneath the sentence are five lettered words or sets of words. Choose the word or set of words for each blank that best fits the meaning of the sentence as a whole.

1. The ------- of the apartment was unbelievable; it was difficult to realize that human beings could live in such -------.

   (A) disorder...isolation
   (B) squalor...filth
   (C) barrenness...confusion
   (D) stench...disarray
   (E) spaciousness...proximity

2. He had taken the shocking news quietly, neither ------- fate nor uttering any word of bitterness.

   (A) conspiring with
   (B) submitting to
   (C) railing against
   (D) dissenting from
   (E) mulling over

3. Old as the continents are, they are apparently not ------- features of the earth but rather secondary features that have formed and evolved during the earth's lifetime.

   (A) inherent
   (B) incongruous
   (C) primordial
   (D) isolated
   (E) unique

4. Although several details of the hypothesis are open to criticism, its general conclusion has not been -------.

   (A) refuted
   (B) determined
   (C) corroborated
   (D) disregarded
   (E) approximated

5. It is a great irony of contemporary history that those friends of judicial autonomy who argue most passionately for creative judicial intervention in the political sphere in effect advocate ------- of an independent, nonelected judiciary.

   (A) abolition
   (B) liberation
   (C) evaluation
   (D) inauguration
   (E) dissemination

6. There is a danger that because Mr. Peters' suggestions are so theatrically -------, readers may treat the book as a performance, enthralling but too ------- to take seriously.

   (A) striking...pedestrian
   (B) bold...overwrought
   (C) plausible...fantastic
   (D) conventional...disturbing
   (E) lacking...histrionic

7. As long as the acquisition of knowledge is rendered habitually -------, so long will there be a prevailing tendency to discontinue it when free from the ------- of parents and teachers.

   (A) repugnant...coercion
   (B) academic...authority
   (C) gratifying...restrictions
   (D) honorable...influence
   (E) irrelevant...custody

Directions: In each of the following questions, a related pair of words or phrases is followed by five lettered pairs of words or phrases. Select the lettered pair that best expresses a relationship similar to that expressed in the original pair.

8. MODERATOR : DEBATE::
   (A) legislator : election
   (B) chef : banquet
   (C) auditor : lecture
   (D) conspirator : plot
   (E) umpire : game

9. DELIRIUM : DISORIENTATION::
   (A) paralysis : immobility
   (B) anorexia : pain
   (C) insomnia : fretfulness
   (D) rash : vaccination
   (E) malaria : relapse

10. GLOSSARY : WORDS::
    (A) catalogue : dates
    (B) atlas : maps
    (C) almanac : synonyms
    (D) thesaurus : rhymes
    (E) lexicon : numbers

11. ARMATURE : STATUE::
    (A) landscape : painting
    (B) framework : building
    (C) arsenal : weapon
    (D) composer : symphony
    (E) apparatus : experiment

12. EPAULET : SHOULDER::
   (A) noose : neck
   (B) tiara : head
   (C) splint : arm
   (D) knapsack : back
   (E) palm : hand

13. LUMBER : BEAR::
   (A) roost : hen
   (B) bray : donkey
   (C) waddle : goose
   (D) swoop : hawk
   (E) chirp : sparrow

14. ENERVATED : VIGOR::
   (A) lax : rigor
   (B) profound : stupor
   (C) pallid : flavor
   (D) ravenous : appetite
   (E) nervous : energy

15. CELERITY : SNAIL::
   (A) indolence : sloth
   (B) cunning : weasel
   (C) curiosity : cat
   (D) humility : peacock
   (E) obstinacy : mule

16. ADULATION : FLATTERY::
   (A) humility : vanity
   (B) credulity : sincerity
   (C) emulation : rivalry
   (D) irascibility : provocation
   (E) castigation : admonishment

Directions: Each passage in this group is followed by questions based on its content. After reading a passage, choose the best answer to each question. Answer all questions following a passage on the basis of what is stated or implied in the passage.

The Quechua world is submerged, so to speak, in a cosmic magma that weighs heavily upon it. It possesses the rare quality of being, as it were, interjected into the midst of antagonistic forces, which in turn implies a whole body of social and aesthetic structures whose innermost meaning must be the administration of energy. This gives rise to the social organism known as the *ayllu*, the agrarian community that regulates the procurement of food. The *ayllu* formed the basic structure of the whole Inca empire.

The central idea of this organization was a kind of closed economy, just the opposite of our economic practices, which can be described as open. The closed economy rested on the fact that the Inca controlled both the production and consumption of food. When one adds to this fact the religious ideas noted in the Quechua texts cited by the chronicler Santa Cruz Pachacuti, one comes to the conclusion that in the Andean zone the margin of life was minimal and was made possible only by the system of magic the Quechua constructed through his religion. Adversities, moreover, were numerous, for the harvest might fail at any time and bring starvation to millions. Hence the whole purpose of the Quechua administrative and ideological system was to carry on the arduous task of achieving *abundance* and staving off shortages. This kind of structure presupposes a state of unremitting anxiety, which could not be resolved by action. The Quechua could not do so because his primordial response to problems was the use of magic, that is, recourse to the unconscious for the solution of external problems. Thus the struggle against the world was a struggle against the dark depths of the Quechua's own psyche, where the solution was found. By overcoming the unconscious, the outer world was also vanquished.

These considerations permit us to classify Quechua culture as absolutely static or, more accurately, as the expression of a mere state of being. Only in this way can we understand the refuge that it took in the germinative center of the cosmic *mandala* as revealed by Quechua art. The Quechua empire was nothing more than a *mandala*, for it was divided into four zones, with Cuzco in the center. Here the Quechua ensconced himself to contemplate the decline of the world as though it were caused by an alien and autonomous force.

17. It can be inferred from the passage that the Quechua world
   (A) aimed at socioeconomic interdependence
   (B) eliminated economic distress
   (C) may be placed in ancient South America
   (D) is located in contemporary Mexico
   (E) was a scene of dynamic activity

18. The term *mandala* as used in the last paragraph most likely means
   (A) an agrarian community
   (B) a kind of superstition
   (C) a closed economic pattern
   (D) a philosophy or way of regarding the world
   (E) a figure composed of four divisions

19. The author implies that the Quechua world was
   (A) uncivilized
   (B) highly introspective
   (C) vitally energetic
   (D) free of major worries
   (E) well organized

20. With which of the following statements would the author most likely agree?

   (A) Only psychological solutions can remedy economic ills.
   (B) The Quechua were renowned for equanimity and unconcern.
   (C) The Quechua limited themselves to realizable goals.
   (D) Much of Quechua existence was harsh and frustrating.
   (E) Modern Western society should adopt some Quechua economic ideas.

   The explosion of a star is an awesome event. The most violent of these cataclysms, which produce supernovae, probably destroys a star completely. Within our galaxy of roughly 100 billion
(5) stars the last supernova was observed in 1604. Much smaller explosions, however, occur quite frequently, giving rise to what astronomers call novae and dwarf novae. On the order of 25 novae occur in our galaxy every year, but only two or
(10) three are near enough to be observed. About 100 dwarf novae are known altogether. If the exploding star is in a nearby part of the galaxy, it may create a ''new star'' that was not previously visible to the naked eye. The last new star of this sort that could
(15) be observed clearly from the Northern Hemisphere appeared in 1946. In these smaller explosions the star loses only a minute fraction of its mass and survives to explode again.
   Astrophysicists are fairly well satisfied that they
(20) can account for the explosions of supernovae. The novae and dwarf novae have presented more of a puzzle. From recent investigations that have provided important new information about these two classes of exploding star, the picture that emerges
(25) is quite astonishing. It appears that every dwarf nova—and perhaps every nova—is a member of a pair of stars. The two stars are so close together that they revolve around a point that lies barely outside the surface of the larger star. As a result the
(30) period of rotation is usually only a few hours, and their velocities range upward to within a two-hundredth of the speed of light.
   Astronomers use the term ''cataclysmic variable'' to embrace the three general classes of
(35) exploding star: dwarf novae, novae and supernovae. A cataclysmic variable is defined as a star that suddenly and unpredictably increases in brightness by a factor of at least 10. Dwarf novae are stars that increase in brightness by a factor of 10 to 100
(40) within a period of several hours and decline to their former brightness in two or three days. In this period they emit some 10.38 to 10.39 ergs of energy. At maximum brilliance a dwarf nova shines about as intensely as our sun; previously it
(45) had been only about a hundredth as bright. The number of outbursts ranges anywhere from three to 30 a year, but for any one star the intervals have a fairly constant value. Moreover, the maximum brightness from outburst to outburst is the same

(50) within a factor of two for a given star. The dwarf novae are often referred to, after their prototypes, as U Geminorum or SS Cygni stars. (The stars of each constellation are designated by letters or numbers.) A subgroup of dwarf novae, called Z Came-
(55) lopardalis stars, do not always descend to minimum brightness between outbursts but may stay at some intermediate level for several months.

21. The author's primary purpose in the passage is to

   (A) compare the characteristics of novae with those of other stars
   (B) explain why supernovae are so much less frequent than novae and dwarf novae
   (C) account for the unpredictability of cataclysmic variables as a class
   (D) describe the nature and range in scale of cataclysmic variables
   (E) explain what happens during the stages of a star's destruction

22. According to the passage, our observations of novae are hampered by their

   (A) extreme brightness
   (B) loss of mass
   (C) speed of rotation
   (D) distance from earth
   (E) tremendous violence

23. Dwarf novae differ from supernovae in which of the following aspects?

   I.   Magnitude of outburst
   II. Frequency of observation
   III. Periodicity of flare-ups

   (A) I only
   (B) II only
   (C) I and II only
   (D) I and III only
   (E) I, II, and III

24. By the term ''new star'' (line 13) the author means one that has

   (A) recently gained in mass
   (B) moved from a distant galaxy
   (C) become bright enough to strike the eye
   (D) not previously risen above the horizon
   (E) become visible by rotating in its orbit

25. The passage suggests which of the following about Z Camelopardalis stars?

   (A) They revert to their original level of brightness more readily than do U Geminorum stars.
   (B) Their outbursts are more frequent than those of other dwarf novae.
   (C) They may lose a proportionally greater fraction of their mass than do SS Cygni stars.
   (D) They may be less frequently observed by astronomers than are supernovae.
   (E) They are distinguishable from other dwarf novae by their lesser degree of brightness.

26. Which of the following topics would most probably be the subject of the paragraph immediately following the last paragraph above?

    (A) The likelihood of our sun's becoming a dwarf nova
    (B) The manner in which the twin stars revolve
    (C) The characteristics of the explosion of a nova
    (D) The origin of the term "cataclysmic variable "
    (E) The nature of the explosions of supernovae

27. The passage provides information that would answer which of the following questions?

    I. In what century were astronomers last able to observe the explosion of a supernova?
    II. Why do the Z Camelopardalis stars remain at intermediate levels of brightness after some outbursts?
    III. How rapidly after outburst do dwarf novae achieve their maximum level of brilliance?

    (A) I only
    (B) III only
    (C) I and II only
    (D) I and III only
    (E) II and III only

Directions: Each question below consists of a word printed in capital letters, followed by five lettered words or phrases. Choose the lettered word or phrase that is most nearly opposite in meaning to the word in capital letters.

Since some of the questions require you to distinguish fine shades of meaning, be sure to consider all the choices before deciding which one is best.

28. FLUSTER:
    (A) soothe
    (B) diminish
    (C) strengthen
    (D) divert
    (E) allow

29. DELETION:
    (A) injury
    (B) delay
    (C) insertion
    (D) permission
    (E) pollution

30. DISPARAGE:
    (A) resemble
    (B) eulogize
    (C) vacillate
    (D) annoy
    (E) appear

31. BALEFUL:
    (A) meager
    (B) beneficent
    (C) indifferent
    (D) uncomfortable
    (E) original

32. SERVILITY:
    (A) resilience
    (B) wickedness
    (C) independence
    (D) righteousness
    (E) humility

33. FELICITOUS:
    (A) inappropriate
    (B) ineffable
    (C) irrational
    (D) atypical
    (E) uncertain

34. PRECIPITOUS:
    (A) cooperative
    (B) cautious
    (C) inaccurate
    (D) formal
    (E) simplistic

35. ASSUAGE:
    (A) wane
    (B) belie
    (C) worsen
    (D) intervene
    (E) presume

36. LATENT:
    (A) prior
    (B) tardy
    (C) devious
    (D) manifest
    (E) astronomical

37. BROACH:
    (A) seal off
    (B) vie with
    (C) unsettle
    (D) stint
    (E) enhance

38. ENCOMIUM:
    (A) prodigality
    (B) denunciation
    (C) sacrifice
    (D) disability
    (E) abbreviation

S T O P

IF YOU FINISH BEFORE TIME IS CALLED, YOU MAY CHECK YOUR WORK ON THIS SECTION ONLY.
DO NOT WORK ON ANY OTHER SECTION IN THE TEST.

Answer Key

Note: The answers to the quantitative sections are keyed to the corresponding review areas in the Mathematics Review (Chapter 11). The numbers in parentheses after each answer refer to the math topic(s) covered by that particular question.

Section 1   Verbal

1.	D	11.	B	21.	B	31.	D
2.	B	12.	C	22.	C	32.	A
3.	B	13.	E	23.	C	33.	B
4.	E	14.	E	24.	A	34.	D
5.	E	15.	C	25.	A	35.	C
6.	D	16.	A	26.	B	36.	A
7.	B	17.	E	27.	B	37.	D
8.	B	18.	C	28.	C	38.	B
9.	C	19.	E	29.	B		
10.	B	20.	C	30.	E		

Section 2   Verbal

1.	C	11.	C	21.	B	31.	B
2.	C	12.	A	22.	B	32.	C
3.	B	13.	B	23.	C	33.	E
4.	C	14.	C	24.	B	34.	A
5.	E	15.	A	25.	C	35.	B
6.	A	16.	B	26.	D	36.	C
7.	D	17.	B	27.	D	37.	D
8.	E	18.	D	28.	C	38.	D
9.	E	19.	E	29.	C		
10.	C	20.	C	30.	A		

Section 3   Quantitative

1.	B (II-G)	9.	C (I-B, II-A)	17.	D (III)	25.	D (II-E)
2.	A (II-B)	10.	C (III-A)	18.	C (I-B)	26.	B (II-A)
3.	A (III-G)	11.	C (I-F)	19.	B (II-B, C)	27.	C (II-E)
4.	C (I-B, II-A)	12.	A (III-D)	20.	D (I-B)	28.	B (III-F)
5.	D (II-G)	13.	B (II-A-3)	21.	B (IV-C)	29.	B (III-D)
6.	B (III-A)	14.	C (III-G)	22.	A (II-E)	30.	A (II-D)
7.	D (III-A)	15.	A (III-D, V)	23.	E (III-F, IV-B)		
8.	C (I-H)	16.	A (I)	24.	C (I-D, IV-B)		

Section 4   Quantitative

1.	C (III-F)	9.	B (II-G)	17.	C (III-D)	25.	D (I-A)
2.	C (II-B)	10.	D (I-H)	18.	D (III-B, D)	26.	C (I-B)
3.	C (III-C)	11.	A (III-A)	19.	A (III-D)	27.	D (III-A)
4.	B (I-B)	12.	C (II-A)	20.	C (II-B)	28.	E (IV-B)
5.	C (III-G)	13.	A (I-B)	21.	E (IV-A)	29.	C (IV-B)
6.	A (I-A)	14.	C (III-D)	22.	D (V-A)	30.	C (IV-B)
7.	A (I-H)	15.	A (III-A)	23.	C (I-A)		
8.	C (III-A)	16.	B (I-B)	24.	B (I-D)		

Section 5   Analytical

1.	A	8.	E	15.	B	22.	D
2.	D	9.	A	16.	D	23.	B
3.	C	10.	B	17.	B	24.	D
4.	E	11.	C	18.	D	25.	C
5.	D	12.	E	19.	B		
6.	B	13.	C	20.	D		
7.	D	14.	A	21.	D		

Section 6   Analytical

1.	D	8.	D	15.	A	22.	C
2.	D	9.	A	16.	E	23.	E
3.	B	10.	D	17.	B	24.	D
4.	C	11.	B	18.	E	25.	C
5.	C	12.	C	19.	D		
6.	E	13.	C	20.	C		
7.	E	14.	B	21.	C		

Section 7   Verbal

1.	B	11.	B	21.	D	31.	B
2.	C	12.	B	22.	D	32.	C
3.	C	13.	C	23.	E	33.	A
4.	A	14.	A	24.	C	34.	B
5.	A	15.	D	25.	C	35.	C
6.	B	16.	E	26.	C	36.	D
7.	A	17.	C	27.	D	37.	A
8.	E	18.	E	28.	A	38.	B
9.	A	19.	B	29.	C		
10.	B	20.	D	30.	B		

Answer Explanations

Section 1

1. **D.** To the cynic (person who expects nothing but the worst of human actions and motives), human actions are *founded* or based upon selfish motives.

2. **B.** The author concedes that the big-bang theory has been changed somewhat: it has undergone *refinement* or polishing. However, he denies that its validity has been threatened seriously by any rival theories: it has *resisted* or defied all challenges.
   The use of the support signal *and* indicates that the first missing word is similar in meaning to "modification." The use of the contrast signal *but* indicates that the second missing word is contrary in meaning to "undergone modification."

3. **B.** Speech that is *hybrid* (made up of several elements) by definition *combines* these elements. The technical term *hybrid* best suits this context because it is a neutral term devoid of negative connotations (which *motley* and *mangled* possess).

4. **E.** Printing *propagates* or disseminates both error (bad books) and *knowledge* (good books). Note how the use of parallel structure demands that the second missing word be a positive term.

5. **E.** One would have to disentangle a *skein* or coiled and twisted bundle of yarn.
   Note how the presence of the verb *disentangle*, which may be used both figuratively and literally, influences the writer's choice of words. In this case, while *line* and *strand* are possible choices, neither word possesses the connotations of twistings and tangled contortions that make *skein* the most suitable choice.

6. **D.** A man too wedded to *orthodox* theories or doctrines can best be described as *doctrinaire* or dogmatic.

7. **B.** The scholar was *eclectic* in his own approach, selecting what he thought was best from the different philosophic schools. However, he did not grant this freedom of selection to others: he was *intolerant of* his colleagues who preached (asserted, averred) what he practiced.
   Note that the use of *illogically* implicitly signals the contrast built into the sentence.

8. **B.** *Fans* or spectators are seated in the *bleachers*. Persons in an *audience* are seated in their *seats*.

   (Defining Characteristic)

9. **C.** An *auger* is a tool that pierces or *bores* holes. A *plane* is a tool that *smooths* surfaces.

   (Function)

10. **B.** A *chameleon*, a kind of lizard, is studied by a *herpetologist* (scientist who studies reptiles and amphibians). A *salmon*, a kind of fish, is studied by an *ichthyologist*.

    (Defining Characteristic)

11. **B.** To *scurry* is to *move* in a brisk and rapid manner. To *chatter* is to *talk* in a brisk and rapid manner.

    (Manner)

12. **C.** A *song* is part of a *cycle* or series of songs. A *sonnet* is part of a *sequence* or series of sonnets.

    (Group and Member)

13. **E.** Someone *obdurate* (unyielding, inflexible) is lacking in *flexibility*. Someone *adamant* (unshakable in opposition) is lacking in *submissiveness*.

    (Antonym Variant)

14. **E.** *Sartorial* by definition means pertaining to the *tailor's* art. *Terpsichorean* by definition means pertaining to the *dancer's* art.

    (Defining Characteristic)

15. **C.** To *skirt* an *issue* is to evade addressing or dealing with it. To *dodge* an *encounter* is to evade meeting the person.
    Beware eye-catchers. *Skirt* here is a verb meaning evade. *Vest* here is a verb meaning to have a legal right or interest in something. Neither here is a noun referring to a garment.

    (Function)

16. **A.** A *feud* or war of revenge is a fight characterized by *acrimony* or bitterness. A *scuffle* or haphazard struggle is a fight characterized by *confusion*.

    (Defining Characteristic)

17. **E.** In this paragraph the author maintains that all forms of government tend to become somewhat dictatorial. He shows how society protects itself from this tendency. Throughout, he demonstrates how people tend to protect or *safeguard* their individual liberties.

18. **C.** The author says that the tendency for a government to encroach upon individual liberty to the extent to which it has the power to do so is "almost a natural law" of politics. Thus, government and individual liberty are *inherently* by their very natures in *opposition* to one another.

19. E.   The final sentence states that the fascist dictatorships "destroyed (*eradicated*) all forms of
social organization which were in any way rivals
to the state."

20. C.   If the fascist dictatorships "are the first truly
tyrannical governments which Western Europe
has known for centuries," then it can be
inferred that centuries ago there were tyrannical or *despotic* governments in Western
Europe.
Thus, the fascist governments represent a
regression or reversion to an earlier form of
government.

21. B.   In the third paragraph, the author mentions the
"restriction of view" imposed by the modern
synthesis, a synthesis he and many of his fellow evolutionists have challenged.
Choice A is incorrect. The author states that the
"modern synthesis works in its appropriate
arena."
Choices C and D are incorrect. It was prior to
the modern synthesis that scientists such as
Bateson found the proposed mechanisms of
evolution *confusing* and *contradictory*.
Choice E is incorrect. According to the author,
he and many other contemporary evolutionists
find the Darwinian synthesis simplistic; they
find the current rethinking of evolutionary theory to be productive.

22. C.   The movement of billiard balls on a pool table
is relatively simple to predict: you can measure
the forces involved and figure out where the
balls will go. Compared to the complexity of
life, the billiard ball example provides *an example of a relatively uncomplicated system.*

23. C.   The opening sentence briefly mentions Darwinian theory's extending its domain, stating
that while it has been doing so some problems
have arisen. This suggests that the author has
just been discussing the *expansion* or extension
of evolutionary theory into new fields.

24. A.   You can answer this question by the process of
elimination.
The author would be likely to agree with Statement I: he cites the confusion and depression
expressed by post-Darwinian biologists unable
to resolve the contradictions inherent in the
then current version of evolutionary theory.
Therefore, you can eliminate Choice B.
The author would be unlikely to agree with
Statement II: he attributes despondency to Darwin's successors, not to Darwin. Therefore,
you can eliminate Choices C and E.
The author would be unlikely to agree with
Statement III: although he quotes Darwin's
comparison of the two systems, he indicates
that Darwin preferred the "wondrous and unpredictable change" of life in its complexity to
the static cycling of the spheres. Therefore,
you can eliminate Choice D.
Only Choice A is left. It is the correct answer.

25. A.   The author poses questions about how well
Darwinism works as a model and provides the
example of *Biston betularia* as an instance of
minor, local, adaptive adjustment. He uses the
metaphor of the pool table, and refers to
Bateson and to Darwin, quoting the latter. He
never *denounces* or censures an opponent.

26. B.   The transformation of certain members of
Biston betularia into black moths can be cate-
gorized as *minor adjustment within populations.* In this instance, the substitution of a
single gene (a minor adjustment) brought about
an adaptive change, a selected response that
made the moths less visible against their
background.

27. B.   The passage states that populations of the moth
Biston betularia turned black, thus gaining the
selective advantage of blending in better with
their soot-darkened environment.
No information is provided to answer the other
questions.

28. C.   The opposite of to *disregard* or ignore is to
heed or pay attention to.
Think of "disregarding a warning."

29. B.   The opposite of *veracity* or truthfulness is *mendacity* or dishonesty.
Word Parts Clue: *Ver-* means truth. *Veracity*
means truthfulness.
Think of "trusting someone's veracity."

30. E.   The opposite of to *bedeck* or ornament pro-
fusely is to *strip.*
Think of someone "bedecked in diamonds and
furs."

31. D.   The opposite of *spurious* (false or fraudulent)
is *genuine.*
Think of forgers selling "a spurious work of
art."

32. A.   The opposite of to *estrange* or alienate is to
reconcile.
Think of "estranged couples" in a divorce.

33. B.   The opposite of *provident* or frugal is *prodigal*
or extravagant.
Think of the fable of the prodigal grasshopper
and the provident ant.

34. D.   The opposite of to *capitulate* or yield is to
resist.
Think of "capitulating without a fight."

35. C.   The opposite of *indigenous* or native is *alien* or
foreign.
Beware eye-catchers. Choice A is incorrect.
Do not confuse *indigenous* or native with *indigent* or poor.

36. A.   The opposite of *salubrity* or healthfulness is
unwholesomeness.
Think of "the salubrity of mountain air."

37. D. The opposite of to *quail* or lose courage is to *become resolute* or firm.
Think of "quailing in fear."

38. B. The opposite of *tantamount* or equivalent in value is *not equivalent*.
Context Clue: "Failure to publish is tantamount to suppression."

Section 2

1. C. The key phrase here is "simplest in structure." In biology, *primitive* life forms are considered simple. Evolved forms are more specialized and do things in more complex ways.

2. C. The leaders would be *apprehensive* in such circumstances that they could not achieve their goal of reconciliation.
Note that the clause "negotiations have reached such a state" generally implies that they have reached a sorry state.

3. B. If we are not *wary* or cautious, even we may be fooled by propaganda. One does not have to be *gullible* or easily deceived to fall for such tricks.

4. C. *Charlatan* is another term for a *quack* or pretender to medical knowledge.

5. E. The statement that "we do not know" whether a gesture indicates devotion or despair suggests that gestures are by their nature *ambiguous* or unclear.

6. A. The common expectation is that *refined* or genteel people would reject evil while *coarse* people would tolerate it. However, the reverse holds true: *paradoxically*, the coarse word *condemns* an evil and the *refined* word excuses or condones it.
Watch out for words like *paradoxically* that signal the unexpected.

7. D. The incongruity here is that one group finds Woolf too feminine for their tastes while another finds her not feminine (or perhaps feminist) enough for theirs.
Note that the word *peculiar* signals that Woolf's destiny is an unexpected one.

8. E. A *dropcloth* protectively covers *furniture*. An *apron* protectively covers *clothing*.

(Function)

9. E. An *archipelago* is a group or chain of *islands*. A *constellation* is a group of *stars*.
Beware eye-catchers. A *garden* does not by definition consist of *flowers*; a garden may comprise vegetables instead.

(Part to Whole)

10. C. To *crow* is to express oneself in a *boastful* manner. To *pout* is to express oneself in a *sulky* manner.

(Defining Characteristic)

11. C. By definition, an *ascetic* (one who practices severe self-discipline) is characterized by *self-denial*. A *zealot* (extreme enthusiast) is characterized by *fanaticism*.
Beware eye-catchers. A *miser* may hoard wealth, but he is not necessarily characterized by *affluence*. Even poor persons may be misers.

(Defining Characteristic)

12. A. To *camouflage* something is to make it difficult to *discern* or perceive. To *encipher* or encode something is to make it difficult to *comprehend*.

(Function)

13. B. A *seer* or prophet is by definition someone gifted in *prophecy*. A *sage* or wise person is by definition someone gifted in *wisdom*.

(Defining Characteristic)

14. C. A *bracket* is a support for a *shelf*. A *strut* is a support for a *rafter*.
Note that you are being tested on an unfamiliar secondary meaning of *strut*. As always in dealing with the more difficult questions at the end of the analogy section, be suspicious when you come across what seems like a familiar word that is being used in an apparently incongruous context. You may be being tested on an unfamiliar secondary meaning of the word.

(Function)

15. A. *Taxonomy* is the science or study of the *classification* of plants and animals. *Etymology* is the science or study of the *derivation* of words.

(Defining Characteristic)

16. B. To be *brusque* or abrupt is to exhibit *unceremoniousness*. To be *obstinate* or stubborn is to exhibit *intractability*.

(Synonym Variant)

17. B. In the third paragraph the author argues that women "have been unified by values, conventions, experiences, and behaviors impinging on each individual." To the extent that they have done this, they have come to constitute a subculture within our society. It is as part of such a subculture that women writers become conscious of their own female literary tradition. Thus, their *assimilation of the values* of their subculture furthers their ability to recognize the female literary tradition.

18. D.   The author opens the paragraph by stating that many literary critics have begun reinterpreting the study of women's literature. She then goes on to cite individual comments that support her assertion. Clearly, she is *receptive* or open to the ideas of these writers, for they and she share a common sense of the need to reinterpret their common field.

Choices A and B are incorrect. The author cites the literary critics straightforwardly, presenting their statements as evidence supporting her thesis.

Choice C is incorrect. The author does not *disparage* or belittle these critics. By quoting them respectfully she implicitly acknowledges their competence.

Choice E is incorrect. The author quotes the critics as acknowledged experts in the field. However, she is quite ready to disagree with their conclusions (as she disagrees with Moers' view of women's literature as an international movement). Clearly, she does not look on these critics with *awe*.

19. E.   Question E is answerable on the basis of the passage. According to lines 7–8, Mills disbelieved in the idea that women "have had a literature of their own all along."

20. C.   The gaps exist in the female literary tradition because once-famous female authors disappear from the records posthumously: they cease to be the subjects of critical discussion, and vanish as if they never had existed. Thus, there is no continuity in the female literary tradition.

21. B.   The writer neither lists (*enumerates*) nor sorts (*classifies*) anything in the opening paragraph.

Choice A is incorrect. The writer likens the female tradition to a lost continent and develops the metaphor by describing the continent "rising...from the sea of English literature."

Choice C is incorrect. The author refers or *alludes* to the classical legend of Atlantis.

Choice D is incorrect. The author quotes Colby and Thompson.

Choice E is incorrect. The author contrasts the revised view of women's literature with Mills' view.

22. B.   If women writers have no history, they have to rediscover the past. In the process, they *create* or forge their consciousness of what their sex has achieved.

Here *forge* is used with its meaning of *fashion* or *make*, as blacksmiths forge metal by hammering it into shape. It is in this sense that James Joyce used *forge* in *A Portrait of the Artist as a Young Man*, whose hero goes forth to "forge in the smithy of [his] soul the uncreated conscience of [his] race."

23. C.   The author both cites Moers' work in support of her own assertions and argues against the validity of Moers' conclusion that women's literature is an international movement. Thus, while she finds Moers' work basically *admirable* and worthy of respect, she considers it *inaccurate* in some of the conclusions it draws.

Choice A is incorrect. The author would not cite Moers as she does in the second paragraph if she believed Moers to be wholly *misleading*.

Choice B is incorrect. Since the author disagrees with at least one of Moers' conclusions, she obviously does not find Moers' work the *definitive* or final word.

Choices D and E are incorrect. Neither is supported by the author's mentions of Moers.

24. B.   Both the author's use of the phrase "a literature of their own" in the opening paragraph and her ongoing exploration of what she means by the female literary tradition in the English novel support this choice.

Choice A is incorrect. It is not the uniqueness of the phenomenon but the traditional nature of the phenomenon that interests the author.

Choice C is incorrect. The passage deals specifically with women's *literary* tradition.

Choice D is incorrect. The passage is concerned with the roots of female writing, not with its present day manifestations.

Choice E is incorrect. The author presents no such choice.

25. C.   The opening paragraph discusses changes in the idea of matter, emphasizing the use of musical terminology to describe the concepts of physics. The second paragraph then goes on to develop the theme of the music of matter.

Choice A is incorrect. Although the author gives examples of the physicists' "strange new language" his chief concern is with the physical concepts themselves, not with their linguistic ramifications.

Choice B is incorrect. Music does not directly influence the interactions of the particles; physicists merely use musical terms to describe these interactions.

Choice D is incorrect. The passage nowhere suggests the quark is to be eliminated.

Choice E is incorrect. The passage says nothing about proving or disproving the existence of matter.

26. D.   The author mentions these terms as examples of what he means by the strange new language or *idiosyncratic nomenclature* of modern particle physics.

27. D.   In his references to the elegance of the newly discovered subatomic structures and to the dance of Creation, the author conveys his *admiration* and *enthusiasm*.

Choice A is incorrect. While the author is clearly sympathetic to the new physics, his attitude is not one of apprehension or *concern*.

Choices B and C are incorrect. The author sees no occasion for *indignation* (resentment) or *derision* (scorn) in the new physics.

Choice E is incorrect. The author views the elegant world of subatomic physics with wonder and delight, not with doubt.

28. **C.** The opposite of to *rectify* or correct is to *make worse*.
    Word Parts Clue: *Rect-* means right; *-ify* means to make. *Rectify* means to make right.
    Think of "rectifying an error."

29. **C.** The opposite of the *apex* or highest point is the *lowest point*.
    Think of being at "the apex of one's career."

30. **A.** The opposite of *prosaic* (dull, matter-of-fact) is *imaginative*.
    Think of "being bored by a commonplace, prosaic job."

31. **B.** The opposite of *dissonance* or discord is *harmony*.
    Word Parts Clue: *Dis-* means apart; *son-* means sound. *Dissonance* is the state of sounding apart (that is, not in harmony).
    Think of an instance of "jarring dissonance."

32. **C.** The opposite of *doltish* or stupid is *clever*.
    Think of "a doltish blockhead."

33. **E.** The opposite of to *chagrin* (disappoint) is to *please*.
    Beware eye-catchers. Choice A is incorrect. *Chagrin* is unrelated to *grin*.
    Think of "being chagrined by a defeat."

34. **A.** The opposite of *disingenuous* or guileful (giving a false impression of naivete) is *naive* or unsophisticated.
    Think of a "disingenuous appearance of candor."

35. **B.** The opposite of *recalcitrance* or stubbornness is *submissiveness*.
    Think of "obstinate recalcitrance."

36. **C.** The opposite of *fecundity* or fruitfulness is *barrenness*.
    Think of "the earth's abundant fecundity."

37. **D.** The opposite of *lugubrious* or melancholy is *jocose* or given to jesting.
    Think of "lugubrious mourners."

38. **D.** The opposite of *animus* or hostility is *amity* or friendliness and good will.
    Beware eye-catchers. Choice A, though tempting, is incorrect. *Hospitality* is an action (the enthusiastic reception of guests), not an emotion: when you speak of someone's hospitality, you are speaking of what he does, not of what he feels.

Section 3

1. **B.** Since the value of the fraction is negative, the denominator must be negative since the numerator has a positive value. Therefore the value of x is less than 1.

2. **A.** $y^2 - 1 = 3$
   $y^2 = 4$
   $y = \pm 2$
   Since $x = 3$, x is larger than y.

3. **A.** The perimeter = 4(2) or 8 feet.
   The area = $(2)^2$ or 4 square feet.

4. **C.** $\dfrac{1}{x} \div \dfrac{1}{\frac{1}{x}} = \dfrac{1}{x} \div \dfrac{x}{1} = \left(\dfrac{1}{x}\right)\left(\dfrac{1}{x}\right) = \dfrac{1}{x^2}$

   $\dfrac{1}{x} \cdot \dfrac{1}{x} = \dfrac{1}{x^2}$

5. **D.** x could be 9, 18, or 27.

6. **B.** Because the measure of $\angle A$ is 70°, the sum of the measures of angles B and C is 110°.
   Since $\angle B = \angle C$ and $x = 27\frac{1}{2}$, the value of y is $180 - 2(27\frac{1}{2})$ or 125. Because $2x = 55$ choice B is correct.

7. **D.** We know that $a + b = 90$, that $90 - b = a$, and that $90 - a = b$. Because we may not assume that $a = b$, choice D is correct.

8. **C.** $\sqrt{\dfrac{2x}{y}} \cdot \sqrt{\dfrac{xy}{2}} = \sqrt{\dfrac{2x^2y}{2y}} = \sqrt{x^2} = x$

9. **C.** $\dfrac{\frac{3}{4}}{1+\frac{1}{2}}$ or $\dfrac{\frac{3}{4}}{\frac{3}{2}}$ or $\dfrac{3}{4} \div \dfrac{3}{2}$ or $\dfrac{\cancel{3}}{\cancel{4}_2} \cdot \dfrac{\cancel{2}}{\cancel{3}} = \dfrac{1}{2}$

10. **C.** If $\frac{1}{2}AC = \frac{1}{2}BC = \frac{1}{2}AB$, then $AC = AB = BC$. The triangle is equilateral and $z = 60$. Since BD divides AC so that $AD = DC$, it is also perpendicular, forming right triangle BDC, and $x = 90$. This question is an application of the Pythagorean theorem.

11. **C.** $AC = 5.6 - 2.8 = 2.8$
    $BD = 6.2 - 3.4 = 2.8$

12. **A.** ABD is equilateral. $x = y = w = 60$. Since $AB \perp BC$, $y + z = 90$, and $z = 30$. BC lies opposite v which equals 120° and DC lies opposite the 30° angle. Therefore, $BC > DC$.

13. B.   The sum of 2 negative integers is negative. The product of 2 negative integers is positive.

14. C.   Because the perimeters are equal, we can say that $4a = 3b = 5c$.
Because equals added to equals results in equals, $5c + 3b$ (Column A) $= 4a + 5c$ (Column B).

15. A.   Since the measure of $\angle C$ is 60, the measure of $\angle A + \angle B$ is 120, and therefore the measure of

$\angle A$ is more than $\dfrac{1}{2}$ of 120, since A is larger

than B (given). Side CB lies opposite the angle with a measure of more than 60 and is therefore larger than side AB, which lies opposite the angle with a measure of 60.

16. A.   Minimum crates $= 3$
Minimum weight $= 125$ pounds
3×125 $= 375$ pounds

17. D. $\angle ADC > \angle ABD$ (the exterior angle of a triangle is greater than either remote interior angle); $\angle ADC > \angle ACD$ (since $\angle ACD = \angle ABD$); $AC > AD$ (In a triangle the larger side is opposite the larger angle.)

18. C.   Examine the problem graphically. $\dfrac{1}{2}$ of 12 (or

6) belong to Club A, but note that 3 of these

belong to both A and B. $\dfrac{1}{3}$ of 12 (or 4) belong

to Club B, but of these 3 also belong to Club A. We have thus accounted for 7 men who are club members. Therefore, 5 men belong to neither club.

19. B.   Since $d > 7$, the charge for the first week, c cents, must be paid plus f cents for each additional day. The number of days over and above 1 week $= (d - 7)$. The charge for these days is $f(d - 7)$. Total cost $=$
$c + f(d + 7)$.

20. D.   Let $\dfrac{2x}{3x}$ = the original fraction.

$$\frac{2x - 6}{3x} = \frac{2}{3}\left(\frac{2x}{3x}\right) \text{[given]}$$
$$\frac{2x - 6}{3x} = \frac{4x}{9x}$$
$$\frac{2x - 6}{3x} = \frac{4}{9}$$
$$18x - 54 = 12x$$
$$6x = 54$$
$$x = 9$$

numerator $= 2x$ or 18

21. B.   I is not correct. The weight of the skeleton and blood = 15,000 grams.

$\dfrac{15,000}{70,000}$ is less than $\dfrac{1}{2}$.

II is correct. The weight of the liver is 1,700 grams. The total body weight is 70,000 grams.

$\dfrac{1,700}{70,000} = \dfrac{17}{700} = 2.4\%$

III is not correct. The weight of the blood in the average adult is half the weight of the skeleton.

22. A.   Set up a proportion.
Let x = total body weight in terms of g.

$\dfrac{\text{weight of skeleton}}{\text{total body weight}} = \dfrac{10,000 \text{ grams}}{70,000 \text{ grams}} = \dfrac{g}{x}$

$\dfrac{1}{7} = \dfrac{g}{x}$

$x = 7g$

23. E. $\dfrac{1000}{2500} = \dfrac{\text{part}}{\text{entire}} = \dfrac{2}{5} = \dfrac{2}{5}$ of $360° = 144°$

24. C. $\dfrac{\text{part}}{\text{whole}} = \dfrac{400}{2,500} = \dfrac{4}{25} = 16\%$

25. D.   Output through kidneys = 1500 cc. (Graph II)
Intake in fluids = 1500 cc. (Graph I)

$\dfrac{1,500}{1,500} = 1 = 100\%$

26. B. a eggs must weigh ab ounces. Minimum weight for all c eggs $= cd$ ounces. Minimum weight for all f eggs $= fg$ ounces. Minimum weight of all eggs $=$
$ab + cd + fg$.

27. **C.** There is a direct proportion between the two types of tumblers.

$$\frac{3 \text{ large tumblers}}{5 \text{ small tumblers}} = \frac{1 \text{ large tumbler}}{x \text{ small tumblers}}$$

$$3x = 5$$

$$x = \frac{5}{3} \text{ or } 1\frac{2}{3}$$

28. **B.** $OA = OB = 4$
$m\angle AOB = \text{arc } AB = 112°$
$m\angle OAB + m\angle ABO = 68°$
$m\angle OAB = m\angle ABO = 34°$

29. **B.** $\angle 1 = \angle 2$ (Vertical angles are equal.)
$\triangle AEB$ is similar to $\triangle DEC$.
Since $\dfrac{CD}{AB} = \dfrac{4}{8}$ or $\dfrac{1}{2}$, then $\dfrac{CE}{EB} = \dfrac{1}{2}$.

Let $x = CE$.
Let $y = EB$.
Then $\dfrac{x}{y} = \dfrac{1}{2}$ and $2x = y$. Since

$$x + y = 4$$
$$x + 2x = 5$$
$$3x = 5$$
$$\text{and } x = \frac{5}{3} \ (CE)$$

In right triangle CED, leg $CD = 4$,
leg $CE = \dfrac{5}{3}$.
By the Pythagorean theorem
$$(CE)^2 + (CD)^2 = (ED)^2$$
$$\left(\frac{5}{3}\right)^2 + 4^2 = (ED)^2$$
$$\frac{25}{9} + 16 = (ED)^2$$
$$\frac{169}{9} = (ED)^2$$
$$\frac{13}{3} = ED$$

If $ED = \dfrac{13}{3}$ then $AE = \dfrac{26}{3}$.

Therefore $AD = \dfrac{39}{3} = 13$.

30. **A.** Note that 7 students take both subjects. 20 students take chemistry only and 15 students take physics only. The ratio of those taking physics only to those taking chemistry only is $\dfrac{15}{20}$ or $\dfrac{3}{4}$ or 3:4.

Section 4

1. **C.** Radii OD and OC are equal legs of right triangle DOC. Area of $DOC = \dfrac{1}{2}$ (leg)(leg) = 12.5 or (leg)² = 25. Therefore, leg = 5. Since leg (or radius) equals 5, the area of the circle equals 25π.

2. **C.** Let $x =$ the price of the item.
$$0.8x + 8 = x$$
$$8x + 80 = 10x$$
$$80 = 2x$$
$$x = 40$$

3. **C.** Since this is a parallelogram, $EH = FG$.

4. **B.** Column A: $\dfrac{2+3}{3} = \dfrac{5}{3} = 1\dfrac{2}{3}$

Column B: $\dfrac{3+4}{4} = \dfrac{7}{4} = 1\dfrac{3}{4}$

Since $1\dfrac{3}{4}$ is greater than $1\dfrac{2}{3}$, choice B is correct.

5. **C.** The area of $ABCD = (BC)(DC)$ or $(2.5\pi)(10)$ or 25π. The area of the circle $= \pi r^2$.
Since the diameter = 10, the radius = 5 and the area $= \pi r^2$, or 25π.

6. **A.** $125R = 81$
$$R = \frac{81}{125}$$
$$5 > R$$

7. **A.** $(-3)^9$ has a negative value (Column B)
$(-3)^8$ has a positive value (Column A)

8. **C.** If the arithmetic mean of b and c is 60, then $b + c = 120$. Therefore $a = 180 - 120$ or 60.

9. **B.** The value of r is between -2 and -9. For any of these values r^7 would be negative. For example, if $r = -2$, then $\dfrac{1}{r^7} = \dfrac{1}{-128}$ or $-\dfrac{1}{128}$.
For any of these values for r, r^6 would have a positive value. For example, if $r = -2$, then
$$\frac{1}{r^6} = \frac{1}{64}.$$
$$\frac{1}{64} > -\frac{1}{128}.$$

10. D. $\dfrac{c^2 d^2 e^2}{c^3 d^3 e^3}$ or $\dfrac{1}{cde}$ may be larger than, smaller

than, or equal to $\dfrac{cde}{3}$ depending upon the

values of c, d, and e.

11. A. Because $b = 125$, $x = 55$, and $y = 180 - (55 + 70)$ or $180 - 125$ or 55, therefore $c = 180 - 55$ or 125 and $a = 180 - 70$ or 110. Thus $c > a$, and choice A is correct.

12. C. $x^2 = xy$. Divide by x and $x = y$.

13. A. $\dfrac{1}{2} + \dfrac{1}{3} = \dfrac{5}{6} = \dfrac{25}{30}$ $\dfrac{2}{5} = \dfrac{12}{30}$

14. C. The measure of $\angle ACB = 180° - 125°$ or $55°$.
The measure of $\angle BAC = 180° - 110°$ or $70°$.
The measure of $\angle ABC = 180° - (55° + 70°)$ or $55°$.
Because angles B and C have equal measures, $AB = AC$.

15. A. Measure of $\angle ABC = 80°$.
Measure of $\angle CAB = 180° - (80° + 30°)$ or $70°$.

Therefore $a = 35$ and $b = \dfrac{1}{2}(80)$ or 40.

Therefore $d = 180 - (35 + 40)$ or 105.

16. B. To compare fractions, change all fractions to fractions with the same numerator or denominator.

$\dfrac{2}{9} = \dfrac{1}{4\frac{1}{2}}$; $\dfrac{3}{11} = \dfrac{1}{3\frac{2}{3}}$; $\dfrac{4}{13} = \dfrac{1}{3\frac{1}{3}}$

$\dfrac{1}{8}$ has the largest denominator.

17. C. Since ABC is equilateral, the measure of $\angle BAC = 60$ and of $ACB = 60$.
$$\begin{aligned} 53 + x &= 60 \\ x &= 7 \\ 72 - y &= 60 \\ -y &= -12 \\ y &= 12 \\ x + y &= 19 \end{aligned}$$

18. D. Since $BE = AE$, the measure of $\angle BAE = ABE = 50$. In triangle BAE, the measure of $\angle AEB = 180 - 100 = 80$. Since $BE \parallel CD$, the measure of $\angle ADC =$ the measure of $\angle AEB = 80$.

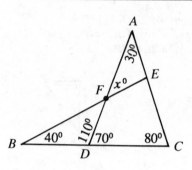

19. A. In $\triangle ADC$, since the measure of $\angle A = 30$ and the measure of $\angle C = 80$, then the measure of $\angle ADC = 70$ and its supplement $\angle FDB = 110$. Then the measure of $\angle BFD = 30$ which $= \angle AFE$ (vertical angles).

20. C. $$\begin{aligned} 2 \oslash a &= 4 + a \\ a \oslash 3 &= 2a + 3 \\ 4 + a &= 2a + 3 \\ 1 &= a \end{aligned}$$

21. E. Using a straightedge at the lowest line of the table, read the figure under the column marked 15.

22. D. In the body of the table, find the payment $50.00, and note that it is to the right of the $5000 row and under the 18-year column.

23. C. In the table, find the row for $5000. Then note that the payment for a 17-year loan is $51.07 per month, while an 18-year loan requires a payment of $50.00 per month. The difference is $1.07 per month.

24. B. The monthly payment is $10.00.

$\dfrac{\$10}{\$1000} = \dfrac{1}{100}$, or 1%.

25. D. At $10.00 a month, or $120.00 per year, the total payments for 18 years would amount to $2160. $2160 - 1000 = \$1160$.

26. C.
$$\frac{\text{number of girls}}{\text{total number of students}} = \frac{\text{part of class made}}{\text{up of girls}}$$
$$= \frac{x}{x + y}$$

27. D. $\angle 1 + \angle 4 = 180°$
$145° + \angle 4 = 180°$
$\angle 4 = 35°$
$\angle 2 + \angle 5 = 180°$
$125° + \angle 5 = 180°$
$\angle 5 = 55°$
$\angle 4 + \angle 5 + \angle 3 = 180°$
(the sum of the angles of a triangle equals 180°)
$35° + 55° + \angle 3 = 180°$
$\angle 3 = 90°$

28. E.
$$4 \text{ quarts} = 1 \text{ gallon}$$
$$16 \text{ quarts} = 4 \text{ gallons}$$
$$2 \text{ pints} = 1 \text{ quart}$$
$$32 \text{ pints} = 16 \text{ quarts}$$
$$\text{or, } 64 \text{ half pints} = 16 \text{ quarts}$$

29. C.   First mixture
$(33¢) (2 \text{ pounds}) = 66¢$
$(24¢) (1 \text{ pound}) = \underline{24¢}$
$\quad\quad 90¢$ is cost of 3 pounds or
$\quad\quad 30¢$ is cost of 1 pound.

Second mixture
$(33¢) (1 \text{ pound}) = 33¢$
$(24¢) (2 \text{ pounds}) = \underline{48¢}$
$\quad\quad 81¢$ is cost of 3 pounds or
$\quad\quad 27¢$ is cost of 1 pound.

The shop will save 3¢ per pound or $3.00 for 100 pounds.

30. C.   Let x = number of minutes allowed for each of the questions other than the mathematics problems. Then $2x$ = number of minutes allowed for each mathematics problem. $(50)(2x)$ or $100x$ = number of minutes allowed for all mathematics problems. $(150)(x)$ or $150x$ = number of minutes allowed for all other questions.
$$100x + 150x = \text{total time} = 3 \text{ hours}$$
$$= 180 \text{ minutes}$$
$$100x + 150x = 180$$
$$250x = 180$$
$$x = \frac{180}{250}$$
$$100x = \frac{180}{250}100 = 72 \text{ minutes}$$

Section 5

1–4.   It would be helpful to make a chart to summarize the information:

Route	Miles	Toll
Bridge	20	$0.75
Tunnel	10	$1.00 + 10¢ each additional passenger
Highway	50 (30 to B, 20 to C)	None

1. A.   The mileage from City B to City C is 20 miles on the highway. The other choices would mean going to City A (30 miles) and then taking either the tunnel (10 miles) or the bridge (20 miles).

2. D.   The mileage on the toll-free highway from City A to City B is 30 miles. The other choices involve going to City C by bridge or tunnel, then from City C for 20 miles to City B.

3. C.   The difference in cost between the bridge toll and the tunnel toll is negligible considering the possible docking of pay due to lateness. Therefore, the most important factor would be traffic conditions, which could cause delays.

4. E.   Generally speaking, the extra 25¢ for using the tunnel would be worth the cost to save the extra 10 miles when crossing the bridge, so IV is not a chief factor. Whether a commuter lived on the outskirts of the city or in its center would affect only the choice of local roads to get to one of the main arteries, so III is not a main consideration. Traffic and road conditions, however, can be expected to influence a driver to choose one means over the other, since delays can cause lateness (I). Also, if the car has many passengers, at 10¢ a passenger, there could be a possible saving in using the bridge (II). Factors I and II are important in choosing between the bridge and the tunnel.

5. D.   The established precedent is the best argument for permitting the church to use the park.

6. B.   The argument in (A) could be used by the church. The correct answer is (B) since there would be some inconvenience to those who are not members of that church. We cannot assume that the church meeting would be excessively noisy (C). We cannot assume that the church people will leave litter to be cleaned up (E).

7. D. The original statement is a conclusion. The correct answer is the argument from which it can be drawn; that is, choice D. If Wilbur were six feet tall or less, he would be seated in the first row. He is not in the first row; therefore, he is not six feet tall or less. (If P, then Q. Not Q; therefore, not P.) We can draw no conclusions from any of the other choices; They all allow the possibility that Wilbur is only 5′11″ tall (or 3′11″ tall, for that matter).

8–12. It would be useful to summarize the information as follows:

Large University	J, K, L
Small College	M, N, O, P

English Literature	J, O, P
Mathematics	K, M
Natural Sciences	L
Latin	N

8. E. J and P cannot serve on the same committee since they both teach English literature I. If J cannot serve then K and L must serve. If K is serving, M may not represent the small college (II). Since L must serve, (III) is correct.

9. A. Committee K, L, M has K and M on the same committee (B). J, K, L has no representative from the small college (C). J, O, N commits two errors. It has two representatives from the small college and it has J and O on the same committee (D). J, K, M has K and M on the same committee (E).

10. B. K and M both teach mathematics (A). O cannot serve with P since they both represent the small college and they both teach English literature (C). J cannot serve with P because they both teach English literature (D). M and N cannot serve with P for they all represent the small college.

11. C. If L is not available then J and K must serve. Since J is serving neither O nor P may serve.

12. E. (I) is incorrect since N and O represent the small college. (II) is correct. M and O represent the small college. (III) is correct. When M serves, K may not serve.

13. C. Both parents of a Brown female are Brown, but her father was born Red. Her mother's mother was Brown, and therefore that grandfather was born Red (I); her father's mother was Red (II), and therefore that grandfather was born Brown (III). Use the following logic: if the parents were born in different groups, and the grandmothers were in the same groups as the parents, the grandfathers must have been in different groups.

14. A. This male's mother is Brown, and his father was born Red. His mother's unmarried brother is Brown, his father's unmarried brother is Red—not to mention married brothers of his parents! Our friend may only marry a Red woman, and their children will be Red (B, C); any persons the children marry must be born Brown (D, E).

15. B. A Red female's mother is Red, and the brother, whether unmarried, divorced, or a widower, is also Red. No Red may marry a Red. The Brown male's father was born Red, so his sister is Red (A). The brother of the man born Red (who as a widow, is Red again) was also born Red, so his wife (now his widow) is Brown (C). Any widower has reverted to his original group, while his wife's sister is in the same group as his wife was (D). Any widow's daughter is in her own group, and the ex-husband, having reverted to the group of his birth, will be eligible (E).

16. D. The woman's mother has the same group as she; the mother's brother was born into this group, but married into the other and, as a widower (according to the changed rules) remains in the second group, so marriage is possible. The dead sister's husband remains in the same group as the dead sister and is not eligible (A). The daughter is in the mother's group and the ex-husband remains in it and so is not eligible (B). The widower retains his married group; his brother, born in the same group as he was, is in the same married group; so is his daughter, and is not eligible (C). The divorced male now has his ex-wife's group; so does the sister, widowed or otherwise, so no marriage is possible (E).

17–22. The trick here is to determine the relative positions of the letters on the basis of the clues, just as if this were a puzzle dealing with persons in a line or any similar situation. Questions 17 and 18 can then be answered immediately; Questions 19–22 involve simple arithmetic which is easy once the relative positions of the letters that stand for the integers are known. Start with the most definite statement, that B is the middle term, and diagram it like this:

$$\_ \ \_ \ \_ \ \overset{\text{B}}{\_} \ \_ \ \_ \ \_$$

The preceding statement, that D is 3 less than

A, gives two possible positions for A (A cannot be where B is or to the left; and it cannot be at the extreme right because then D would be where B is):

_ D _ B A _ _

or

_ _ D B _ A _

The third statement, F is as much less than B as C is greater than D, yields three possibilities: F is 1, 2, or 3 less than B. If F is 1 less than B, C is 1 greater than D. This is not possible in either of the two diagrams above. If F is 3 less than B, C is 3 greater than D. This, too, is not possible in either diagram. If F is 2 less than B, C is 2 greater than D. This is not possible in the first diagram, but it is possible in the second. This, then, must be the correct solution. The two end positions must therefore belong to E and G, and the last statement tells you G must be to the right of F. So you have:

E F D B C A G

The questions are now easy.

17. **B.** By inspection of the diagram.

18. **D.** According to the diagram, A is 4 greater than F, and D is 4 less than G.

19. **B.** Given a value for any of the letters, you can find the values of all the others. If A = 7, E = 2 and G = 8. Their sum is 10. Be careful that you don't assume that A = 7 in the other questions. That is given for this question only.

20. **D.** You might choose E on the reasoning that, if no value is given for any letter, no numerical value can be found for A − F. But this is wrong. You *can* tell that A is 4 greater than F. When any number is subtracted from a second number 4 greater than the first number, the result is 4, no matter what the numbers are.

21. **D.** C is 4 greater than E, so T is 4 greater than C. But this means that T is 3 greater than A. If T = A + E and T = A + 3, E = 3. If E = 3, D = 5.

22. **D.** If the seven integers all fall in the span from 1 to 10, then the highest possible value of C will occur if the seven letters represent the integers 4-10. In this case, C = 8. The smallest possible value of D will occur if the seven letters represent the integers 1-7. In this case, D = 3, and 8 − 3 = 5.

23. **B.** Nancy says that what Ellen reports can't be true and offers, as evidence, Julie's high school grades. The assumption must be that no one who got such grades is likely to flunk out of college. Choice A is wrong because Ellen merely reports what she has heard; by disrupting it, Nancy does not brand her a liar. Nor does Ellen necessarily assume that the rumor is true (C). D is wrong because Nancy does not necessarily claim that Julie has not left college —only that she hasn't flunked out. Ellen has only *heard* something—she *knows* nothing (E).

24. **D.** The president states that any measures required to defeat the "takeover," i.e., to maintain full control, are justified, whether legal or not. This implies D. The president does *not* say that illegal measures *will* definitely be required (A) or allege anything about the union (B). He or she states that *in this case* the workers are trying to take control; E is an unsupported generalization. The president's statements establish only what the president advocates, not what he or she and the Board of Directors will *actually* do if the union wins (C).

25. **C.** Given the statement "If P, then Q," the *only* other statement that can be validly deduced from it is "If not Q, then not P." In this instance, P = presentation of a purple pass; Q = permission to enter the compound. Consequently, only statement III may be validly inferred. You cannot validly deduce "If not P, then not Q" (statement I) or "If Q, then P" (statement II).

Section 6

1–4.   The diagram shown here will make this puzzle much easier to follow.

The top row shows the top office holders; the second row shows the deputies; the third row shows the staffs. Note that these relationships are true no matter which office a given party holds.

1. D. Check the diagram, or reason as follows: the three Offices must always have two Democratic, two Conservative, and Two Justice Party deputies. When the Justice Party holds a top office, one of the deputies in that Office must be a Conservative, so only one of the deputies in the other Offices can be a Conservative. A, B, C, and E all follow logically from the rules and must be true.

2. D. Check the diagram—but remember that the staffs being asked about are not those under the Democratic President, but those under the Prime Minister, who can belong to *either* of the other parties. In each of the other Offices, one of the deputies must be a Democratic Party member who can have no Democratic staff members, while the other deputy *must* have one-half Democratic staff members—for a total of one-fourth the staff members in each office. If the Prime Minister is a Justice Party member, one-half the staff members will be Justice and one-fourth Conservative; if the Prime Minister is Conservative, it will be the other way around. So I must be true, and either II or III must also be true.

3. B. This must always be the case. Since the two deputies in any Office must each have a staff composed half of members of the top office holder's party, exactly half the staff members in any Office must always belong to one party. Choice E is, therefore, logically impossible. The rules for deputies and staffs exclude A and C. Exactly one-third of the total staff members in all three Offices must belong to each party (D).

4. C. The Conservative Chief of Staff has a Justice Department deputy, while the Justice Party Chief of Staff must not; since a Conservative deputy must be brought in, all the Conservative staff members of the fired Justice Party deputy must also be fired; however, the Democratic deputy may retain his or her Conservative staff members, which means only half of the Conservative staff members must be fired. Looking at the diagram, you can see that the Democratic deputy and his or her Justice Party staffers can retain their posts (A); while the Justice deputy must be fired, his or her Democratic staffers can stay (B); the Conservative Chief of Staff had no Conservative deputy (D); one deputy must be fired, but some Conservative staffers may retain their posts (E).

5. C. The statement given is true only if all members of the set "steering committee members" belong to the set "central committee members." (In a diagram, steering committee members would be a circle entirely inside a circle representing central committee members.) Choice A does not rule out the possibility that the steering committee has other members besides those who are on the central committee. B says that Elaine must belong to one of the committees, not necessarily to both. D is a weaker version of A; E establishes no link between central committee membership and steering committee membership.

6. E. If anyone other than a football player wears a football jersey, the conclusion is not valid; so it is valid only if choice D is true. The other choices establish, in various ways, that football players probably or certainly wear football jerseys, but this does not mean that no one else does.

7. E. Evidence of original insights (choice E) would best indicate the presence of what the author most stresses: independent critical thinking. Choice A may display ambition on the student's part; choice B evidences mastery of basic verbal skills; choice C shows a willingness to do hard work. But neither choice A, B, nor C is what the author would find *most* praiseworthy. Choice D is tempting, but simply avoiding clichés and vagueness does not necessarily display independent critical thinking.

8–11. You could make a calendar for these questions, but it would be very complicated. It's easier just to use the times given to make a table showing which possibilities can be scheduled without conflicts.

Course	Days	Time Choice 1	Time Choice 2
L	M–F	9:00 A.M.–11:00 A.M.	2:00 P.M.–4:00 P.M.
S^1	T–Th	12:00 N–3:00 P.M.	
S^2	M, W, F	10:00 A.M.–12:00 N	
A^1	M, W, F	12:30 P.M.–2:00 P.M.	
A^2	T–Th	10:30 A.M.–12:30 P.M.	
C	M–F	4 hours (1 session) between 9:00 A.M. and 4:00 P.M.	2 hours (2 sessions) between 9:00 A.M. and 4:00 P.M.

8. D. The table will tell you that D is impossible; Sanskrit on MWF meets from 10 to 12, which conflicts with Latin. The others are all possible.

9. A. This leaves the hours from 9 to 2 on Tuesday and Thursday free for Celtic Literature. Tom can schedule a 4-hour session at either 9 or 10 on either day (four possibilities), or two-hour sessions starting at 9, 10, 11, or 12 on Tuesday and Thursday (sixteen possible schedules), or two 2-hour sessions in 1 day on either day (four possibilities). The other choices leave either MWF from 2 to 4 or MWF from 12 to 2. In either case, there are only six possibilities for scheduling Celtic Literature.

10. D.   The Friday session must be either from 12 to 2 or from 2 to 4. No schedule leaves both these slots free. It can be 12 to 2 only if Tom takes Sanskrit on MWF and Armenian Literature on TTh. It can be 2 to 4 only if he takes Sanskrit on TTh and Armenian Literature on MWF.

11. B.   This one may be hard without a calendar; you must look back at the times listed, unless you included them in your table. The MWF 11-12:30 slot is open if Tom takes morning Latin (out at 11) and MWF Armenian Literature (starts at 12:30). This doesn't interfere with Celtic Literature. Choices A, C, and D conflict with Sanskrit; E conflicts with Armenian and Celtic Literature.

12–18.   To diagram this puzzle, start with several dashes in a column. These will represent the floors of the building. Start with more than six, so that a wrong guess doesn't push you off your diagram. Use initials and put one person or persons occupying an apartment on each side of a dash representing a given floor. Starting with L (and a blank for his roommate), A/C, M, and R and P fall into place easily. You now have six floors from top to bottom, so R and P must be on floor one. The only floors remaining with two blank spots are two and five; B and F must go on floor two and N must go three floors up, on floor five. The only remaining floor on which J can be three below anyone is floor three; W must be on floor six and E on floor five. You now have:

L/W or L—W
N/E or N—E
—A/C
J—M
B—F
R—P

Note that the diagram for floors five and six reflects the fact that Larry and Willy are on the same floor, as are Ned and Ellen, and may or may not be roommates.

12. C.   By inspection of the diagram. Note that choice D gives a correct list from *top to bottom*— don't get careless and choose this answer.

13. C.   Again by simple inspection of the diagram.

14. B.   The only person mentioned who can live on floor six, and therefore be Larry's roommate, is Willy.

15. A.   By inspection of the diagram, choices B and C also have the wrong persons above or below; choices D and E list the right persons, but Rick can't live on floor four or floor six.

16. E.   No one mentioned is on floor four; Willy *may* live with Larry on floor six.

17. B.   Follow the diagram: Joe goes from floor three to floor one; Rick or Paul goes to floor two; Bob or Frank goes to Ned or Ellen's apartment on floor five, and one of them goes to Joe's old apartment.

18. E.   Dorothy cannot possibly live with Frank, because we are told that he has a *single* apartment. All of the other persons mentioned as possibilities *may* have space available in their apartments.

19–22.   A diagram like the one shown will make it possible to trace the events without becoming confused. The other point to bear in mind is that you must avoid unsupported assumptions; for example, statement (2) doesn't mean that F *always* occurs if B occurs—just that it never occurs without B having occurred. Similarly, statement (1) doesn't mean that B or C *cannot* occur without A—just that *if* A occurs, one of these (but not both) will occur. Finally, statement (3) doesn't mean that D occurs *only* this way—it *may* occur on its own, without B or C, but it will *certainly* occur if B or C occurs. Unless you're clear on this, you'll probably miss some questions.

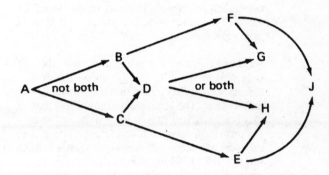

19. D.   A causes B *or* C, but not both. In either case, D occurs (III). F and E can occur *only* if B or C occurs, respectively, so they *cannot* both occur if A occurs (I, II). The other parts of I and II are consistent: G will occur if F occurs; H will occur if E occurs.

20. C.   See statement (3). F *may* occur if B occurs, but may not (choice A); D will occur if B occurs, but D may cause H instead of G (choice B); G occurs if F occurs and may occur if D occurs, but F need not occur if B occurs, while D can lead to H; so G *or* H must occur, but both need not occur (choice D); J *may* not occur even if E or F occurs (choice E).

21. C.   If J occurs, E or F must have occurred—statement (5); thus either B or C must have occurred—statements (2), (4). Since E *or* F, but not both, is required for J, choices A and B are wrong. If E occurs and F does not, G need not occur (choice D). B and C *can* both occur (if one is not caused by A) but both aren't necessary for J; they can lead to E and F, but one of these is all that is required for J to occur (choice E).

22. C.   D *may* occur without B or C; no cause for A is mentioned (I, II); but F occurs *only* if B occurs (statement 2) and so no other cause is possible (III).

23. E.   Statements I and II are plausible explanations for the students' passivity in previous years, but neither one can be inferred definitely (choices A and B); you cannot conclude that one of them must be true (some third explanation is possible) or that they exclude each other (both could be true simultaneously) (choice C). From the students' previous behavior, *no* valid inferences about their response to a new, larger tuition hike are possible (choices D and E).

24. D.   The original statement says that beauty has an objective existence, that is, can exist independently of a person's perceiving it. This would be a rebuttal to the claim made in choice D that beauty is purely subjective and so entirely dependent on its perception by some viewer. None of the other choices is in opposition to the original statement.

25. C.   Examine the structure of the argument: the only reason given for funding the research is that the possibility exists that the substances cure cancer. The unstated assumption is that this is a sufficient reason for providing funds. No probability is mentioned (choice A), and no comparison with other lines of research is made (choice B). D, while probably true, does not provide logical support for the argument about researching this specific possibility. The argument simply says that the government should provide the funds, not that they are definitely unavailable elsewhere (choice E).

Section 7

1. B.   The structure of the sentence indicates that you are looking for two synonyms or near-synonyms, in this case *squalor* and *filth*.

2. C.   To *rail against* fate would be to complain angrily about it or utter words of bitterness about it.
Note how the use of parallel structure (*neither...nor*) indicates that the two participial phrases linked together are similar in meaning.

3. C.   If the continents have formed sometime in the course of the earth's lifetime, then they are not *primordial* features of the earth that have existed from the earth's beginning.
As in the present sentence, inverted word order may sometimes indicate a contrast. The inversion of normal word order in the sentence opening ("Old as the continents are") is concessive: the writer is conceding a point. Rewritten in normal word order, the sentence would begin "Although the continents are old."

4. A.   Some aspects of the hypothesis can be criticized. However, its basic point still appears to hold true: it has not been *refuted* or disproved.

5. A.   It would be *ironic* or the reverse of what was expected for friends of judicial *autonomy* or independence to support the *abolition* or destruction of an independent judiciary.
Note how the use of *irony* implicitly signals the reversal of normal expectations.

6. B.   Readers would be disinclined to take seriously a work they considered *overwrought* or excessive in its *bold* theatricality.
Note how the use of *but* indicates that the second missing word contrasts with *enthralling* (absorbing) in meaning.

7. A.   When an activity is *repugnant* or distasteful, people will discontinue it as soon as they are free to do so. If parents and teachers make the process of getting an education distasteful, children will quit school as soon as they are no longer *coerced* or forced to attend.
Note how the "as long as … happens, so long will … happen" structure indicates cause and effect.

8. E.   A *moderator* presides over a *debate*. An *umpire* presides over a *game*.

(Function)

9. A.   *Delirium* causes *disorientation* or confusion. *Paralysis* causes *immobility* or loss of movement.

(Cause and Effect)

10. B.   A *glossary* or word list is composed of *words*. An *atlas* is composed of *maps*.

(Defining Characteristic)

11. B.   An *armature* is the skeleton that supports a *statue*. A *framework* is the skeleton that supports a *building*.

(Function)

12. B.   An *epaulet* is an ornament worn on the *shoulder*. A *tiara* is an ornament worn on the *head*.

(Defining Characteristic)

13. C.   A *bear* characteristically *lumbers* or moves heavily. A *goose* characteristically *waddles* or moves clumsily.

(Defining Characteristic)

14. A.   Someone *enervated* or weakened is lacking in *vigor* or strength. Someone *lax* or easy-going is lacking in *rigor* or severity.

(Antonym Variant)

15. D.   A *snail* is not noted for *celerity* or speed. A *peacock* is not noted for *humility* or modesty.

(Antonym Variant)

16. E.   *Adulation* or excessive flattery is more extreme than simple *flattery*. *Castigation* or severe reproof is more extreme than an *admonishment* or gentle reproof.

(Degree of Intensity)

17. C.   The references to the Inca empire and to the Andes Mountains, as well as to magical religions and chroniclers, suggest the Quechua world may be placed in ancient South America.

18. E.   The passage compares the Quechua empire to a *mandala* because "it was divided into four parts." Thus, a *mandala* is most likely a *figure composed of four divisions*.

19. B.   The author refers to the Quechua as existing in "a state of unremitting anxiety, which could not be resolved by action" and which a Quechua could deal with only by looking into himself and struggling with the depths of his own psyche. This suggests that the Quechua world was *highly introspective*.

20. D.   Both the unremitting anxiety of Quechua life and the recurring harvest failures that brought starvation to millions illustrate the *harshness and frustration* of Quechua existence.

21. D.   The author states what cataclysmic variables are and describes how the three general classes of exploding stars range in magnitude and other characteristics.
Choice A is incorrect. The author gives far more emphasis to dwarf novae than to novae.
Choice B is incorrect. The author offers no such explanation.
Choice C is incorrect. The author states the unpredictability of cataclysmic variables; he does not explain or account for it.
Choice E is incorrect. The author offers no such explanation.

22. D.   The first paragraph says, …"25 novae occur in our galaxy every year, but only two or three are *near enough* to be observed." Thus, our observations of novae are hampered by their *distance*.

23. E.   You can arrive at the correct answer by the process of elimination.
Statement I is accurate. Dwarf novae explosions are less violent than are those of supernovae. Therefore, you can eliminate Choice B.
Statement II is accurate. Dwarf novae are observed far more frequently than are supernovae. Therefore, you can eliminate Choices A and D.
Statement III is accurate. Dwarf novae, unlike supernovae, flare up periodically rather than flaring up once and being totally consumed. Therefore, you can eliminate Choice C.
Only Choice E is left. It is the correct answer.

24. C.   Lines 11–14 state: "If the exploding star is in a nearby part of the galaxy, it may create a 'new star' that was not previously visible to the naked eye." Thus, a new star is one that has become bright enough to strike the eye.

25. C.   In each explosion, a dwarf nova loses "a minute fraction of its mass" (line 17). By staying at an intermediate level of brightness rather than descending to minimum brightness, Z Camelopardalis stars may use up a proportionally greater fraction of their mass than do the SS Cygni stars, which descend to minimum brightness between outbursts.
Choice A is incorrect. Rather than reverting to some original level of brightness, Z Camelopardalis stars stay at an intermediate level of brightness for a time.
Choice B is incorrect. There is nothing in the passage to suggest it.
Choice D is incorrect. Z Camelopardalis stars are dwarf novae, which are far more frequently observed by astronomers than are supernovae.
Choice E is incorrect. Nothing in the passage suggests that Z Camelopardalis stars are less bright than other dwarf novae.

26. C.   In lines 19–21, the author states that although astrophysicists can account for the explosions of supernovae, "the novae and dwarf novae have presented more of a puzzle." He then proceeds to discuss dwarf novae in detail. He has yet to discuss novae, the other class of puzzling catastrophic variables.

27. D.   You can arrive at the correct answer by the process of elimination.
Question I is answerable on the basis of the passage. Line 5 states that the last supernova was observed in 1604. Therefore, you can eliminate Choices B and E.
Question II is unanswerable on the basis of the

passage. No reason for the phenomenon is given in the passage. Therefore, you can eliminate Choice C.

Question III is answerable on the basis of the passage. Lines 38–41 state that dwarf novae increase in brightness "within a period of several hours" and then decline from this maximum level of brilliance over a period of two to three days. Therefore, you can eliminate Choice A.

Only Choice D is left. It is the correct answer.

28. A.   The opposite of to *fluster* or discompose is to *soothe*.
Think of "being flustered by reporters' questions."

29. C.   The opposite of a *deletion* or removal of material is an *insertion* of material.
Think of "the deletion of objectionable material" from films.

30. B.   The opposite of to *disparage* or belittle is to *eulogize* or praise.
Think of "rival candidates disparaging each other."

31. B.   The opposite of *baleful* (malign, harmful) is *beneficent* or productive of good.
Think of "dangerous baleful influences."

32. C.   The opposite of *servility* or oversubmissiveness is *independence*.
Think of "cringing servility."

33. A.   The opposite of *felicitous* (happily suited to a situation; appropriate) is *inappropriate*.
Think of "a felicitous remark."

34. B.   The opposite of *precipitous* (hasty, rash; steep) is *cautious*.
Think of "a precipitous flight."

35. C.   The opposite of to *assuage* or ease is to *worsen*.
Think of "assuaging someone's grief."

36. D.   The opposite of *latent* (existing in potential; not manifest) is *manifest* or evident.
Think of "latent ability that needs bringing out."

37. A.   The opposite of to *broach* or open up something is to *seal it off*.
Think of "broaching a topic of conversation."

38. B.   The opposite of an *encomium* or statement of praise is a *denunciation* or condemnation.
Think of "a hero receiving an encomium."

Answer Sheet – MODEL TEST 2

Start with number 1 for each new section.
If a section has fewer than 38 questions, leave the extra spaces blank.

Section 1

1. Ⓐ Ⓑ Ⓒ Ⓓ Ⓔ   11. Ⓐ Ⓑ Ⓒ Ⓓ Ⓔ   21. Ⓐ Ⓑ Ⓒ Ⓓ Ⓔ   31. Ⓐ Ⓑ Ⓒ Ⓓ Ⓔ
2. Ⓐ Ⓑ Ⓒ Ⓓ Ⓔ   12. Ⓐ Ⓑ Ⓒ Ⓓ Ⓔ   22. Ⓐ Ⓑ Ⓒ Ⓓ Ⓔ   32. Ⓐ Ⓑ Ⓒ Ⓓ Ⓔ
3. Ⓐ Ⓑ Ⓒ Ⓓ Ⓔ   13. Ⓐ Ⓑ Ⓒ Ⓓ Ⓔ   23. Ⓐ Ⓑ Ⓒ Ⓓ Ⓔ   33. Ⓐ Ⓑ Ⓒ Ⓓ Ⓔ
4. Ⓐ Ⓑ Ⓒ Ⓓ Ⓔ   14. Ⓐ Ⓑ Ⓒ Ⓓ Ⓔ   24. Ⓐ Ⓑ Ⓒ Ⓓ Ⓔ   34. Ⓐ Ⓑ Ⓒ Ⓓ Ⓔ
5. Ⓐ Ⓑ Ⓒ Ⓓ Ⓔ   15. Ⓐ Ⓑ Ⓒ Ⓓ Ⓔ   25. Ⓐ Ⓑ Ⓒ Ⓓ Ⓔ   35. Ⓐ Ⓑ Ⓒ Ⓓ Ⓔ
6. Ⓐ Ⓑ Ⓒ Ⓓ Ⓔ   16. Ⓐ Ⓑ Ⓒ Ⓓ Ⓔ   26. Ⓐ Ⓑ Ⓒ Ⓓ Ⓔ   36. Ⓐ Ⓑ Ⓒ Ⓓ Ⓔ
7. Ⓐ Ⓑ Ⓒ Ⓓ Ⓔ   17. Ⓐ Ⓑ Ⓒ Ⓓ Ⓔ   27. Ⓐ Ⓑ Ⓒ Ⓓ Ⓔ   37. Ⓐ Ⓑ Ⓒ Ⓓ Ⓔ
8. Ⓐ Ⓑ Ⓒ Ⓓ Ⓔ   18. Ⓐ Ⓑ Ⓒ Ⓓ Ⓔ   28. Ⓐ Ⓑ Ⓒ Ⓓ Ⓔ   38. Ⓐ Ⓑ Ⓒ Ⓓ Ⓔ
9. Ⓐ Ⓑ Ⓒ Ⓓ Ⓔ   19. Ⓐ Ⓑ Ⓒ Ⓓ Ⓔ   29. Ⓐ Ⓑ Ⓒ Ⓓ Ⓔ
10. Ⓐ Ⓑ Ⓒ Ⓓ Ⓔ   20. Ⓐ Ⓑ Ⓒ Ⓓ Ⓔ   30. Ⓐ Ⓑ Ⓒ Ⓓ Ⓔ

Section 2

1. Ⓐ Ⓑ Ⓒ Ⓓ Ⓔ   11. Ⓐ Ⓑ Ⓒ Ⓓ Ⓔ   21. Ⓐ Ⓑ Ⓒ Ⓓ Ⓔ   31. Ⓐ Ⓑ Ⓒ Ⓓ Ⓔ
2. Ⓐ Ⓑ Ⓒ Ⓓ Ⓔ   12. Ⓐ Ⓑ Ⓒ Ⓓ Ⓔ   22. Ⓐ Ⓑ Ⓒ Ⓓ Ⓔ   32. Ⓐ Ⓑ Ⓒ Ⓓ Ⓔ
3. Ⓐ Ⓑ Ⓒ Ⓓ Ⓔ   13. Ⓐ Ⓑ Ⓒ Ⓓ Ⓔ   23. Ⓐ Ⓑ Ⓒ Ⓓ Ⓔ   33. Ⓐ Ⓑ Ⓒ Ⓓ Ⓔ
4. Ⓐ Ⓑ Ⓒ Ⓓ Ⓔ   14. Ⓐ Ⓑ Ⓒ Ⓓ Ⓔ   24. Ⓐ Ⓑ Ⓒ Ⓓ Ⓔ   34. Ⓐ Ⓑ Ⓒ Ⓓ Ⓔ
5. Ⓐ Ⓑ Ⓒ Ⓓ Ⓔ   15. Ⓐ Ⓑ Ⓒ Ⓓ Ⓔ   25. Ⓐ Ⓑ Ⓒ Ⓓ Ⓔ   35. Ⓐ Ⓑ Ⓒ Ⓓ Ⓔ
6. Ⓐ Ⓑ Ⓒ Ⓓ Ⓔ   16. Ⓐ Ⓑ Ⓒ Ⓓ Ⓔ   26. Ⓐ Ⓑ Ⓒ Ⓓ Ⓔ   36. Ⓐ Ⓑ Ⓒ Ⓓ Ⓔ
7. Ⓐ Ⓑ Ⓒ Ⓓ Ⓔ   17. Ⓐ Ⓑ Ⓒ Ⓓ Ⓔ   27. Ⓐ Ⓑ Ⓒ Ⓓ Ⓔ   37. Ⓐ Ⓑ Ⓒ Ⓓ Ⓔ
8. Ⓐ Ⓑ Ⓒ Ⓓ Ⓔ   18. Ⓐ Ⓑ Ⓒ Ⓓ Ⓔ   28. Ⓐ Ⓑ Ⓒ Ⓓ Ⓔ   38. Ⓐ Ⓑ Ⓒ Ⓓ Ⓔ
9. Ⓐ Ⓑ Ⓒ Ⓓ Ⓔ   19. Ⓐ Ⓑ Ⓒ Ⓓ Ⓔ   29. Ⓐ Ⓑ Ⓒ Ⓓ Ⓔ
10. Ⓐ Ⓑ Ⓒ Ⓓ Ⓔ   20. Ⓐ Ⓑ Ⓒ Ⓓ Ⓔ   30. Ⓐ Ⓑ Ⓒ Ⓓ Ⓔ

Section 3

1. Ⓐ Ⓑ Ⓒ Ⓓ Ⓔ   11. Ⓐ Ⓑ Ⓒ Ⓓ Ⓔ   21. Ⓐ Ⓑ Ⓒ Ⓓ Ⓔ   31. Ⓐ Ⓑ Ⓒ Ⓓ Ⓔ
2. Ⓐ Ⓑ Ⓒ Ⓓ Ⓔ   12. Ⓐ Ⓑ Ⓒ Ⓓ Ⓔ   22. Ⓐ Ⓑ Ⓒ Ⓓ Ⓔ   32. Ⓐ Ⓑ Ⓒ Ⓓ Ⓔ
3. Ⓐ Ⓑ Ⓒ Ⓓ Ⓔ   13. Ⓐ Ⓑ Ⓒ Ⓓ Ⓔ   23. Ⓐ Ⓑ Ⓒ Ⓓ Ⓔ   33. Ⓐ Ⓑ Ⓒ Ⓓ Ⓔ
4. Ⓐ Ⓑ Ⓒ Ⓓ Ⓔ   14. Ⓐ Ⓑ Ⓒ Ⓓ Ⓔ   24. Ⓐ Ⓑ Ⓒ Ⓓ Ⓔ   34. Ⓐ Ⓑ Ⓒ Ⓓ Ⓔ
5. Ⓐ Ⓑ Ⓒ Ⓓ Ⓔ   15. Ⓐ Ⓑ Ⓒ Ⓓ Ⓔ   25. Ⓐ Ⓑ Ⓒ Ⓓ Ⓔ   35. Ⓐ Ⓑ Ⓒ Ⓓ Ⓔ
6. Ⓐ Ⓑ Ⓒ Ⓓ Ⓔ   16. Ⓐ Ⓑ Ⓒ Ⓓ Ⓔ   26. Ⓐ Ⓑ Ⓒ Ⓓ Ⓔ   36. Ⓐ Ⓑ Ⓒ Ⓓ Ⓔ
7. Ⓐ Ⓑ Ⓒ Ⓓ Ⓔ   17. Ⓐ Ⓑ Ⓒ Ⓓ Ⓔ   27. Ⓐ Ⓑ Ⓒ Ⓓ Ⓔ   37. Ⓐ Ⓑ Ⓒ Ⓓ Ⓔ
8. Ⓐ Ⓑ Ⓒ Ⓓ Ⓔ   18. Ⓐ Ⓑ Ⓒ Ⓓ Ⓔ   28. Ⓐ Ⓑ Ⓒ Ⓓ Ⓔ   38. Ⓐ Ⓑ Ⓒ Ⓓ Ⓔ
9. Ⓐ Ⓑ Ⓒ Ⓓ Ⓔ   19. Ⓐ Ⓑ Ⓒ Ⓓ Ⓔ   29. Ⓐ Ⓑ Ⓒ Ⓓ Ⓔ
10. Ⓐ Ⓑ Ⓒ Ⓓ Ⓔ   20. Ⓐ Ⓑ Ⓒ Ⓓ Ⓔ   30. Ⓐ Ⓑ Ⓒ Ⓓ Ⓔ

Section 4

1. Ⓐ Ⓑ Ⓒ Ⓓ Ⓔ	11. Ⓐ Ⓑ Ⓒ Ⓓ Ⓔ	21. Ⓐ Ⓑ Ⓒ Ⓓ Ⓔ	31. Ⓐ Ⓑ Ⓒ Ⓓ Ⓔ
2. Ⓐ Ⓑ Ⓒ Ⓓ Ⓔ	12. Ⓐ Ⓑ Ⓒ Ⓓ Ⓔ	22. Ⓐ Ⓑ Ⓒ Ⓓ Ⓔ	32. Ⓐ Ⓑ Ⓒ Ⓓ Ⓔ
3. Ⓐ Ⓑ Ⓒ Ⓓ Ⓔ	13. Ⓐ Ⓑ Ⓒ Ⓓ Ⓔ	23. Ⓐ Ⓑ Ⓒ Ⓓ Ⓔ	33. Ⓐ Ⓑ Ⓒ Ⓓ Ⓔ
4. Ⓐ Ⓑ Ⓒ Ⓓ Ⓔ	14. Ⓐ Ⓑ Ⓒ Ⓓ Ⓔ	24. Ⓐ Ⓑ Ⓒ Ⓓ Ⓔ	34. Ⓐ Ⓑ Ⓒ Ⓓ Ⓔ
5. Ⓐ Ⓑ Ⓒ Ⓓ Ⓔ	15. Ⓐ Ⓑ Ⓒ Ⓓ Ⓔ	25. Ⓐ Ⓑ Ⓒ Ⓓ Ⓔ	35. Ⓐ Ⓑ Ⓒ Ⓓ Ⓔ
6. Ⓐ Ⓑ Ⓒ Ⓓ Ⓔ	16. Ⓐ Ⓑ Ⓒ Ⓓ Ⓔ	26. Ⓐ Ⓑ Ⓒ Ⓓ Ⓔ	36. Ⓐ Ⓑ Ⓒ Ⓓ Ⓔ
7. Ⓐ Ⓑ Ⓒ Ⓓ Ⓔ	17. Ⓐ Ⓑ Ⓒ Ⓓ Ⓔ	27. Ⓐ Ⓑ Ⓒ Ⓓ Ⓔ	37. Ⓐ Ⓑ Ⓒ Ⓓ Ⓔ
8. Ⓐ Ⓑ Ⓒ Ⓓ Ⓔ	18. Ⓐ Ⓑ Ⓒ Ⓓ Ⓔ	28. Ⓐ Ⓑ Ⓒ Ⓓ Ⓔ	38. Ⓐ Ⓑ Ⓒ Ⓓ Ⓔ
9. Ⓐ Ⓑ Ⓒ Ⓓ Ⓔ	19. Ⓐ Ⓑ Ⓒ Ⓓ Ⓔ	29. Ⓐ Ⓑ Ⓒ Ⓓ Ⓔ	
10. Ⓐ Ⓑ Ⓒ Ⓓ Ⓔ	20. Ⓐ Ⓑ Ⓒ Ⓓ Ⓔ	30. Ⓐ Ⓑ Ⓒ Ⓓ Ⓔ	

Section 5

1. Ⓐ Ⓑ Ⓒ Ⓓ Ⓔ	11. Ⓐ Ⓑ Ⓒ Ⓓ Ⓔ	21. Ⓐ Ⓑ Ⓒ Ⓓ Ⓔ	31. Ⓐ Ⓑ Ⓒ Ⓓ Ⓔ
2. Ⓐ Ⓑ Ⓒ Ⓓ Ⓔ	12. Ⓐ Ⓑ Ⓒ Ⓓ Ⓔ	22. Ⓐ Ⓑ Ⓒ Ⓓ Ⓔ	32. Ⓐ Ⓑ Ⓒ Ⓓ Ⓔ
3. Ⓐ Ⓑ Ⓒ Ⓓ Ⓔ	13. Ⓐ Ⓑ Ⓒ Ⓓ Ⓔ	23. Ⓐ Ⓑ Ⓒ Ⓓ Ⓔ	33. Ⓐ Ⓑ Ⓒ Ⓓ Ⓔ
4. Ⓐ Ⓑ Ⓒ Ⓓ Ⓔ	14. Ⓐ Ⓑ Ⓒ Ⓓ Ⓔ	24. Ⓐ Ⓑ Ⓒ Ⓓ Ⓔ	34. Ⓐ Ⓑ Ⓒ Ⓓ Ⓔ
5. Ⓐ Ⓑ Ⓒ Ⓓ Ⓔ	15. Ⓐ Ⓑ Ⓒ Ⓓ Ⓔ	25. Ⓐ Ⓑ Ⓒ Ⓓ Ⓔ	35. Ⓐ Ⓑ Ⓒ Ⓓ Ⓔ
6. Ⓐ Ⓑ Ⓒ Ⓓ Ⓔ	16. Ⓐ Ⓑ Ⓒ Ⓓ Ⓔ	26. Ⓐ Ⓑ Ⓒ Ⓓ Ⓔ	36. Ⓐ Ⓑ Ⓒ Ⓓ Ⓔ
7. Ⓐ Ⓑ Ⓒ Ⓓ Ⓔ	17. Ⓐ Ⓑ Ⓒ Ⓓ Ⓔ	27. Ⓐ Ⓑ Ⓒ Ⓓ Ⓔ	37. Ⓐ Ⓑ Ⓒ Ⓓ Ⓔ
8. Ⓐ Ⓑ Ⓒ Ⓓ Ⓔ	18. Ⓐ Ⓑ Ⓒ Ⓓ Ⓔ	28. Ⓐ Ⓑ Ⓒ Ⓓ Ⓔ	38. Ⓐ Ⓑ Ⓒ Ⓓ Ⓔ
9. Ⓐ Ⓑ Ⓒ Ⓓ Ⓔ	19. Ⓐ Ⓑ Ⓒ Ⓓ Ⓔ	29. Ⓐ Ⓑ Ⓒ Ⓓ Ⓔ	
10. Ⓐ Ⓑ Ⓒ Ⓓ Ⓔ	20. Ⓐ Ⓑ Ⓒ Ⓓ Ⓔ	30. Ⓐ Ⓑ Ⓒ Ⓓ Ⓔ	

Section 6

1. Ⓐ Ⓑ Ⓒ Ⓓ Ⓔ	11. Ⓐ Ⓑ Ⓒ Ⓓ Ⓔ	21. Ⓐ Ⓑ Ⓒ Ⓓ Ⓔ	31. Ⓐ Ⓑ Ⓒ Ⓓ Ⓔ
2. Ⓐ Ⓑ Ⓒ Ⓓ Ⓔ	12. Ⓐ Ⓑ Ⓒ Ⓓ Ⓔ	22. Ⓐ Ⓑ Ⓒ Ⓓ Ⓔ	32. Ⓐ Ⓑ Ⓒ Ⓓ Ⓔ
3. Ⓐ Ⓑ Ⓒ Ⓓ Ⓔ	13. Ⓐ Ⓑ Ⓒ Ⓓ Ⓔ	23. Ⓐ Ⓑ Ⓒ Ⓓ Ⓔ	33. Ⓐ Ⓑ Ⓒ Ⓓ Ⓔ
4. Ⓐ Ⓑ Ⓒ Ⓓ Ⓔ	14. Ⓐ Ⓑ Ⓒ Ⓓ Ⓔ	24. Ⓐ Ⓑ Ⓒ Ⓓ Ⓔ	34. Ⓐ Ⓑ Ⓒ Ⓓ Ⓔ
5. Ⓐ Ⓑ Ⓒ Ⓓ Ⓔ	15. Ⓐ Ⓑ Ⓒ Ⓓ Ⓔ	25. Ⓐ Ⓑ Ⓒ Ⓓ Ⓔ	35. Ⓐ Ⓑ Ⓒ Ⓓ Ⓔ
6. Ⓐ Ⓑ Ⓒ Ⓓ Ⓔ	16. Ⓐ Ⓑ Ⓒ Ⓓ Ⓔ	26. Ⓐ Ⓑ Ⓒ Ⓓ Ⓔ	36. Ⓐ Ⓑ Ⓒ Ⓓ Ⓔ
7. Ⓐ Ⓑ Ⓒ Ⓓ Ⓔ	17. Ⓐ Ⓑ Ⓒ Ⓓ Ⓔ	27. Ⓐ Ⓑ Ⓒ Ⓓ Ⓔ	37. Ⓐ Ⓑ Ⓒ Ⓓ Ⓔ
8. Ⓐ Ⓑ Ⓒ Ⓓ Ⓔ	18. Ⓐ Ⓑ Ⓒ Ⓓ Ⓔ	28. Ⓐ Ⓑ Ⓒ Ⓓ Ⓔ	38. Ⓐ Ⓑ Ⓒ Ⓓ Ⓔ
9. Ⓐ Ⓑ Ⓒ Ⓓ Ⓔ	19. Ⓐ Ⓑ Ⓒ Ⓓ Ⓔ	29. Ⓐ Ⓑ Ⓒ Ⓓ Ⓔ	
10. Ⓐ Ⓑ Ⓒ Ⓓ Ⓔ	20. Ⓐ Ⓑ Ⓒ Ⓓ Ⓔ	30. Ⓐ Ⓑ Ⓒ Ⓓ Ⓔ	

Section 7

1. Ⓐ Ⓑ Ⓒ Ⓓ Ⓔ	11. Ⓐ Ⓑ Ⓒ Ⓓ Ⓔ	21. Ⓐ Ⓑ Ⓒ Ⓓ Ⓔ	31. Ⓐ Ⓑ Ⓒ Ⓓ Ⓔ
2. Ⓐ Ⓑ Ⓒ Ⓓ Ⓔ	12. Ⓐ Ⓑ Ⓒ Ⓓ Ⓔ	22. Ⓐ Ⓑ Ⓒ Ⓓ Ⓔ	32. Ⓐ Ⓑ Ⓒ Ⓓ Ⓔ
3. Ⓐ Ⓑ Ⓒ Ⓓ Ⓔ	13. Ⓐ Ⓑ Ⓒ Ⓓ Ⓔ	23. Ⓐ Ⓑ Ⓒ Ⓓ Ⓔ	33. Ⓐ Ⓑ Ⓒ Ⓓ Ⓔ
4. Ⓐ Ⓑ Ⓒ Ⓓ Ⓔ	14. Ⓐ Ⓑ Ⓒ Ⓓ Ⓔ	24. Ⓐ Ⓑ Ⓒ Ⓓ Ⓔ	34. Ⓐ Ⓑ Ⓒ Ⓓ Ⓔ
5. Ⓐ Ⓑ Ⓒ Ⓓ Ⓔ	15. Ⓐ Ⓑ Ⓒ Ⓓ Ⓔ	25. Ⓐ Ⓑ Ⓒ Ⓓ Ⓔ	35. Ⓐ Ⓑ Ⓒ Ⓓ Ⓔ
6. Ⓐ Ⓑ Ⓒ Ⓓ Ⓔ	16. Ⓐ Ⓑ Ⓒ Ⓓ Ⓔ	26. Ⓐ Ⓑ Ⓒ Ⓓ Ⓔ	36. Ⓐ Ⓑ Ⓒ Ⓓ Ⓔ
7. Ⓐ Ⓑ Ⓒ Ⓓ Ⓔ	17. Ⓐ Ⓑ Ⓒ Ⓓ Ⓔ	27. Ⓐ Ⓑ Ⓒ Ⓓ Ⓔ	37. Ⓐ Ⓑ Ⓒ Ⓓ Ⓔ
8. Ⓐ Ⓑ Ⓒ Ⓓ Ⓔ	18. Ⓐ Ⓑ Ⓒ Ⓓ Ⓔ	28. Ⓐ Ⓑ Ⓒ Ⓓ Ⓔ	38. Ⓐ Ⓑ Ⓒ Ⓓ Ⓔ
9. Ⓐ Ⓑ Ⓒ Ⓓ Ⓔ	19. Ⓐ Ⓑ Ⓒ Ⓓ Ⓔ	29. Ⓐ Ⓑ Ⓒ Ⓓ Ⓔ	
10. Ⓐ Ⓑ Ⓒ Ⓓ Ⓔ	20. Ⓐ Ⓑ Ⓒ Ⓓ Ⓔ	30. Ⓐ Ⓑ Ⓒ Ⓓ Ⓔ	

MODEL TEST 2

SECTION 1

Time—30 Minutes

25 Questions

Directions: Each question or group of questions is based on a passage or set of conditions. In answering some of the questions, it may be useful to draw a rough diagram. For each question, select the best answer choice given.

Questions 1–4

Eight varsity baseball players *(G,H,J,K,L,M,N,O)* are to be honored at a special ceremony. Three of these players *(H,M,* and *O)* are also varsity football players. Two of them *(K* and *N)* are also basketball players on the varsity team. In arranging the seats it was decided that no athlete in two sports should be seated next to another two-sport athlete.

1. Which of the following combinations is possible in order to have the arrangement of seat assignments as planned?
   (A) *H G K J*
   (B) *H K J L*
   (C) *J K M N*
   (D) *J L H K*
   (E) *L K N J*

2. To have the proper seating arrangement, *K* should sit between
   (A) *G* and *H*
   (B) *J* and *M*
   (C) *L* and *N*
   (D) *J* and *N*
   (E) *J* and *L*

3. Which of the following cannot sit next to *M?*
   (A) *G*
   (B) *J*
   (C) *G* and *J*
   (D) *K*
   (E) *L*

4. Before all athletes are seated there are two vacant seats on either side of *N*. Which two athletes may occupy these seats?
   (A) *G* and *K*
   (B) *G* and *L*
   (C) *J* and *H*
   (D) *L* and *O*
   (E) *M* and *J*

Questions 5–7

It takes a high degree of courage for a politician to risk her career by introducing federal legislation requiring registration and licensing of gun possession. While many say that the elimination of private ownership of firearms will cure the sociologic ills of our country, the gun lobby in Washington maintains that this would be an invasion of personal liberty.

5. Which of the following is the best argument against national gun registration?
   (A) It would be difficult to enforce.
   (B) It is a violation of rights granted in the Constitution.
   (C) Murderers would ignore gun control legislation.
   (D) Most murders occur between individuals who were acquainted with each other before the shooting.
   (E) Many homicides are committed without the use of guns.

6. Which of the following is the best claim for banning firearms?
   (A) The root causes of violence lie deep in the nature of society.
   (B) The state with the lowest crime rate has a stringent antigun law.
   (C) Many accidents occur in legal hunting and riflery.
   (D) With fewer guns there would be fewer shootings.
   (E) Guns have no place in a civilized country.

7. According to the statement in the passage, why would members of Congress hesitate to introduce gun-control legislation?
   (A) It would never pass.
   (B) It would be declared unconstitutional.
   (C) It would not decrease crime.
   (D) It is unpopular.
   (E) The gun lobby is very strong.

Questions 8–11

To obtain a visa for the Republic of Nimrod, an applicant must appear in person at the Nimrodian Consulate and show a U.S. birth certificate or naturalization papers, a certificate of vaccination for swamp fever, and a notorized bank statement showing a balance in excess of $1,000. Bank statements are available during normal business hours (Monday through Friday, 9 A.M. to 3 P.M. at most banks, which also have a notary on staff). Vaccinations are routinely performed at Alabaster Hospital, adjacent to the Nimrodian Consulate, on Wednesdays from noon to 5 P.M. They are also performed at Beryl Clinic, an hour's travel away from the consulate, on Mondays and Thursdays from 9 A.M. to noon and on Fridays from 4 to 5 P.M. Copies of U.S. birth certificates are issued on Mondays and Thursdays from 9 to 5 and copies of naturalization papers are issued on Tuesdays and Fridays from 9 to 5. The Nimrodian Consulate is open Mondays, Wednesdays, and Fridays from noon to 4 P.M.

8. Which of the following can complete the entire application procedure in the shortest time?

   (A) A native-born U.S. citizen starting Monday
   (B) A naturalized U.S. citizen starting Tuesday morning
   (C) A native-born U.S. citizen starting Wednesday morning
   (D) A naturalized U.S. citizen starting Thursday
   (E) A native-born U.S. citizen starting Friday

9. If a native-born U.S. citizen begins the application procedure by going for a copy of her birth certificate at noon on Thursday, the earliest she can finish will be

   (A) Friday morning
   (B) Friday afternoon
   (C) the following Monday afternoon
   (D) the following Tuesday afternoon
   (E) the following Wednesday afternoon

10. Mr. Nikto's bank, situated in the suburbs one hour's travel time from any other office that must be visited, issues statements only Tuesdays from 4 to 5 P.M. If Mr. Nikto completes the entire application procedure within 30 hours, he is

   (A) a naturalized U.S. citizen who began by getting vaccinated
   (B) a native-born U.S. citizen who began by getting a bank statement
   (C) a naturalized U.S. citizen who began by getting naturalization papers
   (D) a native-born U.S. citizen who began by getting a birth certificate
   (E) a naturalized U.S. citizen who began by getting a bank statement

11. Alabaster Hospital closes because of cuts in government funding. Thereafter, a naturalized U.S. citizen who begins the application procedure at noon on Tuesday can complete it no sooner than

   (A) Tuesday
   (B) Wednesday
   (C) Thursday
   (D) Friday
   (E) Monday

Questions 12–18

The organizer of Local 58 of the hospital workers is forming a five-person team to leaflet a nearby hospital. The team must contain two persons to distribute leaflets, one speaker to address the workers who stop, and a two-person defense squad. A, B, and C are possible leafletters; C, D, and E are possible speakers; F, G, and H are possible members of the defense guard. A and C prefer to work with each other on the same team. E prefers to work only if F works.

12. Which choice of personnel is impossible if all preferences are respected?

   (A) A and B as leafletters, C as speaker
   (B) B and C as leafletters
   (C) A and C as leafletters, F and H on defense
   (D) Either D or E as speaker, with F on defense
   (E) G and H on defense

13. If A and B are leafletters and all preferences are respected, which is (are) true?

   I.   C is the speaker.
   II. F is on defense.
   III. Either F or G is on defense.

   (A) I only
   (B) II only
   (C) III only
   (D) I and II only
   (E) I and III only

14. Which is a possible team if all preferences are respected?

   (A) A, B, C, D, F
   (B) A, C, D, E, F
   (C) A, B, C, F, G
   (D) A, C, E, G, H
   (E) B, C, D, F, G

15. If A is chosen as a member of the team and all preferences are respected, which must be true?

   (A) B must be a leafletter.
   (B) C must be a leafletter.
   (C) F must go.
   (D) Any of the three defense personnel may go.
   (E) Neither D nor E can go.

16. How many different possible teams can the organizer assemble, if all preferences are respected?

   (A) 5   (B) 8   (C) 9   (D) 13   (E) 15

17. Which person(s) must be chosen as part of any team, if all preferences are respected?

   I.   A
   II. E
   III. F

   (A) I only
   (B) III only
   (C) I and II only
   (D) II and III only
   (E) I, II, and III

18. Which person can be part of the smallest number of different possible teams, if everyone's preferences are respected?

    (A) A

    (B) B

    (C) C

    (D) D

    (E) E

Questions 19–22

Delegations from Wallachia and Rumelia are meeting to discuss military, trade, and diplomatic problems. Each delegation consists of a chairperson, two military attachés, and two trade experts. The Wallachian delegation consists of A, B, C, D, and E; the Rumelian delegation of F, G, H, I, and J. Each chairperson is to occupy the middle seat in a row of five on each of two sides of a rectangular table.

(1) A insists on being seated at the opposite end of the table from B.
(2) G, who is deaf in his right ear, must be at the right end of the table.
(3) Neither D nor F is a chairperson.
(4) The Wallachian military attachées, one of whom is B, are seated together, and neither is opposite either of the Rumelian military attachés, neither of whom is G.
(5) C, a trade expert, is seated opposite H.

19. F may be a

    (A) trade expert seated next to I
    (B) military attaché seated next to I
    (C) military attaché seated next to J
    (D) trade expert seated next to H
    (E) trade expert seated opposite B

20. About which of the following do the stated conditions provide the least information?

    (A) The identity of the Wallachian chairperson
    (B) The identity of the Rumelian chairperson
    (C) The identities and seating positions of the Wallachian military attachés
    (D) Which delegate is immediately to the right of the Wallachian chairperson
    (E) Which delegate is immediately to the right of the Rumelian chairperson

21. If J is a military attaché, which of the following must be true?

    I.   The Rumelian chairperson is I.
    II. F is a trade expert.
    III. I is a trade expert.

    (A) I only
    (B) II only
    (C) I and II only
    (D) I or III, but not both
    (E) II or III, but not both

22. Which of the following can be deduced from the introductory paragraph plus statements (1), (2), (4), and (5) only?

    (A) The identities of the Rumelian trade experts
    (B) The identities of the Wallachian military attachés
    (C) The identity of the Wallachian chairperson
    (D) Which two delegates are seated between G and H
    (E) Which two delegates area seated between B and C

Questions 23 and 24

In 1978 Thomas Malthus published "Essay on Population" in which he postulated that food supply can never keep pace with the rate of increase in human population.

23. Which of the following statements, if true, would tend to *weaken* Malthus's argument?

    I.   The total population of humans has risen at a rapid rate partly because of the removal of natural checks on population.
    II. In many nations, the increase in human population has far outstripped the food-producing capacity.
    III. Human population growth may be halted by the use of contraception.
    IV. For many ethnic and religious groups, artificial control of conception is morally unacceptable.

    (A) I only
    (B) I and II
    (C) II only
    (D) II and IV only
    (E) III only

24. Which of the following would be most likely to help limit the demands placed on food supplies?

    (A) Wars
    (B) Conservation of natural resources
    (C) Better farming methods
    (D) Better international relations
    (E) Improved disease control

25. Most people who take the experimental medicine GRE/APT develop headaches; therefore, if Alice does not take GRE/APT, she will probably not develop headaches.

    The argument above most resembles which of the following?

    (A) Most Dobermans are easy to train, so Beth is sure to have no trouble training the Doberman she has just bought.
    (B) Most U.S.-built cars are poorly made; since this car is well made, it was probably not built in the United States.
    (C) Most Broadway plays are very well acted, so *The Logic Game*, which is not a Broadway play, is probably not well acted.
    (D) Most engineers spent many years in school, so Sharon, who has spent many years in school, is probably an engineer.
    (E) All societies known to history have had clearly defined social hierarchies, so there will probably never be a truly nonhierarchical society.

S T O P

IF YOU FINISH BEFORE TIME IS CALLED, YOU MAY CHECK YOUR WORK ON THIS SECTION ONLY.
DO NOT WORK ON ANY OTHER SECTION IN THE TEST.

SECTION 2

Time—30 Minutes

38 Questions

Directions: Each sentence below has one or two blanks, each blank indicating that something has been omitted. Beneath the sentence are five lettered words or sets of words. Choose the word or set of words for each blank that best fits the meaning of the sentence as a whole.

1. No volume on the history of economics can conclude without the hope that the subject will be ------- politics to form again the larger discipline of political economy.

    (A) vindicated by
    (B) segregated from
    (C) reunited with
    (D) recapitulated by
    (E) dependent on

2. Many educators believe that, far from being a temporary stopgap, useful only as a transitional measure, bilingual education has proved to have definite ------- education in any one tongue.

    (A) correlations with
    (B) advantages over
    (C) connotations for
    (D) limitations on
    (E) influence on

3. When facts are ------- and data hard to come by, even scientists occasionally throw aside the professional pretense of ------- and tear into each other with shameless appeals to authority and arguments that are unabashedly *ad hominem*.

    (A) elusive…objectivity
    (B) established…courtesy
    (C) demonstrable…neutrality
    (D) ineluctable…cooperation
    (E) hypothetical…scholarship

4. While the disease is in ------- state it is almost impossible to determine its existence by -------.

    (A) a dormant…postulate
    (B) a critical…examination
    (C) an acute…analysis
    (D) a suspended…estimate
    (E) a latent…observation

5. Woolf ------- conventional notions of truth: in her words, one cannot receive from any lecture "a nugget of pure truth" to wrap up between the pages of one's notebook and keep on the mantlepiece forever.

    (A) anticipates
    (B) articulates
    (C) neglects
    (D) mocks
    (E) rationalizes

6. The term "rare earths" is in fact a -------, for, paradoxically, the rare-earth elements are in actuality -------, being present in low concentration in virtually all minerals.

    (A) truism…essential
    (B) misnomer…ubiquitous
    (C) disclaimer…ephemeral
    (D) metaphor…figurative
    (E) mnemonic…unmemorable

7. That Clement would reclaim psychoanalysis as a healing profession is the ------- of her argument, but it is exactly in this part of her critique, translated to the American psychoanalytic milieu, that her shafts -------.

    (A) crux…fall down
    (B) implication…break down
    (C) basis…strike home
    (D) essence…dig in
    (E) thrust…glance away

Directions: In each of the following questions, a related pair of words or phrases is followed by five lettered pairs of words or phrases. Select the lettered pair that best expresses a relationship similar to that expressed in the original pair.

8. BLEAT : SHEEP ::
    (A) bask : lizard
    (B) preen : peacock
    (C) chirp : sparrow
    (D) slither : snake
    (E) butt : goat

9. CURDLE : MILK ::
    (A) flow : water
    (B) change : oil
    (C) brew : coffee
    (D) decant : wine
    (E) clot : blood

10. MOLT : FEATHERS ::
    (A) slough : skin
    (B) sharpen : talons
    (C) curry : hide
    (D) flutter : wings
    (E) bare : fangs

11. OFFHAND : PREMEDITATION ::
    (A) upright : integrity
    (B) aboveboard : guile
    (C) cutthroat : competition
    (D) backward : direction
    (E) underlying : foundation

12. LARVAL : INSECT ::
    (A) serpentine : snake
    (B) floral : plant
    (C) amphibian : reptile
    (D) embryonic : mammal
    (E) alate : bird

13. POLTERGEIST : APPARITION ::
    (A) dwarf : stature
    (B) witch : familiar
    (C) ogre : monster
    (D) sorceror : spell
    (E) gremlin : mischief

14. AUSTERE : STYLE ::
    (A) controlled : movement
    (B) affluent : wealth
    (C) subservient : demeanor
    (D) inspirational : faith
    (E) pragmatic : speech

15. AVER : AFFIRMATION ::
    (A) proclaim : objection
    (B) denounce : defiance
    (C) nonplus : resistance
    (D) refuse : distress
    (E) demur : protest

16. CHIDE : PILLORY ::
    (A) exalt : venerate
    (B) humor : mollycoddle
    (C) castigate : punish
    (D) quibble : cavil
    (E) sanctify : scourge

Directions: Each passage in this group is followed by questions based on its content. After reading a passage, choose the best answer to each question. Answer all questions following a passage on the basis of what is stated or implied in the passage.

At night, schools of prey and predators are almost always spectacularly illuminated by the bioluminescence produced by the microscopic and larger plankton. The reason for the ubiquitous production of light by the microorganisms of the sea remains obscure, and suggested explanations are controversial. It has been suggested that light is a kind of inadvertent by-product of life in transparent organisms. It has also been hypothesized that the emission of light on disturbance is advantageous to the plankton in making the predators of the plankton conspicuous to their predators! Unquestionably, it does act this way. Indeed, some fisheries base the detection of their prey on the bioluminescence that the fish excite. It is difficult, however, to defend the thesis that this effect was the direct factor in the original development of bioluminescence, since the effect was of no advantage to the individual microorganism that first developed it. Perhaps the luminescence of a microorganism also discourages attack by light-avoiding predators and is of initial survival benefit to the individual. As it then becomes general in the population, the effect of revealing plankton predators to their predators would also become important.

17. The primary topic of the passage is which of the following?

    (A) The origin of bioluminescence in plankton predators
    (B) The disadvantages of bioluminescence in microorganisms
    (C) The varieties of marine bioluminescent life forms
    (D) Symbiotic relationships between predators and their prey
    (E) Hypotheses on the causes of bioluminescence in plankton

18. The author mentions the activities of fisheries in order to provide an example of

    (A) how ubiquitous the phenomenon of bioluminescence is coastally
    (B) how predators do make use of bioluminescence in locating their prey
    (C) how human intervention imperils bioluminescent microorganisms
    (D) how nocturnal fishing expeditions are becoming more and more widespread
    (E) how limited bioluminescence is as a source of light for human use

19. The passage provides an answer to which of the following questions?

    (A) What is the explanation for the phenomenon of bioluminescence in marine life?
    (B) Does the phenomenon of plankton bioluminescence have any practical applications?
    (C) Why do only certain specimens of marine life exhibit the phenomenon of bioluminescence?
    (D) How does underwater bioluminescence differ from atmospheric bioluminescence?
    (E) What are the steps that take place as an individual microorganism becomes bioluminescent?

20. The author's attitude toward the hypothesis that plankton chiefly benefited from their bioluminescence because it made the plankton predators visible to their predators can best be described as

    (A) perplexed
    (B) derisive
    (C) intrigued
    (D) defensive
    (E) dispassionate

The curtain rises; the Cardinal and Daniel de Bosola enter from the right. In appearance, the Cardinal is something between an El Greco cardinal and a Van Dyke noble lord. He has the tall,

(5) spare form—the elongated hands and features—of the former; the trim pointed beard, the imperial repose, the commanding authority of the latter. But the El Greco features are not really those of asceticism or inner mystic spirituality. They are the

(10) index to a cold, refined but ruthless cruelty in a highly civilized controlled form. Neither is the imperial repose an aloof mood of proud detachment. It is a refined expression of satanic pride of place and talent.

(15) To a degree, the Cardinal's coldness is artificially cultivated. He has defined himself against his younger brother Duke Ferdinand and is the opposite to the overwrought emotionality of the latter. But the Cardinal's aloof mood is not one of bland

(20) detachment. It is the deliberate detachment of a methodical man who collects his thoughts and emotions into the most compact and formidable shape—that when he strikes, he may strike with the more efficient and devastating force. His easy

(25) movements are those of the slowly circling eagle just before the swift descent with the exposed talons. Above all else, he is a man who never for a moment doubts his destined authority as a governor. He derisively and sharply rebukes his brother

(30) the Duke as easily and readily as he mocks his mistress Julia. If he has betrayed his hireling Bosola, he uses his brother as the tool to win back his "familiar." His court dress is a long brilliant scarlet cardinal's gown with white cuffs and a white collar

(35) turned back over the red, both collar and cuffs being elaborately scalloped and embroidered. He wears a small cape, reaching only to the elbows. His cassock is buttoned to the ground, giving a heightened effect to his already tall presence.

(40) Richelieu would have adored his neatly trimmed beard. A richly jeweled and oranamented cross lies on his breast, suspended from his neck by a gold chain.

Bosola, for his part, is the Renaissance "familiar"
(45) dressed conventionally in somber black with a white collar. He wears a chain about his neck, a suspended ornament, and a sword. Although a "bravo," he must not be thought of as a leather-jacketed, heavy-booted tough, squat and swarthy.

(50) Still less is he a sneering, leering, melodramatic villain of the Victorian gaslight tradition. Like his black-and-white clothes, he is a colorful contradiction, a scholar-assassin, a humanist-hangman; introverted and introspective, yet ruthless in action;

(55) moody and reluctant, yet violent. He is a man of scholarly taste and subtle intellectual discrimination doing the work of a hired ruffian. In general effect, his impersonator must achieve suppleness and subtlety of nature, a highly complex, com-

(60) pressed, yet well restrained intensity of temperament. Like Duke Ferdinand, he is inwardly tormented, but not by undiluted passion. His dominant emotion is an intellectualized one: that of dis-

gust at a world filled with knavery and folly, but in
(65) which he must play a part and that a lowly, despicable one. He is the kind of rarity that Browning loved to depict in his Renaissance monologues.

21. The primary purpose of the passage appears to be to

(A) provide historical background on the Renaissance church
(B) describe ecclesiastical costuming and pageantry
(C) analyze the appearances and moral natures of two dramatic figures
(D) compare and contrast the subjects of two historical paintings
(E) denounce the corruption of the nobility in Renaissance Italy

22. It can be inferred from the passage that the Cardinal and Bosola

(A) are feuding brothers
(B) are noble lords
(C) together govern the church
(D) are characters in a play
(E) resemble one another in looks

23. In lines 25–27 the author most likely compares the movements of the Cardinal to those of a circling eagle in order to emphasize his

(A) flightiness
(B) love of freedom
(C) eminence
(D) sense of spirituality
(E) mercilessness

24. As used in line 48, the word *bravo* most nearly means

(A) a shout of approbation
(B) a medallion
(C) a clergyman
(D) a humanist
(E) a mercenary killer

25. The author of this passage assumes that the reader is

(A) familiar with the paintings of El Greco and Van Dyke
(B) disgusted with a world filled with cruelty and folly
(C) ignorant of the history of the Roman Catholic Church
(D) uninterested in psychological distinctions
(E) unacquainted with the writing of Browning

26. Which of the following best characterizes the author's attitude toward the Cardinal?

   (A) He deprecates his inability to sustain warm familial relationships.
   (B) He esteems him for his spiritual and emotional control.
   (C) He admires his grace in movement and sure sense of personal authority.
   (D) He finds him formidable both as an opponent and as a dramatic character.
   (E) He is perturbed by his inconsistencies in behavior.

27. According to the passage, the explanation of Bosola's inner suffering lies in his

   (A) highly overwrought excesses of feeling
   (B) resentment against his lack of appropriate rank
   (C) suppression of his intellectual ambitions
   (D) revulsion towards his involvement in ignoble acts
   (E) compassion for those victimized by the Cardinal

Directions: Each question below consists of a word printed in capital letters, followed by five lettered words or phrases. Choose the lettered word or phrase that is most nearly opposite in meaning to the word in capital letters.

Since some of the questions require you to distinguish fine shades of meaning, be sure to consider all the choices before deciding which one is best.

28. AMELIORATION:
   (A) cancellation
   (B) worsening
   (C) forgetfulness
   (D) bribe
   (E) consideration

29. DISARRAY:
   (A) neaten
   (B) empower
   (C) combine
   (D) oscillate
   (E) select

30. DISPUTATIOUS:
   (A) repugnant
   (B) coy
   (C) conciliatory
   (D) infamous
   (E) composed

31. RETICENCE:
   (A) irascibility
   (B) loquaciousness
   (C) quiescence
   (D) patience
   (E) surrender

32. INUNDATE:
   (A) uproot
   (B) channel
   (C) wallow
   (D) embroil
   (E) drain

33. INCONGRUOUS:
   (A) geometric
   (B) prudent
   (C) legitimate
   (D) harmonious
   (E) efficacious

34. APOSTATE:
   (A) laggard
   (B) loyalist
   (C) martinet
   (D) predecessor
   (E) skeptic

35. TOPICAL:
   (A) general
   (B) disinterested
   (C) chronological
   (D) fallacious
   (E) imperceptible

36. FULMINATE:
   (A) authorize
   (B) dominate
   (C) edify
   (D) illuminate
   (E) praise

37. TURBID:
   (A) vigorous
   (B) limpid
   (C) turgid
   (D) viscous
   (E) rancid

38. TYRO:
   (A) zealot
   (B) prodigal
   (C) braggart
   (D) expert
   (E) nihilist

S T O P

IF YOU FINISH BEFORE TIME IS CALLED, YOU MAY CHECK YOUR WORK ON THIS SECTION ONLY.
DO NOT WORK ON ANY OTHER SECTION IN THE TEST.

SECTION 3

Time—30 minutes

30 Questions

Numbers: All numbers used are real numbers.

Figures: Position of points, angles, regions, etc., can be assumed to be in the order shown; and angle measures can be assumed to be positive.

Lines shown as straight can be assumed to be straight.

Figures can be assumed to lie in a plane unless otherwise indicated.

Figures that accompany questions are intended to provide information useful in answering the questions. However, unless a note states that a figure is drawn to scale, you should solve these problems NOT by estimating sizes by sight or by measurement, but by using your knowledge of mathematics (see Example 2 below).

Directions: Each of the Questions 1-15 consists of two quantities, one in Column A and one in Column B. You are to compare the two quantities and choose

> A if the quantity in Column A is greater;
> B if the quantity in Column B is greater;
> C if the two quantities are equal;
> D if the relationship cannot be determined from the information given.

Note: Since there are only four choices, NEVER MARK (E).

Common Information: In a question, information concerning one or both of the quantities to be compared is centered above the two columns. A symbol that appears in both columns represents the same thing in Column A as it does in Column B.

	Column A	Column B	Sample Answers
Example 1:	2×6	$2 + 6$	● Ⓑ Ⓒ Ⓓ Ⓔ

Examples 2-4 refer to $\triangle PQR$.

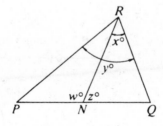

	Column A	Column B	Sample Answers
Example 2:	PN	NQ	Ⓐ Ⓑ Ⓒ ● Ⓔ

(since equal measures cannot be assumed, even though PN and NQ appear equal)

Example 3:	x	y	Ⓐ ● Ⓒ Ⓓ Ⓔ

(since N is between P and Q

Example 4:	$w + z$	180	Ⓐ Ⓑ ● Ⓓ Ⓔ

(since PQ is a straight line)

A if the quantity in Column A is greater;
B if the quantity in Column B is greater;
C if the two quantities are equal;
D if the relationship cannot be determined from the information given.

Column A	Column B
1. $3\frac{1}{2}\%$	$\frac{35}{1000}$

2. The number of posts needed for a fence 144 feet long if posts are placed 12 feet apart

    12 posts

The houses on Jordan Drive are numbered as follows: west side (1801–1837), with consecutive odd numbers; east side has 18 houses.

3. Number of houses on the west side

    Number of houses on the east side

4. $a + b + c + d$ $2x$

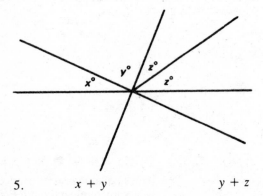

5. $x + y$ $y + z$

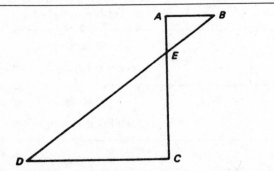

$AC \perp AB, AC \perp DC, AB = 4, EB = 5, DC = 12$

6. AC DC

Column A	Column B

Radius of circle $A = \frac{1}{2}$ radius of circle B

7. Circumference of circle B

    Twice the circumference of circle A

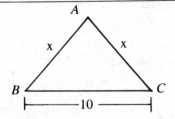

8. $\dfrac{BC}{AB} \cdot \dfrac{AC}{BC}$ 1

$x = 40$

9. Length of side AB Length of side BC

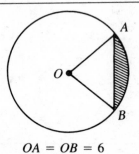

$OA = OB = 6$

10. Area of shaded portion $6\pi - 9\sqrt{3}$

$y = z$ and $x = 100$

11. y 40

A if the quantity in Column A is greater;
B if the quantity in Column B is greater;
C if the two quantities are equal;
D if the relationship cannot be determined from the information given.

Column A	Column B

ABCD is a square.

12. x 8

13. $7(10^4) + 3(10^3) +$ 73,256
     $2(10^2) + 5(10) + 6$

Column A	Column B

$$x + 5 = 7$$
$$y - 5 = 8$$

14. $x + y$ 15

$$\frac{(15)(16)}{x} = (5)(4)(3)$$

15. x 4

Directions: Each of Questions 16–30 has five answer choices. For each of these questions, select the best of the answer choices given.

16. If $K = \dfrac{1}{m + n}$, then $\dfrac{5}{K}$ is equal to

(A) $5(m + n)$

(B) $\dfrac{5}{m + n}$

(C) $\dfrac{m + n}{5}$

(D) $\dfrac{m + n}{5mn}$

(E) $\dfrac{5}{m} + \dfrac{5}{n}$

17. If $r = \sqrt{\dfrac{3V}{\pi h}}$, by what number must we multiply V

in order to multiply r by 9?

(A) 3

(B) $\dfrac{9}{2}$

(C) 9

(D) 18

(E) 81

18. In a group of 15, 7 have studied Latin, 8 have studied Greek, and 3 have not studied either. How many of these have studied both Latin and Greek?

(A) 0   (B) 3   (C) 4   (D) 5   (E) 7

19. If $13 = \dfrac{13w}{1 - w}$, then $(2w)^2 =$

(A) $\dfrac{1}{4}$

(B) $\dfrac{1}{2}$

(C) 1

(D) 2

(E) 4

20. If a and b are positive integers and $\dfrac{a - b}{3.5} = \dfrac{4}{7}$, then

(A) $b < a$
(B) $b > a$
(C) $b = a$
(D) $b \geqq a$
(E) $b \leqq a$

Questions 21–25 refer to the following table. This table shows how much money needs to be invested at a given rate of interest for a given number of years in order to grow to $1000.

Year	Amount of Money (dollars) Invested at:						
	5%	6%	7%	8%	9%	10%	11%
1	952	943	935	926	917	909	901
2	907	890	873	857	842	826	812
3	864	840	816	794	772	751	731
4	823	792	763	735	708	683	659
5	784	747	713	681	650	621	593
6	746	705	666	630	596	564	535
7	711	665	623	583	547	513	482
8	677	627	582	540	502	467	434
9	645	592	544	500	460	424	391
10	614	558	508	463	422	386	352
11	585	527	475	429	388	350	317
12	557	497	444	397	356	319	286
13	530	469	415	368	326	290	258
14	505	442	388	340	299	263	232
15	481	417	362	315	275	239	209
16	458	394	339	292	252	218	188
17	436	371	317	270	231	198	170
18	416	350	296	250	212	180	153
19	396	331	277	232	194	164	138
20	377	312	258	215	178	149	124
21	359	294	242	199	164	135	112
22	342	278	226	184	150	123	101
23	326	262	211	170	138	112	91
24	310	247	197	158	126	102	82
25	295	233	184	146	116	92	74

21. At what rate will an investment double in less than 10 years?

    (A) 5% (B) 6% (C) 7% (D) 8% (E) 9%

22. How much more money must be invested at 5% than at 6% to attain the $1000 goal in 15 years?

    (A) $19
    (B) $55
    (C) $46
    (D) $64
    (E) $100

23. How can an investor make an investment of less than $100 grow to $1000?

    (A) Invest at 8% for 25 years.
    (B) Invest at 8% for 9 years.
    (C) Invest at 9% for 25 years.
    (D) Invest at 10% for 24 years.
    (E) Invest at 10% for 25 years.

24. How much money needs to be invested at 8% to reach the goal of $1000 in 18 years?

    (A) $194
    (B) $212
    (C) $232
    (D) $250
    (E) $317

25. Which of the following investments more than triples in value?

    (A) $339 at 7% for 16 years
    (B) $339 at 7% for 15 years
    (C) $317 at 7% for 17 years
    (D) $317 at 6% for 17 years
    (E) $340 at 8% for 14 years

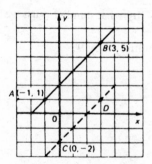

26. In the figure above, in order for the line segment AB to be parallel to the line segment CD, the coordinates of D must be $(3, x)$ with x equal to

    (A) 1 (B) 2 (C) 3 (D) 4 (E) 5

27. A farmer wishes to build a fence around a rectangular field. The field is 100 feet long and 60 feet wide. The fence will be of stone on one long side and of wire on the other three sides. Stone costs $5 a foot, and wire costs $2 a foot. How much will the fence cost?

    (A) $320
    (B) $620
    (C) $760
    (D) $800
    (E) $940

28. In June a baseball team that played 60 games had won 30% of its games played. After a phenomenal winning streak this team raised its average to 50%. How many games must the team have won in a row to attain this average?

    (A) 12   (B) 20   (C) 24   (D) 30   (E) 45

29. A train covers the distance d between two cities in h hours arriving 2 hours late. What rate would permit the train to arrive on schedule?

    (A) $h - 2$

    (B) $\dfrac{d}{h} - 2$

    (C) $\dfrac{d}{h - 2}$

    (D) $dh - 2$

    (E) $\dfrac{d}{h + 2}$

30. M men agreed to purchase a gift for $\$D$. If 3 men drop out, how much more will each have to contribute toward the purchase of the gift?

    (A) $\dfrac{D}{M - 3}$

    (B) $\dfrac{MD}{3}$

    (C) $\dfrac{3D}{M^2 - 3M}$

    (D) $\dfrac{3D}{3M - M^2}$

    (E) $\dfrac{2M + DM}{3M - M^2}$

S T O P

IF YOU FINISH BEFORE TIME IS CALLED, YOU MAY CHECK YOUR WORK ON THIS SECTION ONLY.
DO NOT WORK ON ANY OTHER SECTION IN THE TEST.

SECTION 4
Time—30 minutes
30 Questions

Numbers: All numbers used are real numbers.

Figures: Position of points, angles, regions, etc., can be assumed to be in the order shown; and angle measures can be assumed to be positive.

Lines shown as straight can be assumed to be straight.

Figures can be assumed to lie in a plane unless otherwise indicated.

Figures that accompany questions are intended to provide information useful in answering the questions. However, unless a note states that a figure is drawn to scale, you should solve these problems NOT by estimating sizes by sight or by measurement, but by using your knowledge of mathematics (see Example 2 below).

Directions: Each of the Questions 1-15 consists of two quantities, one in Column A and one in Column B. You are to compare the two quantities and choose

A if the quantity in Column A is greater;
B if the quantity in Column B is greater;
C if the two quantities are equal;
D if the relationship cannot be determined from the information given.

Note: Since there are only four choices, NEVER MARK (E).

Common
Information: In a question, information concerning one or both of the quantities to be compared is centered above the two columns. A symbol that appears in both columns represents the same thing in Column A as it does in Column B.

	Column A	Column B	Sample Answers
Example 1:	2×6	$2 + 6$	● Ⓑ Ⓒ Ⓓ Ⓔ

Examples 2-4 refer to $\triangle PQR$.

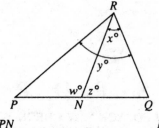

Example 2:	PN	NQ	Ⓐ Ⓑ Ⓒ ● Ⓔ

(since equal measures cannot be assumed, even though PN and NQ appear equal)

Example 3:	x	y	Ⓐ ● Ⓒ Ⓓ Ⓔ

(since N is between P and Q

Example 4:	$w + z$	180	Ⓐ Ⓑ ● Ⓓ Ⓔ

(since PQ is a straight line)

A if the quantity in Column A is greater;
B if the quantity in Column B is greater;
C if the two quantities are equal;
D if the relationship cannot be determined from the information given.

<u>Column A</u>	<u>Column B</u>

$$\frac{1}{x} = \sqrt{0.09}$$

1. x $3\frac{1}{3}$

$$a + 2b = 1\frac{1}{3}$$
$$a - b = \frac{1}{3}$$

2. $3b$ 1

---

3. $\dfrac{x - y}{-z}$ $\dfrac{y - x}{z}$

$$x = 0 \text{ and } y > 0$$

4. $\dfrac{9x^2y^2}{27}$ $\dfrac{1}{3}$

---

5. $\dfrac{4}{5}$ quart $\dfrac{1}{5}$ gallon

$$a{:}b = c{:}d$$

6. $\dfrac{b}{a}$ $\dfrac{d}{c}$

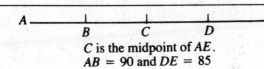

C is the midpoint of AE.
$AB = 90$ and $DE = 85$

7. Length of BC Length of CD

---

8. bh ac

Perimeter of square $ABCD = 4a + 4$

9. Length of side CD a

<u>Column A</u>	<u>Column B</u>

$l = 110$

10. l n

In triangle ABC, side CA is extended to form an exterior angle that measures 80°.

11. Length of side AB Length of side BC

The area of triangle $ABC = 72$. The measure of angle A is equal to the measure of angle C, which is 45 degrees.

12. Length of AB Length of BC

$$(a - 1)(a + 1) = 0$$
$$(b - 2)(b + 2) = 0$$

13. a^2 b^2

$$x > 0$$

14. The arithmetic mean (average) of x
     x, 0, and $\dfrac{3}{2}x$

---

15. x 74

Directions: Each of Questions 16–30 has five answer choices. For each of these questions, select the best of the answer choices given.

16. A rectangular fish tank 25" by 9" has water in it to a level of 2". This water is carefully poured into a cylindrical container with a diameter of 10". How high (in terms of π) will the water reach in the cylindrical container?

(A) 18π

(B) $\frac{\pi}{18}$

(C) $\frac{18}{\pi}$

(D) $\frac{9}{2\pi}$

(E) $\frac{9\pi}{2}$

17. A triangular plot with sides of 28 feet, 35 feet, and 56 feet is to be surrounded by a fence built on posts set 7 feet apart. After posts are placed at each corner, how many additional posts will be needed?

(A) 14
(B) 15
(C) 16
(D) 17
(E) 20

18. A box is made in the form of a cube. If a second cubical box has inside dimensions three times those of the first box, how many times as much does the second box contain?

(A) 3
(B) 6
(C) 9
(D) 12
(E) 27

19. Two hours after a freight train leaves Circleville a passenger train leaves the same station traveling in the same direction at an average speed of 60 miles per hour. After traveling four hours, the passenger train overtakes the freight train. The average speed of the freight train was

(A) 30
(B) 40
(C) 58
(D) 60
(E) 120

20. Which sign inserted in the parentheses will make the following statement correct?

$$\frac{6}{14} \left(\right) \frac{9}{21} = \frac{3}{7}$$

(A) +
(B) −
(C) ×
(D) ÷
(E) =

Questions 21–25 refer to the following graphs.

WHERE THE TAX
DOLLAR GOES

WHERE THE TAX
DOLLAR COMES FROM

21. Which of the following can be inferred from the graphs?
   I. Excise and customs taxes provide more than half of the federal government's revenue.
   II. Corporate taxes and individual income taxes provide more than half the federal government's revenue.
   III. All taxes other than income taxes provide as much revenue as do income taxes.
   (A) I only   (B) II only   (C) III only
   (D) I and III   (E) II and III

22. To accurately draw the sector to show government costs fixed by law the central angle of this sector should be

(A) 22°
(B) 44°
(C) 55°
(D) 60°
(E) 80°

23. What part of all tax revenue comes from income taxes?

(A) $\frac{1}{3}$

(B) $\frac{1}{4}$

(C) $\frac{2}{5}$

(D) $\frac{1}{2}$

(E) $\frac{3}{4}$

24. What percent of the federal government income is derived from individual income taxes?

    (A) 0.0043%
    (B) 0.043%
    (C) 0.43%
    (D) 4.3%
    (E) 43%

25. Of every $1000 received by the federal government, how much is received from sources other than income taxes?

    (A) $260
    (B) $310
    (C) $430
    (D) $570
    (E) $740

26. To which of the following is $\frac{a}{b} - \frac{a}{c}$ equal?

    (A) $\dfrac{a}{b - c}$

    (B) $\dfrac{1}{b - c}$

    (C) $\dfrac{1}{bc}$

    (D) $\dfrac{ab - ac}{bc}$

    (E) $\dfrac{ac - ab}{bc}$

27. The two stars of a basketball team scored 416 points between them during a season. If one of them scored 192 points, what is the ratio of the points scored by this player to those scored by his teammate?

    (A) $\frac{6}{13}$ (B) $\frac{7}{13}$ (C) $\frac{6}{7}$ (D) $\frac{19}{22}$ (E) $\frac{7}{6}$

28. Nancy would like to complete all her homework before 10 P.M. in order to watch an important television program. She has 40-minute assignments in each of her five prepared subjects. What is the latest time at which she can start and still complete her homework in time for the program?

    (A) 6:30 P.M.
    (B) 6:40 P.M.
    (C) 7:10 P.M.
    (D) 7:20 P.M.
    (E) 8:00 P.M.

29. A club purchased novelties for $204.00 for resale at a benefit bazaar. During the first day they made sales amounting to $169.50. The inventory at the end of this day showed that they still had merchandise for which they paid $82.50. The gross profit at the end of the first day of the bazaar was

    (A) $ 34.60
    (B) $ 46.50
    (C) $ 48.00
    (D) $ 48.50
    (E) $121.50

30. Snowhite Paint Company contracts to paint three houses. Mr. Brown can paint a house in 6 days while Mr. Pinter would take 8 days and Mr. Slocum would take 12 days. After 8 days Mr. Brown goes on vacation and Mr. Pinter begins to work for a period of 6 days. How many days will it take Mr. Slocum to complete the contract?

    (A) 7
    (B) 8
    (C) 11
    (D) 12
    (E) 13

S T O P

IF YOU FINISH BEFORE TIME IS CALLED, YOU MAY CHECK YOUR WORK ON THIS SECTION ONLY.
DO NOT WORK ON ANY OTHER SECTION IN THE TEST.

SECTION 5

Time—30 Minutes

38 Questions

Directions: Each sentence below has one or two blanks, each blank indicating that something has been omitted. Beneath the sentence are five lettered words or sets of words. Choose the word or set of words for each blank that best fits the meaning of the sentence as a whole.

1. Criticism that tears down without suggesting areas of improvement is not ------- and should be avoided if possible.

   (A) representative
   (B) constructive
   (C) mandatory
   (D) pertinent
   (E) sagacious

2. As I am not an ardent admirer of the work of George Eliot, simple justice demands a prefatory ------- her many admirable qualities.

   (A) skepticism regarding
   (B) effusion over
   (C) denial of
   (D) tribute to
   (E) dismissal of

3. You may wonder how the expert on fossil remains is able to trace descent through teeth, which seem ------- pegs upon which to hang whole ancestries.

   (A) novel
   (B) reliable
   (C) specious
   (D) inadequate
   (E) academic

4. An essential purpose of the criminal justice system is to enable purgation to take place; that is, to provide a ------- by which a community expresses its collective ------- the transgression of the criminal.

   (A) catharsis...outrage at
   (B) disclaimer...forgiveness of
   (C) means...empathy with
   (D) procedure...distaste for
   (E) document...disapprobation of

5. In the tradition of scholarly -------, the poet and scholar A.E. Housman once assailed a German rival for relying on manuscripts "as a drunkard relies on lampposts, for ------- rather than illumination."

   (A) animosity...current
   (B) discourse...stability
   (C) erudition...shadow
   (D) invective...support
   (E) competition...assistance

6. According to the twelfth-century cosmologists, the natural philosopher must strive to ------- a state of detached objectivity in order to free his capacity for constructing useful hypotheses from the ------- of unquestioned assumptions and accepted opinions about nature.

   (A) capture...contemplation
   (B) achieve...tyranny
   (C) imitate...discipline
   (D) feign...pretense
   (E) attain...confusion

7. Unable to ------- his wholehearted distaste for media events and unnecessary publicity, Dean Brower continued to make ------- comments throughout the ceremony.

   (A) control...garbled
   (B) maintain...copious
   (C) conceal...effusive
   (D) disguise...caustic
   (E) express...vitriolic

Directions: In each of the following questions, a related pair of words or phrases is followed by five lettered pairs of words or phrases. Select the lettered pair that best expresses a relationship similar to that expressed in the original pair.

8. YOLK : EGG::
   (A) rind : melon
   (B) nucleus : cell
   (C) stalk : corn
   (D) duck : fowl
   (E) web : spider

9. WOOD : SAND::
   (A) coal : burn
   (B) brick : lay
   (C) oil : polish
   (D) metal : burnish
   (E) stone : quarry

10. VINDICTIVE : MERCY::
    (A) avaricious : greed
    (B) insightful : hope
    (C) modest : dignity
    (D) skeptical : trustfulness
    (E) pathetic : sympathy

11. RUFFLE : COMPOSURE::
    (A) flounce : turmoil
    (B) flourish : prosperity
    (C) provoke : discussion
    (D) adjust : balance
    (E) upset : equilibrium

12. BOUQUET : WINE::
    (A) chaff : wheat
    (B) aroma : coffee
    (C) yeast : bread
    (D) octane : gasoline
    (E) decanter : brandy

13. SEXTANT : NAUTICAL::
    (A) octet : musical
    (B) therapy : physical
    (C) forceps : surgical
    (D) comet : astronomical
    (E) blueprint : mechanical

14. REFRACTORY : MANAGE::
    (A) redoubtable : impress
    (B) lethargic : stimulate
    (C) pedantic : convince
    (D) officious : arrange
    (E) aggrieved : distress

15. LATENT : MANIFESTATION::
    (A) torpid : hibernation
    (B) patent : appearance
    (C) perfunctory : inspiration
    (D) punctilious : continuity
    (E) dormant : awakening

16. PRECIPICE : STEEPNESS::
    (A) defile : narrowness
    (B) well : shallowness
    (C) plateau : depth
    (D) mountain : range
    (E) marsh : aridity

Directions: Each passage in this group is followed by questions based on its content. After reading a passage, choose the best answer to each question. Answer all questions following a passage on the basis of what is stated or implied in the passage.

Given the persistent and intransigent nature of the American race system, which proved quite impervious to black attacks, Du Bois in his speeches and writings moved from one proposed solution to another, and the salience of various parts of his philosophy changed as his perceptions of the needs and strategies of black America shifted over time. Aloof and autonomous in his personality, Du Bois did not hesitate to depart markedly from whatever was the current mainstream of black thinking when he perceived that the conventional wisdom being enunciated by black spokesmen was proving inadequate to the task of advancing the race. His willingness to seek different solutions often placed him well in advance of his contemporaries, and this, combined with a strong-willed, even arrogant personality made his career as a black leader essentially a series of stormy conflicts.

Thus Du Bois first achieved his role as a major black leader in the controversy that arose over the program of Booker T. Washington, the most prominent and influential black leader at the opening of the twentieth century. Amidst the wave of lynchings, disfranchisement, and segregation laws, Washington, seeking the good will of powerful whites, taught blacks not to protest against discrimination, but to elevate themselves through industrial education, hard work, and property accumulation; then, they would ultimately obtain recognition of their citizenship rights. At first Du Bois agreed with this gradualist strategy, but in 1903 with the publication of his most influential book, *Souls of Black Folk*, he became the chief leader of the onslaught against Washington that polarized the black community into two wings—the "conservative" supporters of Washington and his "radical" critics.

17. The author's primary purpose in the passage is to

    (A) explain how Du Bois was influenced by Washington
    (B) compare the personalities of Du Bois and Washington
    (C) explain why Du Bois gained power in the black community
    (D) describe Du Bois' role in early twentieth century black leadership
    (E) correct the misconception that Du Bois shunned polarization

18. Which of the following statements about W.E.B. Du Bois does the passage best support?

    (A) He sacrificed the proven strategies of earlier black leaders to his craving for political novelty.
    (B) Preferring conflict to harmony, he followed a disruptive course that alienated him from the bulk of his followers.
    (C) He proved unable to change with the times in mounting fresh attacks against white racism.
    (D) He relied on the fundamental benevolence of the white population for the eventual success of his movement.
    (E) Once an adherent of Washington's policies, he ultimately lost patience with them for their inefficacy.

19. It can be inferred that Booker T. Washington in comparison with W.E.B. Du Bois could be described as all of the following EXCEPT

   (A) submissive to the majority
   (B) concerned with financial success
   (C) versatile in adopting strategies
   (D) traditional in preaching industry
   (E) respectful of authority

20. The author's attitude towards Du Bois' departure from conventional black policies can best be described as

   (A) skeptical
   (B) derisive
   (C) shocked
   (D) approving
   (E) resigned

Any successful theory in the physical sciences is expected to make accurate predictions. Given some well-defined experiment, the theory should correctly specify the outcome or should at least assign the correct probabilities to all the possible outcomes. From this point of view quantum mechanics must be judged highly successful. As the fundamental modern theory of atoms, of molecules, of elementary particles, of electromagnetic radiation and of the solid state it supplies methods for calculating the results of experiments in all these realms.

Apart from experimental confirmation, however, something more is generally demanded of a theory. It is expected not only to determine the results of an experiment but also to provide some understanding of the physical events that are presumed to underlie the observed results. In other words, the theory should not only give the position of a pointer on a dial but also explain why the pointer takes up that position. When one seeks information of this kind in the quantum theory, certain conceptual difficulties aries. For example, in quantum mechanics an elementary particle such as an electron is represented by the mathematical expression called a wave function, which often describes the electron as if it were smeared out over a large region of space.

This representation is not in conflict with experiment; on the contrary, the wave function yields an accurate estimate of the probability that the electron will be found in any given place. When the electron is actually detected, however, it is never smeared out but always has a definite position. Hence it is not entirely clear what physical interpretation should be given to the wave function or what picture of the electron one should keep in mind. Because of ambiguities such as this many physicists find it most sensible to regard quantum mechanics as merely a set of rules that prescribe the outcome of experiments. According to this view the quantum theory is concerned only with observable phenomena (the observed position of the pointer) and not with any underlying physical state (the real position of the electron).

It now turns out that even this renunciation is not entirely satisfactory. Even if quantum mechanics is considered to be no more than a set of rules, it is still in conflict with a view of the world many people would consider obvious or natural. This world view is based on three assumptions or premises that must be accepted without proof. One is realism, the doctrine that regularities in observed phenomena are caused by some physical reality whose existence is independent of human observers. The second premise holds that inductive inference is a valid mode of reasoning and can be applied freely, so that legitimate conclusions can be drawn from consistent observations. The third premise is called Einstein separability or Einstein locality, and it states that no influence of any kind can propagate faster than the speed of light. The three premises, which are often assumed to have the status of well-established truths, or even self-evident truths, form the basis of what I shall call local realistic theories of nature. An argument derived from these premises leads to an explicit prediction for the results of a certain class of experiments in the physics of elementary particles. The rules of quantum mechanics can also be employed to calculate the results of these experiments. Significantly, the two predictions differ, and so either the local realistic theories or quantum mechanics must be wrong.

21. This passage was most likely excerpted from a

   (A) physics textbook focused on the mathematical foundations of quantum mechanics
   (B) theoretical physics report urging further experiments to resolve current ambiguities
   (C) scientific journal article informing a general audience of new findings in quantum mechanics
   (D) pamphlet challenging the adequacy of quantum theory as a valid mathematical tool
   (E) student log of a series of controversial experiments in the physics of elementary particles

22. Describing an electron on the basis of its mathematical expression is most like describing a

   (A) paw from the cast of a pawprint
   (B) pebble from the ripples it makes in a pond
   (C) statue on the basis of its armature
   (D) tree trunk from the pattern of its rings
   (E) butterfly on the basis of its chrysalis

23. The author organizes the passage by

   (A) explaining the wide applicability of quantum theory and contrasting it with the inapplicability of local realistic theories
   (B) describing several assumptions underlying quantum theory and then refuting them consecutively
   (C) making distinctions between experimental and nonexperimental methods of representing reality
   (D) making a generalization about scientific theory and then applying it to the theory of quantum mechanics
   (E) stating a specific idea and then moving from it to a sequence of generalizations about quantum theory

24. The author provides information that answers which of the following questions?

I. What are the presuppositions upon which the so-called local realistic theories are based?

II. Which premise of the local realistic theories of nature has been invalidated by current experimental predictions?

III. To what degree can one physically interpret a mathematical expression such as a wave function?

(A) I only
(B) III only
(C) I and II only
(D) I and III only
(E) I, II and III

25. All of the following can be found in the author's discussion of quantum theory EXCEPT

(A) a concrete example of a specific observable phenomenon
(B) a generalization about the criteria for judging the value of a given theory
(C) a hypothesis based on the invalidity of Einstein separability
(D) an enumeration of the fundamental assumptions underlying the local realistic theories of nature
(E) a statement setting the local realistic theories and the quantum theory at variance

26. In terms of its tone and form, this passage can best be described as

(A) a doctrinaire appraisal
(B) a concrete proposal
(C) an iconoclastic observation
(D) a systematic exposition
(E) a cursory examination

27. Which of the following statements concerning physicists is most directly suggested by the passage?

(A) Physicists who gloss over discrepancies between quantum theory and the local realistic theories have yet to account for current experiments in elementary particle physics.
(B) Physicists may have overestimated the ability of quantum mechanics to provide experimental confirmation for theories.
(C) Physicists have not been sufficiently orthodox in their adherence to the three fundamental premises of the local realistic theories.
(D) Physicists see little basis for the conceptual difficulties suffered by laypersons in comprehending the underlying physical state of an observable phenomenon.
(E) Physicists exploring the physics of elementary particles fail to make explicit predictions about their experimental results.

Directions: Each question below consists of a word printed in capital letters, followed by five lettered words or phrases. Choose the lettered word or phrase that is most nearly opposite in meaning to the word in capital letters.

Since some of the questions require you to distinguish fine shades of meaning, be sure to consider all the choices before deciding which one is best.

28. ADULTERATED:
(A) solid
(B) immature
(C) exalted
(D) pure
(E) virtuous

29. DISTEND:
(A) deflate
(B) prolong
(C) commence
(D) forecast
(E) prevent

30. TRANSIENT:
(A) permanent
(B) desultory
(C) spontaneous
(D) subterranean
(E) obsequious

31. ELATED:
(A) crestfallen
(B) inebriated
(C) punctual
(D) insulted
(E) lamented

32. REVILE:
(A) compose
(B) awake
(C) deaden
(D) praise
(E) secrete

33. PROPITIOUS:
(A) adjacent
(B) clandestine
(C) contentious
(D) unfavorable
(E) coy

34. ENSUE:
(A) litigate
(B) precede
(C) arbitrate
(D) accentuate
(E) delay

35. RETROSPECTION:
   (A) introversion
   (B) deliberation
   (C) anticipation
   (D) gregariousness
   (E) equivocation

36. EGRESS:
   (A) deviation
   (B) entrance
   (C) approbation
   (D) dilemma
   (E) renown

37. MAUNDER:
   (A) speak purposefully
   (B) maintain silence
   (C) appear unaware
   (D) evade entanglement
   (E) seek consensus

38. HUBRIS:
   (A) impiety
   (B) insouciance
   (C) apathy
   (D) mendacity
   (E) humility

S T O P

IF YOU FINISH BEFORE TIME IS CALLED, YOU MAY CHECK YOUR WORK ON THIS SECTION ONLY.
DO NOT WORK ON ANY OTHER SECTION IN THE TEST.

SECTION 6

Time—30 Minutes

25 Questions

Directions: Each question or group of questions is based on a passage or set of conditions. In answering some of the questions, it may be useful to draw a rough diagram. For each question, select the best answer choice given.

Questions 1–4

Byram and Adoniram are code clerks at the Pentagon. They are also secret agents for foreign governments. One is in the pay of the Sulgravians and the other is in the pay of the Carolingians. If a document is stolen, it will take four days to reach the Sulgravian government and five days to reach the Carolingian government.

Byram is given top-secret documents to encode on October 19 and 22.

Adoniram is given a top-secret document to encode on October 21.

Byram and Adoniram have lunch together on October 20.

Agents of foreign governments do not transmit documents directly to governments that do not employ them, but may sell documents to an agent of another government. An agent who transmits a document always does so on the day he receives it.

1. If Adoniram is working for the Sulgravians, the Sulgravian government may receive documents on

 I. October 24
 II. October 25
 III. October 26

 (A) I only
 (B) III only
 (C) I and II only
 (D) II and III only
 (E) I, II, and III

2. A top-secret document is received by the Carolingians on October 25. It could have been

 (A) stolen and transmitted by Byram
 (B) stolen and transmitted by Adoniram
 (C) stolen by Adoniram and sold to Byram, who transmitted it
 (D) stolen by Byram and sold to Adoniram, who transmitted it
 (E) stolen by either Byram or Adoniram and sold to the other, who transmitted it

3. If Adoniram is working for the Carolingians, which must be true?

 (A) The Sulgravians may receive documents only on October 23.
 (B) The Carolingians may receive documents only on October 26.
 (C) The Sulgravians may receive documents only on October 24, 26, and 27.
 (D) The Carolingians may receive documents only on October 24, 25, and 26.
 (E) No documents received by the Sulgravians can have been bought at Byram and Adoniram's lunchtime meeting.

4. Which of the following is (are) possible given the conditions as stated?

 I. Documents are received by one of the governments two days in a row.
 II. Documents are received by both governments two days in a row.
 III. Documents are received by one of the governments three days in a row.

 (A) I only
 (B) III only
 (C) I and III only
 (D) I, II, and III
 (E) neither I, II, nor III

5. Although there are no physical differences between the visual organs of the two groups, the inhabitants of the Bilge Islands, when shown a card displaying a spectrum of colors, perceive fewer colors than do most persons in the United States.

 Which of the following conclusions can most reliably be drawn from the information above?

 (A) Human color perception is at least partly determined by factors other than the physical structure of the visual organs.
 (B) The Bilge Islanders are probably taught in childhood to recognize fewer colors than are persons in the United States.
 (C) Differences in social structure probably affect color perception.
 (D) Color perception in humans is influenced by differences in physical environment.
 (E) Bilge Islanders may have fewer terms denoting colors in their language than do English-speaking persons.

Questions 6 and 7

Ms. Brady: Mr. Flynn insists that the only way for our company to increase its profits is to double the advertising budget. That obviously is not the answer. Our two major competitors have operations similar to ours. Both are showing increased profits while spending less on advertising than we presently spend.

6. Ms. Brady's primary method of making her point is to

 (A) suggest a different underlying cause of the problem
 (B) present evidence which was previously overlooked
 (C) point out a logical flaw in Mr. Flynn's reasoning
 (D) draw an analogy
 (E) question Mr. Flynn's competence

7. Which of the following statements would be Mr. Flynn's most effective rebuttal to Ms. Brady's argument?

(A) Our two major competitors do not need to advertise as much as we do, because they are already much better known and have larger shares of the market.
(B) I have been in this business for 30 years, during which time I have repeatedly proven my ability to identify and solve business problems.
(C) The only way for us to increase profits is to sell more of our products; the only way to sell more products is to convince people to buy them; the only way to convince people to buy them is through increased advertising.
(D) You have offered neither statistics to back up your claims nor any proposal for an alternative solution to our problem.
(E) My proposal is not "obviously" wrong. There is only one way to find out if it is wrong, and that is to try it.

Questions 8–12

(1) Ashland is north of East Liverpool and west of Coshocton.
(2) Bowling Green is north of Ashland and west of Fredericktown.
(3) Dover is south and east of Ashland.
(4) East Liverpool is north of Fredericktown and east of Dover.
(5) Fredericktown is north of Dover and west of Ashland.
(6) Coshocton is south of Fredericktown and west of Dover.

8. Which of the towns mentioned is furthest to the northwest?

(A) Ashland
(B) Bowling Green
(C) Coshocton
(D) East Liverpool
(E) Fredericktown

9. Which of the following must be both north and east of Fredericktown?

I.   Ashland
II.   Coshocton
III. East Liverpool

(A) I only
(B) II only
(C) III only
(D) I and II
(E) I and III

10. Which of the following towns must be situated both south and west of at least one other town?

(A) Ashland only
(B) Ashland and Fredericktown
(C) Dover and Fredericktown
(D) Dover, Coshocton, and Fredericktown
(E) Coshocton, Dover, and East Liverpool

11. Which of the following statements, if true, would make the information in the numbered statements more specific?

(A) Coshocton is north of Dover.
(B) East Liverpool is north of Dover.
(C) Ashland is east of Bowling Green.
(D) Coshocton is east of Fredericktown.
(E) Bowling Green is north of Fredericktown.

12. Which of the numbered statements gives information that can be deduced from one or more of the other statements?

(A) (1)
(B) (2)
(C) (3)
(D) (4)
(E) (6)

Questions 13–16

Spelunkers International offers exploring tours in eight caves: Abbott, Benny, Caesar, Dangerfield, Ewell, Fields, Guinness, and Hope.
(1) Class 1 spelunkers may not attempt cave Ewell, Fields, or Hope.
(2) Class 2 spelunkers may not attempt cave Hope.
(3) Class 3 spelunkers may attempt any cave.
(4) Cave Caesar may be attempted only by spelunkers who have previously explored cave Benny.
(5) Cave Fields may be attempted only by spelunkers who have previously explored cave Ewell.
(6) Only two of caves Benny, Caesar, Ewell, Fields, and Hope may be attempted by any explorer in a single tour.

13. Which tour is allowed for a class 2 spelunker who has never explored any of the eight caves before, if the caves are attempted in the order listed?

(A) Abbott, Fields, Ewell, Benny
(B) Dangerfield, Guinness, Caesar, Benny
(C) Guinness, Ewell, Dangerfield, Benny, Abbott
(D) Dangerfield, Ewell, Fields, Abbott, Caesar
(E) Guinness, Ewell, Fields, Dangerfield, Benny

14. A class 2 spelunker who has previously explored cave Ewell may be restricted in choosing a tour by which rule(s)?

    I.   Rule (4)
    II. Rule (5)
    III. Rule (6)

    (A) I only
    (B) II only
    (C) I and III only
    (D) II and III only
    (E) I, II, and III

15. In how many different ways may a class 1 spelunker who has never explored any of the eight caves before set up a tour of three caves, if she wishes to explore caves Abbott and Caesar?

    (A) 2
    (B) 3
    (C) 4
    (D) 5
    (E) 6

16. What is the maximum number of caves that a class 3 spelunker who has previously explored only cave Benny may include in a single tour?

    (A) 4
    (B) 5
    (C) 6
    (D) 7
    (E) 8

Questions 17–22

Mr. Pesth, foreman for Buda Construction Co., is hiring five persons to do wiring and plumbing on a site. He must have a minimum of two electricians. Nine persons are sent by the union hiring hall: Mike, Nick, and Olive are electricians, while Rich, Steve, Tom, Ulysses, Vic, and Wassily are plumbers.

Pesth is unwilling to hire Ulysses and Vic together, because he knows from past experience that they fight all the time.

Steve and Tom are buddies and will only work together.

Olive won't work with Rich, a Moravian, because she despises Moravians.

17. If Mike, Nick, and Olive are hired, the team of plumbers can consist of

    (A) Steve and Tom only
    (B) Steve and Tom or Ulysses and Vic
    (C) Ulysses and Wassily or Vic and Wassily
    (D) Steve and Tom or Ulysses and Wassily or Vic and Wassily
    (E) Steve, Tom, and either Ulysses, Vic, or Wassily

18. Pesth has the greatest number of choices for hiring as plumbers if the electricians he chooses are

    (A) Mike, Nick, and Olive
    (B) Mike and Nick
    (C) Mike and Olive
    (D) Nick and Olive
    (E) Either Mike or Nick, plus Olive

19. If Rich is hired, the other persons hired must be

    (A) Mike, Nick, Steve, and Tom
    (B) Mike, Nick, Olive, and either Ulysses, Vic, or Wassily
    (C) Mike and Nick, together with either Steve and Tom or Ulysses and Wassily
    (D) Mike and Nick, together with either Ulysses and Vic or Vic and Wassily
    (E) Mike and Nick, together with either Steve and Tom, Ulysses and Wassily, or Vic and Wassily

20. Pesth can put together the rest of his crew in the greatest number of different ways if he hires

    (A) Steve and Tom
    (B) Olive
    (C) Ulysses
    (D) Vic
    (E) Wassily

21. If Mike is hired and Nick is not, which of the following statements must be true?

    I. Steve and Tom are hired.
    II. Either Ulysses or Vic is hired, but not both.

    (A) I only
    (B) II only
    (C) either I or II, but not both
    (D) both I and II
    (E) neither I nor II

22. Which of the following statements must be true?

    I.   If only two electricians are hired, the plumbers must include Steve and Tom.
    II. If Olive is not hired, Rich must be hired.
    III. If either Mike or Nick is not hired, Steve and Tom must be hired.

    (A) I only
    (B) II only
    (C) III only
    (D) I and III only
    (E) II and III only

23. The current trend toward specialization in nearly all occupational groups is exactly the opposite of what is needed. World problems today are so diverse, complex, and interrelated that only the generalist stands a chance of understanding the broad picture. Unless our schools stress a truly broad, liberal education, the world will crumble around us as we each expertly perform our own narrow functions.

Each of the following, if true, would weaken the conclusion drawn above, EXCEPT:

(A) Many of the world's problems can be solved only by highly specialized experts working on specific problems.
(B) Relatively few generalists are needed to coordinate the work of the many specialists.
(C) Specialization does not necessarily entail losing the ability to see the broad picture.
(D) Increasingly complex problems require a growing level of technical expertise which can only be acquired through specialization.
(E) Even the traditional liberal education is becoming more highly specialized today.

Questions 24 and 25

All good athletes want to win, and all athletes who want to win eat a well-balanced diet; therefore, all athletes who do not eat a well-balanced diet are bad athletes.

24. If the assumptions of the argument above are true, then which of the following statements must be true?

(A) No bad athlete wants to win.
(B) No athlete who does not eat a well-balanced diet is a good athlete.
(C) Every athlete who eats a well-balanced diet is a good athlete.
(D) All athletes who want to win are good athletes.
(E) Some good athletes do not eat a well-balanced diet.

25. Which of the following, if true, would refute the assumptions of the argument above?

(A) Ann wants to win, but she is not a good athlete.
(B) Bob, the accountant, eats a well-balanced diet, but he is not a good athlete.
(C) All the players on the Burros baseball team eat a well-balanced diet.
(D) No athlete who does not eat a well-balanced diet wants to win.
(E) Cindy, the basketball star, does not eat a well-balanced diet, but she is a good athlete.

S T O P

IF YOU FINISH BEFORE TIME IS CALLED, YOU MAY CHECK YOUR WORK ON THIS SECTION ONLY.
DO NOT WORK ON ANY OTHER SECTION IN THE TEST.

SECTION 7

Time—30 Minutes

30 Questions

Numbers: All numbers used are real numbers.

Figures: Position of points, angles, regions, etc., can be assumed to be in the order shown; and angle measures can be assumed to be positive.

Lines shown as straight can be assumed to be straight.

Figures can be assumed to lie in a plane unless otherwise indicated.

Figures that accompany questions are intended to provide information useful in answering the questions. However, unless a note states that a figure is drawn to scale, you should solve these problems NOT by estimating sizes by sight or by measurement, but by using your knowledge of mathematics (see Example 2 below).

Directions: Each of the Questions 1-15 consists of two quantities, one in Column A and one in Column B. You are to compare the two quantities and choose

        A if the quantity in Column A is greater;
        B if the quantity in Column B is greater;
        C if the two quantities are equal;
        D if the relationship cannot be determined from the information given.

Note: Since there are only four choices, NEVER MARK (E).

Common Information: In a question, information concerning one or both of the quantities to be compared is centered above the two columns. A symbol that appears in both columns represents the same thing in Column A as it does in Column B.

	Column A	Column B	Sample Answers
Example 1:	2×6	$2 + 6$	● Ⓑ Ⓒ Ⓓ Ⓔ

Examples 2-4 refer to △ *PQR*.

Example 2:	*PN*	*NQ*	Ⓐ Ⓑ Ⓒ ● Ⓔ
			(since equal measures cannot be assumed, even though *PN* and *NQ* appear equal)
Example 3:	*x*	*y*	Ⓐ ● Ⓒ Ⓓ Ⓔ
			(since *N* is between *P* and *Q*)
Example 4:	*w* + *z*	180	Ⓐ Ⓑ ● Ⓓ Ⓔ
			(since *PQ* is a straight line)

A if the quantity in Column A is greater;
B if the quantity in Column B is greater;
C if the two quantities are equal;
D if the relationship cannot be determined from the information given.

Column A	Column B		Column A	Column B

$a = 2$ and $b = 3$

1. $a - b$ $b - a$

2. $\sqrt{14.4}$ $\sqrt{1.44}$

3. $DC + AD$ AC

4. Radius of a circle with   Radius of a circle with
    circumference of 9   area of 25

A ———————— C ———————— B

5. The length of the seg-   The length of the seg-
    ment joining the mid-   ment from point A to
    points of AC and CB the midpoint of AB

$\widehat{X}$ is defined by the equation $\widehat{X} = \dfrac{\sqrt{x}}{2}$.

6. $\widehat{100}$ 10

Angle B = Angle C

7. $\dfrac{x}{c}$ $\dfrac{x}{b}$

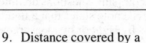

$a^2 + b^2 = 100$
$-6 \leqslant b \leqslant 0$

8. Lowest possible value   0
    of a

9. Distance covered by a   25 miles
    motorist going at 50
    miles per hour from
    10:55 P.M. to 11:25
    P.M. the same evening

$z > 5$

10. $\dfrac{1}{z}$ $\dfrac{1}{z-1}$

$\dfrac{a}{b} = \dfrac{c}{d}$

11. ad bc

$0 < x < y$

12. $3x$ y

13. $\dfrac{1}{4} \div \dfrac{3}{8}$ $1\dfrac{1}{2}$

$x > 0$

14. $(-2)^x$ $(l)^x$

$a = 2b$
$1 < b < 9$

15. a 6

Directions: Each of the <u>Questions 16–30</u> has five answer choices. For each of these questions, select the best of the answer choices given.

16. If $9x - 3y = 12$ and $3x - 5y = 7$, then $6x - 2y$ equals

   (A) -5
   (B) 2
   (C) 4
   (D) 7
   (E) 8

17. The product of 8,754,896 and 48,933 equals

   (A) 428,403,325,965
   (B) 428,403,325,966
   (C) 428,403,325,967
   (D) 428,403,325,968
   (E) 428,403,325,969

18. If $2^{n+2} = 8$, then n equals

   (A) -1
   (B) $+1$
   (C) 2
   (D) 3
   (E) 4

19. If x is an odd integer, which of the following is even?

   (A) $2x + 1$
   (B) $2x + 2$
   (C) $x + x - 1$
   (D) $(x - 2)(x + 2)$
   (E) $2(x + 1)$

20. The price of a garment is reduced by 20 percent. During an "early-bird" special all garments are marked "Take an additional 30 percent off the reduced price." The two reductions are equivalent to a single reduction of

   (A) 25%
   (B) 44%
   (C) 50%
   (D) 56%
   (E) 60%

Questions 21–25 refer to the following graphs.

FLORENCE DRESS SHOP
SALES AND EARNINGS REPORT (1980–1987)

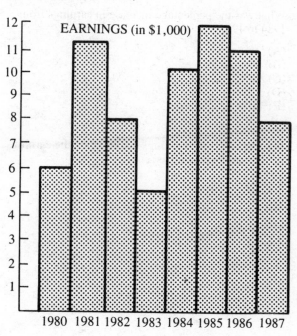

21. What is the average (arithmetic mean) in thousands of dollars of the sales for the period 1982–1985?

    (A) $60.
    (B) $70.
    (C) $72.5
    (D) $80.
    (E) $80.5

22. Which of the following can be inferred from the graphs?
    I.   Sales for 1982 and 1985 were the same.
    II. Sales for 1982 and 1987 were the same.
    III. Earnings for 1985 were twice those for 1980.

    (A) I only   (B) II only   (C) III only
    (D) I and III   (E) II and III

23. What was the ratio of sales to earnings in 1980?

    (A) $\frac{1}{2}$

    (B) $\frac{2}{1}$

    (C) $\frac{1}{5}$

    (D) $\frac{5}{1}$

    (E) $\frac{1}{6}$

24. What was the percentage increase in earnings from 1984 to 1985?

    (A) 2%
    (B) 6%
    (C) 10%
    (D) 12%
    (E) 20%

25. If g represents the earnings in 1980 then the earnings in 1985 are expressed as

    (A) $2g$

    (B) $\frac{g}{2}$

    (C) $g + 2$

    (D) $\frac{2}{g}$

    (E) $3g$

26. R and T are points on straight line PQ on which PR = RT = TQ. What percent of PT is PQ?

    (A) $1\frac{1}{2}\%$

    (B) 50%

    (C) $66\frac{2}{3}\%$

    (D) $33\frac{1}{3}\%$

    (E) 150%

27. Which of the following has the greatest value?

    (A) 0.3

    (B) $\sqrt{0.3}$

    (C) $\frac{2}{5}$

    (D) $\frac{1}{3}$

    (E) 0.01π

28. Mr. Nichols, who owns $66\frac{2}{3}\%$ of a factory, sells half of his share for $33,333. The value of the entire factory is

    (A) $ 9,999
    (B) $ 66,666
    (C) $ 99,999
    (D) $100,000
    (E) $133,332

29. One wheel rotates once every 7 minutes, and another rotates once every 5 minutes. How often will both begin to rotate at the same time?

    (A) every 6 minutes
    (B) every 12 minutes
    (C) every 17.5 minutes
    (D) every 35 minutes
    (E) every 70 minutes

30. An official baseball diamond is a square 90 feet on each side. The shortest distance (to the nearest foot) from third base to first base is

    (A) 90 feet
    (B) 127 feet
    (C) 135 feet
    (D) 180 feet
    (E) less than 90 feet

S T O P

IF YOU FINISH BEFORE TIME IS CALLED, YOU MAY CHECK YOUR WORK ON THIS SECTION ONLY.
DO NOT WORK ON ANY OTHER SECTION IN THE TEST.

Answer Key

Note: The answers to the quantitative sections are keyed to the corresponding review areas in the Mathematics Review (Chapter 11). The numbers in parentheses after each answer refer to the math topic(s) covered by that particular question.

Section 1   Analytical

1.	A	8.	A	15.	D	22.	E
2.	E	9.	C	16.	B	23.	E
3.	D	10.	C	17.	A	24.	A
4.	B	11.	D	18.	E	25.	C
5.	B	12.	B	19.	A		
6.	D	13.	E	20.	E		
7.	E	14.	C	21.	C		

Section 2   Verbal

1.	C	11.	B	21.	C	31.	B
2.	B	12.	D	22.	D	32.	E
3.	A	13.	C	23.	E	33.	D
4.	E	14.	A	24.	E	34.	B
5.	D	15.	E	25.	A	35.	A
6.	B	16.	B	26.	D	36.	E
7.	E	17.	E	27.	D	37.	B
8.	C	18.	B	28.	B	38.	D
9.	E	19.	B	29.	A		
10.	A	20.	B	30.	C		

Section 3   Quantitative

1.	C (I-B, D)	9.	A (III-D)	17.	E (I-H)	25.	C (IV)
2.	A (I)	10.	D (III-F)	18.	B (II-D)	26.	A (III-H, III-B)
3.	A (I)	11.	C (III-D)	19.	C (II-B)	27.	E (III-G)
4.	C (III-A)	12.	B (III-E)	20.	A (I-B, II-G)	28.	C (IV-B)
5.	D (III-A)	13.	C (I-H-2)	21.	D (IV-A)	29.	C (I, V)
6.	C (III-D)	14.	C (II-B)	22.	D (I-A, IV-A)	30.	C (I-B)
7.	C (III-F)	15.	C (I-B)	23.	E (IV-A)		
8.	C (III-D)	16.	A (I-B, II-B)	24.	D (IV-A)		

Section 4   Quantitative

1.	C (I-H)	9.	A (III-G)	17.	A (III-C)	25.	A (IV)
2.	C (II-A)	10.	D (III-A)	18.	E (III-G)	26.	E (I-B)
3.	C (I-B, II-A)	11.	B (III-A)	19.	B (II-C)	27.	C (II-E)
4.	B (II-A)	12.	C (III-A, G)	20.	E (I-B)	28.	B (II-E)
5.	C (I)	13.	B (II-B)	21.	D (IV)	29.	C (I-C)
6.	C (II-A, E)	14.	B (I-G)	22.	E (III, IV)	30.	C (II-C)
7.	B (III-B)	15.	B (III-A)	23.	E (I-B, IV)		
8.	C (III-D, G)	16.	C (III-G)	24.	E (I-D, IV)		

Section 5   Verbal

1.	B	11.	E	21.	C	31.	A
2.	D	12.	B	22.	B	32.	D
3.	D	13.	C	23.	D	33.	D
4.	A	14.	B	24.	A	34.	B
5.	D	15.	E	25.	C	35.	C
6.	B	16.	A	26.	D	36.	B
7.	D	17.	D	27.	A	37.	A
8.	B	18.	E	28.	D	38.	E
9.	D	19.	C	29.	A		
10.	D	20.	D	30.	A		

Section 6   Analytical

1.	C	8.	B	15.	B	22.	C
2.	D	9.	E	16.	B	23.	E
3.	E	10.	D	17.	D	24.	B
4.	A	11.	A	18.	B	25.	E
5.	A	12.	C	19.	E		
6.	D	13.	C	20.	A		
7.	A	14.	C	21.	A		

Section 7   Quantitative

1.	B (II-A)	9.	C (II-C2)	17.	D (I-E)	25.	A (II-C, IV)
2.	A (I-H)	10.	B (I-B)	18.	B (I-H)	26.	E (I-D)
3.	A (III)	11.	C (II-E)	19.	E (I-A)	27.	B (I-B)
4.	B (III-F)	12.	D (II-G)	20.	B (I-D)	28.	C (I-D)
5.	C (III-B)	13.	B (I-B)	21.	C (I-G, IV)	29.	D (I-A)
6.	B (III-A)	14.	D (I-H)	22.	B (IV)	30.	B (III-D)
7.	C (III-A)	15.	D (II-A)	23.	D (II-E, IV)		
8.	B (II-A)	16.	E (II-B)	24.	E (I-D, IV)		

Answer Explanations

Section 1

1–4. Analysis of this situation will indicate that G, J, L must not sit next to each other. The members of the football and the basketball teams must sit next to either G, J, or L.

1. A. In (A) G, J, and L are separated by varsity players on basketball or football teams.

2. E. K may not sit next to H as in (A). K may not sit next to M as in (B), nor N as in (C) or (D).

3. D. M may sit next to either G, J, or L. All others are two-sport athletes.

4. B. The only ones that may sit next to N are G, J, L.

5. B. The gun lobby maintains that our Constitution gives the people (not only the militia) the right to keep and bear arms. It also says that the Fifth Amendment prohibits the confiscation of property without due process and that the Ninth Amendment guarantees all unspecified rights.

6. D. (A) is incorrect since it suggests a cause of violence and not a solution. (B) is incorrect. The fact that a state has the lowest crime rate may be due to factors having nothing to do with antigun laws. In (C) a sport, not a crime, is mentioned. In (E) police protection is not taken into account.

7. E. The passage implies that the gun lobby might destroy the political future of a lawmaker who sponsors a gun control bill.

8–11. You may want to sketch a calendar showing each day of the week and the offices that are open on that day. Or you may want to just make simple notes on the requirements listed and when they can be satisfied, like this:

Birth Cert.	MTh 9-5	
Nat. Papers	TuF 9-5	One of these

Hosp.	A	Wed 12-5
	B	MTh 9-12, F 4-5
Bank		M-F 9-3
Consulate		MWF 12-4
(after all others)		(after all others)

8. A. By starting Monday morning at Beryl Clinic, getting a birth certificate and bank statement before 3 P.M. and proceeding to the Consulate, a native-born citizen can complete the procedure in less than eight hours. The naturalized citizen starting anytime Tuesday (the specifica-tion of Tuesday morning is simply a distracting detail) can't get to the Consulate until Wednesday at noon (B). The applicant in choice C can't get a birth certificate until Thursday; the applicant in choice D can't get naturalization papers until Friday; the applicant in choice E can't complete the procedure until Monday.

9. C. This applicant may acquire a birth certificate and a bank statement on Thursday, but cannot get a vaccination until Friday at 4 (at Beryl Clinic), too late to go to the Consulate before Monday afternoon.

10. C. Mr. Nikto could have acquired naturalization papers as late as Tuesday afternoon and then gone to his bank; he can be vaccinated Wednesday afternoon and get to the Consulate that day. If Mr. Nikto is choice A, the procedure will take from Monday morning to Wednesday afternoon; if he is choice B, from Tuesday at 4 P.M. to Friday afternoon; if he is choice D, from Monday afternoon to Wednesday afternoon; if he is choice E, from Tuesday afternoon until Friday.

11. D. The naturalized citizen can get his or her naturalization papers and bank statement on Tuesday afternoon. Nothing can be accomplished on Wednesday. Thursday morning the applicant can be vaccinated at Beryl Clinic and the procedure could be completed when the Consulate office opens on Friday.

12–18. A "tree" diagram makes everything simple. BC is an impossible leafletting team, since C won't work without A; AC is a possible leafletting team, and so is AB, but only if C is the speaker. (Remember, F is not unwilling to work without E!)

12. B. See the diagram. All other combinations are shown to be all right by the diagram.

13. E. C must be present, and necessarily as a speaker (I); three defense teams are possible—all contain either F or G (III), but one does not contain F (II).

14. C. From the diagram, or even without it—choices A and B contain two speakers, choice D violates E's wishes, and choice E violates both A's and C's wishes.

15. D.   Either team including A can involve any of the three defense personnel. The personnel listed in choices A, B, and C are all possible selections, but others are possible. Choice E is definitely false.

16. B.   The bottom "branches" of the "tree" diagram all represent different possible teams, in combination with the other personnel shown.

17. A.   Only A must be chosen. E is not necessary at all. F becomes a "must" only if E is the speaker.

18. E.   Check the diagram—E appears in only two possible teams (ACEFG, ACEFH); A and C appear in all eight, B and D in three each.

19–22.   Set up five lines symbolizing places at the table; A-E will be seated on one side and F-J on the other. The first three statements give you:

A/B   _____   _____   C/E   _____   _____   A/B
                              H/I/J   G

Statement (4) tells you, first, that the Wallachian military attachés must be opposite the two Rumelian trade experts; second, that the latter must be at the right side of their table and the Wallachian military attachés opposite, on the *left* side from their point of view. From this, you can deduce where B and therefore A sit. You can now fill in this information, plus the uncertain possibilities:

Statement (5) allows you to cross a lot of this out:

That's as much as you can do, but it's enough to answer all the questions.

19. A.   We can't tell exactly who or where F is. But choice A is a possibility. Choices B, C and D are ruled out by the placing of H; choice E is ruled out by the placing of G.

20. E.   Three persons are possibilities. Choices A, C, and D are known exactly; for choice B there are two possibilities, so more is known than in choice E.

21. C.   This supposition eliminates J as Rumelian chairperson (I); since I must be the chairperson, and J is a military attaché, F must be a trade expert (II); III therefore *cannot* be true.

22. E.   Add back into your diagram the uncertainties that were eliminated by statement (3). The Wallachian chairperson can be either D or E; the military attaché seated to the Wallachian chairperson's left can also be either D or E, since only identifying the chairperson as E allowed you to identify the military attaché as D. The Rumelian chairperson can be F as well as I or J. Choice E can be definitely known under these conditions, even though you cannot tell who is in which of the two seats. Choice A cannot be known; it could not be, even *with* statement (3). For choices B and D, there is in each case more than one possibility for one of the slots; for choice C, there are two possibilities.

23. E.   Statements I, II, and IV all tend to *strengthen* Malthus's argument, statements I and IV by helping to explain the causes of the phenomenon Malthus described, statement II by asserting that the phenomenon has, in fact, taken place. Statement III suggests that contraception might be used to invalidate Malthus's prediction; therefore, it does *weaken* Malthus's argument.

24. A.   Malthus mentioned wars, famines, and other catastrophes as population checks. (B) and (C) would tend to increase food supply, but not to limit the demand for food. (D) and (E) would increase population.

25. C.   The first part of the argument contains the premise: most people who do X (take GRE/APT) do Y (get headaches). From this, two possible incorrect conclusions can be drawn: if *anyone* does X, he/she must do Y; and, *only* those who do X can do Y. Choice A contains the first error, but the original argument and choice C both make the second error. Choice B makes a valid inference, whereas the original argument does not. Choice D has the basic structure: If X, then Y—if Y, then X. This is invalid, but it is a different error from the one made in the original argument. Choice E is an invalid inference from past to future, again a different kind of error from that in the original argument.

Section 2

1. C.   The writer hopes that economics and politics will once more form the study known as political economy. Clearly, the subjects have been linked in the past. Thus, he hopes that the two separate fields will be *reunited*.

2. B.   If bilingual education is more than a mere stop-gap (a somewhat negative description), it must possess certain positive qualities. Thus it has *advantages over* education in a single tongue. Note the use of *far from* to signal the contrast between the negative and positive views on bilingual education presented in this sentence.

3. A.   Under certain circumstances scientists attack each other with *ad hominem* arguments (personal attacks) and shameless appeals. When is this likely to occur? When facts are *established* or *demonstrable* or *ineluctable* (unavoidable)? Hardly. Under such circumstances scientists would rely on facts to establish their case. It is when facts prove *elusive* that they lose control and, in doing so, abandon their pretense of *objectivity*.

4. E.   A disease in a *latent* state has yet to manifest itself and emerge into view. Therefore it is impossible to *observe*.
   Remember, in double-blank sentences, go through the answers, testing the *first* word in each choice and eliminating those that don't fit. When a disease is in a *critical* or *acute* state, its existence is obvious. Therefore, you can eliminate Choices B and C.

5. D.   The second clause presents an example of literary *mockery*. The abstract idea of preserving a nugget of pure truth is appealing; the concrete example of setting it up on the mantle makes fun of the whole idea.

6. B.   If the rare earths are actually present to some degree in essentially all minerals, then they are not rare after all. Thus, the term "rare earths" is a *misnomer* (incorrect designation), for the rare earths are actually *ubiquitous* (omnipresent; found everywhere).
   Watch out for words that signal the unexpected. Note the use of "paradoxically" here.

7. E.   Although it is the *thrust* of Clement's argument that psychoanalysis must return to its healing offices, it is precisely here that her argument fails and her shafts *glance away*.
   Be on the lookout for extended metaphors that influence the writer's choice of words. In this case, the use of "shafts" conjures up an image of javelins that do not strike home but instead glance off the foe.

8. C.   A *sheep bleats* in its characteristic call. A *sparrow chirps* in its characteristic call.

   (Defining Characteristic)

9. E.   When *milk curdles*, by definition it coagulates or thickens. Likewise, when *blood clots*, it too coagulates.

   (Definition)

10. A.   A bird *molts* or sheds its *feathers*. A snake casts off or *sloughs* its *skin*.

   (Defining Characteristic)

11. B.   An *offhand* remark is made without forethought or *premeditation*. An *aboveboard* (open) deed is done without trickery or *guile*.

   (Antonym Variant)

12. D.   The *larval* (immature) stage of an *insect* best corresponds to the *embryonic* stage of a *mammal*.

   (Defining Characteristic)

13. C.   A *poltergeist* (noisy, mischievous spirit) is a kind of *apparition* or ghost. An *ogre* is a kind of *monster*.

   (Class and Member)

14. A.   An *austere style* is severely simple and restrained. *Controlled movement* is restrained as well.

   (Defining Characteristic)

15. E.   To *aver* or positively declare something is to indicate *affirmation*. To *demur* or object to something is to indicate *protest*.

   (Action and Significance)

16. B.   To *chide* or scold someone is less extreme than to *pillory* him, exposing him to public scorn. To *humor* or indulge someone is less extreme than to *mollycoddle* or inordinately baby him.

   (Degree of Intensity)

17. E.   The author first states that the reason for bioluminescence in underwater microorganisms is obscure and then proceeds to enumerate various hypotheses.

18. B.   The author does not deny that predators make use of bioluminescence in locating their prey. Instead, he gives an example of human predators (fishers) who are drawn to their prey (the fish that prey on plankton) by the luminescence of the plankton.

19. B.   As the preceding answer makes clear, the phenomenon of plankton bioluminescence does have practical applications. It is a valuable tool for fisheries interested in increasing their catch of fish that prey on plankton.

20. B.   The author's use of both italics and an exclamation mark indicates his extreme scorn of the notion that bioluminescence originated in plankton because it allowed the plankton to expose their predators to the attention of those predators' predators. (Remember the rhyme about little fish having big fish to bite 'em, and so on *ad infinitum*?) Here he derides what he considers an untenable hypothesis.

21. C.   The author provides the reader both with physical details of dress and bearing and with comments about the motivations and emotions of Bosola and the Cardinal.
Choice A is incorrect. The passage scarcely mentions the church.
Choice B is incorrect. The description of ecclesiastical costumes is only one item in the description of the Cardinal.
Choice D is incorrect. The persons described are characters in a play, not figures in paintings.
Choice E is incorrect. The author's purpose is description, not accusation.

22. D.   From the opening lines, in which the curtain rises and the two men "enter from the right" (as a stage direction would say), and from the later references to gaslit Victorian melodrama, we can infer that Bosola and the Cardinal are characters in a play.
Choice A is incorrect. The Cardinal's brother is Duke Ferdinand.
Choices B and C are incorrect. Lines 55-66 describe Bosola as doing the work of a "hired ruffian" and playing a "lowly, despicable" role. He is a servant, not a noble lord or a lord of the church.
Choice E is unsupported by the passage.

23. E.   The eagle is poised to strike "with exposed talons." It, like the Cardinal, collects itself to strike with greater force. The imagery accentuates the Cardinal's *mercilessness*.
Choice A is incorrect. The Cardinal is not *flighty* (light-headed and irresponsible); he is cold and calculating.
Choice B is incorrect. The Cardinal loves power, not freedom.

Choice C is incorrect. An eagle poised to strike with bare claws suggests violence, not *eminence* (fame and high position).
Choice D is incorrect. Nothing in the passage suggests that the Cardinal is spiritual.
Beware eye-catchers. "Eminence" is a title of honor applied to cardinals in the Roman Catholic church. Choice C may attract you for this reason.

24. E.   Although Bosola is not a leather-jacketed hoodlum, he is a hired assassin (despite his scholarly taste).

25. A.   The casual references to the elongated hands and features in El Greco's work and to the trim beards and commanding stances in the work of Van Dyke imply that the author assumes the reader has seen examples of both painters' art.

26. D.   The author's depiction of the Cardinal stresses his redoubtable qualities as a foe (calculation, duplicity, mercilessness) and as a challenge to an actor ("imperial repose," a commanding presence, smooth movements suggesting latent danger).
Choice A is incorrect. The author portrays the Cardinal's relations with his brother and mistress as cold, but he never apologizes for the Cardinal's lack of warmth. Indeed, the author somewhat savors it.
Choices B and C are incorrect. Neither esteem for a nonexistent spirituality nor admiration for a villainous autocracy enters into the author's depiction of the Cardinal.
Choice E is incorrect. A cause of perturbation to others, the Cardinal is never perturbed.

27. D.   Lines 62-66 indicate that Bosola's dominant emotion is disgust at an ignoble world and at himself for his despicable role in that world.
Choice A is incorrect. Not Bosola but Duke Ferdinand suffers from excessive emotionality.
Choice B is incorrect. It is not his lowly rank but his ignoble tasks that rankle Bosola.
Choices C and E are incorrect. They are unsupported by the passage.

28. B.   The opposite of *amelioration* (improvement) is *worsening*.
Think of "a hoped-for amelioration."

29. A.   The opposite of to *disarray* (throw into disorder) is to *neaten*.
Think of "disarraying the blankets."

30. C.   The opposite of *disputatious* (argumentative) is *conciliatory* (pacific, soothing). Note that you can spot the familiar *dispute* in *disputatious*.
Think of "heated disputatious debates."

31. B.   The opposite of *reticence* (uncommunicative-
         ness; restraint in speech) is *loquaciousness*
         (talkativeness).
         Think of "speaking without reticence."

32. E.   The opposite of to *inundate* (flood) is to *drain*.
         Beware eye-catchers. Do not be tempted to
         choose Choice C simply because *inundate* and
         wallow both have something to do with water.
         Think of being "inundated by the rising flood."

33. D.   The opposite of *incongruous* (inconsistent, not
         fitting) is *harmonious*.
         Think of being startled by "incongruous
         behavior."

34. B.   An *apostate* (renegade; person faithless to an
         allegiance) is the opposite of a loyalist.
         Beware eye-catchers. Do not confuse *apostate*
         (renegade) with *apostle* (missionary; reformer).
         Think of "a faithless apostate."

35. A.   *Topical* (local, temporary) is the opposite of
         general.
         Remember that words may be used in several
         different ways. Here *topical* does not mean
         arranged according to topics (as in a topical
         index).
         Think of "a topical anesthetic," one applied
         locally, not generally.

36. E.   To *fulminate* (issue curses or censures;
         explode) is the opposite of to *praise*.
         Context Clue: "The wicked queen fulminated
         against Snow White."

37. B.   The opposite of *turbid* (muddy) is *limpid*
         (clear).
         Word Parts Clue: *Turb-* means disturb. A
         stream is turbid when the silt or sediment is
         disturbed.
         Think of "muddy, turbid waters."

38. D.   The opposite of *tyro* (beginner, novice) is
         expert.
         Think of "a mere tyro in the field."

Section 3

1. C. $3\frac{1}{2}\% = 3.5\% = \frac{3.5}{100} = \frac{35}{1000}$

2. A.   The length of the fence (144 feet) ÷ the dis-
        tance between the posts (12 feet) equals 12
        spaces between posts. However, the first space
        has 2 posts and an additional post will appear
        at each subsequent space.

3. A.   There are 37 houses on the west side. From #1
        to #37 there are 19 odd numbers.

4. C.   The exterior angle of a triangle equals the sum
        of the measures of both remote interior angles.
        Therefore, $x = a + b$ and $x = c + d$. By
        addition, $2x = a + b + c + d$.

5. D.   Note that y is common to both columns. Con-
        sider x and z. No information is given about
        their relationship.

6. C.   Since vertical angles 1 and 2 are equal, right
        triangle ABE is similar to right triangle DEC,
        and $\frac{AB}{DC} = \frac{AE}{EC}$. In ABE, hypotenuse $BE = 5$,
        and $AB = 4$, then leg $AE = 3$. In DEC, if AB
        $= 4$, then $DC = 12$, and since $AE = 3$, then
        $EC = 9$, and $AC = AE + EC = 3 + 9 =$
        12.

7. C.   Circumference $= 2\pi r$. If the radius of $A = \frac{1}{2}$
        radius of B, then circumference of $A = \frac{1}{2}$ cir-
        cumference of B. This may be stated as follows:
        twice the circumference of $A =$ the circumfer-
        ence of B.

8. C. $\frac{BC}{AB} \times \frac{AC}{BC}$
        $\left(\frac{10}{x}\right)\left(\frac{x}{10}\right) = 1$

9. A.   Since $x = 40$, $y = 50$. Since AB lies opposite
        $\angle ACB$, the larger of the 2 acute angles, $AB >$
        BC.

10. D. Since radius $= 6$, area of circle $= 36\pi$, but
        we do not know what part of the circle the seg-
        ment AOB is.

11. C. $z + y = 80$ since $x = 100$
        $y = z = 40$.

12. B. Because $ABCD$ is a square, $AB = AD$.
        Solve: $4x - 3 = 3x + 4$
        $\qquad\qquad x = 7$

13. C.
$$7(10^4) = 70,000$$
$$3(10^3) = 3,000$$
$$2(10^2) = 200$$
$$5(10) = 50$$
$$6 = \underline{\quad 6}$$
Total   73,256

14. C.   Add the 2 equations:
$$x + y = 15$$

15. C.   Since 15 is common to both columns, consider only $\dfrac{16}{x} = 4$. Since $4x = 16$, $x = 4$.

16. A. $K = \dfrac{1}{m+n}$

$\dfrac{1}{K} = m + n$ [reciprocals of equals are equal]

$\dfrac{5}{K} = 5(m + n)$ [multiply by 5]

17. E.   If r is multiplied by 9, V must be multiplied by 81, since $\sqrt{81} = 9$. Recall: If equals are multiplied by equals, the results are equal.

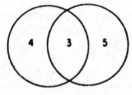

LATIN   GREEK

18. B.   Observe the diagrammatic representation of the Latin and Greek students. Obviously we have accounted for 12 of these students. Three of them studied neither language. Observe that 3 of these classical language students took Latin and Greek.

19. C. $13 = \dfrac{13w}{l - w}$

$13(l - w) = 13w$
$13 - 13w = 13w$
$13 = 26w$

$\dfrac{1}{2} = w$

$(2w)^2 = \left(2 \cdot \dfrac{1}{2}\right)^2 = (1)^2 = 1$

20. A.   Since the relationship of the denominators is 1:2, the relationship of the numerators must be 1:2, so $a - b$ must be 2. Therefore, a is larger than b.

21. D.   Observe that a $500 investment appears in the 9-year row under the 8% column; that is, $500 invested at 8% will grow to $1000 (double) in 9 years.

22. D.   For the 15-year period, the investment at 5% is $481, while at 6% it is $417; $481 − 417 = $64.

23. E.   Investments of less than $100 appear in two places in the table. The 25-year, 11% investment is not included in the answer choices. Therefore, $92 invested for 25 years at 10% is the only possible correct answer.

24. D.   Move across the 18-year row to the number under the 8% column. The correct answer is $250.

25. C. $317 invested at 7% for 17 years increases to $1000, which is more than three times as great as $317.

26. A.   If two lines are parallel, then the distance between the two lines along parallel lines must be equal. The easiest lines to use to calculate distances are lines parallel to the y-axis. The distance along the y-axis from C to AB is 4. AB intersects the y-axis at point $(0,2)$. The distance from D to AB along the line parallel to the y-axis must also be 4. D must have coordinates $(3,1)$, so $x = 1$.

27. E.   The fence will consist of 100 feet of stone and $100 + 60 + 60 = 220$ feet of wire. The cost will be $5(100) + $2(220) = $500 + $440 = $940.

28. C.   To have averaged 30% of 60 games, the team must have won 18 out of 60 games. Let $x =$ number of games played and won during winning streak.

New average: $\dfrac{18 + x}{60 + x} = 50\%$

$\dfrac{18 + x}{60 + x} = \dfrac{1}{2}$

$36 + 2x = 60 + x$
$x = 24$

29. C.   The present time (h hours) must be reduced by 2 hours in order to insure promptness.

$\dfrac{\text{distance}}{\text{time}} = \text{rate}$

$\dfrac{d}{h - 2} = \text{new rate to insure promptness}$

30. C. $\dfrac{\$D}{M}$ = amount each will pay when there are M men

$\dfrac{\$D}{M-3}$ = amount each will pay when there are $M-3$ men

The difference is

$\dfrac{D}{M-3}-\dfrac{D}{M}$

$\dfrac{DM-D(M-3)}{M(M-3)}$

$\dfrac{DM-DM+3D}{M^2-3M}$

$\dfrac{3D}{M^2-3M}$

Section 4

1. C. $\dfrac{1}{x}=\sqrt{0.09}$ and $\dfrac{1}{x}=0.3$

$0.3x=1$
$3x=10$ and $x=3\dfrac{1}{3}$

2. C. $a+2b=1\dfrac{1}{3}$

$-a+b=-\dfrac{1}{3}$ (Multiply by -1)

$\rule{3cm}{0.4pt}$

$3b\ =1$

3. C.   Multiply by $\dfrac{-1}{-1}\cdot\dfrac{x-y}{-z}=\dfrac{-x+y}{z}$ or $\dfrac{y-x}{z}$

4. B.   If $x=$ zero, the numerator equals 0 and the value of the fraction equals 0 regardless of the value of y.

5. C.   4 quarts = 1 gallon

1 quart $=\dfrac{1}{4}$ gallon

$\dfrac{4}{5}$ quart $=\left(\dfrac{4}{5}\right)\left(\dfrac{1}{4}\right)$ or $\dfrac{1}{5}$ gallon

6. C. $a{:}b=c{:}d$ or $\dfrac{a}{b}=\dfrac{c}{d}$. Because reciprocals of equals are equal, $\dfrac{b}{a}=\dfrac{d}{c}$.

7. B. $AC=CE$
$AC-AB=BC$; $AC-90=BC$
$CE-DE=CD$; $CE-85=CD$
$CD>BC$

8. C.   Area of $ABC=\dfrac{bh}{2}$ or $\dfrac{ac}{2}$. Therefore, $bh=ac$.

9. A.   Side of a square $=\dfrac{1}{4}$ of perimeter $\dfrac{1}{4}(4a+4)=$ $a+1$ (length of any side). $a+1>a$

10. D.   We may not assume that this quadrilateral is a parallelogram and we have no basis for determining the value of n, the angle opposite the one with the measure given as 110. We do know that $k+l+m+n=360$.

11. B. $m\angle B+m\angle C=80°$
$\angle BAC>\angle BCA$;
therefore $BC>AB$.

12. C.   Since the measure of $\angle A$ equals the measure of $\angle C$ (45°), $\angle B$ must be a right angle. Sides AB and BC lie opposite equal angles.

13. B. $(a-1)(a+1)=a^2-1=0$; $a^2=1$ (Column A)
$(b-2)(b+2)=b^2-4=0$; $b^2=4$ (Column B)

14. B.   The sum of x, 0, and $\dfrac{3}{2}x=\dfrac{5}{2}x$.

The average $=\dfrac{5}{2}x\div3$ or $\dfrac{5}{6}x$ (Column A)

15. B. $74+x+74\ =180$
$x\ =180-148$
$x\ =32$ (Column A)

16. C.   Volume of water in rectangular tank = $(25")(9")(2")$
Let $x=$ height of this volume of water in cylindrical container.
Volume in cylindrical container
$=(\pi)(\text{radius})^2(\text{height})$ or $(\pi)(5)^2(x)$
or $(25)(x)(\pi)$. Since volumes are equal,

$(25")(9")(2")\ =(25)(x)(\pi)$
$18\ =\pi x$
$\dfrac{18}{\pi}\ =x.$

17. A. *AB* will need 3 additional posts.
AC will need 4 additional posts.
BC will need 7 additional posts.

18. E. Assume *x, y, z* are, respectively, sides of original cube.
Then 3*x*, 3*y*, 3*z* will be sides of enlarged box.
Volume of original box $= xyz$
Volume of enlarged box $= (3x)(3y)(3z)$ or 27*xyz*

19. B. The passenger train traveled 4 hours and covered 240 miles. When it overtook the freight train, the freight train had also covered 240 miles, but it traveled for 6 hours. The average rate of the freight train was $\dfrac{240}{6}$ or 40 miles per hour.

20. E. Since $\dfrac{6}{14} = \dfrac{3}{7}$ and $\dfrac{9}{21} = \dfrac{3}{7}$, the sign to be inserted is $=$.

21. B. I is not correct. Excise and customs taxes yield 22¢ of the tax dollar or 22%.
II is correct. Corporate and individual income taxes yield 74¢ of the tax dollar or 74%.
III is not correct. Taxes other than income taxes yield 4¢ + 16¢ + 6¢ for a total of 26¢ or 26%.

22. E. $\dfrac{22}{100}(360°) = 79.2°$. The closest correct choice is 80°.

23. E. The closest correct choice is $\dfrac{3}{4}$, since $\dfrac{74}{100}$ is close to 75%.

24. E. $\dfrac{43¢}{\$1.00} = \dfrac{43¢}{100¢} = \dfrac{43}{100} = 43\%$

25. A. Income taxes furnish 43¢ + 31¢ or 74¢ of each tax dollar. Therefore 26¢ of each tax dollar comes from other sources.
$$\dfrac{26¢}{\$1.00} = \dfrac{\$0.26}{\$1.00} = \dfrac{\$260}{\$1000}$$

26. E. $\dfrac{a}{b} - \dfrac{a}{c} =$
$\dfrac{ac}{bc} - \dfrac{ab}{bc} =$
$\dfrac{ac - ab}{bc}$

27. C. Ratio $= \dfrac{192}{224} = \dfrac{6}{7}$

28. B. (5)(40 minutes) = 200 minutes
$= 3\dfrac{1}{3}$ hours
= 3 hours and 20 minutes
6:40 P.M. is 3 hours and 20 minutes before 10 P.M.

29. C. Cost of merchandise sold = \$204 − \$82.50
= \$121.50.
Gross profit for day was \$169.50 − \$121.50 or \$48.

30. C. Mr. Brown completes a house and $\dfrac{1}{3}$ of a second house in 8 days. Mr. Pinter does $\dfrac{6}{8}$ or $\dfrac{3}{4}$ of a house in 8 days. Together they have done $1\dfrac{1}{3} + \dfrac{3}{4}$ or $\dfrac{25}{12}$ or 2 houses and $\dfrac{1}{12}$ of the third house.
Mr. Slocum must do $\dfrac{11}{12}$ of the third house. In 1 day Mr. Slocum does $\dfrac{1}{12}$ of a house. He will therefore need 11 days to do $\dfrac{11}{12}$ of the house.

Section 5

1. B. Criticism that suggests areas of improvement is said to be *constructive*.
Remember, before you look at the answer choices, read the sentence and try to think of a word that makes sense.

2. D. *Because* the writer does not personally enjoy Eliot's novels, before he criticizes her he feels he should, to be fair, pay *tribute* to her literary virtues.
Look for signal words or phrases indicating that one thing causes another or logically determines another. In this instance, the conjunction *as* has the meaning *because*.

3. D. If "you may wonder" how the expert reaches his conclusions, it appears that it is questionable to rely on teeth for guidance in interpreting fossils. Choice D, *inadequate*, creates the element of doubt that the clause tries to develop. Choice C, *specious*, also creates an element of doubt; however, nothing in the context justifies the idea that the reasoning is specious or false. Note that here you are dealing with an extended metaphor. Picture yourself hanging a heavy winter coat on a slim wooden peg. Wouldn't you worry that the peg might prove inadequate or flimsy?

4. A.   Here the task is to determine the communal reaction to crime. The writer maintains that the criminal justice system of punishments allows the community to purge itself of its anger, its sense of *outrage* at the criminal's acts. Thus, it provides a *catharsis* or purgation for the community.

Remember, in double-blank sentences, go through the answers, testing the *first* word in each choice and eliminating those that don't fit. In this case, you can readily eliminate Choices B and E: it is unlikely that an *essential* purpose of the criminal justice system would be the provision of either a *disclaimer* (denial or disavowal, as in disavowing responsibility for a legal claim) or a *document*.

5. D.   The key word here is *assailed*. Housman is attacking his rival. Thus he is in the tradition of scholarly *invective* (vehement verbal attack), criticizing his foe for turning to manuscripts merely for confirmation or *support* of old theories and not for enlightenment or illumination. Again, note the use of figurative language, in this case the simile of the drunkard.

6. B.   Unquestioned assumptions and accepted opinions bind the natural philosopher, *tyrannically* restricting his ability to hypothesize freely. Thus, the philosopher must strive to *achieve* detachment in order to free himself from this *tyranny*.

7. D.   Because the Dean was not able to *disguise* his distaste for the P.R. barrage, he failed to stifle his *caustic* or sarcastically biting remarks about the event.

Note the implicit cause and effect relationship between the opening phrase and the central clause of the sentence.

8. B.   Just as the *yolk* is central to the *egg*, the *nucleus* is central to the *cell*.

(Part to Whole)

9. D.   To *sand wood* is to smooth or polish it. To *burnish metal* is to polish it.

(Function)

10. D.   Someone *vindictive* or vengeful is lacking in *mercy*. Someone *skeptical* or suspicious is lacking in *trustfulness*.

(Antonym Variant)

11. E.   To *ruffle* someone's *composure* is to disturb or trouble his self-possession. To *upset* someone's *equilibrium* is to disturb or trouble his balance.

(Function)

12. B.   The *bouquet* of *wine* is its distinctive fragrance. It is analogous to the *aroma* of *coffee*.

(Defining Characteristic)

13. C.   By definition, a *sextant* is a piece of equipment that is *nautical*. Similarly, a *forceps* is a piece of equipment that is *surgical*.

(Defining Characteristic)

14. B.   Someone *refractory* (stubborn; unmanageable) by definition is hard to *manage*. Likewise, someone *lethargic* (sluggish; drowsy) by definition is hard to *stimulate*.

(Definition)

15. E.   Something *latent* has not yet emerged into view but has within it the potential for *manifestation*. Something *dormant* has not yet emerged from its sleep but has within it the potential for *awakening* into activity. As always, consider all the answer choices before making your selection. Choice C, for example, looks tempting: a *perfunctory* (mechanical; cursory) act lacks *inspiration*. However, something *perfunctory* does not necessarily have within it the potential for *inspiration*.

(Antonym Variant)

16. A.   The defining characteristic of a *precipice* (very steep, sheer cliff) is *steepness*. The defining characteristic of a *defile* (long, narrow pass through which one files) is *narrowness*. Note, by the way, that you are dealing with a secondary meaning of *defile*, a meaning in which *defile* is a noun, not a verb. Even if you do not know this meaning of the word, you can still arrive at the correct answer by eliminating those answer choices which are patently incorrect. You know that a *precipice* is by definition characterized by *steepness*. Therefore, you can eliminate Choices C and E: a broad *plateau* is not characterized by *depth*, nor is a damp *marsh* characterized by *aridity* or dryness. Similarly, you can eliminate Choice B: while wells may sometimes be shallow, a *well* is not *by definition* characterized by *shallowness*. Finally, you can eliminate Choice D: *range* is not something that characterizes a *mountain*; a *range* is a chain of *mountains*. Thus, even without knowing the meaning of the noun *defile* you can satisfy yourself that Choice A is the correct answer.

(Defining Characteristic)

17. **D.**   The author first discusses Du Bois in relationship to black leaders in general and then provides the specific example of his relationship to Booker T. Washington.

Choice A is incorrect. The author mentions Du Bois' early support of Washington's gradualist approach in order to contrast it with his later departure from Washington's conservatism.

Choice B is incorrect. The author discusses Du Bois' personality only in passing; he discusses Washington's personality not at all.

Choice C is incorrect. The author's chief concern is to describe Du Bois' position, not analyze what lay behind his achieving this position. He spends more time showing why Du Bois angered his fellow blacks than he does showing why Du Bois attracted his fellow blacks.

Choice E is incorrect. It is unsupported by the passage.

18. **E.**   The last sentence points out that Du Bois originally agreed with Washington's program.

Choice A is incorrect. Nothing in the passage suggests that Du Bois sacrificed effective strategies out of a desire to try something new.

Choice B is incorrect. Du Bois gained in influence, effectively winning away large numbers of blacks from Washington's policies.

Choice C is incorrect. Du Bois' quickness to depart from conventional black wisdom when it proved inadequate to the task of advancing the race shows him to be well able to change with the times.

Choice D is incorrect. Washington, not Du Bois, is described as seeking the good will of powerful whites.

19. **C.**   The author does *not* portray Washington as versatile. Instead, he portrays Du Bois as versatile.

Choice A is incorrect. The author portrays Washington as submissive to the majority; he shows him teaching blacks not to protest.

Choice B is incorrect. The author portrays Washington as concerned with financial success; he shows him advocating property accumulation.

Choice D is incorrect. The author portrays Washington as traditional in preaching industry; he shows him advocating hard work.

Choice E is incorrect. The author portrays Washington as respectful of authority; he shows him deferring to powerful whites.

20. **D.**   Although the author points out that Du Bois' methods led him into conflicts, he describes Du Bois as "often...well in advance of his contemporaries" and stresses that his motives for departing from the mainstream were admirable. Thus, his attitude can best be described as *approving*.

21. **C.**   The extremely general opening paragraphs and the careful use of simple examples imply that the passage most likely has been taken from a scientific journal article intended for a lay audience.

22. **B.**   The mathematical expression of an electron "as if it were smeared out over a large region of space" describes the electron dynamically. Only Choice B possesses an analogous dynamic quality.

23. **D.**   The opening two paragraphs about what is demanded of a physical theory give way to a discussion of quantum mechanics as a successful physical theory.

Choice A is incorrect. While the author cites the wide applicability of quantum theory, nowhere does he openly assert that local realistic theories are inapplicable.

Choice B is incorrect. The author describes the assumptions underlying local realistic theories, not those underlying quantum theory.

Choice C is incorrect. It is unsupported by the passage.

Choice E is incorrect. If anything, the author does the reverse.

24. **A.**   Choice A is correct. You can arrive at it by the process of elimination.

Question I is answerable based on the passage. The fourth paragraph enumerates the premises underlying the local realistic theories of nature. Therefore you can eliminate Choice B.

Question II is unanswerable based on the passage. Nothing in the passage indicates that any premise of the local realistic theories has been invalidated. Therefore you can eliminate Choices C and E.

Question III is also unanswerable based on the passage. Though mathematical expressions such as wave formations are mentioned, no information is given regarding the degree to which one can interpret them physically. Therefore you can eliminate Choice D.

Only Choice A is left. It is the correct answer.

25. **C.**   The author does *not* assume the premise of Einstein separability to be invalid.

Choice A is incorrect. The author gives the position of a pointer on a dial as an example of an observed phenomenon.

Choice B is incorrect. The author's opening paragraph presents such a generalization.

Choice D is incorrect. The author lists the premises underlying local realistic theories.

Choice E is incorrect. The passage concludes with the statement that one theory or the other must be wrong.

26. **D.**   In its explanation of the two conflicting theories and its enumeration of the premises under-

lying the local realistic theories of nature, the passage can best be described as a *systematic exposition*.

27. A.   The author mentions that many physicists find it sensible to limit the scope of quantum mechanics by regarding it "as merely a set of rules that prescribe the outcome of experiments." He then describes this limitation as unsatisfactory, given quantum mechanics' conflict with the so-called local realistic theories of nature and given the differences in predictions resulting from the current experiments he cites. Thus, the physicists who ignore these differences have not yet explained the results of the current experiments in elementary particle physics he cites.

28. D.   *Adulterated* (made impure) is the opposite of *pure*.
Think of "adulterated food."

29. A.   To *distend* (enlarge, as by swelling) is the opposite of to *deflate*.
Word Parts Clue: *Dis-* means apart; *-tend* means stretch. Something distended is enlarged by being stretched apart.
Think of "a distended stomach."

30. A.   *Transient* (fleeting; temporary) is the opposite of *permanent*.
Think of "transient youth."

31. A.   *Elated* (joyful, in high spirits) is the opposite of *crestfallen* (dejected).
Think of "elated by her success."

32. D.   To *revile* (verbally abuse) something is the opposite of *praising* it.
Think of "reviled as a traitor."

33. D.   The opposite of *propitious* (favorable, advantageous) is *unfavorable*.
Think of being pleased by "propitious omens."

34. B.   The opposite of to *ensue* (happen later, follow) is to *precede*.
Think of "the wedding that ensued."

35. C.   *Retrospection* (looking backward; the act of surveying the past) is the opposite of *anticipation* (looking forward).
Word Parts Clue: *Retro-* means backward; *-spect* means look. *Retrospection* means looking backward.
Think of "an old man lost in retrospection."

36. B.   The *egress* (exit) is the opposite of the *entrance*.

Word Parts Clue: *E-* means out; *-gress* means go. The *egress* is the way you go out.
Think of P. T. Barnum's sign, "This way to the egress."

37. A.   To *maunder* (speak disconnectedly; talk without a clear purpose) is the opposite of to *speak purposefully*.
Think of "maundering at random."

38. E.   *Hubris* (overweening arrogance; pride that offends the gods) is the opposite of *humility*.
Think of "conceited hubris."

Section 6

1–4.   To answer these questions, construct a calendar like the one below. The √ mark indicates opportunities for the acquisition of documents; S and C indicate when each government could have received documents acquired on the days shown. B/A indicates the lunchtime meeting of the two traitors.

	19	20	21	22	23	24	25	26	27
B	√			√	S	C		S	C
A			√				S	C	
B/A		√				S	C		

1. C.   Adoniram could acquire documents from Byram (who acquired them on October 19) at their lunch October 20, or on his own on the 21st. The Sulgravians would receive them on the 24th or 25th, respectively (I, II). Adoniram cannot acquire and send any documents on the 22nd, so option III is out.

2. D.   Work backwards from the calendar. On the 25th, the Carolingians can receive a document only if it was acquired on the 20th at lunch. But in that case, Adoniram must have bought it from Byram, since he had not received a document he could sell to Byram.

3. E.   Adoniram can send documents only on the 20th or 21st; they could be received by the Carolingians only on the 25th or 26th. Choice B, therefore, is too narrow, while choice D includes an impossible date. Byram can send documents on the 19th, 20th, or 22nd—to the Sulgravians, who would receive them on the 23rd, 24th, or 26th. So choice A is too narrow and choice C includes an impossible date. But if Adoniram is working for the Carolingians and Byram for the Sulgravians, choice E is correct, since Adoniram had had no opportunity by the 20th to acquire anything to sell Byram.

4. A.   Adoniram can acquire documents from Byram on the 20th and on his own on the 21st, so whichever government he works for can receive documents two days in a row (I). But Byram cannot acquire anything two days in a row, so *both* governments cannot receive documents two days in a row (II). Finally, the calendar should show you that either government could receive documents three days in a row only if they were sent both by Byram and by Adoniram, which is impossible under the rules stated.

5. A.   The only inference that can logically be drawn is the one in choice A; since differences in perception do exist, but no physical differences, perception must depend partly on other factors. Choices B, C, and D all contain unsupported speculations about what those factors might be; choice E is irrelevant, since the data specify that the Bilge Islanders *perceive* fewer colors, not simply that they can name fewer colors. How this was determined we don't know.

6. D.   Brady's sole piece of evidence is the example of the two other companies that are *like* hers, i.e., that are analogous to hers (choice D). She never suggests what might be causing the problem of low profits (choice A). We do not know that the evidence she presents was previously overlooked (choice B). She discusses no flaw in Mr. Flynn's reasoning (choice C). And opposing Mr. Flynn is not the same as questioning his competence (choice E).

7. A.   Since Ms. Brady makes her point by drawing an analogy, Mr. Flynn's most effective rebuttal would be to undermine the strength of the analogy. He could do this by pointing out significant differences between the two situations that are supposed to be alike. That's exactly what

he does in choice A. In choice B, he simply asserts his own expertise, and in choice C he simply restates his argument. In choice D, he merely suggests that Brady's argument may be weak, whereas in choice A he points out a specific weakness. In choice E, he does not even attempt a rebuttal.

8–12.   Your first instinct may be to draw a map and try to place the towns on it directly. You'll go hopelessly wrong if you try. (This is also true for other puzzles that contain *two* sets of ranked variables—John runs faster and jumps higher than Tom, and so on.) First place the towns on a north-south scale and on a separate east-west scale (Diagram 1). Then, if you wish, combine these into a two-dimensional map. This isn't necessary, but it may make the questions a little easier. We've included it (Diagram 2).

Diagram 1:   Diagram 2:

8. B.   Bowling Green is both farthest north and farthest west.

9. E.   Ashland and East Liverpool are north of Fredericktown, while Coshocton is to the south. All three towns are east of Fredericktown.

10. D.   This one may be easier to read from the two-dimensional map, but you can also read it from the two separate scales. Coshocton, Dover, and Fredericktown are all south and west of East Liverpool. Fredericktown is also south and west of Ashland. Bowling Green is not south of any town. Ashland is south of Bowling Green, but east of it.

11. A. The only ambiguous information in the statements concerns the north-south position of Dover. Statements (5) and (6) tell us that Dover and Coshocton are both south of Fredericktown, but not their positions in relation to each other. Choice A would clear this up. Choices B–E can be deduced from the statements as given.

12. C. Dover's north-south position with respect to Ashland can be deduced from statements (1), (4), and (5), without statement (3). Dover's east-west position with respect to Ashland can be deduced from statements (1) and (6). Each of the other choices is necessary to place the town it mentions either on the north-south scale, on the east-west scale, or on both.

13–16. You may not need to create a diagram for this fairly simple problem. If you do, it might look something like this:

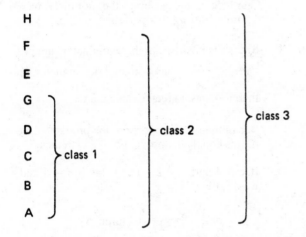

13. C. Choice A violates rules (5) and (6). Choice B violates rule (4). Choice D violates rule (6). Choice E violates rule (6).

14. C. If the spelunker wishes to explore cave Caesar, he or she must first explore cave Benny (I); he or she cannot explore more than two of those listed in rule (6). Rule (5) is no restriction, since it has already been satisfied.

15. B. She must explore caves Abbott, Benny, and Caesar, and she must begin with either Abbott or Benny. If Abbott, she must explore Benny next and then Caesar; if Benny, she can explore Abbott and then Caesar or Caesar and then Abbott.

16. B. He or she can explore any of the caves, provided the order is correct; but three out of the five caves Benny, Caesar, Ewell, Fields, and Hope may not be attempted in one tour. The spelunker may explore Abbott, Dangerfield, Guinness and any two of the restricted five.

17–22. Make a table showing which plumbers can work with which teams of electricians. A useful (but not essential) preliminary is to diagram the permissible combinations. A line shows that two persons must work together; a line with a cross through it, that they *cannot* work together.

Electricians: Plumbers:

In any case, four teams of electricians are possible, with the following possibilities for plumbers in each case:

MNO ST, UW, VW
MN   RST, RUW, RVW, STU, STV, STW
MO   STU, STV, STW
NO   STU, STV, STW

A total of fifteen different combinations is possible, as this table shows. Now read the answers to the questions from the table.

17. D. By inspection of the table. Notice that choice B has an impossible combination—U and V. Also, choice E has a six-person team, which is impossible.

18. B. By inspection of the table.

19. E. Since Olive is too prejudiced to work with Rich, he can work only with Mike and Nick as the two electricians; this eliminates choice B. The three possibilities for the other two plumbers are given in choice E.

20. A. This answer may be surprising—it might seem that filling two slots right away would *reduce* the number of choices. But as the table shows, Steve and Tom appear in eleven possible teams. Olive appears in nine, Wassily in seven, Ulysses and Vic in five each.

21. A.   The electricians are Mike and Olive. Steve and Tom appear in all teams (I), but one team can be made up with neither Ulysses nor Vic (II).

22. C.   Mike, Nick, Rich, Ulysses, Wassily and Mike, Nick, Rich, Vic, Wassily are two-electrician teams without Steve or Tom (I). There are three teams with neither Olive nor Rich (II). If Mike or Nick is not hired, the electricians must be Nick and Olive or Mike and Olive, respectively. Steve and Tom are in all teams which include Mike and Olive or Nick and Olive (III).

23. E.   Choice A exposes the argument's failure to admit that many specific problems may be solved by persons who don't understand the broad picture; choice B exposes the assumption that because generalists are needed, *all* persons should be educated as generalists; choice C exposes the false dichotomy between specialization and seeing the broad picture; and choice D attacks the implicit assumption that fewer specialists are needed. Choice E, however, does not weaken the argument, because the argument is simply calling for *a* broad, liberal education, not necessarily the traditional liberal education.

24. B.   The logic of the argument is valid, and choice B is simply a rephrasing of the conclusion. Therefore, it must be true if the argument is true. It is possible for there to be some bad athletes who want to win (choices A and D), and for some bad athletes to eat a well-balanced diet (choice C). Choice E contradicts the argument's conclusion.

25. E.   The conclusion of the argument states that all good athletes eat a well-balanced diet. Choice E shows that this is not true; there is at least one good athlete who does not eat a well-balanced diet. Choices B and C are both possibly true, but do not weaken the original argument. Choice D can be deduced from the argument.

Section 7

1. B. $a - b = 2 - 3 = -1$; $b - a = 3 - 2 = 1$; -1 is less than 1.

2. A. $\sqrt{14.4} = 3+$ and $\sqrt{1.44} = 1+$

3. A.   A straight line is the shortest distance between two points.

4. B.   Circumference $= \pi d$
$\pi d = 9\pi$
$d = 9$ and radius $= 4.5$
Area $= \pi r^2$
$\pi r^2 = 25\pi$
$r^2 = 25$ and radius $= 5$

5. C.   The segment joining the midpoint of AC to the midpoint of CB consists of $\frac{1}{2}$ of AC plus $\frac{1}{2}$ of CB, or a total of $\frac{1}{2}$ of AB (Column A). The segment from A to the midpoint of AB is also $\frac{1}{2}$ of AB (Column B).

6. B. $\sqrt{100} = \frac{\sqrt{100}}{2} = \frac{10}{2} = 5$ (Column A)

7. C.   Since $b = c$ both fractions have equal denominators.

8. B.   The lowest possible value of a will be reached when b^2 is at a minimum. The minimum value of b^2 is zero, in which case a^2 could equal 100 and a could have a value of -10.

9. C.   Between 10:55 P.M. and 11:25 P.M. 30 minutes or one-half hour elapses. Since the average rate is 50 miles per hour, the motorist covered 25 miles during this period.

10. B.   Since z is positive, both denominators are positive, but $\frac{1}{z-1}$ has a smaller denominator and therefore has a greater value than $\frac{1}{z}$.

11. C.   Recall than in a proportion, the product of the means equals the product of the extremes.

12. D.   If $x = 1$ and $y = 2$, $3x > y$; but if $x = 1$ and $y = 5$, then $3x > y$.

13. B. $\frac{1}{4} \div \frac{3}{8}$ or $\frac{1}{4} \cdot \frac{8}{3} = \frac{2}{3}$ (Column A)
$1\frac{1}{2}$ or $\frac{3}{2} > \frac{2}{3}$

14. D. $(-2)^x$ is negative if x is odd and positive if x is even. 1 raised to any power $= 1$. If x is even, then (-2^x) is greater than 1. If x is odd, then (-2^x) is negative.

15. D.   Possible values of b range from 2 to 8. If $b = 2$, then $2b = 4$, which is less than 6. If $b = 3$, $2b = 6$. If $b = 4$, $2b = 8$, which is more than 6.

16. E.   Call $9x - 3y = 12$ equation 1.
Call $3x - 5y = 7$ equation 2.
Divide equation 1 by 3:
$3x - y = 4$
Multiply by 2:
$6x - 2y = 8$

17. D.   There is no time for lengthy multiplication. Note simply that the correct answer must end with the digit 8.

18. **B.** Since $2^3 = 8$, then $n + 2 = 3$ and $n = 1$.

19. **E.** If 1 is added to an odd integer, the result is an even integer. Twice an even integer yields an even integer.

20. **B.** After a reduction of 20%, the price of the garment is 80% of the original price. The additional redution, 30% of the 80%, results in a price of 56% of the original price (note the incorrect Choice D). For the correct solution, consider that the price of 56% of the original is actually a 44% reduction of the original price.

21. **C.**

YEAR	SALES IN $1,000
1982	80
1983	70
1984	60
1985	80
SUM	$290

$$\text{AVERAGE} = \frac{\$290}{4} = \$72.5$$

22. **D.** I is correct. The sales for both 1982 and 1985 were $80,000. II is not correct. The sales for 1987 were $100,000. III is correct. The earnings for 1980 were $6,000, and the earnings for 1985 were $12,000.

23. **D.** Sales in 1980 were $30,000.
Earnings in 1980 were $6,000.
$$\frac{30}{6} = \frac{5}{1}$$

24. **E.** The increase was from $10,000 to $12,000, or $2,000.
$$\frac{2,000}{10,000} = \frac{1}{5} = 20\%.$$

25. **A.** If $g = \$6,000$, then $2g = \$12,000$.

26. **E.**

$$P \quad\quad R \quad\quad\quad T \quad\quad\quad\quad Q$$

$$\frac{PQ}{PT} = \frac{3 \text{ units}}{2 \text{ units}} = 1\frac{1}{2} = 150\%$$

27. **B.** (A) $0.3 = \frac{3}{10}$

(B) $\sqrt{0.3} = 0.5 +$ or more than $\frac{5}{10}$

(C) $\frac{2}{5} = \frac{4}{10}$

(D) $\frac{1}{3} = \frac{3\frac{1}{3}}{10}$

(E) $\left(\frac{22}{7}\right)\left(\frac{1}{100}\right) = \frac{22}{700} = \frac{3+}{100}$ or $\frac{0.3+}{10}$

28. **C.** $66\frac{2}{3}\% = \frac{2}{3}$

$$\frac{1}{2} \text{ of } \frac{2}{3} = \frac{1}{3}$$

Mr. Nichols sells $\frac{1}{3}$ of the value of the entire factory for $33,333.
Let x = value of entire factory.
$$\frac{1}{3}x = \$33,333$$
$$x = \$99,999$$

29. **D.** The first wheel rotates once every 7, 14, 21, 28, 35, etc., minutes.
The second wheel rotates once every 5, 10, 15, 20, 25, 30, 35, etc., minutes.
They will both begin to rotate every 35 minutes.

30. **B.** Apply the Pythagorean theorem. Let x = distance from first base to third base.

$$x^2 = 90^2 + 90^2$$
$$x^2 = 8100 + 8100$$
$$x^2 = 16200$$
$$x = \sqrt{16200}$$
$$x = 127$$

Answer Sheet – MODEL TEST 3

Start with number 1 for each new section.
If a section has fewer than 38 questions, leave the extra spaces blank.

Section 1

1. Ⓐ Ⓑ Ⓒ Ⓓ Ⓔ
2. Ⓐ Ⓑ Ⓒ Ⓓ Ⓔ
3. Ⓐ Ⓑ Ⓒ Ⓓ Ⓔ
4. Ⓐ Ⓑ Ⓒ Ⓓ Ⓔ
5. Ⓐ Ⓑ Ⓒ Ⓓ Ⓔ
6. Ⓐ Ⓑ Ⓒ Ⓓ Ⓔ
7. Ⓐ Ⓑ Ⓒ Ⓓ Ⓔ
8. Ⓐ Ⓑ Ⓒ Ⓓ Ⓔ
9. Ⓐ Ⓑ Ⓒ Ⓓ Ⓔ
10. Ⓐ Ⓑ Ⓒ Ⓓ Ⓔ

11. Ⓐ Ⓑ Ⓒ Ⓓ Ⓔ
12. Ⓐ Ⓑ Ⓒ Ⓓ Ⓔ
13. Ⓐ Ⓑ Ⓒ Ⓓ Ⓔ
14. Ⓐ Ⓑ Ⓒ Ⓓ Ⓔ
15. Ⓐ Ⓑ Ⓒ Ⓓ Ⓔ
16. Ⓐ Ⓑ Ⓒ Ⓓ Ⓔ
17. Ⓐ Ⓑ Ⓒ Ⓓ Ⓔ
18. Ⓐ Ⓑ Ⓒ Ⓓ Ⓔ
19. Ⓐ Ⓑ Ⓒ Ⓓ Ⓔ
20. Ⓐ Ⓑ Ⓒ Ⓓ Ⓔ

21. Ⓐ Ⓑ Ⓒ Ⓓ Ⓔ
22. Ⓐ Ⓑ Ⓒ Ⓓ Ⓔ
23. Ⓐ Ⓑ Ⓒ Ⓓ Ⓔ
24. Ⓐ Ⓑ Ⓒ Ⓓ Ⓔ
25. Ⓐ Ⓑ Ⓒ Ⓓ Ⓔ
26. Ⓐ Ⓑ Ⓒ Ⓓ Ⓔ
27. Ⓐ Ⓑ Ⓒ Ⓓ Ⓔ
28. Ⓐ Ⓑ Ⓒ Ⓓ Ⓔ
29. Ⓐ Ⓑ Ⓒ Ⓓ Ⓔ
30. Ⓐ Ⓑ Ⓒ Ⓓ Ⓔ

31. Ⓐ Ⓑ Ⓒ Ⓓ Ⓔ
32. Ⓐ Ⓑ Ⓒ Ⓓ Ⓔ
33. Ⓐ Ⓑ Ⓒ Ⓓ Ⓔ
34. Ⓐ Ⓑ Ⓒ Ⓓ Ⓔ
35. Ⓐ Ⓑ Ⓒ Ⓓ Ⓔ
36. Ⓐ Ⓑ Ⓒ Ⓓ Ⓔ
37. Ⓐ Ⓑ Ⓒ Ⓓ Ⓔ
38. Ⓐ Ⓑ Ⓒ Ⓓ Ⓔ

Section 2

1. Ⓐ Ⓑ Ⓒ Ⓓ Ⓔ
2. Ⓐ Ⓑ Ⓒ Ⓓ Ⓔ
3. Ⓐ Ⓑ Ⓒ Ⓓ Ⓔ
4. Ⓐ Ⓑ Ⓒ Ⓓ Ⓔ
5. Ⓐ Ⓑ Ⓒ Ⓓ Ⓔ
6. Ⓐ Ⓑ Ⓒ Ⓓ Ⓔ
7. Ⓐ Ⓑ Ⓒ Ⓓ Ⓔ
8. Ⓐ Ⓑ Ⓒ Ⓓ Ⓔ
9. Ⓐ Ⓑ Ⓒ Ⓓ Ⓔ
10. Ⓐ Ⓑ Ⓒ Ⓓ Ⓔ

11. Ⓐ Ⓑ Ⓒ Ⓓ Ⓔ
12. Ⓐ Ⓑ Ⓒ Ⓓ Ⓔ
13. Ⓐ Ⓑ Ⓒ Ⓓ Ⓔ
14. Ⓐ Ⓑ Ⓒ Ⓓ Ⓔ
15. Ⓐ Ⓑ Ⓒ Ⓓ Ⓔ
16. Ⓐ Ⓑ Ⓒ Ⓓ Ⓔ
17. Ⓐ Ⓑ Ⓒ Ⓓ Ⓔ
18. Ⓐ Ⓑ Ⓒ Ⓓ Ⓔ
19. Ⓐ Ⓑ Ⓒ Ⓓ Ⓔ
20. Ⓐ Ⓑ Ⓒ Ⓓ Ⓔ

21. Ⓐ Ⓑ Ⓒ Ⓓ Ⓔ
22. Ⓐ Ⓑ Ⓒ Ⓓ Ⓔ
23. Ⓐ Ⓑ Ⓒ Ⓓ Ⓔ
24. Ⓐ Ⓑ Ⓒ Ⓓ Ⓔ
25. Ⓐ Ⓑ Ⓒ Ⓓ Ⓔ
26. Ⓐ Ⓑ Ⓒ Ⓓ Ⓔ
27. Ⓐ Ⓑ Ⓒ Ⓓ Ⓔ
28. Ⓐ Ⓑ Ⓒ Ⓓ Ⓔ
29. Ⓐ Ⓑ Ⓒ Ⓓ Ⓔ
30. Ⓐ Ⓑ Ⓒ Ⓓ Ⓔ

31. Ⓐ Ⓑ Ⓒ Ⓓ Ⓔ
32. Ⓐ Ⓑ Ⓒ Ⓓ Ⓔ
33. Ⓐ Ⓑ Ⓒ Ⓓ Ⓔ
34. Ⓐ Ⓑ Ⓒ Ⓓ Ⓔ
35. Ⓐ Ⓑ Ⓒ Ⓓ Ⓔ
36. Ⓐ Ⓑ Ⓒ Ⓓ Ⓔ
37. Ⓐ Ⓑ Ⓒ Ⓓ Ⓔ
38. Ⓐ Ⓑ Ⓒ Ⓓ Ⓔ

Section 3

1. Ⓐ Ⓑ Ⓒ Ⓓ Ⓔ
2. Ⓐ Ⓑ Ⓒ Ⓓ Ⓔ
3. Ⓐ Ⓑ Ⓒ Ⓓ Ⓔ
4. Ⓐ Ⓑ Ⓒ Ⓓ Ⓔ
5. Ⓐ Ⓑ Ⓒ Ⓓ Ⓔ
6. Ⓐ Ⓑ Ⓒ Ⓓ Ⓔ
7. Ⓐ Ⓑ Ⓒ Ⓓ Ⓔ
8. Ⓐ Ⓑ Ⓒ Ⓓ Ⓔ
9. Ⓐ Ⓑ Ⓒ Ⓓ Ⓔ
10. Ⓐ Ⓑ Ⓒ Ⓓ Ⓔ

11. Ⓐ Ⓑ Ⓒ Ⓓ Ⓔ
12. Ⓐ Ⓑ Ⓒ Ⓓ Ⓔ
13. Ⓐ Ⓑ Ⓒ Ⓓ Ⓔ
14. Ⓐ Ⓑ Ⓒ Ⓓ Ⓔ
15. Ⓐ Ⓑ Ⓒ Ⓓ Ⓔ
16. Ⓐ Ⓑ Ⓒ Ⓓ Ⓔ
17. Ⓐ Ⓑ Ⓒ Ⓓ Ⓔ
18. Ⓐ Ⓑ Ⓒ Ⓓ Ⓔ
19. Ⓐ Ⓑ Ⓒ Ⓓ Ⓔ
20. Ⓐ Ⓑ Ⓒ Ⓓ Ⓔ

21. Ⓐ Ⓑ Ⓒ Ⓓ Ⓔ
22. Ⓐ Ⓑ Ⓒ Ⓓ Ⓔ
23. Ⓐ Ⓑ Ⓒ Ⓓ Ⓔ
24. Ⓐ Ⓑ Ⓒ Ⓓ Ⓔ
25. Ⓐ Ⓑ Ⓒ Ⓓ Ⓔ
26. Ⓐ Ⓑ Ⓒ Ⓓ Ⓔ
27. Ⓐ Ⓑ Ⓒ Ⓓ Ⓔ
28. Ⓐ Ⓑ Ⓒ Ⓓ Ⓔ
29. Ⓐ Ⓑ Ⓒ Ⓓ Ⓔ
30. Ⓐ Ⓑ Ⓒ Ⓓ Ⓔ

31. Ⓐ Ⓑ Ⓒ Ⓓ Ⓔ
32. Ⓐ Ⓑ Ⓒ Ⓓ Ⓔ
33. Ⓐ Ⓑ Ⓒ Ⓓ Ⓔ
34. Ⓐ Ⓑ Ⓒ Ⓓ Ⓔ
35. Ⓐ Ⓑ Ⓒ Ⓓ Ⓔ
36. Ⓐ Ⓑ Ⓒ Ⓓ Ⓔ
37. Ⓐ Ⓑ Ⓒ Ⓓ Ⓔ
38. Ⓐ Ⓑ Ⓒ Ⓓ Ⓔ

Section 4

1. (A) (B) (C) (D) (E)	11. (A) (B) (C) (D) (E)	21. (A) (B) (C) (D) (E)	31. (A) (B) (C) (D) (E)
2. (A) (B) (C) (D) (E)	12. (A) (B) (C) (D) (E)	22. (A) (B) (C) (D) (E)	32. (A) (B) (C) (D) (E)
3. (A) (B) (C) (D) (E)	13. (A) (B) (C) (D) (E)	23. (A) (B) (C) (D) (E)	33. (A) (B) (C) (D) (E)
4. (A) (B) (C) (D) (E)	14. (A) (B) (C) (D) (E)	24. (A) (B) (C) (D) (E)	34. (A) (B) (C) (D) (E)
5. (A) (B) (C) (D) (E)	15. (A) (B) (C) (D) (E)	25. (A) (B) (C) (D) (E)	35. (A) (B) (C) (D) (E)
6. (A) (B) (C) (D) (E)	16. (A) (B) (C) (D) (E)	26. (A) (B) (C) (D) (E)	36. (A) (B) (C) (D) (E)
7. (A) (B) (C) (D) (E)	17. (A) (B) (C) (D) (E)	27. (A) (B) (C) (D) (E)	37. (A) (B) (C) (D) (E)
8. (A) (B) (C) (D) (E)	18. (A) (B) (C) (D) (E)	28. (A) (B) (C) (D) (E)	38. (A) (B) (C) (D) (E)
9. (A) (B) (C) (D) (E)	19. (A) (B) (C) (D) (E)	29. (A) (B) (C) (D) (E)	
10. (A) (B) (C) (D) (E)	20. (A) (B) (C) (D) (E)	30. (A) (B) (C) (D) (E)	

Section 5

1. (A) (B) (C) (D) (E)	11. (A) (B) (C) (D) (E)	21. (A) (B) (C) (D) (E)	31. (A) (B) (C) (D) (E)
2. (A) (B) (C) (D) (E)	12. (A) (B) (C) (D) (E)	22. (A) (B) (C) (D) (E)	32. (A) (B) (C) (D) (E)
3. (A) (B) (C) (D) (E)	13. (A) (B) (C) (D) (E)	23. (A) (B) (C) (D) (E)	33. (A) (B) (C) (D) (E)
4. (A) (B) (C) (D) (E)	14. (A) (B) (C) (D) (E)	24. (A) (B) (C) (D) (E)	34. (A) (B) (C) (D) (E)
5. (A) (B) (C) (D) (E)	15. (A) (B) (C) (D) (E)	25. (A) (B) (C) (D) (E)	35. (A) (B) (C) (D) (E)
6. (A) (B) (C) (D) (E)	16. (A) (B) (C) (D) (E)	26. (A) (B) (C) (D) (E)	36. (A) (B) (C) (D) (E)
7. (A) (B) (C) (D) (E)	17. (A) (B) (C) (D) (E)	27. (A) (B) (C) (D) (E)	37. (A) (B) (C) (D) (E)
8. (A) (B) (C) (D) (E)	18. (A) (B) (C) (D) (E)	28. (A) (B) (C) (D) (E)	38. (A) (B) (C) (D) (E)
9. (A) (B) (C) (D) (E)	19. (A) (B) (C) (D) (E)	29. (A) (B) (C) (D) (E)	
10. (A) (B) (C) (D) (E)	20. (A) (B) (C) (D) (E)	30. (A) (B) (C) (D) (E)	

Section 6

1. (A) (B) (C) (D) (E)	11. (A) (B) (C) (D) (E)	21. (A) (B) (C) (D) (E)	31. (A) (B) (C) (D) (E)
2. (A) (B) (C) (D) (E)	12. (A) (B) (C) (D) (E)	22. (A) (B) (C) (D) (E)	32. (A) (B) (C) (D) (E)
3. (A) (B) (C) (D) (E)	13. (A) (B) (C) (D) (E)	23. (A) (B) (C) (D) (E)	33. (A) (B) (C) (D) (E)
4. (A) (B) (C) (D) (E)	14. (A) (B) (C) (D) (E)	24. (A) (B) (C) (D) (E)	34. (A) (B) (C) (D) (E)
5. (A) (B) (C) (D) (E)	15. (A) (B) (C) (D) (E)	25. (A) (B) (C) (D) (E)	35. (A) (B) (C) (D) (E)
6. (A) (B) (C) (D) (E)	16. (A) (B) (C) (D) (E)	26. (A) (B) (C) (D) (E)	36. (A) (B) (C) (D) (E)
7. (A) (B) (C) (D) (E)	17. (A) (B) (C) (D) (E)	27. (A) (B) (C) (D) (E)	37. (A) (B) (C) (D) (E)
8. (A) (B) (C) (D) (E)	18. (A) (B) (C) (D) (E)	28. (A) (B) (C) (D) (E)	38. (A) (B) (C) (D) (E)
9. (A) (B) (C) (D) (E)	19. (A) (B) (C) (D) (E)	29. (A) (B) (C) (D) (E)	
10. (A) (B) (C) (D) (E)	20. (A) (B) (C) (D) (E)	30. (A) (B) (C) (D) (E)	

Section 7

1. (A) (B) (C) (D) (E)	11. (A) (B) (C) (D) (E)	21. (A) (B) (C) (D) (E)	31. (A) (B) (C) (D) (E)
2. (A) (B) (C) (D) (E)	12. (A) (B) (C) (D) (E)	22. (A) (B) (C) (D) (E)	32. (A) (B) (C) (D) (E)
3. (A) (B) (C) (D) (E)	13. (A) (B) (C) (D) (E)	23. (A) (B) (C) (D) (E)	33. (A) (B) (C) (D) (E)
4. (A) (B) (C) (D) (E)	14. (A) (B) (C) (D) (E)	24. (A) (B) (C) (D) (E)	34. (A) (B) (C) (D) (E)
5. (A) (B) (C) (D) (E)	15. (A) (B) (C) (D) (E)	25. (A) (B) (C) (D) (E)	35. (A) (B) (C) (D) (E)
6. (A) (B) (C) (D) (E)	16. (A) (B) (C) (D) (E)	26. (A) (B) (C) (D) (E)	36. (A) (B) (C) (D) (E)
7. (A) (B) (C) (D) (E)	17. (A) (B) (C) (D) (E)	27. (A) (B) (C) (D) (E)	37. (A) (B) (C) (D) (E)
8. (A) (B) (C) (D) (E)	18. (A) (B) (C) (D) (E)	28. (A) (B) (C) (D) (E)	38. (A) (B) (C) (D) (E)
9. (A) (B) (C) (D) (E)	19. (A) (B) (C) (D) (E)	29. (A) (B) (C) (D) (E)	
10. (A) (B) (C) (D) (E)	20. (A) (B) (C) (D) (E)	30. (A) (B) (C) (D) (E)	

MODEL TEST 3

Directions: Each sentence below has one or two blanks, each blank indicating that something has been omitted. Beneath the sentence are five lettered words or sets of words. Choose the word or set of words for each blank that best fits the meaning of the sentence as a whole.

1. The columnist was very gentle when he mentioned his friends, but he was bitter and even ------- when he discussed people who ------- him.

   (A) laconic...infuriated
   (B) acerbic...irritated
   (C) remorseful...encouraged
   (D) militant...distressed
   (E) stoical...alienated

2. Despite her ------- unwillingness, the promoters were still hopeful that, given sufficient diplomacy and flattery on their part, they could ------- her into signing the recording contract.

   (A) patent...entrap
   (B) extreme...intimidate
   (C) apparent...shame
   (D) painful...tantalize
   (E) obvious...inveigle

3. Although he was generally considered an extremely ------- individual, his testimony at the trial revealed that he had been very -------.

   (A) intrepid...valiant
   (B) guileless...hypocritical
   (C) abstemious...temperate
   (D) meek...timorous
   (E) ingenuous...obtuse

4. Reacting to Greene's critical satire by stating that henceforth he will write to please himself, Orlando chooses obscurity; even ------- would be welcome.

   (A) notoriety
   (B) adulation
   (C) parody
   (D) anonymity
   (E) deprecation

5. Whereas off-Broadway theater over the past several seasons has clearly ------- a talent for experimentation and improvisation, one deficiency in the commercial stage of late has been its marked incapacity for -------.

   (A) manifested...spontaneity
   (B) lampooned...theatricality
   (C) cultivated...orthodoxy
   (D) disavowed...histrionics
   (E) betrayed...burlesque

6. The perpetual spinning of particles is much like that of a top, with one significant difference: unlike the top, the particles have no need to be wound up, for ------- is one of their ------- properties.

   (A) revolution...radical
   (B) motion...intangible
   (C) rotation...intrinsic
   (D) acceleration...lesser
   (E) collision...hypothetical

7. She conducted the interrogation not only with dispatch but with -------, being a person who is ------- in manner yet subtle in discrimination.

   (A) elan...enthusiastic
   (B) equanimity...abrupt
   (C) finesse...expeditious
   (D) zeal...doctrinaire
   (E) trepidation...cursory

Directions: In each of the following questions, a related pair of words or phrases is followed by five lettered pairs of words or phrases. Select the lettered pair that best expresses a relationship similar to that expressed in the original pair.

8. REAM : PAPER::
   (A) skin : tissue
   (B) envelope : letter
   (C) cord : wood
   (D) swatch : cloth
   (E) chisel : stone

9. SMART : PAIN::
   (A) grieve : sorrow
   (B) wallow : misery
   (C) afflict : torment
   (D) mollify : anger
   (E) weaken : intensity

10. BAMBOO : SHOOT::
    (A) heather : spray
    (B) holly : shrub
    (C) bean : sprout
    (D) pepper : corn
    (E) oak : tree

11. DEFLECT : MISSILE::
    (A) defend : fortress
    (B) reflect : mirror
    (C) diversify : portfolio
    (D) dismantle : equipment
    (E) distract : attention

12. CLOY : PALATE::
   (A) sniff : nose
   (B) slit : tongue
   (C) surfeit : appetite
   (D) cling : touch
   (E) refine : taste

13. PRATFALL : EMBARRASSMENT::
   (A) deadlock : mortification
   (B) checkup : reluctance
   (C) downfall : penitence
   (D) diehard : grievance
   (E) windfall : jubilation

14. MULISH : PLIANCY::
   (A) piggish : gluttony
   (B) sluggish : reluctance
   (C) kittenish : motility
   (D) apish : servility
   (E) shrewish : amiability

15. MINATORY : THREATEN::
   (A) mandatory : complete
   (B) laudatory : praise
   (C) salutary : greet
   (D) hortatory : listen
   (E) defamatory : publicize

16. CLOUD : SCUD::
   (A) fog : dissipate
   (B) mist : fall
   (C) water : race
   (D) blood : clot
   (E) wave : break

Directions: Each passage in this group is followed by questions based on its content. After reading a passage, choose the best answer to each question. Answer all questions following a passage on the basis of what is stated or implied in the passage.

During the 1930s, National Association for the Advancement of Colored People (NAACP) attorneys Charles H. Houston, William Hastie, James M. Nabrit, Leon Ransom, and Thurgood Marshall charted a legal strategy designed to end segregation in education. They developed a series of legal cases challenging segregation in graduate and professional schools. Houston believed that the battle against segregation had to begin at the highest academic level in order to mitigate fear of race mixing that could create even greater hostility and reluctance on the part of white judges. After establishing a series of favorable legal precedents in higher education, NAACP attorneys planned to launch an all-out attack on the separate-but-equal doctrine in primary and secondary schools. The strategy proved successful. In four major United States Supreme Court decisions, precedents were established that would enable the NAACP to construct a solid legal foundation upon which the Brown case could rest: *Missouri ex rel. Gaines* v. *Canada, Registrar of the University of Missouri* (1938); *Sipuel* v. *Board of Regents of the University of Oklahoma* (1948); *McLaurin* v. *Oklahoma State Regents for Higher Education* (1950); and *Sweatt* v. *Painter* (1950).

In the Oklahoma case, the Supreme Court held that the plaintiff was entitled to enroll in the university. The Oklahoma Regents responded by separating black and white students in cafeterias and classrooms. The 1950 McLaurin decision ruled that such internal separation was unconstitutional. In the Sweatt ruling, delivered on the same day, the Supreme Court held that the maintenance of separate law schools for whites and blacks was unconstitutional. A year after Herman Sweatt entered the University of Texas law school, desegregation cases were filed in the states of Kansas, South Carolina, Virginia, and Delaware, and in the District of Columbia asking the courts to apply the qualitative test of the Sweatt case to the elementary and secondary schools and to declare the separate-but-equal doctrine invalid in the area of public education.

The 1954 *Brown* v. *Board of Education* decision declared that a classification based solely on race violated the 14th Amendment to the United States Constitution. The decision reversed the 1896 *Plessy* v. *Ferguson* ruling which had established the separate-but-equal doctrine. The *Brown* decision more than any other case launched the "equalitarian revolution" in American jurisprudence and signaled the emerging primacy of equality as a guide to constitutional decisions; nevertheless, the decision did not end state-sanctioned segregation. Indeed, the second *Brown* decision, known as *Brown II* and delivered a year later, played a decisive role in limiting the effectiveness and impact of the 1954 case by providing southern states with the opportunity to delay the implementation of desegregation.

The intervention of the federal government and the deployment of the National Guard in the 1954 Little Rock crisis, and again in 1963 when the enrollment of James Meredith desegregated the University of Mississippi, highlight the role of federal power in promoting social change during this era. While black local and national leaders organized and orchestrated the legal struggles, and students joined in freedom rides and staged sit-ins, another equally important dimension of the rights quest took shape: the battle between federal and state authority and the evolution of the doctrine of federalism. The fact remains that the United States Supreme Court lacked the power to enforce its decisions. President Dwight D. Eisenhower's use of federal troops in Little Rock was a major departure from the reluctance of past presidents to display federal power in the South, especially to protect the lives and rights of black citizens.

17. According to the passage, Houston aimed his legislative challenge at the graduate and professional
school level on the basis of the assumption that

(A) the greatest inequities existed at the highest academic and professional levels
(B) the separate-but-equal doctrine applied solely to
the highest academic levels
(C) there were clear precedents for reform in existence at the graduate school level
(D) the judiciary would feel less apprehension at
desegregation on the graduate level
(E) the consequences of desegregation would
become immediately apparent at the graduate
school level

18. The passage suggests that the reaction of the Oklahoma Regents to the 1948 Sipuel decision was one of

(A) resigned tolerance
(B) avowed uncertainty
(C) moderate amusement
(D) distinct displeasure
(E) unquestioning approbation

19. Which of the following best describes the relationship between the McLaurin decision and the 1954
Brown v. *Board of Education* decision?

(A) The McLaurin decision superseded the Brown
decision.
(B) The Brown decision provided a precedent for
the McLaurin decision.
(C) The Brown decision reversed the McLaurin
decision.
(D) The McLaurin decision limited the application
of the Brown decision.
(E) The McLaurin decision provided legal authority
for the Brown decision.

20. To the claim that judicial decisions without executive
intervention would have assured desegregation in
education, the author would most probably respond
with which of the following?

(A) Marked disagreement
(B) Grudging acquiescence
(C) Studied neutrality
(D) Complete indifference
(E) Unqualified enthusiasm

21. The passage suggests that *Brown* v. *Board of Education* might have had an even more significant impact
on segregation if it had not been for which of the
following?

(A) The deployment of the National Guard
(B) The *Plessy* v. *Ferguson* decision
(C) The 1955 *Brown II* decision
(D) James Meredith's enrollment in Mississippi
(E) The *Sweatt* v. *Painter* decision

22. Which of the following titles best describes the content of the passage?

(A) Executive Intervention in the Fight against Seg-
regated Education
(B) The *Brown* Decision and the Equalitarian
Revolution
(C) A Long War: The Struggle to Desegregate
American Education
(D) The Emergence of Federalism and the Civil
Rights Movement
(E) Education Reform and the Role of the NAACP

23. Which of the following statements is most compatible with the principles embodied in *Plessy* v. *Ferguson* as described in the passage?

(A) Internal separation of whites and blacks within
a given school is unconstitutional.
(B) Whites and blacks may be educated in separate
schools so long as the schools offer comparable facilities.
(C) The maintenance of separate professional
schools for blacks and whites is
unconstitutional.
(D) The separate-but-equal doctrine is inapplicable
to the realm of private education.
(E) Blacks may be educated in schools with whites
whenever the blacks and whites have equal
institutions.

24. The aspect of Houston's work most extensively discussed in the passage is its

(A) psychological canniness
(B) judicial complexity
(C) fundamental efficiency
(D) radical intellectualism
(E) exaggerated idealism

One simple physical concept lies behind the formation
of the stars: gravitational instability. The concept is not
new; Newton first perceived it late in the 17th century.
Imagine a uniform, static cloud of gas in space. Imagine then that the gas is somehow disturbed so that one
small spherical region becomes a little denser than the
gas around it so that the small region's gravitational field
becomes slightly stronger. It now attracts more matter to
it and its gravity increases further, causing it to begin to
contract. As it contracts its density increases, which
increases its gravity even more, so that it picks up even
more matter and contracts even further. The process
continues until the small region of gas finally forms a
gravitationally bound object.

25. The primary purpose of the passage is to

(A) demonstrate the evolution of the meaning of a
term
(B) depict the successive stages of a phenomenon
(C) establish the pervasiveness of a process
(D) support a theory considered outmoded
(E) describe a static condition

26. It can be inferred from the passage that the author views the information contained within it as

(A) controversial but irrefutable
(B) speculative and unprofitable
(C) uncomplicated and traditional
(D) original but obscure
(E) sadly lacking in elaboration

27. The author provides information that answers which of the following questions?

I. How does the small region's increasing density affect its gravitational field?
II. What causes the disturbance that changes the cloud from its original static state?
III. What is the end result of the gradually increasing concentration of the small region of gas?

(A) I only
(B) II only
(C) I and II only
(D) I and III only
(E) I, II and III

Directions: Each question below consists of a word printed in capital letters, followed by five lettered words or phrases. Choose the lettered word or phrase that is most nearly opposite in meaning to the word in capital letters.

Since some of the questions require you to distinguish fine shades of meaning, be sure to consider all the choices before deciding which one is best.

28. HAMPER:
(A) feed
(B) animate
(C) facilitate
(D) treat lightly
(E) caution tactfully

29. URBANE:
(A) civic
(B) remote
(C) deceptive
(D) conventional
(E) naive

30. DEMISE:
(A) integrity
(B) irritation
(C) birth
(D) excess
(E) surmise

31. PARIAH:
(A) miser
(B) nomad
(C) servant
(D) idol
(E) renegade

32. PROSTRATE:
(A) divert
(B) strengthen
(C) depreciate
(D) scrutinize
(E) reassure

33. CONTENTIOUS:
(A) amenable
(B) inactive
(C) dispassionate
(D) callow
(E) severe

34. DEBACLE:
(A) effort
(B) success
(C) drought
(D) transience
(E) dominance

35. HAPLESS:
(A) fortuitous
(B) fortunate
(C) fortified
(D) forbidden
(E) forestalled

36. EXACERBATE:
(A) alleviate
(B) bewilder
(C) contemplate
(D) intimidate
(E) economize

37. PROBITY:
(A) fallacy
(B) improbability
(C) conviction
(D) depravity
(E) avidity

38. BANEFUL:
(A) susceptible
(B) incongruous
(C) impulsive
(D) salubrious
(E) desultory

S T O P

IF YOU FINISH BEFORE TIME IS CALLED, YOU MAY CHECK YOUR WORK ON THIS SECTION ONLY.
DO NOT WORK ON ANY OTHER SECTION IN THE TEST.

SECTION 2

Time—30 minutes

38 Questions

Directions: Each sentence below has one or two blanks, each blank indicating that something has been omitted. Beneath the sentence are five lettered words or sets of words. Choose the word or set of words for each blank that best fits the meaning of the sentence as a whole.

1. Even though previous reporters had lampooned the candidate throughout the campaign, he ------- further interviews.

   (A) resisted
   (B) halted
   (C) sidestepped
   (D) welcomed
   (E) dreaded

2. Soap operas and situation comedies, though given to distortion, are so derivative of contemporary culture that they are inestimable ------- the attitudes and values of our society in any particular decade.

   (A) contraventions of
   (B) antidotes to
   (C) indices of
   (D) prerequisites for
   (E) determinants of

3. Perry's critics in the scientific world ------- that many of the observations he has made during more than a decade of research in Costa Rica have been reported as ------- in popular magazines rather than as carefully documented case studies in technical journals.

   (A) intimate…hypotheses
   (B) charge…anecdotes
   (C) applaud…rumors
   (D) claim…scholarship
   (E) apologize…fabrications

4. The homeless wino crouched over the subway grating for warmth, the bag lady groping for recyclable bottles in the garbage can, the line of hungry men waiting at the soup kitchen's door—all these scenes of suffering ------- the ------- of the economic boom proclaimed by the prophets of affluence.

   (A) avouch…existence
   (B) belie…reality
   (C) challenge…legality
   (D) predicate…validity
   (E) minimize…gravity

5. Slander is like counterfeit money: many people who would not coin it ------- it without qualms.

   (A) waste
   (B) denounce
   (C) circulate
   (D) withdraw
   (E) invest

6. Compromise is ------- to passionate natures because it seems a surrender; and to intellectual natures because it seems a -------.

   (A) odious…confusion
   (B) inherent…fabrication
   (C) welcome…fulfillment
   (D) unsuited…submission
   (E) intimidating…dichotomy

7. Although we might ------- Milton's remark that he wrote prose with his left hand as characteristically ironic, we have tended to accept uncritically an apparent Renaissance prejudice against prose, using comments like Milton's to ------- our own prejudices against prose as a less immediately artful medium than poetry or drama.

   (A) refute…countervail
   (B) dismiss…invalidate
   (C) challenge…illuminate
   (D) expurgate…exacerbate
   (E) discount…buttress

Directions: In each of the following questions, a related pair of words or phrases is followed by five lettered pairs of words or phrases. Select the lettered pair that best expresses a relationship similar to that expressed in the original pair.

8. CONFINE : PRISONER::
   (A) impeach : governor
   (B) trace : fugitive
   (C) detain : suspect
   (D) testify : witness
   (E) ambush : sentry

9. SWATCH : FABRIC::
   (A) chip : paint
   (B) slag : metal
   (C) mortar : brick
   (D) essence : perfume
   (E) loaf : bread

10. TENDRIL : VINE::
   (A) trunk : tree
   (B) pollen : flower
   (C) pseudopod : amoeba
   (D) trellis : honeysuckle
   (E) cobra : snake

11. BATTEN : HATCH::
   (A) shatter : window
   (B) unload : cargo
   (C) pack : chest
   (D) latch : door
   (E) repair : cupboard

12. CONTEMPORANEOUS : EVENTS::
   (A) adjacent : objects
   (B) modern : times
   (C) temporary : measures
   (D) gradual : degrees
   (E) repetitive : steps

13. LIMERICK : POEM::
   (A) motif : symphony
   (B) prologue : play
   (C) catch : song
   (D) sequence : sonnet
   (E) epigraph : novel

14. RETAINER : RETINUE::
   (A) servant : mansion
   (B) witch : coven
   (C) director : corporation
   (D) miser : hoard
   (E) vassal : homage

15. HERO : ACCOLADE::
   (A) mentor : advice
   (B) suitor : proposal
   (C) clodhopper : grace
   (D) laughingstock : ridicule
   (E) defendant : indictment

16. RIDER : BILL::
   (A) purchase : receipt
   (B) endorsement : policy
   (C) violation : ordinance
   (D) consignment : invoice
   (E) summons : citation

Directions: Each passage in this group is followed by questions based on its content. After reading a passage, choose the best answer to each question. Answer all questions following a passage on the basis of what is <u>stated</u> or <u>implied</u> in the passage.

With Meredith's *The Egoist* we enter into a critical problem that we have not yet before faced in these studies. That is the problem offered by a writer of recognizably impressive stature, whose work is informed by a muscular intelligence, whose language has splendor, whose "view of life" wins our respect, and yet for whom we are at best able to feel only a passive appreciation which amounts, practically, to indifference. We should be unjust to Meredith and to criticism if we should, giving in to the inertia of indifference, simply avoid dealing with him and thus avoid the problem along with him. He does not "speak to us," we might say; his meaning is not a "meaning for us"; he "leaves us cold." But do not the challenge and the excitement of the critical problem as such lie in that ambivalence of attitude which allows us to recognize the intelligence and even the splendor of Meredith's work, while, at the same time, we experience a lack of sympathy, a failure of any enthusiasm of response?

17. According to the passage, the work of Meredith is noteworthy for its elements of

   (A) sensibility and artistic fervor
   (B) ambivalence and moral ambiguity
   (C) tension and sense of vitality
   (D) brilliance and linguistic grandeur
   (E) wit and whimsical frivolity

18. All of the following can be found in the author's discussion of Meredith EXCEPT

   (A) an indication of Meredith's customary effect on readers
   (B) an enumeration of the admirable qualities in his work
   (C) a selection of hypothetical comments at Meredith's expense
   (D) an analysis of the critical ramifications of Meredith's effect on readers
   (E) a refutation of the claim that Meredith evokes no sympathy

19. It can be inferred from the passage that the author finds the prospect of appraising Meredith's work critically to be

   (A) counterproductive
   (B) extremely formidable
   (C) somewhat tolerable
   (D) markedly unpalatable
   (E) clearly invigorating

20. It can be inferred from the passage that the author would be most likely to agree with which of the following statements about the role of criticism?

   (A) Its prime office should be to make our enjoyment of the things that feed the mind as conscious as possible.

   (B) It should be a disinterested endeavor to learn and propagate the best that is known and thought in the world.

   (C) It should enable us to go beyond personal prejudice to appreciate the virtues of works antipathetic to our own tastes.

   (D) It should dwell upon excellences rather than imperfections, ignoring such deficiencies as irrelevant.

   (E) It should strive both to purify literature and to elevate the literary standards of the reading public.

Genetic variation is also important in the evolution of lower organisms such as bacteria, and here too it arises from mutations. Bacteria have only one chromosome, however, so that different alleles

(5) or variant forms of a gene are not normally present within a single cell. The reshuffling of bacterial genes therefore ordinarily requires the introduction into a bacterium of DNA carrying an allele that originated in a different cell. One mechanism

(10) accomplishing this interbacterial transfer of genes in nature is transduction: certain viruses that can infect bacterial cells pick up fragments of the bacterial DNA and carry the DNA to other cells in the course of a later infection. In another process,

(15) known as transformation, DNA released by cell death or other natural processes simply enters a new cell from the environment by penetrating the cell wall and membrane. A third mechanism, conjugation, involves certain of the self-replicating cir-

(20) cular segments of DNA called plasmids, which can be transferred between bacterial cells that are in direct physical contact with each other.

Whether the genetic information is introduced into a bacterial cell by transduction, transformation

(25) or conjugation, it must be incorporated into the new host's hereditary apparatus if it is to be propagated as part of that apparatus when the cell divides. As in the case of higher organisms, this incorporation is ordinarily accomplished by the

(30) exchange of homologous DNA; the entering gene must have an allelic counterpart in the recipient DNA. Because homologous recombination requires overall similarity of the two DNA segments, it can take place only between structurally

(35) and ancestrally related segments. And so, in bacteria as well as in higher organisms, the generation of genetic variability is limited to what can be attained by exchanges between different alleles of the same genes or between different genes that have

(40) stretches of similar nucleotide sequences. This requirement imposes severe constraints on the rate of evolution that can be attained through homologous recombination.

Until recently mutation and homologous recombina-

(45) tion nevertheless appeared to be the only important mechanisms for generating biological diversity. They seemed to be able to account for the degree of diversity observed in most species, and the implicit constraints of homologous recombination—which prevent the

(50) exchange of genetic information between unrelated organisms lacking extensive DNA-sequence similarity —appeared to be consistent with both a modest rate of biological evolution and the persistence of distinct species that retain their basic identity generation after

(55) generation.

Within the past decade or so, however, it has become increasingly apparent that there are various "illegitimate" recombinational processes, which can join together DNA segments having little or no nucleotide-

(60) sequence homology, and that such processes play a significant role in the organization of genetic information and the regulation of its expression. Such recombination is often effected by transposable genetic elements: structurally and genetically discrete segments of DNA that

(65) have the ability to move around the chromosomes and the extrachromosomal DNA molecules of bacteria and higher organisms. Although transposable elements have been studied largely in bacterial cells, they were originally discovered in plants and are now known to exist in

(70) animals as well. Because illegitimate recombination can join together DNA segments that have little, if any, ancestral relationship, it can affect evolution in quantum leaps as well as in small steps.

21. The passage supplies information for answering which of the following questions?

   I.   Why are interbacterial transfer mechanisms important for genetic variation in bacteria?

   II. What is the role of cell death in the interbacterial transfer of genes?

   III. How do the so-called "illegitimate" recombinational processes differ from homologous recombination?

   (A) I only
   (B) II only
   (C) I and II only
   (D) II and III only
   (E) I, II and III

22. The primary purpose of the passage is to

   (A) examine the evidence supporting the existence of transposable genetic elements in bacteria

   (B) report on the controversy over the use of illegitimate recombinational processes in bacteria

   (C) discuss evolutionary theory and some hypotheses proposed to account for its anomalies

   (D) explain established mechanisms for genetic change and introduce a newly discovered one

   (E) restrict the scope of the investigation of the causes of genetic variation in bacteria

23. The authors use the term "'illegitimate' recombinational processes" (lines 57–58) to refer to

   (A) biological processes outlawed by federal regulation
   (B) processes requiring similarity of nucleotide sequences
   (C) processes that break the rules of homologous recombination
   (D) processes that cannot be found among higher organisms
   (E) processes exceeding the permissible amount of mutation

24. In terms of its tone and form, the passage can best be characterized as

   (A) an angry refutation
   (B) a partisan interpretation
   (C) an equivocal endorsement
   (D) a reflective meditation
   (E) a dispassionate explication

25. A necessary precondition for the process known as transformation to take place is that the cell wall and membrane be

   (A) contiguous
   (B) pliant
   (C) permeable
   (D) homologous
   (E) self-replicating

26. The function of viruses in the mechanism of transduction in bacteria is most like the function of

   (A) caterpillars in the process of metamorphosis
   (B) bees in the process of pollination
   (C) germs in the process of immunization
   (D) pores in the process of perspiration
   (E) atoms in the process of fission

27. It can be inferred from the passage that the paragraph immediately preceding this excerpt most likely dealt with the

   (A) probability of mutations in colonies of bacteria
   (B) significance of genetic diversity in higher organisms
   (C) discovery of transposable genetic elements in plants
   (D) relationship between bacteria and higher organisms
   (E) evidence supporting the theory of evolution

Directions: Each question below consists of a word printed in capital letters, followed by five lettered words or phrases. Choose the lettered word or phrase that is most nearly opposite in meaning to the word in capital letters.

Since some of the questions require you to distinguish fine shades of meaning, be sure to consider all the choices before deciding which one is best.

28. CONDONE:
   (A) denounce
   (B) endure
   (C) imagine
   (D) remember
   (E) grieve

29. ANTITHETICAL:
   (A) qualitative
   (B) unnatural
   (C) deceptive
   (D) supportive
   (E) noncommittal

30. OMNISCIENCE:
   (A) power
   (B) extravagance
   (C) magnanimity
   (D) conscience
   (E) ignorance

31. MOLLIFY:
   (A) acquit
   (B) forbid
   (C) embarrass
   (D) provoke
   (E) demolish

32. GAUCHE:
   (A) grotesque
   (B) tactful
   (C) rightful
   (D) fashionable
   (E) inane

33. DIATRIBE:
    (A) medley
    (B) dilemma
    (C) afterthought
    (D) rebuttal
    (E) praise

34. GAINSAY:
    (A) estimate
    (B) corroborate
    (C) forfeit
    (D) expend
    (E) neglect

35. PROLIXITY:
    (A) proximity
    (B) disinclination
    (C) circuitousness
    (D) extremity
    (E) terseness

36. AVID:
    (A) veracious
    (B) forgetful
    (C) insignificant
    (D) turgid
    (E) loath

37. REPINE:
    (A) endure grudgingly
    (B) maintain composure
    (C) express satisfaction
    (D) arouse hostility
    (E) attract attention

38. SALIENCE:
    (A) insipidity
    (B) immutability
    (C) incongruity
    (D) intransigence
    (E) inconspicuousness

S T O P

IF YOU FINISH BEFORE TIME IS CALLED, YOU MAY CHECK YOUR WORK ON THIS SECTION ONLY.
DO NOT WORK ON ANY OTHER SECTION IN THE TEST.

SECTION 3

Time—30 Minutes

30 Questions

Numbers: All numbers used are real numbers.

Figures: Position of points, angles, regions, etc., can be assumed to be in the order shown; and angle measures can be assumed to be positive.

Lines shown as straight can be assumed to be straight.

Figures can be assumed to lie in a plane unless otherwise indicated.

Figures that accompany questions are intended to provide information useful in answering the questions. However, unless a note states that a figure is drawn to scale, you should solve these problems NOT by estimating sizes by sight or by measurement, but by using your knowledge of mathematics (see Example 2 below).

Directions: Each of the Questions 1-15 consists of two quantities, one in Column A and one in Column B. You are to compare the two quantities and choose

A if the quantity in Column A is greater;
B if the quantity in Column B is greater;
C if the two quantities are equal;
D if the relationship cannot be determined from the information given.

Note: Since there are only four choices, NEVER MARK (E).

Common
Information: In a question, information concerning one or both of the quantities to be compared is centered above the two columns. A symbol that appears in both columns represents the same thing in Column A as it does in Column B.

	Column A	Column B	Sample Answers
Example 1:	2×6	$2 + 6$	● Ⓑ Ⓒ Ⓓ Ⓔ

Examples 2-4 refer to $\triangle PQR$.

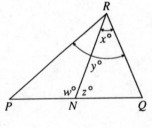

Example 2:	PN	NQ	Ⓐ Ⓑ Ⓒ ● Ⓔ
			(since equal measures cannot be assumed, even though PN and NQ appear equal)

Example 3:	x	y	Ⓐ ● Ⓒ Ⓓ Ⓔ
			(since N is between P and Q)

Example 4:	$w + z$	180	Ⓐ Ⓑ ● Ⓓ Ⓔ
			(since PQ is a straight line)

A if the quantity in Column A is greater;
B if the quantity in Column B is greater;
C if the two quantities are equal;
D if the relationship cannot be determined from the information given.

Column A	Column B

$a = c, f = 50$

1. $c + d$ e

The toll for using the Uniontown Tunnel is $1.50 or 1 token. Tokens are sold in packages of 10 for $12.00.

2. $33\dfrac{1}{3}\%$ The percent saved on 10 trips using the tunnel if a token, rather than $1.50, is used on each trip.

3. $\sqrt{145} + \sqrt{45}$ 18

4. a b

Area of square $ABCD$ = Area of triangle RST

5. ST 6

$-1 < a < 1$
$-1 < b < 0$

6. a b

7. $\dfrac{2x - \dfrac{y-5}{6}}{\dfrac{y-5}{3} - 4x}$ -0.5

Circleville is 23 kilometers from Center City and Centerville is 46 kilometers from Center City

8. Distance from Circleville to Centerville   23 kilometers

Column A	Column B

9. z 45

$8383 = 83x$

10. Value of x 111

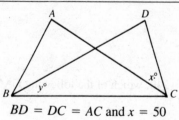

Squares I, II, and III are on the sides of isosceles right triangle ABC, whose area is 12.5.

11. Area of square III   Twice the area of triangle ABC

$x^2 - 5x + 6 = 0$

12. The sum of the roots of the equation   The product of the roots of the equation

Area of triangle ABC + area of square $BCDE$ = 125 and perimeter of square = 40

13. The shortest distance from point A to ED Twice the length of EB

$BD = DC = AC$ and $x = 50$

14. x y

$\dfrac{\text{Radius of circle } A}{\text{Radius of circle } B} = \dfrac{1}{2}$

15. Four times the area of circle A Area of circle B

Directions: Each of the Questions 16–30 has five answer choices. For each of these questions, select the best of the answer choices given.

16. An American tourist in Paris finds that he weights 70 kilograms. When he left the United States he weighed 144 pounds. If 1 kilogram = 2.2 pounds, his net change in weight (in pounds) is

   (A) -31.8
   (B) -10
   (C) 0
   (D) $+10$
   (E) $+31.8$

17. The ratio of boys to girls in a class is $a{:}b$. What part of the class is made up of girls?

   (A) $\dfrac{b}{ab}$

   (B) $\dfrac{a}{ab}$

   (C) $\dfrac{b}{a+b}$

   (D) $\dfrac{a}{b+a}$

   (E) $\dfrac{a+b}{b}$

18. Which of the following is greater than $\tfrac{1}{4}$?

   (A) $(0.25)^2$

   (B) $\sqrt{\dfrac{1}{4}}$

   (C) $\left(\dfrac{1}{4}\right)^4$

   (D) 0.04

   (E) $\dfrac{1}{250}$

19. A piece of paper with an area of 60 square inches is divided into two pieces so that the area of one is $\tfrac{2}{3}$ the area of the other. What is the area (in square inches) of one of the pieces?

   (A) 15
   (B) 20
   (C) 24
   (D) 30
   (E) 45

20. If $xyz = 240$, which of the following CANNOT be a value of y?

   (A) 0
   (B) 2
   (C) 5
   (D) 3
   (E) 8

Questions 21-25 refer to the following graph.

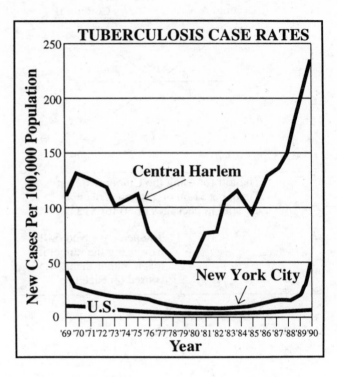

21. How many cases of tuberculosis per 100,000 population were reported for Central Harlem for 1979?

   (A) 50
   (B) 55
   (C) 60
   (D) 65
   (E) 500

22. During what year was there the greatest difference between the cases per 100,000 of tuberculosis in New York City and in the rest of the country?

   (A) 1969
   (B) 1972
   (C) 1980
   (D) 1985
   (E) 1990

23. When did Central Harlem experience the sharpest rise in tuberculosis cases?

   (A) 1972–1973
   (B) 1973–1974
   (C) 1975-1976
   (D) 1976-1977
   (E) 1980-1981

24. When did New York City and the rest of the country have ALMOST the same number of tuberculosis cases per 100,000 population?

    (A) 1975
    (B) 1976
    (C) 1977
    (D) 1978
    (E) 1979

25. In 1990, how many new cases of tuberculosis per 1,000 population occurred in New York City?

    (A) 0.5
    (B) 5.0
    (C) 5.5
    (D) 50.0
    (E) 50.5

26. A rectangle *l* inches long and *w* inches wide is made 3 inches longer. The area (in square inches) has increased by

    (A) 3*w*
    (B) 3*l*
    (C) 3*lw*
    (D) 3(*l* + *w*)
    (E) 3*l* + 3*w* + 9

27. If $x + 2y = 1\frac{1}{3}$ and $x - y = \frac{1}{3}$, then 3*y* =

    (A) $-\frac{1}{3}$

    (B) 0

    (C) $\frac{1}{3}$

    (D) 1

    (E) $1\frac{2}{3}$

28. City X is 200 miles east of City Y, and City Z is 150 miles directly north of City Y. What is the shortest distance (in miles) between X and Z?

    (A) $50\sqrt{7}$
    (B) 175
    (C) 200
    (D) 250
    (E) 300

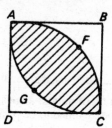

29. In the figure above, *ABCD* is a square of side 10. *AFC* is an arc of a circle with the center at *D* and radius 10. *AGC* is an arc of a circle with the center at *B* and radius 10. What is the area of the shaded region?

    (A) $50\pi - 100$
    (B) $25\pi - 100$
    (C) $100 - 25\pi$
    (D) $100 - 50\pi$
    (E) $100\pi - 100$

30. The price of a balcony seat in a theater is $\frac{1}{3}$ the price of a seat in the orchestra. When the theater is completely sold out, the total receipts from the 600 orchestra seats and the 450 balcony seats are $4,500. What is the price of one orchestra seat?

    (A) $2.00
    (B) $2.30
    (C) $4.00
    (D) $6.00
    (E) $10.00

S T O P

IF YOU FINISH BEFORE TIME IS CALLED, YOU MAY CHECK YOUR WORK ON THIS SECTION ONLY. DO NOT WORK ON ANY OTHER SECTION IN THE TEST.

SECTION 4

Time—30 minutes

30 Questions

Numbers: All numbers used are real numbers.

Figures: Position of points, angles, regions, etc., can be assumed to be in the order shown; and angle measures can be assumed to be positive.

Lines shown as straight can be assumed to be straight.

Figures can be assumed to lie in a plane unless otherwise indicated.

Figures that accompany questions are intended to provide information useful in answering the questions. However, unless a note states that a figure is drawn to scale, you should solve these problems NOT by estimating sizes by sight or by measurement, but by using your knowledge of mathematics (see Example 2 below).

Directions: Each of the Questions 1-15 consists of two quantities, one in Column A and one in Column B. You are to compare the two quantities and choose

A if the quantity in Column A is greater;
B if the quantity in Column B is greater;
C if the two quantities are equal;
D if the relationship cannot be determined from the information given.

Note: Since there are only four choices, NEVER MARK (E).

Common
Information: In a question, information concerning one or both of the quantities to be compared is centered above the two columns. A symbol that appears in both columns represents the same thing in Column A as it does in Column B.

Column A	Column B	Sample Answers
Example 1: 2×6	$2 + 6$	● Ⓑ Ⓒ Ⓓ Ⓔ

Examples 2-4 refer to $\triangle PQR$.

	Column A	Column B	Sample Answers
Example 2:	PN	NQ	Ⓐ Ⓑ Ⓒ ● Ⓔ
			(since equal measures cannot be assumed, even though PN and NQ appear equal)
Example 3:	x	y	Ⓐ ● Ⓒ Ⓓ Ⓔ
			(since N is between P and Q)
Example 4:	$w + z$	180	Ⓐ Ⓑ ● Ⓓ Ⓔ
			(since PQ is a straight line)

A if the quantity in Column A is greater;
B if the quantity in Column B is greater;
C if the two quantities are equal;
D if the relationship cannot be determined from the information given.

<u>Column A</u> <u>Column B</u> <u>Column A</u> <u>Column B</u>

$a \ne b$

1. $90 - b$ $90 - a$

2. $\sqrt{2}$ $\dfrac{4}{\sqrt{2}}$

$s = a - 4$
$t = a + 5$

3. $s + 4$ $t - 5$

Perimeter of square $ABCD = z$

4. $x^2 + y^2$ $\dfrac{z^2}{16}$

5. Circle with area Circle with diameter
25π 10

$AB \perp CD$

6. x y

$0 < x < 99$
x is divisible by 2, 5, 8

7. x 40

In parallelogram $ABCD$, $y = 50$

8. $x + y$ 90

In triangle ABC, the measure of angle A is greater than the measure of angle B, and angle C has a measure of $60°$.

9. Length of side AC Length of side AB

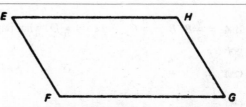

In parallelogram $EFGH$, $EF + EH = 20$

10. $HG + FG$ $\dfrac{1}{2}$ perimeter of $EFGH$

The arithmetic mean (average) of 4, 5, 6, 7, 8, and x is 6.

$x > 0$

11. x 6

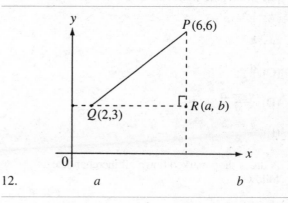

12. a b

$x + y = 9$

13. $2x$ $18 - 2y$

AB, BC, CD are equal lengths of l.

14. The length of $AB + BC$ The length of $AD -$
on line l CD on line l

$a + b = 5$
$a - 3 = 2$

15. a b

Directions: Each of the Questions 16–30 has five answer choices. For each of these questions, select the best of the answer choices given.

16. The wheel of a bicycle is 28 inches in diameter. How many feet will the bicycle cover in 9 turns of the wheel? (Use $\pi = \dfrac{22}{7}$.)

   (A) 66
   (B) 252
   (C) 396
   (D) 462
   (E) 792

17. If $A = \dfrac{2}{3} B$, $B = \dfrac{2}{3} C$, and $C = \dfrac{2}{3} D$, what part of D is B?

   (A) $\dfrac{8}{27}$

   (B) $\dfrac{4}{9}$

   (C) $\dfrac{2}{3}$

   (D) 75%

   (E) $\dfrac{4}{3}$

18. The gasoline tank of an automobile can hold g gallons. If a gallons were removed when the tank was full, what part of the full tank was removed?

   (A) $g - a$

   (B) $\dfrac{g}{a}$

   (C) $\dfrac{a}{g}$

   (D) $\dfrac{g - a}{a}$

   (E) $\dfrac{g - a}{g}$

19. A dress shop marked down all merchandise as follows:

GROUP	REGULAR PRICE	SALE PRICE
A	$60	$50
B	$65	$55
C	$70	$60
D	$75	$65
E	$80	$70

   Which group of merchandise was offered at the greatest rate of discount from its original price?

   (A) A
   (B) B
   (C) C
   (D) D
   (E) E

20. During one year, the highest temperature recorded in a certain city was 22°C, and the lowest temperature recorded was −41°C. What is the absolute value of the difference between the highest and lowest temperature?

   (A) −63
   (B) −19
   (C) 19
   (D) 41
   (E) 63

Questions 21–25 are based on the following table.

HOW YEARLY PERIODIC INVESTMENTS OF EQUAL AMOUNTS GROW TO $1,000

Amount Invested (dollars) at an Interest Rate of:

Year	5%	6%	7%	8%	9%	10%	11%	12%	13%	14%
1	952.38	943.40	934.58	925.93	917.43	909.09	900.90	892.86	884.96	887.19
2	464.58	457.96	451.49	445.16	438.96	432.90	426.97	421.16	415.47	409.90
3	302.10	296.33	290.70	285.22	279.87	274.65	269.56	264.80	259.75	255.03
4	220.96	215.65	210.49	205.48	200.61	195.88	191.29	186.82	182.47	178.25
5	172.36	167.36	162.51	157.83	153.30	148.91	144.66	140.54	136.56	132.70
6	140.02	135.25	130.65	126.22	121.94	117.82	113.85	110.02	106.33	102.77
7	116.97	112.39	107.99	103.77	99.72	95.82	92.09	88.50	85.05	81.75
8	99.74	95.32	91.09	87.05	83.19	79.49	75.96	72.59	69.37	66.29
9	86.37	82.10	78.02	74.15	70.46	66.95	63.61	60.43	57.41	54.53
10	75.72	71.57	67.64	63.92	60.39	57.04	53.88	50.88	48.04	45.36
11	67.04	63.01	59.21	55.63	52.24	49.06	46.05	43.23	40.57	38.07
12	59.83	55.92	52.24	48.79	45.55	42.51	39.66	37.00	34.50	32.17
13	53.77	49.96	46.40	43.08	39.97	37.07	34.37	31.85	29.51	27.34
14	48.59	44.89	41.44	38.24	35.26	32.50	29.94	27.56	25.37	23.34
15	44.14	40.53	37.19	34.10	31.25	28.61	26.18	23.95	21.90	20.01
16	40.26	36.75	33.51	30.53	27.80	25.29	22.99	20.88	18.96	17.21
17	36.86	33.44	30.30	27.43	24.81	22.42	20.24	18.26	16.47	14.84
18	33.85	30.53	27.49	24.72	22.21	19.94	17.88	16.02	14.34	12.83
19	31.19	27.94	25.00	22.34	19.94	17.77	15.82	14.07	12.51	11.11
20	28.80	25.65	22.80	20.23	17.93	15.87	14.03	12.39	10.93	9.64

21. To have periodic investments grow to $1,000 in 7 years, how much more will need to be invested annually at the 7% rate than at the 8% rate?

   (A) $4.05
   (B) $4.09
   (C) $4.20
   (D) $4.22
   (E) $5.00

22. How many years will it take for annual investments of $25.65, invested at 6%, to grow to $1,000?

   (A) 12
   (B) 14
   (C) 16
   (D) 18
   (E) 20

23. At a rate of 14%, how much more is the annual investment for a 10-year period than for a 14-year period?

   (A) $22.
   (B) $23.
   (C) $23.34
   (D) $45.
   (E) $45.36

24. What is the total amount that must be invested at 9% over a period of 4 years to have $1,000 at the end of this period?

   (A) $200
   (B) $352
   (C) $400
   (D) $502
   (E) $802

25. For how many years and at which rate should periodic payments of less than $20 a year be invested in order to grow to $1,000?

   (A) 18 years at 8%
   (B) 18 years at 9%
   (C) 18 years at 10%
   (D) 20 years at 7%
   (E) 20 years at 8%

26. If the perimeter of a square is 16, the area of the square is

   (A)   4
   (B)   8
   (C) 16
   (D) 64
   (E) 256

27. A picture 16 inches × 24 inches has a frame 1 inch wide. About how many times greater than the area of the frame is the area of the picture?

   (A)   1.2
   (B)   4.5
   (C) 12
   (D) 45
   (E) 80

28. $AB = AC$, $DB = DC$, $\angle ABC = \frac{1}{2}\angle DBC$, and $m\angle D = 70$. How many degrees are there in $\angle A$?

   (A)   55
   (B)   70
   (C) 105
   (D) 110
   (E) 125

29. A graduating class of 356 votes to choose a president. With 5 candidates seeking office, what is the least number of votes a successful candidate could receive and yet have more votes than any other candidate?

   (A)   71
   (B)   72
   (C)   89
   (D) 178
   (E) 179

30. In a group of 15, 7 can speak Spanish, 8 can speak French, and 3 can speak neither. What fraction of the group can speak both French and Spanish?

   (A) $\frac{1}{5}$

   (B) $\frac{4}{15}$

   (C) $\frac{1}{3}$

   (D) $\frac{7}{15}$

   (E) $\frac{2}{3}$

S T O P

IF YOU FINISH BEFORE TIME HAS ELAPSED, CHECK YOUR WORK ON THIS SECTION OF THE TEST ONLY. DO NOT GO ON TO THE NEXT SECTION OF THE TEST UNTIL TIME IS UP FOR THIS SECTION.

SECTION 5

Time—30 Minutes

25 Questions

Directions: Each question or group of questions is based on a passage or set of conditions. In answering some of the questions, it may be useful to draw a rough diagram. For each question, select the best answer choice given.

Questions 1–4

John is undecided which of four popular novels to buy. He is considering a spy thriller, a murder mystery, a Gothic romance, and a science fiction novel. The books are written by Rothko, Gorky, Burchfield, and Hopper, not necessarily in that order, and published by Heron, Pigeon, Bluejay, and Sparrow, not necessarily in that order.

(1) The book by Rothko is published by Sparrow.
(2) The spy thriller is published by Heron.
(3) The science fiction novel is by Burchfield and is not published by Bluejay.
(4) The Gothic romance is by Hopper.

1. Pigeon publishes

    (A) the murder mystery
    (B) the science fiction novel
    (C) the spy thriller
    (D) the Gothic romance
    (E) the novel by Rothko

2. The novel by Gorky is

    (A) a science fiction novel published by Bluejay
    (B) a Gothic romance published by Bluejay
    (C) published by Heron and is a murder mystery
    (D) published by Pigeon and is a Gothic romance
    (E) published by Heron and is a spy thriller

3. John purchases books by the two authors whose names come first and third in alphabetical order. He does not buy

    (A) the murder mystery
    (B) the book published by Pigeon
    (C) the science fiction novel
    (D) the book published by Bluejay
    (E) the Gothic romance

4. On the basis of the first paragraph and statements (2), (3), and (4) only, it is possible to deduce that

    I.   Rothko wrote the murder mystery or the spy thriller
    II.   Sparrow published the murder mystery or the spy thriller
    III. the book by Burchfield is published by Sparrow or Pigeon

    (A) I only
    (B) II only
    (C) III only
    (D) I and III only
    (E) I, II, and II

Questions 5–7

When a farmer cultivates his land with an investment of $x for machinery, fertilizer, and labor, his average yield per dollar of investment is 10 bushels of potatoes. The next year he doubles his investment of labor and capital on the same land and he finds that his yield per dollar of investment is 15 bushels of potatoes. The next year he doubles that investment and his yield per dollar of investment is 12 bushels of potatoes.

5. The increase in yield per dollar of investment during the second year was most probably due to

    (A) better, more expensive equipment
    (B) more efficient use of all available soil
    (C) greater incentive to farm workers
    (D) better supervision of larger labor force
    (E) greater efficiency because of higher salaries

6. What accounts for the decrease in yield per dollar during the third year?

    (A) Bad weather reduces profits regardless of efficiency.
    (B) Poor irrigation with crowded crops reduces the size of a crop.
    (C) The limit of efficiency per unit of land was reached.
    (D) Increased costs of production decreased proportionate yield.
    (E) Inflation was a factor.

7. The situation in this passage illustrates the fact that

    (A) farmers must receive federal subsidies
    (B) increasing capital investment results in lower cost of production per unit of product
    (C) there is a point in investment when a greater total yield results, but the increased yield is less than proportionate
    (D) many factors influence profitable farming
    (E) there is a limit to profit in agriculture

Questions 8–12

On Sunday, December 23, four ships were berthed at the New York City Municipal Pier at West 55 Street. All four ships were beginning their series of winter cruises to various ports in the Atlantic and the Caribbean.

Ship W left at 4 P.M. on Sunday, December 23, for a series of 8-day cruises to Bermuda and Nassau.
Ship X left at 4:30 P.M. on Sunday, December 23, for a series of alternating 11- and 13-day cruises.
Ship Y sailed at 5 P.M. on Sunday, December 23, for a series of 5-day cruises to Bermuda.
Ship Z sailed on Monday, December 24, for a series of 7-day cruises to Nassau.

Each cruise officially begins on the day after departure. Each ship is scheduled to return to New York City early in the morning after the last day of the cruise, and leave again late in the afternoon of the same day.

8. On December 31, which ships will be sailing from New York on a New Year's Eve cruise?

   (A) *W* and *X*
   (B) *X* and *Y*
   (C) *W* and *Z*
   (D) *X* and *Z*
   (E) *X, Y,* and *Z*

9. On how many sailing dates between Dec. 24 and Feb. 28 will ship *W* be moored alongside another ship?

   (A) 0
   (B) 2
   (C) 4
   (D) 5
   (E) 6

10. On how many occasions between Dec. 24 and Feb. 28 will three ships be moored at the pier?

   (A) 0
   (B) 1
   (C) 2
   (D) 3
   (E) 4

11. On which day of the week will these four ships make most of their departures?

   (A) Sunday
   (B) Monday
   (C) Tuesday
   (D) Thursday
   (E) Saturday

12. On which days of the week in the period between Dec. 24 and Feb. 28 will the pier be least crowded?

   (A) Tuesday and Friday
   (B) Tuesday and Thurdsay
   (C) Friday and Saturday
   (D) Wednesday and Thursday
   (E) Thursday and Saturday

Questions 13–16

Observance of Memorial Day, which falls on a Saturday this year, will be as follows for the tristate area (New Albion, New Shetland, New Wales):
   Banks and government departments which are normally open on Saturdays will close.
   Those normally closed Saturdays will close as follows:
   Banks will close Friday in New Wales and Monday in New Shetland.
   State government offices will close Friday in New Albion and New Shetland.

Sanitation pick-up in Monday-Wednesday-Friday pickup areas will be cancelled Friday in New Albion and New Shetland, and Monday in New Wales; pickup in Tuesday-Thursday-Saturday areas will be cancelled Saturday in all three states.
   The post office and other federal offices, normally open Monday through Saturday, will be closed Saturday but open Friday and Monday in all three states.
   (Banks are normally open on Saturday only in New Albion; state government offices are normally open Saturday only in Wales.)

13. Which is not available Friday, Saturday, or Monday in New Wales?

   (A) Banking services
   (B) State government office services
   (C) Sanitation pickup in some areas
   (D) Postal services
   (E) Federal government office services

14. Mrs. Semkow goes to the post office, the bank, and the state income tax bureau on Monday. She may live in

   I.   New Albion
   II. New Shetland
   III. New Wales

   (A) I only
   (B) II only
   (C) I or III only
   (D) II or III only
   (E) I, II, or III

15. Mr. Rudolph finds all but one of the listed services available Friday. He lives in

   (A) New Shetland or New Albion
   (B) a Monday-Wednesday-Friday pickup area in New Wales
   (C) any area in New Albion or New Wales
   (D) a Tuesday-Thursday-Saturday pickup area in any of the three states
   (E) a Monday-Wednesday-Friday area in New Albion

16. In which area(s) is there no deviation from normal service on Monday for any of the services listed?

   (A) All of New Albion
   (B) Monday-Wednesday-Friday pickup areas in New Albion and New Wales
   (C) Tuesday-Thursday-Saturday pickup areas in New Shetland and New Wales
   (D) All of New Wales
   (E) Mondays-Wednesday-Friday areas in New Shetland

Questions 17–22

(1) An Airedale, a boxer, a collie, and a Doberman win the top four prizes in the Kennel Show. Their owners are Mr. Edwards, Mr. Foster, Mr. Grossman, and Ms. Huntley, not necessarily in that order. Their dogs' names are Jack, Kelly, Lad, and Max, not necessarily in that order.
(2) Mr. Grossman's dog wins neither first nor second prize.
(3) The collie wins first prize.
(4) Max wins second prize.
(5) The Airedale is Jack.
(6) Mr. Foster's dog, the Doberman, wins fourth prize.
(7) Ms. Huntley's dog is Kelly.

17. First prize is won by

    (A) Mr. Edwards's dog
    (B) Ms. Huntley's dog
    (C) Max
    (D) Jack
    (E) Lad

18. Mr. Grossman's dog

    (A) is the collie
    (B) is the boxer
    (C) is the Airedale
    (D) wins second prize
    (E) is Kelly

19. In which of the following statements are the dogs correctly listed in descending order of their prizes?

    I.   Kelly; the Airedale; Mr. Edward's dog
    II. The boxer; Mr. Grossman's dog; Jack
    III. Mr. Edward's dog; the Airedale; Lad

    (A) I only
    (B) II only
    (C) III only
    (D) I and III only
    (E) II and III only

20. Lad

    (A) is owned by Mr. Foster
    (B) is owned by Mr. Edwards
    (C) is the boxer
    (D) is the collie
    (E) wins third prize

21. On the basis of statements (1), (3), (4), (5), and (6) only, which of the following may be deduced?

    I.   Max is the boxer.
    II. The Doberman is Kelly or Lad.
    III. Jack wins third prize.

    (A) I and II only
    (B) I and III only
    (C) II and III only
    (D) I, II, and III
    (E) Neither I, II, nor III

22. On the basis of statements (1), (2), (3), (4), and (7) only, which of the following may be deduced?

    I.   Mr. Grossman's dog is Jack or Lad.
    II. Mr. Edward's dog wins first or second prize.
    III. Kelly is the collie.

    (A) I only
    (B) II only
    (C) I and II only
    (D) II and III only
    (E) I, II, and III

Questions 23 and 24

(1) All students who major in philosophy wear Clavert Kreem jeans.
(2) None of the students in the Marching and Chowder Society wears Calvert Kreem jeans or majors in history.
(3) If Jack majors in philosophy, Mary majors in history.

23. If the statements above are all true, which of the following must also be true?

    (A) If Jack majors in philosophy, Mary does not wear Calvert Kreem jeans.
    (B) None of the students in the Marching and Chowder Society majors in philosophy.
    (C) If Jack wears Clavert Kreem jeans, he majors in philosophy.
    (D) If Mary majors in history, Jack is not in the Marching and Chowder Society.
    (E) Either Jack or Mary wears Calvert Kreem jeans.

24. The conclusion "Jack does not major in philosophy" could be validly drawn from the statements above if it were established that

    I.   Mary does not major in history
    II. Jack does not belong to the Marching and Chowder Society
    III. Jack does not wear Calvert Kreem jeans

    (A) I only
    (B) II only
    (C) III only
    (D) I and III only
    (E) II and III only

25. Spokesman for a chemical company to residents of a
nearby town: We have conducted tests and have
found no evidence that the fumes leaking from our
waste disposal site are harmful to humans. There is
no reason to be alarmed, much less to begin evacuat-
ing people from their homes.

Which of the following would be the least relevant
question for the head of the residents' committee to
direct to the chemical company spokesman?

(A) What steps are being taken to correct the
        situation?
(B) Are further tests being conducted?
(C) How much will it cost you to stop the leaks?
(D) Do the fumes have an adverse effect on plants
        or animals?
(E) What are the possible long-term effects of expo-
        sure to the fumes?

S T O P

IF YOU FINISH BEFORE TIME IS CALLED, YOU MAY CHECK YOUR WORK ON THIS SECTION ONLY.
DO NOT WORK ON ANY OTHER SECTION IN THE TEST.

SECTION 6

Time—30 minutes

25 Questions

Directions: Each question or group of questions is based on a passage or set of conditions. In answering some of the questions, it may be useful to draw a rough diagram. For each question, select the best answer choice given.

Questions 1–4

(1) All G's are H's.
(2) All G's are J's or K's.
(3) All J's and K's are G's.
(4) All L's are K's.
(5) All N's are M's.
(6) No M's are G's.

1. Which of the following can be logically deduced from the conditions stated?

   (A) No M's are H's.
   (B) No M's that are not N's are H's.
   (C) No H's are M's.
   (D) Some M's are H's.
   (E) No N's are G's.

2. Which of the following is inconsistent with one or more of the conditions?

   (A) All H's are G's.
   (B) All H's that are not G's are M's.
   (C) Some H's are both M's and G's.
   (D) No M's are H's.
   (E) All M's are H's.

3. The statement "No L's are J's" is

   I.   logically deducible from the conditions stated
   II. consistent with but not deducible from the conditions stated
   III. deducible from the stated conditions together with the additional statement "No J's are K's"

   (A) I only
   (B) II only
   (C) III only
   (D) II and III only
   (E) Neither I, II, nor III

4. If no P's are K's, which of the following must be true?

   (A) All P's are J's.
   (B) No P is a G.
   (C) No P is an H.
   (D) If any P is an H it is a G.
   (E) If any P is a G it is a J.

Questions 5 and 6

Ellen to Ralph: I'm not going to play with your cat because I'll be sneezing all afternoon if I do. I've played with your cat three times, and each time I've sneezed all afternoon.

5. The argument above is most like which of the following arguments?

   (A) Empiricism must have developed later than rationalism, because it developed as a reaction to rationalism.
   (B) Drug X increases fertility in humans. Every woman given the drug in tests gave birth to more than one child.
   (C) The dumping of chemicals into the lake two months ago caused the present dying off of the fish. No fish died in the lakes into which no chemicals were dumped.
   (D) The committee's report must have been valid, because it predicted that a crisis would develop, and that is exactly what has happened.
   (E) Joe's fiancee must be allergic to roses. Every time he takes her roses, she becomes weepy.

6. Ellen's argument would be most strengthened if it is also true that

   (A) Ralph also sneezes after playing with his cat
   (B) Ellen never sneezes just before playing with Ralph's cat
   (C) Ellen also sneezes after playing with Dan's dog
   (D) Ellen sneezes only after playing with Ralph's cat
   (E) Ralph's cat also sneezes after playing with Ellen

7. But the number of flights has increased by 30% in the last ten years.

   The statement above would be a logical rebuttal to which of the following claims?

   (A) The airlines must be losing money. The cost of jet fuel has tripled in the last ten years.
   (B) Airline ticket prices have increased so fast in the last ten years that some people who could once afford to fly no longer can.
   (C) Flying is getting more unsafe. The number of airplane accidents per year has increased by over 10% in the last decade.
   (D) More air travelers are taking "short hop," commuter flights. The average number of miles traveled per flight has decreased by 20% in the last ten years.
   (E) The flight industry is being taken over by a few large airlines. There are 25% fewer airlines today than there were ten years ago.

Questions 8–11

At a formal dinner for eight, the host and hostess are seated at opposite ends of a rectangular table, with three persons along each side. Each man must be seated next to at least one woman, and vice-versa.

Allan is opposite Diane, who is not the hostess.

George has a woman on his right and is opposite a woman.

Helga is at the hostess's right, next to Frank.

One person is seated between Belinda and Carol.

8. The eighth person present, Eric, must be

I.   the host
II. seated to Diane's right
III. seated opposite Carol

(A) I only
(B) III only
(C) I and II only
(D) II and III only
(E) I, II, and III

9. If each person is placed directly opposite his or her spouse, which of the following pairs must be married?

(A) George and Helga
(B) Belinda and Frank
(C) Carol and Frank
(D) George and Belinda
(E) Eric and Helga

10. Which person is not seated next to a person of the same sex?

(A) Allan
(B) Belinda
(C) Carol
(D) Diane
(E) Eric

11. George is bothered by the cigarette smoke of his neighbor and exchanges seats with the person four places to his left. Which of the following must be true following the exchange?

I.   No one is seated between two persons of the opposite sex.
II. One side of the table consists entirely of persons of the same sex.
III. Either the host or the hostess has changed seats.

(A) I only
(B) III only
(C) I and II only
(D) II and III only
(E) Neither I, II, not III

Questions 12–18

For a panel of professors to assess the State of the Union Message on public TV, the producer must choose two Republicans and two Democrats. At least one professor must be an economist and at least one a military expert. Available Republicans are Abbott, Bartlett, Catlett, Dorset, and Everett; available Democrats are Fawcett, Gantlet, Helfet, and Insett. Catlett, Fawcett, and Gantlet are economists, Dorset and Insett are military experts. Fawcett will not sit in the same room with Catlett, and will take part only if Abbott is on the panel. Dorset refuses to take part with Gantlet, and Everett refuses to take part with Insett.

12. Which of the following is not an acceptable panel?

(A) Fawcett, Helfet, Abbott, Dorset
(B) Fawcett, Insett, Abbott, Dorset
(C) Gantlet, Helfet, Abbott, Catlett
(D) Gantlet, Insett, Abbott, Catlett
(E) Helfet, Insett, Bartlett, Catlett

13. If Abbott and Bartlett are chosen as the Republicans, who can be chosen as the Democrats?

(A) Fawcett and Insett only
(B) Fawcett and Insett or Gantlet and Insett only
(C) Fawcett and Gantlet or Gantlet and Helfet only
(D) Fawcett and Insett, Gantlet and Insett, or Helfet and Insett
(E) Gantlet and Helfet, Gantlet and Insett, or Helfet and Insett

14. If Gantlett is chosen, which of the following must be true?

I.   Any acceptable panel must contain Insett.
II. Any acceptable panel must contain Abbott.
III. There is no acceptable panel which contains Bartlett.

(A) I only
(B) II only
(C) I and II only
(D) II and III only
(E) I, II, and III

15. How many acceptable panels can the producer put together?

(A) 6
(B) 7
(C) 8
(D) 9
(E) 10

16. Which of the following pairs cannot be part of an acceptable panel?

   I.   Fawcett and Gantlet
   II. Bartlett and Dorset
   III. Catlett and Dorset

   (A) I only
   (B) III only
   (C) I and II only
   (D) II and III only
   (E) I, II, and III

17. Which Republican belongs to the smallest number of different acceptable panels?

   (A) Abbott
   (B) Bartlett
   (C) Catlett
   (D) Dorset
   (E) Everett

18. Which professor belongs to the greatest number of different acceptable panels?

   (A) Abbott
   (B) Bartlett
   (C) Gantlet
   (D) Helfet
   (E) Insett

Questions 19–22

The Hotel Miramar has two wings, the East Wing and the West Wing. Some East Wing rooms, but not all, have an ocean view. All West Wing rooms have a harbor view. The charge for all rooms is identical, except as follows:
   There is an extra charge for all harbor view rooms on or above the third floor.
   There is an extra charge for all ocean view rooms, except those without balcony.
   Some harbor view rooms on the first two floors and some East Wing rooms without ocean view have kitchen facilities, for which there is an extra charge.
   Only the ocean view and harbor view rooms have balconies.

19. A guest may avoid an extra charge by requesting

   (A) a West Wing room on one of the first two floors
   (B) a West Wing room on the fourth floor without balcony
   (C) an East Wing room without an ocean view
   (D) an East Wing room without balcony
   (E) any room without kitchen facilities

20. Which of the following must be true if all the conditions are as stated?

   (A) All rooms above the third floor involve an extra charge.
   (B) No room without an ocean or harbor view or kitchen facilities involves an extra charge.
   (C) There is no extra charge for any East Wing room without an ocean view.
   (D) There is no extra charge for any room without kitchen facilities.
   (E) There is an extra charge for all rooms with an ocean or harbor view.

21. Which of the following must be false if all conditions are as stated?

   (A) Some ocean view rooms do not involve an extra charge.
   (B) All rooms with kitchen facilities involve an extra charge.
   (C) Some West Wing rooms above the second floor do not involve an extra charge.
   (D) Some harbor view rooms do not involve an extra charge.
   (E) Some rooms without a balcony or kitchen facilities involve an extra charge.

22. Which of the following cannot be determined on the basis of the information given?

   I.   Whether there are any rooms without a balcony for which an extra charge is imposed
   II. Whether any room without a kitchen or a view involves an extra charge
   III. Whether two extra charges are imposed for any room

   (A) I only
   (B) II only
   (C) I and III only
   (D) II and III only
   (E) I, II, and III

Question 23 and 24

The people do not run the country; neither do elected officials. The corporations run the country. Heads of corporations routinely and imperiously hand down decisions that profoundly affect millions of people. The people affected do not vote on the decisions, or for the corporate oligarchs. Yet we are supposed to believe we live in a democracy.

23. Which of the following statements, if true, would support the author's views?

    I.   Corporate lobbies strongly influence the introduction and passage of legislation at all levels of government.
    II. Growing numbers of the most talented college graduates are going to work for private corporations rather than for the government.
    III. Few legal requirements are imposed on corporations as to the responsibilities they must fulfill to their employees and their communities.

    (A) I only
    (B) II only
    (C) I and III only
    (D) II and III only
    (E) I, II, and III

24. Which of the following statements most closely parallels the reasoning of the argument above?

    (A) The Police Department just laid off ten patrolmen. Yet we are supposed to believe this is a safe neighborhood.
    (B) He has lied to us many times. Yet we are supposed to believe he is now telling the truth.
    (C) The quality of television programs continues to decline. Yet we are supposed to believe they are still worth watching.
    (D) He has no training or experience in this profession. Yet we are supposed to believe he is qualified for this job.
    (E) We are asked to do nothing but regurgitate facts. Yet we are supposed to believe we are getting an education.

25. Anthony is standing to the right of Beth. Caroline is standing on the opposite side of Beth. Since the opposite of right is wrong, Caroline must be standing on the wrong side of Beth.

    Which of the following logical errors has the author of the argument above committed?

    (A) He has used a single term to mean two different things.
    (B) He has confused cause and effect.
    (C) He has assumed to be true what he wants to prove to be true.
    (D) He has provided no factual evidence for his conclusion.
    (E) He has drawn a general conclusion from an insufficient number of examples.

S T O P

IF YOU FINISH BEFORE TIME IS CALLED, YOU MAY CHECK YOUR WORK ON THIS SECTION ONLY.
DO NOT WORK ON ANY OTHER SECTION IN THE TEST.

SECTION 7

Time—30 minutes

30 Questions

Numbers: All numbers used are real numbers.

Figures: Position of points, angles, regions, etc., can be assumed to be in the order shown; and angle measures can be assumed to be positive.

Lines shown as straight can be assumed to be straight.

Figures can be assumed to lie in a plane unless otherwise indicated.

Figures that accompany questions are intended to provide information useful in answering the questions. However, unless a note states that a figure is drawn to scale, you should solve these problems NOT by estimating sizes by sight or by measurement, but by using your knowledge of mathematics (see Example 2 below).

Directions: Each of the Questions 1-15 consists of two quantities, one in Column A and one in Column B. You are to compare the two quantities and choose

A if the quantity in Column A is greater;
B if the quantity in Column B is greater;
C if the two quantities are equal;
D if the relationship cannot be determined from the information given.

Note: Since there are only four choices, NEVER MARK (E).

Common
Information: In a question, information concerning one or both of the quantities to be compared is centered above the two columns. A symbol that appears in both columns represents the same thing in Column A as it does in Column B.

Column A	Column B	Sample Answers

Example 1: 2×6 $2 + 6$ ● Ⓑ Ⓒ Ⓓ Ⓔ

Examples 2-4 refer to $\triangle PQR$.

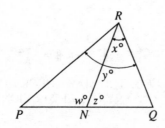

Example 2: PN NQ Ⓐ Ⓑ Ⓒ ● Ⓔ

(since equal measures cannot be assumed, even though PN and NQ appear equal)

Example 3: x y Ⓐ ● Ⓒ Ⓓ Ⓔ

(since N is between P and Q)

Example 4: $w + z$ 180   Ⓐ Ⓑ ● Ⓓ Ⓔ

(since PQ is a straight line)

A if the quantity in Column A is greater;
B if the quantity in Column B is greater;
C if the two quantities are equal;
D if the relationship cannot be determined from the information given.

Column A	Column B		Column A	Column B

Ratio of $2a$ to $5b$ is 3:4.

1. $\dfrac{a}{b}$ $\dfrac{15}{8}$

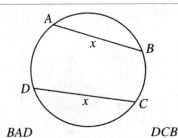

2. BAD DCB

x is positive
$x \neq 1$

3. x^2 $\sqrt{x}$

4. $\sqrt{\dfrac{1}{4}} + \sqrt{\dfrac{1}{25}}$ $\sqrt{\dfrac{1}{4} + \dfrac{1}{25}}$

$x = 3$ and $y = \dfrac{1}{6}$

5. $2x - 18y$ $3x - 36y$

6.   the average of $\sqrt{0.49}$,   75%
$\dfrac{3}{4}$, and 0.8

$B = 0$
$A > 1$
$C > 1$

7. $2B(A + C)$ $A(B + C)$

8. $\dfrac{n + a}{a}$ $\dfrac{n}{a} + 1$

$x + y = 17$
$y + 3 = 13$

9. x y

$x < 0$ and $y < 0$

10. $x + y$ $x - y$

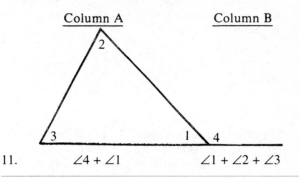

11. $\angle 4 + \angle 1$ $\angle 1 + \angle 2 + \angle 3$

12.   Perimeter RSP $13 + \sqrt{85}$

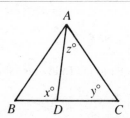

From D, any point on BC, AD is drawn

13. x y

14. $x + y$ $r + s$

Legs EC and EB of right $\triangle BEC$ are equal in length and $ABCD$ is a straight line.

15. x y

Directions: Each of the Questions 16–30 has five answer choices. For each of these questions, select the best of the answer choices given.

16. If a roast that requires 1 hour and 40 minutes of roasting time has been in the oven for 55 minutes, how many more minutes of roasting time are required?

(A) 15
(B) 20
(C) 30
(D) 45
(E) 50

17. City A is 200 miles west of City B and City C is 150 miles directly north of City B. What is the shortest distance (in miles) between City C and City A?

(A) $50\sqrt{7}$
(B) 175
(C) 250
(D) 300
(E) 350

18. A square carpet with an area of 169 square feet must have 2 feet cut off one of its edges in order to be a perfect fit for a rectangular room. What is the area (in square feet) of this rectangular room?

(A) 117
(B) 121
(C) 143
(D) 165
(E) 167

19. A lamp is manufactured to sell for $35.00, which yields a profit of 25% of cost. If the profit is to be reduced to 15% of cost, the new retail price will be

(A) $21.00
(B) $28.00
(C) $31.50
(D) $32.20
(E) $43.00

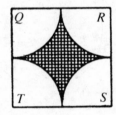

20. In the square $QRST$ above, $QR = 4$. Find the shaded area if Q, R, S, and T are the centers of the arcs that constitute the figure.

(A) 16
(B) 4π
(C) $16 - 4\pi$
(D) $16 - 2\pi$
(E) $16 - 16\pi$

Questions 21–25 refer to the following table and graph.

HOW THE BROWNS SPENT THEIR MONEY LAST YEAR

Item	Amount Expended
Housing (mortgage, taxes, insurance, utilities)	$13,750
Clothing	1,300
Medical insurance	1,500
Medical costs	2,600
Student loan repayments	4,200
Household furniture and appliances	1,700
Contributions (charitable, political)	750
Entertainment	2,200
Food	4,000
Transportation	3,000
Total expenditures	**$35,000**

HOW THE AVERAGE AMERICAN SPENDS MONEY

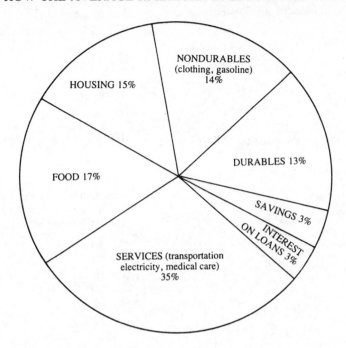

21. For a family with an annual income of $30,000, how much would be put into savings according to the figures for the average American?

   (A) $ 90
   (B) $ 300
   (C) $ 900
   (D) $3000
   (E) $9000

22. How much, out of every dollar spent, does the average American spend for housing?

   (A) 5¢

   (B) $7\frac{1}{2}$¢

   (C) 10¢

   (D) $12\frac{1}{2}$¢

   (E) 15¢

23. How does the expenditure for food by the Browns compare with the way the average American spends for food?

   (A) The Browns spend 5.6% less.
   (B) The Browns spend 5.6% more.
   (C) The Browns spend 9% less.
   (D) The Browns spend 13% less.
   (E) The Browns spend 13% more.

24. What part of the Browns' expenditures is spent for medical care and medical insurance?

   (A) $\dfrac{15}{350}$

   (B) $\dfrac{41}{350}$

   (C) $\dfrac{26}{350}$

   (D) $\dfrac{35}{100}$

   (E) $\dfrac{41}{100}$

25. Which of the following can be inferred from the graph?
   I.   Out of every dollar spent, the average American spends 2¢ less for food than for housing.
   II. The average American spends more for medical care, transportation, and electricity than for food and housing.
   III. The average American saves $3.00 of every $100 earned.
   (A) I only   (B) II only   (C) III only
   (D) I and III   (E) II and III

26. When 6 gallons of gasoline are put into a car, the indicator goes from $\frac{1}{4}$ to $\frac{5}{8}$. The total capacity of the gasoline tank (in gallons) is

   (A) 12
   (B) 14
   (C) 15
   (D) 16
   (E) 30

27. A pile of steel plates is 2.75 feet high. If each plate is 0.375 inch thick, the number of steel plates in this pile is

   (A) 7
   (B) 8
   (C) 14
   (D) 88
   (E) more than 88

28. At c cents per orange, what is the price (in dollars) for 1 dozen oranges?

   (A) $12c$

   (B) $\dfrac{c}{12}$

   (C) $\dfrac{12}{100c}$

   (D) $\dfrac{c}{100}$

   (E) $\dfrac{12c}{100}$

29. A pipe can fill a swimming pool in h hours. What part of the pool is filled in x hours?

   (A) hx

   (B) $\dfrac{h}{x}$

   (C) $\dfrac{x}{h}$

   (D) $h + x$

   (E) $\dfrac{hx}{2}$

30. How many cubic centimeters of water must be added to 100 cc of 80% solution of boric acid to reduce it to a 50% solution?

   (A) 30
   (B) 40
   (C) 50
   (D) 60
   (E) 84

S T O P

IF YOU FINISH BEFORE TIME HAS ELAPSED, CHECK YOUR WORK ON THIS SECTION OF THE TEST ONLY. DO NOT GO ON TO THE NEXT SECTION OF THE TEST UNTIL TIME IS UP FOR THIS SECTION.

Answer Key

Note: The answers to the quantitative sections are keyed to the corresponding review areas in the Mathematics Review (Chapter 11). The numbers in parentheses after each answer refer to the math topic(s) covered by that particular question.

Section 1 Verbal

1.	B	11.	E	21.	C	31.	D
2.	E	12.	C	22.	C	32.	B
3.	B	13.	E	23.	B	33.	A
4.	D	14.	E	24.	A	34.	B
5.	A	15.	B	25.	B	35.	B
6.	C	16.	C	26.	C	36.	A
7.	C	17.	D	27.	D	37.	D
8.	C	18.	D	28.	C	38.	D
9.	A	19.	E	29.	E		
10.	C	20.	A	30.	C		

Section 2 Verbal

1.	D	11.	D	21.	E	31.	D
2.	C	12.	A	22.	D	32.	B
3.	B	13.	C	23.	C	33.	E
4.	B	14.	B	24.	E	34.	B
5.	C	15.	D	25.	C	35.	E
6.	A	16.	B	26.	B	36.	E
7.	E	17.	D	27.	B	37.	C
8.	C	18.	E	28.	A	38.	E
9.	A	19.	E	29.	D		
10.	C	20.	C	30.	E		

Section 3 Quantitative

1.	A (III-A)	9.	C (III-A)	17.	C (I-B)	25.	A (IV-C, II-E)
2.	A (I-D)	10.	B (II-B)	18.	B (II-G)	26.	A (III-G)
3.	A (I-H)	11.	A (III-C, G)	19.	C (II-B)	27.	D (II-B)
4.	C (III-A)	12.	B (II-B-5)	20.	A (I-A)	28.	D (III-D)
5.	A (III-G)	13.	B (III-G)	21.	A (IV-C)	29.	A (III-G)
6.	D (II-G)	14.	B (III-C)	22.	E (IV-C)	30.	D (II-B)
7.	C (I-B, II-A)	15.	C (III-F)	23.	E (IV-C)		
8.	D (III-B)	16.	D (I-F)	24.	D (IV-C)		

Section 4 Quantitative

1.	D (III-A)	9.	B (III-D)	17.	B (I-B)	25.	C (IV-A)
2.	B (I-H)	10.	C (III-C)	18.	C (II-C)	26.	C (IV-C)
3.	C (II-A)	11.	C (I-G)	19.	A (I-D)	27.	B (III-G)
4.	C (III-G)	12.	A (III-H)	20.	E (I-F)	28.	E (III-D)
5.	C (III-G)	13.	C (II-A)	21.	D (IV-A, II-E)	29.	B (II-D)
6.	B (III-A)	14.	C (III-B)	22.	E (IV-A)	30.	A (II-D)
7.	D (II-G)	15.	A (III-B)	23.	A (IV-A)		
8.	C (III-C)	16.	A (III-G)	24.	E (II-E, IV-A)		

Section 5   Analytical

1.	B	8.	C	15.	B	22.	C
2.	E	9.	D	16.	A	23.	B
3.	A	10.	A	17.	B	24.	D
4.	D	11.	B	18.	C	25.	C
5.	B	12.	A	19.	C		
6.	C	13.	C	20.	A		
7.	C	14.	C	21.	D		

Section 6   Analytical

1.	E	8.	C	15.	D	22.	A
2.	C	9.	A	16.	C	23.	C
3.	D	10.	D	17.	E	24.	E
4.	E	11.	A	18.	E	25.	A
5.	B	12.	C	19.	D		
6.	D	13.	B	20.	B		
7.	C	14.	A	21.	C		

Section 7   Quantitative

1.	C (II-E)	9.	B (I-H)	17.	C (III-D)	25.	E (I-D, IV)
2.	D (III-F)	10.	B (II-B)	18.	C (III-G)	26.	D (I-B)
3.	D (I-H)	11.	C (III-D)	19.	D (I-D)	27.	D (I-C)
4.	A (I-H)	12.	C (III-H)	20.	C (III-G)	28.	E (II-E)
5.	C (II-A)	13.	A (III-D)	21.	C (IV)	29.	C (II-C)
6.	C (I-B, I-C, I-G, I-H)	14.	A (III-D)	22.	E (IV)	30.	D (II-C)
7.	B (II-A)	15.	C (III-A)	23.	A (I-D, IV)		
8.	C (II-A)	16.	D (II-E)	24.	B (I-B, IV)		

Answer Explanations

Section 1

1. **B.** The columnist was *acerbic* (bitingly sarcastic) in writing of those who provoked or *irritated* him.
Note the use of *but* to establish the contrast between the two clauses, and the use of *even* to indicate that the missing word is stronger than *bitter*.

2. **E.** By using diplomacy and flattery, the promoters hope to *inveigle* (beguile; cajole) the *obviously* unwilling performer. *Inveigle* has overtones of persuading someone against his or her better judgment.
Choices B and C are clearly incorrect. The use of tact and flattery would not *intimidate* (frighten) or *shame* someone into taking an action. Similarly, Choices A and D are incorrect, since the use of tact and flattery would not necessarily lure the person into a hopeless or compromising position (*entrapment*) or tease and torment that person into giving in (*tantalization*).

3. **B.** In reputation he was a *guileless* or undeceitful person; in real life he showed himself to have been *hypocritical* or deceptive.
Note the use of *although* to signal the contrast.

4. **D.** Orlando shuns criticism, preferring *obscurity* or inconspicuousness. His reaction is so strong that even *anonymity* (obscurity carried to an extreme) would be preferable to further critical exposure.
Note how the intensifier *even* indicates that Orlando's desire is being taken to an extreme.

5. **A.** The off-Broadway and Broadway theaters are contrasted here. The former has *manifested* or shown a talent for improvisation, extemporaneous or spontaneous performance. The latter has manifested no such talent for *spontaneity*.
Note the use of *whereas* to establish the contrast.

6. C.   Particles have no need to be wound up because the property of spinning (*rotation*) is built into their makeup: it is *intrinsic*.

7. C.   That the interrogator is subtle in discrimination or judgment indicates her ability to conduct matters with *finesse*; that she is *expeditious* (efficient and prompt) in manner indicates her ability to conduct matters with "dispatch" (speed).

8. C.   A *ream* is a unit of quantity for *paper*; a *cord* is a unit of quantity for *wood*.

        (Defining Characteristic)

9. A.   To *smart* is to feel *pain*; to *grieve* is to feel *sorrow*. Note that in this instance *smart* is a verb, not an adjective. Remember, you can always tell what parts of speech the capitalized words are by identifying the parts of speech in the answer choices.

        (Action and Significance)

10. C. A new growth of *bamboo* is a *shoot*; a new growth of a *bean* plant is a *sprout*.

        (Defining Characteristic)

11. E. By definition, a *missile* is *deflected* when it turns aside from its original direction. Likewise, someone's *attention* is *distracted* when it turns aside from its original direction.

        (Definition)

12. C. By definition, an excess of once-pleasing flavors *cloys* or sates the *palate* (seat of the sense of taste). An excess of once-tempting foodstuffs *surfeits* or sates the *appetite*.

        (Definition)

13. E. A *pratfall* is a humiliating mishap that causes you to feel *embarrassment*. A *windfall* is an unexpected piece of good fortune that causes you to feel *jubilation*.

        (Cause and Effect)

14. E. Someone *mulish* (stubborn) is not characterized by *pliancy* (readiness to yield). Someone *shrewish* (ill-tempered) is not characterized by *amiability*.

        (Antonym Variant)

15. B. By definition, a *minatory* statement menaces or *threatens*. A *laudatory* statement *praises* or commends.

        (Definition)

16. C. When *clouds scud*, they move swiftly, as if driven.
        When *water races*, it moves swiftly as well.

        (Definition)

17. D. Houston believed that the battle had to begin at the graduate level "to mitigate fear" (relieve *apprehension*) of race-mixing and miscegenation that might otherwise have caused the judges to rule against the NAACP-sponsored complaints.

18. D. Since the Regents responded to their defeat in *Sipuel* v. *Board of Regents of the University of Oklahoma* by separating black and white students in cafeterias and classrooms (thus subverting the effect of the decision), it seems likely that their reaction to the decision was one of *distinct displeasure*.

19. E. The 1950 McLaurin decision was one of the decisions which provided legal precedents for the 1954 Brown decision.
        Choice A is incorrect. *McLaurin* preceded *Brown I*. Therefore, it could not have superseded a decision that had yet to be made.
        Choice B is incorrect. *Brown I* followed *McLaurin*. Therefore, it could not have set a precedent for *McLaurin*.
        Choice C is incorrect. *Brown I* reversed *Plessy* v. *Ferguson*. It built on *Mclaurin*.
        Choice D is incorrect. *McLaurin* preceded *Brown I*. Therefore, it could not have limited the application of a decision that had yet to be made.

20. A. The author states plainly that the United States Supreme Court lacked the power to enforce its decisions and implies that without federal power (intervention by the executive) the desired social changes would not have taken place. Therefore, it seems probable that the author would view such a claim with *marked disagreement*.

21. C. The author states that *Brown II* limited the effectiveness of *Brown I* by allowing southern states a chance to delay desegregating. This suggests that, but for *Brown II*, *Brown I* might have had a more significant impact on segregation.

22. C. Taken as a whole, the passage deals with the entire struggle to desegregate American education, from the NAACP legal maneuvers of the 30's to the executive actions of the 50's and 60's. Only this title is broad enough to cover the passage as a whole.
Choice A is incorrect. The passage deals with the long legal maneuvers far more than it deals with executive intervention.
Choice B is incorrect. The passage deals with much more than *Brown* v. *Board of Education*.
Choices D and E are incorrect. They ignore the central subject of desegregation.

23. B. The separate-but-equal doctrine established by *Plessy* v. *Ferguson* allows the existence of racially segregated schools.

24. A. In assessing the possible effects on judges of race-mixing in the lower grades, Houston was *psychologically canny*, shrewd in seeing potential dangers and in figuring strategies to avoid these dangers.

25. B. The bulk of the passage records step by step what happens in the process of the formation of a star from a small region of interstellar gas. Thus, it *depicts the successive stages* of the process.

26. C. To the author the concept is both simple and traditional, dating as it does from Newton's time.

27. D. You can answer this question by the process of elimination.
Question I is answerable on the basis of the passage. As the region's density increases, its gravitational field increases in strength. Therefore, you can eliminate Choice B.
Question II is not answerable on the basis of the passage. The passage nowhere states what disturbs the gas. Therefore, you can eliminate Choices C and E.
Question III is answerable on the basis of the passage. The end result of the process is the formation of a gravitationally bound object. Therefore, you can eliminate Choice A.
Only Choice D is left. It is the correct answer.

28. C. The opposite of to *hamper* (impede or hinder) is to *facilitate* (make easy).
Think of "hampering progress."

29. E. The opposite of *urbane* (worldly; suave; sophisticated) is *naive* (unsophisticated).
Word Parts Clue: *Urb-* means city. *Urbane* means having the polish of a city-dweller.
Think of "an urbane suavity."

30. C. The opposite of *demise* (death) is *birth*.
Think of "lamenting someone's demise."

31. D. The opposite of a *pariah* or person rejected by society is an *idol* or person greatly loved by society.
Think of being "shunned as a pariah."

32. B. To *prostrate* someone is to overcome him, to weaken him. Its opposite is to *strengthen*.
Note that a quick glance at the answer choices reveals that you are dealing with *prostrate* the verb, not *prostrate* the adjective.
Think of being "prostrated by grief."

33. A. The opposite of *contentious* (quarrelsome, belligerent) is *amenable* (readily brought to yield, tractable).
Note that *contentious* derives from the verb to *contend* (to struggle or argue), not the adjective *content*.
Think of "a contentious argument."

34. B. The opposite of a *debacle* (downfall; failure; collapse) is a *success*.
Think of "the Wall Street debacle of 1987."

35. B. The opposite of *hapless* (unlucky) is *fortunate*.
Think of "hapless unfortunates."

36. A. The opposite of to *exacerbate* (to worsen or make more harsh) is to *alleviate* or lighten.
Think of "exacerbating a quarrel."

37. D. The opposite of *probity* (uprightness; integrity) is *depravity* (debasement; corruption).
Think of "unimpeachable probity."

38. D. The opposite of *baneful* (pernicious; ruinous; deadly) is *salubrious* (healthful; beneficial).
Think of "the baneful effects of slander."

Section 2

1. D. In contrast to what might have been expected, the candidate *welcomed* further interviews.
Note how the use of *even though* indicates a contrast between one idea and another, setting up a reversal of a thought.

2. C.   Soap operas and situation comedies are derivative of contemporary culture: they take their elements from that culture. Therefore, they serve as *indices* (signs or indications) of what is going on in that culture; they both point to and point up the social attitudes and values they portray.
Note that the soap operas and comedies here cannot be *determinants of* our society's attitudes and values: they derive from these attitudes and values; they do not determine them.

3. B.   The critics *charge* that Perry has published only *anecdotes* of his observations and not detailed analyses.
Note that *critics* would be unlikely to *applaud* the publication of *rumors* or *apologize* for Perry's publication of *fabrications* or lies. Thus, you can eliminate Choices C and E. Similarly, *popular magazines* would be unlikely to publish scientific *hypotheses* or examples of *scholarship*. You therefore can rule out Choices A and D as well.

4. B.   The scenes of suffering *belie* (contradict) the *reality* of the proclamations of wealth.

5. C.   Whatever word you choose here must apply equally well both to slander and to counterfeit money. People who would not make up a slanderous statement *circulate* slander by passing it on. So too people who would not coin or make counterfeit money *circulate* counterfeit money by passing it on.
Note how the extended metaphor here influences the writer's choice of words.

6. A.   A passionate nature hates compromise (finds it *odious*) because it seems a surrender. An intellectual nature hates compromise because it seems a *confusion*, mixing together things that to the intellect are inherently distinct.

7. E.   Milton's comment that he wrote prose with his left hand appears to belittle the writing of prose. We might *discount* or lessen the strength of this apparent criticism if we said Milton meant the remark ironically. However, we have not done so. Instead, we have used apparently negative comments like Milton's to *buttress* or support our own prejudices against prose.

8. C.   One *confines* a *prisoner* to keep him in prison. One *detains* a *suspect* to keep him in custody.

(Function)

9. A.   A *swatch* is a sample patch of *fabric*. A *chip* is a sample of *paint*.

(Function)

10. C.   A *tendril* is a slender extension reaching out from a *vine*. A *pseudopod* is a slender extension reaching out from an *amoeba*.

(Part to Whole)

11. D.   One *battens* or fastens a *hatch* (door leading down to a ship compartment) to close it. One *latches* a *door* to close it.

(Function)

12. A.   *Events* that are *contemporaneous* (occurring within the same time frame) exist in temporal reference to one another. *Objects* that are *adjacent* exist in spatial reference to one another.

(Defining Characteristic)

13. C.   A *limerick* is a kind of *poem*. A *catch* is a kind of *song*.
Note how simple the relationship of the original pair of words is. Questions toward the end of an analogy set seldom appear this easy. This should alert you to be on the lookout for something particularly deceptive among the answer choices. In this case, *catch* is used in an uncommon manner.

(Class and Member)

14. B.   A *retainer* or attendant is part of a *retinue* (body of attendants). A *witch* is part of a *coven* (group of witches)

(Group and Member)

15. D.   A *hero* is greeted with an *accolade* or laudatory notice. A *laughingstock* is greeted with *ridicule* or mockery.

(Defining Characteristic)

16. B.   A *rider* is an attachment added to a legislative *bill* to meet a particular purpose. An *endorsement* is an attachment added to an insurance *policy* to meet a particular purpose.
Note the use of secondary meanings of *rider*, *endorsement*, and *bill*.

(Defining Characteristic)

17. D.   The author cites Meredith's intelligence (*brilliance*) and his splendor of language (*linguistic grandeur*).

18. E.   Rather than refuting the claim, the author clearly acknowledges Meredith's inability to evoke the reader's sympathy.
Choice A is incorrect. From the start the author points out how Meredith leaves readers cold.
Choice B is incorrect. The author reiterates Meredith's virtues, citing muscular intelligence and literary merit.
Choice C is incorrect. The author quotes several such imagined criticisms.
Choice D is incorrect. The author indicates that if readers choose to avoid dealing with Meredith they will be doing a disservice to the cause of criticism.
Only Choice E remains. It is the correct answer.

19. E.   Speaking of the "challenge and excitement of the critical problem as such," the author clearly finds the prospect of appraising Meredith critically to be stirring and *invigorating*.

20. C.   The author wishes us to be able to recognize the good qualities of Meredith's work while at the same time we continue to find it personally unsympathetic. Thus, she would agree that criticism should enable us to appreciate the virtues of works we dislike.
Choices A, B, and E are unsupported by the passage.
Choice D is incorrect. While the author wishes the reader to be aware of Meredith's excellences, she does not suggest that the reader should ignore those qualities in Meredith that make his work unsympathetic. Rather, she wishes the reader to come to appreciate the very ambivalence of his critical response.

21. E.   You can answer this question by the process of elimination.
Question I is answerable on the basis of the passage. Because different alleles of a gene are not normally present within a single cell, DNA carrying an allele that originated in a different cell must be introduced into a bacterium via interbacterial transfer mechanisms in order for genetic variation to take place. Therefore, you can eliminate Choices B and D.
Question II is answerable on the basis of the passage. Cell death releases DNA into the environment; this free-floating DNA then makes its way into a new cell through the mechanism of transformation. Therefore, you can eliminate Choice A.
Question III is answerable on the basis of the passage. The illegitimate recombinational processes differ from homologous recombination in their ability to join together DNA segments that have little, if any, ancestral relationship. Therefore, you can eliminate Choice C.
Only Choice E is left. It is the correct answer.

22. D.   The passage serves as an introduction to the concept of illegitimate recombination in cells. To introduce this concept properly, the authors first must explain the other mechanisms which previously seemed to be "the only important mechanisms for generating biological diversity."
Choice A is incorrect. The passage introduces the concept of transposable genetic elements; it does not examine the evidence for their existence.
Choice B is incorrect. The passage indicates no such controversy.
Choice C is incorrect. It is far too vague.
Choice E is incorrect. It is unsupported by the passage.

23. C.   The so-called illegitimate recombinational processes are illegitimate because they do not follow the "legitimate" or accepted patterns for generating biological diversity. They *break the rules* of homologous recombination by joining together DNA segments that are not closely linked by ancestral relationship.

24. E.   The passage objectively explains the nature of a scientific phenomenon. Thus, it can best be described as *a dispassionate explication* (detailed description or exposition).
Choice A is incorrect. The main thrust of the passage is not to *refute* or disprove anything. In addition, its tone is far from *angry*.
Choice B is incorrect. The passage takes no sides; it is not *partisan*.
Choice C is incorrect. The passage does not vacillate; it is not *equivocal*. Neither does it support a position; it is not an *endorsement*.
Choice D is incorrect. The passage is expository and descriptive rather than *meditative*.

25. C.   In transformation, "free-floating" DNA enters a new cell by *penetrating* the cell wall and membrane. Thus, for transformation to occur, the cell wall and membrane must be *permeable*, capable of being penetrated.

26. B.   In transduction, the function of the virus is to "pick up fragments of the bacterial DNA" of one cell and "carry the DNA to other cells." This is analogous to the function of the *bee*, which picks up fragments of pollen from one flower and carries the pollen to other flowers in the process known as *pollination*.

27. B.   The passage opens with the statement that "genetic variation is *also* important in the evolution of lower organisms such as bacteria." From this one can reasonably infer that the authors have just been discussing the importance of genetic variation in the evolution of other sorts of organisms, specifically higher organisms.

28. A. To *condone* is to excuse. Its opposite is to *denounce*.
Think of "condoning a minor offense."

29. D. The opposite of *antithetical* (opposing) is *supportive*.
Think of "warring antithetical elements."

30. E. The opposite of *omniscience* (the quality of knowing everything) is *ignorance*.
Word Parts Clue: *Omni-* means all. *Sci-* means to know. *Omniscience* is the quality of knowing all.
Think of "divine omniscience."

31. D. The opposite of to *mollify* or soothe is to *provoke*.
Think of "mollifying hurt feelings."

32. B. The opposite of *gauche* (awkward; lacking in social grace or tact) is *tactful*.
Think of being embarrassed by "a gauche remark."

33. E. The opposite of a *diatribe* (abusive criticism) is *praise*.
Think of "a bitter diatribe."

34. B. The opposite of to *gainsay* or contradict is to *corroborate* or support.
Beware eye-catchers. To gainsay derives from to say *against*, not from to gain.
Think of "gainsaying an assertion."

35. E. The opposite of *prolixity* (wordiness) is *terseness* or brevity.
Think of "long-winded prolixity."

36. E. The opposite of *avid* (very eager) is *loath* (reluctant). Note that Choice E is the relatively uncommon adjective *loath*, not the verb to *loathe* or detest.
Think of "an avid reader."

37. C. To *repine* is to complain or express discontent. Its opposite is to *express satisfaction*.
Think of "repining the pains of old age."

38. E. The opposite of *salience* (prominence; notice-ableness; emphasis) is *inconspicuousness*.
Think of "striking salience."

Section 3

1. A. $a = d$ (vertical angles), and $c = f$.
$c = f = 50$. $a = d = c = f = 50$.
$b = 180 - 100 = 80$, $b = e = 80$.

2. A. The percent saved on one trip is the same as the percent saved on any number of trips.
Saving $= \dfrac{30¢}{150¢} = \dfrac{1}{5}$ or 20%.

3. A. $\sqrt{144} = 12$, and $\sqrt{145} = 12+$
$\sqrt{45} = 6+$
Sum$= 18+$

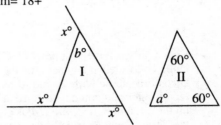

4. C. In triangle I, because the exterior angles have the same measure, each interior angle has the measure $\dfrac{1}{3}$ of 180° or 60°. In triangle II the measure of a is $180 - 120$ or 60°.

5. A. Area of $ABCD = (6)(6) = 36$
Area of $RST = 36$
Let $x = ST$.
$\left(\dfrac{1}{2}\right)(9)(x) = 36$
$9x = 72$
x (or ST) $= 8$

6. D. a could be equal to zero, or some positive fraction less than 1.
b could be some negative fraction more than -1.

7. C. $2x - \dfrac{y-5}{6} \div \dfrac{y-5}{3} - 4x$

$\dfrac{12x - y + 5}{6} \div \dfrac{y - 5 - 12x}{3}$

$\dfrac{12x - y + 5}{\cancel{6}_2} \cdot \dfrac{\cancel{3}^1}{y - 5 - 12x}$

$\dfrac{12x - y + 5}{2} \cdot \dfrac{1}{-12x + y - 5}$

$\dfrac{\cancel{12x - y + 5}}{2} \cdot \dfrac{-1}{\cancel{12x - y + 5}}$

or, $-\dfrac{1}{2}$ or -0.5

8. D.   Center City is located at point O. Circleville could be located at any point on the circumference of the circle with the radius of 23 kilometers. Centerville could be located at any point on the circumference with radius of 46 kilometers. The distance from Circleville and Centerville could be the straight line distance from any point on the circumference of one of these circles to the other circle. Obviously there are innumerable possibilities.

13. B.   Each side of square $BCDE = 10$
Area of $BCDE = 100$
Area of $ABC = 125 - 100$ or 25
Area of $ABC = \frac{1}{2}(BC)(AF) = 25$
$\frac{1}{2}(10)(AF) = 25$
$AF = 5$
$FG = BE = CD = 10$
$AFG = 15$ and $2(EB) = 20$

14. B.   If $BD = DC$, then $y = x + z$ and $y > x$.

9. C.   In right triangle ABC, $x = 45$. In right triangle ADC, $y = 45$. Therefore, $z = 45$.

15. C.   Area of circle $= \pi r^2$
If the radius of circle B is twice the radius of circle A, then area of circle B is four times the area of circle A. Stated differently, four times the area of circle $A =$ the area of circle B.

16. D.   1 kilogram $= 2.2$ pounds
70 kilograms $= (70)(2.2)$ or 154 pounds
$154 - 144 = 10$ pounds increase

10. B. $83x = 8383$
$x = 101$ (Column A)

17. C.   Class consists of $a + b$ pupils.
Class consists of b girls.
$\frac{b}{a + b} =$ part of class made of girls

11. A.   The area of triangle $ABC = \frac{1}{2}(\text{leg} \times \text{leg}) =$
12.5 or $(\text{leg})^2 = 25$. Therefore leg $= 5$.
Area of square I or II $= 5^2$ or 25.
Since $AB = BC = 5$, hypotenuse $AC = 5\sqrt{2}$.
Area of square III $= (5\sqrt{2})^2$ or 50.
Twice the area of $ABC = 25$ (given).

18. B.   (A) $(0.25)^2 = 0.0625$

(B) $\sqrt{\frac{1}{4}} = \frac{1}{2}$

(C) $\left(\frac{1}{4}\right)^4 = \frac{1}{258}$

(D) $0.04 = \frac{4}{100}$

(E) $\frac{1}{250} = \frac{1}{250}$

12. B. $x^2 - 5x + 6 = 0$
$(x - 3)(x - 2) = 0$
$x = 3.2$
The sum of the roots $= 5$.
The product of the roots $= 6$.

19. C.   Let x = area of one piece.
$\frac{2}{3}x$ = area of the other piece.

$$x + \frac{2}{3}x = 60$$
$$3x + 2x = 180$$
$$5x = 180$$
$$x = 36$$

Other piece = $60 - 36 = 24$

20. A.   The product of zero and any whole number is zero. If $y = 0$, then xyz cannot be equal to 240.

21. A.   Using a straightedge, follow the line from the 1979 point to the Central Harlem line.

22. E.   Observe the distance between the lines (for U.S. and for New York City) at the 1990 point. Except for 1969, the difference between the two lines is slight until the mid-80s, when it begins to increase.

23. E.   The dates given in choices A, C, and D show decreases in the number of cases. Choice B shows a very slight rise in cases. In choice E, however, there is a sharp increase from 50 to 75 cases per 100,000 population.

24. D.   The two lower lines almost touch at the 1978 point.

25. A.   Notice that this question refers to *per 1,000 population*, while the chart shows new cases per 100,000 population. In 1990 New York City had 50 cases per 100,000, or 0.5 case per 1000.

26. A.   Area of original rectangle = lw
Area of new rectangle $= (el + 3)(w)$
$= lw + 3w$
Increase = $3w$

27. D.   (1) $x + 2y = 1\frac{1}{3}$

(2) $x - y = \frac{1}{3}$

$-x + y = -\frac{1}{3}$ [multiply (2) by -1]

$x + 2y = 1\frac{1}{3}$ [equation (1)]

$3y = 1$ [addition]

28. D. $(XZ)^2 = (150)^2 + (200)^2$
Or note the ratio of legs:
$$\frac{150}{200} = \frac{3}{4}$$
Therefore, the ratio of the sides of XYZ is 3:4:5. Since $YZ = 3(50)$ and $YX = 4(50)$, then $XZ = 5(50)$ or 250.

29. A.   Draw AC.
Area of right triangle $ADC = \dfrac{10 \times 10}{2}$
$$= 50$$

Area of sector $AFCD = \dfrac{1}{4}$ of the circle, whose center is D, having DA and DC as radii.

Area of this $\dfrac{1}{4}$ of circle = $\dfrac{\pi(10)^2}{4} = 25\pi$

Shaded half above $AC = 25\pi - \triangle ACD$ or $25\pi - 50$
Likewise shaded half below $AC = 25\pi - 50$
Entire shaded area = $50\pi - 100$

30. D.   Let x = price of orchestra seat.
Then $\frac{x}{3}$ = price of balcony seat.
$600x$ = $ from all orchestra seats.

$450\left(\dfrac{x}{3}\right)$ = $ from all balcony seats.

$$600x + 150x = \$4,500$$
$$750x = \$4,500$$
$$x = \$6$$

Section 4

1. D.   We know that $a + b = 90$, that $90 - b = a$, and that $90 - a = b$.
        Because we are told that $a \neq b$, the correct answer is D.

2. B. $\dfrac{4}{\sqrt{2}} \cdot \dfrac{\sqrt{2}}{\sqrt{2}} = \dfrac{4\sqrt{2}}{2} = 2\sqrt{2}$

        $2\sqrt{2} > \sqrt{2}$

3. C.   Because $s = a - 4$, then $a = s + 4$; and since $t = a + 5$, then $a = t - 5$.
        Therefore $s + 4 = t - 5$.
        (Things equal to the same thing are equal to each other)

4. C.   Side $BC = \dfrac{1}{4}$ of the perimeter, or $\dfrac{z}{4}$.

        Apply the Pythagorean theorem:

        $\left(\dfrac{z}{4}\right)^2 = y^2 + x^2$, or $\dfrac{z^2}{16} = y^2 + x^2$

5. C.   A circle with area 25π has radius = 5 and diameter = 10.

6. B. $x = 90 - 80 = 10$
        $y = 90 - 70 = 20$

7. D.   The value of x could be 40 or 80.

8. C.   If $y = 50$, then the measure of $\angle DCB = 100$, the measure of $\angle ABC = 80$, and $x = 40$.
        Therefore $x + y = 90$.

9. B.   The information given tells us that the measure of $\angle A >$ the measure of $\angle B$. Since $A + B = 120$, the measure (in degrees) of $\angle A$ is greater than 60, and $\angle B$ has a measure of less than 60. Side AC lies opposite the smallest angle of the triangle.

10. C. The sum of the lengths of 2 adjacent sides of a parallelogram equals one-half the perimeter.

11. C. The sum $= 30 + x$

        The average $= \dfrac{30 + x}{6} = 6$

        $30 + x = 36$
        $x = 6$

12. A. The distance on the x axis for R is the same as P ($a = 6$).
        The distance on the y axis for R is the same as Q ($b = 3$).

13. C. Since $x + y = 9$, then $x = 9 - y$.
        Multiply by 2: $2x = 18 - 2y$.

14. C. $AB + BC = 2$ units
        $AD - CD = 3$ units $- 1$ unit

15. A. $a = 5$. Substitute $a = 5$: $5 + b = 5$, and $b = 0$.

16. A. The distance covered by a wheel when it makes one revolution is equal to the circumference of the wheel. Note 28 inches $= \dfrac{28}{12}$ feet.

        Circumference $= \pi(\text{diameter})$

        $\left(\dfrac{22}{7}\right)\left(\dfrac{28}{12}\right)\left(\dfrac{9}{1}\right)$ = distance (in feet) covered

        by nine turns.

        $\dfrac{22}{\cancel{7}} \cdot \dfrac{\overset{4}{\cancel{28}}}{\underset{3}{\cancel{12}}} \cdot \dfrac{\overset{3}{9}}{1} = 66$ feet

17. B. Find the value of D in terms of C.

        Since $C = \dfrac{2}{3} D$, then $\dfrac{3}{2} C = D$.

        Since $\dfrac{2}{3} C = B$ (given) we now have values of

        D and B in terms of C. What part of D is B can be found as follows:

        $\dfrac{B}{D} = \dfrac{\dfrac{2}{3}C}{\dfrac{3}{2}C} = \dfrac{\dfrac{2}{3}}{\dfrac{3}{2}}$ or $\dfrac{2}{3} \cdot \dfrac{2}{3}$ or $\dfrac{4}{9}$

18. C. $\dfrac{\text{quantity removed}}{\text{capacity}} = $ part removed $= \dfrac{a}{g}$

19. A. Notice that each group was reduced by \$10. The greatest rate of discount would be for the group which was originally the least expensive.

        $\dfrac{10}{60} = 16.6\%$

        $\dfrac{10}{65} = 15.4\%$

        $\dfrac{10}{70} = 14.3\%$

        $\dfrac{10}{75} = 13.3\%$

        $\dfrac{10}{80} = 12.5\%$

20. E.   The difference is obtained by subtracting the lowest temperature, -41, from the highest, $+22$. In order to subtract -41, change its sign to $+$ and proceed as in addition:

$$+22$$
$$+$$
$$\ominus 41$$
$$\overline{+63}$$

The absolute value is the value without regard to sign; thus, the absolute value of $+63$ is 63. The absolute value of the difference is 63.

21. D.   For the 7-year period at the 7% rate, an annual investment of $107.99 is required. For the same period at 8%, only $103.77 is required. The difference is $4.22.

22. E.   An investment of $25.65 annually is listed under the 6% column in the 20-year row.

23. A.   At 14%, for the 10-year investment the annual amount required is $45.36. At the same rate, a 14-year period requires an annual investment of $23.34. The difference is $22.02. The closest correct answer is A.

24. E.   From the table (9% column, 4% row), the annual investment is $200.61, and over a period of 4 years the sum would be $802.44. The closest correct answer is E.

25. C.   An investment of $19.94 annually at 10% for 18 years will grow to $1,000.

26. C.   If the perimeter $= 16$, each side $= 4$ and the area $= (4)^2$
$$(4)^2 = 16$$

---

27. B.   Area of picture $=$ (24 inches) (16 inches) $=$ 384 sq. in.
Area of picture and frame $=$ (26 inches) (18 inches) $= 468$ sq. in.
Area of frame $= 468 - 384 = 84$ sq. in.
Let $x =$ number of times the area of the picture is greater than the area of the frame.
$$84x = 384$$
$$x = 4.5+$$

28. E. $\angle D = 70°$
$\angle B + \angle C = 110°$
$\angle B = \angle C = 55°$
$\angle ABC = 27°$
$\angle ABC = \angle ACB = 27°$
$\angle ABC = \angle ACB = 55°$
$\angle A = 180° - 55° = 125°$

29. B.   If a candidate received 71 votes, there could be a tie among 4 candidates. If one candidate received 72 votes, there could be no tie, and thus it is possible for that candidate to have received more votes than any other candidate.

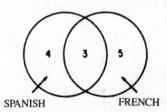

SPANISH   FRENCH

30. A.   We must account for 12 who speak these languages. Note that 3 must speak both languages.
$$\frac{3}{15} = \frac{1}{5}$$

Section 5

1–4.   When all the variables are mentioned in a problem of this kind, there's a very easy way to attach the right names to the right things. Make a chart with three columns: type of book, author, and publisher. As you read through the puzzle, fill in the chart, putting names that belong together on the same line. After reading the four statements, your chart will look like this:

Type	Author	Publisher
	R	S
Spy		H
Sci Fi	B	not B
Gothic	H	

By the process of elimination, you can now fill in the chart completely. The result will look like this:

Type	Author	Publisher
Murder	R	S
Spy	G	H
Sci Fi	B	P
Gothic	H	B

1. B.   By inspection of the completed chart shown above.

2. E.   Can also be read directly from the chart.

3. A.   John buys books by Burchfield and Hopper, and does not buy Gorky and Rothko. Choice A applies to Rothko; all others, to Burchfield or Hopper.

4. D.   The only disadvantage of the chart we constructed above is that you may have to construct it again to solve a question like this. If you do so, leaving out statement (1), you can get options I and III, but for option II, you can't get further than knowing that Sparrow published the mystery, the spy thriller, *or* the Gothic romance.

5–7.   Basically this selection and its questions illustrate the general law of diminishing returns. If increasing amounts of capital are applied to constant amounts of land and labor, the total return may increase, but beyond a certain point the increase will not be in proportion to the inrease in investment.

5. B.   The limit of diminishing returns has not yet been reached.

6. C.   The limit of diminishing returns has been reached.

7. C.   This actually states that the law of diminishing returns is operating in the situation described in the passage.

8–12.   The construction of a calendar for the months of December, January and February may seem to be the best way to answer these questions. However, we may avoid this time-consuming activity by constructing the following table of the days when each ship will be in port. Thus,

Ship W will be in port on days 1, 9, 17, 25, 33, 41, 49, 57, and 65.

Ship X will be in port on days 1, 12, 25, 36, 49, 60, and 73.

Ship Y will be in port on days 1, 6, 11, 16, 21, 26, 31, 36, 41, 46, 51, 56, 61, and 66.

Ship Z will be in port on days 1, 2, 9, 16, 23, 30, 37, 44, 51, 58, and 65.

An examination of this table will enable us to answer the questions.

8. C.   Since December 23 was a Sunday, December 31 will be a Monday and will be the 9th day. Ships W and Z will be in port on December 31.

9. D.   Ship W will be moored alongside ship Z on the 9th day, ship X on the 25th day, ship Y on the 41st day, ship X on the 49th day, and ship Z on the 65th day.

10. A.   On no occasion will three ships be moored at the pier.

11. B.   More departures will take place on Monday than on any other day. Sundays come on days 1, 8, 15, 22, 29, 36, 43, 50, 57, and 64. Including the sailings on December 23, there will be 7 Sunday sailings. Similarly, there will be 13 Monday sailings, 3 Tuesday sailings, 5 Wednesday sailings, 4 Thursday sailings, 3 Friday sailings, and 4 Saturday sailings.

12. A.   From the list above, we can see that Tuesday and Friday will be least busy.

13–16.   This welter of confusing information can be reduced to a table showing what services are available on Friday and Monday in each state. You *don't* have to include Saturday—everything is closed Saturday everywhere.

	Friday:	Monday:
Banks	NA, NS	NA, NW
State gov't offices	NW	NA, NS, NW
Sanit—MWF areas	NW	NA, NS
Sanit—TTS areas	—	—
P.O./fed. offices	NA, NS, NW	NA, NS, NW

---

13. C.   A glance at the table will show you that each service is available on either Friday or Monday, or both, in New Wales, except TTS sanitation pickup.

14. C.   The post office and state government offices are open Monday in all three states, but banks are open only in New Albion and New Wales.

15. B.   For MWF pickup areas in New Wales, all services are available Friday except banking. In MWF pickup areas in the other two states, neither trash pickup nor state government offices are available, though banking is. In TTS areas in all three states, sanitation pickup is not available Friday; banking is not available in new Wales, and state government offices are closed in the other two states. (The fact that sanitation pickup is not normally available Friday in TTS areas is irrelevant—the question states that Mr. Rudolph found all services but one available.)

16. A.   This question is different. Everything is available Monday in New Albion except trash pickup in TTS areas—but this is *not* a "deviation from normal service." The table will confirm that there is some deviation from normal service for all of the other choices given.

17-22.   A four-by-four grid listing prizes, breeds, owners, and dog names will be needed. Using the information given and the process of elimination, you can come up with the following chart:

PRIZE	BREED	OWNER	NAME
1	C	H	K
2	B	E	M
3	A	G	J
4	D	F	L

The questions themselves are fairly straightforward.

17. B.   Once statement (6) identifies the fourth prize winner and you determine that Mr. Grossman's dog therefore won third prize, it follows that, since Max won second prize, Ms. Huntley's Kelly was the collie that won first prize.

18. C.   The same reasoning process used in question 17 makes Mr. Grossman's dog the Airedale that won third prize.

19. C.   Here it's possible for more than one statement to give correct information. It turns out that I is false because Mr. Edwards's dog won second prize and the Airedale third. II is false because Mr. Grossman's dog *is* Jack. III correctly identifies the winners of second, third, and fourth prizes.

20. A.   This can be read from the diagram.

21. D.   The easiest procedure is to jot down the information given in the specified statements:

PRIZE	BREED	OWNER	NAME
1	C		
2			M
	A		J
4	D	F	

Although much remains ambiguous without statements (2) and (7) (for example, who owns which dog), statements I, II, and III all follow by a process of elimination.

22. C.   As for question 21, jot down a simple chart based only on the specified statements:

PRIZE	BREED	OWNER	NAME
1	C		
2			M
3 or 4		G	
1, 3 or 4		H	K

Given the ambiguities arising from the incomplete nature of the information, statement III cannot be deduced. Statements I and II may be deduced, however.

23-24.   Engrave this in your memory indelibly: from a statement in the form "All A are B" or "If A, then B," *one and only one* valid conclusion can be drawn: "If not B, then not A." So: from statement (1), the only valid conclusion is, "A student who does not wear Calvert Kreem jeans does not major in philosophy," and from statement (3), the only valid conclusion is, "If Mary doesn't major in history, Jack doesn't major in philosophy." The statements, "If not A, then not B" and "If B, then A" are *not valid*.

23. B.   Statement (2) says that none of the students in the Marching and Chowder Society wears Calvert Kreem jeans, so they are "not B" in statement (1); the conclusion that they do not major in philosophy is *valid*. Choice A is incorrect: it means only that Mary is not in the Marching and Chowder Society (statement 2) and says nothing about her jeans. Choice C is an "if B, then A" inference, "If Mary majors in history, Jack Majors in philosophy" (and therefore can't be in the Marching and Chowder Society because of his jeans). There's no basis for E.

24. D.   I and III are correct "if not B, then not A" conclusions based on statements (3) and (1), respectively. II can establish only that Jack *may* wear Calvert Kreem Jeans or major in history, neither of which validly implies that he does not major in philosophy.

25. C. The cost to the chemical company (choice C) would be a concern of the company, not of the residents. The residents are primarily concerned about the possible negative effects of the fumes. They might reasonably be expected to be concerned about stopping the fumes (choice A), the adequacy of the original tests (choice B), possible harm to plants and animals (choice D), and possible long-term effects of the fumes (choice E).

Section 6

1-4. The conditions can be diagrammed as in the accompanying figure.

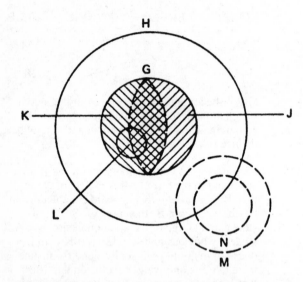

Notice that the positions of two elements (M,N) and the existence of an overlap between J and K are uncertain; these uncertainties are indicated by broken lines.

1. E. From the diagram; statement (6) says that all M's must lie outside the G's; but all N's must lie inside the M's, according to statement (5). Since the only information about the M's is that they are *not* G's, none of the other statements, which attempt to put M's inside or outside the H's, can be deduced.

2. C. This statement is inconsistent with the condition that no M's are G's. Choice A is possible—we could draw the G circle so that it coincided with the H circle. Choices B,D, and E are all possible, since we can draw M anywhere outside G.

3. D. If you thought that statement (2) meant that no J's are K's, you were wrong; it states that all G's are J's or K's, but doesn't exclude the possibility that some G's are both and that J and K overlap. (Consider an analogous statement like

"All voters in my town voted for Republicans or Democrats.") So statement (4) doesn't imply the statement given here, and I is out. It is *possible* that no L's are J's, however, even if J and K do overlap (II). Finally, the additional statement would mean that if L's were K's, they couldn't be J's (III).

4. E. Choice A is not necessarily true, for the reasons given in the answer to number 3. Choices B and C are possible, but not necessarily true. Choice D fails to take the J's into account—it would be true only if the J's and K's overlapped completely. Choice E is correct; statement (2) means that any G that is not a K must be a J. Note that this choice is true even if J's and K's *do* overlap completely—in that case no P can be a G, but the "if then" statement in choice E remains true.

5. B. Ellen assumes a causal relationship on the basis of inference (three times, therefore every time). She commits two logical errors: she fails to exclude alternative causes, and she uses too small a number of "tests" for a valid conclusion. Choice B commits the first error, and may commit the second (we aren't told how many women took the drug). Choice A, a valid argument, concludes that an event must have occurred after its cause. Choice C includes evidence that does tend to rule out alternative explanations. Choice D fails to consider alternative explanations, but involves no inference. Choice E involves sufficient "tests" (she weeps every time) but fails to consider all possible explanations.

6. D. This would tend to rule out alternative explanations (like the other lakes in choice C of question 5), thereby strengthening the argument. Choice A is wrong because Ralph could sneeze for a different reason. Choice B does strengthen the argument (by suggesting that Ellen is not generally sneezy), but not as much as choice D. Choice C weakens the argument (Ellen is sneezy). Choice E implies that Ellen may make herself sneeze.

7. C. If the number of accidents has increased by only 10%, while the number of flights has increased by 30%, then flying is actually getting safer. Thus, the original statement serves to rebut choice C. The increase in the number of flights need not imply that the airlines must be making more money (choice A), that all those who used to fly can still afford to fly (choice B), or that a few large airlines are not taking over the industry (choice E). The only way the statement in choice D could be countered would be to dispute the figure given.

8-11.   To diagram this, just fill in places around the table. Start with Helga, the first person who can be placed definitely. (Make an arbitrary choice as to which end the hostess is at—it will make no difference.) Frank must be at Helga's right. Diane must occupy the third place on Frank and Helga's side of the table because of the seating rule about the sexes, with Allan opposite Diane. You now have:

George cannot be the host, since a man is on the host's right, and he cannot be opposite Frank, so he must be opposite Helga. He is the one person between Belinda and Carol, but we don't know which of these is on his left and which is on his right (in the hostess's chair). But we can fill in this much information and answer the questions.

8. C.   The only slot left for a male is the host's; the host is to Diane's right; but the person opposite him, the hostess, may be either Belinda *or* Carol.

9. A.   George is definitely opposite Helga. He is *not* opposite Belinda (D), nor is Eric opposite Helga (E). Frank may be opposite Belinda *or* Carol, but we don't know which (B,C).

10. D.   By inspection. All the others are next to at least one person of the same sex, no matter where Belinda and Carol are sitting.

11. A.   If you shift George four places to the left, he changes place with Diane. I can be verified, II and III ruled out by inspection of the new, altered diagram.

12-18.   Your basic solution step is to make a table of the possible persons and qualifications on the Democratic side, with the possible combinations on the Republican side. Note that Fawcett insists on Abbott being present, but the reverse is not true. Remember that there *must* be at least one economist and at least one military expert. The valid combinations are as follows:

DEM.	REPUB.
FH	AD
FI	AB,AD
GI	AB, AC, BC
HI	AC, BC, CD

Note that no combinations containing Democrats FG or GH are acceptable because the presence of G would rule out Republican D, the only available military expert. GI is an acceptable pair of Democrats, since I can fill the military expert's role.

12. C.   By inspection of the table.

13. B.   Democrats AB figure in acceptable panels with FI and GI.

14. A.   GI is the *only* pair containing G that may be included in any acceptable panels (I). One of these does *not* contain A (II) and two *do* contain B (III).

15. D.   Count the combinations listed on your table.

16. C.   Republicans CD can serve with Democrats HI. There are no acceptable BD or FG combinations.

17. E.   Republican E figures in *no* acceptable panels; all others can serve on more than one.

18. E.   Democrat I serves on eight acceptable panels (count them).

19-22.   The information becomes a little easier to keep straight with a "tree" diagram showing the various possibilities, like the one given here.

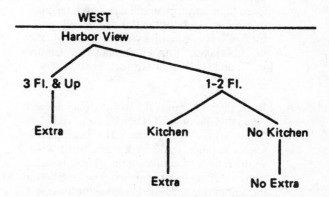

19. **D.** Simply read the information from the diagram. Some rooms described in choices A and C have kitchen facilities; the rooms described in choice B *all* involve an extra charge; and ocean view rooms with balcony but without kitchen facilities (E) involve an extra charge.

20. **B.** The only extra charges are for: ocean view with balcony; harbor view, third floor and up; and rooms with kitchen facilities, no matter where. But some ocean view rooms without balcony and some no-view, no-kitchen East Wing rooms *may* be above the third floor (A). Choices C,D, and E are all false.

21. **C.** This directly contradicts the first extra-charge condition. The other choices are all definitely true.

22. **A.** We don't know whether any West Wing rooms above the second floor or with kitchen facilities have balconies (I). But we do know that East Wing rooms without view or kitchen have no extra charge attached (II) and that all kitchen facilities are in rooms not otherwise subject to an extra charge (III). (Remember, the first paragraph says the charges are identical "except as follows." This means there are no extra charges we weren't told about.)

23. **C.** The author asserts that the corporations, rather than people or elected officials, run the country. The author's evidence is that corporation heads make important decisions without being subject to popular controls. Option I strengthens the conclusion by giving evidence of corporate influence in an area not dealt with in the argument. Option III strengthens the evidence by giving additional data suggesting corporate autonomy. Option II is unrelated to either the evidence or the conclusion.

24. **E.** The original argument contains an implicit but unstated definition of a term—democracy—and depends for its force on the contrast between the definition (popular control of all decisions affecting our lives) and the facts as alleged by the author. Choice E also involves an implicit definition of education as involving more than "regurgitating facts," and depends on the contrast between this and the alleged facts. Choice A involves no definition of "safe neighborhood," implicit or otherwise. Choices B, C, and D all involve direct, explicit contrasts.

25. **A.** First, the author uses the word "right" to mean "the opposite of left." Then he uses "right" to mean "correct" or "proper." This is illogical, as choice A points out. (Technically, this is known as the fallacy of equivocation.) There is no cause or effect to be confused (choice B). And the author does provide evidence for his conclusion (choice D); it's just not very convincing evidence.

Section 7

1. **C.** $\dfrac{2a}{5b} = \dfrac{3}{4}$

   Multiply by $\dfrac{5}{2}$: $\dfrac{5}{2} \cdot \dfrac{\cancel{2}}{\cancel{2}}\left(\dfrac{2a}{5b}\right) = \left(\dfrac{3}{4}\right)\dfrac{5}{2}$

   $\dfrac{a}{b} = \dfrac{15}{8}$

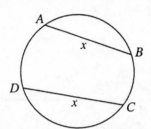

2. **D.** Because chord $AB =$ chord DC, arc $AB =$ arc DC. $B\overset{\frown}{A}D = \overset{\frown}{AB} + \overset{\frown}{AD}$ and $D\overset{\frown}{C}B = \overset{\frown}{DC} + \overset{\frown}{BC}$. $\overset{\frown}{AB} = \overset{\frown}{DC}$, but we may not assume that $\overset{\frown}{AD} = \overset{\frown}{BC}$.

3. **D.** It is possible that x is a fraction. If $x = \dfrac{1}{2}$,

   Column A $= \dfrac{1}{4}$ and Column B $= \dfrac{1}{2}\sqrt{2}$.

   If $x > 1$, other values are possible. If $x = 2$, Column A $= 4$ and Column B $= \sqrt{2}$.

4. **A.** $\sqrt{\dfrac{1}{4}} = \dfrac{1}{2}; \sqrt{\dfrac{1}{25}} = \dfrac{1}{5}; \dfrac{1}{2} + \dfrac{1}{5} = \dfrac{7}{10}$

   $\sqrt{\dfrac{1}{4} + \dfrac{1}{25}} = \sqrt{\dfrac{25}{100} + \dfrac{4}{100}}$

   $= \sqrt{\dfrac{29}{100}} = \dfrac{5+}{10}$

5. **C.** $2x - 18y$

   $2(3) - (18)\left(\dfrac{1}{6}\right)$

   $6 - 3$

   $3x - 36y$

   $(3)(3) - (36)\left(\dfrac{1}{6}\right)$

   $9 - 6$

6. **C.** $\sqrt{0.49} = 0.7; \dfrac{3}{4} = 0.75$. Sum of 0.7, 0.75, and 0.8 $= 2.25$. Average $= 0.75 = 75\%$

7. **B.** Since $B = 0$, $2B(A + C) = 0$. In Column B, A is positive and C is positive. Therefore, $A(B + C)$ or $A(0 + C)$ is positive.

8. C. $\dfrac{n+a}{a} = \dfrac{n}{a} + \dfrac{a}{a}$ or $\dfrac{n}{a} + 1$

9. B. $y = 13 - 3$ or $y = 10$ (Column B)
$x + 10 = 17$ or $x = 7$ (Column A)

10. B. Since x and y have negative values, $x + y$ will be negative. However, in $-x - (-y)$, y will be positive.

11. C. $\angle 4 + \angle 1 = 180$ (supplementary angles)
$\angle 1 + \angle 2 + \angle 3 = 180$ (the measure of the three angles of a triangle)

12. C. $RS = 6$ and $SP = SO + OP$ or $2 + 5 = 7$
For triangle RSP apply the Pythagorean theorem:
$(RS)^2 + (SP)^2 = (RP)^2$, or $(6)^2 + (7)^2 = (PR)^2$
$(PR)^2 = 85$ and $PR = \sqrt{85}$.
Perimeter $= 6 + 7 + \sqrt{85}$

13. A. $\angle ADB$ is an exterior angle of triangle ADC.
$\angle ADB = \angle ACB + \angle BCA$, therefore $x = z + y$. Therefore $x > y$.

14. A. $x + y = 100$
$r + s = 90$

15. C. Since $EB = EC$,
$\angle EBC = \angle ECB$
$\angle ABE$ ($x°$) is the supplement of $\angle EBC$
$\angle DCE$ ($y°$) is the supplement of $\angle ECB$
Thus $x = y$ (supplements of equal angles are equal)

16. D. 1 hour 40 minutes $= 100$ minutes
$100 - 55 = 45$ minutes

17. C. The easiest way to do this type of problem is to draw a diagram like the one here. Note that a 3–4–5 right triangle is formed, with legs 3(50) and 4(50) and the hypotenuse of 5(50) or 250.

18. C. Note that the dimensions of the cut carpet are $(13)(11) = 143$ square feet.

19. D. Find cost and calculate new selling price.
Let $x = $ cost.
$x + \dfrac{1}{4}x = \$35$
$4x + x = 140$
$5x = 140$
$x = \$28$
(Cost) \$28 + (profit) 15% of \$28 or \$4.20 $= \$32.20$

20. C. The 4 arcs (unshaded portion of the square) together constitute 1 circle with radius $= 2$ and area $= 4\pi$. The shaded portion $=$ area $QRST$ minus 4π, or $16 - 4\pi$.

21. C. Either calculate $\$30,000 (0.03) = \$900$ or note that 1% of \$30,000 $= \$300$ and 3% $= \$900$.

22. E. If $15\% = \dfrac{15}{100}$ then $\dfrac{15¢}{100¢}$ or 15¢ out of every \$1.00 is the amount the average American spends for housing.

23. A. The Browns spend $\dfrac{\$4,000}{\$35,000}$ or 11.4%. The average American spends 17%. The difference is 5.6%.

24. B. Medical care includes medical insurance (\$1500) and medical costs (\$2600) for a total of \$4100 out of a total of \$35,000. $\dfrac{\$4,100}{\$35,000} = \dfrac{41}{350}$.

25. E. The data from the graph may be summarized as follows:
The average American spends 15% for housing and 17% for food (I is not true). The average American spends 35% for medical care, transportation, and electricity and 32% for food and housing (II is true). The average American saves 3% of earnings (III is true).

26. D. The rise is $\dfrac{3}{8}$, by the addition of 6 gallons.
Let $x = $ the total capacity.
$\dfrac{3}{8}x = 6$
$x = 16$ gallons

27. D. Note change in units. Change all to inches.

$$\frac{(2.75)(12)}{0.375} = \text{number of steel plates}$$

$$\frac{(2.75)(12)(10)}{0.375} = \frac{(2.75)(\cancel{12})(\cancel{10})}{\cancel{375}} = 88$$

28. E. This is a direct proportion. Observe shift in units. In dollars, price per orange is

$$\frac{\$}{\text{number of oranges}} = \frac{\frac{c}{100}}{1} = \frac{x}{12}$$

$$x = 12\left(\frac{c}{100}\right)$$

$$x = \frac{12c}{100}$$

29. C. In one hour the pipe fills $\frac{1}{h}$ of pool.

In x hours the pipe fills $\frac{x}{h}$ of pool.

30. D. The original solution of 100 cc contains 80% boric acid or 80 cc.
Let x = amount of water to be added to make a 50% solution.
Note that the amount of boric acid (80 cc) remains the same.

$$\frac{80}{100 + x} = 50\%.$$

Answer Sheet – MODEL TEST 4

Start with number 1 for each new section.
If a section has fewer than 38 questions, leave the extra spaces blank.

Section 1

1. Ⓐ Ⓑ Ⓒ Ⓓ Ⓔ	11. Ⓐ Ⓑ Ⓒ Ⓓ Ⓔ	21. Ⓐ Ⓑ Ⓒ Ⓓ Ⓔ	31. Ⓐ Ⓑ Ⓒ Ⓓ Ⓔ
2. Ⓐ Ⓑ Ⓒ Ⓓ Ⓔ	12. Ⓐ Ⓑ Ⓒ Ⓓ Ⓔ	22. Ⓐ Ⓑ Ⓒ Ⓓ Ⓔ	32. Ⓐ Ⓑ Ⓒ Ⓓ Ⓔ
3. Ⓐ Ⓑ Ⓒ Ⓓ Ⓔ	13. Ⓐ Ⓑ Ⓒ Ⓓ Ⓔ	23. Ⓐ Ⓑ Ⓒ Ⓓ Ⓔ	33. Ⓐ Ⓑ Ⓒ Ⓓ Ⓔ
4. Ⓐ Ⓑ Ⓒ Ⓓ Ⓔ	14. Ⓐ Ⓑ Ⓒ Ⓓ Ⓔ	24. Ⓐ Ⓑ Ⓒ Ⓓ Ⓔ	34. Ⓐ Ⓑ Ⓒ Ⓓ Ⓔ
5. Ⓐ Ⓑ Ⓒ Ⓓ Ⓔ	15. Ⓐ Ⓑ Ⓒ Ⓓ Ⓔ	25. Ⓐ Ⓑ Ⓒ Ⓓ Ⓔ	35. Ⓐ Ⓑ Ⓒ Ⓓ Ⓔ
6. Ⓐ Ⓑ Ⓒ Ⓓ Ⓔ	16. Ⓐ Ⓑ Ⓒ Ⓓ Ⓔ	26. Ⓐ Ⓑ Ⓒ Ⓓ Ⓔ	36. Ⓐ Ⓑ Ⓒ Ⓓ Ⓔ
7. Ⓐ Ⓑ Ⓒ Ⓓ Ⓔ	17. Ⓐ Ⓑ Ⓒ Ⓓ Ⓔ	27. Ⓐ Ⓑ Ⓒ Ⓓ Ⓔ	37. Ⓐ Ⓑ Ⓒ Ⓓ Ⓔ
8. Ⓐ Ⓑ Ⓒ Ⓓ Ⓔ	18. Ⓐ Ⓑ Ⓒ Ⓓ Ⓔ	28. Ⓐ Ⓑ Ⓒ Ⓓ Ⓔ	38. Ⓐ Ⓑ Ⓒ Ⓓ Ⓔ
9. Ⓐ Ⓑ Ⓒ Ⓓ Ⓔ	19. Ⓐ Ⓑ Ⓒ Ⓓ Ⓔ	29. Ⓐ Ⓑ Ⓒ Ⓓ Ⓔ	
10. Ⓐ Ⓑ Ⓒ Ⓓ Ⓔ	20. Ⓐ Ⓑ Ⓒ Ⓓ Ⓔ	30. Ⓐ Ⓑ Ⓒ Ⓓ Ⓔ	

Section 2

1. Ⓐ Ⓑ Ⓒ Ⓓ Ⓔ	11. Ⓐ Ⓑ Ⓒ Ⓓ Ⓔ	21. Ⓐ Ⓑ Ⓒ Ⓓ Ⓔ	31. Ⓐ Ⓑ Ⓒ Ⓓ Ⓔ
2. Ⓐ Ⓑ Ⓒ Ⓓ Ⓔ	12. Ⓐ Ⓑ Ⓒ Ⓓ Ⓔ	22. Ⓐ Ⓑ Ⓒ Ⓓ Ⓔ	32. Ⓐ Ⓑ Ⓒ Ⓓ Ⓔ
3. Ⓐ Ⓑ Ⓒ Ⓓ Ⓔ	13. Ⓐ Ⓑ Ⓒ Ⓓ Ⓔ	23. Ⓐ Ⓑ Ⓒ Ⓓ Ⓔ	33. Ⓐ Ⓑ Ⓒ Ⓓ Ⓔ
4. Ⓐ Ⓑ Ⓒ Ⓓ Ⓔ	14. Ⓐ Ⓑ Ⓒ Ⓓ Ⓔ	24. Ⓐ Ⓑ Ⓒ Ⓓ Ⓔ	34. Ⓐ Ⓑ Ⓒ Ⓓ Ⓔ
5. Ⓐ Ⓑ Ⓒ Ⓓ Ⓔ	15. Ⓐ Ⓑ Ⓒ Ⓓ Ⓔ	25. Ⓐ Ⓑ Ⓒ Ⓓ Ⓔ	35. Ⓐ Ⓑ Ⓒ Ⓓ Ⓔ
6. Ⓐ Ⓑ Ⓒ Ⓓ Ⓔ	16. Ⓐ Ⓑ Ⓒ Ⓓ Ⓔ	26. Ⓐ Ⓑ Ⓒ Ⓓ Ⓔ	36. Ⓐ Ⓑ Ⓒ Ⓓ Ⓔ
7. Ⓐ Ⓑ Ⓒ Ⓓ Ⓔ	17. Ⓐ Ⓑ Ⓒ Ⓓ Ⓔ	27. Ⓐ Ⓑ Ⓒ Ⓓ Ⓔ	37. Ⓐ Ⓑ Ⓒ Ⓓ Ⓔ
8. Ⓐ Ⓑ Ⓒ Ⓓ Ⓔ	18. Ⓐ Ⓑ Ⓒ Ⓓ Ⓔ	28. Ⓐ Ⓑ Ⓒ Ⓓ Ⓔ	38. Ⓐ Ⓑ Ⓒ Ⓓ Ⓔ
9. Ⓐ Ⓑ Ⓒ Ⓓ Ⓔ	19. Ⓐ Ⓑ Ⓒ Ⓓ Ⓔ	29. Ⓐ Ⓑ Ⓒ Ⓓ Ⓔ	
10. Ⓐ Ⓑ Ⓒ Ⓓ Ⓔ	20. Ⓐ Ⓑ Ⓒ Ⓓ Ⓔ	30. Ⓐ Ⓑ Ⓒ Ⓓ Ⓔ	

Section 3

1. Ⓐ Ⓑ Ⓒ Ⓓ Ⓔ	11. Ⓐ Ⓑ Ⓒ Ⓓ Ⓔ	21. Ⓐ Ⓑ Ⓒ Ⓓ Ⓔ	31. Ⓐ Ⓑ Ⓒ Ⓓ Ⓔ
2. Ⓐ Ⓑ Ⓒ Ⓓ Ⓔ	12. Ⓐ Ⓑ Ⓒ Ⓓ Ⓔ	22. Ⓐ Ⓑ Ⓒ Ⓓ Ⓔ	32. Ⓐ Ⓑ Ⓒ Ⓓ Ⓔ
3. Ⓐ Ⓑ Ⓒ Ⓓ Ⓔ	13. Ⓐ Ⓑ Ⓒ Ⓓ Ⓔ	23. Ⓐ Ⓑ Ⓒ Ⓓ Ⓔ	33. Ⓐ Ⓑ Ⓒ Ⓓ Ⓔ
4. Ⓐ Ⓑ Ⓒ Ⓓ Ⓔ	14. Ⓐ Ⓑ Ⓒ Ⓓ Ⓔ	24. Ⓐ Ⓑ Ⓒ Ⓓ Ⓔ	34. Ⓐ Ⓑ Ⓒ Ⓓ Ⓔ
5. Ⓐ Ⓑ Ⓒ Ⓓ Ⓔ	15. Ⓐ Ⓑ Ⓒ Ⓓ Ⓔ	25. Ⓐ Ⓑ Ⓒ Ⓓ Ⓔ	35. Ⓐ Ⓑ Ⓒ Ⓓ Ⓔ
6. Ⓐ Ⓑ Ⓒ Ⓓ Ⓔ	16. Ⓐ Ⓑ Ⓒ Ⓓ Ⓔ	26. Ⓐ Ⓑ Ⓒ Ⓓ Ⓔ	36. Ⓐ Ⓑ Ⓒ Ⓓ Ⓔ
7. Ⓐ Ⓑ Ⓒ Ⓓ Ⓔ	17. Ⓐ Ⓑ Ⓒ Ⓓ Ⓔ	27. Ⓐ Ⓑ Ⓒ Ⓓ Ⓔ	37. Ⓐ Ⓑ Ⓒ Ⓓ Ⓔ
8. Ⓐ Ⓑ Ⓒ Ⓓ Ⓔ	18. Ⓐ Ⓑ Ⓒ Ⓓ Ⓔ	28. Ⓐ Ⓑ Ⓒ Ⓓ Ⓔ	38. Ⓐ Ⓑ Ⓒ Ⓓ Ⓔ
9. Ⓐ Ⓑ Ⓒ Ⓓ Ⓔ	19. Ⓐ Ⓑ Ⓒ Ⓓ Ⓔ	29. Ⓐ Ⓑ Ⓒ Ⓓ Ⓔ	
10. Ⓐ Ⓑ Ⓒ Ⓓ Ⓔ	20. Ⓐ Ⓑ Ⓒ Ⓓ Ⓔ	30. Ⓐ Ⓑ Ⓒ Ⓓ Ⓔ	

Remove answer sheet by cutting on dotted line

Section 4

1. Ⓐ Ⓑ Ⓒ Ⓓ Ⓔ	11. Ⓐ Ⓑ Ⓒ Ⓓ Ⓔ	21. Ⓐ Ⓑ Ⓒ Ⓓ Ⓔ	31. Ⓐ Ⓑ Ⓒ Ⓓ Ⓔ
2. Ⓐ Ⓑ Ⓒ Ⓓ Ⓔ	12. Ⓐ Ⓑ Ⓒ Ⓓ Ⓔ	22. Ⓐ Ⓑ Ⓒ Ⓓ Ⓔ	32. Ⓐ Ⓑ Ⓒ Ⓓ Ⓔ
3. Ⓐ Ⓑ Ⓒ Ⓓ Ⓔ	13. Ⓐ Ⓑ Ⓒ Ⓓ Ⓔ	23. Ⓐ Ⓑ Ⓒ Ⓓ Ⓔ	33. Ⓐ Ⓑ Ⓒ Ⓓ Ⓔ
4. Ⓐ Ⓑ Ⓒ Ⓓ Ⓔ	14. Ⓐ Ⓑ Ⓒ Ⓓ Ⓔ	24. Ⓐ Ⓑ Ⓒ Ⓓ Ⓔ	34. Ⓐ Ⓑ Ⓒ Ⓓ Ⓔ
5. Ⓐ Ⓑ Ⓒ Ⓓ Ⓔ	15. Ⓐ Ⓑ Ⓒ Ⓓ Ⓔ	25. Ⓐ Ⓑ Ⓒ Ⓓ Ⓔ	35. Ⓐ Ⓑ Ⓒ Ⓓ Ⓔ
6. Ⓐ Ⓑ Ⓒ Ⓓ Ⓔ	16. Ⓐ Ⓑ Ⓒ Ⓓ Ⓔ	26. Ⓐ Ⓑ Ⓒ Ⓓ Ⓔ	36. Ⓐ Ⓑ Ⓒ Ⓓ Ⓔ
7. Ⓐ Ⓑ Ⓒ Ⓓ Ⓔ	17. Ⓐ Ⓑ Ⓒ Ⓓ Ⓔ	27. Ⓐ Ⓑ Ⓒ Ⓓ Ⓔ	37. Ⓐ Ⓑ Ⓒ Ⓓ Ⓔ
8. Ⓐ Ⓑ Ⓒ Ⓓ Ⓔ	18. Ⓐ Ⓑ Ⓒ Ⓓ Ⓔ	28. Ⓐ Ⓑ Ⓒ Ⓓ Ⓔ	38. Ⓐ Ⓑ Ⓒ Ⓓ Ⓔ
9. Ⓐ Ⓑ Ⓒ Ⓓ Ⓔ	19. Ⓐ Ⓑ Ⓒ Ⓓ Ⓔ	29. Ⓐ Ⓑ Ⓒ Ⓓ Ⓔ	
10. Ⓐ Ⓑ Ⓒ Ⓓ Ⓔ	20. Ⓐ Ⓑ Ⓒ Ⓓ Ⓔ	30. Ⓐ Ⓑ Ⓒ Ⓓ Ⓔ	

Section 5

1. Ⓐ Ⓑ Ⓒ Ⓓ Ⓔ	11. Ⓐ Ⓑ Ⓒ Ⓓ Ⓔ	21. Ⓐ Ⓑ Ⓒ Ⓓ Ⓔ	31. Ⓐ Ⓑ Ⓒ Ⓓ Ⓔ
2. Ⓐ Ⓑ Ⓒ Ⓓ Ⓔ	12. Ⓐ Ⓑ Ⓒ Ⓓ Ⓔ	22. Ⓐ Ⓑ Ⓒ Ⓓ Ⓔ	32. Ⓐ Ⓑ Ⓒ Ⓓ Ⓔ
3. Ⓐ Ⓑ Ⓒ Ⓓ Ⓔ	13. Ⓐ Ⓑ Ⓒ Ⓓ Ⓔ	23. Ⓐ Ⓑ Ⓒ Ⓓ Ⓔ	33. Ⓐ Ⓑ Ⓒ Ⓓ Ⓔ
4. Ⓐ Ⓑ Ⓒ Ⓓ Ⓔ	14. Ⓐ Ⓑ Ⓒ Ⓓ Ⓔ	24. Ⓐ Ⓑ Ⓒ Ⓓ Ⓔ	34. Ⓐ Ⓑ Ⓒ Ⓓ Ⓔ
5. Ⓐ Ⓑ Ⓒ Ⓓ Ⓔ	15. Ⓐ Ⓑ Ⓒ Ⓓ Ⓔ	25. Ⓐ Ⓑ Ⓒ Ⓓ Ⓔ	35. Ⓐ Ⓑ Ⓒ Ⓓ Ⓔ
6. Ⓐ Ⓑ Ⓒ Ⓓ Ⓔ	16. Ⓐ Ⓑ Ⓒ Ⓓ Ⓔ	26. Ⓐ Ⓑ Ⓒ Ⓓ Ⓔ	36. Ⓐ Ⓑ Ⓒ Ⓓ Ⓔ
7. Ⓐ Ⓑ Ⓒ Ⓓ Ⓔ	17. Ⓐ Ⓑ Ⓒ Ⓓ Ⓔ	27. Ⓐ Ⓑ Ⓒ Ⓓ Ⓔ	37. Ⓐ Ⓑ Ⓒ Ⓓ Ⓔ
8. Ⓐ Ⓑ Ⓒ Ⓓ Ⓔ	18. Ⓐ Ⓑ Ⓒ Ⓓ Ⓔ	28. Ⓐ Ⓑ Ⓒ Ⓓ Ⓔ	38. Ⓐ Ⓑ Ⓒ Ⓓ Ⓔ
9. Ⓐ Ⓑ Ⓒ Ⓓ Ⓔ	19. Ⓐ Ⓑ Ⓒ Ⓓ Ⓔ	29. Ⓐ Ⓑ Ⓒ Ⓓ Ⓔ	
10. Ⓐ Ⓑ Ⓒ Ⓓ Ⓔ	20. Ⓐ Ⓑ Ⓒ Ⓓ Ⓔ	30. Ⓐ Ⓑ Ⓒ Ⓓ Ⓔ	

Section 6

1. Ⓐ Ⓑ Ⓒ Ⓓ Ⓔ	11. Ⓐ Ⓑ Ⓒ Ⓓ Ⓔ	21. Ⓐ Ⓑ Ⓒ Ⓓ Ⓔ	31. Ⓐ Ⓑ Ⓒ Ⓓ Ⓔ
2. Ⓐ Ⓑ Ⓒ Ⓓ Ⓔ	12. Ⓐ Ⓑ Ⓒ Ⓓ Ⓔ	22. Ⓐ Ⓑ Ⓒ Ⓓ Ⓔ	32. Ⓐ Ⓑ Ⓒ Ⓓ Ⓔ
3. Ⓐ Ⓑ Ⓒ Ⓓ Ⓔ	13. Ⓐ Ⓑ Ⓒ Ⓓ Ⓔ	23. Ⓐ Ⓑ Ⓒ Ⓓ Ⓔ	33. Ⓐ Ⓑ Ⓒ Ⓓ Ⓔ
4. Ⓐ Ⓑ Ⓒ Ⓓ Ⓔ	14. Ⓐ Ⓑ Ⓒ Ⓓ Ⓔ	24. Ⓐ Ⓑ Ⓒ Ⓓ Ⓔ	34. Ⓐ Ⓑ Ⓒ Ⓓ Ⓔ
5. Ⓐ Ⓑ Ⓒ Ⓓ Ⓔ	15. Ⓐ Ⓑ Ⓒ Ⓓ Ⓔ	25. Ⓐ Ⓑ Ⓒ Ⓓ Ⓔ	35. Ⓐ Ⓑ Ⓒ Ⓓ Ⓔ
6. Ⓐ Ⓑ Ⓒ Ⓓ Ⓔ	16. Ⓐ Ⓑ Ⓒ Ⓓ Ⓔ	26. Ⓐ Ⓑ Ⓒ Ⓓ Ⓔ	36. Ⓐ Ⓑ Ⓒ Ⓓ Ⓔ
7. Ⓐ Ⓑ Ⓒ Ⓓ Ⓔ	17. Ⓐ Ⓑ Ⓒ Ⓓ Ⓔ	27. Ⓐ Ⓑ Ⓒ Ⓓ Ⓔ	37. Ⓐ Ⓑ Ⓒ Ⓓ Ⓔ
8. Ⓐ Ⓑ Ⓒ Ⓓ Ⓔ	18. Ⓐ Ⓑ Ⓒ Ⓓ Ⓔ	28. Ⓐ Ⓑ Ⓒ Ⓓ Ⓔ	38. Ⓐ Ⓑ Ⓒ Ⓓ Ⓔ
9. Ⓐ Ⓑ Ⓒ Ⓓ Ⓔ	19. Ⓐ Ⓑ Ⓒ Ⓓ Ⓔ	29. Ⓐ Ⓑ Ⓒ Ⓓ Ⓔ	
10. Ⓐ Ⓑ Ⓒ Ⓓ Ⓔ	20. Ⓐ Ⓑ Ⓒ Ⓓ Ⓔ	30. Ⓐ Ⓑ Ⓒ Ⓓ Ⓔ	

Section 7

1. Ⓐ Ⓑ Ⓒ Ⓓ Ⓔ	11. Ⓐ Ⓑ Ⓒ Ⓓ Ⓔ	21. Ⓐ Ⓑ Ⓒ Ⓓ Ⓔ	31. Ⓐ Ⓑ Ⓒ Ⓓ Ⓔ
2. Ⓐ Ⓑ Ⓒ Ⓓ Ⓔ	12. Ⓐ Ⓑ Ⓒ Ⓓ Ⓔ	22. Ⓐ Ⓑ Ⓒ Ⓓ Ⓔ	32. Ⓐ Ⓑ Ⓒ Ⓓ Ⓔ
3. Ⓐ Ⓑ Ⓒ Ⓓ Ⓔ	13. Ⓐ Ⓑ Ⓒ Ⓓ Ⓔ	23. Ⓐ Ⓑ Ⓒ Ⓓ Ⓔ	33. Ⓐ Ⓑ Ⓒ Ⓓ Ⓔ
4. Ⓐ Ⓑ Ⓒ Ⓓ Ⓔ	14. Ⓐ Ⓑ Ⓒ Ⓓ Ⓔ	24. Ⓐ Ⓑ Ⓒ Ⓓ Ⓔ	34. Ⓐ Ⓑ Ⓒ Ⓓ Ⓔ
5. Ⓐ Ⓑ Ⓒ Ⓓ Ⓔ	15. Ⓐ Ⓑ Ⓒ Ⓓ Ⓔ	25. Ⓐ Ⓑ Ⓒ Ⓓ Ⓔ	35. Ⓐ Ⓑ Ⓒ Ⓓ Ⓔ
6. Ⓐ Ⓑ Ⓒ Ⓓ Ⓔ	16. Ⓐ Ⓑ Ⓒ Ⓓ Ⓔ	26. Ⓐ Ⓑ Ⓒ Ⓓ Ⓔ	36. Ⓐ Ⓑ Ⓒ Ⓓ Ⓔ
7. Ⓐ Ⓑ Ⓒ Ⓓ Ⓔ	17. Ⓐ Ⓑ Ⓒ Ⓓ Ⓔ	27. Ⓐ Ⓑ Ⓒ Ⓓ Ⓔ	37. Ⓐ Ⓑ Ⓒ Ⓓ Ⓔ
8. Ⓐ Ⓑ Ⓒ Ⓓ Ⓔ	18. Ⓐ Ⓑ Ⓒ Ⓓ Ⓔ	28. Ⓐ Ⓑ Ⓒ Ⓓ Ⓔ	38. Ⓐ Ⓑ Ⓒ Ⓓ Ⓔ
9. Ⓐ Ⓑ Ⓒ Ⓓ Ⓔ	19. Ⓐ Ⓑ Ⓒ Ⓓ Ⓔ	29. Ⓐ Ⓑ Ⓒ Ⓓ Ⓔ	
10. Ⓐ Ⓑ Ⓒ Ⓓ Ⓔ	20. Ⓐ Ⓑ Ⓒ Ⓓ Ⓔ	30. Ⓐ Ⓑ Ⓒ Ⓓ Ⓔ	

MODEL TEST FOUR

Directions: Each sentence below has one or two blanks, each blank indicating that something has been omitted. Beneath the sentence are five lettered words or sets of words. Choose the word or set of words for each blank that best fits the meaning of the sentence as a whole.

1. The dean tried to retain control of the situation on campus, but his attempt was ------- by the board of trustees.

(A) endorsed   (B) frustrated   (C) disclosed
(D) witnessed   (E) justified

2. The current dispute between analytic and nonanalytic philosophers ------- mere ideas, for in academia success in such disputes leads to position and prestige, which lead to control over jobs, money, and publication.

(A) accentuates
(B) transcends
(C) invalidates
(D) exacerbates
(E) precedes

3. Book publishing has long been ------- profession, partly because for younger editors the best way to win a raise or a promotion was to move on to another publishing house.

(A) an innovative
(B) a prestigious
(C) an itinerant
(D) a rewarding
(E) an insular

4. For centuries, physicists have had good reason to believe in the principle of equivalence propounded by Galileo: it has ------- many rigorous tests that ------- its accuracy to extraordinary precision.

(A) endured...compromised
(B) passed...presupposed
(C) borne...postulated
(D) survived...proved
(E) inspired...equated

5. Among contemporary writers of fiction, Mrs. Woolf is ------- figure, in some ways as radical as James Joyce, in others no more modern than Jane Austen.

(A) a doctrinaire
(B) an introspective
(C) a peripheral
(D) a disinterested
(E) an anomalous

6. To the embittered ex-philanthropist, all the former recipients of his charity were -------, as stingy with their thanks as they were wasteful of his largesse.

(A) louts   (B) misers   (C) ingrates
(D) prigs   (E) renegades

7. Physicists dream of a unified theory of matter that could replace the current ------- of mutually inconsistent theories that clutter the field.

(A) bonanza   (B) concord   (C) dearth
(D) integration   (E) welter

Directions: In each of the following questions, a related pair of words or phrases is followed by five lettered pairs of words or phrases. Select the lettered pair that best expresses a relationship similar to that expressed in the original pair.

8. FOOTBALL : GRIDIRON::
(A) soccer : goal
(B) rugby : arena
(C) wrestling : mat
(D) baseball : diamond
(E) bowling : pin

9. LAUREL WREATH : VICTORY::
(A) rosebud : charity
(B) maple leaf : sweetness
(C) blindfold : visibility
(D) palm tree : idleness
(E) olive branch : peace

10. GEOLOGIST : GNEISS::
(A) herpetologist : liver
(B) archaeologist : architectonics
(C) entomologist : anteater
(D) meteorologist : asteroid
(E) botanist : zinnia

11. AGITATOR : FIREBRAND::
(A) miser : spendthrift
(B) renegade : turncoat
(C) anarchist : backslider
(D) maverick : scapegoat
(E) reprobate : hothead

12. CALLOW : MATURITY::
(A) incipient : fruition
(B) eager : anxiety
(C) youthful : senility
(D) apathetic : disinterest
(E) pallid : purity

13. INOCULATION : IMMUNITY::
    (A) talisman : charm
    (B) serum : antidote
    (C) exposure : weathering
    (D) indoctrination : disloyalty
    (E) invasion : fortification

14. DISPASSIONATE : PARTISANSHIP::
    (A) enthusiastic : zealousness
    (B) disconsolate : sorrow
    (C) intemperate : moderation
    (D) volatile : immobility
    (E) ardent : involvement

15. GRISLY : RECOIL::
    (A) sudden : rebound
    (B) tainted : purify
    (C) flagging : invigorate
    (D) heartrending : weep
    (E) craven : quail

16. TOCSIN : DANGER::
    (A) antitoxin : cure
    (B) augury : warning
    (C) oracle : mystery
    (D) clarion : battle
    (E) knell : death

Directions: Each passage in this group is followed by questions based on its content. After reading a passage, choose the best answer to each question. Answer all questions following a passage on the basis of what is stated or implied in the passage.

Mary Shelley herself was the first to point to her fortuitous immersion in the literary and scientific revolutions of her day as the source of her novel *Frankenstein*. Her extreme youth, as well as her sex, have contributed to the generally held opinion that she was not so much an author in her own right as a transparent medium through which passed the ideas of those around her. "All Mrs. Shelley did," writes Mario Praz, "was to provide a passive reflection of some of the wild fantasies which were living in the air about her."

Passive reflections, however, do not produce original works of literature, and *Frankenstein*, if not a great novel, was unquestionably an original one. The major Romantic and minor Gothic tradition to which it *should* have belonged was to the literature of the overreacher: the superman who breaks through normal human limitations to defy the rules of society and infringe upon the realm of God. In the Faust story, hypertrophy of the individual will is symbolized by a pact with the devil. Byron's and Balzac's heroes; the Wandering Jew; the chained and unchained Prometheus: all are overreachers, all are punished by their own excesses—by a surfeit of sensation, of experience, of knowledge and, most typically, by the doom of eternal life.

But Mary Shelley's overreacher is different. Frankenstein's exploration of the forbidden boundaries of human science does not cause the prolongation and extension of his own life, but the creation of a new one. He defies mortality not by living forever, but by giving birth.

17. The primary purpose of the passage is to
    (A) discount Mary Shelley's contribution to the realm of fantastic literature
    (B) trace Mary Shelley's familiarity with the scientific and literary theories of her day
    (C) rehabilitate Mary Shelley's reputation by stressing the innovative qualities in her work
    (D) clarify the nature of the literary tradition to which *Frankenstein* belonged
    (E) demonstrate the influence of Shelley's *Frankenstein* on other examples of the genre

18. The author quotes Mario Praz primarily in order to
    (A) support her own perception of Mary Shelley's uniqueness
    (B) illustrate recent changes in scholarly opinions of Shelley
    (C) demonstrate Praz's unfamiliarity with Shelley's *Frankenstein*.
    (D) provide an example of the predominant critical view of Shelley
    (E) contrast Praz's statement about Shelley with Shelley's own self-appraisal

19. The author of the passage concedes which of the following about Mary Shelley as an author?
    (A) She was unaware of the literary and mythological traditions of the overreacher.
    (B) She intentionally parodied the scientific and literary discoveries of her time.
    (C) She was exposed to radical artistic and scientific concepts which influenced her work.
    (D) She lacked the maturity to create a literary work of absolute originality.
    (E) She was not so much an author in her own right as an imitator of the literary works of others.

20. According to the author, Frankenstein parts from the traditional figure of the overreacher in
    (A) his exaggerated will
    (B) his atypical purpose
    (C) the excesses of his method
    (D) the inevitability of his failure
    (E) his defiance of the deity

The distinction often made between learning and instinct is exemplified by two theoretical approaches to the study of behavior: ethology and behaviorist psychology. Ethology is usually
(5)   thought of as the study of instinct. In the ethological world view most animal behavior is governed

by four basic factors: sign stimuli (instinctively recognized cues), motor programs (innate responses to
cues), drive (controlling motivational impulses)
(10) and imprinting (a restricted and seemingly aberrant
form of learning).

Three of these factors are found in the egg-rolling response of geese, a behavior studied by Kon-
rad Z. Lorenz and Nikolaas Tinbergen, who
(15) together with Karl Frisch were the founders of ethology. Geese incubate their eggs in mound-shaped
nests built on the ground, and it sometimes happens that the incubating goose inadvertently knocks
an egg out of the nest. Such an event leads to a
(20) remarkable behavior. After settling down again on
its nest, the goose eventually notices the errant
egg. The animal then extends its neck to fix its eyes
on the egg, rises and rolls the egg back into the nest
gently with its bill. At first glance this might seem
(25) to be a thoughtful solution to a problem. As it happens, however, the behavior is highly stereotyped
and innate. Any convex object, regardless of color
and almost regardless of size, triggers the response;
beer bottles are particularly effective.
(30) In this example the convex features that trigger
the behavior are the ethologists' sign stimuli. The
egg-rolling response itself is the motor program.
The entire behavior is controlled by a drive that
appears about two weeks before the geese lay eggs
(35) and persists until about two weeks after the eggs
hatch. Geese also exhibit imprinting: during a sensitive period soon after hatching, goslings will follow almost any receding object that emits an
innately recognized "kum-kum" call and thereafter
(40) treat the object as a parent.

Classical behaviorist psychologists see the world
quite differently from ethologists. Behaviorists are
primarily interested in the study of learning under
strictly controlled conditions and have traditionally
(45) treated instinct as irrelevant to learning. Behaviorists believe nearly all the responses of higher
animals can be divided into two kinds of learning
called classical conditioning and operant
conditioning.
(50) Classical conditioning was discovered in dogs by
the Russian physiologist Ivan P. Pavlov. In his
classic experiment he showed that if a bell is rung
consistently just before food is offered to a dog,
eventually the dog will learn to salivate at the
(55) sound of the bell. The important factors in classical
conditioning are the unconditioned stimulus (the
innately recognized cue, equivalent to the ethological sign stimulus, which in this case is food), the
unconditioned response (the innately triggered
(60) behavioral act, equivalent to the ethological motor
program, which in this case is salivation) and the
conditioned stimulus (the stimulus the animal is
conditioned to respond to, which in this case is the
bell). Early behaviorists believed any stimulus an
(65) animal was capable of sensing could be linked, as a
conditioned stimulus, to any unconditioned
response. In operant conditioning, the other major
category of learning recognized by most behaviorists, animals learn a behavior pattern as the result

(70) of trial-and-error experimentation they undertake in
order to obtain a reward or avoid a punishment. In
the classic example a rat is trained to press a lever
to obtain food. The experimenter shapes the behavior by rewarding the rat at first for even partial per-
(75) formance of the desired response. For example, at
the outset the rat might be rewarded simply for facing the end of the cage in which the lever sits.
Later the experimenter requires increasingly precise behavior, until the response is perfected. Early
(80) behaviorists thought any behavior an animal was
capable of performing could be taught, by means
of operant conditioning, as a response to any cue or
situation.

21. The passage is chiefly concerned with

(A) comparing the effectiveness of ethology with
    that of other behavioral theories
(B) presenting a new theory to replace ethology and
    behaviorist psychology
(C) discussing how two differing theories explain
    behavioral processes
(D) disputing the hypotheses of Pavlov and other
    classical behaviorists
(E) explaining the processes that control innate
    behavior

22. The author cites Lorenz, Tinbergen, and Frisch for
their

(A) studies of the egg-rolling response in geese
(B) pioneering work studying instinctual behavior
(C) rejection of imprinting as a form of learning
(D) use of stringently controlled laboratory settings
(E) invalidation of the behaviorist approach

23. It can be inferred from lines 24 – 29 that the goose's
behavior in replacing the egg is "remarkable"
because it

(A) appears purposeful and intelligent
(B) is triggered by the egg
(C) refutes current ethological theories
(D) is a response to sign stimuli
(E) lasts for only four weeks

24. According to the passage, behaviorist learning theories take into account which of the following characteristics of animals?

I.   Their unconditioned response to certain funda-
     mental stimuli, such as food
II. Their ability to learn through being imprinted
     at an early age
III. Their tendency to shun negative stimuli

(A) I only
(B) II only
(C) III only
(D) I and II only
(E) I and III only

25. In exploring these two theoretical approaches to the study of behavior, the author does all of the following EXCEPT

    (A) define a term
    (B) point out functional parallels
    (C) refer to an experimental study
    (D) illustrate through an example
    (E) settle an argument

26. According to the passage, the experimental nature of operant conditioning necessarily involves

    (A) the exposure to punishment of the subject of the experiment
    (B) the introduction of increasingly greater rewards by the experimenter
    (C) an increasing refinement of behavior on the part of the experimental animal
    (D) the use of increasingly subtle cues to trigger the behavioral pattern
    (E) an unwillingness to accept marginal execution of the desired behavior

27. The tone of the author's discussion of the egg-rolling response as an example of instinct is one of

    (A) derision   (B) condescension   (C) neutrality
    (D) exasperation   (E) enthusiasm

Directions: Each question below consists of a word printed in capital letters, followed by five lettered words or phrases. Choose the lettered word or phrase that is most nearly opposite in meaning to the word in capital letters.

Since some of the questions require you to distinguish fine shades of meaning, be sure to consider all the choices before deciding which one is best.

28. SEDATE:
    (A) unify
    (B) immunize
    (C) recuperate
    (D) stimulate
    (E) injure

29. APATHETIC:
    (A) healthy
    (B) sincere
    (C) enthusiastic
    (D) untroubled
    (E) hasty

30. DISLODGE:
    (A) restore
    (B) secure
    (C) wander
    (D) transport
    (E) anticipate

31. CELIBACY:
    (A) informality
    (B) promiscuity
    (C) gluttony
    (D) garrulity
    (E) vanity

32. FLEDGLING:
    (A) experienced
    (B) shy
    (C) cautious
    (D) pedestrian
    (E) fleeting

33. INSIPIDNESS:
    (A) wisdom
    (B) cowardice
    (C) lividity
    (D) savoriness
    (E) tentativeness

34. SEQUESTER:
    (A) precede in sequence
    (B) permit to mingle
    (C) alter in composition
    (D) free from doubt
    (E) attempt to better

35. EQUANIMITY:
    (A) clamor
    (B) disparity
    (C) agitation
    (D) propensity
    (E) indivisibility

36. ANATHEMATIZE:
    (A) appraise
    (B) reciprocate
    (C) patronize
    (D) insinuate
    (E) bless

37. MORIBUND:
    (A) mortal
    (B) vital
    (C) transient
    (D) precarious
    (E) tangential

38. DISTILL:
    (A) provoke
    (B) subordinate
    (C) adulterate
    (D) conjure
    (E) deflate

S T O P

IF YOU FINISH BEFORE TIME IS CALLED, YOU MAY CHECK YOUR WORK ON THIS SECTION ONLY.
DO NOT WORK ON ANY OTHER SECTION IN THE TEST.

SECTION 2

Time—30 minutes

38 Questions

Directions: Each sentence below has one or two blanks, each blank indicating that something has been omitted. Beneath the sentence are five lettered words or sets of words. Choose the word or set of words for each blank that best fits the meaning of the sentence as a whole.

1. Bernard Shaw's goal as an anchorman is ------: when he covered the attempted assassination of President Reagan in 1981, his eyes were not enlarged and his voice was not high-pitched.

    (A) accuracy   (B) eloquence   (C) dispassion
    (D) credibility   (E) sensitivity

2. The epiphyte plants of the rain forest use trees for physical support but do not, like ------, sap nutrients from their hosts.

    (A) fauna   (B) predators   (C) parasites
    (D) insectivores   (E) stumps

3. Although he did not consider himself ------, he felt that the inconsistencies in her story ------ a certain degree of incredulity on his part.

    (A) an apostate...justified
    (B) an optimist...intimated
    (C) a hypocrite...demonstrated
    (D) a charlatan...dignified
    (E) a skeptic...warranted

4. Her employers could not complain about her work because she was ------ in the ------ of her duties.

    (A) derelict...performance
    (B) importunate...observance
    (C) meticulous...postponement
    (D) assiduous...execution
    (E) hidebound...conception

5. Critics were misled by Williams' obvious ------ exaggerated theatrical gestures into ------ his plays as mere melodramas, "full of sound and fury, signifying nothing."

    (A) disinclination for...disparaging
    (B) repudiation of...misrepresenting
    (C) indulgence in...acclaiming
    (D) penchant for...denigrating
    (E) indifference to...lauding

6. Mr. Southern is a historian who has entered so thoroughly into the spirit of the age that even its paradoxes leave him ------.

    (A) nonplussed
    (B) indifferent
    (C) undaunted
    (D) ambivalent
    (E) intransigent

7. What is at the heart of Korzybski's thought is the perception that language, far from being a tool ------ thought and communication, carries within itself a whole body of assumptions about the world and ourselves which go a long way toward shaping and ------ the kinds of thoughts we are able to have.

    (A) incidental to...determining
    (B) requisite for...interpreting
    (C) subordinate to...invalidating
    (D) independent of...correlating
    (E) fundamental to...expurgating

Directions: In each of the following questions, a related pair of words or phrases is followed by five lettered pairs of words or phrases. Select the lettered pair that best expresses a relationship similar to that expressed in the original pair.

8. BARGE : VESSEL::
    (A) cargo : hold
    (B) brake : automobile
    (C) shovel : implement
    (D) squadron : plane
    (E) link : chain

9. RAMSHACKLE : SOUNDNESS::
    (A) garbled : clarity
    (B) decrepit : demolition
    (C) humdrum : monotony
    (D) flimsy : transparency
    (E) steadfast : speed

10. DAMPEN : ENTHUSIASM::
    (A) moisten : throat
    (B) test : commitment
    (C) distract : attention
    (D) reverse : direction
    (E) mute : sound

11. BURST : SOUND::
    (A) ebb : tide
    (B) tinder : fire
    (C) blast : wind
    (D) glimmer : light
    (E) shard : pottery

12. DOVE : COTE::
    (A) sheep : fleece
    (B) pig : sty
    (C) goose : flock
    (D) duck : bill
    (E) fox : den

13. SHOT : SALVO::
   (A) sword : hilt
   (B) ball : musket
   (C) arrow : volley
   (D) flint : powder
   (E) wound : ointment

14. CRAB : CRUSTACEAN::
   (A) salamander : marsupial
   (B) horse : palomino
   (C) swan : cygnet
   (D) spider : arachnid
   (E) aphid : insectivore

15. SKULDUGGERY : SWINDLER::
   (A) surgery : quack
   (B) quandary : craven
   (C) chicanery : trickster
   (D) forgery : speculator
   (E) cutlery : butcher

16. SELF-RESPECTING : VAINGLORIOUS::
   (A) loyal : perfidious
   (B) healthful : salubrious
   (C) querulous : cantankerous
   (D) modest : lascivious
   (E) careful : punctilious

Directions: Each passage in this group is followed by questions based on its content. After reading a passage, choose the best answer to each question. Answer all questions following a passage on the basis of what is stated or implied in the passage.

*There can be no doubt that the emergence of the Negro writer in the post-war period stemmed, in part, from the fact that he was inclined to exploit the opportunity to write about himself. It was more
(5) than that, however. The movement that has variously been called the "Harlem Renaissance," the "Black Renaissance," and the "New Negro Movement" was essentially a part of the growing interest of American literary circles in the immediate and
(10) pressing social and economic problems. This growing interest coincided with two developments in Negro life that fostered the growth of the New Negro Movement. These two factors, the keener realization of injustice and the improvement of the
(15) capacity for expression, produced a crop of Negro writers who constituted the "Harlem Renaissance."

The literature of the Harlem Renaissance was, for the most part, the work of a race-conscious group. Through poetry, prose, and song, the writ-
(20) ers cried out against social and economic wrongs. They protested against segregation and lynching. They demanded higher wages, shorter hours, and better conditions of work. They stood for full social equality and first-class citizenship. The new
(25) vision of social and economic freedom which they had did not force them to embrace the several foreign ideologies that sought to sink their roots in some American groups during the period.

The writers of the Harlem Renaissance, bitter
(30) and cynical as some of them were, gave little attention to the propaganda of the socialists and communists. The editor of the Messenger ventured the opinion that the New Negro was the "product of the same world-wide forces that have brought into
(35) being the great liberal and radical movements that are now seizing the reins of power in all the civilized countries of the world." Such forces may have produced the New Negro, but the more articulate of the group did not resort to advocating the
(40) type of political action that would have subverted American constitutional government. Indeed, the

writers of the Harlem Renaissance were not so much revolting against the system as they were protesting its inefficient operation. In this approach
(45) they proved as characteristically American as any writers of the period. Like his contemporaries, the Negro writer was merely becoming more aware of America's pressing problems; and like the others, he was willing to use his art, not only to contribute
(50) to the great body of American culture but to improve the culture of which he was a part.

It seems possible, moreover, for the historian to assign to the Negro writer a role that he did not assume. There were doubtless many who were not
(55) immediately concerned with the injustices heaped on the Negro. Some contrived their poems, novels, and songs merely for the sake of art, while others took up their pens to escape the sordid aspects of their existence. If there is an element of race in
(60) their writings, it is because the writings flow out of their individual and group experiences. This is not to say that such writings were not effective as protest literature, but rather that not all the authors were conscious crusaders for a better world. As a
(65) matter of fact, it was this detachment, this objectivity, that made it possible for many of the writers of the Harlem Renaissance to achieve a nobility of expression and a poignancy of feeling in their writings that placed them among the masters of recent
(70) American literature.

*Note that this passage is representative of the time it discusses, and therefore uses the terminology commonly accepted in that period.

17. The author is primarily concerned with

   (A) arguing that the literature of the Harlem Renaissance arose from the willingness of black writers to portray their own lives
   (B) depicting the part played by socially conscious black writers in a worldwide ideological and literary crusade
   (C) providing examples of the injustices protested by the writers of the Harlem Renaissance
   (D) describing the social and political background that led to the blossoming of the Harlem Renaissance
   (E) analyzing stages in the development of the New Negro Movement into the Harlem Renaissance

18. In reference to the achievements of the Harlem Renaissance, the passage conveys primarily a sense of

(A) protest   (B) betrayal   (C) nostalgia
(D) urgency   (E) admiration

19. Which of the following is implied by the statement
that the writers of the Harlem Renaissance "were not
so much revolting against the system as they were
protesting its inefficient operation" (lines 41 – 44)?

(A) Black writers played only a minor part in protesting the injustices of the period.
(B) Left to itself, the system was sure to operate
efficiently.
(C) Black writers in general were not opposed to the
system as such.
(D) In order for the system to operate efficiently,
blacks must seize the reins of power in
America.
(E) Black writers were too caught up in aesthetic
philosophy to identify the true nature of the
conflict.

20. With which of the following statements regarding
the writers of the Harlem Renaissance would the
author most likely agree?

(A) They needed to increase their commitment to
international solidarity.
(B) Their awareness of oppression caused them to
reject American society.
(C) They transformed their increasing social and
political consciousness into art.
(D) Their art suffered from their overinvolvement
in political crusades.
(E) Their detachment from their subject matter less-
ened the impact of their works.

21. The information in the passage suggests that the
author is most likely

(A) a historian concerned with presenting socially
conscious black writers of the period as loyal
Americans
(B) a literary critic who questions the conclusions of
the historians about the Harlem Renaissance
(C) an educator involved in fostering creative writing projects for minority youths
(D) a black writer of fiction interested in discovering new facts about his literary roots
(E) a researcher with questions about the validity of
his sources

22. Which of the following statements best describes the
organization of lines 29 – 41 of the passage ("The
writers... constitutional government")?

(A) The author cites an authority supporting a previous statement and then qualifies the original
statement to clarify its implications.
(B) The author makes a point, quotes an observation
apparently contradicting that point, and then
resolves the inconsistency by limiting the
application of his original statement.

(C) The author makes a negative comment and then
modifies it, first by quoting a statement that
qualifies its impact and then by rephrasing his
original comment to eliminate its negative
connotations.
(D) The author summarizes an argument, quotes an
observation in support of that argument, and
then advances an alternative hypothesis to
explain potential contradictions in that
argument.
(E) The author states a thesis, quotes a statement
relevant to that thesis, and then presents two
cases, both of which corroborate the point of
the original statement.

23. The passage supplies information for answering
which of the following questions?

(A) What factors led to the stylistic improvement in
the literary works of black writers in the post-
war period?
(B) Who were the leading exponents of protest literature during the Harlem Renaissance?
(C) Why were the writers of the Harlem Renaissance in rebellion against foreign ideological
systems?
(D) How did black writers in the postwar period
define the literary tradition to which they
belonged?
(E) With what specific socioeconomic causes did
the black writers of the postwar period associate themselves?

(This passage was written before 1967.)

The coastlines on the two sides of the Atlantic Ocean
present a notable parallelism: the easternmost region of
Brazil, in Pernambuco, has a convexity that corresponds
almost perfectly with the concavity of the African Gulf
of Guinea, while the contours of the African coastline
between Rio de Oro and Liberia would, by the same
approximation, match those of the Caribbean Sea.
Similar correspondences are also observed in many
other regions of the Earth. This observation began to
awaken scientific interest about sixty years ago, when
Alfred Wegener, a professor at the University of Ham-
burg, used it as a basis for formulating a revolutionary
theory in geological science. According to Wegener,
there was originally only one continent or land mass,
which he called Pangea. Inasmuch as continental masses
are lighter than the base on which they rest, he reasoned,
they must float on the substratum of igneous rock,
known as sima, as ice floes float on the sea. Then why,
he asked, might continents not be subject to drifting?
The rotation of the globe and other forces, he thought,
had caused the cracking and, finally, the breaking apart
of the original Pangea, along an extensive line represented today by the longitudinal submerged mountain
range in the center of the Atlantic. While Africa seems
to have remained static, the Americas apparently drifted
toward the west until they reached their present position

after more than 100 million years. Although the phenomenon seems fantastic, accustomed as we are to the concept of the rigidity and immobility of the continents, on the basis of the distance that separates them it is possible to calculate that the continental drift would have been no greater than two inches per year.

24. The primary purpose of the passage is to

    (A) describe the relative speed of continental movement
    (B) predict the future configuration of the continents
    (C) refute a radical theory postulating continental movement
    (D) describe the reasoning behind a geological theory
    (E) explain how to calculate the continental drift per year

25. The author's attitude toward Wegener's theory can best be described as

    (A) derisive
    (B) indignant
    (C) judicious
    (D) partisan
    (E) naive

26. It can be inferred from the passage that evidence for continental drift has been provided by the

    (A) correspondences between coastal contours
    (B) proof of an original solitary land mass
    (C) level of sima underlying the continents
    (D) immobility of the African continent
    (E) relative heaviness of the continental masses

27. The passage presents information that would answer which of the following questions?

    (A) In what ways do the coastlines of Africa and South America differ from one another?
    (B) How much lighter than the substratum of igneous rock below them are the continental masses?
    (C) Is the rotation of the globe affecting the stability of the present-day continental masses?
    (D) According to Wegener's theory, in what direction have the Americas tended to move?
    (E) How does Wegener's theory account for the apparent immobility of the African continent?

Directions: Each question below consists of a word printed in capital letters, followed by five lettered words or phrases. Choose the lettered word or phrase that is most nearly <u>opposite</u> in meaning to the word in capital letters.

Since some of the questions require you to distinguish fine shades of meaning, be sure to consider all the choices before deciding which one is best.

28. SMART:
    (A) soothe
    (B) tickle
    (C) support
    (D) shorten
    (E) question

29. LUCID:
    (A) ornate
    (B) arrogant
    (C) embroiled
    (D) hapless
    (E) obscure

30. PERIPHERY:
    (A) authority
    (B) distance
    (C) velocity
    (D) center
    (E) sequence

31. ENIGMATIC:
    (A) frenetic
    (B) genuine
    (C) unambiguous
    (D) vulnerable
    (E) antagonistic

32. REPUDIATE:
    (A) mislead
    (B) minimize
    (C) ascertain
    (D) isolate
    (E) accept

33. ALOOFNESS:
    (A) exaggeration
    (B) simplicity
    (C) concern
    (D) complacency
    (E) disingenuousness

34. EXHUME:
    (A) decay
    (B) inhale
    (C) fertilize
    (D) restrain
    (E) inter

35. DESPOTIC:
    (A) erratic
    (B) impertinent
    (C) reflective
    (D) insouciant
    (E) humble

36. OBFUSCATE:
    (A) insinuate
    (B) exacerbate
    (C) protract
    (D) clarify
    (E) placate

37. PAEAN:
    (A) dirge
    (B) prologue
    (C) chorale
    (D) anthem
    (E) coda

38. CONCATENATE:
    (A) disclaim
    (B) impede
    (C) unlink
    (D) derail
    (E) vacillate

S T O P

IF YOU FINISH BEFORE TIME IS CALLED, YOU MAY CHECK YOUR WORK ON THIS SECTION ONLY.
DO NOT WORK ON ANY OTHER SECTION IN THE TEST.

SECTION 3

Time—30 Minutes

30 Questions

Numbers: All numbers used are real numbers.

Figures: Position of points, angles, regions, etc., can be assumed to be in the order shown; and angle measures can be assumed to be positive.

Lines shown as straight can be assumed to be straight.

Figures can be assumed to lie in a plane unless otherwise indicated.

Figures that accompany questions are intended to provide information useful in answering the questions. However, unless a note states that a figure is drawn to scale, you should solve these problems NOT by estimating sizes by sight or by measurement, but by using your knowledge of mathematics (see Example 2 below).

Directions: Each of the Questions 1-15 consists of two quantities, one in Column A and one in Column B. You are to compare the two quantities and choose

    A if the quantity in Column A is greater;
    B if the quantity in Column B is greater;
    C if the two quantities are equal;
    D if the relationship cannot be determined from the information given.

Note: Since there are only four choices, NEVER MARK (E).

Common
Information: In a question, information concerning one or both of the quantities to be compared is centered above the two columns. A symbol that appears in both columns represents the same thing in Column A as it does in Column B.

	Column A	Column B	Sample Answers
Example 1:	2×6	$2 + 6$	● Ⓑ Ⓒ Ⓓ Ⓔ

Examples 2-4 refer to $\triangle PQR$.

	Column A	Column B	Sample Answers
Example 2:	PN	NQ	Ⓐ Ⓑ Ⓒ ● Ⓔ

(since equal measures cannot be assumed, even though PN and NQ appear equal)

	Column A	Column B	Sample Answers
Example 3:	x	y	Ⓐ ● Ⓒ Ⓓ Ⓔ

(since N is between P and Q)

	Column A	Column B	Sample Answers
Example 4:	$w + z$	180	Ⓐ Ⓑ ● Ⓓ Ⓔ

(since PQ is a straight line)

A if the quantity in Column A is greater;
B if the quantity in Column B is greater;
C if the two quantities are equal;
D if the relationship cannot be determined from the information given.

| Column A | Column B | | Column A | Column B |

$l_1 \| l_2$

1. x 25

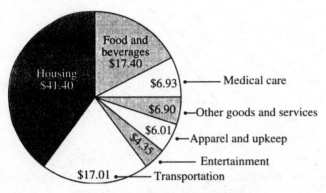

How the average American spends
$100, as measured in late 1992.
Source: U.S. Department of Labor.

2.   Amount (to nearest $)   Amount (to nearest $)
     spent for food and   spent for apparel and
     beverages plus   upkeep plus
     medical care   transportation

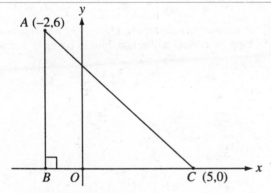

3.   Area of triangle ABC 15

$\overline{AB} \| \overline{CD}$

4. $x + y$ 180

5. The average of $\sqrt{0.81}$,   3

    60%, $1\frac{1}{2}$

$7x = 196$

6. $\dfrac{x}{7}$ 4

7. $(2)(4)(6)(8)(10)(12)(14)$ $(16)(14)(12)(10)(8)(6)$

$A > B$
$B > C$

8. $2A$ $B + C$

$5 \times 5 \times 5 \times 5 = 10 \times 10 \times T$

9. T 10

$\dfrac{\text{Area of circle } A}{\text{Area of circle } B} = \dfrac{1}{4}$

10.   Four times the   The radius of circle B
      radius of circle A

Point O (5,3) is the center of a circle. Point P
(5,7) lies on the circle.

11.   The circumference 8π
      of the circle

ABC and DEF are straight lines
$a = 20$ and $b = 160$

12. $a + x$ $x + y$

Column A	Column B	Column A	Column B

13. x 5

The area of triangle ABC is 12.5.

14.   Length of BC 5

15. $\left(\dfrac{X}{Z}\right)\left(\dfrac{Z}{Y}\right)$ 0

Directions: Each of Questions 16–30 has five answer choices. For each of these questions, select the best of the answer choices given.

16. If $3x - 6 = 1$, then $x - 2 =$

   (A) $\dfrac{1}{3}$

   (B) $\dfrac{1}{2}$

   (C) 2

   (D) $2\dfrac{1}{3}$

   (E) 3

17. If the hypotenuse of isosceles right triangle ABC is $6\sqrt{2}$, then the area of ABC equals

   (A) 6
   (B) 9
   (C) 12
   (D) 18
   (E) 36

18. $(146 \times 117) + (173 \times 146) + (146 \times 210)$ equals

   (A) 69,000
   (B) 70,000
   (C) 71,000
   (D) 72,000
   (E) 73,000

19. If $7x - 5y = 13$, and $2x - 7y = 26$, then $5x + 2y =$

   (A) -39
   (B) -13
   (C) 13
   (D) 19.5
   (E) 39

20. A man covers d miles in t hours. At that rate how long (in hours) will it take him to cover m miles?

   (A) dmt

   (B) $\dfrac{md}{t}$

   (C) $\dfrac{mt}{d}$

   (D) $\dfrac{dt}{m}$

   (E) $\dfrac{d}{t}$

Questions 21–25 refer to the following table.

RELATIVE SWEETNESS OF DIFFERENT SUBSTANCES	
Lactose	0.16
Maltose	0.32
Glucose	0.74
Sucrose	1.00
Fructose	1.70
Saccharin	675.000

21. About how many times sweeter than lactose is fructose?

    (A) 0.09
    (B) 0.1
    (C) 1.54
    (D) 1.86
    (E) 10.6

22. What percent increase in sweetness is obtained by substituting equal amounts of maltose for lactose?

    (A)   16
    (B)   50
    (C) 100
    (D) 200
    (E) 500

23. How many grams of sucrose (to the nearest gram) must be added to one gram of saccharin to make a mixture that will be 100 times as sweet as glucose?

    (A)   7
    (B)   8
    (C)   9
    (D)   10
    (E) 100

24. What is the ratio of glucose to lactose in a mixture as sweet as maltose?

    (A) 8:21
    (B) 21:8
    (C) 25:9
    (D) 29:8
    (E) 32:5

25. Approximately how many times sweeter than sucrose is a mixture of glucose, sucrose, and fructose in the ratio of 1:2:3?

    (A) 0.6
    (B) 1
    (C) 1.3
    (D) 2.3
    (E) 2.9

26. One-half of the student body at Cetco School study French and one-third of the others study Spanish. The remaining 300 do not study any foreign language. How many students are there in this school?

    (A)   360
    (B)   550
    (C)   900
    (D) 1350
    (E) 1800

27. Mr. Jones can mow his lawn in x hours. After 2 hours it begins to rain. What part of the lawn is left unmowed?

    (A) $\dfrac{2 - x}{x}$

    (B) $\dfrac{x}{2}$

    (C) $x - 2$

    (D) $\dfrac{x - 2}{2}$

    (E) $\dfrac{x - 2}{x}$

28. In right triangle ABC, if $\angle A > \angle B > \angle C$, then

    (A) $\angle C > 45°$
    (B) $\angle B = 90°$
    (C) $\angle A > 170°$
    (D) $\angle A > 90°$
    (E) $\angle A = 90°$

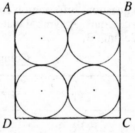

29. In the figure above, the area of each circle is 4π. The perimeter of $ABCD =$

    (A) 16
    (B) 16π
    (C) 32π
    (D) 32
    (E) 64π

30. The area of a square 18 feet on a side is equal to the area of a rectangle with a length of 3 yards. The width of this rectangle (in feet) is

    (A)   2
    (B)   9
    (C) 18
    (D) 27
    (E) 36

S T O P

IF YOU FINISH BEFORE TIME IS CALLED, YOU MAY CHECK YOUR WORK ON THIS SECTION ONLY.
DO NOT WORK ON ANY OTHER SECTION IN THE TEST.

SECTION 4

Time—30 minutes

30 Questions

Numbers: All numbers used are real numbers.

Figures: Position of points, angles, regions, etc., can be assumed to be in the order shown; and angle measures can be assumed to be positive.

Lines shown as straight can be assumed to be straight.

Figures can be assumed to lie in a plane unless otherwise indicated.

Figures that accompany questions are intended to provide information useful in answering the questions. However, unless a note states that a figure is drawn to scale, you should solve these problems NOT by estimating sizes by sight or by measurement, but by using your knowledge of mathematics (see Example 2 below).

Directions: Each of the Questions 1-15 consists of two quantities, one in Column A and one in Column B. You are to compare the two quantities and choose

> A if the quantity in Column A is greater;
> B if the quantity in Column B is greater;
> C if the two quantities are equal;
> D if the relationship cannot be determined from the information given.

Note: Since there are only four choices, NEVER MARK (E).

Common
Information: In a question, information concerning one or both of the quantities to be compared is centered above the two columns. A symbol that appears in both columns represents the same thing in Column A as it does in Column B.

	Column A	Column B	Sample Answers

| Example 1: | 2×6 | $2 + 6$ | ● Ⓑ Ⓒ Ⓓ Ⓔ |

Examples 2-4 refer to $\triangle PQR$.

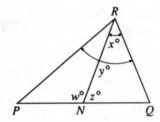

| Example 2: | PN | NQ | Ⓐ Ⓑ Ⓒ ● Ⓔ |

(since equal measures cannot be assumed, even though PN and NQ appear equal)

| Example 3: | x | y | Ⓐ ● Ⓒ Ⓓ Ⓔ |

(since N is between P and Q

| Example 4: | $w + z$ | 180 | Ⓐ Ⓑ ● Ⓓ Ⓔ |

(since PQ is a straight line)

A if the quantity in Column A is greater;
B if the quantity in Column B is greater;
C if the two quantities are equal;
D if the relationship cannot be determined from the information given.

Column A	Column B

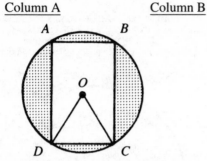

Perimeter of equilateral triangle $ODC = 12$

AD of rectangle $ABCD = 7$

1. Perimeter of $ABCD$ — 22

Nine equal circles are enclosed in square $ABCD$, whose area is 36.

2. Area of each circle — π

$x = 20$

3. $6x$ — y

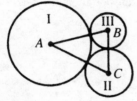

A, C, and B are centers of circles I, II, and III, respectively
Area of circle I $= 25\pi$, area of circle II $= 16\pi$, area of circle III $= 9\pi$

4. Perimeter of triangle ABC — 12

5. $\dfrac{\dfrac{1}{4} - \dfrac{3}{16}}{\dfrac{1}{8}}$ — 2

Column A	Column B

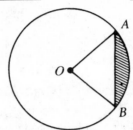

$OA = OB = 6$

6. Area of shaded portion — $6\pi - 9\sqrt{3}$

7. $\dfrac{1}{0.5}$ — $\sqrt{4}$

8. $\left(\dfrac{1}{0.07}\right)^2$ — $\dfrac{1}{7}$

$3^{n+2} = 27$

9. n — 3

$AB \perp BC$

10. y — 45

The average of x, y, and z, three consecutive integers, is M.

11. $x + z$ — $2y$

$-10 < x < 0$

12. $\dfrac{1}{x^5}$ — $\dfrac{1}{x^4}$

$x > 1$ and $y > 1$
$x \neq y$

13. $\dfrac{x}{y} + 1$ — $\dfrac{x + y}{y}$

$x > 0$ and $y > 0$

$\dfrac{x}{y} > 2$

14. $2y$ — x

15. $\sqrt{0.25}$ — $\dfrac{1}{4}$

Directions: Each of the Questions 16–30 has five answer choices. For each of these questions, select the best of the answer choices given.

16. If $xyz = 1$ and $x = z$, $y =$

    (A) $1 - x^2$

    (B) x^2

    (C) $1 - 2x$

    (D) $\dfrac{1}{x^2}$

    (E) $\dfrac{1}{2x}$

17. A piece of cloth y yards long had f feet cut from one end and i inches cut from the other end. The present length (in feet) of the piece of cloth is

    (A) $\dfrac{y}{3}(f + 12i)$

    (B) $3y - f + \dfrac{1}{12}i$

    (C) $3y - \left(f + \dfrac{i}{12}\right)$

    (D) $36y - 12f - i$

    (E) $\dfrac{y}{3} - f + 12i$

18. A sports jacket marked $48 is offered at a discount of 25 percent during a storewide sale. At this reduced price the dealer makes a profit of 20 percent on the cost. The cost to the dealer is

    (A) $29
    (B) $30
    (C) $32
    (D) $36
    (E) $40

19. A company reports that 2,000 electronic parts are found defective. If this represents 6.25 percent of the total shipment, how many of these parts were shipped?

    (A)   3,200
    (B)   17,000
    (C)   32,000
    (D)   34,000
    (E)   320,000

20. On a diagram of a camp site drawn to scale of 1:120, the size of a building is $7\frac{1}{5}$ inches. The actual length (in feet) of this building is

    (A)   7.2
    (B)   72
    (C)   120
    (D)   720
    (E)   864

Questions 21–25 refer to the following graphs.

PORTION OF WAGE EARNERS ENGAGED
IN VARIOUS OCCUPATIONS
IN BONNEVILLE CITY IN 1986
(Number of degrees represent angles on circle graph.)

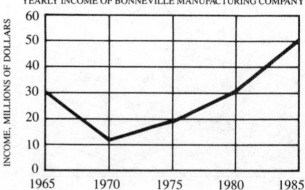

YEARLY INCOME OF BONNEVILLE MANUFACTURING COMPANY

21. What percent of the wage earners in Bonneville were engaged in transportation in 1986?

    (A)   6

    (B) $8\frac{1}{3}$

    (C) $16\frac{2}{3}$

    (D)   30

    (E)   60

22. If 1,980 workers were engaged in commerce, how many were engaged in manufacturing?

    (A) 1,485
    (B) 1,782
    (C) 2,200
    (D) 2,640
    (E) 7,920

23. The average income of professional workers was 50 percent greater than that of the transportation workers. If the total income of the tranportation workers was $2,376,000, what was the total income of the professional workers?

(A) $1,056,000
(B) $2,376,000
(C) $3,168,000
(D) $3,564,000
(E) $7,128,000

24. Which of the following can be inferred from the graphs?
 I. Higher prices were charged by the manufacturing company in 1985 than in preceding years.
 II. The company's income increased more rapidly in the 1980–1985 period than in the preceding 5 years.
 III. The number of sales of the company has been increasing since 1970.
(A) I only   (B) II only   (C) III only
(D) I and III   (E) II and III

25. About what was the average annual income of the company from 1970 to 1980?

(A) $15,000,000
(B) $20,000,000
(C) $25,000,000
(D) $30,000,000
(E) $35,000,000

26. The number of feet in c inches is

(A) $\frac{1}{12c}$
(B) $12c$
(C) $\frac{12}{c}$
(D) $36c$
(E) $\frac{c}{12}$

27. Which of the following represents the area of a rectangle whose length is $x + 1$ and whose width is $x - 1$?

(A) $x^2 + 1$
(B) $2x$
(C) $x^2 - 1$
(D) $4x$
(E) x^2

28. Which of the following must be added to $2x - 4$ to produce a sum of 0?

(A) 0
(B) $x + 4$
(C) $2x + 4$
(D) $x + 2$
(E) $-2x + 4$

29. The expression $\frac{6}{x} \div \frac{3}{x}$ is equivalent to

(A) $\frac{1}{2}$
(B) $2x$
(C) $\frac{x^2}{18}$
(D) $\frac{18}{x^2}$
(E) 2

30. The number line above shows the solution set of which of the following inequalities?

(A) $-3 < x < 5$
(B) $3 \leq x < 5$
(C) $-3 \leq x < 5$
(D) $-3 < x \leq 5$
(E) $-3 \leq x \leq 5$

S T O P

IF YOU FINISH BEFORE TIME IS CALLED, YOU MAY CHECK YOUR WORK ON THIS SECTION ONLY.
DO NOT WORK ON ANY OTHER SECTION IN THE TEST.

SECTION 5

Time —30 minutes

25 Questions

Directions: Each question or group of questions is based on a passage or set of conditions. In answering some of the questions, it may be useful to draw a rough diagram. For each question, select the best answer choice given.

Questions 1–4

In order to conduct the work of a mail order concern it is necessary to have a minimum of three workers each day. The staff consists of five persons who work on a part-time basis. Alice can work on Mondays, Wednesdays, and Fridays. Betty cannot report for work on Wednesdays. Carol can report for work on Tuesdays and Wednesdays only. Dorothy cannot work on Fridays. Edith is available anytime except on the first Monday and Thursday of the month.

1. Which three are available on any Monday?

   (A) Dorothy, Betty, and Alice
   (B) Alice, Edith, and Carol
   (C) Betty, Edith, and Carol
   (D) Edith, Carol, and Dorothy
   (E) Betty, Carol, and Dorothy

2. Which three could you count on to report for work on Friday?

   (A) Alice, Betty, and Dorothy
   (B) Alice, Carol, and Dorothy
   (C) Betty, Carol, and Edith
   (D) Carol, Betty, and Alice
   (E) Alice, Betty, and Edith

3. During which day of the week might it be impossible to obtain a full complement of workers?

   (A) Monday
   (B) Tuesday
   (C) Wednesday
   (D) Thursday
   (E) Friday

4. During which day of the week would it be necessary to call on Alice to complete the full complement of workers?

   (A) Monday
   (B) Tuesday
   (C) Wednesday
   (D) Thursday
   (E) Friday

Questions 5–7

Strict gun control laws cause a decrease in violent crime; in the six months since the city council passed a gun control law, armed robberies in City X have dropped by 18 percent.

5. All of the following, if true, are valid objections to the argument above EXCEPT:

   (A) A decrease in crime in one city does not mean that such a decrease would occur anywhere a gun control law was enacted.
   (B) Other factors may have caused the drop in armed robberies.
   (C) Armed robbery is only one category of violent crime that might be affected by a gun control law.
   (D) The gun control law has made it more difficult for citizens to purchase guns for legitimate purposes of self-defense.
   (E) Since the law was passed, murders involving guns in City X have increased by 22 percent.

6. Which of the following statements, if true, would strengthen the argument above?

   I.   Before the law was passed, the number of armed robberies had been steadily increasing.
   II. The more that laws are used to prevent a crime, the less likely that crime is to occur.
   III. Three-fourths of all violent crimes involve the use of a gun.

   (A) I only
   (B) III only
   (C) I and II only
   (D) II and III only
   (E) I, II, and III

7. Which of the following statements, if true, would weaken the argument above?

   I.   In the six months since the law was passed, 40 percent more police have been hired.
   II. In the six months since the law was passed, accidental deaths by firearms have increased by 10 percent.
   III. Only 30 percent of those indicted under the new law have been convicted.

   (A) I only
   (B) III only
   (C) I and II only
   (D) I and III only
   (E) II and III only

Questions 8–11

(1) Each word in a horizontal row must begin with a successive letter.
(2) Each word in a vertical column must begin with a different letter.
(3) Each word in a horizontal row must have the same number of letters.
(4) Each word in a vertical column must have a different number of letters.
(5) Each word in a vertical column must be the same part of speech. (NOTE: Many English words are more than one part of speech; for example, *cry* is both a noun and a verb.)

	I.	II.	III.	IV.	V.
1.	endear	filter	garish	hotter	intake
2.	chatter	destiny	endless	fester	gradual
3.	bend	calf	death	edge	flow
4.	dread	elbow	fetid	greed	heave
5.	ask	bet	coy	dam	ebb

8. How many rules are not violated by any row or column in the grid?

    (A) 2   (B) 3   (C) 4   (D) 5   (E) 6

9. How many rows and columns satisfy all rules for rows and columns, respectively?

    (A) Four rows and three columns
    (B) Four rows and two columns
    (C) Three rows and two columns
    (D) Three rows and four columns
    (E) Two rows and two columns

10. Word 3 in column III would satisfy all rules if it were changed to

    (A) deter   (B) dirty   (C) deaf
    (D) dash   (E) dry

11. What is the minimum number of words that must be changed for the grid to satisfy all rules?

    (A) 2   (B) 3   (C) 4   (D) 5   (E) 6

Questions 12–18

Only July 4, the Pops Orchestra will perform ten works by nine U.S. composers.
Beach's *Quintet* will be heard immediately after Della Joio's *Fantasies*
Ives's *Fourth of July* will be heard later than the Della Joio. It will be followed immediately by Foster's *Summer Longings.*
The third selection following Copland's *Lincoln Portrait* will be Ellington's *New World A-Coming;* the next will be an aria from Hanson's *Merry Mount.*
Gottschalk's *Grand Tarantelle* will be heard earlier than the Della Joio.
Antes's *Trio* is the second work following the Hanson, and does not end the program.

12. Which of the following lists the composers mentioned in the order in which their works are heard?

    (A) Foster, Ives, Antes, Ellington, Beach, Gottschalk
    (B) Copland, Della Joio, Beach, Ellington, Hanson, Foster
    (C) Gottschalk, Della Joio, Beach, Foster, Antes, Ives
    (D) Copland, Gottschalk, Della Joio, Beach, Ellington, Hanson
    (E) Beach, Ellington, Hanson, Foster, Ives, Antes

13. The Della Joio *Fantasies* is

    (A) the second work on the program
    (B) the second work after the Copland
    (C) the work immediately preceding the Ellington
    (D) followed by two other works before the Hanson aria is heard
    (E) heard immediately following the Gottschalk

14. If the intermission occurs immediately after the Beach *Quintet*, the fourth work after the intermission is by

    (A) Antes   (B) Copland   (C) Ives
    (D) Foster   (E) Hanson

15. The number of works to be heard between the Beach and the Foster is

    (A) 1   (B) 2   (C) 3   (D) 4   (E) 5

16. The soloist who will perform during the Antes, the Gottschalk, and the Ellington must begin tuning up just prior to the start of her first performance. She will begin tuning up

    (A) during the fourth work on the program
    (B) during the Della Joio
    (C) during the sixth work on the program
    (D) during the Hanson
    (E) before the start of the program

17. One composer is represented by two works, separated by four other selections. This composer is

    (A) Antes   (B) Beach   (C) Copland
    (D) Della Joio   (E) Ellington

18. If the total number of works played were eleven instead of ten, which of the following would be possible without violating the stated conditions?

    I.   The Copland *Lincoln Portrait* being played first
    II.   The Antes *Trio* being played after Foster's *Summer Longings*
    III. The Antes *Trio* being played before Gottschalk's *Grand Tarantelle*

    (A) I only
    (B) III only
    (C) I and II only
    (D) II and III only
    (E) I, II, and III

Questions 19–22

A,B,C, or W may cause D.

B,C, or W may cause E.

W or X may cause F.

D or E may cause G or H only if D and E are caused by
    B or C; D or E may cause I only if D and E are caused
    by C.

Only E and F together may cause M or N.

F may cause H only if it is caused by W or X.

19. Which can result from the largest number of imme-
    diately preceding events?

    (A) D
    (B) E
    (C) F
    (D) M
    (E) N

20. Which can result in the smallest number of subse-
    quent events, counting both those that follow imme-
    diately and those that follow after another event?

    (A) A
    (B) B
    (C) C
    (D) W
    (E) X

21. How many different events or combinations of events
    may cause H?

    (A) 5
    (B) 6
    (C) 7
    (D) 8
    (E) 9

22. Which may be a result of the smallest number of dif-
    ferent combinations of events?

    (A) G
    (B) H
    (C) I
    (D) M
    (E) N

Questions 23–25

Statistics indicate that, on the average, women executives' salaries are about 20% lower than the salaries of
men in comparable jobs. This is true in spite of the job
discrimination suits filed by the U.S. government against
firms such as A.T.&T. and the Bank of America in the
early 1970s, as well as the passage of laws forbidding job
discrimination by gender in many states and localities. In
the face of this unrelenting prejudice against women, it
is plain that only an amendment to the U.S. Constitution
can fully remedy the iniquities under which today's
women are laboring.

23. Which of the following is assumed by the author of
    the above argument?

    (A) All women executives are more qualified than
        their male counterparts.
    (B) A constitutional amendment is more likely to
        influence employment practices than sepa-
        rate state laws and court actions.
    (C) Legal remedies for discrimination can be effec-
        tive only when coupled with a sincere desire
        for reform.
    (D) Average salaries are often misleading as indica-
        tors of the real status of a particular social
        group.
    (E) Discrimination against women is as serious and
        widespread as discrimination against mem-
        bers of racial and ethnic minorities.

24. Which of the following would be the most relevant
    question to ask the author of the above argument?

    (A) What employment practices are currently fol-
        lowed by A.T.&T. and the Bank of America
        in relation to their female executives?
    (B) Don't female executives in the United States
        have a far better lot than the millions of im-
        poverished women now living in the under-
        developed nations of the Third World?
    (C) Which states and localities have passed laws
        forbidding job discrimination by gender?
    (D) Isn't "equal pay for equal work" a cardinal prin-
        ciple of law in Slavonia, a well-known totali-
        tarian and repressive state?
    (E) Is a constitutional amendment the most effective
        way to remedy the problem of job discrimina-
        tion by gender?

25. All of the following are weaknesses of the above
    argument except that

    (A) it makes generalizations concerning the status
        of women based on the plight of a single
        group of women
    (B) it draws conclusions from statistical evidence
        which the data themselves may not support
    (C) it disregards efforts being made by some
        employers to end job discrimination within
        their own firms
    (D) it fails to fully consider possible remedies other
        than the one proposed
    (E) it ignores other possible explanations for the
        cited difference in average salaries

S T O P

IF YOU FINISH BEFORE TIME IS CALLED, YOU MAY CHECK YOUR WORK ON THIS SECTION ONLY.
DO NOT WORK ON ANY OTHER SECTION IN THE TEST.

Section 6

Time — 30 minutes

25 Questions

Directions: Each question or group of questions is based on a passage or set of conditions. In answering some of the questions, it may be useful to draw a rough diagram. For each question, select the best answer choice given.

Questions 1–4

Six school board members—Allenby, Broome, Chatsworth, Doggett, Edson, and Fream—are seated at a conference table in the auditorium of Westfield High School, to run a community budget meeting. They take six seats, numbered 1 through 6 from left to right, on the same side of the table. However, there has been some tension among the board members during the current budget crisis, and this affects the seating.

Allenby has openly clashed with Broome over staff cuts, and cannot be seated immediately to the left or immediately to the right of Broome.

Chatsworth has a hearing impairment that only Doggett knows about, and so must be immediately to the left of Doggett.

Fream knows that the angry head of a tax group will be seated on the right side of the auditorium, so he will not occupy seat 6 at the table.

1. Which of the following board members cannot be seated in seat 1?

    (A) Allenby
    (B) Broome
    (C) Chatsworth
    (D) Doggett
    (E) Fream

2. If Doggett is seated in seat 3, Chatsworth must be seated in seat

    (A) 1
    (B) 2
    (C) 4
    (D) 5
    (E) 6

3. If Allenby is seated in seat 5, which of the remaining board members must be seated in seat 6?

    (A) Broome
    (B) Chatsworth
    (C) Doggett
    (D) Edson
    (E) Fream

4. If Fream is seated in seat 3, immediately to the right of Doggett, which of the remaining board members must be seated in seat 5?

    (A) Allenby
    (B) Broome
    (C) Chatsworth
    (D) Doggett
    (E) Edson

5. Gary: I wish you wouldn't drink so much beer. It's bad for your health.
   Nancy: How can you say that? I don't weigh a pound more than I did a year ago.

   Which of the following responses would most strengthen Gary's argument?

    (A) You weigh ten pounds more than you did six years ago.
    (B) Most people who drink a lot of beer do put on weight.
    (C) If you keep drinking so much beer, you will soon put on weight.
    (D) Putting on weight is not the only harmful effect of drinking beer.
    (E) You can put on weight in other ways than by drinking beer.

Questions 6 and 7

Students who are excused from Freshman Composition write better than those who take the course. Thus, we can encourage better writing by our students by dropping the Freshman Composition course.

6. The major flaw in the reasoning used in the argument above is that the author

    (A) bases the argument on a purely subjective judgment
    (B) does not cite evidence for the statements given
    (C) confuses cause and effect
    (D) fails to take into account any long-term effects of the course
    (E) assumes that all Freshman Composition courses are essentially alike

7. Each of the following, if true, would weaken the argument above EXCEPT

    (A) schools with no Freshman Composition course do not generally produce better student writers
    (B) most students who take the Freshman Composition course do not appreciably improve their writing skills
    (C) to be excused from Freshman Composition, a student must pass a rigorous writing test
    (D) each of the English department's best instructors teaches at least one Freshman Composition class each semester
    (E) 65 percent of the students surveyed reported that they learned a great deal about grammar and rhetoric from taking Freshman Composition

Questions 8–12

Five executives of a European corporation hold a conference in Rome.

Mr. A converses in Spanish and Italian.
Mr. B converses in Spanish and English.
Mr. C converses in English and Italian.
Mr. D converses in French and Spanish.
Mr. E, a native Italian, can also converse in French.

8. Which, of the following, can act as interpreter when Mr. C and Mr. D wish to confer?

   (A) Only Mr. A   (B) Only Mr. B
   (C) Only Mr. E   (D) Mr. A or Mr. B
   (E) Any of the other three executives

9. Which of the following cannot converse without an interpreter?

   (A) Mr. B and Mr. E
   (B) Mr. A and Mr. B
   (C) Mr. A and Mr. C
   (D) Mr. B and Mr. D
   (E) Mr. A and Mr. E

10. Besides Mr. E, which of the following can converse with Mr. D without an interpreter?

   (A) Only Mr. A
   (B) Only Mr. B
   (C) Only Mr. C
   (D) Messrs. A and B
   (E) Messrs. A, B, and C

11. If a sixth executive is brought in, to be understood by the maximum number of the original five, he should be fluent in

   (A) English and French
   (B) Italian and English
   (C) French and Italian
   (D) Italian and Spanish
   (E) English and Spanish

12. Of the languages spoken at this conference, which are the two least common?

   (A) English and Spanish
   (B) English and French
   (C) Italian and Spanish
   (D) English and Italian
   (E) French and Spanish

Questions 13–16

All A's, B's, C's, D's, E's, and F's are Q's.
All A's are B's.
No B that is not an A is an F.
Some C's are A's.
All D's are C's.
Some C's are not B's.
No D is an A.
All Q's and only Q's that are neither B's nor C's are E's.

13. Which of the following can be deduced from the information given?

   (A) All F's are A's.
   (B) Some F's are A's.
   (C) Some F's are E's.
   (D) Some F's are C's.
   (E) All F's are A's, C's, or E's.

14. Which must be false if the information given is true?

   (A) No D's are B's.
   (B) Some B's are D's.
   (C) Some F's are both B's and C's.
   (D) Some Q's are neither B's nor E's.
   (E) Some F's are D's.

15. Which cannot be shown to be true or false on the basis of the information given?

   I.   No B or C is an E.
   II.   Some C's are B's but not A's.
   III.   No B is both an A and a D.

   (A) I only
   (B) II only
   (C) III only
   (D) I and II
   (E) II and III

16. P is not a B. Which of the following must be true?

   (A) P is an E.
   (B) If P is a C, it is neither an A nor a D.
   (C) If P is a Q, it is an E or a C.
   (D) If P is not an E, it is a C.
   (E) If P is a Q, it may be a C or an A, but not both.

Questions 17–22

At a congress of the Progressive Federal Party, the seven top party leaders, who are all cabinet ministers, are seated on the platform in order of rank. The Prime Minister, the party leader, is in the center. The closer a person is to the Prime Minister, the higher is his or her rank, with a person on the Prime Minister's right outranking one equidistant from the Prime Minister on her left. The seven leaders are Arning, Brenner, Civili, Dorner, Eckland, Fentz, and Grell.
Fentz is four places to the left of the Minister of Agriculture, who is two places to the right of Civili.
Brenner's neighbors are Arning and the Minister of Agriculture.
Grell is two places to the left of Dorner.
The Ministers of Education, Mining, and Culture are seated together, in that order, from left to right.
The remaining ministers are those of Social Welfare and Defense.

17. The Minister of Culture is

   (A) Arning
   (B) Brenner
   (C) Civili
   (D) Dorner
   (E) Eckland

18. The fifth-ranking person in the party hierarchy is

    (A) Grell, the Minister of Mining
    (B) Fentz, the Minister of Culture
    (C) Dorner, the Prime Minister
    (D) Eckland, the Minister of Defense
    (E) Arning, the Minister of Education

19. The Minister of Social Welfare

    I.   outranks the Minister of Defense
    II. is outranked by the Minister of Mining

    (A) I only
    (B) II only
    (C) I and II only
    (D) I or II, but not both
    (E) Neither I nor II

20. How many of the seven party leaders outrank the
    Minister of Education?

    (A) 2
    (B) 3
    (C) 4
    (D) 5
    (E) 6

21. If, during the congress, the Minister of Agriculture
    and the Minister of Education are ordered to
    exchange positions, which is true?

    (A) Arning will move to a seat six places away from
        his original seat.
    (B) Fentz will move up five places in the leadership
        ranking.
    (C) Eckland will move to a seat three places away
        from his original seat.
    (D) Grell will move up four places in the leadership
        ranking.
    (E) Eckland will move from the Prime Minister's
        left side to his right.

22. If, during the congress, Eckland is demoted two
    places in the party leadership ranking, which is true?

    (A) The Minister of Defense moves up one place in
        the leadership ranking.
    (B) Civili becomes the second-ranking leader in the
        party.
    (C) The Minister of Mining moves up two places in
        the leadership ranking.
    (D) Dorner is demoted within the leadership.
    (E) The positions of five persons within the leader-
        ship remain unchanged.

23. Lillian, who has just celebrated her 107th birthday,
    attributes her longevity to her lifelong habit of drink-
    ing a double shot of whiskey each night and smoking
    three cigars each morning.

    The best way to counter her argument would be to
    point out that

    (A) smoking has been proved to be a causative fac-
        tor in several life-threatening diseases
    (B) other factors besides those mentioned may have
        caused her to live 107 years
    (C) not all centenarians drink alcohol and smoke
        tobacco
    (D) Lillian should not be consuming the substances
        mentioned without medical advice
    (E) alcohol has been shown to kill brain cells

Questions 24 and 25

If Dr. Seymour's theory is correct, then the events she
predicts will happen. The events she predicted did happen. Therefore, her theory must be correct.

24. Which of the following arguments has a logical
    structure that most nearly resembles that of the argu-
    ment above?

    (A) If we win the game, we will be the league
        champions. We won the game; therefore, we
        are the league champions.
    (B) If the fan is running, then the electricity must be
        on. The electricity is on; therefore, the fan
        must be running.
    (C) If the store is open, I will buy a shirt. I think the
        store is open; therefore, I should be able to
        buy a shirt.
    (D) If Alice answers her phone, then my prediciton
        is correct. I predict that she is at home; there-
        fore, she will answer her phone.
    (E) If Ted's flight is delayed, he will miss his
        appointment. He kept his appointment; there-
        fore, his flight must have been on time.

25. The conclusion drawn in the argument above would
    be valid if which of the following were true?

    (A) Only Dr. Seymour's theory fully explains the
        events which happened.
    (B) If the events Dr. Seymour predicted happen,
        then her theory is correct.
    (C) If Dr. Seymour's theory is correct, then the
        events she predicted may happen.
    (D) Only Dr. Seymour predicted the events which
        happened.
    (E) If the events Dr. Seymour predicted happen,
        then Dr. Seymour's theory may be correct.

S T O P

IF YOU FINISH BEFORE TIME IS CALLED, YOU MAY CHECK YOUR WORK ON THIS SECTION ONLY.
DO NOT WORK ON ANY OTHER SECTION IN THE TEST.

SECTION 7

Time - 30 Minutes

38 Questions

1. Because the ice grains in slush are so loosely bonded, it is ------ and thus can cause an avalanche even on gentle slopes.

    (A) compact
    (B) flexible
    (C) interdependent
    (D) paradoxical
    (E) unstable

2. While some of the drawings are well rendered, others are mere ------; nonetheless, nearly all possess a sort of rude ------ that catches the eye.

    (A) portraits...grandeur
    (B) illustrations...finesse
    (C) daubs...vigor
    (D) caricatures...polish
    (E) mementoes...familiarity

3. With their pea-sized brains and giant bodies, dinosaurs became a symbol of lumbering stupidity; their extinction seemed only to ------ their ------ design.

    (A) betray...fundamental
    (B) hypothesize...incongruous
    (C) invalidate...conscious
    (D) embody...ultimate
    (E) confirm...flawed

4. The shortcomings of Mr. Brooks's analysis are ----- his ----- in explaining financial complexity and the sheer importance of this text.

    (A) alleviated by...ineptitude
    (B) offset by...clarity
    (C) magnified by...precision
    (D) demonstrated by...adroitness
    (E) mitigated by...incompetence

5. To a person ------ natural history, his country or seaside stroll is a walk through a gallery filled with wonderful works of art, nine-tenths of which have their faces turned to the wall.

    (A) enamored of
    (B) uninstructed in
    (C) responsive to
    (D) disillusioned with
    (E) dependent on

6. Do not be ------ by that fiery formula which springs from the lips of so many ------ old gentlemen: "I shall write to *The Times* about this outrage!"

    (A) dissuaded...indefatigable
    (B) daunted...irresolute
    (C) intimidated...choleric
    (D) discredited...crotchety
    (E) exasperated...apathetic

7. Despite John's somewhat ------ undergraduate career, as undistinguished by academic brilliance as by dissolute excesses, nothing could convince his anxious though doting mother that her son was neither a genius nor a ------.

    (A) ordinary...prodigy
    (B) colorful...profligate
    (C) anomalous...zealot
    (D) lackluster...libertine
    (E) indifferent...miser

8. STAR : CLUSTER::
    (A) orange : rind
    (B) comet : orbit
    (C) tree : clump
    (D) mirror : reflection
    (E) bulb : lamp

9. GUFFAW : LAUGH::
    (A) sip : drink
    (B) squabble : quarrel
    (C) whimper : cry
    (D) sneeze : cough
    (E) lope : run

10. LOBSTER : POT::
    (A) sardine : tin
    (B) goldfish : bowl
    (C) sparrow : nest
    (D) oyster : shell
    (E) rabbit : snare

11. PISTON : CYLINDER::
    (A) elevator : shaft
    (B) vertex : triangle
    (C) bullet : revolver
    (D) kitchen : colander
    (E) valve : bearing

12. ERUDITE : SCHOLAR::
    (A) remote : hermit
    (B) pliant : beggar
    (C) meandering : traveler
    (D) mendacious : liar
    (E) vindictive : conqueror

13. DRUM : TYMPANI::
    (A) cornet : percussion
    (B) oboe : woodwind
    (C) piano : orchestra
    (D) violin : concerto
    (E) coda : symphony

14. GIBBER : SENSE::
    (A) jabber : noise
    (B) toddle : mobility
    (C) dawdle : deference
    (D) vacillate : resolution
    (E) disobey : order

15. MITIGATE : PUNISHMENT::
    (A) aggregate : wealth
    (B) execute : mandate
    (C) commute : sentence
    (D) collect : fine
    (E) set : penalty

16. SENTENTIOUS : APHORISM::
    (A) redundant : criticism
    (B) deprecatory : panegyric
    (C) allegorical : maxim
    (D) symbolic : adage
    (E) laudatory : eulogy

Directions: Each passage in this group is followed by questions based on its content. After reading a passage, choose the best answer to each question. Answer all questions following a passage on the basis of what is stated or implied in the passage.

(This passage was written prior to 1950.)

We now know that what constitutes practically all of matter is empty space; relatively enormous voids in which revolve with lightning velocity infinitesimal particles so utterly small that they
(5) have never been seen or photographed. The existence of these particles has been demonstrated by mathematical physicists and their operations determined by ingenious laboratory experiments. It was not until 1911 that experiments by Sir Ernest Ruth-
(10) erford revealed the architecture of the mysterious atom. Moseley, Bohr, Fermi, Millikan, Compton, Urey, and others have also worked on the problem.
    Matter is composed of molecules whose average diameter is about 1/125 millionth of an inch. Mole-
(15) cules are composed of atoms so small that about 5 million could be placed in a row on the period at the end of this sentence. Long thought to be the ultimate, indivisible constituent of matter, the atom has been found to consist roughly of a proton, the

(20) positive electrical element in the atomic nucleus, surrounded by electrons, the negative electric elements swirling about the proton.

17. The primary purpose of the passage is to
    (A) honor the pioneering efforts of Sir Ernest Rutherford and his followers
    (B) refute the existence of submicroscopic particles
    (C) illustrate how scientists measure molecular diameter
    (D) summarize the then current findings on the composition of matter
    (E) analyze evidence against one theory of atomic structure

18. According to the passage, all of the following are true of the center of the atom EXCEPT that it
    (A) has not yet been seen by the naked eye
    (B) contains elements that are positively charged
    (C) is very little larger than a molecule
    (D) follows experimentally determinable processes
    (E) is smaller than 1/125 millionth of an inch

19. By referring to the period at the end of the sentence (lines 16–17), the author intends to point up the atom's
    (A) density
    (B) mystery
    (C) velocity
    (D) consistency
    (E) minuteness

20. Which of the following relationships most closely parallels the relationship between the proton and the electrons described in the passage?
    (A) A hawk to its prey
    (B) A blueprint to a framework
    (C) A planet to its satellites
    (D) A magnet to iron filings
    (E) A compound to its elements

No one can be a great thinker who does not realize that as a thinker it is her first duty to follow her intellect to whatever conclusions it may lead. Truth gains more even by the errors of one who, with due
(5) study and preparation, thinks for herself, than by the true opinions of those who only hold them because they do not suffer themselves to think. Not that it is solely, or chiefly, to form great thinkers that freedom of thinking is required. On the con-
(10) trary, it is as much or even more indispensable to enable average human beings to attain the mental stature which they are capable of. There have been, and may again be, great individual thinkers in a general atmosphere of mental slavery. But there
(15) never has been, nor ever will be, in that atmosphere an intellectually active people. Where any people has made a temporary approach to such a character, it has been because the dread of heterodox speculation was for a time suspended. Where

(20) there is a tacit convention that principles are not to be disputed; where the discussion of the greatest questions which can occupy humanity is considered to be closed, we cannot hope to find that gen-
(25) erally high scale of mental activity which has made some periods of history so remarkable. Never when controversy avoided the subjects which are large and important enough to kindle enthusiasm was the mind of a people stirred up from its foundations and the impulse given which raised even persons of
(30) the most ordinary intellect to something of the dignity of thinking beings.

She who knows only her own side of the case knows little of that. Her reasons may be good, and no one may have been able to refute them. But if
(35) she is equally unable to refute the reasons of the opposite side; if she does not so much as know what they are, she has no ground for preferring either opinion. The rational position for her would be suspension of judgment, and unless she contents
(40) herself with that, she is either led by authority, or adopts, like the generality of the world, the side to which she feels the most inclination. Nor is it enough that she should hear the arguments of adversaries from her own teachers, presented as
(45) they state them, and accompanied by what they offer as refutations. That is not the way to do justice to the arguments, or bring them into real contact with her own mind. She must be able to hear them from persons who actually believe them; who
(50) defend them in earnest, and do their very utmost for them. She must know them in their most plausible and persuasive form: she must feel the whole force of the difficulty which the true view of the subject has to encounter and dispose of; else she
(55) will never really possess herself of the portion of truth which meets and removes that difficulty. Ninety-nine in a hundred of what are called educated persons are in this condition; even of those who can argue fluently for their opinions. Their
(60) conclusion may be true, but it might be false for anything they know: they have never thrown themselves into the mental position of those who think differently from them and considered what such persons may have to say; and consequently they do
(65) not, in any proper sense of the word, know the doctrines which they themselves profess. They do not know those parts of the doctrine which explain and justify the remainder; the considerations which show that a fact which seemingly conflicts
(70) with another is reconcilable with it, or that, of two apparently strong reasons, one and not the other ought to be preferred.

21. According to the author, it is always advisable to

(A) have opinions which cannot be refuted
(B) adopt the point of view to which one feels the most inclination
(C) be acquainted with the arguments favoring the point of view with which one disagrees
(D) suspend heterodox speculation in favor of doctrinaire approaches
(E) ignore the accepted opinions of the vast majority

22. According to the author, in a great period such as the Renaissance we may expect to find

(A) acceptance of truth
(B) controversy over principles
(C) inordinate enthusiasm
(D) a dread of heterodox speculation
(E) a suspension of judgment

23. According to the author, which of the following statements is true?

(A) Most educated people study both sides of a question.
(B) Heterodox speculation will lead to many unnecessary errors of thinking.
(C) In debatable issues, we should rely on the opinions of the experts for guidance.
(D) It is wise to hear both sides of a debatable issue from one's teachers.
(E) The majority of those who argue eloquently truly know only one side of an issue.

24. As it is used in line 7 of the passage, the word "suffer" most nearly means

(A) endure
(B) undergo
(C) permit
(D) support
(E) force

25. It can be inferred from the passage that a person who knows only her own side of an issue is regarded by the author as

(A) timorous
(B) opinionated
(C) heterodox
(D) educated
(E) rational

26. According to the author, the person who holds orthodox beliefs without examination may be described in all of the following ways EXCEPT as

(A) enslaved by tradition
(B) less than fully rational
(C) determined on controversy
(D) having a closed mind
(E) unwilling to adopt new ideas

27. It can be inferred from the passage that the author would be most likely to agree with which of the following statements?

(A) A truly great thinker makes no mistakes.
(B) Periods of intellectual achievement are periods of unorthodox reflection.
(C) The refutation of accepted ideas can best be provided by one's own teachers.
(D) Excessive controversy prevents clear thinking.
(E) In a period of mental slavery, no true intellectual thought is possible.

Directions: Each question below consists of a word printed in capital letters, followed by five lettered words or phrases. Choose the lettered word or phrase that is most nearly opposite in meaning to the word in capital letters.

Since some of the questions require you to distinguish fine shades of meaning, be sure to consider all the choices before deciding which one is best.

28. RECOLLECT:
    (A) comprise
    (B) misplace
    (C) settle
    (D) forget
    (E) administer

29. MISAPPREHENSION:
    (A) indignation
    (B) derision
    (C) intense speculation
    (D) approximate estimation
    (E) correct interpretation

30. ABIDE:
    (A) retract an offer
    (B) refuse to endure
    (C) shield from harm
    (D) exonerate
    (E) welcome

31. BENEVOLENT:
    (A) tense
    (B) intrepid
    (C) malicious
    (D) prominent
    (E) disinterested

32. PRECIPITATE:
    (A) intricate
    (B) devious
    (C) posthumous
    (D) dilatory
    (E) contradictory

33. ACERBITY:
    (A) noteworthiness
    (B) hypocrisy
    (C) mildness of temperament
    (D) lack of anxiety
    (E) thirst for pleasure

34. EXTIRPATE:
    (A) dilate
    (B) implicate
    (C) proliferate
    (D) expostulate
    (E) incriminate

35. TORTUOUS:
    (A) merciful
    (B) direct
    (C) dangerous
    (D) legal
    (E) tawdry

36. APLOMB:
    (A) discomposure
    (B) righteousness
    (C) temerity
    (D) disapprobation
    (E) parsimoniousness

37. BEATIFIC:
    (A) unattractive
    (B) arrhythmic
    (C) enormous
    (D) fiendish
    (E) radical

38. ODIUM:
    (A) fragrance
    (B) monotony
    (C) idiosyncrasy
    (D) veneration
    (E) vigilance

S T O P

IF YOU FINISH BEFORE TIME IS CALLED, YOU MAY CHECK YOUR WORK ON THIS SECTION ONLY.
DO NOT WORK ON ANY OTHER SECTION IN THE TEST.

Answer Key

Note: The answers to the quantitative sections are keyed to the corresponding review areas in the Mathematics Review (Chapter 11). The numbers in parentheses after each answer refer to the math topic(s) covered by that particular question.

Section 1 Verbal

1.	B	11.	B	21.	C	31.	B
2.	B	12.	B	22.	B	32.	A
3.	C	13.	C	23.	A	33.	D
4.	D	14.	C	24.	E	34.	B
5.	E	15.	D	25.	E	35.	C
6.	C	16.	E	26.	C	36.	E
7.	E	17.	C	27.	C	37.	B
8.	D	18.	D	28.	D	38.	C
9.	E	19.	C	29.	C		
10.	E	20.	B	30.	B		

Section 2 Verbal

1.	C	11.	C	21.	A	31.	C
2.	C	12.	B	22.	B	32.	E
3.	E	13.	C	23.	E	33.	C
4.	D	14.	D	24.	D	34.	E
5.	D	15.	C	25.	C	35.	E
6.	C	16.	E	26.	A	36.	D
7.	A	17.	D	27.	D	37.	A
8.	C	18.	E	28.	A	38.	C
9.	A	19.	C	29.	E		
10.	E	20.	C	30.	D		

Section 3 Quantitative

1.	C (III-B-2)	9.	B (I)	17.	D (III-D, G)	25.	C (II-E)
2.	A (IV-A)	10.	A (III-F)	18.	E (II-A)	26.	C (I-B)
3.	A (III-H)	11.	C (III-H)	19.	B (II-B)	27.	E (II-A)
4.	C (III-B-2)	12.	C (III-A)	20.	C (II-C)	28.	E (III-D)
5.	B (I-G)	13.	B (III-D)	21.	E (I-C)	29.	D (III-G)
6.	C (II-A)	14.	C (III-H)	22.	C (I-D)	30.	E (III-G)
7.	B (I-A)	15.	A (III-A, D)	23.	B (II-B)		
8.	A (II-G)	16.	A (II-B)	24.	A (II-E)		

Section 4 Quantitative

1.	C (III-G)	9.	B (I-H)	17.	C (II-A)	25.	B (IV-C)
2.	C (III-G)	10.	G (III-A)	18.	B (I-D)	26.	E (II-E)
3.	B (III-AC)	11.	C (II-C)	19.	C (I-D)	27.	C (II-A, III-G)
4.	A (III-G)	12.	B (I-B)	20.	B (II-E)	28.	E (II-A)
5.	B (I-B)	13.	C (I-B)	21.	B (II-E)	29.	E (I-B)
6.	D (III-G)	14.	B (II)	22.	D (IV-B)	30.	C (I-F)
7.	C (I-C)	15.	A (I-B, C, H)	23.	B (IV-A)		
8.	A (I-B, C, H)	16.	D (II-B)	24.	B (IV-C)		

Section 5   Analytical

1.	A	8.	A	15.	E	22.	C
2.	E	9.	C	16.	E	23.	B
3.	D	10.	C	17.	C	24.	E
4.	E	11.	C	18.	C	25.	C
5.	D	12.	B	19.	A		
6.	C	13.	D	20.	A		
7.	A	14.	A	21.	B		

Section 6   Analytical

1.	D	8.	E	15.	B	22.	B
2.	B	9.	A	16.	C	23.	B
3.	D	10.	D	17.	C	24.	B
4.	E	11.	D	18.	A	25.	B
5.	D	12.	B	19.	D		
6.	C	13.	E	20.	E		
7.	B	14.	D	21.	B		

Section 7   Verbal

1.	E	11.	A	21.	C	31.	C
2.	C	12.	D	22.	B	32.	D
3.	E	13.	B	23.	E	33.	C
4.	B	14.	D	24.	C	34.	C
5.	B	15.	C	25.	B	35.	B
6.	C	16.	E	26.	C	36.	A
7.	D	17.	D	27.	B	37.	D
8.	C	18.	C	28.	D	38.	D
9.	B	19.	E	29.	E		
10.	E	20.	C	30.	B		

Answer Explanations

Section 1

1. B.   The use of *but* indicates that the dean's attempt to keep control failed. It did so because it was *frustrated* by the board of trustees. None of the other possible actions of the board of trustees would necessarily have caused the dean's attempt to fail.

2. B.   The dispute goes beyond or *transcends* mere ideas, for it influences the financial and professional futures of the disputants.
Note the use of *mere* to downplay the importance of ideas to the essence of the dispute.

3. C.   The key phrase here is "move on." If editors have to travel from firm to firm to succeed in their field, then publishing can be classified as an *itinerant* profession, a profession marked by traveling.

4. D.   The physicists have had good reason to believe in the principle because it has *survived* rigorous or strict tests. These tests have *proved* that the principle is accurate.
Note how the second clause supports the first, explaining why the physicists have had reason to be confident in the principle.

5. E.   If Mrs. Woolf combines both radical and non-radical elements in her fiction, then she presents *an anomalous* or contradictory image.

6. C.   The embittered benefactor thinks of the recipients as *ingrates* (ungrateful persons) because they do not thank him sufficiently for his generosity. He does not think of them as *misers* (hoarders of wealth): although they are stingy in expressing thanks, they are extravagant in spending money. He certainly does not think of them as *louts* (clumsy oafs), *prigs* (self-righteous fuss-budgets), or *renegades* (traitors): the specific attribute he resents in them is ingratitude, not cloddishness, self-satisfaction, or perfidy.

7. E.   The field is cluttered by a *welter* or chaotic jumble of contradictory theories.
Choice A is incorrect. While *bonanza* means abundance, it is an abundance of good things, a desired abundance. Here the abundance of theories is undesired; it is a confusion, not a blessing.

8. D.   The playing field in *football* is called the *gridiron*. The playing field in *baseball* is called the *diamond*.

(Defining Characteristic)

9. E.   A *laurel wreath* is the symbol of *victory*. An *olive branch* is the symbol of *peace*.
Beware eye-catchers. We may associate *idleness* with the notion of lying under a *palm tree*; however, this is not an essential or necessary relationship.

(Symbol and Abstraction It Represents)

10. E.   A *geologist* studies rocks; *gneiss* is a type of rock. A *botanist* studies plants; a *zinnia* is a type of plant.
Beware eye-catchers. A *meteorologist* deals with weather and other atmospheric phenomena, not with *asteroids* and other astronomical phenomena. Likewise, an *entomologist* deals with ants, not *anteaters*.

(Defining Characteristic)

11. B.   *Agitator* (trouble-maker) is a synonym for *firebrand*. *Renegade* (traitor) is a synonym for *turncoat*.

(Synonym)

12. B.   Someone *callow* is immature and will not reach full development till *maturity*. Something *incipient* is beginning to become apparent and will not reach full development till *fruition*.

(Antonym Variant)

13. C.   *Inoculation* (introduction of a serum or vaccine into a living creature) results in *immunity*. *Exposure* to the elements results in *weathering*.

(Cause and Effect)

14. C.   Someone *dispassionate* or temperate in judgment is lacking in *partisanship* or bias. Someone *intemperate* or immoderate is lacking in *moderation*.

(Antonym Variant)

15. D.   Something *grisly* or gruesome causes one to *recoil* or flinch. Something *heartrending* or severely distressing causes one to *weep*.

(Cause and Effect)

16. E.   A *tocsin* is the ringing of a bell that signals *danger*. A *knell* is the ringing of a bell that signals *death*.
Beware eye-catchers. *Tocsin* and *toxin* sound alike but are unrelated. Similarly, beware tempting marginal relationships. A *clarion* call of a trumpet may summon one to *battle*; it does not *by definition* do so.

(Function)

17. **C.** The author first establishes the general picture of unoriginal, passive Mary Shelley and then goes about demolishing it by bringing out just how innovative Shelley was in departing from the traditional model of the overreacher. Thus, the author's purpose is to *rehabilitate* Shelley's literary reputation.

Choice A is incorrect. Others have discounted Shelley's contribution; this author esteems it.

Choice B is incorrect. The author mentions, but does not trace, Shelley's familiarity with the then current scientific and literary revolution.

Choice D is incorrect. While the author deals with this question, she does so as part of her general attempt to reevaluate Shelley.

Choice E is incorrect. It is unsupported by the passage.

18. **D.** Immediately before quoting Praz, the author states that the general view of Shelley depicts her as "a transparent medium through which passed the ideas of those around her." The quotation from Praz provides an excellent example of this particular point of view.

To answer this question correctly, you do not need to reread the passage in its entirety. Quickly scan the passage for the name Praz; reread only the context in which it appears.

19. **C.** The opening sentence points out that Shelley herself acknowledged the influence of her unplanned immersion in the scientific and literary revolutions of her time. Clearly, the author of the passage concedes this as true of Shelley.

20. **B.** The concluding paragraph distinguishes Frankenstein from the other overreachers in his desire not to extend his own life but to impart life to another (by creating his monster). Thus, his purpose is *atypical* of the traditional overreacher.

To say that someone *parts from* the traditional figure of the overreacher is to say that he *differs* from it. Thus, to answer this question quickly, scan the passage looking for *overreacher* and *different* (or their synonyms).

21. **C.** Choice C is correct. The opening sentence states that ethology and behaviorist psychology (*two differing theories*) illustrate the distinction between learning and instinct (*behavioral processes*). The discussion of these two theories that follows explains the behavioral processes.

Choice A is incorrect. The passage does not suggest that one behavioral theory is more effective than another.

Choice B is incorrect. The passage sums up current theories; it does not propose a new one in their place.

Choice D is incorrect. The passage presents Pavlov's arguments in the course of explaining behaviorist psychology; it does not dispute them.

Choice E is incorrect. The passage is concerned with learned behavior as well as instinctive or innate behavior.

22. **B.** Choice B is correct. In lines 13–16, the author states that Lorenz and Tinbergen were, with Frisch, the founders of ethology (defined in the passage as the study of instinct).

Choice A is incorrect. Only Lorenz and Tinbergen are cited for their work with the egg-rolling response in geese; nothing in the passage suggests that Frisch worked with egg-rolling.

Choice C is incorrect. It is unsupported by the passage.

Choice D is incorrect. Behaviorists, not ethologists, are cited as favoring strictly controlled conditions (lines 42-44).

Choice E is incorrect. Nothing in the passage suggests the ethologists have invalidated the behaviorists' approach.

23. **A.** Choice A is correct. What is remarkable about the goose's response is that "at first glance [it] might seem to be a thoughtful solution to a problem." This suggests that the appearance of *purpose and intelligence* is what makes the act remarkable or noteworthy.

Choice B is incorrect. This is an aspect of the goose's response; it is not what makes the goose's response noteworthy. It is not remarkable for an egg-rolling response to be triggered by an egg.

Choice C is incorrect. The egg-rolling response supports ethological theories; it does not refute or disprove them.

Choice D is incorrect. This is an aspect of the goose's response, not what makes the goose's response noteworthy.

Choice E is incorrect. It is both inaccurate factually (the response lasts longer than four weeks) and not an aspect of the goose's response that would be noteworthy.

24. **E.** Choice E is correct. You can arrive at it by the process of elimination.

Statement I is true. Behaviorists such as Pavlov worked with the unconditioned responses of animals. Therefore, you can eliminate Choices B and C.

Statement II is untrue. Imprinting is a term current among ethologists, not behaviorists (lines 36-40). Therefore, you can eliminate Choice D.

Statement III is true. Behaviorists assume animals act in order to obtain rewards or avoid punishments (*shun negative stimuli*). Therefore, you can eliminate Choice A.

Only Choice E is left. It is the correct answer.

25. **E.** The author does *not* settle any arguments; he merely presents differing theories without attempting to resolve their differences.

Choice A is incorrect. The author defines terms throughout the entire passage.

Choice B is incorrect. The author points out equivalents (*functional parallels*) between the two systems (lines 55-64).

Choice C is incorrect. The author refers to experimental studies involving both classical and operant conditioning.

Choice D is incorrect. The author uses the example of beer bottles to illustrate what sort of convex objects evoke the egg-rolling response from geese (lines 27-29,

26. C.   The trial-and-error method of experimentation first rewards the animal for even partial performance of the desired response but later rewards only increasingly precise behavior. Thus, this method requires *an increasing refinement of behavior* from the experimental animal.

Choice A is incorrect. Although both rewards and punishments may be used in operant conditioning, the animal does not have to be exposed to punishment for the experiment to succeed.

Choice B is incorrect. The experimenter asks for increasingly precise behavior. Nothing suggests he or she gives increasingly greater rewards.

Choice D is incorrect. Nothing suggests that the cues necessarily change.

Choice E is incorrect. At the onset of the experiment, the experimenter rewards *even partial performance* of the desired behavior.

27. C.   Although the author reports that behaviorists view instinct as "irrelevant to learning," his description of the egg-rolling process shows no such bias against the ethologists' point of view. Instead, he focuses on pointing out correspondences between the two approaches to behavior in an unbiased, dispassionate manner; the tone of his discussion is one of *neutrality*.

28. D.   The opposite of to *sedate* or *tranquillize* is to *stimulate* or arouse.
Beware eye-catchers. Note the abundance of medical terms among the answer choices here.
Think of "sedating a restless patient."

29. C.   The opposite of *apathetic* or indifferent is *enthusiastic*.
Word Parts Clue: *A-* means without; *path-* means feeling. Someone *apathetic* is without feeling; he or she does not care.
Think of "sadly apathetic voters."

30. B.   The opposite of to *dislodge* or cause something to shift is to *secure* or fasten it in place.
Think of "dislodging a boulder" from its position.

31. B.   The opposite of *celibacy* or chastity is *promiscuity* or indiscriminate sexual union.
Think of "vows of celibacy."

32. A.   The opposite of *fledgling* or untried is *experienced*. The image is of a young bird just capable of leaving the nest.
Think of "fledgling pilots trying their wings."

33. D.   The opposite of *insipidness* or lack of flavor is *savoriness*, the quality of being flavorsome.
Think of the "insipidness of overcooked boiled cabbage."

34. B.   The opposite of to *sequester* or segregate is to *permit to mingle*.
Word Parts Clue: *Se-* means apart. To *sequester* someone means to set him apart.
Think of "sequestered jurors."

35. C.   The opposite of *equanimity* (emotional balance or composure) is *agitation*.
Word Parts Clue: *Equ-* means even; *anim-* means mind or spirit. *Equanimity* is an evenness of mind; composure.
Think of "something shattering one's equanimity."

36. E.   The opposite of to *anathematize* or curse is to *bless*.
Think of "anathematizing one's foes."

37. B.   The opposite of *moribund* or approaching death is *vital* or full of life.
Word Parts Clue: *Mori-* means die. *Moribund* means dying.
Think of "a moribund patient."

38. C.   The opposite of to *distill* or concentrate in purity is to *adulterate* or make impure (as by adding inessentials).
Think of "distilling strong brandy."

Section 2

1. C.   While all the answer choices are plausible goals for an anchorman, only one is acceptable in light of the second clause: *dispassion* or calm. Shaw's maintenance of his composure is illustrated by his ability to maintain the normal pitch of his voice.

2. C.   By definition, *parasites* sap or drain nutrients from their hosts.

3. E.   Inconsistencies in a story would *warrant* or justify disbelief or incredulity on anyone's part, whether or not he considered himself a *skeptic* (doubter).

4. D.   The *assiduous* or diligent *execution* of one's job would give one's employer no cause for complaint.

5. D.   It was Williams' *penchant* or liking for the-
        atricality that caused critics to *denigrate* or
        belittle his plays as mere melodrama.
        Note how the use of *mere* and the sense of the
        Shakespearean quotation convey the idea that
        Williams' plays have been sullied or belittled.

6. C.   Because Mr. Southern so understands the spirit
        of the age, he is unafraid of or *undaunted by* its
        paradoxes.
        To say that a historian has entered thoroughly
        into the spirit of an age is a compliment. Thus,
        the missing word must be complimentary in
        meaning.

7. A.   If language shapes and *determines* the very
        thoughts we are able to have, then it is certainly
        far more than merely *incidental* to or acciden-
        tally linked with thought and communication.
        Note how the phrase *far from being* signals the
        basic contrast of the sentence.

8. C.   A *barge* is a kind of *vessel* or ship. A *shovel* is
        a kind of *implement* or tool.

        (Class and Member)

9. A.   Something *ramshackle* or rickety lacks *sound-
        ness* or solidity. Something *garbled* or jumbled
        lacks *clarity*.

        (Antonym Variant)

10. E. To *dampen enthusiasm* is to diminish it. To
        mute (muffle) *sound* is to diminish it.
        Note that Choice C is incorrect: to *distract
        attention* is not to diminish it but to divert it in
        a new direction.

        (Defining Characteristic)

11. C. A *burst* is a sudden violent outbreak of *sound*.
        A *blast* is a sudden violent outbreak (heavy
        gust) of *wind*.
        Beware eye-catchers. Choice D is incorrect. A
        glimmer is a feeble or intermittent *light*, not a
        sudden violent flare or blast of light.

        (Degree of Intensity)

12. B. Domesticated *doves* are kept in an enclosure
        called a *cote*. Domesticated *pigs* are kept in an
        enclosure called a *sty*.
        Note that Choice E is incorrect. While *foxes*
        live in *dens*, foxes are not domestic animals
        and dens are not manmade enclosures.

        (Defining Characteristic)

13. C. A *shot* is part of a *salvo* (a simultaneous dis-
        charge of shots). An *arrow* is part of a *volley* (a
        simultaneous discharge of arrows).
        Beware eye-catchers. *Salvo* is unrelated to
        salve or *ointment*.

        (Part to Whole)

14. D. A *crab* is an example of a *crustacean*. A *spi-
        der* is an example of an *arachnid*.

        (Class and Member)

15. C. *Skulduggery* or dishonest, unscrupulous behav-
        ior is the mark of the *swindler*. *Chicanery* or
        trickery is the mark of the *trickster*.

        (Defining Characteristic)

16. E. *Self-respecting* is less extreme than *vainglo-
        rious* or excessively proud. *Careful* is less
        extreme than *punctilious* or excessively atten-
        tive to fine points.

        (Degree of Intensity)

17. D. The concluding sentence of the opening para-
        graph mentions factors that produced the crop
        of black writers who made up the Harlem Ren-
        aissance. The subsequent paragraph continues
        the discussion of these social and political
        factors.
        Choice A is incorrect. Although the opening
        sentence indicates that the willingness of black
        writers to portray their own lives was a contrib-
        uting factor to the Harlem Renaissance, the
        next sentence makes it clear that this willing-
        ness was only *part* of what was going on.
        Choice B is incorrect. The author is concerned
        with these writers as part of an American liter-
        ary movement, not a worldwide crusade.
        Choice C is incorrect. The author cites exam-
        ples of specific injustices in passing.
        Choice E is incorrect. It is unsupported by the
        passage.

18. E. The author's use of such terms as "nobility of
        expression" and "masters of recent American
        literature" makes it clear his attitude is one of
        admiration.

19. C. The fact that the writers were more involved
        with fighting problems in the system than with
        attacking the system itself suggests that funda-
        mentally they *were not opposed to* the demo-
        cratic system of government.
        Choice A is incorrect. The fact that the writers
        did not revolt against the system does not nec-
        essarily imply that they played a minor part in
        fighting abuses of the system.
        Choices B, D, and E are incorrect. None is
        suggested by the statement.

20. C.   In lines 8-10, the author mentions the growing interest in social and economic problems among the writers of the Harlem Renaissance. They used poetry, prose, and song to cry out against social and economic wrongs. Thus, they transformed their growing social and political interest into art.
Choice A is incorrect. The author distrusts the "foreign ideologies" (lines 26–27) with their commitment to international solidarity.
Choice B is incorrect. The author states that the writers wished to improve American culture.
Choices D and E are incorrect. Neither is implied by the author.

21. A.   Both the author's reference to historical interpretations of the Negro writer's role (lines 52-54) and the author's evident concern to distinguish Negro writers from those who "embraced" socialist and communist propaganda (lines 24-28) suggest he is a historian interested in presenting these writers as loyal Americans.
Choice B is incorrect. The author touches on literature only in relationship to historical events.
Choices C, D and E are incorrect. There is nothing to suggest any of these interpretations in the passage.

22. B.   The author's point is that the writers essentially ignored socialist and communist propaganda. This is apparently contradicted by the *Messenger* quote asserting that the New Negro (and thus the new black writer) was *produced* by the same forces that produced socialism and communism. The author gives qualified assent to that assertion ("Such forces *may* have produced the New Negro").

23. E.   The passage cites the battles for better working conditions, desegregation, and social and political equality, among others.
Choice A is unanswerable on the basis of the passage. The passage mentions an "improvement in the capacity for expression" in the period, but cites no factors leading to this stylistic improvement.
Choice B is unanswerable on the basis of the passage. It mentions no specific names.
Choice C is unanswerable on the basis of the passage. The passage states the writers did not "embrace the several foreign ideologies that sought to sink their roots" in America. However, it nowhere suggests that the writers were *in rebellion* against these foreign ideologies.
Choice D is unanswerable on the basis of the passage. No such information is supplied.

24. D.   The author takes the reader through Wegener's reasoning step by step, describing what led Wegener to reach his conclusions.

25. C.   The author both notes that Wegener's theory is revolutionary and indicates that it defies our conventional notions of the rigidity and immobility of the continents. At the same time, he presents Wegener's reasoning fully and objectively, neither mocking him nor adulating him. Thus, the author displays a *judicious* attitude, a level-headed, academically respectable approach to a then controversial theory.

26. A.   Since the existence of the correspondences between the various coastal contours was used by Wegener as a basis for formulating his theory of continental drift, it can be inferred that the correspondences provide evidence for the theory.
Choice B is incorrect. The passage does not indicate that Pangea's existence has been proved.
Choice C is incorrect. It is the relative heaviness of sima, not the level or depth of sima, that suggested the possibility of the lighter continents drifting.
Choice D is incorrect. Mobility rather than immobility would provide evidence for continental drift.
Choice E is incorrect. The continents are lighter than the underlying sima.

27. D.   Choice D is answerable on the basis of the passage. The next-to-the-last sentence of the second paragraph states that the Americas "apparently drifted toward the west."

28. A.   The opposite of to *smart* or cause a sharp stinging pain is to *soothe*.
Think of "a cut that smarts."

29. E.   The opposite of *lucid* (clear) is *obscure*.
Think of "lucid thinking."

30. D.   The opposite of the *periphery* (outward boundary) is the *center*.
Think of the "periphery or outskirts of a city."

31. C.   The opposite of *enigmatic* (puzzling; mysterious) is *unambiguous* or clear.
Think of the Mona Lisa's "enigmatic smile."

32. E.   The opposite of to *repudiate* (disown; refuse to acknowledge) is to *accept*.
Think of "repudiating a debt."

33. C.   The opposite of *aloofness* (remoteness, indifference) is *concern*.
Think of "haughty aloofness."

34. E.   The opposite of to *exhume* or disinter is to bury or *inter*.
Word Parts Clue: *Ex-* means out. *Humus* means earth. To *exhume* is to dig out of the earth.
Think of "exhuming a corpse."

35. E.   The opposite of *despotic* (imperious, domi-
          neering) is *humble*.
          Think of "a despotic tyrant."

36. D.   The opposite of to *obfuscate* or confuse is to
          clarify.
          Word Parts Clue: *Ob-* means completely; *fusc-*
          means dark; *-ate* means to make. To *obfuscate*
          is to becloud or make completely dark.
          Think of "obfuscating the issue."

37. A.   The opposite of a *paean* or song expressing
          exultation is a *dirge* or song expressing grief.
          Think of "a triumphant paean."

38. C.   The opposite of to *concatenate* or link together
          is to detach or *unlink*.
          Word Parts Clue: *Con-* means together; *catena-*
          means chain. *Concatenate* means to link
          together as in a chain.
          Think of "sonnets concatenated in a sequence."

Section 3

1. C.   Because alternate angles have the same mea-
         sure, $x = 3x - 50$; then $50 = 2x$ and $x = 25$.

2. A.   Column A: $17.40 + \$6.93 = \$24.33$
         Column B: $\$6.01 + \$17.01 = \$23.02$

3. A. $AB = 6, BO = 2, OC = 5$
         $BC = BO + OC = 7$

         Area of triangle $ABC = \dfrac{1}{2}\,(6)\,(7) = 21$

4. C. $a + y = 180$ (angles on the same side of the
         transversal)
         $a = x$ (vertical angles)
         Therefore $x + y = 180$

5. B. $\sqrt{0.81} = 0.9$
         $60\% = 0.6$
         $1\dfrac{1}{2} = \dfrac{1.5}{3.0}$
         Sum average $= \dfrac{3.0}{3} = 1$

6. C. $7x = 196$
         $x = 28$
         $\dfrac{x}{7} = 4$

7. B.   Both columns have in common: 14, 12, 10, 8,
         and 6. Column A has, in addition, $(2)(4)$ or 8.
         Column B has, in addition, 16.

8. A.   From the given information $2A > 2B$. But
         $2B > B + C$, since $C < B$.

9. B. $5^4 = 625$
         $625 = 100T$
         $6.25 = T$
         Therefore, $10 > T$.

10. A.   If the area of a circle is four times a smaller cir-
          cle its radius is two times as much.

11. C.   The distance from $(5,3)$ to $(5,7) = 4$. The
          radius of the circle is 4 and the circumference
          is 8π.

12. C.   If $a = 20$ then $x = 160$
          If $b = 160$ then $y = 20$
          $a + x = 180$
          $y + x = 180$

13. B.   The triangle is a 3-4-5 triangle.
          Hypotenuse $= 2x + x = 3x$
          Hypotenuse $= 5$
          $3x = 5$
          $x = \dfrac{5}{3}$ (Column A)

14. C.   Since the measure of $\angle C = 45°$, the measure
          of $\angle A = 45°$ and $AB = BC$.
          Let $x = AB = BC$
          Area $ABC = \dfrac{1}{2}(x)(x) = 12.5$
          $x^2 = 25$ and $x = 5$
          $AB = 5; BC = 5$

15. A. $\left(\dfrac{X}{Z}\right)\left(\dfrac{Z}{Y}\right) = \dfrac{X}{Y}$

          X and Y are opposite equal angles and therefore
          $X = Y$ and $\dfrac{X}{Y} = 1$

16. A.   (1) $3x - 6 = 1$
          (2) $x - 2 = ?$
          Observe equation (2) $= \dfrac{1}{3}$ of equation (1)
          $x = \dfrac{1}{3}(3x)$
          $-2 = \dfrac{1}{3}(-6)$
          $? = \dfrac{1}{3}(1)$
          $? = \dfrac{1}{3}$

17. D.   Let $x = AB = BC$.
          By the Pythagorean theorem,
          $x^2 + x^2 = (6\sqrt{2})^2$
          $2x^2 = (36)(2)$
          $x^2 = (36)$
          $x = 6$
          Area $= \dfrac{(6)(6)}{2}$ or 18
          Or, recall that in 45°, 45° right triangles, the
          hypotenuse $=$ leg $\sqrt{2}$.

18. E.   Factor out 146.
         146(117 + 173 + 210)
         146(500) = 73,000

19. B.   (1) $7x - 5y = 13$
         (2) $2x - 7y = 26$
         (3) $5x + 2y =$
         Observe equation (3) is the difference between
         equation (1) and (2). Therefore $13 - 26 = -13$.

20. C.   Rate $= \dfrac{\text{distance}}{\text{time}}$ or $\dfrac{d}{t}$
         Let x = time required to cover m miles.
         Distance = rate × time
         $m = \dfrac{d}{t} \times x$
         $m = \dfrac{dx}{t}$ or $\dfrac{mt}{d} = x$

21. E.   Lactose = 0.16
         Fructose = 1.70
         Fructose is about 10.6 times sweeter.

22. C.   The increase is from 0.16 to 0.32.
         Change is 0.16.
         $\dfrac{\text{change}}{\text{original}} = \dfrac{0.16}{0.16} = 1 = 100\%$

23. B.   100 times as sweet as glucose = 74
         Let x = number of grams of sucrose to be
         added to saccharin.
         1 gram of saccharin = 675
         x grams of sucrose = $(1.00)(x) = x$
         $\dfrac{\text{sweetness}}{\text{number of grams}} = \dfrac{x + 675}{1 + x} = 74$
         $74 + 74x = x + 675$
         $\phantom{74 + {}}74x = 601$
         $\phantom{74 + {}}x = 8.2$ grams

24. A.   Obviously we must use less of the glucose than
         lactose to get 0.32, since glucose is sweeter
         than lactose. Observe the answers.

25. C.   To make mixture:
         1 gram glucose = 0.74
         2 grams sucrose = 2.00
         3 grams fructose = 5.10
         Total of 6 grams = 7.84
         1 gram sucrose = 1.00
         6 grams sucrose = 6.00
         Let x = number of times mixture is sweeter
         than sucrose.
         $7.84 = 6x$
         $1.3 = x$

26. C. $\dfrac{1}{2}$ study French.
         $\dfrac{1}{3}$ of $\dfrac{1}{2}$ or $\dfrac{1}{6}$ study Spanish.
         The remainder $\left(\dfrac{2}{6}\right)$ or $\dfrac{1}{3}$ do not study any for-
         eign language.

Let x = the total number of students in this
school.
$\dfrac{1}{3}x = 300$
$\phantom{\dfrac{1}{3}}x = 900$

27. E.   In 2 hours Mr. Jones completed $\dfrac{2}{x}$ part of the
         lawn. He left unmowed $1 - \dfrac{2}{x}$ or $\dfrac{x - 2}{x}$.

28. E.   Since $\angle A$ is the largest angle and since this is a
         right triangle, $\angle A = 90°$.

29. D.   Since the area of each circle is 4π, the radius
         of each circle is 2 ($\pi r^2 = 4\pi$). The diameter
         of each circle is 4. Since each side of $ABCD$
         equals two diameters, $AB = BC = DC = AD$
         $= 8$ and the perimeter of $ABCD = (4)(8)$ or 32.

30. E.   Area of square = 324 square feet
         Area of rectangle = 324 square feet
         Length of rectangle = 3 yards = 9 feet
         Let x = width of rectangle.
         Area of rectangle = $9x = 324$ $x = 36$.

Section 4

1. C.   Since ODC is equilateral, $DC = \dfrac{1}{3}$ of 12 or 4.
        Since $AB = DC$, and $BC = AD$, perimeter
        $ABCD = 22$.

2. C.   If the area of $ABCD = 36$, each side = 6, the
        length of 6 radii = 6, and each radius = 1. The
        area of each circle = $(1)^2\pi$ or π.

3. B.   Since $x = 20$, $\angle FCD = 40$
        $\angle FCB = 140$ (supplement)
        $\angle FAB = \angle FCB$ (opposite angles of a
        parallelogram)
        Therefore, $y = 140$ and $y > 6x$

4. A.   Radius of I = 5
        Radius of II = 4
        Radius of III = 3
        $AB = 5 + 3 = 8$
        $BC = 3 + 4 = 7$
        $AC = 5 + 4 = 9$
        Perimeter of $ABC = 24$

5. B. $\dfrac{\dfrac{1}{4} - \dfrac{3}{16}}{\dfrac{1}{8}} = \dfrac{\dfrac{4}{16} - \dfrac{3}{16}}{\dfrac{1}{8}} = \dfrac{\dfrac{1}{16}}{\dfrac{1}{8}} = \dfrac{1}{\cancel{16}_2} \cdot \dfrac{\cancel{8}^1}{1} = \dfrac{1}{2}$

6. D. Since radius = 6, area of circle = 36π, but we do not know what part of the circle the segment *AOB* is.

7. C. $\dfrac{1}{5} = \dfrac{10}{5} = 2$ and $\sqrt{4} = 2$

8. A. $\left(\dfrac{1}{0.07}\right)^2 = \dfrac{1}{0.0049} = 204 +$

$204 > \dfrac{1}{7}$

9. B. $3^{n+2} = 27$ or $3^3 = 27$
Since $n + 2 = 3$, $n = 1$
$3 > 1$

10. C. $y + x = 180$
$z + x = 180$
$y + z = 90$ (given)
$y = z$
$y = 45$

11. C. In any 3 consecutive integers, the sum of the first and third is equal to twice the second.

12. B. Since x has a negative value, x^5 will have a negative value and $\dfrac{1}{x^5}$ will have a negative value. In Column B, x^4 will have a positive value.

13. C. $\dfrac{x+y}{y} = \dfrac{x}{y} + \dfrac{y}{y} = \dfrac{x}{y} + 1$

14. B. The fraction $\dfrac{x}{y}$ has a positive value since the numerator and the denominator are positive. If this fraction were equal to 2, then x would equal $2y$. However, since the fraction is equal to more than 2, then x is greater than $2y$.

15. A. $\sqrt{0.25} = 0.5 = \dfrac{1}{2}$
$\dfrac{1}{2} > \dfrac{1}{4}$

16. D. $xyz = 1$
Since $x = z$
$xyz = 1$
$x^2y = 1$
$y = \dfrac{1}{x^2}$

17. C. Change all dimensions to feet.
Piece of cloth was $3y$ feet long; f feet and $\dfrac{i}{12}$ feet were cut.

The present length is $3y - \left(f + \dfrac{i}{12}\right)$.

18. B. \$48.00 (market price) $- \dfrac{1}{4}$ (\$48.00) or
\$12.00 = \$36.00 selling price
Let x = cost.

(cost) x + profit $\left(\dfrac{1}{5}x\right)$ = \$36

$x + \dfrac{x}{5} = 36$
$5x + x = 180$
$6x = 180$
$x = \$30$

19. C. Let x = number of articles shipped.
$0.0625x = 2,000$
$625x = 20,000,000$
$x = 32,000$

20. B. $\left(7\dfrac{1}{5}\text{ inches}\right)(120) = 864$ inches $= 72$ feet

21. B. $30° = \dfrac{30°}{360°} = \dfrac{1}{12} = 8\dfrac{1}{3}\%$

22. D. This is a direct proportion. Let x = number of workers engaged in transportation.
$\dfrac{90°}{1980} = \dfrac{120°}{x}$
$90x = (120)(1980)$
$x = \dfrac{(120)(1980)}{90}$

$x = \dfrac{\overset{4}{\cancel{(120)}}\overset{660}{\cancel{(1980)}}}{\underset{(30)}{\cancel{(30)}} \; \underset{(3)}{\cancel{(3)}}} = 2640$

23. B. There are 50% more transportation workers (30° on chart) than professional workers (20° on chart). The 50% greater income of the professional workers makes their total income equal to the transportation workers' total income.

24. B I is not correct. The increased company income in 1985 (\$50 million) did not necessarily result from price increases.
II is correct. The increase for the 1980–1985 period over the previous period was \$20 million. In the preceding 5 years the increase was \$11 million.
III is not correct. The increase in income could be due to other factors, such as price increases.

25. B. \$30 million + \$11 million = \$41 million $\div$ 2 = \$20$\dfrac{1}{2}$ million. The closest choice is (B).

26. E. There are 12 inches in one foot. To change inches to feet, we would have to divide the inches into groups of 12. Thus, 36 inches contains $36 \div 12$, or 3 groups of 12, or 3 feet. In like manner, c inches contains $c \div 12$ or $\dfrac{c}{12}$ feet.

27. C. $(x + 1)(x - 1) = x^2 - 1$

28. E.   If the sum of two numbers is known (here it is 0), subtracting one of the numbers from the sum will give the other number: Subtract:

$$0$$
$$\underline{2x - 4}$$

To subtract polynomials, change the signs of the subtrahend (polynomial being subtracted) and proceed as in addition:

$$0$$
$$\underline{-2x + 4}$$

The other number is: $-2x + 4$

29. E.   To divide two fractions, invert the divisor $\left(\text{here, the divisor is } \dfrac{3}{x}\right)$, and change the operation to multiplication:

$$\frac{6}{x} \cdot \frac{x}{3}$$

"Cancel" or divide numerator and denominator by factors that will go evenly into both. In this case, 3 and x are such factors. Note that $x \div x = 1$:

$$\frac{\overset{2}{\cancel{6}}}{\cancel{x}} \cdot \frac{\cancel{x}}{\cancel{3}}$$
$$\quad 1 \quad 1$$

Multiply together the remaining factors of the numerator to obtain the numerator of the answer, and multiply together the remaining factors of the denominator to obtain the denominator of the answer.

$$\frac{2}{1} \cdot \frac{1}{1}$$

Simplify: 2

30. C.   The darkened line extends to the right of –3 and includes –3. Therefore, the solution set contains numbers greater than or equal to –3. The darkened line extends to the left of 5, but the open, unshaded dot at 5 indicates that 5 is not included in the solution set; therefore, numbers less than 5 but not including 5 are in the solution set.
If x stands for any member of the solution set, the two conditions above may be represented by $-3 \leqq x < 5$.

Section 5

1-4.   Summarize the availability of the staff.

Monday Alice, Betty, Dorothy, Edith (except first Monday of month)
Tuesday Carol, Betty, Dorothy, Edith
Wednesday Alice, Carol, Dorothy, Edith
Thursday Betty, Dorothy, Edith (except first Thursday of month)
Friday Alice, Betty, Edith

1. A.   Observe that Alice, Betty, and Dorothy are available on any Monday.

2. E.   Observe summary above.

3. D.   Dorothy and Betty are available on any Thursday but Edith is available on all Thursdays except the first Thursday of the month.

4. E.   Observe summary. Only Alice, Betty, and Edith are available on Fridays.

5. D.   The argument states that gun control laws reduce violent crime; the evidence is a drop in armed robberies in one city. This involves unwarranted generalizations (A, C), a failure to consider alternative explanations (B), and a possible failure to consider contrary evidence (E). D, however, raises an objection to gun control laws unrelated to either the validity of the evidence or the validity of the conclusion in the argument.

6. C.   Option I partly answers the objection given in choice B above; this makes it appear more likely that the law directly caused the drop in armed robberies. Option II strengthens the argument in a somewhat more general way; if this statement is true, those violent crimes committed with a gun will be more strongly deterred by the additional punishment mandated for violation of the gun control law. Option III would strengthen the argument *only if* an additional assumption were made, that gun control laws make gun crimes less likely.

7. A.   Option I weakens the argument by suggesting an alternative explanation for the drop in the crime rate. Option II has nothing to do with the crime rate. Option III does not, in itself, suggest that the gun control law is an ineffective *deterrent*.

8-11.   You might first examine the grid and circle the words which seem to violate one or more rules. They are: *death* [violates rules (3) and (4), as well as (5), because it is not an adjective]; *hotter* [violates rule (5), since all other words in column IV are either nouns or verbs; violates rule (4) unless *fester* is changed]; *fester* [violates rule (3); violates rule (4) unless *hotter* is changed — but if *fester* is changed to satisfy rule (3), it will no longer violate rule (4), may violate rule (5), depending on whether *dam* and *edge* are read as nouns or verbs]; *greed* [may violate rule (5), depending, again, on *dam* and *edge*]; *gradual* [violates rule (5)]. Now you should be able to answer the questions dealing only with the trouble spots in the grid.

8. A.   Rules (1) and (2) are not violated by any row or column; the others are (see above).

9. C. Two rules, (1) and (3), apply to rows; rule (1) is satisfied by all rows, rule (3) by rows 1, 4, and 5. Three rules, rules (2), (4), and (5), apply to columns. Rule (2) is satisfied by all columns; rules (4) and (5) only by columns I and II.

10. C. *Death* must be changed to a four-letter word, according to rule (3); this will also bring it into conformity with rule (4); and the new word must be an adjective, according to rule (5).

11. C. This is tricky. *Death* and *gradual* must be changed (*deaf* and *glitter* will do). *Hotter* must be changed to the right part of speech—but what is that? If *dam* and *edge* are verbs, *hotter* can become *hanker*, but *greed* must become a verb (*groan*), while *fester* must become a seven-letter verb (*flicker*). This is a total of five changes. But if *dam* and *edge* are nouns, *hotter* can be a noun (*heater*), *fester* can become a seven-letter noun (*failure*), and *greed* can remain unchanged. This is a total of four changes. Of course, you are not required to supply words which will fit the rules; the examples we've given are simply to clarify the puzzle for you.

12-18. The various statements result in two lists of musical works, which can then be put together because the total number of works is specified. This also becomes important in the last question. The statements about Beach, Ives, and Gottschalk give you:

> G . . . D B . . . I F

The dots indicate that we don't know how many works intervene. The other statements yield:

> C — — E H — A

The three dashes indicate that a precise number of works intervene. *Within a limit of ten works in all*, these two patterns can be put together in only one way:

> G C D B E H — A I F

Note that one space is still blank. We know that ten works will be heard, but only nine composers and works are named, so this is logical.

12. B. This can be answered by inspection of the diagram. Note that choice A is correct *in reverse order*.

13. D. This can also be answered by inspection. Note that choice C contradicts a stated condition.

14. A. This can also be answered by inspection.

15. E. Again, simply inspect the diagram. Five works, including one whose name we don't know, will be heard between the Beach and the Foster.

16. E. Since the soloist's first performance will be during the Gottschalk—the first work to be heard—she will begin tuning up before the start of the program.

17. C. This is just a matter of counting back from the blank space. Works H, E, B, and D are the four that intervene.

18. C. This is the only really hard item in this set. Inserting G into the blank following C, we would have: C G—E H—A D B I F, a total of 11 (I). Inserting I and F into the blanks after C, we would have: G D B C I F E H—A—, a total of 11 (remember that Antes can't end the program) (II). But if A preceded G (III), six composers would precede A and five would follow, for a total of 12.

19-22. A diagram showing which events may lead to which will help you here. We have used broken and dotted lines with B, C, and the events which follow from them in order to distinguish which combinations lead to which results. Your diagram need not be this elaborate (or neat); you are the only person who must be able to read it.

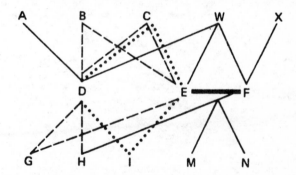

19. A. D results from A, B, C, or W. E results from B, C, or W; F from W or X; M or N from E + F. Your only problem might have come if you failed to notice the stipulation of *immediately preceding* events—so you can't count C or W among the causes of M in this question.

20. A. A results in D only; but D may cause another event only if it is caused by B or C, so no subsequent event follows after the AD sequence. B, C, and W all have more than one immediate result; X has only one, F, but F caused by X may cause H.

21. B. BDH, BEH, CDH, CEH, WFH, and XFH are the combinations that cause H. Notice that H may not result from any of the immediately preceding events unless these resulted from an earlier event.

22. **C.**   I results from two combinations only—CDI and CEI. G results from four combinations—BDG, BEG, CDG, CEG. H results from six, as we just saw. M and N result from either five or six combinations—in the case of M, BEXFM, CEXFM, WEXFM, BEWFM, CEWFM, and possibly WEWFM (we don't know if W can act twice, but it doesn't matter —choice C is still lowest by far).

23. **B.**   This can be deduced from the fact that the author believes that a constitutional amendment will succeed where lawsuits and local statutes have failed.

24. **E.**   This question raises an issue the author has failed to address adequately: given the fact that job discrimination by gender is a real problem, does it necessarily follow that only a constitutional amendment can solve the problem?

25. **C.**   The fact that some employers do not discriminate against women does not undermine the argument as presented, since it does not imply that no problem of discrimination exists.

Section 6

Questions 1–4

1. **D.**   Seat 1 is the leftmost seat; and since Doggett must have Chatsworth seated immediately to his left, he can't sit in seat 1.

2. **B.**   Chatsworth must be seated immediately to the left of Doggett, so he must sit in seat 2 if Doggett is in seat 3.

3. **D.**   Broome cannot sit next to Allenby, so Broome cannot be in seat 6. Since Chatsworth must have Doggett to his right, and seat 6 is the rightmost seat, Chatsworth is eliminated. Doggett, who must have Chatsworth, not Allenby, to his left, is eliminated. Fream refuses to sit in seat 6, so Edson is the only remaining choice.

4. **E.**   If Fream is in seat 3 and Doggett is in seat 2, then Chatsworth, who must sit to the left of Doggett, must be in seat 1. Allenby, Broome, and Edson remain as candidates for seats 4–6. If Allenby occupied seat 5, Broome would have to be next to him; if Broome occupied seat 5, Allenby would have to be next to him—both impossible since Allenby and Broome will not sit next to each other. This means that Edson must occupy seat 5.

5. **D.**   Analyze Nancy's logic: she assumes that the only harmful effect of beer drinking is gaining weight. The best way to strengthen Gary's argument and refute Nancy's is to dispute this assumption. D points out the obvious and explodes her argument. The other choices all fail to challenge Nancy's illogical reasoning.

6. **C.**   It is most likely that students are excused from Freshman Composition if they demonstrate superior writing ability. Thus, being excused is an effect, not a cause, of their writing well; but the argument, in assuming that dropping the course will improve everyone's writing, treats it as if it were a cause. Choice A is incorrect—the first sentence in the argument is a factual statement, whether true or false. Choice B is incidental—the reasoning would be invalid even if the statements were backed by miles of evidence. Choices D and E similarly focus on incidental features which might be important *if* the basic reasoning were valid.

7. **B.**   All choices except choice B suggest that Freshman Composition has educational value and can help to improve writing skills. Choice B suggests just the opposite.

8-12.   Summarize the facts.
Spanish is spoken by 3—A,B,D.
Italian is spoken by 3—A,C,E.
English is spoken by 2—B,C.
French is spoken by 2—D,E.

8. **E.**   When C and D converse they can use English, Italian, French, and Spanish between them. Mr. A speaks Spanish and Italian. Mr. B speaks English and Spanish. Mr. E speaks French and Italian.

9. **A.**   Mr. B understands English and Spanish, while Mr. E speaks two other languages, French and Italian.

10. **D.**   Mr. A and Mr. B can converse in Spanish.

11. **D.**   Three executives speak Spanish (Messrs. A, B, and D). The other executives (Messrs. C and E) speak Italian.

12. **B.** English is spoken by two executives (Messrs. B and C) and French is spoken by two executives (Messrs. D and E). English and Spanish are spoken by 5. Italian and Spanish are spoken by 6. English and Italian are spoken by 5. French and Spanish are spoken by 5.

13-16. Problems like this, which are almost impossible to figure out without a diagram, become relatively simple with a circle diagram like the one shown. Broken lines are used for uncertain relations; shading is used for E; F is shown in various possible positions.

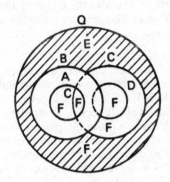

13. **E.** All we know about F's is that they are Q's and that the non-A part of the B circle does not contain any. They must be A's, C's, or E's because these groups define the rest of the Q's. Choice A can be seen to be wrong from the diagram. Choices B, C, and D are all possible, but not necessarily true.

14. **D.** B's, C's, and E's define all the Q's. Choices A and B are possible, but not necessarily true. Choice C would fit an F that was within the A/C overlap. Choice E seems false only if you are hypnotized by the F we have drawn in the A circle, which is also a B. Remember that F is only one possibility.

15. **B.** E's are defined as not B or C, so I is definitely true. III is true because no D is an A. II cannot be known; the fact that C's appear both outside the B's and inside the A's does not mean that there are any in the non-A part of B, where our broken line shows them.

16. **C.** The question does not say P is a Q, so choice A is out. Choice B is only a possibility—P could be in the non-B portion of the D circle as drawn. Choice C is correct—E and C together define the non-B portions of Q (remember that A's are B's). Choice D fails to account for the fact that P may be outside Q altogether. If not a B, P *cannot* be an A (choice E).

17-22. As usual with puzzles about seating arrangements, begin with a series of blanks—at first, more than you will eventually need. You might put initials above the blanks and cabinet positions below. The statement about Fentz gives:

$$\underline{\quad} \quad \underline{F} \quad \underline{\quad} \quad \underline{\quad} \quad \underline{C} \quad \underline{\quad} \quad \underline{\quad} \quad \underline{\quad}$$
$$\text{Ag.}$$

Brenner must be to the right of the Minister of Agriculture since, if he or she were to the left, Civili would be one of his or her neighbors. This gives you a stretch of seven persons between Fentz and Arning, and so you can trim the ends of your diagram. Put the Prime Minister in the center spot. Grell can be two places to the left of Dorner only if Dorner is the Prime Minister. The three ministers seated in a row must be on the left of the Prime Minister, since the Agriculture Minister is on the right. Eckland is placed by elimination. We cannot determine which of the two right-hand places the last two ministers occupy. The completed diagram looks like this:

F	G	C	D	E	B	A
Educ.	Min.	Cult.	P.M.	Ag.	SW or D	SW or D

17. **C.** This information may be easily gleaned from the diagram.

18. **A.** Remember the rules about rank. The top five leaders are Dorner, Eckland, Civili, Brenner, and Grell.

19. **D.** We don't know whether Brenner or Arning is Minister of Social Welfare. If Brenner, he outranks the Minister of Defense, who (by elimination) is Arning. If Arning, he is outranked by the Minister of Mining, Grell. Thus, either I or II may be true. Both together (C) is impossible.

20. **E.** The extreme left-hand seat is the lowest in rank.

21. **B.** According to the question, Minister of Education Fentz will exchange positions with Minister of Agriculture Eckland. As a result, Fentz will move up from seventh to second in the leadership ranking. Choice E would be correct if the directions mentioned were reversed.

22. **B.** Eckland, previously second in rank, becomes fourth; Civili, previously third, becomes second; and Brenner, previously fourth, becomes third. The positions of the Ministers of Defense, Mining, and Education, who rank lower than fourth, and Dorner, who ranks first, are unaffected.

23. **B.** Lillian's argument is flawed because she fails to consider all the possible factors that could explain her longevity; B points this out. Choices A and C do not weaken Lillian's argument, because they do not prove that tobacco and whiskey have bad effects in all cases (choice E may even be considered an *ad hominem* argument!). Choice C doesn't directly answer Lillian, because it proves only that other factors may explain *other* centenarians' survival. Choice D does not get to the flaw in Lillian's reasoning—and besides, she may have had medical advice.

24. **B.** The logical structure of the argument is: If P, then Q; Q, therefore P. This is fallacious reasoning, and we're asked to find the same fallacious reasoning in one of the choices. Choice B commits exactly the same error. Choice A says: If P, then Q; P, therefore Q (which is valid). Choice E says: If P, then Q; Not Q, therefore not P (also valid). Neither of these structures matches that of the original argument. Neither choice C nor choice D can be symbolized using just two letters; thus neither can match the original.

25. **B.** Choice B states the hidden assumption on which the original, fallacious argument was based. If it were true, the original conclusion ("her theory must be correct") would be valid.

Section 7

1. **E.** The *unstableness* of slush makes it unlikely to cling to even gentle slopes. Instead, it starts to slide; it may even cause an avalanche.
   Things that are tightly bonded stick together securely; things that are loosely bonded stick together less well. Note that the loose bonding of the ice grains lessens their stability.

2. **C.** The writer contrasts well-rendered works of art with poorly executed *daubs* or crude pictures. However, he qualifies his criticism by stating that almost all these artworks possess a *vigor* or liveliness that attracts the viewer.

3. **E.** Extinction or destruction of the species appears to *confirm* a *flawed* design that combines an extremely small brain in an extremely huge body. (Actually, current studies of reptiles indicate that the dinosaur's brain was in proper proportion to its body mass.)

4. **B.** *Clarity* in explaining complicated financial matters would do a great deal to *offset* or compensate for shortcomings in a text.
   Note the use of *and* linking the positive phrase "sheer importance of his text" with the second blank. This indicates that the second missing word must be a positive term.

5. **B.** If nine tenths of the works of art in the gallery have their faces turned to the wall, then the visitor to the gallery has no clue whatsoever to what wonders they contain. Similarly, a person *uninstructed in* natural history wanders through the world with no clue whatsoever to nine tenths of the natural wonders that surround him.

6. **C.** *Choleric* or irascible old men are likely to issue fiery proclamations. However, such formulas should not *intimidate* or frighten anyone. The use of terms such as "fiery formula" and "outrage" conveys the image of an elderly gentleman who gets hot under the collar or *choleric*.

7. **D.** John's mother is at once excessively optimistic and excessively pessimistic. Optimistically she thinks her son is a genius (person showing "academic brilliance"). Pessimistically she thinks he is a *libertine* (person given to "dissolute excesses"). In both instances she is wrong: John's career has not been distinguished by genius or depravity; it has merely been *lackluster* (dull, uninspired).
   Note that an undergraduate career undistinguished by genius and depravity would not be likely to be described as either *colorful* or *anomalous* (abnormal). Thus, you could immediately eliminate choices B and C.

8. **C.** A *cluster* is a group of *stars*. A *clump* is a group of *trees*.

   (Group and Member)

9. **B.** To *guffaw* is to *laugh* in a noisy manner. To *squabble* is to *quarrel* in a noisy manner.

   (Manner)

10. **E.** A *lobster* is trapped by lobstermen in a *pot*. A *rabbit* is trapped by hunters in a *snare*.

   (Function)

11. **A.** A *piston* moves up and down within a *cylinder*. An *elevator* moves up and down within a *shaft*. Beware eye-catchers. A *bullet* is fired from a *revolver*; it does not merely move up and down the barrel of the revolver.

   (Location)

12. **D.** *Erudition* or learnedness characterizes the *scholar*. *Mendacity* or dishonesty characterizes the *liar*.

   (Defining Characteristic)

13. **B.** A *drum* is an instrument in the *tympani* or percussion section of an orchestra. An *oboe* is an instrument in the *woodwind* section of an orchestra.

(Class and Member)

14. **D.** To *gibber* (chatter foolishly) is to speak without *sense*. To *vacillate* (waver) is to act without *resolution* (firmness of resolve).

(Antonym Variant)

15. **C.** To *mitigate* a *punishment* is to lessen or reduce it. To *commute* a *sentence* is to lessen or reduce it.

(Function)

16. **E.** An *aphorism* or concise formulation of a truth is by definition *sententious* (pithy; concise). A *eulogy* or expression of praise is by definition *laudatory*.

(Defining Characteristic)

17. **D.** In the opening and closing sentences of the passage, the author sums up what "we now know" and informs the reader what "has been found" about the composition of matter (what constitutes matter).

18. **C.** The passage states that molecules are made of atoms; logically, therefore, an atom is smaller, not larger, than the molecule to which it belongs.
Choice A is incorrect. Line 5 states atoms "have never been seen or photographed."
Choice B is incorrect. Lines 19-20 mention the presence of positive electric elements.
Choice D is incorrect. Lines 5-8 note the ingenious laboratory experiments that determine the atom's operations or processes.
Choice E is incorrect. Lines 13-14 mention the average diameter of a molecule is 1/125 millionth of an inch. Atoms are smaller yet.

19. **E.** The comparison emphasizes the smallness or *minuteness* of atoms.

20. **C.** The satellites *circle* the planet. The electrons *swirl around* the proton. As depicted, the relationships are comparable.
Choice A is incorrect. A hawk *swoops down* upon its prey. The proton does not swoop down upon the electrons.
Choice B is incorrect. A blueprint is an outline or plan. A framework is a skeletal structure, possibly constructed in accordance with a blueprint. The relationships are not comparable.
Choice D is incorrect. Iron filings are *drawn or attracted* to a magnet. Electrons *swirl around* a proton.
Choice E is incorrect. A compound is *made up of* elements. A proton is not made up of electrons.

21. **C.** In the second paragraph, the author emphasizes the need for being able to refute the arguments of the opponents of the side of an issue which an individual supports.

22. **B.** In the next-to-the-last sentence of the first paragraph we are told that when principles cannot be disputed, a period of history cannot achieve the level of brilliance which has made some periods of history so noteworthy.

23. **E.** The second paragraph states that "ninety-nine in a hundred" of so-called educated people do not have a full sense of the force of the arguments that favor their opponents' side.

24. **C.** The opening sentence states that it is a duty to follow one's intellect to whatever conclusions it may lead. Those who do not do so are not suffering or *permitting* themselves to think.

25. **B.** The third sentence of the second paragraph states that the kind of person described in this question "has no ground for preferring either opinion." If she chooses either side, she is acting out of bias or prejudice, and so is opinionated.

26. **C.** A person who holds orthodox ideas without subjecting them to examination cannot be *determined on controversy* (bent on getting into an argument), for her ideas will not be in conflict with those of a majority of her contemporaries.

27. **B.** If it is the suspension of the dread of heterodox speculation that characterizes such periods of intellectual achievement, then such periods must be characterized by unorthodox thought and reflection.

28. **D.** The opposite of to *recollect* or remember is to *forget*.
Think of "recollecting someone's name."

29. **E.** The opposite of a *misapprehension* or incorrect understanding is a *correct interpretation*.
Think of "being under an unfortunate misapprehension."

30. **B.** The opposite of to *abide* or bear patiently is to *refuse to endure*.
Think of being "unable to abide punk rock."

31. **C.** The opposite of *benevolent* or well-meaning is *malicious* or wicked.
Word Parts Clue: *Bene-* means well; *vol-* means wish. Someone *benevolent* wishes people well.
Think of "a benevolent philanthropist."

32. **D.** The opposite of *precipitate* or hasty is *dilatory* or tardy.
Think of "a precipitate departure."

33. C.   The opposite of *acerbity* or sharpness of temper is *mildness of temperament*.
Think of "biting acerbity."

34. C.   The opposite of to *extirpate* or eradicate is to *proliferate* or cause to increase in numbers.
Think of "extirpating endangered species."

35. B.   The opposite of *tortuous* or winding is *direct*.
Beware eye-catchers. *Tortuous* has nothing to do with *torture*.
Think of "a tortuous mountain road."

36. A.   The opposite of *aplomb* (equanimity or poise) is *discomposure* or agitation.
Think of "the aplomb of a diplomat."

37. D.   The opposite of *beatific* or saintly is *fiendish*.
Beware eye-catchers. Choice A is incorrect. *Beatific* is not a synonym for beautiful.
Think of "beatific angels."

38. D.   The opposite of *odium* or detestation is *veneration* or great respect.
Beware eye-catchers. Choice A is incorrect. *Odium* is unrelated to odor.
Think of "despicable odium."

Answer Sheet – MODEL TEST 5

Start with number 1 for each new section.
If a section has fewer than 38 questions, leave the extra spaces blank.

Section 1

1. Ⓐ Ⓑ Ⓒ Ⓓ Ⓔ	11. Ⓐ Ⓑ Ⓒ Ⓓ Ⓔ	21. Ⓐ Ⓑ Ⓒ Ⓓ Ⓔ	31. Ⓐ Ⓑ Ⓒ Ⓓ Ⓔ
2. Ⓐ Ⓑ Ⓒ Ⓓ Ⓔ	12. Ⓐ Ⓑ Ⓒ Ⓓ Ⓔ	22. Ⓐ Ⓑ Ⓒ Ⓓ Ⓔ	32. Ⓐ Ⓑ Ⓒ Ⓓ Ⓔ
3. Ⓐ Ⓑ Ⓒ Ⓓ Ⓔ	13. Ⓐ Ⓑ Ⓒ Ⓓ Ⓔ	23. Ⓐ Ⓑ Ⓒ Ⓓ Ⓔ	33. Ⓐ Ⓑ Ⓒ Ⓓ Ⓔ
4. Ⓐ Ⓑ Ⓒ Ⓓ Ⓔ	14. Ⓐ Ⓑ Ⓒ Ⓓ Ⓔ	24. Ⓐ Ⓑ Ⓒ Ⓓ Ⓔ	34. Ⓐ Ⓑ Ⓒ Ⓓ Ⓔ
5. Ⓐ Ⓑ Ⓒ Ⓓ Ⓔ	15. Ⓐ Ⓑ Ⓒ Ⓓ Ⓔ	25. Ⓐ Ⓑ Ⓒ Ⓓ Ⓔ	35. Ⓐ Ⓑ Ⓒ Ⓓ Ⓔ
6. Ⓐ Ⓑ Ⓒ Ⓓ Ⓔ	16. Ⓐ Ⓑ Ⓒ Ⓓ Ⓔ	26. Ⓐ Ⓑ Ⓒ Ⓓ Ⓔ	36. Ⓐ Ⓑ Ⓒ Ⓓ Ⓔ
7. Ⓐ Ⓑ Ⓒ Ⓓ Ⓔ	17. Ⓐ Ⓑ Ⓒ Ⓓ Ⓔ	27. Ⓐ Ⓑ Ⓒ Ⓓ Ⓔ	37. Ⓐ Ⓑ Ⓒ Ⓓ Ⓔ
8. Ⓐ Ⓑ Ⓒ Ⓓ Ⓔ	18. Ⓐ Ⓑ Ⓒ Ⓓ Ⓔ	28. Ⓐ Ⓑ Ⓒ Ⓓ Ⓔ	38. Ⓐ Ⓑ Ⓒ Ⓓ Ⓔ
9. Ⓐ Ⓑ Ⓒ Ⓓ Ⓔ	19. Ⓐ Ⓑ Ⓒ Ⓓ Ⓔ	29. Ⓐ Ⓑ Ⓒ Ⓓ Ⓔ	
10. Ⓐ Ⓑ Ⓒ Ⓓ Ⓔ	20. Ⓐ Ⓑ Ⓒ Ⓓ Ⓔ	30. Ⓐ Ⓑ Ⓒ Ⓓ Ⓔ	

Section 2

1. Ⓐ Ⓑ Ⓒ Ⓓ Ⓔ	11. Ⓐ Ⓑ Ⓒ Ⓓ Ⓔ	21. Ⓐ Ⓑ Ⓒ Ⓓ Ⓔ	31. Ⓐ Ⓑ Ⓒ Ⓓ Ⓔ
2. Ⓐ Ⓑ Ⓒ Ⓓ Ⓔ	12. Ⓐ Ⓑ Ⓒ Ⓓ Ⓔ	22. Ⓐ Ⓑ Ⓒ Ⓓ Ⓔ	32. Ⓐ Ⓑ Ⓒ Ⓓ Ⓔ
3. Ⓐ Ⓑ Ⓒ Ⓓ Ⓔ	13. Ⓐ Ⓑ Ⓒ Ⓓ Ⓔ	23. Ⓐ Ⓑ Ⓒ Ⓓ Ⓔ	33. Ⓐ Ⓑ Ⓒ Ⓓ Ⓔ
4. Ⓐ Ⓑ Ⓒ Ⓓ Ⓔ	14. Ⓐ Ⓑ Ⓒ Ⓓ Ⓔ	24. Ⓐ Ⓑ Ⓒ Ⓓ Ⓔ	34. Ⓐ Ⓑ Ⓒ Ⓓ Ⓔ
5. Ⓐ Ⓑ Ⓒ Ⓓ Ⓔ	15. Ⓐ Ⓑ Ⓒ Ⓓ Ⓔ	25. Ⓐ Ⓑ Ⓒ Ⓓ Ⓔ	35. Ⓐ Ⓑ Ⓒ Ⓓ Ⓔ
6. Ⓐ Ⓑ Ⓒ Ⓓ Ⓔ	16. Ⓐ Ⓑ Ⓒ Ⓓ Ⓔ	26. Ⓐ Ⓑ Ⓒ Ⓓ Ⓔ	36. Ⓐ Ⓑ Ⓒ Ⓓ Ⓔ
7. Ⓐ Ⓑ Ⓒ Ⓓ Ⓔ	17. Ⓐ Ⓑ Ⓒ Ⓓ Ⓔ	27. Ⓐ Ⓑ Ⓒ Ⓓ Ⓔ	37. Ⓐ Ⓑ Ⓒ Ⓓ Ⓔ
8. Ⓐ Ⓑ Ⓒ Ⓓ Ⓔ	18. Ⓐ Ⓑ Ⓒ Ⓓ Ⓔ	28. Ⓐ Ⓑ Ⓒ Ⓓ Ⓔ	38. Ⓐ Ⓑ Ⓒ Ⓓ Ⓔ
9. Ⓐ Ⓑ Ⓒ Ⓓ Ⓔ	19. Ⓐ Ⓑ Ⓒ Ⓓ Ⓔ	29. Ⓐ Ⓑ Ⓒ Ⓓ Ⓔ	
10. Ⓐ Ⓑ Ⓒ Ⓓ Ⓔ	20. Ⓐ Ⓑ Ⓒ Ⓓ Ⓔ	30. Ⓐ Ⓑ Ⓒ Ⓓ Ⓔ	

Section 3

1. Ⓐ Ⓑ Ⓒ Ⓓ Ⓔ	11. Ⓐ Ⓑ Ⓒ Ⓓ Ⓔ	21. Ⓐ Ⓑ Ⓒ Ⓓ Ⓔ	31. Ⓐ Ⓑ Ⓒ Ⓓ Ⓔ
2. Ⓐ Ⓑ Ⓒ Ⓓ Ⓔ	12. Ⓐ Ⓑ Ⓒ Ⓓ Ⓔ	22. Ⓐ Ⓑ Ⓒ Ⓓ Ⓔ	32. Ⓐ Ⓑ Ⓒ Ⓓ Ⓔ
3. Ⓐ Ⓑ Ⓒ Ⓓ Ⓔ	13. Ⓐ Ⓑ Ⓒ Ⓓ Ⓔ	23. Ⓐ Ⓑ Ⓒ Ⓓ Ⓔ	33. Ⓐ Ⓑ Ⓒ Ⓓ Ⓔ
4. Ⓐ Ⓑ Ⓒ Ⓓ Ⓔ	14. Ⓐ Ⓑ Ⓒ Ⓓ Ⓔ	24. Ⓐ Ⓑ Ⓒ Ⓓ Ⓔ	34. Ⓐ Ⓑ Ⓒ Ⓓ Ⓔ
5. Ⓐ Ⓑ Ⓒ Ⓓ Ⓔ	15. Ⓐ Ⓑ Ⓒ Ⓓ Ⓔ	25. Ⓐ Ⓑ Ⓒ Ⓓ Ⓔ	35. Ⓐ Ⓑ Ⓒ Ⓓ Ⓔ
6. Ⓐ Ⓑ Ⓒ Ⓓ Ⓔ	16. Ⓐ Ⓑ Ⓒ Ⓓ Ⓔ	26. Ⓐ Ⓑ Ⓒ Ⓓ Ⓔ	36. Ⓐ Ⓑ Ⓒ Ⓓ Ⓔ
7. Ⓐ Ⓑ Ⓒ Ⓓ Ⓔ	17. Ⓐ Ⓑ Ⓒ Ⓓ Ⓔ	27. Ⓐ Ⓑ Ⓒ Ⓓ Ⓔ	37. Ⓐ Ⓑ Ⓒ Ⓓ Ⓔ
8. Ⓐ Ⓑ Ⓒ Ⓓ Ⓔ	18. Ⓐ Ⓑ Ⓒ Ⓓ Ⓔ	28. Ⓐ Ⓑ Ⓒ Ⓓ Ⓔ	38. Ⓐ Ⓑ Ⓒ Ⓓ Ⓔ
9. Ⓐ Ⓑ Ⓒ Ⓓ Ⓔ	19. Ⓐ Ⓑ Ⓒ Ⓓ Ⓔ	29. Ⓐ Ⓑ Ⓒ Ⓓ Ⓔ	
10. Ⓐ Ⓑ Ⓒ Ⓓ Ⓔ	20. Ⓐ Ⓑ Ⓒ Ⓓ Ⓔ	30. Ⓐ Ⓑ Ⓒ Ⓓ Ⓔ	

Section 4

1. Ⓐ Ⓑ Ⓒ Ⓓ Ⓔ	11. Ⓐ Ⓑ Ⓒ Ⓓ Ⓔ	21. Ⓐ Ⓑ Ⓒ Ⓓ Ⓔ	31. Ⓐ Ⓑ Ⓒ Ⓓ Ⓔ
2. Ⓐ Ⓑ Ⓒ Ⓓ Ⓔ	12. Ⓐ Ⓑ Ⓒ Ⓓ Ⓔ	22. Ⓐ Ⓑ Ⓒ Ⓓ Ⓔ	32. Ⓐ Ⓑ Ⓒ Ⓓ Ⓔ
3. Ⓐ Ⓑ Ⓒ Ⓓ Ⓔ	13. Ⓐ Ⓑ Ⓒ Ⓓ Ⓔ	23. Ⓐ Ⓑ Ⓒ Ⓓ Ⓔ	33. Ⓐ Ⓑ Ⓒ Ⓓ Ⓔ
4. Ⓐ Ⓑ Ⓒ Ⓓ Ⓔ	14. Ⓐ Ⓑ Ⓒ Ⓓ Ⓔ	24. Ⓐ Ⓑ Ⓒ Ⓓ Ⓔ	34. Ⓐ Ⓑ Ⓒ Ⓓ Ⓔ
5. Ⓐ Ⓑ Ⓒ Ⓓ Ⓔ	15. Ⓐ Ⓑ Ⓒ Ⓓ Ⓔ	25. Ⓐ Ⓑ Ⓒ Ⓓ Ⓔ	35. Ⓐ Ⓑ Ⓒ Ⓓ Ⓔ
6. Ⓐ Ⓑ Ⓒ Ⓓ Ⓔ	16. Ⓐ Ⓑ Ⓒ Ⓓ Ⓔ	26. Ⓐ Ⓑ Ⓒ Ⓓ Ⓔ	36. Ⓐ Ⓑ Ⓒ Ⓓ Ⓔ
7. Ⓐ Ⓑ Ⓒ Ⓓ Ⓔ	17. Ⓐ Ⓑ Ⓒ Ⓓ Ⓔ	27. Ⓐ Ⓑ Ⓒ Ⓓ Ⓔ	37. Ⓐ Ⓑ Ⓒ Ⓓ Ⓔ
8. Ⓐ Ⓑ Ⓒ Ⓓ Ⓔ	18. Ⓐ Ⓑ Ⓒ Ⓓ Ⓔ	28. Ⓐ Ⓑ Ⓒ Ⓓ Ⓔ	38. Ⓐ Ⓑ Ⓒ Ⓓ Ⓔ
9. Ⓐ Ⓑ Ⓒ Ⓓ Ⓔ	19. Ⓐ Ⓑ Ⓒ Ⓓ Ⓔ	29. Ⓐ Ⓑ Ⓒ Ⓓ Ⓔ	
10. Ⓐ Ⓑ Ⓒ Ⓓ Ⓔ	20. Ⓐ Ⓑ Ⓒ Ⓓ Ⓔ	30. Ⓐ Ⓑ Ⓒ Ⓓ Ⓔ	

Section 5

1. Ⓐ Ⓑ Ⓒ Ⓓ Ⓔ	11. Ⓐ Ⓑ Ⓒ Ⓓ Ⓔ	21. Ⓐ Ⓑ Ⓒ Ⓓ Ⓔ	31. Ⓐ Ⓑ Ⓒ Ⓓ Ⓔ
2. Ⓐ Ⓑ Ⓒ Ⓓ Ⓔ	12. Ⓐ Ⓑ Ⓒ Ⓓ Ⓔ	22. Ⓐ Ⓑ Ⓒ Ⓓ Ⓔ	32. Ⓐ Ⓑ Ⓒ Ⓓ Ⓔ
3. Ⓐ Ⓑ Ⓒ Ⓓ Ⓔ	13. Ⓐ Ⓑ Ⓒ Ⓓ Ⓔ	23. Ⓐ Ⓑ Ⓒ Ⓓ Ⓔ	33. Ⓐ Ⓑ Ⓒ Ⓓ Ⓔ
4. Ⓐ Ⓑ Ⓒ Ⓓ Ⓔ	14. Ⓐ Ⓑ Ⓒ Ⓓ Ⓔ	24. Ⓐ Ⓑ Ⓒ Ⓓ Ⓔ	34. Ⓐ Ⓑ Ⓒ Ⓓ Ⓔ
5. Ⓐ Ⓑ Ⓒ Ⓓ Ⓔ	15. Ⓐ Ⓑ Ⓒ Ⓓ Ⓔ	25. Ⓐ Ⓑ Ⓒ Ⓓ Ⓔ	35. Ⓐ Ⓑ Ⓒ Ⓓ Ⓔ
6. Ⓐ Ⓑ Ⓒ Ⓓ Ⓔ	16. Ⓐ Ⓑ Ⓒ Ⓓ Ⓔ	26. Ⓐ Ⓑ Ⓒ Ⓓ Ⓔ	36. Ⓐ Ⓑ Ⓒ Ⓓ Ⓔ
7. Ⓐ Ⓑ Ⓒ Ⓓ Ⓔ	17. Ⓐ Ⓑ Ⓒ Ⓓ Ⓔ	27. Ⓐ Ⓑ Ⓒ Ⓓ Ⓔ	37. Ⓐ Ⓑ Ⓒ Ⓓ Ⓔ
8. Ⓐ Ⓑ Ⓒ Ⓓ Ⓔ	18. Ⓐ Ⓑ Ⓒ Ⓓ Ⓔ	28. Ⓐ Ⓑ Ⓒ Ⓓ Ⓔ	38. Ⓐ Ⓑ Ⓒ Ⓓ Ⓔ
9. Ⓐ Ⓑ Ⓒ Ⓓ Ⓔ	19. Ⓐ Ⓑ Ⓒ Ⓓ Ⓔ	29. Ⓐ Ⓑ Ⓒ Ⓓ Ⓔ	
10. Ⓐ Ⓑ Ⓒ Ⓓ Ⓔ	20. Ⓐ Ⓑ Ⓒ Ⓓ Ⓔ	30. Ⓐ Ⓑ Ⓒ Ⓓ Ⓔ	

Section 6

1. Ⓐ Ⓑ Ⓒ Ⓓ Ⓔ	11. Ⓐ Ⓑ Ⓒ Ⓓ Ⓔ	21. Ⓐ Ⓑ Ⓒ Ⓓ Ⓔ	31. Ⓐ Ⓑ Ⓒ Ⓓ Ⓔ
2. Ⓐ Ⓑ Ⓒ Ⓓ Ⓔ	12. Ⓐ Ⓑ Ⓒ Ⓓ Ⓔ	22. Ⓐ Ⓑ Ⓒ Ⓓ Ⓔ	32. Ⓐ Ⓑ Ⓒ Ⓓ Ⓔ
3. Ⓐ Ⓑ Ⓒ Ⓓ Ⓔ	13. Ⓐ Ⓑ Ⓒ Ⓓ Ⓔ	23. Ⓐ Ⓑ Ⓒ Ⓓ Ⓔ	33. Ⓐ Ⓑ Ⓒ Ⓓ Ⓔ
4. Ⓐ Ⓑ Ⓒ Ⓓ Ⓔ	14. Ⓐ Ⓑ Ⓒ Ⓓ Ⓔ	24. Ⓐ Ⓑ Ⓒ Ⓓ Ⓔ	34. Ⓐ Ⓑ Ⓒ Ⓓ Ⓔ
5. Ⓐ Ⓑ Ⓒ Ⓓ Ⓔ	15. Ⓐ Ⓑ Ⓒ Ⓓ Ⓔ	25. Ⓐ Ⓑ Ⓒ Ⓓ Ⓔ	35. Ⓐ Ⓑ Ⓒ Ⓓ Ⓔ
6. Ⓐ Ⓑ Ⓒ Ⓓ Ⓔ	16. Ⓐ Ⓑ Ⓒ Ⓓ Ⓔ	26. Ⓐ Ⓑ Ⓒ Ⓓ Ⓔ	36. Ⓐ Ⓑ Ⓒ Ⓓ Ⓔ
7. Ⓐ Ⓑ Ⓒ Ⓓ Ⓔ	17. Ⓐ Ⓑ Ⓒ Ⓓ Ⓔ	27. Ⓐ Ⓑ Ⓒ Ⓓ Ⓔ	37. Ⓐ Ⓑ Ⓒ Ⓓ Ⓔ
8. Ⓐ Ⓑ Ⓒ Ⓓ Ⓔ	18. Ⓐ Ⓑ Ⓒ Ⓓ Ⓔ	28. Ⓐ Ⓑ Ⓒ Ⓓ Ⓔ	38. Ⓐ Ⓑ Ⓒ Ⓓ Ⓔ
9. Ⓐ Ⓑ Ⓒ Ⓓ Ⓔ	19. Ⓐ Ⓑ Ⓒ Ⓓ Ⓔ	29. Ⓐ Ⓑ Ⓒ Ⓓ Ⓔ	
10. Ⓐ Ⓑ Ⓒ Ⓓ Ⓔ	20. Ⓐ Ⓑ Ⓒ Ⓓ Ⓔ	30. Ⓐ Ⓑ Ⓒ Ⓓ Ⓔ	

Section 7

1. Ⓐ Ⓑ Ⓒ Ⓓ Ⓔ	11. Ⓐ Ⓑ Ⓒ Ⓓ Ⓔ	21. Ⓐ Ⓑ Ⓒ Ⓓ Ⓔ	31. Ⓐ Ⓑ Ⓒ Ⓓ Ⓔ
2. Ⓐ Ⓑ Ⓒ Ⓓ Ⓔ	12. Ⓐ Ⓑ Ⓒ Ⓓ Ⓔ	22. Ⓐ Ⓑ Ⓒ Ⓓ Ⓔ	32. Ⓐ Ⓑ Ⓒ Ⓓ Ⓔ
3. Ⓐ Ⓑ Ⓒ Ⓓ Ⓔ	13. Ⓐ Ⓑ Ⓒ Ⓓ Ⓔ	23. Ⓐ Ⓑ Ⓒ Ⓓ Ⓔ	33. Ⓐ Ⓑ Ⓒ Ⓓ Ⓔ
4. Ⓐ Ⓑ Ⓒ Ⓓ Ⓔ	14. Ⓐ Ⓑ Ⓒ Ⓓ Ⓔ	24. Ⓐ Ⓑ Ⓒ Ⓓ Ⓔ	34. Ⓐ Ⓑ Ⓒ Ⓓ Ⓔ
5. Ⓐ Ⓑ Ⓒ Ⓓ Ⓔ	15. Ⓐ Ⓑ Ⓒ Ⓓ Ⓔ	25. Ⓐ Ⓑ Ⓒ Ⓓ Ⓔ	35. Ⓐ Ⓑ Ⓒ Ⓓ Ⓔ
6. Ⓐ Ⓑ Ⓒ Ⓓ Ⓔ	16. Ⓐ Ⓑ Ⓒ Ⓓ Ⓔ	26. Ⓐ Ⓑ Ⓒ Ⓓ Ⓔ	36. Ⓐ Ⓑ Ⓒ Ⓓ Ⓔ
7. Ⓐ Ⓑ Ⓒ Ⓓ Ⓔ	17. Ⓐ Ⓑ Ⓒ Ⓓ Ⓔ	27. Ⓐ Ⓑ Ⓒ Ⓓ Ⓔ	37. Ⓐ Ⓑ Ⓒ Ⓓ Ⓔ
8. Ⓐ Ⓑ Ⓒ Ⓓ Ⓔ	18. Ⓐ Ⓑ Ⓒ Ⓓ Ⓔ	28. Ⓐ Ⓑ Ⓒ Ⓓ Ⓔ	38. Ⓐ Ⓑ Ⓒ Ⓓ Ⓔ
9. Ⓐ Ⓑ Ⓒ Ⓓ Ⓔ	19. Ⓐ Ⓑ Ⓒ Ⓓ Ⓔ	29. Ⓐ Ⓑ Ⓒ Ⓓ Ⓔ	
10. Ⓐ Ⓑ Ⓒ Ⓓ Ⓔ	20. Ⓐ Ⓑ Ⓒ Ⓓ Ⓔ	30. Ⓐ Ⓑ Ⓒ Ⓓ Ⓔ	

MODEL TEST 5

SECTION 1

Time—30 Minutes

38 Questions

Directions: Each sentence below has one or two blanks, each blank indicating that something has been omitted. Beneath the sentence are five lettered words or sets of words. Choose the word or set of words for each blank that <u>best</u> fits the meaning of the sentence as a whole.

1. Language, culture, and personality may be considered independently of each other in thought, but they are ------ in fact.

   (A) autonomous (B) pervasive (C) equivocal
   (D) inseparable (E) immutable

2. Since depression seems to result when certain cells in the brain receive too little of two key chemicals, the neurotransmitters norepinephrine and serotonin, one goal of treatment is to make more of the chemicals ------ the nerve cells that need them.

   (A) analogous to (B) dependent on
   (C) available to (D) regardless of
   (E) interchangeable with

3. Wildlife managers and conservationists have gradually come to recognize that ------ methods of protecting the flock by maintaining refuges and regulating hunting are no longer sufficient, and in their dissatisfaction they are ------ a new approach.

   (A) radical...incapable of
   (B) innovative...cognizant of
   (C) conventional...pressing for
   (D) previous...chagrined by
   (E) conservative...dubious of

4. Neutron stars are believed to be the highly compressed remnants of exploding stars (supernovas) and thus ------ of one of the most ------ processes in nature.

   (A) causes...cataclysmic
   (B) products...violent
   (C) examples...equivocal
   (D) justifications...harsh
   (E) precursors...dynamic

5. The sudden shift from ------ to ------ in Hugo's novels can startle readers, especially when he abruptly juxtaposes a scene of chaste and holy love with one of coarse and profane licentiousness.

   (A) devotion...frivolity
   (B) piety...ribaldry
   (C) vulgarity...adultery
   (D) decorum...salubrity
   (E) purity...maturity

6. Isozaki's eye for detail is apparent everywhere in the new museum, but fortunately the details are ------ to the building's larger formal composition, which is ------ by the busyness of much recent architecture.

   (A) important...harmed
   (B) irrelevant...fragmented
   (C) appropriate...echoed
   (D) subordinated...unencumbered
   (E) incidental...nullified

7. Instead of taking exaggerated precautions against touching or tipping or jarring the costly bottle of wine, the waitress handled it quite ------, being careful only to use a napkin to keep her hands from the cool bottle itself.

   (A) fastidiously
   (B) capriciously
   (C) nonchalantly
   (D) tentatively
   (E) imprudently

Directions: In each of the following questions, a related pair of words or phrases is followed by five lettered pairs of words or phrases. Select the lettered pair that best expresses a relationship similar to that expressed in the original pair.

8. LODGE : BEAVER::
   (A) sty : pig
   (B) nest : bird
   (C) shell : turtle
   (D) pelt : rabbit
   (E) walnut : squirrel

9. RUSTLE : CATTLE::
   (A) bleat : sheep
   (B) swim : fish
   (C) pan : gold
   (D) speculate : stock
   (E) hijack : cargo

10. GLAND : ENZYME::
    (A) muscle : spasm
    (B) generator : current
    (C) organ : kidney
    (D) brain : cortex
    (E) silo : grain

11. JUG : CROCKERY::
    (A) wine : vineyard
    (B) hospital : surgery
    (C) hat : millinery
    (D) tankard : brewery
    (E) kiln : ceramics

12. GLINT : LIGHT::
    (A) blare : sound
    (B) whiff : scent
    (C) shade : color
    (D) glut : food
    (E) wave : tide

13. DOGGEREL : POET::
    (A) symphony : composer
    (B) easel : painter
    (C) caption : cartoonist
    (D) soliloquy : playwright
    (E) potboiler : novelist

14. FERAL : DOMESTICATION::
    (A) arable : cultivation
    (B) viral : infection
    (C) crude : refinement
    (D) frugal : economy
    (E) pliable : molding

15. SCOTCH : RUMOR::
    (A) divert : traffic
    (B) broach : topic
    (C) quash : riot
    (D) singe : fire
    (E) spread : gossip

16. QUALIFY : PARTICULAR::
    (A) restrain : effusive
    (B) flout : arbitrary
    (C) acknowledge : specific
    (D) mollify : agreeable
    (E) burnish : dull

Directions: Each passage in this group is followed by questions based on its content. After reading a passage, choose the best answer to each question. Answer all questions following a passage on the basis of what is stated or implied in that passage.

The notion of a tranquil abyss had been so generally held that many investigators were initially reluctant to accept the evidence for strong currents and storms in the deep sea. The first argument for the existence of such currents came from theory. Cold water is denser than warm water, and models of ocean circulation showed that the sinking of cold water near the poles should generate strong, deep and steady currents flowing toward the Equator. Subsequent observations not only confirmed the presence of the deep currents but also disclosed the existence of eddies on the western side of ocean basins that can be some 300 times as energetic as the mean current. Photographs of the sea floor underlying the deep currents also revealed extensive graded beds indicative of the active transport of sediment. The final evidence for dynamic activity at great depths came from direct measurements of currents and sediments in the North Atlantic carried out in the HEBBLE program.

Before we describe the HEBBLE findings in some detail let us briefly review the sources and sinks of deep-sea sediments and the forces that activate the global patterns of ocean circulation. The sediments that end up on the ocean floor are of two main types. One component is the detritus whose source is the weathering of rocks on continents and islands. This detritus, together with decaying vegetable matter from land plants, is carried by rivers to the edge of the continent and out onto the continental shelf, where it is picked up by marine currents. Once the detritus reaches the edge of the shelf it is carried to the base of the continental rise by gravitational processes. A significant amount of terrestrial material is also blown out to sea in subtropical regions by strong desert winds. Every year some 15 billion tons of continental material reaches the outlets of streams and rivers. Most of it is trapped there or on the continental shelves; only a few billion tons escapes into the deep sea.

The second major component arriving at the sea floor consists of the shells and skeletons of dead microscopic organisms that flourish and die in the sunlit waters of the top 100 meters of the world's oceans. Such biological material contributes to the total inventory at the bottom about three billion tons per year. Rates of accumulation are governed by rates of biological productivity, which are controlled in part by surface currents. Where surface currents meet they are said to converge, and where they part they are said to diverge. Zones of divergence of major water masses allow nutrient-rich deeper water to "outcrop" at the sunlit zone where photosynthesis and the resulting fixation of organic carbon take place. Such belts of high productivity and high rates of accumulation are normally around the major oceanic fronts (such as the region around the Antarctic) and along the edges of major currents (such as the Gulf Stream off New England and the Kuroshio currents off Japan). Nutrient-rich water also outcrops in a zone along the Equator, where there is a divergence of two major, wind-driven gyres.

17. The primary purpose of the passage is to
    (A) contrast surface currents with marine currents
    (B) question the methods of earlier investigators
    (C) demonstrate the benefits of the HEBBLE program
    (D) describe a replicable laboratory experiment
    (E) summarize evidence supporting oceanic circulation

18. Which of the following best describes the attitude of many scientists when they first encountered the theory that strong currents are at work in the deep sea?
    (A) Somber resignation
    (B) Measured approbation
    (C) Marked skepticism
    (D) Academic detachment
    (E) Active espousal

19. According to the passage, the earliest data supporting the idea that the sea depths were dynamic rather than placid came from
    (A) underwater photographic surveys
    (B) the activities of the HEBBLE program
    (C) analysis of North Atlantic sea-bed sediments
    (D) direct measurement of undersea currents
    (E) models showing how hot and cold water interact

20. This passage most likely would be of particular interest to
    (A) navigators of sailing vessels
    (B) students of global weather patterns
    (C) current passengers on ocean liners
    (D) designers of sea-floor structures
    (E) researchers into photosynthesis

21. As defined in the passage, the second type of deep-sea sediment consists of which of the following?
    I. Minute particles of rock
    II. Fragmentary shells
    III. Wind-blown soil

    (A) I only
    (B) II only
    (C) I and II only
    (D) I and III only
    (E) I, II, and III

22. In the passage the authors do all of the following EXCEPT
    (A) approximate an amount
    (B) refer to a model
    (C) give an example
    (D) propose a solution
    (E) support a theory

23. The style of the passage can best be described as
    (A) oratorical
    (B) epigrammatic
    (C) expository
    (D) digressive
    (E) metaphorical

Unlike the carefully weighted and planned compositions of Dante, Goethe's writings have always the sense of immediacy and enthusiasm. He was a constant experimenter with life, with ideas, and with forms of writing. For the same reason, his works seldom have the qualities of finish or formal beauty which distinguish the masterpieces of Dante and Virgil. He came to love the beauties of classicism but these were never an essential part of his make-up. Instead, the urgency of the moment, the spirit of the thing, guided his pen. As a result, nearly all his works have serious flaws of structure, of inconsistencies, of excesses and redundancies and extraneities.

In the large sense, Goethe represents the fullest development of the romanticist. It has been argued that he should not be so designated because he so clearly matured and outgrew the kind of romanticism exhibited by Wordsworth, Shelley, and Keats. Shelley and Keats died young; Wordsworth lived narrowly and abandoned his early attitudes. In contrast, Goethe lived abundantly and developed his faith in the spirit, his understanding of nature and human nature, and his reliance on feelings as man's essential motivating force. The result was an all-encompassing vision of reality and a philosophy of life broader and deeper than the partial visions and attitudes of other romanticists. Yet the spirit of youthfulness, the impatience with close reasoning or "logic-chopping," and the continued faith in nature remained his to the end, together with an occasional waywardness and impulsiveness and a disregard of artistic or logical propriety which savor strongly of romantic individualism. Since so many twentieth-century thoughts and attitudes are similarly based on the stimulus of the Romantic Movement, Goethe stands as particularly the poet of modern times as Dante stood for medieval times and as Shakespeare for the Renaissance.

24. The title that best expresses the ideas of this passage is
    (A) Goethe and Dante
    (B) The Characteristics of Romanticism
    (C) Classicism versus Romanticism
    (D) Goethe, the Romanticist
    (E) Goethe's Abundant Life

25. A characteristic of romanticism NOT mentioned in this passage is its
    (A) elevation of nature
    (B) preference for spontaneity
    (C) modernity of ideas
    (D) unconcern for artistic decorum
    (E) simplicity of language

26. It can be inferred from the passage that classicism has which of the following characteristics?

   I. Sensitivity toward emotional promptings
   II. Emphasis on formal aesthetic criteria
   III. Meticulous planning of artistic works

   (A) II only   (B) III only   (C) I and II
   (D) II and III   (E) I, II, and III

27. The author's attitude towards Goethe's writings is best described as

   (A) unqualified endorsement
   (B) lofty indifference
   (C) reluctant tolerance
   (D) measured admiration
   (E) undisguised contempt

Directions: Each question below consists of a word printed in capital letters, followed by five lettered words or phrases. Choose the lettered word or phrase that is most nearly opposite in meaning to the word in capital letters.

Since some of the questions require you to distinguish fine shades of meaning, be sure to consider all the choices before deciding which one is best.

28. SUPERFICIAL:
   (A) profound
   (B) exaggerated
   (C) subjective
   (D) spirited
   (E) dense

29. NAIVETE:
   (A) originality
   (B) sensitivity
   (C) sophistication
   (D) antipathy
   (E) vigor

30. TETHER:
   (A) fetch
   (B) demand
   (C) estrange
   (D) neglect
   (E) loose

31. PANDEMONIUM:
   (A) amusement
   (B) indolence
   (C) deceleration
   (D) tranquillity
   (E) tolerance

32. ENERVATE:
   (A) aggravate
   (B) stimulate
   (C) edify
   (D) applaud
   (E) disregard

33. DESTITUTION:
   (A) civilization
   (B) recompense
   (C) affluence
   (D) reformation
   (E) parsimony

34. BEREAVE:
   (A) commiserate
   (B) antagonize
   (C) restore
   (D) evade
   (E) clarify

35. ESCHEW:
   (A) gnaw
   (B) reproach
   (C) transform
   (D) preserve
   (E) seek

36. RECONDITE:
   (A) immediate
   (B) opportune
   (C) inherent
   (D) obvious
   (E) diverse

37. OBVIATE:
   (A) becloud
   (B) necessitate
   (C) rationalize
   (D) execute
   (E) assuage

38. CONTUMACIOUS:
   (A) laudatory
   (B) taciturn
   (C) fastidious
   (D) impassive
   (E) tractable

S T O P

IF YOU FINISH BEFORE TIME IS CALLED, YOU MAY CHECK YOUR WORK ON THIS SECTION ONLY.
DO NOT WORK ON ANY OTHER SECTION IN THE TEST.

SECTION 2

Time—30 Minutes

30 Questions

Numbers: All numbers used are real numbers.

Figures: Position of points, angles, regions, etc., can be assumed to be in the order shown; and angle measures can be assumed to be positive.

Lines shown as straight can be assumed to be straight.

Figures can be assumed to lie in a plane unless otherwise indicated.

Figures that accompany questions are intended to provide information useful in answering the questions. However, unless a note states that a figure is drawn to scale, you should solve these problems NOT by estimating sizes by sight or by measurement, but by using your knowledge of mathematics (see Example 2 below).

Directions: Each of the Questions 1-15 consists of two quantities, one in Column A and one in Column B. You are to compare the two quantities and choose

   A if the quantity in Column A is greater;
   B if the quantity in Column B is greater;
   C if the two quantities are equal;
   D if the relationship cannot be determined from the information given.

Note: Since there are only four choices, NEVER MARK (E).

Common
Information: In a question, information concerning one or both of the quantities to be compared is centered above the two columns. A symbol that appears in both columns represents the same thing in Column A as it does in Column B.

	Column A	Column B	Sample Answers
Example 1:	2×6	$2 + 6$	● Ⓑ Ⓒ Ⓓ Ⓔ

Examples 2-4 refer to $\triangle PQR$.

	Column A	Column B	Sample Answers
Example 2:	PN	NQ	Ⓐ Ⓑ Ⓒ ● Ⓔ
			(since equal measures cannot be assumed, even though PN and NQ appear equal)
Example 3:	x	y	Ⓐ ● Ⓒ Ⓓ Ⓔ
			(since N is between P and Q)
Example 4:	$w + z$	180	Ⓐ Ⓑ ● Ⓓ Ⓔ
			(since PQ is a straight line)

A if the quantity in Column A is greater;
B if the quantity in Column B is greater;
C if the two quantities are equal;
D if the relationship cannot be determined from the information given.

Column A	Column B

1. $\dfrac{7+7+7}{-7-7-7}$ | 1

$0 < x < 100$
x is divisible by 2, 3, 5

2.   30 | x

Two science classes share microscopes numbered 4 to 16.

3. The number of microscopes used in Classroom A, where microscopes with odd numbers are used | The number of microscopes used in Classroom B, where microscopes with even numbers are used

There are 30 members on the varsity football squad, 20 on the varsity baseball squad, and 10 varsity players who are on both squads.

4. The ratio of the number on both squads to the number on the baseball squad | The ratio of the number on the baseball squad but not on the football squad to the number on the football squad but not on the baseball squad

5. The distance covered in 20 minutes at the average rate of 30 miles per hour | The distance covered in 30 minutes at the average rate of 20 miles per hour

$\overset{\frown}{AB} = \overset{\frown}{AC} = \overset{\frown}{BC}$
$BD = DC$

6. $\dfrac{AC}{DC}$ | 2

Column A	Column B

$AB \parallel DC$, and $AD \parallel BC$
$y = 50$

7. z | 90

8. a | b

$AB = AC$ and $EC = ED$
$x = 40$ and $y = 80$

9. $3x$ | $2z$

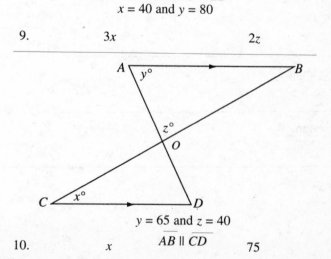

$y = 65$ and $z = 40$
$AB \parallel CD$

10. x | 75

A if the quantity in Column A is greater;
B if the quantity in Column B is greater;
C if the two quantities are equal;
D if the relationship cannot be determined from the information given.

Column A   Column B   Column A   Column B

Martin is 5 times as old as Sara.

Michael's age is $\frac{1}{6}$ of Martin's age.

13.   Michael's age   Sara's age

The average weight of Mark, Philip, and Lori
is 50 pounds.

14. Weight of Mark and Lori   Weight of Philip and
                                          Lori

$AB = BC = AC$
$BD \perp AC$

11. $\frac{x}{y}$ 3

In a shipment of electronic parts 0.01 percent is
defective. ABC Electronics received a shipment of
10,000 of these parts.

$$x > \frac{y}{3} > 0$$

12. The number of   1
     defective parts in this   15. x y
     shipment

Directions: Each of the Questions 16–30 has five answer choices. For each of these questions, select the best of the
answer choices given.

16. What is the radius of the largest circular disc that   18. How many 5¢ stamps can be purchased for c cents?
     can be cut from a strip of metal 15″ × 21″?
                                                                     (A) $5c$
     (A) 7″   (B) $7\frac{1}{2}$″   (C) 15″
                                                                     (B) $\frac{c}{5}$
     (D) $15\frac{1}{2}$″   (E) $157\frac{1}{2}$″
                                                                     (C) $\frac{5}{c}$

                                                                     (D) $500c$

                                                                     (E) $\frac{5c}{100}$

17. In the figure above, if $BC = 26$, $AE = 4$,   19. By how much is $\frac{3}{7}$ larger than 20 percent of 2?
     $AB = DC = 5$, $AE \perp BC$ and AD is parallel to BC;
     $AD = ?$ (A) $\frac{1}{35}$

     (A) 3   (B) $\frac{1}{7}$
     (B) 6
     (C) 20   (C) $\frac{4}{7}$
     (D) 23
     (E) none of these   (D) $3\frac{3}{7}$

                                                                     (E) $3\frac{4}{7}$

20. Points *B* and *C* lie on line *AD* so that $AB = BC = CD$. What part of *AD* is *AC*?

(A) $\frac{1}{4}$ (B) $\frac{1}{3}$ (C) $\frac{2}{4}$ (D) $\frac{2}{3}$ (E) $\frac{3}{4}$

Questions 21-25 refer to the following table and graph.

YOUR PROPERTY TAX BILL

Tax Levy Description	Tax Rate per $100 of Taxable Value
School	24.856
Community College	0.654
Library	1.458
Police	6.815
Water Supply	0.380
Sewer Maintenance	0.674
Sewage Disposal	1.211
Parks	0.039
General County	3.683
General Town	0.860
Fire	0.640

WHERE THE SCHOOL TAX GOES

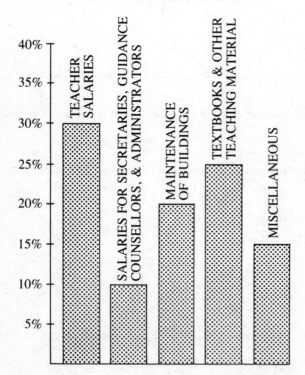

21. What is the ratio of taxpayers' money spent for teachers' salaries to taxpayers' money for the salaries of other school personnel?

(A) 1:2
(B) 1:3
(C) 3:1
(D) 2:3
(E) 3:2

22. How many times greater is the tax rate for schools than the tax rate for the community college?

(A)   4
(B)   6
(C) 24
(D) 38
(E) 48

23. What is the annual tax paid for schools by a property owner whose house has a taxable value of $10,000?

(A) $24.85
(B) $248.50
(C) $2,485.00
(D) $24,850.00
(E) $248,500.00

24. If the amount of money spent for maintenance of school buildings is represented by $D, then the amount of money spent for miscellaneous school items is expressed as

(A) $20D

(B) $15D

(C) $\frac{3}{4}$D

(D) $\frac{4}{3}$D

(E) $1\frac{1}{3}$D

25. What part of the school budget is allocated for textbooks and other teaching material?

(A) $\frac{1}{25}$

(B) $\frac{1}{5}$

(C) $\frac{1}{4}$

(D) $\frac{1}{8}$

(E) $\frac{3}{8}$

26. In the figure above, how many square units are there in the shaded triangle?

(A)   4
(B)   6
(C)   8
(D)   9
(E) 12

27. How many 3-gallon cans can be filled with the milk from 165 one-pint containers? (2 pints = 1 quart; 4 quarts = 1 gallon)

    (A) 3
    (B) 4
    (C) 5
    (D) 6
    (E) 7

28. If $3x = \dfrac{5}{6}y$, then $5y =$

    (A) $\dfrac{1}{2}x$

    (B) $2x$
    (C) $3.6x$
    (D) $5x$
    (E) $18x$

29. The size of the smaller angle between the hands of the clock at half past six, expressed in degrees, is

    (A) $7\dfrac{1}{2}$

    (B) 15

    (C) $22\dfrac{1}{2}$

    (D) 30

    (E) more than $22\dfrac{1}{2}$ but less than 30

30. How many ounces of water must be added to 48 ounces of alcohol to make a solution that is 25% alcohol?

    (A) 16
    (B) 48
    (C) 64
    (D) 144
    (E) 192

S T O P

**IF YOU FINISH BEFORE TIME IS CALLED, YOU MAY CHECK YOUR WORK ON THIS SECTION ONLY.
DO NOT WORK ON ANY OTHER SECTION IN THE TEST.**

SECTION 3

Time—30 Minutes

25 Questions

Directions: Each question or group of questions is based on a passage or set of conditions. In answering some of the questions, it may be useful to draw a rough diagram. For each question, select the best answer choice given.

Questions 1–4

Mrs. F, official hostess of New York City, has invited several wives of delegates to the United Nations for an informal luncheon. She plans to seat her eleven guests so that each lady will be able to converse with at least the person directly to her right or left. She has prepared the following list.

Mrs. F speaks English only.
Mrs. G speaks English and French.
Mrs. H speaks English and Russian.
Mrs. J speaks Russian only.
Mrs. K speaks English only.
Mrs. L speaks French only.
Mrs. M speaks French and German.
Mrs. N speaks English and German.
Mrs. O speaks English and French.
Mrs. P speaks German and Russian.
Mrs. Q speaks French and German.
Mrs. R speaks English only.

1. Which of the following arrangements will meet Mrs. F's requirement?

   I.   FOLMPJHKGQNR
   II. FRNLPKHJGMQO
   III. FRGJHOLMQPKN

   (A) I only
   (B) II only
   (C) III only
   (D) I and II only
   (E) I and III only

2. If the ladies seated to the right of Mrs. P are, respectively, MGHKFO, who must sit at Mrs. P's left hand?

   (A) J
   (B) L
   (C) N
   (D) Q
   (E) R

3. If seven of the ladies have seated themselves in the following order: NGFROMQ, who must be the next lady seated?

   (A) H
   (B) J
   (C) K
   (D) L
   (E) P

4. Mrs. F has decided upon the following seating arrangement:

   R K G Q N F O L M P J H

   At the last minute, Mrs. H and Mrs. P inform the hostess that they will not be able to attend. Which of the following adjustments will allow Mrs. F's seating requirements to be met?

   I.   Seat Mrs. J between Mrs. K and Mrs. G
   II. Seat Mrs. J between Mrs. Q and Mrs. F
   III. Seat Mrs. J to the right of Mrs. N

   (A) I only
   (B) III only
   (C) I or II only
   (D) II or III only
   (E) Neither I, II, nor III

5. Senator Johnson: No argument for this bill is valid, because no one would argue for this bill without having an ulterior motive: namely, the desire for personal gain.

   The bill's sponsors would be committing the same error in reasoning as Senator Johnson if they responded by saying:

   (A) Of course we have ulterior motives. It is perfectly reasonable to support a bill in order to promote our personal interests.
   (B) The fact that passing a bill would benefit its sponsors does not mean that the bill should not be passed.
   (C) The fact that Senator Johnson has substituted a personal attack for a discussion of the merits of the bill leads us to suspect that he can offer no strong arguments against it.
   (D) Senator Johnson has no valid reason for opposing our bill; he is doing so only because we helped defeat his pork-barrelling bill last month.
   (E) Everyone is always motivated in part by a desire for personal gain; Senator Johnson is no exception.

6. Father: My daughter could be a star on Broadway if she could only get one big break. Why, you should see the rave reviews she received when she was the lead in her high school play.

The best way to counter the argument above would be to point out that

(A) big breaks are hard to come by on Broadway
(B) one big break does not ensure continued success in the theater
(C) the standards on Broadway are much higher than they are at the high school level
(D) fewer plays are being produced on Broadway today than in the past
(E) relatively few aspiring actors ever become Broadway stars

7. Most persons who oppose gun control are conservatives; therefore, since Kathleen favors gun control, she is probably not a conservative.

The above argument most resembles which of the following?

(A) Most sociology professors are liberals; therefore Dr. Williams, who is a liberal, is probably a sociology professor.
(B) Most corporation presidents own country homes; if Ms. Steeples is a corporation president, she may or may not have a country home.
(C) Few major publishing firms publish much poetry; since Flame Press publishes only poetry, it is probably not a major publishing firm.
(D) Most sports cars are extremely expensive; since the new Venus Leopard is not a sports car, it is probably inexpensive.
(E) Most desert plants are cacti; therefore the cholla, a desert plant, is probably a cactus.

Questions 8–11

The Homer Museum of American Art is open daily except Monday from 11 A.M. to 5 P.M. Tuesdays and Thursdays the museum remains open until 8 P.M. The spring special exhibitions are: "Albert Pinkham Ryder, A Retrospective," which is on view from Friday, April 24, through Sunday, May 31, in the Pollock Wing; "Precursors of Thomas Eakins," from Friday, May 8, through Sunday, July 6, in the Third Floor Gallery; and "The Hudson River School," in the John Twachtman Gallery, which is closed Tuesdays, from Friday, May 1, through Sunday, May 24 only. The Pollock wing is closed Thursdays during May.

8. If Dan can visit the museum only after 5 P.M. or on Saturday, and does not wish to view more than one special exhibition in a day, he can see all three special exhibitions in the briefest time by starting with

(A) "The Hudson River School" on a Thursday
(B) the Ryder Retrospective on a Saturday
(C) "Precursors of Eakins" or the Ryder Retrospective on a Tuesday
(D) "Precursors of Eakins" on a Thursday
(E) any exhibition on a Saturday

9. Ellen wishes to visit the three special exhibitions on successive Thursdays. This is possible only if she visits

I.   the Ryder Retrospective in April
II. "The Hudson River School" second
III. "Precursors of Eakins" immediately following the Ryder Retrospective

(A) I only
(B) II only
(C) I and II only
(D) II and III only
(E) I, II, and III

10. Ralph can visit all three special exhibitions on one day if he goes on

I.   any Saturday in May
II. the second, third, or fourth Saturday in May
III. any Tuesday or Friday between May 5 and May 22

(A) I only
(B) II only
(C) III only
(D) I and III only
(E) II and III only

11. Terry visits the museum on an afternoon six days after the opening of "The Hudson River School." Which of the special exhibitions may he visit?

I.   The Ryder Retrospective
II. "Precursors of Eakins"
III. "The Hudson River School"

(A) I only
(B) III only
(C) I and II only
(D) II and III only
(E) I, II, and III

Questions 12–18

At a symposium on the possible dangers of the industrial chemical PBX, three pro-industry spokespersons are to be seated to the left of the moderator and three critics of PBX to the right of the moderator. The speakers are Drs. Albert, Burris, Cathode, Durand, Ettis, and Felsenstein.

(1) The person delivering the paper "Epidemiological Aspects of PBX" is seated immediately between Dr. Albert and Dr. Durand.
(2) The persons delivering "Public Health and PBX" and "Radiological Aspects of PBX" are close friends and insist on sitting together.
(3) Felsenstein is placed two seats to the left of the moderator.
(4) As heavy smoking is repugnant to the moderator, she insists that the person delivering "PBX: Benign or Malignant," a heavy smoker, be seated at one end of the table.
(5) Cathode, delivering "The Impact of PBX on the Environment," is seated to the left of Felsenstein.
(6) Albert, a critic of PBX, is seated to the left of Ettis.

12. The pro-industry spokespersons are

(A) Albert, Felsenstein, Durand
(B) Felsenstein, Burris, Albert
(C) Cathode, Felsenstein, Ettis
(D) Albert, Burris, Durand
(E) Cathode, Felsenstein, Burris

13. The person seated immediately to the left of the moderator is

(A) Albert
(B) Burris
(C) Cathode
(D) Durand
(E) Ettis

14. Assuming it is one of the papers delivered at the symposium, "PBX and the Digestive Tract" must be by

(A) Albert
(B) Burris
(C) Durand
(D) Ettis
(E) Felsenstein

15. Which of the following cannot be determined on the basis of the information given?

I.   The author of "Public Health and PBX"
II. The title of the paper delivered by Durand
III. The identity of the two friends who insist on being together

(A) I only
(B) II only
(C) III only
(D) I and II only
(E) II and III only

16. Given the seating rules as stated, which of the numbered statements are logically sufficient to establish the position of Dr. Ettis and the title of the paper she delivers?

(A) 1, 3, 4
(B) 1, 2, 3, 4
(C) 1, 3, 5, 6
(D) 1, 4, 5, 6
(E) 1, 3, 4, 5

17. The symposium is expanded to include a seventh speaker. If he is seated exactly midway between Cathode and the moderator, he will sit

(A) to the left of the author of "Radiological Aspects of PBX"
(B) one seat to the right of the moderator
(C) two seats to the right of Durand
(D) three seats to the left of Albert
(E) four seats to the left of the author of "PBX: Benign or Malignant"

18. The symposium is expanded to include two more speakers. If the eighth speaker is seated exactly midway between Durand and the author of "Public Health and PBX," which of the following must be true?

(A) The eighth speaker must be seated at one end of the table.
(B) Burris must be the author of "Radiological Aspects of PBX."
(C) The eighth speaker must be seated on the same side of the moderator as Felsenstein.
(D) The moderator must be seated next to the author of "Public Health and PBX."
(E) The eighth speaker must be seated immediately to the left of Ettis.

Questions 19–22

A is the father of two children, B and D, who are of different sexes
C is B's spouse.
E is the same sex as D.
B and C have two children: F, who is the same sex as B, and G, who is the same sex as C.
E's mother, H, who is married to L, is the sister of D's mother, M.
E and E's spouse, I, have two children, J and K, who are the same sex as I.
No persons have married more than once and no children have been born out of wedlock. The only restrictions on marriage are that marriage to a sibling, to a direct descendant, or to more than one person at the same time is forbidden.

19. F is

(A) G's brother
(B) G's sister
(C) B's daughter
(D) D's niece or nephew
(E) the same sex as H

20. According to the rules, D can marry

    (A) F only
    (B) G only
    (C) J only
    (D) J or K only
    (E) F, J, or K

21. If L and H divorced, H could marry

    I.   D only
    II.   F
    III.   D or G

    (A) I only
    (B) II only
    (C) III only
    (D) I or II, but not both
    (E) II or III, but not both

22. If the generation of F and K's parents and their siblings contains more females than males, which of the following must be true?

    (A) There are more females than males in F and K's generation.
    (B) J is male.
    (C) A is the same sex as D
    (D) K and G are the same sex.
    (E) D is H's nephew.

Questions 23–25

The internal combustion engine, which powers all private motorized vehicles, should be banned. It burns up petroleum products that are needed to produce plastics, synthetics, and many medicines. Once all the oil is gone, we will no longer be able to produce these valuable commodities. Yet we do not have to burn gasoline to satisfy our transportation needs. Other kinds of engines could be developed if the oil companies would stop blocking research efforts.

23. The argument above depends on which of the following assumptions?

    I.   We are in imminent danger of running out of oil.
    II.   Alternative methods of producing plastics will not be found before the oil runs out.
    III.   If they so desired, the oil companies could develop methods of transporation not based on the burning of petroleum.

    (A) I only
    (B) II only
    (C) I and II only
    (D) II and III only
    (E) I, II and III

24. The argument above would be most weakened by the development of which of the following?

    (A) An internal combustion engine that operated on one-tenth the gasoline used in a normal engine
    (B) A car that operated on solar energy stored in special batteries
    (C) A method of producing plastic that used no petroleum products
    (D) A synthetic oil with all the properties of natural oil
    (E) A means of locating numerous undiscovered oil fields

25. The argument above would be most strengthened if which of the following were true?

    (A) One of the oil companies has suppressed the discovery of an engine that burns only alcohol.
    (B) Some of the medicines that require petroleum for their production help to control and cure several of the world's most deadly diseases.
    (C) The world's current oil reserves are about half of what they were 30 years ago.
    (D) In high-pollution areas, automobile exhaust fumes have been shown to cause high rates of lung cancer and heart disease.
    (E) When gasoline is burned inside an auto engine, less than one-fourth of the energy produced is used to propel the vehicle.

S T O P

IF YOU FINISH BEFORE TIME IS CALLED, YOU MAY CHECK YOUR WORK ON THIS SECTION ONLY.
DO NOT WORK ON ANY OTHER SECTION IN THE TEST.

SECTION 4

Time—30 Minutes

30 Questions

Numbers: All numbers used are real numbers.

Figures: Position of points, angles, regions, etc., can be assumed to be in the order shown; and angle measures can be assumed to be positive.

Lines shown as straight can be assumed to be straight.

Figures can be assumed to lie in a plane unless otherwise indicated.

Figures that accompany questions are intended to provide information useful in answering the questions. However, unless a note states that a figure is drawn to scale, you should solve these problems NOT by estimating sizes by sight or by measurement, but by using your knowledge of mathematics (see Example 2 below).

Directions: Each of the <u>Questions 1-15</u> consists of two quantities, one in Column A and one in Column B. You are to compare the two quantities and choose

A if the quantity in Column A is greater;
B if the quantity in Column B is greater;
C if the two quantities are equal;
D if the relationship cannot be determined from the information given.

Note: Since there are only four choices, NEVER MARK (E).

Common
Information: In a question, information concerning one or both of the quantities to be compared is centered above the two columns. A symbol that appears in both columns represents the same thing in Column A as it does in Column B.

	Column A	Column B	Sample Answers
Example 1:	2×6	$2 + 6$	● Ⓑ Ⓒ Ⓓ Ⓔ

Examples 2-4 refer to $\triangle PQR$.

	Column A	Column B	Sample Answers
Example 2:	PN	NQ	Ⓐ Ⓑ Ⓒ ● Ⓔ

(since equal measures cannot be assumed, even though PN and NQ appear equal)

	Column A	Column B	Sample Answers
Example 3:	x	y	Ⓐ ● Ⓒ Ⓓ Ⓔ

(since N is between P and Q)

	Column A	Column B	Sample Answers
Example 4:	$w + z$	180	Ⓐ Ⓑ ● Ⓓ Ⓔ

(since PQ is a straight line)

A if the quantity in Column A is greater;
B if the quantity in Column B is greater;
C if the two quantities are equal;
D if the relationship cannot be determined from the information given.

<u>Column A</u>   <u>Column B</u>

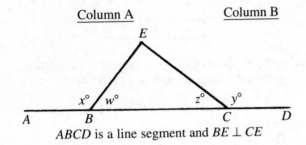

ABCD is a line segment and *BE* ⊥ *CE*

1. $x + y$ 90

___

Area of circle = $\dfrac{\pi}{4}$

2.   Radius of circle   0.5

___

$a = b = c$

3. $a + b$ $b + c$

___

4. The number of inte-   The number of integers from −5 to 5   gers from 5 to 15
inclusive   inclusive

___

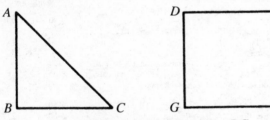

AB = *BC*, and *DE* = *EF* = *FG* = *DG*
Area of right triangle *ABC*
equals area of square *DEFG*.

5. $\dfrac{AB}{DG}$ $\sqrt{2}$

___

m is parallel to *n*.

6.   Area of ABC   Area of ABD

___

$\overset{\frown}{AB} = \overset{\frown}{AC} = \overset{\frown}{BC}$
BD = *DC*

7. $\dfrac{AC}{DC}$ 2

___

<u>Column A</u>   <u>Column B</u>

8. The time required to   The time required to

cover $\dfrac{1}{2}$ mile traveling   cover $\dfrac{1}{3}$ mile traveling

at 20 miles per hour   at 30 miles per hour

___

9. The number of revolu-   The number of revolutions made by the   tions made by the
wheel of a bicycle   wheel of a motorcycle

(diameter of $\dfrac{7}{\pi}$ feet)   (diameter of $\dfrac{10}{\pi}$ feet)

covering a distance of   covering a distance of
70 feet   100 feet

___

$X + Y + Z = 350$
$X + Y = 100$
All unknowns > 0

10.   Z   X

___

Distance from X to Y = 3 miles
Distance from Y to Z = 2 miles

11. Distance from X to Z   Distance from X to Y

___

$9x^2 = y$
x is a nonzero integer.

12.   x   y

___

Area of *ABC* = 18

13.   AB   BC

___

ABCD is a parallelogram

14.   AD + BC   AB + DC

___

AB = *BC*, and *DE* = *EF* = *FG* = *DG*
Area of right triangle *ABC* = area of square *DEFG*

15. $\dfrac{AB}{DG}$ $\sqrt{2}$

Directions: Each of the Questions 16–30 has five answer choices. For each of these questions, select the best of the answer choices given.

16. The ingredients for making 5 dozen cookies, as given in a recipe, are 1 egg, $\frac{1}{2}$ cup shortening, $\frac{3}{4}$ cup sugar, 1 teaspoon flavoring, $1\frac{1}{2}$ cup sifted flour. How much flour would be needed in order to make 20 cookies?

(A) $\frac{1}{4}$ cup

(B) $\frac{1}{2}$ cup

(C) $3\frac{3}{4}$ cups

(D) $4\frac{1}{2}$ cups

(E) 6 cups

17. Potassium nitrate is composed of 39 parts potassium, 14 parts nitrogen, and 48 parts oxygen. Find the percentage (to the nearest %) of potassium in potassium nitrate.

(A) 14
(B) 39
(C) 45
(D) 48
(E) 62

18. A rectangular field 100 feet long is twice as long as it is wide. The number of feet of fencing needed to enclose the field is

(A) 150
(B) 300
(C) 400
(D) 500
(E) 600

19. In the triangle above, BC equals one half of AB. The area of right triangle ABC equals 64 square feet. To the nearest foot, what is the length of hypotenuse AC?

(A) 12
(B) 14
(C) 18
(D) 24
(E) 32

x	5	$\frac{5}{9}$
y	3	?

20. In the figure above, if $x = ky$, and k is a constant, what is the missing value of y in the table?

(A) $\frac{1}{27}$ (B) $\frac{1}{3}$ (C) $\frac{25}{27}$

(D) $\frac{27}{25}$ (E) 3

Questions 21–25 refer to the following chart.

NUTRITIONAL VALUE OF SOME DAIRY PRODUCTS

	SIZE OF PORTION	CALO-RIES	PROTEIN (grams)
Milk, whole	1 glass (8 oz.)	160	9
Milk, skim or buttermilk	1 glass (8 oz.)	90	9
Milk, chocolate drink . . .	1 glass (8 oz.)	190	8
Cheese, American or	1" cube or med. slice		
Swiss	(1 oz.)	110	8
Cheese foods, Cheddar-type	2 tablespoons (1 oz.)	90	6
Cheese, cottage, creamed	2 tablespoons (1 oz.)	30	4
Cheese, cream	2 x 1 x ½" or 2 tbsp.	110	2
Butter	1 tablespoon (½ oz.)	100	–
Butter	1 teaspoon or small pat . .	35	–
Cream, light, table	2 tablespoons	60	1
Cream, heavy, whipped	1 heaping tablespoon	50	–
Half-and-half	¼ cup	80	2
Ice cream, vanilla	¼ pint (½ cup)	145	3
Ice cream, as for a la mode	Medium scoop (⅓ pint) . .	115	2
Sherbert	½ cup	130	1

21. How many tablespoons of light cream have the same number of calories as 8 ounces of buttermilk?

(A) 2
(B) 3
(C) 4
(D) 5
(E) 6

22. How many calories of cream cheese would there be in the amount needed to furnish the same number of grams of protein as there are in 4 ounces of chocolate milk?

(A) 55
(B) 95
(C) 110
(D) 220
(E) 330

23. Which of the following has the greatest number of calories per pound?

    (A) Whole milk
    (B) Buttermilk
    (C) Swiss cheese
    (D) Cottage cheese
    (E) Chocolate milk

24. Which of the following has the smallest number of calories per ounce?

    (A) Cottage cheese
    (B) Cheddar-type cheese
    (C) Swiss cheese
    (D) Butter
    (E) Whole milk

25. Which of the following furnishes the greatest number of grams of protein per unit weight?

    (A) Whole milk
    (B) Cottage cheese
    (C) Butter
    (D) Chocolate milk
    (E) American cheese

26. Which of the following statements is (are) always true?

    I.   A root of a negative number may be a real number.
    II. The positive square root of a number is smaller than the number.
    III. A binomial multiplied by a binomial yields a trinomial.

    (A) I only
    (B) II only
    (C) III only
    (D) II and III only
    (E) all are true

27. Which of the following numbers does *not* have a reciprocal?

    (A) 1
    (B) -2
    (C) $\frac{1}{3}$
    (D) 0
    (E) 3

28. If $x + y = 16$, then $x - z =$

    (A) $z + 16$
    (B) 8
    (C) $16 - y$
    (D) $z(16 - y)$
    (E) $16 - y - z$

29. If a and b are positive integers and $\frac{a - b}{3.5} = \frac{4}{7}$, then

    (A) $b < a$
    (B) $b > a$
    (C) $b = a$
    (D) $b \geqq a$
    (E) $b \leqq a$

30. 10^x means that 10 is to be used as a factor x times, and 10^{-x} means $\frac{1}{10^x}$. A very large or very small number, therefore, is frequently written as a decimal multipled by 10^x, where x is a positive or a negative integer. Which, if any, of the following is false?

    (A) $470{,}000 = 4.7 \times 10^5$
    (B) 450 billion $= 4.5 \times 10^{11}$
    (C) $0.00000000075 = 7.5 \times 10^{-10}$
    (D) 86 hundred-thousandths $= 8.6 \times 10^{-2}$
    (E) None of these

S T O P

IF YOU FINISH BEFORE TIME IS CALLED, YOU MAY CHECK YOUR WORK ON THIS SECTION ONLY.
DO NOT WORK ON ANY OTHER SECTION IN THE TEST.

SECTION 5

Time—30 Minutes

30 Questions

Numbers: All numbers used are real numbers.

Figures: Position of points, angles, regions, etc., can be assumed to be in the order shown; and angle measures can be assumed to be positive.

Lines shown as straight can be assumed to be straight.

Figures can be assumed to lie in a plane unless otherwise indicated.

Figures that accompany questions are intended to provide information useful in answering the questions. However, unless a note states that a figure is drawn to scale, you should solve these problems NOT by estimating sizes by sight or by measurement, but by using your knowledge of mathematics (see Example 2 below).

Directions: Each of the Questions 1-15 consists of two quantities, one in Column A and one in Column B. You are to compare the two quantities and choose

A if the quantity in Column A is greater;
B if the quantity in Column B is greater;
C if the two quantities are equal;
D if the relationship cannot be determined from the information given.

Note: Since there are only four choices, NEVER MARK (E).

Common
Information: In a question, information concerning one or both of the quantities to be compared is centered above the two columns. A symbol that appears in both columns represents the same thing in Column A as it does in Column B.

Column A	Column B	Sample Answers

Example 1: 2×6 $2 + 6$ ● Ⓑ Ⓒ Ⓓ Ⓔ

Examples 2-4 refer to △ *PQR*.

Example 2:   *PN*   *NQ*   Ⓐ Ⓑ Ⓒ ● Ⓔ

(since equal measures cannot be assumed, even though *PN* and *NQ* appear equal)

Example 3:   *x*   *y*   Ⓐ ● Ⓒ Ⓓ Ⓔ

(since *N* is between *P* and *Q*)

Example 4: $w + z$ 180   Ⓐ Ⓑ ● Ⓓ Ⓔ

(since *PQ* is a straight line)

A if the quantity in Column A is greater;
B if the quantity in Column B is greater;
C if the two quantities are equal;
D if the relationship cannot be determined from the information given.

Column A	Column B

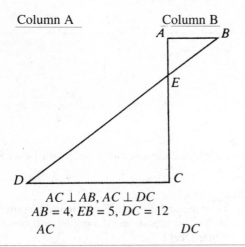

$AC \perp AB, AC \perp DC$
$AB = 4, EB = 5, DC = 12$

1. AC DC

Radius of circle $A = \dfrac{1}{2}$ radius of circle B

2. Circumference of circle B Twice the circumference of circle A

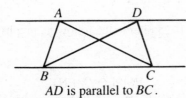

AD is parallel to BC.

3.   Area of ABC Area of DBC

$AB = AC$

4. $\dfrac{b}{c}$ $\dfrac{c}{b}$

$BA = BC$, $\angle x = 60°$, and $\angle y = 100°$

5.   Value of z $140°$

$a = 3, b = 9$

6. $a^2 - b$ $b - a^2$

Column A	Column B

7. The area of the lot on the corner of Chester Street and Newport Avenue   200,000 square feet

$a < b$

8. $-2a$ $-2b$

q is the smallest of nine consecutive integers.

9.   The average of these nine integers $q + 4$

10. $(1813)\left(\dfrac{1}{2} + \dfrac{1}{3}\right)$ 1813

$x > 0$ and $y > 0$
$xy = 1$

11. $\dfrac{x}{y}$ x^2

$x < 0$

12. $\dfrac{1}{x}$ x^2

Three gold coins and 1 silver coin are worth as much as 5 silver coins and 2 gold coins.

13.   4 of these silver coins   1 of these gold coins

Column A	Column B

The lines are parallel.

14. a b

_____

Column A	Column B

$$2a - b = 3$$
$$a + b = -6$$

15. a b

_____

Directions: Each of Questions 16–30 has five answer choices. For each of these questions, select the best of the answer choices given.

16. A $41\frac{1}{2}$-foot string is to be cut into 6 approximately equal lengths. The average length of each piece will be

(A) 6′1″
(B) 6′9″
(C) 6′11″
(D) 7′9″
(E) 8′3″

17. A shirt marked $12.50 was sold for $10.00. The rate of discount on the marked price was

(A) 2%
(B) 2.5%
(C) 20%
(D) 25%
(E) 80%

18. A radio marked $96 is offered for $72. The percent discount is

(A) 4%
(B) 24%
(C) 25%
(D) $33\frac{1}{3}\%$
(E) $66\frac{2}{3}\%$

19. A car uses a gallon of gasoline in traveling 15 miles. Another automobile can travel m miles on a gallon of gasoline. How many miles can the second travel on the amount of gasoline required by the first car in going 60 miles?

(A) $\frac{m}{4}$
(B) m
(C) $4m$
(D) $\frac{m}{9}$
(E) $9m$

20. How many gallons of paint should be purchased to cover 760 square feet if a gallon will cover 200 square feet?

(A) 3
(B) 4
(C) 5
(D) 6
(E) 7

Questions 21–25 refer to the following graphs.

EMPLOYMENT
BASED ON SEASONALLY ADJUSTED NONAGRICULTURAL PAYROLLS.
(Figures represent millions of jobs.)

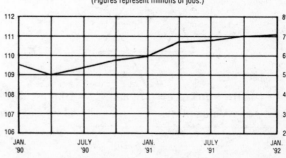

UNEMPLOYMENT
BASED ON SEASONALLY ADJUSTED NONAGRICULTURAL PAYROLLS.
(Figures represent millions of jobs.)

Source: Bureau of Labor Statistics

21. How many jobs (in millions) were reported for July 1990?

    (A) 50
    (B) 108
    (C) 109
    (D) 110
    (E) 150

22. In April 1992 the Labor Department reported that the unemployment rate for the previous month remained at a seven-year high. What was the unemployment rate for March 1992?

    (A) 5%
    (B) 6%
    (C) 7%
    (D) 7.3%
    (E) 10.9%

23. According to the Bureau of Labor Statistics, which of the following months showed the healthiest state of economy?

    (A) July 1990
    (B) October 1990
    (C) January 1991
    (D) April 1991
    (E) July 1991

24. For the 1990–1992 period what was the maximum number of jobs (in millions) held during any one particular month, as reported by the Bureau of Labor Statistics?

    (A) 109.5
    (B) 110
    (C) 110.5
    (D) 111
    (E) 112

25. When the two graphs are compared, which statement best describes their general trends?

    (A) As one rises, the other also rises.
    (B) As one rises, the other falls.
    (C) They remain parallel.
    (D) As one falls, the other also falls.
    (E) None of the above.

26. What is a percent of b divided by b percent of a?

    (A) a
    (B) b
    (C) 1
    (D) 10
    (E) 100

27. Which of the following fractions is next smaller in value than one-half?

    (A) $\frac{1}{5}$

    (B) $\frac{1}{4}$

    (C) $\frac{2}{5}$

    (D) $\frac{16}{25}$

    (E) $\frac{3}{10}$

28. The fraction $\frac{t + n}{n}$ equals

    (A) $\frac{t}{n} + n$

    (B) $\frac{t + n}{t}$

    (C) $\frac{t}{n} + 1$

    (D) $t^2 + 1$

    (E) t

29. A cow is grazing in a pasture bordered by two fences more than 10 feet long that meet at an angle of 60°. If the cow is tethered by a 10-foot-long rope to the post at which the two fences meet, it can graze in an area of

    (A) 20π

    (B) $\frac{5\pi}{3}$

    (C) $\frac{20\pi}{3}$

    (D) $\frac{50\pi}{3}$

    (E) 100π

30. A certain recipe makes enough dough to fill two cake tins, each 7 inches in diameter and 1 inch deep. How many inches deep will the cake dough be if put into one cake tin 10 inches in diameter?

    (A) 0.51
    (B) 0.71
    (C) 0.98
    (D) 1.02
    (E) 1.40

S T O P

IF YOU FINISH BEFORE TIME IS CALLED, YOU MAY CHECK YOUR WORK ON THIS SECTION ONLY.
DO NOT WORK ON ANY OTHER SECTION IN THE TEST.

SECTION 6

Time - 30 Minutes

38 Questions

Directions: Each sentence below has one or two blanks, each blank indicating that something has been omitted. Beneath the sentence are five lettered words or sets of words. Choose the word or set of words for each blank that best fits the meaning of the sentence as a whole.

1. With few exceptions, explorers now are not individuals setting out alone or in pairs to some remote destination but are instead members of ------, often international, undertaking.

    (A) a singular
    (B) a collaborative
    (C) an objective
    (D) an insular
    (E) a private

2. Anthropologists who have dismissed Villa's notion of prehistoric "social cannibalism" ------ that Villa's research was carefully done but stress that other interpretations of the evidence are possible.

    (A) deny
    (B) ignore
    (C) preclude
    (D) refute
    (E) grant

3. Surprisingly to those who view the ocean floor as a uniformly ------ waste, each vent in the floor, where sea water is heated by the earth's interior magma, has been found to be an island-like ------ with its own distinctive fauna.

    (A) teeming...habitat
    (B) lifeless...enclave
    (C) barren...oasis
    (D) sunken...grotto
    (E) hazardous...environment

4. Rather than allowing these dramatic exchanges between her characters to develop fully, Ms. Norman unfortunately tends to ------ the discussions involving the two women.

    (A) exacerbate
    (B) protract
    (C) augment
    (D) truncate
    (E) elaborate

5. A ------ of recent cases of scientific fraud in which gross errors of fact and logic have slipped past the review panels that scrutinize submissions to journals suggests that the review system is seriously ------.

    (A) plethora...intended
    (B) lack...strained
    (C) dearth...compromised
    (D) spate...taxed
    (E) preponderance...substantiated

6. Egocentric, at times vindictive when he believed his authority was being questioned, White could also be kind, gracious, and even ------ when the circumstances seemed to require it.

    (A) authoritarian
    (B) taciturn
    (C) vainglorious
    (D) self-deprecating
    (E) self-assured

7. Many of Updike's characters live to ------ the assurances they give one another glibly or sincerely; they define themselves by their betrayals of their spouses or their children or their parents.

    (A) flaunt   (B) underscore   (C) fulfill
    (D) deplore   (E) belie

Directions: In each of the following questions, a related pair of words or phrases is followed by five lettered pairs of words or phrases. Select the lettered pair that best expresses a relationship similar to that expressed in the original pair.

8. BOOK : CHAPTER::
    (A) painting : frame
    (B) sentence : verb
    (C) building : story
    (D) tree : root
    (E) movie : scenario

9. INAUGURATE : PRESIDENT::
    (A) abdicate : king
    (B) promote : student
    (C) campaign : candidate
    (D) install : officer
    (E) succeed : governor

10. ADJUST : TINKER::
    (A) invent : design
    (B) improve : hamper
    (C) throw : hurl
    (D) analyze : repair
    (E) write : scribble

11. ZINC : ELEMENT::
    (A) gold : bullion
    (B) uranium : fission
    (C) quark : particle
    (D) electron : molecule
    (E) light : photosynthesis

12. UPROARIOUS : AMUSING::
    (A) treacherous : steadfast
    (B) tumultuous : windy
    (C) menacing : aghast
    (D) repugnant : disagreeable
    (E) devious : clever

13. FORENSIC : DEBATE::
    (A) empirical : argument
    (B) judicious : law
    (C) histrionic : theater
    (D) sophomoric : humor
    (E) philosophic : temperament

14. LIMPET : DETACH::
    (A) porpoise : sound
    (B) hummingbird : hover
    (C) chameleon : disguise
    (D) tick : extract
    (E) eel : wriggle

15. COUNTENANCE : APPROVAL::
    (A) uphold : delay
    (B) disclaim : obligation
    (C) traduce : reputation
    (D) propound : distinction
    (E) air : expression

16. INSOUCIANT : DISTURB::
    (A) supererogatory : require
    (B) laconic : interpret
    (C) distraught : ruffle
    (D) incredulous : convince
    (E) egregious : obtrude

Directions: Each passage in this group is followed by questions based on its content. After reading a passage, choose the best answer to each question. Answer all questions following a passage on the basis of what is stated or implied in that passage.

Paralleling the growth of interest among professional historians during the early 1960s was a simultaneous groundswell of popular interest in the Afro-American past that was directly stimulated by the drama of the protest movement. Sensing the "Negro Mood," the journalist Lerone Bennett wrote a series of articles on Afro-American history for *Ebony* and soon after brought them together in his popular volume, *Before the Mayflower* (1962). As the nonviolent direct action movement attained its crest in 1963-64, movement activists introduced black history units into the curricula of the "freedom schools" that accompanied the school integration boycotts. Meanwhile, boards of education began to address themselves to "the racial imbalance and neutralism of pusillanimous textbooks designed to appeal to Southern as well as Northern school adoption committees." In 1964 New York City's school board published *The Negro in American History*; Detroit's social studies teachers produced *The Struggle for Freedom and Rights: Basic Facts about the Negro in American History*. Franklin, surveying the activities among publishers, teachers, and school boards, called these beginnings of curriculum revision "one of the most significant by-products of the current Civil Rights Revolution."

The relationship between these developments at the grass roots level and what was occurring in the scholarly world is of course indirect. Yet given the context of social change in the early 1960s, Negro history was now the object of unprecedented attention among wide segments of the American population, black and white. In academe nothing demonstrated this growing legitimacy of black history better than the way in which certain scholars of both races, who had previously been ambivalent about being identified as specialists in the field, now reversed themselves.

Thus Frenise Logan, returning to an academic career, decided to attempt to publish his doctoral dissertation on blacks in late nineteenth-century North Carolina. A 1960 award encouraged him to do further research, and his expanded *The Negro in North Carolina, 1876–1894* appeared in 1964. It is true that as late as 1963 a white professor advised John W. Blassingame to avoid black history if he wanted to have "a future in the historical

profession." Yet more indicative of how things were going was that 1964–65 marked a turning point for two of Kenneth Stampp's former students—Nathan Huggins and Leon Litwack. The changing intellectual milieu seems to have permitted Huggins, whose original intention of specializing in African and Afro-American history had been overruled by practical concerns, to move into what became his long-range commitment to the field. By 1965 when his interest in intellectual history found expression in the idea of doing a book on the Harlem Renaissance, the factors that earlier would have discouraged him from such a study had dissipated. For Litwack the return to Negro history was an especially vivid experience, and he recalls the day he spoke at the University of Rochester, lecturing on Jacksonian democracy. Some students in the audience, sensing that his heart was just not in that topic, urged him to undertake research once again in the field to which he had already contributed so significantly. He settled on the study that became *Been in the Storm So Long* (1979). In short, both Huggins and Litwack now felt able to dismiss the professional considerations that had loomed so large in their earlier decision to work in other specialties and to identify themselves with what had hitherto been a marginal field of inquiry.

17. The author indicates that the growth of scholarly involvement in the study of black history was

    (A) unappreciated in academic circles
    (B) encouraged by the civil rights movement
    (C) systematically organized
    (D) unaffected by current events
    (E) motivated by purely financial concerns

18. The author's account is based on all of the following EXCEPT

    (A) personal anecdotes
    (B) magazine articles
    (C) curricular materials
    (D) public opinion polls
    (E) scholarly publications

19. The author cites Logan, Huggins, and Litwack for their

    (A) work on curriculum reform in the public schools
    (B) participation in the Freedom Summer in Mississippi
    (C) return to the field of Afro-American history
    (D) research on blacks in nineteenth century North Carolina
    (E) identification with nonviolent direct action

20. The author suggests that the advice given to John W. Blassingame was

    (A) meant maliciously
    (B) inappropriate to the times
    (C) acted on in good faith
    (D) vital to his career
    (E) verified by research

21. Which of the following best describes the purpose of the passage?

    (A) To document the sacrifices made by black and white scholars in the field
    (B) To defend the validity of black history as a legitimate scholarly pursuit
    (C) To investigate the origins of Afro-American studies in American universities
    (D) To encourage the return to the study of black history at the grass roots level
    (E) To describe black history's coming of age as an academically respectable field

22. The passage suggests that Bennett's work was similar to Logan's work in which of the following ways?

    I.   Both Bennett's and Logan's books recorded a then relatively unfamiliar aspect of Afro-American history.
    II. Both Bennett's and Logan's work were designed to appeal to a primarily academic audience.
    III. Both Bennett's and Logan's work were published in a variety of formats.

    (A) I only
    (B) III only
    (C) I and II only
    (D) I and III only
    (E) II and III only

23. It can be inferred that prior to 1950 for a historian to choose to specialize in black history

    (A) was encouraged by the academic establishment
    (B) established his academic conventionality
    (C) afforded him special opportunities for publication
    (D) was detrimental to his professional career
    (E) enhanced his contact with his colleagues

A few species demonstrate conditions which are neither complete hibernation nor aestivation. Instead of going into a long "sleep" during the most adverse season, they become torpid for a few hours each day. This kind of behavior is known in other animals — bats become torpid during daytime, and hummingbirds at night. The first time I appreciated this phenomenon was while working with fat mice (*Steatomys*) in Africa. These mice, incidentally, have a most appropriate name, for their bodies are so full of fat they resemble little furry balls. Fat storage as a method of survival has rebounded to some extent as far as the fat mice are concerned. They are regarded as a succulent delicacy by many African tribes who hunt them with great tenacity; when captured, the mice are skewered and fried in their own fat. A captive fat mouse was once kept without food or water for thirty-six days; at the end of that time it had lost a third of its weight but appeared quite healthy. During the dry season, some captives spent the day in such a deep state of torpor that they could be roughly handled without waking. The body temperature was a couple of degrees above room temperature and the respiration was most irregular, several short pants being followed by a pause of up to three minutes. Just before dusk the mice woke up of their own accord and respired normally. In this case the torpid state was not induced by shortage of food or abnormal temperatures. The forest dormouse of southern Asia and Europe also undergoes periods of torpidity during the day; this species has been recorded as having pauses of up to seventeen minutes between breaths. There is also a record of a leaf-eared mouse of the Peruvian desert which became torpid under severe conditions.

24. The primary focus of the passage is on

    (A) the inhumane treatment of laboratory specimens
    (B) irregularities of respiration in mammals
    (C) conditions that induce rodents to hibernate
    (D) species that exhibit brief periods of dormancy
    (E) the similarities among rodent species

25. It can be inferred from the passage that fat storage as a method of survival "has rebounded" for fat mice for which of the following reasons?

    (A) It has enabled them to go without food and water for long periods of time.
    (B) It has made them particularly tempting to human predators.
    (C) It has made them so spherical they cannot move easily.
    (D) It has caused them to adopt abnormal patterns of sleep.
    (E) It has made them susceptible to abnormal temperatures.

26. This passage would most likely appear in which of the following types of publications?

    (A) A geographical atlas
    (B) A history of African exploration
    (C) A textbook on rodent biology
    (D) A guide to the care of laboratory animals
    (E) A general-interest periodical

27. It can be inferred that in the paragraph preceding this passage the author most likely discussed

    (A) his initial journey to Africa
    (B) the problem caused by sleep deprivation
    (C) other types of dormant states
    (D) the physical appearance of rodents
    (E) methods for measuring rodent respiration

Directions: Each question below consists of a word printed in capital letters, followed by five lettered words or phrases. Choose the lettered word or phrase that is most nearly opposite in meaning to the word in capital letters.

Since some of the questions require you to distinguish fine shades of meaning, be sure to consider all the choices before deciding which one is best.

28. SAP:
    (A) divert
    (B) educate
    (C) invigorate
    (D) liquefy
    (E) polish

29. UNFEIGNED:
    (A) pretentious
    (B) cautious
    (C) simulated
    (D) controlled
    (E) designed

30. VACILLATION:
    (A) coarseness
    (B) simplicity
    (C) retraction
    (D) firmness
    (E) tedium

31. SWATHE:
    (A) fondle
    (B) nourish
    (C) anoint
    (D) unwrap
    (E) refresh

32. COGNIZANCE:
    (A) ignobility
    (B) disbelief
    (C) impotence
    (D) illegality
    (E) unawareness

33. NEBULOUS:
    (A) hypothetical
    (B) querulous
    (C) lamentable
    (D) piquant
    (E) distinct

34. DENIGRATE:
    (A) emancipate
    (B) examine
    (C) desecrate
    (D) mollify
    (E) extol

35. DECORUM:
    (A) lucidity
    (B) flexibility
    (C) impropriety
    (D) duplicity
    (E) severity

36. CONDIGN:
    (A) intentional
    (B) unbiased
    (C) obdurate
    (D) inevitable
    (E) unmerited

37. PUISSANCE:
    (A) effortlessness
    (B) powerlessness
    (C) recklessness
    (D) timeliness
    (E) wholeness

38. PALLIATE:
    (A) exacerbate
    (B) immunize
    (C) oscillate
    (D) rarefy
    (E) precipitate

S T O P

**IF YOU FINISH BEFORE TIME IS CALLED, YOU MAY CHECK YOUR WORK ON THIS SECTION ONLY.
DO NOT WORK ON ANY OTHER SECTION IN THE TEST.**

SECTION 7

Time - 30 Minutes

25 Questions

Directions: Each question or group of questions is based on a passage or set of conditions. In answering some of the questions, it may be useful to draw a rough diagram. For each question, select the best answer choice given.

Questions 1–5

In a certain society, only two forms of marriage are recognized. In *Prahtu* marriage, several brothers marry a single woman, while in *Brihtu* marriage, several sisters marry a single man. All members of a given married group are regarded as the parents of any children of the marriage. Marriage between male and female children of the same parents is forbidden.
  E is a son of A.
  G is a daughter of B.
  F is a daughter of C.
  E, F, M, and N have a daughter, H.
  E and F have the same paternal grandmother, Q.
  A and B are the only grandfathers of H; C, J, K, and
    L are the only grandmothers of H.
  No one has married more than once; all children were
    born in wedlock.

1. G is a sister of

    (A) N only
    (B) M only
    (C) E
    (D) F
    (E) E or F, but not both

2. N is a sibling of

    I.   M only
    II. M and E
    III. M and F

    (A) I only
    (B) II only
    (C) III only
    (D) II or III, but not both
    (E) Neither I, II, nor III

3. One of Q's children may be

    (A) A
    (B) C
    (C) J
    (D) K
    (E) M

4. Which of the following is an offspring of a *Brihtu* marriage?

    (A) H
    (B) E
    (C) A
    (D) B
    (E) J

5. If E, F, M, and N had not married, which would be a permissible marriage?

    (A) N marries M and others of M's sex.
    (B) N and M marry E.
    (C) N and M marry G and F.
    (D) G marries E only.
    (E) E marries G and F.

Questions 6–9

Seven varsity basketball players are to be honored at a special luncheon. The players will be seated on the dais along one side of a single rectangular table.
Adams and Goldberg have to leave the luncheon early and so must be seated at the extreme right end of the table, which is closest to the exit.
Baker will receive the Most Valuable Player's trophy and so must be in the center chair to facilitate the presentation.
Cooper and D'Amato, who were bitter rivals for the position of center during the basketball season, dislike one another and should be seated as far apart as is convenient.
Edwards and Farley are best friends and want to sit together.

6. Which of the following may not be seated at either end of the table?

    (A) Cooper
    (B) D'Amato
    (C) Goldberg
    (D) Farley
    (E) Adams

7. Which of the following pairs may not be seated together?

    (A) Cooper and Farley
    (B) Baker and D'Amato
    (C) Edwards and Adams
    (D) Goldberg and D'Amato
    (E) Edwards and Cooper

8. Which of the following pairs may not occupy the seats on either side of Baker?

    (A) Farley and D'Amato
    (B) D'Amato and Edwards
    (C) Edwards and Goldberg
    (D) Farley and Cooper
    (E) Cooper and Edwards

9. If neither Edwards nor D'Amato is seated next to Baker, how many *different* seating arrangements are possible?

   (A) 1
   (B) 2
   (C) 3
   (D) 4
   (E) 5

Questions 10–15

Number series questions provide psychologists with a means of testing a person's ability to determine quantitative patterns. Below are seven number series:

   I.   4, 64, 5, 125, 6, x
   II. 6, 37, 7, 50, 8, 65, 9, x
   III. 5, 25, 125, 7, 49, 343, 9, 81, x
   IV. 9, −7, 18, −18, 31, x
   V.   4, 16, 80, 480, 3360, x
   VI. 25, 24, 22, 19, 15, 10, x
   VII. 100, 81, 64, 49, 36, x

10. In which of the above number series is the third power of a number the determining factor?

    (A) I and III
    (B) I, IV, and V
    (C) I, III, and VII
    (D) II, III, and VI
    (E) I, III, IV, and VII

11. In which of the above number series is the use of powers of a number NOT a determining factor?

    (A) I
    (B) II
    (C) IV
    (D) V
    (E) VII

12. In which of the above number series is the determining factor the addition and subtraction of squares?

    (A) II
    (B) IV
    (C) VI
    (D) VII
    (E) None

13. In which of the above number series is $n^2 + 1$ the determining factor?

    (A) II
    (B) III
    (C) V
    (D) VII
    (E) None

14. In which of the above number series is the recognition of increasing multiples significant?

    (A) II
    (B) V
    (C) VI
    (D) II and IV
    (E) II and VI

15. In which of the above number series is it necessary to consider a pattern of three elements?

    (A) I
    (B) II
    (C) III
    (D) IV
    (E) V

Questions 16–20

Mr. Pict must accommodate seven tour group passengers in two four-person cabins on the *S.S. Gallia*. Each passenger in a cabin must be able to converse with at least one other passenger, though not necessarily in the same language.
   A, an Etruscan, also speaks Gothic and Hittite.
   B and F are Hittites and speak only that language.
   C, an Etruscan, also speaks Gothic.
   D and G are Goths and speak only Gothic.
   E, an Etruscan, also speaks Hittite.
   Hittites refuse to share rooms with Goths.

16. Which combination of passengers in one of the cabins will result in a rooming arrangement that satisfies all conditions for both cabins?

    (A) B, C, F
    (B) D, E, G
    (C) A, D, E, G
    (D) C, D, E, G
    (E) A, B, C, F

17. Which CANNOT be true, given the conditions as stated?
    I.   C cannot room with A.
    II. Any cabin containing three persons must include A.
    III. E must always room with a Hittite.

    (A) I only
    (B) II only
    (C) I and III only
    (D) II and III only
    (E) I, II, and III

18. How many different combinations of cabin mates satisfy all conditions?

    (A) 2
    (B) 3
    (C) 4
    (D) 5
    (E) 6

19. If E objects to sharing a cabin with A, with whom can Mr. Pict place him in order to arrive at an arrangement that satisfies all conditions?

   I.   D and G, with no fourth cabin mate
  II.   B and F, with no fourth cabin mate
III.   C, D, and G

   (A) I only
   (B) II only
   (C) I and III only
   (D) II and III only
   (E) Neither I, II, nor III

20. At the last minute, a new person applies to join the group. Mr. Pict can place her with any of the following except

   (A) C, D, and G if she is a Goth
   (B) A, B, and F is she is an Etruscan
   (C) B, E, and F if she is a Hittite
   (D) C, D, and G if she is an Etruscan
   (E) B, E, and F is she is a Goth

Questions 21–25

In the days of sailing ships fresh food was not available, and at the end of long trips many sailors came down with scurvy. Many attempts were made to seek a cure for this condition.

  1. John Hall cured several cases of scurvy by administering an acidic brew made of a certain grass and watercress.
  2. William Harvey suggested that the sailors take lemon juice to prevent scurvy. He thought the specific acid (citric acid) in lemon juice would prevent the disease.
  3. James Lind experimented with 12 sick sailors to find out whether the acid was responsible for the cure. Each was given the same diet except that four of the men were given small amounts of dilute sulfuric acid, four others were given vinegar (acetic acid), and the remaining four were given lemons. Only those given lemons recovered from the scurvy.

21. Credit for solving the problem described in the passage belongs to

   (A) Hall because he devised a cure for scurvy
   (B) Harvey because he first proposed a solution of the problem
   (C) Lind because he used the scientific experimental method
   (D) Harvey and Lind because they found that lemons are more effective than Hall's brew
   (E) All three men because each made some contribution

22. How many controls did James Lind use?

   (A) One
   (B) Two
   (C) Three
   (D) Four
   (E) None

23. The hypothesis tested by Lind was that

   (A) lemons contain some substance not present in vinegar
   (B) the citric acid of lemons is effective in treating scurvy
   (C) lemons contain some unknown acid that cures scurvy
   (D) the substance to cure scurvy is found only in lemons
   (E) some specific substance, rather than acids in general, is needed to cure scurvy

24. Which question did Lind's experiment NOT answer?

   (A) Will lemons cure scurvy?
   (B) Will either sulfuric acid or vinegar cure scurvy?
   (C) Will citric acid alone cure scurvy?
   (D) Are lemons more effective than either sulfuric acid or vinegar in the treatment of scurvy?
   (E) Are all substances that contain acids equally effective as treatments for scurvy?

25. A possible cause of scurvy is

   (A) lack of watercress
   (B) lack of acidity
   (C) lack of fresh food
   (D) lengthy sea voyages
   (E) lack of lemon juice

S T O P

IF YOU FINISH BEFORE TIME IS CALLED, YOU MAY CHECK YOUR WORK ON THIS SECTION ONLY.
DO NOT WORK ON ANY OTHER SECTION IN THE TEST.

Answer Key

Note: The answers to the quantitative sections are keyed to the corresponding review areas in the Mathematics Review (Chapter 11). The numbers in parentheses after each answer refer to the math topic(s) covered by that particular question.

Section 1   Verbal

1.	D	11.	C	21.	B	31.	D
2.	C	12.	B	22.	D	32.	B
3.	C	13.	E	23.	A	33.	C
4.	B	14.	C	24.	D	34.	C
5.	B	15.	C	25.	E	35.	E
6.	D	16.	D	26.	D	36.	D
7.	C	17.	E	27.	D	37.	B
8.	B	18.	C	28.	A	38.	E
9.	E	19.	E	29.	C		
10.	B	20.	D	30.	E		

Section 2   Quantitative

1.	B (I-B)	9.	C (III-A, D)	17.	C (III-G)	25.	C (I-B, IV)
2.	D (I-A)	10.	C (III-A)	18.	B (II-E)	26.	B (III-H)
3.	B (I-A)	11.	C (III-A, D)	19.	A (I-D)	27.	D (II-E)
4.	C (II-E)	12.	C (I-D)	20.	D (I-B, III)	28.	E (II-B)
5.	C (II-C-2)	13.	B (II-C)	21.	C (II-E, IV)	29.	B (III-F)
6.	C (III-F)	14.	D (II-C)	22.	D (I, IV)	30.	D (I-D)
7.	C (III-A, C)	15.	D (I-B, II-A)	23.	C (I-A, IV)		
8.	D (III-A)	16.	B (III-F)	24.	C (II-ED, IV)		

Section 3   Analytical

1.	E	8.	C	15.	A	22.	B
2.	A	9.	C	16.	C	23.	B
3.	D	10.	B	17.	D	24.	D
4.	E	11.	B	18.	B	25.	B
5.	D	12.	E	19.	D		
6.	C	13.	B	20.	E		
7.	D	14.	A	21.	E		

Section 4   Quantitative

1.	A (III-A, D)	9.	C (III-G)	17.	B (I-D)	25.	E (III-D)
2.	C (III-G)	10.	A (II-A)	18.	B (III-G)	26.	A (I-H, II-A)
3.	C (II-B)	11.	D (III-B)	19.	C (III-D)	27.	D (I-B)
4.	C (I-A)	12.	B (II-A)	20.	B (II-E)	28.	E (II-A)
5.	C (III-G)	13.	D (III-G)	21.	B (II-B)	29.	A (II-G)
6.	C (III-B)	14.	D (III-C)	22.	D (II-C)	30.	D (I-H)
7.	C (III-F)	15.	C (III-G)	23.	C (I-B)		
8.	A (II-C2)	16.	B (II-E)	24.	E (II-A)		

Section 5   Quantitative

1.	C (III-B)	9.	C (I-G)	17.	C (I-D)	25.	B (IV)
2.	C (III-F)	10.	B (I-B)	18.	C (I-D)	26.	C (I-D)
3.	C (III-G)	11.	C (II-A)	19.	C (II-E)	27.	C (I-B)
4.	C (IV-D)	12.	B (II-A)	20.	B (I-A)	28.	C (II-A)
5.	C (III-A)	13.	C (II-C)	21.	D (IV-C)	29.	D (III-G)
6.	C (I-A)	14.	B (III-A)	22.	D (IV-C)	30.	C (III-G)
7.	A (III-G)	15.	A (II-B)	23.	A (IV-C)		
8.	A (II-G)	16.	C (I-A)	24.	C (IV-C)		

Section 6   Verbal

1.	B	11.	C	21.	E	31.	D
2.	E	12.	D	22.	D	32.	E
3.	C	13.	C	23.	D	33.	E
4.	D	14.	D	24.	D	34.	E
5.	D	15.	E	25.	B	35.	C
6.	D	16.	D	26.	C	36.	E
7.	E	17.	B	27.	C	37.	B
8.	C	18.	D	28.	C	38.	A
9.	D	19.	C	29.	C		
10.	E	20.	B	30.	D		

Section 7   Analytical

1.	D	8.	C	15.	C	22.	B
2.	D	9.	B	16.	D	23.	E
3.	A	10.	A	17.	E	24.	C
4.	B	11.	D	18.	C	25.	C
5.	E	12.	B	19.	D		
6.	D	13.	A	20.	E		
7.	C	14.	B	21.	E		

Answer Explanations

Section 1

1. **D.** The statement asserts that the three are not in fact independent or separate but are instead *inseparable*.

2. **C.** If depression arises when nerve cells get too little of certain chemicals, it makes sense to have these cells get more of the chemicals. This can be done by making more of the chemicals *available to* the cells.

3. **C.** *Conventional* or traditional methods no longer are adequate to protect wild creatures. Conservationists wish to protect wildlife. Therefore, they are *pressing for* a new approach.

4. **B.** If neutron stars are the remnants or remaining traces of exploding stars, then they are the *products* or results of *violent* natural processes.
   Choice A is incorrect. The neutron stars did not cause the explosions; they were *caused by* the explosions.
   Choice C is incorrect. There is nothing *equivocal* or inconclusive about the explosion of a star.
   Choice D is incorrect. Nothing in the statement suggests that the creation of neutron stars *justifies* or vindicates the explosion of a star. In addition *harsh* is far too weak a word to describe a stellar explosion.
   Choice E is incorrect. Neutron stars come into existence *after* a supernova explodes. Thus, they are not *precursors* or forerunners of the explosion.

5. **B.** The contrast in Hugo is between *piety* or devotion ("a scene of chaste and holy love") and *ribaldry* or indecency (a scene of "coarse and profane licentiousness").
   Note that the sentence's parallelism demands that the two missing words be antonyms or near-antonyms.

6. **D.** The key word here is *busyness*, used to indicate a state of having many intricate details that do not coordinate into a harmonious whole.
   Because the details were *subordinated* or made less important than the building's total design, the building was *unencumbered* or unhampered by a sense of busyness.

7. **C.** The waitress omits taking *exaggerated* precautions. However, this does not imply that in doing so she was either rash (*imprudent*) or erratic (*capricious*). She was merely being *nonchalant* or poised, undisturbed by any untoward agitation over the performance of an everyday task.

8. **B.** A *lodge* is a place of shelter constructed by a *beaver*. A *nest* is a place of shelter constructed by a *bird*.
   (Defining Characteristic)

9. **E.** To *rustle cattle* is to steal them. To *hijack cargo* is to steal it. Note that you are dealing with a secondary meaning of the verb *rustle* here.
   (Defining Characteristic)

10. **B.** A *gland* produces *enzymes*. A *generator* produces electric *current*.
    Beware eye-catchers. Choices A, C, and D are incorrect although they contain biological terms.
    (Function)

11. **C.** A *jug* is an example of *crockery* or earthenware. A *hat* is an example of *millinery* or the hatmaker's ware.
    (Class and Member)

12. **B.** A *glint* is a small gleam of *light*. A *whiff* is a slight puff of *scent*.
    (Degree of Intensity)

13. **E.** *Doggerel* is trivial or inferior verse produced by a *poet*. A *potboiler* is a trivial or inferior literary work produced by a *novelist*.
    (Defining Characteristic)

14. **C.** Something *feral* or wild lacks *domestication* or taming. Something *crude* or rough lacks *refinement* or polish.
    (Antonym Variant)

15. **C.** To *scotch* or block a *rumor* is to suppress it. To *quash* or quell a *riot* is to suppress it.
    (Defining Characteristic)

16. **D.** To *qualify* something is to make it less general and more *particular*. To *mollify* something is to make it less harsh and more *agreeable*.
    (Defining Characteristic)

17. **E.** By providing background on how the theory of a dynamic abyss came to take hold in the scientific community and on how the forces that activate the global patterns of ocean currents actually work, the passage serves to "summarize evidence supporting oceanic circulation."

18. **C.** The opening sentence states that "many investigators were initially reluctant" to accept the evidence in favor of this controversial hypothesis. Committed to the belief that the depths of the ocean were calm ("the notion of the tranquil abyss"), these scientists at first viewed the idea that the abyss could be dynamic with *marked skepticism* (distinct doubt).

19. E.   The passage states that the *first* argument for the existence of dynamic currents in the deep sea came from theory, based on "models of ocean circulation" involving the tendency of cold water to sink.

20. D.   Because they need to take into account the effects of strong sea-floor currents on the structures they plan to build, *designers of sea-floor structures* are most likely to be interested in this particular article.

21. B.   Both minute particles of rock and grains of wind-blown soil belong to the first type of sediment discussed ("detritus whose source is the weathering of rocks on continents and islands"). Only the *fragmentary shells* of dead microscopic organisms belong to the second type.

22. D.   The authors approximate an amount ("about three billion tons per year"), refer to a model of ocean circulation, give several examples ("such as the..."), and list evidence to support a theory. They never *propose a solution* to a problem.

23. A.   The authors are objective and factual. Their tone can best be described as *dispassionate* (unemotional).

24. D.   In the two paragraphs of this passage, we find the justification for Choice D. In the first paragraph, we are told that Goethe loved the elements of classicism but could not adhere to its requirements. In the second paragraph we are shown how Goethe embodied the elements of romanticism in his writings.
        Choice A is incorrect. The passage fails to give equal weight to both writers.
        Choice B is incorrect. The passage focuses on Goethe, not on romanticism.
        Choice C is incorrect. The passage refers to the differences between classicism and romanticism in order to explain Goethe's writings.
        Choice E is incorrect. The passage deals with Goethe's art, not his life.

25. E.   The author never mentions *simplicity of language* as a characteristic of romanticism.
        Choice A is incorrect. The passage refers to a "continued faith in nature" as one aspect of Goethe's romanticism.
        Choice B is incorrect. The passage refers to impulsiveness or *spontaneity* as savoring strongly of romantic individualism.
        Choice C is incorrect. Since romanticism has *formed* so many modern attitudes, one finds in romanticism ideas that seem noteworthy for their modernity.
        Choice D is incorrect. The passage refers to "a disregard of artistic or logical propriety" as characteristic of romanticism.

26. D.   You can arrive at the correct answer by the process of elimination.
        Sensitivity towards emotional promptings is characteristic of romanticism; it is an unlikely characteristic of classicism. Therefore, you can eliminate Choices C and E.
        Emphasis on formal aesthetic criteria is a likely characteristic of classicism. The passage talks of the formal beauty that distinguishes the classical works of Dante and Virgil. Therefore, you can eliminate Choice B.
        Meticulous planning of artistic works is a likely characteristic of classicism. The passage talks of the carefully planned compositions of the classicist Dante; it also tells of the structurally flawed compositions of the romantic Goethe. Therefore, you can eliminate Choice A.
        Only Choice D is left. It is the correct answer.

27. D.   The author both admires Goethe's writings and notes their flaws; his attitude is one of *measured admiration*.

28. A.   The opposite of *superficial* or shallow is *profound*.
        Think of "superficial ideas."

29. C.   The opposite of *naivete* or lack of worldliness is *sophistication*.
        Think of "innocent naivete."

30. E.   The opposite of to *tether* or fasten is to *loose*.
        Think of "tethering a horse to the hitching post."

31. D.   The opposite of *pandemonium* or tumultuous uproar is *tranquillity* or calm.
        Word Parts Clue: *Pan-* means all; *demon-* means evil spirit. Hell or *Pandemonium*, the place where all the evil spirits dwell, is a place of noise and uproar.
        Think of "pandemonium breaking loose."

32. B.   To *enervate* (weaken or enfeeble) is the opposite of to *stimulate* or energize.
        Think of being "enervated by the heat."

33. C.   The opposite of *destitution* (privation; lack of life's necessities) is *affluence* or wealth.
        Think of "the poor living in destitution."

34. C.   The opposite of to *bereave* (deprive or dispossess, especially by death) is to *restore*.
        Think of being "bereaved of all hope."

35. E.   The opposite of to *eschew* or shun is to *seek*.
        Beware eye-catchers. Choice A is incorrect. *Eschew* is unrelated to chewing or gnawing.
        Think of "eschewing violence and seeking peace."

36. D. The opposite of *recondite* (obscure; difficult to comprehend) is *obvious*.
Context Clue: "Many consider quantum theory a recondite subject."

37. B. The opposite of to *obviate* something (make it unnecessary) is to require or *necessitate* it. Think of "obviating a need."

38. E. The opposite of *contumacious* (insubordinate; stubbornly disobedient) is *tractable* (docile; obedient).
Think of "contumacious rebels."

5. C. Distance = rate × time

Distance = $(30 \text{ m.p.h.})\left(\frac{1}{3}\text{ hour}\right) = 10$ miles

Distance = $(20 \text{ m.p.h.})\left(\frac{1}{2}\text{ hour}\right) = 10$ miles

6. C. Because the arcs are equal, ABC is an equilateral triangle. AE bisects BC (given); therefore,

DC is $\frac{1}{2}$ of any side of ABC.

7. C. Since $y = 50$, the measure of $\angle DBC = 100$. Since this is a parallelogram, the measure of $\angle ABC = 80$ and $x = 40$. In the triangle formed, since $x + y = 90$, the measure of z, the vertex angle, is 90 because the sum of all the angles is a straight angle.

8. D. We may conclude that $a = 80$ but we have no information to determine the value of b, since we may not assume that any lines are parallel.

Section 2

1. B. $\dfrac{7+7+7}{-7-7-7} = \dfrac{21}{-21} = -1$

2. D. The value of x may be 30 or 60 or 90.

3. B. The 13 microscopes are divided so that Classroom A uses 6 odd-numbered microscopes and Classroom B uses 7 even-numbered ones.

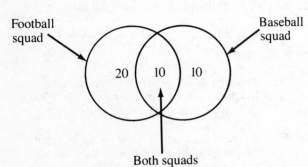

Football squad

Baseball squad

20   10   10

Both squads

4. C. The number of those on both squads = 10.
The number on the baseball squad = 20.
The number on the baseball squad but not on the football squad = 10.
The number on the football squad but not on the baseball squad = 20.
Column A: 10:20 or 1:2
Column B: 10:20 or 1:2

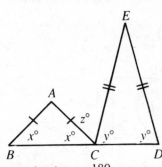

9. C.
$$
\begin{aligned}
x + y + z &= 180 \\
40 + 80 + z &= 180 \\
z &= 60 \\
3x &= 120 \\
2z &= 120
\end{aligned}
$$

10. C.
$$
\begin{aligned}
z + y + \angle ABC &= 180° \\
40 + 65 + \angle ABC &= 180° \\
\angle ABC &= 75° \\
m\angle OCD &= m\angle ABC \\
&\quad \text{(alternate interior angles)} \\
x &= 75
\end{aligned}
$$

11. C. Since $BD \perp AC$, $x = 90$
Since ABC is equilateral, $z = 60$
Therefore, $y = 30$

$\dfrac{x}{y} = \dfrac{90}{30} = 3$

12. C. 0.01 percent = 0.0001
(0.0001) (10,000) = 1.0

13. B. Since Martin is 5 times as old as Sara, Sara's

age is $\frac{1}{5}$ of Martin's age.

Michael is younger since his age is $\frac{1}{6}$ of

Martin's age.

14. D. The only information we have is that the sum
of the weights of the 3 children is 150 pounds.

15. D. We may assume that x and y have positive
values but only that x is greater than $\frac{1}{3} y$. Note
the many possibilities.
If $x = 3$ and $y = 2$, 3 is greater than $\frac{2}{3}$.
If $x = 4$ and $y = 5$, 4 is greater than $\frac{5}{3}$.

16. B. (See diagram)

17. C. Draw $DF \perp BC$
$DF = AE = 4$
Therefore, $FC = 3$

$BE = 3$
$EF = 26 - 6 = 20$
$AD = 20$

18. B. This is a direct proportion. Let x = number of
postage stamps that can be purchased for c
cents.
$$\frac{1 \text{ stamp}}{5 ¢} = \frac{x \text{ stamps}}{c ¢}$$
$$5x = c$$
$$x = \frac{c}{5}$$

19. A. $20\% \left(\text{or } \frac{1}{5} \right)$ of $2 = \frac{2}{5}$

$$\frac{3}{7} - \frac{2}{5} = \frac{15}{35} - \frac{14}{35} = \frac{1}{35}$$

20. D.

$$\frac{AC}{AD} = \frac{2 \text{ equal segments}}{3 \text{ equal segments}} = \frac{2}{3}$$

21. C. Teachers' salaries represent 30% of the budget.
Salaries of other school personnel represent
10% of the budget.
30%:10% or 3:1

22. D. Tax rate per $100 for schools = 24.856
Tax rate per $100 for community college
= 0.654
$$\frac{24.856}{0.654} = 38 +$$

23. C. $10,000 = 100 ($100)
($100)(24.856) = $2485.60

24. C. If $D = 20% of the budget then
$$\frac{\$D}{20\%} = \frac{?}{15\%}$$
$$(20\%)(?) = 15(\$D)$$
$$? = \$\frac{15}{20}D = \$\frac{3}{4}D$$

25. C. $25\% = \frac{1}{4}$

26. B. Area of triangle $= \frac{1}{2}$ (base)(altitude)

Area of triangle $= \frac{1}{2}$ (6 units)(2 units) $=$
6 units

27. D. 3 gallons = 12 quarts = 24 pints
165 pints = 6.8 (3-gallon cans)
Only six 3-gallon cans will be *filled*.

28. E. A time-consuming method would be to solve
for y in terms of x and to substitute that value in
$5y$. A superior method would be to multiply
both sides of the equation by 6 in order to
obtain a value of $5y$.
$$3x = \frac{5}{6}y$$

$$(6)(3x) = \left(\frac{5}{6}y \right)(6)$$

$$18x = 5y$$

29. **B.** One-minute unit on the clock $= \dfrac{360°}{60°} = 6°$

At half-past six the large hand of the clock is midway between 6 and 7 ($2\frac{1}{2}$ units) or 15°.

30. **D.** Let $x =$ number of ounces of water to be added to make a 25% alcohol solution.

$$\frac{\text{amount of alcohol}}{\text{amount of solution}} = \frac{1}{4}$$
$$\frac{48}{48 + x} = \frac{1}{4}$$
$$48 + x = 192$$
$$x = 144$$

Section 3

1-3. A quick reading of the three questions will reveal that the student is not asked to prepare a seating arrangement. The student should examine what is presented.

1. **E.** Choice I is satisfactory.

Choice III is also satisfactory.

Choice II is unsatisfactory.

Having discovered that Mrs. L will not be able to communicate with either Mrs. N or Mrs. P, the student need not continue examining the remaining ladies' abilities to communicate with their neighbors.

2. **A.** Since Mrs. J speaks Russian only, she must sit alongside Mrs. P or Mrs. H. Mrs. H is already seated; the only place left for Mrs. J is alongside Mrs. P.

3. **D.** An examination of the list of guests reveals that five ladies speak French. Four have already seated themselves in this group of seven. Mrs. L speaks only French and therefore must be seated alongside Mrs. Q.

4. **E.** It is not really necessary to examine statements I, II, and III. A glance at the chart should reveal that Mrs. J, who speaks Russian only, will have no one to converse with, since the only other Russian-speaking women—Mrs. H and Mrs. P—will not be in attendance. Choice E is the only possible answer.

5. **D.** Johnson makes two claims: (1) anyone supporting the bill must have an ulterior motive, and (2) therefore, there are no valid grounds for supporting the bill. Choice D makes the same two claims about Johnson. Choice B is the best response to Johnson, and does *not* make the error in reasoning that he makes; choice A grants Johnson's claims and does not attack him; choice C attacks Johnson's argument rather than attacking his motives; and choice E attacks Johnson but doesn't claim that motivation discredits his argument.

6. **C.** This deluded father is basing his whole argument about his daughter's talents on the rave reviews from a single high school play. The best way to counter his argument would be to point out the inadequacy of that evidence, which is what choice C does. All the other choices refer to the stiff competition for jobs on Broadway and the high odds against succeeding. They do not directly counter the father's line of reasoning.

7. **D.** The original argument states that most X (opponents of gun control) are Y (conservatives); therefore, someone who is not X is probably not Y. The flaw in this reasoning is that many persons other than X may also be Y. Choice D makes the same error: most X (sports cars) are Y (expensive), so a non-X is probably not Y. But many kinds of cars other than sports cars may be expensive. The other arguments have logical structures different from that of the original argument. Choice A wrongly argues: most X are Y, therefore a Y is probably X. Choices B, C, and E are all logically valid.

8-11. Since this problem involves both days of the week and calendar dates, make a calendar. Keep it simple. It doesn't have to show all days of the week—only one choice in one question involves a day other than Tuesday, Thursday, or Saturday—and it doesn't have to go all the way through May. It will look like this:

	RYDER	EAKINS	HUDSON RIVER
Th. 4-30	√	—	—
Sat. 5-2	√	—	√
Tu. 5-5	√	—	—
Th. 5-7	—	—	√
Sat. 5-9	√	√	√
Tu. 5-12	√	√	—
Th. 5-14	—	√	√
Sat. 5-16	√	√	√
Tu. 5-19	√	√	√
Th. 5-21	—	√	√
Sat. 5-23	√	√	√

(ends 5-24)

8. C. The conditions mean Dan can go to the museum only on Tuesday, Thursday, or Saturday. By starting on Tuesday, he can complete the three visits in five days, whereas by starting on Thursday or Saturday he must take six days. This is enough to get you to choice C. Dan must go to the Eakins or Ryder exhibition first, since the Twachtman Gallery is closed Tuesdays.

9. C. Since the Pollock Wing is closed Thursdays during May, Ellen must see the Ryder exhibition first, on Thursday, April 30 (I); she must, then, see "The Hudson River School" second, on May 7, since the "Precursors of Eakins" does not open until May 8 (II). This excludes choice III.

10. B. Your calendar tells you that all three exhibitions can be seen on Saturday, May 9, 16, or 23 (II)—not on Saturday, May 2, because the "Eakins" is not yet open, and not on May 30, because "The Hudson River School" is closed (I). III is out both because the Twachtman Gallery is closed Tuesdays and because the Eakins exhibition does not open until May 8.

11. B. Terry's visit falls on Thursday, May 7 (six days after the May 1 opening of "The Hudson River School"). A glance at the calendar shows that "The Hudson River School" is the only special exhibition open on that date.

12-18. To diagram this one, start with seven blanks for the seats. Put the moderator in the middle; put the initials of the speakers under the blanks and abbreviated titles over the blanks. (Of course, your diagram may be slightly different. Any clear and readable system will do.) Starting with statements (3) and (5), you have:

Impact						
C	F		Mod.			

The person delivering "Epidemiological Aspects" must be in a middle seat, and it must be on the right because Cathode, not Albert or Durand, is in an end seat on the left. Given this information, Albert and Durand must be in the two other seats on the right, while the two friends in statement (2) must be in the two remaining seats on the left, although in each case we don't know who is in which seat. Since the person in statement (4) is delivering "Benign," not "Impact," he or she must be in the end seat on the right. Finally, statement (6) tells us that Ettis is in the middle on the right, with Albert to her left. You now have:

Impact	Pub/Rad	Pub/Rad			Epidem	Benign
C	F		Mod.	A	E	D

By elimination, Burris is in the last available seat. We still don't know the title of Albert's paper, nor do we know which paper is to be delivered by Felsenstein, which by Burris.

12. E. By inspection of the diagram. Notice that choices A and B include Albert as pro-industry, while statement (6) says that he or she is a critic.

13. B. By inspection of the diagram.

14. A. Albert is the only person the title of whose paper is unknown.

15. A. We've seen that I remains ambiguous. II and III can be read from the diagram.

16. C. Statement (1) establishes the title of the paper. Statements (3) and (5), along with (1), put the author in the middle seat on the right. Statement (6) establishes the name of the person in that seat. Statements (2) and (4) aren't needed.

17. D. The diagram shows that, if the seventh speaker is to sit midway between Cathode and the moderator, he must sit between Felsenstein and Burris.

18. B. If the eighth speaker is to sit exactly midway between Durand and the author of "Public Health and PBX," then the latter must be Felsenstein, not Burris, since otherwise there would be no vacant spot *exactly* midway between the two. Therefore, Burris must be the author of "Radiological Aspects of PBX." The eighth speaker will sit between the moderator and Albert.

19-22. We've drawn a diagram similar to the traditional "family tree" diagram used in history books and genealogies. Since so many persons are of uncertain sex, we've used m for male, f for female, and x and y for unknowns. We know, for example, that G is the same sex as C, so we label both x; B and therefore F are the opposite sex from C, so we label both y, and so on. Horizontal lines indicate marriage, vertical or diagonal lines indicate children.

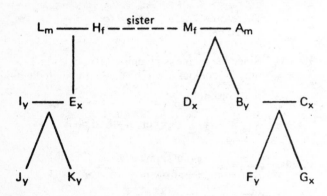

19. D. This question orients you, in case you made an unwarranted assumption about the sexes. Since we do not know B's sex for sure, we don't know F's; this rules out all the wrong choices —including E, since we *do* know H's sex. As the child of D's sibling B, F is D's niece or nephew.

20. E. D is an x, and can therefore marry any unmarried y.

21. E. H is female. If x = male, H can marry D *or* G, so I is out. If y = male, H can marry F. Clearly H cannot marry both. (J and K are ruled out, since they are H's direct descendants.)

22. B. This generation (the middle generation) contains three x's and two y's. If the more numerous x's are female, J, who is a y, must be male. If x = female, choices A, C, and E are untrue. Choice D can never be true.

23. B. Statement I is *not* assumed. The author assumes only that we are in danger of running out of oil *eventually*. Statement II *is* assumed. The author's claim is that we *must* use oil to produce plastics and other goods. Statement III is *not* assumed. The author assumes only that *someone* could develop alternative methods of transportation, not that the oil companies are in a position to do this themselves.

24. D. The author's only basis for advocating the banning of the internal combustion engine is that the oil it burns is needed for other purposes. If a synthetic oil were developed that did every-

thing natural oil does, the author's complaint would lose its force. All the other choices describe events which would ameliorate the problem without eliminating it.

25. B. The author claims that the oil we are burning is needed to produce many important commodities. Choice B underscores both the value of some of those items and the necessity of using oil to produce them. Choice A supports the author's secondary point that other methods of transportation could be developed, but does not directly support the main conclusion that the internal combustion engine should be banned. Choice C emphasizes the urgency of the problem, but the original argument makes no claims about time. Choices D and E provide bases of other arguments for the banning of gasoline-burning cars, but have no effect on the original argument.

Section 4

1. A. Angle *BEC* is a right angle. Therefore $w + z = 90$. Since $w + x + z + y = 360$ and $w + z = 90$, then $x + y = 270$.

2. C.
$$\text{Area} = \pi r^2 = \frac{\pi}{4}$$
$$r^2 = \frac{1}{4}$$
$$r = \frac{1}{2} \text{ or } 0.5$$

3. C. If equal quantities are added to equal quantities the sums are equal.

4. C. From –5 to zero inclusive there are 6 integers, and from 1 to 5 there are 5 more integers, for a total of 11 integers. From 5 to 15 inclusive there are also 11 integers.

5. C. Let s = side of square
Then area of square = s^2
s^2 = area of triangle *ABC* (given)
Therefore, $AB = BC = s\sqrt{2}$ for $s^2 =$
$$\frac{(s\sqrt{2})(s\sqrt{2})}{2}$$
Therefore, $\dfrac{AB}{DG} = \dfrac{s\sqrt{2}}{s}$ or $\sqrt{2}$

6. C. Area of a triangle = $\dfrac{1}{2}$ (base)(altitude). Both triangles share the same base (*AB*). Since distances between parallel lines are the same, the two triangles have equal altitudes.

7. C.   Because the arcs are equal, *ABC* is an equilateral triangle. *AE* bisects *BC* (given); therefore

DC is $\frac{1}{2}$ of any side of *ABC*.

8. A.   Time = $\dfrac{\text{distance}}{\text{rate}}$

Time = $\dfrac{\frac{1}{2}\text{ mile}}{20\text{ miles per hour}} = \dfrac{1}{40}$ hour

Time = $\dfrac{\frac{1}{3}\text{ mile}}{30\text{ miles per hour}} = \dfrac{1}{90}$ hour

9. C. $\dfrac{\text{Distance}}{\text{Circumference}}$ = number of revolutions

$\dfrac{70\text{ feet}}{7\text{ feet}}$ = 10 revolutions

$\dfrac{100\text{ feet}}{10\text{ feet}}$ = 10 revolutions

Circumference = πd

Circumference = $\cancel{\pi} \cdot \dfrac{7}{\cancel{\pi}} = 7$ (Column A)

Circumference = $\cancel{\pi} \cdot \dfrac{10}{\cancel{\pi}} = 10$ (Column B)

10. A.   If $X + Y = 100$
then $100 + Z = 350$
and $Z = 250$
If $X + Y = 100$
then $X < 100$ and $Z > X$

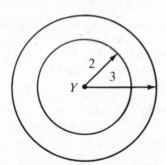

11. D.   If *Y* is at the center of both circles, then *Z* could be anywhere on the circumference of the circle with radius = 2, and *X* could be at any point on the circumference with radius = 3. There are many possibilities for the location of *X* in respect to the location of *Z*.

12. B. $x < y$ because when x is squared and multiplied by 9 it has the same value as y.

13. D.   From the information given, we can only deduce that $\frac{1}{2}$ the product of these two values equals 18.

14. D.   We may conclude only that $AD = BC$ and $AB = DC$.

15. C.   Let s = side of square. Then
Area of square = s^2
s^2 = area of triangle *ABC* (given)
Therefore, $AB = BC = s\sqrt{2}$

for $s^2 = \dfrac{(s\sqrt{2})(s\sqrt{2})}{2}$

Therefore, $\dfrac{AB}{DG} = \dfrac{s\sqrt{2}}{s}$ or $\sqrt{2}$

16. B.   Since the recipe is given for 60 cookies and only 20 cookies are to be made, the ingredients must be cut by $\frac{1}{3}$.

$\dfrac{1}{3} \cdot 1\dfrac{1}{2} = \dfrac{1}{3} \cdot \dfrac{3}{2} = \dfrac{1}{2}$ cup of sifted flour

17. B. $\dfrac{\text{potassium}}{\text{potassium + nitrogen + oxygen}}$
$= \dfrac{39}{39 + 14 + 48} = \dfrac{39}{101}$
= approximately 39%

18. B.   The width is 50, since the length is twice the width. Perimeter = 50 + 50 + 100 + 100 = 300 feet.

19. C.   Let $x = BC$; then $AB = 2x$.
Area of triangle *ABC* = $\dfrac{1}{2}(b)(h)$

or $\left(\dfrac{1}{2}\right)(x)(2x)$ or x^2.

Area is given equal to 64 square feet.
$x^2 = 64$
$x = 8$
$BC = 8; AB = 16$
$(8)^2 + (16)^2 = (AC)^2$ (Pythagorean theorem)
$64 + 256 = (AC)^2$
$(AC)^2 = 320$
$AC = \sqrt{320}$
or approximately 18 feet

20. B. $x = ky$ $\therefore \dfrac{5}{9} = \dfrac{5}{3} \cdot y$
$5 = 3k$
$k = \dfrac{5}{3}$ $y = \dfrac{1}{3}$

21. B. 8 ounces buttermilk = 90 calories
2 tablespoons light cream = 60 calories
3 tablespoons light cream = 90 calories

22. D. 4 ounces chocolate milk = 4 grams of protein
4 tablespoons cream cheese = 4 grams of protein
4 tablespoons cream cheese = 220 calories

23. C. (A) whole milk = 320 calories
(B) buttermilk = 180 calories
(C) Swiss cheese = 1760 calories
(D) cottage cheese = 480 calories
(E) chocolate milk = 380 calories

24. E. (A) cottage cheese = 30 calories
(B) cheddar-type cheese = 90 calories
(C) Swiss cheese = 110 calories
(D) butter = 200 calories
(E) whole milk = 20 calories

25. E. In 8 ounces, the number of grams of protein is:
(A) whole milk, 9
(B) cottage cheese, 32
(C) butter, none
(D) chocolate milk, 8
(E) American cheese, 64

26. A. I is true; e.g., $\sqrt[3]{-8} = -2$.

II is false; $\sqrt{\dfrac{1}{4}}$ is not smaller than $\dfrac{1}{4}$;

$\sqrt{\dfrac{1}{4}} = \dfrac{1}{2}; \dfrac{1}{2}$ is larger than $\dfrac{1}{4}$.

III is false; $(A - B)(A + B) = A^2 - B^2$.

27. D. The reciprocal of 0 is $\dfrac{1}{0}$. Any number with a zero in the denominator does not exist, since division by zero is meaningless or undefined. Therefore, 0 does not have a reciprocal.

(A) The reciprocal of 1 or $\dfrac{1}{1}$ is 1.

(B) The reciprocal of -2 or $\dfrac{-2}{1}$ is $\dfrac{1}{-2}$.

(C) The reciprocal of $\dfrac{1}{3}$ is $\dfrac{3}{1}$ or 3.

(E) The reciprocal of 3 is $\dfrac{1}{3}$.

28. E. $x + y = 16$
$x = 16 - y$
$(16 - y) - z = 16 - y - z$

29. A. $\dfrac{a - b}{3.5} = \dfrac{4}{7}$

Since $3.5 = \dfrac{1}{2}$ of 7, then $a - b = \dfrac{1}{2}$ of $4 = 2$.
Since $a - b = 2$, $b < a$.

30. D. $10^x = \underbrace{(10)(10)(10) \dots\dots\dots\dots 10}_{x \text{ times}}$

$10^{-x} = \dfrac{1}{\underbrace{(10)(10)(10) \dots\dots (10)}_{x \text{ times}}}$

(A) is true.
$470,000 = (4.7)(10)(10)(10)(10)(10)$
$= 4.7 \times 10^5$
(B) is true. 450 billion $= 4.5 \times 10^{11}$
(C) is true. $0.00000000075 = 7.5 \times 10^{-10}$
(D) is not true. $\dfrac{86}{100,000} = \dfrac{8.6}{10,000} \; 8.6^{-4}$

Section 5

1. C. Since vertical angles 1 and 2 are equal, right triangle ABE is similar to right triangle DEC,

and $\dfrac{AB}{DC} = \dfrac{AE}{EC}$.

In ABE, hypotenuse $BE = 5$, and $AB = 4$; then leg $AE = 3$.
In DEC, if $AB = 4$, and $DC = 12$, and since $AE = 3$, then $EC = 9$, because $\dfrac{4}{12} = \dfrac{3}{EC}$,

$4EC = 36$, $EC = 9$.
$AC = AE + EC = 3 + 9 = 12$.

2. C. Circumference $= 2\pi r$. If radius of A $=$ $\dfrac{1}{2}$ radius of B, then circumference of $A =$ $\dfrac{1}{2}$ circumference of B. This may be stated as follows: twice the circumference of A equals the circumference of B.

3. C. Both triangles share the same base and they have equal altitudes, since AD is parallel to BC.

4. C. Since $b = c$, each fraction equals 1.

5. C.   Since $BA = BC$,
$\angle A = \angle C$. Since $\angle x = 60°$, $\angle A + \angle C = 120°$.
(The sum of the angles of a triangle equals
180°.) Therefore $\angle C = 60°$. Since $\angle y = 100°$,
$\angle CGH = 80°$, because these angles are supplementary. In triangle CGH, since $\angle C = 60°$ and
$\angle CGH = 80°$, $\angle CHG$ must equal 40°. Since
$\angle z$ is the supplement of $\angle CHG$, the $\angle z = 180°$
$- 40°$, or 140°.

6. C. $a^2 = 9$, $b = 9$; $a^2 - b = 0$.
$b = 9$; $a^2 = 9$; $b - a^2 = 0$.

7. A.   Draw EC. $EC = AB = 400$ feet. Area of
square $ABCE = (400)^2$, or 160,000 square
feet. Area of triangle $EDC = \frac{1}{2}(400)(300)$, or
60,000 square feet. Area of entire lot =
160,000 + 60,000, or 220,000 square feet
(Column A).

8. A.   Multiply the expression $a < b$ by -2. The result
is $-2a > -2b$. Recall that, when you multiply
each side of an inequality by the same negative
expression, the inequality is reversed.

9. C.   The numbers are q, $q + 1$, $q + 2$, $q + 3$,
$q + 4$, $q + 5$, $q + 6$, $q + 7$, $q + 8$. The sum
of the numbers is $9q + 36$. The average is
$\frac{9q + 36}{9}$, which is $q + 4$.

10. B. $\frac{1}{2} + \frac{1}{3} = \frac{5}{6}$

$\left(\frac{5}{6}\right)(1813) < 1813$

11. C. $xy = 1$
$y = \frac{1}{x}$ (divide by x)
$\frac{x}{y} = \frac{x}{\frac{1}{x}}$ (substitution)
$\frac{x}{y} = x^2$

12. B.   Since x is negative, $\frac{1}{x}$ is negative and x^2 is
positive.

13. C.   Let g = value of each gold coin, and let s =
value of each silver coin. Then
$3g + 1s = 5s + 2g$ (given)
$1g = 4s$

14. B. $b° = 120$ (corresponding angles of parallel
lines)
$a° + 120 = 180°$
$a° = 60$

15. A.   Add the two equations.
$3a = -3$ and $a = -1$.
$-1 + b = -6$
$b = -5$
-1 is greater than -5, so a is greater than b.

16. C. $\frac{41.5 \text{ feet}}{6} = 6.91 +$ feet, or each string is just
under 7 feet. Checking each answer for the clos-
est figure is more rapid than changing 41 feet to
498 inches, dividing by 6, and converting the
answer to feet and inches.

17. C. $\frac{\text{difference}}{\text{original}} = \frac{\$2.50}{\$12.50} = \frac{1}{5} = 20\%$

18. C. $\frac{\text{difference}}{\text{original}} = \frac{\$24}{\$96} = \frac{1}{4} = 25\%$

19. C.   Since the first car uses 1 gallon for 15 miles, it
will use 4 gallons for 60 miles. Since the second car uses 1 gallon for m miles, it will go $4m$
miles on 4 gallons.

20. B. $\frac{760}{200} = 3.8$ gallons. It will be necessary to purchase 4 gallons.

21. D.   Using the upper graph, follow the July 1990
point to the 110 mark.

22. D.   In March 1992, the unemployment rate was
slightly more than 7%.

23. A.   During July 1990 there were a low unemployment rate (5%) and a high employment rate
(110 million), indicative of a fairly healthy
economy.

24. B.   The upper chart shows that the highest peak
was reached in July 1990, when 110 million
people were employed.

25. B.   Logically one would expect to find unemployment decreasing as the number of people employed increases.

26. C. $\left(\dfrac{ab}{100}\right) \div \left(\dfrac{ba}{100}\right) = \left(\dfrac{ab}{100}\right) \cdot \left(\dfrac{100}{ba}\right) = 1$

27. C. (A) $\dfrac{1}{5} = 0.2$

(B) $\dfrac{1}{4} = 0.25$

(C) $\dfrac{2}{5} = 0.4$

(D) $\dfrac{16}{25} = 0.64 \left(\text{which is more than } \dfrac{1}{2}\right)$

(E) $\dfrac{3}{10} = 0.3$

28. C. $\dfrac{t+n}{n} = \dfrac{t}{n} + \dfrac{n}{n}$ or $\dfrac{t}{n} + 1$

29. D. If the cow were tethered by a ten-foot-rope in a pasture without fences, it could graze in a circular area of 100π. Since the fences form an angle of $60°$, the cow will be confined to $\dfrac{60}{360}$ or $\dfrac{1}{6}$ of that circle, or $\dfrac{1}{6}$ of 100π or $\dfrac{50\pi}{3}$.

30. C. Radius = $\dfrac{7}{2}$ inches, and the area of the bottom of the smaller tin = $\pi\left(\dfrac{7}{2}\right)\left(\dfrac{7}{2}\right)$ square inches.

The volume of each small tin = $\pi\left(\dfrac{7}{2}\right)\left(\dfrac{7}{2}\right)(1)$ cubic inches.
The volume of the two small tins =
$2\pi\left(\dfrac{7}{2}\right)\left(\dfrac{7}{2}\right)(1)$ cubic inches.

Let x = depth of dough in the larger tin. Since the radius of the larger tin = 5 inches, the volume of dough in the larger tin = $(5)(5)(\pi)(x)$ or $25\pi x$.

$25\pi x = \dfrac{49}{2}\pi$ (the amount of dough is the same)

$25x = \dfrac{49}{2}$

$x = \dfrac{49}{50}$ or 0.98

Section 6

1. B. The writer contrasts the individualistic nature of early explorations with the *collaborative* nature of present day ones.

2. E. The anthropologists have dismissed Villa's theory. Nevertheless, they still must stress that other interpretations of the evidence are possible. Why? Because they have not been able to dismiss his evidence. Thus, they are forced to *grant* or concede that his research was carefully done.

3. C. Rather than being *barren* or devoid of life, the vent regions are like *oases* that support life.
Choice A is incorrect. A *waste* by definition is not *teeming* but *barren*.
Choice B is incorrect. The vent region would not be described as an *enclave* (tract enclosed within a foreign territory).
Choice D is incorrect. A *grotto* would not be described as island-like.
Choice E is incorrect. Nothing in the sentence justifies the use of the term *hazardous*.

4. D. Instead of allowing the exchanges to develop fully, the playwright cuts short or *truncates* them.

5. D. A *spate* or flood of examples of fraud suggests that the review system intended to catch such frauds is severely *taxed* or burdened.

6. D. Despite his self-centeredness, White could be kind to others. He could even go beyond kindness and do what for someone egocentric was harder still—*deprecate* or belittle himself. Note the use of *even* as an intensifier here.

7. E. Characters who define themselves by their betrayals *belie* or contradict any assurances they have given others of their good faith.
Choices A, B and D are incorrect. Nothing in the sentence suggests they *flaunt* (parade), *underscore* (emphasize) or *deplore* (lament) the promises they have made.
Choice C is incorrect. Updike's characters break their promises; they do not *fulfill* them.

8. C. A *book* consists of several *chapters*. A *building* consists of several *stories*.

(Part to Whole)

9. D. To *inaugurate* a *president* is to introduce him or her into office. To *install* an *officer* is to do the same.

(Function)

10. E. To *tinker* is to *adjust* or repair something in an unskilled manner. To *scribble* is to *write* or draw something in an unskilled manner.

(Manner)

11. C. *Zinc* is a specific example of an *element*. A *quark* is a specific example of a *particle*.

(Class and Member)

12. D. Something *uproarious* is by definition extremely *amusing*. Something *repugnant* is by definition extremely *disagreeable*.

(Degree of Intensity)

13. C.   *Forensic* means pertaining to the art of *debate*. *Histrionic* means pertaining to the art of the *theater*.

Beware eye-catchers. Choice A is incorrect. An argument may be empirical or based on fact; however, arguments are not necessarily empirical.

(Defining Characteristic)

14. D.   A *limpet* (mollusk that adheres strongly when disturbed) is difficult to *detach*. A *tick* (parasite that burrows into its host) is difficult to *extract*.

(Defining Characteristic)

15. E.   To *countenance* or allow something is to give it *approval*. To *air* or voice something is to give it *expression*.

Note that *air* here is used with a less familiar, secondary meaning.

(Synonym Variant)

16. D.   Someone *insouciant* (nonchalant; unconcerned) is difficult to *disturb*. Someone *incredulous* (skeptical; disbelieving) is difficult to *convince*.

(Antonym Variant)

17. B.   The opening sentence maintains the growth of scholarly activity was stimulated by the protest movement. The protest movement caused an upsurge of popular interest in the Afro-American past. It also created a climate in which professional studies of black history were legitimized.

18. D.   The author cites no public opinion polls in the passage. However, he does cite personal anecdotes (Logan's and Litwack's experiences), magazine articles (Bennett's series in *Ebony*), curricular materials (both the freedom schools' materials and those developed for the New York and Detroit public schools) and scholarly publications (Logan's and Litwack's texts).

19. C.   The three men are cited as examples of scholars who were encouraged to resume their earlier researches in black history.

Choices A, B and E are incorrect. None of the three men was identified in the passage with these concerns.

Choice D is incorrect. Only Logan is identified with research on blacks in nineteenth-century North Carolina.

20. B.   Since the advice was not actually "indicative of how things were going" in the field, it was inappropriate to the times or out of keeping with the current state of cultural and professional development.

21. E.   The author is describing what occurred during the period to change black history from a marginal field to a vital field of specialization.

22. D.   You can arrive at the correct answer by the process of elimination.

Statement I is supported by the passage. At the time Bennett and Logan wrote, both the pre-Mayflower period of black history and the nineteenth-century life of blacks in North Carolina were relatively unexplored. Therefore, you can eliminate Choices B and E.

Statement II is unsupported by the passage. Bennett's work was a popularization intended for a wide general audience. It was not aimed at academics. Therefore, you can eliminate Choice C.

Statement III is supported by the passage. Bennett's work appeared first as a series of magazine articles, then as a book. Logan's work first appeared as a doctoral thesis, then (with revisions) as a book. Therefore, you can eliminate Choice A.

Only Choice D is left. It is the correct answer.

23. D.   According to the passage, prior to the early 1960s Negro history was not an object of particularly great renown in academe. In the 1950s, the advice given to Blassingame to avoid black history if he desired "a future in the historical profession" seemed wise — graduate students of the caliber of Huggins and Litwack felt an ambivalence about entering the field because of "practical concerns." What these concerns boiled down to was the sense that to choose black history as one's specialization would be *detrimental* or harmful to one's career.

24. D.   The author is discussing the behavior of various rodents that become *dormant* or inactive for brief periods of time.

25. B.   Fat storage has worked against the fat mouse's survival because it has led to the mouse's being considered a succulent delicacy by African hunters.

26. C.   This detailed account of a particular aspect of rodent behavior clearly belongs in a *textbook on rodent biology*.

27. C.   In the opening sentence the author refers to hibernation and aestivation, two other types of dormant states. This suggests he has just been discussing these dormant states in some detail.

28. C.   The opposite of to *sap* or weaken is to *invigorate* or strengthen.

Think of "sapping one's energy."

29. C.   The opposite of *unfeigned* or not pretended is *simulated* or feigned.
Beware eye-catchers. Choice A is incorrect. *Pretentious* means ostentatious, showy, or ambitious. It does not mean pretended or feigned.
Think of welcoming someone "with unfeigned delight."

30. D.   The opposite of *vacillation* or wavering is *firmness*. Think of "indecisive vacillation."

31. D.   The opposite of to *swathe* or cover up is to *unwrap*.
Beware eye-catchers. Though babies are sometimes described as *swathed* in swaddling clothes and injured persons are sometimes described as *swathed* in bandages, *swathing* is related to wrapping, not to nurturing or anointing.
Think of "swathed in blankets."

32. E.   The opposite of *cognizance* (conscious knowledge, awareness) is *unawareness*.
Word Parts Clue: *Cogn-* means know. *Cognizance* means knowledge.
Context Clue: "He had no cognizance of the crime."

33. E.   The opposite of *nebulous* (vague, cloudy) is *distinct*.
Think of "a nebulous memory."

34. E.   The opposite of to *denigrate* (belittle or defame) is to *extol* or praise.
Think of "denigrating someone's efforts."

35. C.   The opposite of *decorum* (correctness, good taste) is *impropriety* or unseemliness.
Think of "a proper degree of decorum."

36. E.   The opposite of *condign* or due (as in exactly deserved) is *unmerited*.
Think of "condign punishment."

37. B.   The opposite of *puissance* or power is *powerlessness*.
Beware eye-catchers. Choice A is incorrect. The opposite of power is a lack of power, not a lack of effort.
Think of "the puissance of the emperor."

38. A.   The opposite of to *palliate* or moderate in severity or intensity is to *exacerbate* or increase in severity.
Think of "efforts to palliate a disease."

Section 7

1-5.   In this extremely tricky problem, the first five statements will tell you only who is in what generation and some of the relationships, but the last two statements clarify everything. Using solid horizontal lines for marriages, circles for married groups, broken lines for sibling relationships, and vertical lines for parent-child relationships, we first get the following diagram:

We know that N and M must be brothers of E *or* sisters of F, but we never find out which. We don't yet know the relationships among A, B, and C, although we *do* know that C and A aren't married (because their male and female children marry). We don't know exactly who Q's children are. The next two statements tell us. A and B are male; the paternal grandmother of E and F must be the mother of their fathers, so A and B must be brothers. *But* if they are the only grandfathers of H, they must be the fathers of her father E and her mother F. Since C is F's mother, B and C must be married, and G must be F's sister. Since A and C can't be married, A must be married in *Brihtu* marriage to several sisters (remember, A and B are H's *only* grandfathers), while B is married in *Brihtu* marriage to C and her sister or sisters. J, K, and L are the wives of A and B, but we don't know who is the wife of which of them. All this gives us the following completed diagram:

The questions are now easy.

1. D.   This can be read from the diagram. G is definitely *not* a sister of E, since she is a sister of F who is married to E. Since F may be the sister of N and M, G may be their sister as well; but she would be the sister of both, which eliminates choices A and B.

2. D.   N *must* be the sibling of more than one person, since he or she is married to three people. The possibilities are: M and E, if N is male; M and F, if N is female—but not both.

3. A.   A is definitely one of Q's children; C, J, and K cannot be, since they are married to Q's children (A and B); M must be a sibling of one of Q's grandchildren

4. B.   The only *Brihtu* marriages we are sure of are those of A and B. The marriage of N, M, E, and F, of which H is the daughter, could be either. We don't know whom Q married, so we can't tell what kind of marriage A and B are children of. We don't know who J's parents might have been.

5. E.   We know that E is eligible to marry F, and that G is F's sister. N cannot marry M (choice A), since they are the same sex—there would be either no male or no female in the marriage. Choice B *may* be permissible, but we don't know. Choice C is impermissible: assuming that N and M are E's brothers, this would mean that two brothers married two sisters, which is neither *Brihtu* nor *Prahtu* marriage. Choice D is a monogamous marriage, which is definitely out in the society under consideration.

6-9.   The players must be seated as shown in the following diagram:

Cooper	Edwards	Edwards	Baker
or	*or*	*or*	
D'Amato	Farley	Farley	

Cooper	Adams	Adams	
or	*or*	*or*	
D'Amato	Goldberg	Goldberg	

Note that all the seats except for the center seat *may* be occupied by either of two individuals. Take this into account when answering the questions.

6. D.   In order for Farley and Edwards to be seated together, they must occupy the second and third seats from the left, in either order.

7. C.   Since Edwards is in either the second or third seat from the left, he cannot be next to Adams, who is in either the first or second seat from the right.

8. C.   Goldberg is in one of the two seats nearest the exit, and therefore cannot be on either side of Baker.

9. B.   If neither Edwards nor D'Amato is seated next to Baker, then Baker must be flanked by Farley on the left and Cooper on the right. This means that the table must be seated as follows (left to right): D'Amato, Edwards, Farley, Baker, Cooper, and, in the last two seats, Adams and Goldberg in either order. The fact that Adams and Goldberg may be seated in either order results in the two possible seating arrangements for the table as a whole.

10-15.   An examination of the seven number series reveals

I.   64 is the third power of 4 ($4 \times 4 \times 4$); 125 is the third power of 5 ($5 \times 5 \times 5$). The next number should be the third power of 6 ($6 \times 6 \times 6$).

II.   This is a more difficult series. The square of 6 is 36. 37 is the square of $6 + 1$. The square of 7 is 49. 50 is the square of $7 + 1$. The square of 8 is 64. 65 is the square of $8 + 1$. We may assume that x in this series will equal $9 \times 9 + 1$ or 82.

III.   Here we find a pattern of three elements. $25 = 5 \times 5$; $125 = 5 \times 5 \times 5$. Similarly $49 = 7 \times 7$; $343 = 7 \times 7 \times 7$. We may assume that x will equal $9 \times 9 \times 9$.

IV.   The difference between 9 and –7 is 16 (4×4). The difference between –7 and 18 is 25 (5×5). The difference between 18 and –18 is 36 (6×6). The difference between –18 and 31 is 49 (7×7). We should also notice that these squares alternately use plus and minus signs. The next number (x) should be $31 - (8 \times 8)$ or –33.

V. $16 = 4 \times 4$. $80 = 16 \times 5$. $480 = 80 \times 6$. $3360 = 480 \times 7$. The next number should be 3360×8. Here the pattern is increasing multipliers of the preceding number.

VI.   Increasing units of subtraction. The pattern is number $- 1, - 2, - 3, - 4$, etc.

VII.   Descending order of squares. 100 is 10×10. 81 is 9×9. $64 = 8 \times 8$. $49 = 7 \times 7$. $36 = 6 \times 6$. The next number should be 25 (5×5).

10. A.   Questions involving the third power occur in I and III.

11. D.   Choice V does not involve the use of second or third powers of numbers.

12. B.   See analysis of IV above.

13. A.   See analysis of II above.

14. B.   See analysis of V above.

15. C.   Example III cannot be solved unless we see that 5, 25, and 125 make a pattern which is repeated with 7, 49, and 343.

16-20. Make a table of the rooming possibilities. Since Hittites and Goths must be separated, D and G must always be in one cabin, while B and F are in the other. In the first three lines of the following table, D and G are placed consecutively with A, C, and E, while whichever two of these three remain are placed in the other cabin with B and F. Then, B and F are put with A, B, and C in turn, the two remaining being put with D and G in the other cabin. The √ mark shows combinations in which everyone in each cabin can talk, whether directly or with one person translating. The X mark shows combinations where this is impossible.

DGA	BFCE	√
DGC	BFAE	√
DGE	BFAC	X
DGCE	BFA	√
DGAE	BFC	X
DGAC	BFE	√

16. D. The combination of DGCE and BFA is satisfactory. BFC is impossible, because B and F speak only Hittite and C speaks only Etruscan and Gothic. Likewise, DGE is out, because E speaks no Gothic. The other two choices are fine by themselves, since A speaks all languages; but they represent the four-person second cabins corresponding to the two impossible choices given in choices A and B.

17. E. There is one acceptable rooming arrangement that places C with A (I). There are two acceptable arrangements in which A is not in the three-person cabin (II). In one acceptable arrangement, DGCE and BFA, E does not room with a Hittite (III).

18. C. If your table has been set up correctly, just count.

19. D. D, E, and G are *not* part of any acceptable arrangement (I); B, E, F and C, D, E, G are (II, III).

20. E. B, E, and F—an acceptable combination previously, since E speaks Hittite—becomes impossible now, since Goths won't room with Hittites. The others all place the newcomer with persons of her own nationality.

21. E. While Lind used the scientific method, the contributions of Hall and Harvey set the stage for his experiment. Credit for the discovery must be given to all three men.

22. B. The group receiving the dilute sulfuric acid and the group receiving vinegar were the control groups. These sailors received the same diets as the third group except for the substance tested.

23. E. Hall and Harvey seemed to have established the fact that acids are effective, but Lind's experiment was to find out whether it was acidity or some specific substance perhaps associated with acids that cured scurvy. Today we know this substance is ascorbic acid. Hall's brew and Harvey's lemon juice must have contained ascorbic acid.

24. C. Lind did not use pure citric acid. Lemon juice contains other substances besides citric acid.

25. C. The passage indicates that lack of fresh food was the cause of scurvy.

14 The Computerized GRE Option

- ■ What Is the Computerized GRE Option I've Heard Mentioned?
- ■ Are There Advantages to Taking the GRE in Computerized Form?
- ■ What Are the Disadvantages to Taking the Computerized GRE?
- ■ How Can I Determine Whether or Not to Take the Computerized GRE?
- ■ A Final Word of Advice

What Is the Computerized GRE Option I've Heard Mentioned?

Back in March 1992, the Graduate Record Examination Board announced a new option for test-takers: the computerized GRE. The initial version of the computerized test, offered first in October 1992, resembled the current paper-and-pencil test in length and format: 186 questions, divided into six sections (two verbal, two analytical, two quantitative), plus one experimental section in one of the three tested areas. (As in the pen-and-pencil test, the experimental section was not counted in the scoring.) These standard computerized test sections grouped questions by type (e.g., sentence completion, analogy, antonym) and by level of difficulty.

How did this initial computerized GRE test work? First, you went through a tutorial module that acquainted you with the skills you needed to take the test: how to keep track of the time, how to move from question to question, how to mark an answer, how to locate unanswered questions, and so on. Using a mouse* to enter your answers on the computer screen, you were expected to respond to as many questions as you could within the

standard 3.5-hour time limit. Within each section of the test you were able to review previously answered questions and, if you wished, to change your answers. You could also skip questions that were slowing you down, marking them so that you could return to them easily. No matter how few questions you answered on any given area of this skip-and-change test, the program was set up to calculate your score.

In October 1993, however, the computerized exam changed markedly. It became primarily an interactive or adaptive test, customized to each student's level of skill. Here is how the test works.

The new computerized test is divided into five sections. Two of these sections (usually the first two you face), like the sections on the initial computerized test, are not adaptive. These two sections test a single subject area: there are two verbal sections, two math sections, or (currently the most likely) two analytical sections. The function of these two nonadaptive sections appears to be to check how accurately the adaptive test assesses your performance in a particular subject area. Unlike the old experimental section, however, these nonadaptive sections may count in the scoring. In particular, if you earn a higher score on the two nonadaptive sections of the test you take than you do on the adaptive section in the same subject area, then the nonadaptive sections count. For any subject area in which you have earned two separate scores, the computer reports only the higher score. For an example, see the following charts.

*An input device connected to the computer by a wire.

Example of Scoring on the New Computerized GRE

	Analytical Reasoning		Verbal	Quantitative
	Nonadaptive	Adaptive	Adaptive	Adaptive
Score Earned	620	570	580	610
Score Reported	620		580	610

	Analytical Reasoning		Verbal	Quantitative
	Nonadaptive	Adaptive	Adaptive	Adaptive
Score Earned	570	620	580	610
Score Reported	620		580	610

How do the interactive or adaptive sections of the new test work? In these sections, you mark an answer to a question. Before you move on to the next question, however, you must confirm that you're sure that this is the answer you want. Once you click the mouse to confirm your answer, that's it. You can no longer change your mind. If you've answered the question correctly, the program then steers you to a more difficult question; if you've answered it incorrectly, the program steers you to an easier one. Essentially, the computer adapts the test to reflect how you perform.

In this portion of the test, you <u>must</u> enter an answer to every question the computer throws at you. If you try to move on to the next question without marking an answer to the question currently on the screen, a message appears instructing you to select an answer choice. You no longer have the option of going back to an earlier question to change your answer, or the option of skipping from one type of question to another within a section. In essence, you are no longer in control of how you work your way through a test section; the computer is in control.

On the adaptive sections, different types of questions pop up in no particular order: on a verbal section you may answer an analogy question and then face three antonym questions in a row. Occasionally a group of questions come up that all relate to a single passage or situation: two reading comprehension questions based on the same 150-word paragraph, or three or four math questions based on the same chart or graph. For the most part, however, you never know what sort of question is coming up next. You just know you have to mark down an answer for every question you face.

To get a score on an adaptive section of the test, you must answer 80 percent of the questions on that section. In other words, to get a score on the 28-question math section, you must mark answers to 23 questions, although you don't have to answer all these 23 questions correctly. (If you answer only 22 questions, the computer will record No Score as your math score, even if you've answered all 22 questions correctly.) See the table below for a summary of this information.

The Adaptive Sections

Section	Number of Questions	Time Allowed (minutes)	Number of Questions You <u>Must</u> Answer to Earn a Score
Analytic	35	60	28
Verbal	30	30	24
Math	28	45	23

Are There Advantages to Taking the GRE in Computerized Form?

Obviously, there are pluses and minuses to the computerized GRE. One plus is availability: rather than being administered five times a year, the computerized GRE is available several days a week by appointment. If you're late applying to graduate school and need to get your test scores to your college in a hurry, you can arrange to take the test within a few days by calling 1-800-967-1100 (if you pay by Visa or MasterCard). Your score reports will go out to the schools you indicate 10–15 days after you take the test. Another plus is immediate feedback: the computer calculates your score within minutes of your finishing the test. You know right away how well you have done.

Yet another plus to the computerized GRE is its setting. Most computerized GREs are administered at the private Sylvan Learning Centers. Before the test, you and the few other test-takers scheduled that hour get an informal briefing on what to expect from a Sylvan employee. Then, after putting your personal belongings in a locker and being photographed, you proceed to a small computer lab where, seated at an individual desk, you take the test in a relatively comfortable, quiet environment. Proctoring is done via overhead video cameras; if you need fresh scratch paper or want to leave the lab, you signal by raising your hand.

What Are the Disadvantages to Taking the Computerized GRE?

Cost

One big minus is cost: the current version of the computerized test costs nearly $100, about twice as much as the paper-and-pencil test. You're paying a premium for the comfortable setting and the speedy feedback.

Problems with Starting

There are also other, more serious drawbacks. Students unfamiliar with computers are at a distinct disadvantage in taking the new computerized GRE. Before you take the test, you do have a chance to work through a tutorial module that teaches you about the various icons or symbols that appear on the screen and gives you a chance to familiarize yourself with using a mouse. The tutorial is untimed; you can repeat parts of it over and over again until you feel somewhat comfortable with the mechanics of the computerized test. However, no amount of practice time on the test day will make working with icons and mice second nature to complete computer novices. There's a good chance you will wind up marking an incorrect answer or two by inadvertently clicking the mouse on the wrong spot. In addition, you may use up so much time practicing using the computer that you will tire yourself out before you ever get to the actual GRE.

Problems with Scrolling

If you are a computer novice, you may have a particularly tough time handling the reading passages, most of which are too lengthy to fit on a single screen. The tutorial section "How to Scroll" gives you a chance to practice using a mouse to scroll through a reading passage, clicking the mouse to move up or down the screen. However, scrolling with a mouse takes a lot more time than scanning a printed page visually. Also, it's easy to click on the wrong part of the scroll bar, jump to the end of the text, and lose the author's train of thought. In short, if you're unaccustomed to working with a mouse, you may find the process distracting; it's hard to concentrate on the content of a passage as a whole when you're having trouble getting from one sentence to the next.

Problems with Speeding

If you are a computer hotshot, particularly a video games whiz, you also may run into trouble with the computerized GRE. You're used to working in a computer environment in which speed pays off: the faster you click onto the menu, the faster you get to the file you want; the faster you click Super Mario's controller, the faster he dodges the bad guys. But the swift reaction time that works for you on video games can work against you on the computerized GRE. When you see an answer that looks good, you should not just click on it instantly and then click to confirm your choice automatically. Take time to think things through. If you find that you're racing through a section, make yourself slow down. Take a second look at the answer choices, this time starting with E and working your way back up to A. Give yourself enough time so that, when you click to confirm an answer, you're sure you've made the right choice.

Problems with Seeing

If you wear glasses or contact lenses, you may discover that your current prescription is inappropriate for middle-distance viewing: you may run into trouble reading material on a computer screen. Taking the GRE is stress enough; you don't want to complicate matters with eyestrain.

Problems with Strategies

As an experienced test-taker, you may find that the new computerized GRE severely handicaps you. You lose the opportunity to mark up your test booklet, underlining significant words in reading passages and crossing out answers you can eliminate as wrong. You also miss out on the chance to maximize your score by skipping over tough questions and concentrating on easier, less time-consuming ones. Most demoralizing of all, you lose a sense of control over the test situation.

It is possible that scores on the computerized GRE do give a fairly accurate picture of a test-taker's abilities. However, is a fairly accurate picture of your abilities what you really want? After all, when you had your yearbook photograph taken, were you satisfied with just a pretty good likeness of your face? Not on your life; what you wanted was the best possible image you could present to the world—no wrinkles, no blemishes. Only flattering camera angles were allowed. Similarly, when you take the GRE, you want the best possible scores you can get to present to your graduate school. You want to use every strategy available to come out looking good to those fellowship and admission committees.

How Can I Determine Whether or Not to Take the Computerized GRE?

If, at this point, you are still considering taking the computerized GRE, remember that this form of the test is only an <u>option</u>. Please take one last minute to assess whether it's a good option for <u>you</u>.

If you answer "YES" to the following questions, you possibly may profit from taking the computerized GRE:

1. Do you usually achieve high scores on standardized assessment tests?

2. Is there a personal computer in your home?

3. Are you familiar with working with a mouse?

4. Have you ever played video games?

5. As an undergraduate, did you take advantage of opportunities for computer-assisted instruction?

6. In taking standardized multiple-choice tests, do you customarily work straight through each section, <u>without</u> backtracking and without leaving many questions blank?

7. In writing down your answers on standard multiple-choice tests, do you tend to mismark answer sheets, for example, putting the answer to question 22 in the space for the answer to question 23?

If you are a "friendly user" of computers or a testing ace, you may welcome the computerized GRE. You will certainly approach the test positively, and your score may well reflect your positive attitude.

If you answer "YES" to the following questions, you probably are better off avoiding the computerized GRE:

1. Do you feel nervous when you have to work with unfamiliar software or machines?

2. Are you accustomed to writing term papers in longhand or on a typewriter rather than on a word processor?

3. Do your eyes feel strained after you've spent some time reading words on a computer screen?

4. In taking standardized multiple-choice tests, do you find it helpful to underline or highlight key words or phrases in reading passages?

5. Do you customarily make marks in your test booklet to indicate answer choices you've eliminated?

6. Do you follow the tactic of skipping the difficult questions at the end of each set and coming back to them after you've answered all the easy questions ahead?

7. Would it bother you to have to mark down a random guess in answer to a question that stumped you, just so that you could move on to the next question without wasting too much time?

If you prefer the printed page to the CRT and are happy with the strategies you have worked out to capitalize on the printed form, you should probably stick to what works for you.

If you are still unsure whether or not to take the computerized GRE, you need to take some time to learn about yourself as a test-taker. As you go through our model tests, see how helpful tactics like underlining key words, crossing out answer choices that you've eliminated, and leapfrogging over tough questions are to you in maximizing your score. Then make your decision about whether the computerized GRE is right for you.

A Final Word of Advice

On the whole, we do <u>not</u> recommend that you take the computerized GRE. Of course, if you are a superbrain who will ace the GRE no matter how it's packaged, you might find taking the test on a computer fun. But our experience is that, if you take the computerized GRE, you give up more than you gain.